STUDIES IN THE CONTRACT LAWS OF ASIA II: FORMATION AND THIRD PARTY BENEFICIARIES

Studies in the Contract Laws of Asia II

Formation and Third Party Beneficiaries

Edited by

MINDY CHEN-WISHART

Professor of the Law of Contract, Oxford University, Tutorial Fellow in Law at Merton College, Oxford, and Professor of Law, National University of Singapore

ALEXANDER LOKE

Professor, School of Law, City University of Hong Kong and Adjunct Research Professor at the Centre for Banking & Finance Law, National University of Singapore

STEFAN VOGENAUER

Director at the Max Planck Institute for European Legal History in Frankfurt

OXFORD
UNIVERSITY PRESS

OXFORD
UNIVERSITY PRESS

Great Clarendon Street, Oxford, OX2 6DP,
United Kingdom

Oxford University Press is a department of the University of Oxford.
It furthers the University's objective of excellence in research, scholarship,
and education by publishing worldwide. Oxford is a registered trade mark of
Oxford University Press in the UK and in certain other countries

First Edition published in 2018

Impression: 1

Published in the United States of America by Oxford University Press
198 Madison Avenue, New York, NY 10016, United States of America

British Library Cataloguing in Publication Data
Data available

Library of Congress Control Number: 2017950176

ISBN 978–0–19–880811–4

Printed and bound by
CPI Group (UK) Ltd, Croydon, CR0 4YY

To my parents Peter and Jean Chen, and my sons James, Zachary, and Max, whose encouragement to embark on this project brought me back to my origins: Luodong, Taipei, Christchurch, Dunedin, Oxford, Asia.

Mindy Chen-Wishart

To the Almighty who grants strength, mercy, and grace, and to my beloved Constance, Benjamin, and Grace.

Alexander Loke

To Johannes Benedikt Vogenauer

Stefan Vogenauer

Foreword

This volume forms the second part of what will ultimately provide a wide-ranging comparative analysis of the contract laws of Asia. It is a ground-breaking project and its accomplishment will be a remarkable achievement.

This part covers the important topics of contract formation and third party beneficiaries in 13 Asian countries, whose combined population is nearly one half of the world's total population. The contributors were wisely given a detailed common brief identifying the particular matters which they were asked to address, as the editors explain in the Introduction, their principal aims being to facilitate conversations: (a) between Asian jurisdictions and (b) between Asian and 'Western' jurisdictions by up-to-date scholarly study of the contract laws of the different jurisdictions. (As an exception to the general methodology, the chapter on the law of Myanmar comes from the recent independently published work of Professors Andrew Burrows and Adrian Briggs, as the editors explain. Its inclusion in the present survey of the contract laws of Asia is a fine example of academic cooperation and particularly welcome as Myanmar is going through the process of reconstructing and revitalizing its legal system after years of military rule.) The individual chapters illustrate the value of the project for academics, practitioners, and judges. They show that there is not only a wide variety of approaches in the contract laws of Asia, but that there is singularly little regional cross-fertilization, each country looking rather towards the laws of others with which it shares its inherited legal tradition. This striking feature is highlighted in Professor Loke's lucid concluding chapter, which in itself is a masterly summary of the values of comparative legal studies.

The value of the work lies in its capacity not only to inform but, in so doing, to provide an educated basis for stimulating debate and influencing legal development at a number of levels. At a simple level, practitioners and others who want to know the relevant contract law in a particular part of Asia will find this a valuable source book. A party negotiating a contract with a counter-party in a particular country will be helped by an understanding of the assumptions which the other is likely to have. More widely, increased regional commerce has led in many areas to an increase in legal regional arrangements, and this process is helped by understanding the different players' legal culture.

Besides the importance of familiarity with the core principles of other legal systems in the development of cross-border legal relations, whether through bilateral contracts or regional arrangements, a proper understanding of other legal systems' principles and practical functioning can deepen and sharpen insight into one's own legal system. It can foster critical analysis, and study of how a problematic area is addressed in other jurisdictions may encourage (or indeed discourage) the adoption of a parallel approach. For that reason and from past experience, the Law Commission habitually includes a comparative study in its examination of any branch of the law.

The editors and contributors are to be warmly congratulated for providing an original, valuable, and timely extension of the literature of comparative legal studies to an area which has been previously neglected, despite its size and increasing global significance.

Lord Roger Toulson
Former Justice of the Supreme Court of the United Kingdom
(1946–2017)

Acknowledgements

A project that involves so many participants and contributors incurs many debts of gratitude, which we eagerly acknowledge here. First and foremost, this volume was made possible by Research Grant R-241-000-130-112 made under the Ministry of Education (Singapore) Academic Research Fund (Tier 1). The grant supported the Conference on the 'Formation and Third Party Beneficiaries', which was held at the Law Faculty of the National University of Singapore (NUS). The grant also funded the employment of copy-editors, who helped to get the manuscripts ready for publication. Working dinners, which enabled the participants to build on and sustain the momentum of the discussions, were sponsored by the NUS Centre for Law & Business, and the NUS Centre for Asian Legal Studies (which also funded the attendance of two contributors to a future volume). We hope that this volume advances the research agendas of the research centres. We also acknowledge research support funding from the Law Faculty of Oxford University, Merton College, Oxford, and the Max Planck Institute for European Legal History.

We are indebted to the commentators who critiqued the papers presented at the colloquium and whose insightful comments helped improve the quality of the papers: Yeo Tiong Min, Akira Kamo, Hiroyuki Kihara, Sandra Booysen, Tan Zhong Xing, Christian Hofmann, Kelry Loi, Kelvin Low, Michael Furmston, Tan Lee Cheng, and Ibrahim Sjarief Assegaf. We are, of course, hugely thankful to the contributors to this volume for their hard work and patience through the many steps required to bring the volume to its final form.

We would also like to thank the managers and administrators at the Law Faculty of the NUS for their knowledgeable, helpful, and resourceful planning of the Conference. Special thanks to Elizabeth Chua, Kris Zhao, and the team of support staff for managing the logistics of the event with such professionalism, skill, and efficiency. Special thanks are due to Liew Yuit Leng and Jasmine Foo for their methodical, dependable, and tireless editorial assistance in preparing the manuscripts for publication. The journey to publication has been an arduous one, and they have demonstrated patience and utmost professionalism in managing 19 authors across Asia. Thanks also to Jodi Gardner for determined assistance at the proofs stage. We are grateful to the team at Oxford University Press for their faith in this project and their key role in bringing it to an international audience. We are also grateful to Lord Toulson for his interest in and support for our project. It is with deep shock and sadness that we learnt of his unexpected passing.

Finally, we acknowledge the support of our families and friends, whose encouragement and patience sustained us in the completion of this project.

Mindy Chen-Wishart
Alexander Loke
Stefan Vogenauer

Table of Contents

THAILAND: CONTRACTS FOR THE BENEFIT OF THIRD PARTIES

VIETNAM: CONTRACT FORMATION AND CONTRACTS FOR THE BENEFIT OF THIRD PARTIES

MYANMAR: CONTRACT FORMATION AND CONTRACTS FOR THE BENEFIT OF THIRD PARTIES

CONCLUSION

Table of Cases

AUSTRALIA

CHINA

EUROPEAN UNION

HONG KONG

INDIA

MALAYSIA

MYANMAR

NETHERLANDS

NEW ZEALAND

NORWAY

SINGAPORE

UNITED KINGDOM

UNITED STATES

VIETNAM

Table of Legislation

Secondary Legislation

HONG KONG

INDIA

INDONESIA

JAPAN

KOREA

MALAYSIA

MYANMAR

SINGAPORE

TAIWAN

VIETNAM

NETHERLANDS

NEW ZEALAND

SWITZERLAND

UNITED KINGDOM

UNITED STATES

List of Contributors

Gary BELL Director of the Asian Law Institute (ASLI), National University of Singapore

Gary F Bell is an Associate Professor at the Faculty of Law of the National University of Singapore (NUS) and is the Director of its Asian Law Institute (ASLI). He received degrees in both civil law and common law from McGill University and in American law (LLM) from Columbia University. At NUS he teaches courses on Indonesian Law, International Commercial Arbitration, and the International Sale of Goods. He is a Fellow of the Chartered Institute of Arbitrators and has acted as an arbitrator in many commercial disputes particularly when the governing law is that of a civil law jurisdiction. He Clerked for Justice Stevenson of the Supreme Court of Canada.

Nilima BHADEBHADE Consultant

Dr Nilima Bhadbhade was, until recently, Associate Professor at ILS Law College, Pune, India, where she taught the laws of contracts, evidence, insurance, and transfer of property. She has designed and conducted workshops about contracting for persons from industry and young lawyers. At ILS Law College, she oversaw mooting and advocacy skills activities for more than 15 years. Dr Bhadbhade is the author of a 300-page monograph on Contract Law in India for the *International Encyclopedia of Laws* (Kluwer Law International, The Hague, four editions 2009–2015), and the books *Contract Law in India* and *Specific Enforcement of Contract Terms: The Tests of Inadequacy and Effective Enforcement*. She has revised three editions of the 100-year-old treatise *Pollock and Mulla's Indian Contract and Specific Relief Acts* (Butterworths India and Lexis-Nexis India 2001–14); and *Halsbury's Laws of India, Vol 9: Contract* (2nd edn, Lexis-Nexis India 2015). Her other articles and works are available on her page at <http://www.academia.edu>.

Adrian BRIGGS Oxford University

Adrian Briggs is the Sir Richard Gozney Fellow and Tutor at St Edmund Hall. He has been teaching in Oxford since 1980. His main interest has always been in private international law, and within that, in questions of civil jurisdiction and the effect of foreign judgments. He spent 15 years as one of the editors of Dicey, Morris and Collins, *The Conflict of Laws*, but his own perspective on the subject, in its increasingly European guise, was published as *Private International Law in English Courts* (2014) and took its place alongside his several other books on private international law, of which *Civil Jurisdiction and Judgments* is the most established. No doubt when the dust settles, and it is possible to see the outlines of private international law after secession from the European Union, it will be time to return to the task of writing monographs on the subject. In the meantime, he has published *Private International Law in Myanmar* and *The Law of Contract in Myanmar*. He also practises from chambers in the Temple.

Andrew BURROWS Oxford University

Andrew Burrows, QC (Hon), FBA, DCL, is Professor of the Law of England in the University of Oxford and a Fellow of All Souls College, Oxford. Between 1994 and 1999, he was Law Commissioner for England and Wales. He has a part-time practice at the English Bar through his membership of Fountain Court Chambers, London. He has written many books and articles, especially on contract, tort, and unjust enrichment. In recent years, he has principally been working on novel projects to produce Restatements of areas of English law. These have involved working with advisory groups of academics, judges, and practitioners to formulate statute-like provisions which attempt to capture the best interpretation of the law. The essential aim is to enhance our understanding of the common law and to make it more accessible. Two Restatements have so far been published by OUP: *A Restatement of the English Law of Unjust Enrichment* and *A Restatement of the English Law of Contract*. Professor Burrows has been heavily involved in the Oxford–Burma/Myanmar law programme and has taught in Myanmar. He was President of the Society of Legal Scholars (2015–16).

Lei CHEN City University of Hong Kong

Lei Chen is Associate Professor and Associate Dean of City University of Hong Kong Law School. His research areas are property theory, contract law, comparative legal method, and Chinese legal history. He is also Associate Director of the Center for Chinese and Comparative Law. In 2011, he was elected an Associate Member of the International Academy of Comparative Law and a Fellow of the European Law Institute. He is also a fellow of the Hong Kong Institute of Arbitrators and the panel arbitrator in Hong Kong International Arbitration Centre, CIETAC, BAC, and SCIA.

Mindy CHEN-WISHART Oxford University

Mindy Chen-Wishart is Professor of the Law of Contract and Associate Dean of Graduates at Oxford University. She is also Fellow in Law at Merton College. She holds a fractional professorship at the National University of Singapore and holds or has held visiting professorships at Hong Kong University, the National University of Taiwan, Otago University, Auckland University, Canterbury University, and Göttingen University. She is author of *Contract Law* (6th edn, OUP 2018), an editor of *Chitty on Contracts* (32nd edn), and was a member of the Advisory Group on *A Restatement of the English Law of Contract* by Professor Burrows. Mindy has lectured to the Judicial College of England and Wales and to the Judicial Academy in Taiwan and Hong Kong. She delivered the Fourth Annual Lecture of the International and Comparative Law Quarterly as author of the best paper.

DING Chunyan City University of Hong Kong

Ding Chunyan is Associate Professor of City University of Hong Kong. She has an LLB and LLM from Peking University, an LLM from University College London, and a PhD from the University of Hong Kong. She became a qualified PRC lawyer in 2000. Before joining the Law School, she was a Fulbright research fellow at Harvard Law School, where she conducted research on comparative health law and tort law during 2008–9. Her primary areas of research and teaching are tort law, medical law, contract law, and comparative law.

David FUNG Alex Pang & Co.

David Fung is an advocate practising civil litigation in Sabah, Malaysia. He heads the litigation practice of the firm Alex Pang & Co. His practice and academic interests are contract, unjust enrichment, torts, property, remedies, and constitutional rights. He is the author of *Pre-Contractual Rights and Remedies* (Sweet & Maxwell Asia 1999) which is based on his dissertation for the SJD degree with the University of Sydney. He is a member of the editorial board of the Journal of Contract Law.

Lusina HO University of Hong Kong

Lusina Ho is Harold Hsiao-Wo Lee Professor in Trust and Equity at the University of Hong Kong. Her research interests are trusts, equity, restitution, and comparative trusts. She is the author of *Trust Law in China* (2003) and, with Rebecca Lee, the editor of *Trust Law in Asian Civil Law Jurisdictions: A Comparative Analysis* (2013). She serves as a member of the international board of editors of the Journal of Equity and as a country representative for China of Trusts and Trustees. She is also an invited member of the International Academy of Estate and Trust Law and the Society of Trust and Estate Practitioners.

JAN Sheng-lin The Constitutional Court of Taiwan, National Taiwan University

Sheng-Lin Jan graduated from National Taiwan University (LLB, LLM) and Frankfurt University am Main, Germany (Dr iur). He joined the College of Law, National Taiwan University in August 1992 and was a distinguished Professor and Fu Ssu-Nien Memorial Chair Professor of the University. His teaching and research areas include comparative civil law, consumer protection law, and government procurement law. In October 2016, Professor Jan was appointed Justice of the Constitutional Court of Taiwan from 1 November 2016. He remains an adjunct professor at National Taiwan University, College of Law.

KWON Youngjoon Seoul National University

Youngjoon Kwon is a Professor of Law at Seoul National University. He teaches and researches in the field of civil law, mainly on contract, tort, property, and secured transaction. He was previously a Judge-advocate in the Republic of Korea Navy, and a Judge in various courts before he joined the faculty. He earned his LLB, LLM, and PhD from Seoul National University, and LLM from Harvard Law School. He has been the Associate Dean at Seoul National University School of Law, the

Director at Law and Technology Center, a committee member in various governmental committees including the Committee for the Civil Code Reform, and a delegate to the UNCITRAL Working Group IV (Secured Transaction). He has authored and co-authored numerous books and articles in the field of civil law and intellectual property law both in Korean and in English, and received numerous prizes and awards for his research and teaching.

Dr LE Net LNT & Partners Law Firm

Le Net heads the LNT & Partners Law Firm's Banking & Finance practice group. He also acts in matters under the firm's Real Estate & Infrastructure practice group, having represented major Vietnamese companies and the Vietnamese Government in significant infrastructure projects. He is a lecturer of civil law at the Ho Chi Minh City University of Law, and has authored textbooks that have been published abroad and in Vietnam. Dr Le is also an arbitrator at the Vietnam International Arbitration Centre (VIAC) and acts as counsel at the Financial and Commercial Centre for Arbitration (FCCA). Prior to co-founding LNT & Partners, Dr Le practised at Baker & McKenzie. In 2017, Dr Le was shortlisted by the *Financial Times* as one of five innovative lawyers of Asia.

Alexander LOKE City University of Hong Kong

Alexander Loke is currently Professor at the School of Law, City University of Hong Kong and Adjunct Research Professor at the Centre for Banking & Finance Law, National University of Singapore. Until December 2014, Loke was Associate Professor at the NUS Faculty of Law where he was convenor of the foundational Contract Law course. Between July 2013 and December 2014, Loke was Deputy Director of the Centre for Banking & Finance Law; during this period, Loke oversaw the creation of the researcher program and a research eco-system attractive to researchers, the scholarly community, the regulators, and the banking and legal professionals. Loke was also the founding editor of the Asian Journal of Comparative Law, which received an 'A' ranking in the Australian Research Council Ranking of world journals 2009. Loke's research interests lie in contract law, banking and finance law, and international capital markets and securities regulation. Loke authored the chapters on 'Remedies' and 'Discharge by Breach and Repudiation' of *Halsbury Laws of Singapore: Contract.* Other representative publications include: 'Tainting Illegality' (2014) 34 Legal Studies 560, 'Rethinking the Transplantation of TSC Industries v Northway in Singapore' (2013) 28 Australian Journal of Corporate Law 253; 'Mounting Hurdles in lokeSecurities Litigation—Addressing the Funding and Collective Action Issues' (2010) 22 Sing Ac L J 660; 'From the Fiduciary Theory to Information Abuse: The Changing Fabric of Insider Trading Law in the U.K., Australia and Singapore' (2006) 54 Am J Comparative L 123.

LY Tayseng HBS Law

LY Tayseng is the Managing Director of HBS Law Firm. He is also a Lecturer in Law at the Royal School of Administration and Royal University of Law and Economics. Mr Tayseng was formerly the Secretary General of the Bar Association of the Kingdom of Cambodia.

Lee MASON Former Lecturer, University of Hong Kong

Lee Mason spent several years lecturing law, including at the University of Hong Kong on the JD, LLB, and LLM programmes, serving as Course Convenor for both 'Law of Contract' and 'Construction of Commercial Contracts'. He has written extensively in the area of contract law and has been invited to present various conference papers and lectures on the subject, locally and internationally, both for the academic and legal professions. Further to this, he was invited to provide Consultation Paper comments to the Hong Kong Department of Justice and deliver submissions in deputation to the Bills Committee of the Hong Kong Legislative Council, regarding reform to the doctrine of privity of contract, prior to the passing of the Contracts (Rights of Third Parties) Ordinance (Cap 623). Lee Mason is called to the Bar of England and Wales and is both a CEDR and HKMAAL Accredited Mediator.

Nigam NUGGEHALLI Azim Premji University

Nigam Nuggehalli is an Associate Professor at the School of Policy and Governance at Azim Premji University in Bangalore, India. Prior to this, Nigam was a Principal Lecturer at BPP University,

London, UK where he developed an international and comparative tax law postgraduate studies programme. Nigam also developed the first senior level jurisprudence module at BPP University. Nigam's expertise is in commercial law, tax law and policy, as well as wider issues in legal philosophy and governance. He has led a team of academics in delivering undergraduate programmes in jurisprudence and postgraduate programmes in commercial law and international tax law. Nigam also taught tax law at the National Law School of India University (NLSIU) in 2003–4. Prior to that, Nigam was an international tax lawyer working in New York, US. Nigam worked as an associate at the New York office of a Canadian law firm and worked on cross-border tax issues.

Masami OKINO University of Tokyo

Masami Okino is Professor of Law at the University of Tokyo Graduate Schools for Law and Politics (since 2010). She graduated from the University of Tokyo Faculty of Law (Bachelor of law) in 1987 and the University of Virginia School of Law (LLM) in 1996. She was previously a Research Associate at the University of Tokyo (1987–90), Lecturer at Tsukuba University (1990–3), Associate Professor at Gakushuin University (1993–9), Professor at Gakushuin University (1999–2007), and Professor at Hitotsubashi University (2007–10). Professor Okino teaches civil law (covering general principles, contracts, torts, law of obligations in general, property, family law and law of successions), consumer law, and trust law. Her main study areas are contracts and juridical acts, law of obligations, trust law, and consumer contract law. She has been an associate member of the Legislative Council of the Ministry of Justice, Civil Law Subcommittee (Obligations) (2009–15), Civil Law Subcommittee (Inheritance) (2015–present), and Trust Law Subcommittee (2004–present).

Burton ONG National University of Singapore

Burton Ong (LLB) (NUS), BCL (Oxon) (Vinerian Scholar), DPhil (Oxon), LLM (Harv) is an Associate Professor at the Faculty of Law, National University of Singapore (NUS). He is also an Advocate and Solicitor in Singapore, and an Attorney and Counsellor at Law in New York State. He teaches and researches in the areas of contract law, intellectual property, and competition law. He is a Director (Competition Law) of the Centre for Law and Business at NUS and course convenor for the Law of Contract module that is taught as part of the first-year core curriculum at the NUS Law Faculty. He was one of the general editors of Vol 1 of *Studies in the Contract Laws of Asia: Remedies for Breach of Contract* (OUP 2016) and was one of the principal investigators behind the project that received the research grant to study the extent to which the performance interest of contracting parties was protected under the contract law regimes of ten Asian jurisdictions.

Angkanawadee PINKAEW Chulalongkorn University

Angkanawadee Pinkaew is Lecturer at the Faculty of Law, Chulalongkorn University. She studied for her advanced degrees at L'Université de Nantes, France. She teaches tort, contract, and business law. Her research focuses on damages, contract, professional liability, and remedies.

TAN Cheng Han, SC National University of Singapore

Professor Tan Cheng Han is Chairman, EW Barker Centre for Law & Business at the Faculty of Law of the National University of Singapore (NUS). He is also Chairman of the Public Accountants Oversight Committee, Chairman of Singapore Exchange Regulation Pte Ltd, a board member of the Accounting and Corporate Regulatory Authority, a Council member of Sport Singapore, a member of the Appeal Advisory Panel to the Singapore Minister for Finance, and a member of the Governing Board of the International Association of Law Schools in the US. Professor Tan has also been a Visiting Professor at Bucerius Law School, the East China University of Political Science and Law, National Taiwan University, and Peking University.

TAY Pek San University of Malaya

Tay Pek San is an Associate Professor at the Faculty of Law, University of Malaya. She is also the legal advisor to the University of Malaya, Centre of Innovation & Commercialisation, a committee member of the Intellectual Property Chapter of the International Chamber of Commerce (Malaysia), and a committee member for the Evaluation of Intellectual Property of the University of Malaya. Dr Tay has taught the law of contract for more than 15 years. She also teaches intellectual property law at undergraduate level and trade mark law at postgraduate level. Prior to joining the academia, she practised law for five years, specializing in commercial law transactions and disputes. Dr Tay has published extensively. She is the co-author of the book *Introduction to Cyberlaw in Malaysia* (Advanced Professional Courses 2004) and author of *Protection of Well-Known Trade Marks in Malaysia* (Sweet & Maxwell Asia 2007) and *Intellectual Property Law in Malaysia* (Sweet & Maxwell Asia 2013). She has contributed chapters to many academic publications and has also written many articles for legal journals. She obtained the double degrees of BSC/LLB from the University of Sydney and her LLM as well as PhD from the University of Malaya.

Pattarapas TUDSRI McGill University

Pattarapas Tudris has a BA from Cambridge University, UK and an LLM from McGill University, Canada. He was a lecturer of law at Chulalongkorn University from 2011–13; responsible mostly for comparative private law courses. His research interests are primarily in the areas of civil law and private international law. During the course of his tenure at Chulalongkorn, Mr Tudsri's research focused on the powers to revest title following a defective transfer; the interaction between property, equity, and unjust enrichment; and private international law. At present, he is a doctoral candidate at McGill University. His thesis aims to trace the normative foundations of the principle of unjust enrichment. It questions the legitimacy of the generalizations and taxonomy of the principle and argues that these often overlook the normative concerns that underpin the restitutionary liability in the paradigm mistaken payment case.

Stefan VOGENAUER Max Planck Institute for European Legal History

Stefan Vogenauer is Director at the Max Planck Institute for European Legal History in Frankfurt/Main and Chair of Max Planck Law, the network of 11 law-related institutes in the Max Planck Society covering all areas of law from legal anthropology to tax. From 2003 to 2015 he held the Chair in Comparative Law at the University of Oxford where he was also the Director of the Institute of European and Comparative Law. He has held visiting positions at the universities of Melbourne, Paris II, and Stellenbosch, and also at Bucerius Law School, National Law University Delhi, Louisiana State University (LSU), National Taiwan University (NTU), New York University (NYU), and the University of Texas at Austin. He works mostly in the areas of European legal history, comparative law, and transnational private law. His publications, partially co-authored and co-edited, in the area of comparative, European, and transnational contract law include *Ius Commune Casebooks on the Common Law of Europe: Cases, Materials and Text on Contract Law* (2nd edn, 2010); *The Common European Sales Law in Context: Interactions with English and German Law* (2013); *English and European Perspectives on Contract and Commercial Law: Essays in Honour of Hugh Beale* (2014); *Commentary on the UNIDROIT Principles of International Commercial Contracts* (2nd edn, 2015).

WU Ying-Chieh National Taiwan University, Singapore Management University

Ying-Chieh Wu (DPhil, Oxon) was an Assistant Professor of civil law at National Taiwan University, College of Law. His main teaching and research areas are obligations, property, trusts, and comparative private law (especially the comparison between civil law and common law). He also serves as Deputy Director of the International Office of the Faculty of Law. Before joining the faculty, he conducted his doctoral research on comparative trusts law at the University of Oxford, UK and previously taught at Korea University, School of Law, Republic of Korea, where he won a best teaching award. He recently received an excellent teaching award from National Taiwan University, Republic of China. His articles and book chapters have been written in English, Chinese, and Korean. Japanese civil law is also within the scope of his comparative research. He has just assumed a new post at the Singapore Management University.

Yoshikazu YAMASHITA Gakushuin University

Yoshikazu Yamashita undertook an LLB at the University of Tokyo, graduating in 1996. He was previously a Research Associate at the University of Tokyo (1996–9). He then became a lecturer at Gakushuin University in Tokyo in 1999, an Associate Professor in 2001, and Professor in 2008. His research areas are contract law and trust law.

List of Abbreviations

BGB	*Bürgerliches Gesetzbuch* 1900 (German Civil Code)
BGH	*Bundesgerichtshof* (German Federal Supreme Court)
CA	Contract Act 1872 (Myanmar)
CA 1950	Contracts Act 1950 (Malaysia)
CCL	Chinese Contract Law of 1999
CECO	Control of Exemption Clauses Ordinance (Cap 71) (Hong Kong)
CESL	Common European Sales Law (European Union)
CISG	United Nations Convention on Contracts for the International Sale of Goods 1980
CLA	Civil Law Act 1956 (Malaysia)
CPA 1999	Consumer Protection Act 1999 (Malaysia)
CPO	Conveyancing and Property Ordinance (Cap 219) (Hong Kong)
CRTPA	Contracts (Rights of Third Parties) Act 2001 (Singapore)
DCFR	Draft Common Frame of Reference (European Union)
Decree No 38	Decree No 38 on Contract and other Liabilities (Cambodia)
DLP	deed of limited partnership
DMC	deed of mutual covenant
GPCL	General Principles of Civil Law of 1986 (China)
ICA	Indian Contract Act 1872
Interpretation II	Interpretation II of the Supreme People's Court of Several Issues Concerning the Application of the Contract Law of the People's Republic of China 2009
ITA	Information Technology Act 2000 (India)
JCC	Japanese Civil Code 1898
JICA	Japanese International Cooperation Agency
KCC	Korean Civil Code 1960
KUHPer	*Kitab Undang-Undang Hukum Perdata* (Indonesian Civil Code)
LES	Chinese Law on Electronic Signature 2004
MCA 1950	Malaysian Contracts Act 1950
MOU	memorandum of understanding
NPCSC	Standing Committee of the National People's Congress (China)
PACL	Principles of Asian Contract Law project
PECL	Principles of European Contract Law
PICC	UNIDROIT Principles of International Commercial Contracts 2010
PRC	People's Republic of China
SPC	Supreme People's Court (China)
Taiwan CC	Taiwan Civil Code 1929
Thai CCC	Thai Civil and Commercial Code 1925
UCC	Uniform Commercial Code 1952 (United States)
VCC	Vietnamese Civil Code

1

Introduction

*Mindy CHEN-WISHART, Alexander LOKE, & Stefan VOGENAUER**

I. Genesis and Objectives of the Project

This project has resulted in part from the experience of two of the editors, Mindy Chen-Wishart and Alexander Loke, on the Principles of Asian Contract Law ('PACL') project,[1] initially, as representatives of Singapore, but later, in Mindy's case, as a joint chief editor.[2] The PACL experience revealed a glaring gap in the Asian literature of the sort that has underwritten the European efforts at harmonization that have borne fruit in the Principles of European Contract Law ('PECL'), the Draft Common Frame of Reference ('DCFR'), and the Common European Sales Law ('CESL'). While there is a long history of comparative contract law studies in Europe, along with concerted efforts to encourage regional harmonization of the contract laws, the same cannot be said of Asia. Regional integration within Asia has, for various historical and socio-political reasons, not been a priority for many Asian jurisdictions.[3] Consequently, the bulk of the literature in the field of contract law is confined to texts and commentaries aimed at domestic audiences and in the local language. With increasing global focus on the rising power and emerging markets of Asia and an increasing interest within Asia to harmonize their contract laws, the gaps need to be addressed.

This project has two main aims: to facilitate conversations *between* Asian jurisdictions, and between them and 'Western' jurisdictions by providing (in English) up-to-date and scholarly literature on the contract laws of many Asian jurisdictions and on comparative Asian contract law. A bibliography for each jurisdiction will also assist further study. This will lay the groundwork for those interested in exploring the possibility of regional harmonization within the commercial law sphere of Asia. It will also open up the channels of communication between contract law academics, policy-makers, law-makers, and practitioners in Asia and those in the 'West' with great potential for enhancing mutual understanding and fruitful collaborations. The project may also promote the development and teaching of courses on comparative Asian contract law in law schools worldwide.

To these ends, there will be six titles in this series on the contract law regimes of key Asian jurisdictions and their comparative dimension, with each thematic volume addressing core legal issues that are encountered by contract lawyers in all jurisdictions. These are:

I. Remedies for Breach of Contract (published in 2016)
II. Formation and Third Party Beneficiaries

* This chapter is based on, and borrows from, M Chen-Wishart, A Loke, & B Ong, 'Introduction' in M Chen-Wishart, A Loke, & B Ong (eds), *Studies in the Contract Laws of Asia: Remedies for Breach of Contract* (Oxford: OUP 2016) 1; cite as M Chen-Wishart, A Loke, & S Vogenauer, 'Introduction' in Chen-Wishart, Loke, & Vogenauer, *Studies in the Contract Laws of Asia Vol II: Formation and Third Party Beneficiaries* (Oxford: OUP 2017).

[1] Shiyuan Han, 'Principles of Asian Contract Law: An Endeavor of Regional Harmonization of Contract Law in East Asia' (2013) 58 Villanova L Rev 589–599.

[2] Neither of us remain involved with PACL.

[3] eg Shiyuan Han (n 1) 591, has described the current relationship between China, Japan, and Korea to be 'politically cold, but economically warm'.

III. The Contents of Contracts
IV. Invalidity
V. Ending and Changing Performance
VI. Public Policy and Illegality.

In each volume, there are typically two contributions per jurisdiction directed to a fairly detailed brief provided by the editors. These include: 'issues to be addressed' and hypotheticals involving commonly encountered problems. In addition, a concluding chapter analyses the contributions from a comparative perspective, and draws out the common themes and the theoretical underpinnings of the convergences and divergences revealed.

Most Asian countries have private law systems transplanted from European legal systems, sometimes as a legacy of colonialism, sometimes consciously imported by local elites. Thus, English law provides the common law roots of the legal systems in Singapore, India, Malaysia, Myanmar, and Hong Kong, while German law's civil law model forms the basis of the contract law in Japan, Korea, and Taiwan. Indeed, some jurisdictions are the result of 'double transplants'. Four jurisdictions in this volume which fall within this category are Thailand and Cambodia (which have adopted many Japanese provisions), and Malaysia and Myanmar (which have imported the Indian Contract Act). In addition, Vietnamese contract law is largely based on the French Civil Code, while Indonesian contract law is based on pre-1992 Dutch law, which is itself an adaptation of French law. Consequently, this project will not only bring Asian voices into the international comparative law scholarship, but can also yield insights into the phenomenon of 'legal transplant', namely, how laws developed in one jurisdiction evolve and are interpreted after they are transplanted into another jurisdiction.

This volume examines the contract laws of 13 Asian jurisdictions: Cambodia, China, Hong Kong, India, Indonesia, Japan, Korea, Malaysia, Myanmar, Singapore, Taiwan, Thailand, and Vietnam. The overarching questions are: first, what transactions are recognized as enforceable contracts in each jurisdiction? Second, when can recognized contracts be enforced by a third party beneficiary who is not a party to the contract?

II. The Asian Jurisdictions Covered in this Volume

Asia is a vast continent with almost 50 states. It is impossible to attempt to cover all these jurisdictions within the scope of this project. Instead, we chose to focus on a representative sample of countries selected from some of the more dynamic economies in East, Southeast, and South Asia. These are all countries whose legal systems have long-standing historical ties either with the English common law or the European civil law traditions. Many of them also have the experience of borrowing from the jurisprudence of one another. The largest economies by population size in East Asia are represented by the chapters on China, Korea, Japan, and Indonesia while smaller jurisdictions are represented by the chapters on Singapore, Hong Kong, and Cambodia.

The juxtaposition of the contract laws of China, Hong Kong, and Taiwan present an interesting study of contrasts between three territories with close political, cultural, and economic ties, with the Hong Kong and Taiwan legal systems heavily influenced by the laws of their former colonial history (involving England and Japan respectively). India, the largest country in South Asia, is important not only economically, but also historically, because it was the test bed for many codifications of the common law, which were exported to other British colonies, including Malaysia and Myanmar. Thailand, one of the few states in the region that was never colonized by a Western power, is included because its contract law reflects the legal influences from French, German, and Japanese civil law traditions.

Table 1.1 Population and GDP per capita of subject jurisdictions

Country/Territory	Population size (2015)	GDP per capita (2015) (US$)
China	1,371,220,000	7,820.00
Japan	127,338,621	38,492.00
Korea (South)	50,219,669	25,977.00
Taiwan[4]	23,373,517	20,952.00
Hong Kong	7,187,500	38,124.00
India	1,252,139,596	1,499.00
Thailand	67,010,502	5,779.00
Malaysia	29,716,965	10,514.00
Singapore	5,399,200	55,182.00
Indonesia	257,563,815	3,346.50
Vietnam	91,703,800	2,111.10
Cambodia	15,577,899	1,158.70
Myanmar	53,897,154	1.160.00
Total	3,352,348,238 (45.6% of the world population of 7,346,633,040)	
Average		$17,580 (compared with the world average GDP of $10,004.90)

Cambodia has recently adopted a new Civil Code (December 2011) with the assistance of Japanese legal experts. Its law purports to take account of the global trends in harmonization of contract laws by reference to international instruments including the PECL, the UNIDROIT Principles of International Commercial Contracts ('PICC'), and the United Nations Convention on Contracts for the International Sale of Goods ('CISG'). In contrast, Indonesia's law seems a little anachronistic and bewildering, having three contract laws operating simultaneously. These are: the indigenous laws of different ethnic groups; different varieties of Islamic contract law; and a Civil Code which is a direct transplant from the Dutch law of 1846 that is still in the Dutch language when 98 per cent of lawyers and judges do not understand Dutch or French, and when the Dutch law itself was substantially reformed in 1992.[5] This is particularly notable since Indonesia has the fourth largest population in the world and is the most populous Muslim majority country in the world.

The socio-economic diversity of the selected Asian jurisdictions represented in this volume is reflected in this table of statistics representing the situation in 2015:[6]

III. Methodology

The PACL experience revealed certain particularities with legal scholarship in the countries covered in this project, including: proficiency in scholarly and legal English, the different structure of relationships (being more hierarchical and loyalty-based), the different styles of

4 Source: Republic of China (Taiwan) Statistical Bureau <http://eng.stat.gov.tw>.
5 See G Bell, 'Formation of Contract and Stipulations for Third Parties in Indonesia', ch 18.
6 Source (for all countries apart from Taiwan): World Bank <http://data.worldbank.org>.

scholarship (leaning more towards doctrinal exposition rather than policy and theoretical discussions), and an expectations gap in what amounts to publishable quality. We put in place a number of measures to meet these challenges.

First, the difficulty of finding the right contributors from so many jurisdictions cannot be overestimated. The editors came to know some contract scholars in Asia through their participation in the PACL project and other scholarly projects, others through their involvement in the Asian Law Institute, and yet others through the *Asian Journal of Comparative Law*. This is the starting point for the selection of serious scholars with relative proficiency in English. However, we were also reliant on recommendations. The final result is some unevenness which we then worked extremely hard to iron out in the editorial process.

Second, contributors received very detailed terms of reference with the aims of providing sufficient guidance to ensure that the papers cover the same issues and address the same themes to enable fruitful comparisons. At the same time, we sought to encourage contributors to explore issues that have been the subject(s) of particular attention or controversy in their jurisdictions, and to address the normative dimensions that may inform law reform. Contributors were also provided with a mini-reading list on comparative materials to get a feel of the issues that are generally discussed in these contexts in the European systems; the hope was that the material would help contributors approach their own legal systems with various different models in mind. Given the confines of this volume, the aim is not to provide an exhaustive account of the law in each jurisdiction, but to give an outline of the shape and form of the law and a taster of some of the issues that preoccupy that jurisdiction. The Bibliography provides a starting point for readers who seek to explore particular issues further.

Third, this volume, like the preceding volume, was facilitated by a colloquium involving all the contributors, editors, and invited commentators, practitioners, and judges. The first draft was submitted by the contributors six weeks before the colloquium to enable the editors to review each paper and revert with 'talking points' for each contributor to address at the colloquium. This allowed the editors to highlight common issues, unusual features of the particular law, gaps in the paper, and areas for further explanations. This gave contributors time to consider how to respond at the colloquium and forewarning of what would need to be addressed in redrafting the paper.

Fourth, at the colloquium, each contributor addressed his or her 'talking points', followed by a commentator's remarks, and open discussion. The colloquium yielded fruitful comparisons, raised further questions for consideration, and generally facilitated a better sense of the common endeavour. We also had a dedicated session on the publication process to impress on contributors the substantial revisions that would be necessary in most cases. After the colloquium, the editors wrote again to each contributor with detailed comments on the draft and suggestions for revision.

Lastly, once the second drafts were submitted, the editors reviewed and reverted again on any issues still outstanding and worked to resolve them with the contributors. This turned out to be a very significant enterprise for the editors in respect of some papers.

We need to say a particular word about the chapter on Myanmar contract law. It has been excised from the work of Professors Adrian Briggs and Andrew Burrows of the Oxford Law Faculty, *The Law of Contract in Myanmar* (2017),[7] with their kind permission. The work is a major project of the Oxford–Burma/Myanmar Law Programme, instituted to assist

[7] Freely available at <https://www.law.ox.ac.uk/sites/files/oxlaw/briggsburrowsbook_thelawofcontractinmyanmar.pdf>.

Myanmar law schools and the wider community in the aftermath of the end of military rule and the introduction of democratic reforms after 2011. It is the first book to look in detail at Myanmar contract law, which clearly self-identifies as a common law system. So this is the only chapter in this book that was not written by authors from the jurisdiction in question. However, the authors rely primarily on the Myanmar Contract Act 1872 (which is essentially identical to the Indian Contract Act 1872 and regarded as a codification of the English common law) and on the relevant Burmese/Myanmar case law. They sought to identify, read, and understand all the reported decisions on contract of the courts of Burma/Myanmar since the enactment of the 1872 Act until about 1968 after which the Myanmar law reports are in the Burmese language only. The authors' 'research and writing was primarily carried out in Oxford using facilities of the Bodleian Law Library and electronic databases' in addition to short teaching visits to Yangon where they spoke with law faculty, practitioners, and judges about the Myanmar law of contract.[8] We are extremely pleased to be able to showcase their work in this collection of Asian contract law. We hope to add the Myanmar law on the remedies for breach (covered in Volume I of this series on specific performance and damages) in Volume V: the ending and changing of contracts, which will partly deal with a remedy for breach, namely, termination of contract.

IV. Guidance Provided to Chapter Contributors

For ease of exposition, discussion of each jurisdiction is typically divided into two chapters—one dealing with the formation of contract and the other dealing with third party beneficiaries. In four cases (Korea, Indonesia, Vietnam, and Cambodia), the authors combined both areas of discussion into single chapters. We sent the contributors the following terms of reference:

The principles governing contract formation demarcate the line between contractual responsibility and freedom from that responsibility. In doing so, they determine when the law will deem individuals to have assumed contractual liability and so allow them to organize their affairs accordingly. The distinctive basis of liability in contract lies in the voluntariness of the obligations undertaken. However, not all voluntary undertakings are enforceable. The boundaries of enforceability will vary between jurisdictions according to the particular legal system's conception of the nature of a contract, considerations of practicality in the administration of justice, efficiency, public policy, and maybe even of fairness. An intriguing question is whether modernity and international commerce are producing any functional convergences in the contract laws of Asia, and if so, what implications this has for the theoretical foundations of the contract laws of Asia?

A related question to that of contract formation is the question of '*who* can sue on the contract?' Can third party beneficiaries who are neither the promisees nor (where this matters) the providers of consideration sue on the contract? What are the parameters of third party rights vis-à-vis the contract parties? How are any such rights theoretically justified?

In exploring these issues, we hope to understand the current critiques and debates taking place in the subject jurisdictions and the possible trajectory of development.

In writing your papers, please:

- Highlight any *similarities* or *differences* you think are especially notable between your law and the laws of other Asian jurisdictions.

[8] <https://www.law.ox.ac.uk/research-and-subject-groups/the-myanmar-law-of-contract>.

- Highlight any *controversial* issues in your jurisdiction. How is the law on this topic likely to develop in the next ten years?
- Analyse and comment on the *principles/interests/values/policies* that underlie your law.
- *Give examples* to illustrate your points.

In your respective papers, please cover the following issues, although they need not be in the order presented here.

I. Contract formation

Note that your paper does *not* cover deficiencies of consent discussed under the doctrines of mistake, fraud, duress and so on. These will be dealt with in Volume IV on Invalidity. On the other hand, formalities will be covered in this volume.

A. Please give a *brief* introduction to the historical background to the modern law in your jurisdiction.

B. Is the test of intention objective or subjective? What background information is taken into account in determining intention? Please explain *with examples.*

C. Formality requirements:

   - When must enforceable contracts satisfy formality requirements?
   - What are the formality requirements?
   - What are the consequences of non-compliance? Is parties' reliance protected?
   - What is/are the justification/s for the formality requirements (eg evidentiary, ensuring serious intention, consumer protection)?

D. Are offers binding in your jurisdiction (ie can they be revoked before acceptance)?

   - If binding, how are attempted revocations of offers remedied?
   - If not binding, how does your law protect the offeree's reliance (eg in the tender process)?
   - Does your jurisdiction recognize any obligation (whether expressed by the parties or imposed by law) to negotiate in good faith? If so, what is the content of such an obligation and remedies for its breach?
   - Are there any other pre-contractual duties (eg disclosure)? If so, what remedies are available for their breach?

E. What are the requirements of acceptance or agreement? What determines the *time* of acceptance when there is a delay between the sending and arrival of the communication of acceptance (eg by letter/post, answering machines, voicemail)? Which party bears the risk of delay or loss of the communication?

F. When one party makes an offer on one set of terms, the other purports to accept on a different set of terms, *and performance begins* (also known as a 'battle of forms' at common law), how does your jurisdiction resolve disputes as to the governing terms, or to any unjust enrichment?

G. What is the approach of your jurisdiction if the terms of the agreement are vague or uncertain? What if there are gaps so that the agreement is incomplete?

H. Does your jurisdiction have special rules for contracts concluded through electronic means? If so, what types of electronic communication are covered (eg emails, internet 'forms', instant messaging, bulletin boards)? How do these rules alter the general principles of contract formation? Does your jurisdiction adopt a different approach for the formation of standard form or consumer contracts?

I. Is there a formal test of serious intention to create legal relations? What does this involve?

J. Are gratuitous (sometimes called 'unilateral' by civil law jurisdictions) promises enforceable (whether with or without formalities)? If they are enforceable, what is the justification and what are the requirements (eg formalities)? Are the remedies for non-performance and grounds of invalidity (or vitiation) the same as for onerous (or 'bilateral') contracts?

K. How does your jurisdiction deal with 'bilateral' contracts (also described in terms of exchange, onerous, synallagmatic, 'consideration')? What is the justification? If an exchange is required, how does your law protect the gratuitous promisee's reliance?

L. How would your jurisdiction deal with the following case?
The delayed building work: X contracts for Y to refurbish 27 flats for £20,000. However, Y ran into difficulties. X was concerned about having to pay a penalty under the head contract, and promised to pay Y an extra £10,300 to complete the work on time. Can Y enforce the additional £10,300?

II. Contracts for the benefit of third parties

Please highlight the current doctrinal and theoretical debates concerning the contractual rights of third parties in your jurisdiction.

A. Does your jurisdiction recognize a privity rule, which (generally) prevents those who are not parties to the contract from acquiring enforceable rights under the contract? Please give the rationale for your answer.

B. Can contract parties make a contract for the benefit of a third party enforceable *by* the third party in a *contractual* action?

- If so, in what precise circumstances? Eg must the parties *expressly* confer a right to sue on the third party, or is something less sufficient? If the latter, what?
- Can allowing third party action in contract be regarded as filling a gap in the law of tort in your jurisdiction?
- What is the principle or theory justifying the law?

C. Is the third party who can enforce the contract in as good a position as a promisee would be? What is the nature of available *remedies* (eg performance, damages (expectation or reliance), termination)?

D. What is the nature of the debtor-promisor's available *defences*? Can the debtor rescind the contract against the third party (eg if the third party had induced the contract by making a misrepresentation to the debtor)?

E. In what circumstances can the contract parties vary or rescind the benefit to the third party?

F. Can a contract for the benefit of a third party be *indirectly* enforceable by the third party (eg via tort; specialized areas of commercial law should only be mentioned in passing)?

- If so, briefly list the circumstances.
- Broadly, how much use is made of these techniques to circumvent the privity rule?

G. To what extent are contracts for the benefit of third parties enforceable by the promisee-contract party?

- For example, can performance remedies be ordered against the promisor, or damages awarded for losses suffered by the promisee, or suffered by the third party (if the latter, does the promisee owe a duty to hand over the damages awarded), or any other judicial remedy?
- Is there a hierarchy between the claims of the promisee and any claims available to the third party (ie is the loss regarded as more properly belonging to one party)?
- How is any potential risk of double liability to the promisor dealt with?

H. How would your jurisdiction deal with the following case?
Exemption clauses for stevedores: X contracts with Y to transport X's goods using Y's ship to a foreign market. The contract for the carriage of goods by sea between X and Y contains an exemption of liability provision which purports to protect Z, the stevedores hired to unload X's goods from Y's ship once it arrives at the docks. As a result of Z's carelessness, X's goods are damaged while they are being unloaded from the ship and X wants to sue Z for negligence to recover damages for the losses suffered by X. Can Z rely on the exemption of liability provision in the contract between X and Y?

I. How would your jurisdiction deal with the following case?
Selling bread: X leases two adjoining properties to Y and Z. The lease between X and Y barred Y from selling bread because Z sold bread from his leased property. Can X and Y agree to lift the bar?

J. How would your jurisdiction deal with the following case?
The stolen shop takings: X bank makes a contract for Y security company to collect Z store's takings. The contract requires Y to use armoured vehicles and take out insurance. Y failed to do these and the takings were stolen while being collected in an ordinary car. Can Z sue?

There will predictably be questions that you may like to raise for discussion, which are not set out above. We therefore welcome your feedback on the above questions. Your thoughts on how the questions may be refined and further questions to be addressed will enrich the discussion we shall have.

V. Chapter Overviews

This volume covers 13 jurisdictions in 21 chapters, preceded by this introductory chapter and followed by a concluding chapter. The contributions are individually interesting for the light they shed on commonly occurring questions as well as the values which underpin the approach taken for their resolution. Valuable comparative insights, whether on legal transplantation or legal culture, can also be obtained by reading different combinations of the chapters. It will be for our readers to decide how best to tackle these chapters, depending on their specific interest in the contract laws of Asia; some suggestions to this effect were made in the Introduction to the first volume of the *Studies in the Contract Laws of Asia*.[9]

[9] Chen-Wishart, Loke, & Ong (n *) 20.

In **Chapter 2**, *DING Chunyan* discusses the law on **contract formation in Chinese law** which largely follows the 1980 CISG and the 1994 PICC. An objective approach is adopted in determining the parties' intentions. Exceptions are allowed where parties have not accurately expressed their true agreement, where the contract is a sham, or where one party's intentional false expression is known to the other. For a contract to be binding, its 'essential elements' must be agreed (namely, the names of the parties, the subject matter, and the quantity; other terms may be agreed by the parties *after* the conclusion of the contract or, failing that, determination by the court). In reality, however, courts use soft laws and the nature of the contract to augment what is required. The law states that a purported acceptance which makes a 'non-material' alteration to the content of the offer can bind the offeror unless the offeror rejects such alterations by timely objection. However, courts have defined 'materiality' broadly leaving little scope for non-materiality. Nevertheless, even a materially varied acceptance can bind if the original offeror's performance amounts to acceptance by conduct or trade custom indicates such. There is no general requirement of form for a valid contract, although exceptionally, laws or administrative regulations may require writing (failure to comply means there is no contract unless one of the parties has already performed the main obligations and the other party has accepted the performance), or approval/registration (where failure to comply cannot be perfected by performance). There is no general requirement of consideration; gratuitous contracts are enforceable. However, the latter attract far less legal force than onerous contracts since: the donor can rescind in a wide range of circumstances; the donor is not liable for losses caused by defective performance except for intentional concealment or gross negligence; and the creditor under the onerous contract can apply for the revocation of the gift if that is necessary to protect its contractual rights against the donor. An offer is irrevocable only if it is an option or if the offeree reasonably believes the offer is irrevocable and has made preparations for the performance of the contract. An acceptance takes effect only when it arrives. A late acceptance is ineffective unless the offeror gives timely notice of its intention to ratify the acceptance. Electronic means of communication are treated in the same way as paper-based communications with specific rules to determine the time and place of contract formation. Reliance-based pre-contractual liability (which may be reduced for contributory negligence) may be imposed, on the basis of the requirement of good faith, for example: negotiating with no intention of concluding a contract, intentional concealment of material facts, or breach of confidentiality.

In **Chapter 3**, *CHEN Lei* examines the position of **third party beneficiaries in Chinese law**. Article 64 of the Chinese Contract Law ('CCL') states that where a contract for the benefit of a third party is breached, the debtor is liable to the creditor. Chen Lei regards this as leaving unanswered the question of whether the *third party* has a right of direct action against the debtor. He advocates a positive answer based on policy reasons, foreign laws, and international instruments. Chen Lei draws a distinction between 'genuine' and 'incidental' third party contracts, where the former aims to confer a substantive benefit on the third party, whereas the latter merely directs performance to the third party in discharging the obligation to the creditor (as where A agrees to pay B by paying into B's bank, C). One school of thought regards the third party as having the right to sue for the benefit, whether the third party contract is genuine or incidental, although this right (originally included in the draft) was ultimately excluded from the CCL for reasons unknown. The second view, supported by an Interpretation of the Supreme People's Court, is that Article 64 does not provide a right of action for a third party, whether the third party contract is genuine or incidental, but merely prescribes performance in 'incidental' third party contracts. This leaves open the position in respect of 'genuine' third party contracts. The third view then, supported by a judgment, is that there is a third party right of action in cases of 'genuine' third party contracts, in order to avoid a legal lacunae. The problem is that the definition of a 'genuine' third party contract is somewhat circular. Nevertheless, nothing prevents the parties from *expressly* creating third party rights in the contract. Courts are unlikely to recognize a third party action where the contract merely purports to confer a benefit on the third party. Where a third party *can* sue, it can access all of the promisee's remedies (aside from termination) and is subject to all of the defences, set-offs, and counterclaims against the promisee (including the withholding of performance) and to defences as if it were a party to the contract. The *promisee* may also enforce the contract by claiming specific performance, the agreed sum, restitution, or damages. Courts must guard against double liability. Damages awarded to the creditor are likely to be nominal, but where they are substantial, they should be held for the benefit of the third party where the claim is for the third party's loss (eg where a homeowners' association obtains damages against a property developer, they must then be shared amongst the third party homeowners); otherwise, they can be kept by the promisee (eg where the contract stipulates agreed damages). As a matter of good faith, where the third party has communicated its assent to either of the contract parties, the latter should not be able to vary or rescind the third party benefit without the third party's consent. The situation in the absence of assent but in the presence of reasonable reliance is uncertain. Specific statutes in commercial law have sidestepped privity of contract, for example in agency, assignment, insurance, carriage of goods by sea, trust, and construction. The tort of negligence may also allow a third party to sue for breach but only where there has been fault, only for the reliance loss, only for pure economic loss in limited circumstances, and only where the highly contested causation requirement is satisfied. Looking to the reform of the Civil Code, Chen Lei calls for greater clarity in recognizing a third party right to sue on the contract made for its benefit.

In **Chapter 4**, *Nigam NUGGEHALLI* examines the law on the **formation of contracts in India**. The Indian Contract Act 1872 ('ICA 1872') is significant as it is the product of the first successful attempt to codify the English common law of contract in the British Commonwealth. The Act was then transplanted to other jurisdictions in the British Commonwealth, including Malaysia. As Nuggehalli points out, the preamble of the ICA 1872 makes it clear that it is intended to 'define and amend *certain* parts of the law relating to contract'; as such, the Act does not exhaustively set out the rules of contract law. Interesting issues follow relating to the precise ambit of the ICA, and the areas where there continues to be room for common law development, whether novel and unique to India, or adopted into Indian law after considering the common law developments in other jurisdictions. One such issue relates to section 4 of the ICA 1872, which is seen to state the postal acceptance rule—except that it does not state that it is an exception to the instantaneous communication rule. Instead, section 4 merely sets out when the offeror is bound ('when [the communication of acceptance] is put in the course of transmission, so as to be out of the power of the acceptor') and when the offeree is bound ('when it comes to the knowledge of the [offeror]'). The question which thereby arises is whether section 4 sets out a general rule or whether it is merely an exceptional one operating against the unstated instantaneous communication rule. Though the Indian Supreme Court in *Bhagwandas Goverdhandas Kedia v Girdharilal Parshottamdass*[10] indicated that it is the latter, the matter seems as yet unsettled in Malaysia, which has a cognate provision. Another issue relates to whether the ICA 1872 permits the accommodation of a subsequent development in the English common law. An example is the element of intention to create legal relations, which today is regarded as integral to the analysis of contract

[10] AIR 1966 SC 543.

formation in the English, Singapore, and Hong Kong common law. The Indian courts seem to doubt the existence of this as an independent element, whereas Malaysia has embraced the presumptions that accompany the element. A notable area where Indian contract law has embraced a common law development and moved ahead of developments in the home jurisdiction is promissory estoppel. The Indian Supreme Court made clear its preference for the notion of 'inequitability' to 'detriment' even before the English courts reached a clear position on the matter. Significantly, the use of promissory estoppel is expressly permitted as a cause of action and not merely as a defence.

In **Chapter 5**, *Nilima BHADBHADE* explores the **Indian law** relating to whether **third party beneficiaries** of a contract can enforce its terms. The chapter usefully sets out the reception of English law into India prior to the ICA 1872, in particular how the broad instruction to courts in the Act of 1781 to act according to 'justice, equity and good conscience' formed the basis for the early application of English law in India. Hence, even though the ICA 1872 does not state the privity rule, the rule has been regarded as so firmly embedded in the received law that it is regarded as being infused into the very fabric of the ICA 1872. Despite early uncertainty over whether the rule should be regarded as a matter of procedure rather than substance, Indian law has settled on the latter orthodox position. With the privity rule as the overarching general rule, the ensuing discussion necessarily relates to how parties can utilize existing doctrines to circumvent the obstacle posed by the privity rule. Many of these devices will be familiar to the common lawyer acquainted with the coping strategies adopted in England prior to the Contracts (Rights of Third Parties) Act 1999. An exception peculiar to India pertains to marriage and family settlements and compromises where, as an outworking of the respect given to the personal laws of Muslims and Hindus, beneficiaries of such settlements and compromises are accorded enforcement rights. The privity rule does not therefore apply to such settlements and compromises. Another noteworthy exception occurs under the Consumer Protection Act 1986, in which the beneficiary, who uses goods or takes the benefit of services with the approval of the buyer of goods and services, is entitled to claim relief under the Act similar to that available to the buyer. After a failed attempt at reforming the privity rule in 1958, fresh recommendations were made in October 2016 to reform the rule.

In **Chapter 6**, *TAY Pek San* examines the **formation of contract under Malaysian law**. The Malaysian Contracts Act 1950 ('MCA 1950') is modelled on the Indian Contract Act 1872. In common with the ICA 1872, the analytical structure for the formation of contract is strikingly similar to that of English law, if mediated by unique statutory definitions introduced by the ICA 1872. A proposal, upon acceptance by the person to whom the proposal is directed, becomes a promise; reciprocal promises which constitute consideration for each other result in an agreement; upon the satisfaction of the other conditions for the formation of contract, a contract is constituted. The continuing influence of the English common law on Malaysian law is expressly provided by sections 3 and 5 of the Civil Law Act 1956; these form the statutory basis for the reception of the doctrine of promissory estoppel which is noticeably absent in the statutory text of the MCA 1950. Where the MCA 1950 does not preclude the adoption of English legal developments, the Malaysian courts have shown themselves ready to adopt such developments. A good example is the element of intention to enter into legal relations, which has been accommodated within the Malaysian analytical structure for the formation of contract. Yet, even if there is much similarity between Malaysian contract law and English law, its unique features are notable. Like the cognate provision in the ICA 1872, section 64 of the MCA 1950 renders a promise to accept lesser payment of a debt enforceable. In doing so, it honours debt compromises between creditors and debtors, and overcomes the problem with legal consideration predicated by *Pinnel's* case[11] and *Foakes v Beer*.[12] The good Samaritan exception (section 26(b)) represents another notable exception to the operation of the consideration doctrine, rendering enforceable a promise to reward after the performance of what would ordinarily be regarded as a gratuitous act. The doctrine of promissory estoppel was embraced and developed slightly beyond its ambit in the English common law to operate as part of a cause of action, and not merely as a defence. In doing so, it not only finds company with developments in other common law jurisdictions like India and Australia, but also raises the question whether the English limitation on its use as a cause of action should be reconsidered. The codification of common law rules occasionally results in gaps of which transaction planners should be mindful. Section 4 of the MCA 1950, which is in *pari materia* with section 4 of the ICA, posits different times at which the offeror and offeree are bound. The offeror is bound when the offeree posts his acceptance, whereas the offeree is bound when the acceptance comes to the knowledge of the offeror. The offeree is *ex facie* afforded an opportunity to retract an earlier acceptance by a speedier mode of communication before the acceptance reaches the offeror. If contracting parties do not desire such a result, they will have to devise conditions to the terms of the offer which avoid such an outcome. Special note should also be made of a contract made by a person of unsound mind; the Act prescribes that the contract is void whereas the common law regards it as voidable.

In **Chapter 7**, *David FUNG* examines the **Malaysian position on privity and third party beneficiaries**. Given that the MCA 1950 is virtually a copy of the ICA 1872, the issues are, unsurprisingly, similar. The absence of a clear statement of the rule in the MCA meant that its existence was susceptible to challenge. It was only in *Kepong Prospecting Ltd v Schmidt*,[13] when the Privy Council pronounced on the fundamentality of the privity rule, that the matter was finally settled. Fung's chapter demonstrates both the ingenuity as well as the limitations of the common law. The strategy of finding an express trust of a promise finds a familiar trajectory in the use of that strategy in England. The need to prove the three certainties—of intention to create a trust, beneficiaries, and subject matter—emphasizes the clear intention to create *property* rights. This is not something to be inferred lightly. An alternative explored by Fung relates to the institutional constructive trust; though somewhat malleable for delivering a just solution, it nonetheless requires a proprietary base by which the constructive trust may be found. Fung's discussion of the problems presented by the privity doctrine—such as a promisee's claims on behalf of third parties—provides a useful backdrop for appreciating how legislation facilitating third party enforcement of contractual rights found in Singapore and now Hong Kong helps overcome many of these problems.

In **Chapter 8**, *TAN Cheng Han* observes that the **Singapore law on contract formation** largely replicates the English law which it inherited from colonial days and is maintained by the Application of English Law Act 1993 'so far as it is applicable to the circumstances of Singapore and its inhabitants and subject to such modifications as those circumstances may require'. The offer and acceptance approach to contract formation is mediated through the objective test of intentions which takes account of the circumstances in which the words or conduct are to be interpreted; but if one party's mistaken expression is known to the other, there is no valid contract. However, even where an offer and acceptance analysis is difficult, courts are prepared to imply contracts or perfect contracts if the parties' intention to contract is clear. An offer is distinguished from an 'invitation to treat' since the former evinces an intention to be bound by acceptance, while the latter does not. However, some rules (which may seem counter-intuitive) govern the classification in specific situations (eg that

[11] (1602) 5 Co Rep 117a, 77 ER 237. [12] (1883–84) LR 9 App Cas 605. [13] [1968] 1 MLJ 170.

shop displays are merely invitations to treat). An offer can be revoked at any time before acceptance and, in the absence of consideration, even before the expiration of the time for which the offer is stated to be open (although a willing court could easily find consideration to keep the offer open). A unilateral offer is a promise for a completed act. In some circumstances, this may be irrevocable once the offeree has commenced performance. An acceptance must mirror the offer; where it does not, it turns into a counter-offer that can be accepted by the other party's performance; this is the 'last-shot' approach. The offer, its revocation, and acceptance must be actually communicated to the other party. However, an acceptance can be inferred from conduct or, exceptionally, waived. Moreover, where post is a reasonable method of acceptance, the acceptance takes effect when it is posted unless the offeror stipulates otherwise. The postal rule is largely overtaken by instantaneous methods of communication; here, Singapore courts have leaned towards the actual receipt rule. This is confirmed by the rules on contracts made by electronic communications. There is no valid contract if its terms are too vague or incomplete to be cured by judicial interpretation. There is no general requirement of form for contracts, subject to exceptions (eg the sale of land); non-compliance with formalities requirements renders the contract void or unenforceable, although this is mitigated by the estoppel-based part-performance doctrine. Consideration is required for a valid contract unless the agreement is under seal; there is no need for consideration to be adequate. Historically, this rendered unenforceable agreements to vary existing contracts by one party's promise to pay more. But courts now recognize the 'practical benefit' of a reciprocal promise to perform the pre-existing contractual duty to render such variations enforceable in the absence of duress. This is symptomatic of the modern trend for downplaying the importance of consideration, especially where parties modify an *existing* contract, although consideration is unlikely to be abolished any time soon. In the absence of consideration, where one party promises not to enforce its strict legal rights against the other who has relied on that promise, the doctrine of promissory estoppel will give some effect to that promise to prevent detriment to the promisee. However, promissory estoppel cannot be used as a cause of action, only as a defence to one. The requirement of an intention to create legal relations allows parties to regulate the bindingness of their undertakings and operates to keep courts out of dealings in the private domain.

In **Chapter 9**, *Burton ONG* observes that the **Singapore law on third party beneficiaries** has stayed faithful to the English law, adopting the privity of contract rule, various common law exceptions to the rule, and a statutory regime to empower third parties to enforce contractual terms in prescribed circumstances. The privity rule confines the benefits and burdens under the contract to the contract parties; only they have given consideration and only they can sue and be sued under it. However, various reasons support the third party beneficiary having some right to enforce that benefit and a range of common law mechanisms allow the third party to do this. Some of these are true exceptions, typically by the operation of other branches of law, such as shipping, banking, and agency. Others operate by changing the status of the third party into that of a primary party, thereby eliminating the lack of privity (eg collateral contract or the tort of negligence). In the latter case, the third party can sue the promisor, if its breach also amounts to negligence, since Singaporean law (unlike English law) freely allows claims for pure economic loss. In most types of contracts the Contract (Rights of Third Parties) Act 2001 ('CRTPA') confers on the third party beneficiary the right to enforce the benefit if: the contract expressly confers this right, or alternatively, unless the contract indicates otherwise, if it 'purports to confer a benefit' on the third party. The latter has been widely interpreted (although an incidental benefit is excluded) and where the parties are silent, the default position is to allow the third party to sue. This is said to give effect to the contract parties' intentions. Unless the contracting parties stipulate to the contrary in the contract, they cannot vary or rescind the benefit to the third party without the third party's consent where: (1) the third party has communicated his assent to the promisor; (2) the promisor knows that the third party has relied on the term; or (3) the promisor can reasonably be expected to have foreseen the third party's reliance. In the case of (2) and (3), it is irrelevant that the third party does not know the precise terms involved. The third party can seek any legal remedy (damages, injunctions, specific performance, and so forth) that would have been available had it been a party to the contract. At the same time, the promisor can raise against the third party: (1) any defences that it could have raised against a contract party; and (2) any defences that could have been raised against the third party had it been a contracting party. Where the third party seeks to benefit from an exemption clause in the contract, the promisor can rely on the Unfair Contracts Terms Act to challenge its validity. But the third party cannot appeal to the same Act where the contract exempts the promisor's negligence liability, since the Act only protects contract parties and the third party is not treated as such under the CRTPA. Logically, other legislation that applies to contract parties also cannot apply in favour of the third party. Since the common law continues to develop the promisee's remedial rights, courts must be vigilant to guard against imposing double liability on a promisor. The promisee may enforce the benefit for the third party by claiming specific performance where this is available, but damages are problematic since the promisee is deemed to have suffered no loss. To fill this 'legal black hole' courts have recognized two exceptions: the first (the *Albazero* exception) allows the promisee to claim on behalf of the third party in certain circumstances, although this may be largely overtaken by the CRTPA where its operation is not excluded by agreement; and the second recharacterizes the promisee's loss as the loss of performance itself (rather than the economic loss caused by the loss of performance). The latter raises the spectre of double liability for the promisor although it may be resolved by joining the third party to the action; it has yet to be successfully claimed. The relationship between these two exceptions and the third party's claim under the CRTPA has yet to be precisely delineated, as have the rights and obligations between the promisor, the promisee, and the third party.

In **Chapter 10**, *Lusina HO* examines the law on **contract formation in Hong Kong** which is closely modelled on the English common law but adapts the English solutions to the local context if and when required. The test for ascertaining the parties' meeting of the minds is objective, the agreement (an offer with a matching acceptance) must be certain, complete, and made with the intention to create legal relations—the latter being presumed to be present in a commercial context and absent in a familial or social context. Offers are freely revocable although the reliance of the offeree is protected in exceptional circumstances. Acceptances become effective as soon as they are dispatched. In the 'battle of forms' scenario, the Hong Kong courts follow the traditional 'last-shot' rule although an important nuance was suggested in the lower courts: if the last set of standard terms communicated by one of the parties differs materially from the initial contract the provider of those terms has to give notice of the differences. There is no general duty to negotiate in good faith under Hong Kong law, and even agreements to negotiate in good faith are normally unenforceable for lack of certainty. As a general rule, contracts can be validly made without adhering to any formal requirement: even online contracts will normally be valid and enforceable. A number of legislative formality requirements pertain to certain types of transaction and stipulate a range of legal responses for non-compliance. Most of them mirror the respective English rules. In the case of contracts for the sale and disposition of land, the solution of the Statute of Frauds (abolished in England in 1989) still prevails. Such contracts do not have to be wholly in writing (as in England) but merely have to be evidenced by a written and signed memorandum of the agreement. While the courts initially adopted a fairly relaxed attitude to the question whether a given document constituted a sufficient memorandum, they became more restrictive when the Hong Kong property market started booming in the 1990s. Since then, the memorandum of agreement has had to explicitly mention the property, parties, and price, as well as the date of completion. Finally, the Hong Kong courts remain firmly wedded to the doctrine of consideration where they take their lead from English law on all important aspects, including the relaxation in *Williams v Roffey*, where additional payment promised for the same work was regarded as a 'practical benefit' sufficient to constitute consideration. Interestingly, the Hong Kong courts extended this analysis to the converse scenario where one of the parties agrees to receive less pay for the same work; whereas the English courts, in *Re Selectmove*, had considered themselves barred from doing so by *Foakes v Beer*. A promise not supported by consideration may still be considered binding under the doctrine of promissory estoppel which the Hong Kong courts apply in much the same manner as in English law; it seems that the Australian example of broadening the scope of the doctrine was eschewed after some experimentation, but some uncertainty remains.

In **Chapter 11**, *Lee MASON* analyses the law on **third party beneficiaries in Hong Kong** that was long characterized by strict adherence to the traditional common law doctrine of privity. The law relating to third party rights was only reformed by way of Ordinance in 2016, very much along the lines of the equivalent statutory reform of English law in 1999. Only a small number of specifically enumerated types of contract are excluded from the scope of the Ordinance (and in these instances the traditional common law subterfuges for circumventing the doctrine of privity may still be deployed); all other contracts may be concluded so as to confer enforceable contractual rights on third parties. Whether a third party may enforce a term of a contract depends on the interpretation of the contract: if the third party right was not expressly conferred there is a presumption that the conferral was intended; the presumption will only be rebutted if the parties made it clear that they did not intend the term to be enforceable by the third party. The third party must be expressly identified in the contract either by name, as a member of a class, or answering a particular description, although it need not be in existence at the time when the contract was formed. The third party may claim the same remedies for breach that would have been available to it had it been an actual party to the contract. The promisor may in turn assert the defences against the third party that it has against the promisee. The promisee may enforce the promise to benefit the third party, subject to the limited availability of specific performance. The promisee may also recover substantial damages for the third party's loss in cases where the *Albazero* exception applies, with the risk of the promisor's double liability being explicitly excluded by the Ordinance. After the reform, there are only very few differences between the laws of Hong Kong and England with regard to contracts for the benefit of third parties. First, covenants relating to land are explicitly excluded from the scope of the Hong Kong Ordinance. Second, clauses in the main contract which exclude or limit the promisor's liability to the third party for breach of a contractual duty of care are subject to a reasonableness test in Hong Kong, while the applicability of this test is explicitly excluded by the English Act. Third, the Hong Kong Ordinance expressly deals with exclusive jurisdiction clauses. Fourth, it explicitly allows for a third party to assign its right to enforce a term under the contract, unless otherwise provided.

In **Chapter 12**, *Yoshikazu YAMASHITA* provides insights into the law on **contract formation in Japan**. The Japanese approach is traditional, requiring an agreement which, in turn, normally requires an offer and a matching acceptance, according to the 'mirror image rule'. Both of these 'declarations of intent' are understood objectively, unless it can be shown that both parties shared the same intention and this intention did not correspond to the objective meaning of their words or conduct. If only one of the parties had a subjective intention that did not correspond to the objective meaning of its words or conduct it might be able rely on the rules on mistake. Once offers become effective (ie when they reach the offeree) the 1898 Japanese Civil Code ('JCC') severely restricts their revocability: if they specify a period for acceptance, they may not be revoked during that period; if they do not specify such a period, they may (in contracts *inter absentes*) only be revoked after the lapse of a reasonable period. All of this is very much in tune with the mostly German origins of Japanese contract law. However, the drafters of the JCC deliberately followed the common law in one respect: the offeree's acceptance becomes effective as soon as it is dispatched. This reception of the 'mailbox rule' is highly controversial. In 2001, it was abolished for acceptances by electronic means which now have to reach the offeror to become effective. The major reform of Japanese contract law of 2017 finally extended this solution to all contracts and thus abolished the mailbox rule for good. Once the offer has been accepted, the contract will normally be concluded. Japanese law has no doctrine of consideration and has traditionally eschewed formal requirements as a prerequisite for the validity or enforceability of contracts. Only more recently have formalities been introduced by way of legislation, first for certain consumer contracts, then for contracts of suretyship. A particular feature of Japanese law pertaining to contract formation is the strong duty to negotiate in good faith that is imposed on the parties: if a party breaks off the negotiations in an unreasonable fashion the court may hold that the party is nevertheless bound to the contract or, at the very least, liable for the negative interest. Moreover, the duty to act in accordance with good faith during the negotiations imposes far-reaching duties of disclosure on the parties, particularly on businesses in consumer contracts and on parties that enjoy a particular position of trust. Breaches of a duty of disclosure may entail liability in tort.

In **Chapter 13**, *Masami OKINO* discusses the law on **third party beneficiaries in Japan**. This is mostly characterized by adherence to the German model that still bears an imprint on Japanese contract law. Thus there is neither a doctrine of consideration nor any other justification for a general doctrine of privity in Japanese contract law, and contracts for the benefit of third parties are generally enforceable as a matter of course. Whether an enforceable right on the part of a third party is actually created is simply a matter of interpretation of the contract. If the third party right is not provided for expressly, the court will take into account a number of circumstances in the process of interpretation, such as the relationship between the promisee and the third party, the expenditure made by the promisee, the determinability of the third party, custom, and trade practices. While the interpretation of the contract is always made on a case-by-case analysis, there are a number of typical scenarios where the courts have normally found the existence (or non-existence) of a contract for the benefit of a third party. In the recent debate on the reform of Japanese contract law, wide-ranging suggestions were made for a revision of the provisions on contracts for the benefit of third parties in the JCC. However, the actual legislative changes in this area of contract law were ultimately confined to a very limited codification of established case law. One of the proposed changes concerned a remnant of Japan's old, French law-inspired Civil Code that was maintained in the JCC (ie the requirement that the third party declare its intention to enjoy the benefit of the acquisition of the right). The legal nature of this 'acknowledgement' has never been clear, and it sits uncomfortably with the other provisions of the JCC that are modelled on German law and thus presume that the right of the third party accrues directly from the contract between the promisee and the promisor. Moreover, specific legislation for particularly relevant types of contract for the benefit of third parties, such as life insurance contracts, does not require the third party's acknowledgement. Yet, at present it looks as if this requirement will survive the reform. Another transplant that the drafters of the JCC borrowed from France, in deliberate deviation from the German model, is the wide and generous liability flowing from tort law. Japanese contract lawyers therefore have little incentive to push the boundaries of contractual liability in order to cover losses caused to a third party that was never intended to acquire a right to performance against the promisor, as is done under the German doctrine of 'contracts with protective effect towards third parties'.

In **Chapter 14**, *KWON Youngjoon* reports on the rules on **contract formation and third party beneficiaries in Korea**. These can be found in the Korean Civil Code of 1960 ('KCC') that is closely modelled on the Japanese Civil Code, so many of its solutions can be ultimately traced back to German law. For a binding contract to be made, Korean law only requires an agreement which is normally constituted by an offer and a matching acceptance; there is no requirement of consideration, and as a general rule there is freedom of form—only limited statutory exceptions impose formal requirements for specific types of contract. Offers must be sufficient and sufficiently definite, and they must be made with the intention to be legally bound. They become effective once they reach the offeree. From then on they are, in principle, irrevocable—a position that is only slightly softened by a 2014 Ministry of Justice draft to amend the KCC. The same draft also suggests abolishing the common law-style 'mailbox rule' that the KCC inherited from the JCC: in the future, acceptances *inter absentes* shall only be effective when they reach the offeror, not at the point when they are dispatched by the offeree. In the pre-contractual phase, Korean law imposes certain duties on the parties. First, if one of the parties has actual or constructive knowledge that the objective of the contract is unattainable, the other party is entitled to reliance damages. Second, there is a duty to negotiate in good faith, and if a party breaks off negotiations in a manner contrary to good faith and fair dealing the other party may have a claim in tort. Third, the principle of good faith may impose on one of the parties a duty to disclose certain information, and breach of this duty normally triggers tortious liability.

The KCC explicitly recognizes contracts for the benefit of third parties. A third party is endowed with a contractual right to performance or damages against the promisor if the agreement of the two original parties contains a 'third party beneficiary clause'. Whether such a clause exists, either expressly or impliedly, is a matter of interpretation of the agreement. Sometimes the finding of an implied third party beneficiary clause has the result that a third party that is not yet in existence or only identifiable in general terms acquires a directly enforceable right against the promisor and can thus claim contractual damages in the event of breach (eg a foetus against the doctor who contracted with the mother or the wife against the security service that contracted with her husband). The KCC follows the JCC in that the right only comes into existence once the third party has declared its intention to benefit from the contract; and, again like Japanese law, Korean law has statutory exceptions from this requirement for insurance contracts and other types of contract. Until the third party has made this declaration, the two original parties are free to modify or terminate their contract and thus limit or extinguish the third party right. Once the right has accrued, the promisee retains the right to claim specific performance to the third party, and if the promisor has defences against the promisee, the promisor may also assert those against the third party.

In **Chapter 15**, *WU Ying-Chieh* starts by examining the rules of offer and acceptance in the **formation of contract in Taiwan law**. An offer is binding unless: the offer states otherwise, the revocation reaches the offeree before or at the same time as the offer, or if the offeree does not respond within a reasonable time. A display in a shop window with prices is an offer, but a price list is not. An acceptance only becomes effective when it reaches the offeror. The postal rule does not apply, but if the postal acceptance is delayed for reasons not attributable to the offeree, the offeror who knows of the delay must inform the offeree of it, otherwise the offeror will be bound at the time that the acceptance would normally have arrived. In a 'battle of forms' situation where B attempts acceptance on different terms from that offered by A, there is no binding contract if the different terms are core (rather than ancillary) to the contract. B has really made a counter-offer which may be accepted by A's performance or acceptance of B's performance. Where the variations are ancillary, the court will choose between A and B's terms that can be supported by some other objective and extrinsic resources available to the court such as the context and purpose of the contract, the parties' words exchanged during negotiations, the relevant commercial practice, the good faith principle, or the parties' subsequent conduct. Silence may amount to acceptance if communication of acceptance is waived by the offeror or by custom, or acceptance by conduct can be inferred. Taiwan law looks for the parties' 'real intentions'. However, this is interpreted from objective evidence including the purpose of the contract, conventions, or custom of the market and the principle of good faith. Subjectivity is nevertheless relevant where the parties have mistakenly recorded their true agreement. There is no general requirement of form for a valid contract, but exceptionally, formalities are necessary (eg for the lease of land). The 'acquisition, creation, loss or alternation of rights in rem' must be in writing and registered, but there was no formality requirement to create a contractual right or obligation in respect of land. Notarization has been required since 1999, but its implementation has yet to be activated. Gratuitous promises are enforceable; no consideration is required for the formation or the modification of a contract. However, with certain promises (eg to lend and to keep), the promisor can change her mind until the subject matter is delivered or possessed. A gift can be revoked before performance unless it is notarized. However, a promisor can revoke a notarized gift if her economic conditions have deteriorated such that performance would seriously affect her livelihood or hinder her duty to maintain others. Furthermore, the donee's remedies for defective performance are severely curtailed. Contracts can be made electronically, and there are rules stipulating when communications become effective. The Taiwan Civil Code provides for reliance-based damages for breaches of a general duty to negotiate in good faith, such as deliberate concealment (triggering a duty to disclose) or fraud in response to a question, the intentional or reckless divulgence of the other party's secrets, the untimely breaking off of negotiations, or harm to person or property caused in the process of negotiations.

In **Chapter 16**, *Sheng-Lin JAN* discusses the position of **third party beneficiaries in Taiwan law**. He notes that the principle of privity of contract is well established. However, article 269 of the Taiwan Civil Code confers the right on the third party to sue for performance so long as the parties have at least impliedly agreed to this. This is a 'causal contract' for the benefit of third parties and applies, for example, where parents buy property for their children, children employ someone to look after an elderly parent, or couples make provision for their minor children on divorce. This should be distinguished from a 'spurious contract' for the benefit of third parties where there is no agreement to permit the third party to claim. Both the aggrieved party and the third party beneficiary can sue on the contract; there is no priority of claims. But where damages are claimed, each can only claim for its own loss. Against the third party, the debtor may rely on all defences that would have been available to him in an action brought by the other party. In appropriate cases, the debtor may also withhold his own performance where the creditor has not performed. However, where the contract is terminated or avoided after the benefit has been conferred on the third party, only the creditor (and not the third party) is liable to give restitution. The debtor can only set off on a counterclaim arising from its legal relationship with the third party (and not one with the creditor). Where the third party coerces the debtor into the contract, the contract can be avoided but where the third party induces the debtor to contract with the creditor by misrepresentation, the debtor can only avoid the contract if the creditor knows or ought to have known of the misrepresentation. Once the third party has indicated expressly or impliedly its acceptance of the benefit (to either contract party) the parties cannot modify or revoke the contract, although the contract can still be terminated for the breach of one of the parties. While German law has implied a contract to benefit third parties to circumvent the limited scope of tortious liability of a master for the acts of its servants, this technique has not been necessary in Taiwan law because, in practice, courts rarely exculpate the master for the acts of its servants and limited protection of pure economic loss is accepted.

In **Chapter 17**, *LY Tayseng* gives an overview of the law on **contract formation and third party beneficiaries in Cambodia**. Much of his discussion is tentative since the new Cambodian Civil Code only entered into force in December 2011 and there is very little case law and academic writing fleshing out its provisions. The Code was drafted with the technical assistance of Japanese lawyers and owes much to the Japanese Civil Code of 1898. Like the latter, it does not have a requirement of consideration and hardly imposes formal requirements for the making of contracts; there are only a few statutory exceptions from the principle of freedom from form. All that is required for a binding contract is the agreement of the parties which normally results from an offer and a matching acceptance. The offer must be made with the intention to create a legally binding obligation, and it becomes effective once it reaches the offeree. It is binding to the extent that it can only be revoked after the expiry of the period specified for acceptance or, where no such period was specified *inter absentes*, after the expiry of a reasonable period of time. The acceptance must match the offer and, in contrast to the solution under the JCC, only becomes effective when it reaches the offeror. The new Cambodian Civil Code explicitly provides that the parties to the contract may agree to confer a right arising under the contract upon a third party. This right accrues directly from their agreement; thus, in another notable deviation from the Japanese model, it is not required that the third party declare its intention to accept the right. However, until such a declaration is made, the promisor is entitled to modify or revoke the conferral of the right upon the third party.

In **Chapter 18**, *Gary F BELL* notes that **Indonesia** is one of the most legally diverse, and consequently legally complex, countries in the world. It practises legal pluralism with three types of contract law in force: adat (customary) contract laws, Islamic contract laws (mostly related to banking), and the Civil Code (the *Kitab Undang-Undang Hukum Perdata*, 'KUHPer') transplanted from Dutch law which is itself largely based on French law. The KUHPer effectively governs all commercial transactions (excluding land and certain security transactions). It remains in Dutch despite 98 per cent of judges and lawyers not understanding Dutch, and remains almost totally as it was when transplanted in 1847 although both the Dutch and French Civil Codes have since been substantially reformed. In addition, Indonesian contract law is not well developed; there are few treatises, the judgments do not have a high reputation and are unilluminating, and most large commercial disputes are settled by arbitration. The four requirements of a valid contract are: consent, capacity, specific object, and cause. The test of intention is subjective insofar as the literal interpretation of words can be trumped by the parties' common intention, and mistaken offers and gentlemen's agreements are not binding. Although the Indonesian language is legally required to be used in memoranda of understanding or agreements involving government institutions, private Indonesian institutions, or citizens, no sanction is stated. Nevertheless, the Supreme Court has invalidated a contract that infringed this language requirement. There is no general requirement of form for a valid contract but this is subject to stated exceptions (eg settlements out of court (but surprisingly no category of consumer contracts)). Some contracts must be executed as an authentic (or notarial) deed to be valid (eg gifts and some transactions involving land). A notarial deed constitutes conclusive evidence of its contents and all contract parties may employ the device. Written contracts must be stamped, otherwise the document cannot be entered into evidence—the contract is valid but unenforceable; however, it can be stamped after formation by the payment of a small penalty (US$1). Electronic transactions are binding; communications are received when they enter the electronic system of the recipient. Offers are binding if they are stated to be open for a fixed period. There is no concept of an 'invitation to treat'. A display is an offer but may be interpreted as not made to a certain sector of the population. A valid contract of sale must include the price agreed by the parties or to be determined by a third party. If the third party is unable or unwilling to do so, there is no contract; the courts cannot step in to fix a reasonable price. However, courts can infer the parties' true intention from the circumstances, and can fill gaps with usage or what is required by equity and fairness. There is an obligation to perform contracts in good faith but not explicitly to make contracts in good faith, although this would be a small step to take and would be consistent with Dutch and French law. An acceptance must mirror the offer. Commentators reject the postal acceptance rule as inconsistent with Dutch law; postal acceptance, as with all other communications, is effective only on receipt. There is no requirement of consideration. Gratuitous contracts are binding. However, gifts of things (but not of services or delivered things) need to be notarized, and loans for consumption and deposits are treated as unilateral (in the sense that only one party has an obligation) real contracts that only become binding by delivery. Gifts and exchanges yield the same remedies for breach and are subject to the same grounds of invalidity except that, additionally, a gift is revocable if the donee commits a crime against the donor or refuses to support the donor who has subsequently fallen on hard times.

Although Indonesian law recognizes the principle of relativity (or privity), article 1317 KUHPer provides such a wide exception that the principle is substantially undermined. It allows stipulations in contracts made for the benefit of a third party to be enforceable by the third party. Article 1317 KUHPer had conditioned such enforcement on the following: (1) the creditor must also get something in return from the debtor; or (2) the creditor must also give a gift to the debtor. But following French and Dutch decisions, these odd conditions have been dispensed with. Where the third party has declared his intent to rely on the benefit, the stipulation cannot be revoked; it is unclear whether the parties can vary or revoke the benefit with the third party's consent. The third party can access the same remedies as the creditor could and would be subject to the same defences as can be raised against the creditor, but it is unclear whether a defence can be raised against the *third party* for reasons specific to the third party. Since Indonesian law allows direct suit by the third party, there is no need for the promisee to enforce the benefit for the third party. Indonesian law allows recovery for pure economic loss; therefore, third party actions in contract cannot be regarded as filling any gap in tort law.

In **Chapter 19**, *Pattarapas TUDSRI* and *Angkanawadee PINKAEW* examine the issues that relate to the **formation of contract** under the law of **Thailand**. The chapter usefully begins by discussing the background to the enactment of the Thai Civil and Commercial Code 1925 ('Thai CCC') and the foreign influences on the drafting of its provisions; this explains the necessarily peripatetic references to French and German legal concepts found in the later discussion. Readers will find a fascinating segment dealing with the interpretation of intention, which is integral to the notion of a juristic act for the creation of contractual obligations. The direction in section 171 to discern the true intention, combined with notions of fictitious intention and concealed juristic act (section 155), invites the court to recharacterize transactions according to their true intention. A financing transaction couched in the form of a sale and repurchase agreement may thus be recharacterized as a concealed loan. Foreign contracting parties operating in jurisdictions which accord much respect to the form chosen by the parties to achieve purposes not usually associated with those forms have thus to be extremely mindful of the recharacterization risks present in Thai law. The segment on formalities will dispel any notion that the subject matter is a dry one. Through the power to 'transform a void act' (section 174), a court may declare an act valid otherwise void for non-compliance with formalities governing one kind of juristic act, if it complies with the requirements of another juristic act. Accordingly, a failed *inter vivos* gift may take effect as a testamentary gift, and an unregistered contract for sale of land without a title deed may be interpreted as a contract for the delivery of possession of that land. The differences in Thai and German institutions (eg the notary) have resulted in adjustments to the formality requirements in Thailand. The adjustments do not detract from the broad requirement for writing and registration found in section 456; apart from applying to immovable property generally, the requirement for formalities also extends to movable property where the agreed price is 20,000 baht (approx US$560) or more. For transactions that have not fully complied with the formalities required, the German concept of *Vorvertrag* or pre-contract should assume heightened significance since the pre-contract can form the basis for the court to order execution of the principal contract. The authors pose the puzzle why the Thai judges have not discussed or developed the concept. The binding nature of promises proceeds from a conception of autonomy that is consistent with the sensibilities of Civilian lawyers. A promisor will be held to his promise to hold an offer open for a stipulated period of time. This, suggest the authors, holds the potential for curtailing the broad freedom to decide whether to proceed further after a tender exercise. The segment on how Thai law works out the battle of forms is also interesting for revealing the judicial reluctance to find agreement where it is disputed.

In **Chapter 20**, *Pattarapas TUDSRI* and *Angkanawadee PINKAEW* examine the allowance for **third party beneficiaries** to enforce contracts under section 374 of the **Thai** CCC. The provision illustrates a point made in the introduction of the earlier chapter—that the urgency for enactment of the Thai CCC came at the expense of depth and intricacy. Whereas the German Civil Code (*Bürgerliches Gesetzbuch*, 'BGB') expressly provides that the third party's entitlement to enforce the provisions of a contract may be inferred from the circumstances, such a provision is absent in the Thai CCC. The predicate to the third party's entitlement is simply stated as: 'If a party by contract agrees to make a performance to a third person . . .' While the intention of parties should be capable of being inferred from the contract, the Thai courts have demonstrated reluctance to reading section 374 broadly; compelling evidence is thus required before the third party is found to acquire rights under a contract. Apart from the four categories of contracts where the courts more readily find third party rights—insurance, compromise, a contract to discharge a debt owed by a third party, and a contract to confer an option on a third party—parties are likely to find it difficult to invoke section 374. Underlying the judicial attitude is the strong grip of the privity rule, or to use the German-inspired term, the 'relativity of contract'. The restrictive approach carries through to the interpretation of 'performance'—for the term does not include conferment of benefits such as the exemption or limitation of liability. The judicial preference for the literal approach to interpretation means that parties who intend to provide for the right, to revoke the right conferred on the third party, would be well advised to ensure that clear provision is made.

In **Chapter 21**, *LE Net* examines the recent changes to the **Vietnamese** Civil Code ('VCC') and its impact on **contract formation and third party beneficiaries**. A number of matters stand out in Le's discussion. First, since the enactment of the first modern civil code in 1995, major revisions have been made every ten years. The VCC 2015, for example, repeals more than 50 per cent of the VCC 2005; this represents more than 300 articles of the VCC 2005. Concepts like apparent authority were only recognized in 2005, while the notion of an offer to the world (rather than to specific parties) was only recognized recently in the VCC 2015. Second, the VCC 1995 is a product of the move from a planned economy to a socialist-oriented market economy. Any notion that the French Civil Code was used as the model should be dispelled immediately, as the draftsmen of the VCC 1995 were trained in the socialist legal tradition and looked first to Eastern Europe for inspiration. The revisions found in the VCC 2005 and the VCC 2015 are interesting in reflecting the progressive adoption of legal concepts otherwise unexceptional in market economies but which the Vietnamese legal system saw fit to adopt only in stages. Third, the strength of the socialist norms means that an accurate picture of how the law operates can only be obtained by inquiring how state interest and regulatory concerns operate to modify the norms of contractual freedom found in the VCC. While such an inquiry should also be made in laissez-faire economies, the pervasiveness of the state interest in Vietnam means that it is a necessary second step in understanding how contract law operates in Vietnam. It explains the many prescribed form contracts, as well as the formality and registration requirements seen as integral to the planning of the socialist market economy. These features provide a new complexion to the formation rules and the provision for third party beneficiaries to enforce contractual terms, which otherwise look similar to those found in other jurisdictions.

In **Chapter 22,** *Adrian BRIGGS* and *Andrew BURROWS* set out the **Myanmar law on contract formation and third party beneficiaries**. Myanmar law of contract largely comprises the Myanmar Contract Act 1872 ('CA', which is identical to the Indian Contract Act 1872 subject to some factual changes in the illustrations). It was drafted by English lawyers but appears to have been essentially regarded as a statutory codification of the English common law of contract. In addition, section 13(3) of the Burma Laws Act 1898 allows or requires a court to fill in gaps in the written laws by the application of the principles of justice, equity, and good conscience. For a contract to be recognized in law, the first requirement is a 'proposal' (an unconditional willingness to be bound by a simple conforming acceptance, ie an offer). A proposal may be revoked at any time prior to its acceptance (by: notice to the acceptor, lapse of time, the acceptor's failure to fulfil a condition precedent, or the acceptor's knowledge of the proposer's death or insanity), unless consideration has been given for an agreement to keep the proposal open for a stipulated time (ie an option). Second, acceptance of the proposal, either by expression of agreement (the postal acceptance rule applies unless otherwise specified) or by (perhaps the start of) performance of the specified condition, converts the proposal into a 'promise'. Third, consideration (in the form of a counter-promise to do, or actually, doing or abstaining from doing something 'at the desire of the promisor') is necessary to convert an agreement into an enforceable contract, so long as the parties are competent and the agreement is lawful. Sometimes, the facts have to be forced uneasily into the analysis. Under section 62 CA the parties can substitute a new contract and thus circumvent the consideration problem where one party agrees to pay more or to accept less from the other. Section 63 expressly permits one party to release the other from partial or whole performance; no consideration is necessary. Section 25 CA subjects the consideration requirement to three exceptions: (a) an agreement made in writing between parties who are in a close relationship, for reasons of natural love and affection, and satisfying the Registration Act 1909 or other legislation providing for the registration of documents; (b) a promise for past consideration; (c) a written and signed promise to pay a debt which would otherwise be irrecoverable by reason of the Limitation Act 1909 or other statutory provision.

There is no general formality requirement. While there is no technical requirement of 'intention to create legal relations' in the sense of a presumption against enforcement of agreements within the private domain, this must be the law consistent with 'justice, equity and good conscience' under section 13(3) of the Burma Laws Act 1898. The parties' intentions are judged objectively. Courts will fill any gaps in the parties' contracts via implication, especially if the parties have started performance, unless this is impossible. Courts will also resolve any uncertainties in the agreement by objective interpretation if they are 'capable of being made certain' under section 29 CA, otherwise the contract is void.

Myanmar contract law does not contain a doctrine of privity of contract. The question, therefore, of who is bound by, and who entitled by, a contract is most conveniently considered as an aspect of the construction of the terms of the contract. At common law the burdens of contracts cannot be imposed on those who are strangers to the contract; nothing in the CA suggests that Myanmar law takes a different view. However, Myanmar law does not adopt the common law view that only the parties can enforce the contract, thus leaving third parties free to enforce contracts made for their benefit. However, it remains unclear how a qualifying third party should be identified (a question of contractual interpretation), and how any compensation should be measured. This is complicated by section 2(d) which treats something desired by the promisor moving from a third party as consideration.

In **Chapter 23**, *Alexander LOKE* draws out the insights and lessons that the contributions in this volume reveal. A broad divide in the philosophical foundations of contract can be found in the bargain theory of contract and the theory of contract as the concordant expression of wills. These help make sense of the starting points adopted by jurisdictions situated in different legal traditions, though the final resolution might very well take surprising turns given that jurisdictions tend to be pluralistic in selecting the rules to be transplanted. At the same time, functional convergence often occurs despite disparate analytical approaches, whether because of a common sense of the just solution, the influence of international norms, or the imperative to honour parties' agreements. A useful operating precept is to be conscious of the forces of convergence while being alert to the values and policy considerations which finally determine the legal outcomes.

These chapters introduce the diversity and commonalities between the contract law regimes of the different Asian jurisdictions and aim to enhance the conversations between the Asian jurisdictions and with the rest of the world.

2

Contract Formation under Chinese Law

*DING Chunyan**

I. Introduction

Since the promulgation of the 1999 Contract Law of the People's Republic of China ('CCL'),[1] the issue of contract formation has not aroused much enthusiasm among Chinese legal scholars.[2] This is partially because many understand the issue merely as a matter of black letter law since Chapter 2 of the CCL, titled 'Contract Formation', provides a set of provisions on contract formation, which to a large extent follows the relevant provisions of the 1980 UN Convention on Contracts for the International Sale of Goods ('CISG') and the 1994 UNIDROIT Principles of International Commercial Contracts. However, controversies surrounding contract formation have arisen from judicial practice, therefore Part One of the 2009 Interpretation II of the Supreme People's Court of Several Issues Concerning the Application of the Contract Law of the People's Republic of China ('Interpretation II')[3] provides supplementary provisions on contract formation to tackle some legal loopholes. Nevertheless, little literature has given a deep analysis of the principles of contract formation under Chinese law.

This chapter focuses on three fundamental issues of contract formation under Chinese law: conditions for conclusion of a contract, offer and acceptance, and pre-contractual obligations. Although the major sources of Chinese contract law are the CCL and the Supreme People's Court's three sets of judicial interpretations concerning the application of the CCL,[4] this chapter also reviews the relevant provisions on contract formation scattered throughout other laws, administrative regulations, and judicial interpretations. Judicial decisions, though not legally binding in Chinese law, also shed light on the practical understanding of the principles of contract formation.

* Cite as C Ding, 'Contract Formation under Chinese Law' in Chen-Wishart, Loke, & Vogenauer, *Studies in the Contract Laws of Asia Vol II: Formation and Third Party Beneficiaries* (Oxford: OUP 2017) ch 2.

[1] [中华人民共和国合同法] (made by the National People's Congress on 13 March 1999; effective on 1 October 1999).

[2] The author's search in the China Academic Journals Full-Text Database found only six articles on contract formation in the 21 core law journals published since the promulgation of the CCL. There is little English literature on contract formation under Chinese law. Only two articles on the topic were found in the HeinOnline Database.

[3] [最高人民法院关于适用《中华人民共和国合同法》若干问题的解释(二)] (made by the Supreme People's Court ('SPC') on 24 April 2009; effective on 13 May 2009).

[4] Besides Interpretation II, the other two include the 1999 Interpretation I of the SPC on Several Issues Concerning the Application of the CCL [最高人民法院关于适用《中华人民共和国合同法》若干问题的解释(一)] and the 2012 Interpretations of the SPC on Issues Concerning the Application of Law for the Trial of Cases on Sale Contract Disputes [最高人民法院关于审理买卖合同纠纷案件适用法律问题的解释].

Contract Formation Under Chinese Law. Ding Chunyan.

II. Conditions for Conclusion of a Contract

Under Chinese law, contract is one of the sources of obligations,[5] and it is defined as an agreement whereby natural persons, legal persons, or other organizations, as equal parties, establish, modify, or extinguish relationships of civil rights and obligations.[6] Concluding a contract is a juristic act, which is intended to have legal effect; it must satisfy three conditions: the parties must have 'capacity to perform juristic act',[7] they must intend to be legally bound,[8] and they must have reached an agreement.[9] Under Chinese law, a contract generally does not need to be concluded in writing or meet any other formality requirement, unless the parties have agreed otherwise or special laws governing certain types of contracts provide otherwise.[10] Neither does a contract nor a modification require consideration; gratuitous contracts are recognized in Chinese law.

1. Construction of Declarations of Intention

Concluding a contract is a juristic act requiring a meeting of minds that is demonstrated in the declarations of intention of each party.[11] Deciding whether the parties have an intention to be legally bound or whether they have reached an agreement is essentially a matter of construction of declarations of intention. In the course of concluding a contract, for a party's declaration of intention to take effect, it must be communicated to and reach the other party and the latter will have reliance thereon. Therefore, one party's autonomy and the other party's reliance need to be fully considered and balanced,[12] and an objective approach is preferred in construing the parties' declarations of intention.[13]

Although the 1986 General Principles of Civil Law of the People's Republic of China ('GPCL') does not provide any rules on the construction of declarations of intention, Article 125(1) of the CCL[14] stipulates the approach for the interpretation of contract terms that may, by analogy, be used to construe the parties' declarations of intention. Specifically, relevant considerations include: the words and expressions used by a particular party to

[5] Art 84, 1986 General Principles of Civil Law of the People's Republic of China ('PRC') [中华人民共和国民法通则, 'GPCL'] (made by the National People's Congress on 12 April 1986; effective on 1 January 1987; amended in 2009).

[6] Art 2, CCL excludes the making of any agreement concerning civil status, eg marriage, adoption, and guardianship from the CCL's purview.

[7] Art 9, CCL provides that a person without full capacity to perform a juristic act needs a legal representative to conclude a contract on his behalf or consent to conclusion of a contract. Arts 11–13, GPCL set general rules on capacity to perform a juristic act.

[8] When the promisor has no intention to be legally bound (eg in a domestic or social agreement), it is merely a gentlemen's agreement, and not a contract: Wang Zejian [王泽鉴], Zhaifa yuanli vol 1 [*Principles of Law of Obligation Vol 1* 债法原理第一册] (Taipei: San Min Book 1999) 223. Moreover, Art 2, Interpretation II emphasizes the parties' intention to conclude a contract as the gist of a contract.

[9] Art 2, CCL. [10] Art 10, CCL.

[11] Han Shiyuan [韩世远], Hetong fa zonglun (*General Principles of Contract Law* 合同法总论) (Beijing: Law Press 2008) 2.

[12] Some courts have mentioned the offeree's reliance interest when construing the offeror's declaration of intention, eg *Zhihang Branch in Wuhan Province of a Bank Corporation v Luan, Zhou & Ors* ((2013) 鄂武昌民商初字第00127号, which is the case docket number) and *Shandong Shengbang Lvye Huaxue Co Ltd v Kunming Shuaibang Jingmao Co Ltd and Yang Xiaofeng* ((2014) 天商园初字第155号).

[13] Wang Zejian [王泽鉴], Minfa zongze [*General Provisions of Civil Law* 民法总则] (Taipei: San Min Book 2000) 438.

[14] Art 125(1), CCL provides that if there is a dispute between the parties over the understanding of a term of the contract, the true meaning of that term shall be determined in the light of the words and expressions used in the contract, the related terms in the contract, the purpose of the contract, the usage of transaction, and the doctrine of good faith.

declare his intention, the circumstances at the moment of the declaration, the purpose of the declaration, the 'usage of transaction',[15] and the doctrine of good faith. Thus, the parties' intention to be legally bound and whether they have reached an agreement are to be ascertained objectively. A party whose real intention differs from the construed intention remains legally bound to it, although Article 54(1) of the CCL allows that party to apply for modification or rescission of a contract when he has made a 'significant mistake' as to the content of the contract in the course of concluding the contract.[16]

In *Danzhou Chunjiang Nanhua Tangye Co Ltd v Danzhou Branch of Bank of China Corporation & Danzhou Branch of China Construction Bank Corporation & Ors*,[17] a third party company, which was established owing to the local government's policy on attracting overseas investments, submitted a report to the two defendants, explaining its shortage of cash and applying to purchase sugar on credit from the plaintiff, a state-owned enterprise. The bank president of the two defendants took the local government's advice and gave written approval to the credit purchase stated in the report. The report was passed to the plaintiff, who agreed to the sale and delivered 1,000 tons of sugar to the third party company. As the third party company made no payment of the price of RMB 3.9 million, the plaintiff sued the two defendants for breach of contract. One issue was whether the two defendants were a party to the contract for the sale of sugar. To decide their intention, the Supreme People's Court considered a number of factors, including the wording of the bank president's written approval, the invoices and records of the transaction, the delivery method of sugar, the plaintiff's actual knowledge of the defendants' subjective intention, the state economic system at that time, the circumstances of the transaction, and the purpose of the contract. The court found that the two defendants had no intention to be the purchaser of sugar or to assume the obligation for payment; they were not a contracting party and were not liable for breach of contract.

The GPCL does not have a provision similar to Article 98 of the Taiwanese Civil Code, which provides that the real intention of the parties must be sought rather than just accepting the literal meaning of the words as declarations of intention. Nevertheless, in special situations Chinese courts may give effect to a party's subjective intention which differs from his words and expressions. First, where parties have used words or expressions different from what they have agreed (ie an unintentional false demonstration), the courts will give effect to the subjective intentions of the parties according to the doctrine of *falsa demonstratio non nocet*.[18] Second, if it is a false demonstration in conspiracy, the courts will ascertain the hidden subjective intentions of the parties so as to displace the inference raised by their words or expressions. For example, the Supreme People's Court has clarified that 'a contract of factoring in name but of loan in reality'[19] and 'a contract of joint operation in name but of loan in reality'[20] shall be construed as a loan contract. Third, where the offeror has intentionally made a false demonstration of intention and the offeree knows this at the

[15] It is defined by Art 7, Interpretation II as 'the practice which is universally adopted at the place of transaction or in a certain field or sector and is known or should be known by the other party to the transaction when the contract is concluded' and 'the course of dealings between the parties'.

[16] When a party makes a mistake as to the terms of a contract, which is known to the other party, they arguably have not agreed on the relevant terms according to the objective test of intention.

[17] (2011) 民提字第318号.

[18] It is defined as 'a false designation; an erroneous description of a person or thing in a legal instrument. Generally, a simple error in description, grammar, or spelling will not void an instrument or even a single provision in it (eg a bequest by will)': see BA Garner, *Black's Law Dictionary* (9th edn, St Paul, MN: West Publishing 2004) 677.

[19] See the 7th issue of the 2015 Opinions of the SPC on Several Specific Issues Concerning the Current Work of the Commercial Cases Trial [最高人民法院关于当前商事审判工作中的若干具体问题].

[20] See the 4th issue of the 1990 Replies of the SPC on Several Issues Concerning the Trial of Cases on Joint Operation Contract Disputes [最高人民法院关于审理联营合同纠纷案件若干问题的解答].

time of acceptance,[21] Chinese courts have upheld the offeror's subjective intention over his inconsistent words or expressions, because this upholds his autonomy and because the offeree with knowledge has not relied on the offeror's false demonstration.[22]

2. A Sufficient Agreement

(a) *Essential elements of a contract*

To conclude a contract, the parties must agree upon the 'essential elements' of the contract. Thus, a contract is considered to have been concluded even though the parties are silent on the 'subsidiary elements' of the contract. It is therefore critical to define the essential elements of a contract in each case. Article 12 of the CCL provides that the content of a contract to be agreed upon by the parties shall generally include the following eight elements: (1) business names or names and addresses of the parties; (2) subject matter; (3) quantity; (4) quality; (5) price or remuneration; (6) time, place, and manner of performance; (7) liability for breach of contract; and (8) means of dispute resolution. Article 12 is suggestive not mandatory, and not all the listed elements are essential elements of a contract.[23]

Article 1 of Interpretation II clarifies that a contract is concluded if the court is able to determine the names of the parties, the subject matter, and the quantity (ie the three elements), unless otherwise provided by laws or agreed upon by the parties. It further provides that the parties may agree upon the subsidiary elements *after* the conclusion of the contract, and if they fail to reach agreement, the court shall make a determination thereof in accordance with Articles 61, 62, and 125(1) of the CCL,[24] which contain the gap-filling principles of contract interpretation. Therefore, Chinese law has set the names of the parties, the subject matter, and the quantity as the bottom line of a contract's essential elements.[25] This shows a legal policy which is in favour of upholding the parties' agreement, thereby providing the parties with much flexibility in contract formation. On the other hand, such a liberal approach has two disadvantages. First, it may establish a contractual relationship with too much uncertainty between the parties, thus sowing the seeds of dispute therein. Second, it gives the courts too much power and discretion in supplementing the subsidiary elements of a contract; it may lead to inconsistency in judicial practice and result in the courts largely making contracts for the parties.

Article 1 of Interpretation II states that laws may provide or the parties may agree upon more elements of a contract as essential.[26] For example, Article 18 of the 1995 Insurance

[21] If the offeree is unaware of the offeror's intentional false demonstration, the offeror's intention is to be ascertained according to his words or expressions, despite his different subjective intention: confirmed in *Zhihang Branch in Wuhan Province of a Bank Corporation v Luan, Zhou & Ors* ((2013) 鄂武昌民商初字第00127号) and *Zhu Yufeng v Li Gongzheng and Jiang Pinzhen* ((2014) 苏中民终字第02932号).

[22] eg *Shenyang Jilongyuan Wuliu Co Ltd v Gu Yushuang, Gu Yu, and Wang Zhenzhong* ((2013) 于民三初字第01752号) and *Chen Xuefei v Chen Weiwei* ((2015) 沪一中民二(民)终字第2964号).

[23] The CCL also suggests main contractual terms for contracts for the supply and use of electricity, water, gas, and heat (Art 117), loan contracts (Art 197), lease contracts (Art 213), financial leasing contracts (Art 238), contracts for work (Art 252), construction project contracts (Art 275), and technology contracts (Art 324). They are all suggestive provisions.

[24] See n 14 for the text of Art 125(1), CCL.

[25] eg *Li Yunchang v Zhao Xiang, Ding Zhengmei, and Qin Zhilan* ((2015) 渝二中法民终字第01037号), where the No 2 Intermediary People's Court of Chongqing held that a property sale contract was not concluded because the parties failed to agree on the essential terms concerning the property to be sold and the size of the property.

[26] Art 1, Interpretation II does not address the situation where one party refuses to conclude a contract unless the parties have agreed upon some specific matter other than the three essential elements. There will nevertheless be no contract if agreement on that matter has not been reached, because otherwise it would be against that party's intention.

Law of the People's Republic of China[27] requires the parties to agree on more than the above three essential elements for an insurance contract,[28] and Article 10 of the 1997 Several Provisions on Changes in Equity Interests of Investors in Foreign-Invested Enterprise[29] does the same for an equity interests transfer agreement.[30]

In practice, Chinese courts use, first, soft laws to augment the essential elements of a particular type of contract. For example, in *Kunming Fengqing Guoji Lvyou (Group) Co Ltd v Beijingshi Yuanhua Guoji Lvyou Co Ltd*,[31] the High People's Court of Sichuan Province took into account the standard 'Outbound Travel Contract' jointly introduced by the National Tourism Administration and the State Administration of Industry and Commerce in 2007 although it is not law in the strict sense. The court concluded that the essential elements of a travel contract should include travel expenses, the trip itinerary, the rights and obligations of the parties, liability for breach of contract, and means of dispute resolution. The parties failed to agree upon these essential elements and therefore they did not reach a sufficient agreement to conclude a travel contract.

Second, the courts decide the essential elements of a contract according to the nature of the contract. For example, in *Cheng Guangyi v Heilongjiang Xingyun Fangdichan Kaifa Co Ltd*,[32] the Dongfeng District People's Court of Jiamusi City of Heilongjiang Province held that the essential elements of a sale of property contract should also include the price of the property and the delivery time. Despite the absence of a legal basis for deciding that the essential elements are based upon the nature of the contract, judicial practice implies that the three essential elements of a contract set forth in Article 1 of Interpretation II (names of the parties, subject matter, and quantity) do not fit all contracts and the nature of the contract is a relevant factor in determining the essential elements of a contract.

(b) 'Battle of forms'

The problem with the battle of forms arises where the parties disagree on a certain term of their contract and both clearly declare what they mean by that term; sometimes they nevertheless proceed to perform. This raises two related issues. The first is the 'formation' issue: is a contract concluded when each of the parties, either making the offer or purporting to accept the offer, refers to its own terms? If a contract is concluded, the second is the 'term' issue: which party's term will prevail?

The doctrine of party autonomy aligns with the common law mirror image rule, which requires a clear and unequivocal offer to be matched or 'mirrored' by an equally clear and

[27] [中华人民共和国保险法] (made by the Standing Committee of the National People's Congress ('NPCSC') on 30 June 1995; effective on 1 October 1995; amended in 2002, 2009, 2014, and 2015).

[28] They include insurance liability and liability exemption, duration of insurance and time of commencement of insurance liability, insured amount, premium and payment method, liability for breach of contract, and means of dispute resolution: see Fan Qirong [樊启荣], 'Baoxian hetong chengli yinan wenti yanjiu' [Study on Difficult Issues Concerning Conclusion of Insurance Contract保险合同成立疑难问题研究] (2008) 126 Fashang yanjiu [*Study on Law and Commerce*法商研究] 61, 62.

[29] [外商投资企业投资者股权变更的若干规定] (issued by the Ministry of Foreign Trade and Economic Cooperation (revised) and the State Administration for Industry and Commerce on 28 May 1997).

[30] The essential terms of an equity interests transfer agreement include names and residences of transferors and transferees and names, posts, and nationalities of their legal representatives; amount of equities to be transferred and prices, time limit, and method for delivery of the equities to be transferred; rights and responsibilities of transferee as specified in the contracts and articles of association of enterprises; liabilities for breach of contract; applicable law; means of dispute resolution; effectuation and termination of agreements; and time and venue of concluding the agreement. Though some argue that not all the above terms are essential elements of an equity interests transfer contract, but factually they are essential because the public authority will refuse to approve a contract that fails to contain all the listed terms.

[31] (2013) 川民申字第2525号.

[32] (2014) 东民初字第120号.

unequivocal acceptance to conclude a contract.[33] This also aligns with the civil law conformity of declarations of intention rule, which requires perfect identity between the contents of the two declarations of intention of the parties (ie offer and acceptance) for the conclusion of a contract.[34] If there is any difference between offer and acceptance, the purported acceptance counts as a rejection of the offer and a new offer or counter-offer. In the battle of forms, the party who fires the 'last shot' may take advantage of the other party's performance as the acceptance of the last-shot offer; a contract is thus concluded on the terms of the last-shooter.

The CCL has no particular provision dealing with the battle of forms, but Articles 30 and 31 of the CCL are relevant. Unlike § 2-207 of the US Uniform Commercial Code ('UCC'), which abrogates the mirror image rule,[35] Article 30 of the CCL confirms that the content of the acceptance shall accord with that of the offer, but it relaxes the mirror image rule by further providing that only a purported acceptance which makes a *material* change to the content of the offer amounts to a new offer.[36] Article 31 of the CCL states that a purported acceptance which makes a non-material change to the content of the offer remains an effective acceptance; the terms of the contract shall accord with those of the acceptance, unless the offeror expresses his objection to the alteration in a timely manner or the offer expressly limits acceptance to the content of the offer.

Articles 30 and 31 of the CCL basically follow Article 19 of the CISG except that they are not limited to sale of goods contracts. Because Article 30 of the CCL defines broadly the term 'material alteration of the content of the offer' as 'any alteration of the subject matter of the contract, quantity, quality, price or remuneration, time of performance, place or manner of performance, liability for breach of contract, means of dispute resolution and so forth', the relaxation of the mirror image rule is unlikely to result in many enforceable contracts. This non-exhaustive list of what constitutes material alteration provided in Article 30 of the CCL also gives the courts discretion as to what other terms may be considered material in individual cases.

Turning to the cases on battle of forms, according to Article 31 of the CCL, when the parties merely disagree upon a non-material term, the last-shooter, as the offeree, has effectively accepted the other party's offer with *non-material* alteration. The form of the last-shooter then becomes the contractual terms legally binding both parties unless the offeror expresses his objection to the alteration in a timely manner or expresses in his offer that the acceptance may not make any change to the content of the offer. More often, the parties in the battle of forms will disagree upon a *material* term. According to Article 30 of the CCL, the last-shooter's terms are thus considered a new offer and no contract has yet been concluded. Nevertheless, if the parties begin performance, the issue arises whether the performance of the other party will amount to an acceptance or the parties' performance and acceptance of performance will suffice to conclude a contract.

Articles 22 and 26(1) of the CCL require an acceptance to be made by the giving of notice, and the acceptance takes effect when the notice reaches the offeror. However, the usage of transaction or the express terms of the offer may allow the offeree to opt out of the notice requirement so that an act that is allowed by the usage of transaction or permitted by the offer may amount to an acceptance. Therefore, even without notice of acceptance from the offeree, it is possible for the last-shooter's variation of material terms to be accepted by

[33] E McKendrick, *Contract Law* (10th edn, London: Palgrave Macmillan 2013) 22.

[34] F Vergne, 'The "Battle of the Forms" Under the 1980 United Nations Convention on Contracts for the International Sale of Goods' (1985) 33 Am J Comp L 233, 247.

[35] D Keating, 'Exploring the Battle of the Forms in Action' (1999–2000) 98 Mich L Rev 2678, 2684.

[36] It also terminates the offer: see Art 20(4), CCL.

the offeree's conduct of performance where: (1) there is a usage of transaction in the relevant industry or sector that a contract of that kind can be made by performance; or (2) the last-shooter has indicated assent in his form to acceptance by conduct of performance, then a contract will be concluded on the terms of his form when the other party conducts the performance.

In the absence of either of these two situations, no contract is concluded in a case on battle of forms although the parties have performed a transaction. However, where there have been performance and acceptance of the performance, it is unrealistic to find no contract between the parties. As there are very few typical battle of forms cases in China,[37] it is unclear whether Chinese courts will strictly apply the CCL in such cases. However, it is more likely that they will take a pragmatic view and find a contract, even in *material* alteration cases: (1) based on the parties' acts of performance; or (2) by recognizing an acceptance by the offeree's conduct of performance in more situations than Article 22 of the CCL ostensibly allows.[38]

For example, in *Sheyang Yuanxin Fuzhuang Co Ltd v Jiangsu Suhao Hongrui Jinchukou Co Ltd*,[39] the defendant signed and sealed a formal contract for processing clothes and passed it to the plaintiff, who subsequently signed and sealed it but with an alteration to the term on time of delivery. Later the plaintiff denied the existence of the contract. The Sheyang County District People's Court of Jiangsu Province held that the formal contract signed and sealed by the plaintiff was a new offer because it made a material alteration of the content of the original contract. Although the defendant did not overtly accept the new offer, the court held that the contract was established by the performance of the plaintiff (who started and continued processing the clothes for two months until their dispute) and the defendant's acknowledgement of that performance.

Although this is not a typical battle of forms case, it involves the same legal issue: whether the performance of the two parties per se is sufficient to establish the existence of a contract when their writings did not establish a contract due to a material alteration of the content of the offer. The court in this case found a contract made by the parties' acts of performance, an approach that resembles § 2-207(3) of the UCC.[40] The case only addressed the formation issue for the purpose of settling a dispute over forum. But, if the court had to resolve the term issue, it was likely that the court would replace the conflicting time of delivery term with a supplementary term, on the basis of the principles of contract interpretation, similar to the gap-filling approach of Article 1 of Interpretation II in dealing with the 'essential elements of a contract' problem.

In addition, courts have shown their willingness to recognize acceptance by conduct of performance in more situations than Article 22 of the CCL allows. For example, in *Dongguanshi Xinyu Chaoshengbo Jixie Co Ltd v Shenzhenshi Ankexun Dianzi Zhizao Co Ltd*,[41] the plaintiff faxed a written 'sale contract' of a welding machine to the defendant, who faxed back the contract with a note 'trial of a sample machine' besides the words 'sale contract' and a statement that 'our company will pay logistic costs if we decide not to buy the machine'. The plaintiff immediately delivered a machine to the defendant after receiving the

[37] The author searched the database of 'China's Judgments Online' [中国裁判文书网] (initiated by the SPC, <http://wenshu.court.gov.cn> accessed on 31 July 2016) and found no typical battle of forms cases.

[38] Whether the courts have legal basis to do so is a controversial subject.

[39] (2015) 射商初字第00731号.

[40] § 2-207(3) UCC provides that '[c]onduct by both parties which recognizes the existence of a contract is sufficient to establish a contract for sale although the writings of the parties do not otherwise establish a contract. In such case the terms of the particular contract consist of those terms on which the writings of the parties agree, together with any supplementary terms incorporated under any other provisions of this Act'.

[41] (2013) 深中法商终字第1332号.

latter's reply. The parties later disputed the nature of the contract, among other issues. The Shenzhen Intermediate People's Court of Guangdong Province held that the defendant's reply was a new offer because it made a material alteration to the content of the plaintiff's offer by changing the nature of the contract from a sale contract to a sale on approval contract, and the plaintiff accepted the new offer by delivering the machine. Although this case involved neither of the two situations mentioned in Article 22 of the CCL (ie the usage of transaction or the express terms of the offer recognize acceptance by conduct), the court found an acceptance by the offeree's conduct of performance.[42]

Similarly, although this case does not involve a typical battle of forms problem, it raises the same legal issue: whether the last-shooter's terms can be accepted by the other party's conduct of performance. When Chinese courts are willing to recognize an acceptance by the conduct of performance beyond the scope of application described in Article 22 of the CCL in battle of forms cases, there will be more contracts concluded on the terms of the last-shooter, which share similar legal effects as well as criticisms with the last-shot doctrine.[43]

3. Formality Requirement

In principle, Chinese law has no formality requirement for conclusion of a contract, as Article 10(1) of the CCL provides that the parties may conclude contracts in written, oral, or another form, thus leaving the choice of formality to party autonomy. Here, 'written form' is defined as 'a form capable of expressing the content in a tangible manner such as formal contracts,[44] letters, and data messages including telegrams, telexes, facsimiles, electronic data interchange and electronic mail'.[45] The term 'data messages' is further defined as 'information generated, sent, received or stored by electronic, optical, magnetic or similar means' in Article 2(2) of the 2004 Law on Electronic Signature of the People's Republic of China.[46] 'Another form' may include notarization, attestation, or any other form agreed upon by the parties.

Moreover, Article 2 of Interpretation II provides that when the parties have not concluded a contract in written or oral form, the courts may on the basis of their juristic acts find an intention to make a contract and deduce that a contract has been concluded in 'another form',[47] unless it is otherwise provided by law. Although it seems far-fetched that 'no form but the parties' intentions to conclude a contract inferred from their juristic acts'—in Article 2 of Interpretation II—is treated as a contract concluded in 'another form', Article 2 shows that Chinese law has in general a soft view towards the formality requirement and that it takes a flexible approach to questions of evidence of the existence of a contract.

Laws or administrative regulations may require a contract to be concluded in written form.[48] For example, the CCL requires the following 'named contracts' to be in writing:[49]

[42] Other examples include *Zhejiang Yongtai Zhiye (Group) Co Ltd by Shares v Liu Rongquan, Zhangzhoushi Taiya Gongmiao Co Ltd and Zhangzhoushi Rongxing Gongmiao Co Ltd* ((2015) 浙杭商终字第1381号) and *Beijing Zhonghe Jiuye Co Ltd v Weifang Xingye Huanbao Keji Co Ltd* ((2015) 二中民(商)终字第10152号).

[43] D Keating, 'Exploring the Battle of the Forms in Action' (1999–2000) 98 Mich L Rev 2678, 2684.

[44] A formal contract must be signed or sealed. A fingerprint has the same legal effect as a signature or seal: see Art 5, Interpretation II.

[45] Art 11, CCL.

[46] [中华人民共和国电子签名法] (made by the NPCSC on 28 August 2004; effective on 1 April 2005).

[47] eg in *Sichuansheng Taiyu Shihua Co Ltd v Chongqing Xijiang Jianshe (Group) Co Ltd* ((2014) 川民终字第209号), despite the lack of a written contract, the High People's Court of Sichuan Province found that there existed a contract between the parties based on their intentions to conclude the contract as shown by the plaintiff's supply of asphalt and the defendant's receipt and use of the asphalt for its business.

[48] Art 10(2), CCL.

[49] Named contracts [有名合同] refer to contracts for which the CCL provides special provisions.

loan contracts involving a non-natural person, lease contracts of over six months' duration, financial leasing contracts, construction project contracts, mandate contracts for supervision, contracts for technological development, and contracts for the transfer of technology.[50]

In addition, other laws and administrative regulations require seven types of contracts to be in written form:

(1) contracts regarding real estate transactions[51]—such as contracts for the transfer of urban-land use rights, the transfer of real estate ownership, mortgage of real estate, lease of real estate,[52] rural-land use rights, trading rural-land use rights,[53] the transfer or disposition of use rights of land for construction, and easements;[54]

(2) contracts regarding security interests—such as contracts of guarantee, deposit,[55] floating charge, mortgage, and pledge;[56]

(3) contracts concluded through tendering and bidding processes;[57]

(4) contracts regarding intellectual property—such as copyright licence contracts,[58] contracts for the transfer of patent application rights or patent rights,[59] and franchising contracts;[60]

(5) contracts regarding establishment of business entities—such as partnership agreements,[61] Chinese–foreign equity joint venture agreements,[62] and Chinese–foreign contractual joint venture agreements;[63]

(6) employment contracts[64] and agent-organized tour contracts;[65] and

(7) advertisement contracts[66] and fresh milk sale contracts.[67]

[50] Arts 197, 215, 238(2), 270, 276, 330(3), and 243(2), CCL.

[51] As Chinese law treats civil aircraft and ships as real estate by analogy, contracts for the transfer of or disposition of property right in these special movable properties are required to be in writing.

[52] Arts 15, 41, 50, and 54, 1994 Law on Urban Real Estate Administration of the PRC [中华人民共和国城市房地产管理法] (made by the NPCSC on 5 July 1994; effective on 1 January 1995; amended in 2007 and 2009).

[53] Arts 21 and 37, 2002 Law on Rural Land Use of the PRC [中华人民共和国农村土地承包法] (made by the NPCSC on 29 August 2002; effective on 1 March 2003; amended in 2009).

[54] Arts 138, 144, and 157, 2007 Property Law of the PRC [中华人民共和国物权法] (made by the NPCSC on 16 March 2007; effective on 1 October 2007).

[55] Arts 13 and 90, 1995 Security Law of the PRC [中华人民共和国担保法] (made by the NPCSC on 30 June 1995; effective on 1 October 1995).

[56] Arts 181, 185, and 210, 2007 Property Law.

[57] Art 46(1), 1999 Law on Tendering and Bidding of the PRC [中华人民共和国招标投标法] (made by the NPCSC on 30 August 1999; effective on 1 January 2000).

[58] Art 25, 1990 Copyright Law of the PRC [中华人民共和国著作权法] (made by the NPCSC on 26 February 1990; effective on 1 June 1991; amended in 2001 and 2010).

[59] Art 10(3), 1984 Patent Law of the PRC [中华人民共和国专利法] (made by the NPCSC on 12 March 1984; effective on 1 April 1985; amended in 1992, 2002, and 2008).

[60] Art 11, 2007 Regulations on the Administration of Commercial Franchises [商业特许经营条例] (issued by the State Council on 6 February 2007; effective on 1 May 2007).

[61] Art 4, 1997 Partnership Enterprise Law of the PRC [中华人民共和国合伙企业法] (made by the NPCSC on 23 February 1997; effective on 1 August 1997; amended in 2006).

[62] Art 3, 1979 Law on Chinese–Foreign Equity Joint Ventures of the PRC [中华人民共和国中外合资经营企业法] (made by the National People's Congress on 8 July 1979; amended in 1990 and 2001).

[63] Art 5, 1988 Chinese–Foreign Contractual Joint Ventures of the PRC [中华人民共和国中外合作经营企业法] (made by the National People's Congress on 13 April 1988; effective on the same day; amended in 2000). This type of contracts, although requiring only the public authority's review and approval of the agreement, also needs a written form for the agreement.

[64] Art 10, 2007 Labour Contract Law of the PRC [中华人民共和国劳动合同法] (made by the NPCSC on 29 June 2007; effective on 1 January 2008; amended in 2012).

[65] Art 58, 2013 Tourism Law of the PRC [中华人民共和国旅游法] (made by the NPCSC on 25 April 2013; effective on 1 October 2013).

[66] Art 30, 1994 Advertisement Law of the PRC [中华人民共和国广告法] (made by the NPCSC on 27 October 1994; effective on 1 February 1995; amended in 2015).

[67] Art 23, 2008 Regulations on the Supervision and Administration of the Quality and Safety of Dairy Products [乳品质量安全监督管理条例] (issued by the State Council on 9 October 2008).

The requirement of written form for conclusion of a contract is intended to play four major functions in Chinese law.[68]

- The most significant is the cautionary function as a written contract reminds the parties of the importance of the transaction that they are entering into (eg contracts in categories (1), (3), and (5)) or of the substantial obligations that they are about to assume (eg contracts in category (2)).
- The second function is the evidentiary function as in disputes a written contract provides evidence of the existence and content of the contract;[69] this is especially important in transactions involving multiple parties or complicated commercial arrangements (eg contracts in categories (3), (4), and (5)).
- The third function is the informing function as a written contract explicates and informs the weaker party who is likely to suffer information asymmetry of their rights and the other party's obligations (eg contracts in category (6)).
- The fourth function is the supervisory function as a written contract facilitates supervision of business activities and transactions by public authorities (eg contracts in categories (5) and (7)). This kind of contract is often subject to the requirement not only of written form, but also of administrative review and approval.

Non-compliance with the formality requirement can mean, for example, that a formal contract which has not been properly signed by the parties[70] is not a concluded contract. However, according to Articles 36 and 37 of the CCL, the written form for conclusion of a contract that is either required by laws or administrative regulations or agreed upon by the parties may be dispensed with if one of the parties has already performed the main obligations and the other party accepts the performance. Such an exemption may be justified on two grounds. First, a large number of contracts that failed to meet the formality requirement have nevertheless been performed.[71] It is unrealistic and inefficient to deny the existence of an executed contract merely for the reason of its not satisfying the formality requirement. Second, the performance of the main obligations of the contract and the acceptance of that performance between the parties have rendered the most significant (cautionary) function of the formality requirement useless.

Nevertheless, a concluded contract may remain ineffective and unenforceable because it has not met a certain formality requirement under Chinese law.[72] According to Article 44 of the CCL,[73] a contract legally concluded enters into effect at the time of its conclusion; however, it will not become effective until the formality requirement (such as approval or registration) is satisfied when laws or administrative regulations provide for such a requirement.[74]

[68] When parties voluntarily agree upon a certain form for conclusion of their contract, they may intend that form to play other functions, such as the ritual, the publicity, or the enforceability function of a notarized contract.

[69] That is why business contracts are often made in written form even though it is not a mandatory requirement.

[70] eg *Wang Junfeng v Gaomishi Zhongya Nuantong Shebei Co Ltd and Teng Guiliang* ((2014) 鲁民提字第174号).

[71] As in the following cases: *Bama Zuyan Keji Co Ltd v Lei Shaoning* ((2012) 桂民三终字第20号); *Mianyangshi Wanshan Shiyan Co Ltd v Mianyang Huaxia Fangdichan Kaifa Co Ltd, Sichuan Xinma Jianshe Co Ltd, and Li Meihua* ((2013) 川民提字第160号); *Wang Aizhu & Ors v Zhongguo Jianzhu Diqi Gongchengju Co Ltd* ((2014) 浙温民终字第835号).

[72] In Chinese law, 'conclusion of the contract' and 'effectuation of the contract' are two different legal concepts: the former focuses on a meeting of the minds of the parties, while the latter concerns the effectiveness and enforceability of the contract. A concluded contract may remain ineffective in one of the following situations: (1) the formality requirement for effectuation of the contract has not been met (Art 44, CCL); (2) the 'condition for the effectuation of the contract' agreed upon by the parties has not been fulfilled (Art 45, CCL); or (3) the 'time of effectiveness' agreed upon by the parties has not arrived (Art 46, CCL).

[73] Also see Art 9(1), Interpretation I.

[74] Legal liability for failure to satisfy the formality requirement is discussed in section IV.

Examples of such contracts include: contracts for the transfer of urban-land use rights separated from the ownership of the building thereon;[75] contracts for the transfer, lease, or mortgage of the allocated urban-land use right;[76] Chinese–foreign equity joint venture agreements and any modification to the agreements;[77] contracts for the transfer or mortgage of assets, rights, or interests of a wholly foreign-invested enterprise;[78] contracts for the transfer of exploration rights or mining rights;[79] and contracts for the transfer of patent application rights or patent rights.[80] All these contracts take effect after the approval of the relevant public authority has been given or upon registration. However, there has been a trend for reducing such formality requirements. For example, previously neither sale of real estate contracts, nor mortgage contracts and pledge contracts of shares or intellectual property took effect before registration,[81] but now these contracts become effective and enforceable at the time of their conclusion.[82]

4. Gratuitous Contract

Chinese law recognizes gratuitous contracts where one party (the debtor) promises to perform some obligations without any consideration while the other party (the creditor) merely obtains the benefits.[83] A typical named gratuitous contract is a gift contract, with special rules set forth in Chapter 11 of the CCL and applicable to other gratuitous contracts[84] by analogy.

However, because of the lack of consideration, the enforceability of a gratuitous contract and legal protection of the creditor's contractual rights is therefore much less than in cases of onerous contracts under Chinese law. First, although a gift contract has no formality requirement and becomes effective at the time of its conclusion, the debtor is entitled to rescind the contract without reason before the rights in the gift pass, unless the gift contract is made in the public interest (such as one for disaster and poverty relief), made out of a moral obligation, or has been notarized.[85] Moreover, if the debtor refuses to deliver the gift, the creditor cannot demand its delivery. In short, gift contracts are not enforceable except for those made in the public interest or made out of a moral obligation or those that have been notarized.[86]

Second, even where the rights in the gift have passed, if the creditor seriously harms the debtor or the debtor's close relatives, or fails to perform a duty of maintenance towards the

[75] Art 25, 1990 Interim Regulations on the Assignment and Transfer of the State-Owned Urban-Land Use Right of the PRC [中华人民共和国城镇国有土地使用权出让和转让暂行条例] (issued by the State Council on 19 May 1990).

[76] Art 45, 1990 Interim Regulations on the Assignment and Transfer of the State-Owned Urban-Land Use Right.

[77] Art 14, 1983 Regulations of the Implementation of the Law on Chinese–Foreign Equity Joint Ventures of the PRC [中华人民共和国中外合资经营企业法实施条例] (issued by the State Council on 20 September 1983; amended in 1986, 1987, 2001, and 2014).

[78] Art 23, 1990 Detail Rules on the Implementation of the Law on Wholly Foreign-Owned Enterprises of the PRC [中华人民共和国外资企业法实施细则] (issued by the State of Council on 12 December 1990; amended in 2001 and 2014).

[79] Art 10(3), 1998 Measures on the Administration of the Transfer of Exploration Rights and Mining Rights [探矿权采矿权转让管理办法] (issued by the State Council on 12 February 1998; amended in 2014).

[80] Art 10(3), 1984 Patent Law.

[81] Arts 41, 78, and 79, 1995 Security Law.

[82] Art 15, 2007 Property Law.

[83] Under Chinese law, a bilateral contract is not necessarily a gratuitous contract, but a gratuitous contract must be a bilateral contract; eg when a loan contract is concluded through the lender's disbursement and payment of the loan to the borrower, the borrower is the party who alone has obligations to repay the loan and interest. This is a bilateral but onerous contract.

[84] eg contracts for lending property without charge, gratuitous deposit contracts, and gratuitous mandate contracts.

[85] Art 186, CCL.

[86] Art 188, CCL.

debtor, the debtor is also entitled to rescind the gift contract within one year from the date when he knows or ought to know of the cause of rescission.[87] The debtor's obligation under a gift contract may also be dispensed with if his economic conditions deteriorate significantly, thereby seriously affecting his production and business operation or his family life.[88] The debtor's right of rescission with reason and his right to exemption apply to all gift contracts, including those made in the public interest, or made out of a moral obligation, or those that have been notarized.

Third, the debtor is not liable for any defect in the gift; however, he will be liable to compensate for the creditor's losses resulting from the defect if he intentionally conceals the defect from the creditor or he warrants that the gift is free from defects.[89] Similarly, the debtor depositary under a gratuitous deposit contract is not liable to compensate for the damaged or lost deposited articles unless he has been grossly negligent;[90] the mandatary under a gratuitous mandate contract is not liable for the mandator's losses except for those caused by the intentional act or gross negligence of the mandatary.[91] Thus, in a gratuitous contract, the debtor's liability for defective performance is significantly reduced due to the lack of consideration.

Last but not least, the creditor under a gift contract has less protection than a creditor to whom the debtor owes obligations in an onerous contract, because the CCL allows the creditor under the onerous contract to apply to the court for revocation of the gift contract if transfer of the rights in the gift reduces the debtor's assets and thus damages the creditor's contractual rights against the debtor.[92] As an exception to the privity of contract doctrine, a competing creditor under an onerous contract may request the court to revoke a gift contract.

III. Offer and Acceptance

A contract is formed by means of offer and acceptance.[93] An offer must have specific and definite content and indicate the offeror's intention to be legally bound to the content of the offer if the offeree accepts it, and an acceptance must contain an expression of assent to the content of the offer.[94] Both offer and acceptance are declarations of intention that must be made and must reach the other party in order to take effect ('the arrival rule').[95] Upon receipt, an offer becomes effective and a period for acceptance commences, and a contract is concluded when an acceptance reaches the offeror within the period in normal cases.[96] However, controversy may arise as to whether the offeror may revoke the offer after the period starts ('revocation of offer') and whether the offeree may accept after the period lapses ('late acceptance'). As more and more parties make offer, acceptance, and other declarations of intention (such as withdrawal, revocation, and rejection) by electronic means, this medium also gives rise to issues of time, place, and signature in the formation of contract.

1. Revocability of Offers

(a) Revocable offers

An offer shows the offeror's intention to be bound in the case of its acceptance, which is different when the offeror's intention is to be irrevocably bound by his offer.[97] In principle,

[87] Art 192, CCL. [88] Art 195, CCL. [89] Art 191, CCL. [90] Art 374, CCL.
[91] Art 406(1), CCL. [92] Art 94, CCL. [93] Art 13, CCL. [94] Arts 14 and 21, CCL.
[95] Arts 16 and 26(1), CCL. [96] Art 25, CCL.
[97] B Vural, 'Formation of Contract According to the CISG' (2013) 6 Ankara Bar Review 125, 131.

an offer may be revoked as long as the offer is not irrevocable and the notice of revocation reaches the offeree *before* he dispatches the notice of acceptance according to Article 18 of the CCL. Although theoretically the offeror is entitled to revoke his offer until a contract is concluded, revocation is no longer available after dispatch of the acceptance; this is analogous to the common law 'postal rule'. Since it is practically difficult for the offeror to know the exact time when the notice of acceptance is dispatched,[98] he normally revokes the offer anyway and leaves the offeree to argue that the revocation is ineffective because the notice of revocation arrived too late. This inevitably creates uncertainty as to the existence of a contract between the parties.

Given the wording of Article 18 of the CCL, it seems that revocation of an offer is limited to situations where the offeree makes its acceptance through a notice. However, an acceptance may be made by conduct if the usage of transaction accepts or the express terms of the offer permit it according to Articles 22 and 26(1) of the CCL. As there is little reason why the offeror cannot revoke the offer when acceptance is made by conduct, Article 18 of the CCL should be broadly interpreted to cover acceptance by conduct.

Article 18 of the CCL implies that the revocation of offer shall be made by notice, but the means by which the notice is given is not necessarily the same as that used for making the offer. In *Zhang Chenglin v Dalian Shunda Fangwu Kaifa Co Ltd*,[99] the defendant land developer made an offer regarding sale discounts to the public through advertisements online and in a newspaper, and later revoked the offer by a poster at its sales office. The plaintiff argued that the defendant must use the same means of notice (ie advertisements) to revoke its offer. The High People's Court of Liaoning Province disagreed; it held that the CCL does not require this and the poster at the defendant's sales office was sufficient notice to revoke the offer. However, the court did not investigate the critical issue of whether the notice of revocation reached the plaintiff before he dispatched his acceptance to purchase the property. If the answer is negative, the notice of revocation by that poster arguably did not take effect in this case. In order to reduce potential disputes regarding effectiveness of revocations, it would be better for the law to clarify that an offer made to the public should be revoked by the same means as that used for making the offer.

(b) Irrevocable offers

An offer may be irrevocable if it shows that the offeror intends to be irrevocably bound by the offer despite the absence of consideration. However, it may be difficult to ascertain whether the offeror has made such a commitment; this will ultimately depend on the court's interpretation of his declaration of intention. Article 19(1) of the CCL stipulates that an offer becomes irrevocable if the offeror has expressly indicated, by fixing a period of time for acceptance or otherwise, that the offer is irrevocable. This clarification reduces uncertainty in the construing of the offeror's intention.

Furthermore, Article 19(2) of the CCL provides that an offer becomes irrevocable if the offeree has reason to believe that the offer is irrevocable and has already made preparations for performance of the contract. The critical issue is whether the offeree's reliance is reasonable and this needs to be determined on a case-by-case basis. There are hardly any judicial decisions involving revocation of an offer based upon Article 19(2) of the CCL;[100] it is therefore unclear how the courts are likely to determine the question of reasonableness.

[98] Especially when an offer is made to the public.

[99] (2014) 辽审四民申字第577号.

[100] No such cases were found in the database of 'China's Judgments Online'.

2. Late Acceptance

Late acceptance occurs when the acceptance arrives after the period for acceptance has lapsed. Articles 28 and 29 of the CCL are relevant to this issue. As Article 28 of the CCL provides, an acceptance that is dispatched after expiration of the period for acceptance is a new offer, unless the offeror notifies the offeree in a timely manner that the acceptance is effective. It is understood that when the period expires with no acceptance made to the offeror, an offer ceases to be effective in accordance with Article 20(3) of the CCL. That is, there is no offer open for acceptance when the offeree purports to do so. Therefore, a late acceptance dispatched after expiration of the period is logically a new offer and the original offeror, who now becomes the offeree, may accept this new offer and conclude a contract. But Article 28 of the CCL allows the original offeror to ratify the ineffective acceptance by giving a timely notice of his intention to the offeree;[101] the late acceptance is retrospectively validated and a contract is concluded at the time and place that the late acceptance arrives.

The wording 'the acceptance is dispatched' used in Article 28 of the CCL, which differs from the wording 'the notice of the acceptance is dispatched',[102] implies that the provision applies equally to late acceptance by conduct. In practice, the courts have recognized that late acceptance may be ratified by conduct instead of notice. For example, in *Chu Jiang v Kaidan Zhidi (Chengdu) Co Ltd*,[103] the defendant-offeror required the offer to be accepted by the paying of earnest money of RMB 30,000. The plaintiff-offeree transmitted the money to the defendant's bank account after the period for acceptance had expired. The defendant did not return the earnest money but continued to negotiate with the plaintiff on the details of their transaction. The District People's Court of the High-Tech Industrial Development Zone of Chengdu held that although the defendant did not send a notice to the plaintiff that the late acceptance by conduct was effective, his conduct sufficiently showed that he had ratified the plaintiff's late acceptance.

Article 29 of the CCL provides that if the offeree has dispatched the acceptance within the period for acceptance and under normal circumstances, it would have reached the offeror in due time, but in consequence of other factors, it reaches the offeror after the expiration of the period, the acceptance is effective, unless the offeror notifies the offeree in a timely manner that he does not accept the acceptance due to its late arrival. When the lateness of arrival cannot be attributed to the offeree, the risk of delay in transmission of the acceptance falls on the offeror; the late acceptance remains effective for concluding a contract upon the offeror's receipt of the acceptance unless the offeror gives timely notice of his rejection of the acceptance to the offeree. As a declaration of intention, such a notice of the offeror is effective upon receipt; therefore, the law actually requires the notice to reach the offeree in a timely manner. For example, in *Lu Qiling v Zhang Huihong and Guangzhoushi Decheng Zonghe Shichang Co Ltd*,[104] Zhang offered to sell her company shares to shareholder Lu and set a three-day period for acceptance. The acceptance was dispatched by Lu within the required duration but it arrived in the early morning of the fourth day due to an unforeseen delay in transmission. Zhang sent a letter to Lu refusing Lu's late acceptance on the fifth day. However, the letter was sent via a third party who passed the letter to Lu two months later. The High People's Court of Guangdong Province held that Zhang's letter failed to reach Lu

[101] A request by the offeror for a seal to be added on to an already signed formal contract which arrived late may be treated as a notice to ratify the ineffective acceptance: see *Zhejiang Wede Jinchukou Co Ltd v Taizhoushi Fenghua Gongmao Co Ltd* ((2015) 浙甬商终字第888号).

[102] Art 18, CCL uses the wording 'the notice of the acceptance is dispatched'.

[103] (2013) 高新民初字第2135号.

[104] (2013) 粤高法民二申字第560号.

in a timely manner, therefore the late acceptance was effective and the share transfer contract was validly formed.

The offeror should check the dispatch time of the late acceptance indicated by the letter's date or postmark, etc to determine whether the late arrival was caused by an unforeseen delay in transmission. Where the cause of late acceptance is difficult to determine, the offeror should, in any event, inform the offeree that he rejects the late acceptance so as to avoid the risk of being bound. The CCL does not define the term 'in a timely manner', which is left to the courts' discretion. Since the law imposes the risk of delay in transmission of the acceptance on the offeror, who would otherwise have no duty to declare that the late acceptance is ineffective, the courts should interpret the term 'in a timely manner' generously in order to consider the interests of the offeror. Furthermore, Article 29 of the CCL does not exclude the possibility that the offeror may give notice to the offeree, that he rejects any late acceptance on account of delay in transmission, *before* arrival of the acceptance (and even in the original offer itself and so opt out of Article 29 of the CCL).

Articles 28 and 29 of the CCL do not address a situation where the acceptance was dispatched to the offeror within the period for acceptance but it arrives late because the offeree failed to take into account or miscalculated the time needed for transmission. Given that this is the offeree's fault, the purported acceptance should be ineffective by analogy to a purported acceptance after expiration of the period for acceptance, dealt with by Article 28 of the CCL.

3. Formation by Electronic Means of Communication

Article 2(2) of the 2004 Law on Electronic Signature of the People's Republic of China ('LES') defines 'data messages' as 'information generated, sent, received, or stored by electronic, optical, magnetic or similar means', including but not limited to telegrams, telexes, facsimiles, electronic data interchange, and electronic mail.[105] Chinese law recognizes that data messages may be used for the purpose of forming a contract.[106] The parties may make any declarations of intention by means of data messages in the formation of contract, unless otherwise agreed by the parties.[107] However, Article 3(2) of the LES *disallows* the use of data messages for three types of legal documents that deal with: (1) civil status matters such as marriage, adoption, and guardianship; (2) transfer of rights and interests in land or building; and (3) termination of water supply, heat supply, gas supply, power supply, and other public utility services.

Electronic means of communication are treated as equivalent to paper-based communication in the formation of contract under Chinese law; they are treated as one type of written form as long as they are capable of expressing the content in a tangible manner.[108] Article 4 of the LES adds another requirement before the mode of communication can be treated as written form, namely, that the content is capable of being retrieved and presented for review and use whenever it is required. How are the rules on contract formation adapted to suit an electronic environment in relation to the time and place of dispatch and receipt of data messages, and the validity of electronic signatures?

[105] Art 11, CCL. Data exchanges through a social networking service may be recognized as data messages in contract formation; eg in *Yang Zhiming v Guo Xianyong* ((2014) 浙金商终字第2145号), the Jinhua Intermediate People's Court of Zhejiang Province recognized the offer and the counter-offer exchanged between the parties through 'WeChat'.

[106] Art 11, CCL. [107] Art 3(1), LES. [108] Art 11, CCL.

(a) *Time and place of dispatch and receipt of data messages*

According to Article 11(1) of the LES, the time of dispatch of a data message is the time it enters into an information system outside the control of the originator, such as an information system of the intermediary or of the addressee. If dispatch occurs when a data message enters into an information system of the addressee, the data message is dispatched and received simultaneously. If a data message reaches but fails to enter an information system outside the control of the originator, it cannot be considered as having been dispatched. As a special rule, Article 24 of the CCL provides that the time of dispatch of a telegram is the date the telegram is handed in for dispatch.

Article 11(2) of the LES and Articles 16(2) and 26(2) of the CCL establish the default rule for time of receipt of data messages: (1) if the addressee has designated an information system for the purpose of receiving data messages, the time of receipt of a data message is the time it enters the designated information system, such as the designated email address of the addressee; and (2) if the addressee has not designated any information system for receiving data messages, the time of receipt of a data message is the time it enters any information system of the addressee for the first time.

When an acceptance is made by means of data messages, the time of receipt of that data message is the effective time of the acceptance as well as the conclusion of the contract.[109] For greater legal certainty, the parties may agree that receipt of the data message be acknowledged and the data message is treated as though it has not arrived until the acknowledgement is received. Furthermore, Article 33 of the CCL provides that if parties form a contract by means of data messages, they may request execution of a confirmation note before the contract is formed, as a consequence of which the contract is formed when the confirmation note is executed.

According to Article 12 of the LES and Article 34(2) of the CCL, the place of dispatch and receipt of data messages is the place where the originator and the addressee have their principal places of business or their habitual residences if there are no principal places of business. Thus, it is possible that the place of dispatch and receipt of data messages differs from the place of business of the originator or the addressee that has the closest relationship to the contract concerned, or from the place where the information system or service provider of the originator or the addressee is located. The rationale behind this rule is that it is easier to ascertain the place of dispatch and receipt of a data message, especially when the data message contains the acceptance, thus providing certainty in the contract.

(b) *Electronic signature*

When data messages are seen as one type of written form in contract formation, an electronic signature is equivalent to a handwritten signature in the traditional paper-based environment. An electronic signature carries much importance because electronic means of communication make it difficult for one party to verify the identity of the other. Despite the silence of the CCL on electronic signature, Article 2(1) of the LES defines it as electronic data included in or attached to data messages and used for identifying the signatory and indicating the signatory's approval of the content in the data messages. Thus, electronic signature performs two functions: identifying the signatory and indicating assent.

Moreover, Article 13 of the LES lays down four requirements for 'a reliable electronic signature' (ie 'enhanced electronic signature')[110] in order to give greater security and certainty

[109] Art 25, CCL.

[110] CT Poggi, 'Electronic Commerce Legislation: An Analysis of European and American Approaches to Contract Formation' (2000–1) 41 Va J of Int'l L 224, 252.

to the users of electronic signature technology: (1) it is uniquely linked to the signatory; (2) it is created using means over which the signatory has sole control; (3) any subsequent change to the electronic signature is detectable; and (4) any subsequent change to the content and form of the data to which it relates is detectable. Only a reliable electronic signature is recognized by the LES as capable of satisfying the requirement of a signature in relation to data messages for the purpose of contract formation, and given the same legal effect as a handwritten signature or a seal.[111]

IV. Pre-Contractual Obligations

The pre-contractual relationship of the parties in the period immediately preceding an agreement inhabits the borderland between contract law and tort law. The pre-contractual obligations of the parties as contained in the CCL are based upon the general doctrine of good faith.[112] Because pre-contractual obligations are imposed by law (and not by the contract) for the purpose of balancing the parties' autonomy and reliance in the pre-contractual period, they differ essentially from the obligations under 'a contract to make a contract'.[113] In other words, pre-contractual obligations do not require the parties to make a contract. The parties retain freedom to negotiate and are not liable for failure to reach an agreement; however, they are required to negotiate in good faith.

1. Breach of Pre-Contractual Obligations

Article 42 of the CCL provides that a party is liable to compensate for the other party's losses caused by any of the following:

(1) his negotiating in bad faith under the pretext of concluding a contract—this involves a party who has no intention of making a contract but fraudulently misrepresents otherwise to induce the other party to engage in negotiations. Bad faith of the breaching party herein is understood as 'deceit malice', that is, knowledge of the falsity of a statement sufficiently constitutes malice;[114]

(2) his intentional concealment of a material fact relevant to the conclusion of the contract or his provision of false information in the course of concluding the contract; or

(3) his engagement in any other act that violates the doctrine of good faith in the course of concluding the contract.

Clause 3 is a catch-all provision, which grants the courts great flexibility and discretion in determining breach of pre-contractual obligations in individual cases. It is understood as establishing a fault-based liability, so much so that breach of a pre-contractual obligation may also be called 'liability for fault in concluding a contract'.[115]

[111] Art 14, LES. [112] Art 6, CCL.

[113] 'Contract to make a contract' is mentioned in Art 2, 2012 Interpretations of the SPC of Issues Concerning the Application of Law in the Trial of Cases on Sale Contract Disputes and the 2007 Provisions on Causes of Action in Civil Cases [民事案件案由规定] (issued by the SPC in 2007; amended in 2011).

[114] A typical case is *Nong'an Shengxiang Yumi Co Ltd v Jilin Branch of Agriculture Development Bank of China and Changchunshi Kangrun Shengwu Keji Co Ltd* ((2014) 吉民二终字第106号), where the defendant bank had no intention to make a RMB 20 million loan contract with the plaintiff, but induced the plaintiff to engage in negotiation and restructuring of the Kangrun Company for the purpose of clearing off its problematic loan to the Kangrun Company. The High People's Court of Jilin Province found that the defendant bank breached its pre-contractual obligations under Art 42(1), CCL.

[115] [缔约过失责任]; it is a term frequently used in judicial decisions. The author searched the database of 'China's Judgments Online' and found over 4,500 such judicial decisions in the past four years.

Article 43 of the CCL establishes, as part of their pre-contractual obligations, the parties' obligation of confidentiality not to disclose or improperly use trade secrets procured in the course of concluding a contract, whether or not the contract is concluded, otherwise the breaching party is liable to compensate for loss caused to the other party. To establish a breach of this obligation, fault is not required to be proved.

The concept of breach of pre-contractual obligations covers the period between conclusion of the contract and effectuation of the contract. Article 8 of Interpretation II provides that when a contract does not take effect until the formality requirement of approval or registration is satisfied, the party who is obliged to apply for approval or registration but fails to do so has committed an 'act that violates the doctrine of good faith in the course of concluding the contract' noted in Article 42(3) of the CCL. He shall be liable to compensate for the expenses incurred in the application for approval or registration and for the actual losses suffered by the other party.

In practice, the courts normally adopt a two-stage analysis: first, to identify the specific content of the pre-contractual obligation of the alleged liable party in the circumstances of the case and, second, to determine whether the party has breached the pre-contractual obligation. For example, in *Xingye Quanqiu Jijin Guanli Co Ltd v Jiangsu Rongsheng Zhonggong Co Ltd*,[116] the Supreme People's Court held that the pre-contractual obligations of the defendant should first be determined in the light of the nature and purpose of the contract in question and the relevant usage of transaction. As the plaintiff, one of the majority shareholders of the target company of the defendant's takeover attempt, was in negotiation with the defendant for a purchase of shares in the target company, the main pre-contractual obligation of the defendant was to keep the plaintiff updated with the latest information on its takeover attempt because the plaintiff relied heavily on the defendant's information in deciding whether to continue holding the shares of the target company. At the second stage, the court found that the defendant had fulfilled that duty and that there was no breach of the pre-contractual obligation. The court held that application for the public authorities' approval for the takeover attempt was not part of the defendant's pre-contractual obligations. The defendant was free to contract and its decision to withdraw its application for approval and cancel its takeover attempt did not violate the doctrine of good faith in the course of concluding the contract with the plaintiff.

2. Liability for Breach of Pre-Contractual Obligations

Breach of pre-contractual obligations gives rise to liability for compensation of the aggrieved party's reliance interest. In *Anhui Shuili Kaifa Co Ltd by Shares v Huaiyuanxian Chengshi Touzi Fazhan Co Ltd*,[117] the plaintiff-bidder submitted to the defendant-tenderer a proposal to undertake a construction project. After accepting the plaintiff's bid, the defendant refused to execute a written construction project contract with the plaintiff, who then sued the defendant for breach of pre-contractual obligations. The High People's Court of Anhui Province confirmed that no construction project contract was concluded due to the defendant's failure to meet the formality requirement for conclusion of the contract.[118] The court considered the defendant's refusal to execute a written contract as coming within an 'other act that violates the doctrine of good faith in the course of concluding the contract' as provided in Article 42(3) of the CCL and held that the defendant had breached his pre-contractual obligation to the plaintiff. However, the court rejected the plaintiff's claim for loss of his

[116] (2013) 民申字第1881号. [117] (2014) 皖民二终字第00659号. [118] See Art 270, CCL.

expectation interest and clarified that the liability for breach of a pre-contractual obligation was limited to the plaintiff's actual losses associated with his reliance on the defendant's execution of a written contract after the acceptance; loss of profits expected from the contract was beyond the scope of compensation. Finally, the court ordered the defendant to compensate the plaintiff's expenses of purchasing the bidding documents and the interest on the plaintiff's bidding deposit of RMB 50 million which the defendant retained for 421 days. Although the plaintiff did not claim it, his expenses in bidding were also recoverable as part of his actual losses.

By the same token, the court rejected an aggrieved party's claim of liquidated damages in a pre-contractual obligation case.[119] Moreover, when the aggrieved party is also at fault for the occurrence of his loss, the courts may reduce the breaching party's liability for breach of pre-contractual obligations. For example, in *Changzhou Branch of Huaxia Bank Co Ltd by Shares v Changzhoushi Shenli Moju Co Ltd and Changzhou Yatai Fangzhi Ranzheng Co Ltd*,[120] the High People's Court of Jiangsu Province reduced the first defendant's liability for breach of pre-contractual obligations to 10 per cent of the plaintiff's loss of reliance interest. Although the court did not give any legal basis for its decision on this matter, it seems that it applied by analogy the doctrine of contributory fault established in Chinese tort law.[121]

3. Functions of the Law of Pre-Contractual Obligations

Pre-contractual obligations evidently show that parties in negotiating for a contract have a special relationship before a contract is concluded. The law of pre-contractual obligations applies once the parties embark on the process of negotiation; it is not dependent on the conclusion of the contract. A failure to conclude a contract does not put an end to the pre-contractual obligations; on the contrary, pre-contractual obligation claims are often litigated when parties fail to reach an agreement after negotiation.

Under Chinese law, pre-contractual obligations contain 'a bundle of obligations' that regulate the negotiating parties. The first is an obligation on a party not to fraudulently misrepresent his intention to make a contract or any material fact relating to the conclusion of a contract under Article 42(1) and (2) of the CCL. If the parties conclude a contract thereafter, the aggrieved party who decides to rescind the contract may claim compensation on the basis of breach of pre-contractual obligations under Article 42(1) of the CCL or fraudulent misrepresentation under Articles 54(2) and 58 of the CCL. However, when a contract is not concluded between the parties,[122] or the aggrieved party for some reason decides not to rescind the contract for fraudulent misrepresentation, or he is unable to rescind the contract due to expiration of the time limitation for rescission,[123] or rescission

[119] See *Beipiaoshi Shengxin Jinkuang Co Ltd v Tianjin Tianshengxiang Kuangye (Group) Co Ltd and Beipiaoshi Tianlong Kuangye Co Ltd* ((2015) 辽民三终字第00299号), where a concluded contract between the plaintiff and the defendant Tianlong Company did not take effect because the latter refused to apply to the public authority for an approval to a transfer of mining rights after its shareholder changed. The High People's Court of Liaoning Province confirmed the defendant's liability for breach of pre-contractual obligations.

[120] (2013) 苏商终字第0078号.

[121] Art 131, GPCL and Art 26, 2009 Tort Liability Law [侵权责任法] (made by the NPCSC on 26 December 2009; effective on 1 October 2010).

[122] eg *Xu Wencai v Xinjiang Guoda Fangdichan Kaifa Co Ltd & Anor* ((2014) 新民二终字第6号), where the High People's Court of Xinjiang Uygur Autonomous Region upheld the plaintiff's claim for breach of pre-contractual obligations when the parties' lease of commercial real estate contract was not concluded due to the non-existence of the subject matter, which the defendant intentionally concealed from the plaintiff in the course of concluding the contract. As the tort of deceit is not clearly recognized by Chinese tort law, a claim for breach of pre-contractual obligations is more important in such cases.

[123] Art 55(1), CCL sets a one-year time limitation for rescission of contract.

of contract is meaningless because he has already performed his contractual obligation before discovering the fraudulent misrepresentation,[124] then the law of pre-contractual obligations plays an important role in providing the aggrieved party with a legal basis to recover his loss of reliance interest.

Under Article 43 of the CCL, the second pre-contractual obligation is a confidentiality obligation regarding trade secrets imparted in the course of concluding a contract, which overlaps with the duty of confidentiality under tort law.[125] In terms of breach of confidentiality by the negotiating parties, the law of pre-contractual obligations adds little to the claim in tort law and even provides fewer types of remedies than tort law, although it gives the aggrieved party another concurrent cause of action for seeking compensation.

The third pre-contractual obligation is a fault-based obligation to take reasonable care of each other in the course of concluding a contract based upon the doctrine of good faith under Article 42(3) of the CCL. This obligation consists of two duties. First, each party has a duty to take care of the other party's person and property in the course of concluding a contract.[126] This obligation overlaps with certain fault-based liabilities in tort law, such as occupier's and organizer's duty to maintain safety under Article 37(1) of the 2009 Tort Liability Law.[127] Second, the parties have a duty to take care to avoid pure economic loss to each other in the course of concluding a contract; that is, a duty to facilitate the conclusion and effectuation of a contract.[128] Accordingly, negotiating parties are required to give proper notice and information,[129] apply for approval or registration to satisfy the formality requirement for effectuation of the contract,[130] or provide assistance and cooperation as required in the circumstances.[131] The standard of care may gradually increase as the positions of parties draw closer and their reliance on each other becomes greater. Although pure economic losses are arguably recoverable in tort law, the law of economic torts and economic negligence is undeveloped under Chinese tort law. The second duty under the third obligation is therefore of great importance because it provides negotiating parties with a certain and convenient legal basis for claiming pure economic losses arising in the context of contract negotiation.

[124] eg *Bingzhou Branch of Shanghai Pudong Fazhan Yinhang Co Ltd by Shares v Hunan Biye Co Ltd and Hunan Mayang Youse Jinshu Co Ltd & Ors* ((2015) 湘高法民二终字第227号), where under a contract of financing under assignment of monetary demand, the plaintiff paid RMB 22 million to the third party creditor in reliance on the defendants' fraudulent statement that they owed receivable accounts over the above amount to the third party. It was too late for the plaintiff to rescind the contract, and the High People's Court of Hunan Province upheld his claim for breach of pre-contractual obligations against the defendants.

[125] Art 2, 2009 Tort Liability Law.

[126] eg *Gao Weizhong v Wang Xinfang* ((2014) 沁民一初字第00347号), where the defendant was held liable for breach of pre-contractual obligations and ordered to compensate the plaintiff for the injury he suffered when he was investigating the water leakage problem at the defendant's premises in the course of concluding a contract for work with the defendant.

[127] Art 37(1), 2009 Tort Liability Law states that the manager of a public venue (eg a hotel, shopping centre, bank, station, or place of entertainment) or the organizer of a mass activity shall incur tortious liability for any harm caused to another person as the result of his failure to fulfil the legal duty to maintain safety.

[128] Most pre-contractual obligation cases involve this duty.

[129] eg *Feng Jun v Baoshan Hengyi Shangye Guanli Co Ltd* ((2015) 云高民三终字第35号), where the parties concluded and partly performed their lease contract before the plaintiff found that the defendant had negligently provided material information in the course of concluding the contract, thereby causing loss to the plaintiff. The High People's Court of Yunnan Province held that the defendant breached its pre-contractual obligation to reasonably provide information and explanation, and thus ordered it to compensate RMB 20,000 based on the defendant's degree of fault that contributed to the plaintiff's loss.

[130] Art 8, Interpretation II.

[131] eg *Yang Qianyuan and Li Qingsong v Wang Dachang* ((2015) 黔高民申字第491号), where the defendant failed to assist the plaintiff in applying for approval to the transfer of mining rights and was held liable for breach of pre-contractual obligations.

V. Conclusion

Since the promulgation of the CCL, Chinese law has provided individuals and entities with more freedom with respect to contract formation; this is primarily evidenced by the relaxed formality requirements for conclusion and effectuation of a contract. Meanwhile, Chinese law has demonstrated a strong willingness to uphold an agreement and facilitate the conclusion of a contract. The approach of Chinese contract law concerning the essential elements of a contract, the pragmatic view that inclines towards finding a contract in the battle of forms cases, the recognition of late acceptance when it is caused by an unforeseen delay in transmission, and the recognition of the use of electronic means of communication in forming a contract are good examples of a liberal legal policy. Moreover, Chinese contract law has made efforts to strike a balance between one party's autonomy and the other party's reliance in the course of concluding a contract by its adoption of an objective approach to the construction of declarations of intention, the restriction of the offeror's right to revoke the offer, and the imposition of pre-contractual obligations on negotiating parties. It is also well observed that the principles of contract formation presented in the CCL and the Supreme People's Court's judicial interpretations have been continuously enriched and developed by judicial decisions in China.

3

Relaxations of Contractual Privity and the Need for Third Party Rights in Chinese Contract Law

*CHEN Lei**

I. Introduction: Chinese Position on Contractual Privity

This chapter discusses the principle of privity of contract and the operation of third party rights in Chinese law. For the sake of consistency and clarity, whenever the relevant parties are referred to, the terms 'promisor', 'promisee', and 'third party'[1] are used throughout this chapter. In the following discussion, the writer addresses a distinctive element of Chinese law: the legislature's affirmation of the principle of contractual privity in the absence of explicit recognition of third party rights.[2] Many of the discussions in this chapter refer to academic debates, judicial practice, and comparative studies. Even so, without clear statutory backing, writing on third party rights in China is like 'treading in the dark'. The upside to the story is that one cannot err seriously in depicting the Chinese law position due to the statutory lacunae in this area of law. The downside may be that the views expressed would generate heated academic debate or criticisms. Nevertheless, quoting a Chinese poem, '山不让尘，川不辞盈' meaning the mountain is gorgeous as it never resists dust and the river is magnificent as it is confluent with small waters, it is hoped that this chapter will heighten visibility of the views on third party rights in Chinese contract law.

1. Rules

Simply put, the principle of privity dictates that a contract generally has no legal effect beyond the parties to the contract.[3] To be specific, the principle of privity consists of two general rules. First, a third party cannot be subject to a burden by a contract to which he is not a party. There is no controversy about this. It would be irrational and unreasonable for a law to allow two contracting parties to impose a burden on a third party. The second rule

* Cite as L Chen, 'Relaxations of Contractual Privity and the Need for Third Party Rights in Chinese Contract Law' in Chen-Wishart, Loke, & Vogenauer, *Studies in the Contract Laws of Asia Vol II: Formation and Third Party Beneficiaries* (Oxford: OUP 2017) ch 3.

[1] Other terms are intentionally not used, such as 'creditor', 'debtor', and 'third party beneficiary'.

[2] Yin Tian [尹田], Lun sheta qiyue-jianping hetongfa di 64 tiao, Di 65 tiao zhiguiding ['Discussion on Contracts Involving Third Parties and Discussion on Articles 64 and 65' 论涉他契约—兼评合同法第64条、第65条之规定] (2001) 1 Fa Xue Yan Jiu [CASS Journal of Law 《法学研究》] 33, 47–49; Wu Xuli [吴旭莉], Hetong disanren cunzai qingxingde shizheng fenxi—jianping disanren liyi hetong zai woguo cunzai yufou zhizheng ['A Case Analysis of Third Party Rights in Certain Situations' 合同第三人存在情形的实证分析——兼评第三人利益合同在我国存在与否之争] (2012) 5 Xia Men Da Xue Xue Bao (Zhexue Shehui Kexue Ban) [Journal of Xiamen University (Arts & Social Sciences) 《厦门大学学报(哲学社会科学版)》] 75.

[3] S Vogenauer, 'The Effects of Contracts on Third Parties: the Avant-projet de réforme in a Comparative Perspective' in J Cartwright, S Vogenauer, and S Whittaker (eds), *Reforming the French Law of Obligations* (Oxford: Hart Publishing 2009).

is that a third party, an outsider to a contract, cannot enforce the promised performance, even when the contract is concluded with a clear intention of benefiting him. This rule is controversial as it has been criticized for causing hardship, and is therefore not conducive to commercial life.[4]

The fundamental argument in support of the latter rule is that a contract is a *vinculum iuris* (a bond of law) binding contracting parties. This is true even if the contracting parties agree that each of them may discharge their liability by rendering performance to someone else. If the buyer, at the seller's request, pays the price to the seller's creditor instead of the seller himself, in rendering performance to the seller's third party creditor, the buyer is performing an obligation he owes *to the seller*, a party to the contract, and not to the third party creditor. Nonetheless, what if the seller's creditor wants to demand payment in his own name from the buyer? Here we need to address the Chinese position on contracts for the benefit of third parties.

2. Chinese Position

The rule of privity mentioned in the preceding paragraph is widely understood and accepted. Being a civil law jurisdiction inspired by continental European systems,[5] the Chinese legal system explicitly established the civil law concept of relativity (privity)[6] of contract in its contract law.[7] Article 8(1) of the 1999 Chinese Contract Law ('CCL') provides that 'a lawfully established contract shall be legally binding on the parties thereto, each of whom shall perform its own obligations in accordance with the terms of the contract . . .' This is a clear expression of the Roman legal maxim *stipulatio alteri non potest* (a contract purporting to benefit a third party would be invalid).

The principle of privity of contract can be further inferred from Article 121 of the CCL. This provides that 'if a party breaches the contract due to a cause attributable to a third person, he shall bear liability for breach of contract to the other party. The dispute between the party and the third party shall be resolved in accordance with provisions of law or their agreement'. While this article mentions the third party in a given contractual relationship, it does not explicitly provide the third party with a right of action to demand the promisor's performance. Similarly, Article 224(1) of the CCL states that 'with the lessor's consent, the lessee may sublease the premises to a third person. In the case of sublease, the lease contract between the lessee and the lessor shall remain in effect; if the third party causes damage to the premises, the lessee shall be liable for damages.' The legislation does not recognize the

[4] Liming Wang, *Studies on Contract Law* (Beijing: Renmin University of China Press 2002) 130; E McKendrick, *Contract Law* (11th edn, London: Palgrave 2015) 113–115; B Markesinis, H Unberath, and A Johnston, *The German Law of Contract* (2nd edn, Oxford: Hart Publishing 2006) 181–183.

[5] Lei Chen, 'The Historical Development of the Civil Law Tradition in China: A Private Law Perspective' (2010) 78 Legal History Review 159–181.

[6] Chinese law, due to its civil law tradition, has an overarching principle of relativity of obligatory relationships, including privity of contract. That said, other obligation systems, such as tort, unjust enrichment, and *negotiorum gestio* (management of another's affairs) are also subject to the privity principle. However, to ensure clarity and consistency, this chapter deals only with privity of contract. The common law concept of 'privity of contract' is taken to be more or less synonymous with its civil law counterpart.

[7] Wang Liming [王利明], Tongyi hetong fa zhiding zhong de ruogan yinan wenti de tangao (shang) ['Discussion on the Difficult Issues in the Process of the Legislation of Unified Contract Law (1st Volume)' 统一合同法制订中的若干疑难问题的探讨(上)] (1996) 4 Zhengfa Luntan [Journal of CUPL 《政法论坛》] 49, 51; Xi Xiaoming [奚晓明] (ed), Zuigao renmin fayuan guanyu maimai hetong sifa jieshi lijie yu shiyong [*Understanding and Applying the Judicial Interpretation Concerning the Sale of Goods Contract Disputes by the Supreme People's Court*最高人民法院关于买卖合同司法解释理解与适用] (Beijing: People's Court Press 2012) 299–300. For an account of the legislative history before the PRC was founded, see Sheng-Lin Jan, 'Contracts for the Benefit of Third Parties under the Taiwan Civil Code', ch 16, section I.

third party's right of action. In each case, the promisor's legal relationship is only with the promisee and not with the third party.

The main rationale for keeping the privity principle is twofold. First, contractual rights and obligations are relative or personal to those who voluntarily create them.[8] Defining them in this way entails three elements, namely: (1) the contract creates the legal relation between the specific contracting parties only;[9] (2) only the contracting parties are bound by the contract;[10] and (3) the liability for breach of contract is owed only to the contracting parties.[11] Consequently, as a matter of principle, the right of enforcement by a third party should be disallowed. This has long been accepted as a distinguishing feature of the law of obligations, in contrast to property rights which are absolute in that they generally bind the whole world. Second, there was a fear among the draftsmen of the CCL that without the privity principle, anyone could potentially enforce a contract, thus opening the floodgate for unnecessary litigation. In a similar vein, without the principle, the draftsmen also cautioned that Chinese courts could potentially order any third party to join the litigation and to pay damages for which the contracting parties were not liable.[12] This would essentially impose an unfettered burden on a third party. To fend off potential abuses of third party rights and obligations in court proceedings, it is necessary to comply with the privity of contract principle.

II. Right of Action to Enforce Contract by Third Party

1. Direct Right of Claim by Third Party?

Can the contractual parties provide a benefit to a third party that is directly enforceable by the third party in a contractual action? A negative answer may cause inconvenience and hardship. First, it totally disregards the real intentions of contracting parties who create such third party rights.[13] Second, it may sometimes leave lacunae in the law on remedies for the third party and unjustly enrich the contract-breaker.[14] This is because the promisee can sue but obtains no meaningful remedy as the promisee suffers no recognized loss, but the third party who suffers the loss cannot sue. Third, it creates difficulties and increases transaction costs in the commercial context,[15] which are especially apparent in insurance situations where X pays a premium to insurer Y for the beneficiary Z. Comparative law analysis suggests that almost all the Western codified systems of contract laws from the French Code Civil of 1804 contain articles recognizing third parties' rights, not by assignment or other

[8] Wang Liming [王利明], He tong fa yan jiu [*Study on Contract Law* 合同法研究] (Beijing: Renmin University of China Press 2011) 117–120.

[9] Art 84, 1986 General Principles of Civil Law ('GPCL').

[10] Art 8(1), CCL. [11] Arts 121, 224, 253, 254, CCL.

[12] Liang Huixing [梁慧星], Liang Huixing jiao shou tan he tong fa [*Professor Liang on Law of Contract*, Internal Trial Guidance by the High Court of Sichuan Province] (98) No 174, 150–151 (internally circulated publication in Chinese) 梁慧星教授谈合同法，四川省高级人民法院印，川新出内(98)字第174 号] 150–151.

[13] Xue Jun [薛军], Yisi zizhi yu falu xingwei she ta xiaoli de moshi xuanze ['Private Autonomy and the Model Choice of Legal Behaviour's Third-Party Effect' 意思自治与法律行为涉他效力的模式选择] (2008) 5 Shanghai Caijing Daxue Xuebao [Journal of Shanghai University of Finance and Economics (Arts & Social Science edition) 《上海财经大学学报(哲学社会科学版)》] 25, 31.

[14] Yin Tian [尹田], Lun sheta qiyue-jianping hetongfa di 64 tiao, di 65 tiao zhiguiding ['Discussion on Contracts Involving Third Parties and Discussion on Articles 64 and 65' 论涉他契约—兼评合同法第64条、第65条之规定] (2001) 1 Fa Xue Yan Jiu [CASS Journal of Law 《法学研究》] 33, 47–49; S Smith, 'Contracts for the Benefit of Third Parties: In Defence of the Third Party Rule' (1997) 17 OJLS 645.

[15] A Burrows, 'The Contracts (Rights of Third Parties) Act 1999 and Its Implication for Commercial Contracts' [2000] LMCLQ 553.

juridical acts over the contract, but by provision in the contract itself.[16] It is unsurprising that such third party rights are recognized in the UNIDROIT Principles of International Commercial Contracts ('PICC'), the Principles of European Contract Law ('PECL'), and the Draft Common Frame of Reference ('DCFR').[17] In the common law world, the New York Court of Appeals in the United States took the lead in recognizing third party rights in contracts in the mid-nineteenth century.[18] Other parts of the common law world followed suit and abandoned the rigid privity rule, notably: the Contracts (Privity) Act 1982 in New Zealand, the Contracts (Rights of Third Parties) Act 1999 in England, the Contracts (Rights of Third Parties) Act 2001 in Singapore, and the Contracts (Rights of Third Parties) Ordinance 2014 in Hong Kong.[19] In the major mixed jurisdictions such as Scotland and South Africa, third party rights have long been recognized.[20]

Back to Chinese law, there are two articles in the CCL that pertain to contract performance where a third party is involved. Article 64 governs a contract to be performed for the benefit of a third party (向第三人履行的合同) while Article 65 addresses contracts that need to be performed *by* a third party (由第三人履行的合同).

Article 64 of the CCL provides:

> Where the parties agree that the promisor shall perform the obligation to a third party, and if the promisor fails to perform the obligation to the third party or if his performance is not in conformity with the agreement, the promisor shall be liable to the promisee for breach of contract.

Article 65 of the CCL provides:

> Where the parties agree that a third party shall perform the obligation to the creditor, the debtor shall be liable to the creditor for breach of contract if the third party fails to perform or if his performance is not in conformity with the agreement.

Articles 64 and 65 of the CCL appear to suggest that a third party does not have a direct right of action. But these two articles do not explicitly rule out the possibility of a third party right when the contracting parties agree to confer it on the third party. In other words, whether the third party has a direct right to demand performance is left unanswered in Chinese legislation.[21] There is no stated exception in Article 8(1) of the CCL (rule of privity) or elsewhere in the CCL that sets out the way in which a third party's right to enforce performance can be given. This is different from the approach taken by Article 1121 of the French Civil Code and §§ 328–335 of the German Civil Code (*Bürgerliches Gesetzbuch*, 'BGB'), both of which provide that a contracting party may stipulate that the other party performs for the benefit of a third party and that the third party has a direct right of action.

[16] HL MacQueen, 'Third Party Rights in Contract: A Case Study on Codifying and Not Codifying' in Lei Chen and CH van Rhee (eds), *Towards a Chinese Civil Code: Comparative and Historical Perspectives* (Leiden: Brill 2012) 309–334.

[17] Arts 5.2.1–6 PICC; Art 6:110 PECL; Arts II.-9:301–303 DCFR.

[18] *Lawrence v Fox*, 20 NY 268 (1859).

[19] For Singapore, see Yeo Tiong Min, 'When Do Third Party Rights Arise under the Contracts (Rights of Third Parties) Act 1999 (UK)?' (2001) 13 SAcLJ 43. For other common law jurisdictions, see the Consultation Paper by the Hong Kong Law Reform Commission on the Privity of Contract, 2005 <http://www.hkreform.gov.hk/en/publications/privity.htm> accessed 7 July 2016.

[20] P Sutherland, 'Third-Party Contracts' in HL MacQueen and R Zimmermann (eds), *European Contract Law: Scots and South African Perspectives* (Edinburgh: Edinburgh University Press 2006) 203.

[21] Drafts of the earlier versions of contract law by academic groups explicitly recognized the third party's right to demand performance directly from the promisor. But the final version of the CCL took this out. See the details in Han Shiyuan, 'A Snapshot of Chinese Contract Law from an Historical and Comparative Perspective' in Lei Chen and CH van Rhee (eds), *Towards a Chinese Civil Code: Historical and Comparative Perspectives* (Leiden: Brill 2012) 247–248.

Chinese law appears to remain silent on this, thus triggering debates among legal scholars and the courts.

Before we explore different views on whether a third party has a directly enforceable claim, it is necessary to appreciate the difference between genuine third party contracts and merely incidental third party contracts. The genuine third party contract ('Genuine TPC') is made for the benefit of the third party. The incidental third party contract is made where contracting parties consent to delivery of performance to a third party ('Incidental TPC').[22] The Incidental TPC only provides a way by which a promisor discharges an obligation to a promisee, while in the Genuine TPC, the contractual parties agree to directly confer a benefit (a direct right of action) on a third party.[23] For example, an Incidental TPC is created if A enters into a contract with B whereby A undertakes to pay the agreed sum to C, B's bank; the bank is not a third party beneficiary if A's payment to C is seen by the parties merely as a discharge of A's debt to B. In other words, the contracting parties A and B intend the third party C to be only a passive recipient of the performance and C does not have a direct right of claim against A, the promisor.[24] More importantly, the intentions of the contractual parties are different. In Incidental TPCs, the parties merely intend to deliver the performance to the third party, whereas in Genuine TPCs, in addition to that, the parties intend the delivery of performance to benefit the third party and also to be enforceable by him.[25] Hence, in Incidental TPCs, the promisor still owes the obligation to the promisee, and the third party has no right of action. But in Genuine TPCs, the promisor owes the obligation to the third party, who can enforce delivery of the performance.[26]

Interpretations of Articles 64 and 65 are divided broadly into three. The first view is that Article 64 grants the third party a right of action against the promisor in cases of non-performance whether the third party contract is genuine or incidental. This is so despite the fact that the third party's right to enforce performance is not explicitly provided for.[27] According to this view, a third party is a beneficiary only if he, for whose benefit the contract is created, can enforce it against the promisor. Cui Jianyuan maintained that the initial versions of Article 64 provided the third party a right to enforce the performance.[28] However, due to some unknown reason, possibly an oversight, the enforcement right of the third party was omitted or deleted from Article 64. It is notable that the legislature's law-drafting committee expressed the same view in a commentary.[29] In *Zhang Yong v Guangxi*

[22] Wang Liming [王利明], Hetong fa yanjiu (di yi juan) [*Discussion on Contract Law* (1st Volume) 合同法研究(第一卷)] (Beijing: Renmin University of China Press 2002) 55.

[23] Zhu Yan [朱岩], Liyu di san ren hetong yanjiu ['Studies on Contracts in Favour of the Third Party' 利于第三人合同研究] (2005) 5 Falu Kexue [Science of Law《法律科学》] 55, 56.

[24] Ling Bing, *Contract Law in China* (Hong Kong: Sweet & Maxwell Asia 2002) 253.

[25] Xue Jun [薛军], Lun < zhonghua renmin gongheguo hetong fa > di 64 tiao de dingxing yu jieshi ['The Nature and Interpretation of Article 64 of Contract Law of People's Republic of China' 论<中华人民共和国合同法>第64条的定性与解释] (2010) 2 Fashang yanjiu [Studies in Law and Business《法商研究》] 51, 52.

[26] Wu Xuli [吴旭莉], Hetong di san ren cunzai qingxing de shizheng fenxi – jian ping di san ren liyi hetong zai woguo cunzai yu fou zhi zheng ['Empirical Analyses on the Existence of Third Parties and Discussion of Third-Party Contracts in China' 合同第三人存在情形的实证分析—兼评第三人利益合同在我国存在与否之争] (2012) 5 Xiamen Daxue Xuebao (Zhexue Shehui Kexue Ban [Journal of Xiamen University (Arts & Social Sciences)《厦门大学学报(哲学社会科学版)》] 75, 77.

[27] Hu Kangsheng [胡康生], Zhonghua renmin gongheguo hetong fa shiyi [*The Interpretation of the Contract Law of the People's Republic of China* 中华人民共和国合同法释义] (Beijing: Law Press 1999) 112, 113.

[28] Cui Jianyuan, Wei di san ren liyi hetong de guige lun ['Discussion on Third-Party Contracts—From the Perspective of Article 64' 为第三人利益合同的规格论] (2008) 1 Zhengzhi Yu Falu [Political Science and Law《政治与法律》] 68, 72.

[29] See Hu Kangsheng [胡康生], Zhonghua renmin gongheguo hetong fa shiyi [*The Interpretation of the Contract Law of the People's Republic of China* 中华人民共和国合同法释义] (Beijing: Law Press 1999) 112, 113. (Hu Kangsheng was chairman of the legislative drafting department of the National People's Congress.)

Hengxin Movable Houses Co Ltd,[30] the court held that the contract in dispute was a Genuine TPC, but it sidestepped the question of whether Article 64 recognizes third party rights.

The second view is that Articles 64 and 65 do not provide a right of action for a third party,[31] whether the third party contract is genuine or incidental. The reasoning is that as Article 64 is contained in the chapter on Contract Performance of the CCL, it merely provides a method of contractual performance in an Incidental TPC, rather than creating a new right of action as in the case of a Genuine TPC.[32] In other words, Article 64 merely states that the performance of a third party contract in full compliance with the contractual terms is to deliver the promised performance to the third party. By delivering the performance to a third party, the obligation owed to the promisee has been discharged. Therefore, it is argued that the CCL does not address third party enforcement rights.[33] This is supported by the outright refusal of the Supreme People's Court ('SPC') to recognize third party rights in Article 16 of Interpretation II of the CCL:

> [t]he People's Court may, as the case may be, list a third party as described in Articles 64 and 65 of the Contract Law as a third party without a direct right of claim, but shall not, ex officio, list such a third party as a defendant or a third party with a direct right of claim to the action.[34]

This is despite attempts by lower level courts to allow rights of suit by third parties and severe academic criticism of the absence of a right to action by a third party in a Genuine TPC.

Article 16 of Interpretation II is, in essence, a civil procedure issue. However, the implication is that the SPC took a conservative stance by not recognizing third parties as having a direct right of action. Nonetheless, similar to the approach taken by Article 64, this provision does not explicitly rule out the possibility of third party rights of action when the contracting parties confer such a right of action on the third party. So whether third parties have a direct right of action still appears to be an open question.

The third view is a derivative of the first one by holding that a third party has a right of enforcement in Genuine TPCs.[35] First, although Article 64 is silent on whether the third party has a direct claim, it needs to be interpreted to the effect that there is a direct obligation owed to the third party in genuine TPCs. If Article 64 is only used to indicate that the promisor's obligation is owed to the promisee, it would be a repetition of the principle of privity of contract contained in Article 8(1).[36] Second, parliamentary minutes concerning the deliberation of the contract law drafts show that enforceability by the third party was provided for,[37] but was subsequently deleted with no explanation given.[38] Third, if Article

[30] The Judgment of the Nanning Intermediate People's Court (2011) Nan Shi Min No 2 Zhong No 132 (南宁市中级人民法院民事判决书2011南市民二终字第132号).

[31] Yin Tian [尹田], Lun sheta qiyue-jianping hetongfa di 64 tiao, di 65 tiao zhiguiding ['Discussion on Contracts Involving Third Parties and Discussion on Articles 64 and 65' 论涉他契约—兼评合同法第64条、第65条之规定] (2001) 1 Fa Xue Yan Jiu [CASS Journal of Law《法学研究》] 47–49.

[32] Ye Jinqiang [叶金强], Di san ren liyi hetong yanjiu ['A Study of the Third Party Beneficiary Contract' 第三人利益合同研究] (2001) 4 Bijiao Fa Yanjiu [Journal of Comparative Law《比较法研究》] 70.

[33] Xue Jun [薛军], Lita hetong de jiben lilun wenti ['The Basic Theory of Third-Party Contract' 利他合同的基本理论问题] (2006) 4 Faxue Yanjiu [Chinese Journal of Law 《法学研究》] 116, 125.

[34] Art 16, SPC's 2009 Judicial Interpretation No II on Certain Questions Concerning the Application of the Contract Law.

[35] Han Shiyuan [韩世远], *The Law of Contract* 合同法 (3rd edn, Beijing: Law Press China 法律出版社 2011) 303–306.

[36] Han Shiyuan [韩世远], Shi lun xiang di san ren luxing de hetong – dui woguo <hetong fa> di 64 tiao de jieshi ['Discussion on Contracts with the Performance to Third Parties' 试论向第三人履行的合同—对我国<合同法>第 64 条的解释] (2004) 6 Falu Kexue [Science of Law 《法律科学》] 100, 104.

[37] Wang Cheng [王成], 'The Opinions for the Contract Law Draft' (1999) 1 Peking University Law Journal《中外法学》97.

[38] 'The Consultation Paper of the Draft Contract Law' published by the Legislative Working Committee of the 9th National People's Congress of PRC in 1999 <http://www.npc.gov.cn/wxzl/gongbao/2000-12/06/content_5007083.htm> accessed 2 July 2016.

64 excludes third party rights, it would inevitably lead to a statutory lacuna in contract law, which should be avoided.[39] Therefore, a right of action by a third party should be given.[40] This view is taken in *Sheng Qiaohong & Ors v Chu Wen Hua*.[41] The court held that a third party could enforce the contract under Article 64 in certain types of contracts. The difficulty with the third view is that the definition of a Genuine TPC is riddled with circularity. The distinguishing feature of a Genuine TPC is that the parties intend the third party to have the right of action. But the reason for asking whether the contract concerned is a Genuine TPC is precisely in order to determine whether a direct right of action is available. Therefore, it can be argued that nowhere, perhaps, is the imperfect logic of Chinese contract law more apparent than in its attempt to stipulate third party rights.

In summary, Article 64 of the CCL does not explicitly provide a right to a third party in enforcing the performance. At first glance, Article 64 seems not to address whether a direct right of action by a third party exists in Chinese law. This is because the phrase 'the promisor shall be liable to the promisee for breach of contract' can be understood as a method of discharging the contractual obligation between the contracting parties. So, it would be far-fetched and even illogical to argue that Article 64 confers de facto third party rights where the law itself seems to be framed in such a way as to exclude it. The second view seems to hold, and it has been supported by the SPC in its 2009 Judicial Interpretation. As a result, third party rights could be created by agreement of the contracting parties, and not from provisions of law.[42] The third view takes a pragmatic approach by distinguishing a Genuine TPC from an Incidental TPC. A Genuine TPC provides a direct right of claim but an Incidental TPC does not. However, this view is not immune to criticism. If introducing third party rights in the CCL was supported by contract law scholars in drafting the bill, why did the final version of the CCL omit it, thus causing debate and discrepancies? This is left unanswered.

Nonetheless, despite the imperfect definition and the lack of provisions in the CCL, direct rights of action by third parties have, in practice, been given in certain circumstances. Chinese contract law does not prevent contracting parties from creating a third party right if they expressly provide for it in the contract.[43] The next section describes the precise circumstances when third parties can enforce the performance in their own right.

2. Basis of Third Party Claims

A third party's right of action is determined by the intention of the contracting parties.[44] The fact that no clear answer was provided in either the CCL or the Judicial Interpretations

[39] Han Shiyuan [韩世远], Shi lun xiang di san ren luxing de hetong – dui woguo <hetong fa> di 64 tiao de jieshi ['Discussion on Contracts with Performance to Third Parties' 试论向第三人履行的合同—对我国<合同法>第64条的解释] (2004) 6 Falu Kexue [Science of Law《法律科学》] 106.

[40] See the ruling by the SPC in the case of *Wuhan Zhongheng Electronics Co v Wuhan Xiahuazhongheng Electronics Co and Xiamen Huaqiao Co* (2005) Min 2 Zhong No 90. It is notable that the ruling itself seems to contradict the position taken in the SPC's Judicial Interpretation No II on Certain Questions Concerning the Application of the Contract Law in 2009.

[41] The Judgment of the Chongqing High People's Court (2011) Yu Gao Fa Min Zhong No 00119 (重庆市高级人民法院民事判决书2011渝高法民终字第00119号).

[42] Ling Bing, *Contract Law in China* ((Hong Kong: Sweet & Maxwell Asia 2002) 254.

[43] Cui Jianyuan, Wei di san ren liyi hetong de guige lun ['Discussion on Third-Party Contracts—From the Perspective of Article 64' 为第三人利益合同的规格论] (2008) 1 Zhengzhi Yu Falu [Political Science and Law 政治与法律] 71.

[44] Wang Liming and Ye Jinqiang, 'Discussion on Third-Party Contracts' (2001) 4 Journal of Comparative Law 73; Xi Xiaoming [奚晓明] (ed), Zuigao renmin fayuan guanyu maimai hetong sifa jieshi lijie yu shiyong [*Understanding and Applying the Judicial Interpretation Concerning the Sale of Goods Contract Disputes by the Supreme People's Court*最高人民法院关于买卖合同司法解释理解与适用] (Beijing: People's Court Press 2012) 303.

highlights the need for the parties to make their intention explicit in the contract. A third party may be given a right of action in two situations. The first is much less controversial than the second.

The first situation arises where the contract *expressly* stipulates that the third party may enforce the performance. In other words, a third party may require performance of a contractual obligation when such a right of action has been expressly agreed between the promisor and the promisee. So, the right of action exists without requiring the third party to accept it.[45] In *China Pacific Insurance (Group) Co Ltd v China COASCO Shipping Corporation Ltd and Hainan Office of Haima Automobile Group Co Ltd* ('*China Pacific Insurance (Group) Co Ltd*'),[46] the defendant-promisor and the promisee made a carriage of goods by sea contract whereby the promisor agreed to ship the goods for the benefit of the third party claimant. The promisor agreed to be liable for any loss to the claimant. When the promisor failed to perform, the third party sued in its own right to enforce the performance. The SPC supported this view as the contract expressly provided that the third party claimant who enjoyed the benefit of the contract for shipping goods, had the right to enforce against the defendant.[47] In the absence of statutory provisions for third party rights, this case is striking, as it shows the SPC beginning to recognize third party rights when such a right is expressly provided for in the contract.

Two related issues are not addressed in this case. First, the contracting parties can express clearly their intention *not* to confer a right of claim on the third party or they can set a condition precedent to the third party's acquisition of the right of claim. That is, the contracting parties can contract out of the third party right. Second, what if the third party renounces the right of claim? It is suggested that due consideration should be given to the approach taken by the PECL and the Taiwan Civil Code, which stipulates that if the third party expresses to either of the parties his intent not to take the benefit of the contract, he is deemed never to have acquired any right under the contract.[48]

The second situation arises where the contracting parties do not express their intention but the contract term can be construed as purporting to confer a benefit on the third party, ie a Genuine TPC. This situation is less straightforward. In order for a term to purport to confer a benefit on the third party, it is arguable that the main purpose of the parties' bargain must be to benefit the third party. For example, in the *China Pacific Insurance (Group) Co Ltd* case,[49] the third party beneficiary under an insurance policy has a right of action against the insurance company in cases of breach even though the contract has not expressly conferred the right of action on him. Otherwise, the nature and purpose of the contract would be frustrated. However, the example relates to a peculiar type of contract, which already falls within a statutory exception to the privity rule. At a general level, the difficulty remains that of discerning the intention of the parties where they have not expressed it. Although the *China Pacific Insurance (Group) Co Ltd* approach has been suggested by the SPC in its Commentary on the 2012 *SPC's Judicial Interpretation Concerning the Sale of Goods Contract Disputes*,[50] how ready Chinese courts are to confer third party rights merits

[45] It has been argued that the third party right becomes effective only when the third party declares his intention to accept it. See Ling Bing, *Contract Law in China* (Hong Kong: Sweet & Maxwell Asia 2002) 254.

[46] The Judgment of the Supreme People's Court of the People's Republic of China (2011) Min Ti Zi No 12 (最高人民法院民事判决书2011民提字第12号) (published by the SPC).

[47] ibid. [48] Art 269(3), Taiwan CC and Art 6:110(2) PECL.

[49] The Judgment of the Supreme People's Court of the People's Republic of China (2011) Min Ti Zi No 12 (最高人民法院民事判决书2011民提字第12号) (published by the SPC).

[50] Xi Xiaoming [奚晓明] (ed), Zuigao renmin fayuan guanyu maimai hetong sifa jieshi lijie yu shiyong [*Understanding and Applying the Judicial Interpretation Concerning the Sale of Goods Contract Disputes by the Supreme People's Court*最高人民法院关于买卖合同司法解释理解与适用] (Beijing: People's Court Press 2012) 303.

an empirical survey. A cursory survey of the SPC's case database[51] shows that if a contract only contains a delivery of performance to a third party but does not expressly provide for the third party right, Chinese courts will deny the third party right under the doctrine of privity.

Nonetheless, two decisions have allowed a third party right of action when the contracts did not expressly so provide. In *Sheng Qiaohong & Ors v Chu Wen Hua*,[52] the promisor-defendant agreed to transfer his shares in the third party claimant company to the promisee in order to settle the claimant's debt to the promisee before finalizing the transfer of shares. The court held that as the claimant benefited from having its debt obligation discharged, the third party right therefore arose. In *Zhang Yong v Guangxi Hengxin Movable Houses Co Ltd*,[53] the promisor-defendant agreed to compensate the third party claimant for its unrealized credit owed by others. The court opined that this contract, by its nature and purpose, was a genuine third party contract. Therefore, the court allowed the claimant to enforce its right against the defendant for compensation.

The conferral of a third party right depends on the intention of the contracting parties. The third party need not assent to the contract in order to take the benefit. The guiding principle is the autonomy of the contracting parties. The contract between the contracting parties stipulates the nature and content of the third party's benefit. If the third party renounces the right of action, the right is deemed never to have been created. The assent of the third party to the contract is relevant only in the context of variation and rescission of a third party contract, which is discussed in section V.[54]

III. Third Party's Remedies and Promisor's Defences

In essence, under Chinese law, the right which a third party might be able to acquire is the right to enforce the contractual terms subject to the defences which would have been available to the promisor had he been sued by the promisee.[55] The rules governing damages, specific performance, injunctions, and other remedies will apply to the third party's right of action.[56] For example, the rules on remoteness and mitigation (by the third party) will be applicable when the third party claims damages.

The third party is said to stand in no better position than the promisee, and it cannot exercise the right to terminate the contract. This is mainly because the right to terminate the contract, by its nature, belongs to either of the contracting parties only, since the third party is not one of the parties to the contract.[57] It is therefore advisable for the promisor and the promisee to decide whether or not to terminate the contract if there is a breach by one party to the contract.

[51] China Judgments online <http://wenshu.court.gov.cn/>.

[52] The Judgment of the Chongqing High People's Court (2011) Yu Gao Fa Min Zhong Zi No 00119 (重庆市高级人民法院民事判决书2011渝高法民终字第00119号).

[53] The Judgment of the Nanning Intermediate People's Court (2011) Nan Shi Min No 2 Zhong No 132 (南宁市中级人民法院民事判决书2011南市民二终字第132号).

[54] Ye Jinqiang [叶金强], Di san ren liyi hetong yanjiu ['A Study of the Third Party Beneficiary Contract' 第三人利益合同研究] (2001) 4 Bijiao Fa Yanjiu [Journal of Comparative Law《比较法研究》] 74.

[55] Yin Tian [尹田], Lun sheta qiyue-jianping hetongfa di 64 tiao, di 65 tiao zhiguiding ['Discussion on Contracts Involving Third Parties and Discussion on Articles 64 and 65' 论涉他契约—兼评合同法第64条、第65条之规定] (2001) 1 Fa Xue Yan Jiu [CASS Journal of Law 《法学研究》] 49.

[56] Zhu Yan, [朱岩], Liyu di san ren hetong yanjiu ['Studies on Contracts in Favour of the Third Party' 利于第三人合同研究] (2005) 5 Falu Kexue [Science of Law《法律科学》] 61–62.

[57] Han Shiyuan [韩世远], *The Law of Contract* 合同法 (3rd edn, Beijing: Law Press China 法律出版社 2011) 272; Ling Bing, *Contract Law in China* (Hong Kong: Sweet & Maxwell Asia 2002) 254.

While there is no explicit provision in the CCL, it is generally agreed that *if* a third party can bring an action against the promisor, the promisor may invoke all the defences, set-offs, and counterclaims which would have been available to him if the action had been brought by the promisee.[58] The third party does not acquire an absolute right to have the contract performed. The promisor can raise any defence against the third party, such as fraud or duress, that would have been valid against the promisee since the defences are derived from the agreement between the contracting parties that gives rise to the third party right in the first place.

The contracting parties may contract out of this general position. They may expressly agree that the promisor will not raise any defence or set-off that would have been available against the promisee. Allowing this would reduce uncertainty for the third party and render the third party right much stronger. In the case of a bilateral contract in favour of a third party where the parties undertake reciprocal obligations,[59] the usual defences available to a promisor, such as the right to withhold performance, would also apply against the third party when it is plain that there will be non-performance by the promisee when that performance is due.[60]

Can the promisor have defences or counterclaims against the third party that he would not have against the promisee? The answer is positive under Chinese law. The promisor may defeat the third party's claim in the following situations: (1) where the third party induced the promisor to make the contract by misrepresentation or any other ground of invalidity such as coercion, exploitation, evident unfairness, or significant misconception or (2) where the third party was indebted to the promisor under another transaction, ie a set-off against the third party. While there is no provision in the 1986 General Principles of Civil Law ('GPCL') or the CCL that deals with these situations, the principle of good faith in Article 6 of the CCL is likely to allow the promisor to raise against the third party the latter's misrepresentation (or other ground of invalidity) or existing debts as if the third party had been a party to the contract. In other words, rules that govern misrepresentation and set-off[61] in Chinese contract law generally apply in these circumstances. If the misrepresentation is intentional, the contract is voidable under Article 52(1) of the CCL. If there is a negligent misrepresentation, pursuant to Article 54 of the CCL, the contract is only voidable if it leads to a substantial misunderstanding by the promisor (重大误解).

IV. Rights of Promisee

1. Extent of Promisee's Rights

Where A makes a contract with B, B can enforce the contract even where C is given the right to enforce the contractual terms against A. This is because B is a party to the contract. Therefore, under Chinese law, on A's failure to perform in favour of C, B may be able to claim the agreed sum, specific performance, damages (likely to be nominal), or restitutionary relief. The remedies could be awarded to the promisee against the promisor in the sense that the promisor will be ordered to perform the contract terms in favour of the third party rather than the promisee himself.

[58] § 334 BGB; Art 539, Japanese Civil Code; Art 270, Taiwan Civil Code. The rule of set-off is provided in Art 83, CCL.

[59] Obligations are reciprocal when a party undertakes an obligation only in exchange for the other party undertaking another obligation.

[60] Han Shiyuan [韩世远], *The Law of Contract* 合同法 (3rd edn, Beijing: Law Press China 法律出版社 2011) 275.

[61] Art 99, CCL concerns the rule of set-off.

The person who has the main interest in enforcing the promise made for the benefit of a third party is the third party himself. The contract was made in his favour and without enforcement the third party is the one who suffers the loss. There could be cases, however, where the promisee has a strong performance interest or where it is impractical for the third party to enforce the contract. For example, in a service contract signed between a homeowners' association of a high-rise building and a property management company, if the service provided is not up to the expectation of the homeowners, who are the third party beneficiaries, the individual homeowners may take action against the service provider. However, an individual homeowner taking action against the promisor would be unlikely in view of the modest gain that would be received relative to the substantial litigation costs involved in bringing such an action. The homeowners' association, being the promisee, is better placed to enforce the performance. Once the homeowners' association has obtained damages, it would hold the compensation for the homeowners. The homeowners' association may either distribute the monetary compensation to the individual homeowners in proportion to the share value allocated or offset the compensation against the monthly management charges next due.

It is also possible for the promisee to recover his own loss without prejudice to the third party's claim. For example, A contracts with B to buy B's flat and registers it under C's name. The contract between A and B states that: (1) an agreed sum would be payable if the contract is breached; and (2) C has a right to claim the title transfer. A breaches the contract by transferring the flat's title to D. Both B, the promisee, and C, the third party, may now have an action against the promisor, A. Chinese courts are likely to hold that both B and C are entitled to claim for damages. C can sue because the contract is a Genuine TPC and C's benefit has been clearly stipulated. C may claim as compensation the market value of the flat in fulfilment of his expectation interest. Besides, B may sue for the agreed sum as a compensatory penalty and keep it.

Finally, under Chinese law, there seems to be no hierarchy between the claims of the promisee and any claims available to the third party. However, it appears that Chinese courts will only allow the promisee to recover his own loss, which he can keep.[62] Compensation is compensation for loss. Even when the promisee is well positioned to claim substantial damages against the promisor, as in the homeowners' association case, the promisee would hold the compensation for the third party because it is compensation for the third party's loss. If damages have already been awarded to the third party, the promisee should not be able to make a claim to recover the same loss suffered by the third party. It is advisable for this approach be adopted in the future Chinese Civil Code so as to reduce the risk of double liability.

2. Avoiding Double Liability

The conferral of a third party right does not preclude the promisee from availing himself of remedies under the contract. Both the third party and the promisee may bring an action against the promisor when the contract is breached; this raises the issue of potential double liability for the same loss on the part of the promisor. Where the third party has already recovered damages from the promisor, Chinese courts are unlikely to support the promisee's claim because the promisee is unlikely to be able to prove that he has suffered substantial loss (as the third party is the one who suffers the expectation loss).

[62] Zhu Yan [朱岩], Liyu di san ren hetong yanjiu ['Studies on Contracts in Favour of the Third Party' 利于第三人合同研究] (2005) 5 Falu Kexue [Science of Law《法律科学》] 58.

However, where the promisee has recovered damages from the promisor first, whether the third party can be awarded damages to compensate his financial loss merits some discussion. If the third party could still obtain damages from the promisor after the promisor has paid damages to the promisee, that would be an obvious case of double liability. This should be avoided for the sake of fairness and justice. Unfortunately, Chinese law is not clear on this, but in order to shield the promisor from double liability it is sensible to refer to the English law approach that in any subsequent proceedings brought by the third party the court shall reduce any award to the third party to such extent as it thinks just and fit in order to take into account the amount which has already been recovered by the promisee.[63] In brief, the promisee can only recover his own loss. If the promisee brings an action ahead of the third party in an attempt to recover the latter's loss, the damages which the promisee obtains are held by him for the third party.

The first question that Chinese courts need to address in these situations relates to the identification of the party who has in fact suffered the loss. If *both* the promisee and the third party suffer loss, they are perfectly entitled to sue for their own loss and double liability is not relevant here. If the promisee suffers no substantial loss but brings an action first, Chinese courts could direct the third party to join the litigation. This rarely happens as the promisee has no incentive to sue since he would receive no damages. In the event that it does happen, as the promisee is not deprived of the right to sue as a party to the contract, the promisee's action should be stayed until the court is satisfied that the third party has failed to commence proceedings in time or has otherwise failed to sue for damages. In so doing, it ensures that the promisor is protected against double liability when both the promisee and the third party are allowed to enforce the same term.

V. Modification and Cancellation by Contracting Parties

An alteration may operate not only to the third party's prejudice, but also to his advantage, such as increasing the payment amount to the third party. Two points seem to be quite settled in Chinese law. First, the contracting parties can modify or rescind third party rights before the third party communicates his assent to take the benefit of the contract to either the promisor or the promisee. This is because the contracting parties' right to modify and terminate the contract and the conditions for exercising the right are expressly provided for in Article 77(1) of the CCL, which stipulates that the parties may modify the contract upon reaching a consensus by consultation.[64] Furthermore, Article 93(1) of the CCL provides that the parties may terminate the contract upon reaching a consensus by consultation.[65]

Second, after the third party has notified his consent to the variation and cancellation of the contract to the contracting parties, the variation and cancellation of the contract become possible. This makes sense since the principle of good faith contained in Article 6 of the CCL would require the contracting parties to exercise their rights to modify or rescind reasonably so that the third party's interest would not be impaired.[66]

If the contracting parties could at any time modify or rescind the contract where the third party is the designated beneficiary, third party rights would be significantly limited. It would not serve the purpose of recognizing third party rights. A sensible legal approach would strike a balance between preserving the freedom of the contracting parties and permitting the creation of effective third party rights which provides certainty for third parties.

[63] s 5, Contracts (Rights of Third Parties) Act 1999 (UK).
[64] Art 77(1), CCL. [65] Art 93(1), CCL.
[66] Art 6, CCL states that 'the parties shall observe the principle of good faith in the exercise of their rights and performance of their duties'.

Chinese statutory provisions remain silent on this. It has been argued that the contracting parties *cannot* modify or rescind third party benefits once the third party has communicated his assent to at least one of the contracting parties.[67] If the assent is sent by post, it shall be accepted as communicated when received by the promisor or the promisee.

Another view is that whether the third party's assent to the rescission or modification has been communicated to the promisor or the promisee, the contracting parties have the right to rescind or modify the contract.[68] However, Han Shiyuan argues that 'if the third party suffers the loss due to the promisor's breach, his direct right of action will not be extinguished or adversely affected just because the promisee rescinds the contract'.[69] Following this argument it can be inferred that a third party's right of action can still exist regardless of whether the contract between the promisor and the promisee has been cancelled. So if the third party's right of action cannot be divested when the contract has been cancelled, it seems that the contracting parties can exercise the right of cancellation or modification regardless of whether the third party's assent has been sought. Therefore, if understood correctly, Han Shiyuan seems to argue that there is no need for the contracting parties to obtain the third party's assent in order to modify or rescind the contract. Does this mean that a direct right of action could be regarded as an independent contract? That is, an independent right of action by the third party can still exist without the principal contract. This may seem to suggest that once the third party has communicated his assent to the modification or rescission to the promisor or promisee, his right to claim is irrevocable and the contracting parties cannot between themselves divest the third party of his right. Chinese law seems unsettled on this matter and therefore it is still subject to academic debate; legislation is needed. It is suggested that the rules be simplified by stating that without the third party's consent, the contracting parties may not modify or rescind the contract so that the third party's benefits would be affected only if assent to the modification or rescission by the third party has been communicated to the contracting parties.

More difficult is the situation where the third party has not declared or communicated his consent to the contracting parties but has relied on the term. In this situation, the third party should bear the burden of proving that he has relied upon the term. However, it may be exceedingly difficult for the third party to prove that the promisor or the promisee is aware of his reliance or is reasonably expected to have foreseen his reliance. In this instance the third party's position looks vulnerable given the evidential difficulties. The fact that it is no easy task for the third party to prove the promisor's or promisee's knowledge of his reliance underlines the need for the third party to communicate his assent to the contract expressly. The final point is that despite the default rule, the contracting parties should be free to reserve in the contract the right to modify or rescind the contract without the consent of the third party. Chinese law, again, needs to address this particular point.

VI. Using Existing Legal Mechanisms to Circumvent Principle of Privity

1. Special Areas of Commercial Law

Under Chinese law, some statutes on commercial law, such as agency, insurance, carriage of goods by sea,[70] trust, and construction,[71] etc, have sidestepped privity of contract in certain situations.

[67] Zheng Yubo [郑玉波], Minfa zhai bian zong lun [*Civil Obligations* 《民法债编总论》 (15th edn, Taipei: Sanmin Bookstore 1996) 393.

[68] Han Shiyuan [韩世远], *The Law of Contract* 合同法 (3rd edn, Beijing: Law Press China 法律出版社 2011) 275.

[69] ibid 276.

[70] Art 46, Maritime Law of the PRC.

[71] Art 272, CCL.

In agency contracts, the principal has given authority to the agent to act on his behalf; the agent may receive the performance from the promisor on behalf of the principal, or he may make the contract with the promisor on behalf of the principal. In the latter case, the contract will bind the principal if the agent acts in the name of the principal and the other party, ie the promisor knows or has reason to know either from the agent or from the circumstances that the principal will be bound by the contract, that is the principal acquires rights and incurs liability.[72] Strictly speaking, the principal is not a third party as his existence is known to the other party throughout the process where the agent has actual authority. However, under the principle of apparent authority where the principal is not clearly disclosed but the agent is acting within the apparent authority, the principal may still have a right to sue and be sued.[73] In insurance, the beneficiary can directly enforce the benefit provided by the insurer.[74]

The third party may rely on a property right to claim directly, for example via trust law. The third party beneficiary has the right to enforce the performance against the trustee.[75] The basis of the third party's claim is his proprietary interest in the subject matter. He does not rely on any contract made by others.

Under Chinese law, the third party can enforce a contract for his benefit if the right has been assigned to him. Assignment is a process of transferring a contractual right to the third party by the original promisee without the consent of the original promisor.[76] It is an exception to the principle of privity. It may happen either by operation of law, such as succession[77] and subrogation,[78] or by agreement between assignor and assignee. It is notable that the CCL has introduced subrogation rights in Article 73. This means that a contractual right can be enforced against the promisor by a person to whom the promisee owes an obligation if the promisee neglects to enforce the contract against the promisor when the obligation is due.[79] In consequence, the promisor may discharge his obligation by performing to that person.[80] In the case of agreement, a third party is the assignee of the contractual right, and he has a direct right of claim against the promisor.

2. Role of Tort Law

In other situations, the third party who cannot rely on the contract may be able to circumvent the privity principle by suing in tort where he has suffered loss, caused by the promisor's negligent conduct. It is necessary to note the conceptual difference between contractual and tortious actions. First, tortious liability is determined by the existence of negligence while contractual liability is usually strict. Second, in a tort action the third party cannot recover any expectation interest while a contract claim can fulfil the third party's expectation interest.

While Chinese tort law provides a long list of protected interests, it does not cover relative (ie contractual) rights.[81] Therefore, pure economic loss cannot generally be recovered

[72] Art 88(2), Judicial Interpretation Concerning the Implementation of the GPCL. [73] Art 49, CCL.

[74] Arts 21, 22, and 23, Insurance Law of the PRC (2015 Amendment); Art 76, Road Traffic Safety Law of the PRC; Art 168, Civil Aviation Law of the PRC.

[75] Art 43, Trust Law of the PRC. [76] Arts 81–83, CCL. [77] Art 3(7), Succession Law of the PRC.

[78] Art 73, CCL; and Art 11, Judicial Interpretation I Concerning the 1999 CCL.

[79] An exception to the principle of privity is created by granting a third party, the creditor of the promisee, the right of action. This mechanism is so designed in order to deal with the situation where the third party creditor's interest may be damaged if the promisee neglects to exercise the right of enforcement against the promisor.

[80] Art 73, CCL.

[81] Chen Lei [陈磊], Chuncui jingji sunshi: Putong fa xi de shijiao ['Recovery of Pure Economic Loss: Experiences and Lessons from Common Law' 纯粹经济损失：普通法系的视角] (2010) 5 Qinghua Faxue [Tsinghua Law Review《清华法学》] 116.

in a tort action under Chinese law. It can only be recovered in exceptional circumstances, such as in cases concerning the disappointed beneficiary whose loss is caused by negligent lawyers or auditors.[82] Given the very limited recovery of pure economic loss in tort actions, it has been argued that contract law should expand the scope of protection for pure economic loss.[83] One way of doing this is perhaps to recognize a third party's direct right of action.

An expansive application of Chinese tort law compensates for the rigidity of contract law with regard to third party rights. In the Chinese Tort Liability Law, Article 2 provides for liability for the violation of a wide range of protected interests, including the right to life, the right to health, personality rights such as reputation, dignity, the right to one's image, the right to privacy, the right to marital autonomy, the right to guardianship, ownership rights, usufruct, copyright, patent rights, exclusive rights to use trade marks, discovery rights, equity rights, and inheritance rights. So, there are not many problems in finding a tort claim in Chinese law as there may be in German law.[84] However, while it is relatively easy for the third party to claim loss in a tort action, it is not equally easy for the third party to succeed in the claim. The main control device in Chinese tort law is the requirement of causation. This is different from English law where causation is rarely a problem in practice. In practice, causation is only disputed in common law when a number of separate acts by different people contributed to the harmful result, or where the harm occurred in an unusual set of circumstances.[85] In Chinese law, causation is a highly contested area because there is no functional equivalent of the 'duty of care' rule. So, there is no need for the claimant to prove that the wrongdoer owes him a legal duty or a duty of care arising from their relationship.

Under Chinese law, the tort of negligence provides an exception to the doctrine of privity. The most difficult hurdle for the third party claimant to overcome is the proof of causation between the negligent conduct and the harm caused. Insofar as causation is proved, the third party may obtain remedies in tort. That in part explains why the Chinese legislature has been slow to recognize third party rights in contract. However, given the fundamental differences between tort remedies and contract ones, there is a dire need to fill the gap with a third party contract right where tort remedies would be inadequate.

VII. Case Illustrations—How Would Chinese Law Deal with the Following Cases

1. Exemption Clauses for Stevedores

X contracts with Y to transport X's goods using Y's ship to a foreign market. The contract for the carriage of goods by sea between X and Y contains an exemption of liability provision which purports to protect Z, the stevedores hired to unload X's goods from Y's ship once it arrives at the docks. As a result of Z's carelessness, X's goods are damaged while they are being unloaded from the ship and X wants to sue Z for negligence to recover damages for the losses suffered by X. Can Z rely on the exemption of liability provision in the contract between X and Y?

[82] Cheng Xiao [程啸], Qinquan zeren fa jiaocheng [*An Introduction to Tort Law*侵权责任法教程] (Beijing: Renmin University of China Press 2009) 205.

[83] Zhang Xinbao [张新宝] and Li Qian [李倩], Chuncui jingji sunshi peichang guize ['The Compensation Rule of Pure Economic Loss, Theory, Practice and Legislative Choice' 纯粹经济损失赔偿规则] (2009) 1 Faxue Luntan [Legal Forum 《法学论坛》] 7.

[84] § 823(1) BGB lists only life, body, health, freedom, property, and other rights. This does not allow recovery in tort for negligently inflicted pure economic loss.

[85] HLA Hart and T Honoré, *Causation in the Law* (2nd edn, Oxford: Clarendon Press 1985) ch 6.

The CCL provisions do not provide a straightforward answer to this question. However, under the current Chinese law, Z would have a strong case for relying on the exemption of liability provision if Z is regarded as an agent or employee of Y.

If the privity principle is applied rigidly, the stevedores would lose because they could not have been protected by the terms of the bill of lading without being in any contractual relationship with X, the cargo owner. The question is whether the stevedores could succeed because they were beneficiaries, even if they were not a party. The contract between X and Y provided expressly for the protection of Z under the exemption of liability clause. So there are two lines of possibility. First, if Z was clearly identified as a beneficiary in the contract with a protective benefit, Z should be able to have the benefit of the defence against X's claim. Second, if Z was not clearly identified but Z was described as Y's 'employee', 'agent', or 'subcontractor' rather than as an 'independent contractor', Z would also very likely be able to rely on the exemption clause as a defence in a tort action.

There are three policy reasons for favouring this holding. First, to decide otherwise would cause liability to rest on minor individuals (the subcontractors) with a weak position in a large company (the carrier) that is protected by the exemption clause. Second, to hold the stevedores liable would have a significant implication for the insurance industry in that area of business. The standard practice in carriage of goods by sea is that the cargo owner's insurance will cover the loss above the financial limits contained in the contract, whether the loss is caused by the carrier, its employee, or a subcontractor. If this insurance arrangement could not achieve its purpose, insurance companies' business might be adversely affected, as there would be no need for the insurance if Z were held liable. Third, the facts of the case indicate that: (1) X knew that Z would actually unload X's goods from Y's ship; and (2) X intended to protect Z with such an exemption of liability clause. While Z was not a party to the contract, it would be odd to contradict the intentions of the promisor and the promisee. It would therefore be sensible for X to sue Z for negligence.

If Z was an agent or a subcontractor of Y, the Chinese judiciary would hold that the contract itself covered the protection for Z; so the tort claim would not be accepted. This is because Article 58 of the Chinese Maritime Law contains a Himalaya clause which protects any persons who are not parties to the bill of lading contract provided that the persons are the carrier's servants, employees, or agents. But this protection is not extended to independent contractors.

Article 58 of the Chinese Maritime Law stipulates:

> The defence and limitation of liability provided for shall apply to any legal action brought against the carrier with regard to the loss of or damage to or delay in delivery of the goods covered by the contract of carriage of goods by sea, whether the claimant is a party to the contract or whether the action is founded in contract or in tort. The provisions shall apply when the action referred to is brought against the carrier's servant or agent. The carrier's servant or agent proves that his action was within the scope of his employment or agency.

A Chinese case decided by the Guangzhou Maritime Court in 2003 is similar to the hypothetical scenario.[86] The claimant company contracted with COSCO Container Lines Co Ltd ('COSCO') to transport the claimant's manufacturing equipment using COSCO's ship from Italy to Guangzhou port. The stevedores hired by Guangzhou Container Co Ltd ('GCC')

86 *Contractual Disputes over Goods Damage between Fujian Tingyi Food Co, COSCO Container Lines Co Ltd v Maritime Transportation* Fujian ding yi shipin youxian gongsi su zhongyuan jizhuangxiang yunshu youxian gongsi deng haishang huowu yunshu hetong huosun peichang jiufen an福建顶益食品有限公司诉中远集装箱运输有限公司等海上货物运输合同货损赔偿纠纷案(2003) Guang Hai Fa Chu Zi Di 171 Hao [the Judgment of the Guangzhou Maritime Court (Trial) No 171 广海法初字第171号].

carelessly damaged the goods when unloading them from COSCO's ship. Note, however, that there was no exemption of liability clause in the contract between the claimant and the carrier. The claimant first brought an action against both COSCO and GCC claiming the loss suffered. The Guangzhou Maritime Court held that GCC was not a party to the carriage of goods contract, so GCC was not liable for the loss. Subsequently, the claimant brought a negligence tort claim against GCC. In the first trial, the Guangzhou Maritime Court held that since GCC was an agent or a subcontractor of the carrier, COSCO, and applying the Himalaya clause contained in Article 58 of the Chinese Maritime Law, GCC was not liable. On appeal, the Guangdong High Court overturned the first instance ruling as GCC was an independent contractor so the Himalaya clause was not applicable;[87] GCC was liable in negligence.

In sum, under Chinese law it seems that Z might rely on the exemption of liability provision in the contract between X and Y as a defence against X if Z was clearly identified as a beneficiary in the contract. In addition, since there is a Himalaya clause contained in Article 58 of the Chinese Maritime Law, Z would be protected if Z was regarded as an agent, a servant, or an employee of Y, but not if Z was an independent contractor.

2. Selling Bread

X leases two adjoining properties to Y and Z. The lease between X and Y barred Y from selling bread because Z sold bread from his leased property. Can X and Y agree to lift the bar?

This question is whether restrictions on the business of tenants may be enforced by other tenants. As the case is fact-sensitive, it is necessary to assume that this is not a novation contract signed by the three parties X, Y, and Z with a protective benefit for Z.

The ruling therefore hinges upon the existence of a third party right under the lease contract between X and Y. If there was no express provision in the contract between X and Y clearly identifying Z as the beneficiary of this restriction, it is hard to prove that the parties intended to confer a benefit on Z. This is particularly so in view of the lack of third party rights in Chinese contract law. Assuming this is the case, Z only enjoys a derivative interest (反射利益); this cannot justify his direct right to claim a third party right. Would Chinese courts attempt to establish that a common intention to benefit Z by X and Y could be found from the surrounding or attendant circumstances? In other words, would Chinese courts try to find, by exercising their discretion, that restricting Y from selling bread could only have been intended to benefit the lessee of the neighbouring shop, Z? Given the SPC's restrictive stance on third party rights, it is unlikely that Chinese courts would do so.

Nonetheless, if Z's benefit was clearly mentioned in the contract between X and Y, then Z's right of action has been given. The next key issue would become whether X and Y can modify or rescind the contract. Here Z needs to prove: (1) Z has communicated his assent to the modification or rescission expressly to X or Y; (2) X or Y is aware that Z has relied on the term; or (3) X or Y can reasonably foresee Z's reliance upon the term.

Assuming that Z has not expressed his assent to X or Y, it could be ascertained with reasonable certainty from the surrounding circumstances that Z has relied on the term. It is

[87] *Contractual Disputes over Goods Damage between Fujian Tingyi Food Co, COSCO Container Lines Co Ltd v Maritime Transportation* Fujian ding yi shipin youxian gongsi su zhongyuan jizhuangxiang yunshu youxian gongsi deng haishang huowu yunshu hetong huosun peichang jiufen an福建顶益食品有限公司诉中远集装箱运输有限公司等海上货物运输合同货损赔偿纠纷案(2003) Guang Gao Fa Er Zi Di 233 Hao [the Judgment of the Guangdong High Court (Second) No 233 广高法二字第233号].

notable that reliance itself is enough, and there is no need to prove that Z acted to his detriment. For example, let us assume that it is a long lease and Z had been a tenant of the shop for ten years, as had his father before him. Also, it may be the case that X himself enjoys an easement right prohibiting Y's property from being used to run a bread business before X leased to Z. Chinese law knows of no law of restrictive covenant which exists under the common law but servitude is recognized. In the absence of a straightforward third party right, the principle of good faith and fair dealing set out in Article 6 of the CCL could be used to argue that if reliance by the third party has been proved, then the contracting parties may not by agreement rescind or modify the contract without the third party's consent. In other words, without Z's consent to the lifting of the bar, Z would be able to enforce the restrictive term and perhaps claim compensation for any loss suffered.

3. The Stolen Shop Takings

X bank makes a contract for Y security company to collect Z store's takings. The contract requires Y to use armoured vehicles and take out insurance. Y failed to do these and the takings were stolen while being collected in an ordinary car. Can Z sue?

Z could sue Y to claim for the loss he suffered due to the negligent promisor's conduct. Z only needs to prove the causal link between Z's loss and Y's breach arising from his negligent conduct. Insofar as causation between Y's conduct of negligence and the harm suffered by Z is proved, Y, the civil wrongdoer, is held liable.

In the domain of contract law, the discussion is relatively straightforward. A fundamental issue is at stake—whether there is a stipulation for the benefit of a third party, namely, Z store. As the facts provided suggest, the contract between X bank and Y security company explicitly requires Y to use armoured vehicles and take out insurance in order to successfully collect Z store's takings. Here Z store has been mentioned in the contract. But does this mean that both X and Y have a common intention to confer a benefit on Z if the contract does not expressly state this? This is a matter of contract interpretation. The objective of using armoured vehicles and taking out insurance is to ensure the safe carriage of the takings in consideration of the payment of an agreed service fee to Y security company. In brief, all these measures agreed by X and Y to ensure the safe carriage of Z's takings are indicative of the intention to confer the benefit on Z. In the contract performance, Y had full knowledge of the terms. It should not be difficult to argue that both X and Y intended the contract to benefit Z. Therefore, when Y breached the contract causing Z store a loss, Z has a direct claim to recover the loss.

VIII. Conclusion

Chinese statutory law is silent on third party rights. There is no mention of third party rights, if any, in the CCL other than what is briefly set out in the two loosely framed provisions, Article 64 and Article 65 in the CCL stating the obvious: that the promisor is liable to the promisee when the promisor fails to perform a contract for the third party's benefit; and that the promisor is liable to the promisee if the third party fails to perform the obligation. Article 64 does not recognize third party rights in the sense that a third party beneficiary is given a direct right to enforce the performance agreed by the contracting parties. Given this, Chinese courts tend to apply the privity rule strictly and third party rights are generally disallowed. Nevertheless, in certain circumstances, third party rights may be recognized if they are expressly provided for in the contract. Obviously, this situation is unsatisfactory as it: (1) contradicts the contracting parties' intentions and causes injustice to the third party;

(2) leads to inconvenience and difficulties in commercial life; and (3) causes uncertainty and unpredictability. Therefore, China is still in limbo, for it has no explicit third party rights in spite of fast-growing business transactions. Article 64 of the CCL was poorly drafted leaving loopholes. It is increasingly becoming a source of discrepancies in judicial decisions in China. As a matter of necessity, therefore, clear third party rights should be recognized and introduced in Chinese law by way of legislative amendments.

In the legislative drafting process, some contract law scholars were invited to participate but it seems that they had little say in the final product of law-making. A third party right was in the academic draft under parliamentary deliberation but, insidiously, it was taken out of the final version and nobody seems to know the reason behind it. Curiously, it has been argued that third party rights *have* been recognized despite the lack of an unambiguous provision in the CCL.[88] The reasons given were, first, market forces necessitate it; second, there was a provision recognizing third party rights in the original draft of the CCL. Neither of these reasons is convincing. It seems that despite the legislative loophole, some academics try to create a legal fiction in order to protect third parties. This is not only unacceptable but also dangerous. It is market forces and commercial practice that call for reform. Action to reform needs to be taken rather than maintaining the status quo and justifying the unsophisticated legislation. To do so would frustrate the purpose of introducing third party rights. More than that, the fiction would set an unwelcome precedent and generate a scramble in the Chinese contract law system. If Article 64 can be interpreted as giving a green light to third party rights, the courts will sidestep the law on paper, a hard law, and turn to academic commentaries, a soft law, in practice. This would allow academics, combined with the judiciary, to undermine and usurp the legislature's power. In view of this, one cannot assume that the initial academic provisions which were deleted in the final version should be used as a source of law in court proceedings.[89] Because of these three reasons, we need to face reality and call for long-awaited legislative reform.

When third party rights are reformed in Chinese contract law, not only should a rule recognizing third party rights be declared, a set of rules should also be introduced setting out the relationship between tort actions and third party contracts, the defences available to the promisee, when variation and cancellation of the contract are permitted, and how to avoid the promisor's double liability. Additionally, a framework should be designed to interpret the contracting parties' common intention to confer on the third party a right to sue where the contracting parties have not clearly expressed that right. All in all, as a later bloomer, China, taking into consideration its own social, economic, and cultural contexts, needs to learn from experienced jurisdictions and avoid dysfunctional practices in this area of law.

[88] Han Shiyuan [韩世远], Shi lun xiang di san ren luxing de hetong – dui woguo <hetong fa> di 64 tiao de jieshi ['Discussion on Contracts with Performance to Third Parties' 试论向第三人履行的合同—对我国<合同法>第64 条的解释] (2004) 6 Falu Kexue [Science of Law 《法律科学》] 105–106; Cui Jianyuan, Wei di san ren liyi hetong de guige lun ['Discussion on Third-Party Contracts—From the Perspective of Article 64' 为第三人利益合同的规格论] (2008) 1 Zhengzhi Yu Falu [Political Science and Law 《政治与法律》] 73.

[89] Zhang Jiayong [张家勇], Wei di san ren liyi de hetong de zhidu gouzao [*Designing a Third Party Contract Rule*为第三人利益的合同的制度构造] (Beijing: Law Press 2007) 361–365.

4

Contract Formation in India: Law and Practice

*Nigam NUGGEHALLI**

I. Introduction

Unlike the United Kingdom, where the law on contract formation is contained primarily in the common law, the Indian law on formation of contracts is for the most part regulated by the Indian Contract Act 1872 ('ICA'). The ICA is a colonial era enactment intended to codify the English common law on contracts. Consequently, Indian courts tend to rely on English common law principles to interpret the ICA. A preliminary question relates to the impact of the English common law on Indian contract law after the enactment of the ICA. The ICA's preamble states that the Act has been enacted because 'it is expedient to define and amend certain parts of the law relating to contracts', thus making it clear that the ICA is not meant to be exhaustive of the law on contracts in India.

On matters that have been expressly dealt with by the ICA, it is clear that the rules of the ICA would reign supreme. In other areas, the courts have adopted language that varies slightly from case to case. In *Naresh Chandra Guha v Ram Chandra Samanta*,[1] the Calcutta High Court held that in the case of disputes on matters not covered by the ICA, the case should be decided on 'established English principles *not inconsistent* with principles of equity, justice and good conscience'.[2] This case suggests that gaps in the application of the ICA would be filled by English common law principles as long as these are not opposed to the principles of equity, justice, and good conscience. Such an approach in practice gives primary consideration to English common law principles in cases where the ICA provisions are not applicable.

However, other cases have taken a different approach and applied the 'principles of equity, justice and good conscience' to achieve 'complete justice'.[3] The difference in terminology is not merely academic. In order to do complete justice, the courts might deviate from English case law in appropriate circumstances.[4] In practice, Indian courts generally tend to follow the lead of the English common law.[5] However, in cases where the ICA has diverged from the English common law,[6] Indian courts have not hesitated to depart from the traditional English principles of contract formation in interpreting the ICA.

* Cite as N Nuggehalli, 'Contract Formation in India: Law and Practice' in Chen-Wishart, Loke, & Vogenauer, *Studies in the Contract Laws of Asia Vol II: Formation and Third Party Beneficiaries* (Oxford: OUP 2017) ch 4. I thank Professor Michael Furmston, Professor Mindy Chen-Wishart, Professor Stefan Vogenauer, Professor Alexander Loke, and Rachel Chenchiah for their thoughtful comments on this chapter.

[1] AIR 1952 Cal 93 (HC). [2] ibid para 12.

[3] *Deb Narayan Dutt v Chunilal Ghose* (1914) ILR 41 Cal 137 (HC) para 3.

[4] Refer to the discussion on Promissory Estoppel in section IX.3.

[5] See the Supreme Court's comments in *Bhagwandas Goverdhandas Kedia v Girdharilal Parshottamdass & Ors* AIR 1966 SC 543 (SC) para 13. According to the court, the expressions 'justice, equity and good conscience' are expressions that 'have been consistently interpreted to mean the rules of English common law, so far as they are applied to the Indian society and circumstance'.

[6] eg refer to the discussion on s 63 in section IX.4.

Contract Formation in India: Law and Practice. Nigam Nuggehalli.

Indian contract law begins with the idea of an 'agreement'. The path to an agreement begins with a proposal,[7] which if accepted,[8] results in a promise. Every promise, or a set of promises, is an agreement.[9] The ICA makes it clear that not all agreements are contracts. Only those agreements that are *enforceable by law* are contracts.[10] Therefore, the ICA makes a distinction between agreements and contracts. A legal relationship between two persons might qualify as an agreement under the ICA but might still fail to be recognized as a contract under the ICA. It follows that a legal relationship can fail the contract formation test on two counts under the ICA. The legal relationship may not reach the stage of an *agreement* and even if it did, might not otherwise be *enforceable by law* and is therefore devoid of contractual force.

Section 10 of the ICA is the primary provision that is concerned with the identification of agreements that are enforceable by law. Under section 10, all agreements are contracts 'if they are made by the *free consent* of parties *competent* to contract, for a *lawful consideration* and with a *lawful object*, and are not hereby expressly declared to be *void*' (emphasis added). Section 10 does not require that all contracts have to be reduced to writing in order to be enforceable.[11]

The rest of this chapter will discuss the main features of the Indian law on contract formation. Given the breadth of the topic, the discussion of case law will be selective. The case law discussed in this chapter provides a flavour of the debates and controversies in this area while also acquainting the reader with the main themes and trends in the Indian law on contract formation.

II. Intention

Contract formation involves intentional actions on the part of the persons entering into the contract in the form of proposals (offers) and acceptances. Must the parties to an agreement really intend to enter into an agreement, or is it sufficient if it looks to a reasonable third person that the parties intended to enter into an agreement? In other words, should the test of intentional action in contracts be subjective or objective?

In applying English law, the English courts have adopted the objective approach to the issue of contract formation. In one of the leading cases on this point, the House of Lords pointed out that the relevant test of an intention to enter into a legal relationship is that which would be understood by a reasonable person in the shoes of the person receiving the proposal.[12]

In India, the situation is made clear by the statute itself. The ICA deals separately with the idea of a communication of a proposal and an acceptance. Section 3 of the ICA states that the communication of a proposal and an acceptance is deemed to be made by an act or omission of the party proposing or accepting 'by which he intends to communicate such proposal, acceptance…or *which has the effect of communicating it*' (emphasis added). The ICA thus explicitly accounts for an objective test. This has been confirmed in the Supreme Court case of *Commissioner of Wealth Tax, Bhopal v Abdul Hussain Mulla Muhammad Ali.*[13]

[7] s 2(a), ICA defines a proposal, discussed further in section III.
[8] s 2(b), ICA defines an acceptance, discussed further in section IV.
[9] s 2(e), ICA. [10] s 2(h), ICA.
[11] s 10 states that 'Nothing herein contained shall affect any law in force in India and not hereby expressly repealed, by which any contract is required to be made in writing or in the presence of witnesses, or any law relating to the registration of documents.'
[12] *Paul Wilson & Co v Partenreederei Hannah Blumenthal (The Hannah Blumenthal)* [1983] 1 ALL ER 34 (HL) 48–49.
[13] AIR 1988 SC 1417 (SC) para 5.

Abdul Hussain was a case of the imposition of a wealth tax in India, the incidence of which depended on the legal enforceability of a debt. If the debt was enforceable in law, the creditor would have been subject to a wealth tax on the value of the debt. The creditor claimed that the debt was an agreement made in good faith between the parties and that the agreement could not reasonably be construed as an agreement intended to have any legal consequences.[14] The creditor even adduced a declaration from the debtor that the loan did not impose any obligations on the debtor.[15] The Supreme Court ignored the declaration and explicitly adopted an objective test to the question of whether the agreement was intended to have legal consequences.[16] It decided that the debt did indeed objectively fulfil the criteria for a legally enforceable agreement under the ICA.[17]

III. Offers

Offers, along with acceptances, are the building blocks of contracts. An *agreement* under Indian contract law is reached by way of an *offer* from one party that is *accepted* by another party. As discussed later, the ICA has detailed rules on offers and acceptances. One question that frequently arises is whether an offer, by itself, has any legal implications. This question arises usually in two contexts. In the case of tender offers, it is in some instances argued that an offer, once made, ought not to be withdrawn as it would lead to undue hardship for the person who floated the tender. Similarly, in some contexts where parties are negotiating with each other, it is argued that offers ought not to be withdrawn as parties are under an obligation to negotiate in good faith. Both issues will be addressed in this section.

The ICA uses the nomenclature 'proposal' to signify an offer. According to section 2(a) of the ICA, when one person signifies to another his willingness to do or to abstain from doing anything, with a view to obtaining the assent of that other person to such act or abstinence, he is said to make a proposal. The ICA defines an acceptance in the following manner (section 2(d)): when the person to whom the proposal is made signifies his assent thereto, the proposal is said to be accepted. A proposal, when accepted, becomes a promise. A promise or a set of promises comprises an agreement (section 2(e)).

It is clear from the above description that an offer needs to be assented to before it can become a promise and provided it fulfils the other conditions of the ICA, is a constituent element of a contract. This legislative structure explicitly allows for an offer to be revoked before its acceptance. According to section 5 of the ICA, a proposal may be revoked at any time before the communication of its acceptance is complete as against the proposer, but not afterwards.[18]

1. Tender Offers

The ICA's provisions allowing revocation of offers might create some difficulty in the case of tender offers. The tender process begins with a person, usually the government in the

[14] ibid paras 2 and 9. [15] ibid para 1.

[16] ibid para 10. The Supreme Court's observations are instructive of its objective approach:

> Here, one partner has lent a large sum to the other to be utilised as capital in the partnership venture. The transaction is in the context of a commercial venture. The presumption is that legal obligations are intended. The onus is on the parties asserting the absence of legal obligations and the test is not subjective to the parties; but is an objective one.

[17] ibid paras 11 and 12. [18] Communication of acceptances is considered in section IV.2.

Indian context, inviting offers (tenders) for the supply of goods or services to the government. In response, there might be tender offers from more than one person in which case the government accepts one of the tender offers based on some criteria (usually the offer with the lowest price). The tender offer, like any other proposal under the ICA, can be revoked by the proposer before the proposal is accepted. In some cases, the Indian Government has tried to enforce the tender offer even after the tender offer has been withdrawn. However, the courts have held that in tender offer situations, much like in the case of any other offer under the ICA, the tender offer can be withdrawn before it is accepted, and this is the case even if the tender rules promulgated by the government state that a tender offer cannot be withdrawn.[19]

2. Duty to Negotiate in Good Faith

There are no Indian decisions on the duty to negotiate in good faith. It is likely that Indian courts would follow *Walford v Miles*,[20] and decline to recognize such a duty in a commercial context. English law has traditionally been indifferent to the idea of recognizing qualitative standards for commercial negotiations. Many English decisions base their indifference in this area to the uncertainties inherent in policing the quality of negotiations when offers are going back and forth. Consequently, good faith arguments are rarely successful in regulating the manner in which parties negotiate with each other.

Therefore, at least in purely commercial circumstances where two unrelated parties are bargaining with each other at arm's length, it is unlikely that the withdrawal of an offer would be seen by Indian courts as violating any good faith duties.[21] An allied issue is the legal position of agreements that expressly include the language of negotiations. For example, two parties might enter into an 'agreement to agree'. English law has refused to give legal effect to such agreements particularly when the terms of the agreement left open for future negotiations relate to important elements of the contract such as the price.[22] The same position is likely in Indian law as the ICA voids agreements if such agreements contain terms that are uncertain.[23]

[19] *Rajendra Kumar Verma v State of Madhya Pradesh & Ors* AIR 1972 Madhya Pradesh 131 (HC). For the proposition that an offer can be withdrawn even if an offer has been provisionally accepted, see *Somasundaram Pillai v The Provincial Government of Madras* AIR 1947 Mad 366 (HC). This case involved a public auction conducted under conditions of sale that prohibited the withdrawal of offers once the offers were provisionally accepted. The Madras High Court held that such a prohibition was ineffective in preventing the withdrawal of offers under the ICA. The court made it clear that, under the ICA, an offer could be withdrawn at any time until the time of its unconditional (not provisional) acceptance (para 14).

[20] [1992] 2 AC 128 (HL). In *Walford*, the good faith argument was brought into the picture in a somewhat convoluted manner. Walford and Miles negotiated a sale of Miles's business. Miles and Walford agreed that if Walford provided a comfort letter from his bank supporting the acquisition of Miles's business, Miles would desist from negotiating with other purchasers. Walford procured the comfort letter; however, Miles continued to negotiate with other buyers and sold his business to another buyer. Walford's argument was that Miles was under an implied duty to negotiate in good faith, which he had violated. The court rejected this argument. The key reasoning behind the court's decision was that a duty to negotiate in good faith was impossible to police. It was difficult to police because the parties could change their positions at any time and, keeping in mind the inherently adversarial position of parties that is assumed in English contract law, there was no way in which the courts could identify a particular negotiating tactic as a violation of good faith dealing between the parties. Notice in particular [1992] 2 AC 128, 138 where Lord Ackner said,'[h]ow is a vendor ever to know that he is entitled to withdraw from further negotiations?'

[21] This chapter does not consider contracts with public authorities. Public authorities in India are subject to constitutional obligations in the process of contract negotiations with private parties. These constitutional obligations mandate that the government must not act arbitrarily and must conform to principles of natural justice in contracting with private parties. See eg the case of *Mahabir Auto Stores v Indian Oil Corporation* (1990) 3 SCC 752 (SC).

[22] See eg *Courtney and Fairbairn Ltd v Tolani Brothers (Hotels) Ltd* [1975] 1 WLR 297 (CA Civ).

[23] s 29, ICA: 'Agreements, the meaning of which is not certain, or capable of being made certain, are void.'

IV. Acceptance

1. Requirements of Acceptance

The ICA covers the mechanics of acceptance in four sections. Section 3 is concerned with the communication of acceptances. Section 4 focuses on when the communication of an acceptance would be complete. Section 7 insists that an acceptance has to be absolute. Section 8 provides that a proposal can be accepted through conduct rather than through a verbal or written communication. This segment will consider some issues arising under section 3. The next segment will consider certain timing issues in acceptances that arise under section 4.

Section 3 states than an acceptance can occur through an act or omission that intends to communicate such an acceptance *or* which has the effect of communicating such an acceptance. This is a fairly liberal rule but even such a rule has its limitations. For instance, it appears to exclude silence as a form of communicating an acceptance. One might argue that an 'omission' can manifest itself in silence in certain instances. However, there are so many complexities involved in introducing silence as a mode of acceptance that, barring exceptional circumstances, the law both in the UK and in India has tended to be quite strict in considering silence as a mode of acceptance. The English common law has followed the famous case of *Felthouse v Bindley*,[24] in which a person who offered to sell a horse could not argue for a binding agreement merely because his proposal stated that silence as a response to the proposal would be deemed as an acceptance of the proposal.

Likewise, Indian courts have generally tended to look unfavourably at silence as a mode of acceptance. An example is the Supreme Court case of *Life Insurance Corporation of India v Raja Vasireddy Komalavalli Kamba & Ors*,[25] in which the legal dispute concerned the formation of a life insurance contract. The putative insured made an offer to the insurers. The insurers did not communicate their acceptance of the offer. The insurers, however, accepted the payment of some insurance premiums from the putative insured. The Supreme Court held that without a communication of an unconditional acceptance from the insurers, there was no binding agreement. Mere receipt of insurance premiums would not amount to acceptance. The court made it clear that the insurance officials must communicate their acceptance through words or some positive actions to signify their assent to the offer. A passive acceptance of insurance premiums could not constitute acceptance for the purposes of contract formation.[26] This case was not a case of silence *simpliciter* as there was some form of conduct by the insurers (passive acceptance of premiums) in response to the offer of the putative insured. However, the Supreme Court treated a mere passive acceptance of insurance premiums as equivalent to silence *simpliciter*. Presumably, the Supreme Court's decision was based on protecting an insurer from contractual liability unless there has been a clear and unconditional positive act of acceptance from the insurer.

However, the judicial hostility towards silence as a mode of communication also has its limits. A case in point is *Ramji Dayawala & Sons (P) Ltd v Invest Import*,[27] which concerned a dispute between parties about a contract containing an arbitration clause that referred disputes between the parties to a foreign arbitrator in Paris. One of the parties had objected to the arbitration clause during the negotiations stage. However, the arbitration clause made its way into the final signed agreement. Immediately after signing the agreement, the party that had objected to the arbitration clause ('the objecting party') wrote twice to the other party to the effect that the arbitration clause was unacceptable to them and should be

[24] (1862) 11 CBNS 869, 142 ER 1037.
[25] AIR 1984 SC 1014 (SC).
[26] ibid para 18.
[27] AIR 1981 SC 2085 (SC).

deleted from the agreement. The other party did not reply to these communications from the objecting party but continued to otherwise transact with the objecting party under the contract.

Subsequently, when the question of the arbitration clause came up in judicial proceedings, the Supreme Court ruled that the arbitration clause was not part of the contract that came into existence between the parties. It arrived at this conclusion in the following manner. The arbitration clause had been disputed by one of the parties. The party that objected to the arbitration clause made a counter-offer to the effect that the contract ought not to have the arbitration clause in question. The other party, through its silence, accepted this counter-offer.[28]

This might appear to be a surprising conclusion but is consistent with the facts leading up to the case. One of the parties had always disputed the arbitration clause and this disputation also continued immediately after the signing of the contract. It is the consistent denial of a contractual clause taken by one of the parties that led the Supreme Court to consider silence from the other party as acceptance of a certain kind of contractual bargain.[29]

2. Timing of Acceptance

The timing of the acceptance of a proposal is important in Indian contract law. Once a proposal is accepted, the proposal cannot be revoked, and provided other conditions are fulfilled, a contract comes into place. The general rule in section 4 of the ICA is: 'The communication of a proposal is complete when it comes to the knowledge of the person to whom it is made.' However, as is common in the case of contracts concluded through the post, what happens if a proposal is revoked in the time period between the sending of the proposal and the receipt of its acceptance?

The ICA has detailed rules regarding this question. According to section 4 of the ICA:

> The communication of an acceptance is complete:-
>
> as against the proposer, when it is put in the course of transmission to him, so as to be out of the power of the acceptor;
>
> as against the acceptor, when it comes to the knowledge of the proposer.

Curiously, in the case of a delay between the transmission and the receipt of the communication of an acceptance, the position of the acceptor has been strengthened vis-à-vis that of the proposer. As soon as the acceptance is put in the course of transmission, for example by post, the communication of the acceptance is complete as against the proposer. Since this rule applies mainly to postal communication, it has come to be known as the 'postal rule'. One implication of the postal rule is that *the proposer cannot revoke his offer after the acceptance has entered the course of transmission*. Thus, the risk of delay or loss of the acceptance is on the proposer rather than the acceptor. This rule was invoked in *JK Enterprises v State of Madhya Pradesh*[30] in which the Madhya Pradesh High Court considered the case of a proposer trying to withdraw his offer after the acceptance had already been sent by post. The court made it clear that a valid contract had come into place the moment the acceptance was posted.

[28] ibid para 17.

[29] The Supreme Court also considered this issue from another perspective by treating, in the alternative, the arbitration clause as severable from the rest of the contract. Since there was no *consensus ad idem* regarding the arbitration clause, the arbitration clause never came into existence. See *Ramji Dayawala* (n 27) para 17 for a discussion on this point.

[30] AIR 1997 MP 68 (HC).

The postal rule in section 4, while incorporating the English common law on the same point, is arguably more liberal. As the provision predicates that the communication of an acceptance is complete as against the acceptor when it comes to the knowledge of the proposer, it allows the acceptor to revoke his acceptance even after he has posted his acceptance as long as his revocation reaches the proposer before the acceptance reaches him by post. In English law, there is no decision specifically on this issue. However, it is commonly assumed that the moment of contract under the postal acceptance rule is at the point the letter is posted. One English authority has said that the acceptor ought not to be allowed to revoke his acceptance after he posts his acceptance.[31]

In the case of instantaneous communication, ie where there is no delay between the transmission and the receipt of the communication of an acceptance, there has been some debate in Indian law on the application of section 4. In *Bhagwandas Goverdhandas Kedia v M/s Girdharilal Parshottamdass & Ors*,[32] the Supreme Court considered this issue in the case of an acceptance given over the telephone. The proposer and the acceptor were in two places; the proposer was in Ahmedabad and the acceptor was in Khamgaon. The acceptance took place over the phone. The place of the conclusion of the contract was important because it would determine the court in which the parties would litigate their contractual differences. The proposer argued that the contract was completed when the acceptance was intimated to him at Ahmedabad (over the phone). The acceptor argued that the contract was completed as soon as he accepted over the phone at Khamgaon.

The Supreme Court, following the English common law rule laid down in *Entores Ltd v Miles Far East Corporation*,[33] ruled that the postal rule was not applicable to instantaneous communications.[34] The normal rule is that the communication of an acceptance would be complete when it is intimated to the proposer. Therefore, it was held that the contract was concluded when the acceptance was intimated to the proposer at Ahmedabad, and the court in Ahmedabad had jurisdiction to try any contractual disputes between the parties.[35]

V. The Battle of Forms

Frequently, both parties to a purported contract try to ensure that the contract is formed on their respective standard terms. This is known as the 'battle of forms'. The genesis of the battle of forms lies in the traditional common law principle that offers and acceptances in contracts have to mirror each other for a valid contract to come into existence. Section 7 of the ICA statutorily incorporates this principle in the following way: 'In order to convert a proposal into a promise the acceptance must be absolute and unqualified'.

Butler Machine Tool Co Ltd v Ex-Cell-O Corp (England) Ltd[36] exemplifies the common law approach to the battle of forms issue. Two parties (the seller and the buyer) negotiated with each other on their respective standard contractual terms. However, during the course of the negotiations, the buyer made an offer (by placing an order) to the seller accompanied by an acknowledgement receipt meant for the seller to sign that stated: 'We accept your order on the terms and conditions stated therein…' The seller signed the acknowledgement receipt and sent it back. It was held that in the negotiations back and forth, as soon as an

[31] See J Beatson, A Burrows, and J Cartwright, *Anson's Law of Contract* (29th edn, Oxford: OUP 2010) 52, where the authors state: 'This, it is argued, is both the logical and fair conclusion; otherwise the offeree could blow both hot and cold, having the benefit of certainty in the postal acceptance, and the opportunity to revoke it if the offer turned out suddenly to be disadvantageous.'

[32] AIR 1966 SC 543 (SC).

[33] [1955] EWCA Civ 3, [1955] 2 QB 327 (CA).

[34] *Bhagwandas* (n 32) para 17.

[35] ibid para 18.

[36] [1977] EWCA Civ 9.

offer is accepted without any objections, a contract comes into place.[37] By unconditionally accepting the offer of the buyer (signing the acknowledgement slip), the seller had entered into a contract on the standard terms of the buyer. Thus, at the moment that an offer is accepted as such by the party to which the offer is made, contractual obligations are created, as long as other conditions of contractual validity are fulfilled. The ICA has statutorily recognized this traditional principle of acceptance in section 7 as it provides validity only to absolute and unqualified acceptances of proposals, ie proposals that are accepted without any objection by the other party.[38]

VI. Uncertain and Incomplete Contracts

According to section 29 of the ICA, agreements, the meaning of which is not certain, *or capable of being made certain*, are void. The Indian law on vague or incomplete contractual terms follows the English common law on the same point, ie a contract that is silent or ambiguous about important terms such as the price or (in some instances) the time of performance would fail to create any contractual obligations.[39] The most pertinent question in the context of section 29 is what makes uncertain agreements 'capable of being made certain'? In some instances, even a liberal interpretation of an agreement cannot overcome the uncertainty in the agreement. For example, in *NK Giriraja Shetty v NK Parthasarathy Shetty*,[40] the plaintiff attempted to enforce an agreement of sale of land. However, the precise details of the property that was the subject matter of the sale were not clear and the plaintiff could not adduce sufficient evidence to provide certainty to the terms.[41] The Karnataka High Court held that the agreement was too uncertain to be enforced.

The *Giriraja* case can be contrasted with the case of *Rajkishor Mohanty v Banabehari Patnaik*,[42] where the parties had not mentioned the price at which the sale of land would take place. Normally the absence of price would be fatal to such a contract but the court was willing to imply a reasonable price in the circumstances of the case. The sale of land was part of a complex arrangement that settled a property dispute. Given that the parties clearly intended to transfer land between themselves, the court was willing to imply a 'reasonable' price in the contract to give effect to the parties' intentions.[43]

In addition to contracts that are incomplete, Indian courts have also had to consider the effect of *ambiguous* terms in contracts which might potentially make the contract uncertain and therefore void under section 29. Indian courts have tried to forestall voiding such contracts by looking to the commercial context in which the contract was made. A case in point is the Supreme Court case of *Dhanrajamal Gobindram v Shamji Kalidas*.[44]

In *Dhanrajamal*, the contract was for the purchase of African raw cotton. The contract was subject to the 'usual Force Majeure clause'. When the buyers did not perform their part of the contract, the sellers sued on the contract. The buyers argued that the phrase 'the usual Force Majeure clause' was vague and uncertain[45] and therefore voided the contract. The court disagreed because of two related but distinct reasons. First, the phrase 'force majeure' itself was not vague; it denoted, even if taken in its widest amplitude, the

[37] ibid para 5.

[38] See *Rajasthan State Electricity Board v Dayal Wood Work* AIR 1998 AP 381 (HC) for an example of Indian contract law's insistence on offers and acceptances matching each other perfectly. When a purchase order contained additional terms and conditions that had not been agreed to by the other party, it was held that no contract came into existence.

[39] *Scammell v Ouston* [1941] AC 251 (HL), dealing with the sale of a vehicle on 'hire purchase terms', is an example of a contract that was not enforced due to its uncertain terms.

[40] AIR 2006 Kant 180 (HC). [41] ibid paras 29, 39. [42] AIR 1951 Ori 291 (HC).

[43] ibid paras 5–6, 9. [44] AIR 1961 SC 1285 (SC). [45] ibid para 18.

'intention to save the performing party from the consequences of anything over which he has no control'.[46]

Further, the use of the word 'usual' meant that the clause could be made more certain by the parties adducing evidence that in their past dealings with each other or in the trading business in British East Africa, a certain kind of force majeure clause was usually adopted.[47] The Supreme Court emphasized that section 29 itself accounted for contracts that are 'capable of being made certain'; consequently, additional evidence could be allowed to make clear those clauses of the contract that are unclear at first blush.[48]

VII. Electronic Contracts

Electronic contracts are contracts that are concluded without the exchange of paper between the parties. This can include contracts concluded via email or by the customer signing a contract online. Strictly speaking, electronic contracts do not include contracts concluded by telephone. In the case of contracts concluded by telephone, the contract is memorialized neither in paper form nor in electronic form.

Electronic contracts pose at least two problems in the area of formation of contracts. First, they raise issues as to how electronic communication ought to be authenticated, and in this sense the issue is more evidential than substantive. Second, electronic communication raises issues as to where and when the contract was formed, and in this sense the second set of issues are more familiar to us from our study of the more traditional forms of contracts.

In India, electronic contracts are addressed primarily in the Information Technology Act 2000 ('ITA') which draws from the UNCITRAL Model Law on Electronic Commerce 1996. The ITA authenticates electronic signatures and legitimizes the practice of customers buying products online.[49] From the point of view of contract formation, the impact of the ITA lies in its analysis of contracts concluded through an exchange of emails. Section 10A of the ITA states the following:

> Where in a contract formation, the communication of proposals, the acceptance of proposals, the revocation of proposals and acceptances, as the case may be, are expressed in electronic form or by means of an electronic record, such contract shall not be deemed to be unenforceable solely on the ground that such electronic form or means was used for that purpose.[50]

Section 10A specifies that transactions leading to contract formation without the exchange of paper would be treated on a par with transactions of contract formation that involve an exchange of paper.

However, section 10A leaves untouched the rules on formation of contract to be determined by general law. For example, an important issue often discussed in this context is the application, to electronic contracts, of the postal rule relating to the communication of proposals and acceptances. Where two parties correspond with each other through the post, the proposer might revoke his proposal before he receives (by post) the acceptance of his proposal but after the acceptance has been posted to him. Under the postal rule, now enshrined in section 4 of the ICA, a communication of an acceptance (responding to a proposal) is complete such as to bind the proposer the moment the acceptance is mailed by the

[46] ibid para 19. [47] ibid para 23. [48] ibid para 23.
[49] Pt II of the ITA, ss 3 and 3A.
[50] s 10A was introduced by an amendment to the ITA in 2008.

acceptor. After that time, the proposer cannot revoke his proposal even though he might not have yet received the acceptance by post.

Should the postal rule apply to electronic contracts? An electronic contract is a term that can encompass two kinds of contracts. One kind of contract, sometimes termed as 'click-wrap' contracts, involves customers clicking their acceptance on designated online forms. The other kind of contract is a contract that is completed through a series of email exchanges ('email contracts').[51] The two kinds of contracts just described are likely to have different rules for the communication of offers and acceptances, as seen below.

The ITA does not address the communication of offers and acceptances explicitly. However, section 13 of the ITA, by providing rules on the time at which electronic records[52] are received, shapes how traditional rules on offer and acceptance are applied to electronic contracts.

Section 13 has different rules on the receipt of an electronic record depending on whether the addressee of the electronic record has designated a certain computer resource[53] for the purpose of receiving computer records. If the addressee has designated such a computer resource, section 13 provides that the receipt of an electronic record occurs when it enters the designated computer resource. If the addressee has designated a computer resource (eg an email account) but the electronic record has been sent to another computer resource of the addressee (eg to some other email account), the receipt of the electronic record occurs when the electronic record is retrieved by the addressee (ie the email is opened by the addressee).

It is not clear how these rules interact with the traditional contract law rules on the communication of proposals, acceptances, and revocations. It does appear from section 13 that it is concerned with the non-instantaneous form of electronic contracts, namely the email contracts mentioned previously, for in the case of at least some click-wrap contracts, there is usually no transfer of electronic records back and forth; all relevant contract-related communications happen instantaneously on the website of the e-commerce vendor.[54]

In the case of email contracts, does section 13 affect the way the law conceives of effective communication of offers and acceptances? Some commentators are of the opinion that section 13 does not make any difference to the extant rules on contract formation and in fact should be read along with section 4 of the ICA. For example, the following legal consequence has been suggested in the context of 'receipts' for electronic contracts:

> The communication of an acceptance is complete as against the offeror, when the electronic record is dispatched such that it enters a computer resource outside the control of the originator (acceptor) and as against the acceptor, when the electronic record enters any information system

[51] See AK Pandey, 'E-Contracts: Mail Box Rule and Legal Impact of the Information Technology Act' (2000) I(IV) RLR <http://rostrumlegal.com/blog/e-contracts-mail-box-rule-and-legal-impact-of-the-information-technology-act-2000-by-atul-kumar-pandey/> (accessed 11 March 2014) for a description of click-wrap contracts and email contracts; D Kamat, 'Information Technology Act, 2000: A Contractual Perspective' (2004) 1 SCC (Jour) 11 where the author makes a similar distinction between the two kinds of contracts but terms click-wrap contracts as 'web-click' contracts.

[52] Rule 2 of the Information Technology (Use of Electronic Records and Digital Signatures) Rules 2004 specifies that 'electronic record' means data, record, or data-generated, image or sound stored, received, or sent in an electronic form, or microfilm, or computer-generated microfiche.

[53] A computer resource has been expansively defined in s 2(k), ITA as a 'computer, computer system, computer network, data, computer database or software'. Although it is not clear, an email account of the addressee can be considered as a computer resource.

[54] The instantaneous nature of the communication would depend on the transaction. The customer who clicks on 'confirm order' sends a communication which is usually (but not always) received by the counterparty. How long this takes depends on what is being processed and the complexity of the transaction. If, eg, a payment instruction requires verification by third party payment intermediaries (eg PayPal/Visa/bank), it cannot be said to be instantaneous.

> designated by the offeror for the purpose, or, if no system is designated for the purpose, when the electronic record enters the information system of the offeror, or, if any information system has been designated, but the electronic record is sent to some other information system, when the offeror retrieves such electronic record.[55]

Other commentators disagree. It has been suggested, for example, that section 13 of the ITA has replaced section 4 of the ICA when it comes to deciding when the communication of an acceptance is complete in the case of electronic contracts. Recall that the postal rule in section 4 looks at the communication of acceptances from two perspectives. As against the proposer, the communication of the acceptance of his offer is complete when the acceptance is put in the course of transmission so as to be out of the power of the acceptor. As against the acceptor, the communication of his acceptance is complete when the acceptance comes to the knowledge of the proposer. It has been argued that when it comes to email contracts, section 13 of the ITA has now made it the case that the communication of an acceptance is complete as against both the proposer and the acceptor when the acceptance email enters a 'designated' computer resource, if the proposer has designated a computer resource. If the proposer has designated a computer resource but the acceptance email has been sent to another computer resource of the proposer, the communication of the acceptance is complete when the acceptance email is retrieved by the proposer.[56]

The Supreme Court, in the case of *Trimex International FZE Ltd Dubai v Vedanta Aluminium Ltd, India*, appears to confirm that email communications of acceptances ought not to be treated on a par with instantaneous communications.[57] A mere delivery of email is not evidence of the recipient having read it. In *Trimex*, the Supreme Court did not elaborate on its reasons for indicating that email acceptances are not to be treated as instantaneous communications. This issue was not crucial to the primary issue in *Trimex*, which was concerned with the identification of a concluded contract between the parties, and not when or where it was concluded. The question of when the communication of an email acceptance is complete awaits further judicial elaboration along with the application of the ITA to the traditional rules on offers and acceptances under the ICA.

VIII. Formality Requirements

The general rule in Indian contract law is that there are no formality requirements for contract formation. This is evident from the provisions on the communication of offer and acceptance under the ICA. Section 3 of the ICA states that proposals and acceptances can be made by any act or omission that has the effect of communicating such proposals or acceptances. Therefore, the ICA is flexible enough to recognize oral as well as written contracts.

[55] CM Abhilash, 'E-Commerce Law in Developing Countries: An Indian Perspective' (2002) 11 Info & Comm Tech L 269, 274.

[56] F Ahmad, 'Electronic Commerce, An Indian Perspective' (2001) 9 Int'l JL & Info Tech 133, 151 where it is stated:

> The communication of acceptance is complete against the acceptor as well as the offeror at the time when acceptance enters into the designated computer resource or where no computer resource has been designated, the computer resource of the addressee.

[57] (2010) 3 SCC 1 (SC) para 10 where the Supreme Court stated, without further elaboration:

> As rightly pointed out by the learned senior counsel for the petitioner, when Mr. Swaminathan of Trimex opened the email of Mr. Swayam Mishra of Vedanta at 3.06 PM on 16.10.2007, *it came to his knowledge* that an irrevocable contract was concluded…

thus indicating that a contract was in place even before the recipient of the email acceptance had knowledge of the email acceptance.

Similarly, section 10 of the ICA makes it clear that all agreements are contracts if they are made by the free consent of parties competent to contract and for a lawful consideration and lawful object. Thus, the default rule is that of flexibility in the form of the contracts. However, section 10 makes it clear that the ICA's liberal rule in this regard is subject to other statutes that might require contracts to be in written form or might require witnesses or registration.[58]

In India, various statutory enactments have provided that certain contracts have to be in writing. In the main, these are contracts relating to company formation, subscription and transfer of shares, arbitration agreements, and transfers of immovable property.[59] Some contracts that are required to be in writing have to be registered as well. The most common of these are contracts relating to transfers of immovable property.[60] Certain contracts ought to be written, registered, and have stamp duty payable for them to have any legal effect.[61] If contracts are invalidated due to lack of compliance with formality requirements, the resulting issue is the legal protection of the legitimate expectation of the contracting parties, which is discussed in a separate section of this chapter.[62]

The formality requirements in Indian contract law exist for a variety of reasons, as explained in Pollock and Mulla's treatise on Indian contract law. The law is interested in ensuring that parties enter into binding agreements on certain matters only after due consideration and serious thought. In the event of any disputes between the parties, the law would like to enable any future adjudicatory authorities to distinguish between pre-contractual negotiations and the actual contract between the parties. In some cases, by insisting on certain formalities relating to contract formation, the law also attempts to protect the more vulnerable party to the contract.[63] In the case of stamp duties, one of the important reasons, as highlighted by the Law Commission in its report on the Indian Stamp Act, is to raise revenue.[64]

An example of a statute that uses the requirement of formality to introduce terms for the protection of the vulnerable party to the contract is the Cine-Workers and Cinema Theatres Workers (Regulation of Employment) Act 1981 ('CW Act'). Section 3 of the CW Act requires contracts between cine-workers and film producers to be in writing and prescribes a detailed format for the content of the contract. For instance, it requires the contract to specify the nature of assignment of the employee, his hours of work, wages and other benefits (including benefits by way of provident fund,[65] if any) to which he is entitled, the mode of payment of such wages and contributions to such provident fund, and all other terms and conditions of employment.

[58] s 10 of the ICA states: 'Nothing herein contained shall affect any law in force in India, and not hereby expressly repealed, by which any contract is required to be made in writing or in the presence of witnesses, or any law relating to the registration of documents.'

[59] Agreements relating to formation of companies and transfer of shares are required to be in writing under the Indian Companies Act 2013, s 3. Arbitration agreements are required to be in writing under the Arbitration and Conciliation Act 1996, s 7(3). Agreements regarding sale of immovable property are required to be in writing under the Transfer of Property Act 1882, s 54.

[60] s 17, Indian Registration Act 1908 lists documents for which registration is compulsory. The most prominent of these documents are those that pertain to transfers concerning immovable property.

[61] s 54, Transfer of Property Act 1882 and s 17, Indian Registration Act 1908 require the agreements relating to the sale of immovable property to be written and registered. The stamp duty applicable to such agreements is imposed by the state (provincial) jurisdiction in which the property is located, eg the Karnataka Stamp Act 1957 provides for the imposition of duties on the transfer of immovable property located in Karnataka.

[62] See section XI on Quasi-Contractual Obligations.

[63] Pollock and Mulla, *The Indian Contract Act 1872* (14th edn, Nagpur: LexisNexis Butterworths Wadhwa Nagpur 2013) 232.

[64] Law Commission, *Sixty-Seventh Report on the Indian Stamp Act 1899*, pp 3–4 <http://lawcommissionofindia.nic.in/51-100/report67.pdf> accessed 23 November 2014.

[65] A statutory fund created as a pension fund for certain employees.

IX. Consideration and Gratuitous Promises

1. Introduction

Promises are broadly of two types: promises supported by consideration and gratuitous promises, ie promises that are given without consideration. Indian law takes consideration to be an integral part of the formation of contracts. The ICA's provisions on consideration are contained mainly in sections 10 and 25. Section 10 states that an agreement would be enforceable as a contract only if it is made for a lawful consideration. Section 25 denies contractual validity to gratuitous promises, subject to certain narrow exceptions:

> An agreement made without consideration is void, unless—
>
> (1) it is expressed in writing and registered under the law for the time being in force for the registration of documents, and is made on account of natural love and affection between parties standing in a near relation to each other, or unless
>
> (2) it is a promise to compensate, wholly or in part, a person who has already voluntarily done something for the promisor, or something which the promisor was legally compellable to do, or unless,
>
> (3) it is a promise, made in writing and signed by the person to be charged therewith, or by his agent generally or specially authorized in that behalf, to pay wholly or in part a debt of which the creditor might have enforced payment but for the law for the limitation of suits.

There are three enumerated exceptions to the invalidity of gratuitous promises. The first exception refers to contracts in writing, registered, and made out of natural love and affection between near relatives; the second exception refers to contracts made to recompense for past consideration; and the third exception refers to written contracts made to pay a time-barred debt. The protection of the legitimate expectations of parties when contracts are voided for lack of consideration is discussed separately.[66] Section 25 is an integrated aspect of the doctrine of consideration under which only those agreements that are supported by consideration are considered as contracts enforceable under the ICA. Section 2(d) of the ICA defines consideration as follows:

> When, at the desire of the promisor, the promisee or any other person has done or abstained from doing, or does or abstains from doing, or promises to do or abstains from doing, something, such act or abstinence or promise is called a consideration for the promise.

The Indian position on consideration follows the UK common law position. International instruments on contract law differ from the common law on this point. For example, Article 2:101 of the Principles of European Contract Law ('PECL') states:

> (1) A contract is concluded if:
>
> (a) the parties intend to be legally bound, and
> (b) they reach a sufficient agreement
>
> without any further requirement.[67]

Although Indian law insists on consideration, the definition of consideration in section 2(d) is wide enough to include a variety of actions, forbearances, and promises as long as

[66] See section XI on Quasi-Contractual Obligations.

[67] <http://www.jus.uio.no/lm/eu.contract.principles.parts.1.to.3.2002/> accessed 1 February 2015. Similar language appears in Art 3.1.2, Unidroit Principles of International Commercial Contracts 2010 ('PICC 2010'): 'A contract is concluded, modified or terminated by mere agreement of the parties, without any further requirement.'

some 'valuable benefit' is transferred or is expected to be transferred between the contracting parties.[68] What makes a benefit valuable? The courts tend to look at value in terms of money or money's worth.[69] Therefore, as long as what is transferred or expected to be transferred between the parties has some monetary value, the benefit transferred is likely to be considered as consideration under the ICA. Similar to the common law rule that consideration need not be adequate, the ICA does not require that the benefits mutually transferred between the parties in an agreement be equal or even proportionate in value, as long as the benefits have some real monetary value.[70] Consideration must consist of benefits that are 'real' rather than illusory. As the Madras High Court pointed out, while discussing the definition in section 2(d) of the ICA in *Muthukaruppa Mudali & Ors v Pi Mu Kathappudayan & Ors*:[71]

> The above definition is couched in the widest possible words, but it has been always held that the 'something' which the promisee has done cannot be a merely illusory thing. For instance, if B asks his friend A to take Rs. 5 from A's left-hand pocket and put it into A's right-hand pocket and A accordingly transfers the money from his left-hand pocket into his right-hand pocket, A suffers no detriment at all by complying with that request of B. It would be against common sense to hold that A's above act at B's request will be good consideration for B's signing a promissory note in favour of A for Rs. 1000.[72]

The insistence on consideration being 'real' rather than 'illusory' raises interesting conceptual questions about the nature of consideration under Indian law. If, as the ICA insists, consideration is to be adjudged by whether it is 'at the request of the promisor', it can be argued that nothing more needs to be said about the 'value' of the consideration. However, as the observations quoted above suggest, Indian law appears to be imposing a valuation from its own perspective. The use of the phrase 'illusory' suggests that Indian courts will view the consideration offered as of no value only in rare circumstances, circumstances that, as Treitel has commented (see paragraph below), in effect suggest that the parties did not intend to enter into a contract at all.

Treitel, while noting the capacious definition of consideration under English contract law, makes the point that if 'the consideration as a matter of arithmetic be worth less than the performance of the counter-promise, there would seem to be no contract'.[73] Treitel gives the example of A promising to pay B a hundred pound sterling in return for one pound sterling to be paid by B. This agreement, according to Treitel, is no contract at all, presumably due to the illusionary nature of the putative consideration.[74] The example of an unworkable consideration given by the Madras High Court, where a person transfers money from his left-hand pocket to his right-hand pocket in return for monetary compensation, is

[68] See *Sonia Bhatia v State of UP* AIR 1981 SC 1274 (SC) para 19. The court in this case looked into the meaning of transactions that involve consideration in order to distinguish such transactions from gifts.

[69] ibid paras 19–21.

[70] Since neither English law nor Indian law insists on the adequacy of consideration, one might question the relevance of the doctrine of consideration in contract law, given that the classical doctrine of consideration is meant to preserve the bargain element in a contract. On this point, see the debate between Treitel and Atiyah in PS Atiyah, 'Consideration: A Restatement' in *Essays on Contract* (Oxford: Clarendon Press 1986) 181 reprinted with revisions to meet the criticism of Treitel in *Essays on Contract* (Oxford: Clarendon Press 1986) 179 and G Treitel, 'Consideration: A Critical Analysis of Professor Atiyah's Fundamental Restatement' (1976) 50 ALJ 439. For the argument that the ICA 1872 takes an extremely broad view of consideration, see S Swaminathan, 'Eclipsed by Orthodoxy: The Vanishing Point of Consideration and the Forgotten Ingenuity of the Indian Contract Act 1872' (2017) Asian J Comp L 141–165.

[71] (1914) 24 MLJ 249 (HC). [72] ibid para 5.

[73] G Treitel, *The Law of Contract* (11th edn, London: Thomson Sweet & Maxwell 2003) 75.

[74] ibid 75.

similarly illusionary in nature, and suggests that the parties did not really intend to enter into a contract.

2. At the Desire of the Promisor

Section 2(d) of the ICA requires that the consideration must be such that it is given *at the desire of the promisor*. This provision underscores the bargain element in contracts. The requirement of consideration moving from one party to another pursuant to the desire of the other party appears to include the idea of past consideration, ie a promise or an act done for one of the parties before any agreement took place between the parties. Further, section 25(2) of the ICA states that an agreement without consideration is nevertheless valid if the agreement contains a promise that was voluntarily provided. This is a curious requirement as, on the face of it, it is difficult to conceive of a situation where an agreement contains a promise that has not been voluntarily provided. Yet, as the *Raja of Venkatagiri*'s case shows,[75] this is a possibility.

The *Raja of Venkatagiri*'s case involved some complex facts about adoptions in a royal setting but can be summarized in the following manner (with some simplification and modification of the facts for explanatory reasons). A made a legally binding promise to B that he would pay the expenses of a certain litigation involving B. A and B were both interested in obtaining a favourable result in the litigation. B gave a promissory note promising to repay the amount advanced by A if the litigation had a favourable result. When the litigation was successfully completed, A sued on the promissory note. The Privy Council held that the promissory note failed to give rise to a contractual obligation for lack of consideration. The facts of the case precluded A from claiming that the money advanced towards the litigation was the consideration for the promissory note. The crucial factor was the binding nature of the undertaking to pay the litigation expenses. Once that was established, it followed that the money advanced for the litigation was not at the 'desire' of B; instead the money was advanced because A felt himself obligated to advance the money (as a result of his undertaking). Thus, section 2(d) of the ICA did not apply. Similarly, the money advanced for the litigation was not advanced 'voluntarily' by A, as A had advanced the money under a binding undertaking.[76] Consequently, A was precluded from taking advantage of the exception in section 25(2).

3. Promissory Estoppel

The doctrine of promissory estoppel has had a long and illustrious history in India. The main elements of the doctrine were delineated in 2012 by the Supreme Court in *Monnet Ispat & Energy Ltd v Union of India*.[77] Of the court's observations, three are especially relevant for their elaboration on the doctrine of promissory estoppel in India.[78]

The first related to the general features of the doctrine of promissory estoppel. The Supreme Court followed the lead of an earlier case, *Motilal Padampat Sugar Mills v Union of India*,[79] where the court stated the following principle:[80]

> Where one party has by his words or conduct made to the other a *clear and unequivocal promise* which is *intended to create legal relations or affect a legal relationship* to arise in the future, knowing or intending that it would be acted upon by the other party to whom the promise is made

[75] *Raja of Venkatagiri v Krishnayya Rao* (1948) 50 BOM LR 517 (PC). [76] ibid paras 31–32.
[77] (2012) 11 SCC 1 (SC). [78] ibid para 146. [79] 1969 SCR (3) 75.
[80] Relied on *Central London Property Trust Ltd v High Trees House Ltd* [1947] KB 130.

> and it is, in fact, so acted upon by the other party, the promise would be binding on the party making it and he would not be entitled to go back upon it, if it would be inequitable to allow him to do so having regard to the dealings which have taken place between the parties, and this would be so irrespective of whether there is any pre-existing relationship between the parties or not. [Emphasis added]

The first observation on promissory estoppel followed closely the doctrine as it is traditionally understood in England.

However, in its second observation, the Supreme Court made it clear that the doctrine's application in India is of much wider import. The court stated that promissory estoppel in India can serve as an independent *cause of action*.[81] The English common law has generally been reluctant to accord a strong juristic basis to promissory estoppel. Subsequent to *High Trees*, many English judgments have pointed out that promissory estoppel cannot be used to found a cause of action; it can be a shield but not a sword.[82] However, a long line of Indian cases have considered promissory estoppel as giving rise to a cause of action, and the Supreme Court emphasized that this was a point of departure from English decisions.

Finally, the Supreme Court mentioned an often overlooked feature of promissory estoppel. The invocation of promissory estoppel does not require that the promisee ought to have suffered a detriment as a result of the promise. It is enough if the promisee has changed his position as a result of the promise.[83] This greatly expands the reach of promissory estoppel. The point about detriment was of particular importance in *Motilal Padampat Sugar Mills v Union of India*.[84]

In *Motilal*, the state of Uttar Pradesh promised a sales tax exemption to a company if it established a presence in Uttar Pradesh. The company invested in Uttar Pradesh on the basis of that promise. However, the government later reneged on its promise of a sales tax exemption. The company sued on the basis of promissory estoppel. One of the objections of the state of Uttar Pradesh was that the company had not suffered any detriment as a result of the promise. The company was promised something it was not owed previously (exemption of sales tax) and, therefore, could not be said to have suffered a detriment if such an exemption was not provided. The Supreme Court rejected this contention and confirmed the point, already well known in English law, that for promissory estoppel to be effective all that is needed is that the promisee alters his position on the faith of the promise.

In India, the issue of promissory estoppel has been litigated either in the context of government commitments to provide tax subsidies for industrial investment (on which the government has backtracked subsequently) or in the context of subscriptions to charities, where the subscriber has failed to fulfil his promise subsequently. The government commitment cases have been mentioned previously. An example of the subscription cases is *The Nair Service Society v Krishna Pillai Kunjukrishna Pillai & Ors*.[85]

In *Nair Service Society*, the defendant promised a certain sum of money to a charity that wanted to build a college. On the faith of the promise, and with the knowledge of the defendant, the charity began work on the construction of the college building. When the defendant did not pay the promised subscription, the charity sued him to recover the promised subscription. The suit ultimately failed because it exceeded the time limit specified in the Indian Limitation Act 1908. However, the Kerala High Court was of the opinion that if the suit had not exceeded the limitation period, the promise would have been enforceable under the doctrine of promissory estoppel.

[81] *Monnet Ispat* (n 77) para 146.
[82] *Combe v Combe* [1951] 2 KB 215. See the Supreme Court's comments on this point: *Monnet Ispat* (n 77) para 138.
[83] *Monnet Ispat* (n 77) para 146. [84] 1969 SCR (3) 75. [85] AIR 1964 Ker 265 (HC).

The doctrine of promissory estoppel is key to subscription cases because in some instances it is difficult to find consideration in these cases, even if the concerned charity has, in anticipation of the subscription, done something, such as starting work on constructing a building. Recall that the definition of consideration in section 2 of the ICA requires that *at the desire* of the promisor, the promisee has done or promises to do something. Therefore, even if the charity has done something (by beginning construction) such actions must be at the desire (or request) of the promisor of subscriptions. However, a person might commit to make a subscription to a charity without at the same time having any particular desire that the charity should do something with his money. Note that this is different from a person having some knowledge that the charity will do something with his money.

When the element of desire (or request) is missing, one might argue that there is no consideration.[86] However, the doctrine of promissory estoppel, as discussed through US case law in *Nair Service Society*, does not entail any element of a desire or request from the promisor in connection with his promise.[87] As long as the promisor ought to have reasonably expected that the promisee would change his position in reliance on the promise, promissory estoppel would apply. Hence, in *Nair Service Society*, the court, in recognizing a case of promissory estoppel, focused in the main on whether any steps were taken to construct the college building pursuant to the subscription promise. The motivations or desires of the promisor were not relevant to the question of promissory estoppel.

4. Promise Given for Existing Contractual Obligation

The doctrine of consideration focuses on the bargain element in contracts. A promise flowing from one party to another must be in return for the other party doing something or obliging himself (through a reciprocal promise) to do something. In some instances, one party promises to do something in return for the other party doing something that it was already contractually obliged to perform.

Promises given for existing contractual obligations exist in two versions. In the first version (the 'benefits' version), a benefit is provided by one party to the other party in order to motivate the other party to complete his performance under an existing contract between the two parties. For example, A, the landlord, agreed with B, the painter, to pay an extra sum of money to B to induce B to complete his painting work on time. In the second version (the 'concessions' version), a concession is made by one party to the contract to motivate the other party to complete his performance under an existing contract between the two parties. For example, A, a moneylender, agrees with B, the debtor, to accept a sum of money in repayment of the debt that is less than that lent to B originally, in order to induce B to repay A.

Traditionally, English contract law has looked unfavourably at both versions of such promises as they do not conform to the bargain element in consideration. If anything, such situations appear to be one party taking advantage of another party.[88] In recent times, English courts have tended to take a more liberal approach towards the 'benefits' version of such promises. A case in point is *Williams v Roffey*[89] where the promisor committed to pay

[86] See *Doraswami Iyer v Arunachala Ayyar* AIR 1936 Mad 135 (HC) (discussion of consideration in paras 2–3) for the proposition that a promise is not supported by consideration unless the promisee has done something *at the request* of the promisor.

[87] *Nair Service Society* (n 85) para 7.

[88] See KM Teeven, 'Consensual Path to Abolition of Pre existing Duty' (1999) 34 Val UL Rev 43, 48–51 for an analysis of the reasons for English contract law's hostility to promises given for existing contractual obligations.

[89] *Williams v Roffey Bros & Nicholls (Contractors) Ltd* [1991] 1 QB 1, para 24 (CA Civ).

the promisee an extra sum of money to perform the contract as the promisee's performance of the contract was a key step in the promisor's obligations to a third party.

The Court of Appeal held that as the promisor had received a practical benefit in return for the promise (performance of the contract on time) there was sufficient consideration for the promise to pay an additional sum of money. However, this liberalization of the consideration rule has not been extended to the concessions version of such promises. For example, in the case of a debt, a promise to accept a lesser sum in repayment of the debt would not be binding if there is no other consideration for such a promise.[90]

The situations described previously must be understood in the light of the technical rules of contract law. For example, the problem of consideration arises in the practical benefit and the debt example because the parties have purported to make an additional contract that depends on consideration that flows from an earlier contract. If A agrees with B to provide an additional sum of money to motivate B to complete his work under a contract between them, A can be seen as entering into an additional contract to pay a sum of money in return for B completing his obligation under a pre-existing contract with A. If analysed in this manner, the problem of consideration in the second contract between A and B is apparent, as consideration for A's promise is something that B is obliged to do in any case under another contract.

Indian contract law follows the approach of the English law except that it appears to make a distinction between the two versions (*benefits* and *concessions*) of the promises discussed previously. Traditionally, Indian law does not recognize the contractual effect of promises that provide benefits in return for existing contractual obligations. For example, in *Ramachandra Chintaman v Kalu Raju*,[91] a lawyer and his client agreed to an extra amount of money to be paid to the lawyer (under an *Inam Chithi* or a letter of reward) if the lawyer succeeded in winning his client's case. When the suit was concluded in favour of the client, the client did not pay the extra sum of money to the lawyer.

The lawyer sued for the extra sum but his claim failed due to lack of consideration. The Bombay High Court ruled that the lawyer was already contractually obligated to provide his professional services under a *Vakalatnama* (contract for the provision of legal services) and, therefore, the client's promise to pay an extra sum was without consideration. It remains to be seen if the Indian judiciary would follow the more liberal approach demonstrated in *Williams v Roffey*.[92] One might argue that the *Inam Chithi* provides a practical benefit to the client as it would serve as an additional motivating factor for the lawyer. However, there might be public policy reasons why courts would be reluctant to recognize the validity of promises that provide additional benefits to lawyers who are already bound to represent their client to the greatest degree possible. This is an instance of traditional contract law (eg consideration), functioning as a proxy for public policy. In their zeal to sustain the sanctity of a lawyer's duty to clients, the courts have used the doctrine of consideration to underscore the importance of this public duty.

[90] *Penny v Cole* (*Pinnel's* case) (1602) 5 Co Rep 117a and *Foakes v Beer* [1884] UKHL 1. *Williams v Roffey* (CA Civ) could not extend the practical benefit analysis to debt cases because *Foakes v Beer* [1884] UKHL 1 is a House of Lords decision. Also note that in England the doctrine of promissory estoppel has been used to address the debt fact-pattern, as seen in *Collier v P & MJ Wright (Holdings) Ltd* [2007] EWCA Civ 1329 (Mary Arden LJ).

[91] (1878) ILR 2 Bom 362 (HC).

[92] One might query whether the Indian definition of consideration allows the 'practical benefit' approach to consideration adopted in *Roffey*, particularly since the ICA's definition of consideration requires that it be given *at the desire of the promisor*. Since the presumption under the practical benefit rule is that A has performed his part of the contract in response to B's *desire* to obtain more certainty about A's performance, the ICA's definition is sufficiently capacious to absorb the *Roffey* principle.

In section 63, the ICA departs from English law when it comes to the concessions version of the promises discussed previously. Section 63 states the following:

> Every promisee may dispense with or remit, wholly or in part, the performance of the promise made to him, or may extend the time for such performance, or may accept instead of it any satisfaction which he thinks fit.

Section 63 does not specify how a promisee may dispense with or remit the performance of the promise made to him. Presumably section 63 would cover both unilateral concessions from the promisee as well as situations in which the promisee agrees with the promisor in remitting the performance of the promisor. If this is the case, section 63 has done away with the requirement of consideration when it comes to concessionary promises. Concessionary promises disqualified under the *Pinnel* principle in England would be valid in India by virtue of section 63. Since there is no difference in principle between the two versions (*benefits* and *concessions*) of the promises described previously, section 63 creates an anomaly in the case of promises given in return for existing contractual obligations.

Some High Court decisions in India have diluted the potential impact of section 63. These courts have made a distinction between a remission *in praesenti* and an agreement to remit *in future*.[93] A remission *in praesenti* is an immediate 'act of grace'[94] by the promisee excusing the performance of the promisor whereas an agreement to remit in future is an agreement between the parties to the effect that one party's performance under the contract would be excused completely or partially *in the future*. The courts have held that a remission *in praesenti* is covered by section 63 whereas an agreement to remit *in the future* would require consideration and would fail to impose any contractual obligations if no consideration can be identified.[95]

The courts' approach recognizes the two mechanisms envisaged under the ICA through which the contracting parties can modify or extinguish their contractual performances. Under section 62,[96] the parties can agree to substitute a new contract or to rescind or to alter the existing contract, with the result that the original contract need not be performed. However, section 62 requires consideration.[97]

Another way to achieve the same result (with respect to remissions) is for the contracting parties to unilaterally or bilaterally excuse, completely or partially, a contracting party's performance under the contract. This mechanism is recognized by section 63 and does not require consideration. However, such remissions have to have immediate effect. If A owes a sum of money to B, section 63 will sanctify a remission only if B agrees with A, that A would pay B immediately, a smaller sum of money in satisfaction of the entire debt. If on the other hand, B agrees with A that A would pay a lesser sum of money over a number of instalments provided the instalments are paid on time, section 63 will not operate to sanctify such an agreement. In the latter example, there is no remission but only an agreement to remit in the future provided that A pays his instalments on time. Such an agreement to remit would require consideration.

[93] See eg the comments of the Andhra Pradesh High Court in *Mirriyala China Subbaraidu v Kallarsu Mahadeva Rao* AIR 1965 AP 171, paras 12–17. The point of distinction was articulated in this manner in F Pollock and D Mulla on the *Indian Contract and Specific Relief Acts: with a commentary, critical and explanatory* (8th edn, Bombay: NM Tripathi 1957) 380, which the court quoted with approval.

[94] Words to this affect were used by the Madras High Court in *Balasundra v Ranganatha* AIR 1929 Mad 794, 797. An act of grace leads to, as the Madras High Court recognized in this case, the conclusion that s 63 is meant to apply to unilateral remissions and not agreements. If this is the case, the impact of s 63 is further diluted.

[95] *Mirriyala China Subbaraidu* (n 93) paras 12–17.

[96] s 62, ICA: 'Effect of novation, rescission, and alteration of contract—If the parties to a contract agree to substitute a new contract for it, or to rescind or alter it, the original contract need not be performed.'

[97] *Union of India v Kishorilal Gupta & Bros* AIR 1953 Cal 642 (HC) para 22.

The limited impact of section 63 can be seen in *Rudra Pratap Singh v Ballabh Das*.[98] In an action to enforce a mortgage, the mortgagor claimed that the mortgagee had agreed to reduce the interest payable on the mortgage in return for regular interest payments on the mortgage. The court ruled that this agreement was without contractual force as it lacked consideration. Although the court did not discuss it, presumably section 63 was not applicable because the partial remission of interest took place over a number of interest payments.

X. Test of Intention to Create Legal Relations

The ICA does not lay down a formal test of an intention to create legal relations. The ICA's definition of a proposal (which if accepted becomes a contract) does not lay down the 'intention to create a legal relationship' rule explicitly. Instead, it states the following: 'When one person signifies to another his willingness to do or to abstain from doing anything, with a view to obtaining the assent of that other to such act or abstinence, he is said to make a proposal.'[99]

This definition does not refer to any particular intention in the course of making a proposal. However, several commentators on the ICA have always assumed that such a test exists in Indian law.[100]

The Supreme Court in the *Abdul Hussain* case[101] considered, in passing, whether Indian contract law requires an intention to create legal relations as an independent element in the formation of contracts, in addition to other elements such as consideration.[102] Although the Supreme Court did not express a definitive opinion on this point, it appears that the court rather doubted the validity of an intention to create legal relations as an independent element in contract formation. The court stated that although English common law had accepted this requirement, it was not unanimously accepted even in England.[103]

Pollock and Mulla refer tangentially to two Indian cases under the heading 'Intention to Create Legal Relations'.[104] The reference is tangential with good reason: neither of these two cases considers in detail the issue of intention to create legal relations. In the first, *Nalini v Somasundaram*,[105] the Madras High Court discussed the entitlement of a wife to stay in the matrimonial home after divorce. The court assumed the existence of a contractual relationship and did not delve into the requirement of the intention to create a legal relationship. In the second case, *Nandganj Sihori Sugar Co Ltd v Badri Nath Dixit*,[106] the Supreme Court denied contractual status to a letter from the chairman of a company suggesting an appointment to a certain position. In the discussion on this issue, the Supreme Court did not discuss the issue of an intention to create legal relations explicitly, it was instead eager to point out that such a letter cannot purport to create a contractual right in the person mentioned in the letter.

[98] AIR 1948 Oudh 152 (HC) paras 9–10.

[99] s 2(a), ICA.

[100] SV Joga Rao, *Computer Contracts and Information Technology Law* (Nagpur: LexisNexis Butterworths 2005) 257; Pollock and Mulla (n 63) 46–48.

[101] See *Commissioner of Wealth Tax, Bhopal v Abdul Hussain Mulla Muhammad Ali* AIR 1988 SC 1417, discussed in section II.

[102] ibid para 11. The Supreme Court stated: 'The arguments of learned counsel proceeds on the general proposition that in addition to the existence of an agreement and the presence of consideration there is also a third contractual element in the form of intention of the parties to create legal relations.'

[103] The court, at para 11, stated that the test of *intention to create legal relations* 'has not passed unchallenged' and quoted Professor Williston for the proposition that the 'separate element of intention is foreign to the common law'.

[104] Pollock and Mulla (n 63) see fn 56 and 66, pp 47 and 48.

[105] AIR 1964 Mad 52 (HC).

[106] AIR 1955 SC 1525.

XI. Quasi-Contractual Obligations

The ICA has a chapter devoted to 'Relations Resembling those Created by Contract', ie obligations that arise out of what several commentators have termed as 'quasi-contracts'. The ICA addresses the issue of quasi-contracts through five situations. All these situations are concerned with an obligation to pay when the conferment of benefits between two persons was not intended to be gratuitous. The first situation involves a claim for necessaries supplied to persons incapable of contracting (section 68), the second involves reimbursing a person for paying money due by another (section 69), the third refers to the obligation of a person enjoying the benefit of a non-gratuitous act (section 70), the fourth lays out the responsibilities of the finder of goods (section 71), and the fifth is concerned with the liability of a person to whom money is paid or a thing is delivered by mistake or under coercion (section 72).

Although at first blush the notion of quasi-contracts might be construed as referring to situations of purported contracts that have failed to result in contractual obligation for one reason or another, the intention of the ICA's quasi-contractual obligations is not to address failed contracts but certain *enumerated* situations of unjust enrichment or restitution.[107] The concept of unjust enrichment is meant to provide recourse in situations where one person has unjustly enriched himself at the expense of another. In such situations, the person who has provided the benefit (enrichment) to another is entitled to receive recompense either in terms of the property transferred or its equivalent. It is not surprising that in some situations of failed contracts such as contracts that are inoperative due to lack of stamp duties, the courts have refused to allow quasi-contractual provisions to come to the aid of the contracting parties.[108]

Of the aforementioned five sections, sections 69 and 70 are the most typical of situations of unjust enrichment. Section 69 states the following: 'A person who is interested in the payment of money which another is bound by law to pay, and who therefore pays it, is entitled to be reimbursed by the other'. Section 69 envisages a situation in which one person (the 'payor') pays money that is meant to be paid by another (the 'beneficiary') and therefore requires recompense for his payment. However, the two trigger factors in section 69 are that the payor must be *interested* in the payment of money and that the beneficiary must be *bound by law* to pay.

A typical case that brings out the importance of the payor being interested in the payment of money is *Secretary of State v S Rangaswami and Co.*[109] The plaintiff in this case entered into a contract with the defendant for the supply of coal by a third party. The third party was to supply coal by rail to the plaintiff. The contract between the plaintiff and the defendant stipulated that the defendant would pay for the rail freight. When the coal arrived by rail, the rail authorities contacted the plaintiff for the payment of the freight charges and the plaintiff obliged.

Subsequently, in a suit brought by the plaintiff to recover the freight charges, the Madras High Court ruled that section 69 would not be of any assistance to the plaintiff. The plaintiff was not interested in the payment of the freight charges as under the contract the defendant was to pay the freight charges.[110] While the plaintiff could have rejected the consignment of coal, instead, it had chosen to pay the freight charges. The court was of the opinion that the

[107] Pollock and Mulla (n 63) 1043.

[108] *Lothamasu Sambasiva Rao v Thadwarthi Balakotiah* AIR 1973 AP 342 (HC), discussed in more detail in this section.

[109] AIR 1928 Mad 198 (HC).

[110] ibid para 3.

plaintiff's payment of the freight charges was voluntary and not in pursuance of a prior interest that it might have had in such a payment. However, the court's reasoning in holding that the plaintiff did not have any interest in the payment of freight charges seems erroneous. If the plaintiff-payor is interested in a continuous supply of coal and this is secured by the payment to the supplier, why does the plaintiff-payor not have an interest in the payment obligation? There have been cases such as *Suradhani Debi v Hari Charan Mahton*[111] which have indicated that 'mere apprehension founded upon an impression that one's interest will be adversely affected is sufficient'.[112] It is reasonable to interpret section 69 in a way that recognizes a party's economic interest in paying a sum of money on behalf of other parties. It is clear from the facts that the plaintiff in *Rangaswami* had an economic interest in paying the freight to guarantee its access to the coal.[113]

Section 70 has the closest connection with issues of contract formation and contractual liability. Section 70 states the following:

> Where a person lawfully does anything for another person or delivers anything to him, not intending to do so gratuitously, and such another person enjoys the benefit thereof, the latter is bound to make compensation to the former in respect of, or to restore, the thing so done or delivered.

Section 70 appears to include agreements that would have contractual force but for some defect in their formation such as lack of capacity or consideration, absence of registration, or insufficient stamp duties. However, the reach of section 70 in situations that resemble contracts is controversial. In the instances mentioned previously, there is an agreement in place between the parties but contract law does not provide the agreement with legal validity because of some defect with the agreement relating to capacity (eg one of the parties is a minor)[114] or consideration (one of the parties has not provided a benefit or suffered a detriment) or lack of formalities (the agreement is not in written form as required by legislation). In such instances, it is, at least on the face of it, odd that on the one hand, the ICA refuses legal force to such agreements and, on the other hand, provides that parties to such agreements are entitled to compensation.

This contradictory push and pull of the ICA was addressed by the Supreme Court in *State of West Bengal v BK Mondal and Sons*.[115] The plaintiffs were a group of contractors that constructed buildings for the benefit of the State of West Bengal, the defendant. Unfortunately, the government officials that they dealt with were not authorized to contract on behalf of the defendant. Section 175 of the Government of India Act 1935 (the language of which was later incorporated in the Indian Constitution) provided that all contracts made in the exercise of the executive authority of a province (eg the State of West Bengal) shall be 'executed on behalf of the Governor by such persons and in such manner as he may direct or authorise'. The government officials who entered into the contract with the plaintiffs were not authorized by the governor. The defendant took the position that since a contract could not have come into force between the unauthorized government officials and the plaintiffs, section 70 was inapplicable as well. Enforcing section 70 would amount to ignoring the unlawful nature of the agreement between the plaintiffs and the government officials.

In *BK Mondal*, the Supreme Court recognizing the distinct juristic field of quasi-contracts, stated that under section 70 of the ICA, the cause of action was not the breach of an

[111] AIR 1922 Pat 337 (HC). [112] ibid para 8. [113] *S Rangaswami* (n 109) para 3.

[114] s 11, ICA: 'Who are competent to contract.—Every person is competent to contract who is of the age of majority according to the law to which he is subject, and who is of sound mind and is not disqualified from contracting by any law to which he is subject.'

[115] AIR 1962 SC 779 (SC).

agreement; the cause of action lay in one person's work for another having been accepted voluntarily by the other person *and* enjoyed by that person.[116] Since the cause of action under section 70 was on a juristic basis that was different from that of a contract, the court saw no contradiction in recognizing a party's right to compensation under an invalid contract.

It must be noted that the courts have not always been consistent in recognizing the implications of the different juristic bases for contracts and quasi-contracts. A case in point is the Andhra Pradesh High Court decision in *Lothamasu Sambasiva Rao v Thadwarthi Balakotiah*.[117] *Lothamasu* involved a loan given via a promissory note that was not stamped. Under the law as it applied to that case, an unstamped promissory note was not admissible in proof of a loan nor could the loan be proved through oral evidence. The plaintiff argued that section 70 would be applicable to the case. The court declined to apply section 70 as in the eyes of the law there was no loan at all.[118]

Perhaps this case can be explained not as a case of a denial of a quasi-contractual juristic basis but as an example of evidential proof that is applicable to contracts and quasi-contracts alike. If a certain loan transaction cannot be proved at all using oral or written evidence, then the elements needed to prove either an obligation in contract or an obligation in quasi-contract are missing and, therefore, a claim under such a loan transaction would fail under both contract law principles as well as under section 70.

XII. Contract Formation Issues in Arbitration Agreements: Contemporary Trends

As discussed in this chapter, the Indian jurisprudence on contract formation is rooted in and draws strongly from the English common law. Courts have tended to rely on the English courts' reasoning in this area, and the position of law on contract formation is well established. The notable recent exception in this regard has been cases involving arbitration clauses in contracts, where the Indian courts are required to craft a position on contract formation guided by Indian arbitration law and the motivations of Indian commercial law.

This section discusses some fundamental issues in contract formation, foregrounded in arbitration law, and issues of resolving ambiguities in the language of arbitration agreements, which dovetail with earlier discussions on the judicial attitude towards vague language in contracts. Arbitration law in India has been the site for judicial innovation in recent times. Since the arbitration legislation in India specifically impacts fundamental issues in the formation of contractual agreements between parties, any discussion of contemporary issues in contract formation in Indian law must take notice of judicial interpretations of Indian arbitration law.

Arbitration clauses are increasingly commonplace in most sophisticated commercial contracts in the Indian context. When there is a dispute, one party to the contract invariably challenges the ability of the other party to invoke the arbitration clause. Frequently, this challenge invokes arguments about contract formation, and takes two forms—one, that the commercial agreement in which the arbitration clause is housed is not a contract as the requirements of contract formation have not been fulfilled and, two, that the arbitration clause itself is too vague and incomplete and, therefore, unworkable as an incubator of contractual responsibility. Therefore, there are two distinct arguments relating to the creation of contractual responsibility here—one that relates to whether there is consensus on essential

[116] ibid para 15. [117] AIR 1973 AP 342 (HC). [118] ibid para 57.

terms of the contract of which the arbitration clause forms a part; and, two, whether the terms of the arbitration clause are too vague to generate contractual responsibility.

On both these issues, as recent cases have demonstrated, the Indian courts tend to uphold the arbitration process, and their approach is founded on legislation that tries to forestall arguments of contractual formation in arbitration agreements. Most recently, the Supreme Court had occasion to consider these issues in the *Enercon India* case.[119] In *Enercon*, two companies had a long-standing legal relationship as licensor and licensee of technical know-how. When the technical know-how transfer agreement came to an end, the two companies entered into negotiations with each other regarding a new Intellectual Property Licence Agreement (the 'IPLA'). The parties also entered into a 'Heads of Agreement on the proposed IPLA' under which the parties 'irrevocably' agreed to settle their disputes through arbitration.

While the parties acknowledged in their emails to each other that the finer points of the IPLA were still subject to negotiation, they actually signed the IPLA, thus complicating future discussions about the existence of a contractual relationship between the two parties. Ultimately, the licensor stopped providing any further supplies to the licensee. The licensee filed a civil suit to secure the supplies. In response, the licensor filed an arbitration notice under the IPLA.

A preliminary objection raised by the licensee against the arbitration notice was that since there was no concluded IPLA (ie no concluded contract), the arbitration clause in the IPLA would not have any legal effect whatsoever. The argument was that the parties were in dispute about the essential terms of the IPLA and it was never the case that the draft IPLA constituted a concluded contract between the parties. In response, the licensor argued that the validity of the arbitration clause did not depend on the contractual status of the IPLA.

Another objection of the licensee took aim at the arbitration clause itself. The arbitration clause stated the following regarding the appointment of arbitrators:

> Arbitral Tribunal to consist of three (3) arbitrators, of whom one will be appointed by each of the Licensor and the Licensee and the arbitrator appointed by the Licensor shall also act as the presiding arbitrator.

It is clear that something went wrong in the drafting of this arbitration clause. While the clause envisaged three arbitrators, it accounted for the appointment of only two arbitrators, one of whom would act as the presiding arbitrator. The licensor argued that this infirmity could be rectified by the court and it only related to the machinery of the arbitration rather than a substantive element of the arbitration. The licensee argued that the infirmity was serious enough to make the arbitration clause vague and unworkable and that the court could not rectify the infirmity without redrafting the arbitration clause in its entirety.

The Indian Arbitration and Conciliation Act 1996 ('Arbitration Act') recognizes that arbitration is a voluntary process which *requires an agreement between parties* to resolve their dispute through a mechanism that serves as an alternative to the regular judicial process.[120] The Arbitration Act envisages an arbitration to occur in circumstances where the parties are not in a contractual relationship with each other. Nevertheless, the existence of an agreement between the parties to refer their disputes to arbitration is a sine qua non for a binding arbitration process. Arbitration is not a top-down dispute resolution procedure that is mandatorily imposed by legislation; the legislation recognizes the process of arbitration only after the parties have mutually consented to abide by the arbitral process.

[119] *Enercon (India) Ltd & Ors v Enercon Gmbh & Anr* AIR 2014 SC 3152 (SC).

[120] s 7, Arbitration Act defines an arbitration agreement as an agreement (in writing) by the parties to submit to arbitration all or certain disputes which have arisen or which may arise between them in respect of a defined legal relationship, whether contractual or not.

Section 16(1) of the Arbitration Act states the following:

The arbitral tribunal may rule on its own jurisdiction, including ruling on any objections with respect to the existence or validity of the arbitration agreement, and for that purpose:-

a. an arbitration clause which forms part of a contract shall be treated as an agreement independent of the other terms of the contract; and
b. a decision by the arbitral tribunal that the contract is null and void shall not entail ipso jure the invalidity of the arbitration clause.

Section 16 embodies the severability doctrine in arbitration law. A liberal reading of this doctrine, the reading that, as observed later, the Supreme Court adopted, would indicate that the status of the arbitration clause as a generator of contractual responsibility is not dependent on whether the overall document of which it is a part succeeds or fails in generating contractual responsibility. Read in this manner, section 16 appears to engineer absurd consequences for parties. Parties that do not have a contractual relationship either because there was no offer and acceptance of terms between them or the offer and acceptance did not correspond might still be stuck with an enforceable arbitration agreement because the documents that passed back and forth between the parties contained an arbitration clause. The absurdity of such a consequence is anticipated to some extent by the Arbitration Act; an arbitration agreement has been defined under section 7 of the Arbitration Act such that it presupposes a 'defined legal relationship' between the parties. However, the contours of a defined legal relationship are hazy. In *Enercon*, the Supreme Court, following the definition of an international commercial arbitration agreement in the Arbitration Act, stated that there was a legal relationship between the parties as long as the relationship was considered as commercial under the laws in force in India.[121] This is a very wide test and would include circumstances where the parties, despite having entered into negotiations with each other, have not yet agreed on any essential commercial matters.

In *Enercon*, the Supreme Court gave two independent reasons for upholding the validity of the arbitration clause. First, the parties in their heads of agreement (akin to a memorandum of understanding) had irrevocably agreed to settle their disputes through arbitration and had expressly clarified that the part that included the reference to arbitration was intended to be legally binding. As a result, the Supreme Court identified a legally enforceable arbitration agreement between the parties.[122]

The heads of agreement or a memorandum of understanding or letters of intent traditionally do not result in contractual obligations under English law, and Indian cases have tended to follow English law in this respect. However, this is not the case if the parties expressly delineate certain provisions in the heads of agreement as contractually binding. In recognizing the contractual validity of the arbitration clause, the Supreme Court in *Enercon* was giving effect to the wishes of the parties expressly mentioned in the heads of agreement.

The Supreme Court, however, gave another reason for upholding the validity of the arbitration clause. According to the Supreme Court, whether the IPLA led to contractual obligations was not a question relevant to whether the arbitration clause created a contractual obligation to refer disputes to arbitration. The court stated that under section 16 of the Arbitration Act, the arbitration clause was considered as an agreement independent of such a contract. A necessary corollary of such independence is that even if the IPLA was not a concluded agreement, it would not result in the invalidation of the arbitration clause housed therein.[123]

121 *Enercon* (n 119) para 75. 122 ibid paras 76–77. 123 ibid paras 79–81.

There is, however, an alternative way of reading section 16. The manner in which section 16 is drafted gives us an idea of its primary purpose. Its title is 'Competence of the Arbitral Tribunal to rule on its jurisdiction'. Section 16 was included in the Arbitration Act to secure the competence of the arbitrators to decide whether they have the competence to arbitrate in a dispute.

Section 16 secures the competence of the arbitrators to decide their own jurisdiction by first deeming the arbitration clause as a separate contract independent of the other terms of the contract and then protecting the arbitral decision even if the overall contract is declared invalid or void. It is interesting to note that the two clauses of section 16 refer to the agreements of which the arbitration clause is a part as 'contracts'. The way to read section 16 is to understand it as applying only to situations in which the relationship between the parties can *purport* to be a contractual relationship.

One understands from the ICA that not all commercial relationships can qualify to become contractual relationships. Only agreements can obtain the status of contracts (section 2(h)). In order for commercial dealings between parties to be recognized as an agreement, a promise or promises supported by consideration must have passed between the parties (section 2(e)). A promise requires a proposal from one party and its acceptance by the other party (section 2(b)). Therefore, the ICA's view of a promise is that of a proposal that is accepted by the person to whom the proposal is made. Mere unilateral proposals will not make the grade of a promise under the ICA. The ICA also makes it clear that in order for a proposal to be upgraded to a promise, its acceptance by the other party has to be absolute and unqualified (section 7).

It is the last requirement of an absolute and unqualified acceptance that ensures that not all commercial dealings can purport to be contracts. Only promises as envisaged by the ICA can purport to be contracts; however, a proposal from one party cannot become a promise unless it has been absolutely and unqualifiedly accepted by the party to whom the proposal was made. In *Enercon*, the argument of the licensee (the person denying the legal force of the arbitration agreement) was precisely on the point that the commercial dealings between the parties could not purport to be contracts at all. According to the licensee, the IPLA was merely a contract draft that was undergoing changes as the negotiations between the parties continued and, thus, there was no *consensus ad idem* between the parties.

The argument on lack of *consensus ad idem* was considered by the Supreme Court as irrelevant to the issue of the validity of the arbitration clause. However, the alternative reading of section 16 allows a party to challenge the existence of the arbitration clause by arguing that the relationship between the parties did not purport to be a contract at all. In fact, in previous cases, the courts have considered such arguments, but these cases were decided under the old arbitration legislation which did not deem the arbitration clause to be valid independent of the rest of the contract.

A prominent example of the courts' approach under the earlier arbitration legislation is the Supreme Court case of *UP Rajkiya Nirman Nigam Ltd v Indure Pvt Ltd & Ors.*[124] In this case, two parties purported to enter into an agreement prior to a joint tender application. The proposal and counter-proposal passing between the parties differed materially from each other on important terms such as the joint liability of the parties and the performance of the contract. Even though the purported agreement contained an arbitration clause, the Supreme Court ruled that since the relationship between the parties could not achieve the status of a legally enforceable agreement, the arbitration clause did not have any force either.

[124] AIR 1996 SC 1373 (SC).

The alternative reading of section 16 might be objected to on the ground that section 16 might lose its bite if it is interpreted to allow arguments about contract formation. However, this objection can be met if one understands that challenges to contract formation are of two types. The first type refers to one party alleging that its legal relationship with the other party is not of a type that can give rise to a promise as that term is recognized in Indian contract law. In other words, the objection is that the legal relationship between the parties does not even purport to be a contract. The other type refers to the objection that even though there is a promise or a set of promises as understood under the Indian contract law, the promise or set of promises do not form a contract because the formalities of contract formation are missing. Two important formalities are sometimes missed by parties to a contract: registration and payment of stamp duty. Under the alternative view, only the first type of argument can be raised under section 16. The second type is precluded by the application of section 16. This issue was discussed in the Supreme Court case of *M/S SMS Tea Estates Pvt Ltd v M/s Chandmari Tea Co Pvt Ltd.*[125] In *SMS Tea Estates*, the two litigating parties had entered into a lease deed which also contained an arbitration clause. However, the lease deed had not been registered, as was required under the Indian Registration Act 1908. If registration requirements are not complied with, the property interest would not be transferred and the lease deed could not be included as evidence of a transfer of property in any legal proceedings. One of the exceptions to this rule is that the lease deed can be used as evidence to demonstrate the existence of collateral transactions provided those collateral transactions themselves do not require registration.

The court considered the arbitration clause as a collateral transaction the existence of which could be proved through the submission of the lease deed.[126] The court was able to identify the arbitration clause as constituting a collateral transaction because the arbitration clause has a status that is independent of the contract of which it is a part. The court referred to section 16 of the Arbitration Act to buttress its point on the separability principle, ie that the validity of the arbitration clause is not affected by the validity of the overall contract of which it is a part.[127] Note that this is a case of the overarching contract failing to form a contractual relationship between the parties because of a violation of registration conditions. This case is different from a situation where the parties have failed to reach a consensus on important contractual matters.

The second argument propounded in *Enercon* was that the arbitration clause was too vague to be workable and, therefore, failed to create an obligation on the parties to refer their disputes to arbitration.[128] The wording of the arbitration clause was somewhat unfortunate. While it mentioned that three arbitrators would decide the dispute, it referred to only two arbitrators when it laid down the composition of the tribunal. The argument of the licensee was that the language of the clause made it unworkable. The court disagreed with this argument and held that the absence of a provision providing for a third arbitrator would not make the arbitration clause unworkable. The court gave three broad reasons for its decision. First, the Arbitration Act mandates the court to follow a non-interventionist policy towards arbitration proceedings and, therefore, the court must interpret arbitration agreements in such a way that it does not frustrate the arbitration process.[129] Second, the general principles of contract law interpretation allow the courts a certain degree of flexibility in construing contracts.[130] The court must interpret the contracts as a reasonable

[125] (2011) 4 SCC 66 (SC). [126] ibid para 7. [127] ibid para 7.
[128] See section VI for a general discussion on how the courts have resolved issues of uncertainty in contracts.
[129] *Enercon* (n 119) paras 76–78. [130] ibid para 83.

business person would and in this process, it must not interpret the contracts in such a way that it leads to absurd results or is contrary to the intentions of the contracting parties.

Finally, the court stated that the number of arbitrators on the panel related to a procedural mechanism and any defect in that respect would not affect the contractual status of the arbitration clause.[131] In classifying the matter of the number of arbitrators as a matter relating to the procedural mechanism rather than the substance or essence of the contract, the court signalled the course adopted by the House of Lords in similar situations.

In *Sudbrook Trading Estate Ltd v Eggleton*,[132] the House of Lords had to contend with a pricing mechanism in a real estate contract. The lessees had the option to convert their lease into a freehold at a price to be fixed by two valuers and, in the event of a deadlock, by a third party umpire. Both the lessees and the lessors had the right to appoint a valuer. The lessees decided to convert their lease into a freehold and appointed a valuer. The lessors decided not to appoint a valuer and brought matters to a head. The lessors argued that the contract was uncertain because there was no price mentioned in the contract. The contract instead had a price-fixing mechanism but that mechanism had failed to generate a price (albeit because of the intransigence of the lessors).

The House of Lords decided that the uncertainty in pricing did not nullify the contractual obligations of the parties and, thus, heralded what was (at least in appearance) a new approach to inchoate contractual provisions. The House of Lords said that price-fixing mechanisms that were subsidiary to the main purpose of the contract would not make the contract void for uncertainty.[133] In the same vein, the Supreme Court in *Enercon*, rightly in this commentator's opinion, decided that uncertainty regarding the number of arbitrators was merely subsidiary to the main purpose of the contract between the parties, which was to refer their disputes to arbitration.

XIII. Conclusion

Indian contract law began with an experiment in colonial times that was intended to bring the main principles of English common law into legislative form. In terms of longevity and stability, this experiment has succeeded with the legislative provisions on contract law, particularly those pertaining to contract formation, remaining largely unchanged over the past century and a half. The ICA provisions on contract formation are arranged sequentially through a series of definitions starting with what constitutes a proposal, its acceptance, a promise, an agreement, and finally a contract.

Indian contract law adopts an objective approach to the question of the formation of contracts and, therefore, asks whether a reasonable person would consider the parties to have entered into an agreement. Such an objective appraisal extends to whether offers and acceptances mirror each other. Offers can be revoked but are subject to the complex postal communication rules that are familiar to English scholars of contract law. The ICA's rules on the communication of offers and acceptances are now subject to new rules under the Information Technology Act 2000 though it is unclear whether the ITA has in fact made any difference to the traditional rules on offers and acceptances.

The ICA has detailed rules on consideration. While it follows the English common law on consideration, the ICA has created some statutory exceptions that have no parallel in English common law.[134] Another novel feature of Indian contract law in this area relates to promissory estoppel where a more liberal approach, as opposed to its English counterpart, is followed. Under Indian law, promissory estoppel can be used as a cause of action, and

[131] ibid para 85. [132] [1983] 1 AC 444 (HL). [133] ibid 483. [134] See s 63, ICA.

therefore can act as a shield as well as a sword. In situations where a contract has not been formed owing to an absence of consideration or formalities, the ICA's quasi-contractual provisions that prevent unjust enrichment could still be of assistance to the parties.

The major contemporary debates in Indian contract law now tend to arise in the area of arbitration clauses in commercial agreements. In *Enercon*, the Supreme Court considered issues that arose at the intersection of contract formation and arbitration law, thus showcasing the kind of legal puzzles that can arise when traditional contract law principles are modified through statutory interventions. In *Enercon*, by applying the severability doctrine enshrined in the Arbitration Act, the Supreme Court recognized the legal effect of an arbitration clause even though the arbitration clause was part of an agreement the existence of which was in dispute. This case is an example of how issues of contract formation can in some cases be impacted by legislation on the resolution of commercial disputes.

While Indian contract law is mainly statutory in form, it includes a fascinating mix of English common law principles interspersed with some limited modifications designed to make Indian contract law provisions more progressive and suitable for Indian conditions. By and large, the law in this area demonstrates the extent to which English common law has shaped the Indian law on contract formation. Prominent Indian cases on contract law that make new and substantial statements of doctrine are actually fewer in number than one would expect in such a litigious field. The lack of judicial activism in this area owes as much to the sturdy and stable legislative framework for contract law in India as to the influence that English common law principles continue to exert on contract law jurisprudence in India.

5

Contracts for the Benefit of Third Parties: The Indian Perspective

*Nilima BHADBHADE**

I. Introduction

The doctrine of privity states that a contract cannot confer rights and obligations arising under it to anyone other than the parties to it. In this chapter, the privity rule is discussed with reference to the first aspect: that a person cannot claim the benefit conferred upon him by a contract to which he is not a party. It is referred to in this chapter as the privity rule.

The privity rule is a foundational rule in Indian contract law. It was applied in India even before[1] English law recognized it in 1861 in the case *Tweddle v Atkinson*.[2] Despite being a rule of English law at the time of its enactment, the privity rule was not stated in express words in the Indian Contract Act 1872 ('ICA'). The rule has been recognized not only as a principle of common law, but also from an analysis of the provisions of the ICA. Unlike English or Singapore law, Indian law does not have any statute conferring such a right on third parties. Indian law also recognizes exceptions to the privity rule. Most of these exceptions (viz trusts and settlements, charges) are derived from English law. The privity rule and exceptions have been acknowledged and accepted by the Supreme Court of India in the case of *MC Chacko v State Bank of Travancore*.[3]

This chapter elaborates on the privity rule in Indian law. Section II discusses Indian contract law, its background and the close association of Indian contract law with English law, the distinct rule in the ICA that allows a stranger to provide consideration but does not affect the privity rule, and the source of the privity rule in the ICA. Section III analyses the privity rule as a rule of substance or of procedure. Section IV discusses the application of the privity rule in Indian law in allowing enforcement by a third party or allowing it to take the benefit of exclusion clauses in a contract. Section V states and discusses the exceptions to the privity rule developed through case law, and provided in statutes. Section VI examines the rights and remedies of parties. Section VII discusses the call for law reform.

II. Indian Contract Law

The ICA deals with general principles applicable to all contracts.[4] These are provisions about formation of agreements, rules of offers and acceptances, conditions of validity, rules

* Cite as N Bhadbhade, 'Contracts for the Benefit of Third Parties: The Indian Perspective' in Chen-Wishart, Loke, & Vogenauer, *Studies in the Contract Laws of Asia Vol II: Formation and Third Party Beneficiaries* (Oxford: OUP 2017) ch 5.

[1] Agreements have effect only between the parties: discussed on the bases of judgments of lower British courts in India before 1864 by W Macpherson, *Outlines of the Law of Contracts as administered by the Courts of British India not established by Royal Charter* (London: RC LePage and Co 1864) 69–73.

[2] (1861) 1 B & S 393 (QB).

[3] AIR 1970 SC 504, 1969 (2) SCC 343.

[4] ss 1–75, ICA give general provisions.

about performance of promises, discharge of contracts by agreement, impossibility, valid rescission and other circumstances, and the remedy of compensation. Particular contracts have special provisions stated in separate chapters in the ICA,[5] and others in independent statutes.[6] The ICA does not have express provisions, either to enable or to prohibit the enforcement of contracts by persons other than its parties.

To the extent the ICA (or any statute affecting particular contracts) does not make any provision, courts will enunciate principles, often by reference to English law. The association of Indian contract law with English law is discussed in section II.1. Indian courts also refer to statutory provisions or judge-made principles from other jurisdictions.[7] Contract law evolves through such principles.

The doctrine of precedent and *stare decisis* apply in India. Contract law is also made by decisions of superior courts: the Supreme Court and the 24 High Courts that are located in the capital cities of states.[8] Only judgments of these courts are reported. Principles affecting contracts derived in the course of judgments of each High Court bind the courts subordinate to it.[9] The law laid down by the Supreme Court of India binds all courts in the territory of India.[10] High Courts are likely to differ in their views about any aspect of law, thereby leading to conflicting judgments. A High Court is not bound to follow any principle laid down by another High Court. Each subordinate court is bound to apply any principle stated by the High Court to which it is subordinate, until the subject is settled by a judgment of the Supreme Court. Different High Courts have from time to time taken different approaches towards the privity rule. These are discussed later in the chapter.[11]

A civil suit for breach of contract is filed in the lowest civil court having jurisdiction. Commercial courts will try commercial disputes under a recent law.[12] Any civil suit for breach of contract will usually go through at least one appeal before it reaches the High Court.[13] It can be expected that if the amount involved in a dispute is small, or an unsuccessful party does not wish to continue proceedings in an appeal, or in the High Court for reasons of time, expense, or distance to the location of the High Court,[14] then very few contract matters will reach the High Court. Reports of the superior courts are therefore not truly indicative of the doctrines and principles of contract law applied in India, especially the prevalent and applied doctrines put into practice by subordinate courts in contract law-related matters before them. A subordinate court[15] deciding a contract dispute that faces an issue not covered by statute or precedent, will deal with it based on the judge's understanding

[5] Contracts of indemnity, guarantee, bailment, pledge, and agency.

[6] eg Sale of Goods Act 1930; Indian Partnership Act 1932; Carriage of Goods by Sea Act 1925; Carriage by Road Act 2007.

[7] *Bhagwandas Goverdhandas Kedia v Girdharlal Parshottamadas and Co* AIR 1966 SC 543 (communication of acceptance); *Central Inland Water Transport Corporation Ltd v Brojo Nath Ganguly* AIR 1986 SC 1571 (unconscionable terms in contract are against public policy); *Renusagar Power Co Ltd v General Electric Co* AIR 1994 SC 860 (recognition of foreign award).

[8] Some High Courts also have benches in other locations in the state.

[9] ie the civil courts and district courts.

[10] Art 141, Constitution of India.

[11] See section III (Privity Rule: of Substance or Procedure).

[12] Under the Commercial Courts, Commercial Division and Commercial Appellate Division of High Courts Act 2015, in force with effect from 31 December 2015, Commercial Courts have been set up at district level for deciding 'commercial disputes'. High Courts will have a Commercial Division for similar disputes, and will also hear appeals from judgments from Commercial Courts. Under s 2(1)(c) of this Act, 'commercial disputes' include those arising from ordinary transactions of merchants, carriage of goods, import or export of merchandise and services, shareholders agreements, agreements for sale of goods, etc.

[13] Most High Courts have original jurisdiction for matters arising in the city or town where the High Court is located.

[14] Which may be 1,000 kms or more.

[15] India has 16,839 subordinate courts (source: National Judicial Data Grid) <http://njdg.ecourts.gov.in/njdg_public/main.php> accessed 26 October 2016.

of contract principles, or with reference to English law, or laws of foreign jurisdictions. Judgments of subordinate courts are not visible or reported.[16]

1. Association with English Law

The ICA defines, amends, and codifies certain parts of contract law. It draws heavily upon English law of that time. The ICA is not a complete code, and does not cover the whole field of contract law.[17] It attempts to 'codify—that is to say, arrange clearly and systematically, the principal rules relating to the formation, ratification and discharge of all agreements enforceable by law, made between two or more persons, by which rights are acquired by one or more of them to acts or forbearances on the part of others'.[18] It departs from English law on some essential principles, viz a promisee can sue on a contract even though he has not supplied consideration for the promise, a full or part remission by a promisee does not require consideration, past consideration is valid consideration, and agreements in restraint of trade are void even if restraint is partial.

The development of the principles of contract law influence the discussion and development of the privity rule in Indian law within the jurisdictions of the various High Courts.

Codification in India started in 1833,[19] and mainly from 1853.[20] British courts at the time were free to decide disputes with very few guidelines or law. This was a period of judicial creativity. The principles of Hindu or Muslim contract law applied, and courts took assistance from persons learned in those laws. Bombay, Calcutta, and Madras were Presidency Towns, and other areas were termed the 'mofussil', ie the provincial and rural areas. The laws in these two areas took different courses.

In the Presidency Towns of Calcutta, Madras, and Bombay, matters of contract were directed to be regulated by the personal law of the party, ie Muslim and Hindu law.[21] Thus, English law would apply to all except to Hindus and Muslims, who would be governed by their law. Nevertheless, the Supreme Court of Bombay ignored the Hindu law, and applied English law in contract cases.[22]

In the mofussil, there was no express provision for contracts until the Declaratory Act of 1781 which laid down that the courts were to act according to 'justice, equity and good conscience'. This gave the judges substantial discretion. There was no body of law to turn to. They were free to adopt any rule or custom which they considered reasonable, or apply a body of principles that appeared to do substantial justice between the parties. Judges did not have legal training. They were English administrative officers and not acquainted with local customs. They took assistance from native law officers, the Muslim *kazis*, and the Hindu *pandits*, and applied the Hindu or the Muslim law.[23]

In 1833, the Privy Council became the final court of appeal for matters from India. The judges of the Privy Council, naturally,[24] drew from the basic principles of English law when

[16] Judgments of subordinate courts from the past decade are now available on the internet, but they are not reported, nor have they been discussed or analysed.

[17] C Ilbert, *The Government of India: Being a Digest of the Statute Law relating thereto with Historical Introduction and Explanatory Matter* (3rd edn, London: Clarendon Press 1915) 364.

[18] W Stokes, *The Anglo-Indian Codes* (Oxford: Clarendon Press 1887) vol 1, 491.

[19] Charter Act 1833: Governor General became the sole authority to promulgate laws for persons and courts.

[20] Charter Act 1853: Legislative Council was established.

[21] Declaratory Acts 1781 (21Geo 3, c 70) and 1797 (37 Geo 3, c 142).

[22] MP Jain, 'The Law of Contract before its Codification' (1972) 14 (Special Issue) JILI 178, 189.

[23] See generally W Macpherson, *Outlines of the Law of Contracts as administered by the Courts of British India not established by Royal Charter* (London: RC LePage and Co 1864); MP Jain, 'The Law of Contract before its Codification' (1972) 14 (Special Issue) JILI 178, 190.

[24] MC Setalvad, *The Common Law in India* (London: Stevens & Sons Ltd 1960) 23.

there were no provisions of statute law to apply. After 1862,[25] the High Courts and the lower courts had judges and lawyers trained as barristers in English law who were familiar with principles of English common law. These two factors explain why principles of English common law and equity found their way into Indian contract jurisprudence, especially in the application of the principles of 'justice, equity and good conscience'.[26]

It has been observed:

> An Englishman would naturally interpret these words as meaning such rules and principles of English law as he happened to know and considered applicable to the case; and thus, under the influence of English judges, native law and usage were, without express legislation, largely supplemented, modified, and superseded by English law.[27]

After many judgments of High Courts applying English law as the principles of 'justice, equity and good conscience', the Privy Council settled the question in *Waghela Rajsanji v Shekh Masludin*,[28] where Hobhouse J observed that these principles shall be 'generally interpreted to mean the rules of English law if found applicable to Indian society and circumstances'. Courts applied English law to the extent that it was suitable for Indian conditions.[29] It has been observed:

> In proposing to apply the juristic rules of a distant time or country to the conditions of a particular place at the present day regard must be had to the physical, social and historical condition to which that rule is to be adapted.[30]

Thus, the Privy Council departed from English law to enforce agreements of a champertous nature,[31] and in other cases. It also departed from the English rule of privity in *Tweddle v Atkinson*[32] in a case involving similar facts.[33]

Tweddle v Atkinson that represents the doctrine of privity in the common law intertwines the two doctrines of consideration and privity. A plaintiff in a similar case will not be barred under Indian law for lack of consideration. The two doctrines operate in different fields as discussed below.

2. Privity Rule and Doctrine of Consideration

The rule as to who shall provide consideration must be distinguished from the privity rule. The two rules reflect separate issues of policy. The rule of privity relates to who can enforce the contract, and that of consideration is about the types of promises which can be enforced.[34] Thus, whether a stranger to consideration can sue is a question distinct from whether a stranger to contract can sue.

[25] Indian High Courts Act 1861.

[26] See AC Patra, 'Historical Background of the Indian Contract Act, 1872' (1962) 4 JILI 373, 393.

[27] C Ilbert, *The Government of India: Being a Digest of the Statute Law relating thereto with Historical Introduction and Explanatory Matter* (3rd edn, London: Clarendon Press 1915) 360.

[28] (1887) 14 IA 89, 96, [1887] UKPC 9.

[29] For discussion of the approach of courts, see BK Acharyya, *Codification in British India* (Calcutta: SK Banerji and Sons 1914) 130; AC Patra 'Historical Background of the Indian Contract Act, 1872' (1962) 4 JILI 373.

[30] *Raja Srinath Roy v Dinabandhu Sen* (1914) 41 IA 221, 243, [1914] UKPC 64 <http://www.bailii.org/uk/cases/UKPC/1914/1914_64.pdf> at p 24 (Sumner J) (a case about river rights), accessed 17 January 2017.

[31] *Chedambara Chetty v Ranja Krishna Muttu Naicker* (1874)1 IA 241, [1874] UKPC 34; *Ram Coomar Coondoo v Chander Canto Mookerjee* [1876] 4 IA 23, [1874] UKPC 54.

[32] (1861) 1 B & S 393 (QB).

[33] *Nawab Khwaja Muhammad Khan v Nawab Husaini Begam* (1910) 37 IA 152, [1910] UKPC 25.

[34] J Beatson, A Burrows, and J Cartwright, *Anson's Law of Contract* (29th edn, Oxford: OUP 2010) 616; Law Commission, *Privity of Contract: Contract for the Benefit of Third Parties*, Pt VI (Law Com No 242, 1996) (UK).

In Indian law, the requirement of consideration is a matter of substantive validity of contract. Consideration for a contract can move from the promisee or any person other than the promisee. Also, past consideration can support a contract. This is a vital departure from English law. Thus, if X and Y agree that in consideration of Z paying to Y Rs 100, Y will repair X's house, X can enforce the contract against Y, who cannot object that he received the money from Z and not from X. But in a contract where A agrees with B to provide services to B the charges of which B shall pay to C, C cannot enforce the contract.

Clause (d) of section 2 defines 'consideration' as follows:

> When, at the desire of the promisor, the promisee *or any other person* has done or abstained from doing, or does or abstains from doing, or promises to do or to abstain from doing, something, such act or abstinence or promise is called a consideration for the promise...[35]

This clause widens the definition of 'consideration' beyond its terms under English law 'so as to enable a party to a contract to enforce the same in India in certain cases in which the English Law would regard that party as the recipient of a purely voluntary promise and would refuse to him a right of action on the ground of nudum pactum'.[36] The effect of section 2(d) of the Act is that if a promisee wishes to enforce the contract, the promisor cannot object that the consideration has proceeded from a third party.

Such a question arose in the early case of *Chinnaya v Ramayya*.[37] X made a gift of her property to her daughter Y with a direction that she should continue to pay to Z, X's brothers, an annuity that X had been paying, until a village could be given to them that would yield them income. On the same day Y executed an agreement in favour of Z covenanting to carry out the terms of the deed of gift. Y did not comply, and Z sued for the annuity under the terms of the agreement. The main question before the court was whether Z had the right to sue, being a stranger to consideration. Innes J held that Z could sue since consideration moved indirectly from them wholly or partly. Kindersley J agreed, and also held that the two documents formed one transaction, and the consideration was provided in the deed of gift by X, who was not a party to the agreement sought to be enforced.

In this analysis, the third party beneficiary can sue the promisor on an independent promise or agreement with the promisor.[38] Similarly, collateral contracts, such as manufacturer's warranties, can be enforced directly.

3. Privity Rule and Indian Contract Act

The privity rule has its source in English common law, particularly in the decision of *Tweddle v Atkinson*:[39] one will find reference to the common law principle and this judgment in most decisions of superior courts that deal with this issue. The rule precedes the ICA. In his book written in 1864, William Macpherson states that agreements have no effect except between the contracting parties.[40]

It is now accepted in Indian law that the rule arises from an interpretation of the ICA. The ICA does not make any provision conferring the right of enforcement on the third party for whose benefit a contract is made. Nor does it restrict enforcement by a person who is not a party to a contract. Although the ICA does not make any provision about this question, the

[35] Emphasis added.

[36] *Krishna Lal Sadhu v Promila Bala Dasi* AIR 1928 Cal 518, 522 (Calcutta HC) (Rankin CJ).

[37] (1881) 4 Mad 137 (Madras HC).

[38] Recognized in *Jamna Das v Ram Autar Pande* (1911) 39 IA 7 (PC), [1911] UKPC 69.

[39] (1861) 1 B & S 393 (QB).

[40] W Macpherson, *Outlines of the Law of Contracts as administered by the Courts of British India not established by Royal Charter* (London: RC LePage and Co 1864) 69.

rule is implicit within the definitions of proposal, acceptance, promisor, promisee, promise, and agreement stated in the ICA.[41]

This absence of provision generated many views in earlier judgments. One view suggests that a third party cannot enforce a contract to which he is not a party unless a statute provides that he can. On this view, no rule can be implied from the language of the Act. It has been observed: 'if the rule is to be introduced into this country that any person may sue upon a contract, if he takes a benefit under it, although a stranger to such contract,...the rule must be introduced by the legislature, and not by the Courts'.[42] On another view, enforcement by the third party beneficiary is possible because there is nothing in the Act 'which prevents recognition of a right in a third party to enforce a contract made by others'.[43] A third view recognizes that in the absence of any express provision in the statute, it is within the courts' powers to do justice between the parties and adjudicate between the parties before them.[44]

The prevalent view, however, is that the privity rule is implied from the language of the ICA. As is observed: '[I]t is wrong to say that there is no provision in Indian law in support of this principle [of privity], which has been well-established in England from very old times'.[45]

Under the ICA,[46] a proposal is an expression of willingness to do something with a view to getting the assent of the addressee. It is made to the person who indicates his assent. This becomes a promise. The person expressing willingness to do or not to do something is the promisor. The person stating assent is the promisee. Every promise and every set of promises, forming the consideration for each other, is an agreement between those two persons.

As far back as 1913, the Bombay High Court refused[47] to enforce the payment of a life insurance policy to a wife, its nominated beneficiary, relying on an analysis of the ICA. It held that: (1) there was no evidence that the plaintiff-wife was a promisor or a promisee and therefore a party to the agreement; and (2) there was nothing in the ICA to show an intention that a person not a party to the contract could sue on it; and (3) clause (i) of section 2 was an indication to the contrary.[48] In 1926, a Full Bench of the Allahabad High

[41] F Pollock and D Mulla, *The Indian Contract Act* (2nd edn, Bombay: NM Tripathi & Co 1909).

[42] *National Petroleum Co Ltd v Popatlal Mulji* AIR 1936 Bom 344, 346 (Bombay HC) (Beaumont CJ).

[43] *Khirod Behari Dutt v Man Govinda* AIR 1934 Cal 682, 689 (Calcutta HC) (Lort-Williams J).

[44] *Post Master General Patna v Ram Kripal Sahu* AIR 1955 Pat 442, 444 (Patna HC) (Sinha J): 'it is not necessary for the Legislature to intervene for the purpose of enabling the plaintiff, not party to a contract, to sue on the contract'.

[45] *National Petroleum Co Ltd v Popatlal Mulji* AIR 1936 Bom 344, 351 (Bombay HC) (Rangnekar J).

[46] Indian Contract Act 1872, s 2:

> In this Act the following words and expressions are used in the following senses, unless a contrary intention appears from the context:
>
> (a) When one person signifies to another his willingness to do or to abstain from doing anything, with a view to obtaining the assent of that other to such act or abstinence, he is said to make a proposal;
> (b) When the person to whom the proposal is made signifies his assent thereto, the proposal is said to be accepted. A proposal, when accepted, becomes a promise;
> (c) The person making the proposal is called the 'promisor', and the person accepting the proposal is called 'promisee';
> (d) When, at the desire of the promisor, the promisee or any other person has done or abstained from doing, or does or abstains from doing, or promises to do or to abstain from doing, something, such act or abstinence or promise is called a consideration for the promise;
> (e) Every promise and every set of promises, forming the consideration for each other, is an agreement;
> (i) An agreement which is enforceable by law at the option of one or more of the parties thereto, but not at the option of the other or others, is a voidable contract.

[47] *Shankar Vishwanath Vagh v Umabai Sadashiv Wagle* (1913) 37 Bom 471 (Bombay HC).

[48] Under cl 2(i), an agreement which is enforceable by law at the option of one or more of the parties thereto, but not at the option of the other or others, is a voidable contract; indicating thereby that a contract is enforceable at the instance of parties only.

Court followed the same analysis and held that since a proposal should be made to the promisee who must indicate his assent to it, it follows that a stranger cannot enforce the contract to which he is not a party.[49] In *Krishna Lal Sadhu v Promila Bala Dasi*,[50] Rankin CJ observed: 'the idea that contracts can be enforced by a person who is not a party to the contract…is rightly excluded by the definition of "promisor" and "promisee"'.[51] In *MC Chacko*'s case, the Supreme Court accepted this analysis.[52]

In the Malaysian case of *Kepong Prospecting Ltd v Schmidt*,[53] the Privy Council took a similar view.

III. Privity Rule: Of Substance or Procedure

The nature of relief that a court may give to a third party might be affected by classification of the privity rule as one of substance or of procedure. If it is a substantive rule, a civil court will not have the power to get around it.

There have been attempts to classify the privity rule as one of procedure. This allows courts to take a very wide approach and give relief to a third party by resorting to the rules of 'justice, equity and good conscience'.[54] These are the principles a court may resort to where there is no specific rule of law applicable to the case. Some later cases do not agree with such a wide view.[55]

When viewed as a rule of procedure, a civil court is able to give relief in a suit by a third party especially when the promisor, the promisee, and the third party are all parties to the proceedings.[56] Thus:

> where a Court has before it all persons and is in a position to do complete justice to the case, it would be straining the law to hold that the suit should fail on the ground that the defendant [promisor] did not contract with the plaintiff [third party] to pay the amount which he contracted to pay on his [the promisee's] behalf.[57]

It has also been suggested that the technical plea of privity can be avoided by making or joining the promisee as a co-plaintiff.[58] In these cases, the third party is not a volunteer, and the promisor has undertaken to fulfil the promisee's obligation towards the third party.

If the privity rule is a rule of procedure, a court can resort to the principle that requires avoiding multiplicity of litigation.[59] As observed: 'all the parties were before the Courts

[49] *Mittar Sain v Data Ram* AIR 1926 All 194 (Allahabad HC) (Linsdsay J); *Iswaram Pillai v Tharagan* AIR 1914 Mad 701 (Madras HC).

[50] AIR 1928 Cal 518 (Calcutta HC). [51] ibid 522.

[52] *MC Chacko v State Bank of Travancore* AIR 1970 SC 504, 1969 (2) SCC 343.

[53] [1968] AC 810 (PC), [1967] UKPC 22.

[54] *Deb Narayan Dutt v Chunilal Ghose* (1914) ILR 41 Cal 137 (Calcutta HC); *Dwarika Nath Ash v Priya Nath Malki* AIR 1918 Cal 941 (Calcutta HC); *Khirod Behari Dutt v Man Govinda* AIR 1934 Cal 682 (Calcutta HC); *Bhujendra Nath Biswas v Sushmoyee Basu* AIR 1936 Cal 67 (Calcutta HC); *A Singarayya v A Subbayya* AIR 1924 Mad 861 (Madras HC); *Post Master General Patna v Ram Kripal Sahu* AIR 1955 Pat 442 (Patna HC); *Babu Ram Budhu Mal v Dhan Singh Bishan Singh* AIR 1957 Punj 169 (Punjab HC).

[55] *Iswaram Pillai v Tharagan* AIR 1914 Mad 701 (Madras HC); *Gauri Shankar v Mangal* AIR 1933 Lah 178 (Lahore HC); *Mangal Sen v Muahammad Hussain* (1915) 37 All 115 (Allahabad HC); *National Petroleum Co Ltd v Popatlal Mulji* AIR 1936 Bom 344 (Bombay HC) (Rangnekar J); *District Board v Rai Bahadur Chandra Ketu Narayan* AIR 1937 Cal 625 (Calcutta HC).

[56] *Iswaram Pillai v Tharagan* AIR 1914 Mad 701 (Madras HC); *Dwarika Nath Ash v Priya Nath Malki* AIR 1918 Cal 941(Calcutta HC); *Torabaz Khan v Nanak Chand* AIR 1932 Lah 566 (Lahore HC); *Khirod Behari Dutt v Man Govinda* AIR 1934 Cal 682 (Calcutta HC).

[57] *A Singarayya v A Subbayya* AIR 1924 Mad 861, 862 (Madras (HC) (Devadoss J).

[58] *Hashmatmal v Pribhdas* AIR 1929 Sind 117 (Sind HC).

[59] *Khirod Behari Dutt v Man Govinda* AIR 1934 Cal 682 (Calcutta HC); *Bibhuti Bhusan Ghose v Baikuntha Nath Mondal* (1935) 62 CLJ 55 (Calcutta HC).

below and are before us, and neither common sense nor convenience, equity nor good conscience require me to force the parties into further and unnecessary litigation.'[60]

The power of the civil courts to enable enforcement with a view to avoiding multiple litigation actually enables relief to be given to a third party without any further exercise of the powers of the court. If all three are parties to the suit, and relief is granted to the third party, the interests of all parties are protected. The third party gets what is expected and promised under the terms of the contract, to which the promisee need not have objection. The promisee can avoid taking steps for enforcement. By application of the principles of *res judicata*, the promisee will not be able to file another suit for the promise. The promisor will not face the prospect of being doubly liable. All parties will stand discharged as contemplated by the contract. The need for impleading all parties has also been justified thus:[61]

> [A] person who is not a party to the contract cannot be permitted to enforce it without being subject to all the equities which would be present between the parties themselves, and this would almost *invariably necessitate that all the parties to the contract should be impleaded in the suit*: the question whether the contract is revocable at the option of either of the parties or whether it has been altered by mutual consent or been performed in part, whether the parties can be restored to their original position and other similar questions would have to be considered and would affect the third party's claim.

In *Thirumulu Subbu Chetti v Arunachalam Chettiar*,[62] the Full Bench of the Madras High Court digressed from this view. In this case, a sale deed of immovable property contained a stipulation directing the purchaser to pay off the seller's creditor. The creditor sued the seller for the debt, and also the purchaser to enforce the stipulation. It was argued that since all the parties to the contract were before the court, and complete justice could be done between them, the court was not prevented from giving a decree to a person although he was not a party to the contract, and that this exception should be created and grafted on to the rule in *Tweddle v Atkinson*. The Full Bench of the Madras High Court held that the creditor could not recover from the purchaser, and adding the seller as a party to the suit did not make any difference. It observed:

> [I]t is no answer to say that all the parties are before the Court.... There should be a right to relief in respect of the transaction set out in the plaint before a party can be added as defendant. The addition of others would not so far as he is concerned alter his rights... there is [no] legal basis for holding that the mere joinder of the original parties to the contract would give the plaintiff a cause of action which does not exist before the suit.[63]

Here, the privity rule is recognized as one of substance. If it relates to the rights of parties as stated above by the Full Bench of the Madras High Court, only such person can be made party to a suit who has a right or is liable. It is necessary for the plaintiff-third party to have a right before filing the suit. The Allahabad High Court has held that a court cannot grant a decree against a person who is not liable in law, only for avoiding multiplicity of litigation.[64]

That the rule is substantive is also seen from its application in relation to claims in insolvency proceedings. Thus, where X sold goods to Y and kept the price with Y to be paid to Z (X's creditor), to whom X was indebted, and X was declared insolvent, Z could not resist the claim of the Official Receiver to the amount because Z was not entitled to enforce

[60] *Khirod Behari Dutt v Man Govinda* AIR 1934 Cal 682, 690 (Lort-Williams J).

[61] *Iswaram Pillai v Tharagan* AIR 1914 Mad 701, 706 (Tyabji J) (emphasis added).

[62] AIR 1930 Mad 382 (Madras HC) (FB); see also *New Bank of India Ltd v Union of India* (1977) 2 Del 672 (Delhi HC) (seller's creditor could not enforce although all parties were before the court).

[63] AIR 1930 Mad 382, 389 (Madras HC) (FB) (Kumarswami Sastri J).

[64] *Mangal Sen v Muahammad Hussain* (1915) 37 All 115 (Allahabad HC).

the contract between X and Y.[65] Moreover, failure by the promisor to perform his promise to pay a third party did not amount to an act of insolvency. It has been observed: 'in insolvency proceedings, creditors can[not] claim benefits under a contract which benefits would not be available to them in action by suit'.[66]

The Full Bench of the Madras High Court[67] and the Division Bench of the Allahabad High Court[68] are of the view that the privity rule cannot be ignored even though the promisee is also party to the suit, or to avoid multiplicity of litigation. Views of other High Courts continue to have force within their jurisdictions.

IV. Privity Rule in Indian Law

The rule that a third party on whom a contract confers a benefit cannot enforce it, has been applied in India in diverse situations.

MC Chacko v State Bank of Travancore[69] is an important judgment of the Supreme Court recognizing the rule. In this case, Highland Bank had an overdraft account with Kottayam Bank, merged later into the State Bank of Travancore. K, the father of Chacko, guaranteed the amount. In 1951 he executed a deed of partition of his properties among his relatives, where he provided:

> If in pursuance of the letter given by me to the Kottayam Bank at the request of my eldest son, Chacko, for the purpose of the High Land Bank Ltd., ... any amount is due and payable to the Kottayam Bank, that amount is to be paid from the High Land Bank by my son, Chacko. If the same is not so done and any amount becomes payable (by me) as per my letter, ... my eldest son, Chacko and the properties in Schedule A alone will be answerable for that amount ...[70]

The plaintiff claimed against Chacko on the basis of the above provision in the deed to which the plaintiff was not a party. An alternative claim[71] lay under a charge that it alleged was created in its favour by the terms of the deed. The trial court and the High Court decreed the suit against Chacko. The Supreme Court first held that the language in the deed did not create any charge over the property in favour of the plaintiff. On the question whether the plaintiff could claim as a beneficiary under the above provision, it held that the plaintiff not being a party to the deed, could not claim under the deed. The Supreme Court observed:

> It must ... be taken as well settled that except in the case of a beneficiary under a trust created by a contract or in the case of a family arrangement, no right may be enforced by a person who is not a party to the contract.[72]

The privity rule has been applied in a large number of cases where X sold or transferred property to Z with a stipulation that Z should pay off Y (X's creditor), to deny relief to Y. For example, in *Thirumulu Subbu Chetti v Arunachalam Chettiar*,[73] a creditor sought to enforce a stipulation in a sale deed that directed the purchaser to pay the amount due to the creditor out of the consideration of the sale. The creditor sued the seller for the debt, and the

[65] *Gurdit Singh v Chuni Lal* AIR 1932 Lah 66 (Lahore HC).
[66] *Rijhumal Nandiram v Jan Mahomed* AIR 1943 Sind 190, 192 (Sindh HC) (Weston J).
[67] *Thirumulu Subbu Chetti v Arunachalam Chettiar* AIR 1930 Mad 382 (FB) (Madras HC).
[68] *Mangal Sen v Muahammad Hussain* (1915) 37 All 115 (Allahabad HC).
[69] AIR 1970 SC 504, 1969 (2) SCC 343. [70] ibid 506; 1969 (2) SCC 343.
[71] The suit for the amount due was filed against High Land Bank as its debtor, K as the guarantor, and against Chacko under the provisions of the deed. The claim under the guarantee was barred by limitation.
[72] *MC Chacko v State Bank of Travancore* AIR 1970 SC 504, 508 (Shah CJ), 1969 (2) SCC 343.
[73] AIR 1930 Mad 382 (Madras HC) (FB); see also *Ganesh Das v Banto* AIR 1935 Lah 354 (Lahore HC); *Jnan Chandra Mukherji v Mano Ranjan Mitra* AIR 1942 Cal 251 (Calcutta HC).

purchaser as the promisor of the stipulation. After analysis of all judgments (which the court found difficult to reconcile), the Full Bench of the Madras High Court held that the creditor could not sue the purchaser.

Thus, where X bank makes a contract with Y security company for collection of Z store's takings, under which Y must use armoured vehicles, Z cannot sue Y if the takings are stolen while being collected in an ordinary car.

The nominated beneficiary of insurance policies could not claim under the policy.[74] An employee could not claim his remuneration from anyone other than his employer, even though his services have been lent under an arrangement.[75] Where a party to a contract agrees to indemnify the other party against all his debts, the creditor of the other party cannot sue the indemnifier under such a contract (ie the obligation is owed to the person indemnified, not to the creditor).[76]

1. Benefit of Exclusion Clauses in Contracts

Can a person seek the benefit of an exclusion clause agreed in a contract to which he is not a party? In the case *Midland Silicones Ltd v Scruttons Ltd*,[77] Lord Reid suggested that the stevedores could take advantage of the exemption clause agreed in a contract between the shipper and the charterer provided certain conditions were met. Later, in *The Eurymedon*,[78] the Privy Council gave effect to an exclusion clause in a bill of lading relied on by the third party stevedores by applying an analysis of an offer by the shipper of a unilateral contract to the stevedores accepted by the stevedores when the latter commenced work; and the Privy Council also stated the importance of such recognition in the commercial context.

This issue has not been decided by the High Court or the Supreme Court in any Indian case. In the hypothetical concerning enforcing exemption clause by stevedores,[79] the exclusion clause would not enure to the benefit of the stevedores under the privity principle. But such a clause will bind the shipper when the stevedores commence work in response to the proposal of the shipper to be bound by it.[80]

Courts have adhered to the privity rule and refused to grant the benefit of other types of clauses to *or against* third parties.

In *Jahandar Baksh Mallick v Ram Lal Hazra*,[81] the plaintiff held land from the government under a condition that he would not increase the rent receivable from his tenants beyond a certain amount. He then made agreements with his tenants, the defendants, for enhanced rent, and sued to recover it. The tenants relied on the condition alleging that the condition was inserted for their benefit and protection. The plaintiff contended that the defendants could not enforce the condition because they were not parties to his engagement

[74] *Shankar Vishwanath Vagh v Umabai Sadashiv Wagle* (1913) 37 Bom 471 (Bombay HC); *Krishna Lal Sadhu v Promila Bala Dasi* AIR 1928 Cal 518 (Calcutta (HC); *Pokkunuri Balamba v Kakaraparti Krishnayya* (1914) 37 Mad 483 (Madras HC) (FB); but see s 39, Insurance Act 1938, under which a nominee can claim the amount from the insurer.

[75] *UK Seal v ARA Aramugam Chettyar* AIR 1938 Rang 35 (Rangoon HC); *State of Bihar v Charanjitlal Chadha* AIR 1960 Pat 139 (Patna HC).

[76] *National Petroleum Co Ltd v Popatlal Mulji* AIR 1936 Bom 344 (Bombay HC).

[77] [1962] AC 446 (HL), [1961] UKHL 4.

[78] *New Zealand Shipping Co Ltd v AM Satterthwaite & Co Ltd* [1975] AC 154 (PC), [1974] UKPC 4.

[79] See Chen-Wishart, Loke, & Vogenauer, 'Introduction', ch 1, section IV.

[80] s 8, Indian Contract Act 1872 provides:

> Performance of the conditions of a proposal, or the acceptance of any consideration for a reciprocal promise which may be offered with a proposal, is an acceptance of the proposal.

[81] (1910) 5 IC 565 (Calcutta HC) (the plaintiff did succeed on the basis of rights under the rent control statute).

with the government. It was held that the defendants could not take the benefit of this condition.

As regards jurisdiction clauses, a clause restricting jurisdiction to the courts at a specified place cannot prevent a third party from filing proceedings in the courts in another place. In *East India Transport Agency v National Insurance Co Ltd*,[82] a consignment note provided for the exclusive jurisdiction of the Calcutta courts in matters arising from the consignment. The goods were damaged in transit and the insurer paid out under the insurance policy. The insurer and the consignor of goods filed a suit in Hyderabad to recover the amount from the carrier. The carrier objected to the jurisdiction. It was held that the suit was correctly filed because the clause could not bind the insurer (a third party) unless it was shown that the attention of the third party was drawn to the clause.

V. Exceptions to the Privity Rule

The Privy Council,[83] the Supreme Court,[84] and the High Courts[85] in India have reiterated time and again that a third party can enforce a contract in his favour only if his claim falls within the exceptions to the privity rule. It has been stated: '[u]nless something over and beyond a mere contract can be inferred, the suit cannot lie'.[86] The recognized exceptions have been derived from English law: trusts and settlements, and agency. Some exceptions properly belong to the subject of property law: charges and assignments. Some additional exceptions are recognized in Indian law: family arrangements, partitions and compromises of rights, and pre-incorporation contracts. A third party can also enforce contracts under statutory provisions. Enforcement in situations of agency, and of covenants running with the land, are covered by statutes. These exceptions are discussed below.

1. Trusts

Where A contracts with B to pay a sum of money to C, the latter cannot sue A merely on the basis of such a contract. C can sue where, by such contract, A intends to create a trust over the payment obligation with C as the beneficiary of the trust. This exception stems from the law of trusts; the four certainties to constitute a trust must therefore be satisfied: (1) an intention to create a trust; (2) a purpose of the trust; (3) the beneficiary; and (4) the trust property, and transfer of the trust property to the trustee.[87]

[82] AIR 1991 AP 53 (Andhra Pradesh HC).

[83] *Nawab Khwaja Muhammad Khan v Nawab Husaini Begam* (1910) 37 IA 152 (PC), [1910] UKPC 25; *Alice Marie Vandepitte v The Preferred Accident Insurance Co of New York* AIR 1933 PC 11 (PC), [1932] UKPC 68; *Dan Kuer v Sarla Devi* AIR 1947 PC 8 (PC), [1932] UKPC 68.

[84] *MC Chacko v State Bank of Travancore* AIR 1970 SC 504, 1969 (2) SCC 343.

[85] Some cases are *Thirumulu Subbu Chetti v Arunachalam Chettiar* AIR 1930 Mad 382 (FB) (Madras HC); *Mittar Sain v Data Ram* AIR 1926 All 194 (Allahabad HC); *Veeramma v Appayya* AIR 1957 AP 965 (Andhra Pradesh HC); *Shankar Vishwanath Vagh v Umabai Sadashiv Wagle* (1913) 37 Bom 471 (Bombay HC); *National Petroleum Co Ltd v Popatlal Mulji* AIR 1936 Bom 344 (Bombay HC); *Jiban Krishna Mullick v Nirupama Gupta* AIR 1926 Cal 1009 (Calcutta HC); *Desraj v Ralli Ram* AIR 1957 J & K 10 (Jammu and Kashmir HC); *Maghi Mal v Darbara Singh* AIR 1933 Lah 695 (Lahore HC); *N Devaraje Urs v M Ramakrishniah* AIR 1952 Mys 109 (Mysore HC); *Saraswatibai v Haibatrao Ramji Patil* AIR 1945 Nag 261 (Nagpur HC); *Janaki Bala Debya v Maheshwar Das* AIR 1942 Pat 460 (Patna HC); *Suraj Prasad Oja v Ram Lal Singh* AIR 1947 Pat 131 (Patna HC); *Babu Ram Budhu Mal v Dhan Singh Bishan Singh* AIR 1957 Punj 169 (Punjab HC); *Ram Dhan v L Chauthmal* AIR 1935 Oudh 496 (Oudh HC); *UK Seal v ARA Aramugam Chettyar* AIR 1938 Rang 35 (Rangoon HC); *Hashmatmal v Pribhdas* AIR 1929 Sind 117 (Sind HC).

[86] *Seth Bhabhootmal Seth Nathmal Oswal v Moolchand Munnalal Sagotia* AIR 1943 Nag 266, 268 (Nagpur HC) (Bose J).

[87] s 6, Indian Trusts Act 1882.

Such a trust may be created in express and clear words. Thus, a statement in the instrument of transfer or contract that the money is retained by the transferor 'in trust' for payment to a third party shows the existence of a trust.[88] In addition, the question whether a trust is created depends on the construction of the terms of the contract, and other circumstances.

Sri Rajah Inuganti Kasturamma Bahadur Zamindarini v Chelikani Venkatasurayya Garu[89] discusses the principles for deciding the existence of a trust that would entitle its beneficiary to claim as a third party to the arrangement creating it. The decision has been followed in many later judgments. In this case, the plaintiff and his father rendered services to a Zamindar,[90] who agreed to give to the plaintiff a salary during the plaintiff's lifetime. The Zamindar paid the salary as agreed. The Zamindar made a usufructuary mortgage in favour of his wife, the defendant. The mortgage deed directed the defendant to pay this salary to the plaintiff. The defendant also paid the salary to the plaintiff as directed for some time, and later stopped the payment. The plaintiff claimed as a beneficiary of this direction. The court first held that a mere direction in a document to which the plaintiff was not a party was not enough to create a trust. An intention to create a trust was necessary. The plaintiff could recover because the intention to create a trust could be gathered from various circumstances in the case, viz the prior contract by the Zamindar indicated the motive for creating the trust, the amount was actually paid by the Zamindar and his wife (the defendant) until some time after the Zamindar died, and the arrangement was not revocable.

Some factors might defeat such an intention, viz the claim is sought against the will of the alleged trustee,[91] the alleged trustee is free to utilize the amount for his own purpose, or for any purpose, or to mix them up with his own money.[92] The third party can enforce under the trust exception if the direction to pay is for his benefit (and not of the promisee),[93] or the direction constitutes him the nominee of the promisee.[94]

The trust is constituted when the trustee acquires title over the trust property. As such, where the subject matter for the trust is transferred to the trustee, a trust is constituted.[95] There is no trust if no property is transferred,[96] or no money is entrusted.[97] A promise to create a trust, as distinguished from a complete trust, cannot be enforced by a third party.[98] But a trust that is executed can be enforced, though the trustees have agreed to act in the future.[99] A third party cannot enforce the contract against his promisor merely because the money is kept as a deposit with the promisor, or that the promisor has retained in his hands the money under an express or implied agreement to pay to the third party.[100] There is no

[88] *Desraj v Ralli Ram* AIR 1957 J & K 10 (Jammu and Kashmir HC).

[89] (1915) 29 Mad LJ 538 (Madras HC).

[90] A feudal landlord in British India paying the government a fixed revenue.

[91] *Iswaram Pillai v Tharagan* AIR 1914 Mad 701 (Madras HC).

[92] *National Petroleum Co Ltd v Popatlal Mulji* AIR 1936 Bom 344 (Bombay HC).

[93] *Adhar Chandra Mondal v Dologobinda Das* AIR 1936 Cal 663 (Calcutta HC); *UK Seal v ARA Aramugam Chettyar* AIR 1938 Rang 35 (Rangoon HC); *Jnan Chandra Mukherji v Mano Ranjan Mitra* AIR 1942 Cal 251 (Calcutta HC).

[94] *Jiban Krishna Mullick v Nirupama Gupta* AIR 1926 Cal 1009 (Calcutta HC); *District Board v Rai Bahadur Chandra Ketu Narayan* AIR 1937 Cal 625 (Calcutta HC); *Suraj Prasad Oja v Ram Lal Singh* AIR 1947 Pat 131 (Patna HC).

[95] *Sundararaja Aiyangar v Lakshmiammal* (1915) 38 Mad 788 (Madras HC).

[96] *Iswaram Pillai v Tharagan* AIR 1914 Mad 701 (Madras HC).

[97] *Mittar Sain v Data Ram* AIR 1926 All 194 (Allahabad HC).

[98] *Iswaram Pillai v Tharagan* 1914 Mad 701 (Madras HC).

[99] *Jang Bahadur v Rana Uma Nath Baksh Singh* AIR 1937 Oudh 99 (Oudh HC), affd in *Rana Uma Nath Bakhsh Singh v Jang Bahadur* AIR 1938 PC 245 (PC), [1938] UKPC 44.

[100] *Jamna Das v Ram Autar Pande* (1911) 39 IA 7 (PC), [1911] UKPC 69 (PC); *Babu Ram Budhu Mal v Dhan Singh Bishan Singh* AIR 1957 Punj 169 (Punjab HC); *Maghi Mal v Darbara Singh* AIR 1933 Lah 695 (Lahore HC); *Sudama Devi v Ram Kishan Lal* AIR 1954 All 348 (Allahabad HC).

trust merely because a life insurer promised to pay the sum insured to the beneficiary named in the policy.[101]

2. Marriage and Family Settlements, and Compromises

A person beneficially entitled under a contract in a settlement on marriage, or a family settlement, or on a compromise of doubtful rights between family members can enforce his claim under such transactions. His claim is also recognized for grant of specific performance in the Specific Relief Act 1963.[102] Such settlements or compromises need not relate to any property.

This exception is special to Indian law. In *Nawab Khwaja Muhammad Khan v Nawab Husaini Begam*,[103] a Muslim woman filed a suit against her father-in-law to recover an allowance of Rs 500 per month under the terms of a registered agreement he made with her father prior to and in consideration of her marriage with his son. The Privy Council made an observation that has guided many later cases:[104]

> Their Lordships desire to observe that in India and among communities circumstanced as the Mahomedans, among whom marriages are contracted for minors by parents and guardians, it might occasion serious injustice if the common law doctrine was applied to agreements or arrangements entered into in connection with such contracts.[105]

A Hindu Joint Family is an entity traditionally having as its members the males in a family, with limited rights for the female members.[106] Members can divide and separate their shares by effecting partition of property. Such partition may be made orally, or by a document called the deed of partition. Although such a partition deed is made between those who have shares in the family property or business, it is usual to find provisions for maintenance and support of other persons, viz mother, brothers and sisters, collaterals staying with the family, elder members of the family, etc. In one such partition deed between Y, the husband of Z, and his father and sons, it was settled that Y would maintain Z and her children from the property. It was held that Y knew that the deed was for the benefit of Z. Z had a beneficial interest, and could claim maintenance.[107] Where two brothers divided the family property between them, and agreed that they would invest in equal shares a certain sum of money for maintenance of their mother, the mother could enforce such investment.[108]

[101] *Shankar Vishwanath Vagh v Umabai Sadashiv Wagle* (1913) 37 Bom 471 (Bombay HC).

[102] s 15(c), Specific Relief Act 1963; s 23(c), Specific Relief Act of 1877 (repealed by the 1963 Act) provided: '[S]pecific performance of a contract may be obtained by . . . (c) where the contract is a settlement on marriage, or a compromise of doubtful rights between members of the same family any person beneficially entitled thereunder.'

[103] (1910) 37 IA 152 (PC), [1910] UKPC 25.

[104] As discussed in section V.4 (Charges), the plaintiff in this case could successfully claim as beneficiary of a charge created on the property by a registered document.

[105] (1910) 37 IA 152, 159 (PC), [1910] UKPC 25 (Ameer Ali J). In many later cases, this observation has been interpreted to mean that the doctrine in *Tweddle v Atkinson* (1861) 1 B & S 393 (QB) did not apply in India, and that Indian courts were free to allow enforcement by third parties because courts could apply principles of justice, equity, and good conscience. See the observation of Sir Lawrence Jenkins J in *Deb Narayan Dutt v Chunilal Ghose* (1914) ILR 41 Cal 137 (Calcutta HC): 'the administration of justice in these Courts is not to be in any way hampered by the doctrine laid down in *Tweddle v. Atkinson* . . .', and therefore '[i]n India we are free from these trammels and are guided in matters of procedure by the rule of justice, equity and good conscience' (at 131) (Jenkins and Mookerjee JJ). See also *Dwarika Nath Ash v Priya Nath Malki* AIR 1918 Cal 941 (Calcutta HC); *Khirod Behari Dutt v Man Govinda* AIR 1934 Cal 682 (Calcutta HC); *Bibhuti Bhusan Ghose v Baikuntha Nath Mondal* (1935) 62 CLJ 55 (Calcutta HC); *Bhujendra Nath Biswas v Sushmoyee Basu* AIR 1936 Cal 67 (Calcutta HC); *A Singarayya v A Subbayya* AIR 1924 Mad 861 (Madras HC); *Post Master General Patna v Ram Kripal Sahu* AIR 1955 Pat 442 (Patna HC); *Babu Ram Budhu Mal v Dhan Singh Bishan Singh* AIR 1957 Punj 169 (Punjab HC).

[106] Since 2015, daughters have the same rights as sons in such family property or business.

[107] *Rakhmabai v Govind Moreshwar* (1904) 6 Bom LR 421 (Bombay HC).

[108] *Shuppu Ammal v Subramaniyan* (1910) 33 Mad 238 (Madras HC) (held that the money was also charged on the property).

In a similar situation, the father's concubine could also recover the maintenance secured.[109] A sister was entitled to sue for a provision made for her benefit,[110] or for an arrangement for performance of her marriage[111] which was made in a partition deed between her brothers. It has been stated:

> I should consider that if the rule is subject to exceptions a very proper class of exceptions would be where coparceners in a Hindu family agree that payments should be made to female members for maintenance, and the exception need not be confined to cases where the maintenance provided is in favour of persons who have a strict legal right to it.[112]

Similarly, if a contract is intended to secure a benefit to a third party as a beneficiary under a family arrangement, such party can sue in his own right to enforce it.[113] A 'family arrangement' results from a compromise of doubtful rights between members of a family. It could settle existing debts or could be made to avoid future disputes.[114] It is not necessary that the third party claiming under such a settlement should have a legal right to maintenance;[115] the term 'family' is very wide, and will include illegitimate members and persons yet to be born,[116] or to be adopted.[117]

3. Pre-Incorporation Contracts

A contract made by promoters of a company before its incorporation can be enforced by the company after it is formed if the contract is made for the purposes of that company, is warranted by the terms of incorporation, and the company has accepted the contract, and communicated its acceptance to the other party to the contract.[118] The company can also sue for specific performance.[119] At first blush, this appears to be an issue of agency.[120] But the company does not sue as principal of its agents, the promoters, because it was not in existence when the contract was made. Nor can it ratify acts of the promoters.[121] Moreover, the contract does not bind automatically the company unless the company has accepted it.

4. Charges

A charge[122] on property created in favour of a third party can be enforced by the charge holder, even if he is not party to the transaction that created the charge.[123]

[109] *Arumuga Gounden v Chinnammal* (1911) 21 Mad LJ 918 (Madras HC).
[110] *Kosuri Rajagopala Raju v Datla Radhayya* (1922) 22 Mad LJ 159 (Madras HC).
[111] *Sundararaja Aiyangar v Lakshmiammal* (1915) 38 Mad 788 (Madras HC) (also held that a trust was created).
[112] *Arumuga Gounden v Chinnammal* (1911) 21 Mad LJ 918 919 (Madras (HC) (Sundara Aiyar J).
[113] *Dan Kuer v Sarla Devi* AIR 1947 PC 8 (PC), [1946] UKPC 27 holds this as a rule that undoubtedly has prevailed in India. In this case, a mother claimed under a compromise deed made between her two sons.
[114] *Jang Bahadur v Rana Uma Nath Baksh Singh* AIR 1937 Oudh 99 (Oudh HC), affd in *Rana Uma Nath Bakhsh Singh v Jang Bahadur* AIR 1938 PC 245 (PC), [1938] UKPC 44.
[115] *Arumuga Gounden v Chinnammal* (1911) 21 Mad LJ 918 (Madras HC).
[116] *Jang Bahadur v Rana Uma Nath Baksh Singh* AIR 1937 Oudh 99 (HC), affd in *Rana Uma Nath Bakhsh Singh v Jang Bahadur* AIR 1938 PC 245 (PC), [1938] UKPC 44.
[117] *Shanmugan v PLAPL Annamalai Chettiar* AIR 1935 Mad 141 (Madras (HC).
[118] *Jai Narain Parasrampuria v Pushpa Devi Saraf* (2006) 7 SCC 756.
[119] s 15(h), Specific Relief Act 1963.
[120] For discussion, see section V.6(a) (Agency).
[121] *Surrendro and Co v Liquidator Punjab Tannery Co Ltd* AIR 1923 Lah 100 (Lahore HC); *Ramkumar Potdar v Sholapur Spinning and Weaving Co Ltd* AIR 1934 Bom 427 (Bombay HC).
[122] A charge over immovable property must be registered: s 100, Transfer of Property Act 1882; s 17, Registration Act 1963.
[123] *Nawab Khwaja Muhammad Khan v Nawab Husaini Begam* (1910) 37 IA 152 (PC), [1910] UKPC 25; see also *Narayani Devi v Tagore Commercial Corpn Ltd* AIR 1973 Cal 401 (Calcutta HC); *Shuppu Ammal v Subramaniyan* (1910) 33 Mad 238 (Madras HC).

Two brothers partitioned a property and created a charge over the property for a sum of money until they invested the money for maintenance of their mother. The mother could enforce this charge.[124] In *Nawab Khwaja Muhammad Khan v Nawab Husaini Begam*,[125] a Muslim woman filed a suit against her father-in-law to recover an allowance of Rs 500 per month under the terms of a registered agreement he made with her father prior to and in consideration of her marriage with his son. This amount was payable out of certain properties which the father-in-law charged for this payment. The agreement also gave her the power to enforce that charge. It was held that she was the only person beneficially entitled under it, and the father-in-law had specifically charged immovable property to secure the payment in her favour, which she could enforce.

A charge may be express or implied from the terms of the instrument. A charge cannot be implied unless the intention is clearly seen from the terms of the instrument.[126] Thus, the clause in a deed of partition in *MC Chacko*'s case[127] did not create a charge.

5. Assignment

An assignment is an immediate transfer of a debt, a contractual right, or any other intangible right by the assignor to the assignee. The assignee can enforce such debt or right against the debtor or promisor of the contract. The right of a contracting party to assign the contract (benefits and burdens) is recognized. In *Khardah & Co Ltd v Raymon & Co (India) Pvt Ltd*,[128] the Supreme Court held that rights under a contract are assignable unless the contract is personal in its nature or the rights are incapable of assignment, eg personal licences. Thus, assignability of contract rights is the rule and the contrary an exception.[129] An assignee cannot sue in his own name; he must join his assignor as a party,[130] unless he has such a right under a statute.[131] An assignee can also claim specific performance, as a 'representative-in-interest' of the contracting party.[132] The assignee's right is a right as owner of property.

An assignee or endorsee of a consignment note or bill of lading[133] can sue the carrier for damage done to goods. A consignee can sue if he has acquired ownership of goods.[134] A consignor does not lose his rights to seek compensation after the endorsement and even if ownership has passed to the consignee.[135]

6. Statutory Exceptions

Many statutes allow third parties to enforce contracts. These are stated below.

[124] *Shuppu Ammal v Subramaniyan* (1910) 33 Mad 238 (Madras HC).
[125] (1910) 37 IA 152 (PC), [1910] UKPC 25.
[126] *Akolla Suryanarayana Rao v Dwarapundi Basivireddi* AIR 1932 Mad 457 (Madras HC).
[127] See text to n 70 in section IV (Privity Rule in Indian Law) for text of the clause.
[128] AIR 1962 SC 1810.
[129] *Ram Baran Prasad v Ram Mohit Hazra* AIR 1961 Cal 152 (Calcutta HC).
[130] *PR Viswanatha Iyer v A Muthukumaraswami Pillai* AIR 1948 Mad 139 (Madras HC); *JH Tod v Lakhmidas Purshotamdas* (1892) ILR 16 Bom 441 (Bombay HC).
[131] s 130, Transfer of Property Act 1882 (assignment of actionable claims); s 38, Insurance Act 1938 (assignment of insurance policies).
[132] s 15(b), Specific Relief Act 1963; *Habiba Khatoon v Ubaidul Huq* AIR 1997 SC 3236; *Shyam Singh v Daryao Singh* AIR 2004 SC 348.
[133] *Laxmi Board and Paper Mills Ltd v MV 'Seacrest Achiever'* AIR 1992 Bom 86 (Bombay HC); *Syndicate Bank v Africana Co* AIR 1977 Ker 103 (Kerala HC).
[134] *Union of India v West Punjab Factories Ltd* AIR 1966 SC 395; *Morvi Mercantile Bank Ltd v Union of India* AIR 1965 SC 1954.
[135] *Shamji Bhanji & Co v North Western Railway Co* AIR 1947 Bom 169 (Bombay HC).

(a) Agency

The Indian Contract Act 1872 states the law of agency. The principal can enforce contracts made by an agent within the scope of his authority.[136] The principal can ratify and enforce contracts made by an agent exceeding his authority or acting outside the scope of his authority.[137] Where a person contracts with an agent, and neither suspects nor knows that he is an agent, the principal can enforce the contract, but he can only obtain performance subject to the rights and obligations subsisting between the agent and the other party to the contract.[138]

(b) Arbitration

The Arbitration and Conciliation Act 1996 empowers a judicial authority to refer parties to arbitration in matters of enforcement of foreign awards at the request of one of the parties or *any person* claiming through or under him.[139] In *Chloro Controls India (I) P Ltd v Severn Trent Water Purification Inc*,[140] the Supreme Court held that reference to arbitration can be sought by persons who are not signatories to an arbitration agreement. Such person will have to show that he claims 'through' or 'under' a signatory to the agreement. Thus, an arbitration agreement can bind affiliates in a group of companies, or in other circumstances that disclose an intention of such parties. The burden of showing that an agreement binds a non-party is a heavy one. The court should examine such a plea with great caution.

(c) Carriage

Unless otherwise provided by statute, a consignee can sue the carrier only if property has passed to him, or in other limited circumstances. This is discussed above.[141] However, when goods are carried by sea, the consignee named in a bill of lading, and every endorsee of a bill of lading, can sue as if the contract in the bill of lading has been made with himself.[142] When goods are carried by rail, the consignee or endorsee of the rail receipt has all the rights of the consignor.[143]

(d) Consumer protection

The Consumer Protection Act 1986 cuts through the web of the doctrine of privity. A beneficiary of a contract is also a consumer and can seek remedies against the seller of goods or supplier of services, and also the manufacturer or original supplier. A beneficiary is one who uses goods or takes the benefit of services with the approval of the buyer of goods and services.[144] Such user or beneficiary can claim all reliefs under the Act, ie refund of price, compensation for negligence, replacement, repair, or performance (called removal of deficiency under the Act), etc.[145] Such user or beneficiary must prove the original purchase or hiring of services, and his standing: that he uses goods or takes benefit of services, and does so with the approval of the purchaser.

In a case where a child was admitted to a hospital for treatment, his parents were consumers having actually hired the services of the hospital, and the child was also a consumer-beneficiary of such services. Hence, both could claim compensation from the hospital for

[136] s 226, ICA 1872. [137] ibid s 196. [138] ibid ss 231 and 232.
[139] s 45, Arbitration and Conciliation Act 1996. [140] AIR 2012 SC (Supp) 1017, (2013) 1 SCC 641.
[141] See section V.5 (Assignment). [142] s 1, Indian Bills of Lading Act 1856.
[143] s 74, Railways Act 1989. [144] s 2(d), Consumer Protection Act 1986. [145] ibid s 14.

deficiency in services.[146] Members of a housing society that had been allotted land by a statutory board were beneficiaries of the services of the board, and hence consumers. They were entitled to refund of earnest money deposited under the terms of the contract between the housing society and the board.[147]

(e) Insurance

Where a policy of insurance effected by a married man on his own life, and expressed on the face of it to be for the benefit of his wife, or of his wife and children, or any of them, it will enure and be deemed to be a trust for such beneficiary, and will not be subject to the control of the husband, or of his creditors, or form part of his estate.[148] In other cases, the beneficiary of an insurance policy cannot sue the insurance company unless the policy is assigned in his favour or a trust has been declared by the insured. This is true even where the beneficiary is the wife of the person effecting the policy.[149]

A policyholder of a life insurance policy on his own life can nominate a person to receive the policy amount upon his death, and the insurer must pay the policy amount to such nominee, and it is discharged on such payment.[150] The nominee, however, is a mere 'collector', and is liable to hand over the amount to the heirs or legatees of the deceased policyholder.[151] An amendment in 2015[152] modified this position. If such policyholder nominates a close relative (his parents, spouse, children), such nominee shall be beneficially entitled to the policy amount, unless it can be proved that the policyholder, having regard to the nature of his title to the policy, could not have conferred any such beneficial title on the nominee.

The Motor Vehicles Act 1988 provides a scheme of compulsory insurance for vehicles plying for trade in a public place. Under its provisions, an award of a Motor Accidents Claims Tribunal ordering payment of compensation for the death of or personal injury to a person from the use of such a motor vehicle shall be directly satisfied by the insurer of the vehicle involved in that accident.[153] A victim of an accident is not, otherwise than under the Motor Vehicles Act 1988,[154] entitled to recover the insurance money from the insurer of the vehicle that has caused the accident.[155] Nor can the victim claim under the terms of an arbitration clause in the insurance contract between the owner of the car and the owner's insurer.[156]

A mortgagee, consignee, or other person having an interest in the insured subject matter may insure on behalf and for the benefit of other persons interested as well as for his own benefit.[157] Thus, if a person with a limited interest takes out insurance, he can sue for the entire insurance money, and retain for the benefit of other interested persons any amount that exceeds his own loss. Every assignee of a policy of insurance against fire, in whom the property in the subject insured shall be absolutely vested at the date of assignment, shall

[146] *Spring Meadows Hospital v Harjol Ahluwalia* AIR 1998 SC 1801.

[147] *Chandigarh Housing Board v Avtar Singh* AIR 2011 SC 130.

[148] s 5, Married Women's Property Act 1874.

[149] *Shankar Vishwanath Vagh v Umabai Sadashiv Wagle* (1913) 37 Bom 471 (Bombay HC); see also *Pokkunuri Balamba v Kakaraparti Krishnayya* (1914) 37 Mad 483 (Madras HC) (FB) (claim of a daughter); *Krishna Lal Sadhu v Promila Bala Dasi* AIR 1928 Cal 518 (Calcutta HC).

[150] s 39, Insurance Act 1938.

[151] *Sarbati Devi v Usha Devi* AIR 1984 SC 346.

[152] Insurance Laws (Amendment) Act 2015.

[153] ss 146, 147, and 149, Motor Vehicles Act 1988.

[154] *New India Assurance Co Ltd v Rula* AIR 2000 SC 1082.

[155] *Alice Marie Vandepitte v The Preferred Accident Insurance Co of New York* AIR 1933 PC 11 (PC), [1932] UKPC 68 (case from Canada); *British India General Insurance Co Ltd v Janardan Vishwanath Naik* AIR 1938 Bom 217 (Bombay HC).

[156] *Des Raj Pahwa v Concord of India Insurance Co* AIR 1951 Punj 114 (Punjab HC).

[157] s 16(2), Marine Insurance Act 1963.

have all rights of suit on the policy.[158] An assignee of a policy of marine insurance is entitled to sue in his own name, although a defendant would have any defence he would be entitled to make if the suit had been brought in the name of the person effecting the policy.[159]

(f) Negotiable instruments

A promissory note, bill of exchange, or cheque can be negotiated (transferred) by endorsement and delivery.[160] Such transferee, called the holder, is entitled in his own name to receive or recover the amount due on the instrument from the parties to it.[161] If the holder has obtained it in good faith and for consideration before the date due for payment, he is a holder in due course,[162] and every prior party to a negotiable instrument is liable thereon until the instrument is satisfied.[163]

(g) Transfer of property

Negative covenants that restrain the enjoyment of immovable property can be enforced against the transferor if such restriction is for the beneficial enjoyment of another piece of property of the transferor. These can also be enforced against the transferor's transferees without consideration and with notice of the obligation.[164] Thus, in the hypothetical case where X leases two adjoining properties to Y and Z, and the lease between X and Y bars Y from selling bread because Z sold bread from his leased property, Z will not be able to enforce the restriction found in the lease between X and Y because of the privity rule. Nor can he enforce it as a restrictive covenant affecting property unless he can show that it was for the beneficial enjoyment of X's other property (including his leasehold).[165]

A right of a person to receive maintenance or provision for advancement of marriage from the profits of immovable property can be enforced against a transferee of that property who takes such property without consideration and with notice of such right.[166] A transferee from a lessor of immovable property possesses all the rights of the lessor, but the lessor's liabilities do not cease unless the lessee elects to treat the transferee as liable to him.[167] The transferee of an actionable claim has all the rights and remedies of the transferor, whether by way of damages or otherwise, but he is subject to the claims that the defendant may have against the transferor of the actionable claim.[168]

VI. Rights and Remedies of Parties

Application of the privity rule involves three parties. (1) The promisor, who has promised to render performance to the third party. His interest lies in protection against double claims. (2) The promisee, who is entitled to claim that the performance be rendered to a third person indicated in the contract. His interest lies in seeing that such performance is rendered. He is therefore entitled to the remedies for enforcing such a promise, ie specific

[158] s 135, Transfer of Property Act 1882. [159] s 52(2), Marine Insurance Act 1963.

[160] ss 46 and 48, Negotiable Instruments Act 1881; some instruments can be negotiated by delivery only.

[161] ibid s 8. [162] ibid s 9. [163] ibid s 36. [164] s 40, Transfer of Property Act 1882.

[165] See *Sanjeev Mittal v Tirupati Infraprojects Pvt Ltd* (unreported) decided by Delhi High Court on 4 March 2014: a lessor of a shop given on lease for vending liquor promised the lessee that the lessor would not transfer any other shop in the premises for selling liquor. The court refused to grant interim relief of injunction, inter alia, because the plaintiff lessee had not shown that the restriction was for the beneficial enjoyment of another piece of property (of the lessor).

[166] s 39, Transfer of Property Act 1882. [167] ibid s 109. [168] ibid s 130.

performance, injunction, or compensation. (3) The third party indicated in the contract expects that the promisor shall give him the performance. The privity rule prevents such performance subject to exceptions already discussed earlier. In these exceptional situations, he has the same remedies as the promisee. These aspects are discussed below.

1. Remedies Available to Third Party

As a general rule, the third party cannot seek specific performance of a contract made for his benefit; the promisee can seek specific performance of the promise that the act be performed for the benefit of the third party.[169]

In circumstances in which a third party can enforce the contract, he can claim specific performance, injunction, compensation, or the agreed sum. The right of a third party to seek specific performance in situations of exceptions to the privity rule has been stated in section 15 of the Specific Relief Act 1963. Apart from the parties to the contract, specific performance can be sought by a principal (for contracts made by his agent), an assignee or other representative-in-interest, a person beneficially entitled under a contract that is a settlement on marriage or compromise of doubtful rights between members of a family, and a company formed after amalgamation. A company can also specifically enforce a pre-incorporation contract under specified conditions described elsewhere in this chapter.[170] These persons can also seek an injunction to restrain breach of that contract.[171] Courts have allowed a third party's claim for monies promised under a contract, viz annuity,[172] maintenance,[173] or similar payments,[174] and also value of goods secured for maintenance.[175]

Some High Courts have granted relief to a third party because all the parties were before the court. This was discussed earlier.[176] In these cases, relief was granted in favour of the third party, jointly against the promisee as well as the promisor.[177] An order was also granted against the promisor in the first instance, and against the promisee for any balance.[178]

2. Remedies Available to Promisee

The promisee can claim specific performance, injunction, agreed amount, or compensation for the loss he has suffered.

The promisee does not lose his right to enforce because a contract purports to confer the right on a third party. Thus, an official receiver in insolvency could recover the amount due to the insolvent despite the claim of the third party entitled to his benefit under a contract.[179] The promisee can sue the promisor if the promisor fails to perform.[180] In *Dorasinga*

[169] *Seth Bhabhootmal Seth Nathmal Oswal v Moolchand Munnalal Sagotia* AIR 1943 Nag 266 (Nagpur HC).

[170] See section V.3 (Pre-Incorporation Contracts).

[171] s 38(2), Specific Relief Act 1963 under which provisions for grant of specific performance apply to grant of injunctions.

[172] *Chinnaya v Ramayya* (1881) 4 Mad 137 (Madras (HC).

[173] *Rakhmabai v Govind Moreshwar* (1904) 6 Bom LR 421 (Bombay HC).

[174] *Nawab Khwaja Muhammad Khan v Nawab Husaini Begam* (1910) 37 IA 152 (PC), [1910] UKPC 25.

[175] *Arumuga Gounden v Chinnammal* (1911) 21 Mad LJ 918 (Madras HC).

[176] See section III (Privity Rule: Of Substance or Procedure).

[177] *Gauri Shankar v Mangal* AIR 1933 Lah 178 (Lahore HC); *Khirod Behari Dutt v Man Govinda* AIR 1934 Cal 682 (Calcutta HC).

[178] *Khirod Behari Dutt v Man Govinda* AIR 1934 Cal 682 (Calcutta HC).

[179] *Gurdit Singh v Chuni Lal* AIR 1932 Lah 66 (Lahore HC).

[180] *UK Seal v ARA Aramugam Chettyar* AIR 1938 Rang 35 (Rangoon HC); *Jnan Chandra Mukherji v Mano Ranjan Mitra* AIR 1942 Cal 251 (Calcutta HC); *Raghunatha Chariar v Sadagopa Chariar* (1911) 36 Mad 348 (Madras HC).

Tevar v Arunachalam Chetti,[181] where the sub-lessee-promisor agreed in consideration of the sub-lease to pay the debt due by his lessor-promisee under his mortgage to the mortgagee-third party, and failed to do so within a reasonable time, the promisee could recover the amount although he had not paid it himself, and it was not necessary to show that he had been damnified. The promisee can recover compensation,[182] being equal to the amount of the debt,[183] or the value of the property lost because of such non-payment.[184]

The promisor cannot resist the promisee's claim on the ground that the obligation is owed by the promisor to the third party. In *Raghunatha Chariar v Sadagopa Chariar*,[185] the promisee transferred his property to the promisor in consideration of the promisor agreeing to pay a sum of money to the third party. The promisor failed to pay the amount. The promisee paid it to the third party and filed a suit against the promisor to recover the amount. The promisor contended that it was the promisor's obligation to pay the amount, and the promisee could not claim the amount in variance of the contract, especially without proving actual damage. It was held that this arrangement was for the benefit of the promisee, who was entitled to pay it off and claim from the promisor. If the arrangement was for the benefit of the promisor, it was possible to say that the promisee would not be able to alter the mode of payment agreed. The court also observed:

> It may also be conceded that when on the faith of the original direction the assignee [promisor] has entered into direct relations with the third party and rendered himself liable to make the payment to him, the assignor [promisee] could no longer require the assignee [promisor] to pay the consideration to himself.[186]

The promisee can claim return of money or loss suffered, whichever is higher. Thus, where a transferee-promisor promised to pay the debts to the third party to whom the transferor-promisee was indebted, and the transferee-promisor did not pay, the transferor-promisee could claim the higher of the amount of debts or loss suffered.[187] The promisee's remedy in such cases depends on the nature of the transaction, described by a Full Bench of the Allahabad High Court in *Naima Khatun v Basant Singh*:[188]

> (i) The amount left in the hands of the vendee may be a part of the purchase money remaining unpaid, in which case it is obviously money belonging to the vendor and if not paid as directed is still due to be paid to the vendor; or (ii) it may amount to a covenant with an undertaking to relieve the vendor from his existing liability, in which case a suit on the covenant may lie; or (iii) it may be a mere promise to perform an act for consideration, or a contract of indemnity, in which case a suit for damages incurred on the breach of the contract would lie under Section 125, [Indian] Contract Act; but it must be proved that loss has been sustained.[189]

A question arises whether in a transfer, an express promise by the transferee-promisor that he will pay to a third party a sum of money owed by the transferor-promisee to the third party, and if he does not do so, to be liable to compensate the transferor-promisee, is an absolute covenant to pay the amount or a contract of indemnity. This depends on the construction of the document. Such a promise by itself is a contract to pay money, even if there

[181] (1898) 23 Mad 441 (Madras HC); see also *W Srinivasavaradachariar v Dasu Reddiar* AIR 1944 Mad 330 (Madras HC).
[182] *W Srinivasavaradachariar v Dasu Reddiar* AIR 1944 Mad 330 (Madras HC) (awarded in the alternative).
[183] *Dorasinga Tevar v Arunachalam Chetti* (1898) 23 Mad 441 (Madras HC).
[184] *Komu Kutti v Kumara Menon* (1918) 35 Mad LJ 692 (Madras HC).
[185] (1911) 36 Mad 348 (Madras HC).
[186] ibid 350 (Abdul Rahim and Sundara Ayyar JJ).
[187] *W Srinivasavaradachariar v Dasu Reddiar* AIR 1944 Mad 330 (Madras HC).
[188] AIR 1934 All 406 (Allahabad HC).
[189] ibid 420 (Sulaiman J).

is a provision to pay compensation in the case of default, and its breach entitles the transferor-promisee to claim compensation from the transferee-promisor.[190]

While making an order in favour of the third party plaintiff, the court can make provision for protecting the interests of the contracting parties. Thus, in *Okara Grain Buyers Syndicate Ltd v United Commercial Bank Ltd*,[191] the court ordered the third party to give to the promisor an indemnity that would cover any potential claims of the promisee, who was not party to the suit. In *Dorasinga Tevar v Arunachalam Chetti*,[192] the court also ordered that the decree for compensation in favour of the lessor-promisee should protect the interest of the sub-lessee promisor that would be prejudiced in any suit by the mortgagee-third party against the property sub-leased.

In all these cases, the promisee was entitled to claim his loss only, and not the losses suffered by the third party.

3. Protection of Promisor against Double Claims

In Indian law, discharge of a contract by a third person is effectual, and it does not need the ratification or authorization of the promisor.[193] Section 41 of the ICA provides: 'When a promisee accepts performance of the promise from a third person, he cannot afterwards enforce it against the promisor.' Thus, a promisee cannot claim performance from the promisor if he has received it from the third party. A promisee cannot have double satisfaction of his claim from the promisor as well as a third party. This provision gives protection to the promisor against double claims.

This is best explained with reference to the underlying contract for the performance of which the current contract is made. X is indebted to Y. X sells or leases land to Z, and Z retains some money promising to pay it to Y. If Y receives the amount from Z, he cannot claim the amount once again from X. The promisee (Y being the promisee *in the contract between X and Y*) who has accepted satisfaction from the third person (Z in this case), cannot insist on the satisfaction of his claim from the promisor (X in this case) as well.[194] This rule applies only when a contract has in fact been performed by such third person.[195]

Nor can the third party claim from the promisee (ie promisor under his underlying contract) if he has received performance from the promisor. In the above example, if Y receives the amount from X, the promise is discharged. He cannot claim it once again from Z.

VII. Law Reform

Time and again the courts have refrained from recognizing the rights of enforcement of a third party taking a benefit under a contract, because such provision is appropriate for legislation.[196] The Bombay High Court has observed:

[190] *Dorasinga Tevar v Arunachalam Chetti* (1898) 23 Mad 441 (Madras HC); *Komu Kutti v Kumara Menon* (1918) 35 Mad LJ 692 (Madras HC).

[191] AIR 1961 Punj 66 (Punjab HC), upheld in *United Commercial Bank Ltd v Okara Grain Buyers Syndicate Ltd* AIR 1968 SC 1115.

[192] (1898) 23 Mad 441 (Madras HC).

[193] *Lala Kapurchand Godha v Mir Nawab Himayatali Khan* AIR 1963 SC 250, 254.

[194] s 41, Indian Contract Act 1872; F Pollock and D Mulla, *The Indian Contract Act* (2nd edn, Bombay: NM Tripathi & Co 1909).

[195] *Sri Sarada Mills Ltd v Union of India* AIR 1966 Mad 381 (Madras HC), affd in *Union of India v Sri Sarada Mills* AIR 1973 SC 281.

[196] See eg *Tobacco Friends Union v State of Uttar Pradesh* AIR 1958 All 688 (Allahabad HC); *National Petroleum Co Ltd v Popatlal Mulji* AIR 1936 Bom 344 (HC) (Beaumont CJ).

> [I]f the rule is to be introduced into this country that any person may sue upon a contract, if he takes a benefit under it, although a stranger to such contract, . . . such rule must be introduced by the legislature, and not by the Courts. From the point of view of practical convenience, . . . quite as much [can] be said against the introduction of such a rule, as in favour of it.[197]

The Law Commission of India, in its 13th Report of 1958, undertook the task of recommending amendments to the Indian Contract Act 1872. It recommended adding a new provision to the Act in the chapter relating to performance of contracts:

> **37A. Benefits conferred on third parties:**
>
> (1) Where a contract expressly confers a benefit directly on a third party, then, unless the contract otherwise provides, it shall be enforceable by the third party in his own name, subject to any defences that would have been valid between the contracting parties.
>
> (2) Where a contract expressly conferring a benefit directly upon a third party has been adopted, expressly or impliedly, by a third party, the parties to the contract cannot substitute a new contract for it or rescind or alter it so as to affect the rights of the third party.

The amendment proposed by the Law Commission recognized the right of a third party to enforce a contract made for his benefit. He cannot enforce it if the contract provides otherwise. He can do this only if the contract conferred on him a benefit. He can enforce only if such benefit was conferred directly on him. He can sue to enforce it in his own name and, hence, it is supposed, he need not sue in the name of the promisee of the contract, nor need he make the promisee a party to his suit. His rights are subject to the defences that the parties would have against each other. Even if a contract confers a direct benefit on a third party, the contracting parties can substitute a new contract for it or rescind or alter it, although it may affect the rights of the third party. But if the third party has adopted the contract, expressly or impliedly, the parties cannot substitute, rescind, or cancel it so as to affect the rights of the third party. These recommendations have not yet become law.

In 2016, an Expert Committee appointed by the Government of India, Ministry of Law and Justice, recommended an amendment to the law recognizing rights of third parties.[198] Action on the report is awaited.

VIII. Conclusion

The rule of privity that prevents a third party from enforcing a contract to which he is not a party is very much a part of Indian law, and expressly recognized by the Supreme Court in *MC Chacko v State Bank of Travancore*.[199] This rule has stood its ground despite attempts to dilute it by resorting to the principles of justice, equity, and good conscience. Exceptions recognized generally follow those recognized in English law. A special exception recognized as suitable for Indian conditions is the enforcement of family arrangements and settlements. Many statutes also make exceptions.

There is a demand for enabling third parties' rights to enforce. The Law Commission of India has already recommended this change, and it is hoped that the legislature will take the lead in allowing enforcement by persons not parties to a contract.

[197] *National Petroleum Co Ltd v Popatlal Mulji* AIR 1936 Bom 344, 346 (Bombay (HC) (Beaumont CJ).

[198] Note of the Press Information Bureau, Government of India, Ministry of Law and Justice, dated 20 June 2016 <http://pib.nic.in/newsite/PrintRelease.aspx?relid=146360> accessed 26 October 2016.

[199] AIR 1970 SC 504, 1969 (2) SCC 343.

6

The Legal Landscape of Contract Formation: Towards a Distinct Malaysian Jurisprudence?

*TAY Pek San**

I. Introduction

Malaysian contract law is statutorily embodied in the Contracts Act 1950 (Revised 1974) ('CA 1950').[1] The Act is modelled on the Indian Contract Act 1872 with minor modifications. The Indian Contract Act is, to a large extent, a codification of the English common law of contract and rules of equity, although there are some areas of departure. It follows from this that Malaysian contract law shares many areas of commonality with English law on contract. As a result of section 3 of the Civil Law Act 1956 (Revised 1972)[2] which provides for the general reception of English law and section 5 which provides for the reception of English law in commercial matters, Malaysian contract law has also been shaped by English judicial decisions. The reception of English law as administered in England on certain dates under sections 3 and 5 has been discussed extensively in Malaysian texts on contract law.[3] English decisions decided after those dates are not binding in Malaysia and are of persuasive value only.

II. Traditional Analysis for Formation of Contract

In Malaysia, the determination as to whether a contract is formed follows the traditional analysis of whether the elements for the existence of a contract exist.[4] The elements are offer, acceptance, consideration, intention to create legal relations, and capacity of the parties to contract.[5] The presence of an offer and its acceptance brings into existence a promise.[6] And when a promise given by one party becomes the consideration for the promise by the other

* Cite as PS Tay, 'The Legal Landscape of Contract Formation: Towards a Distinct Malaysian Jurisprudence?' in Chen-Wishart, Loke, & Vogenauer, *Studies in the Contract Laws of Asia Vol II: Formation and Third Party Beneficiaries* (Oxford: OUP 2017) ch 6. I would like to thank Professor Alexander Loke for his extremely helpful comments on an earlier draft of this chapter.

[1] Act 136. [2] Act 67.

[3] V Sinnadurai, *Law of Contract* (4th edn, Petaling Jaya: Sweet & Maxwell 2011) 16–22; A Mohaimin Ayus, *Law of Contract in Malaysia*, Vol 1 (Petaling Jaya: Sweet & Maxwell 2009) 2–15; MF Cheong, *Contract Law in Malaysia* (Petaling Jaya: Sweet & Maxwell 2010) 11–13.

[4] *Bekalan Sains P&C Sdn Bhd v Bank Bumiputra Malaysia Bhd* [2011] 5 MLJ 1 [53]–[59] (HC); Cheong, ibid 60.

[5] *Preston Corporation Sdn Bhd v Edward Leong* [1982] 2 MLJ 22 (FC); *Ka Wah Bank Ltd v Nadinusa Sdn Bhd & Anor* [1998] 2 CLJ 486 (FC); *Khaw Poh Chhuan v Ng Gaik Peng & Yap Wan Chuan & Ors* [1996] 1 MLJ 761 (FC).

[6] CA 1950, s 2(b) states as follows:

> [W]hen the person to whom the proposal is made signifies his assent thereto, the proposal is said to be accepted: a proposal, when accepted, becomes a promise.

The Legal Landscape of Contract Formation: Towards a Distinct Malaysia Jurisprudence? Tay Pek San.

party, an agreement is formed.[7] An agreement that is enforceable by law is a contract.[8] In order to bring about an enforceable agreement, the parties must have the intention that their agreement is legally binding and they must be competent to contract.[9] Accordingly, a unilateral declaration cannot amount to a contract.[10] Neither can any agreement arise without an identifiable offer and acceptance. In a similar vein, the CA 1950 does not recognize a contract under seal.[11] In the light of the general principle laid down in section 26 of the CA 1950 that an agreement made without consideration is void and the exceptions in the section, there is no room to import the English common law principle that a promise under seal is enforceable.

A contract can be concluded in writing, orally, or by way of conduct.[12] The requirements for contract formation are the same, whether the contract is concluded orally, in writing, or by conduct. Contracts that are made orally or by conduct are binding in the same manner as written contracts. Be that as it may, there are some statutes that impose certain formalities such as a contract must be written or registered with the relevant authority.[13] Also, parties to a contract may themselves agree that an enforceable contract will only come into existence when it is put into writing.

Some judges, instead of undertaking an analysis of the elements of a contract, have adopted an objective approach by considering whether a reasonable person in the circumstances of the case would have concluded that the parties had reached an agreement.[14] This approach places emphasis on the words exchanged between the parties and their conduct during the negotiation rather than on any meticulous determination of whether the elements of a contract exist. The objective approach takes cognizance of the reality that many commercial transactions are rarely straightforward and that it may be artificial to require all the five elements to be proved for there to be an enforceable contract. For instance, in *Floral Trends Ltd v Li Onn Floral Enterprise (M) Sdn Bhd*,[15] the grant of a friendly loan by the plaintiff to the first defendant to assist him in his floral business was made orally without any formal agreement being entered into between the parties. The High Court stated that regardless of whether a contract was entered into orally or in writing, there must be a meeting of the minds between the contracting parties and this is determined through an objective approach. According to the court, it is difficult to ascertain a person's subjective

[7] CA 1950, s 2(e) states as follows:

> [E]very promise and every set of promises, forming the consideration for each other, is an agreement.

Although the definition in s 2(e) operates within the framework of a promise being met with a reciprocal promise which would culminate in a bilateral contract, the Malaysian contract law also recognizes unilateral contracts. This recognition is derived from English common law cases and s 8, CA 1950.

[8] CA 1950, s 2(h).

[9] CA 1950, s 10(1) states as follows:

> All agreements are contracts if they are made by the free consent of parties competent to contract, for a lawful consideration and with a lawful object, and are not hereby expressly declared to be void.

[10] *Guthrie Waugh Bhd v Malaippan Muthucumaru* [1972] 1 MLJ 35 (FC).

[11] Except where the matter falls within s 26(a), CA 1950. Section 26(a) states as follows:

> An agreement made without consideration is void unless it is expressed in writing and registered under the law (if any) for the time being in force for the registration of such documents, and is made on account of natural love and affection between parties standing in a near relation to each other.

In *Guthrie Waugh Bbd v Malaippan Muthucumaru* ibid 39, Sharma J observed that in Malaysia, no question of contract under seal arises unless the matter is covered by s 26(a).

[12] *Syed Jaafar bin Syed Ibrahim v Maju Mehar Singh Travel & Tours Sdn Bhd* [1999] 4 MLJ 413 (HC).

[13] This is discussed in section III of this chapter.

[14] See eg *Ahmad Zaini bin Japar v TL Offshore Sdn Bhd* [2002] 7 MLJ 604 (HC); *Floral Trends Ltd v Li Onn Floral Enterprise (M) Sdn Bhd* [2006] MLJU 339 (HC).

[15] ibid.

intentions; in the interests of fairness, certainty, and commercial convenience, the parties are deemed to have reached an agreement if, viewed objectively, they appear to have agreed.[16]

Unlike English common law, the CA 1950 makes a distinction between an agreement and a contract.[17] Under the CA 1950, although an agreement is formed when there exists mutual promises that become the consideration for the agreement, the agreement may not qualify as a contract. It is only when the agreement is legally enforceable that it is recognized as a contract. For instance, an agreement that is forbidden by law is an illegal agreement but not a contract.

In the light of the traditional scheme of analysing whether a contract is formed by establishing the existence of each of the five elements mentioned previously, namely, offer, acceptance, consideration, intention to create legal relations, and capacity to enter into a contract, this chapter will discuss the law on formation of contract in Malaysia by examining each of these elements in turn. In addition, this chapter will also discuss three other matters which are closely linked to contract formation, namely, exceptions to the no formality rule on contract formation, good faith negotiation, and formation of electronic contracts.

1. Offer

The CA 1950 does not use the word 'offer' but provides for the corresponding term 'proposal'. Nevertheless, almost invariably, Malaysian judges use the word 'offer' in their written judgments in the same manner as the term is used in English cases. Both terms are treated as synonymous by Malaysian judges. A proposal is defined in section 2(a) of the CA 1950 as follows:

> [W]hen one person signifies to another his willingness to do or to abstain from doing anything, with a view to obtaining the assent of that other to the act or abstinence, he is said to make a proposal.

The essence of a proposal as an indication of a person's willingness to enter into a legally binding contract was emphasized by the Federal Court when it explained the meaning of an 'offer' in *Preston Corporation Sdn Bhd v Edward Leong & Ors.*[18] In this case, the court stated that an offer was an intimation of willingness by an offeror to enter into a legally binding contract.

As with the position in English law, an offer may be made by words or conduct or a combination of both. Pursuant to section 9 of the CA 1950, where a proposal is made in words and is accepted by the offeree, the promise is said to be express. On the other hand, if the promise is made otherwise than in words, the promise is said to be implied. An offer must be clear in its meaning so that the offeree knows what obligations the offeror is willing to undertake. An offer may be made to a specific individual, a group of individuals, or the world at large.

[16] ibid [14]. Similarly, the Court of Appeal in *Cipta Cermat Sdn Bhd v Perbandaran Kemajuan Negeri Kedah* [2007] 2 MLJ 746 also adopted the objective approach to arrive at the conclusion that the parties had reached a final agreement even in the absence of a formal contract. More recently, the High Court in *Singham Sulaiman Sdn Bhd (t/a Jones Lang Wootton) v Mega Palm Sdn Bhd* [2014] 7 MLJ 476 [112], referring to the Singapore case of *Colliers International (Singapore) Pte Ltd v Senkee Logistics Pte Ltd* [2007] 2 SLR (R) 230 (HC), again pointed out that an objective test will be applied to determine whether an agreement has been reached between any two prospective contracting parties and that the parties' subjective belief was irrelevant unless it assisted in ascertaining the objective understanding between them.

[17] *Beca (Malaysia) Sdn Bhd v Tan Choong Kuan & Anor* [1986] 1 MLJ 390 (FC) 394.

[18] [1982] 2 MLJ 23 (FC).

(a) Offer distinguished from invitation to treat

An offer is to be distinguished from an invitation to treat. What amounts to an invitation to treat is not defined in the CA 1950, but this concept is entrenched in Malaysian contract law, and its scope is the same as in English common law. Essentially, an invitation to treat is an invitation by a person to another to make an offer; it has no binding effect at law. The established guiding principles developed in English contract law are used by Malaysian judges in resolving whether a statement amounts to an offer or an invitation to treat. The facts of each case and the intention of the parties are important considerations.[19]

(b) Offer must be communicated

An offer becomes effective only when it is communicated to the offeree. By section 3, the communication of an offer may be made by any act or omission of the offeror which has the effect of communicating it. Section 4(1) provides that the communication of an offer is complete when it comes to the knowledge of the offeree. It follows from this that an offer which is sent by ordinary mail, electronic mail, or text messaging service does not become effective until the offeree has knowledge of the offer.

No acceptance of an offer can take place until and unless the communication of the offer is complete. In *Madam Loh Sai Nyah v American International Assurance Co Ltd*,[20] two days prior to his death, the deceased Chye Kee Jin paid the premium for a personal accident insurance policy. The premium payment was made to an insurance agent who only forwarded it to the respondent a day after the death of the deceased. The proposal form was received by the respondent four days after the deceased's death. The appellant, who was the widow of the deceased, brought legal proceedings to demand the insured sum. The respondent denied liability on the ground that no contract of insurance was formed between the deceased and the respondent on the date the deceased died. According to the respondent, they had not accepted the proposal because the proposal form was only received by them four days after his death. The matter was argued before the Sessions Judge who found that no contract existed between the deceased and the respondent. On appeal to the High Court, the judge, agreeing with the Sessions Judge, referred to section 4(1) and held that it was clear that the proposal had not come to the knowledge of the respondent as it was only received by them after the deceased had died. On further appeal to the Court of Appeal, the court dismissed the appeal on the ground that there was no contract of insurance between the deceased and the respondent on the date of the deceased's death. The court also held that the insurance agent was an ordinary agent who was authorized to act on the respondent's behalf only to the extent of collecting the proposal form and payment; he had no authority to accept the offer of the proposer.[21]

When offers in identical terms cross in the post, neither party can be said to have accepted the offer because no acceptance can be made by any person who does not have knowledge of the offer. Accordingly, cross-offers which are identical in terms cannot result in an enforceable contract.[22]

[19] *Hui Jia Hao v Perdana Park City Sdn Bhd & Anor* [2012] 8 MLJ 385 (HC) 389.
[20] *Madam Loh Sai Nyah v American International Assurance Co Ltd* [1998] 2 MLJ 310 (CA).
[21] See the criticism of this decision in A Nurjaanah, 'Law and Ethics in the Malaysian Insurance Industry—A Review of Selected Practices' (2004) 31 JMCL 87, 91.
[22] *Tinn v Hoffman & Co* (1873) 29 LT 271.

(c) Revocation of offer

Offers are revocable at any time provided acceptance has not yet taken place. Once acceptance has taken place, the offer is legally binding and can no longer be revoked. However, an offer is irrevocable in the situation where the offeree gives the offeror consideration to make the offer irrevocable, as in the case of an option where the grantor, for consideration, agrees with the grantee to keep the offer open for a period of time.[23] In the absence of consideration, the offer is revocable even before the expiry of the prescribed duration for acceptance. This is because there is no consideration for the offeror's promise to keep the offer open.

A difficult issue arises with regard to the revocation of offers in unilateral contracts. Unilateral contracts, which arise where one party promises to do or refrain from doing something in return for an act, are recognized in section 8 of the CA 1950. The section provides that performance of the conditions of an offer is acceptance of the offer. Instances include offers of reward to the public for providing certain information and simple contracts of estate agency where commission is only paid to an estate agent when a sale is concluded with the buyer introduced by the agent. The issue is whether an offeror can revoke his offer just before the offeree's completion of the act but after the offeree has expended time, effort, and financial resources to perform the act mentioned in the offer. The CA 1950 is silent on this, and there is no Malaysian case law dealing with this point. However, it is submitted that the offeror in a unilateral contract may revoke his offer at any time before the completion of the act. This view appears to receive some support in *Inch Kenneth Kajang Rubber Public Ltd Co v Tor Peng Sie (t/a Pacific Landmark Real Estate Agents)*,[24] although the case does not deal directly with this point. In this case, the appellant appointed the respondent as its sales agent to secure buyers to purchase some pieces of the appellant's land. The respondent introduced a buyer to the appellant and, eventually, a sale and purchase agreement was entered into. However, the appellant refused to pay the respondent the agency fee, arguing that the appellant's obligation to pay the fee only arose if the land was sold at a certain minimum price. The appellant contended that this condition was not fulfilled. The respondent successfully sued the appellant before the High Court to recover the agency fee. Based on the evidence adduced, the trial judge was not convinced that the parties had agreed to any term that the land was to be sold at a certain minimum price. The appellant appealed unsuccessfully to the Court of Appeal. In dismissing the appeal, the court stated that the principal's liability to pay commission depended on whether the event upon which the commission was to be paid had happened. Since the sale and purchase had materialized, the appellant's liability to pay the agency fee had arisen. In coming to this decision, Mah Weng Kwai JCA referred to the earlier Federal Court decision in *Tang Chiok Sing v Lian Fatt Sawmill*.[25] Although the Federal Court in that case did not refer to the concept of unilateral contract, the reasoning in essence adopted the principle that under a unilateral contract, an agent's commission was only payable upon satisfaction of the conditions agreed by the parties. Indeed, the court stated that no obligation was imposed on the agent to do anything and that the principal–agent contract was essentially a promise binding on the principal to pay a sum of money upon the rendering of some service by the agent. The court in *Tang Chiok Sing* also stated that there was nothing to prevent the principal from terminating the contract at any time before the agent accomplished what he had undertaken to do.

[23] *Yap Sze Peng v Great Eastern Life Assurance (Malaysia) Berhad & Anor* [2011] 2 AMCR 276 (HC) 287.
[24] [2014] 1 MLJ 118 (CA). [25] [1976] 2 MLJ 241 (FC).

An offer may be revoked by the offeree's rejection or counter-offer.[26] Further, section 6 provides four other ways by which an offer may be revoked. These are:

(1) by the communication of a notice of revocation by the offeror to the other party;
(2) by the lapse of the time prescribed in the offer for its acceptance, or by the lapse of a reasonable time where no time for acceptance is prescribed;
(3) by the failure of the acceptor to fulfil a condition precedent to acceptance; or
(4) by the death or mental disorder of the offeror provided that the acceptor has knowledge of this before acceptance.

(1) Revocation by offeror

As provided in section 6(a), an offer may be revoked by the offeror communicating the revocation to the offeree. Revocation in this manner can only be done prior to acceptance by the offeree. This is stated in section 5(1) which provides that an offer may be revoked at any time before the communication of its acceptance is complete as against the offeror, but not afterwards. Section 5(1) has to be read with section 4(2)(a) which defines the time when communication of an acceptance is complete as against the offeror. Pursuant to section 4(2)(a), the communication of an acceptance is complete as against the offeror when it is put in a course of transmission to him so as to be out of the power of the acceptor to retract that acceptance. In other words, an offer may be revoked at any time by the offeror before the acceptance has been sent to him. For example: if A sends his offer by post to B, A may revoke his offer at any time before or at the moment when B accepts the offer, but not afterwards.

Pursuant to section 4(3)(b), the communication of revocation of an offer only binds the offeree when it comes to his knowledge. Thus, if A revokes his offer by post but before the letter of revocation reaches B, B accepts the offer not knowing that it has been revoked by A, the acceptance is valid. This legal position is consistent with the English decision in *Byrne & Co v Leon Van Tienhoven & Co*[27] which requires revocation of an offer to be communicated to the offeree so that he has knowledge of the revocation.

Whether communication of notice of revocation can be made by a third party who is a stranger to the transaction is unclear. The wording of section 6(a) seems to suggest that only the offeror can communicate the notice of revocation of the offer, although this runs counter to the old English decision in *Dickinson v Dodds*[28] which found that the revocation of an offer was effective even though the notification was communicated by a third party. Nevertheless, the generally accepted view is that, for reasons of certainty, communication of revocation of an offer cannot be made by a third party who has no connection with the transaction.[29]

(2) Revocation by lapse of time

Pursuant to section 6(b), where time for acceptance is stipulated in the offer and no acceptance has taken place within that time, the offer is revoked by the lapse of the prescribed time. In *Yusof b Rahmat v Bumiputra-Commerce Bank Berhad*,[30] the court held that the revocation of an offer was not automatic, and that the offeror could waive the right to revoke

[26] *Malayan Flour Mills Bhd v Saw Eng Chee (Administrator of the Estate of Saw Cheng Chor, deceased) & Anor* [1997] 1 MLJ 763 (HC).
[27] [1874–80] All ER 1432 (CPD). [28] (1876) 2 Ch D 463 (CA Civ).
[29] A Mohaimin Ayus, *Law of Contract in Malaysia*, Vol 1 (Petaling Jaya: Sweet & Maxwell 2009) 330; MF Cheong, *Contract Law in Malaysia* (Petaling Jaya: Sweet & Maxwell 2010) 32.
[30] [2006] MLJU 474 (HC).

for the benefit of the offeree. The court in that case also held that the effect of stating a time frame for acceptance was to create a rebuttable presumption that the offeror reserved the right to revoke the offer after the lapse of the prescribed time. In that case, the plaintiff offered the defendant an overdraft facility through a letter of offer dated 3 May 1995. Pursuant to the letter, the defendant was requested to indicate his acceptance within 30 days from 3 May 1995. However, the defendant did not accept within that time frame but did so only on 6 June 1995. Nevertheless, the plaintiff granted the overdraft facility to the defendant. Subsequently, the defendant defaulted and the plaintiff commenced action to recover the sum owing. Counsel for the defendant contested the validity of the agreement because the acceptance by the defendant was beyond the 30-day period prescribed in the plaintiff's letter of offer. The High Court held that the time frame of 30 days created a rebuttable presumption that the offeror reserved the right to revoke the offer after that date, but that did not preclude the offeror from waiving the right for the benefit of the offeree. It was held that the presumption was rebutted because the plaintiff proceeded to grant the overdraft facility even though the defendant's acceptance was beyond the time frame given. The reasoning of the court raises some doubt because section 6 states in unequivocal terms that an offer is revoked by the lapse of the time prescribed for its acceptance. To infuse the notion of a rebuttable presumption that the offeror reserves the right to revoke the offer upon expiry of the time stipulated is contrary to the clear words of the provision. It is submitted that a more plausible reasoning to support the validity of the agreement is to argue on the basis that upon revocation of the express offer, there is an implied offer by the plaintiff on the same terms to the defendant. This implied offer is externally manifested by the conduct of the parties, that is, the defendant's acceptance and the plaintiff's release of the monies subsequently. This argument would appear to accord more with commercial convenience and reality.

Where no time for acceptance is prescribed by the offeror, the offeree must accept within a reasonable time. What amounts to a reasonable time is a question of fact which depends on the circumstances of each case, the nature of the business, and the conduct of the parties after the offer was made.[31] In *Macon Works & Trading Sdn Bhd v Phang Hon Chin & Anor*,[32] the court stated that an offer would lapse after a reasonable time not because this was implied in the offer but because failure to accept within a reasonable time implied rejection by the offeree.

(3) Failure of acceptor to fulfil condition precedent to acceptance

Pursuant to section 6(c), an offer is revoked if the acceptor fails to fulfil the condition precedent stipulated in the offer prior to acceptance. Section 6(c) deals with a condition that affects the formation of a contract and not a condition that relates to an obligation of an already binding contract.[33] In *Kopeks Holdings Sdn Bhd v Bank Islam Malaysia*,[34] the defendant, by a letter, offered banking facilities to the plaintiff. The offer was a conditional offer in that it required all the legal documents spelt out in the letter of offer to be executed before a contract could come into existence. In addition, the letter of offer required the plaintiff to forward to the defendant its Memorandum and Articles of Association as well as its Board of Directors' resolution accepting the facilities. The plaintiff purported to accept the letter of offer but did not forward the documents to the defendant nor execute any of the legal documents. Subsequently, the defendant revoked the letter of offer on the ground of

[31] *Macon Works & Trading Sdn Bhd v Phang Hon Chin & Anor* [1976] 2 MLJ 177 (CA).
[32] ibid.
[33] V Sinnadurai, *Law of Contract* (4th edn, Petaling Jaya: Sweet & Maxwell 2011) 116, para 2.71.
[34] [2012] 4 MLJ 337 (CA).

certain non-disclosure of facts by the plaintiff. In an action against the defendant for breach of contract, an issue arose with regard to the legal significance of the non-fulfilment by the defendant of the conditions precedent stipulated in the letter of offer. The court held that the conditions precedent could not be disregarded and that the fulfilment of those conditions was a prerequisite to the creation of a legally binding contract. The court referred to section 6(c) and concluded that the letter of offer would only bind the defendant if and when the conditions precedent had been fulfilled.

(4) Death or mental disorder of offeror prior to acceptance

Pursuant to section 6(d), an offer is revoked by the death or mental disorder of the offeror provided that this fact comes to the knowledge of the acceptor prior to his acceptance. It would appear that if the acceptor is unaware of the offeror's death, section 6(d) does not apply and the offer is not revoked. In such a case, section 38(2) requires the representative of the offeror to be bound by the contract unless a contrary intention appears from the contract. Such a contrary intention would arise where the offer concerns personal performance by the offeror, for instance his performing on stage or writing a book.

2. Acceptance

The acceptance of an offer results in a promise which creates legal rights and obligations. In section 2(b) of the CA 1950, an acceptance is defined as follows:

> [W]hen the person to whom the proposal is made signifies his assent thereto, the proposal is said to be accepted: a proposal, when accepted, becomes a promise.

(a) Acceptance to be absolute and unqualified

An offeree must unconditionally agree to accept all the terms of the offer. This is provided in section 7(a) which requires an acceptance to be absolute and unqualified. This is in line with the position under English law where the acceptance must be absolute and must correspond to the terms of the offer. Thus, cross-offers, which are identical offers made by the offeror and offeree in ignorance of each other's offer, cannot amount to acceptance since a person cannot be said to unconditionally agree to the terms of an offer which he is not aware of.[35] Similarly, counter-offers which are made in response to an earlier offer but which add to or vary the terms of that earlier offer, do not amount to acceptance.[36]

In 'battle of forms' cases where, during the course of negotiation, one party makes an offer on a set of terms while the other purports to accept on another set of terms and, subsequently, performance begins, the question as to which set of terms applies is determined based on when the parties are in complete agreement on the essential terms of the contract. The court will adopt an objective approach based on the correspondence between the parties and the documents before the court. In many cases, the parties would have exchanged a series of letters or correspondence prior to concluding a contract but it does not necessarily follow that the last document contains the prevailing terms. In *Tan Geok Khoon & Gerard Francis Robless v Paya Terubong Estate Sdn Bhd*,[37] the plaintiff, who had since passed away, made an offer by way of a letter to buy land belonging to the defendants at a certain price and forwarded a deposit of $6,000. This was not accepted by the defendants but, subsequently,

[35] *Guiness Anchor Marketing Sdn Bhd v Chellam Joe Vetha Thya Singh* [1999] 3 AMR 2735 (HC) 2764, relying on the English case of *Tinn v Hoffman & Co* (1873) 29 LT 271.

[36] *Quality Talent Sdn Bhd v Lee Joo Guan & Ors* [2011] MLJU 645 (HC).

[37] [1988] 2 MLJ 672 (HC).

they offered to sell the land if the entire purchase price was paid within 14 days. The court construed this to be a counter-offer. The plaintiff accepted the counter-offer and, at the same time, paid the balance of the purchase price. The defendants then issued a receipt acknowledging payment. Later, in their letter to the plaintiff, the defendants stated that their solicitors would prepare the agreement for sale which would be forwarded to the plaintiff when it was ready. The court referred to the decision of Lord Diplock in *Gibson v Manchester City Council*[38] where it was held that in determining whether a contract had been made by a valid offer and acceptance during the course of correspondence, the court would look at the documents relied upon as constituting the contract and determine whether upon their true construction there was to be found in them a contractual offer to sell and an acceptance of that offer. On the facts before the court, the judge found that when the defendants issued the receipt of payment, the contract was made because the parties were *ad idem* as to the terms of the contract. The terms were to be determined based on the correspondence between the parties and documents that existed at that time. The defendants' subsequent letter about the drafting of an agreement of sale was merely the expression of a desire to have the agreement put into due form by a solicitor and was to be disregarded in determining the terms of the agreement.

(b) Acceptance 'subject to contract'

At times, the agreement between the parties may contain a phrase to the effect that the acceptance is subject to a formal contract to be prepared and executed by the parties. Where an acceptance is made 'subject to contract', the Supreme Court in *Ayer Hitam Tin Dredging Malaysia Bhd v YC Chin Enterprises Sdn Bhd*[39] held that the existence or otherwise of a contractual relationship depended on whether the parties intended to be bound at the time when the acceptance was made or at a later time upon the occurrence of some further event, such as the execution of a formal agreement.[40] According to the court, the general rule is that when an arrangement is made containing the phrase 'subject to contract' or similar expressions, the parties are still in a state of negotiation and do not intend to be bound unless and until a formal contract is exchanged.[41]

In *Ayer Hitam*, the respondent entered into negotiations to construct low-cost houses for the appellant's workers. The appellant wrote a letter to the respondent accepting its proposal for the project, subject to various terms and conditions. One of the conditions was that the terms stated in the letter were to be constituted in the form of an agreement between them. Relying on that letter, the respondent proceeded to make arrangements for the project's end-financing and commenced preliminary works on the site. The respondent also appointed architects, engineers, and surveyors although no formal agreement had been executed. Subsequently, a draft agreement was forwarded to the respondent for its approval but, since the parties were still negotiating, no such approval was given. Eventually, the negotiations broke down and the appellant instructed the respondent to cease all works on the site. The issue was whether the appellant's letter of acceptance to the respondent embodied any contractual obligations between the parties. The court held that this depended on the intention of the parties. An objective test would be applied to determine the intention of a reasonable man in the shoes of the parties to the alleged contract. The court placed emphasis on the

38 [1979] 1 WLR 294 (HL). 39 [1994] 2 MLJ 754 (SC).

40 Similarly, see the Privy Council decision in *Daiman Development Sdn Bhd v Mathew Lui Chin Teck* [1981] 1 MLJ 5.

41 See also the Supreme Court decision in *Kam Mah Theatre Sdn Bhd v Tan Lay Soon* [1994] 1 MLJ 108 and the Federal Court decision in *Lim Chia Min v Cheah Sang Ngeow & Anor* [1997] 1 MLJ 127 for cases to the same effect.

phrase 'subject to the following terms and conditions' found in the letter and held that as several essential matters still remained to be settled between the parties, the letter did not constitute a binding contract between the parties. Instead, the court found that the letter was only a record of the terms which the parties had agreed would be a basis for the negotiation of a contract.

However, 'subject to contract' does not necessarily mean that a formal agreement must be executed before the contract comes into existence. If the conduct or correspondence of the parties indicates that they have come to an agreement to which they intend to be bound, the courts have been prepared to find a legally enforceable contract, the failure to execute the formal contract notwithstanding. In the Federal Court decision in *Charles Grenier v Lau Wing Hong*,[42] it was found that despite the phrase 'subject to the sale and purchase agreement', an enforceable contract had come into existence as that was the result intended by the parties. The case concerned the sale by the appellant of two shophouses to the respondent. In the letter accompanying the payment of the 10 per cent deposit, the respondent's estate agents stated that the deposit was paid 'subject to the sale and purchase agreement'. The Federal Court examined the correspondence between the parties as well as the aim of the transaction and concluded that the phrase in the estate agent's letter did not point to an intention that no contract was to come into existence until a formal sale and purchase agreement had been prepared and executed. Rather, the court found that the correspondence and aim of the transaction indicated an intention to merely formalize the agreement already concluded between the parties. The parties had identified with sufficient clarity the property, the price, and the terms they considered essential.

(c) Communication of acceptance

Acceptance must be communicated to the offeror so that he is aware that his offer has been accepted and he is, accordingly, bound by the acceptance. This follows from the English landmark case of *Entores Ltd v Miles Far East Corporation*.[43] Pursuant to section 3 of the CA 1950, the communication of an acceptance may be made by any act or omission of the acceptor which has the effect of communicating the acceptance. Acceptance can be communicated by an acceptor or any person authorized by him.[44] Depending on the terms of the offer, an acceptance may be made orally, in writing, or by conduct. Section 8, which affirms that acceptance may be made by conduct, states that performance of the conditions of a proposal is an acceptance of the proposal.

While section 3 contemplates that acceptance may be made by an omission of the acceptor, Malaysian courts have followed the old English cases of *Felthouse v Bindley*[45] and *Fraser v Everett*[46] that the offeror cannot impose silence as a manner of acceptance.[47] In *Alex Ting Kuang Kuo @ Alex Ting Kwang Kuo (trading under the style and firm name of WTS Konsultant) v Arab-Malaysian Corporation Builders Sdn Bhd*,[48] the plaintiff, a professional engineer, was given a draft letter of appointment by the defendant to be its engineer for a project. The plaintiff replied that he wished to make changes to the draft letter but the defendant did not agree to the changes suggested. Subsequently, the defendant handed the

[42] [1996] 3 MLJ 327 (FC).
[43] [1955] 2 QB 327 (CA).
[44] *Mega First Corporation Berhad v Tepat Intan Sdn Bhd* [2010] MLJU 927, affd on appeal to the Court of Appeal in *Tepat Intan Sdn Bhd v Mega First Corp Bhd* [2014] 1 MLJ 573.
[45] (1862) 11 CBNS 869, 142 ER 1037.
[46] (1889) 4 Ky 512.
[47] Cases that affirmed the general rule that silence cannot constitute acceptance include *Chan Kok Thin @ Chan Kok Cheng & Anor v Chan Yock Cher@ Chan Yock Kher & Ors* [2000] AMEJ 0216 (HC), and *Chan Yuet Chun @ Chan Oi Lin v Martego Sdn Bhd* [1996] MLJU 573 (HC).
[48] [2013] 4 BLR 248 (HC).

plaintiff another draft letter of appointment which was in exactly the same terms as the original draft. The plaintiff accepted the defendant's letter of appointment but added that the acceptance was subject to the changes that he had requested earlier. In addition, the plaintiff added new terms to his appointment and stated that if he did not hear from the defendant by a specified date, he would assume that the defendant had agreed with the plaintiff's letter and the contents were to be read as part of the plaintiff's letter of appointment. The defendant did not reply. Disputes subsequently arose between them. One of the issues was whether there was an agreement between the plaintiff and the defendant to engage the former as its engineer. The court, referring to *Felthouse v Bindley*, held that as a general rule, acceptance of an offer could not be implied from mere silence on the part of the offeree. However, the court recognized that 'it may be going too far, however, to say that silence can never be unequivocal evidence of consent'.[49] On the facts of the case, the court found that the general rule was not displaced because the defendant's earlier rejection of the plaintiff's attempt to change the terms of the defendant's draft letter of appointment was inconsistent with the claim by the plaintiff that the defendant's silence amounted to an acceptance of his counter-offer. The rule that silence does not constitute acceptance may be displaced in circumstances where reasonable opportunities exist to reject the offer but the acceptor fails to do so.[50] The English cases of *Weatherby v Banham*[51] and *Re Selectmove*,[52] where silence was recognized as constituting acceptance in exceptional circumstances, are likely to be followed in Malaysia in the light of section 3 which provides that acceptance may be made by an omission.

Although an offeror cannot unilaterally impose the rule that silence constitutes acceptance, section 7(b) allows the offeror to prescribe the manner in which the offer is to be accepted. According to section 7(b), an acceptance must be expressed in some usual and reasonable manner unless the proposal prescribes the manner in which it is to be accepted. The section further states that if the offeror prescribes the manner in which it is to be accepted, and the acceptance is not made in that manner, the offeror may within a reasonable time after the acceptance is communicated to him, insist that his proposal shall be accepted in the prescribed manner and not otherwise. However, if the offeror fails to do so within a reasonable time, he is deemed to have accepted the acceptance. To the extent that section 7(b) places the onus on the offeror who has prescribed the manner of acceptance to insist that the acceptance be made in that manner, the position departs from the English case of *Manchester Diocesan Council for Education v Commercial & General Investments Ltd*[53] where it was held that the offeror would not be bound unless the acceptance was made in the manner prescribed.

Section 7(b) was raised in *Leong Mun Chiew & Anor v Glenmarie Cove Development Sdn Bhd*[54] which concerned the sale and purchase of a bungalow lot. In this case, the plaintiffs, having heard over the radio that the defendant was conducting a sale of bungalow lots, approached the defendant to hand over a cheque for part of the 10 per cent of the purchase price with the view to buying a bungalow lot. A temporary receipt was issued to the plaintiffs by the defendant. The plaintiffs also signed a document which stated that their offer to purchase would only be deemed accepted upon issuance of the developers' official receipt. The document additionally stated that no other acts would constitute acceptance. Subsequently, the defendant realizing that the lots had already been reserved by the defendant's directors, returned the plaintiffs' payment to them. The plaintiffs argued that a contract had come into existence and that it was breached by the defendant. In dismissing the plaintiffs' claim, the

49 ibid [65].
50 MF Cheong, *Contract Law in Malaysia* (Petaling Jaya: Sweet & Maxwell 2010) 56.
51 (1832) 5 C & P 228.
52 [1995] 2 All ER 531 (CA).
53 [1970] 1 WLR 241 (Ch).
54 [2010] 7 AMR 688 (HC).

court held that no contract had been reached between the parties because the plaintiffs were merely making an offer to purchase the bungalow lot. By the terms of the document signed between the parties at the time when the plaintiffs made the first payment, acceptance would only be made if the developers' official receipt was issued. Pursuant to section 7(b), the defendant only issued a temporary receipt and this could not constitute acceptance on the part of the defendant.

(d) Completion of communication of acceptance

Section 4(2), which deals with the time when the communication of an acceptance is complete, provides for different times in which an acceptance is complete against the proposer and the acceptor. Section 4(2) states as follows:

> The communication of an acceptance is complete –
>
> (a) as against the proposer, when it is put in a course of transmission to him, so as to be out of the power of the acceptor; and
>
> (b) as against the acceptor, when it comes to the knowledge of the proposer.

Where the communication of an acceptance is non-instantaneous, such as in the case of acceptance by post or by courier, section 4(2)(a) dictates that the offeror is bound by the acceptance when the letter is placed in the post box or handed over to a courier company. Section 4(2)(a) is the equivalent of the postal rule under English law where acceptance by post takes effect when it is posted.[55] However, by section 4(2)(b), the acceptor is only bound by his acceptance when the acceptance letter comes to the knowledge of the offeror. This can lead to an anomalous situation where an offeror is bound by the acceptance at a time when he does not yet have knowledge of the acceptance but is nevertheless no longer legally able to revoke his offer. On the other hand, since the acceptor is not bound by his acceptance until it reaches the knowledge of the offeror, the acceptor is legally able to revoke his acceptance in the interim period. An unfair conclusion can at times result from this because the acceptor can blow hot and cold since his acceptance would have already bound the offeror but the acceptor continues to have the opportunity to revoke his acceptance until it reaches the offeror.

The predecessor to the current section 4(2)(a) of the CA 1950, which is section 4 of the Contracts Enactment 1899, was applied by the Court of Appeal in *Ignatius v Bell*.[56] In this case, the defendant granted to the plaintiff an option to purchase his land. The agreement stated that the option had to be exercised on or before 20 August 1912 by a notice in writing to the defendant. The plaintiff exercised the option by sending a notice in a registered letter addressed to the defendant on 16 August. Unfortunately, the letter was not delivered to the defendant until 25 August. The issue was whether the plaintiff had exercised his option when he mailed the letter by registered post. Applying section 4 of the Contracts Enactment, the court held that the acceptance by the plaintiff was complete when it was put in a course of transmission to the defendant on 16 August and the defendant was bound by the plaintiff's acceptance.

While it is clear that section 4(2) applies where the acceptance is by non-instantaneous means, the position is less clear where the acceptance is by instantaneous communication, such as by telephone or facsimile. This issue is addressed in two different ways by Malaysian courts. As yet, this issue has not been specifically argued before the Malaysian court. There is divergence in the Malaysian judicial precedents on whether section 4(2) should be applied

[55] *Adams v Lindsell* (1818) 1 B & Ald 681.

[56] (1913) 2 FMSLR 115 (CA).

to determine whether acceptance of an offer is complete or whether the English common law rule in *Entores Ltd v Miles Far East Corp*[57] should be used instead. On the one hand, there are cases that rely on the principle in *Entores* that for instantaneous communications such as telephone, facsimile, or face-to-face communication, acceptance is complete when it is brought to the knowledge of the offeror. Malaysian cases that have relied on *Entores* include the Court of Appeal decision in *YK Fung Securities Sdn Bhd v James Capel (Far East) Ltd*[58] which held that a contract by telephone or facsimile is deemed to be made at the place where the offeror hears from the offeree about the acceptance.

On the other hand, there are cases that have relied on section 4(2) for determination of whether acceptance is complete in instantaneous communications, presumably on the basis that section 4(2) is worded in a manner that is not dependent on the mode of communication used by the acceptor. In most situations, the application of this provision to straightforward instantaneous communications where the acceptance is instantaneously heard by the offeror will lead to the same result as an application of the principle in the *Entores* case. However, there are exceptional circumstances where the result may be different, as in the example given by Lord Denning in *Entores* where his lordship said that no contract was formed if a man shouted an offer to another across a river but could not hear his reply because it was drowned out by an aircraft flying overhead. Yet, if section 4(2) was applied to this example, the offeror would be bound by the acceptance under section 4(2)(a) but not the acceptor. An application of section 4(2) can therefore lead to an awkward result especially where the acceptance, for some reason, fails to reach the offeror. Accordingly, it is submitted that the better approach is to apply the principle in *Entores* in a situation where instantaneous communications are used by the parties. An instance of a Malaysian case that referred to section 4(2) where acceptance was by way of instantaneous communication is *Mega First Corporation Berhad v Tepat Intan Sdn Bhd*[59] which concerned an offer by the defendant to purchase the plaintiff's shares in a certain company. The plaintiff, through its representative, had a meeting with a director of the defendant and verbally informed him that the plaintiff had accepted the offer. However, the defendant then informed the plaintiff's representative that the defendant had changed its mind and was revoking the offer. The communication of acceptance was instantaneous in this case since it was carried out in a face-to-face setting. The court applied section 4(2) to hold that a contract had come into existence between the parties since the acceptance had already been communicated to the defendant. The question whether it would be appropriate to apply section 4(2) or the principle in *Entores* to instantaneous communications was not argued before the court. Nevertheless, it appears from the judgment that the court took the view that whether an acceptance is complete is to be determined by reference to section 4(2) alone in both instantaneous and non-instantaneous communications.

The application in *Mega First Corporation* of section 4(2) to situations involving instantaneous communications is to be contrasted with the Indian case of *Bhagwandas Goverdhandas Kedia v M/s Girdharilal Parshottamdas & Co & Ors*,[60] which is of persuasive authority in Malaysia. In the *Bhagwandas* case, the majority in the Supreme Court of India applied the *Entores* rule to a case where the acceptance involved telephone communications. The court considered whether section 4 of the Indian Contract Act 1872, which is *in pari materia* with section 4 of the Malaysian CA 1950, would apply in cases of acceptance by instantaneous communication and, by majority, concluded that it did not. According to Shah J, who delivered the judgment for the majority, there was no statutory provision dealing

[57] [1955] 2 QB 327 (CA). [58] [1997] 2 MLJ 621 (CA). [59] [2010] MLJU 927 (HC).
[60] AIR 1966 SC 543 (SC).

with contracts made by instantaneous communication under the Indian Contract Act 1872 and, therefore, Indian courts would be guided by English common law on this issue. In other words, for acceptance by instantaneous communication, the acceptance is complete when it comes to the knowledge of the offeror, following the rule in *Entores*. On the other hand, Hidayatullah J in his dissenting judgment adopted a view to the contrary. He held that section 4 of the Indian Contract Act should apply to all modes of communication of acceptance because the language of the section was worded in a technologically neutral manner such that it was able to cover communication by post, telegraph, telephone, or wireless.

Although *Bhagwandas* is merely of persuasive authority in Malaysia, it demonstrates that section 4(2) of the CA 1950 is amenable to two possible interpretations, which at the present moment have not been settled by the courts. Nevertheless, it is submitted that the better view is the view of the majority in *Bhagwandas*, which is that the principle in *Entores* would apply to contracts made by instantaneous communications. This follows from section 3 of the Civil Law Act 1956 ('CLA') which provides that English law is applicable in Malaysia unless there are provisions to the contrary made by any written law in Malaysia and so far as the circumstances of Malaysia and its inhabitants permit. As the CA 1950 is silent on when acceptance is complete where instantaneous communications are involved, section 3 of the CLA 1956 would pave the way for the application of the principle in *Entores*.

(e) Revocation of acceptance

The time in which an acceptance may be revoked is provided in section 5(2). The section states that an acceptance may be revoked at any time before the communication of the acceptance is complete as against the acceptor, but not afterwards. As mentioned previously, section 4(2)(b) provides that the communication of an acceptance is complete as against the acceptor when it comes to the knowledge of the offeror. In other words, an acceptance may be revoked at any time before the acceptance comes to the knowledge of the offeror.

The time when the revocation of an acceptance is complete is provided in section 4(3) which states as follows:

> The communication of a revocation is complete–
>
> (a) as against the person who makes it, when it is put into a course of transmission to the person to whom it is made, so as to be out of the power of the person who makes it; and
>
> (b) as against the person to whom it is made, when it comes to his knowledge.

For instance, if the acceptor revokes his acceptance by post, he is bound by the revocation as soon as it is put in the post. However, the offeror is only bound by the revocation when it comes to his knowledge.

3. Consideration

Consideration is an essential element in the formation of a contract. Section 26 provides that an agreement made without consideration is void. In *Macon Works & Trading Sdn Bhd v Phang Hon Chin & Anor*,[61] the defendants, for a consideration of \$1, gave a written option to one Kong Yoke Sam to purchase a piece of land. Subsequently, disputes arose and it was proved that the \$1 consideration was never paid or received. The court held that the option

[61] *Macon Works & Trading Sdn Bhd v Phang Hon Chin & Anor* [1976] 2 MLJ 177 (CA).

was void for lack of consideration. Apart from section 26, section 10(1) states that all agreements are contracts if they are made, inter alia, for a lawful consideration.

Mutual promises, which result from a promise made by one party in return for a promise made by another, can also constitute consideration. This is recognized in section 2(e) which provides that every promise and every set of promises, forming the consideration for each other, is an agreement. Also, section 2(f) states that promises which form the consideration for each other are called reciprocal promises. For instance, where A agrees to sell a house to B for a certain sum, the promise by B to pay the sum is the consideration for A's promise to sell the house, and A's promise to sell the house is the consideration for B's promise to pay the money.[62]

Consideration is defined in section 2(d) as:

> [W]hen, at the desire of the promisor, the promisee or any other person has done or abstained from doing, or does or abstains from doing, or promises to do or to abstain from doing, something, such act or abstinence or promise is called a consideration for the promise.

Consideration, therefore, entails the existence of an act or abstinence or promise to act or to abstain from doing something. In *Guthrie Waugh Bhd v Malaippan Muthuchumaru*,[63] it was held that forbearance, which is a type of abstinence, involved forgoing the exercise of a legal right. The consideration lay in the detriment to the party who had a right to resort to court action and the corresponding benefit to the other party who was saved from having to defend legal proceedings.

As is evident from the statutory language of section 2(d), to constitute consideration, the act or abstinence must be done 'at the desire of the promisor'. Similarly, if the act involves a promise to do or to abstain from doing something, the promise must be made at the desire of the promisor. In other words, the mere fact that an act is done voluntarily or a promise to do an act is voluntary cannot amount to consideration.

An issue that arises from section 2(d) concerns the legal implication of the phrase 'at the desire of the promisor' when read together with 'the promisee or any other person has done or abstained from doing' something. The old English cases, namely, *Re McArdle*[64] and *Lampleigh v Brathwait*[65] may be alluded to in order to shed light on the scope of section 2(d). In *Re McArdle*, it was held that past consideration could not be good consideration for a contract. An exception is made where the act was done 'at the request' of the promisor, as in *Lampleigh*'s case. In *Lampleigh*, it was held that a promise by the defendant to pay the plaintiff for a past act that was carried out at the request of the defendant could be enforced because the past act constituted good consideration. The definition of consideration in section 2(d) is sufficiently broad to encompass the rule in *Lampleigh*'s case. This is affirmed by the Supreme Court in *South East Asia Insurance Berhad v Nasir Ibrahim*[66] where Gunn Chit Tuan SCJ noted that the phrase 'has done or abstained from doing' showed that the CA 1950 recognized the principle laid down in *Lampleigh*'s case. In *South East Asia Insurance Berhad*, the appellant, at the request of the respondent, issued a performance bond to a company for a certain sum of money guaranteeing the performance of a contract by a housing developer. The performance bond was dated 9 August 1986. On 19 December 1986, the respondent executed a third party indemnity under which the respondent undertook to indemnify the appellant against all claims arising out of the guarantee. The main issue that arose was whether the third party indemnity executed by the respondent was invalid on the

[62] See s 24, Illustration (a) which was referred to by the Federal Court in *K Murugesu v Nadarajah* [1980] 2 MLJ 82, 83 as an example of promises which form the consideration for each other.

[63] [1972] 1 MLJ 35 (FC).

[64] [1951] Ch 669 (CA).

[65] (1615) Hob 105 (KB).

[66] [1992] 2 MLJ 355 (SC).

ground of past consideration because the performance bond was signed by the appellant on 9 August 1986 whereas the indemnity was signed on 19 December 1986. The Supreme Court held that the appellant, by giving the performance bond, had taken upon itself some burden or detriment. The detriment undertaken by the appellant, which was a past performance, was sufficient consideration since the act previously done was at the request of the respondent. According to the court, consideration accommodated past consideration so long as the 'desire' requirement was satisfied. Since the guarantee was given at the request of the indemnifier, the court held that the third party indemnity was valid. It follows from this that where a loan is fully disbursed prior to the execution of a guarantee, the guarantee can only be enforced if the loan is given at the desire of the guarantor.[67]

English law on past consideration has developed further as seen in *Pao On v Lau Yiu Long*[68] where the Privy Council states that a past act can be consideration for a promise if three conditions are met. First, the act must have been done at the request of the promisor. Second, it must have been understood that payment should be made for the act. Third, the payment must have been legally enforceable had it been promised in advance.[69] The second and third conditions are additional to that laid down in *Lampleigh*'s case. It is submitted that section 2(d) is sufficiently broad to encompass the three conditions in *Pao On* because the requirements are essentially linked as one complete transaction.[70] The transaction begins with a request by the promisor to the promisee to carry out the act and this is subsequently followed by a promise to pay. Indeed, in *South East Asia Insurance Berhad*, the Supreme Court stated that one should not take a strictly chronological view in deciding whether consideration was past.[71] The court also stated that it should not matter in what order the promise to pay was given where the circumstances were such that the consideration and the promise to pay were substantially one transaction.

(a) Consideration given by promisee or any other person

Under English law, consideration must move from the promisee only, although it need not move to the promisor.[72] The position is different in Malaysia because section 2(d) provides that 'the promisee or any other person has done or abstained from doing, or does or abstains from doing…' Consideration may, therefore, be given by the promisee or someone else who is not a party to the contract. This was affirmed by the Privy Council in *Kepong Prospecting Ltd v Schmidt*.[73]

(b) Sufficiency of consideration

The position in English law that consideration, though a necessary element in the formation of a contract, need not be adequate also represents the law in Malaysia.[74] Explanation 2 of section 26 states that an agreement to which the consent of the promisor is freely given is not void merely because the consideration is inadequate. However, pursuant to Explanation 2,

[67] *Hongkong and Shanghai Banking Corporation v Syarikat United Leong Enterprise Sdn Bhd & Anor* [1993] 2 MLJ 449 (HC).

[68] [1980] AC 614 (PC).

[69] E Peel, *Treitel on the Law of Contract* (13th edn, London: Sweet & Maxwell 2011) para 3-019.

[70] A Phang Boon Leong, *Cheshire, Fifoot and Furmston's Law of Contract* (2nd Singapore and Malaysia edn, Singapore: Butterworths Asia 1998) 154.

[71] [1992] 2 MLJ 355 (SC) 363.

[72] *Tweddle v Atkinson* (1861) 1 B & S 393 (QB). The impact of the case has been altered by the Contracts (Rights of Third Parties) Act 1999 (UK).

[73] [1968] 1 MLJ 170, [1968] AC 810 (PC).

[74] *Phang Swee Kim v Beh I Hock* [1964] MLJ 383 (FC).

the inadequacy of the consideration may be taken into account by the court in determining whether the consent of the promisor is freely given.

Even though consideration need not be adequate, it must be sufficient. In *Thong Guan Co (Pte) Ltd v Lam Kong Co Ltd (No 2)*,[75] it was held that so long as consideration has some value in the eyes of the law, it is sufficient and the court will not inquire into its adequacy. In *Aspac Lubricants (M) Sdn Bhd v Ketua Pengarah Hasil Dalam Negeri*,[76] the issue before the Court of Appeal was whether promotional items in the form of mugs, T-shirts, and umbrellas which were given free to the appellant's customers could constitute valid consideration in addition to the purchase price when they bought the appellant's products. The court, referring to the established English case of *Chappell & Co Ltd v Nestle Co Ltd*,[77] held that the items given free by the appellant were valid consideration even though they had little value to the appellant's customers.

In *Aspac Lubricants*, the court also stated that a practical advantage obtained by a promisor in a bargain was good consideration. This is consistent with the definition of consideration in section 2(d), which is sufficiently broad in scope to encompass any act done at the desire of the promisor, and this includes an advantage conferred on him. The court referred to, inter alia, the English Court of Appeal decision in *Williams v Roffey Bros & Nicholls (Contractors) Ltd*[78] in support of this view. For instance, X contracted with Y to have the latter refurbish 27 flats for RM 2 million. Y subsequently ran into difficulties. X was concerned about having to pay a penalty under the head contract and promised to pay Y an extra RM 100,000 to complete the work on time. Y could enforce payment of the additional RM 100,000 because X had obtained a practical advantage of timely completion and, hence, avoided any liability to pay the penalty under the head contract.

(c) *Exceptions to principle that agreements without consideration are void*

Although gratuitous promises are not enforceable, there are exceptions to this. One exception is found in section 26(a) of the CA 1950 which provides that an agreement that is made on account of natural love and affection may be enforced if it is in writing and registered under the law requiring such registration, if any. In addition, the agreement must be made between parties standing in a near relation to each other. Registration is required only if, owing to the nature of the transaction, the law imposes some form of registration as a formality. For instance, a transfer of land, whether on account of natural love and affection or otherwise, is required to be registered with the Land Registry under the National Land Code 1965.[79] Whether natural love and affection exists is determined by reference to the evidence adduced and the surrounding circumstances.[80] In the case of a mother and her son, it is presumed that natural love and affection exist, and that the transfer of land by way of gift from the mother to the son is on account of natural love and affection. Natural love and affection is presumed to exist among biological brothers.[81]

Another exception is provided in section 26(b), which is a promise to compensate a person who has voluntarily done something for the promisor. As discussed previously, section 2(d) only recognizes the validity of a past act as consideration if it was done at the desire of the promisor. However, by section 26(b), where a promise is made to compensate a person who has already voluntarily done something for the promisor, the promise can be enforced even though the past act which was voluntarily carried out would not qualify as

[75] [1998] 7 MLJ 720 (HC). [76] [2007] 6 MLJ 65 (CA). [77] [1960] AC 87 (HL).
[78] [1991] 1 QB 1 (CA Civ). [79] Act 56.
[80] *Tang Meng Hock v Tang Ming Seng* [2010] 1 MLJ 33 (CA) [18]. [81] ibid.

consideration. In *JM Wotherspoon & Co Ltd v Henry Agency House*,[82] it was held that an act done at the suggestion of another had not been done voluntarily. To constitute a voluntary act, it must be done at the person's initiative or on his own free will, impulse, or by his choice.[83]

A further exception is embodied in section 26(c), which provides that a promise to pay a debt barred by limitation law can be enforced. Pursuant to section 6(1) of the Limitation Act 1953,[84] the limitation period for debts is six years from the date the cause of action accrued. The effect of section 26(c) is that a debtor who promises in writing and signs a document to repay a loan that is barred by limitation may be sued by the creditor based on the promise although it was made without consideration.

Apart from the above, scholarship agreements may be enforced even though they lack consideration. This is provided in section 4(c) of the Contracts (Amendment) Act 1976.[85] The section only applies to scholarship agreements within the meaning of section 2 of the Act, that is, agreements between an appropriate authority and a scholar. An 'appropriate authority' is defined in section 2 to mean the Federal Government or a State Government, a statutory authority, or an approved educational institution as declared by the Minister.

Section 64 of the CA 1950 provides another exception to the principle that agreements without consideration are void. Pursuant to section 64, every promisee may dispense with or remit, wholly or in part, the performance of the promise made to him, or may extend the time for such performance, or may accept instead of it any satisfaction which he thinks fit. Section 64 is a departure from the common law in England as represented in *Pinnel's* case where it was held that payment of a smaller sum could not satisfy the obligation to pay a larger sum unless the payment was made on an earlier date than was due or was payable at a different place or was made in a different mode.[86] In the Indian case of *Chunna Mal Ram Nath v Mool Chand Bhagat*,[87] the Privy Council held that section 63 of the Indian Contract Act 1872, which is *in pari materia* with section 64 of the CA 1950, did not require any consideration for its application provided it was clear that the promisee dispensed with the performance of the promisor by a voluntary act which must be an affirmative act on his part.

(d) Promissory estoppel

Under the doctrine of promissory estoppel, if a person makes a promise that is not supported by consideration with the intention that the other person acts on it and the other person does act upon the promise, the promisor is not allowed to go back on his promise.[88] The doctrine has been applied by Malaysian judges to enforce obligations that are made without consideration. In *Sim Siok Eng v Government of Malaysia*,[89] the appellant entered into a contract for the construction of a building for the respondent. During the construction period, the appellant had difficulty obtaining building materials to complete the work. The respondent then promised to supply the appellant with construction materials for the building but after some time the supply stopped without any notice to the appellant. As a result, the appellant stopped work and his contract was terminated. The Federal Court, in applying the doctrine of estoppel enunciated by the House of Lords in *Hughes v Metropolitan*

[82] [1962] MLJ 86 (HC). [83] ibid. [84] Act 254. [85] Act A329.

[86] *Kerpa Singh v Bariam Singh* [1966] 1 MLJ 38 (FC); *Associated Pan Malaysia Cement Sdn Bhd v Syarikat Teknikal & Kejuruteraan Sdn Bhd* [1990] 3 MLJ 287 (SC).

[87] AIR 1928 PC 99. [88] *Central London Property Trust Ltd v High Trees House Ltd* [1947] KB 130.

[89] [1978] 1 MLJ 15 (FC).

Railway Co,[90] held that the appellant's obligations under the original contract were suspended until sufficient notice was given to him to enable him to resume his obligations under the original contract. For the doctrine of promissory estoppel to apply, the promise, whether express or by way of conduct, must be clear and unambiguous. Promissory estoppel is suspensory in operation in the sense that the promisor's rights are suspended and not extinguished altogether except in situations where the promisee's original position can no longer be restored. In a number of cases, Malaysian judges have taken a liberal approach when elucidating the parameters of the doctrine, mainly because the flexibility of this equitable doctrine allows fair and just results to be achieved in deserving situations. This is demonstrated in the court's approach to many aspects of the doctrine. First, although it is sometimes assumed that the doctrine of promissory estoppel only applies to contractual obligations, Lord Wilberforce in *Bank Negara Indonesia v Philip Hoalim*[91] observed that the existence of a contractual relationship is not necessary for promissory estoppel to apply. In *Philip Hoalim*'s case, the respondent, who was the appellants' monthly tenant of a room in a building under the Control of Rent Ordinance, was asked by the appellants to vacate the premises. Upon the respondent's refusal to vacate, the appellants suggested that he move to the new third floor of the building and assured him that they would not ask him to leave the premises as long as he continued to practise his profession there. With this assurance, the respondent moved to the third floor. A few years later, the appellants served him with a notice to quit. The respondent relied, inter alia, on the defence that the appellants were estopped from claiming possession of the premises based on the assurance they made to him. Lord Wilberforce noted that the rights which the appellants had against the respondent were not strictly pre-existing contractual rights but rights that came into existence upon the change in the respondent's situation which was induced by the appellants' assurances. Nevertheless, his lordship opined that the same equitable principles for governing the doctrine of promissory estoppel applied even if the relationship between the parties was non-contractual in nature.

Second, English law has closely adhered to the Court of Appeal decision in *Combe v Combe*[92] that the doctrine operates only as a defence and not as a cause of action. Hence, the phrase 'used as a shield and not as a sword' is often used to describe this aspect of the doctrine. In *Boustead Trading (1985) Sdn Bhd v Arab-Malaysian Merchant Bank Bhd*,[93] the Federal Court adopted a liberal approach to the rule laid down in *Combe*'s case and stated that the availability of the doctrine was not limited to defendants only but that plaintiffs could also have recourse to the doctrine in order to assist the main cause of action. If invoked by a plaintiff, the effect is to prevent the defendant from denying the existence of some fact essential for the plaintiff to establish the cause of action or to prevent the defendant from raising any defences to destroy the plaintiff's cause of action. Similar statements to the effect that promissory estoppel can be used as part of a cause of action but not the cause of action itself were also made in the later High Court case of *Hong Leong Leasing Sdn Bhd v Tan Kim Cheong*.[94]

Third, the Federal Court in *Boustead*'s case observed that there was no requirement that in relying on the promise, the promisee had to show that he had acted to his detriment. According to the court, it would be sufficient to show that it was unjust to permit the promisor to insist upon his strict legal rights. The court further stated that in assessing where the justice of the case should lie, the judge could take into account the conduct of the litigant

[90] (1877) 2 App Cas 439 (HL). [91] [1973] 2 MLJ 3 (PC). [92] [1951] 2 KB 215 (CA).
[93] [1995] 3 MLJ 331 (FC). [94] [1994] 1 MLJ 177 (HC).

raising the estoppel, which included whether he had altered his position, although such alteration need not be to his detriment.

Fourth, the court in *Boustead*, following the English case of *Amalgamated Investment and Property Co Ltd v Texas Commerce International Bank Ltd*,[95] stated that there was no requirement for the party invoking the doctrine of promissory estoppel to prove that he was induced by the conduct of the promisor to act in a particular way. It was sufficient if he proved that from the facts of the case, it may fairly be drawn that he was influenced by the promisor's encouragement or representation such that it would be unconscionable for the promisor thereafter to enforce his strict legal rights.

4. Intention to Create Legal Relations

For a contract to be legally enforceable, it is essential that the parties intend to enter into a legal relationship. The intention to create legal relations means that the parties intend to be legally bound, that is, to subject themselves to be legally sued and to sue. The significance of the intention to enter into a legal relationship is also underscored by the fundamental characteristic of an offer as an indication of a person's willingness to enter into a legally binding contract.

In determining whether intention exists, the court adopts an objective test.[96] The court is not concerned with the subjective intention of the parties because it is usually not possible to ascertain a person's subjective intention when bargaining for a contract. It was stated in *Floral Trends Ltd v Li Onn Floral Enterprise (M) Sdn Bhd*[97] that in the interests of fairness, certainty, and commercial convenience, the parties are deemed to have reached an agreement if, viewed objectively, they appear to have agreed. The assessment would be made in relation to a reasonable person in the position of the offeree.[98] The question for determination is whether the law will imply, from the circumstance of the case, a common intention that the agreement is to be attended with legal consequences. The court takes into account various factors including the following: the nature of the agreement, whether there was a written expression of the parties' arrangements, the language and circumstances of the agreement, and the certainty of the terms used in the agreement.[99]

The court adopts two rebuttable presumptions in determining whether intention exists. First, it is presumed that where domestic and social agreements are concerned, the parties do not have an intention to enter into legal obligations.[100] Such agreements are by their nature unsuitable for legal enforcement. Second, in commercial agreements, it is presumed that the parties intend to be legally bound.[101] This presumption is necessary to ensure certainty in commercial transactions. These are presumptions of fact which can be rebutted by evidence to the contrary.

The mere fact that the parties intend that their agreement be subject to the execution of a formal contract is not conclusive of an absence of legal intention to be bound.[102] In *Daiman*

[95] [1982] 1 QB 84.

[96] *Floral Trends Ltd v Li Onn Floral Enterprise (M) Sdn Bhd* [2006] MLJU 339 (HC).

[97] ibid.

[98] ibid. On this point, the court referred to the English cases of *Smith v Hughes* (1871) LR 6 QB 597, 607 and *Cambridge Nutrition Ltd v BBC* [1990] 3 All ER 523 (CA) 542.

[99] *Phiong Khon v Chonh Chai Fah* [1970] 2 MLJ 114 (FC).

[100] *Choo Tiong Hin & Ors v Choo Hock Swee* [1959] MLJ 67 (CA); *Tan Hung Sang v Tan Hung Khim & Anor* [2008–9] MLJU 888 (HC); *Sim Soi Lek @ Sim Kuan Hua v Sim Sui Tee & Sim Ah Boi @ Sim Kwong Wee* [2014] AMEJ 0878 (HC).

[101] *AHT Properties Sdn Bhd (Company No 460683-X) & Ors v Tan Yee Hee & Ors* [2010] MLJU 1597 (HC), citing the English case of *Edwards v Skyway Ltd* [1964] 1 WLR 349 (QB).

[102] *Ayer Hitam Tin Dredging Malaysia Bhd v YC Chin Enterprises Sdn Bhd* [1994] 2 MLJ 754 (SC).

Development Sdn Bhd v Mathew Lui Chin Teck & Anor,[103] the court held that where the intention of the parties was clearly established, a binding contract may exist even though the parties agreed to execute a formal document subsequently.

5. Capacity

A party to a contract must have the capacity to enter into the contract. This is provided in section 10(1) which states that parties must be competent to contract.[104] Pursuant to section 11, every person is competent to contract if he is of the age of majority according to the law to which he is subject, is of sound mind, and is not disqualified from contracting by any law to which he is subject. In *Heng Poh Glass Sdn Bhd v Chong Lan Moy & Anor*,[105] it was held that a bankrupt is a competent person to enter into contracts despite his bankruptcy. If any of these requirements is not met, the person is not competent to enter into a contract. However, where minors are concerned, exceptions to the general rule that they are not competent to contract exist, as discussed below.[106] Even though by the wording of section 11, all the three requirements are to be met conjunctively, section 1(2) of the CA 1950 makes it clear that the Act shall not affect any written law or any usage or custom of trade. Accordingly, exceptions to section 11, that have been created either by the legislature or the court, do not contravene the provision.

Prior to the enactment of the Age of Majority Act 1971, the age of majority was either 18 or 21 years depending on whether the individual was a Muslim or non-Muslim. But, with the passing of the Age of Majority Act 1971, which consolidated the law relating to the age of majority, section 2 provides for a uniform age of majority that is applicable throughout the Federation, which is 18 years old.

(a) Effect of agreement by incompetent person

The CA 1950 is silent on the effect of an agreement entered into by an incompetent person. Although it has been said that this is an obvious lacuna in the Act,[107] it is now settled law that agreements entered into by minors are void. In the Indian case of *Mohori Bibee v Dharmodas Ghose*,[108] the Privy Council considered both sections 10 and 11 of the Indian Contract Act 1872 (which are *in pari materia* with sections 10 and 11 of the CA 1950) and held that both sections made it essential that all contracting parties should be competent to contract. According to the Privy Council, any contract in which a minor is a party is void. The case, along with its reasoning, has been followed in Malaysia in cases such as the Federal Court decision in *Leha binti Jusoh v Awang Johari bin Hashim*[109] and the High Court decision in *Government of Malaysia v Gurcharan Singh & Ors.*[110]

Pursuant to section 11, a person who enters into a contract must be of sound mind. Section 12(1) provides that a person is of sound mind for the purpose of making a contract if, at the time when he makes it, he is capable of understanding it and of forming a rational judgment as to its effect upon his interests. Currently, the law in Malaysia is not settled as to the consequence of an agreement entered into by a person of unsound mind. Some judges have followed English law on this point in holding that agreements entered into by a person of unsound mind are voidable at his option provided two conditions are satisfied. First, the person of unsound mind was not capable of understanding his actions at the time of

[103] [1981] 1 MLJ 56 (PC).
[104] See n 9 for text of s 10(1).
[105] [2014] 9 MLJ 628 (HC).
[106] See section II.5(b).
[107] *Ng Mei Kheng v JB Securities Sdn Bhd* [1998] MLJU 75 (HC).
[108] (1902–3) LR 30 IA 114 (PC).
[109] [1978] 1 MLJ 202 (FC).
[110] [1971] 1 MLJ 211 (HC).

making the contract. Second, the party with whom he was contracting was aware of his condition. Such cases include *Chemsource (M) Sdn Bhd v Udanis bin Mohammad Nor*[111] and *Asia Commercial Finance (M) Bhd v Yap Bee Lee.*[112] On the other hand, in *Sim Kon San Peter (administrator of the estate of Chong Yu Tai, decd) v Datin Shim Tok Keng,*[113] the court took the view that since section 11 covered not only cases relating to the age of majority but also cases of unsoundness of mind, an agreement made by a person of unsound mind is void and not merely voidable. It is submitted that the latter view is to be preferred for two reasons. First, if a person is of unsound mind, he is not competent to contract and any agreement entered into with him is thus void. There is no room to introduce the concept of voidable contract, as suggested by the first view. Second, subsections (2) and (3) of section 12 amply provide for the situation where a person is sometimes of unsound mind and, therefore, there does not appear to be any need to judicially introduce additional conditions in this context. Pursuant to section 12(2), a person who is usually of unsound mind, but occasionally of sound mind, may make a contract when he is of sound mind. Section 12(3) provides that a person who is usually of sound mind, but occasionally of unsound mind, may not make a contract when he is of unsound mind.

(b) Exceptions to the principle in Mohori Bibee

There are exceptions to the rule that agreements entered into by minors are void. In *Rajeswary & Anor v Balakrishnan & Ors,*[114] it was held that a contract of marriage by a minor is valid and does not fall within the *Mohori Bibee* principle which concerned a business contract. Hence, a minor can sue or be sued for a breach of promise to marry. According to Good J, serious consequences might result if the common law position in *Mohori Bibee* was applied to marriage contracts. The court stated that it was the common practice and custom of some communities in Malaysia to arrange marriages between children who were under-age. Since it could not have been the intention of the Indian legislature, when enacting sections 10 and 11 of the Indian Contract Act 1872 that the sections would have any application to marriage contracts, the same reasoning would apply in Malaysia when Parliament enacted the corresponding provisions of the CA 1950. However, in the light of social developments that have taken place in Malaysia since the *Rajeswary* case, it is doubtful whether the reasoning in the case remains valid today. Although a contract to marry can validly be entered into by a minor, the solemnization of the marriage can only take place after the parties attain 18 years of age. This is provided in section 10 of the Law Reform (Marriage and Divorce) Act 1976 which provides that any marriage purported to be solemnized in Malaysia shall be void if, at the date of the marriage, either party is under the age of 18 years.[115]

Another exception concerns scholarship agreements. Pursuant to section 4 of the Contracts (Amendment) Act 1976, no scholarship agreement shall be invalidated on the ground that the scholar entering into such an agreement is not of the age of majority. The scholarship agreements that fall within the ambit of this Act are mentioned in section II.3(c).

Employment contracts under the Children and Young Persons (Employment) Act 1966[116] are valid even though they involve minors. Section 13 of the Act provides that any

[111] [2002] 6 MLJ 273 (HC). [112] [1991] 1 CLJ 271 (HC). [113] [1994] 2 MLJ 517 (HC).

[114] (1958) 3 MC 178.

[115] In the case of a female party, a licence authorizing the solemnization of the marriage may be granted by the Chief Minister under s 21(2), Law Reform (Marriage and Divorce) Act 1976 (Act 164).

[116] Act 350.

child or young person shall be competent to enter into a contract of service, although he cannot be an employer. Under the Act, a 'child' means any person who has not completed his 14th year of age or who is of such age as the Yang di-Pertuan Agong may by notification in the Gazette prescribe; a 'young person' means any person who, not being a child, has not completed his 16th year of age. While allowing minors to enter into employment contracts, the Act extends a certain level of protection to minors. According to section 13, a minor may sue as plaintiff to enforce the contract without his next friend or defend any action without a guardian *ad litem*. The section further provides that no damages or indemnity shall be recoverable from a minor even though he terminated his contract of employment without notice. In the usual case of employment contracts with adults, section 12 of the Employment Act 1955[117] requires a notice in writing of a certain duration to be given to the affected party or, as provided in section 13, an indemnity in lieu of notice to be paid.

Insurance contracts entered into by minors are an exception to the principle in *Mohori Bibee*. Pursuant to section 128, Schedule 8, paragraph 4(1) of the Financial Services Act 2013,[118] a minor who has attained the age of ten years but has not attained the age of 16 years may, with the consent in writing of his parent or guardian, effect a life policy upon his own life or upon another life in which he has an insurable interest. Paragraph 4(2) states that a minor who has attained the age of 16 years may effect a life policy without written consent from his parent or guardian.

(c) Agreements for supply of necessaries

Where an agreement for the supply of necessaries is entered into by an individual who is incapable of entering into a contract, section 69 of the CA 1950 provides that the person supplying the necessaries is entitled to be reimbursed from the property of such incapable person. The section applies even if the agreement is for the supply of necessaries not to the incapable person himself but to anyone whom the incapable person is legally bound to support. Except for the express requirement in section 69 that the necessaries supplied must be suited to the incapable person's condition in life, the CA 1950 is silent on the meaning of necessaries. In *Government of Malaysia v Gurcharan Singh*,[119] the High Court cited passages from, inter alia, the English decisions of *Roberts v Gray*[120] and *Nash v Inman*[121] when determining the scope of necessaries under section 69. In *Gurcharan Singh*'s case, the Government of Malaysia sued the first defendant for breach of an agreement for training at the Malayan Teachers' Training Institution. The first defendant was alleged to have breached his agreement to serve the government as a teacher for five years after his training. The court held that the scholarship agreement was void[122] as it was entered into during the first defendant's minority but proceeded to consider whether education and training qualified as necessaries under section 69. The court held that the term 'necessaries' must be construed broadly and regard must be given to the facts of each case, the conditions and circumstances in which the supply was made, and the purpose which is served. It was argued by the defendant that the notion of necessaries applied only to the provision of goods, articles, and other services but did not extend to education. This argument was dismissed by the judge who held that the provision of professional or vocational training was a provision for necessaries.

[117] Act 265. [118] Act 758. [119] [1971] MLJ 211 (HC). [120] [1913] 1 KB 520 (CA).
[121] [1908] 2 KB 1 (CA).
[122] With the enactment of the Contracts (Amendment) Act 1976 (Act A329), such agreements would be valid under s 4 of the Act.

(d) False representation by minors as to age

The law's protection of minors against their immaturity and inexperience in the course of entering into agreements extends to the situation where a minor falsely represents that he is of full age. In *Natesan v Thanaletcumi & Anor*,[123] it was held that a minor who misrepresents his age is not estopped from pleading his minority. Again, the Privy Council in *Mahomed Syedol Ariffin v Yeoh Ooi Gark*,[124] which was an appeal from Penang, held that a minor who induced an adult to lend him money by falsely representing that he was of full age could not be estopped from pleading his minority and avoiding the agreement he signed.

III. Exceptions to Rule That No Formality is Required for Contract Formation

While the general rule is that there is no requirement for any formality in the form of writing or signature when making a contract, there are several exceptions which are imposed by statutes. Some instances of statutes which impose formality requirements for contract formation are as follows: pursuant to section 26(a) of the CA 1950, an agreement which is made without consideration is enforceable if it is expressed in writing, registered under the law (if any), and made on account of natural love and affection between parties standing in a near relation to each other.[125] Also, section 26(c) provides that a promise made in writing and signed by a person to pay a debt which is barred by the law of limitation is enforceable even though consideration is absent. Apart from the CA 1950, section 4A(1) of the Hire-Purchase Act 1967[126] states that a hire-purchase agreement in respect of goods specified in the First Schedule shall be in writing, failing which the agreement is void. Under section 16 of the Moneylenders Act 1951,[127] no moneylending agreement shall be enforceable unless the agreement has been signed by all the parties to the agreement and a copy of the agreement has been duly stamped or delivered to the borrower by the moneylender before the money is lent. In respect of land dealings, the National Land Code 1965 requires contracts for sale of land, grant of leases exceeding three years in duration, and grant of easements[128] to be carried out by prescribed registered instruments and registered with the Land Registry. Bills of sale are required by section 4(1) of the Bills of Sale Act 1950[129] to be attested and registered under the Act within seven days after their execution failing which they shall be void. Pursuant to section 27(3) of the Copyright Act 1987,[130] no assignment of copyright and no licence to do an act the doing of which is controlled by copyright shall have effect unless it is in writing. Under section 39(3) of the Patents Act 1983,[131] no assignment of a patent application or patent shall be recorded in the Register of Patents unless it is in writing and signed by or on behalf of the contracting parties. If the assignment of a patent application or patent is not recorded in the register, section 39(4) states that the assignment shall not have any effect against third parties.

IV. No Duty on Parties to Negotiate in Good Faith

In negotiating for a contract, the general rule is that there is no obligation on the part of the parties to negotiate in good faith. There are some exceptions to this general principle such

[123] [1952] 1 MLJ 1 (HC). [124] [1916] 2 AC 575 (PC). [125] See n 11 for text of s 26(a), CA 1950.
[126] Act 212. [127] Act 400.
[128] s 282(1), National Land Code 1965 (Act 56) states that an 'easement' means any right granted by one proprietor to another, in his capacity as such and for the beneficial enjoyment of his land.
[129] Act 268. [130] Act 332. [131] Act 291.

as the negotiation of insurance contracts[132] and contracts between a director and his company.[133] In the 2014 Court of Appeal decision in *Aseambankers Malaysia Bhd & Ors v Shencourt Sdn Bhd & Anor*,[134] it was held that an obligation of good faith could not be interposed in a borrower–lender relationship because the transactions contained very detailed and precise terms. According to the court, the banking industry was best guided when disputes between parties could be resolved by reference to the actual written terms in the contract documents without interposing them with an overarching and uncertain perceived equitable obligation of good faith. The case concerned the issue of good faith performance in administering a syndicated loan but the court stated, obiter, that in the context of whether there existed a duty to negotiate in good faith, the English case of *Walford v Miles*[135] applied. In *Walford*'s case, it was held that the concept of a duty to carry on negotiations in good faith was unworkable in practice and inherently repugnant to the adversarial position of the parties when involved in negotiations.

Although there is no duty placed on the parties to negotiate in good faith, the Consumer Protection (Amendment) Act 2010,[136] which inserted Part IIIA into the Consumer Protection Act 1999[137] ('CPA 1999'), was enacted to regulate standard form contracts and consumer contracts by ensuring that they do not contain unfair terms. Pursuant to section 3 of the CPA 1999, a consumer contract is one in which the consumer acquires goods or services for personal, domestic, or household purposes or consumption. This is in contrast to commercial contracts where the consumer acquires the goods or services for trade, manufacturing, or other commercial purposes. For standard form contracts and consumer contracts, Part IIIA, entitled 'Unfair Contract Terms' and encompassing sections 24A to 24J, introduced the notions of procedural and substantive unfairness. Under section 24G(1), a court or the Tribunal for Consumer Claims may declare unenforceable or void a term that is either procedurally or substantively unfair or both. Part IIIA does not alter the general principles of contract formation but is concerned with the protection of consumers from unfair contract terms, particularly those that may be found in standard form contracts. Procedural unfairness refers to the unfairness that occurs at the stage when the parties are in the negotiation process. Pursuant to section 24C(1) of the parent Act, a contract is procedurally unfair if it has resulted in 'an unjust advantage to the supplier or unjust disadvantage to the consumer on account of the conduct of the supplier or the manner in which or circumstances under which the contract has been entered into'. The circumstances that may be taken into account to determine whether procedural unfairness exists are stated in section 24C(2) and these include the following: the knowledge and understanding of the consumer in relation to the meaning of the terms of the contract, the bargaining strength of the parties, the reasonable standards of fair dealing, the opportunity for negotiation with regard to the terms of the contract prior to its formation, the legibility of the expressions contained in the contract and the ease of understanding the expressions, the ability of the consumer to protect his own interests or appreciate adequately the terms of the contract by reasons of matters such as age, sickness, mental or linguistic disability, and the opportunity to obtain independent legal or expert advice. Substantive unfairness, which is dealt with in section 24D(1), refers to a term of the contract which is harsh, oppressive, unconscionable, excludes or restricts liability for negligence, or excludes or restricts liability for breach of a term of the contract without adequate justification.

[132] Pt 2 of Sch 9, s 4 of the Financial Services Act 2013 (Act 758) requires both parties to a contract of insurance to disclose honestly and truthfully all that they know to be material to the acceptance or rejection of the application.

[133] s 131, Companies Act 1965 (Act 125) requires a director who is interested in a contract or proposed contract with the company to disclose the nature and extent of any direct or indirect interest in the contract.

[134] [2014] 4 MLJ 619 (CA). [135] [1992] 2 AC 128 (HL). [136] Act A1381. [137] Act 599.

V. Contracts Concluded Through Electronic Means

Contracts which are concluded through electronic means are valid under the Electronic Commerce Act 2006.[138] The Act, which is based on the UNCITRAL Model Law on Electronic Commerce (1996),[139] provides for the legal recognition of electronic messages in commercial transactions in order to facilitate e-commerce. Section 6(1) states that any information shall not be denied legal effect, validity, or enforceability on the ground that it is wholly or partly in an electronic form. Further, section 7(1) provides that in the formation of a contract, the communication and acceptance of proposals as well as their revocation may be expressed by an electronic message. The validity of contracts entered into via electronic means is reiterated in section 7(2) which stipulates that a contract shall not be denied legal effect, validity, or enforceability on the ground that an electronic message is used in its formation.

The Act applies to all electronic messages which are generated, sent, received, or stored by electronic means.[140] In turn, the word 'electronic' is defined broadly in section 5 as 'the technology of utilizing electrical, optical, magnetic, electromagnetic, biometric, photonic or other similar technology'. The Act does not alter the rules on the formation of contract provided in the CA 1950, and those rules apply with equal force to electronic contracts.

In electronic contracts, the notions of 'writing' and 'signature', which are familiar in the paper-based world, have to be redefined in the electronic world. To this end, section 8 of the Electronic Commerce Act 2006 provides that where any law requires information to be in writing, the requirement is fulfilled if the information is contained in an electronic message that is accessible and intelligible so as to be usable for subsequent reference.

In the case of 'signature' of the parties or witnesses, section 9 clarifies that an electronic signature is sufficient to meet the requirement of the law provided the conditions spelt out in the section are met. The phrase 'electronic signature' is defined in section 5 to mean any letter, character, number, sound, or any other symbol, or any combination thereof created in an electronic form adopted by a person as a signature. Where digital signatures are used as electronic signatures in commercial transactions, the legality of the signatures is governed by the Digital Signature Act 1997.[141] Section 2 of the Act defines a 'digital signature' as:

> a transformation of a message using an asymmetric cryptosystem such that a person having the initial message and the signer's public key can accurately determine whether the transformation was created using the private key that corresponds to the signer's public key; and whether the message has been altered since the transformation was made.

VI. Conclusion

This chapter has provided a summary of the law on contract formation in Malaysia. While there are Malaysian judges who have approached the question of whether a contract is formed through an analysis of the existence of offer, acceptance, consideration, intention to create legal relations, and capacity, other judges prefer to adopt a more holistic approach by assessing whether a reasonable person in the circumstances of the case would conclude that a contract exists. It seems clear that regardless of the approach adopted, the purpose is to

[138] Act 658.

[139] See <http://www.uncitral.org/uncitral/en/uncitral_texts/electronic_commerce/1996Model.html> accessed 20 June 2016.

[140] Electronic Commerce Act 2006 (Act 658), s 5.

[141] Act 562.

determine whether the parties, by their negotiations, intended to enter into a legally binding relationship with each other; and this is ultimately an objective assessment.

Malaysia has the benefit of a contract statute which contains provisions dealing with fundamental principles of contract formation. Principles of communication and revocation of offer and acceptance are provided in the CA 1950. Similarly, the notion of consideration and capacity are dealt with by the Act. Perhaps for this reason, Malaysian judges have thus far managed to resolve issues on contract formation and the creation of contractual responsibility in Malaysia generally in an uncontroversial manner. This stability is further boosted by sections 3 and 5 of the Civil Law Act 1956[142] which provide for the reception of English law prior to specified cut-off dates. Instances of this may be seen in the similarities with English law in the concepts of an invitation to treat, communication of acceptance in instantaneous communications, intention to create a legal relationship, and the absence of the need for any party to negotiate in good faith. As a result of the close similarities between the CA 1950 and the Indian Contract Act 1872, Malaysian judges are also receptive to decisions of Indian courts and are willing to be persuaded by the rationale underlying those decisions. A clear example is the adoption in Malaysia of the decision in the Indian case of *Mohori Bibee*[143] which held that agreements entered into with minors are void. This again provides support to Malaysian courts to achieve a relatively clear and stable structure of the law on contract formation. Given that the CA 1950 was enacted in the days prior to the advent of electronic communications, the formation of electronic contracts is specifically given legal recognition by the Electronic Commerce Act 2006.[144]

[142] Act 67. [143] (1902–3) LR 30 IA 114 (PC). [144] Act 658.

7

Contracts for the Benefit of Third Parties in Malaysia

*David FUNG**

Privity of contract is a doctrine that is regarded as fundamental and is well entrenched in Malaysia. Only persons who are parties to the contract can sue and be sued in contract. Third parties who have been conferred a benefit under a contract cannot institute a contractual action to enforce the benefit. Third parties who are strangers to the contract similarly cannot have burdens imposed upon them by a contract. There is no statute of general application to vest in a third party a legal right intended under a contract for him if he is not a party to the contract. However, the Malaysian courts have depended on principles of common law and equity emanating from other areas of law to avoid the undesirable consequence of a doctrine that is implicit on a view of contract as essentially a legally enforceable promise between the parties to the bargain. This 'classic' model of contract was inherited from English common law, a legacy of Malaysia's colonial past.

This chapter looks at third parties' rights within the rubric of the privity rule as it is and as it might be adjudged in Malaysia. How well or poorly Malaysian law has fared will invariably be considered in this chapter against a backdrop where every Asian country represented in this volume, save for India and China, has a regime of law that allows for, or vests, a right in a third party to claim for a contractual benefit as intended by the contracting parties.

I. Privity of Contract in Malaysia

The doctrine of privity of contract, as understood by English judges in the last century, was pronounced as governing Malaysian contract law. Lord Wilberforce in the Privy Council decision of an appeal originating from Malaysia, *Kepong Prospecting Ltd v Schmidt*,[1] remarked:

> Their Lordships need, on this point, do no more than state their agreement with the judgment of the Federal Court which correctly stated the law from well-known passages in the opinions of the House of Lords in *Dunlop Pneumatic Tyre Co Ltd v Selfridge & Co Ltd* [1915] AC 847 at p 853 and *Scruttons Ltd v Midland Silicones Ltd* [1962] AC 446 at p 468. But it was suggested that in this respect the law of Malaysia differed from the law of England in admitting the principle of *jus quaesitum tertio*. Their Lordships are of opinion that the appellant company failed to make good this contention. Their Lordships were not referred to any statutory provision by virtue of which it could be said that the Malaysian law as to contracts differs in so important a respect

* Cite as D Fung, 'Contracts for the Benefit of Third Parties in Malaysia' in Chen-Wishart, Loke, & Vogenauer, *Studies in the Contract Laws of Asia Vol II: Formation and Third Party Beneficiaries* (Oxford: OUP 2017) ch 7. I am most grateful to Professor Alexander Loke, an editor of this work, for his detailed and perceptive comments which have benefited me immensely and saved me from certain errors, but responsibility for this chapter remains solely mine.

[1] [1968] 1 MLJ 170, 174, [1968] AC 810 (PC) 825–826.

> from English law. It is true that section 2(d) of the Contracts (Malay States) Ordinance gives a wider definition of 'consideration' than that which applies in England particularly in that it enables consideration to move from another person than the promisee, but the appellant was unable to show how this affected the law as to enforcement of contracts by third parties, and it was not possible to point to any other provision having this effect. On the contrary paragraphs (a), (b), (c) and (e) support the English conception of a contract as an agreement on which only the parties to it can sue.

In *Kepong Prospecting*, Mr Schmidt rendered services to Mr Tan in obtaining mining permits from the state government to extract iron ore. A company Kepong Prospecting Ltd was formed to take over the extraction of the iron ore from the mines. In 1954, Kepong and Tan initially agreed that Schmidt would be paid 1 per cent of the value of the iron ore extracted and sold from the mines. An agreement in 1955 between Kepong and Schmidt 'supplemented' the earlier agreement and stipulated that Kepong would pay the 1 per cent of the value of ore extracted. The privity rule disallowed any claim by Schmidt against Kepong under the 1954 agreement.

One might be forgiven for thinking that the Privy Council's judgment that the privity rule is applicable to contract law in Malaysia is unhelpfully curt. This was especially so, since section 2(d) permits consideration for the promise to be supplied by a third party besides the promisee, Indian authorities on the same section gave opposing views as to the applicability of the privity rule, and there is also no statutory provision to say that the English privity rule shall apply. Despite its conciseness, the judgment delivered by Lord Wilberforce reveals that the privity rule was applied by complying with the basic theoretical assumptions that underpinned the understanding of contract law in England at that time and which the statutory provisions do not dispel but coalesce.

Lord Wilberforce stated that it is for the party wanting to show that the third party has a right to a contractual claim for a benefit under the contract—*a jus quaesitum tertio*—to show that there is a statutory provision in the contract statute to admit such a principle since it differs fundamentally from English law. The unstated assumption is that the principles of contract law as developed by English common law are still the law applicable to the contract unless express provisions of the Malaysian Contracts Act 1950 state otherwise. This is by and large the 'default' premise in contract dispute resolutions in Malaysia. In *Ooi Boon Leong v Citibank NA*,[2] Lord Brightman for the Privy Council stated that the freedom of contract, as the principle is known in English law, cannot be curtailed by the general wording in section 1(2) of the Contracts Act 1950,[3] and express clear statutory provisions are required to do so.[4]

The language of subsections (b), (c), (d), (e), and (h) of section 2[5] affirms the English conception of contract. The unconditional acceptance of a proposal, an offer as it is commonly called, constitutes a promise between the promisor and promisee. A promise

[2] [1984] 1 MLJ 222 (PC) 226. Their lordships' reasoning here was consistent with and supported by the Privy Council's earlier judgment in the Indian appeal on the same section under the Indian Contract Act 1872 in *Irrawady Flotilla Co v Bugwandass* (1890) 18 IA 121 (PC).

[3] (Rev 1974) Act 136.

[4] s 1(2) reads:

> Nothing herein contained shall affect any written law or usage or custom of trade, or any incident of any contract, not inconsistent with this Act.

[5] s (2)(b), (c), (d), (e), and (h) read:

> (b) when the person to whom the proposal is made signifies his assent thereto, the proposal is said to be accepted: a proposal, when accepted, becomes a promise;
> (c) the person making the proposal is called the 'promisor' and the person accepting the proposal is called the 'promisee';

supported by consideration is an agreement enforceable by law: a contract. As the promise or agreement is between the promisor and promisee, only they *being privy to the promise* can enforce it.

The element of consideration is distinct from the privity rule and in this sense privity is primal to it. The consideration for the promise, which subsection (d) defines, is that which clothes the promise with legal enforceability provided that the other element developed by the common law, intention to contract, which is also not stipulated in the statute, is satisfied. It follows that though consideration for the promise could move from a third party under Malaysian law, this difference does not obviate the more primal privity rule.[6]

The privity rule eventually came to be considered by Malaysia's highest court, the Federal Court,[7] in *Badiaddin bin Mohd Mahidin v Arab Malaysian Finance Bhd*.[8] This case witnessed an extraordinary procession of multiple judicial proceedings and pronouncements through the superior courts over a relatively straightforward transaction involving a third party charge over titled lands reserved only for Malays to a financial institution in giving a loan to a borrower. In its final rendition before the Federal Court, after the court confirmed that such a charge was unlawful since such dealings were prohibited by law, the issue arose as to whether the financial institution could obtain restitution of the loan to the borrower after the third party charge agreement was found to be illegal and unenforceable. The loan advanced by the financial institution was obviously a benefit to the borrower, but the financial institution wanted restitution from the third party chargor in the wake of the discharge

(d) when, at the desire of the promisor, the promisee or any other person has done or abstained from doing, or does or abstains from doing, or promises to do or to abstain from doing, something, such act or abstinence or promise is called a consideration for the promise;

(e) every promise and every set of promises, forming the consideration for each other, is an agreement;

...

(h) an agreement enforceable by law is a contract;

[6] It is against the background of this strict conception of the 'classic' contract as fundamentally a promise between parties privy to it that critics have accused the UK Law Commission of reforming the privity rule, without taking into account the apparent distortion to its fundamental conception. See P Kincaid, 'The UK Law Commission's Privity Proposals and Contract Theory' (1994) 8 JCL 51, 54–55.

[7] The Malaysian hierarchy of superior courts comprises the High Court, the Court of Appeal (an intermediate appellate court since 24 June 1996), and the Federal Court (a final court of appeal much like the UK Supreme Court).

[8] [1998] 1 MLJ 393 (FC). The other reported Malaysian cases which followed *Kepong* in applying the privity rule are as follows: *Fima Palmbulk Services Sdn Bhd v Suruhjaya Pelabuhan Pulau Pinang* [1988] 1 MLJ 269 (HC); *Oversea-Chinese Banking Corp Ltd v Woo Hing Brothers (M) Sdn Bhd* [1992] 2 MLJ 86 (HC); *Punca Klasik Sdn Bhd v All persons in occupation of the wooden house erected on a portion of land held under Grant No 26977 for Lot 4271 in the Township of Johor Bahru, Johor* [1996] 5 MLJ 92 (HC); *Golden Court Hotel Sdn Bhd v Pejabat Pemegang Harta Malaysia* [1995] 4 MLJ 708 (HC); *Punca Klasik Sdn Bhd v Foh Chong & Sons Sdn Bhd* [1998]1 CLJ 601 (HC); *Phua Siong Hoe v RHB Bank Bhd* [2001] 6 CLJ 326 (HC); *TSC Education Sdn Bhd v Kolej Yayasan Pelajaran Mara* [2002] 2 CLJ 581(HC); *Bel Realty Sdn Bhd v Kumpulan Lanjut Budi (M) Sdn Bhd* [2004] 8 CLJ 34 (HC); *Low Lain Koon v Meng Fong Realty Sdn Bhd* [2004] 8 CLJ 391 (HC); *Hospital Pantai Keroh Sdn Bhd v Lu Wei Hong* [2005] 4 MLJ 153 (HC); *Mok Yong Chuan v Mok Yong Kong* [2006] 7 MLJ 526 (HC); *Law Kam Loy v Boltex Sdn Bhd* [2005] 3 CLJ 355 (CA); *Brilliant Team Management Sdn Bhd v South East Pahang Oil Palm Sdn Bhd* [2006] 2 CLJ 1218 (HC); *Seremban Golf Resort Bhd v Amerfab Sdn Bhd* [2006] 5 CLJ 114 (HC); *KM Quarry Sdn Bhd v Ho Hup Construction Co Bhd* [2006] 7 MLJ 203 (HC); *Sulisen Sdn Bhd v Kerajaan Malaysia* [2006] 7 CLJ 247 (HC); *Amer Singh Bhatt v Kelana Resorts Sdn Bhd* [2007] 4 CLJ 557 (HC); *Suwira Sdn Bhd v Government of the State of Sabah* [2008] 1 CLJ 123 (FC); *Tropical Profile Sdn Bhd v Kerajaan Malaysia Jabatan Kerja Raya Malaysia* [2008] 1 CLJ 513 (HC); *Razshah Enterprise Sdn Bhd v Arab Malaysian Finance Bhd* [2009] 2 MLJ 102 (CA); *Ngan & Ngan Holdings Sdn Bhd v Central Mercantile Corporation (M) Sdn Bhd* [2010] 3 CLJ 818 (CA); *Koey Sher Ling v Sanctuary Management Corporation Sdn Bhd* [2012] 1 CLJ 249 (HC); *Tsang Yee Kwan v Majlis Perbandaran Batu Pahat* [2011] 8 CLJ 913 (CA); *Bacom Enterprises Sdn Bhd v Jong Chuk* [2011] 5 MLJ 820 (CA); *Tg Choong Yuan Sdn Bhd v Yeap Geok Kee Sdn Bhd* [2012] 6 CLJ 786 (HC); *Ong Siew Keet v Wan Ariff Wan Hamzah* [2012] 5 CLJ 404 (CA); *Boustead Naval Shipyard Sdn Bhd v DynaForce Corporation Sdn Bhd* [2015] 1 MLJ 284 (CA); *Kapten Lam Chee Keong v Malaysian Airline System Bhd* [2015] 4 CLJ 1089 (HC); *Aneka Melor Sdn Bhd v Seri Sabco (M) Sdn Bhd* [2016] 2 CLJ 563 (CA).

of the unlawful charge agreement, and in support of its claim relied on section 66 of the Contracts Act 1950.[9]

The financial institution argued that 'any person' appearing in section 66 could include persons who received a benefit or advantage but were not parties to the void contract. It relied on two Indian authorities on an identical section 65 of the Indian Contract Act 1872, *Giraj Baksh v Kazi Hamid Ali*[10] and *Devi Prasad v Mehdi Hasan*.[11] It was noted by his lordship Gopal Sri Ram that those authorities relied on reasoning from section 2(d) of the Indian Contract Act that since consideration can be supplied not only by the promisee but 'any other person', that has the effect of abolishing the doctrine of privity of contract and would apply to section 65 of the Indian Contract Act. However, in Malaysia, *Kepong* has conclusively ruled that section 2(d) does not abolish the privity rule. The Federal Court observed that the third party chargor was not a party to the loan agreement under which the benefit passed to the borrower from the financial institution. As for the charge contract, no benefit passed from the financial institution either, but the chargor suffered a detriment as his land was put at risk. Gopal Sri Ram JCA (as he then was) said: [12]

> *Kepong Prospecting* is therefore authority for the proposition that the words 'or any other person' appearing in s 2(d) of the Contracts Act 1950 are not to be wide enough to exclude the doctrine of privity of contract. It follows, by parallel reasoning, that the identical words used by s 66 do not include persons who are not parties to a contract under which a benefit passed. In my judgment, there is no justification, in principle or policy, to extend the terms of the action by means of an interpretation that runs counter to settled jurisprudence. It follows that *only the parties to a contract may claim or become liable to make restitution under that section.* Any other construction would produce an anomaly because, while only parties to a contract may sue upon it, yet, when the very same contract is discovered to be void, anyone, including persons who cannot enforce it may recover any benefit received by one of the parties thereto.

This analysis is correct, for the restitution claim following discharge of the illegal contract would have to be from the contract party at whose expense the benefit was conferred on the other contract party. The two Indian cases were rightly not followed. The judgment has rightly interpreted the ambit of section 66 as only applicable to a relationship of contract parties following discharge of their contract which has become void.

All agree that it was only after the House of Lords' decision in *Tweddle v Atkinson*[13] that English law came down on the side that did not recognize *jus quaesitum tertio*.[14] A third party cannot sue on a contract made for his benefit. The literature on what exactly the doctrine of privity of contract entails ambles between two views. The first view is that there are two rules that prevent the third party from suing on the contract made for his benefit: the third party did not supply any consideration to the bargain; and the third party is not a party to the contract.[15] The second view is that the two rules are actually one rule: the third party is a stranger to the consideration, as he did not supply the consideration.[16]

[9] s 66 reads:

> When an agreement was discovered to be void, or when a contract becomes void, any person who has received any advantage under the agreement or contract is bound to restore it, or make compensation for it, to the person from whom he received it.

[10] (1886) ILP 9 All 340 (HC).
[11] AIR 1940 Pat 81 (HC).
[12] [1998] 1 MLJ 393 (FC) 431 (emphasis added).
[13] (1861) 1 B & S 393 (QB).
[14] *Scruttons Ltd v Midland Silicones Ltd* [1962] AC 446 (HL) 473 (Lord Reid); A Phang Boon Leong, *Cheshire, Fifoot and Furmston's Law of Contract* (2nd Singapore and Malaysian edn, Singapore: Butterworths Asia 1998) 775.
[15] *Dunlop Pneumatic Tyre Co Ltd v Selfridge & Co Ltd* [1915] AC 847 (HL) 853 (Viscount Haldane LC).
[16] See the discussion in Windeyer J's judgment in *Coulls v Bagot's Executor & Trustee Co Ltd* (1967) 119 CLR 460 (HC Aus) 494.

Malaysian contract law simply takes the doctrine of privity as stating that a party who is not a party to the contract cannot sue or be sued on it.[17] Section 2(d) of the Contracts Act 1950 recognizes that the consideration can move from another person besides the promisee, and so could be supplied by a third party. This is a wider definition of consideration than that allowed under English common law. In Malaysia, if the relationship of promisor and promisee is established then the promise, clothed with consideration from a third party, can constitute a contract. A promises B that he will clean B's car if C pays him RM 50. C pays A the money but A does not clean B's car. B can enforce the promise against A. The privity of contract is between A (promisor) and B (promisee); C (third party) is outside that relationship but supplies the consideration for A's promise, since the consideration need not be supplied by the promisee but by 'any other person'. The promise is not *nudum pactum* and is enforceable as a contract by the promisee.[18] In India, which shares the same section 2(d), the court in *Samuel Pillai v Ananthanatha Pillai*[19] allowed a creditor to claim on a promissory note against an heir for a proportionate part of a debt owed by the estate since the administratrix had permitted the heir to have his full share of the estate without paying his portion of the debt in exchange for his promissory note.

In our example, if C does not pay the RM 50, the privity rule does not prevent B from attempting to enforce the promise against A. But the privity rule will prevent B from enforcing the promise against C who *did not promise B* that he would clean the car. Let us assume slightly different facts. At the time when A promises B that he will clean B's car if C pays him RM 50, C also accepted the promise but later declined to pay A. The privity rule as applied in Malaysia should in principle allow B to enforce the promise against C because the promise was supported by consideration that moved from A. C's acceptance of A's promise to B meant that C's promise to pay A was made jointly to A and B. Therefore, B can also claim against C but will face the separate argument that he suffered no real loss. In this way, a burden is imposed on C. Under English law, B, a party to the promise but who has not given consideration, will not be able to enforce the promise.

Now let us assume the facts were that A promises B that he will clean *C's car* if B pays him RM 50. C, a third party and not the promisee and who is conferred a benefit under the contract, will not be able to enforce the promise which is supported by consideration from B. However, if C accepted the promise when it was made and was thus a party and joint promisee, C would be able to enforce the promise against A. It can be expected that contract drafters under this regime will adequately provide for such third party rights to be protected in a tripartite agreement.

This commentator notes that the Malaysian concept of contract, in following the classic contract paradigm, mirrors the idea of contract argued for by Professor Charles Fried in his admirable book *Contract as Promise*.[20] Promise is central to contract. And in both the Indian and Malaysian Acts, it is acceptance of the offer that is defined as 'Promise'. This conception heightens the sense that for a promise to be morally binding, there is to be invoked a belief and trust in someone that it is to be performed. Otherwise, according to Fried, a

[17] *Kepong Prospecting Ltd v Schmidt* [1968] 1 MLJ 170 (PC) 174; *Sulisen Sdn Bhd v Kerajaan Malaysia* [2006] 7 CLJ 247 (HC) 263; and *Boustead Naval Shipyard Sdn Bhd v Dynaforce Corp Sdn Bhd* [2015] 1 MLJ 284 (CA) 306–307. See also E Clarence, 'Contracts for the Benefit of Third Parties—Will our Common Law see the Demise of Privity of Contract?' [2000] 4 MLJ i, v.

[18] See Rankin CJ's pertinent remarks in *Krishna Lal Sadhu v Promila Bala Dasi* AIR 1928 Cal 518 (HC), which was cited with approval by the Malaysian High Court in the unreported judgment of *Syed Mansor bin Syed Hassan v The Official Administrator (for the estate of Saud bin Haji Adam, deceased)* decided by KC Vohrah J on 1 June 1995 in suit No 139 of 1979 [1995] 1 LNS 239.

[19] (1883) ILR 6 Mad 351 (HC).

[20] C Fried, *Contract as Promise* (Cambridge, MA/London: Harvard University Press 1981).

promise to oneself is a vow and if it is made to God, this makes the case that it has to be placed before another person, a promisee, who holds the obligation. It comes before the need for consideration. In Fried's discussion of the third party's rights in this contract conundrum of a basically bilateral relationship where A and B can change their intentions of benefiting C, he is of the view that:

> [N]ot only reliance but also C's 'acceptance' of the promise will cause C's rights to vest, preventing A and B from undoing what they have done... It is the very operative act of acquiescing in the promissory benefit that... is necessary to complete a binding promise.[21]

In both *Kepong* and *Badiaddin*, consideration was supplied by a third party to the bargain. It was in *Kepong* that the privity rule prevented the third party from claiming under the contract, whereas in *Badiaddin* it was a claim in restitution after discharge of the illegal contract that failed and the privity rule was applied in the context of the parties to the restitution claim. In *Kepong*, the inclusion of Mr Schmidt as a party into the 1954 agreement which conferred the benefit on him would have given him a right to sue in contract. In *Badiaddin*, the motivation for the financial institution was not to enforce the illegal contract but to claim for restitution of benefits transferred therein after discharge of the contract for illegality. For the loan contract, the chargors of the land were not a party, and for the charge contract, the detriment of charging the lands to the financial institution did not result in the transfer of a benefit to the chargors.

The Contracts Act 1950 is a statute that governed to a large extent the development of contract law in Malaysia. It is a progeny of the Indian Contract Act 1872.[22] Both India and Malaysia being former colonies of the British Empire inherited a contract Act that though not a replication of English common law rules on contract[23] has nevertheless an indelible imprint of the English concept of contract as an enforceable promise (or agreement) between parties who of their own free will entered into it for their purposes. The privity rule is thus derived. For Malaysia, a relatively young nation, the rule has been applied in this sense ever since British rule until now without much judicial dissension. It is a rule that had been faithfully applied in Malaysia without the introspection and the criticism which in the UK had led to a law commission and, eventually, legislative intervention to allow a third party who has been conferred benefits under the contract to sue the promisor directly on the contract.[24] In India, following a law commission[25] a new provision, section 37A, was proposed to be added to the Contract Act 1872, but the proposed section never came into effect:

> **37 A *Benefits conferred on third parties***
>
> (1) Where a contract expressly confers a benefit directly on a third party, then, unless the contract otherwise provides, it shall be enforceable by the third party in his own name, subject to any defences that would have been valid between the contracting parties.
>
> (2) Where a contract expressly conferring a benefit directly upon a third party has been adopted, expressly or impliedly, by the third party, the parties to the contract cannot substitute a new contract for it or rescind or alter it so as to affect the rights of the third party.

[21] ibid 45. cf s 2(1)(a), (b), and (c) of Contracts (Rights of Third Parties) Act 1999 (UK).

[22] See RR Sethu, 'The History, Impact and Influence of the Indian Contracts Act 1872' (2011) 28 JCL 31; V Sinnadurai, *Law of Contract* (4th edn, Kuala Lumpur: LexisNexis 2011) 12.

[23] See V Niranjan, 'Specific and Agreed Remedies for Breach of Contract in Indian Law: A Code of English Law?' in Chen-Wishart, Loke, & Ong, *Studies in the Contract Laws of Asia: Remedies for Breach of Contract* (Oxford: OUP 2016) ch 4.

[24] Law Commission, *Privity of Contract: Contracts for the Benefit of 3rd Parties* (Law Com No 242, 1996) which led to the enactment of the Contracts (Rights of Third Parties) Act 1999 (UK).

[25] Law Commission of India, *Thirteenth Report (Contract Act, 1872)* published in 1958.

Judicial criticisms of the doctrine have been distinctly mild in Malaysia. The strongest was that of his lordship PS Gill JCA in *Ramli bin Shahdan v Motor Insurers' Bureau of West Malaysia*[26] where he said:

> On our part we are aware that the doctrine of privity, while not an irrational doctrine from the nature of a contract, has in particular incidence caused injustice and proved inadequate to modern needs. In such circumstances, it is not surprising that various attempts have been made to induce courts to sanction evasions of the doctrine.

Abdul Malik Ishak JCA spoke more in a resigned tone in *Razshah Enterprise Sdn Bhd v Arab Malaysian Finance Bhd*[27] that *Kepong* has set the gloomy scene that the doctrine still applies in Malaysia. Academics have criticized the privity rule as antiquated and liable to cause injustice to third parties' rights under the contract because they are unable under the present law to have a direct contractual action to enforce their rights.[28]

II. Circumventing the Privity Rule

Since the privity rule is followed strictly, though parties to the contract can provide benefits to a third party under the contract, the latter would not be able to claim against the promisor in an action in contract either for specific performance or for damages arising from breach of the contract. Not being a party of the contract, he is unable to claim for the right, benefit, or immunity conferred in the contract in an action based on the contract against a contract party.

As a result, third parties who might have reason to rely upon or claim for benefits in a contract would have to resort to other legal bases to claim for such benefits under the contract. These are more accurately described *as other legal bases by which the third party acquires enforceable rights* rather than true exceptions to the privity rule (though judges used this phrase) for the third party's cause of action is independent of an action founded on the contract, which cannot found the third party's claim because of the privity rule, and some other legal principles are depended upon for the third party action.[29] The privity rule has to be circumvented by the claimant because it is fundamental in Malaysian contract law.[30] It is usually raised, whenever the opportunity is available, as a defence to defeat the claim and is a formidable argument against the claimant whose strategy is best to acknowledge it and circumvent the obstacle presented. Parliament has only stepped in under specific areas of the law to create exceptions to the privity rule, for example for claims on life insurance policy by the beneficiaries,[31] or for claims by the third party who suffered loss in a motor vehicle accident.[32] Assignments of a debt or chose of action are also statutorily recognized under section 4(3) of the Civil Law Act 1956.[33] The negotiation of a bill of exchange and the right of a holder to sue on the bill in his own name are allowed: sections 31 and 38 of the Bills of Exchange Act 1949.[34]

[26] [2006] 2 MLJ 116 (CA) 129. [27] [2010] 2 CLJ 457 (CA) 476.

[28] E Clarence, 'Contracts for the Benefit of Third Parties—Will our Common Law see the Demise of Privity of Contract?' [2000] 4 MLJ i; Tan Pei Meng, 'Circumventing the Privity Rule in Malaysia' (2009) 4 JICLT 262.

[29] See Lord Reid in *Scruttons Ltd v Midland Silicones Ltd* [1962] AC 446 (HL) 473; Brennan J in the Australian High Court decision of *Trident General Insurance Co Ltd v McNiece Bros Pty Ltd* (1988) 80 ALR 574, 593.

[30] See Tan Pei Meng, 'Circumventing the Privity Rule in Malaysia' (2009) 4 JICLT 262.

[31] s 23, Civil Law Act 1956 (Rev 1972) (Act 67) and the Insurance Act 1996 (Act 553).

[32] s 90, Road Transport Act 1987 (Act 333) which made insurance to cover risk of damage to third parties compulsory.

[33] (Rev 1972) Act 67. [34] (Rev 1978) Act 204.

1. Agency

The third party would not be the party named in the contract. He becomes or is treated as the contracting party because the contract has been formed in his stead by his agent. He could stand in this position whether he is a disclosed or undisclosed principal. If the relationship of agency is established, the third party would come under the regime of the contract and with it the rights, privileges, immunities, and obligations which the contract carries in relation to the other party of the contract.[35] Section 179 of the Contracts Act 1950 states the common law rule.[36]

The contractual claim or reliance on terms of the contract is dependent first on the establishment of the agency, or else the party remains a stranger to the contract and cannot sue on it. The issue of whether a cargo owner, whose goods were damaged by seawater during carriage, could claim damages against the shipowner in the *Viva Ocean*[37] for breach of its contractual duty to take reasonable care of the cargo turned on the question: was the contract of carriage made between the cargo owner and the shipowner? The shipowner argued that there was no privity of contract with the cargo owner who shipped the cargo. The bill of lading was issued to the cargo owner by an agent called Dooyang Line Company Ltd for the carriage of cargo from Ulsan Port, South Korea to Tawau Port, Malaysia. Clause 15 of the bill of lading stated that if the ship was not owned by or chartered by demise to Dooyang Line, the bill of lading shall take effect as a contract with the shipowner as principal made through Dooyang Line which acted as agent with no personal liability. The trial judge Richard Malanjum J (now Chief Judge of Sabah and Sarawak) found there was privity of contract between the cargo owner and the shipowner and granted an award of damages which included loss of profit shown to be a natural consequence of the breach of contract.

The cargo owner's expectation interest is protected through a contractual claim.[38] If privity of contract were not established and if the cargo owner were to sue under the tort of negligence, the measure of damages would not include loss of profit.

Staying on this factual context, exemption clauses for stevedores have attracted much litigation in the Commonwealth. X contracts with Y to transport X's goods using Y's ship to a foreign market. The contract for the carriage of goods by sea between X and Y contains an exemption of liability provision which purports to protect Z, the stevedores hired to unload X's goods from Y's ship once they arrive at the docks. As a result of Z's carelessness, X's goods are damaged while they are being unloaded from the ship and X wants to sue Z under the tort of negligence to recover damages for the losses suffered by X. Can Z rely on the exemption of liability provision in the contract between X and Y?

This commentator does not know of any Malaysian decision in this fact situation. However, there is obiter dicta by the High Court in *Ramachandran a/l Mayandy v Abdul Rahman bin Ambok Laongan*,[39] a case in a different fact situation, to the following effect:

> *Scruttons Ltd v Midland Silicones Ltd*... established the now famous rule that a principal may be able to claim the benefit of the terms of a contract made by his agent which limit the agent's liability for tortious acts.

[35] See the insurance cases of *Anvest Corporation Sdn Bhd v Wong Siew Choong Sdn Bhd* [1998] 2 CLJ 245 (CA) and *Anika Insurance Sdn Bhd v Public Bank Bhd* [2004] 6 CLJ 282 (HC).

[36] The section reads:

> Contracts entered into through an agent, and obligations arising from acts done by an agent, may be enforced in the same manner, and will have the same legal consequences as if the contracts had been entered into and the acts done by the principal in person.

[37] [2004] 6 MLJ 134 (HC).

[38] See LL Fuller and WR Perdue Jr, 'The Reliance Interest in Contract Damages' (1936) 46 Yale LJ 52, 373.

[39] [1997] 4 MLJ 237 (HC) 246.

The rule propounded by Lord Reid in *Scruttons*[40] is as follows:

> I can see a possibility of success of the agency argument if (first) the bill of lading makes it clear that the stevedore is intended to be protected by the provisions in it which limit liability, (secondly) the bill of lading makes it clear that the carrier, in addition to contracting for these provisions on his own behalf, is also contracting as agent for the stevedore that these provisions should apply to the stevedore, (thirdly) the carrier has authority from the stevedore to do that, or perhaps later ratification by the stevedore would suffice, and (fourthly) that any difficulties about consideration moving from the stevedore were overcome.

The exemption clause came to be known as the '*Himalaya*' clause, and in the Privy Council's cases of *New Zealand Shipping Co Ltd v AM Satterthwaite & Co Ltd (The Eurymedon)*[41] and *Port Jackson Stevedoring Pty Ltd v Salmond & Spraggon (Australia) Pty Ltd (The New York Star)*[42] their lordships were prepared to hold that the stevedores could rely on the exemption clauses in the contracts of carriage through the carrier acting as their agent. Lord Reid's rule was applied. The reasoning in *The Eurymedon*, as explained by Lord Wilberforce for the majority, is as follows. The contract of carriage assumes an obligation to transport the goods and discharge them at the port of destination. It is contemplated that discharge is by X or its servants or independent contractors; here it is Z. The bill of lading brought into existence a bargain, initially unilateral but capable of becoming mutual, between X and Z. This contract was made through Y as agent for Z. The exemption is intended to cover the whole carriage from loading to discharge, by whomsoever it is performed. The contract comes into its own when Z performed services by unloading the goods, which is also the consideration Z furnishes for X agreeing that Z should have the benefit of the exemption of liability contained in the bill of lading.

In *The New York Star*,[43] a unanimous decision for the stevedores, Lord Wilberforce found additional support in Barwick CJ's reasoning in the High Court of Australia on the possible bases of liability ventilated in *The Eurymedon*. The X–Z agreement was a bilateral contract, brought into existence through the agency of Y when X accepted the bill of lading. However, according to Barwick CJ in the High Court of Australia, that agreement lacked consideration which was only subsequently supplied when Z performed the act of unloading X's goods. Although the parties were *ad idem*, this was not a situation where promises were exchanged between X and Z, for Y had not at that stage promised the stevedores.[44]

If such a case should be decided in Malaysia, the first three of Lord Reid's conditions would have been decided as in *The Eurymedon* and *The New York Star*. The fourth condition for consideration to move from Z so as to enjoy the benefit of the exemption clause would be more liberally handled.[45] Since consideration, as defined in section 2(d), need not move from Z in exchange for the benefit of the exemption clause and could be supplied by 'any other person', Y's promise to carry and discharge X's goods at the port of arrival could furnish the consideration for the X–Z agreement formed through the agency of Y. In discharging X's goods on arrival, either Y or Z would have performed to fulfil the promise to discharge the goods 'at the desire' of X.[46]

[40] [1962] AC 446 (HL) 474. [41] [1975] AC 154 (PC). [42] [1980] 3 All ER 257 (PC).

[43] ibid 261.

[44] *Port Jackson Stevedoring Pty Ltd v Salmond & Spraggon (Australia) Pty Ltd* (1978) 18 ALR 333 (HC Aus) 344. See also the comments by Lord Goff in another Privy Council decision, *The Mahkutai* [1996] AC 650 (PC) 663.

[45] See section I above.

[46] See s 2(d), Contracts Act 1950; *Borneo Housing Mortgage Finance Bhd v Personnel Representatives of the Estate of Lee Lun Wah Maureen* [1994] 1 MLJ 209 (HC); A Phang Boon Leong, *Cheshire, Fifoot and Furmston's Law of Contract* (2nd Singapore and Malaysian edn, Singapore: Butterworths Asia 1998) 163 expressing the view that the 'joint promisee doctrine' propounded by the High Court of Australia in *Coulls v Bagot's Executor and Trustee Co Ltd* (1967) 119 CLR 460 is 'statutorily embodied' in Malaysia.

2. Trust of Promise for Third Party/Beneficiary, and Constructive Trust

Where X promises Y in a contract that he will confer a benefit on Z, the early English cases relying on equity to do what the common law could not, did not take long to find that Y, *the promisee*, held a *trust of the promise* for the benefit of Z, the beneficiary. Y could sue X for specific performance of the promise. Implicit in the trust concept is that should Y refuse to sue X, then Z as the beneficiary could enforce his equitable right by suing Y the trustee and X the promisor as joint defendants in the action.[47] The privity rule is thus avoided. By emphasizing that there must be affirmative evidence of an intention to create an express trust, later English cases were not so ready to find an express trust.[48] To create an express trust, the three certainties must be satisfied: (1) the settlor must intend to benefit the beneficiaries by way of a legally enforceable trust, not by gift, loan, contract, or any other way; (2) the subject matter of the trust property must be certain; and (3) the identity of the beneficiaries must be certain.[49] The reluctance of English courts to make use of the trust device in this context has been attributed to its artificiality, the emphasis on an intention to create a trust to be clearly shown, and a concern that the irrevocable nature of a trust could prevent the contracting parties from varying the contract terms.[50]

The trust of the promise was found to have been created in *Malaysian Australian Finance Co Ltd v The Law Union & Rock Insurance Co Ltd*.[51] The applicant was a finance company and the owner of the vehicle which was under hire purchase to the insured. The applicant wanted the High Court to determine whether it had rights coextensive with the insured in commencing claims in its own name for the loss covered under the insurance policy with the respondent. The insurance policy was issued by the respondent to the insured. A particular feature of the insurance contract was an endorsement in it which stated the applicant's ownership of the vehicle under hire purchase to the insured. The endorsement also stated that the applicant was 'interested in any monies' for loss or damage to the vehicle which but for the endorsement could be payable to the insured, *and* that the monies should be paid to the applicant as owner whose receipt would be a full discharge to the respondent. In the proposal form submitted to the respondent, it was disclosed that the vehicle was the subject of a hire-purchase agreement and the applicant was named the owner. Under the hire-purchase agreement between the applicant and the insured, the latter was obligated to insure the vehicle on terms acceptable to both the respondent and the applicant.

On those facts, Mohamed Azmi J (as he then was) found that the insurance was bought by the named insured on behalf of and for the benefit of the applicant. That the applicant had the prior right to receive the money under the policy showed further that the insurance was taken up for it. The fact that the respondent disclaimed any liability to the insured's claim did not affect the applicant's insurable interest in the policy; money could still be

[47] See A Phang Boon Leong, *Cheshire, Fifoot and Furmston's Law of Contract* (2nd Singapore and Malaysian edn, Singapore: Butterworths Asia 1998) 785–786. There is a helpful discussion of the trust device in the early English case of *Gregory and Parker v Williams* (1817) 3 Mer 582, 36 ER 224 and a recall of Maitland's definition (FW Maitland, *Equity* (Cambridge: University Press 1936) 44):

> Where a person has rights which he is bound to exercise on behalf of another or for the accomplishment of some particular purpose, he is said to have those rights in trust for another or for that purpose, and he is called a trustee.

[48] eg *Green v Russell* [1958] 2 QB 226.

[49] *Knight v Knight* (1840) 3 Beav 148, 173.

[50] See A Phang Boon Leong, *Cheshire, Fifoot and Furmston's Law of Contract* (2nd Singapore and Malaysian edn, Singapore: Butterworths Asia 1998) 787–788. The Contracts (Rights of Third Parties) Act 1999 (UK), s 2(3) specifically provides that the contracting parties, who would otherwise be prohibited under subs (1) from varying the contract by agreement without the consent of the third party, can vary the contract if the contract *expressly* provides that they may do so without the consent of the third party.

[51] [1972] 2 MLJ 10 (HC).

payable under the policy to the applicant. Therefore, he found that the applicant was a party to the contract and that it could institute a claim against the respondent in its own name.

He went on to find that, even if the applicant was not a party to the insurance contract and the privity rule would not allow it to sue on the contract, the fact that the respondent had promised in the endorsement to pay the money under the insurance policy directly to the applicant and the fact that the policy was effected for the applicant's benefit, the respondent 'should be regarded as trustee and/or agent for the applicant'.[52]

Three observations are necessary. First, the judge's reasoning that the applicant was a party to the insurance contract is difficult to follow. The better analysis is this. The respondent promised to pay the insurance money directly to the applicant vehicle-owner if the insured vehicle-hirer were to pay the premium to the respondent. There was express acceptance of the promise in the insurance contract and payment of premium by the insured; and implied acceptance by the applicant as shown in the endorsement which was included at the applicant's request. Since section 2(d) of the Contracts Act 1950 permitted consideration to move from 'another person', the applicant who was privy to the promise could sue on the insurance contract; the applicant's right was coextensive with that of the insured because they were joint promisees of the promise.[53]

Second, as regards the alternative claim based on trust of a promise, it would be more precise to say that the respondent entered into the insurance contract with the insured where the respondent's promise to pay the insurance money was held on trust by the insured, who was the promisee, for the applicant beneficiary. The trust created was that of *the respondent's promise* to pay the money directly to the applicant.

Third, there is nothing in the endorsement which showed that there was an intention to create a trust of the insurance money for the applicant. There must be a *clear intention to constitute one as trustee over a specified property for an identified beneficiary*, and these requirements also apply to trusts informally made: *Re Kayford Ltd*[54] and *Paul v Constance*.[55] There is no affirmative evidence that the insured-promisee had intended to create a trust of the promise, that is, expressly constitute oneself as a trustee over specified property for the third party beneficiary. An intention to benefit the third party does not translate into an intention to *create* a trust. That the court managed to find the respondent to be the trustee, instead of the insured-promisee, proves the point.

The decision in *Malaysian Australian Finance* showed the liberal approach in contrast to another decision of the High Court, *GR Nair v Eastern Mining & Metals Co Sdn Bhd*,[56] which showed the stricter approach to the question of whether an *express trust* has been created. In *GR Nair* the High Court rejected the plaintiffs' claim that the insurance contract was taken out by their employer, the defendant, together with the insurance proceeds paid to the defendant, as trustee for their benefit. The defendant had contracted for a Group All

[52] ibid 12. His lordship relied on and quoted two relevant passages on the *Law of Trusts* from *Halsbury's Laws of England* (3rd edn, London: Butterworths 1962) Vol 38 as support for his opinion. From pp 809–810:

> When a person has property or rights which he holds or is bound to exercise for or on behalf of another or others, or for the accomplishment of some particular purpose or particular purposes, he is said to hold the property or rights in trust for that other or those others, or for that purpose or those purposes, and he is called a trustee. A trust is a purely equitable obligation and is enforceable only in a court in which equity is administered.

And from p 822 dealing with contracts for the benefit of third parties:

> There must be a trust of a contract. If one of two contracting parties contracts as trustee for another person, that third person can enforce the trust. A clear intention to create such a trust must be shown to render it enforceable.

[53] See section I above.
[54] [1975] 1 All ER 604 (Ch D).
[55] [1977] 1 All ER 195 (CA Civ).
[56] [1974] 1 MLJ 176 (HC).

Sickness Policy for its employees which included the plaintiffs. The court followed the Privy Council's opinion in *Vandepitte v Preferred Accident Insurance Corporation of New York*,[57] *Cleaver v Mutual Reserve Fund Life Association*,[58] and *Green v Russell*.[59] The court quoted with approval the words of Lord Wright in *Vandepitte*:[60]

> The intention to constitute the trust must be affirmatively proved: the intention cannot necessarily be inferred from the mere general words of the policy.

The court held that there was nothing in the terms of the insurance contract to show that the contract was for the benefit of the plaintiffs. The premium was paid by the defendant who was the insured and any insurance payment was to be made to the defendant. If the contract is determined, the refund of the premium is stated to be paid to the defendant. The court was of the view that even if the insurance was for the plaintiffs' benefit, that was not sufficient to satisfy affirmatively that the defendant had intended to create a trust of its contractual rights under the insurance policy. The court also found that there was no constructive trust for the insurance proceeds. The defendant's conduct in paying over some of the insurance proceeds for seven disabled employees showed that the plaintiffs might have been paid, but the defendant had informed that those payments were gratuitously made. The judge accepted the defendant's reason in purchasing the insurance policy which was for its own financial planning to meet the contingencies of claims and also to make voluntary payments in hard cases even when there was no liability to pay.

An analysis of the Malaysian cases dealing with the trust of a promise reveals that the Malaysian courts do not adopt a consistent approach.[61] They seemed to follow the inconsistency that had been reflected between the earlier and later English decisions. Given the inconsistency of the law in this area, criticism has been levelled at the Court of Appeal's pronouncement in *Bank Bumiputra Malaysia Bhd v Mohamed Salleh*[62] that based on the law of trust any employee would be able to lodge a claim against the insurance company in a group insurance policy bought by the employer who 'is entitled to receive any benefit due to [the employee.] Once received it will hold the monies as trustee for [the employee].'

The statement has been criticized for begging the critical question of just how such a trust arose, and the court merely supported its argument that it was based on the 'ordinary principles governing the law of trust'.[63] The court probably meant its statement as a reference to the constructive trust, for it went on to say that the constructive trust could not be implied (more accurate to say imposed) unless there was a clear intention to create a trust.[64] Such instability of description and use has contributed to a confused legal basis of trust of a promise for the provision of a remedy for the third party. The trust of a promise arising from an express trust, which can either be formally or informally created, being in essence consensual and promise-based, has metamorphosed into a variety of something that is imposed by law—and thus, not necessarily consensual and promissory.

Recent cases have used the constructive trust to avoid the privity rule; whereas the older cases sought to find an express trust based on an intention to create a trust of the promise, which could be founded expressly in words or inferred from clear words showing such an

[57] [1933] AC 70 (PC). [58] [1892] 1 QB 147. [59] [1959] 2 QB 256.

[60] *Vandepitte v Preferred Accident Insurance Corporation of New York* [1933] AC 70 (PC) 79–80.

[61] See Tan Pei Meng, 'Circumventing the Privity Rule in Malaysia' (2009) 4 JICLT 266–268. The learned author listed *Kishabai v Jaikishan* [1981] 2 MLJ 289 (HC) and *ESPL (M) Sdn Bhd v Radio & General Engineering Sdn Bhd* [2005] 2 MLJ 422 (CA) as finding that a trust of the contract was created for there was an intention to create a trust, and *Anuar bin Ismail v Tan Sri Tan Chin Tuan* [1992] 1 MLJ 155 (HC) as ruling that a trust had not been created.

[62] [2000] 2 CLJ 13 (CA) 15.

[63] Tan Pei Meng, 'Circumventing the Privity Rule in Malaysia' (2009) 4 JICLT 267.

[64] *Bank Bumiputra Malaysia Bhd v Mohamed Salleh* [2000] 2 CLJ 13 (CA) 17.

intention. The recent cases extend the use of equity's principles by using the constructive trust, which can but need not be dependent on an intention to create a trust of the promise.[65] The Federal Court recognizes that in Malaysia the constructive trust could in principle arise either as an institutional constructive trust or a remedial constructive trust: *RHB Bank Bhd v Travelsight (M) Sdn Bhd*.[66] The distinction between the two varieties that the Federal Court adopted is in the explanation given by Lord Browne-Wilkinson in *Westdeutsche Landesbank Girozentrale v Islington London Borough Council*:[67]

> Under an institutional constructive trust, the trust arises by operation of law as from the date of the circumstances which give rise to it: the function of the court is merely to declare that such trust has arisen in the past. The consequences that flow from such trust having arisen (including the possibly unfair consequences to third parties who in the interim have received the trust property) are also determined by rules of law, not under a discretion. A remedial constructive trust, as I understand it, is different. It is a judicial remedy giving rise to an enforceable equitable obligation: the extent to which it operates retrospectively to the prejudice of third parties lies in the discretion of the court.

In the context of the cases considered here, it is the institutional constructive trust that is imposed by the court: the constructive trust would have arisen at the time the facts occurred, and the courts would declare the existence of a constructive trust based on the rules of law relating to third parties' rights without resort to discretion in this regard. The courts have relied on English authorities, and the conventional view is that English law does not recognize the remedial constructive trust.[68] There are early signs that the Malaysian courts would be relying more on the constructive trust and general principles in equity to resolve issues which, invariably to some extent at least, engage with the privity rule. Two recent Federal Court decisions are important.

The first is *Takako Sakao v Ng Pek Yuen*.[69] The plaintiff, a Japanese national living in Japan, decided to partner with the defendant, a Malaysian, to operate a Japanese restaurant in Kuala Lumpur. In the course of their business, they reached an agreement in 1992 to purchase the building where their restaurant was sited. It was their intention that the building be purchased and registered under their joint names in equal shares. The plaintiff had contributed various sums towards the purchase price of the building totalling RM 194,610. In the same year, the building was purchased for RM 950,000 but registered in the defendant's name only. The purchase price was partly financed by a bank loan.

In the middle of 1996, the defendant sold the building to Glamour Land Sdn Bhd, a co-defendant in the action, for RM 1,930,000; this sale was partly financed by another bank. The defendant's husband controlled Glamour Land. The plaintiff had by this time lodged a caveat on the title to the building, and commenced a writ action in the High Court to enforce the trust she claimed had arisen in her favour. The defendant applied to the High Court to remove the caveat. Both actions were tried together.

The High Court ordered the removal of the plaintiff's caveat, dismissed her claim for enforcement of a trust, and ordered the defendant to refund a sum of RM 65,450 with interest.

[65] See also G Elias, *Explaining Constructive Trusts* (Oxford: Clarendon Press 1990). The author has helpfully offered an explanation of constructive trusts, which defies definition, by rationalization of the rules that govern them through three aims called 'the perfection aim', 'the restitution aim', and 'the reparation aim'.

[66] [2015] 1 CLJ 309 (FC) 326, 331 (Jeffrey Tan FCJ).

[67] [1996] AC 669, 714–715. cf J McGhee (ed), *Snell's Equity* (33rd edn, London: Sweet & Maxwell 2015) 697.

[68] See *Re Polly Peck International plc (No 2)* [1998] 3 All ER 812 (CA Civ) 830–832 (Nourse J), but the future possibilities of the imposition of a remedial constructive trust under English law are left open: *London Allied Holdings Ltd v Lee* [2007] EWHC 2061 (Ch), Etherton J citing the Court of Appeal's dicta in *Methall and Rohstaff AG v Donaldson Lufkin & Jenrette Inc* [1990] 1 QB 391, 479.

[69] [2009] 6 MLJ 751 (FC), [2009] 4 MLJ 66 (CA).

The plaintiff's argument proceeded on the footing that a resulting trust could be implied because of her contribution to the purchase price. The plaintiff's appeal to the Court of Appeal was dismissed. In the Court of Appeal, their lordships remarked that the plaintiff's claim was only against the defendant and not against Glamour Land or the bank, who were both 'strangers to the agreement' between the plaintiff and the defendant in respect of the property (ie 'the privity issue').[70]

The Federal Court allowed the plaintiff's appeal. Their lordships were of the opinion that a constructive trust had arisen by operation of law over the building with the defendant holding as trustee for the plaintiff's beneficial interest, her one-half share in the property. The Federal Court reasoned as follows. First, being partners meant that the plaintiff and defendant were fiduciaries one to the other, and they should act with utmost good faith towards each other. The defendant acted in breach of fiduciary duty when she acquired the property pursuant to her agreement with the plaintiff but put it in her sole name and then sold it to Glamour Land at a higher price to deny the plaintiff's right to a half share in it. Following Edmund Davies LJ in *Carl Zeiss Stiftung v Herbert Smith & Co*[71] and Millett LJ's 'first class of case' of constructive trust in *Paragon Finance plc v DB Thakerar & Co*,[72] the court would impose a constructive trust in this fact situation: the fiduciary or trustee, in breach of trust or by conduct which is considered unconscionable, would hold the property on constructive trust for the true beneficiary.[73] The constructive trust yielded a proprietary remedy for the beneficiary, the plaintiff, who may also enforce her proprietary remedy to the trust property through the process of following and tracing.

On the second leg of their reasoning and which engaged with the privity rule—whether the trust in favour of the plaintiff could be enforced against Glamour Land who was not a party to the agreement—the Federal Court answered it in the affirmative. The court was of the view that the trial judge's finding that Glamour Land was *not* a bona fide purchaser of the trust property, and the effect of section 26(b) of the Specific Relief Act 1950[74] were both overlooked by the Court of Appeal. Since Glamour Land could not prove it was a bona fide purchaser, the plaintiff's equitable interest in the property, which is already protected by the constructive trust, could be enforced by specific performance directly in contract, and it is also enforceable against the co-defendant Glamour Land.[75]

Moreover, the court found that there is another ground on the privity issue. Once it was recognized that the obligation sought to be enforced was a trust, following *Beswick v Beswick*[76] trusts are an exception to the common law rule of privity of contract.[77]

The second decision is that in *Datuk M Kayveas v See Hong Chen & Sons Sdn Bhd*,[78] where a political party's intention to purchase a property and the manner it had proceeded with the purchase led to the present litigation. The plaintiff sued in a representative capacity for the People's Progressive Party of Malaysia against altogether seven defendants in the action for the return of shares which he held for the Party in the fifth defendant. In August

[70] [2009] 4 MLJ 66 (CA) 75.
[71] [1969] 2 Ch 276, 300.
[72] [1999] 1 All ER 400, 409.
[73] [2009] 6 MLJ 751 (FC) 763.
[74] s 26, Specific Relief Act 1950 (Rev 1974) (Act 137) reads:

> Except as otherwise provided by this Chapter, specific performance of a contract may be enforced against –
>
> (a) either party thereto;
> (b) any other person claiming under a party to the contract by a title arising subsequently to the contract, except a transferee for value who has paid his money in good faith and without notice of the original contract.

[75] See also *Ramli bin Shahdan v Motor Insurers' Bureau of West Malaysia* [2006] 2 MLJ 116 (CA) 129–130.
[76] [1968] AC 58 (HL).
[77] *Takako Sakao v Ng Pek Yuen* [2009] 6 MLJ 751 (FC) 773.
[78] [2014] 4 MLJ 64 (FC).

2003, the plaintiff purchased a piece of land which it had been occupying since 1998 at a public auction for RM 2,673,000. The plaintiff paid the deposit at 10 per cent of the price with its own funds. The balance purchase price of RM 2,405,700 was raised through a friendly loan from the first defendant to the fifth defendant, and paid before the property was registered in the name of the fifth defendant, an investment company of the plaintiff and the designated entity to hold the property. It was agreed between the plaintiff and the first defendant that as security for the loan the only two shares issued at that time by the fifth defendant would be transferred to the first defendant 'on trust until the full repayment of the loan' for the plaintiff as beneficiary. Upon full repayment, the two shares would be re-transferred to the plaintiff's nominees and in the meantime the first defendant would not do anything to affect the interest of the two shares.

However, after the transfer of the two shares to him and having the full control of the fifth defendant, in March 2005 the first defendant increased the equity of the fifth defendant from two to 100,000 by issuing 99,998 fresh shares to himself. The two shares which the first defendant was holding as bare trustee he transferred to his nominees, the second and third defendants who were appointed to the fifth defendant's board of directors. Then in November 2005, the first defendant together with the second and third defendants entered into a share sale and purchase agreement with the fourth defendant for a supposed consideration of RM 2,500,000. Consequently the fourth defendant controlled the fifth defendant and with that, the property. It was only in July 2008 that the plaintiff knew something had gone wrong when it was served with the fourth defendant's notice to vacate the property followed by a trespass action.

The High Court allowed the plaintiff's claim for a breach of trust and the return of the shares in the fifth defendant to the plaintiff. The Court of Appeal allowed the fourth, fifth, sixth, and seventh defendants' appeal and set aside the High Court order. The Court of Appeal was of the view that the trial judge had erred in ruling that there was an express trust created in 2003 when according to their lordships there was no evidence of any transfer of the shares on trust, nor could there be an express trust of the 99,998 shares in 2003 when these shares were only created in 2005. Without proof of the existence of the express trust, the plaintiff's action on breach of trust collapsed.

The Federal Court's decision on the variance of the finding of fact by the courts below on the existence of the trust in 2003 was as follows. The plaintiff's pleaded case was that there was a trust of the two shares transferred to the first defendant for him to hold as security until his loan was fully paid. The plaintiff did not state that it was an express trust. In reaching his decision that there was a trust of the two shares and then the additional 99,998 shares, the trial judge did not decide or say in his judgment that it was an express trust. Even before the Court of Appeal, the defendants who appealed did not in their grounds of appeal complain that the trial judge had erred on the ground that he had ruled that an express trust of the entire 100,000 shares was created. Therefore, it was wrong for the Court of Appeal to go outside the appeal case before it and to overturn a finding of the trial judge which in fact he did not make.

This commentator makes five points. First, the use of the trust device in avoiding the privity rule and giving the plaintiff a proprietary remedy would import some of the more controversial issues in trust law and equity into the present area of law under study. If, indeed, there was no express trust informally constituted in 2003, the fact that a constructive trust could arise through the common intention of the plaintiff and the first defendant under their agreement for the initial transfer of the only two shares to the first defendant for him to hold on trust as security for the loan until it was fully repaid means that the common-intention constructive trustee is really a trustee like one created under an express trust but unlike it in another aspect, as the constructive trust is imposed by law because there was no express trust. This would be the preferred explanation for the creation in 2003 of the trust of the two shares. However, when the first defendant unconscionably issued another 99,998 shares to himself and then transferred the total 100,000 shares to his nominees, he held the shares on a constructive trust for the plaintiff, whose beneficial interest is good against all those who would subsequently take a transfer of the 100,000 shares with notice of the trust. This later constructive trust would have arisen irrespective of the parties' intention, premised on the first defendant's unconscionable conduct in respect of the unlawful issuance of the additional shares and the transfer of all the shares to his nominees, and it is again imposed by the law.

Second, the Federal Court followed the equitable principle that the plaintiff as the beneficiary has in equity a proprietary interest in the trust property, which is enforceable against all subsequent holders, except a bona fide purchaser for value without notice of the trust.[79] The fourth defendant needed to show clean title to the trust property by proving it was: (1) a bona fide purchaser for value; and (2) one without notice. The fourth defendant failed on both counts. The Federal Court agreed with the trial judge that the fourth defendant, which was not a bona fide purchaser for value, took a transfer of all the shares in the fifth defendant with notice that the shares were trust property.

Third, the Federal Court also relied on a separate principle in equity developed in *Tulk v Moxhay*[80] that equity will not permit a defendant who knew of a restrictive covenant on land to disregard the negative obligation affecting the land which he took over as purchaser. The vendor sold the land minus the right stipulated by the negative covenant to the original purchaser who could not thence sell the land without the limitation of the negative covenant; to do so would be inequitable, for the original purchaser would be selling and benefiting more than what he had. It is in this manner that Equity treated the equity or interest to run with the land.[81] Their lordships in *Kayveas* then endorsed the view that an equitable remedy would be granted by the court to prevent a breach of a restrictive covenant relating to property (the shares) by the other defendants who would otherwise be strangers to the agreement between the plaintiff and the first defendant—and for which proposition they followed Knight-Bruce LJ in *De Mattos v Gibson*[82] and approved by the House of Lords in *Lord Strathcona Steamship Co Ltd v Dominion Coal Ltd.*[83]

Take the selling bread hypothetical, where X leases two adjoining properties to Y and Z. The lease between X and Y barred Y from selling bread because Z sold bread from his leased property. Can X and Y agree to lift the bar? The bar is a restrictive covenant on Y's leased property and is in the X–Y lease contract to protect, and is for the benefit of, Z. Being adjoining properties and the fact that the bar was inserted in the X–Y lease provides good evidence that both X and Y knew of the bar and its intended purpose to protect and benefit Z. If Z had entered into its lease with X with the intention that such a negative condition would be stipulated in a lease with the adjoining property, such an equity is attached to X's property and X would have leased the adjoining property to Y minus the right of the tenant to sell bread on the leased land. Following *Kayveas*, which approves of the principle in *Tulk v Moxhay*, X and Y would most likely *not* be allowed to lift the restrictive covenant on X's property (leased to Y) though the covenant is only between X and Y, for it is an equity

[79] Following Lord Browne-Wilkinson in *Westdeuthsche Landesbank Girozentrale v Islington London Borough Council* [1996] 2 All ER 961 (HL) 988; Lord Millett in *Foskett v McKeown* [2000] 3 All ER 97 (HL) 122.

[80] [1843–60] All ER Rep 9 (Ch D).

[81] See *Rhone v Stephens* [1994] 2 AC 310 (HL) 317–318 for Lord Templeton's affirmation and explanation of the rule of equity in *Tulk v Moxhay*.

[82] [1843–60] All ER Rep 803 (QB).

[83] [1926] AC 108 (HL).

attached to Y's leased property, which being a limitation of proprietary rights for the benefit of the neighbouring property is enforceable by its neighbour, Z. To enforce the equity, Z could successfully apply for injunctions to restrain both X and Y from lifting the restrictive covenant that ran with the X–Y land. Z could also arguably claim damages on the tort of interfering with Z's business by unlawful means, that is, the lifting of the bar which X and Y were not at liberty to commit. Both these causes of action are not based on an action in contract but are dependent on other legal bases, one on an equity or interest created in property and the other on the law of torts, to protect Z's economic interest against interference.

The privity rule would continue to apply to prevent a stranger from enforcing a positive covenant contained in a contract on a purchaser of the land with notice of the positive covenant, since both the common law and equity would not enforce a positive obligation to perform an action on a third party who had not contracted to do so: *Wilson Parking (M) Sdn Bhd v JW Marriott Hotel, Kuala Lumpur*.[84]

Fourth, the Federal Court acknowledged that these principles of equity were adequate 'to circumvent the privity of contract hurdle' in pursuing the fourth, fifth, sixth, and seventh defendants 'who were far removed' from the plaintiff.[85] From the above exercise, it is hard not to note that the Malaysian courts have been quick to fasten on to equity to go where the common law cannot. The genius of equity, as developed by English law, in creating the concept of Trust, and with that the creation and division of property into legal and equitable interest, having the characteristics of transferability and excludability, has seen both the trust concept and the fact of its recognition as property bypass the common law doctrine of privity of contract.[86] For both trust and property, by their very nature, transcend privity of contract: they present the right *in rem* that is enforced through the application of equitable remedies as a right *in personam* to protect the trust property or a mere equity. Where there is a conflict between the common law and equity over the same matter, equity shall prevail subject to statute providing otherwise.[87]

Fifth, in all the cases discussed in this section, the plaintiff's expectation interest in the agreement has been protected by the remedy granted by the courts. The plaintiff's expectation interest that was contained in the agreement, where he was a stranger, could be enforced by either an express trust or a constructive trust (and the distinction is sometimes lost) of the promise against the promisor who is in reality a constructive trustee, imposed by the courts. Or the plaintiff's expectation interest contained in the agreement is enforced against a stranger to the agreement who violated or denied the plaintiff's equitable right in the trust property and which because it is a trust property with attendant contractual rights, the stranger who violated the right could well bear the force of the court's arsenal of enforcement remedies to protect the plaintiff's expectation interest.

III. Adequacy or Lack of Common Law Solutions

1. Promisee's Remedy for Damages to Protect its Performance Interest

(a) Disappointing family holidays

Take the facts of a disappointing family holiday that were the facts in *Jackson v Horizon Holidays Ltd*[88] and ask how a Malaysian court would deal with such a claim. X purchases a package holiday for X and her family, which includes Z, from Y's travel agency. The holiday

[84] [2011] 2 CLJ 136 (HC) following *Rhone v Stephens* [1994] 2 AC 310 (HL). See also *Kean Yick Enterprise Sdn Bhd v Cherating Development Sdn Bhd* [2012] 3 CLJ 741, 760–761 (HC).
[85] [2014] 4 MLJ 64 (FC) 82.
[86] See S Worthington, *Equity* (Oxford: OUP 2003) 219.
[87] s 3(2), Civil Law Act 1956 (Rev 1972) Act 67.
[88] [1975] 3 All ER 92 (CA).

turns out to be an absolute disaster, with poor-quality accommodation, lousy meals, uncomfortable journeys, and numerous delays attributable to Y's poor planning.

Z was not a party to the contract. The purchase of the holiday was made by X for herself and her family. X would have contracted for herself as the principal for a holiday that would benefit her and her family. The fact that it was the intention of the contracting parties, X and Y, that the purchase price paid for the enjoyable family holiday ought to have benefited X's family members does not create a right in Z, a family member, to sue for breach of contract. Can X sue for damages suffered by Z, a third party? The general rule is that X can only claim for damages suffered by her. This rule would apply in Malaysia.[89] However, it is probable that X could successfully sue Y for breach of contract and claim damages for the loss to herself and her family including Z's by using a broad conception of damages suffered by X.[90] When X purchased the holiday package she had purchased it for herself and her family, and Y had entered into the contract with the knowledge that any loss X suffered would also include her family's loss. Lord Russell in *Woodar Investment v Wimpey Construction UK Ltd*[91] thought that the damages the plaintiff recovered in *Jackson v Horizon Holidays Ltd* were recovered because of the failure to supply *him* with the high-class family holiday he had purchased. That is, the damages were awarded for X's loss.

(b) Building works for subsidiary company

X contracts for Y, a construction firm, to erect a building on land belonging to Z, a subsidiary company wholly owned by X. Numerous defects are subsequently discovered in the building constructed by Y. If X were to sue Y for breach of contract, would X be entitled to recover substantive damages against Y in respect of those building defects found on Z's land?

If there is no relationship of agency between X and Z, the very interesting question arises—whether X can sue Y for breach of contract for substantial damages in respect of those building defects on Z's land. The widely accepted general principle in English law is that the plaintiff can only claim for substantial damages for a loss suffered by him or else he could only obtain nominal damages.[92] Where, as in this fact situation, the defective building is located on land belonging to Z, the defective works are then seen as a loss arising from the breach of contract by Y but suffered by Z, a third party, and not X, the contracting party. Since Z is not a party to the contract, the privity doctrine would prevent Z from suing Y for the loss caused by having the defective building. The substantial loss or damage could be formulated either as the costs of rectifying the defects, that is, the costs of cure or, alternatively, as the diminution in value of the defective building. If X could only claim nominal damages for the breach of contract since the defective building does not belong to it and if Z, the owner of the defective building, could not claim any damages because of the privity rule, such lack on the law's part to provide a just remedy has been metaphorically described as the disappearance of a substantial claim into a 'legal black hole'.[93]

Perceived thus mainly as a privity of contract problem, the common law solution is to develop an exception known as the rule in *Dunlop v Lambert*[94] and rationalized by Lord

[89] See section III(1)(b) below. [90] ibid. [91] [1980] 1 All ER 571 (HL) 585.

[92] See *Albacruz (cargo owners) v Albazero (owners) (The Albazero)* [1976] 3 All ER 129 (HL) 136 (Lord Diplock).

[93] See *Alfred McAlpine Construction Ltd v Panatown Ltd* [2001] 1 AC 518 (HL) 529, 567–568; A Loke, 'The "Broad Ground" and the Not-So-Narrow Ground in Singapore: *Chia Kok Leong v Prosperland Pte Ltd*' (2007) 23 JCL 148, 148.

[94] (1839) 6 Cl & Fin 600, 7 ER 824 (HL).

Diplock in *The Albazero*,[95] both of which were suits by the consignor of cargo against the shipowner for lost or damaged cargo during the sea carriage. In those instances the risk or title in the goods would have passed to the consignee when the bill of lading was endorsed and delivered to the consignee. The exception to the privity rule works this way. The consignor has the right to claim for the loss and damage to the goods as it had entered into the carriage of goods contract with the shipowner, and it was intended that it was the consignor who would claim the loss for which it was accountable to the consignee provided that the consignee has no separate right to claim against the shipowner.

This exception to the general rule was then extended by the House of Lords to yield a remedy for substantial damages to the employer of a contractor for services and materials in a construction contract for buildings belonging to a third party in *Linden Gardens Trust Ltd v Lenesta Sludge Disposals Ltd, St Martin's Property Ltd v Sir Robert McAlpine & Sons*,[96] *Darlington Borough Council v Wiltshier Northern Ltd*,[97] and *Alfred McAlpine Construction Ltd v Panatown Ltd*.[98] In *Panatown*, their lordships addressed this exception as the 'narrow ground' for X to sue Y to claim substantial damages for the defective building in contradistinction to the 'broad ground', which was the preferred ground of Lord Griffiths in *Linden Gardens*. The broad ground states that X can claim substantial damages for the defective building from Y for a contract essentially for services and materials, as Y had not performed its part of the bargain with X who has thus suffered damage in that the performance of the bargain was not as bargained for and not as expected to be.

The minority in the House of Lords in *Panatown*, Lord Goff and Lord Millett, was of the opinion that the broad ground was not an exception to the privity rule since it does not relate to the problems posed by the privity rule, but was an issue which dealt with the general principles governing damages for breach of contract and reform of such principles where they are lacking.

A survey of cases right up to the writing of this chapter showed that this debate has passed by Malaysia. How would a Malaysian court at present resolve such a dispute? This commentator is of the view that Malaysian courts would be inclined to allow X's claim for substantial damages in making good the building defects against Y for breach of the X–Y contract though the building is on Z's land, based on the broad ground as clarified by Lord Goff in *Panatown*. Five reasons are suggested.

First, although the privity doctrine is not mentioned in the Malaysian Contracts Act 1950, it is basic to Malaysian contract law. The model of the contract that is adopted and followed until today is what contract scholars have described as the 'classic' model. Professor Patrick Atiyah has described it as the bilateral executory agreement.[99] It is an exchange of promises, which are intended to be legally binding. Once the contract is formed, the promisee can sue for damages for breach of contract if the promisor fails to perform his promise, although no part of the bargain has been performed and the promisor has not received any benefit from the contract.

Second, the general principle governing damages is the intent of contract damages to put the promisee in the position he would have been in if the contract had been performed, as pronounced by Parke B in *Robinson v Harman*[100] and Lord Blackburn in *Livingstone v Rawyards Coal Co.*[101] This has been explained as the normal contract measure of damages or expectation damages. Such a paradigm of contractual damages is arguably a consequence

[95] [1976] 3 All ER 129 (HL). [96] [1993] 3 All ER 417 (HL). [97] [1995] 3 All ER 895 (CA Civ).
[98] [2001] 1 AC 518 (HL). [99] PS Atiyah, *Essays on Contract* (reprinted edn, Oxford: OUP 1990) 11–12.
[100] (1848) 1 Exch 850 (Ex Ct).
[101] (1880) 5 App Cas 25 (HL). The Federal Court in *Tan Sri Khoo Teck Puat v Plenitude Holdings Sdn Bhd* [1995] 1 CLJ 15, 22–23 endorsed and followed these general principles of contract damages.

of the 'classic' model of contract that governs contract law in Malaysia. The Contracts Act 1950, together with its provisions which have not been amended since inception, virtually a replica of the Indian Contract Act 1872, is an omnipresent reminder of contract doctrines from that era.

Section 74(1) of the Contracts Act 1950 in effect codifies the principles of contract damages that were expounded in *Hadley v Baxendale*.[102] The section comes with an extensive list of illustrations to display how the section would work in different scenarios. Although the illustrations do not comprise part of the section, they should not be ignored as they are helpful in the application of the section: *Muralidhar Chatterjee v International Film Co*.[103] Illustrations (f) and (l) do show that the promisee's expectation interest, or more accurately the performance interest of the contract, is protected by adequate damages.[104] It is admittedly true that the illustrations do not characterize the present fact situation where a third party stands to suffer loss because of the promisor's failure to perform adequately or at all. Assuming that, nevertheless, the aim of the damages under section 74(1) as illustrated shows that damages as a remedy for the breach of contract do protect the performance interest.

Third, Professor Brian Coote[105] has insightfully noted that the debate on this point has failed to distinguish between the two types of benefit conferred by the performance of a contract. The contractual performance might confer upon a third party de facto benefits which are incidental to those legal benefits which are bargained for. In the present fact situation, the construction of the building by Y as promised to X is the legal bargained-for benefit and the use and enjoyment by Z are the de facto benefits incidental to the performance of the bargain. The performance interest that contract law would seek to protect is the promise made by Y to X that it would construct a free-from-defects building on Z's land. X had bargained for this promise and the failure to perform by Y has resulted in damages suffered by X for the costs of cure or the diminution in value of the defective building though it is on Z's land, since the promise of the bargained-for benefit was made to X.

Fourth, since the protection of X's performance interest in the X–Y contract by an award of damages to X would and is the appropriate remedy, there is neither necessity nor room for the application of the narrow ground in this fact situation.[106]

Fifth, the narrow ground derived from the rule in *Dunlop v Lambert* and rationalized by Lord Diplock in *The Albazero* has not been accepted as the law in Malaysia as an exception to the privity rule. In *The SS Hwa Lung*,[107] the Federal Court considered whether the consignor of cargo who was holder and endorsee of the bill of lading had a cause of action for

[102] (1854) 9 Exch 341 (Ex Ct).

[103] (1942) 70 IA 35, a decision of the Privy Council on the Indian Contract Act 1872, which was followed by the Malaysian Court of Appeal in *Poh Geok Sing v HB Enterprise Sdn Bhd* [2006] 1 CLJ 765 and the Federal Court in *Berjaya Times Square v M-Concept Sdn Bhd* [2010] 1 CLJ 269.

[104] (f) *A* contracts to repair *B's* house in a certain manner, and receives payment in advance. *A* repairs the house, but not according to contract. *B* is entitled to recover from *A* the cost of making the repairs conform to the contract.

...

(l) *A*, a builder, contracts to erect and finish a house by the 1st of January, in order that *B* may give possession of it at the time to *C*, to whom *B* has contracted to let it. *A* is informed of the contract between *B* and *C*. *A* builds the house so badly that, before the 1st of January it falls down and has to be rebuilt by *B*, who in consequence, loses the rent which he was to have received from *C*, and is obliged to make compensation to *C* for the breach of his contract. *A* must make compensation to *B* for the costs of rebuilding the house, for the rent lost and for the compensation made to *C*.

[105] B Coote, 'Contract Damages, *Ruxley*, and the Performance Interest' (1997) 56 Camb LJ 537.

[106] See A Loke, 'The "Broad Ground" and the Not-So-Narrow Ground in Singapore: *Chia Kok Leong v Prosperland Pte Ltd*' (2007) 23 JCL 148, 153.

[107] *Mahawangsa Holdings Sdn Bhd v The SS 'Hwa Lung' (The SS Hwa Lung)* [1977] 2 MLJ 132 (FC).

loss of the cargo against the shipowner. Their lordships applied the English Court of Appeal's reasoning in *The Albazero*[108] and treated the suit by the consignor who was the contracting party as one decided on the privity of contract to yield a cause of action to the consignor, and were not concerned with where the title or risk lay.[109] The Federal Court's treatment of the issue of a contracting party suing for substantial loss for breach of contract where ownership might have passed to a third party shows that the Malaysian judges are not overly concerned with the fact that X was claiming for substantial damages on a contract in which Z, being the owner of the property, could claim to have suffered the loss. It is an irony that the strict application of the privity rule accentuates the 'classic' contract model, breach of which in turn would yield a right in the promisee to expect the substantial performance of the promise by the promisor.

2. Expansion of Law of Torts

Where a promisee to a contract has rights which a third party has interfered with or threatens to interfere with, the promisee's economic interest is protected by the law of torts. The promisee has no contractual relationship with the third party and so cannot sue him in contract. However, the law of torts will protect an interference with the plaintiff's economic interest with remedies such as damages and injunction.

The plaintiff in *Yong Sze Hong v Pan KA General Agencies Sdn Bhd*[110] was given exclusive rights to sell a horse-racing sweepstake in designated territories in one of the Malaysian states. The defendant was alleged to have infringed those contractual rights by selling tickets in the designated areas. When the defendant was sued for damages for breach of the contractual right by the plaintiff, the defendant raised lack of privity of contract to strike out the claim. The High Court was of the view that the tort of deliberate and direct interference of the performance of the contract by a third party who induces a breach, without the need for actual breach, was the reasonable cause of action.

The tort of negligence has expanded into an area which would have been covered by contract if contractual remedies were available to enable a third party who has been conferred a benefit under the contract with a vested right of action—a *jus quaesitum tertio*. The Atkinian 'neighbour' principle developed in *Donoghue v Stevenson*[111] has covered much territory in the private law of obligations to plug the hole left in the law of obligations, even where the interest to be protected is purely economic. The better view in Malaysia is that pure economic loss is protected by the tort of negligence, as decided by the Federal Court in *Majlis Perbandaran Ampang Jaya v Steven Phoa Cheng Loon*,[112] and since the duty of reasonable care is imposed under the common law incrementally on a case-to-case basis, it could expand to cover fact situations involving third parties who are not privy to the contract but had been conferred a benefit under the contract.

The hypothetical presented by the stolen shop takings is a good example to illustrate how Malaysian courts would cope with providing a remedy in that factual context. X bank makes a contract for Y security company to collect Z store's takings. The contract requires Y to use

[108] [1975] 3 All ER 21 (CA). The House of Lords' decision, reported in [1976] 3 All ER 129, overturning the Court of Appeal's decision, which would have been just published, was not referred to the Federal Court where the respondent was not represented.

[109] *The SS Hwa Lung* [1977] 2 MLJ 132 (FC) 133, 134.

[110] [1994] 1 CLJ 555 (HC).

[111] [1932] AC 562 (HL).

[112] [2006] 2 CLJ 1 (FC). In *Loh Chiak Eong v Lok Kok Beng* [2012] 9 CLJ 699, 723 the Court of Appeal pointed out that in those situations where economic loss was pronounced to be recoverable, the plaintiffs had also suffered damage to their properties.

armoured vehicles and take out insurance. Y failed to do these and the takings were stolen while being collected in an ordinary car. Can Z sue? There is little doubt that Y has committed a breach of the X–Y contract in failing first to use an armoured vehicle, and second to take out insurance. Z, whose proceeds of sale—presumably in banknotes and coins—were transported in an ordinary car with no insurance cover, were stolen and Z has suffered loss of the total sum of money that was taken into possession by Y. There is arguably a non-contractual bailment between Z and Y, for Y as bailee has taken possession of the money in a bag or envelope to be delivered to X. During the time after taking possession of the money and before delivery to X, or as it transpired here, the money was stolen, the takings have not passed into circulation yet and could constitute chattels. Any right of action by Z would advisedly be a personal action against Y, the bailee, and perhaps X.

There is no right vested in Z to claim the benefit of the contractual term in the X–Y contract, which was breached; Z has no cause of action in contract to claim damages caused by breach of that term.

It is in the tort of negligence taken together with the bailment, or on its own, that Z could claim against Y. Under the relationship of bailment, Y, the bailee, even under a gratuitous bailment owes a duty to Z, to take as much care of the goods bailed to it as a person of ordinary prudence would in such circumstances take care of its own goods.[113] As against X, a duty of care may be argued to be imposed by the law against it in relation to Z its customer, for the loss is reasonably foreseeable, the proximity of the relationship is close, and it is reasonable and just that such a duty is imposed. Z would argue that were it not for its reliance on the security offered by Y, which X had assumed responsibility to ensure a safe and careful passage of its takings from Z's store to X's vault, it would not have placed its money into Y's possession for the trip. As envisaged in *Donoghue v Stevenson*,[114] the expansion of the tort of negligence—which is not privity-rule bound—would make inroads into the law of obligations where there is no contract.

IV. Concluding Remarks

Although the Malaysian courts have been able to negotiate their way around the privity rule, the solutions employed are in some instances artificial, relying more on a legal fiction (eg an express trust when there is scant evidence of an intention to create a trust), and have not resulted in consistent decisions. The recent use of the constructive trust serves different aims. The imposition of the common-intention constructive trust can accord with the aim to grant the third party a remedy corresponding to the expectation of the promisee. However, where the constructive trust is imposed because of the defendant's unconscionable conduct, as in *Takako* and *Kayveas* (the issuance of an additional 99,998 shares and then the transfer of 100,000 shares), then the aim of the action is further removed from an enforcement of promise situation to one which is more closely related to granting a proprietary remedy in an equitable wrong situation. This is not a fact situation of a third party beneficiary claiming on the trust of a promise for the benefit intended under the contract against the promisee-trustee or promisor or both.

In a regime of law, following English law, where equity's principles are drawn upon, it can be expected that the unique creature of Equity—the trust—is used to provide a solution. The map of third party's contractual rights in a civil law system, without the role played by

[113] s 104, Contracts Act 1950; *Port Swettenham Authority v TW Wu and Co (M) Sdn Bhd* [1978] 2 MLJ 137 (PC).
[114] [1932] AC 562 (HL).

Equity's trust, would exhibit a different landscape.[115] A judicial attitude hospitable to Equity's role in this area has perhaps in part seen less of an impetus for third parties' rights to be resolved under the facility of Contract. There is nothing wrong for equity to provide the remedy where the facts of the case, for instance, do constitute an express trust of the promise for the benefit of the third party beneficiary in accordance with the principles of trust law. However, the temptation to stretch orthodoxy in order to provide the remedy in the immediate case which deserves judicial redress[116] would do more harm than good in the long run if left undetected where the fiction gains ascendency over truth. A coherent system of clear legal principles must surely be the aim of any rational legal system. The inconsistency of the decisions is a verdict that there are justified limits to their application.

The indirect manner in which a non-contractual party with a chose in action or immunity conferred in a contract has to protect or enforce his right has led to the expansion of other areas of the law. A law of torts that protects pure economic loss has a bigger role to play in giving a remedy to a non-contractual third party. The hypothetical examples and cases have shown that much dexterity in handling legal concepts in other areas of the law is required to avoid the quagmire of litigation quicksand. This would likely result in higher transaction costs for the parties: the costs of litigation caused by uncertainty and complexity in the law would contribute to the transaction costs.

Malaysia's neighbour, Singapore, which shared a common legal heritage, has followed the way of the UK. Save for some differences, Singapore has adopted the English Contracts (Rights of Third Parties) Act 1999 by having its own similar statutory regime to vest third parties with a direct right to claim for benefits conferred in a contract intended for it under the Contract (Rights of Third Parties) Act (Cap 53B) enacted in 2001. Another nearby jurisdiction that has recently introduced similar legislation is Hong Kong, through its Contracts (Rights of Third Parties) Ordinance (Cap 623).

The motivation to reform Malaysia's law in this area so that it is comparable with the overwhelming majority of countries may prove irresistible since it is in the interest of commerce (if there is such a push there) that harmonious laws apply to the transaction between contracting parties and third parties who are conferred a benefit under the contract. Reform of the law in Malaysia should be by statute very much along the lines of the seminal English statute. The motivation for statutory reform should be weighed up against the views of the doubters.[117]

The statute would grant a direct remedy to the third party provided the statutory conditions are satisfied. The statutory conditions would operate like 'facilitative' rules enabling contracting parties if they so intend, to create such rights to vest in a third party. Unlike the other rights acquired by a third party to claim for benefits which have been considered here, this would be a right created by a statute of general application, as a true exception to the privity rule, to contracts in general save for specific contracts which are excluded. It is here that Malaysia—with a promise-centred theoretical structure of contract and a generous definition of consideration under the Contracts Act 1950—has to decide what are the 'facilitative' rules that would vest the right in the third party and that are consistent with the contract which birthed the third party right in the first place. This commentator thinks that

[115] See K Zweigert and H Kotz, *An Introduction to Comparative Law* (Oxford: OUP 1998) ch 34; VV Palmer, 'Contracts in Favour of Third Parties in Europe: First Steps Toward Tomorrow's Harmonization' [2003] 1 Euro Rev Priv L 8, 20–21.

[116] I am grateful for this helpful point made by the commentator Mr Tan Zhong Xing, Sheridan Fellow with the National University of Singapore, Faculty of Law, at the colloquium in January 2015.

[117] P Kincaid, 'Privity and Private Justice in Contract' (1997) 12 JCL 47; R Stevens, 'The Contracts (Rights of Third Parties) Act 1999' (2004) 120 LQR 292.

the 'facilitative' rules in the English statute would be suitable, as the Malaysian liberal position on consideration has left the door ajar in that the consideration required to form the contract, the enforceable promise, need not be supplied by the promisee. If therefore the contract, being formed, already envisages 'any other person' besides the contracting parties to be part of the creation process, it is not a big step to take in saying that had the contracting parties intended that a third party may enforce a term of that contract, then he may do so. Put differently, first, since contract formation allows consideration to proceed from a third party and, second, if a contract thus formed intended that any third party suitably identified shall be able to enforce a term of the contract then, third, an exception is made to the privity rule to allow the third party to enforce the term of the contract. The statutory exception only comes in at the third stage.[118] There should also be the freedom to opt out of the statutory regime by clear contractual provisions to show the contracting parties' intention. It is then seen as an additional right that can be conferred on the third party; it does not abolish the privity rule that is basic to the Contracts Act 1950. It is a positive right vested in the third party. Freedom of contract remains.

[118] See ss 1 and 2 of the Contracts (Rights of Third Parties) Act 1999 (UK).

8

Contract Formation in Singapore

*TAN Cheng Han**

I. Introduction

Contract law in Singapore is largely comprised of case law. This is because Singapore is a former British colony and therefore adopted a common law system based on English law that was introduced to Singapore in 1826 when the Second Charter of Justice was promulgated. This was confirmed in *R v Willans*.[1]

In 1993, Singapore enacted the Application of English Law Act.[2] Section 3(1) of the Act states that the 'common law of England (including the principles and rules of equity), so far as it was part of the law of Singapore immediately before 12th November 1993, shall continue to be part of the law of Singapore'. Section 3(2) adds that the common law 'shall continue to be in force in Singapore, as provided in subsection (1), so far as it is applicable to the circumstances of Singapore and its inhabitants and subject to such modifications as those circumstances may require'. English cases therefore continue to be regarded as highly persuasive and are frequently cited and applied by Singapore courts.[3] Since the 1990s, Singapore courts have also increasingly referred to judicial decisions from other Commonwealth countries for guidance. Notwithstanding this, in many areas of commercial law, including contract law, Singapore continues to closely follow English law not only for historical reasons but for the certainty that this provides to foreign entities that conduct business in Singapore. There are signs, though, that the courts in Singapore may be more prepared to depart from English law in certain areas (see the discussion on the doctrine of consideration in section X below). This is because of a maturing judiciary and a desire to promote Singapore as a preferred venue for dispute resolution, particularly those involving Asian parties.

Section 4 of the Act also provides that certain English enactments will, with necessary modifications, apply or continue to apply in Singapore. In the context of contract law, three important English statutes that continue to apply in Singapore are the Misrepresentation Act 1967, the Unfair Contract Terms Act 1977, and the Sale of Goods Act 1979. These English statutes supplement the common law on contract in Singapore.[4]

II. The Objective Test of Agreement

As a general principle, a contract between two or more persons comes into existence when there is agreement between all the parties to such contract, as to the terms of the contract.

* Cite as CH Tan, 'Contract Formation in Singapore' in Chen-Wishart, Loke, & Vogenauer, *Studies in the Contract Laws of Asia Vol II: Formation and Third Party Beneficiaries* (Oxford: OUP 2017) ch 8.

[1] (1858) 3 Ky 16, where it was held that the Second Charter of Justice introduced English law into the Straits Settlements which comprised Malacca, Penang, and Singapore.

[2] Cap 7A, 1994 Rev Ed.

[3] This explains the large number of English cases cited in this chapter. Where there are no Singapore cases on a particular point, judges and lawyers will frequently look to English law as a starting point.

[4] Others include the Corporate Bodies' Contracts Act 1960 and the Minors' Contracts Act 1987.

Contract Formation in Singapore. Tan Cheng Han.

The process by which such agreement is reached can be relatively straightforward, or it may involve protracted negotiations. Nevertheless, in order to create a framework within which it can be determined whether a contract has been formed, Singapore law generally requires a congruence of offer and acceptance. An enforceable agreement is formed (subject to other requirements such as consideration) when an offer made by one party is accepted by another.[5] Without this basic requirement being met, no contract comes into existence. Singapore law considers an agreement to have been reached when an objective ascertainment of all the relevant circumstances of the case points towards the existence of an agreement.[6] In other words, when determining whether offer and acceptance have taken place, this is ascertained objectively from the surrounding circumstances and is not based on the subjective intentions of the parties. The Singapore Court of Appeal has therefore said that the existence of any contract must be culled from the written correspondence and contemporaneous conduct of the parties at the material time.[7] Accordingly, an agreement may be held to have been formed even if one of the parties subjectively did not have any such intention. The courts will not give effect to the unexpressed reservations of a party but will construe the intentions of the parties based on their conduct from an objective standpoint.[8]

While the law requires both an offer and an acceptance, it can sometimes be difficult to determine which party has made the offer and that the conduct of the other party amounts to an acceptance. For example, there may be proposals and counter-proposals going back and forth so it may not be clear at which point the parties came to a consensus. Furthermore, the parties may not even consider any consensus to have been reached to give rise to a contract, because their respective legal advisors have yet to set out the terms in a written contract that is to be executed by the parties, whereupon the agreement will take effect. As such an agreement only takes effect upon execution, and if both parties sign the contract simultaneously or within seconds of each other, it is difficult to determine an offer from one party to the other.

Where it is clear from the execution of the written contract by both parties that they clearly intended there to be a binding agreement, pragmatic courts will not be troubled by the difficulty of fitting the formation of such an agreement into the traditional framework of offer and acceptance.[9] The framework is therefore important only when the facts on their face do not clearly point to the existence (or non-existence) of a contract, thereby necessitating an inquiry into whether there was finality in the negotiations, giving rise to a consensus between the parties.

Courts may also imply a contract from the parties' conduct and from the circumstances of the case, as in *Blackpool and Fylde Aero Club Ltd v Blackpool Borough Council.*[10] An instance of an implied contract in Singapore, where the courts found an implied retainer

[5] *Overseas Union Insurance Ltd v Home and Overseas Insurance Co Ltd* [2002] SGHC 109, [2002] 2 SLR(R) 1 (HC); *Trans-World (Aluminium) Ltd v Cornelder China (Singapore)* [2003] SGHC 56, [2003] 3 SLR(R) 501 (HC) [155].

[6] *Bakery Mart Pte Ltd (in receivership) v Sincere Watch Ltd* [2003] SGCA 36, [2003] 3 SLR(R) 462 (CA) [22]; *Aircharter World Pte Ltd v Kontena Nasional Bhd* [1999] SGCA 36, [1999] 2 SLR(R) 440 (CA) [30]; *Zurich Insurance (Singapore) Pte Ltd v B-Gold Interior Design & Construction Pte Ltd* [2008] SGCA 27, [2008] 3 SLR(R) 1029 (CA) [125]–[126]; *Gay Choon Ing v Loh Sze Ti Terence Peter* [2009] SGCA 3, [2009] 2 SLR(R) 332 (CA) [47].

[7] *Tribune Investment Trust Inc v Soosan Trading Co Ltd* [2000] SGCA 33, [2000] 2 SLR(R) 407 (CA) [39].

[8] *Aircharter* (n 6) [30].

[9] It could be said that the draft written contract that is to be signed by the parties amounts to a mutual offer to each other which both accept when they sign the contract. This is not the traditional sequential understanding of offer and acceptance involving an offer made by one party that is subsequently accepted by the other party.

[10] [1990] 1 WLR 1195 (CA). This case is discussed in greater detail in section IV.2 below.

between a solicitor and a client is the case of *Anwar Patrick Adrian v Ng Chong Hue LLC*.[11] The Singapore Court of Appeal found that although the plaintiffs did not communicate directly with the defendant firm of solicitors, the conduct and documents objectively pointed towards the existence of an implied retainer between the parties.[12]

III. Offers

In relation to an offer, the application of the objective test means that a party must have objectively expressed a willingness to contract on specified terms, and be bound by such terms if, while the offer is open, it is accepted, by the person to whom the offer is communicated.[13] That is, the expression of willingness or consent to contract must be one which would reasonably be construed as such by a person in the position of the offeree, rather than any subjective intention present in the offeror's mind that may differ from that.[14]

Although the test is an objective one, there is one aspect of it that contains a subjective element. Where an offeree knows, despite the objective appearance of willingness to contract, that the offeror had no intention to do so, the offeror is not bound. The objective test gives way here to the subjective knowledge of the offeree because the offeree, knowing of the offeror's real intention,[15] cannot assert that there was *consensus ad idem*.[16] For this reason, the Court of Appeal has stated that 'the objective test of agreement is not wholly objective, but is in fact partly objective and partly subjective'.[17]Another possibility arises where the offeree neither believes that the offeror intends to make a binding offer nor knows that there is no such intention despite the offer being one which would meet the objective test. In most instances, this question will not arise because it is unlikely that an offeree will have any doubt over the offeror's intention if a reasonable person in the offeree's position would construe the offeror's actions as expressing a willingness to contract. However, in exceptional cases this issue can arise as the offeree may be uncertain or has no view over the meaning of the offeror's words, or is aware of facts which causes him (the offeree) to be uncertain of the actual intention of the offeror.[18] English cases have differed on this issue.[19] In Singapore, the Court of Appeal in *Aircharter World Pte Ltd v Kontena Nasional Bhd* mentioned the issue but did not discuss the opposing views as it was not relevant to the case at hand.[20] The court may nevertheless have implicitly preferred the view that the offeror should only be bound if the offeree actually believed that the offeror intended to contract. First, the court took note[21] that a leading English contract law text stated that the objective test 'should not apply' to this possibility because there was, by reason of the offeree's state of mind, no risk of his

[11] [2014] 3 SLR 761 (CA).

[12] Professor Yeo Tiong Min in his response at the 2015 colloquium characterized this case as an instance of an 'inferred contract' which comes into existence without the usual rules of offer and acceptance being applied.

[13] *Aircharter* (n 6) [47].

[14] *Tribune* (n 7) [40]; *Projection Pte Ltd v The Tai Ping Insurance Co Ltd* [2001] SGCA 28, [2001] 1 SLR(R) 798 (CA) [15]; *Chia Ee Lin Evelyn v Teh Guek Ngor Engelin* [2004] SGHC 193, [2004] 4 SLR(R) 330 (HC) [43].

[15] *Aircharter* (n 6) [31].

[16] *Chwee Kin Keong v Digilandmall.com Pte Ltd* [2005] SGCA 2, [2005] 1 SLR(R) 502 (CA) [31].

[17] *Aircharter* (n 6) [32], citing *Smith v Hughes* (1871) LR 6 QB 597, 607.

[18] eg the offeree had read an article in a business publication that a third party was purchasing the very item being offered to the offeree.

[19] *Paul Wilson & Co A/S v Partenreederei Hannah Blumenthal (The Hannah Blumenthal)* [1983] 1 AC 854 (HL) expressed the view that the objective test is met if the offeror's acts could be reasonably regarded as giving rise to the requisite intention and the offeree also held the belief that the offeror intended to contract. A different view was expressed by Staughton J in *Excomm Ltd v Guan Guan Shipping (Pte) Ltd (The Golden Bear)* [1987] 1 Lloyd's Rep 330. Staughton J's view was approved by Bingham LJ in *Food Corporation of India v Antclizo Shipping Corporation (The Antclizo)* [1987] EWCA Civ J0407-1, [1987] 2 Lloyd's Rep 130 (CA) 143, but doubted by Nicholls LJ at 146–147.

[20] *Aircharter* (n 6) [30].

[21] ibid [31].

suffering any prejudice as a result of the objective appearance of the offeror's intention.[22] Second, the court cited[23] *Paul Wilson & Co A/S v Partenreederei Hannah Blumenthal (The Hannah Blumenthal)* where Lord Diplock stated that the necessary *consensus ad idem* would be present where a reasonable person would understand the communication as giving rise to an offer, and the offeree did in fact understand the communication in that manner.[24] In other words, the offeree must as a matter of fact have understood that the offeror intended to contract on specified terms.[25]

It is suggested that this is the better position. The policy rationale for the objective test is that it facilitates certainty in commercial transactions. It would be inconvenient for commercial affairs to be subject to the uncertainty of a party's unexpressed subjective intention. Such reasoning is not applicable where the offeree is uncertain about or has no view about the offeror's intention to contract. If the offeree is uncertain, then it behoves him to make further inquiries if he wishes to be certain of the offeror's intention. If the offeree chooses to proffer an acceptance despite uncertainty over the offeror's intention to contract, the offeree takes a chance and cannot claim that he has suffered any prejudice.[26]

IV. Invitations to Treat as Distinguished from Offers

In applying the objective test of whether an agreement had been reached between the parties, the common law often draws a distinction between an offer and an invitation to treat. An invitation to treat is merely an invitation to others to make an offer. It is 'an attempt to initiate negotiations, to induce offers' and as such 'a response to an "invitation to treat" can never result in a concluded contract'.[27] It is usually part of the process of negotiation that may eventually lead to an agreement between the parties. Whether an act or expression amounts to an offer or is only an invitation to treat will be assessed objectively in the light of all the relevant circumstances from the standpoint of a reasonable person in the offeree/invitee's position. Usually the distinction will be clear but difficult cases can sometimes arise. For example, in *Michael Gerson (Leasing) Ltd v Wilkinson* one question was whether the statement: 'I am willing to make an outright sale for £319,000 plus VAT' amounted to an offer.[28] Clarke LJ said it seemed to him that this was merely an invitation to treat but also recognized that it was capable of being regarded as an offer. In any event, it was held that there was no acceptance.

Where a person has indicated clearly that he does not yet wish to be bound by the statement he has made (eg when he qualifies his words with the phrase 'subject to contract') no contract can arise from any acceptance by the person to whom the statement has been made. The objective test may also negative any finding of an offer even where the word 'offer' has been used if it is clear from an objective interpretation of the facts that no offer had been intended.[29]

To provide greater commercial certainty, there are specific situations where a prima facie rule of law applies as to whether an offer has arisen or if there was only an invitation to treat. Such rules are presumptive and can be negatived by evidence to the contrary. These rules

[22] A Guest (ed), *Chitty on Contracts* (27th edn, London: Sweet & Maxwell 1994) para 2-002. In the most recent edition, H Beale (ed), *Chitty on Contracts* (31st edn, London: Sweet & Maxwell 2012), the proposition is set out at para 2-004 where it is submitted that the objective test 'should not apply'.

[23] *Aircharter* (n 6) [32].

[24] [1982] UKHL J1202-1, [1983] 1 AC 854 (HL) 915–916.

[25] This is the position preferred by the leading Singapore contract law textbook, A Phang (ed), *The Law of Contract in Singapore* (Singapore: Academy Publishing 2012) para 03.027.

[26] See also E Peel, *Treitel on the Law of Contract* (13th edn, London: Sweet & Maxwell 2011) para 2-003.

[27] *Gay Choon Ing* (n 6) [48].

[28] [2000] EWCA Civ J0731-21, [2000] QB 514 (CA) 530.

[29] *Datec Electronic Holdings Ltd v United Parcels Service Ltd* [2007] UKHL 23, [2007] 1 WLR 1325 (HL).

are not necessarily inconsistent with the objective test as they may well reflect what reasonable persons would have understood.[30] It will not be possible to discuss all the situations where such presumptions arise and only two will be mentioned.[31]

1. Priced Goods on Display

The first relates to priced goods that are on display whether in a shop window or in a self-service store.

English common law generally regards goods on display as invitations to treat and not offers.[32] One stated rationale is that otherwise, the customer's act of putting an item in a shopping basket would constitute acceptance and the customer could not thereafter substitute such item for another that he preferred.[33] Another is that 'the vendor might otherwise find himself bound to a series of contracts that he would be quite unable to fulfil'.[34] These reasons are not convincing.[35] It is possible to regard the acceptance as arising only when the customer brings the item to the cashier for payment rather than merely placing it in a shopping basket.[36] Similarly, the vendor could be protected from having to fulfil every order because it could be implied that its offer is 'subject to availability'.

Although there are no Singapore cases on point, there are obiter statements that assume the position in England is valid in Singapore.[37] However unintuitive such a position may be to a non-legally trained person,[38] it is unlikely that Singapore courts would wish to adopt a different approach given that the English position has generally been accepted by the legal community and has not apparently caused any problems for the retail sector while a more 'consumerist' approach (which would prevent the trader from refusing to sell on the terms advertised or displayed), being untested, may lead to unforeseen issues.

2. Calls for Tender

The second presumptive situation to be discussed involves calls for tender. The general rule is that they are invitations to treat and not offers.[39] They are intended to invite others to submit offers that fulfil the objectives of the person calling the tender. The latter may then decide whether and if so which offer to accept. Tenders are used in a wide variety of circumstances, and often used where price may not be the overriding factor because of other qualitative considerations such as the reputation of the tenderer, the materials to be used, and so on.

However, the presumption that a call for tenders is not an offer can be displaced, for example if on an objective interpretation of the call document, the caller agrees to be bound

[30] Phang (n 25) para 03.035. Though it will be suggested below that the default rule in relation to goods on display may not reflect the view of ordinary consumers.

[31] Others not discussed include auctions and advertisements.

[32] *Pharmaceutical Society of Great Britain v Boots Cash Chemists (Southern) Ltd* [1953] EWCA Civ J0205-5, [1953] 1 QB 401 (CA); *Fisher v Bell* [1961] 1 QB 394.

[33] *Pharmaceutical Society* (n 32).

[34] *Esso Petroleum v Commissioners of Customs and Excise* [1975] UKHL J1210-2, [1976] 1 WLR 1 (HL) 11.

[35] Peel (n 26) para 2-009.

[36] That this is the point at which acceptance could take place is alluded to in *Chua Kian Kok v Public Prosecutor* [1999] SGHC 65, [1999] 1 SLR(R) 826 (HC) [59].

[37] ibid; *Chwee Kin Keong v Digilandmall.com Pte Ltd* [2004] SGHC 71, [2004] 2 SLR(R) 594 (HC) [94]; affd in *Digilandmall* (CA) (n 16) without comment on this issue.

[38] In *Chua Kian Kok* (n 36) [59], Yong Pung How CJ opined: 'The common perception would be that the shop was offering these items at the marked prices and [the customer] was accepting the offer by bringing it to the checkout counter and paying for it.'

[39] *Spencer v Harding* (1870) LR 5 CP 561; *UOL Development (Novena) Pte Ltd v Commissioner of Stamp Duties* [2007] SGHC 173, [2008] 1 SLR(R) 126 (HC) [14].

by the highest price.[40] It is also possible that a call for tenders may be expressed in such manner or (as was the case in *Blackpool and Fylde Aero Club Ltd v Blackpool Borough Council*) it may be implied from the format and circumstances in which the tender was called that there is a contractual obligation on the caller to consider all tenders received that comply with the conditions set, even though it does not have to accept any of them.[41] In such circumstances, an offer to consider all tenders received in good order is made when the caller issues the tender documents, and this limited offer is accepted by the tenderer who submits the tender documents in accordance with the stipulated conditions. However, implying any such obligation raises the possibility of uncertainty,[42] and consequently such cases ought to be rare and limited to their facts.[43] The Singapore Court of Appeal has said that facts supporting the existence of implied contracts should be subject to the same level of scrutiny as express contracts.[44] Such contracts ought not lightly to be implied.[45] All the requirements for the formation of a contract, such as offer and acceptance, consideration, and intention to create legal relations, must be satisfied before the court will imply the existence of a contract.[46] It is also open to inviters of tenders to expressly exclude any obligations whatsoever on their part in the tender documents.

V. Communication and Termination of Offer

An offer must be communicated to an offeree because without this the offer will be incapable of being accepted. The offer need not, however, be communicated to specific offerees as an offer can be made to the whole world or to a class of persons. Thus, in *Carlill v Carbolic Smoke Ball Co*[47] it was held that an advertisement addressed to the world at large was capable of being and did amount to an offer. While there are no Singapore cases to the same effect, many Singapore cases have cited the *Carbolic Smoke Ball* case[48] and this proposition can be considered to represent the law in Singapore.

After an offer has been communicated to the offeree, it may be terminated or revoked at any time before acceptance but not after the offer has been accepted. This is the position in England and while there do not appear to be any Singapore cases directly on point, the position in Singapore is unlikely to be different.[49] The reason for this is because an offer

[40] ibid; *Harvela Investments Ltd v Royal Trust of Canada (CI) Ltd* [1985] UKHL J0711-1, [1986] AC 207 (HL).

[41] *Blackpool and Fylde Aero Club Ltd v Blackpool Borough Council* [1990] EWCA Civ J0525-1, [1990] 1 WLR 1195 (CA). The issue of how to quantify the damage suffered was not discussed. Damages are likely to be assessed on the basis of the 'loss of a chance' as to which see Phang (n 25) paras 21.026–21.031.

[42] See Phang (n 25) paras 03.052–03.055.

[43] It is suggested that the implied contract in *Blackpool* may be justified on the basis that the invitation prescribed a familiar procedure. Indeed, the plaintiff had for an unbroken period since 1875 been able to secure the concession to operate pleasure flights from the airport managed by the defendant council. Accordingly, the failure to consider the plaintiff's tender was probably in breach of the standard procedure that had been in operation for a lengthy period and thus contrary to the assumption on which the inviter and tenderers operated.

[44] *Cooperatieve Centrale Raiffeisen-Boerenleenbank BA (trading as Rabobank International), Singapore Branch v Motorola Electronics Pte Ltd* [2010] SGCA 47, [2011] 2 SLR 63 (CA) [46].

[45] See also *Lian Hwee Choo Phebe v Tan Seng Ong* [2013] 3 SLR 1162 (CA).

[46] *Cooperatieve* (n 44) [46].

[47] [1893] 1 QB 256.

[48] eg *Alrich Development Pte Ltd v Rafiq Jumabhoy* [1995] SGCA 53, [1995] 2 SLR(R) 340 (CA) and *Gay Choon Ing* (n 6).

[49] Arguably, *Dickson Trading (S) Pte Ltd v Transmarco Ltd* [1987] SGHC 59, [1987] SLR(R) 674 (HC) at [39] implicitly accepts the common law position in England. Chan Sek Keong JC was there making the point that the offeror in a unilateral contract has an obligation not to revoke the offer after the offeree has embarked on the performance of the condition. While this statement was made in the context of a unilateral contract (which will be discussed later in this section), the reference to an obligation not to revoke the offer once performance has been embarked on indicates that the general position is that offers are revocable as long as acceptance has not taken place.

does not of itself carry an implied promise that it will be kept open for any period of time. Even where there is such an express or implied promise, the offer may be withdrawn if the promise is not supported by consideration[50] from the offeree.[51] An offeree who wishes to have the benefit of a binding offer that is kept open for a stipulated period must offer consideration to support the promise to keep the offer open.

For an offer to be terminated, the termination must be communicated to the offeree such that if it is sent by post the termination takes effect only when the letter reaches the offeree.[52] It may not, however, be necessary for the communication to the offeree to come from the offeror,[53] provided the source of the information is reliable.[54]

The position in Singapore (and England) can cause unfairness to offerees who have relied on the offer by incurring time and expense in determining whether to accept an offer. Where offerees have not, through the provision of consideration, obtained for themselves an express promise to keep the offer open for a stipulated time, it is possible in exceptional circumstances for a court to find that there was nevertheless consideration from the offeree because the offeree promised to undertake the due diligence for the proposed transaction in return for the offeror's promise to keep the offer open for a period of time. Another possibility, though untested in Singapore, is that the offeror's promise and the offeree's subsequent action have given rise to an estoppel against the offeror such that the offeror cannot rely on the lack of consideration as a defence against a claim for breach of contract should the offeree accept the offer within the prescribed time.[55] Essentially, the offeree would sue on the promise to keep the offer open and rely on promissory estoppel to prevent the offeror from raising the absence of consideration as a defence.[56]

A more established area in which the offeree is afforded greater protection against withdrawal arises in cases of unilateral contracts. A unilateral contract is one where the offeror makes a promise, usually to pay a sum of money, to another if the latter performs an act which the latter accepts by fully performing such act. For example, the offeror may promise to pay a bonus to employees if they remain in employment at a certain date.[57] Unlike a bilateral contract which involves the mutual exchange of promises that bind all the parties immediately, the offeror in a unilateral contract is not seeking a promise to perform an act but instead is binding himself to do something only *if* the stipulated act is completed. The completion of the act constitutes acceptance and until this takes place the offeree is under no obligation to do so and if he has started, can stop at any time.[58]

However, if the offeror can withdraw the offer at any time prior to the fulfilment of the condition, this can cause great injustice to the offeree if he has already begun attempting to fulfil the condition set out by the offeror. Accordingly, it is generally thought that once there has been a degree of part performance that is not *de minimis*, the offeror should not be allowed to withdraw the offer. There are two possible justifications for this, both of which

[50] Consideration, broadly speaking, is the giving of something in return for a promise. This is discussed in section X below.

[51] *Dickinson v Dodds* (1876) 2 Ch D 463 (CA).

[52] *Byrne & Co v Van Tienhoven* (1880) 5 CPD 344. There are exceptions to this rule, eg where the letter is received but the addressee has omitted to read it or disposed of it by mistake, see *Eaglehill Ltd v J Needham (Builders) Ltd* [1973] AC 992 (HL) 1011.

[53] *Dickinson* (n 51).

[54] See MP Furmston, *Cheshire, Fifoot and Furmston's Law of Contract* (15th edn, Oxford: OUP 2007) 74.

[55] See the discussion on promissory estoppel in section XI below.

[56] This would be an extension of the traditional understanding of promissory estoppel which is that it cannot be used as a 'sword' but only as a 'shield'. This is discussed further in section XI.

[57] *Brader Daniel John v Commerzbank AG* [2014] 2 SLR 81 (HC).

[58] Thus, there is no need for any acceptance to be communicated to the offeror, *Carbolic Smoke Ball* (n 47).

have judicial support.[59] The first is that the offeror in fact makes two offers, the principal one and a collateral or implied offer to keep the offer open once performance has begun. The latter offer is accepted by beginning performance.[60] The second justification is that there is only one offer which is accepted when performance begins.[61]

While both approaches will lead to the same outcome, and it does not appear that one approach will lead to superior results over the other, it is suggested that the 'two-offer' approach provides a better justification for the offeror's inability to withdraw once performance has commenced. This is because although performance may have begun, neither party is bound on the principal promise until the act has been completed. Given that no primary contract arises, all that exists is an implied collateral contract to keep the primary offer open. Accordingly, the offeree may cease performance at any time without being in breach of contract.

English law as well as Singapore law[62] appears to assume that the primary offer is irrevocable once acceptance by performance has begun. As a matter of principle, though, it is submitted that depending on the circumstances, there can be situations where the right to revoke the offer without any adverse consequences may be implied. For example, a person may have offered a reward for a lost item but if there has been no success after a lengthy period of time despite third parties embarking on a search, it seems reasonable that the offeror should be entitled to call off the search by withdrawing the reward, for example where the passage of time may render the identification of the lost item especially difficult or raise the prospect of counterfeiting.

This appears to be the position in Australia. In *Mobil Oil Australia Ltd v Wellcome International Pty Ltd*,[63] the court expressed the view that as the respective positions of the offeror and offeree can vary greatly from one unilateral contract to another, it did not accept that it was universally unjust for an offeror to be at liberty to revoke once the offeree had commenced performance. Further, even if an ancillary contract not to revoke should be implied in all cases, this did not mean that a revocation would be ineffective. It would simply give rise to the normal remedy of an award of damages.[64]

VI. Acceptance

In *Gay Choon Ing v Loh Sze Yi Terence Peter*, the Court of Appeal cited the following description of 'acceptance':[65] 'An acceptance is a final and unqualified expression of assent to the terms of an offer.'[66] Consistent with the objective test of agreement, whether there has been an acceptance of an offer is determined objectively from the relevant surrounding circumstances.[67] The facts must show that the acceptor has agreed without qualification to the terms of the offer. There are two elements to this. First, an acceptor cannot accept an offer with amendments or qualifications; this amounts to a counter-offer which only gives rise to a contract if the original offeror accepts such amendments or qualifications. There must be

[59] See Peel (n 26) para 2-053; Phang (n 25) paras 03.085–03.090.

[60] See *Daulia Ltd v Four Millbank Nominees Ltd* [1977] EWCA Civ J1124-1, [1978] Ch 231 (CA) 239; *Dickson Trading* (n 49) [39].

[61] *Errington v Errington and Woods* [1952] 1 KB 290 (CA) 295.

[62] See *Dickson Trading* (n 49) [39]; *Brader* (n 57) [66].

[63] (1998) 81 FCR 475 (Federal Court).

[64] This was also canvassed in Phang (n 25) para 03.090.

[65] *Gay Choon Ing* (n 6) [47]. See also *Aircharter* (n 6) [31].

[66] The citation was from the 12th edition of *Treitel on Law of Contract*. The 14th edition contains the same description at para 2-016.

[67] *Midlink Development Pte Ltd v The Stansfield Group Pte Ltd* [2004] SGHC 182, [2004] 4 SLR(R) 258 (HC) [47]; *Gay Choon Ing* (n 6); *Inland Revenue Commissioners v Fry* [2001] STC 1715 (HC); *Michael Gerson (Leasing) Ltd v Wilkinson* [2000] QB 514, 530, CA.

precise correspondence between the offer and the acceptance.[68] Second, the fact of acceptance must be clear. There is no unqualified assent where it is not clear what the acceptor is assenting, for example where a tenderer submitted two offers, one based on a fixed price and the other on a variable price, and the tender was accepted without specifying which of the two offers was being accepted.[69]

Acceptance can be inferred from conduct. The conduct must objectively point to an unequivocal acceptance of the offer.[70] For example, in *Midlink Development Pte Ltd v The Stansfield Group Pte Ltd*[71] it was held that even if there had not been a concluded agreement between the parties after a meeting, when the landlord subsequently forwarded new tenancy agreements and the tenant paid the revised rental set out therein, there had been acceptance by the tenant's conduct.

Acceptance can also be waived,[72] and even silence can give rise to acceptance though such cases will be exceptional as silence is generally equivocal.[73] Accordingly, an offer stipulating that the offeree's silence will constitute acceptance will generally not yield a binding contract. The law will not impose an obligation on the offeree to reject an offer.[74] In *Felthouse v Bindley*, an uncle wrote to his nephew offering to buy the nephew's horse at a certain price, stating that he would consider the horse to be his if he heard no more from the nephew.[75] The nephew intended that the uncle should have the horse at the price offered, and did not respond. Nevertheless, it was held that there was no acceptance as the uncle had no right to impose on his nephew the sale of the horse unless the nephew chose to specifically repudiate the uncle's offer.[76]

However, in some cases there could be a duty to respond, arising from the parties' existing relationship[77] or the way they have dealt with each other. For example, in *Rust v Abbey Life Assurance Co Ltd*, the court found a valid offer and acceptance, but went on to say that if such analysis was incorrect, when the defendant issued the insurance policy to the plaintiff, the plaintiff's conduct in holding on to such policy for seven months must lead to the 'inevitable inference' that the plaintiff had accepted the policy as a valid contract.[78] Although the court spoke of conduct, such 'conduct' amounted to no more than inaction or silence. The decision is correct given that it was the plaintiff's acts that led to the policy being sent to her—she had completed the application form and paid over a cheque in favour of the insurers. In this context, if the sending of the policy to her was the offer, her silence in the context of her earlier acts could objectively point to there being an unequivocal acceptance.

In Singapore, it has been held that contracts can be effectively concluded via electronic means over the internet. Specifically, programmed computers sending out automated

[68] *Stuttgart Auto Pte Ltd v Ng Shwu Yong* [2005] 1 SLR(R) 92 (HC); *Compaq Computer Asia Pte Ltd v Computer Interface (S) Pte Ltd* [2004] 3 SLR(R) 316 (CA).

[69] *Peter Lind & Co Ltd v Mersey Docks & Harbour Board* [1972] 2 Lloyd's Rep 234, HC.

[70] *Midlink* (n 67).

[71] [2004] SGHC 182, [2004] 4 SLR(R) 258 (HC). See also *Brogden v Metropolitan Railway Co* (1877) 2 App Cas 666 (HL) where deliveries were accepted by a railway company even though amendments proposed by the merchant to a draft agreement were never expressly agreed to by the railway company. It was held that there was an agreement on the terms of the amended agreement once the railway company accepted deliveries. For a case where it was held that there was no contract, see *Colliers International (Singapore) Pte Ltd v Senkee Logistics Pte Ltd* [2007] SGHC 18, [2007] 2 SLR(R) 230 (HC) as there had been no agreement on an important term.

[72] *Brader* (n 57).

[73] *Midlink* (n 67) [47]–[52].

[74] Other possible reasons for the rule include the disinclination of the common law to impose legal liability on individuals for omissions, and the contractual theory of the common law that a binding contract must be mutually achieved, see *Empirnall Holdings Pty Ltd v Machon Paull Partners Pty Ltd* (1988) 14 NSWLR 523 (CA) 527–528.

[75] (1862) 142 ER 1037.

[76] See also *Southern Ocean Shipbuilding Co Pte Ltd v Deutsche Bank AG & Anor* [1993] SGHC 221, [1993] 3 SLR(R) 86 (HC).

[77] *Midlink* (n 67) [51].

[78] [1979] EWCA Civ J0330-3, [1979] 2 Lloyd's Rep 334 (CA) 340.

responses can bind the sender where it is objectively clear that there has been a coincidence of offer and acceptance.[79] Communication through email can also lead to the conclusion of a contract[80] and it is submitted that the position should be no different for instant messaging.[81]

1. Battle of the Forms

Commercial parties typically use standard printed contract forms. Where both parties to an agreement purport to contract on the basis of their respective standard forms, the question is which form prevails. As the general principle is that there must be a correspondence between offer and acceptance, a party that purports to use its standard form to accept an offer based on the offeror's standard form does not accept the offer but instead makes a counter-offer. Should the original offeror then accept the counter-offer, the second standard form prevails and governs the terms of the agreement.[82] When parties negotiate through a series of offers and counter-offers, whether these are exchanged orally or through standard form contracts or in some other manner, the question is whether any particular act during the negotiations can be identified as objectively accepting an offer.

The classic case is *Butler Machine Tool Co Ltd v Ex-Cell-O Corp (England) Ltd*;[83] there, the seller offered to supply a machine for a stated price on the seller's standard conditions which included a clause stating that goods would be charged at prices prevailing at the delivery date. The buyer replied by placing an order on its standard form contract which did not contain a price variation clause. The buyer's standard form contract contained a tear-out acknowledgement slip which was to be used to accept the buyer's order on the terms and conditions set out in their standard form. The seller returned the acknowledgement form duly completed, but with a covering letter stating that delivery would be in accordance with its earlier offer. Delivery and acceptance duly took place but a dispute arose when the seller purported to rely on the price variation clause as costs had increased.

One possibility was that the seller's last act was a counter-offer which the buyer accepted when it took delivery. However, the court instead took the view that despite the covering letter, the seller had accepted the buyer's counter-offer by returning the acknowledgement form. The court said that when the seller referred to its earlier offer this was only intended to identify the *subject matter* of the sale and not the *terms* of that offer. Such an interpretation of the seller's final written communication is unconvincing.[84] However, the result cannot be faulted if this interpretation was correct.

Lord Denning MR said that in many cases the following approach would be preferable to the traditional offer and acceptance approach:

> The better way is to look at all the documents passing between the parties—and glean from them, or from the conduct of the parties, whether they have reached agreement on all material points—even though there may be differences between the forms and conditions printed on the back of them.[85]

However, it is not clear that this is indeed a better approach. Even if all the documents and circumstances were viewed as a whole (and they should even with the traditional

[79] *Digilandmall* (HC) (n 37) [91], [134]; affd in *Digilandmall* (CA) (n 16).
[80] *Digilandmall* (HC) (n 37) [97], [136].
[81] See further the discussion in section VI.2 below on contracts entered into electronically.
[82] *British Road Services Ltd v Arthur V Crutchley Ltd* [1967] EWCA Civ J1215-2, [1967] 1 WLR 835 (CA).
[83] [1977] EWCA Civ J0425-1, [1979] 1 WLR 401 (CA).
[84] A similar reservation is expressed in Phang (n 25) para 03.109.
[85] *Butler Machine* (n 83) 404. See also Port Sudan Cotton Co v Govindaswamy Chettiar & Sons [1977] EWCA Civ J0308-3, [1977] 2 Lloyd's Rep 5 (CA) 10.

approach[86]), it would still be necessary to determine the point at which there was finality in the negotiations and a commitment to be bound. Indeed, the Singapore Court of Appeal has questioned whether there is any real difference between Lord Denning's approach and the traditional approach. The court also opined that the traditional approach is probably the approach that has hitherto been adopted in the Singapore context.[87]

2. Communication of Acceptance

As a general rule, acceptance must be communicated to the offeror as it would be unfair for an offeror to be bound by an acceptance that the offeror knew nothing of.[88] Thus, if the acceptance is drowned out by an aircraft flying overhead, or if the telephone line is cut off before the acceptance is made, or if the communication is so indistinct that it was not heard by the offeror, there is no contract.[89] There is also no communication where the offeree's conduct is not such as would allow the offeror to reasonably infer that acceptance had taken place.[90] The acceptance need not, however, be communicated by the acceptor and can be brought to the attention of the offeror by a third party acting with the authority of the acceptor or if the facts are such as to indicate that the offeror must have known of the acceptance.[91] Where the failure to receive the acceptance was due to the offeror's fault, for example where the offeror did not fully comprehend what the acceptor said but did not seek a clarification[92] or where the acceptance was communicated to the offeror's agent authorized to receive such an acceptance, an agreement will come into existence.[93]

Where acceptance has been made by post, Singapore law has adopted the 'postal acceptance rule'.[94] This rule provides that where acceptance is made by post, such acceptance takes place at the time of posting rather than at the time it was read by the offeror, or received by the offeror, or when it would in the ordinary course of events have been received by the offeror.[95] The rule applies even if the acceptance was lost in the post.[96] The postal acceptance rule is beneficial to acceptors[97] and it is suggested that the rule is best understood as the common law's attempt to balance matters in favour of the acceptor against the general rule that an offer may be withdrawn at any time.

The postal acceptance rule only applies where it is reasonable for the acceptance to be communicated by post. It is clearly reasonable if the offer itself was sent by post. Even if the offer was communicated orally, it may be reasonable to accept by post if the parties live some distance from each other.[98] It will not be reasonable to communicate acceptance by post if the terms of the offer exclude such means of acceptance, or where the offer has been made by email or telephone.[99] In such circumstances, the offeree should communicate acceptance through a more instantaneous form of communication.

[86] See *Gay Choon Ing* (n 6) [61]–[63] which affirmed the traditional approach.

[87] *Gay Choon Ing* (n 6) [63]. It should be noted, though, that the Court of Appeal in an earlier decision endorsed Lord Denning's approach, see *Projection* (n 14) [16].

[88] *Holwell Securities Ltd v Hughes* [1973] EWCA Civ J1105-4, [1974] 1 WLR 155 (CA) 157.

[89] *Entores Ltd v Miles Far East Corp* [1955] EWCA Civ J0517-1, [1955] 2 QB 327 (CA) 333.

[90] *Brader* (n 57), though it was held that a contract had been formed because the offeror had waived acceptance and the offer was also one relating to a unilateral contract.

[91] *Re International Contract Coy, Levita's Case* (1867) LR 3 Ch App 36 (CA).

[92] *Entores* (n 89) 333.

[93] *Henthorn v Fraser* [1892] 2 Ch 27 (CA) 33.

[94] *Lee Seng Heng v The Guardian Assurance Co Ltd* [1932] MLJ 17, [1932] SSLR 110 (Supreme Court).

[95] ibid; *Stevenson, Jacques & Co v McLean* (1880) 5 QBD 346.

[96] *Household Fire and Carriage Accident Insurance Co v Grant* (1879) 4 Ex D 216.

[97] There is a valid acceptance upon posting even if the offeror has already posted a letter withdrawing the offer, provided the offeror's letter has not reached the offeree before the posting of the acceptance, see *Henthorn* (n 93); *Re London & Northern Bank* [1900] 1 Ch 200.

[98] *Henthorn* (n 93).

[99] Peel (n 26) para 2-032.

The postal acceptance rule is probably of little importance today given the widespread use of instantaneous and electronic communications. Commercial parties are likely today to communicate acceptances by phone, fax, teleconference, email, and perhaps even through some form of instant messaging. The postal acceptance rule should clearly have no application to such forms of communication which are virtually instantaneous. There is no issue of which party ought to bear the risk of a material time lag between communication and receipt. In Singapore, the High Court has leaned towards the receipt rule for these modern forms of communication rather than the postal acceptance rule, at least as the starting point.[100]

VII. Contracts Entered into Electronically

In addition to the foregoing, the Electronic Transactions Act must also be noted when considering contracts entered into in the online world.[101] Section 11(1) of the Act provides '[f]or the avoidance of doubt' that an offer and acceptance 'may be expressed by means of electronic communications'. The words 'for the avoidance of doubt' indicate that the Act is not intended to change the common law and simply confirms that electronic communications are a form of communication to which the common law rules of offer and acceptance are applicable.

Likewise, section 12 states that '[a]s between the originator and the addressee of an electronic communication, a declaration of intent or other statement shall not be denied legal effect, validity or enforceability solely on the ground that it is in the form of an electronic communication'. Under section 13(1) of the Act, the time of dispatch of an electronic communication is the time when it leaves the information system under the control of the originator of the communication, or the time when it is received if the electronic communication has not left an information system under the control of the originator.[102] The time of receipt of an electronic communication is the time when the electronic communication becomes capable of being retrieved by the addressee at an electronic address designated by the addressee.[103] This provision is probably only intended to deal with the question of when messages are dispatched and received, without changing the common law. Thus, if the receipt rule is the proper rule to apply in an email acceptance, the time of receipt where an electronic address has been designated is the time when the electronic communication becomes capable of being retrieved at such electronic address. Where no electronic address has been designated but an acceptance has been sent by email to the offeror's email address, section 13(3) of the Act states that the time of receipt is the time when the electronic communication becomes capable of being retrieved by the addressee at that address *and* the addressee becomes aware that the electronic communication has been sent to that address.

The Act also provides that a proposal to conclude a contract made through one or more electronic communications which is not addressed to one or more specific parties, but is generally accessible to parties making use of information systems, including a proposal that makes use of interactive applications for the placement of orders through such information systems, is to be regarded as an invitation to treat, unless it clearly indicates the intention of the party making the proposal to be bound in the case of acceptance.[104]

When transacting through a website, it is common for automated messages to be used. The Act provides that the use of automated messages does not preclude a contract from being

[100] *Digilandmall* (HC) (n 37) [98]–[100]. See also Phang (n 25) paras 03.203–03.206.
[101] Cap 88, 2011 Rev Ed. [102] eg leaving a comment on an internet website.
[103] Electronic Transactions Act (n 101) s 13(2). [104] ibid s 14.

formed[105] and this indeed was the position arrived at in *Chwee Kin Keong v Digilandmall.com Pte Ltd*.[106]

The above provisions of the Electronic Transactions Act do not apply to any rule of law requiring writing or signatures in any of the matters specified in the second column of the First Schedule to the Act.[107] These include the creation or execution of a will, any contract for the sale or other disposition of immovable property, and the conveyance of immovable property. This does not necessarily mean that electronic communications cannot be relied on in these matters if the law, apart from the Electronic Transactions Act, allows it. Thus, it has been held in the context of contracts relating to the sale of land that electronic communications fulfil the need for such contracts to be evidenced in writing.[108]

VIII. Certainty of Terms and Completeness of Agreement

Although offer and acceptance may have taken place, if the terms of the agreement are too vague, or material terms do not exist, no enforceable contract arises.

An agreement will be too vague to enforce if its material terms are such that the court cannot give the agreement a practical meaning.[109] For an agreement to be enforceable, its 'terms must be so definite, or capable of being made definite without further agreement of the parties, that the promises and performances to be rendered by each party are reasonably certain'.[110] In determining this, the court will interpret the words used broadly and non-technically[111] and it is only where the words fail to evince any definite meaning that the court will have no choice but to find that there was no contract.[112] Accordingly, simply agreeing to purchase goods 'on hire purchase' was found to be too uncertain as there were many different types of hire-purchase agreements with different terms.[113]

Where the parties have not reached agreement on all the material terms of the contract, there is no binding obligation. Accordingly, there is no contract if a material term is neither settled nor implied by law[114] and the document contains no machinery for ascertaining it.[115] As the parties have not come to a complete agreement, no enforceable contract comes into existence and the courts will not fill in matters that the parties have left unsettled. To do so would be to impose on the parties an agreement that they did not conclude themselves.[116] Conversely, where all the material terms have been agreed, the contract will be enforceable even if certain minor terms have been left out. The question is whether the

105 ibid s 15. 106 *Digilandmall* (HC) (n 37).

107 Electronic Transactions Act (n 103) s 4. 108 Discussed in section IX on 'Formalities'.

109 It may be possible for an agreement to have vague terms but for such terms to be regarded by the court as minor or meaningless such that the uncertainty of such terms does not vitiate the entire contract because all material terms of the agreement are to be found in the contract entered into, see eg *Nicolene Ltd v Simmonds* [1953] EWCA Civ J0305-1, [1953] 1 QB 543 (CA) where it was held that a term that was unascertainable could be ignored because it was meaningless and could be severed from an otherwise complete agreement.

110 *G Scammell & Nephew Ltd v Ouston* [1940] UKHL J1216-2, [1941] AC 251 (HL) 269. This approach has been accepted in Singapore in *T2 Networks Pte Ltd v Nasioncom Sdn Bhd* [2007] SGHC 193, [2008] 2 SLR(R) 1 (HC) and *Soon Kok Tiang v DBS Bank* [2012] 1 SLR 397 (CA).

111 Many agreements are not entered into with legal advice and may therefore lack legal precision. Accordingly, Singapore courts will endeavour to uphold contracts rather than striking them down, see *Gardner Smith (SE Asia) Pte Ltd v Jee Woo Trading Pte Ltd* [1998] SGHC 94, [1998] 1 SLR(R) 950 (HC) [10]; *Rudra Minerals Pte Ltd v MRI Trading Pte Ltd* [2013] 4 SLR 1023 (HC) [32].

112 *G Scammell* (n 110) 268; followed in *Soon Kok Tiang* (n 110) [39]. 113 *G Scammell* (n 110).

114 eg in contracts of employment the employee impliedly undertakes that the employee will serve the employer faithfully, see *Hivac Ltd v Park Royal Scientific Instruments Ltd* [1946] 1 Ch 169 (CA).

115 *Foley v Classique Coaches Ltd* [1934] 2 KB 1 (CA) 13.

116 *Grossner Jens v Raffles Holdings Ltd* [2003] SGHC 290, [2004] 1 SLR(R) 202 (HC) where it was held that there was no agreement as crucial terms such as remuneration and scope of services had not been agreed.

parties by their words and conduct have made it clear, objectively, that they intended to be bound despite the unsettled terms.[117]

Even where what would ordinarily be material terms have been omitted, or there is apparent vagueness in the terms used, a contract may nevertheless be enforceable if the gaps can be filled or vagueness resolved from an objective ascertainment of all the facts. For example, this may be the case if there is a custom, trade usage, or previous course of dealings that allows the incomplete terms to be ascertained or the vagueness to be resolved,[118] or if the words used are common in a particular industry and therefore can be ascertained by expert evidence.[119]

IX. Formalities

Singapore law, as is the case in English law, generally allows contracts to be formed without any formality.[120] It is usually not necessary for contracts to be concluded in any particular form or even to be in writing. This common law position is, however, subject to a number of statutory exceptions. Some contracts must be in a specified form[121] or may simply need to be made or evidenced in writing.[122] For such contracts, it is considered desirable that there should be more formality so as to engender certainty over the terms, prevent fraudulent evidence of an oral contract being adduced, or perhaps engender greater reflection over the agreement before it is entered into.

While it is beyond the scope of this chapter to consider all the statutory exceptions, a note should however be made of section 6 of the Civil Law Act. This provides that unless a promise or agreement, or some memorandum or note thereof, is in writing and signed by a party or some other person lawfully authorized by him, no action shall be brought against such party in relation to certain transactions, the most important of which relates to 'any contract for the sale or other disposition of immovable property, or any interest in such property'.[123]

In addition, section 7(1) states that a declaration of trust respecting any immovable property or any interest in such property must be manifested and proved by some writing signed by some person who is able to declare such trust or by his will. Further, a disposition of an equitable interest or trust subsisting at the time of the disposition must be in writing signed by the person disposing of the same or by his agent lawfully authorized in writing or by will.[124] The requirement of writing does not apply, however, to trusts that may be said to arise by operation of law such as resulting, implied, or constructive trusts.[125]

In the context of electronic communications, section 7 of the Electronic Transactions Act provides that '[w]here a rule of law requires information to be written, in writing, to be presented in writing or provides for certain consequences if it is not, an electronic record satisfies that rule of law if the information contained therein is accessible so as to be usable for subsequent reference'.[126] Even without such a provision, the courts in Singapore have taken the view that email and other electronic records can be considered to be 'in writing', at least for the purpose of section 6 of the Civil Law Act.[127]

[117] *Pagnan SpA v Feed Products Ltd* [1987] 2 Lloyd's Rep 601 (CA); *The Rainbow Spring* [2003] SGCA 31, [2003] 3 SLR(R) 362 (CA) [20]; *Rudhra Minerals Pte Ltd v MRI Trading Pte Ltd* [2013] 4 SLR 1023 (HC) [27].

[118] *Grossner* (n 116) [18]. [119] *Ashburn Anstalt v Arnold* [1989] Ch 1 (CA).

[120] For a more detailed treatment of this topic generally, see A Phang (ed), *The Law of Contract in Singapore* (Singapore: Academy Publishing 2012) ch 8.

[121] eg Merchant Shipping Act (Cap 179, 1996 Rev Ed) s 18, Conveyancing and Law of Property Act (Cap 61, 1994 Rev Ed) s 53, and Hire Purchase Act (Cap 125, 1999 Rev Ed) s 3.

[122] See eg Civil Law Act (Cap 43, 1999 Rev Ed) ss 6 and 7.

[123] ibid s 6(d). [124] ibid s 7(2). [125] ibid s 7(3). [126] n 101.

[127] *SM Integrated Transware Pte Ltd v Schenker Singapore (Pte) Ltd* [2005] SGHC 58, [2005] 2 SLR(R) 651 (HC) [76]; *Joseph Mathew v Singh Chiranjeev* [2009] SGCA 51, [2010] 1 SLR 338 (CA).

Where there has been non-compliance with formalities, the legislation may state that the contract is *void*. Thus, a conveyance of any estate or interest in land other than a lease for a period not exceeding seven years at a rack rent is void at law unless it is by deed in the English language.[128] Where a contract is void it is a complete nullity and has no legal effect whatsoever.

Alternatively, the effect of the legislation may be that non-compliance with formalities simply renders the contract *unenforceable* rather than void. In such circumstances, the contract is valid but neither party can enforce it in a court of law. This will mean that no party can derive any benefit from the contract if the other party refuses to perform because a court of law will not allow an action to be brought against the non-performing party. It has been held in England that non-compliance with provisions equivalent to section 6 of the Civil Law Act does not render the contract void but only unenforceable.[129] This means that if the contract was performed and title has passed, it is not open to the vendor to recover the property. In the case of a void contract, the vendor may yet be able to recover the conveyed property.

While one purpose of provisions rendering contracts unenforceable when not in writing is to protect parties from wrongful claims that they have entered into such contracts orally, it is possible that such provisions may themselves be used unscrupulously to lead counterparties on before subsequently relying on the lack of writing to defeat the counterparty's contractual expectations. Thus, English law developed the doctrine of part performance which provides that if a party to an agreement stands by and lets the other party incur expense or prejudice his position on the faith of the agreement being valid, the former will not be allowed to assert that the agreement is unenforceable.[130] The doctrine of part performance is part of Singapore law and in *Seah Boon Lock v Family Food Court*, it was stated that the basis for this doctrine was the 'ground of estoppel to prevent a defendant from sheltering behind the statute'.[131]

Traditionally, the part performance being relied upon comprises the *plaintiff's* performance of his obligations under the oral contract. The defendant is precluded from relying on the lack of formalities because it would be unfair to the plaintiff. However, a number of Singapore cases appear to have extended the doctrine of part performance to the *defendant's* acts such that a plaintiff can rely on a *defendant's* part performance of an oral contract to overcome the lack of formalities.[132] For example, in *Joseph Mathew v Singh Chiranjeev* the Court of Appeal accepted that the first defendant's conduct in accepting the plaintiffs' cheque amounted to part performance,[133] though arguably this can also be seen as a case of part performance by the plaintiffs in issuing the cheque that was accepted.

X. Consideration

At common law, for a promise to have binding force there must be consideration provided by the promisee. Consideration is regarded as something of value in the eyes of the law given in exchange for a promise. The doctrine of consideration requires there to be reciprocity for contracts to become binding. This usually arises from a benefit provided or a

[128] Conveyancing and Law of Property Act (n 121) s 53(1).
[129] *Maddison v Alderson* (1883) 8 App Cas 467 (HL) 488.
[130] *Steadman v Steadman* [1976] AC 536 (HL) 540.
[131] [2007] 3 SLR(R) 362 (HC) [28]; cf Phang (n 25) para 08.144.
[132] For a critique, see Phang (n 25) para 08.149 fn 409.
[133] *Joseph Mathew* (n 127) [63]. See also *Midlink* (n 67) [67].

detriment incurred.[134] Gratuitous promises are not, therefore, as a general principle, enforceable at common law.

Consideration arguably serves a valuable purpose in placing some limits on the types of promises that have legal effect.[135] In life, promises are often made and it is undesirable for every promise to be potentially enforceable especially those made in a social or family setting. It is likely, therefore, that most developed legal systems will set some constraints on the types of promises that are enforceable. At common law, this role is played mainly by the doctrine of consideration.[136] Reciprocity provides a strong indicator of the seriousness of the promises being made.

It should be noted, though, that consideration is unnecessary where an agreement has been executed under seal,[137] which today is little more than signing a document referred to as a deed to which a red circular sticker is affixed next to the signatures of the parties. This suggests that the common law is not entirely wedded to the requirement of reciprocity. Rather, the additional formality undertaken when executing a document under seal sufficiently signifies the seriousness of the promise being made. The common law also does not look at the adequacy of consideration as it is for the parties to decide what is a sufficient benefit or detriment for the promise, though the consideration must have some, even if nominal, economic value.

An example of a situation where consideration would be absent is one where a promise is made to a person who is already under an existing contractual obligation to perform the act in question. As consideration must have some economic value, a promise to perform what one is already under an obligation to perform has no such value. Accordingly, in the well-known English decision of *Stilk v Myrick*, a promise by the captain of a ship to his crewmen that the wages of two deserters would be paid to them if the remaining crewmen continued to perform their duties was held to be unenforceable.[138] One rationale for this is that the remaining crewmen were already under a contractual obligation to perform their duties regardless of the desertion.

Yet it has also been recognized that there may be circumstances where a rigid adherence to the doctrine of consideration may not be ideal. In *Williams v Roffey Bros & Nicholls (Contractors) Ltd*, the defendant, a contractor, hired the plaintiff as carpentry subcontractors for a building project.[139] The plaintiff subsequently ran into financial difficulty as the subcontract amount was inadequate. The defendant, fearing a delay which would have led to penalty payments by the defendant under the main contract, agreed to pay the plaintiff an additional sum for the plaintiff to complete the work already agreed upon under the subcontract. It was held that there was sufficient consideration to support the defendant's promise of additional payment because 'there was clearly a commercial advantage to both sides from a pragmatic point of view',[140] and the defendant received 'practical benefits'[141] even though the plaintiff was already contractually bound to perform the work. This would not traditionally have constituted consideration which would have required there to be either a benefit that the promisor was not already entitled to under the existing contract, or a detriment that was not already imposed on the promisee. All three judges also stated that given the developments in the area of economic duress, this may be a better basis for testing the validity of the second agreement rather than reliance on lack of consideration.[142] On the

134 *Currie v Misa* (1875) LR 10 Ex 153, 162. 135 *Gay Choon Ing* (n 6) [98].

136 This explains why the other possible limiting factor, namely the requirement that parties must intend to enter into legal relations, is relatively undeveloped at common law.

137 *Gay Choon Ing* (n 6) [65]. 138 170 ER 1168 (HC).

139 [1989] EWCA Civ J1123-4, [1991] 1 QB 1 (CA). 140 ibid 22. 141 ibid 11.

142 ibid 14–15, 18, 21.

facts, there was no duress or fraud on the part of the plaintiff, so the promise of extra payment could be enforced.

Although the court in *Williams v Roffey* affirmed the correctness of *Stilk v Myrick* and considered it to continue to represent the law in England, it is clear that the decisions are not easily reconcilable.[143] Accordingly, it has been observed by the Singapore High Court that the notion of a factual or practical (as opposed to a legal) benefit in *Williams v Roffey*, together with the doctrine that consideration need not be adequate, means that consideration will be easily found between contracting parties thereby rendering consideration redundant for the most part.[144] Nevertheless, *Williams v Roffey* has been applied in Singapore.[145]

Williams v Roffey signals a substantial relaxation in the doctrine of consideration because there is a modern tendency to question its relevance and thereby to downplay its significance. For example, in Singapore it has been said that 'the time may have come for the common law to shed the pretence of searching for consideration to uphold commercial contracts. The marrow of contractual relationships should be the parties' intention to create a legal relationship.'[146] Nevertheless, it does not appear that the doctrine of consideration will be abolished at any time soon in Singapore. The Court of Appeal, while acknowledging the weaknesses of the doctrine, has expressed the view that the existence of a combination of the doctrine together with other doctrines such as duress and promissory estoppel[147] may most practically enable the courts to effectively ascertain which promises ought to be enforceable in a just and fair manner.[148]

Since consideration as a doctrine remains a key feature of Singapore contract law, the question therefore is how *Williams v Roffey* can be reconciled with the general doctrine. The broadest explanation of it is that a *legal* benefit or detriment is no longer necessary to give rise to consideration as long as there is some *factual* or *practical* benefit that is conferred. It is unlikely that such a radical approach was contemplated by the court in *Williams v Roffey* or the Singapore cases that have applied it.[149] It is suggested that the approach in *Williams v Roffey* should therefore be applicable only to one-sided contract modifications which was the factual situation that the court was called upon to adjudicate. Under this approach, the law should be slow to upset bargains made by persons who have negotiated in good faith where they are *already* in a contractual relationship and the new bargain is regarded by them as mutually beneficial despite the absence of consideration.[150]

We have already seen that the common law's commitment to the idea of reciprocity in contracting is a weak one given that consideration can be nominal and altogether unnecessary in the case of a deed. In addition, one of the objectives behind consideration is to ensure that parties are aware of the seriousness of the promises being made. Where the parties are already in a contractual relationship and are seeking to modify it, it is likely that

[143] M Chen-Wishart, *Contract Law* (5th edn, Oxford: OUP 2015) 134 states that while *Williams v Roffey* affirms the need for fresh consideration to enforce an additional promise, it has overruled *Stilk v Myrick* on what counts as fresh consideration.

[144] *Sunny Metal & Engineering Pte Ltd v Ng Khim Ming Eric* [2006] SGHC 222, [2007] 1 SLR(R) 853 (HC) [30].

[145] *Fong Holdings Pte Ltd v Computer Library (S) Pte Ltd* [1991] SGHC 61, [1991] 1 SLR(R) 834 (HC); *Sharon Global Solutions Pte Ltd v LG International (Singapore) Pte Ltd* [2001] SGHC 139, [2001] 2 SLR(R) 233 (HC); *Teo Seng Kee Bob v Arianecorp Ltd* [2008] SGHC 81, [2008] 3 SLR(R) 1114 (HC). See also *Sea-Land Service Inc v Cheong Fook Chee Vincent* [1994] SGCA 103, [1994] 3 SLR(R) 250 (CA) where it was held that *Williams v Roffey* did not apply on the facts.

[146] *Digilandmall* (HC) (n 37) [139].

[147] On promissory estoppel, see section XI on 'Promissory Estoppel'.

[148] *Gay Choon Ing* (n 6) [117]–[118].

[149] As pointed out by Chen-Wishart (n 143) 132–33 this would 'dilute the consideration requirement to the point of extinction'.

[150] CH Tan, 'Contract Modifications, Consideration and Moral Hazard' (2005) 17 SAcLJ 566.

the negotiations and eventual agreement will be made with due deliberation without the need for the doctrine of consideration. Not applying the doctrine of consideration in such circumstances is also unlikely to lead to a deluge of plaintiffs asking the court to enforce promises. Thus, it is suggested that not requiring consideration in this context does no great violence, in principle, to the doctrine.[151] Rather, the courts should guard against the possibility that a contracting party may hold the other party to ransom if such other party faces severe consequences should there be a breach of contract. Other tools such as economic duress can guard against such fears and consideration may have served this purpose in the past when the doctrine of economic duress was less developed.[152]

XI. Promissory Estoppel

The doctrine of promissory estoppel provides another avenue to ameliorate the unenforceability of promises that are not supported by consideration. The doctrine prevents a person from going back on a promise not to enforce his strict legal rights even when such promise is not supported by consideration, provided it would be inequitable to allow such person to resile from his promise. It will usually be inequitable if the other party has relied on the promise.[153] Thus, a landlord who makes an implied promise to a tenant that time for effecting repairs will not run while negotiations over the sale of a lease are ongoing, cannot forfeit the lease when negotiations break down and the repairs were not made within the original time period, even though there was no consideration to support the promise.[154] The landlord must give the tenant extra time to make the repairs. Promissory estoppel is therefore a possible alternative means of arriving at the same outcome as that in *Williams v Roffey*.

The difficulty with promissory estoppel in this context is that orthodoxy does not allow the doctrine to create a cause of action but only to provide a defence against a claim brought by another.[155] Thus, in the landlord–tenant situation discussed above, the inability of the tenant—the promisee—to bring a claim is unimportant because the tenant does not need to do so to enjoy the benefit of the promise. It is the landlord who must bring a claim if the landlord wishes to terminate the lease for failure to make repairs within the period provided for in the contract.

However, in a *Williams v Roffey* situation the promisee must bring an action against the promisor on the gratuitous promise itself. As the estoppel does not create a cause of action but merely a defence, promissory estoppel cannot be used to compel performance (or to obtain damages for breach) of such a promise. This orthodox position was departed from in Australia in *Waltons Stores (Interstate) Ltd v Maher*.[156] In Singapore, the Court of Appeal has acknowledged the different approaches and said that the issue would have to be considered when relevant.[157] It is suggested that Singapore courts should adopt the position in

[151] This was the approach adopted in New Zealand in *Antons Trawling Co Ltd v Smith* [2003] 2 NZLR 23.

[152] *Williams v Roffey* (n 139) 13–15, 21; *Gay Choon Ing* (n 6) [107].

[153] *Fu Loong Lithographer Pte Ltd v Mun Hean Realty Pte Ltd* [1989] SGHC 18, [1989] 1 SLR(R) 194 (HC); *Abdul Jalil bin Ahmad bin Talib v A Formation Construction Pte Ltd* [2006] SGHC 171, [2006] 4 SLR(R) 778 (HC); *Tee Soon Kay v Attorney-General* [2007] SGCA 27, [2007] 3 SLR(R) 133 (CA) [112]; *Lam Chi Kin David v Deutsche Bank AG* [2010] SGCA 42, [2011] 1 SLR 800 (CA) [40].

[154] *Hughes v Metropolitan Railway Co* (1877) 2 App Cas 439 (HL). See also *Central London Property Trust Ltd v High Trees House Ltd* [1947] 1 KB 130 (KB); *Kodrat Suradji v Banque Nationale de Paris* [1992] SGHC 50, [1992] 1 SLR(R) 470 (HC); *QBE Insurance (International) Ltd v Winterthur Insurance (Far East) Pte Ltd* [2005] SGHC 11, [2005] 1 SLR(R) 711 (HC) [24]–[25].

[155] *Combe v Combe* [1951] 2 KB 215 (CA). Thus, it is often said that promissory estoppel can be used only as a shield and not as a sword.

[156] [1988] HCA 7, (1988) 164 CLR 387 (HCA).

[157] *Tee Soon Kay* (n 153) [114].

Australia as it is somewhat capricious that a person's legal position should depend on whether he needs to take active steps to enforce the promise.

XII. Intention to Create Legal Relations

Under Singapore law, a contract is formed not only when there has been offer and acceptance supported by consideration, there must in addition be an intention on the part of the parties to enter into or create a legal relationship. The parties must by their conduct, objectively construed, have intended 'that the transaction entered into was to *have legal effect* before a valid contract can be said to have been formed'.[158]

It is questionable whether the common law requires both the doctrines of consideration and intention to create legal relations since, the idea of reciprocity aside, both play similar roles in providing evidence of the seriousness of the promises made. One advantage of consideration is that its presence or absence will usually be clear and it is therefore an efficient mechanism to determine when promises are enforceable. A test premised only on intention to create legal relations, while more attractive in principle, means that many gratuitous promises that are sued upon will have to be resolved after a full judicial hearing as to the presence or absence of such intention.[159]

This, in turn, raises the issue of the relevance of intention to create legal relations given that it plays a much less important role than consideration. Yet, as consideration may be more easily located (or disregarded) today, particularly where the parties are already in an existing contractual relationship, there may be an increasing need for an alternative doctrine to filter enforceable promises from the unenforceable.[160] There are also reasons why an independent doctrine of intention to create legal relations is relevant despite the fact that it could already be implicitly located within offer and acceptance. Implied contracts can arise without the mechanism of offer and acceptance and for such contracts contractual intention is essential for an enforceable contract to arise.[161] Parties may also expressly (or impliedly) exclude their intention to be bound in the context of a commercial relationship and the courts have given effect to this even where the other formation elements were present. For example, the courts have in cases involving 'letters of comfort' held that such letters do not give rise to any binding obligation on issuers.[162] As such, the doctrine has relevance beyond presumptively excluding domestic relationships from binding contractual obligations.[163]

In general, because of the doctrine of consideration and the fact that most contracts are made in a commercial context, the issue of whether the parties had the requisite intention to create legal relations rarely arises in practice. It would be very difficult to argue that the

[158] *Gay Choon Ing* (n 6) [71].

[159] One possible solution is to subsume consideration under intention to create legal relations, in that the absence or presence of consideration will, absent exceptional circumstances, indicate objectively the absence or presence respectively of the requisite intention. This allows much of the existing law to continue to be relevant, abolishes consideration as a separate requirement while still keeping in place an efficient mechanism to determine when promises are enforceable, and focuses attention on the real issue which is whether the requisite intent to form a legal relationship exists.

[160] *Gay Choon Ing* (n 6) [71].

[161] *Blackpool and Fylde Aero Club v Blackpool Borough Council* [1990] EWCA Civ J0525-1, [1990] 1 WLR 1195 (CA) 1202.

[162] *Malayan Banking Berhad v Jurong Engineering Ltd* [1999] SGHC 240 (HC); *Hong Kong & Shanghai Banking Corp Ltd v Jurong Engineering Ltd* [2000] SGHC 20, [2000] 1 SLR(R) 204 (HC), and see also *Rose and Frank Co v JR Crompton & Bros Ltd* [1923] 2 KB 261 (CA); affd on this point in *Rose and Frank Co v JR Crompton & Bros Ltd* [1924] UKHL J1205-1, [1925] AC 445 (HL).

[163] See below on agreements in a social or family context. The exclusion of domestic relations could be regarded as a manifestation of public policy and treated as such without a separate doctrine of contractual intention.

requisite intention was not present even where there was consideration and the contract was a commercial one. Indeed, the law presumes that there was such an intention for agreements made in a business context.[164] The opposite presumption applies to agreements made in a social or family context,[165] such as an agreement between a father and his adopted sons.[166] These presumptions may, of course, be displaced by evidence to the contrary.[167]

XIII. Conclusion

As a small jurisdiction that depends significantly on commerce and foreign investment, Singapore's approach to law in this context is to have a body of rules that is familiar to, and has credibility with, the international business community. This explains the continued importance of English contract law to Singapore and why Singapore contract law will continue to retain much of the English architecture. Nevertheless, in commercial law in general and contract law in particular[168] there have been and will continue to be departures from English law. In the area of contract formation the Singapore courts appear to be prepared to consider taking slightly different approaches in the areas of consideration and promissory estoppel. It is therefore hoped that appropriate cases will come before the courts in the near future.

[164] *Gay Choon Ing* (n 6) [72].

[165] ibid [72]; *Choo Tiong Hin v Choo Hock Swee* [1959] 1 MLJ 67 (CA).

[166] *Choo Tiong Hin* (n 165).

[167] eg in the commercial context see *Rose and Frank* (n 162), *Malayan Banking Berhad* (n 162); *Hong Kong & Shanghai Banking Corp Ltd* (n 162).

[168] eg see *RDC Concrete Pte Ltd v Sato Kogyo (S) Pte Ltd* [2007] SGCA 39, [2007] 4 SLR(R) 413 (CA) on the law relating to discharge by breach.

9

Contracts for the Benefit of Third Parties: The Singapore Law Perspectives

*Burton ONG**

I. Introduction

While Singapore marked its 50th year of independence from England in 2015, its contract law roots remain firmly anchored to the English common law even as the Singapore courts have, in recent years, begun to make subtle but significant deviations from contemporary English contract law doctrine.[1] Where contracts for the benefit of third parties are concerned, Singapore has, for the most part, stayed faithful to the position taken under English contract law: adopting the privity of contract rule, various common law exceptions to the rule—many of which are really doctrinal techniques of avoiding or circumventing the privity rule—as well as a statutory regime to empower third parties to enforce contractual terms in specifically prescribed circumstances. This chapter will seek to provide an overview of this area of Singapore contract law with a view towards analysing the legal boundaries that define the rights of third parties and promisees to pursue legal claims against promisors who have made contractual promises to confer benefits upon them. To obtain legal recourse against the contracting party who has promised to confer these benefits (the 'promisor-debtor'), the third party who stands outside the contract (the '3P-creditor') must successfully navigate his way around the privity rule, which only permits contracting parties to enforce contractual obligations, to establish an extra-contractual common law or statutory cause of action or, alternatively, enlist the assistance of the other contracting party—the promisee—to take action against the promisor-debtor on the 3P-creditor's behalf.

The privity of contract doctrine only permits those who are party to the contract, to whom promises have been made (ie promisees), to enforce the terms of the contract and to seek contract law remedies for breaches of the contract. A third party has no right to sue upon a contract, even if that contract was made for his benefit; neither may the contract impose legal obligations upon the third party even if such burdens were contemplated by the contracting parties. The rationale behind the privity rule resides within one of the core defining features of contract law rights and obligations: they arise from the voluntary participation of individual actors who have elected to bring themselves together within a consensual, reciprocal, and *exclusive* legal relationship. The parties to a contract are thus in a fundamentally different position from third parties. Unlike the promisees in a contract,

* Cite as B Ong, 'Contracts for the Benefit of Third Parties: The Singapore Law Perspectives' in Chen-Wishart, Loke, & Vogenauer, *Studies in the Contract Laws of Asia Vol II: Formation and Third Party Beneficiaries* (Oxford: OUP 2017) ch 9.

[1] eg in the previous volume of this series, Associate Professors Dora Neo and Alexander Loke explore the doctrinal innovations introduced by the Singapore courts in the areas of specific and monetary remedies for breach of contract. See D Neo, 'Specific Remedies and the Performance Interest in Singapore Contract Law' and A Loke, 'The Performance Interest and Monetary Awards for Breach of Contract under Singapore Law' in Chen-Wishart, Loke, & Ong, *Studies in the Contract Laws of Asia: Remedies for Breach of Contract* (Oxford: OUP 2016).

no promises have been made *to* third parties who may or may not even be aware of the existence of the contract. This distinction between promisees and third parties underpins why the legally enforceable rights in the contract may accrue to the former instead of the latter. From the promisor-debtor's perspective, the privity rule serves a vital role in circumscribing the scope of his legal obligations under the contract. However, there may be circumstances where justice requires the promisor-debtor to be held legally accountable to the 3P-creditor for failing to perform his contractual promise to the promisee, when the latter is unwilling or unable to take action. Making such legal actions available to the 3P-creditor would, in particular circumstances, give effect to the objective intentions of the contracting parties and prevent the promisor-debtor from evading his end of the bargain without legal consequence. In Singapore, the doctrine of privity of contract has been recognized by the courts as one of the basic rules of Singapore contract law that is distinct from the common law doctrine of consideration.[2] At the same time, the importance of ensuring that defaulting promisor-debtors can be brought to task (both by promisees and 3P-creditors) has led the Singapore courts to embrace various common law techniques to support such claims against them. Similarly, the Singapore legislature has mirrored the legislative efforts of the UK Parliament to enact the Contracts (Rights of Third Parties) Act 2001[3] ('CRTPA') to allow third parties to bring statutory claims to enforce specific contractual terms for benefits that contracting parties have intended for them to receive.

Section II of this chapter will examine the exceptions to the privity rule which enable the third party to *directly* enforce a contract or, more precisely, a specific contractual term which purports to confer a benefit upon the third party. Section III will introduce alternative non-contract-based legal channels available to third parties that might be explored to *indirectly* enforce a contract that would have produced a benefit to the third party if the promisor had not been in breach of contract. Section IV will focus on how a contract made for the benefit of a third party may be enforced, independently, by a *promisee* against the promisor-debtor and the circumstances in which substantial damages may be recovered from the latter for his failure to confer contractually stipulated benefits upon a third party.

II. Direct Enforcement of Contracts by Third Parties

English law has developed a wide range of 'exceptions' to the privity rule that have found their way into Singapore's common law system. Some of these are true exceptions, in the sense that the third party is entitled to sue under the contract notwithstanding his third party status—typically by the operation of another branch of the law, such as shipping law, banking law, and agency law. Others are not, strictly speaking, exceptions but rather common law mechanisms for changing the status of the third party into that of a contracting party, thereby eliminating the lack of privity problem altogether. Finally, and perhaps most significantly, there has been a general statutory exception to the privity rule since 1 January 2002 when the CRTPA came into force.

[2] A Phang and Y Goh, *Contract Law in Singapore* (Alphen aan den Rijn: Kluwer Law International 2012) § 1216. Third parties are precluded from enforcing contracts made for their benefit for two distinct, though often closely associated, reasons: first, they are not privy to these contracts and, second, they have not furnished consideration for the contractual promises they seek to enforce. See *Tweddle v Atkinson* (1861) 121 ER 762. An example of the Singapore courts explicitly treating the privity rule as a separate principle from the doctrine of consideration can be found in *Vaswani Lalchand Challaram v Vaswani Roshni Anilkumar* [2005] SGHC 110, [2005] 3 SLR(R) 625 (HC) [10] where Choo J accepted that 'the doctrine of privity is one of the strictest rules in the common law, and it remains a useful rule, especially when we can distinguish between a *plain privity* rule and a *privity to the consideration* rule'.

[3] Cap 53B, 2002 Rev Ed.

1. True Exceptions to the Privity Rule

True exceptions to the privity rule result from the operation of well-established legal principles from the law of agency, property law, and trust law, as well as via the relevant legal frameworks governing industry-specific contracts such as negotiable instruments. Under agency law principles, a third party who is a principal in a principal–agent relationship may step into the shoes of his agent if the latter enters into a contract on the former's behalf. Contracts made by the agent for his principal are, as a result, regarded as contracts made between the third-party-turned-principal and the other contracting party.[4] This exception can be quite far-reaching as it extends also to undisclosed principals—where the contracting party dealing with the agent has no idea of the existence of the principal.[5] Different areas of property law also have a significant impact on the non-operation of the privity rule. Restrictive covenants found in conveyancing contracts may be enforced by third parties who subsequently acquire ownership of the real property to which these covenants are attached,[6] while personal property law regards contractual promises as a form of property—choses in action—that are capable of being transferred by assignment to, and hence enforced by, third parties.[7] Likewise, trust law also recognizes that a beneficiary who has beneficial ownership of the contractual subject matter, that is held on trust for the beneficiary, may bring an action to enforce his rights notwithstanding the fact that the beneficiary was not a contracting party, though the courts have traditionally demanded extremely clear evidence of an intention to create a trust arrangement before allowing the third party's action to succeed.[8]

2. Collateral Contracts as a Doctrinal Device to Circumvent the Privity Rule

Another common law 'exception' which permits a third party to directly enforce a contract made for his benefit lies in the collateral contract doctrine, a well-established contract law device which connects the 3P-creditor directly to the promisor-debtor in an implied contractual relationship. The Singapore courts have acknowledged collateral contracts as a legitimate means of circumventing the privity doctrine that would enable the 3P-creditor to ground his legal claim as a contracting party to a separate ancillary contract. This *ancillary* contract is distinct from the *main* contract which purports to confer the benefit on the third party, and all the traditional doctrinal requirements relating to contractual formation—

[4] See FMB Reynolds, *Bowstead and Reynolds on Agency* (19th edn, London: Sweet & Maxwell 2010) and CH Tan, *The Law of Agency* (Singapore: Academy Publishing 2010).

[5] *Family Food Court (a firm) v Seah Booh Lock* [2008] SGCA 31, [2008] 4 SLR(R) 272 [29] where the Singapore Court of Appeal declared that '[I]t is now well accepted as a general principle that the undisclosed principal can sue and be sued on a contract made by its agent, although it is not a party to the contract', referring to FMB Reynolds, *Bowstead and Reynolds on Agency* (18th edn, London: Sweet & Maxwell 2006) para 8-071 which explains the doctrine of undisclosed principal as an exception to the privity of contract rule that is 'unusual…and…is probably best explained as one of commercial convenience, and its justice is disputable'.

[6] The lack of privity of contract is made up for by the concept of privity of estate—a land law concept unique to real property. See Phang and Goh (n 2) para 1223.

[7] See YL Tan, 'Choses in Action: Still More Contract than Property?' (2010) 26 JCL 160. Apart from voluntary assignments of contractual benefits by contracting parties to third parties, third parties may also acquire rights under contracts by operation of law—eg in bankruptcy and garnishee proceedings, where third party rights in contracts emerge without the consent of both or either of the original contracting parties. Similarly, a third party may also step into the shoes of a contracting party via the equitable doctrine of subrogation—where, eg, a third party guarantor in a loan arrangement pays out on the guarantee, the guarantor will become subrogated to the claims of the lender against the borrower. The doctrine empowers the third party with the contractual rights which the lender had under its contract with the borrower.

[8] See Phang and Goh (n 2) paras 1225, 1226.

offer, acceptance, and consideration—have to be satisfied before such an implied collateral contract between the promisor-debtor and the 3P-creditor is recognized.[9]

The implied collateral contract is frequently invoked in the carriage of goods by sea context, where an exemption clause is included in a contract between the owner of the goods (X) and the carrier (Y) with the clause purporting to confer a benefit on a third party (Z)—stevedores who will unload the goods when they arrive at their destination—in the form of an exemption of liability from X for the protection of Z. Such a contractual exemption of liability can be relied upon by Z in the event the goods are damaged while they are unloaded, even though he is not a party to the contract between X and Y which contains this contractual clause. Z is allowed to enforce this exemption clause if an implied, ancillary, and unilateral collateral contract can be established directly between himself and X where this collateral contract contains, as one of its terms, the same exemption of liability term found in the main contract between X and Y. These cases involve what are referred to as *Himalaya* clauses,[10] developed from a line of well-known English cases including the House of Lords decision in *Scruttons v Midland Silicones Ltd*[11] and the Privy Council case of *The Eurymedon*,[12] where the third party could take the benefit of an exemption clause in a contract that he was not a party to if five cumulative conditions were satisfied:

(1) the bill of lading makes it clear that the contracting parties intended for the third party stevedore to be protected by the exemption clause;
(2) it is clear that the carrier-contracting party is contracting both on his own behalf as well as on behalf of the third party stevedore as the latter's agent;
(3) the carrier has authority from the third party stevedore to act on the latter's behalf;
(4) that the third party stevedores could be said to have provided consideration for the exemption of liability; and
(5) that the relevant provisions from the statute governing such commercial arrangements (ie the Bills of Lading Act) applied.

Taken collectively, satisfying these requirements would enable the court to find an offer of a unilateral contract by X to Z, through Y as Z's agent, to exempt Z from liability in return for Z unloading the goods. Z's act of unloading the goods would constitute both the acceptance of X's offer as well as the consideration which Z furnishes to X in exchange for X's exemption of liability. Z would thus be able to rely on the exemption clause, found in the contract between X and Y, by enforcing it as a term of an implied collateral contract between X and Z. This collateral contract line of reasoning has been adopted by the Singapore Court of Appeal to permit a cargo handling agent to enforce a limitation of liability clause in a cargo freight forwarding contract between a freight forwarding agent and an airline carrier.[13]

Satisfying the strict qualifying criteria laid out in the English case law would require X and Y to include very detailed and elaborately worded clauses in their contracts to give effect to their common intention to protect Z.[14] Deploying the collateral contract as a doctrinal

[9] See eg *Jiang Haiying v Tan Lim Hui* [2009] SGHC 42, [2009] 3 SLR(R) 13 [52] which referred to the classic English decision on collateral contracts in *Shanklin Pier v Detel Products* [1951] 2 KB 854.

[10] See *Adler v Dickson (The Himalaya)* [1955] 1 QB 158.

[11] [1962] AC 446.

[12] *New Zealand Shipping Co Ltd v AM Sattherwaite & Co (The Eurymedon)* [1975] AC 154.

[13] *Yusen Air & Sea Service (S) Pte Ltd v Changi International Airport Services Pte Ltd* [1999] SGCA 62, [1999] 3 SLR(R) 95.

[14] A sample clause would read something like this: 'It is hereby expressly agreed that no servant or agent of the carrier (including every independent contractor from time to time employed by the carrier) shall in any circumstances whatsoever be under any liability whatsoever to the shipper, consignee or owner of the goods or to any holder of this Bill of Lading for any loss, damage or delay of whatsoever kind arising or resulting directly or indirectly from any act, neglect or default on his part while acting in the course of or in connection with his

device, in the manner described above, just to achieve the goal of circumventing the privity of contract rule also seems highly artificial even if it is motivated by a desire on the part of the courts to reflect established commercial reality and practice.[15] A far more elegant and straightforward solution to the privity problem can be found in the statutory exception to the CRTPA, further discussed in the following section, which expressly preserves the possibility of a third party using the statutory mechanism to avail himself of a contractual exclusion or limitation of liability clause.[16]

3. A General Statutory Exception: The Contracts (Rights of Third Parties) Act 2001

Modelled closely after the UK Contracts (Rights of Third Parties) Act 1999 (the 'UK Act'), and introduced in Singapore just two years after the UK enacted this statute, the CRTPA represents the most systematic and structured qualification to the privity of contract rule. Like its English counterpart, the CRTPA was part of a legislative reform[17] effort that was directed, not at abrogating the common law privity rule, but rather at providing a facilitative framework under which contracting parties are empowered to create (if they so wish) enforceable rights for third parties.[18] One small, but significant, substantive difference between the two statutes lies in section 2(5) of the CRTPA and section 1(5) of the UK Act which both provide that the third party, when exercising his right under the statute to enforce a term of a contract, is to be given the same range of remedies that would have been available to him in an action for breach of contract if he had been a party to the contract. The Singapore Act goes further to *expressly* state that the third party should not be denied contractual remedies 'on the ground that, as against the promisor, the third party is a volunteer'. In contrast, the notion that a lack of consideration moving from the third party cannot be an obstacle to the third party using the statute as a basis for enforcing rights under the contract is only *implied* in the UK statute.[19]

Under the CRTPA, a 3P-creditor can invoke the statutory exception to the privity rule and acquire enforceable rights under a contract against the promisor-debtor if he can meet two basic threshold criteria laid down in section 2 of the Act. First, he must be expressly identified in the contract, whether by name or as a member of a class or answering to a particular description, though it is not necessary for the third party to be in existence at the time the contract was entered into (the 'identification requirement').[20] Second, the contracting

employment and, without prejudice to the generality of the foregoing provisions of this clause, every exemption, limitation, condition and liberty herein contained and every right, exemption from liability, defence and immunity of whatsoever nature applicable to the carrier or to which the carrier is entitled hereunder shall also be available and shall extend to protect every such servant or agent of the carrier acting as aforesaid and for the purpose of all the foregoing provisions of this clause the carrier is or shall be deemed to be acting as agent or trustee on behalf of and for the benefit of all persons who are or might be his servants or agents from time to time (including independent contractors as aforesaid) and all such persons shall to this extent be or be deemed to be parties to the contract in or evidenced by this Bill of Lading.'

[15] Phang and Goh (n 2) paras 1243–1244.

[16] See proviso to CRTPA 2001, s 7(4), which is identical to the UK Contracts (Rights of Third Parties) Act 1999, s 6(5).

[17] In the run-up to the enactment of the CRTPA, the Law Reform and Revision Division Committee of the Singapore Attorney-General's Chambers produced a report which articulated a preference for legislative reform of the privity rule over relying entirely on judicially created exceptions to the privity rule. See Law Reform and Revision Division, AGC, *Report on the Contracts (Rights of Third Parties) Bill (2001)* (LLRD No 2/2001) para 3.1.3.

[18] TM Yeo, 'When Do Third Party Rights Arise Under the Contracts (Rights of Third Parties) Act 1999 (UK)?' (2001) 13 SAcLJ 34, 53.

[19] UK Law Commission, *Privity of Contract: Contracts for the Benefit of Third Parties* (Law Com CP No 242, Cm 3329, 1996) para 6.8, fn 8.

[20] CRTPA 2001, s 2(3).

parties must have intended to confer upon him enforceable rights under the contract, either by expressly providing so in the contract[21] or, in the alternative, by implication via the fact that the contract purports to confer a benefit upon the third party (the 'contractual intention requirement'),[22] unless a proper construction of the contract indicates that the contracting parties did not intend the contractual term to be enforceable by the third party.[23] Subject to the qualifications found elsewhere in the statute, a third party who meets these eligibility criteria can unlock the statutory exception to the privity rule and acquire a direct right of enforcement in contract against the promisor-debtor for breach of contract. The spirit of the statute is animated by a legislative intention to realize the objective contractual intentions of the parties to the contract, neutralizing the privity rule in circumstances where allowing third parties to pursue claims under the contract would bring about what the contracting parties had agreed upon.

(a) Eligibility criteria for third parties seeking to use the CRTPA

The first (identification) requirement of the CRTPA is comparatively straightforward and is satisfied as long as the identities of the third parties, or the means for identifying them, are disclosed with sufficient clarity and certainty.[24] Express identification of the third party would, ideally, occur within an express term found within the written contract. However, such a term could just as easily be part of a collateral contract, the oral part of a partly written and partly oral contract or the result of a proper construction of the contractual terms that is consistent with common business sense.[25]

The second (contractual intention) requirement is bifurcated by design and relies primarily on a contextual construction of the contract, inevitably introducing some degree of unpredictability that arises when the language of the contract has to be interpreted by the courts. This requirement is satisfied either by showing that the 'contract expressly provides that [the third party] may [in his own right, enforce a term of the contract]' (section 2(1)(a)), or that 'the term purports to confer a benefit on [the third party]... [unless] it appears that the parties did not intend the term to be enforceable by the third party' (sections 2(1)(b) and 2(1)(c)). Determining if the third party has a statutory claim under either section 2(1)(a) or section 2(1)(b) boils down to a matter of *construction* of contracting parties' intentions. For instance, an exclusion clause that is drafted to cover third parties might plausibly fall under section 2(1)(b), since it does confer a 'benefit' on the third party, yet one might just as easily consider it to fall within section 2(1)(a) since such a clause would be meaningless unless it was legally enforceable by its intended beneficiaries.[26] While the boundaries between these two limbs of section 2(1) of the CRTPA may not be sharply defined, one Singapore commentator has pointed out that a conceptual distinction can nevertheless be maintained: the first limb looks for the meaning of the words expressed in the terms, while the second limb looks for the parties' intention beyond the meaning of those words (inferring from the purported benefit that has been conferred on the third party and other surrounding circumstances).[27]

[21] ibid s 2(1)(a). [22] ibid s 2(1)(b). [23] ibid s 2(2).

[24] Though there is some debate about whether the courts should recognize the designation of a third party by the use of the words 'or his nominee... can enforce the contract' as satisfying the express identification criterion. See TM Yeo (n 18) 38–42.

[25] See *Starlight Shipping Co v Allianz Marine And Aviation Versicherungs AG & Ors* [2014] EWHC 3068 (Comm), [2014] 2 Lloyd's Rep 579.

[26] This was the view of the UK Law Commission (n 19) para 7.18. [27] See TM Yeo (n 18) 43.

The main practical difference between these alternative limbs lies in the additional analytical step involved in the application of section 2(1)(b) that is not triggered if the third party qualifies under section 2(1)(a). Invoking section 2(1)(b) requires the third party to show, first, that a term of the contract 'purports to confer a benefit' on him and that, second, based on the further qualification found in section 2(2), nothing from 'a proper construction of the contract' indicates that the parties 'did not intend the term to be enforceable by the third party'.[28] The rationale behind the combination of sections 2(1)(b) and 2(2) is to limit the scope of the statutory exception to situations where the conferral of benefits upon a third party via the contract, when objectively interpreted together with the other terms of the contract, supports an *implied contractual intention* to give the third party enforceable rights under the contract. Such an implied intention requires, at the very least, the third party to have been an *intended* beneficiary under the contract rather than merely an *incidental* beneficiary.[29] It is thus not enough that the third party is to receive a factual or legal benefit under the contract. The term in question, which reflects the collective will of the contracting parties, must actually *purport* to confer this benefit on this third party. So if X bank makes a contract with Y security company to collect Z store's takings, where the contract requires Y to use armoured vehicles and to take out insurance, would Y be open to an action from Z under the CRTPA via section 2(1)(b) read with section 2(2) if Y does not make these arrangements and Z store's takings are stolen in the collection process? It is submitted that the contractual term requiring Y to adopt these additional security and insurance measures is likely to be construed as purporting to confer benefits on X (the other contracting party) rather than on the third party Z because X's principal contractual interest is to manage *its own risks* that arise from its obligation to ensure the secure conveyance of Z's takings. While Z may also benefit from these additional measures taken by Y, these benefits should be regarded as incidental in nature. Alternatively, even if these security and insurance terms of the contract are characterized as purporting to confer a benefit on Z for the purposes of section 2(1)(b), engaging in a 'proper construction of the contract' might indicate that X (and Y, for that matter) did not intend for Z to enforce these terms directly. This is because there is likely to be a contractual arrangement between X and Z for the former to provide money transportation services to the latter as part of a wider package of commercial banking services, such that the risks associated with such activities are assumed by X rather than Z—hence the need for X to engage Y and include these security and insurance obligations in the X–Y contract. Given this risk-allocation arrangement between X and Z, logic and commercial sense would suggest that the primary intended beneficiary of the these security and insurance contractual terms is X and that, taking into account the chain of contracts between X and Z, a proper construction of these terms should indicate that X and Y did not intend for Z to enforce these terms against Y.

The Singapore Court of Appeal had the opportunity to interpret sections 2(1)(b) and 2(2) of the CRTPA in *CLAAS Medical Centre Pte Ltd v Ng Boon Ching*.[30] The court affirmed that whether a term of the contract purports to confer a benefit on a third party is ultimately a matter of contractual interpretation which required an objective interpretation of the contract with appropriate consideration given to the background facts.[31] Satisfying the

[28] In the UK, one of the Law Commissioners behind the UK Act has explained that adopting a structured statutory test of benefit (where there was no express contractual provision in the contract for third party enforcement) would provide greater certainty than a 'roving search for an implied intention'. See A Burrows, 'Reforming Privity of Contract: Law Commission Report No 242' [1996] LMCLQ 467, 472.

[29] UK Law Commission (n 19) para 3.2.2.

[30] [2010] 2 SLR 386. The SGCA also cited with approval one of the seminal English cases—*The Laemthong Glory (No 2)* [2005] 1 Lloyd's Rep 688, which interpreted the equivalent provisions in the UK Act.

[31] *CLAAS Medical Centre* (n 30) [37].

requirements of section 2(1)(b) raises a rebuttable presumption in favour of the third party such that the promisor-debtor—the party seeking to invoke section 2(2)—bears the burden of proving that, on a proper construction of the contract, the contracting parties did not in fact intend—at the time the contract was formed—for the term concerned to be enforceable by the third party.[32] The absence in the contract of an express statement that the third party is to have a right of enforcement does not automatically rebut this presumption to bar the pursuit of a third party claim; neither should the contractual silence be construed as an indication that the contracting parties lacked any intention to give the third party enforceable rights under the contract.[33] The case before the court involved a contract between a group of medical doctors who were shareholders in a joint venture company they incorporated to run their Aesthetic Medicine practice. The contract contained a restraint of trade provision which precluded the signatories from practising in the business of Aesthetic Medicine for as long as they remained shareholders in the company and for a period of three years thereafter. In the event they defaulted, the contracting parties agreed to pay the company—who was not party to this particular agreement—liquidated damages. One key issue was whether the company, as a third party, was entitled to enforce this liquidated damages clause under the CRTPA. In the absence of any express term of the contract that provided the company with such a right of enforcement, the only statutory route available to the third party company was section 2(1)(b) and it was clear that the liquidated damages clause was one that would inure to the benefit of the third party company. In finding that this contractual term met the 'purports to confer a benefit on [the third party]' threshold, the court explained that it was not necessary to show that benefiting the third party was *the predominant* purpose or intent behind the term—so long as it was *a* purpose of the parties.[34] This gave rise to a rebuttable presumption that the contracting parties had intended to give the third party enforceable rights under the contract.

The trial judge in *CLAAS Medical Centre* had concluded that the inclusion of express rights of termination and restrictions on the assignment of contractual rights or benefits in the contract, exercisable by the contracting parties without the concurrence of the third party, rebutted this presumption because they evinced an intention of the parties not to make the liquidated damages clause enforceable by the third party. However, the Court of Appeal reversed this decision and held that the presumption in favour of the third party created by section 2(1)(b) was *not rebutted* by the presence of such provisions in the contract. The Court of Appeal's conclusion rested on the presence of other statutory provisions within the CRTPA dealing with the crystallization of third party rights and the limits placed on the freedom of the contracting parties to vary or rescind the contract without the third party's consent. If the mere presence of a reservation of a right of the contracting parties to terminate or vary the contract meant that there was no intention to confer enforceable rights upon a named third party, then there would have been no need for the elaborate provisions in section 3 of the CRTPA—in particular, section 3(3) which explicitly preserves the freedom of the contracting parties to include express contract terms which permit rescission or variation of their contract such that the benefits they have provided for the third party can be taken away without the third party's consent.[35] There was thus nothing inconsistent about express termination rights coexisting with terms purporting to confer benefits on third parties that the contracting parties had objectively intended to be enforceable by such third parties; neither was it inconsistent to conclude that the contracting parties objectively intended to give enforceable rights to third parties while simultaneously

[32] ibid [29]. [33] ibid [37]. [34] ibid [28]. [35] ibid [33].

placing general restrictions on the assignment of benefits by the individual signatories.[36] In reaching its conclusion that the threshold requirements of the CRTPA had indeed been met, the Singapore Court of Appeal adopted a commercially pragmatic approach:

> In short, the fact that the parties' objective of entering into the contract was to benefit themselves, the shareholders of the [joint venture company], does not rebut the presumption that the parties intended the term to be enforceable by the [joint venture company], a corporate vehicle they had established to advance and protect their interests. To adopt the other view...would mean that the parties had entered into an agreement providing for liquidated damages for a breach of the covenant which are neither enforceable by the [joint venture company] nor the parties (as [the contract clause] does not confer a right to recover liquidated damages upon the parties), a totally senseless arrangement.[37]

(b) Rights granted to eligible third parties under the CRTPA

Section 2(5) of the CRTPA provides that an eligible 3P-creditor is entitled to enforce a term of the contract by seeking any legal remedy (damages, injunctions, specific performance, and so forth) that would have been available to him had he been a party to the contract, notwithstanding the fact that the third party has not furnished any consideration to the promisor-debtor. The 3P-creditor's enforcement rights are also qualified by section 2(4) which states that they have to be exercised 'subject to and in accordance with any other relevant terms of the contract'. Section 2(6) specifically provides for 3P-creditors to enforce contractual exclusion or limitation clauses, making it clear that the Act is intended to provide a more straightforward alternative to the circuitous common law collateral contract route discussed above in the hypothetical scenario involving third party stevedores.[38]

Section 3 of the CRTPA provides for situations where the 3P-creditor's rights in the contract via the CRTPA have crystallized—meaning that these rights cannot be altered or extinguished without the 3P-creditor's consent. Section 3(1) precludes the contracting parties from varying or rescinding the contract without the 3P-creditor's consent in three scenarios:

(a) when the third party has communicated his assent to the promisor;[39]

(b) when the promisor is aware that the third party has relied on the term (whether or not the third party has knowledge of its precise terms); and

(c) when the promisor can reasonably be expected to have foreseen that the third party would rely on the term and the third party has in fact relied on it (whether or not the third party has knowledge of its precise terms).

These provisions are identical to the corresponding provisions in the UK Act, except that the Singapore legislators thought it appropriate to clarify scenarios (b) and (c) with the additional particulars in parentheses to underscore the applicability of the CRTPA's provisions even when the 3P-creditor is not fully aware of the precise terms of the contract. However, the crystallization of the third party's rights in a contract via the CRTPA is, by virtue of section 3(3) of the Act, subject to express terms of the contract which preserve the freedom of the contracting parties to vary or rescind the contract without seeking the prior consent of the third party.

[36] ibid [35]–[36]. [37] ibid [39]. [38] See discussion above at text accompanying nn 9–16.

[39] CRTPA 2001, s 3(2) explains that the 'assent' referred to here may be communicated to the promisor by words or conduct, and if the 3P-creditor communicates by post or other means, the assent shall only be regarded as communicated to the promisor upon receipt by the promisor.

In *CLAAS Medical Centre*, the 3P-creditor's right to receive payment of liquidated damages under a contract entered into only by its shareholders was found to have crystallized under section 3(1)(a) of the CRTPA because the terms of this contract were set out as an appendix to an earlier contract to which the 3P-creditor was a signatory, with the Court of Appeal reasoning that the 3P-creditor had in fact assented to the terms of the later contract as it was 'patently clear that the [3P-creditor] had worked out what were to be the terms of the [later contract] and had agreed to them'.[40] Since there was no express term in the later contract which triggered the operation of section 3(3) of the CRTPA, the contracting parties were 'no longer at liberty to take away the benefits provided in favour of the [3P-creditor]... without the consent of the [third party debtor]'.[41]

So in the hypothetical scenario where a landlord (X) leases two properties to two adjoining tenants (Y and Z), and includes a term in the X–Y tenancy contract that bars Y from selling bread on the property because Z sells bread from the other property, if we assume that the restrictive covenant against the sale of bread in the X–Y contract purports to confer a benefit on Z and there is nothing to indicate that X and Y did not objectively intend for this contractual term to be enforceable by Z, then the issue of whether X and Y can effectively lift the bar by varying the X–Y tenancy contract (without Z's consent) will depend on whether Z's third party rights have crystallized under one of the limbs of section 3(1) CRTPA. If Z was aware of this restriction in the X–Y tenancy contract at the time he entered into the X–Z tenancy contract, his conduct in taking up the X–Z tenancy may be construed as *conduct which communicates his assent* to the term of the contract to X and Y, thereby triggering section 3(1)(a) CRTPA—in which case, Z's consent will be required for X and Y to vary the X–Y tenancy contract and lift the bar.[42] Alternatively, Z's conduct in taking up the X–Z tenancy, with the knowledge that commercial interests have been catered for in the X–Y contract, may be characterized as an *act of reliance* on the term by Z which X and Y were aware of, or which they could reasonably be expected to have foreseen, thereby triggering either section 3(1)(b) or 3(1)(c) CRTPA with the same consequence.

The third party rights created by sections 2 and 3 of the CRTPA are further qualified by various provisions aimed at protecting the interests of the contracting parties, particularly the promisor-debtor, which will be discussed in the next section. Whilst the CRTPA has introduced a general statutory exception to the privity rule, the legislation is careful to exclude from its ambit certain categories of specialized contracts with well-established legal frameworks:[43] contracts involving negotiable instruments within the field of banking law, limited liability partnership agreements and contracts between companies and their members regulated by statute, employment contracts, and carriage of goods contracts[44] are specifically excluded from the scope of the CRTPA. Furthermore, the statutory reforms introduced by the CRTPA are not intended to replace or change the common law principles that predate it. What the Act does is to *add to* the pre-existing rights and remedies available to 3P-creditors,[45] potentially (and perhaps unintentionally) altering the broader dynamics

[40] *CLAAS Medical Centre*, (n 30) [34]. [41] ibid [34].

[42] Alternatively, there may be other ways in which Z might enforce this term directly. The restrictive covenant preventing Y from selling bread might find its way into the X–Z tenancy contract as an implied term, with X promising Z that he would include such a term in the X–Y tenancy contract for the benefit of Z. Alternatively, there might be a collateral contract between X and Z containing this restrictive term, the consideration for which is Z entering into the X–Z tenancy contract.

[43] See CRTPA 2001, s 7.

[44] See ibid s 7(4), save for exclusion or limitation of liability clauses found in such contracts—discussed above at text accompanying n 16 above.

[45] See CRTPA 2001, s 8(1).

of this area of Singapore's contract law beyond the range of third party legal actions discussed in this section.[46]

(c) *Limitations on third party rights granted under the CRTPA*

Apart from the definitional limits identified above, the CRTPA also contains various statutory provisions which curtail the 3P-creditor's rights of action in order to balance their interests against those of the promisor-debtor. Fairness to the promisor-debtor means that the third party should not be placed in a better position than the promisee. This translates into the provision of statutory defences available to the promisor-debtor that might be raised against the 3P-creditor who relies on the CRTPA to enforce a term of the contract. Defences that the promisor-debtor could have raised against the promisee had the promisee sued on the contract (eg if the contract was tainted by illegality) can also be raised against the 3P-creditor.[47] In the same vein, defences that could have been raised against the third party had the third party been a contracting party (eg if the third party had committed a misrepresentation which induced the promisor to enter into the contract) can also be raised against the 3P-creditor.[48]

Where the 3P-creditor is seeking to enforce a term of a contract which, in particular, purports to exempt or limit his liability, the CRTPA treats the third party as if he were a contracting party trying to rely on an exclusion clause,[49] thereby permitting the promisor-debtor to challenge the validity of such clauses under the Unfair Contracts Terms Act[50] framework. However, the 3P-creditor is not treated as a contracting party for the purposes of any other written law.[51] He may not, for example, avail himself of the remedies potentially available to promisees under the Misrepresentation Act[52] or the Frustrated Contracts Act.[53] Similarly, when a 3P-creditor is seeking to enforce a term of the contract under section 2 of the CRTPA, where the breach of contract involves negligence on the part of the promisor-debtor, and the contract contains an exclusion clause, the 3P-creditor is statutorily barred from invoking section 2(2) of the Unfair Contract Terms Act to challenge the validity of the exclusion clause.[54]

The 3P-creditor's right to recover damages from the promisor-debtor for breach of contract via the CRTPA enforcement action is also qualified by a statutory provision which seeks to protect the promisor-debtor from double liability, given that the CRTPA does not affect the rights of the promisee to enforce any term of the contract against the promisor.[55] Section 6 of the CRTPA directs the courts to 'reduce any award to the third party to such

[46] See discussion below in section IV which discusses the legal principles governing the contract enforcement actions potentially available to the promisee against the promisor-debtor.

[47] See CRTPA 2001, s 4(3). [48] See ibid s 4(4). [49] See ibid s 4(6).

[50] Cap 396, 1994 Rev Ed. [51] See CRTPA 2001, s 8(4).

[52] Cap 390, 1994 Rev Ed. Eg a misrepresentation from the promisor-debtor may have simultaneously: (1) induced the promisee into entering the contract; and (2) prompted the 3P-creditor (who knows that he is to receive a benefit under this contract) to incur expenses. An operative misrepresentation would entitle the promisee to pursue damages under the auspices of the Misrepresentation Act, while the 3P-creditor would be limited to his enforcement rights under the CRTPA (and only if the contract has not been rescinded) and claims in tort law (if any).

[53] Cap 115, 2014 Rev Ed. A 3P-creditor who has incurred expenses in anticipation of receiving payment (or some other benefit) from the promisor-debtor under the contract would not be entitled to recover such expenses via the Frustrated Contracts Act if a frustrating event occurred and discharged the contract before the latter made payment to the former (or conferred the expected benefit upon the former).

[54] See CRTPA 2001, s 8(2). The Unfair Contract Terms Act framework contemplates challenges to the reasonableness of exclusion clauses being made by the actual parties to a contract, requiring an assessment of factors such as an analysis of the relative bargaining positions of the contracting parties—an exercise that cannot be carried out between the promisor-debtor (a contracting party) and the 3P-creditor (a stranger to the contract).

[55] See CRTPA 2001, s 5.

extent as it thinks appropriate to take into account the sum recovered by the promisee', where the promisee has recovered from the promisor a sum 'in respect of (a) the third party's loss in respect of the term; or (b) the expense to the promisee of making good to the third party the default of the promisor'. The statutory impulse to protect the promisor-debtor from double liability is clearly necessary in this area of contract law, where the promisor is potentially exposed to actions from both the promisee and a third party beneficiary, and this policy interest in fairness towards the promisor-debtor is echoed elsewhere in the common law principles governing the recoverability of substantial damages by the promisee against the promisor-debtor.[56]

(d) Residual issues with the CRTPA

The CRTPA has carved out a substantial exception to the privity rule that permits the creation of third party rights of action, thereby giving effect to the actual or presumed intentions of parties to contracts governed by Singapore law. Just as contracting parties are free to create contractual rights that are enforceable by third parties via the CRTPA, they are equally free to override the operation of some or all of its legislative provisions according to their particular needs and interests. While it must be considered a highly significant piece of legislative reform, the CRTPA is not without its imperfections. Some of these have been alluded to in the discussion above, due in part to the uncertain scope of some of its provisions,[57] but nothing that cannot be ironed out by the courts over time via conventional modes of statutory interpretation. However, the Act itself—a static framework of rules—is situated at the crossroads of various strands of common law contract principles that have continued to evolve organically, creating the potential for gaps in the legislation when doctrinal shifts occur at common law. This is best illustrated with reference to the double liability provisions just discussed: the CRTPA allows a court to make reductions to the damages awarded to 3P-creditors where the promisee has already recovered damages from the promisor-debtor 'in respect of… *the third party's loss* in respect of the term…', but no mention is made of situations where the promisee has recovered damages from the promisor-debtor in respect of his *own (ie the promisee's) loss*.[58] This omission is understandable given

[56] See discussion below in sections IV.1 and IV.2.

[57] See eg n 24 and accompanying text.

[58] See discussion below in section IV on the recoverability of damages under the 'broad ground' principles at n 89 and accompanying text. Professor Yeo Tiong Min, who commented on an earlier draft of this chapter at the symposium when it was first presented, takes the view that proviso (b) of s 6—which instructs the court to consider 'the expense to the promisee of making good to the third party the default of the promisor' when awarding damages to the third party bringing an action under the CRTPA—could, possibly, be interpreted widely enough to encompass the 'broad ground' principle on which a promisee's claim for substantial damages against the promisor may be based. In his view, s 6(b) encompasses damages recovered by the promisee for the loss to his performance interest arising from the third party being deprived of the contractual benefit—regardless of whether such damages are awarded on a cost of cure, diminution of value, or loss of amenity basis. This would entail a non-literal interpretation of the word 'expense', which one would more readily associate with expenditures incurred to rectify the harm suffered by the third party as a result of the promisor's breach of contract. However, damages awarded to the promisee under the 'broad ground' principle belong to the promisee alone, and it is entirely up to him to decide if he wants to apply them for the benefit of the third party. Even if Professor Yeo's interpretation of s 6(b) is correct, this still would not protect promisors from double liability to the fullest extent possible. This is because the promisee may have recovered damages in respect of his own losses that are not within the scope of the 'broad ground' principle—damages which reflect the harm to his performance interest (eg disappointment and non-pecuniary losses) quite apart from the loss associated with the deprivation of the third party (ie damages recoverable by way of the 'broad ground' principle) that could have been recovered in two-party cases. Maximum protection for the promisor from being unfairly saddled with 'double liability' should entail permitting the court, when faced with a third party claim under the CRTPA after the promisee has already obtained damages separately from the promisor, to factor in *all damages for breach of contract that have been awarded to the promisee* before determining what would be a reasonable, additional, measure of damages that the promisor should have to pay the third party.

that the legislation was enacted before the relevant English case law developed the notion of permitting a promisee to recover substantial damages from the promisor (on the basis of the 'broad ground' principle)—where the latter's breach consists of a failure to confer a benefit upon a third party—on the basis of protecting the promisee's performance interest in the contract.[59] What this means is that it remains imperative for the courts, when interpreting and applying the provisions of the CRTPA, to keep an eye on surrounding contemporary doctrinal developments in the common law of contracts that are relevant to the statutory provisions of the CRTPA and that seek to balance the interests of promisor-debtors, promisees, and 3P-creditors.

III. Indirect Enforcement of Contracts by Third Parties

In the event that the third party is unable to circumvent the privity rule or qualify for one of the exceptions to the privity rule that have been outlined above, he will have no choice but to resort to alternative non-contract-based legal avenues (if any are available) to pursue his claim against the promisor. In Singapore, the most obvious alternative route is via the law of torts. Singapore tort law differs substantially from English tort law where the tort of negligence is concerned. Unlike the position in the UK, pure economic losses may be recovered in Singapore under the tort of negligence so long as the requisite factual and legal proximity is established between the claimant (the 3P-creditor, in this case) and the negligent tortfeasor (the promisor-debtor).[60] So in a typical three-party scenario where a builder (promisor) contractually promises a housing developer (promisee) to construct new homes that will be subsequently sold to various property buyers (third parties), if a third party who purchases one of these homes suffers economic loss arising from workmanship defects caused by the promisor's negligence, the third party may potentially have a negligence claim against the promisor. The availability of this cause of action transposes what was originally a contractual obligation owed by the promisor to the promisee into a tortious duty of care owed to the injured third party, enabling the third party to hold the promisor accountable for his defective performance and, arguably, indirectly enforcing the home-building contract.

Where the third party is a disappointed beneficiary who ends up not receiving an inheritance from a testator's estate because of a solicitor's negligent will-drafting, English law allows for the tort of negligence to be made available to the injured third party when the privity rule operates as an insurmountable obstacle to an action under the testator–solicitor contract. The principle in *White v Jones*[61] was intended to achieve a just result by making the solicitor legally accountable to the third party, via an exceptional extension to the tort of negligence, given that any action for breach of contract, if any were pursued, could only be pursued by the testator's estate which would have great difficulty proving that the estate has suffered any substantial losses from the solicitor's breach of contract. This extension to the tort of negligence causing pure economic loss was explicitly endorsed by the Singapore Court of Appeal in a 2014 decision[62] and offers yet another legal avenue for the third party to claim against the promisor, yielding a remedial result that is similar to the outcome if the

[59] *Alfred McAlpine Construction Ltd v Panatown Ltd* [2001] 1 AC 518 (HL). See discussion below in section IV.2.

[60] See *Spandeck Engineering (S) Pte Ltd v Defence Science & Technology Agency* [2007] SGCA 37, [2007] 4 SLR(R) 100 where the Court of Appeal held that a single test should determine the imposition of a duty of care in all claims arising out of negligence, irrespective of the type of the damages claimed, and that there was no justification for a general exclusionary rule against recovery of all economic losses.

[61] [1995] 2 AC 207 (HL).

[62] *Anwar Patrick Adrian & Anor v Ng Chong & Hue LLC & Anor* [2014] SGCA 34.

third party had been permitted to directly enforce the contract against the promisor. It is submitted, however, that tort-based causes of action that serve as indirect means to enforce the promisor-debtor's obligations under a contract should be considered inferior substitutes for the various direct third party actions in contract that have been examined in section II above. Third party claims in contract are typically concerned with strict obligations, whereas claims in tort are generally fault-based, potentially placing a 3P-creditor who can only access tort-based claims in a strategically weaker position than a 3P-creditor who is able to launch a direct contract-based claim against the promisor-debtor.

IV. Enforcement of Contracts for the Benefit of Third Parties by Promisees

Enforcement actions by promisees against promisors where the breach of contract involves a failure by the latter to confer a benefit on a third party can take the form of either an action for specific performance, injunction, or an action for damages. The primary remedy available to the promisee is a claim for damages for breach of contract, though he will have to prove that he has suffered actual loss as a result of the breach of contract. Alternatively, specific performance (or a stay of proceedings, where the benefit purportedly conferred on the third party consists of a promise not to sue the third party) may be sought, requiring the promisor to carry out his promise to benefit the third party, but only as a secondary remedy if damages would not be adequate. In either case, the enforcement action is driven solely by the promisee, rather than the third party, and the pursuit of such claims is entirely dependent on the willingness and ability of the promisee to commence proceedings against the promisor.

One of the doctrinal obstacles towards claims for damages by promisees against promisors in contracts that confer benefits on third parties lies in the principle that damages are compensatory in nature, such that a promisee is only entitled to recover losses which he has *actually* suffered. A contracting party may not recover damages for breach of contract in relation to the losses suffered by a third party. If the promisee is unable to prove that *he* has suffered a real loss from the promisor's contractual breach, all he is entitled to recover are nominal damages. When this damages rule is applied alongside the privity rule, which precludes claims under the contract by third parties, their combined effect is to produce what common lawyers have described as a 'legal black hole'—where the promisor is not held accountable, either to the promisee or the third party, for his failure to perform his contractual promise to benefit a third party. This has led the English courts to develop two sets of common law principles that facilitate a promisee's claims for substantial damages for breach of contract in order to close the 'legal black hole'. First, a promisee may in some circumstances recover substantial damages on behalf of the third party. This is an *exception* to the damages rule and is known as the 'narrow ground' of recovery. Second, a promisee may also recover substantial damages in respect of his own loss, where his performance interest in the contract has been undermined by the promisor's failure to benefit the third party in accordance with the terms of the contract. This involves a change in the way the promisee's loss is characterized, and is referred to as the 'broad ground' of recovery. Both the 'narrow ground' and 'broad ground' bases for substantial damages have been judicially endorsed by the Singapore Court of Appeal in *Chia Kok Leong v Prosperland*[63] and *Family Food Court v Seah Boon Lock*.[64]

[63] [2005] SGCA 12. [64] *Family Food Court* (n 5).

1. Damages—The 'Narrow Ground'

Under the classic formulation of the narrow ground of recovery, a promisee may recover substantial damages on behalf of the third party, in an action for breach of contract against the promisor, where the conditions identified in *The Albazero*[65] are satisfied: (1) it was in the contemplation of the contracting parties that the proprietary interest in the goods may be transferred to a third party after the contract has been entered into, but before the breach which causes the loss or damage occurs; and (2) it was within the intentions of both contracting parties to treat the promisee as entering into the contract for the benefit of all persons who have or may acquire an interest in the goods before they are damaged. This exception was subsequently extended from the carriage of goods context to the construction context,[66] where ownership in real property rather than goods was transferred, and further expanded to cases where there was no transfer of proprietary interest at all,[67] with ownership of the contractual subject matter remaining with the third party throughout. These developments to the common law were endorsed by the House of Lords in *Alfred McAlpine Construction Ltd v Panatown*[68] where the narrow ground principles were restated by Lord Browne-Wilkinson along with two important qualifications:

> [W]here A enters into a contract with B [the promisor] relating to property and it is envisaged by the parties that ownership of that property may be transferred to a third party, C, so that the consequences of any breach of contract will be suffered by C, A has a cause of action to recover from B the loss suffered by C. However... [f]irst, A is accountable to C for any damages recovered by A from B as compensation for C's loss...Second, the exceptional principle does not apply (because it is not needed) where C has a direct remedy against B.[69]

Accepting these statements of the principles governing the narrow ground exception, the Singapore Court of Appeal in *Family Food Court* emphasized that the rationale behind them was to respond to the 'legal black hole' problem. However, there would be no black hole if the third parties were given a direct cause of action against the promisor (as was the case in *Panatown* where there as a Duty of Care Deed issued by the promisor which the third party could sue upon), making it unnecessary to allow the promisee to recover substantial damages on the third party's behalf. The scope of the narrow ground exception is thus dependent on the scope of this qualification—the more things that qualify as direct remedies that the third party may pursue against the promisor, the less room for invoking the narrow ground exception. However, in *Prosperland*, the Singapore Court of Appeal held that only a contract-like remedy available to the third party (such as the Duty of Care Deed in *Panatown*) would counter the legal black hole, thus allowing a promisee to rely on the narrow ground exception as a basis for recovering substantial damages from the promisor even though the third party could potentially sue the promisor under the tort of negligence:[70]

> To deprive a building employer [the promisee] of The Albazero exception, there has to be an express contractual right in favour of [the] third party or something akin to it, as in the case of an indorsee of a bill of lading under the [Bills of Lading Act 1855].

This 'robust approach' of the Court of Appeal has been welcomed by one of Singapore's leading contract law scholars, who explains that maintaining the breadth of this exception 'provides assurance that the narrow ground continues to safeguard the efficacy of contractual

[65] [1977] AC 774 (HL) 847.
[66] *Linden Gardens Trust Ltd v Lenesta Sludge Disposals Ltd* [1994] 1 AC 85 (HL).
[67] *Darlington Borough Council v Wiltshire Northern Ltd* [1994] EWCA Civ J0628-8, [1995] 1 WLR 68.
[68] [2001] 1 AC 518 (HL).
[69] ibid 575.
[70] *Prosperland*, (n 63) [43]–[45].

obligations despite the existence of rights to sue in tort' because tort law liability is fault-based and susceptible to various defences that do not apply to contract-based claims.[71] Professor Loke also highlights an important contrast between English and Singapore law which results from this approach. In property development cases, UK tort law does not permit negligence claims by subsequent third party buyers for pure economic loss unlike their Singapore counterparts.[72] Thus, a Duty of Care Deed would have to be negotiated as part of the contractual arrangements in the UK context if the goal is to protect the third party by giving him a direct cause of action against the building contractors. But doing so would close the legal black hole and bar the employers from claiming substantial damages under the narrow ground. Only one or the other can take action against the promisor. In contrast, Singapore law permits *both* the subsequent third party purchaser *and* the employer to claim against the promisor without incurring the transaction costs associated with negotiating or drafting a Duty of Care Deed—one able to sue in tort, and one able to sue in contract since the legal black hole remains unfilled—though subject to procedural safeguards requiring the third party to be joined together with the promisee in the same action to protect the promisor from double liability.[73]

However, one issue which remains unresolved by the Singapore courts and contract law commentators, is the extent to which the availability of third party rights of action under the CRTPA might be regarded as filling the legal black hole: is the narrow ground exception to the damages rule still necessary, or justifiable, in the light of this legislative reform? If the third party can bring a direct statutory claim under the Act against the promisor—an option that was not available at the time the English courts developed the exception in the line of cases that sprung from *The Albazero*—then perhaps there is no longer a basis for permitting the promisee to recover substantial damages on the third party's behalf. It should be noted, however, that it is common commercial practice for contracting parties to expressly exclude the operation of the CRTPA in their contractual arrangements, so this issue may be more conceptual than of practical significance.

Another issue about the narrow ground exception which remains unclear is whether *Panatown* fully accepted the extension of this principle to situations where the third party was the owner of the damaged property from the start of the contract, given that Lord Browne-Wilkinson's restatement still required the contemplation on the part of the contracting parties that the proprietary interest in the goods may be transferred from one owner to another after the contract has been entered into and before the breach which causes the loss or damage occurs. This was discussed in obiter dicta by the Court of Appeal in *Family Food Court* where no satisfactory conclusion was reached.[74] It is thus unclear exactly how narrow this 'narrow ground' exception—which is already confined to cases where the breach of contract causes *loss to property* owned by a third party—actually is. What *is* clear from the *Family Food Court* decision is that the narrow ground exception is *not* applicable to situations involving third parties who are undisclosed principals because the promisor would have been 'totally unaware of the existence of the third party', making

[71] A Loke, 'The "Broad Ground" and the Not-So-Narrow Ground in Singapore: *Chia Kok Leong v Prosperland Pte Ltd*' (2007) JCL 148. In the later case of *Family Food Court* (n 5) [47], the Court of Appeal reiterated the point: '[A]n alternative cause of action in *tort* that may be available to the third party does not mean that the "legal black hole"... is eradicated or filled up. A claim in tort (subject to all the usual limitations and defences in tort) is not the same as a claim in contract, and, thus, the existence of an alternative cause of action in tort does not render the narrow ground inapplicable.'

[72] *RSP Architects v Ocean Front* [1995] SGCA 79, [1996] 1 SLR 113; *RSP Architects v MCST Plan 1075 (Eastern Lagoon)* [1999] SGCA 30, [1999] 2 SLR 449.

[73] *Prosperland* (n 63) [56], where reference was also made to the 'practical solutions' suggested by Lord Millett in *Panatown* (n 68) 595.

[74] *Family Food Court* (n 5) [40] and [56].

it impossible for the contracting parties to have contemplated any transfer of proprietary interest between the promisee (agent) and the third party (undisclosed principal).[75] However, even if the narrow ground exception is not available to permit the promisee to recover the third party's losses from the promisor in such cases, agency law still permits the third party who is an undisclosed principal to sue the promisor directly under the contract.

2. Damages—The 'Broad Ground'

The broad ground of recovery involves a reconceptualization of the meaning of the 'loss' which the promisee has suffered as a result of the breach of contract, where loss has traditionally been understood in purely economic terms. If the breach caused loss to a third party's property, then the traditional approach was to treat the promisee as having suffered no 'real' loss and to award him nominal damages only. However, if the loss suffered by the promisee was understood as a loss of his *performance interest* in the contract—that the promisor has failed to deliver the performance contracted for by the promisee who intends to benefit a third party—then the promisee should always, in principle, be entitled to recover substantial damages for the losses *he has suffered* from the promisor's breach of contract. This principle has its origins in the *Linden Gardens* case, where Lord Griffiths expressed the view that the promisee should be entitled to substantive damages even if he did not have a proprietary interest in the damaged property, and that the appropriate measure of damages would be the cost to the promisee of securing an alternative performance of the bargain.[76] The Law Lords in *Panatown* subsequently endorsed the broad ground principle, albeit with varying degrees of enthusiasm and with significant variations in its breadth of application, with the majority declining to invoke this principle to permit the promisee to recover substantial damages because actual damage to his performance interest had not been satisfactorily established.[77]

The Singapore Court of Appeal in *Prosperland* was more unequivocal in its adoption of the broad ground principle, describing it as 'probably more consistent with principle' than the narrow ground exception, discussed above, on the basis that the promisee's entitlement to substantial damages flows from the fact 'that he did not receive what he had bargained and paid for'.[78] This position was affirmed in *Family Food Court* where the same court reiterated 'the performance interest approach to contractual damages as the foundation of the broad ground' and that, unlike the narrow ground exception, 'the plaintiff/promisee [pursuing a claim under the broad ground] is recovering substantial damages for his own loss, and not on behalf of the third party'.[79]

The broad ground has nothing to do with 'filling' up the legal black hole[80]—it actually *prevents* the black hole problem from materializing by modifying the damages rule, which previously limited the promisee in such three-party scenarios to recovering only nominal damages. On the 'broad ground' approach, the promisee's unsatisfied performance interest *is* the *loss* he suffers from the breach of contract. In *Family Food Court*, the court noted that 'the performance interest claimed ... must be a genuine one ... [This would require] the court [to] apply an objective test of reasonableness to the performance interest claimed so

[75] ibid [58]. Even if the transfer of a proprietary interest between the promisee and the third party after the time of the contract, but before the occurrence of the breach, is not one of the essential requirements of the narrow ground exception, it should be apparent that the promisor must have had—at the very least—some form of knowledge or awareness of the existence of the third party before it would be fair to allow the promisee to recover damages, *on behalf of* the third party, for losses suffered by the third party as a result of the promisor's breach of contract.

[76] *Linden Gardens* (n 66) 96–97.

[77] See discussion in *Family Food Court* (n 5) [50]–[51].

[78] *Prosperland*, (n 63) [53].

[79] *Family Food Court* (n 5) [52].

[80] *Prosperland* (n 63) [55].

as to curb what would otherwise be a windfall accrued to the plaintiff/promisee'.[81] This is consistent with the position that the court took earlier in *Prosperland* that it is unnecessary for the promisee to always demonstrate an intention to utilize the damages sought to benefit the third party before he is entitled to claim for substantial damages from the promisor.[82] Nevertheless, while indicating its readiness to permit promisees to invoke the broad ground to recover substantial damages from defaulting promisors, the Court of Appeal was also careful to emphasize that it was important to guard against the promisor being made to compensate twice over for the same damage—once in an action brought by the promisee, and once in an action brought by the third party. Judicial attention was given to the civil procedure rules which allow third parties to be joined to the proceedings brought by promisees, thereby allowing double liability concerns to be allayed by determining the rights and liabilities of all interested parties at the same time.[83] The power of the court to order third parties to join in proceedings brought by the promisee was also considered in the *Family Food Court* decision as a procedural solution to the unresolved question of whether the broad ground principle could apply to situations involving promisees acting on behalf of undisclosed principals.[84]

What is interesting about the Singapore position is that even as the Court of Appeal showed its 'eagerness . . . to provide a disappointed [promisee] with a substantial remedy for defective performance' (by readily embracing *both* the broad and narrow grounds as common law responses to the 'legal black hole' problem),[85] it was at the same time critically aware that they 'are *conceptually inconsistent* with each other . . . [and] although . . . are commonly discussed together in the same case . . . they *cannot apply simultaneously*'.[86] The application of the broad ground means that the promisee can recover substantial damages from the promisor, thereby forestalling the legal black hole which the narrow ground exception seeks to fill.[87] While the Court of Appeal has flagged the issue without expressing a definitive opinion, suggesting that 'there ought to be an objective legal point which, when reached, will result in the broad ground being applied in place of the narrow ground', it was not prepared to say anything more about the relationship between the broad ground and the narrow ground in the *Family Food Court* decision since this was not a 'live issue' in that case.[88] It is submitted that if and when this issue is revisited by the Singapore courts in

[81] *Family Food Court* (n 5) [53].

[82] *Prosperland*, (n 63) [57], where Chao JA held that '[a]t the end of the day, the entire circumstances of the case must be considered to determine whether the claim [for substantial damages against the promisor under the broad ground] made was reasonable or was made with a view to obtaining an uncovenanted benefit'—this means that that an inquiry into the intentions of the promisee (whether or not he intended to realize his performance interest by using the damages to benefit the third party) is merely a relevant, rather than conclusive, factor for the court to consider when deciding how much to award the promisee.

[83] *Prosperland* (n 63) [54]–[56], where reference was made to Order 15 rule 6 of the Rules of Court (Cap 322, R 5, 2004 Rev Ed).

[84] *Family Food Court* (n 5) [63]–[67]. Strictly speaking, all of the discussion relating to undisclosed principals in the Court of Appeal was obiter dictum because it had already held, at [26]–[27], that there was no undisclosed principal in this case. It was thus unnecessary for the court to consider the question of whether the broad ground principle should apply to cases involving third party undisclosed principals, and it was inconsequential that this question was not conclusively determined. Hence, at [62], it observed that '[n]otwithstanding the conflicting arguments for and against the application of the broad ground in the context of an undisclosed principal, we are of the view that there is no need to determine conclusively which set of arguments should prevail and, in the process, descend into the legal controversy surrounding the application of the broad ground. The relevant rules of civil procedure render the potential difficulties vis-à-vis the extent of recovery of damages available to a plaintiff/agent a moot point in most cases in light of the act that these rules permit the court to order the undisclosed principal to be joined to the proceedings if the latter chooses not to intervene of its own accord.'

[85] See Loke (n 71) 153.

[86] *Family Food Court* (n 5) [56].

[87] As Professor Loke has eloquently put it: 'The acceptance of the broad ground must undercut the premises of the narrow ground . . . as the broad ground increases in currency, the narrow ground will foreseeably diminish'. See n 71, 153.

[88] *Family Food Court* (n 5) [56].

future cases, the examination of the scope of the broad ground of recovery must be considered alongside the statutory framework of the CRTPA. When such an opportunity arises, the courts will need to consider how the performance interest of the promisee is affected if at all, by the availability of a third party statutory action to enforce a term of the contract and, more specifically, how the promisee's right to recover substantial damages in respect of his *own* losses via the broad ground relates to section 6 of the CRTPA ('Protection of promisor from double liability').[89]

3. Specific Performance

In theory, the promisee may also seek to enforce the promise to confer a benefit on a third party by way of an order of specific performance, provided that it can convince the court to exercise its discretion to award this secondary remedy on the basis that damages would be inadequate and none of the bars to equitable relief apply. The classic case here is the English decision of *Beswick v Beswick*,[90] where a third party was able to enforce a contract in her capacity as the personal representative of the deceased promisee, thereby overcoming the privity rule obstacle, and succeeded in obtaining specific performance of the contract under which she was to be paid by the promisor a weekly annuity after the promisee had, before his death, assigned his business assets to the promisor. The House of Lords held that damages would have been an inadequate remedy as the promisee's estate, having suffered 'no loss', would only have recovered nominal damages, and it would have been inequitable to allow the promisor, having already taken the benefits of the contract, to escape the bargain that he had made with the promisee to pay the third party a sum of money on a weekly basis.

Whether an order of specific performance is necessary to achieve an equitable result in situations involving contracts for the benefit of a third party requires an evaluation of multiple factors, two of which have been subject to very significant legal developments since *Beswick v Beswick* was decided. The first factor relates to whether the third party has the option of pursuing a direct cause of action against the promisor; if so, then the necessity of granting an order of specific performance to the promisee fades away. So the Singapore High Court refused to grant specific performance to the promisee in *Indulge Food Pte Ltd v Torabi Marashi Bahram*, where the promisor had agreed to pay sums of money to a third party, because the third party, who was privy to another contract with the promisor, 'could [have sued the promisor] in its own right, and was unable to do so only because of [the promisee's] procedural omission to join it as a party to the proceedings'.[91] Furthermore, the potential availability of third party statutory actions under the CRTPA could also diminish the willingness of the courts to grant specific performance to the promisee. The second factor relates to whether an award of damages would provide an 'adequate' remedy for the breach of contract. When *Beswick v Beswick* was decided, the common law had a very parochial understanding of the promisee's 'loss' when the breach of contract consisted of the promisor's failure to confer a benefit on a third party; the promisee was then only entitled to nominal damages. Moreover, there were no well-developed exceptions to the damages rule which would have allowed the promisee to recover damages in respect of the losses suffered by the third party. From the discussion above,[92] it should be clear that the common law in this area has evolved significantly, introducing both the narrow ground exception and the broad ground basis as mechanisms for a promisee to recover substantial damages for breach of contract in such situations, thus making it quite unlikely for a court faced with

[89] See discussion above at text accompanying nn 56–58.
[90] [1968] AC 58 (HL).
[91] [2010] SGHC 22, [2010] 2 SLR 540, [35].
[92] See sections IV.1 and IV.2 above.

a request for specific performance to conclude that an award of damages to the promisee would be 'inadequate'. Given the extensive legislative and common law developments that have emerged from this area of the law, it is submitted that the specific performance remedy will not be awarded to the promisee in the majority of these sorts of cases.

V. Conclusion

Even as the Singapore courts have had the opportunity to grapple with the technical and doctrinal intricacies of this area of contract law, which substantially intersects with other fields of private law (tort law, in particular) and specialized branches of commercial law, it is submitted that the law relating to contracts for the benefit of third parties is still at a relatively nascent stage of development. Broad statements of principle have been articulated by the Singapore courts, which have clearly accepted the promisee's right to claim substantial damages for the loss of his performance interest when the third party does not receive the benefit which the promisor had contracted to provide. The availability of statutory actions under the CRTPA for third parties has also been examined by the Singapore courts, mapping out the basic contours of the rights that 3P-creditors have against promisor-debtors; however the opportunity to *simultaneously* consider the promisor's liabilities towards the promisee (at common law) and the third party (under the statute) has not yet arisen. If and when such an opportunity arises, the courts need to approach the claims of each party against the promisor with careful precision. As the discussion above has, hopefully, illustrated, this is an area of law with many moving parts—common law, statute, and equity—making it essential that judges who engage with the doctrinal machinery always keep an eye on how adjustments to one component might have an impact elsewhere within the wider framework of legal rules and principles.

10

Contract Formation in Hong Kong

*Lusina HO**

I. Introduction

Contractual rules on the creation of an enforceable contract crucially determine which class of promises a legal system chooses to enforce and what standard of behaviour governs the negotiation process; in doing so, they reflect if not reinforce the social values and commercial needs of society. In Hong Kong, the relevant rules were transplanted in its early colonial days from English law by the proclamation of the Charter of the Colony of Hong Kong on 5 April 1843.[1] This broad stroke of legislative pen imported the precepts of the common law that were developed from a tradition and a society dramatically different from the fishing village that Hong Kong was. The relevant provision was improved by a series of legislation that culminated in the now repealed section 3(1) of the Application of English Law Ordinance 1966, which provided that the common law and the rules of equity shall be in force in Hong Kong so far as they are applicable to the circumstances of Hong Kong or its inhabitants, and subject to amendment by legislation or modifications as circumstances may require.[2] This was the standard formula used by the British Empire in transplanting the common law to its colonies; one can find similar legislation in the early colonial periods of neighbouring Asian countries such as Malaysia, Singapore, Myanmar, India, and Brunei.

By 1997, when Hong Kong returned to China, it had grown to become a leading financial centre in Asia and a gateway to China. To preserve the economic success in Hong Kong, which is due in great part to an effective legal system and independent judiciary, China gave assurance for the continuity of existing laws and the capitalist system for 50 years. Hence, despite the resumption of sovereignty by China, a civil law country, the rules of common law and equity were kept in place by Article 8 of the Basic Law, Hong Kong's constitution promulgated in 1997.[3] These rules provide the primary source of contract law in Hong Kong, albeit there are modifications in sporadic areas by specific legislation, such as the Contracts (Rights of Third Parties) Ordinance that is the focus of the following chapter. Most of these legislative instruments were enacted to dovetail the English statutes, and often

* Cite as L Ho, 'Contract Formation in Hong Kong' in Chen-Wishart, Loke, & Vogenauer, *Studies in the Contract Laws of Asia Vol II: Formation and Third Party Beneficiaries* (Oxford: OUP 2017) ch 10. I am most grateful to Tom Ng and Victor Lui for their research assistance. All errors are mine.

[1] For detailed accounts of the reception of English law, see S Lo and WH Chui, *The Hong Kong Legal System* (Singapore: McGraw Hill Education (Asia) 2012) 3–9; P Wesley-Smith, *An Introduction to the Hong Kong Legal System* (3rd edn, Hong Kong: OUP 1988) 38–40. See also C Munn, *Anglo-China: Chinese People and British Rule in Hong Kong, 1841–1880* (Richmond: Curzon Press 2001) 165–166; MK Chan, 'The Imperfect Legacy: Defects in the British Legal System in Colonial Hong Kong' (1997) 18 U Penn J Int'l Econ L 133, 156; E Marcks, 'English Law in Early Hong Kong: Colonial Law as a Means for Control and Liberation' (2000) 35 Texas Int'l LJ 265, 266.

[2] Application of English Law Ordinance (Cap 88), repealed on 1 July 1997.

[3] Basic Law of the Hong Kong Special Administrative Region of the People's Republic of China, Art 8, provides that the laws previously in force in Hong Kong (including common law and equity) shall be maintained. See also Basic Law, Arts 5, 18, and 84.

Contract Formation in Hong Kong. Lusina Ho.

a few years if not a decade or so after its English pioneer.[4] Thus, Hong Kong contract law—as well as most areas of law that are heavily based on judge-made law—resembles closely English law before the impact of European Union regulations becoming applicable in the UK.

After the handover, the Court of Final Appeal is the highest court in Hong Kong, and is at liberty to apply judicial authorities from any common law jurisdiction, whereas previously the highest court in Hong Kong was the Judicial Committee of the Privy Council, and the Hong Kong Court of Appeal was bound by decisions of the Judicial Committee.[5] Thus, even before 1997, courts in Hong Kong were never bound by decisions of the English House of Lords,[6] Court of Appeal, or lower courts, albeit they almost invariably followed English law, often as if it were binding.[7] After 1997, Privy Council decisions on appeal from Hong Kong remain binding until they are departed from by the Hong Kong Court of Final Appeal,[8] but all post-1997 Privy Council decisions and UK Supreme Court (formerly House of Lords) decisions are of persuasive authority,[9] as are decisions of other common law jurisdictions. The establishment of the Court of Final Appeal in Hong Kong thus gives its highest court a fresh opportunity to consider the immense range of common law jurisprudence available for the vibrant financial centre that Hong Kong has become. These choices include the relatively hard-nosed English approach that caters for international commerce, and by way of contrast the domestically oriented Australian approach that emphasizes consumer protection.

Interestingly, not only has Hong Kong jurisprudence adhered to the English approach, at times it has gone further in laying down shrewd and bright-line rules to govern contractual negotiation and performance. There is also significant emphasis, probably greater than in English law, on the written words of the contract or instruments used by parties in the run-up to the conclusion of the contract, and greater reluctance to rely on open-ended discretionary principles to resolve disputes. Such an approach is often justified on the grounds of commercial certainty which is needed for the unique, cut-throat property market and thriving construction and financial industries in Hong Kong. In an '(in)famous' decision on contractual performance, *Union Eagle Ltd v Golden Achievement Ltd*,[10] all three levels of courts held that when a contract for the sale and purchase of land stipulated the completion time of 5 pm to be 'of the essence', the vendor could legitimately terminate the contract on breach even though the purchaser turned up just 10 minutes after 5 pm to complete the contract due to traffic delay. Lord Hoffmann, who delivered the unanimous decision of the Privy Council on one of the last appeal cases from Hong Kong, steadfastly refused to allow equity to intervene, on the grounds of 'practical considerations of business' and the need for parties to 'know with certainty that the terms of the contract will be enforced'.[11] The same judicial attitude, of giving primacy to the written document, permeates the law relating to the formation of contracts.

Having said that, within these parameters and preferences, the courts have tried their best to provide a level playing field between contractual parties, and are constantly fine-tuning it to strike the balance. In this process, the Court of Final Appeal has on several occasions overturned decisions of lower courts that merely followed traditional English law

[4] eg the Misrepresentation Ordinance 1977.

[5] On questions of English law applicable in Hong Kong, the Hong Kong Court of Final Appeal is also bound by decisions of the House of Lords.

[6] ibid. [7] Wesley-Smith (n 1) 83–86. [8] Basic Law, Art 82.

[9] *Solicitor (24/07) v Law Society of Hong Kong* (2008) 11 HKCFAR 117 (CFA) [17].

[10] [1997] AC 514, discussed in ME Kowalski, 'Good Faith, Greed and Time of the Essence' (2000) 30 HKLJ 476.

[11] ibid 518.

as if it was binding, and made a conscious effort to carve its own path. It also regularly marshals the breadth of case law in major common law jurisdictions in order to resolve disputes at hand.

This chapter will examine contract formation rules in Hong Kong. It argues that the Hong Kong courts have endeavoured to adapt common law rules transplanted from a society that is radically different culturally and commercially in order to resolve multidirectional policy tensions and lay down rules of fair play between parties. The aspects where such adaption is particularly noteworthy typically involve negotiation conduct that may be considered morally unscrupulous, such as: attempts to enforce terms in a contract to which one party knows the other party never meant to agree; breaking off negotiations in a fluctuating property market; refusing to honour agreements to negotiate in good faith; renegotiating for additional or lower pay for the same work; and refusing to honour gratuitous promises.

II. Requirements for a Valid Contract

Hong Kong law follows its English heritage in, first, ascertaining the existence of a contract upon what objectively appears to a reasonable person (the objective intention) and, second, requiring the basic elements of offer, acceptance, consideration, intention to create legal relation, and certainty, to create a binding contract. Over the years, detailed rules have been developed to flesh out the requirements for these elements. To find a binding contract, judges need to categorize and analyse the facts under the tests established for each of these elements. In this way, commercial certainty is promoted, as there is very little room for a court to assess the facts in the round to infer that the parties have come to an agreement. It also contrasts with the typical civilian approach of identifying an agreement between the parties based on a general inference about their intention.[12]

1. The Objective Intention

Hong Kong law adopts the English principle, which has been well established since *Smith v Hughes*,[13] that the meaning of the contract is that which objectively appears to a reasonable person, and is so understood by the contracting party. Such a principle ensures that a contractual party is only bound by what a reasonable person would understand the contract to be, and not what the other party subjectively (and perhaps also unilaterally) believes it to be. In Hong Kong, the principle has been utilized most effectively to fend off an attempt by a party to impose a contract to which it knew the other party never meant to agree. In *Shanghai Tongji Science & Technology Industrial Co Ltd v Casil Clearing Ltd*,[14] after detailed (and exclusive) reference to English authorities and treatises, the Court of Final Appeal affirmed the objective principle. In this case, a fraudster successfully played two parties against each other before disappearing with the benefits from the fraud. From the plaintiff, she procured the issue of a letter of credit in favour of the defendant by making it believe that the defendant was the purported seller. From the defendant, who was actually her moneylender, she obtained a further loan by using the proceeds of the letter to pay for outstanding loans. When the purported goods never reached the plaintiff, it sued the defendant for non-delivery of goods. Since no written contract was ever executed between the plaintiff and defendant, the plaintiff sought to argue that a contract was concluded by the

[12] See Y Kwon, 'Contract Formation and Third Party Beneficiaries in Korea', ch 14.
[13] (1871) LR 6 QB 597.
[14] 7 HKCFAR 79, [2004] 2 HKLRD 548 (CFA).

conduct of issuing and negotiating the letter of credit. Ribeiro PJ categorically held that in applying the objective approach to infer a contract from conduct, it was not sufficient that the conduct was *capable* of constituting a contract, but that it must be consistent *only* with there being a contract. His lordship considered the lack of any previous contact between the two parties and the common practice of naming financial intermediaries in letters of credits as fatal to such inference. Significantly, he further relied on the subjective qualification of the objective approach and considered it fatal that the defendant never intended to be bound by any underlying sale contract with the plaintiff and the plaintiff knew of the defendant's state of mind.[15]

The same objective principle (and its concomitant subjective qualification) was affirmed in 2013 in *Kowloon Development Finance Ltd v Pendex Industries Ltd*.[16] In this case, the parties had entered into consent orders which failed to reflect a term of the loan resettlements agreed between them, namely that the servicing of the loan did not discharge the outstanding balance. When the defendant sought to rely on the second consent order to argue that the loan was discharged by its partial repayments, Lord Hoffmann NPJ found it possible to construe the consent order objectively as including the omitted term. His lordship referred to the classic English approach laid down in *Smith v Hughes*,[17] and reiterated that one party's knowledge of the other's state of mind aside, 'objective interpretation of contractual agreements is a fundamental principle of the common law'.[18]

The plaintiffs in both decisions attempted to enforce a contract in terms on which they knew the other party never meant to agree, and the courts were able to achieve the just result by applying the objective theory of contract and the subjective qualification. As Hoffmann NPJ remarked in *Kowloon Development Finance*, a civilian system would deal with such reprehensible conduct by the principle of good faith in contractual negotiations, whereas common law would tackle it by 'a number of individual rules which provide remedies against specific forms of bad faith', such as the subjective qualification in the objective principle and rectification for unilateral mistake.[19]

2. Offer and Acceptance

The principles of offer and acceptance in Hong Kong law are similar to those in English law. In English law, an offer is 'an expression of willingness to contract on specified terms, made with the intention that it is to become binding as soon as it is accepted by the person to whom it is addressed'.[20] The same definition is adopted in Hong Kong.[21]

Since both English and Hong Kong law allow the revocation of the offer before it is accepted, there is significant room for a party to make offers to multiple parties as a negotiation tactic and drop less favourable deals at any time before they are accepted in order to maximize his bargain. For example, an offer can be revoked at any time before it is accepted, even though the offeror has promised to keep the offer open for a specified time, because such a promise is not supported by consideration.[22] If the offeror makes a second offer that

[15] ibid [50]–[57]. *Shanghai Tongi* has been applied in the lower courts in eg *Etacol (Hong Kong) Ltd v Sinomast Ltd (No 2)* [2007] 2 HKC 73 (CFI).

[16] (2013) 16 HKCFAR 226 (CFA) [8] and [14], observed in L Mason, 'Restatement of the Law on Rectification: Equitable Relief for Mistakes in Contractual Documents' [2014] ICCLR 26. See *The Harriette N* [2008] EWHC 2257 (Comm).

[17] *Smith* (n 13). [18] *Kowloon* (n 16) [22].

[19] cf ibid [20] citing *Interfoto Picture Library Ltd v Stiletto Visual Programmes Ltd* [1989] QB 433.

[20] E Peel, *Treitel on The Law of Contract* (14 edn, London: Sweet & Maxwell 2015) 10.

[21] *Lee Siu Fong Mary v Ngai Yee Chai* [2005] HKCA 484, [2006] 1 HKC 157, 161.

[22] For a specific scenario provided by legislation, ie the Sales of Goods Ordinance (Cap 26), s 60(b): in an auction, an offer can be revoked before it is accepted.

contains terms that are materially inconsistent with the first, the first offer is revoked by the second, so the parties will need to start afresh. Similarly, a counter-offer destroys an offer.[23] Thus, bids are offers to purchase the auctioned property; if a bid is withdrawn, it does not revive an earlier bid; the bidding needs to restart. As the court puts it in *Hoie Sook Fong v Ismail Halima*, 'all the bids amount to conditional offers and acceptance is conditional on the reserve price being reached or exceeded'.[24] These general rules are tempered by a few important exceptions to protect offerees who have relied on the offer. In particular, judges in Hong Kong have displayed great acumen in utilizing the English rules to strike a balance between negotiating vendors and purchasers in the heated and volatile Hong Kong property market.

First, a unilateral offer cannot be revoked once the offeree has started to perform the requested act, unless the latter abandons performance or is unable to complete it.[25]

Second, revocation of the offer must be communicated to the offeree to be effective, and for this purpose the postal rule does not apply. Equally, even if an offer has been revoked by a counter-offer, if the original offeror still puts the original offer forward, it will form a binding contract once it is accepted. Where parties are haggling over a series of communications over a short space of time, there is much room for the parties' protestations as to whether the offers are rejected, withdrawn, or accepted. *Maxbase Investments Ltd v Chan Chui Ping* provides a neat illustration of how the court takes a holistic view of the parties' behaviour in applying these old rules of offer and acceptance to property transactions in a heated market.[26] The parties were negotiating over the sale of a flat. The purchaser offered to buy it at $7.1 million and, following standard practice, placed a cheque of the deposit with the estate agent as an earnest of his interest. The offer was revoked by the vendor's counter-offer to sell it at no less than $7.15 million. The purchaser allowed the estate agent time to negotiate the price down and had not withdrawn the cheque, but subsequently changed his mind when the agent secured the vendor's signature to the $7.1 million offer by forfeiting $0.05 million of her own commission. The court considered that even though the original offer of $7.1 million was revoked by the counter-offer, it was put forward again when the purchaser did not recall the cheque or expressly instruct the agent to terminate the negotiation.

Third, another way to protect the offeree's reliance especially in a tendering process is to treat the promise in a tender that it will remain valid for a certain period of time as a binding contract, and that the inviter of the tender will consider all timely and conforming tenders before the end of the period. This important exception to the general rule that an offer can be revoked at any time before it was accepted, was affirmed in *City University of Hong Kong v Blue Cross (Asia Pacific) Insurance Ltd*,[27] which applied the landmark English decision of *Blackpool and Fylde Aero Club Ltd v Blackpool Borough Council*.[28]

Fourth, the postal rule applies to acceptance of offers. Where parties reasonably anticipate the use of the postal service to communicate acceptance, an offer is accepted once the

[23] *Lee Siu Fong Mary* (n 21). *Wealthy Century Investment Ltd v DBS Bank (HK) Ltd* [2010] HKDC 101, [2010] HKEC 1386 (DC); *Capacious Investments Ltd v Secretary for Justice* [2001] HKCFI 1104, [2001] 1 HKC 219 (CFI): when the plaintiff accepted the government's offer of compensation to resume certain land owned by it but added that it reserved its right to claim interest, it was held to have included a new term and given a counter-offer; *Leung Lai Bun v Sam Woo Bore Pile Foundation Ltd* [2003] HKCFI 917, [2003] 1 HKLRD D8 (CFI): when an employee who was paid less than his entitlement accepted pay as full and final settlement but upon protest and clarification that he was entitled to a higher sum, the court held that it was a counter-offer and there was no acceptance of the reduced pay; *Combi (Singapore) Pte Ltd v Winston Camera & Radio Co Ltd* [1988] HKCA 269, [1988] 1 HKC 151 (CA): when a purported purchaser replied to an offer to sell but implicitly added that the seller should open a letter of credit, the purported purchaser made a counter-offer that rejected the offer.

[24] [2009] HKCFI 177, [2009] 1 HKC 326 (CFI) 330.

[25] *Carlill v Carbolic Smoke Ball* [1893] 1 QB 256.

[26] [2011] HKDC 130, [2011] HKEC 592 (DC).

[27] [2001] HKCFI 1356.

[28] [1990] EWCA Civ 13, [1990] 1 WLR 1195.

letter of acceptance is posted. Such a rule puts the risks of delay in postal service on the offeror, as he has chosen this mode of communication. The postal rule does not apply, however, if instantaneous means of communication such as faxes are used.[29]

3. Battle of Forms

In the earlier case law, in *OKA Electronics Ltd v Manohar Chugh (t/a Electric & Electronics Industries)*,[30] the courts in Hong Kong followed the more conservative 'last-shot' doctrine favoured by Lawton and Bridge LJJ in *Butler Machine Tool Co Ltd v Ex-Cell-O-Corp (England) Ltd*.[31] This was somewhat tempered by the observation in the District Court in *Headwin Engineering Ltd v United Soundfair Engineering Co Ltd*, that the last-shot doctrine should be displaced if the 'last shot' contract differed materially from the initial contract, such that it would be unjust for the sender to take advantage of the differences without telling the receiver.[32] This requirement to give notice of material differences from the initial contract provides a significant fine-tuning of the last-shot doctrine, albeit *Headwin Engineering* is a District Court decision and may not be seen to have qualified the position of *OKA Electronics Ltd v Manohar Chugh (t/a Electric & Electronic Industries)*.

4. Certainty and Completeness

The requirement of certainty stipulates that the objective agreement between the parties must contain all the essential terms and must not be so vague as to be unworkable unless substantially rewritten.[33] If the court is satisfied that the parties had agreed upon the essential terms and intended to create legal relations, it will endeavour to find practical meaning in the parties' commercial agreement to avoid having to strike it down on uncertainty. *New World Development Co Ltd v Sun Hung Kai Securities Ltd* is a case on point. Here, the defendant was held to have agreed during a telephone conversation to contribute some HK$80 million (approx US$10 million) towards a joint venture project to redevelop hotels in Malaysia. Representatives of the two companies had been long-standing friends since childhood and had cooperated in many previous ventures. The Court of Final Appeal also found that the presumed intention to enter into a legal relationship was not rebutted, and there was sufficient certainty of terms, albeit they were simple.[34]

This contrasts sharply with the situation where the parties have not agreed on the essential terms, as any filling in of such terms will involve the court writing a contract for the parties. The Hong Kong Court of Final Appeal made a conscious departure from the traditional English doctrine,[35] where in cases pertaining to an 'open' contract in the purchase of land, once the parties agree to the three Ps (parties, price, and place), the court will be prepared to fill out the missing terms by implication. Even though the English doctrine had been invoked from time to time in the lower courts in Hong Kong,[36] the Court of Final Appeal categorically preferred a departure from the English approach, on the ground that it

[29] *Susanto Wing Sun Co Ltd v Yung Chi Hardware Machinery Co Ltd* [1989] HKCFI 8, [1989] 2 HKC 504.

[30] [1991] HKCA 266.

[31] [1977] EWCA Civ 9, [1979] 1 WLR 401.

[32] [2008] HKDC 103, [2008] HKEC 591.

[33] *G Scammell & Nephew Ltd v Ouston* [1941] AC 251 (HL); *Hillas & Co Ltd v Arcos Ltd* (1932) 43 Ll L Rep 359 (HL), cited in *New World Development Co Ltd v Sun Hung Kai Securities Ltd* (2006) 9 HKCFAR 403, [2006] 3 HKLRD 345 (CFA) [31]–[32].

[34] (2006) 9 HKCFAR 403, [2006] 3 HKLRD 345 (CFA).

[35] *Perry v Suffields* [1916] 2 Ch 187 (CA).

[36] *Wong Chim Ying v Cheng Kam Wing* [1991] 2 HKLR 253 (CA); *Lee Kenny v Wong Kwok Yan* [1994] 2 HKC 309 (CA); *Active Keen Industries Ltd v Fok Chi Keong* [1994] 1 HKLR 396 (CA); *Grandwide Ltd v Bonaventure Textiles Ltd* [1990] 2 HKC 154 (CA).

fails to serve the unique needs of the property market in Hong Kong.[37] The court's consideration of Hong Kong's unique situation will be considered in section V below.

5. Intention

Hong Kong law follows English law in relation to the need to show an intention to create legal relations, albeit unlike civil law jurisdictions, intention plays a relatively minor role and is often tackled by the use of presumptions depending on the context in which the agreement is made. Two aspects pertaining to this issue are of interest. First, the extent to which the simple bifurcation between family and commercial contexts in English law (which is adopted in Hong Kong law) can embrace the predominance of family businesses in Asian culture (where family and business relationships often overlap) is put to question. In both English and Hong Kong law, these presumptions serve the purpose of filtering out promises made in a familial or social context from contractual enforcement, unless there is evidence of an intention to create legal relations or the family members are no longer on amicable terms, such as when a couple breaking-up reach an agreement on maintenance provisions. The court also fine-tunes the strength of the presumptions to take into account the nature and consequence of the transaction, such as the seriousness of its consequence on the parties and whether it was executed. Hence, if the agreement has been partially executed by one side, the court will be more willing to find that the presumption against contractual intention is rebutted. Where the value of the subject matter of the 'agreement' is on a more social scale, such a presumption is less likely to be rebutted.

The contrary presumption in favour of an intention to create legal relations is applied to contracts entered into in commercial contexts, even if amongst business partners who have been long-standing friends. The burden of proof lies with the party who asserts that no legal effect was intended, and it is a heavy burden.[38] This simple dichotomy between family and commercial settings does not fully reflect the complexity of situations in Hong Kong, where family members often contribute towards the family business and in pursuing their common enterprise may enter into contractual relationships with each other. Thus far, arguments made to the court to deny the existence of an intention to create legal relations on the ground that the parties purportedly entering into an agreement were family members, have not met with much success, let alone been given serious attention by the court.[39]

Moreover, in commercial contexts, negotiating parties often seek to hold each other's interest in the potential bargain while avoiding a final commitment. Thus to avoid the contractual intention from applying, parties will expressly indicate that their understanding is a 'letter of intent' or 'letter of comfort', or is 'subject to contract'. The significance the courts attach to these labels varies, and perhaps because of their overwhelming emphasis on the written words and commercial certainty, the Hong Kong courts tend to pay strict adherence to these terms, especially in conveyancing contexts. Thus, a letter of intent sent by a parent company to the debtor of the subsidiary expressing a willingness to take full responsibility for the subsidiary's accounts and to provide full financial support for the subsidiary's business was held to lack sufficient certainty and contractual intention.[40] In the much-cited decision of *Attorney General of Hong Kong v Humphrey's Estate (Queen's Gardens) Ltd* on

[37] *Kwan Siu Man Joshua v Yaacov Ozer* [1999] 1 HKLRD 216, [1999] 1 HKC 150 (CFA) (Litton PJ).

[38] *New World Development* (n 34); *Ever-Long Securities Co Ltd v Wong Sio Po* [2003] HKCA 418, [2004] 2 HKLRD 143, [2004] 1 HKC 702 (CA).

[39] *Bel Nickel Resources Ltd v Eastbourne Trading Pte Ltd & Ors* [2010] HKCFI 772; *Hung Chung Chi Johnny v Tang Jian* [2008] HKCA 405; *Wong Kwong Lung v Wong Ming Yau* [2014] HKCFI 1610.

[40] *Toppan Printing Co v Chinese United Press Ltd* [2005] HKCFI 354, [2005] HKCU 614 (CFI).

estoppel,[41] where the Hong Kong Government entered into a substantial transaction with a property developer 'subject to contract', and the parties acted upon the agreement and partly performed it, save for the execution of the necessary document, the Privy Council held that the developer was estopped from going back on the transaction. Throughout the stages of litigation, the assumption, that the phrase 'subject to contract' had the effect of preventing a binding contract from arising, was never challenged, which thus necessitated the court's reliance on the doctrine of estoppel to resolve the dispute. Since then, even though the phrase 'subject to contract' is not a conclusive magic phrase, it is not likely to be ignored unless the court finds that the phrase had no meaning in the documents that contain it,[42] or when the parties' conduct (eg entry into a provisional agreement)[43] has unequivocally shown that they had treated the phrase as expunged from such documents.[44]

III. Duty to Negotiate in Good Faith

Considerations of certainty have also been cited by the courts of Hong Kong as a basis for not embracing a doctrine to negotiate in good faith. In line with its English heritage, it employs disparate doctrines such as rectification for unilateral mistake,[45] claims for *quantum meruit*,[46] material non-disclosure, or tortious actions such as fraud or negligent misrepresentation to deal with unacceptable conduct in negotiation. There has, however, been a fleeting willingness to enforce a duty to negotiate in good faith, albeit orthodoxy was quickly restored. In *Hyundai Engineering and Construction Co Ltd v Vigour Ltd*, Reyes J held that an agreement between parties to a construction dispute to use their best endeavours to negotiate and to mediate was enforceable in principle.[47] His Honour undertook a detailed survey of international jurisprudence and was confident that with a long tradition in European courts in considering issues of good faith in commercial contracts, it should not be difficult for a common law court such as Hong Kong to deal with an agreement to negotiate in good faith. The decision was overturned, however, in the Court of Appeal,[48] which affirmed the historical position laid down by the House of Lords in *Walford v Miles* that an agreement to negotiate in good faith is generally unenforceable on the ground of uncertainty.[49] There is also no broader acceptance of the duty of good faith in other aspects such as the performance of contract in Hong Kong.

Nonetheless, the *Walford v Miles* position is not absolute. It will not be too uncertain to enforce a duty to negotiate in good faith in 'an open-ended and multifarious context' where the court may find a party's negotiation tactics unjustifiable.[50] If the procedures for submitting to good faith negotiation have been clearly set forth, as in *Cable & Wireless plc v IBM*

[41] [1986] UKPC 58, [1981] AC 114. See also *Darton Ltd v Hong Kong Island Development Ltd* [2001] HKCFA 25, [2001] 4 HKC 575.

[42] *Hong Kong Housing Authority v Hung Pui* [1987] HKCFI 248, [1987] 3 HKC 495.

[43] *Au Wing Cheung v Roseric Ltd* [1992] HKCA 277, [1992] 1 HKC 149; *Lam Tam Yi v Chak Wai Man* [1993] 1 HKC 537 (HC).

[44] *Tevanan v Norman Brett (Builders) Ltd* (1972) 223 EG 1945.

[45] *Kowloon* (n 16).

[46] *Profit Boat Development Ltd v Craft Projects (HK) Co Ltd* [2007] HKEC 1615 (CFI); *Four Seas Union Holdings Ltd v Hong Kong & Macau Scent On Engineering & Construction Ltd* [2003] HKCFI 953, [2003] 1 HKLRD 653 (CFI); *Professional Associates v Polytek Engineering Co Ltd* [1985] HKCFI 521, [1986] HKLR 20 (CFI).

[47] [2004] HKCFI 205, [2004] 3 HKLRD 1, applying *Coal Cliff Collieries Pty Ltd & Anor v Sijehama PTY Ltd & Anor* (1991) 24 NSWLR 1 (HC Aus) (Kirby J).

[48] *Hyundai Engineering and Construction Co Ltd v Vigour Ltd* [2005] HKCA 52, [2005] 1 HKC 579, [2005] 3 HKLRD 723. cf David Bateson and Kim Barton, 'Hong Kong: Enforceability of Agreements to Negotiate and Mediate—Where Does Hong Kong Stand?' (2006) 23 ICLR 266.

[49] [1992] 2 AC 128.

[50] *Secretary for Justice v Hong Kong and Yaumati Ferry Co Ltd* [2006] HKCFI 1456, [2006] HKCU 2148 (CFI) (Reyes J).

United Kingdom Ltd,[51] or the subject matter of the negotiation can be assessed objectively to determine whether the parties have acted in good faith, as in *Petromec Inc v Petroleo Brasileiro*,[52] the court will find it sufficiently certain to enforce such clauses. In 2012, the Hong Kong Court of Appeal distinguished its own decision in *Hyundai* to imply an obligation to negotiate in good faith. In *Hong Jing Co Ltd v Zhuhai Kwok Yuen Investment Co Ltd*, the plaintiff and defendant agreed on a scheme to restructure debts of some HK$800 million owed by the defendant's subsidiaries to a third party, Bank of China Group Investment Co Ltd (BOCI).[53] Under the agreement, the defendant would negotiate with BOCI to purchase the debts at the target price of HK$700 million, and on-sell them with underlying security to the plaintiff investor for $810 million. The defendant undertook not to deal with any other party for resale of the debt during an exclusivity period. As it transpired, the defendant was unable to purchase the debt from BOCI at the target price until one week after the expiry of the exclusivity period, but it then immediately sold the debt to another party at $872 million. The Court of Appeal had little difficulty implying a duty on the part of the defendant to use reasonable endeavours in good faith to reach an agreement with BOCI.[54] Cheung JA noted that the implied duty was necessary to give efficacy to the agreement between the parties. Similarly, although the issue was not resolved in *World Sport Group Pte Ltd v Asian Tour International Ltd*,[55] the Court of First Instance did not rule out as unenforceable a contractual term which gives an existing contractual party the first right to match a third party's offer to renew an existing distribution agreement and to negotiate in good faith. Clearly, in both cases, the defendants deliberately ran the clock down to the end of the exclusivity period in order to frustrate the plaintiff's rights agreed under the contract, so the court showed much greater willingness to imply a duty to use best endeavours to negotiate in good faith.

IV. Online Contracts

An online contract is one in which the offer and acceptance are sent and received in part or in full by electronic means.[56] This typically happens through email correspondence or online website purchases, as well as instant messaging (eg SMS and WhatsApp). In Hong Kong, the Electronic Transactions Ordinance was enacted to place electronic records and digital signatures on the same legal platform as with documents and paper signatures. Section 17 of the Ordinance puts in place the non-discrimination principle of the UNCITRAL Model Law on Electronic Commerce, in stating that unless otherwise agreed by the parties, the validity or enforceability of a contract will not be affected on the sole ground that part or all of it is formed by means of an electronic record.[57] Section 19 further specifies that if the offeror has designated an information system for receiving email, acceptance by email is effective when the message is received by the offeror's email server.[58] The section does not define a 'designated information system'. One can only assume that by sending the offer through an information system, the offeror designates the same information system for receiving emails. If the offeror has not designated an information system for

[51] [2002] EWHC 2059 (Comm). [52] [2005] EWCA Civ 891, [2006] 1 Lloyd's Rep 121 (CA Civ).
[53] [2012] HKCA 296, [2013] 1 HKLRD 441 (CA). [54] ibid [37.18] [55] [2009] HKCFI 98.
[56] R Ribeiro (ed), *Chitty on Contracts: Hong Kong Specific Contracts* (3rd edn, Hong Kong: Sweet & Maxwell 2013) para 14-027. C Wright, W McAuliffe, and A Gamvros, *Internet Law in Hong Kong* (Hong Kong: Sweet & Maxwell Asia 2002).
[57] See UNCITRAL Model Law of Electronic Commerce, Art 7, which was also incorporated in Arbitration Ordinance (Cap 609), s 19, by providing that an arbitration agreement in writing can be made by electronic communication.
[58] Electronic Transactions Ordinance (Cap 553) s 19(2)(a)(i).

receiving email, or if he has designated an information system but the email is not sent to that designated system, then acceptance only takes place when it comes to the offeror's knowledge, which was determined in *Bernuth Lines Ltd v High Seas Shipping Ltd* as when he would have read it in the ordinary course of business.[59] Acceptance is presumed to take place at the offeror's place of business, even if the email is read by the company at a place outside Hong Kong.[60] The Ordinance also does not stipulate when the contract is concluded, but only when acceptance is received, leaving it to general contract law to decide whether such receipt amounts to the conclusion of the contract. There has been considerable academic literature on the operation of the Ordinance, albeit there has not yet been any decision in Hong Kong pertaining to the application of these two sections.[61]

V. Formality

As a default rule, contracts not supported by consideration are enforceable only if they are made in the form of a deed, whereas contracts supported by consideration can be oral or written.

1. Scope and Range of Formality Requirements

In line with most common law jurisdictions, depending on the seriousness of the risks and consequences of informality, a progressive range of formality requirements is imposed. At the most stringent level is the requirement that the contract be created by deed. This applies to: a lease of land for three years or more (land is traditionally and still is a principal source of wealth and economic activity in society);[62] a power of attorney and an enduring power of attorney (because of the extensive powers it endows on the donee and the need to protect the vulnerable party);[63] and the grant of an authority to execute a deed (except if the donor is a foreign corporation incorporated in a state that does not impose a similar requirement).[64] The next level is the requirement that the contract be made entirely in writing, which applies to contracts creating or disposing of equitable interests in land,[65] bills of exchange, promissory notes,[66] assignment of copyright,[67] memorandum and articles of association of companies,[68] and agreements to submit disputes to arbitration.[69] The important economic interests involved in the subject matter of these contracts speak for themselves. At the third level is the requirement that the contract be evidenced in writing, which means that the contract can be made orally but that it is enforceable only if it is evidenced by a memorandum in writing signed by the party to be charged for performance. This requirement, now set forth in section 3(1) of the Conveyancing and Property Ordinance ('CPO'), dates back to the English Statutes of Frauds 1677 and applies to contracts for the sale and disposition

[59] ibid s 19(2)(a)(ii) and (3); [2005] EWHC 3020 (QB), [2006], 1 CLC 403 (QBD).

[60] Electronic Transactions Ordinance (Cap 553) s 19(4).

[61] E Fong, 'E-Commerce: A Legislative Initiative in the Hong Kong SAR' [2000] JIBL 75; S Anil, 'The Regulation of Electronic Commerce in Asia: An Exploration' [2001] JIFM 220; D Seng, 'The Singapore Electronic Transactions Act and the Hong Kong Electronic Transactions Ordinance' (2008) 5 DE & ESLR 7; R Ong, 'Consumer Based Electronic Commerce: A Comparative Analysis of the Position in Malaysia and Hong Kong' (2004) 12(1) IJLIT 101.

[62] Conveyancing and Property Ordinance (Cap 219) s 4(1).

[63] Powers of Attorney Ordinance (Cap 31) s 2(1); Enduring Powers of Attorney Ordinance (Cap 501) s 3, specifying the use of a prescribed form and requisite signatures.

[64] Law Amendment and Reform (Consolidation) Ordinance (Cap 23) s 26.

[65] Conveyancing and Property Ordinance (Cap 219) ss 3–5, 15(e), 19(1) and (2), 20(1), and 26.

[66] Bills of Exchange Ordinance (Cap 19) ss 3(1), 89(1), 17(2), 73.

[67] Copyright Ordinance (Cap 528) s 216.

[68] Companies Ordinance (Cap 622) Pt 3, Division 2, ss 75–99, 121.

[69] Arbitration Ordinance (Cap 609) s 19.

of land. It has remained on Hong Kong's statute books even though the evidentiary constraint that was addressed by its seventeenth-century heritage is no longer applicable.[70] A better way forward is to require the whole agreement to be in writing, as section 2(8) of the Law of Property (Miscellaneous Provisions) Act 1989 did some three decades ago. This will also remove the oddity that contracts to dispose land only need to be evidenced in writing, whereas contracts to create a lease of land for three years or more need to be entirely in writing.

Although very little has been said of the underlying justifications for these formality requirements, as most of them are derived from their English heritage, it appears that two factors are most important: the subject matter of the contract and the respective bargaining powers of the contractual parties. Where land or other important economic goods (eg copyright, negotiable instruments, and shares) are concerned, formality requirements are tightened notwithstanding the respective bargaining powers of the parties. As an additional protection, if none of these economic goods are involved but the economic interest at stake is still substantial (eg loans by moneylenders, insurance contracts, and apprenticeship), *and* one of the parties is particularly vulnerable (eg donors of powers of attorney, borrowers from moneylenders, and apprentices), formality requirements are also imposed. These factors show that the main purposes behind formality are to prevent fraud and to protect consumers.

2. Content of Formality Requirements

Rather than recounting the details of these formality requirements, which are ably summarized in treatises and textbooks on Hong Kong contract law,[71] this chapter focuses on the requirement in section 3(1) of the CPO that sale of land must be evidenced in writing. The Hong Kong jurisprudence is particularly interesting, as it shows how the courts grapple with the operation of an inadequate and antiquated provision in the vibrant and volatile property market that Hong Kong is. Section 3(1) stipulates that:

> [N]o action shall be brought upon any contract for the sale of or other disposition of land unless the agreement upon which such action is brought, or *some memorandum or note thereof, is in writing and signed by the party to be charged* or by some other person lawfully authorised by him for that purpose.[72]

As a provision that governs the sale of what is unequivocally the most important asset in the Hong Kong economy, section 3(1) is far from adequate. It asks for the existence of a written and signed memorandum of the agreement, but omits to stipulate the most crucial test as to what constitutes a sufficient memorandum of such agreement. It is only clear from the 1918 decision of *Roe v RA Naylor Ltd* that the memorandum must contain the material terms of

[70] The statute sought to allow a party charged to submit written evidence of an oral agreement to counter perjured evidence by witnesses produced by the opposing party.

[71] Under the Electronic Transactions Ordinance, the requirement of 'in writing' can be satisfied by an electronic record which is accessible for subsequent reference. The requirement of signature can be satisfied by an electronic signature. A document purporting to be a deed is presumed to be sealed. Delivery refers to an act which evinces an intention to be bound, and not necessarily physical transfer to the other party. Delivery under escrow means that the delivery is made subject to condition, ie it becomes binding when the condition is fulfilled. For moneylenders, repayment of money lent by a moneylender is not enforceable, unless a note/memorandum in writing is made before the money is lent. However, the court has discretion to enforce it, subject to modifications as are equitable.

[72] CPO (emphasis added). The document can be signed by writing, typing, or a chop if there was sufficient intention of the maker (*Hoie Sook Fong* (n 24)) but unlikely so by SMS message unless permitted by the Electronic Transactions Ordinance (Cap 553) s 6(1) (*Distinct Fortune Ltd v Hyndland Investment Co Ltd* [2011] 1 HKLRD 817 (CFI)).

the bargain and without the addition of any fresh terms.[73] The Statute of Frauds was enacted at a time when land ownership in England was limited to the noble gentry and transacted within an exclusive stratum of society for family preservation rather than traded as a key asset for profit-making as in the modern world and particularly in Hong Kong. While the vagueness of the provision was tolerable in the previous era, it is debilitating in modern-day Hong Kong: the case law has also shown an increasing tightening of the requirements for a sufficient memorandum as the property market continues to boom. Three judicial decisions illustrate the change.

In *JN Roland Deneault v Yangtzekiang Garment Manufacturing Co Ltd*,[74] a decision in the 1970s when the economy and land prices were on the cusp of taking off, the vendors had orally agreed to sell their co-owned plot of land to a purchaser, who owned the adjacent land, for HK$2.2 million. Correspondence in the week that immediately followed led to the parties' signing of a letter recording the fact of the agreement and the purchase price, but no further terms that had been orally agreed such as deposit, vacant possession, and architect's fees. When the purchaser signed and returned the draft agreement for sale to the vendors for signature, the latter called off the deal. The purchaser sued for breach of contract. Prima facie, the letter signed by the vendor (the party charged) did not amount to a sufficient memorandum required by *Roe v RA Naylor Ltd*, as it did not fully reflect the terms orally agreed. Another memorandum required a deposit to be remitted to the vendors forthwith even though the oral contract did not contain the word 'forthwith'. To overcome these gaps, the Hong Kong Court of Appeal held that the vendor's defence and counterclaim to such an action was an sufficient memorandum of the oral agreement;[75] and also that the reference to 'forthwith' was immaterial and could be ignored. A letter to a third party by the defendant in an action for breach of contract could be a sufficient memorandum for section 3(1) of the CPO. In a similar vein, in *Chan Yat v Fung Rubber Manufacturing Factory*, Pickering J (who later became Pickering JA in *JN Roland Deneault v Yangtzekiang*), held that a letter by the purported lessee to its own bankers setting out the terms of the oral agreement for a lease constituted a sufficient memorandum to bind him.[76]

Such a sympathetic attitude of the court in the 1960s and 70s was considered to be 'an extreme case' by the Court of Final Appeal in 1998, when the property market in Hong Kong had already started booming.[77] Instead, the court emphasized the need to find a concluded oral agreement on all essential terms, particularly that on the time of completion, before identifying a memorandum that contains all of them. In *Kwan Siu Man Joshua v Yaacov Ozer*,[78] the parties were former landlord and tenant who had an ongoing litigation about the latter's overdue rent. The tenant claimed that at a chance meeting in the lift lobby, the landlord agreed to sell the property to him for $4.25 million, and sought to use a subsequent piece of correspondence from the landlord as memorandum of that oral contract, even though the series of correspondence revealed continuing negotiation between the parties. The Court of Final Appeal held that with the volatile property market in Hong Kong where property prices fluctuated dramatically by the month, a concluded contract for the sale of property could only come into existence when there was agreement on not just the property, parties, and prices (the three Ps), but also the date of completion. As the oral agreement in this case did not include the date of completion, there was no concluded

[73] (1918) 119 LT 359 (EWCA Civ) 361 (Swinfen Eady MR). [74] [1977] HKLR 320 (CA).

[75] Huggins JA preferred to see the subsequent exchange as revealing an agreement. The purchaser discontinued the first action to start a second one, and used the vendors' defence to the first action as memorandum of the agreement for the purposes of the second one.

[76] [1967] HKLR 364 (OJ). [77] *Kwan Siu Man Joshua* (n 37). [78] ibid.

contract for which a memorandum would be evidence. Significantly, Litton PJ remarked on the need to interpret section 3(1) of the CPO to suit the needs of Hong Kong:

> Further, as is common knowledge in Hong Kong, the property market is highly volatile. Whatever might have been the position in England in the last century—when the concept of an 'open contract' was first developed in a climate of a stable pound sterling and no inflation—in the Hong Kong of today, the date of completion is an essential term of any contract for the sale and purchase of land.

His lordship warned of the danger of turning the logic of section 3(1) on its head if the court was satisfied with a memorandum as long as it contained the three magic ingredients of property, parties, and price.

The Court of Final Appeal also put the last nail in the coffin of the traditional English concept of an open contract in the purchase of land. Under this doctrine, once the parties agree on the three Ps, the court will find a binding contract and imply terms into the contract.[79] The court was adamant that in Hong Kong the completion date must be an essential term of such contracts. Given that property prices in Hong Kong may easily go up or down by a significant percentage between the date of the purchase agreement and completion, there is much to be said for this position, otherwise the court would be allocating risks between the parties.

3. Non-Compliance with Formal Requirements and the Doctrine of Part Performance

The effect of non-compliance varies depending on the legislative stipulation concerned. For example, informal contracts to dispose of equitable interests in land are void.[80] Informal declarations of trust respecting land and contracts for the sale of land are not void but unenforceable.[81] Informal leases of land not exceeding three years take effect as agreements for leases, which should satisfy section 3(1) of the CPO; the agreement for a lease in respect of which the court will grant specific performance creates an equitable interest under the doctrine of *Walsh v Lonsdale*.[82]

Section 3(2) of the CPO expressly retains the doctrine of part performance, whereby parol evidence was admissible to prove all of a contract's terms once it has been partly performed. This is a long-established doctrine in English law to prevent the formality statute from being used as an instrument of fraud, albeit that it was in effect abolished in England by the legislative reform that required all the terms of contracts for sale of land to be included in one written document.[83]

The doctrine should be applied only after, first, an oral contract has been concluded between the parties; second, the contract is not evidenced by a sufficient memorandum; and, third, there are acts which when viewed on their own are unequivocal about the existence of the contract,[84] or which when viewed in their surrounding circumstances are probably referable to a contract.[85] In applying the doctrine in the cut-throat property market in

[79] *Perry v Suffields* [1916] 2 Ch 187, applied in *Wong Chim Ying* (n 36); *Lee Kenny* (n 36); *Active Keen Industries* (n 36); *Grandwide* (n 36).

[80] CPO, s 4. [81] ibid. [82] (1882) 21 Ch D 9 (CA).

[83] Law of Property (Miscellaneous Provisions) Act 1989, s 2, repealing Law of Property Act 1925, s 40. See UK Law Commission report on the transfer of land, *Formalities for Contracts for Sale etc of Land* (Law Com No 164, 1987); *Actionstrength Ltd v International Glass Engineering* [2003] UKHL 17, [2003] 2 AC 541.

[84] *Maddison v Alderson* (1882–3) 8 App Cas 467.

[85] See the relaxation by Lords Reid and Dilhorne in *Steadman v Steadman* [1976] AC 536 (HL) 541–542 (Lord Reid).

Hong Kong, the courts have taken care to prevent the use of this doctrine to jump the gun and find the existence of a contract from what really is still an ongoing negotiation process.

In the clearest scenario, the acts point unequivocally to the existence of a contract, as in *Wu Koon Tai v Wu Yau Loi*, where the parties had followed procedures in customary law for conveying a piece of land which did not meet the requirement of section 3(1), but had delivered possession in exchange of payment of the full purchase price.[86] Here, the court had little difficulty enforcing the contract on the doctrine of part performance.[87] Significantly, the Privy Council held that the Land Registration Ordinance should not be trumped by customary law, but since the delivery of possession and receipt of the purchase price were the clearest possible acts of part performance, the doctrine of part performance could be called to the rescue.

On the other side of the line falls the attempt to argue that a tenant's vacation from the rented premises was a sufficient act of part performance referable to the existence of an oral contract to surrender the tenancy. In *Take Harvest Ltd v Liu*,[88] there was indeed such an oral contract, but before the agreed date when the surrender was due the landlord retracted from the oral agreement and informed the tenant that the lease should continue. When the tenant nonetheless sought to surrender and vacated from the premises, the landlord refused and sued for outstanding rent. The Privy Council rejected the tenant's argument that the oral contract was partly performed, as the delivery of vacant possession was 'equally consistent with the existence or non-existence of a contract to surrender the tenancy'.[89]

Equally, acts done during the negotiation process in anticipation of an agreement are rightly discarded as not amounting to part performance, since there is no established contract in the first place. In *Shun Lin Weaving Factory Ltd v Siu Cheng Yee Wah Eva*, the court held that it was not part performance to instruct solicitors to prepare a sale and purchase agreement, since such instructions were not referable to the existence of the contract, but could be consistent with preparation for reaching a concluded agreement.[90] The same care was taken by the Court of Final Appeal in *The World Food Fair Ltd v Hong Kong Island Development Ltd* even where more extensive expenses were incurred.[91] In this case, the potential landlord had orally agreed in principle to grant a tenancy of a section of commercial premises to the tenant to operate a food court, albeit protracted negotiation about essential terms such as the commencement date and rent period still continued over the following few months. During that period, the potential landlord gave vacant possession and took an initial deposit from the latter, who incurred numerous expenses for fitting-out works in the premises. Ribeiro PJ of the Court of Final Appeal was categorical that the giving of possession to allow builders access to the premises was ambiguous as to the existence of the contract as well as acts done in anticipation of a legally binding agreement. Equally, the demand for an initial but not full deposit in the context of a lengthy pre-contractual negotiation may suggest that the parties had not reached final agreement, as the landlord had no assurance that there was already a binding contract.[92] The principle that emerges from these three decisions which rejected the doctrine of part performance was that a party who has orally agreed to an informal land contract remains free to change his mind unless there are acts probably referable to the existence of such a contract and, where the parties are still in the process of negotiation, acts done that are also consistent with pre-contractual

[86] [1997] AC 179 (PC).

[87] See also *Silver Hope Ltd v Chan Kwai Wah Alice* [2013] 1 HKLRD 823 (CFI), where the party had gone into possession and provided the entire purchase price; *Hoie Sook Fong* (n 24), where part performance was satisfied upon payment of 10 per cent deposit and 1 per cent of the purchase price.

[88] [1993] AC 552 (PC).

[89] ibid 571 (Sir Christopher Slade).

[90] (1980) 10 HKLJ 213.

[91] [2007] 1 HKLRD 498 (CFA).

[92] ibid [29] and [32].

expenses in anticipation of an agreement should not be used to create a contract under the guise of part performance, even if the expenses incurred were considerable.

VI. Consideration and the Protection of Non-Bargained for Promises

In Hong Kong law, as in English law, non-bargained for promises are enforced or protected only if they are made by deed or if a gift is completed. Similar to English law, only bargained-for promises as objectively assessed and so relied on are enforceable; promises to make gifts or grant rights are unenforceable.[93] Thus, in *Ian Hung Wai v Cheung Sau Kuen*, a retiree in his late 50s who made gifts to his cohabitee partner 18 years younger than him, allegedly in contemplation of marriage, was found on the facts to have made them free from any condition (of marriage), and hence could not recover them when their relationship broke up.[94]

If there is neither a deed nor an executed gift, a promise must be supported by consideration for it to be binding. Hong Kong jurisprudence does not differ from English law. To establish sufficient consideration, there must be something of value conferred upon the promisor or a detriment suffered by the promisee.[95] This can take the form of non-monetary benefits (wrappers in *Chappell & Co Ltd v Nestle Co Ltd*,[96] commemorative coins in *Esso Petroleum Co Ltd v Commissioners of Customs and Excise*[97]) or it can be a promise for a promise. Consideration was found, for example, from: a party's forbearance from legal action;[98] compromise of a disputed claim, as long as the party honestly believes the case to be arguable, even though it turns out to be unjustified;[99] procuring a third party creditor to refrain from enforcing a judgment debt against the promisor;[100] and the performance of a private duty owed to third parties;[101] to name but a few.

Hong Kong also adopts the English doctrine of past consideration, namely that consideration must not be given after the promise has already been made independently of the consideration: past consideration is no consideration.[102] Several decisions illustrate the courts' pragmatic approach to prevent its use as a technicality to deny a promise. Lawyers in the common law jurisdictions are familiar, for example, with *Pao On v Lau Yiu Long*, a Privy Council decision on appeal from Hong Kong, which held that past consideration could be good consideration if the act is done on request, and the request carries with it an implied promise to compensation.[103] In *Chong Cheng Lin Courtney v Cathay Pacific Airways Ltd*, Cathay Pacific amended its contract with existing cabin attendants by replacing the retirement grant with retirement travel benefits that offered discounts to retired staff and eligible dependants. The plaintiff was one of the affected parties, but on her departure was refused the retirement travel benefits (as well as the retirement grant) on the ground that

[93] *Smith v Hughes* (1870) LR 6 QB 597 (QBD) 607; *Shogun Finance Ltd v Hudson* [2004] 1 AC 919 (HL); *Paal Wilson & Co A/S v Partenreederei Hannah Blumenthal (The Hannah Blumenthal)* [1983] 1 AC 854 (HL); *VTB Capital plc v Nutritek International Corp* [2013] UKSC 5, [2013] 1 All ER 1296 (SC).

[94] [2011] 3 HKLRD 459 (CA). A gift made by a party in anticipation of marriage is recoverable if the agreement to marry is terminated, and the fact that he is the party who terminates the agreement does not bar his request to return the gift: Law Amendment and Reform (Consolidation) Ordinance (Cap 23) s 25.

[95] *Currie v Misa* [1875] LR 10 Ex 153. [96] [1960] AC 87 (HL). [97] [1976] 1 WLR 1 (HL).

[98] *On Hing Paper Agency Ltd v Best Tri Colour Printing & Packaging Co Ltd* [2010] HKCU 722 (CFI); *Yeung Chee-Kiu v Lam Chee t/a Yau Fat Furniture Co* [1996] HKDCLR 65 (DC); *Fine Master Ltd v Nippon Circuits Ltd* [2013] HKCU 564 (CFI).

[99] *Cosmo Sea Freight (HK) Ltd v Gold King Consolidator Ltd* [1994] HKLR 225 (SC).

[100] *Padilla Chien Mateo v Chan Choi Hing* [1997] HKLRD 539 (HC).

[101] *Fong Huen v Anthony Wong* [1975] HKLR 21 (OJ).

[102] *Eastwood v Kenyon* [1835-42] All ER Rep 133 (QB): promise by a husband to pay off loans already incurred by his wife's guardian to raise the wife.

[103] [1980] AC 614 (PC).

she had only provided past consideration (past service) for this new promise. The court held that in refraining from exercising her right to resign from Cathay Pacific, the plaintiff has provided fresh consideration.[104] In a similar vein, the court also rejected the argument of a purchaser who argued that because an estate agent had shown him an apartment before signing the agency agreement with regard to commission, there was past consideration.[105]

For the sake of completeness, it might also be noted that the rigorous debate in Singaporean jurisprudence sparked off by the learned judgment of Phang JA in *Gay Choon Ing v Loh Sze Ti Terence Peter* about the abolition of the doctrine of consideration has not taken place in Hong Kong.[106]

1. Renegotiating Contractual Terms

In the hypothetical scenario where X pays $10,300 extra to Y to complete renovation work on time in order to avoid a penalty (which he will suffer under the head contract if the work is not completed on time), an interesting policy issue is raised as to the scope a party has to renegotiate his contractual terms. The English solution in *Williams v Roffey Bros & Nicholls (Contractors) Ltd*,[107] which adopted a liberalized notion of consideration to include practical benefits, was also adopted in Hong Kong. In *UBC (Construction) Ltd v Sung Foo Kee Ltd*, the facts were practically on all fours with the above scenario. The court held that the promisor's ability to secure the practical benefit of timely completion and avoid the disbenefit of incurring liability for liquidated damages to a third party and finding alternative subcontractors provided fresh consideration for the varied contract.[108]

Williams v Roffey involves giving additional payment for the same work, but it was also applied in Hong Kong in the converse situation where a party accepted a lower payment for the same work. This happens in the employment context during economic downturns where employees accept reduced or deferred pay in return for continued employment. Here, the rule in *Foakes v Beer*[109] is directly relevant, and has been affirmed in Hong Kong to hold that a promise to accept part payment of a loan, or full payment of a loan by instalments, is not sufficient consideration.[110] However, in *Yeung Kin Ha v El Grande Holdings Ltd*[111] and *Chiu Wing Hang v BG Lighting Ltd*,[112] where the employees accepted reduced or deferred pay, the court applied *Williams v Roffey* to find fresh consideration in having received the practical benefit of keeping their jobs during an economic downturn or a continued harmonious work environment and averting the disbenefit of lawful termination of their employment. *Foakes v Beer* was not cited. Given that the employers in both cases had the right to terminate the employment contracts, a better analysis, which is in line with *Foakes v Beer*, is to treat the parties as having varied the existing contracts, where the variation was supported by fresh consideration in the promise of the new salary in return for work. It would not have been necessary to invoke *Williams v Roffey*.[113]

[104] [2011] 1 HKLRD 10 (CA), [2010] HKCA 338.

[105] *L & D Associates v Chan Man Chon Madalena* [1987] 2 HKC 237 (CA); see also *Ng Luk Mui v Shiu Tsun Wai Vincent* [2011] 5 HKLRD 707 (CA).

[106] [2009] 2 SLR(R) 332, discussed in M Chen-Wishart, 'Consideration and Serious Intention' [2009] SJLS 434.

[107] [1991] 1 QB 1.

[108] [1993] 2 HKLR 207 (CFI); applied in Hong Kong in *SKK (Hong Kong) Co Ltd v Hon Fung Engineering Ltd* [2005] HKCU 74 (CFI); *Sai Man Logistics Ltd v Packers Express Ltd* [2012] HKEC 908 (DC).

[109] (1884) 9 App Cas 605.

[110] *Vinson Engineering Ltd v Kin Shing Engineering (HK) Co Ltd* [2007] 5 HKC 441 (DC); *Fortis Bank Asia HK v Queensmill Investment Ltd* [2001] HKLRD (Yrbk) 224 (CFI).

[111] [2004] 2 HKLRD G4 (CFI). cf *Attrill v Dresdner Kleinwort Ltd* [2011] EWCA Civ 229, [2012] All ER (D) 97 (CA).

[112] (CFI, 8 March 2000; HCLA 67/1999).

[113] I am grateful to Sandra Booysen for this point.

2. Refusing to Honour Contractual Promises

Short of a deed, a perfected gift, and consideration, a gratuitous promisee may argue for legal obligations on the part of the promisor by relying on the doctrine of estoppel by convention,[114] estoppel by representation, promissory estoppel, or the law of unjust enrichment. If the promise is to grant a right in real property, he may also invoke the doctrine of proprietary estoppel[115] or common intention constructive trust. The present chapter will focus on promissory estoppel, as the other doctrines fall within the province of other areas of law.

Save for one problematic decision, which should properly be seen as an example of proprietary estoppel, the doctrine of promissory estoppel has been recognized by Hong Kong courts in much the same manner as in English (as opposed to Australian) law. There are two main differences between the English and Australian approaches: first, English law requires the existence of a pre-existing contract between the promisor and promisee, whereas Australian law does not; second, in Australia, promissory estoppel can be invoked as a cause of action, a sword, but it can only be invoked as a shield in English law to estop a claimant from reneging on his promise.[116]

The Hong Kong courts have established that promissory estoppel applies where, in the course of an existing legal relationship, one party promises or represents to the other party that he will not enforce his strict legal rights arising out of that relationship as against the other party, and intends the other party to act upon the promise. If the other party is thus induced to act in reliance upon it such that it will be inequitable for the promisor to renege on his words, the latter will be estopped from acting inconsistently with his promise.[117]

Thus, there must be a clear and unequivocal representation, such that the court will not infer a representation to withhold legal proceedings to enforce a loan merely from the lender's conduct in agreeing to accept interim partial repayment before funds are said to be forthcoming to pay off the loan. The acceptance of partial payment itself is but an indulgence.[118] In exceptional circumstances, however, where there was a legal duty on the promisor to make a statement to the other and he remained silent, he could be estopped. In *Victory Star Ltd v Ng Fung Ying*, the plaintiff purchaser asked the defendant vendor to remove a structure in the property to be sold to him; however, when the vendor wrote to confirm that he would do so if he did not hear from the purchaser by a certain date, the purchaser did not reply. Instead, he waited for the structure to be removed and sought to rescind the contract on the ground that a term of the purchase agreement was varied. The court held that exceptionally a representation was found upon his silence, as in that case, the purchaser owed a duty to respond and refrained from doing so.[119]

114 For illustration of its application in Hong Kong, see *Newmark Capital Corp Ltd v Coffee Partners Ltd* [2007] 1 HKLRD 718 (CFI) (elements of estoppel by convention laid down); *Kaisilk Development Ltd v Urban Renewal Authority* [2004] 1 HKLRD 907 (CA) (the doctrine can only be used as a shield).

115 For a Hong Kong illustration in the commercial context, see *Attorney General of Hong Kong v Humphrey Estates (Queen's Gardens) Ltd (Hong Kong)* [1987] AC 114 (PC); for one in the domestic context, see *Li Yuk Ying v Wong Yuet Kam* [2013] 1 HKLRD 967 (CFI) (agreeing to bear a third child can be detriment); *Cheung Pak Chuen v Au Yeung Wing Chi* [2013] HKEC 721 (CFI) (expenditure of money to set up business in the promised property and looking after parents who reside in the premises); *Mak Ho Fung v Mak Kai* [2013] HKEC 1924 (CA) (living with and looking after aunts).

116 *Walton Stores (Interstate) Ltd v Maher* (1988) 164 CLR 387 (HCA); *Combe v Combe* [1951] 2 KB 215 (CA); *Central London Property Trust Ltd v High Trees House Ltd* [1947] KB 130 (KBD).

117 *Newmark Capital* (n 114) [55]; *Luo Xing Juan v Estate of Hui Shui See* (2009) 12 HKCFAR 1 (CFA) 21 (Ribeiro PJ).

118 *Fortis Bank Asia HK v Queensmill Investment Ltd* (n 110); cf *Chan Wing v Chow Lee Wah* [2004] 1 HKLRD 1051 (CFI) (a landlord estopped from claiming full payment of rent during the period he had promised to accept a lower rent).

119 [2004] 2 HKLRD 518, [2003] 4 HKC 677.

There must also have been detrimental reliance on the promise. Hong Kong courts have not required that the act of reliance must be independently detrimental, but it has been clarified that the necessary reliance must be such as to render it inequitable for the promisor to renege on his words. In *Newmark Capital Corp Ltd v Coffee Partners Ltd*,[120] Recorder Shieh, SC at the Court of First Instance held that to establish detrimental reliance, which does not differ in substance from that in estoppel by convention,[121] the court needs to examine closely: (1) the nature of the acts of reliance; and (2) the way in which a party is seeking to renege and the consequence of his doing so. Thus, when a plaintiff who had agreed to purchase shares from the defendants and purported to have submitted to an arbitration clause later sought to take action in court on the latter's failure to issue such shares, and the defendant sought to estop him from doing so, the court held that there was no detrimental reliance, because: (1) the acts of reliance by the defendant were but correspondence that proceeded on the assumption that the plaintiff was a shareholder and bound by the arbitration clause in the company's memorandum of association; and (2) the plaintiff's attempt to resolve the dispute by litigation rather than arbitration was of little consequence to the defendant.

While most of the Hong Kong cases that apply the doctrine of promissory estoppel abide by its traditional (English) contours, the Court of Final Appeal decision of *Luo Xing Juan v Estate of Hui Shui See Willy, Deceased*[122] appeared to have adopted the progressive approach in *Walton Stores (Interstate) Ltd v Maher*[123] and even gone further in the remedial aspect. However, it is submitted that the court was in substance invoking proprietary estoppel in a domestic context when it was technically prevented from doing so, and the decision must be read in the light of a more recent, orthodox decision by the same judge. In *Luo Xing Juan*, the testator had promised to give his fiancée a 35 per cent share in a property in contemplation of their marriage; as the property was owned through a company and was its only asset, he transferred the same percentage of company shares to the plaintiff, but passed away shortly afterwards. On his death, his estate (through the company) sought to evict the fiancée. This is a classic fact pattern for proprietary estoppel or common intention constructive trust, but the court was unable to invoke those doctrines because the legal owner of the property was the company and the representation was made by the testator, who was merely the controlling shareholder of the company. Ribeiro PJ invoked the doctrine of promissory estoppel, and held that, first, the requirement of a pre-existing legal relationship between the parties as laid down in English law, which Hong Kong was more inclined towards than the Australian approach, was satisfied.[124] This was because the requirement is not limited to a relationship of pre-existing rights and duties, but also powers between the parties. Thus, even though the controlling shareholder (the deceased) has no direct right over the ordinary shareholder (his fiancée), he has power to make a decision on the company that affects the rights of the ordinary shareholder (eg to evict her). Second, applying *Walton Stores* and its emphasis on the underlying rationale of preventing unconscionability, the court had a wide discretion to fashion the minimum remedy to satisfy the equity, which would be to fulfil the fiancée's expectation interest in a case such as this where a clear-cut promise has been made and relied upon. The court then granted the fiancée a 35 per cent interest in the proceeds from the sale of the property, which translated to a few million dollars, and undisturbed occupation pending disposal of the property. This far exceeded her detrimental

[120] *Newmark Capital* (n 114) [62]. [121] ibid [62]–[64].

[122] *Luo Xing Juan* (n 117), noted by L Ho and R Lee, 'Disputes over Family Homes Owned Through Companies: Constructive Trust or Promissory Estoppel?' (2009) 125 LQR 25; K Low, '*Luo Xing Juan Angela v Estate of Hui Shui See Willy, Deceased*: Family Property & interposed companies' [2009] Conveyancer and Property Lawyer 524.

[123] *Walton Stores* (n 116). [124] *Luo Xing Juan* (n 117) [72].

reliance in continuing to reside with her fiancé, not pursuing employment opportunities, and paying a mortgage instalment of HK$40,000. Interestingly, this achieved the just solution of providing her with a roof over her head in the interim and providing sufficient funds to purchase a smaller property in the future, but at the expense of making bad law.

In both of these aspects, the court has stretched the scope of promissory estoppel beyond its English boundary of requiring a pre-existing contractual relationship (one that the court chose to bind itself to) and the Australian boundary of limiting relief to protecting the detrimental reliance of the promisee. The doctrine of promissory estoppel was also invoked in another domestic case involving a company-owned property, albeit the court did not find a sufficient representation in that case.[125] It is submitted that the *Luo Xing Juan* approach should not be treated as laying down any change of direction in Hong Kong's approach to promissory estoppel, as the doctrine was only utilized as an expedient substitute for proprietary estoppel. Besides, in the subsequent decision of *Unruh v Seeberger*, Ribeiro PJ rejected the adoption of a single overarching principle of estoppel, and endorsed Handley JA's extrajudicial observation that promissory estoppel is a defensive equity.[126]

VII. Conclusion

The rules on offer and acceptance, consideration, and formality may seem routine if not mundane to most lawyers, probably because they have been well settled for centuries and any room for innovation is limited. When placed within a fast-changing property market in Hong Kong, where negotiation tactics are key to many successful conveyancing deals and protracted construction disputes are a common phenomenon, these rules take on a new significance. The brief survey in this chapter hopes to show that while the lower courts in Hong Kong are generally content with applying English law almost exclusively and in a perfunctory manner, as if it were binding even after the handover, the Court of Final Appeal has utilized the occasion available to it to examine the suitability of these rules in the Hong Kong context. At times, it makes a decisive departure from English law, such as in relation to the doctrine of open contract, the application of section 3(1) of the CPO, and the primeval importance it places on the phrase 'subject to contract'. Most of the time, it prefers the English approach over competing approaches in Australia or continental Europe. These can be seen in its treatment of the duty to negotiate in good faith; protection of offerees in the tendering process; renegotiation of contractual terms; and the doctrine of estoppel, to name but a few. In these instances, even if English law was followed, there has generally been deliberation as to the reasons for doing so. One only hopes that the care, subtlety, and independent evaluation displayed in the Court of Final Appeal can also be adopted in the lower courts in the years to come.

[125] *Hong Kong Hua Qiao Co Ltd v Cham Ka Tai* [2013] HKEC 1182 (CFI).
[126] (2007) 10 HKCFAR 31, [2007] 2 HKLRD 414 (CFA) [127].

11

Contracts for the Benefit of Third Parties: Hong Kong

*Lee MASON**

I. Introduction

On 1 January 2016, the Contracts (Rights of Third Parties) Ordinance (Cap 623) ('the Ordinance') which enables contracting parties to confer enforceable contractual rights on third parties, came into force.[1] Until this time, the common law doctrine of privity was fully recognized and operated to prevent a third party to a contract from acquiring and enforcing a right which was intended to have been conferred on it by the contracting parties. Given that almost every other common law jurisdiction already has third party contractual rights legislation in place, it seems that the Ordinance was long overdue. For example, the UK passed the equivalent legislation in 1999[2] ('the 1999 UK Act') and Singapore in 2001.[3] The reason for Hong Kong lagging behind most other common law jurisdictions in this way may be due, in part, to the fact that Hong Kong, as a former colony of the UK, was returned to the People's Republic of China in July 1997, that is over two years prior to the passing of the 1999 UK Act. Perhaps if the UK had passed that Act whilst Hong Kong was still a colony, it may have prompted the passing of equivalent legislation in Hong Kong, as had hitherto been the general trend.[4]

It was not until 2005 that the Hong Kong Law Reform Commission published a report[5] recommending reform of the doctrine of privity by legislation, albeit not its complete abolition.[6] This eventually led to a bill being drafted by the Hong Kong Department of Justice in 2013 which was, in November 2014, almost a decade after the recommendations of the Law Reform Commission, passed by the Hong Kong Legislative Council. Now in force, more than 15 years behind the 1999 UK Act, the Ordinance allows third parties the ability to directly enforce rights intended to be conferred on them by the contracting parties where, and to the extent that, the Ordinance applies. To this end, it should be noted that certain contracts fall outside the scope of the Ordinance[7] and the contracting parties are

* Cite as L Mason, 'Contracts for the Benefit of Third Parties: Hong Kong' in Chen-Wishart, Loke, & Vogenauer, *Studies in the Contract Laws of Asia Vol II: Formation and Third Party Beneficiaries* (Oxford: OUP 2017) ch 11.

[1] Contracts (Rights of Third Parties) Ordinance (Cap 623). Available at <https://www.elegislation.gov.hk/hk/cap623> accessed 11 November 2016.

[2] Contracts (Rights of Third Parties) Act 1999.

[3] Contracts (Rights of Third Parties) Act 2001. See also Australia (Western Australia Property Law Act 1969, Queensland Property Law Act 1974 and Northern Territory Law of Property Act 2000), New Zealand (Contracts (Privity) Act 1982) and Canada (New Brunswick Law Reform Act 2000).

[4] eg the UK Sale of Goods Act 1893 was followed by the Sale of Goods Ordinance 1896 in Hong Kong; the UK Misrepresentation Act 1967 was followed by the Misrepresentation Ordinance 1969 in Hong Kong; and the UK Unfair Contract Terms Act 1977 was followed by the Control of Exemption Clauses Ordinance 1989 in Hong Kong.

[5] Law Reform Commission of Hong Kong, *Report on Privity of Contract* (2005) ('the LRC Report') <http://www.hkreform.gov.hk/en/docs/rprivity-e.pdf> accessed 11 November 2016.

[6] ibid 25 and 31. [7] The Ordinance (n 1) s 3. cf the 1999 UK Act, s 6.

Contract for the Benefit of Third Parties: Hong Kong. Lee Mason.

free to 'contract out' of the Ordinance.[8] As such, the following discussion will take account of both the common law doctrine of privity and the recent legislative reform as and where they apply in Hong Kong.

II. Recent Reform to the Law Relating to Third Party Rights

1. Rationale for the Hitherto Full Recognition and Operation of the Doctrine of Privity

The reasons for Hong Kong's recognition of the doctrine of privity precluding the enforceability of contractual rights by third parties were, essentially, those which justified the doctrine in the UK up until the introduction of 1999 UK Act. These reasons were, to a large extent, identified by the Law Reform Commission in its 2005 Report.[9] The first justification was based on the absence of consideration provided by a third party, insofar as it would be unreasonable to place a third party in a better position than a promisee since a promisee can only acquire rights under a contract where that promisee has provided consideration.[10] Second, a contract can be seen as a personal transaction, between the parties who agree on its terms and scope, insofar as those parties provide a requisite element of consent, through offer and acceptance, neither of which has been made by a third party.[11] Third, allowing a third party to enforce a contractual right would have the undesirable consequence of making the promisor potentially liable to litigation on two fronts, that is susceptible to being sued by both the promisee and the third party. A fourth reason for justifying the privity doctrine was the otherwise unjust consequence of a third party being able to sue on a contract but not, itself, be sued on it. Finally, if a third party can enforce a contractual benefit conferred on it, the freedom of the promisor and promisee to vary or rescind the contract would be affected, as well as subjecting the promisor to a wide range of possible third party claimants.

2. The Lead-Up to Reform

Although Lord Goff in the 1996 Privy Council case of *The Mahkutai*[12] (on appeal from Hong Kong) considered, obiter, the possibility of a 'fully-fledged exception'[13] to the doctrine of privity, this suggestion was not effectuated by any subsequent Hong Kong judicial or legislative development. Indeed, in the 2000 Court of Appeal case of *B + B Construction Ltd v Sun Alliance and London Insurance Plc*,[14] Godfrey VP made clear that, despite judicial developments in the relaxation of the privity doctrine elsewhere,[15] the doctrine still stands firm in Hong Kong:

> [I]n Hong Kong, the law remains as magisterially stated by Viscount Haldane LC in *Dunlop Pneumatic Tyre Company Ltd v Selfridge and Co Ltd*[[16]]: '...only a person who is a party to a contract can sue on it. Our law knows nothing of a *jus quaesitum tertio* arising by way of contract.'[17]

[8] The Ordinance (n 1) s 4(3). cf the 1999 UK Act, s 1(2).

[9] LRC Report (n 5) paras 2.2–2.11.

[10] Except, of course, for contracts by deed. Supporters of this view have included the Hong Kong Federation of Insurers (LRC Report (n 5) para 2.2).

[11] Again, this view has been supported by the Hong Kong Federation of Insurers (LRC Report (n 5) para 2.4).

[12] [1996] 2 HKLR 199 (PC) (Privy Council on appeal from Hong Kong).

[13] [1996] 2 HKLR 199 (CA) 208.

[14] [2000] 2 HKC 295 (CA).

[15] In particular, *Trident General Insurance Co Ltd v McNiece Bros Pty* (1988) 165 CLR 107 (HC Aus).

[16] [1915] AC 847 (HL) 853.

[17] *B + B Construction* (n 14) [15].

As such, prior to the consideration of the Ordinance at the Legislative Council's Bills Committee in 2014, there had been no significant open debate—at least none within the local academic literature—with regard to reform of the doctrine of privity. Rather, the issue was only meaningfully considered in 2005 by the Law Reform Commission, instigated by the Secretary for Justice and the Chief Justice from whom the Law Reform Commission received its terms of reference: '[t]o examine the doctrine of privity of contract and its exceptions, and the justifications for and against its retention, and to make such recommendations for reform as appropriate.'[18]

Ultimately, as noted above,[19] the Law Reform Commission recommended reform of the doctrine of privity by legislation, albeit not its complete abolition so as not to preclude the ability of the contracting parties to choose to confer a benefit on a third party which is *un*enforceable by that third party.[20] The Law Reform Commission found the arguments in favour of reform 'compelling'[21] and that there should be 'a simple and clear mechanism'[22] whereby a third party can enforce a right or benefit which the contracting parties intended to confer on it.

3. The Rationale for Reform

The first reason for recommending reform of the privity doctrine is that the doctrine frustrates the contracting parties' intention to benefit a third party.[23] Indeed, according to the Law Reform Commission, this is the 'foremost'[24] reason for reform:

> [I]f the parties to a contract wish to confer a benefit on a third party, they should have the freedom to do so...The fact that the privity doctrine prevents effect from being given to the contracting parties' intention runs counter to the underlying theory of contract...[25]

The second argument is that the doctrine of privity has caused the law relating to it to become 'unduly complex'[26] due to the courts' attempts to mitigate its harshness by developing ways to circumvent it, which in itself, is evidence of the injustice that the doctrine causes.[27] Such complexity from artificial, and inevitably uncertain, mechanisms designed to deal with the perceived injustice further calls into question the doctrine's coherency and, indeed, prompted the UK Privy Council (as noted in section II.2) to call for a 'fully-fledged exception' to the doctrine of privity.[28]

The third argument cited for reforming the doctrine is that the doctrine can lead to a 'perverse and unjust result'[29] in that the party that has suffered the loss (the third party) *cannot* sue, whereas the party that has suffered no loss (the promisee) *can* sue.[30]

The fourth argument in favour of reform is based on the injustice caused to a third party that has relied on the promisor's promise and changed its position in expectation of receiving the benefit promised, particularly where it changed its position to its detriment.

The final reason for reforming the doctrine of privity (as cited by the Law Reform Commission)[31] is based on the widespread criticisms of the doctrine, noting that no other

[18] LRC Report (n 5) 1. [19] ibid 25 and 31. [20] ibid para 2.30. [21] ibid para 2.33.
[22] ibid para 2.33. [23] See eg *Tweddle v Atkinson* (1861) 1 B & S 393. [24] LRC Report (n 5) 2.13.
[25] ibid para 2.33. [26] ibid para 2.15.
[27] *New Zealand Shipping Co Ltd v AM Satterthwaite & Co Ltd (The Eurymedon)* [1975] AC 154 (PC) (Privy Council on appeal from New Zealand). Eg through the use of agency, collateral contracts, and trusts.
[28] Lord Goff in *The Mahkutai* (n 12) 208, criticized the solution devised in *The Eurymedon* as being too technical and that the courts should recognize a 'fully-fledged exception' to the privity doctrine so as to avoid these technical and complex solutions.
[29] LRC Report (n 5) para 2.20. [30] *Beswick v Beswick* [1968] AC 58 (HL).
[31] LRC Report (n 5) para 2.23.

doctrine of English contract law (upon which Hong Kong contract law was founded) has been subjected to more criticism by the senior judiciary.[32] Indeed, as was noted by the Law Reform Commission, Steyn LJ (as he then was) thought that there was 'no doctrinal, logical, or policy reason'[33] for not allowing a third party to enforce a promise made in its favour by the contracting parties. The Law Reform Commission further took account of the fact that the doctrine has been reformed elsewhere within the common law.[34]

These arguments in favour of reform, and the subsequent recommendations of the Law Reform Commission, led to the Department of Justice proposing a bill in 2013 and, ultimately, the passing of the Ordinance by the Legislative Council in 2014. Nevertheless, it is important to remember that the common law doctrine of privity has not been abolished but still exists and operates in third party contractual situations unless, and to the extent that, the Ordinance applies.

III. The Contracts (Rights of Third Parties) Ordinance: The Tests of Enforceability

First, it should be noted that certain contracts will fall outside the scope of the Ordinance.[35] Examples of contracts to which the Ordinance does not apply include bills of exchange,[36] covenants relating to land,[37] and contracts for the carriage of goods by sea.[38] Nevertheless, all other contracts will fall within the ambit of the Ordinance, allowing a third party to have a directly enforceable right, subject to satisfying either of the two limbs to the test of enforceability.

Essentially, a third party may enforce a term of a contract where: (1) this is 'expressly' provided for in the contract by the contracting parties;[39] or (2) the term 'purports' to confer a benefit on the third party.[40] This second (alternative) limb, however, is not satisfied if, 'on a proper construction' of the contract, it is clear that the contracting parties did *not* intend that term to be enforceable by the third party.[41] In any event, in order to have an enforceable right at all under the Ordinance, the third party must be expressly identified in the contract either by name, as a member of a class, or answering a particular description,[42] but need not be in existence at the time when the contract was formed.[43]

1. Exceptions to, and Circumventions of, the Doctrine of Privity

Despite the continued existence of the doctrine of privity in Hong Kong, there are certain circumstances (both at common law and under statute) where the doctrine does not apply, or is at least effectively circumvented, so that a contract for the benefit of a third party is, at least, *indirectly* enforceable by that third party. At common law, perhaps the most common

[32] eg Lords Denning, Reid, Scarman, Diplock, Goff, and Steyn (as noted in A Burrows, 'The Contracts (Rights of Third Parties) Act 1999 and its Implications for Commercial Contracts' [2000] LMCLQ 540, 540).

[33] *Darlington Borough Council v Wiltshier Northern Ltd* [1995] 1 WLR 68 (CA) 76.

[34] LRC Report (n 5) para 2.24 (see also nn 2 and 3). Albeit, the Hong Kong Federation of Insurers thought that this did not constitute an acceptable reason for amending such a fundamental doctrine (LRC Report (n 5) para 2.32).

[35] s 3. cf 1999 UK Act, s 6.

[36] s 3(2)(a). cf 1999 UK Act, s 6(1).

[37] s 3(2)(c). Note that there is no equivalent provision in the 1999 UK Act.

[38] s 3(2)(d). However, s 3(3) provides an express exception to s 3(2)(d) in relation to exemption clauses. cf 1999 UK Act, s 6(5)(a).

[39] s 4(1)(a). cf 1999 UK Act, s 1(1)(a).

[40] s 4(1)(b). cf 1999 UK Act, s 1(1)(b).

[41] s 4(3). Clearly, this allows for the contracting parties to simply 'contract out' of the legislation by using an express term (or even, perhaps inadvertently, if such a term can be implied). cf 1999 UK Act, s 1(2).

[42] s 4(2). cf 1999 UK Act, s 1(3).

[43] s 4(6). cf 1999 UK Act, s 1(3).

example of circumventing the privity doctrine is assignment. A third party may enforce a benefit which, although originally conferred by one contracting party on another contracting party, was transferred by that other party to the third party by way of assignment. This is a common feature of commercial practice, particularly in the context of debt. Another relatively common example of circumventing the doctrine of privity is by way of agency whereby, for example, a third party can enforce rights against the agent's principal. Even if it is argued that the agent acts merely as an 'instrument' of the principal so that, technically, the principal is the real party with whom the third party contracts, such an argument is doubtful—and so seems more like an exception to the privity doctrine—in situations where the agent acts without actual but with 'usual' authority[44] or where the principal's identity is not disclosed,[45] for example.

Claims through the tort of negligence also operate to defy the doctrine of privity whereby a third party may sue a promisor for negligence where that promisor owed a duty of care to the third party. However, this method of circumventing the privity doctrine seems to be restricted to claims based on a third party's loss by way of physical injury or property damage.[46] With regard to pure economic loss by a third party, this seems to be restricted to testamentary dispositions.[47] Another, albeit seldom-utilized, method of circumventing the doctrine is by way of a collateral contract between the promisor and a third party whereby, for example, the court may recognize that the third party has a right to sue the promisor for breach of a warranty to that third party which was given by the promisor in consideration of the third party's agreement with another party that that other party would enter into a contract with the promisor.[48] However, given the requirements of offer, acceptance, intention to create legal relations, and consideration, it seems that the courts will not readily recognize the existence of a collateral contract as a means of circumventing the doctrine of privity,[49] particularly where the situation involves experienced commercial parties which could have created a direct contractual relationship but, for whatever reason, chose not to do so.[50]

A further circumstance at common law where the effect of the privity doctrine can be avoided, albeit very rarely, is by way of a trust of a contractual right.[51] An example would be where a promisee agrees to hold its contractual right (against the promisor) on trust for a third party which the third party, as a beneficiary, can assert, as a property right, against the promisor if the promisor interferes with it.[52] However, using the trust as a device to circumvent the doctrine of privity appears to have its limits, not least due to the fact that it may be difficult to establish the requisite intention to create a trust by the promisee in favour of the

[44] *Watteau v Fenwick* [1893] 1 QB 346 (QBD) (note that this principle was doubted in *Bonus Garment Co v Karl Rieker GmbH & Co KG* [2001] HKCA 335 (CA) and *Greatworth Industrial Ltd v Sun Fook Kong Construction Ltd* [2006] HKCA 460 (CA)).

[45] *Siu Yin Kwan v Eastern Insurance Co Ltd* [1994] 2 AC 199, [1994] 1 HKLR 77 (PC) (Privy Council on appeal from Hong Kong).

[46] *Donoghue v Stevenson* [1932] AC 562 (HL).

[47] *White v Jones* [1995] 2 AC 207 (HL). Defects in property causing economic loss to a third party are unlikely to be successful in the wake of criticisms of *Junior Books Ltd v Veitchi Co Ltd* [1983] 1 AC 520 (HL) (noted in *Sunface International Ltd v Meco Engineering Ltd* [1990] 2 HKLR 193 (CFI)). See also *Yuen Kun-yeu v Attorney General of Hong Kong* [1988] AC 175, [1987] HKLR 1154 (PC) (Privy Council on Appeal from Hong Kong) and *Leon Engineering & Construction Co Ltd v Ka Duck Investments Ltd* [1989] 2 HKLR 537.

[48] *Shanklin Pier Ltd v Detel Products Ltd* [1951] 2 KB 854 (KBD).

[49] *Independent Broadcasting Authority v EMI Electronics Ltd* (1980) 14 BLR 1 (HL) (with regard to a finding of no intention); cf *The Eurymedon* (n 27) (with regard to a flexible approach to finding an offer, acceptance, and consideration).

[50] *Fuji Seal Europe Ltd v Catalytic Combustion Corp* [2005] EWHC 1659 (TCC).

[51] *Dunlop Pneumatic Tyre Co Ltd v Selfridge and Co Ltd* [1915] AC 847 (HL) 953.

[52] *Les Affreteurs Reunis v Walford* [1919] AC 801 (HL).

third party.[53] Further, given the irrevocable nature of a trust, it is unlikely that it could even be implied that the contracting parties would want to give up their freedom to vary or rescind their contractual obligations.[54] Moreover, it seems that the trust device in the third party context, at present, is confined to promises to pay money or to transfer property. Finally, at common law, although it is possible for a third party to enforce a covenant, made by its predecessor in title, against a party who acquires an interest in land that, to its knowledge, is subject to such a covenant, it is only possible where that third party can show that the covenant in question was originally imposed for the benefit of neighbouring land owned by that third party.[55] In this regard, this exception to the privity doctrine is very narrow and very seldom applicable.

The operation of the privity doctrine is also subject to specific statutory exceptions, most notably the Ordinance.[56] Other than this, there are other legislative limitations on the operation of the doctrine. The Conveyancing and Property Ordinance (Cap 219) allows a third party to enforce a covenant as a successor in title, assignee, lessee, and mortgagee, notwithstanding the fact that the third party was not the original covenantee or a named party to the instrument.[57] The Third Parties (Rights Against Insurers) Ordinance (Cap 273) allows for a third party, in certain circumstances, to directly enforce rights against an insurer as if that third party was the insured, such as where the party insured against liabilities to the third party becomes bankrupt or is wound up.[58] The Bills of Exchange Ordinance (Cap 19) allows for a third party, as holder of a bill of exchange, to sue on the bill in its own name.[59] The Bills of Lading and Analogous Shipping Documents Ordinance (Cap 440) allows a third party holder of a bill of lading to enforce all rights of suit under a contract of carriage, despite not being party to the contract of carriage.[60] The Married Persons Status Ordinance (Cap 182) allows for a third party spouse or child to enforce a benefit of a life insurance policy made in its favour by the insured by virtue of that policy creating a trust in favour of that third party spouse or child.[61] Under the Marine Insurance Ordinance (Cap 329), a third party which has an interest in a subject matter that has been insured by another party which also has an interest in that same subject matter, and which insured the subject matter for the (part) benefit of that third party, may recover under the insurance policy notwithstanding the fact that that third party was not privy to the insurance contract.[62] Finally, the Motor Vehicle Insurance (Third Party Risks) Ordinance (Cap 272) allows a third party, as judgment creditor, to enforce the benefit of insurance in respect of third party risks.[63]

2. Remedies Available to a Promisee: Enforcing the Promise to Benefit the Third Party

Contracts for the benefit of a third party may be enforceable by the promisee as against the promisor. However, to the extent that the doctrine of privity is applicable, there are

[53] *Re Schebsman* [1944] Ch 83 (Ch); *Swain v Law Society* [1983] 1 AC 598 (HL) 620; *Shiu Yeuk Yuen v Hong Kong Solicitors Indemnity Fund Ltd* [2010] 4 HKLRD 296 (CFI).

[54] *Re Schebsman* (n 53) 104 (followed in *THH and TWK v The Commissioner of Estate Duty* [1990] 2 HKLR 333 (HC)).

[55] *Tulk v Moxhay* (1848) 2 Ph 774, (1848) 47 ER 1345 (Ct of Ch) and *Wong King Lim v Incorporated Owners of Peony House* [2013] 4 HKC 295 (CA).

[56] That is the Contracts (Rights of Third Parties) Ordinance (Cap 623) (n 1).

[57] ss 41 and 26. cf UK Law of Property (Miscellaneous Provisions) Act 1994, Pt I and UK Law of Property Act 1925, ss 77–84 and 56(1).

[58] s 2. cf UK Third Parties (Rights Against Insurers) Act 1930, s 1.

[59] s 38(a). cf UK Bills of Exchange Act 1882, s 38(1).

[60] s 4(1). cf UK Carriage of Goods by Sea Act 1992, s 2(1).

[61] s 13. cf UK Married Women's Property Act 1882, s 11.

[62] s 14(2). cf UK Marine Insurance Act 1906, s 14(2).

[63] s 10. cf UK Road Traffic Act 1988, s 151.

difficulties attached to the apparent remedies open to the promisee. The first is in relation to the equitable remedy of specific performance. Although this remedy is arguably the best remedy for the third party, via the promisee, insofar as it would realize the benefit as originally agreed by the contracting parties, it is nevertheless a discretionary remedy and subject to certain restrictions.[64] Although specific performance in favour of the third party will not be excluded simply on the basis that damages would provide an adequate remedy for the promisee,[65] or on the basis that the remedy would not have been available in a two-party situation,[66] it seems unlikely to be ordered where the promisor's obligation to the third party is to render a personal service[67] or where such an order would offend against the requirement of mutuality.[68]

However, where the promisor has contracted to pay a sum of money to the third party, the promisee may be able to specifically enforce the third party's right, by way of a common law action for the agreed sum. Although it might be argued that such an action would be to force the promisor to do that which it had never contracted to do, that is to pay the promisee as opposed to the third party, and that the promisee therefore should not be able to sue for the agreed sum,[69] such an argument seems to lose its potency where the promisor is in no way prejudiced by having to pay the promisee as opposed to the third party, provided that such a payment constitutes full discharge of that promise to pay the third party. Indeed, allowing the promisee to claim the agreed sum owed to the third party may be justified through contractual construction insofar as the contract is interpreted as providing for payment to the third party or as directed by the promisee.[70]

A related issue, here, arises in the context of a promisor actually performing (voluntarily or involuntarily) its contractual obligation to the third party, such as paying the agreed sum, and the promisee then arguing that the third party is not entitled to retain the sum for its own benefit but, rather, holds that sum on behalf of the promisee. Such an argument is most likely to actually come from the promisee's trustee in bankruptcy or executor.[71] However, the promisee will only be able to claim such sums if, on a true construction of the contract, those sums were paid by the promisor to the third party as nominee for the promisee.[72]

The promisee may be able to base a claim in restitution against the promisor to restore the promisee with the consideration that it provided to the promisor, albeit only where there has been a total failure of consideration by that promisor.[73] However, the most apparent remedy available to the promisee is damages. Where the promisor's failure to perform in favour of the third party results in loss to the promisee, the promisee may claim damages.[74] Such loss may stem from the promisee itself, having to provide the agreed benefit to the third party, such as making a payment which would have discharged the promisee's

[64] *Co-operative Insurance Society Ltd v Argyll Stores (Holdings) Ltd* [1998] AC 1 (HL) 16.

[65] *Beswick* (n 30) 88.

[66] *Gurtner v Circuit* [1968] 2 QB 587 (CA) (specific performance could be ordered to enforce a promise to pay a lump sum to a third party, even though it would be more apposite to enforce this promise through a common law action for the agreed sum in a two-party situation).

[67] *Johnson v Shrewsbury and Birmingham Rlwy* (1853) 3 DM & G 358, (1853) 43 ER 358 (HC); cf *Giles v Morris* [1972] 1 WLR 307 (Ch) and *Tito v Waddell* [1977] Ch 106 (Ch) (noted in *Anstalt Nybro v Hong Kong Resort Co Ltd* [1978] HKLR 414 (CA) 428).

[68] *Ogden v Fossick* (1862) DF & J 426, (1862) 45 ER 1249 (Ct of Ch) (followed in *Chan Kam Ming (No 2) v Kwong Lin* [1959] HKLR 544 (CA), 556).

[69] *Coulls v Bagot's Executor and Trustee Co Ltd* [1967] ALR 385 (HCA) 409–411.

[70] *The Spiros C* [2000] 2 Lloyd's Rep 319 (CA) 331.

[71] *Beswick* (n 30) 71 and 96.

[72] *The Spiros C* (n 70) 331.

[73] *Fibrosa Spolka Akcyjna v Fairbairn Lawson Combe Barbour Ltd* [1943] AC 32 (HL) (endorsed in *Shanghai Tongji Science & Technology Industrial Co Ltd v Casil Clearing Ltd* [2004] 2 HKLRD 548 (CFA)).

[74] *De Jongh Weill v Mean Fiddler Holdings Ltd* [2005] All ER (D) 331 (QBD) (the promisor failed to grant share warrants to the third party nominee, thereby causing loss to the promisee).

obligation to make if the promisor had, as agreed, made such payment instead. Indeed, where the promisee suffers loss from the promisor's failure to fulfil its obligation to the third party, the promisee can claim damages, even where it has an obligation to pay such damages to the third party.[75]

However, where there is no loss suffered by the promisee, it can only recover nominal damages.[76] This means that, as a general rule, a promisee cannot recover damages for losses suffered by a third party from the promisor's breach of a contract for that third party's benefit.[77] This position has been criticized as possibly leading to 'unsatisfactory'[78] results and 'legal black holes'[79] so that the third party's cause of action has 'completely disappeared'.[80] The general rule is, nevertheless, subject to the *Albazero* exception which allows a promisee to recover substantial damages purely for the third party's loss in certain circumstances, that is where 'at the time when the contract was made the parties actually contemplated that an identified third party would or might suffer damage in the event of a breach of contract'.[81]

> [K]nowledge that an identified third party would or might suffer damage if there were a breach of contract ought to be capable of being readily demonstrated, and the possibility of loss would have been known at the time the contract was made.... it [gives] effect to the contemplation of the contracting parties and provide[s] a means of compensating the third party for whose benefit, at least in part, the relevant contractual obligation was undertaken.[82]

To this end, it seems that where a promisee *can* (by virtue of the *Albazero* exception) make a claim to recover substantial damages for loss incurred purely by the third party from the promisor's breach, the promisee will hold those damages on trust for the third party.[83] Where, however, the *Albazero* exception is inapplicable, the third party has no rights of action against the promisee to recover damages (in whole or in part) which have been awarded to the promisee to compensate the promisee for its *own* loss.[84]

However, where the Ordinance applies, the remedies available to the third party are the same as those which would have been available to it, in an action for breach of contract, if it had been an actual party to the contract.[85] Clearly, this would include damages, being the primary remedy in the common law for breach of contract,[86] but also *expressly* includes 'a

[75] *Chappell v Somers & Blake (a firm)* [2003] EWHC 1644 (Ch). It may also be possible for the promisee to recover damages to cover losses incurred from the promisee making a *voluntary* alternative provision in favour of the third party (*Banco de Portugal v Waterlow & Sons Ltd* [1932] AC 452 (HL)).

[76] eg the lack of loss suffered by the uncle's estate in *Beswick* (n 30).

[77] *Kinetics Medical and Health Group Co Ltd v Dr Tse Ivan Cheong Yau* [2013] HKCFI 1645 (CFI) [34] (citing *Woodar Investment Development Ltd v Wimpey Construction UK Ltd* [1980] 1 WLR 277 (HL)).

[78] *Kinetics Medical* (n 77) [34].

[79] ibid [34].

[80] ibid [34] (albeit not, of course, where there is a satisfactory alternative remedy, such as in *Beswick* (n 30) (for the promisee against the promisor by way of specific performance) and *Alfred McAlpine Construction Co Ltd v Panatown Ltd* [2001] 1 AC 518 (HL) (for the third party against the promisor by way of damages under a separate contract)).

[81] ibid [35].

[82] ibid [35] (noting endorsement from *Alfred McAlpine* (n 80)). See *The Albazero* [1977] AC 774 (HL) (albeit the principle was not applied in that case). For examples of its operation, see *Rolls Royce Power Engineering Plc v Ricardo Consulting Engineers Ltd* [2003] EWHC 2871 (TCC) [116] (in relation to a trust); *Dunlop v Lambert* (1839) 6 Cl & F 600 (HL) 626–627 (in relation to carriage of goods); *Siu Yin Kwan v Eastern Insurance Co Ltd* (n 45) 85 (in relation to agency); and *Linden Gardens Trust v Lenesta Sludge Disposals Ltd* [1994] 1 AC 85 (HL) (in relation to a building contract).

[83] *The Albazero* (n 82) 845.

[84] This, of course, includes any restitution awarded to the promisee as being a recovery of the consideration provided to the promisor by the promisee. Furthermore, in any event, the third party has no right to insist that the promisee take any action to enforce the promise at all (see *Beswick* (n 30) and *Gurtner* (n 66) 599 and 606).

[85] s 5(1). cf 1999 UK Act, s 1(5).

[86] *Photo Production Ltd v Securicor Transport Ltd* [1980] AC 827 (HL) 847. This is particularly important for a third party which, if bringing its claim in tort, as a result of the application of the privity doctrine, could not claim for pure economic loss, other than as a disappointed beneficiary in the context of a negligently drafted will (see

remedy under the rules of equity',[87] that is specific performance and injunction. The Ordinance further makes clear that any rights or remedies which are available as part of the exceptions to the doctrine of privity are still in force and operative.[88] However, the Ordinance also enables a promisor to rely on any defence or set-off which would have been available to the promisor: (1) if the third party had been a party to the contract;[89] or (2) had the claim been made by the promisee *and* which either (a) arises from, or in connection with, the contract which is relevant to the term in question[90] or (b) is made expressly available to the promisor in the case of proceedings brought by the third party.[91] Furthermore, a promisor may counterclaim against the third party for a matter not arising from the contract that would have been available to the promisor if the third party had been a party to the contract.[92]

To the extent that the doctrine of privity applies to the contract, there seems to be no risk of the promisor facing double liability, to both the promisee and the third party, for failing to make good its promise to benefit the third party. Indeed, the undesirability of potentially subjecting a promisor to two actions for the same breach was one of the arguments cited in support of a fully recognized and operative privity doctrine in Hong Kong.[93] Nevertheless, where the Ordinance applies, the potential risk of double liability is specifically dealt with.[94] Essentially, the Ordinance provides that, where a promisor has wholly or partly performed its obligations to the third party, the promisor is discharged from the obligations it owed to the promisee to the extent of having performed those same obligations to the third party.[95] Further, where the third party brings a claim against the promisor for breach of the promisor's obligations to that third party, the court (or arbitral tribunal) must reduce—to the extent to which that court (or arbitral tribunal) thinks appropriate—any award made to the third party to take into account any sum already recovered by the promisee in respect of the third party's loss or the expense to the promisee of making good to the third party the promisor's breach.[96]

However, this provision has attracted some criticism.[97] For example, the provision only protects a promisor insofar as preventing double recovery (by the promisee and the third party) for the *same* loss. There may, however, be occasional circumstances where the promisee suffers *personal* loss as a result of the promisor's breach and this loss is *separate* to the

White (n 47)). On this point, note that, according to the LRC's recommendations, a solicitor's contractual obligation to use reasonable care in drafting a will would not, in relation to the beneficiaries, fall within the scope of the Ordinance because such a term does not purport to confer a benefit on the beneficiaries; rather, the benefit to them derives from the testator, not from the solicitor whose only role is to enable its client to confer a benefit on the beneficiaries (see LRC Report (n 5) para 4.35). As such, disappointed beneficiaries would still have to bring their action in tort.

[87] s 5(3). However, since s 5(2) states that '[a]ny law relating to the remedy applies accordingly', it is not entirely clear how this sits with the equitable maxim that 'equity will not assist a volunteer' given that the third party will not have provided any consideration. cf 1999 UK Act, s 1(5).

[88] s 5(4). cf 1999 UK Act, s 7(1). See above for examples.

[89] s 8(2)(c) (subject to any express term restricting the available defences and set-offs: s 8(4)). cf 1999 UK Act, ss 3(4)(a) and 3(5).

[90] s 8(2)(a) (subject to any express term restricting the available defences and set-offs: s 8(4)). cf 1999 UK Act, ss 3(2) and 3(5).

[91] s 8(2)(b). cf 1999 UK Act, s 3(3).

[92] s 8(3) (subject to any express term restricting the available counterclaims: s 8(4)). cf 1999 UK Act, ss 3(4)(b) and 3(5).

[93] LRC Report (n 5) para 2.6.

[94] s 11. cf 1999 UK Act, s 5.

[95] s 11(1) and (2). Note that there are no equivalent provisions in the 1999 UK Act, although they might be implied.

[96] s 11(3) and (4). cf 1999 UK Act, s 5.

[97] L Mason, 'Comments on the Bill submitted to the Bills Committee on the Contract (Rights of Third Parties) Bill' (14 May 2014) <http://www.legco.gov.hk/yr13-14/english/bc/bc102/papers/bc1020507cb4-672-1-e.pdf> accessed 29 November 2016; and the Administration's Responses of the Department of Justice (June 2014) <http://www.legco.gov.hk/yr13-14/english/bc/bc102/papers/bc1020616cb4-815-1-e.pdf> accessed 29 November 2016.

third party's loss or the making good to the third party of the breach. In this regard, the promisor is exposed to litigation on two fronts, albeit not arising from the same loss but, nevertheless, from the same breach of the same obligation. Presumably, any personal loss claimed by the promisee will not be taken into account by the court (or arbitral tribunal) when making an award to the third party given that such loss is separate to the losses for which the promisee may recover, as stipulated elsewhere in the provision,[98] and which *will* be taken into account by the court (or arbitral tribunal) when determining the sum to be awarded to the third party.[99] However, this is not entirely clear from the provision. Furthermore, the provision does not address the situation where the third party claims and recovers damages *first*, prior to the promisee. Again, presumably the promisee can still recover damages for any personal loss caused by the promisor's breach which is separate to that already recovered by the third party.

Another criticism of the provision in the Ordinance which deals with double liability is that, whereas it prescribes that the sum to be awarded to the third party, where so claimed by that third party, should take into account any recovery (for the same loss) by the promisee, there is no express provision dealing with the promisee's duty to account to the third party for those damages recovered in relation to the third party's loss. The response of the Department of Justice (the drafters of the Ordinance) to this criticism is simply that no other common law jurisdiction which has enacted legislation reforming the privity doctrine has introduced such an express provision on this issue and that the view of the Law Reform Commission is being followed, that is that it should be for the court (or arbitral tribunal), rather than the legislature, to determine the circumstances under which a promisee may have to account to the third party for sums recovered by the promisee.[100] However, although this could, indeed, reasonably be left to the common law as a restitutionary claim by the third party against the promisee, an express provision that the promisee will account to the third party for such damages would make the position clearer and, arguably, reduce the likelihood of litigation.

Finally, to the extent that the doctrine of privity applies in full, another method by which a promisee may be able to enforce a promise for the benefit of a third party is by way of a stay of proceedings. For example, where a promisor promises not to sue the third party, the promisee may seek a stay of the proceedings if the promisor does bring an action against the third party.[101] However, in order to obtain the stay, the promisee must satisfy the court that: (1) there was a clear promise, by the promisor to the promisee, not to sue the third party; and (2) the promisee has a sufficient interest in the enforcement of that promise to justify the granting of the stay.[102]

3. Case Studies

(a) Exemption clauses for stevedores

X contracts with Y to transport X's goods using Y's ship to a foreign market. The contract for the carriage of goods by sea between X and Y contains an exemption of liability provision

[98] s 11(3)(b). cf 1999 UK Act, s 5. [99] s 11(4). cf 1999 UK Act, s 5.

[100] Administration's Responses of the Department of Justice (June 2014) <http://www.legco.gov.hk/yr13-14/english/bc/bc102/papers/bc1020616cb4-815-1-e.pdf> accessed 29 November 2016; LRC Report (n 5) para 4.143.

[101] High Court Ordinance (Cap 4), s 16(3). The promisee would *not* be able to bring a second action for an injunction to restrain the promisor from bringing an action against the third party since multiplicity of legal proceedings is to be avoided: High Court Ordinance (Cap 4), s 16(2)(b). cf UK Senior Courts Act 1981, ss 49(3) and 49(2)(b).

[102] *Gore v Van Der Lann* [1967] 2 QB 31 (CA) (followed in *Kanematsu-Gosho (HK) Ltd v Lee Boon-Chean* [1986] HKLR 59 (HC)).

which purports to protect Z, the stevedores hired to unload X's goods from Y's ship once it arrives at the docks. As a result of Z's carelessness, X's goods are damaged while they are being unloaded from the ship and X wants to sue Z for negligence to recover damages for the losses suffered by X. Can Z rely on the exemption of liability provision in the contract between X and Y?

In this scenario, if X and Y have contracted out of the Ordinance so that the common law doctrine of privity applies, assuming Y is the party which hired Z, Z would nevertheless be able to rely on the exemption clause provided that it could satisfy the following conditions: (1) the bill of lading makes clear that Z is intended to be protected by the exemption clause; (2) the bill of lading makes it clear that Y, in addition to contracting for the exemption clause on its own behalf, is also contracting as agent for Z that the exemption clause should apply to Z; (3) Y has authority from Z to so contract on Z's behalf (or if Z later ratifies this); and (4) there are no difficulties concerning the movement of consideration from Z.[103] With regard to the fourth condition, the fact that Z is already under a duty to Y (by virtue of the Y–Z contract) to unload X's goods with due care (express or implied), the performance of such a duty would also be consideration for a separate contract which exempts Z from liability to X.[104] Further, and in relation to that separate contract between Z and X, although it could be argued that that contract might not be bilateral in nature, the X–Y contract can be viewed as resulting in X making an offer by way of a unilateral contract insofar as offering to exempt from liability anybody which undertakes to unload X's goods.[105]

However, assuming that the Ordinance applies, Z would be able to directly enforce the benefit of the exemption clause against X, albeit on a much simpler analysis than under the common law doctrine. The stevedores were expressly identified (in this case, as members of a class)[106] and the right to rely on the exemption clause was expressly extended to them.[107] Although the Ordinance expressly excludes contracts for the carriage of goods by sea from its scope,[108] it nevertheless provides an express *exception* to this in relation to exemption clauses.[109]

(b) Selling bread

X leases two adjoining properties to Y and Z. The lease between X and Y barred Y from selling bread because Z sold bread from his leased property. Can X and Y agree to lift the bar?

In this scenario, the common law doctrine of privity applies because the Ordinance expressly excludes covenants relating to land from its scope of applicability.[110] As such, X and Y are free to agree to lift the bar (or restrictive covenant) notwithstanding any detriment to be suffered by Z.[111] However, Z may have a claim against X if this restrictive covenant forms part of his own lease agreement with X, or where X has otherwise made a representation or collateral warranty to that effect.

[103] *Scruttons Ltd v Midland Silicones Ltd* [1962] AC 446 (HL) (giving rise to what became known as a '*Himalaya*' clause); *The Eurymedon* (n 27); *The Mahkutai* (n 12); and *Bewise Motors Co Ltd v Hoi Kong Container Services Ltd* [1998] 2 HKLRD 645 (CFA).

[104] *Scotson v Pegg* (1861) 6 H & N 295 (Exch Ct) and *The Eurymedon* (n 27).

[105] *The Eurymedon* (n 27). Note that it was these very complexities and artificial reasonings which led Lord Goff in *The Mahkutai* (n 12) 208 to criticize the device used in *The Eurymedon* to circumvent the privity doctrine and which were referred to by the LRC as one of the arguments justifying reform of the privity doctrine (LRC Report (n 5) paras 2.15–2.19).

[106] s 4(2). cf 1999 UK Act, s 1(3).

[107] s 4(1)(a). cf 1999 UK Act, s 1(1)(a).

[108] s 3(2)(d). cf 1999 UK Act, s 6(5)(a).

[109] s 3(3). cf 1999 UK Act, s 6(5).

[110] s 3(2)(c). Note that there is no equivalent provision in the 1999 UK Act.

[111] *Real Honest Investment Ltd v Attorney-General* [1997] 2 HKC 436 (PC).

(c) *The stolen shop takings*

X bank makes a contract for Y security company to collect Z store's takings. The contract requires Y to use armoured vehicles and take out insurance. Y failed to do these and the takings were stolen while being collected in an ordinary car. Can Z sue?

In this scenario, presumably X will have a contract with Z for the collection and banking of Z's takings. If so, Y (which has contracted with X for the collection of Z's takings) can be regarded as the agent of X, thereby making X vicariously liable for Y's negligence, resulting in the loss of the takings, by breaching a contractual duty of care (express or implied) owed to Z by virtue of the X–Z contract. Indeed, the provisions in the X–Y contract (that Y should use an armoured vehicle and take out insurance) cannot be said to confer, or purport to confer, a benefit on Z: those provisions can only be said to confer a benefit on X since X is already in a contractual relationship with Z (its customer) to collect Z's takings. As such, it seems clear that all the risk falls on X (as Z's bank, charged with collecting Z's money) and that is why X has employed Y (as a security company), requiring Y to use an armoured vehicle and take out insurance. Therefore, the law relating to third party rights (whether at common law under the doctrine of privity or by virtue of the Ordinance) is not applicable and Z can sue X for the lost takings.

IV. Critique of the Recent Legislative Reform

1. How is the Ordinance Different from the 1999 UK Act?

Although the Ordinance is substantially the same as the 1999 UK Act, there are some notable differences. One particularly notable difference between the Ordinance and the 1999 UK Act is in relation to the *scope* of the Ordinance insofar as it excludes covenants relating to land.[112] The Ordinance also specifically excludes a particular type of land covenant which is especially relevant to Hong Kong land law, that is a deed of mutual covenant ('DMC').[113] Various reasons were cited by the drafters of the Ordinance for excluding land covenants generally, and DMCs specifically, including the 'unique and intricate' legal regime of Hong Kong land law which sets clear limits on the enforceability of such covenants, particularly the law relevant to building management and enforcement of rights under a DMC.[114] For example, a third party co-owner in a building (as successor in title) can enforce its rights under a DMC against another third party co-owner (as a fellow successor in title) and, further, a DMC entails not only rights but also burdens being conferred on third parties. Furthermore, the Department of Justice noted that the local legal framework for enforcing a DMC has, over many years, developed specifically in response to the needs of regulating the occupation and management of multi-storey buildings and estate developments in Hong Kong and that any changes to the DMC regime would affect a large number of people which, therefore, makes such amendments 'inappropriate' without a full consultation aimed specifically at reforming the DMC regime.[115]

[112] s 3(2)(c).

[113] s 3(2)(b). A DMC is defined in the Building Management Ordinance (Cap 344), s 2, as 'a document which—(a) defines the rights, interests and obligations of [land] owners [and mortgagees in possession] among themselves; and (b) is registered in the Land Registry'.

[114] Legislative Council Secretariat, 'House Committee Meeting Paper: Report of the Bills Committee on Contracts (Rights of Third Parties) Bill' <http://www.legco.gov.hk/yr14-15/english/hc/papers/hc20141114cb4-145-e.pdf> accessed 29 November 2016.

[115] Legislative Council Secretariat, 'House Committee Meeting Paper: Report of the Bills Committee on Contracts (Rights of Third Parties) Bill', para 29 <http://www.legco.gov.hk/yr14-15/english/hc/papers/hc20141114cb4-145-e.pdf> accessed 29 November 2016.

Although there are no equivalent provisions in the 1999 UK Act, the reason for this, speculated by the Department of Justice, may be that there are relatively fewer multi-storey buildings in the UK and, as such, relatively fewer DMCs drawn up.[116] Interestingly, however, there are also no equivalent provisions in the Singapore Contracts (Rights of Third Parties) Act 2001 despite Singapore, like Hong Kong, having many multi-storey buildings. The Department of Justice simply attributed this, without elaboration, to the circumstances between Hong Kong and Singapore being 'different'.[117]

Perhaps most striking, however, is the fact that the Law Reform Commission did *not* recommend the exclusion of such covenants from the Ordinance; rather, the Commission considered the potential impact of the legislation on the building management regime to be 'only minimal'.[118] This view was vehemently opposed by the Hong Kong Bar Association[119] which considered that allowing third parties to enforce a covenant in situations where the current law does not, may have 'far reaching and unintended consequences'.[120] In the context of DMCs under the current law in Hong Kong, in order for a third party to enforce a covenant, the covenant must 'touch and concern' the land *and* the third party must be a successor in title of the original covenantee. This, according to the Hong Kong Bar Association, provides an 'important safeguard against exploitation by unscrupulous developers' which would be substantially weakened or lost if DMCs were not excluded from the scope of the Ordinance.[121] The Department of Justice agreed with the view of the Bar Association[122] and, as such, land covenants (including DMCs) are excluded from the scope of the Ordinance so as not to contradict or prejudice the existing regime which is specific to Hong Kong.

Another evident difference between the Ordinance and the 1999 UK Act is that, where there is an exemption clause in the main contract which excludes or limits the promisor's liability to the third party for breach of a contractual duty of care,[123] this clause will be subject to the 'reasonableness test' in the Control of Exemption Clauses Ordinance (Cap 71) ('CECO').[124] According to section 7(2) of the CECO:

> In the case of other loss or damage, a person cannot so exclude or restrict his liability for negligence except in so far as the term or notice satisfies the requirement of reasonableness.

In other words, section 7(2) of the CECO is wide enough to possibly prevent the promisor from excluding or limiting its liability to the third party for breach of a contractual duty of care if the relevant exemption clause fails to satisfy the reasonableness test laid out in section 3(1) of the CECO. By contrast, in the 1999 UK Act, there is a provision[125] specifically disapplying the UK's equivalent of section 7(2) of the CECO,[126] thereby preventing the third party from having the promisor's exemption clause avoided for being 'unreasonable'. There is no such equivalent provision in the Ordinance which disapplies section 7(2) of the CECO.

It has been argued that, although the Ordinance may appear more third-party-friendly, it creates uncertainty for the contracting parties, most particularly the promisor whose liability to the third party may ultimately *not* be exempted, despite the promisor and the

[116] ibid. [117] ibid. [118] LRC Report (n 5) para 4.168.

[119] Hong Kong Bar Association, 'Further Views on Consultation Paper on the Contracts (Rights of Third Parties) Bill 2013' (January 2014) <http://www.legco.gov.hk/yr13-14/english/panels/ajls/papers/aj1126cb4-328-1-e.pdf> accessed 29 November 2016.

[120] ibid para 6. [121] ibid para 7. [122] Legislative Council Secretariat (n 115) para 7, fn 1.

[123] Control of Exemption Clauses Ordinance (Cap 71), s 2(1)(a) defines negligence as being a breach of any of any obligation, arising from the terms of a contract, to take reasonable care or exercise reasonable skill in the performance of the contract.

[124] CECO, ss 7(2) and 3(1). [125] s 7(2). [126] UK's Unfair Contract Terms Act 1977, s 2(2).

promisee having freely agreed that it should.[127] This appears to run contrary to the main driving force for privity reform: namely, giving effect to the intentions of the contracting parties.[128] Given that the contracting parties are able to decide whether to give a third party an enforceable right *at all*, it is arguably only fair that they should also be able to exclude or limit those rights if they do indeed decide to confer such rights on a third party. Therefore, it would seem contrary to the goal of respecting the intentions of the contracting parties if a statutory reasonableness test could be relied on by the third party (which had had its conferred right deliberately restricted by the contracting parties) so as to strike out a clause (agreed on by the contracting parties) which exempted the promisor's liability to it for loss or damage (other than death or personal injury)[129] as a result of the promisor's negligence.[130] Essentially, since section 7(2) of the CECO is not disapplied, the promisor is actually open to more potential liability than it contractually bargained for with the promisee. Nevertheless, in response to this criticism, the drafters of the Ordinance considered that there was 'no compelling reason for distinguishing promisees from third parties' in respect of the protection afforded by section 7(2) of the CECO so that it should apply where the third party sues the promisor for negligence amounting to a breach of contract.[131]

A further notable distinction with the 1999 UK Act (and, indeed, with any other third party legislation in any other common law jurisdiction) is the inclusion in the Ordinance of a provision expressly dealing with exclusive jurisdiction clauses.[132] However, it has been argued that the problem or, at least, uncertainty with this provision seems to be in the context of exemption clauses where the promisor brings an action in tort against a third party.[133] If the third party wants to rely on an exemption clause (which was conferred on it for its benefit), it could mean that such a third party is subject to the burden of being forced to defend itself in the jurisdiction agreed in the main contract. Since reform of the privity doctrine is not intended to allow burdens to be conferred on third parties,[134] it must mean that, although the promisor is bound to sue in the stipulated jurisdiction, the third party is not bound to submit to that jurisdiction (but may opt to do so). If the third party chooses not to submit to that jurisdiction, the court of that jurisdiction would (unless that court is able to find jurisdiction on some other ground) have to stay the proceedings, thereby resulting in the promisor only having the option of bringing the proceedings in a court which does have jurisdiction over the dispute.[135] Nevertheless, the actual position is unclear as this provision in the Ordinance does not have a tried-and-tested legislative equivalent in the other common law jurisdictions, though the response of the drafters of the Ordinance is to simply 'leave the matter to be determined according to the jurisdiction rules of the relevant court'.[136]

[127] L Mason, 'Comments on the Bill' (n 97).

[128] Indeed, despite the LRC considering that the 'foremost criticism' of the privity doctrine was that it thwarted the intentions of the contracting parties (see LRC Report, para 2.13), the LRC then went on to *withdraw* their initial recommendation to disapply s 7(2) of the CECO (see LRC Report, para 4.127).

[129] In which event, liability in negligence cannot be exempted (see CECO, s 7(1)).

[130] Note that there does not appear to be a problem with the *other* provisions in the CECO since, other than the ones which cannot be excluded or limited in any event whatsoever (eg in s 7(1)), the CECO only deals with exemption clauses as between the *contracting* parties.

[131] Administration's Responses (n 97).

[132] s 13. However, based on academic opinion, although not expressly provided for, the 1999 UK Act is thought to cover exclusive jurisdiction clauses: eg R Merkin, *Privity of Contract: The Impact of the Contracts (Rights of Third Parties) Act 1999* (London: LLP Professional Publishing 2000) para 5.124; C Macmillan, 'A Birthday Present for Lord Denning: The Contracts (Rights of Third Parties) Act 1999' (2000) 63 MLR 721, 733.

[133] L Mason, 'Comments on the Bill' (n 97).

[134] LRC Report (n 5) 2.

[135] Of course, it seems that the third party may choose to make use of the jurisdiction clause if it is being sued by the promisor in a jurisdiction different to the one agreed in the main contract.

[136] Administration's Responses (n 97).

A final observable difference between the Ordinance and the 1999 UK Act is the inclusion in the Ordinance of a specific provision dealing with assignment.[137] This seems relatively uncontroversial, the Law Reform Commission agreeing with the English Law Commission's view that there was 'no good reason'[138] for not allowing the assignment of third party rights given that they are 'closely analogous'[139] to contractual rights, although the English Law Commission considered that no legislative provision was necessary.[140] The provision in the Ordinance essentially allows for a third party to assign its right to enforce a term under the contract[141] except where the contract expressly provides otherwise[142] or where, on a proper construction of the contract, that right is not assignable.[143] However, the provision has received criticism from the Hong Kong Federation of Insurers which thinks that it would be more 'practical' for the legislation to adopt an 'opt-in' approach rather than an 'opt-out' approach, particularly in the case of a life insurance policy where assignment may create difficulties for the insurer in verifying the authenticity and validity of such an assignment.[144]

Nevertheless, since such an assignment is expressly provided for under the Ordinance, it raises two related questions in the context of variation and rescission. First, whether it would be the action (assent or reliance)[145] of the third party *or* the *assignee* that would bring an end to the contracting parties' right to vary or rescind the contract (without the consent of the third party).[146] Second, whether, where the contracting parties have expressly reserved their right to vary or rescind the contract, they should bring such an express term to the attention of the third party *or the assignee*.[147] According to the Law Reform Commission, the 'natural and logical' answer to these two questions depends on whether the contracting parties have been notified of the assignment: if they have, then the answer to both of the above questions would be the assignee.[148]

2. Does the Ordinance have the Potential to Confer a Burden on a Third Party?

A potentially problematic provision under the Ordinance is section 12 which deals with arbitration agreements. The problem with this provision concerns the interplay between

[137] s 14.

[138] Law Commission, *Privity of Contract: Contracts for the Benefit of Third Parties* (Law Com No 242, 1996) ('ELC Report') para 14.6.

[139] ibid para 14.6 and LRC Report (n 5) para 4.188.

[140] ibid para 14.7. Note that the current law allowing for contracting parties to assign contractual rights was put forth by the Hong Kong Federation of Insurers as an argument for not needing to reform the privity doctrine, ie contracting parties could simply *assign* contractual rights to third parties (eg under a life insurance policy). However, the LRC pointed out that the reform would: (1) avoid the need for a promisee and third party to enter into a separate contract of assignment; as well as (2) enable the promisor to ascertain the identity of the third party before deciding whether to confer a benefit on it, unlike with an assignment which does not require the assent of the promisor (LRC Report (n 5) para 2.31).

[141] s 14(1). [142] s 14(2)(a). [143] s 14(2)(b).

[144] Letter from the Hong Kong Federation of Insurers to the Bills Committee on Contracts (Rights of Third Parties) Bill (7 May 2014) <http://www.legco.gov.hk/yr13-14/english/bc/bc102/papers/bc1020507cb4-644-1-e.pdf> accessed 30 November 2016.

[145] s 6(2)(a) and (b). cf 1999 UK Act, s 2(1)(a)–(c). [146] s 6(1) and (2). cf 1999 UK Act, s 2(1).

[147] s 6(3) and (4). Note that although s 6(3) of the Ordinance is the equivalent of s 2(3) of the 1999 UK Act, there is no equivalent of s 6(4) of the Ordinance in the 1999 UK Act. In this regard, the Ordinance provides greater protection for the third party since, in order for the contracting parties to expressly 'contract out' of the need for the third party's consent to vary or rescind the contract, they must show that they brought this express term to the third party's attention (or took reasonable steps to) *before* the third party assented to or relied on the term conferring the benefit.

[148] LRC Report (n 5) para 4.189.

exemption clauses and third parties.[149] In other words, how a third party can realize a negative right which has been conferred on it but which has been made subject to an arbitration agreement for its enforcement. This problem has been highlighted, most recently, in the 2013 English Court of Appeal case of *Fortress v Blue Skye*[150] which involved section 8(1) of the 1999 UK Act (which deals with arbitration agreements and is substantively identical to section 12(1) and (2) of the Ordinance) and section 9 of the UK Arbitration Act 1996 (which deals with stay of legal proceedings and is substantially similar to section 20 of Hong Kong's Arbitration Ordinance (Cap 609)).

Essentially, section 9 of the Arbitration Act 1996 provides that, where the parties have included an arbitration clause in their contract (ie where they have agreed to submit any disputes—relating to the contract—to arbitration), one party can obtain a stay of any court proceedings brought by the other party. Section 8(1) of the 1999 UK Act provides that, where a contractual term confers a benefit (a substantive benefit, including an exemption clause) on a third party and the enforcement of that benefit is subject to an arbitration agreement,[151] then the third party will be treated as a party to that arbitration agreement for the purposes of any dispute between the promisor and the third party which relates to the enforcement of that benefit. This 'conditional' substantive benefit results in the third party having both the procedural *benefit* of being entitled to enforce the substantive benefit by way of arbitration (as opposed to choosing not to enforce it at all) but also the procedural *condition* of being bound to enforce its substantive benefit by way of arbitration (if it does so choose to enforce it).

The facts in *Fortress v Blue Skye* illustrate the potential problem with including a provision on arbitration agreements in third party rights legislation. The claimant (Fortress) was the assignee of one of four limited partners of an investment structure (called the Blue Skye Fund) which was regulated by a deed of limited partnership ('DLP'). The claimant brought court proceedings against the three other partners and the managers of the Blue Skye Fund, based in tort, alleging conspiracy, unlawful interference, procuring breach of the DLP, and dishonest assistance—essentially, that they had been operating a dishonest scheme as to the way the Blue Skye Fund was run, to the detriment of the partner which had assigned its interest to Fortress (the claimant). Since the DLP contained an arbitration clause (which covered any claims 'arising out of or in connection with' the DLP or its 'breach'), the other partners (who were being sued by the claimant) were able to obtain a stay of the court proceedings, pursuant to section 9 of the Arbitration Act 1996. However, the managers of the Blue Skye Fund (who, being responsible for the day-to-day running of the fund, were also being sued by the claimant) were not able to rely on the arbitration clause in order to obtain a stay of the court action because they were not privy to the DLP contract (which contained that clause). Therefore, the managers (as defendants) appealed against this first instance refusal to stay the claimant's court action against them.

The defendant managers argued that their ability to rely on an exclusion clause contained in the DLP (the benefit to which they were undisputedly entitled) was subject to the arbitration agreement (also contained in the DLP) and, as such, that the claimant could only bring proceedings against them in arbitration. In other words, they argued that *all* the terms of the DLP were subject to the arbitration agreement, including the term excluding the liability of the

[149] L Mason, 'Legislating for Third Party Contractual Rights: Two Potentially Problematic Provisions' (Obligations VII conference: Divergence and Convergence, The University of Hong Kong, 18 July 2014).

[150] *Fortress Value Recovery Fund I LLC & Ors v Blue Skye Special Opportunities Fund LP & Ors* [2013] EWCA Civ 367.

[151] 1999 UK Act, s 1(4), and the Ordinance, s 4(4), allows for the placing of *conditions* on conferred third party rights.

defendant managers. Since this dispute (the tort action) concerned the availability of the exclusion clause as a defence,[152] the defendant managers were to be treated as parties to the arbitration agreement (in accordance with section 8(1) of the 1999 UK Act) and so could not enforce their right to rely on the exclusion clause *if* the claimant pursued court proceedings; rather, the defendant managers argued, they could only enforce their substantive benefit (the exclusion clause) by way of arbitration—and, as such, they argued that they were entitled to a stay of the court proceedings (so that the matter could be dealt with through arbitration).

The English Court of Appeal considered that if a promisor chooses to bring a court action against a third party (to which the third party claims to have the ability to rely on an exclusion clause conferred on it as a defence), then the third party must be entitled to rely on that contractual right in its defence in those court proceedings. According to the Court of Appeal, it would be nonsense (and contrary to the purpose of section 8(1) of the 1999 UK Act) to interpret section 8(1) as preventing the third party from being entitled to rely on that contractual defence in a situation where the promisor had chosen to sue the third party in court. Indeed, the Court of Appeal thought that if the third party could only rely on that contractual defence through arbitration, it would run contrary to the principle that arbitration is a consensual process because the third party (who had not initiated the proceedings) would have the burden of having no choice but to submit to arbitration in order to invoke its exclusion clause defence. If this were so, the Court of Appeal thought, it would make for a 'striking outcome'.[153] According to Tomlinson LJ:

> It is . . . to impute to the parties a really *very far reaching* intention if it is to be inferred that they positively intended to bring about the result that third parties would be bound by the outcome of arbitration proceedings which they had not themselves initiated in order to secure a benefit apparently conferred upon them by the Agreement.[154]

However, it would be different if the third party was the one initiating the proceedings (to enforce a positive right, such as an indemnity conferred on it) because it would be doing no more than realizing the conditional benefit—that is, that it can enforce the benefit against the promisor but *only* on the condition that it uses arbitration to do so. Either way, the third party has a choice whether to arbitrate.

As such, even though the third party defendant managers in the *Fortress* case *wanted* to arbitrate, section 8(1) could not be interpreted so as to *require* them to arbitrate in order to invoke the exclusion clause defence. Indeed, the court recognized the irony because, since the defendants were not bound by the arbitration agreement, it meant that they could not compel the claimant to pursue its claim in arbitration—which was what the defendants actually wanted. Nevertheless, the court maintained that section 8(1) could not be interpreted so as to require the third party to arbitrate in order to realize the protection of an exclusion clause otherwise the 1999 UK Act would be conferring a *burden* on third parties and it would increase the prospect of fragmented dispute resolution (insofar as once the arbitral tribunal has decided that the defendant managers cannot rely on the exclusion clause, then the claimant can go to court to sue over other disputes, outside the arbitrator's jurisdiction). Alternatively, if section 8(1) did not allow for the claimant to go to court, later (ie did not allow fragmented dispute resolution), then the entirety of the dispute could only be dealt with through arbitration, even though: (1) the third party had never agreed to arbitrate (therefore making such arbitration *non-consensual*); and (2) there were aspects about the dispute which were not connected to the question of whether the third party could rely

[152] ie whether they were *grossly* negligent or reckless.

[153] *Fortress v Blue Skye* (n 150) [29].

[154] ibid [36] (emphasis added).

on the exclusion clause. This, as noted by the Court of Appeal, would make for a 'very odd and unprincipled outcome'.[155]

Either way, it has been argued[156] that this conclusion was based purely on the court's interpretation of the contractual clause in question: meaning, therefore, that it is still possible that, by the use of 'very clear language',[157] a promisor can draft a clause in such a way as to result in a burden being conferred on a third party, insofar as the third party being forced to arbitrate in particular situations with regard to realizing its negative right—that is an exclusion from liability.

Therefore, the inclusion of the provision on arbitration agreements in the Ordinance creates the potential problem of a third party having the burden of being forced to arbitrate in order to defend itself through use of its right to rely on an exclusion clause. Such a binding of the third party to arbitrate not only confers a burden on it (therefore contradicting the central philosophy of the legislative reform) but also runs contrary to the principle of arbitration as a *consensual* process (since the third party had never agreed to be bound by the arbitration agreement and therefore submit to arbitration).

In fact, this was the initial concern of the English Law Commission where, in its 1996 Report on third party contract rights,[158] the Commission actually opposed the introduction of a provision dealing with third party rights in the context of arbitration agreements. However, during the UK parliamentary debate on the bill, the Law Commission appeared to resile from its earlier position and so the provision eventually made its way into the 1999 UK Act. Nevertheless, as Tomlinson LJ noted in the *Fortress* case, 'this case demonstrates that the [Law] Commission's fears were not unfounded'.[159]

This, however, has not deterred the drafters of the Ordinance from including the arbitration agreement provision in the legislation and, despite the potential problems having been drawn to their attention,[160] they have seemingly sidestepped these issues raised in deputation before the Bills Committee.[161] This has prompted the criticism that the drafters of the Ordinance have taken a 'rigid adherence' approach to the 2005 recommendations of the Law Reform Commission which, themselves are, to some extent, a 'copy and paste' of the English Law Commission's 1996 recommendations.[162]

V. Conclusion

Despite the resumption of sovereignty over Hong Kong by the People's Republic of China on 1 July 1997, Hong Kong remains a common law jurisdiction as it was under the colonial rule of the UK.[163] It is no surprise, therefore, that statutory developments in the UK continue to shape the law reform agenda in Hong Kong, such as with regard to legislation of third party rights. Indeed, not only is the Ordinance substantially similar to the 1999 UK

[155] ibid [30]. [156] L Mason, 'Legislating for Third Party Contractual Rights' (n 149).

[157] *Fortress v Blue Skye* (n 150) [36]. [158] ELC Report (n 138) para 14.15.

[159] *Fortress v Blue Skye* (n 150) [1]. Note that the facts in the *Fortress* case are a little peculiar since it would normally be the promisor seeking a stay of court proceedings brought by a third party which is trying to enforce the benefit that has been conferred on it. However, in this case, the promisor sued the third party (in tort) and so it was the third party who sought a stay of court proceedings (the third party managers wanting the arbitral tribunal to determine whether they could rely on the exclusion clause, ie to determine whether they were grossly negligent or reckless).

[160] L Mason, 'Comments on the Bill' (n 97). [161] Administration's Responses (n 97).

[162] L Mason, 'Legislating for Third Party Contractual Rights' (n 149).

[163] 1842–1941 and 1945–97. Such continuance of the common law is safeguarded—at least until 2047—under the Hong Kong Basic Law, Arts 5, 8, 18, and 84. (The Basic Law is officially entitled 'The Basic Law of the Hong Kong Special Administrative Region of the People's Republic of China' and is, essentially, regarded as Hong Kong's constitution.)

Act but the 2005 Law Reform Commission Report is, in essence, the same as the 1996 English Law Commission Report. Even before the Ordinance came into operation (and, even still, where the Ordinance does not apply), the Hong Kong Court of Appeal has made clear that the law on privity in Hong Kong remains as that stated by the UK House of Lords in *Dunlop Pneumatic Tyre Co Ltd v Selfridge and Co Ltd.*[164] As such, there does not appear to be anything discernibly Chinese (or Asian) about the values and policies underlying the current law on third party rights.[165] Indeed, one of the arguments in favour of legislative reform cited by the Law Reform Commission was the fact that the doctrine of privity had been reformed elsewhere, including the UK.[166] In fact, it is probably safe to speculate that future Hong Kong judicial interpretations of specific provisions of the Ordinance, with regard to legal scenarios not yet tested in the Hong Kong courts, will be influenced largely by English judicial interpretations of the equivalent provisions in the 1999 UK Act, as has been the general trend within the realm of contract law both before and after China's resumption of sovereignty.[167]

[164] See nn 14 and 17.

[165] Indeed, perhaps the only specifically 'Hong Kong' aspect of the Ordinance is in relation to covenants of land falling outside the scope of the Ordinance (s 3(2)(b) and (c)). However, as noted in section IV.1, this is simply a response to the unique land law of Hong Kong, particularly relating to issues of ownership in multi-storey buildings.

[166] See n 34.

[167] Certainly, English case law has always been, and continues to be, highly persuasive in Hong Kong, not least due to the historical ties (albeit it was never binding). Indeed, although the Hong Kong Basic Law allows the Hong Kong courts to refer to precedents 'of other common law jurisdictions' (Art 84), former Chief Justice Andrew Li has stated, judicially, that post-1997 UK Privy Council decisions (on appeal from any jurisdiction) and decisions of the UK Supreme Court (formerly House of Lords) will be 'treated with great respect' (*Solicitor (24/07) v Law Society of Hong Kong* (2008) 11 HKCFAR 117 (CFA) [17]).

12

Formation of Contract in Japan

*Yoshikazu YAMASHITA**

I. Introduction

In 1853, Japan started moving away from its seventeenth-century isolationist policy, and the feudal society ruled by the samurai came to an end with the advent of a new government in 1868, modelled on the West. Under the pressure of Western imperialism and colonialism, the new government embarked on the construction of a Western-style legal system and adapted its infrastructure to enable Japan, as a Far Eastern country, to operate as an equal trading partner with the West. The Japanese Government sent its young lawyers to Europe to study the Western legal systems, and asked a French law professor, Gustave Émile Boissonade, to draft a civil code based on the European model.

The civil code drafted by Boissonade was based on the French Civil Code but was modified with his own ideas. However, some Japanese lawyers were not satisfied with the resulting bill, and called for a proper Japanese civil code drafted by the Japanese themselves. After lengthy debate, the bill was fundamentally changed, and three young legal academics (Kenjiro Ume, Masa-akira Tomii, and Nobushige Hozumi) were chosen upon their return from Europe to draft a new civil code.

The three ambitious young lawyers had studied as many European civil codes as they could, alongside the common law of England. Fortunately, a new German Civil Code was being drafted just at that time. The newest draft produced by Friedrich Carl von Savigny, based on the theory of will (the theory of the declaration of intent), was so sophisticated that it seemed to the Japanese lawyers easy to understand and sensible. They accordingly decided to follow German legal thinking and codified the systematic rules in the *Pandekten* order, as the German Civil Code did, even though they chose each rule individually, picking those most suited to Japanese society, custom, and morals.

As a result, the Japanese civil law codified in 1898 defines contract as a juristic act (*Rechtsgeschäft* in German) that can be legally enforced because of the declaration of intent (*Willenserklärung*) by the contracting party. Because the Japanese Civil Code introduced the will theory, according to which the declaration of intent is enough to enforce the contract in its purest form, it makes no distinction between a gratuitous contract and an onerous contract, although some formal requirements remain, as we will see in section V.

The emphasis on reliance on the declaration of intent is likewise one of the foundations of the Japanese Civil Code. The aim of protecting that reliance has been reinforced by case law, since it was in harmony with Japanese business practice. The notion of good faith and a flexible law of torts also support that tendency, as we will see in section IV.

A salient feature of the traditional Japanese law on contract formation is the combination of two fundamental principles—the will theory and the protection of reliance; the balance of which will be slightly changed in the ongoing reformation of the code.

* Cite as Y Yamashita, 'Formation of Contract in Japan' in Chen-Wishart, Loke & Vogenauer, *Studies in the Contract Laws of Asia Vol II: Formation and Third Party Beneficiaries* (Oxford: OUP 2017) ch 12.

Formation of Contract in Japan. Yoshikazu Yamashita.

II. Principles of Contract Formation

1. Rejection of Formalism

The Japanese Civil Code contains no provision on the general principle of contract formation. The requirements for the formation of typical contracts are set out in the first provision of each chapter on typical contracts. Generally speaking, because of the influence of the will theory in Japanese law, the requirement for the formation of a contract is basically the agreement of two declarations of intent (offer and acceptance). In theory, an oral agreement is enough to create an enforceable contract.

Exceptionally, for very few types of contract (eg a loan or bailment (deposit)) the actual transfer of the money or property is required for the formation of a contract, according to the Civil Code,[1] simply because the drafters were loath to change the Roman law tradition. However, later lawyers unanimously condemned this as a shortcoming, insisting that a loan agreement should be enforceable even prior to the transfer of the loan, if the contracting parties so agree. The Japanese Supreme Court relaxed the formalism for loan contracts as early as 1913.[2]

After lengthy discussions, the recent reform of the Civil Code has just been concluded. Chapter 13 of volume book contains some more information on the process. As a result of the reform, the requirement to transfer property for the conclusion of contracts of bailment has been abandoned. At the same time, no change has been made to the requirement of transfer of money for the conclusion of loan contracts in order to prevent debtors, mainly consumer debtors, from carelessly agreeing on harsh or unnecessary loan conditions. Given that the reason for the requirement of the transfer is to ensure that the intent of the debtor is confirmed, it can thus be substituted by other formalities. The new code which is enacted in 2018 stipulates that the loan contract may be concluded before the transfer if the contract is made in writing (Article 587-2).[3]

2. Reliance on the Expression of Intent

If the agreement of two declarations of intent is the only requirement for contract formation, the problem then arises of how to judge that agreement. In Japan, the question is whether an agreement requires two external declarations to coincide, or whether the intention may be internal.

[1] Translations of articles of the Japanese Civil Code in this chapter are taken from the homepage of the Ministry of Justice, <http://www.moj.go.jp/content/000056024.pdf> accessed 2 February 2017. However, a major amendment of the Civil Code was enacted on 2 June 2018 and will be brought into force within three years. The new rules on formation of contracts are very different from the old ones in some respects; especially, the rules on distance communication have changed considerably, and some provisions mentioned in this chapter were deleted. The reasons for this particular aspect of the reform are explained in section III of this chapter.

> Art 587 (Loans for Consumption):
>
> A loan for consumption shall become effective when one of the parties receives money or other things from the other party by promising that he/she will return by means of things that are the same in kind, quality and quantity.
>
> Art 657 (Deposit):
>
> A deposit shall become effective when one of the parties receives a certain thing by promising that he/she will retain it for the other party.

[2] 大判大正2年5月8日民録19輯312頁 (Fomer Supreme Court, Judgment, 8 May Taisyo 2 (1913), Civil Reports, Vol 19, p 312). The system of the Supreme Court in Japan was fully changed after the Second World War, but its decisions are sometimes still referred to as an authority, especially in contract law.

[3] New Art 587–2 (author's translation):

> Notwithstanding the previous provision (Article 587), the loan contract in writing shall become effective when one of the parties promises to transfer the money or other things to the other party and the latter promises that he/she will return by means of things that are the same in kind, quality, and quantity.

In a case in the mid-twentieth century, the applicant sold a licence for the production of silk (this was during the Second World War) to the defendant. The price of the licence was 10,290 yen. However, the defendant thought he had to pay only 8,290 yen, as he had already paid 2,000 yen to the association of silk producers which he believed to be included in the transaction. However, the applicant insisted the defendant pay 10,290 yen, claiming that the 2,000 yen already disbursed did not form part of the price, although he refunded the same amount from the association. The Supreme Court held that there was no agreement, hence no contract, if the two internal intentions of the contract parties could not be made to coincide.[4]

However, a majority of lawyers criticized this judgment, arguing that the contract was concluded in the case at issue, since two declarations of intent matched, but that there was the possibility of invalidity of the contract due to mistake. According to Article 95 on mistake, the declaration of intent is invalid in the event of mistake in respect of an important element of the contract where there is no serious fault on the part of the mistaken party.[5] Hence, most Japanese lawyers believe that the contract was validly made even though there was only superficial, or at least objective, agreement of the declarations of intent, with one party carelessly expressing its intention to contract and the other depending or relying on that declaration.

3. Subjective or Objective?

Although constantly disputed among academic lawyers today, the rules of contract formation in Japan may be summarized as follows.

(1) If an offer meets with both internal (at the level of intention) and external (at the level of manifestation) acceptance, the contract is concluded. There are no further formal requirements. Writing is important only because the written form could later be adduced in evidence of the coincidence of the declarations of intent.

(2) If the internal intention of the offeror does not meet that of the offeree, but the two declarations of intent coincide, uncertainty arises as to whether there is a contract or not. However, if one of the parties carelessly expressed a mistaken intention and the other party relied on it, the contract is concluded and is fully enforceable.

(3) When two internal intentions are in accord but the declarations of intent seem to be different, uncertainty again arises. From the point of view of the will theory, there is no reason to deny the contract formation. However, since the accordance of internal intentions is not so apparent, the practising lawyer might hesitate to recognize the agreement.

These uncertainties notwithstanding, Japanese courts appear to make little effort to deal with problems of contract formation. One reason seems to be that the rule on negotiating in good faith can fill the gap to decide between conclusion and non-conclusion of a contract, as we will see later.

[4] 大判昭和19年6月28日民集23巻387頁 (Former Supreme Court, Judgment, 28 June Syowa 19 (1944), Civil Reports, Vol 23, p 387).

[5] Old Art 95 (Mistake):

> Manifestation of intention has no effect when there is a mistake in any element of the juristic act in question; provided, however, that the person who made the manifestation of intention may not assert such nullity by himself/herself if he/she was grossly negligent.

This provision has been rewritten entirely in the recent reform, but the substance of the rule on mistake is unchanged.

III. Distance Communications

1. Binding Offer and Speedy Formation

Until 2018 the Japanese Civil Code had no general provision on contract formation,[6] it only had provisions on contract formation by distance communication. Under the recent reforms, the rules on distance communication were completely revised but the new provisions are not in force yet. I will mostly explain the old rule and the problems arising under it, and then the new rule.

According to Article 523 of the Civil Code, an offer that specifies a period for acceptance is irrevocable, although the offer is without effect if the offeror does not receive notice of acceptance within that period.[7] However, the offeror had a duty to inform the offeree of the late arrival of the notice of acceptance if, in normal circumstances, the notice could have arrived within the period set, so that the offeree would assume the contract to be concluded. If the offeror neglected this duty, the notice of acceptance was deemed to have arrived within the period set, such that the contract was concluded (old Article 522).[8] Alternatively, the offeror was entitled to deem the delayed acceptance to constitute a new offer (old Article 523).[9]

On the other hand, an offer that does not specify a period for acceptance may not be revoked until a reasonable time for the offeror to receive a notice of acceptance has lapsed (old Article 524).[10] Additionally, according to old Article 526(1), a contract between persons at a distance was formed at the time when the notice of acceptance was dispatched. This was an exception to the general principle of the declaration of intent, because Article 97(1) provided that the effect of the declaration of intent was triggered when the notice of

[6] In 2018, a new general rule on contract formation will be adopted. New Art 522 (author's translation):

(1) A contract is made if one party manifests the intention to make a contract showing the contents of it and the other party accepts.

[7] Art 523 (Offers that Specify Period for Acceptance):

(1) An offer which specifies a period for acceptance may not be revoked. [However, the offeror retains the right to revoke.]
(2) If an offeror does not receive notice of acceptance of the offer set forth in the preceding paragraph within the period referred to in the same paragraph, the offer shall cease to be effective.

This article largely corresponds to old Art 521; the sentence in brackets was added.

[8] Art 522 (Late Arrival of Notice of Acceptance):

(1) Even in cases where the notice of acceptance of the offer under Paragraph 1 of the preceding Article arrives after the lapse of the period referred to in the same paragraph, if the offeror is in a position to know that the notice was dispatched at a time which, under normal circumstances, would have allowed the notice to arrive within that period, the offeror must dispatch a notice of late arrival to the other party without delay; provided, however, that this shall not apply when the offeror dispatches the notice of delay before the arrival of the notice of acceptance.
(2) When the offeror fails to give the notice of late arrival referred to in the main clause of the preceding paragraph, the notice of acceptance shall be deemed to have arrived within the period referred to in Paragraph 1 of the preceding Article.

This article was deleted in 2018 in the recent reform of the Civil Code (see section III.3).

[9] This article is moved to new Art 524.

[10] Old Art 524 (Offers that do not Specify Period for Acceptance):

An offer made to a person at a distance without specifying a period for acceptance may not be revoked until the lapse of a reasonable period for the offeror to receive a notice of acceptance.

This article was moved to Art 525(1) in the recent reform of the Civil Code and specific rules on verbal communication were added.

New Art 525:

(2) Nevertheless, an offer to the interlocutor may be revoked while the negotiation is being continued.
(3) An offer to the interlocutor ceases to be effective if the offeror does not receive the acceptance while the negotiation is being continued, unless the offeror declares otherwise.

the declaration reached the other distant party.[11] The drafters argued that a special rule was needed for the formation of a contract because the rule permitting the offeror to revoke the offer after the offeree has dispatched the notice of acceptance might cause unexpected loss on the part of the offeree.[12]

Even after the lapse of a reasonable time, the offer remains effective unless it is revoked. If the offeror's notification of revocation of the offer does not reach the offeree before the latter has dispatched its notification of acceptance, the contract is effectively formed. An exception was found in old Article 527, which provided that in the event of late arrival of the notice of revocation, the offeree should inform the offeror that the revocation was unsuccessful. If it does not do so, the offeror was deemed to have revoked the declaration successfully.[13]

2. Too Strict a Rule for the Offeror?

The old rule that acceptance made the contract as soon as the notice of acceptance was dispatched meant that the offeree bore none of the risk of delay or loss of communication. Even in cases where the offeror was entitled to specify the period for receipt of acceptance (old Article 521) and where the notice of acceptance accidentally arrived after that period had lapsed, the offeror had to give notice of late acceptance to the offeree without delay; otherwise the contract was deemed to be concluded.

In brief, Japanese law protected the reliance of the offeree on the formation of the contract. The old rules could be understood as meaning that the offeror's declaration of intent was binding as soon as the offeree placed reliance on it.

However, these old rules on offer and acceptance were perhaps too strict from the offeror's point of view. One Japanese professor maintained that it was unfairly advantageous for the offeree to be given a choice as to whether to accept the offer or not without bearing any of the risk of miscommunication, whereas the offeror had no alternative to revoke its offer.[14] He pointed out that the binding offer rule was similar to German law and the rule on the timing of contract formation was in keeping with the common law, but that the combination of these two rules was unusual from a comparative standpoint.

3. New Rules

In addition to the imbalance between offeror and offeree, it was often asserted that new methods of communication lower the risk of miscommunication, and that the interval of

[11] Art 97 (Manifestation of Intention to Person at a Distance):

(1) Manifestation of intention to a person at a distance shall become effective at the time of the arrival of the notice to the other party.

[12] 梅謙次郎『民法要義　巻之三　債権編』(有斐閣) (Ume Kenjiro, *The Essence of Civil Code 3 (Law of Obligations)* (Tokyo: Yuhikaku 1901)) 382–386.

[13] Art 527 (Late Arrival of Notice of Revocation of Offer):

(1) Even if a notice to revoke an offer arrives after the dispatch of the acceptance notice, if the offeree is in a position to know that the notice was dispatched at a time which, under normal circumstances would have allowed the notice to arrive before the dispatch of the acceptance notice, the offeree must dispatch a notice of the late arrival to the offeror without delay.
(2) If the offeree fails to give the notice of late arrival referred to in the preceding paragraph, it shall be deemed that no contract was formed.

This article was deleted in the recent reform of the Civil Code (see section III.3).

[14] 能見善久=四宮和夫、"民法総則" (第8版、2010年　弘文堂) (Nomi Yoshihisa and Shinomiya Kazuo, *General Provisions of the Civil Code* (8th edn, Tokyo: Kobundo 2010)) 254–256.

communication is so short that the merit of speedy formation of contracts seems less relevant.

For all these reasons, the traditional Japanese rules, especially those dealing with the timing of contract formation, were changed. Some of the changes were made by means of a special Act in 2001, and the imminent amendment of the Civil Code will change the face of this body of rules entirely.

The special Act of 2001 concerns acceptance of an offer by electronic means.[15] The Act covers acceptance by the use of computer, facsimile, telex, or telephone. If the offeree uses such devices for its notice of acceptance, the contract is formed when the notice of acceptance reaches the offeror.

At last, the Civil Code itself was changed in 2018. The old provisions stating that the contract is concluded as soon as the notice of acceptance is dispatched were deleted. As a result, the general principle with regard to declarations of intent applies to the timing of formation of contract which means that the acceptance takes effect and the contract is formed when the declaration reaches the offeror.

IV. Good Faith in Contract Formation

1. Negotiation in Good Faith

The principle of good faith was introduced into the Japanese Civil Code in 1947, but was already well documented in the case law and scholarly writings. The current provision of the Civil Code provides that the exercise of rights and the performance of duties must be carried out in good faith,[16] such that the principle of good faith seems to be applied only to the 'exercise of rights' or the 'performance of duties'. However, good faith is now regarded as a fundamental principle across the spectrum of the law, especially in contract law. In a case in 1984, the Japanese Supreme Court suggested that the principle of good faith should also be applied in contractual negotiations.[17]

The case at issue concerned the sale of an apartment. The applicant planned to build and sell apartments. The defendant, a dentist, was interested in buying one of these for use as a dental clinic. The defendant began negotiations with the applicant, indicating however that he would only buy the apartment if the electrical capacity was sufficient for his medical tools. The applicant, in the expectation of selling the apartment, changed the building plans to increase the electrical capacity. However, the defendant had already decided not to buy the apartment while the applicant was still in the process of changing the building plans, but never notified the applicant of his decision. The applicant sued the defendant, asserting that a contract of sale had already been concluded.

The Supreme Court upheld the judgment of the High Court which denied that a contract had been concluded but nevertheless ordered the defendant to pay to the applicant the cost of changing the building plans. The Supreme Court held that the defendant had breached the duty of care in contract negotiations grounded in the principle of good faith. This case is regarded as the leading case in respect of the failure of a contracting party to negotiate in good faith, thereby causing damage due to the other party's reliance on the contract.

[15] The Act regarding the Special Provision of the Civil Code on Electronic Consumer Contract and the Notice of Acceptance by Telecommunication.

[16] Art 1(2).

[17] 最判昭和59年9月18日判例時報142号311頁 (Supreme Court, Judgment, 18 September Syowa 59 (1984), Law Cases Reports, Vol 142, p 311).

2. Duty of Disclosure

The other cases that discuss the principle of good faith in negotiations concern the duty of disclosure. For example, in transactions involving consumers and a professional party or other contracting party in a special position of trust, the latter often has a duty to disclose important information related to the contract to the other party. This duty derives from the principle of good faith in negotiations.

In Japan, there are many cases dealing with the duty of disclosure in transactions involving financial products. It is generally held that a retail distributor of financial products has a duty to disclose grave risks attached to such products. Before the Retail of Financial Products Act 2000 imposed a duty of disclosure on the retailer, Japanese courts had already introduced such a duty on the basis of good faith, holding the retailer liable in breach of the duty to pay damages in tort.

Another example concerns franchise marketing. A franchiser has more information than the franchisee as to the prospects of a business. If the franchiser invites a layperson into the franchise business but does not disclose the prospects of that business, the franchiser is liable in tort.

In these cases, the courts use tort liability as the measure to sanction violation of the duty. A precondition of such intervention is the flexibility of tort liability. Because of the simplicity of the wording of the Japanese Civil Code provision,[18] tort liability may be applied in cases of economic loss arising from another's breach of duty in contractual negotiations.[19] The damages allowed in such cases usually involve the payment of financial products (money), so the restitution of reliance damages in contractual matters is settled by torts.

3. The Battle of Forms in the Japanese Context

(a) Relation between contract formation and the duty of good faith

Because of the duty to negotiate a contract in good faith and the flexible torts provision, in Japan a contracting party is liable to compensate the damage of another party who relies on the negotiation even before the contract is formed. This seems to be why there are not many disputes relating to the timing of contract formation, the so-called 'battle of forms'.

According to Article 528, a contract cannot be formed if the acceptance does not coincide perfectly with the offer.[20] The so-called mirror image rule is applied in the Japanese Civil Code. However, it is usual in Japan for a contracting party to start performing the contract before the final contract documents are exchanged. In these circumstances, opinion is that the contract might be concluded by the implicit manifestation of intention of acceptance on the side of performer but the contents of the contract are interpreted only when the last form is sent by the other side. An academic explains that Article 528 is the provision providing for the case where the contracting parties investigate all conditions of the contract and finally agree; in other words, there is a lack of specific provision to manage

[18] Art 709 (Damages in Torts):

> A person who has intentionally or negligently infringed any right of others, or legally protected interest of others, shall be liable to compensate any damages resulting in consequence.

[19] Academics have discussed the nature of pre-contractual liability for many years (see H Kihara, *Tort Law in Japan* (The Hague/Boston: Kluwer Law International 2015) 26–27), but the courts tend to classify it as tortious liability caused by the breach of duties arising from good faith.

[20] Art 528 (Acceptances which Modify the Offer):

> If the offeree has accepted the offer by adding any condition or by making any other modification, it shall be deemed that the offeree has refused the offer and has made a new offer.

the situation of battle of forms, so the contents of the contract should comply with the custom, default rules, and principle of good faith.[21]

A Supreme Court case in 2007 concerned contractual negotiations between a slot machine developer (the defendant) and a slot machine manufacturer (the applicant).[22] A slot machine distributor approached the defendant to develop a new machine and the latter approached the applicant to manufacture it. The applicant and defendant exchanged several written documents on the contractual terms, but no final contract was made. The applicant began production, but the distributor pulled out and the negotiations between the applicant and the defendant were broken off.

The Supreme Court held that although the contract between the applicant and the defendant had not yet been concluded, the defendant had breached its duty of care to negotiate in good faith, since its conduct throughout the negotiations was such as to create an excessive expectation on the part of the applicant that the contract would be concluded. The court ordered the defendant to pay damages.

It is a fact that Japanese courts rarely recognize the formation of a contract before the final contract papers are exchanged between the two parties. Rather, it prefers to order payment of damages for breach of the duty of good faith in negotiating the contract. This tallies with Japanese business practice. Even before a final agreement on the contract is reached, a contracting party incurs costs to meet the requirements of the other party; such outlay places the business relationship on a more solid footing and lays the foundations for a long-term trade relationship. Japanese case law is in line with that custom in that it protects the reliance of the negotiating parties.

(b) Why the battle of forms is rare in Japan

The aforementioned case explains why the battle of forms is not a crucial issue in Japanese legal tradition. Even though the applicant and the defendant had exchanged several documents about the terms of the contract, the court was loath to recognize the final agreement establishing the contract. Instead, it applied the principle of good faith and resolved the dispute as one involving a breach of the duty to negotiate in good faith.

The battle of forms is widely discussed amongst Japanese scholars and in the standard legal textbooks. It would appear that an increasing number of Japanese companies are sensitive to the issue of ensuring that a contract is put into final form, especially when they are negotiating with an international company, where contractual interpretation might give rise to problems.

Even so, if we look at purely domestic transactions in Japan, the battle of forms rarely seems to occur. This may be explained in many ways. In a nutshell, however, the reason may simply be that the Japanese do not put a contract into its final form until the negotiations have been completed: no form, no battle.

(c) Do the Japanese dislike formal writings?

I do not mean to suggest that ordinary people dislike and avoid stipulating their rights and duties because they place importance on verbal communication or underestimate the

[21] 内田貴、"民法　2" （第3版、2011年、東京大学出版会） (Uchida Takashi, *Civil Code II* (3rd edn, Tokyo: Tokyo University Press 2011)) 33–34. He refers to § 2-207(3) of the US Uniform Commercial Code ('UCC').

[22] 最判平成19年2月27集民223号343頁 (Supreme Court, Judgment, 27 February Heisei 19 (2007), Civil Reports, no 223, p 343).

importance of written evidence. Certainly, socio-legal research sometimes points out that some types of contract, such as long-term contracts prevalent in *Keiretsu* relationships, do not generally involve making a contract in written form. However, even if that is the case, it does not explain the court's decision in the slot machine case, where the court denied that a contract had been concluded because, even though the details of the contract had been certified by both parties, the actual formal contract was not made until the day after the negotiations were completed. The court justified its denial of the existence of a contract on the ground that there was no final formal contract.

Most Japanese do make formal contracts, especially in high-value transactions such as those involving immovable property. This is probably much the same as in Western jurisdictions. In such situations, the Japanese prefer the traditional custom of formalism. When they conclude a contract, they prepare the form of the contract, sign it, and stamp a seal on it. These stamps are regarded as the most important identification tools for the Japanese; everyone has their own stamp and those involved in high-value transactions usually have an original stamp made and registered with the official registry system in order to combat forgery.

(d) Final forms are not complete contracts

I use the phrase 'the Japanese do not put a contract into its final form until the negotiations have been completed' because the Japanese often draft the formal contract just before the conclusion of the contract. No formal contracts are drafted in the course of the negotiations; instead, Japanese contracting parties exchange several memoranda (覚書, *Oboegaki*), which are made for the purpose of certifying the rights and obligations of each party.

Such memoranda are different from draft formal contracts, because they are made for each individual contract term. Each memorandum employs one or several terms indicating that both parties agree on the topic they have just negotiated. As such, they are not drafts of the final formal contract because each contains just one fragment of the contractual agreement.

Furthermore, the agreements described in such memoranda are often not inserted into the formal contract. The contracting parties often write only the most standard or important terms of agreements into the formal contract. In other words, the memoranda exchanged before the day the contract is made are not reflected in the terms of the contract.

However, such memoranda do sometimes play an important role in court proceedings, especially in cases involving interpretation of a contract. Since the Japanese contracting parties will not be familiar with the full panoply of the terms of their agreement, the memoranda made in the course of negotiations should be considered as evidence of what both parties really intended when they signed and stamped the final contract forms. Each memorandum is usually signed and sealed by both parties, in order to certify the negotiation process.

These business practices explain the court's decision in the slot machine case that the contract was not concluded even though the applicant began manufacturing the machines after several documents had been exchanged between the parties and the framework of the contractual agreement had been fixed: the documents exchanged between the contracting parties are not drafts of the formal contract, but mere memoranda. These business practices also explain why the battle of forms is rare in Japan: there is no incentive to set the terms of the contract 'in concrete'. To the Japanese, signing and sealing the final, formal contract only serves the purpose of ensuring that the small agreements cumulatively certified in many memoranda come into effect at the end of the negotiations.

V. Gratuitous Contract or Consumer Contract

1. Gift and Formalism

Because the enforceability of a contract is a matter depending on the intention and reliance of the contracting parties, there is no reason to deny the enforceability of gratuitous contracts. Even though a contract is gratuitous, if one contracting party intends to undertake the obligation, and the other party has the intention to receive (or rely on) the interest, this is sufficient reason to make the contract enforceable.

This can be seen in the following hypothetical scenario where building works are delayed: let us assume that X contracts for Y to refurbish 27 flats for £20,000, but Y runs into difficulties and X is concerned about having to pay a penalty under the head contract. He therefore promises to pay Y an extra £10,300 to complete the work on time. Here, Y can enforce the payment of the additional £10,300: even if a contract includes an additional undertaking of obligation, it is enforceable if there is an agreement. Of course, the contract might be invalid or voidable if Y's bad faith in the negotiation deformed X's intention (by fraud or duress), or Y might be liable in tort if its bad faith was excessive. For example, if Y intentionally stops work in order to increase the fee, X may revoke the contract for fraud or duress. However, this does not seem to be at issue here.

Overall, there is no theoretical reason to make a distinction between the effect of a gratuitous contract and that of an onerous contract. The drafters of the Japanese Civil Code held that the provisions on gifts should be placed in the chapter on contracts.[23]

However, a gift not in written form is revocable by the donor before its (partial or full) execution.[24] The drafters did consider whether a notarial deed should be a requirement of a gift contract, but the idea was abandoned because the notarial system was not popular in nineteenth-century Japan, and the requirement of writing was thought sufficient to prevent lack of seriousness on the part of donors, future difficulties, and instability of the contract.

As a result, the written form is not regarded as a prerequisite for the formation of a gift contract, merely as a step to confirm the intention of the donor and to strengthen the enforceability of the contract. Since it is regarded merely as confirmation, the courts do not require the formal contract to use the word 'gift'. Even a letter from the donor to the third party is enough to establish irrevocability if it proves the donor's serious intention.[25]

2. Gift and Intention

In addition to the requirement of writing, the enforceability of gifts is mitigated in case law. A famous case was *Café Marutama*,[26] where a man (the defendant) promised a female waitress (the applicant) in a coffee shop in Osaka a great deal of money to help her. After making the promise, the defendant made a novation from gift to loan (so the gift contract was executed and irrevocable). The applicant brought the suit, when the defendant refused to pay the money.

[23] Art 549 (Gifts):

Gifts shall become effective by the manifestation by one of the parties of his/her intention to give his/her property to the other party gratuitously, and the acceptance of the other party thereof.

[24] Art 550 (Revocation of Gift Not in Writing):

Gifts not in writing may be revoked by either party; provided, however, that this shall not apply to any portion of the gift for which performance has been completed.

[25] 最判昭和60年11月29日民集39巻7号1719頁 (Supreme Court, Judgment, 29 November Syowa 60 (1985), Civil Reports, Vol 39, no 7, p 1719).

[26] 大判昭和10年4月25日新聞3835号5頁 (Fomer Supreme Court, Judgment, 25 April Syowa 10 (1935), Law Paper, no 3835, p 5).

Although both the District Court and the High Court found for the applicant, the Supreme Court remanded the case. It suggested that the applicant had a right to keep the money if the defendant voluntarily executed the contract, but the obligation from such a contract was unenforceable. Today, this case is understood as an example of moral or natural obligation, or as a version of mental reservations. One possible explanation is that the defendant's intention to make a gift was not serious and that the applicant knew this, so it was felt that the reliance of the donee need not be protected.

Another example is that of a gift in a family setting. Gift is used here as an alternative to succession between family members, and old people often make a gift *inter vivos* to younger relatives of cohabitants, in return expecting the latter to care for them for the rest of their lives. If the care given by the donee is agreed to be the condition or burden of the gift, failure to provide care becomes a ground for cancelling the gift as a bilateral contract.[27] However, in some cases the donor does not clearly express their expectations. In such situations, the court often recognizes the implied condition or burden of the gift and finds for the donor, by cancelling the contract on the basis of the donee's betrayal or faithlessness.

To sum up, even though theoretically there is no distinction between gratuitous and onerous contracts, the court relaxes the enforceability of gifts in various contexts. The background of the donor's intention, or motive behind the gift, seems to be a consideration in such cases.

3. Other Gratuitous Contracts

We now turn to other gratuitous contracts. Of late, Japanese legal scholars seem to be taking the typology of contracts more serious than the purity or unity of contract theory. The distinction between gratuitous contracts and onerous contracts is also being re-evaluated from a practical point of view. One example is a contract of surety made by individuals.

Contracts of surety are used in many situations in Japan. The most popular incidence is, of course, the loan—the creditor usually requires a third party to secure repayment by the debtor—but this is by no means the only scenario. In an employment contract, an employer will often ask an employee's family to secure all damage caused by the employee. In real estate lease contracts, the lessor usually requires the lessee to find someone who guarantees the lessee's payment of rent. Usually, those who guarantee a debt are relatives or close friends; they undertake the obligation of surety based on kinship or friendship.

Although this custom goes back a long way in Japan, it seems to cause serious problems since the person who voluntarily undertakes the obligation of surety could be liable for an unexpectedly heavy debt. This is why the 2004 amendment of the Civil Code introduced the requirement of written form for the formation of surety contracts.[28] This formalism has now come back as a safeguard against rash intention and reckless reliance.

[27] Art 553 (Encumbered Gift):

With respect to gifts with burden, in addition to the provisions of this Section, the provisions regarding bilateral contracts apply mutatis mutandis, to the extent that these provisions are not inconsistent with the nature of gifts with burden mutatis mutandis.

[28] Art 446 (Responsibility of Guarantor):

(1) A guarantor shall have the responsibility to perform the obligation of the principal obligor when the latter fails to perform such obligation.
(2) No contract of guarantee shall be effective unless it is made in writing.
(3) If a contract of guarantee is concluded by electromagnetic record (meaning a record produced by electronic means, magnetic means, or any other means unrecognizable by natural sensory functions that is for computer data-processing use) which records the contents thereof, the contract of guarantee is deemed to be made in writing, and the provision of the preceding paragraph shall apply.

VI. Conclusion

The requirements of formalism are being reintroduced into Japanese law which once abandoned it because intention and reliance were thought to be sufficient reason to enforce a contract. However, in my view, this does not mean a move away from the Japanese legal tradition. Through a combination of the will theory and the reliance theory, Japanese law is changing the way in which it justifies the enforceability of contracts, in the context of negotiations. It seems to me that the formalism in surety contracts is a natural reaction in a situation where surety given by individuals is so embedded in the Japanese social context that the law cannot confirm their intention or reliance without a formal requirement.

Finally, combined with the flexibility of tort liability discussed earlier, formalism is now spreading across a specific area of contract law—consumer contracts. There are many administrative acts that require professionals to make a formal contract with consumers or clients. Although the primary sanctions of violations of the formality requirement are administrative, such as administrative dispositions or fines, the courts often regard such a violation as a sign of breach of the duty of disclosure that justifies compensatory damages to consumers. In other words, the lack of form does not cause the absence or invalidity of agreement in consumer contracts, but it is sanctioned not only administratively, but also privately. This is another example of the principle of good faith in negotiations.

13

Contracts for the Benefit of Third Parties in Japan

*Masami OKINO**

I. The History of the Japanese Civil Code

1. Making of the Japanese Civil Code

The establishment of a 'modern' (or Westernized) set of laws and a contemporary legal system, in particular, a judicial system, was a matter of crucial importance to the Japanese Government in the Meiji era (1868–1912), after the feudal system gave way to the Meiji restoration. The main reason for haste was the need to revise the treaties concluded on the eve of the Meiji restoration. These treaties gave extraterritorial jurisdiction to the countries of the West but deprived the Japanese Government of tariff autonomy. Another prime goal was the need to achieve unification and turn Japan into a single nation after the decline of the feudal system and to set in place policies that would give the country the wealth and military power that had been difficult to accomplish without a solid legal system.

In the early stages of the Meiji era, the government started work on a modern civil code. It first translated the Napoleonic Civil Code of 1804, inviting legal experts from France to assist in understanding Western law, drafting, and codification. Several attempts to draft the provisions of a civil code turned out to be unsuccessful, leaving various fragmental drafts; then at last the task of drafting the code was entrusted to a French scholar, Dr Gustave Émile Boissonade de Fontarabie, Professor at the University of Paris. Dr Boissonade drafted the Japanese Civil Code except for the part on family law, an area where tradition and custom are paramount. This part was drafted by Japanese drafters. The Japanese Civil Code was promulgated in 1890 and was supposed to take effect on 1 January 1893 (that Civil Code is referred to as the 'Old Civil Code' (*kyu-minpou*). However, vociferous objections and heated debate meant a bill had to be passed in 1892 to postpone enactment of the (Old) Civil Code until the necessary changes could be made. Three Japanese professors were appointed as drafters: Dr Nobushige Hozumi, Dr Masaakira Tomii, and Dr Kenjiro Ume.

As to structure, the Old Civil Code basically followed the French Civil Code (*Institutionen* system). By contrast, the so-called *Pandekten* system was adopted following the first draft of the German Civil Code (*Bürgerliches Gesetzbuch*, 'BGB'), more precisely the Civil Code of Saxony, which consisted of five books: General Principles, Rights *in rem*, Rights *in personam* (Claims/Obligations), Family, and Inheritance. The first three books of the Civil Code were completed and promulgated in 1896, followed in 1898 by the remaining two, to be enacted together in 1898. This Code is the current Japanese Civil Code ('JCC'). It is occasionally called the 'Meiji Civil Code' (*Meiji minpou*) because the last two books (on family and inheritance) were wholly revised in 1947 after the enactment of a new constitution following the Japanese defeat in the Second World War, and are now called 'Showa Civil Code' (*Showa minpou*).

* Cite as M Okino, 'Contracts for the Benefit of Third Parties in Japan' in Chen-Wishart, Loke, & Vogenauer, *Studies in the Contract Laws of Asia Vol II: Formation and Third Party Beneficiaries* (Oxford: OUP 2017) ch 13.

Contracts for the Benefit of Third Parties in Japan. Masami Okino.

In drafting the JCC, the three scholars researched the civil laws of many jurisdictions, such as French, Italian, German, and Belgian civil law, and that of Montenegro, as well as the English common law, etc. Some provisions take their cue from the common law, such as Article 416 dealing with the scope of damages due to default of obligations based on the English case of *Hadley v Baxendale*. However, by far the most influential were French and German law. Because of the structure of the JCC and several institutions then uniquely observed in the German Civil Code (more particularly, its first and second drafts), the JCC appears to be a daughter of the (then draft) German Civil Code. Nevertheless, many of the JCC's provisions were taken from the Old Civil Code and there were similarities with the French Civil Code. It is reported that Dr Boissonade drafted the outline of the Old Civil Code with reference to the French Civil Code and the then Italian Civil Code, and that some of its provisions were originally created by Dr Boissonade himself. For instance, the system of transfer of claim, general principles of torts, and many other rules were taken from French law and contrast with German law. The JCC is therefore said to be a product of comparative law research and described as having French and German law as parents.

2. A Strong Inclination for German Law and Literature and the Backlash

With its enactment in 1900, the German Civil Code was regarded as the most advanced code at the time. Especially after the influence of the drafters of the JCC faded, legal scholars turned their attention almost exclusively to German law and literature. Most civil law scholars went to Germany to study. They tended to interpret the provisions of the JCC as though they were the same or similar to those of the German Civil Code regardless of any difference in phrasing, overlooking their origins. This penchant for German law and the attitudes and arguments that went with it also affected the courts. Dominant views were formed that are currently regarded as traditional. This trend continued in the face of objections and opposing trends, until an epoch-making article by Professor Eiichi Hoshino in the 1960s highlighted the influence of French law on the JCC.[1] Professor Hoshino had studied in France, and civil law scholars began to turn to France and other countries to study in preference to Germany.

Because of its roots and history, any arguments involving the JCC are often based on comparative law study. The influence of German law and literature may have grown fainter, but it is still one of the main sources of reference. French law and literature are now as often referred to and Anglo-American laws are also referred to in scholarly works.

3. Revision of the Civil Code

In contrast to the last two books of the JCC, which underwent a complete rewrite in 1947, to bring them in line with the new, post-Second World War constitution, the first three books of the JCC remained essentially untouched for over 100 years. The contract law-related provisions in Part 1 of the JCC (general provisions) and Part 3 (the law of obligations) have been basically unchanged. New problems have arisen, and social and economic change has occurred since the JCC was enacted over a century ago in 1898. These new situations have been addressed through the development of case law and specific legislation falling outside the JCC.

[1] 星野英一「日本民法典に与えたフランス民法の影響」同『民法論集』第1巻 (有斐閣, 1970) 所収 (1965初出) (Eiichi Hoshino, 'The Influence of French Civil Law on the Japanese Civil Code' in id, *Essays on Civil Law*, vol 1 (Tokyo: Yuhikaku Publishing Co 1970) (first published 1965)).

Finally, the Japanese Government (the Ministry of Justice) was reported to have commenced preparatory work in 2006 on a revision of the JCC's provisions on contracts and obligation-related issues. In 2009, the Minister of Justice launched an inquiry with the Legislative Council of the Justice Ministry and asked the latter to present an outline of such a revision. This marked the start of the official process of reform of the JCC (on obligation-related provisions). The Subcommittee on the Civil Code (Obligation-related provisions) of the Legislative Council was set up in 2009. The Subcommittee worked for five years, during which it identified possible issues for revision, and published its interim report in April 2011, followed by interim proposals for the outline of the revision in February 2013, tentative proposals for the outline in August 2014, and a draft outline of the revision in February 2015. The latter was approved by the general assembly of the Legislative Council of the Justice Ministry and submitted to the Minister of Justice in February 2015. The Ministry of Justice had in the meantime carried out preparatory work on a bill while the Subcommittee was deliberating, and a bill to revise the Civil Code was approved by the Cabinet and submitted to the Diet at the end of March 2015. The bill was submitted to a law committee of the Diet for deliberation, but as a result of the political situation and because of other bills with priority status, the bill to revise the Civil Code (contracts and obligation-related provisions) had to be suspended. The Diet started its examination of the bill at its special session in the autumn of 2016. Finally, after discussion in two consecutive sessions, the Diet passed the bill on the 26 May 2017 without any change in substance. It was promulgated on 2 June 2017, as law no 44 of 2017. It will come into effect within three years of promulgation, with the specific date to be set by a Cabinet ordinance.

II. Provisions of the JCC on Contracts for the Benefit of Third Parties

1. General Remarks

The JCC specifically provides that a third party may derive rights from a contract made between other parties. This solution was much debated when the JCC was first promulgated; however, the rule is now taken for granted. Cases and academic discussions on contracts for the benefit of third parties are relatively scarce. This is probably because of the existence of relevant provisions in the Code and the general tenor of Japanese scholarly works, and also the rules available in adjacent areas of law such as tort. Moreover, there is no requirement of cause or consideration for contracts, and tort liability has a wide scope.

2. Provisions of the JCC

There are three provisions in the JCC on contracts for the benefit of third parties, Articles 537 to 539, which are placed in Subsection 2 ('Effect of Contracts'), Section 1 ('General Provisions'), Chapter 2 ('Contracts'), Part 3 ('Obligations/Claims') of the JCC. They run as follows:[2]

Contracts for the Benefit of Third Parties
Article 537

(1) If one of the parties promises in a contract that he/she will tender a certain performance to any third party, the third party shall have the right to claim that performance directly from the obligor.

[2] The English translation of the Civil Code in this chapter is taken from the 'Japanese Law Translation Database System', an unofficial translation offered by the Ministry of Justice Japan <http://www.japaneselawtranslation.go.jp/law/detail/?re=01&yo=%E6%B0%91%E6%B3%95&ft=2&ky=&page=3> accessed 31 January 2017.

(2) In the cases set forth in the preceding paragraph, rights of the third party shall accrue when the third party has expressed his/her intention to the obligor to enjoy the benefit of the contract under that paragraph.

Determination of Rights of the Third Party
Article 538
After rights of the third party have come into existence in accordance with the provisions of the preceding Article, the parties may not modify or extinguish those rights.

Obligors' Defense
Article 539
The obligor may raise the defense founded on the contract referred to in Paragraph 1 of Article 537 against a third party who is to enjoy the benefit of the contract.

As shown in Article 537, the JCC specifically provides that a third party other than the parties to the contract is entitled to seek performance against the promisor who is one of the parties to the contract when the parties agree to give such a right to the third party and that the third party acknowledges the right. This is regarded as an exception to the general principle that the effect and force of contracts are limited to the parties to the contract: the principle of relative effect of contracts (the word 'privity' is not commonly used in Japanese civil law, which refers to it rather as the 'relativity principle of contract effects'). Article 537 of the JCC was a break from the position of the Old Civil Code. Articles 537 to 539 of the JCC were introduced by amending the corresponding provisions of the Old Civil Code of 1890 which, in the part on property law, provided as follows:[3]

Article 323
When a promisee to an agreement has no legitimate interest the monetary value of which can be estimated, the agreement is void due to the lack of a cause.

When a promise is made for the benefit of any third party but no penalty clause is provided for the breach, the promisee is deemed to have no interest the monetary value of which can be estimated.

Notwithstanding the previous paragraph, a promise for the benefit of a third party is effective if it is made secondarily to the promise made by the promisee for its own benefit, or if it is the secondary condition of the gift made to the promisor.

In the previous two situations, the promisee is entitled to exercise an action to terminate the agreement or an action to seek performance of the penalty clause if the secondary condition is not fulfilled.

Article 345
The convention shall produce no effect other than between the parties and their successors; provided that it shall produce effect against third parties only when the law so provides and the conditions required by the law are met.

As is clear from the face of the Old Civil Code provisions, the position, influenced by French law, is not to allow any third party to acquire rights and to deny any entitlement to seek performance against the promisor except in very few situations. The principle of the relative effect of the contract was stressed.

The drafters of the JCC, however, departed from the Old Civil Code and provided that a third party may acquire rights against the promisor under the contract. This ultimately became the current law. The change from the old Code was partly because there is no longer any reason to void a contract without a cause that can be estimated in monetary value, either because: (1) the cause requirement was abolished; or (2) the object of the claim/

[3] Author's translation.

obligation is not limited to something the monetary value of which may be estimated.[4] Furthermore, one of the drafters commented that this shift would be convenient from a practical point of view and meet the intention of the parties, and that acknowledging the third party's right would do no harm.[5] The position (ie that the third party may acquire a right immediately and lose it when he renounces it) taken by the draft German Civil Code (BGB) and the Swiss Law of Obligations was referred to. The drafters of the JCC also felt it was inappropriate for a third party to acquire a right without its knowledge.[6]

Although the change from the position of the Old Civil Code—modelled on the French Civil Code which strictly limited or basically denied contracts for the benefit of third parties—was influenced by German law (the draft BGB) and the Swiss Law of Obligations, unlike these two texts, the JCC took the position that the third party would not acquire its right automatically but was required to make manifest its intention to enjoy the benefit. The drafters of the JCC explained that the position of the Code in this regard took a middle road between French and German/Swiss law.

III. Characteristics of the JCC

The following three points may be regarded as characteristic of the JCC. One concerns the provision on contacts for third parties itself, while the other two relate to the system adjacent to contracts for third parties: one on contracts, the other on torts.

1. Between French Law and German/Swiss Law

As just mentioned, the provisions of the JCC were deliberately situated between French law and German/Swiss law. The JCC provisions are characteristic on two counts: (1) the JCC widely admits the third party beneficiary's right against the promisor, who is a party to the contract; (2) the third party is required to declare its intention to enjoy the benefit of the acquisition of the right by the third party ('acknowledgement').[7]

The reasons why the drafters of the JCC took this middle road are less clear. As to the first feature, they probably wished to stress respect for the intention of the parties to the contract. As to the second (ie the requirement of the third party's declaration of intent to enjoy the benefit or, in other words, the denial of automatic accruement of the right to the third party), the drafters of the JCC explained that it would be too much if the third party were to acquire a right without knowing about it, since he might not even want it—automatic acquisition is not suited to the 'Japanese way of thinking'. The point was not debated further.

Two issues arose in the course of the discussions on this provision. The first point concerned admittance of contracts for the benefit of third parties (or acquisition of the right by a third party); the second dealt with how and when the third party's right arises. The discussions, following the explanation by Dr Tomii, who presumably drafted the provision, were focused on the former issue. Dr Tomii cited an example of a building contract for the benefit of a third party to deal with the former issue. While arguing that this would rest on the

[4] JCC, Art 399: 'Even a matter for which no monetary value can be estimated may be the subject of a claim'.

[5] 梅謙次郎『民法要義』第3巻434頁(大正元年復刻版、有斐閣、1985年) (Kenjiro Ume, *A Commentary on the Civil Code*, vol 3 (Tokyo: Yuhikaku Publishing Co 1985, 1912 edn reprinted) 434).

[6] 民法修正案理由書536条 (Explanatory Statement of the Draft to Revise the Civil Code, Art 536).

[7] The requirement of the third party's manifestation of intent to enjoy a benefit is occasionally referred to or translated as 'acceptance'. However, it would be better to use a word other than acceptance in view of issues as to what the acquisition of the right by a third party should be based on, and one argument concerns the offer(-and-acceptance) doctrine, which is not the dominant view in Japan. If we use the word acceptance, the offer doctrine might be inferred to be the base.

acknowledgement requirement of the third party, the drafters pointed out that from a practical viewpoint, insurance is the type of contract with the most practical use; although it is precisely insurance contracts that form the exception to the positive acknowledgement requirement.

As to the meaning of 'the Japanese way of thinking', what may have been referred to was perhaps the 'samurai spirit': it is against samurai ethics or even disgraceful to believe that it is acceptable to give someone a benefit without the recipient signifying its intention or assent just because it is to the latter's benefit. The 'samurai spirit' is cited in the commentary by one of the drafters, Dr Ume, to explain a distinct issue of performance or payment by the third party (Article 474), where the third party 'who has no interest in an obligation' may not perform the obligation against the will of the obligor. This has been taken up subsequently by academics, to extend the principle to other provisions which deny a benefit to an obligor if given against its will.[8] Although the 'samurai spirit' may explain the acknowledgement requirement of the third party beneficiary, this attitude is not coherently adopted throughout the JCC.

It should be noted that, where necessary, special provisions in specific acts are established as an exception to the acknowledgement requirement—the requirement of the third party's manifestation of intention to enjoy the benefit. Two areas where it would be inconvenient from a practical standpoint to impose the acknowledgement requirement are covered by specific legislation, such as trust in the Trust Act of 1921 and the life insurance contract in insurance contract law (originally in the Commercial Code).[9] Now, justification is sought not for the acknowledgement requirement, but rather for the exceptional treatment afforded in situations involving trust or insurance.

As to the nature of the acknowledgement and the mechanism for the acquisition of the third party beneficiary's right, the drafters defended different views in their writings after the Code was enacted. One of the drafters, Dr Ume, seemed to regard the third party's declaration of intent to enjoy the benefit as akin to acceptance, whereas another drafter, Dr Tomii, explained that the third party's declaration of intent to enjoy the benefit is the condition precedent to acquisition, not acceptance in an offer–acceptance scenario. The difference resides in the understanding of the legal nature of the declaration of intent by the third party. Dr Ume seemed to regard it as a fundamental element of the contract for the benefit of a third party, whereas Dr Tomii viewed it as a mere condition. According to a scholarly analysis, Dr Ume's position is called the 'acceptance doctrine', influenced by French law; while Dr Tomii's position is referred to as the 'direct acquisition of the right doctrine', influenced by German law.[10] In both viewed, however, the contract itself is effectively formed before the declaration of intent by the third party is made. It is not a requirement or condition for the formation or effectiveness of the contract itself.

Later generations of lawyers have rationalized the rule in Article 537(2) of the JCC on the basis of Dr Tomii's argument. In general, these eras were heavily influenced by German law and scholarship, hence so was the argument on the mechanism and legal nature of the contract for the benefit of a third party.

[8] For further details, see 中田裕康『債權総論(第3版)』(岩波書店、2013年) 325頁 (Hiroyasu Nakata, *Law of Obligations in General* (3rd edn, Tokyo: Iwanami Shoten 2013) 325).

[9] This treatment of automatic acquisition of a right by a third party beneficiary continues in the current legislation, in the first sentence of the Trust Act of 2006, Art 88 and in the Insurance Act of 2008, Arts 8 and 42. For further information, see text to nn 39–42 below.

[10] 春田一夫『第三者のためにする契約の法理』(信山社, 2002) 152–154頁 (Kazuo Haruta, *A Theory on the Contract for the Benefit of Third Parties* (Tokyo: Shinzansha 2002) 152–154).

Once it is established that the third party is to acquire its right directly from and based on the contract (the agreement of the parties), and all other explanations such as offer–acceptance, agency, transfer, or *negotiorum gestio* (management of the affairs of another) are put aside as historical issues, the question of justification of the contract for the benefit of a third party becomes less relevant. The issue is no longer a matter of debate in scholarly works. The mechanism of the acquisition of a right by a third party is still controversial, yet recent scholarship seems to have lost interest in this issue.

In sum, it is now unanimously understood that the third party acquires its right or entitlement directly from the contract and that the declaration of intent of the third party is a prerequisite for the acquisition of the right or accruement of the right, and that it is not a condition for the formation or effectiveness of the contract. The declaration of intent by the third party is simply a type of declaration of intent in general, and the third party acquires the right by declaring such intention. Therefore, the explanation goes, the third party has a so-called formative right. It is now also the dominant view that any agreement to give a right to a third party is typically an ancillary agreement to the contract such as a sale contract, gift, or suchlike.

2. No Requirement of Cause or Consideration

The right of the third party arises from the contract (ie the agreement of the parties). The fact that the third party provides no consideration does not bar it from acquiring the right to demand performance against the promisor since consideration is not required for ordinary two-party agreements to be enforceable (eg a gift is an executory contract).[11]

3. Wide Coverage of Tort Liability

It should be noted that tort liability is covered quite extensively in Japanese civil law.

(a) General (not categorically limited) conditions of liability

First, the core provision on torts, Article 709 of the JCC, which takes after French civil law, is a general provision, that is to say, it does not simply list several categories where tort liability arises.

> **Damages in Torts**
> **Article 709**
> A person who has intentionally or negligently infringed any right of others, or legally protected interest of others, shall be liable to compensate any damages resulting in consequence.[12]

[11] eg a gift orally agreed is an executory contract. The donee is entitled to demand the performance of the donor, although the donor may revoke the contract if it is not in writing, to the extent that its performance is not complete (JCC, Arts 549 and 550). The text in Art 550 which bars the party to the contract from revoking it, is interpreted as meaning that any text suffices insofar as it indicates the intent of the parties.

[12] In addition, in respect of employer's liability, courts interpret the exemption provision strictly and would not actually grant exemption under Art 715 of the JCC. This shows that the provision is similar to the corresponding provision of the German Civil Code rather than that of the French Civil Code, but that its actual administration by the courts rather resembles that of the French Civil Code.

JCC, Art 715(1) provides:

> A person who employs others for a certain business shall be liable for damages inflicted on a third party by his/her employees with respect to the execution of that business; provided, however, that this shall not apply if the employer exercised reasonable care in appointing the employee or in supervising the business, or if the damages could not have been avoided even if he/she had exercised reasonable care.

(b) Scope of damages

Second, the scope of damages recoverable based on torts is not covered in a specific article. Article 416 of the JCC, which provides the scope of damages based on breach of an obligation, is applicable by analogy to tort damages.[13]

> **Scope of Damages**
> **Article 416**
>
> (1) The purpose of the demand for the damages for failure to perform an obligation shall be to demand the compensation for damages which would ordinarily arise from such failure.
>
> (2) The obligee may also demand the compensation for damages which arise from any special circumstances if the party/parties did foresee, or should have foreseen, such circumstances.

According to Article 416, what is recoverable is to be determined by the ordinary loss and foreseeability test. For instance, 'pure economic loss' could be recoverable if it falls within the category of 'ordinary loss' or 'special foreseeable loss', that is to say, it is not categorically excluded from coverage, even if the provision is applied to a tort situation.[14]

(c) Losses incurred by a person other than the direct victim

Third, the loss incurred by so-called indirect victims may be recoverable under Articles 709 and 416 of the JCC (applied by analogy). There are several situations where indirect victims seek damages.

One is the so-called 'substitution loss' case, in which family members or relatives pay a victim's medical fees or attend the hospital to care for the victim, leaving work and incurring expenses that result in losses. In such cases, the direct victim may seek compensation for such expenses and losses together with its own (or else the family members or relatives may seek compensation as their own losses). For instance, when a mother was injured in a traffic accident and her daughter, who was studying abroad, flew back and forth to see and take care of her mother, the cost of the airline tickets was regarded as an ordinary loss, hence recoverable in a tort action as part of the mother's loss.[15] Alternatively, the family members or relatives themselves (in the above case, the daughter) may seek compensation for their outlay as their own loss.

Another example would be a case when a husband, who supports his family (wife and children), is killed in a car accident. In that case, his surviving wife and children may seek damages for their loss of support.[16]

A third example is when injury or death of a person would cause losses to the company that employed him and the company sues for damages. The Supreme Court has granted

[13] In scholarly writings, this position taken by the case law is criticized as making inappropriate use of the rule typically meant for cases of breach of contract where parties to the contract agree to share the risk.

[14] For a detailed analysis of the characteristics of Japanese private law compared with German and French law, see 能見善久「比較法的にみた現在の日本民法——経済的利益の保護と不法行為法(純粋経済損失の問題を中心に)」広中俊雄・星野英一編『民法典の百年Ⅰ』619頁(有斐閣、1998) (Yoshihisa Nomi, 'The Current Japanese Civil Law in Comparative Law Perspective—The Protection of Economic Interests and Torts Law (Focusing on the Question of Pure Economic Loss') in Toshio Hironaka and Eiichi Hoshino (eds), *The Centennial of the Civil Code*, I (Tokyo: Yuhikaku Publishing Co 1998) 619).

[15] Decision of 25 April 1969 of the Supreme Court of Japan (published in *Minshu* [Supreme Court civil case reports] vol 28, no 3, p 447).

[16] Typically, in the case of the husband's death, they (the wife and children) would seek damages for their own pain and suffering as well as for losses incurred by the direct victim (the husband), such as loss of future income through succession of the right of the direct victim. Instances where the indirect victims who were supported by the direct victim seek damages for the loss of support as their own loss, rather than inheriting the right of the direct victim's right of damages for the loss of the future income, include those where these victims waive their right to succession or they are not heirs (non-married couple, parents who are not successors, etc).

damages only in very limited circumstances, where it is impossible for the company to substitute the direct victim and where the latter is economically inseparable from the company.[17] The court did not rest its decision on the 'indirect victim' doctrine, but dealt with the question as one of scope of damages. Unlike German law, Article 709 of the JCC does not specify to whom the wrongdoer must make compensation, or whose damages he has to compensate. Views are divided on this issue. One school of thought treats the question of establishing who can seek damages as one belonging to the 'indirect victim' doctrine, while another sees it as a question of scope of damages.

(d) Liability of experts

An expert may be liable based on tort, beyond the contract, against third parties other than the contracting party. The construction industry is a case in point.

One example is the decision of the Supreme Court of 6 July 2007 (heisei 19).[18] A buyer bought a newly constructed nine-storey building two months after the building was completed, from the owner of the building who had ordered the work and made a construction contract with the construction company. The buyer subsequently discovered numerous defects in the building and sued for damages against the construction company, as well as the company who made a contract with the construction company to design and supervise the work.

The court of second instance, Fukuoka High Court, dismissed the buyer's claim on the ground that the seller had not assigned to the buyer (the plaintiff and appellant) the contractual status of the construction contract which is necessary for the buyer to seek fulfilment of a warranty against defects from the construction company (one of the defendants and respondents). It further held that the existence of defects in a building does not necessarily raise a tortious liability on the part of the constructor or the person in charge of designing the building or supervising the work, and that a tort liability can be admitted only where the defects are plainly illegal—for instance, where the constructor has produced a defective building deliberately, with the positive intention of infringing the client's rights, where the nature of the defects is anti-social or unethical, or where the degree or substance of the defects in the building is so serious that the very existence of the building poses a danger to society. The court found none of these circumstances in this case.

The Supreme Court overruled the High Court. It held that the designer, constructor, and construction supervisor involved in the construction of buildings must, in constructing a building, bear the duty of care to ensure the fundamental safety expected of a building, not only towards the party to the contract but also towards those using the building—including residents and neighbours and passers-by who are not in a contractual relationship with them. If negligence of this duty has resulted in defects in the building that undermine its fundamental safety, thereby endangering the life, limb, or property of residents etc, the designer etc, is liable under the tort provision of the Civil Code (Article 709) to pay damages caused by such defects, unless there are special circumstances where, for example, the person claiming the tort liability has purchased the building while knowing of and taking into account the existence of the defects.

[17] Decision of 15 November 1968 of the Supreme Court of Japan (published in *Minshu* [Supreme Court civil case reports] vol 22, no 12, p 2614).

[18] Published in *Minshu* [Supreme Court civil case reports] vol 61, no 5, p 1769. Unofficial English translation provided by the Supreme Court at <http://www.courts.go.jp/app/hanrei_en/detail?id=898> accessed 31 January 2017.

In the above case, the buyer had other remedies at its disposal, such as the remedy of seeking damages against the seller based on the seller's liability (Articles 570 and 566 of the JCC) and, if the seller is insolvent, to exercise the creditor's right of subrogation (Article 423 of the JCC) and seek damages against the contractor (the contractual relief the seller as an owner and a party to the construction contract has) (Article 634 of JCC). In that case, however, the contractual limitation would apply, since the damages constitute contractual relief.

Concern is expressed in scholarly works about this judgment. It gives the third party, including a subsequent buyer, relief based on tort, insofar as the defect concerns the fundamental safety expected of a building. As a result, it might override a contractual arrangement on risk-sharing between the contractor and the company designing and supervising the work, or between the owner and the contractor.

(e) Availability of tort claim with contractual claim

Unlike French law, Japanese law admits that the claimant may seek damages based on torts and/or contracts at the choice of the claimant when the requirements for both causes of action are met. In practice, the claimant will often insist on both as the cause of the lawsuit. Also, it is not rare even for courts to refer to both as in 'based on torts or default of obligations' for this grounds of decision—for example, in medical malpractice cases.

(f) Contracts with protective effect towards third parties

The German doctrine of 'contracts with protective effect towards third parties' (*Vertrag mit Schutzwirkung für Dritte*) is known to, but not accepted uncritically by, Japanese academics. One example is malpractice in a medical contract involving childbirth, in which a newborn child injured during delivery may claim compensation for injury against the obstetrician or hospital as a third party beneficiary to the contract between its mother and the doctor/hospital. Under current law, the acknowledgement of the beneficiary is required and it was construed to mean that the mother manifested her intention to acknowledge the right, as the child's statutory agent, once it had been born. It is argued that such construal is too technical and that, as a matter of legislative policy, automatic acquisition of the right by the child (beneficiary) is desirable.

In this context, for instance, it is argued that there is no need to regard such contracts as contracts for the benefit of third parties, and that their effect would extend to the child based on the spirit or purpose of the contract, referring to the doctrine of 'contracts with protective effect towards third parties'.

That doctrine is indeed referred to in scholarly works but it is also pointed out that most of the situations could be covered by tort liability, including malpractice in the childbirth case since the general rule of tort liability has wide coverage, and because, for the purposes of tort law, a foetus is deemed to be born.[19] This doctrine is viewed as somewhat superior to tort, especially from a burden of proof point of view, even though its coverage may come within the ambit of tort liability.

In a hypothetical scenario in which bank X made a contract for security services company Y to collect store Z's takings, where the contract required Y to use armoured vehicles and take out insurance, and where Y failed to fulfil these obligations so that the takings were

[19] JCC, Art 721 provides:

> An unborn child shall be deemed to have been already born with respect to the right to demand compensation for damages.

stolen while being collected in an ordinary car, Z should have no problem suing Y based on tort in view of Y's negligence.

IV. Particular Issues

1. Finding a Contract for the Benefit of a Third Party

Whether a contract is found to be one for the benefit of a third party has been a key issue and focal point for the JCC. The question that needs to be answered is whether the parties to the contract agreed that the contract would be for the benefit of a third party, and the answer is to be found through interpretation of the contract. For instance, if A promises to sell A's property to B and B in return promises to pay a certain amount of money to C in the agreement between A and B, this could be interpreted as a contract for the benefit of a third party in which C has a right to demand performance (payment) from B, or it could be a contract not for the benefit of a third party in which C is simply the designated recipient who might benefit but has no enforceable right. Which of the two options prevails is a matter of interpretation of the contract between A and B and depends on what they, as parties to the contract, intended, and whether they had the common intention to give a right to C rather than merely some benefit.

The Code offers no concrete guidance as to how this should be done, either with regard specifically to contracts for the benefit of a third party or, more generally, in respect of the interpretation of the contract.

There are no specific provisions in the Code on the interpretation of a contract, and the issue will be discussed in more detail in Volume III of this series. At this stage, suffice it to say that there have been debates on the interpretation of the manifestation of intent, in particular the question of whether this should explore the objective or subjective meaning of the manifestation of intent. Most now agree that the apparent tension between objective and subjective tests as to the interpretation of contracts is not as severe as might seem. The trend is now to stress that the basic idea of a contract is that the parties determine their relationship and that it is what the parties intend that counts. The language used by the parties is the expression of their common intention, and therefore the primary task of the interpretation of contracts is to find the common meaning given by the parties. As a rule, the ordinary meaning of the manifestation of intent (the objective meaning, so to speak) would be the meaning given by the parties, but should what the parties intended or meant in common be found to be different from the objective meaning of the language used, the meaning given by the parties should be adopted. If the common meaning is not clear, what it would be reasonable to conclude the parties' intended should be explored; and this can be done by resorting to various factors. It should be noted, to begin with, that what is sought to be established in interpreting the contract is the common intention of the parties, not each party's innermost thoughts, and this provides some objectivity in itself. Second, there is no writing requirement for the contract formation (except in respect of suretyship) and no parol evidence rule.

According to one analysis[20] (with reference to a number of lower court cases and academic works), in exploring the common intention of the parties as to the specific question of whether the parties intended to give a third party a right or only a factual benefit, consideration should be given to such factors as: (1) the expenditure made by the promisee, and its relation to the benefit to the third party (eg whether giving such a financial interest is the

[20] 平井宜雄『債権各論Ⅰ上契約総論』185–186頁(弘文堂、2008) (Yoshio Hirai, *Law of Obligations in Specific, I-1 Contracts in General* (Toyko: Kobundo 2008) 185–186).

condition or consideration for the benefit to the third party, in situations such as those where A promises to give B A's property in order for alimony to be paid to C); (2) the certainty of the third party (its existence or certain existence in the near future);[21] and (3) custom and trade practices not limited to the parties to the contract but including the trade practices and custom existing between the third party and the promisee.

2. Examples of Contracts for the Benefit of a Third Party

(a) Insurance contracts and annuities contracts

The drafters of the Code had in mind insurance contracts and annuities contracts as typical examples of contracts for the benefit of a third party, and the legislative council debated a hypothetical case involving a construction contract.

(b) Other examples of contracts held to be contracts for the benefit of third parties

The concept of a contract for the benefit of a third party is well known and there are plenty of cases, other than insurance contracts, in which the courts have found the contractual relation to be such. The following are examples of cases where the courts recognized the contractual relationship as one made for the benefit of a third party, where the third party (C) is entitled to demand performance directly of one of the parties to the contract (B).[22]

(1) Cumulative assumption of obligation: A owes an obligation to C, and B agrees with A to assume the obligation.[23] Such an assumption is often observed in the situation where a business is transferred, and a critical issue may be whether the third party declared its intention to enjoy the benefit (see section IV.2(d)).[24]

(2) Joint and several suretyship: B agrees with A to guarantee A's obligation against C.[25]

(3) Power to collect a debt: C loans money to A (contractor) for the purpose of carrying out construction work and A and C agree that C may collect A's remuneration claim against B arising from a construction contract between A and B. B agrees with A to make the payment directly to C. Here, the agreement between A and B is the contract for the benefit of C and C has a right to seek payment from B not in the name of A, based on a mandate between A and C, but in his own right, although C's manifestation of acknowledgement precedes the agreement between A and B.[26]

(4) Deposit for performance: A deposits money with the official depository (B), designating C as a recipient in order to perform A's obligation to C. Although the consensual relationship between A and B had a public law element because of the public service represented by the official depository, the court held it appropriate to apply by

[21] The contrary proposal is currently envisaged by the Legislative Council of the Ministry of Justice.

[22] For details of the court decisions (after 1945), see新堂明子「第三者のためにする契約法理の現代的意義(2・完)」法学協会雑誌115巻11号1740–1773頁(1998) (Akiko Shindo, 'On the Doctrine of Contracts for the Benefit of Third Parties—A Comparison Between Common Law and Japanese Civil Law' (1998) 115(11) J Jurisprudence Assoc 1740–1773).

[23] Tokyo High Court 7 August 1975 (showa 50), Hanrei Jiho 798-86; Supreme Court 29 June 2012 (heisei 24), Hanrei Jiho 2160-20.

[24] Supreme Court 29 June 2012 (heisei 24), Hanrei Jiho 2160-20; Supreme Court 30 September 2011 (heisei 23) Hanrei Jiho 2131-57. For details and the lower court decisions, see 渡辺達徳「判批」判例時報2196号149頁判例評論657号11頁 (Tatsunori Watanabe, 'Case Note to the Decision of the Supreme Court 29 June 2012 (heisei 24)', Hanrei Jiho 2196-149 (Hanrei Hyoron 657-11)).

[25] Supreme Court 16 July 1968 (showa 43), Kinyu Shoji Hanrei 124-2.

[26] Kobe District Court, Tatsuno Branch 6 November 1961 (showa 36), Kaminshu (lower court civil law reports) 12-11-2659.

analogy the rules in the Civil Code on deposit contracts for the benefit of third parties.[27]

(5) Retirement payment: company A seconds its employee C to subsidiary company B, arranging for C later to quit A and work for B as B's employee. A and B agree that retirement payment for C will be assumed respectively by A, during the period that C was seconded by A, and thereafter by B, and that the total sum will be paid by B to C.[28]

(6) Agreement between labour union and employers: cooperative B made up of manufacturing companies makes an agreement with labour union A in which B promises to create new jobs for designated employees C1 and others, and to pay money in an amount equivalent to salaries until they are actually employed. C1 and other workers sought payment from B.[29]

(7) Promise of inaction in a sales contract: landowner B sells part of his land to contractor A, who builds houses on it and sells them together with the land to C. B keeps another part of his land for his own use. The sales contract between A and B include a clause where B promises not to erect any gates or barriers between the two parcels of land, since they inconvenience C. Later, B announces he will be erecting a fence on the border and C requested B not to do so.[30]

(8) Malpractice in medical contracts: a newborn child accidentally injured during delivery may demand compensation for injury against the obstetrician or hospital as a third party beneficiary to the contract between its mother A and doctor/hospital B.[31]

(9) Product liability: A buys contaminated food from B and A's family member C, who eats it, suffers symptoms of food poisoning. In the judgment, it was pointed out that seller B owes a duty not to endanger the life, limb, or property of buyer A and his family or housemates, that may reasonably be expected to use or consume the product, and that buyer A may be assumed to have concluded a contract with seller B for the benefit of a third party.[32]

(10) Finance lease contract: supplier/seller B sold a computer system to a leasing company/buyer A which on-lent it to user C. The agreement between A and B included a guarantee clause according to which B guaranteed to buyer A and lessee C that the system was in conformity with C's intended use and B promised to respond to requests by A and C as to termination, repairs, delivery of substitutes, or compensation for damage. This is regarded as a contract between A and B for the benefit of third party C.[33]

(c) Contracts involving electronic fund/money transfer

On the other hand, there are cases in which it was argued that the contractual relationship was one for the benefit of a third party but where the courts found otherwise. The most

[27] Nagoya District Court 9 July 1966 (showa 41), Hanrei Jiho 464-23.

[28] Sendai District Court 22 January 1989 (heisei 1), Rodou Minshu 42-1-1, Hanrei Times 771-145.

[29] Osaka District Court 30 October 1989 (heisei 1), Rodo Minshu 40-4/5-585, Hanrei Times 730-119.

[30] Tokyo District Court 19 July 1985 (showa 60), Hanrei Jiho 1211-74.

[31] Tokyo District Court 24 April 1979 (showa 54), Hanrei Times 388-147; Yokohama District Court 30 April 1982 (showa 57), Hanrei Jiho 1060-116; Nagoya District Court 17 February 1989 (heisei 1), Hanrei Times 703-204. There are a few cases in which damages were granted based on the legal qualification as contracts for the benefit of third parties, however, the majority of cases rely on tort or simple breach of obligations.

[32] Gifu District Court Ogaki Branch 27 December 1973 (showa 48), Hanrei Jiho 725-19. Although the court referred to contracts for the benefit of a third party, this was just one way of explaining the matter.

[33] Osaka High Court 27 April 1988 (showa 63), Hanrei Times 685-241.

famous and heavily debated was one involving an electronic fund/money transfer, where the Supreme Court held this was not a contract for the benefit of a third party. There have been several other cases, but the facts in the most famous case were as follows. Company E, a customer of bank A in Iwate (in northern Japan) asked bank A to send money by money order for his employee C in Kyoto (western Japan). Bank A had no branch in Kyoto, and therefore asked bank B to make the payment based on the money order contracts between them. E notified C of the money order in electronic form. C was staying at his friend D's house in Kyoto and E's notification was received by D rather than by C, who was absent. D went to bank B, Kyoto branch, presented the notification and received the money. C demanded payment and sued B.

The question was whether C had any right to demand payment of B, as a third party beneficiary to the contract for the electronic fund transfer by money order between bank A and B.

The courts both of first and second instance held that the contract was a contract for the benefit of a third party and granted the request. However, the Supreme Court[34] (like the old Supreme Court of Judicature)[35] found no contract for the benefit of a third party that entitled the designated recipient C to request payment from B,[36] since: (1) there was no express or implied reference in the agreement to indicate it was a contract for the benefit of a third party; and (2) it had been customary among banks operating the money order system that bank B did not pay before bank A (sending bank) designated bank B and that despite the request of C, banks A and B could overturn and return the money based on E's request if it were done before the payment by B was made; such operations presuppose that the contract is not for the benefit of a third party that gave C a right to demand payment of bank B; (3) bank B owes a duty to bank A to make payment to the designated recipient, but does not owe any duty to C, that is to say, in relation to C, bank B has the power to make payment on the account of bank A.

Although there was strong support for this position, the courts' position and reasoning were criticized in several scholarly works on the grounds that: (1) the purpose of an electronic fund transfer contract is to send money to the recipient quickly and safely and for this purpose it would be natural to regard bank B as owing a duty to pay to C; (2) interbank practices or custom are not conclusive when it comes to the legal nature of contracts involving not only banks but their customers, as well.

The Supreme Court has stuck to its position and the Supreme Court likewise holds that a fund transfer to an account between banks is not a contract for the benefit of a third party but a mandate, and that fund transfers to an account are a complex matter involving three contracts.

(d) *Other examples of contracts held not to be contracts for the benefit of third parties*

There have been other cases in which it was argued that a given contract was a contract for the benefit of a third party yet the court found otherwise.

[34] Decision of 5 December 1968 of the Supreme Court of Japan (showa 43) (published in *Minshu* vol 22, no 13, p 2876).

[35] Old Supreme Court judgment 29 September 1922, *Minshu* (Supreme Court civil case reports) 1–557.

[36] The case was remanded twice and the Supreme Court passed judgment three times. For a detailed analysis of the reasoning of each judgment, including those of lower courts, see Shindo (n 22) 1744–1749.

(1) Promise of inaction: realty company A sold land for housing purposes to B, C1, and others. Each sales agreement featured a clause stating that the buyer would not build or build nothing higher than two storeys or indeed build anything that might annoy the neighbours. Buyer B planned to build a three-storey reinforced concrete building. Company A and other buyers of neighbouring lands (C1 and others) sought a preliminary injunction against B to stop construction. The court granted relief to A based on the contractual clause but denied it to C1 and others, stating that it was not a contract for the benefit of a third party. However, together with the assertion based on the contractual clause between A and B, C1 and others also sought an injunction based on the assertion that the construction would damage the residential environment of C1 and others to an extent beyond endurance. The court granted an injunctive order based on the infringement of property rights on the land.[37]

(2) Pollution control agreement: local government A agreed with power plant company B that B would control the amount and temperature of water emission from the plant to keep it below a certain level. Residents C1 and others demanded that company B observe the agreement, arguing that C1 and other residents were third party beneficiaries to the agreement between A and B. The court found that this was not a contract for the benefit of a third party.[38]

3. Types of 'Benefit'/Right/Entitlement of the Third Party

The basic model of a contract for the benefit of a third party is a contract where the third party acquires a claim (obligation right/personal right) such as a right to payment so that it is entitled to demand performance of the promisor. The types of benefit or right/entitlement which the third party acquires are not limited to a claim.

It is also recognized that: (1) the third party acquires a right with ancillary burdens; (2) the third party may acquire a property right such as ownership in an asset; (3) the benefit of the third party may be the release from an existing obligation to the promisor (so there is no situation in which the third party can demand performance); (4) the third party may acquire the right to a price such as ownership in consideration for payment (eg ownership of an asset for a price, or right of lease for rent)—in this later case (4), the courts arguably recognize it as one type of contract for the benefit of a third party, in which the third party's benefit is similar to an option to conclude a contract. It is also pointed out in scholarly works that (5) the practice of an exemption clause or other contractual clause for the benefit of a third party could be explained as a reference to or within the conceptual framework of a contract for the benefit of a third party.

4. The Acquisition of the Right by the Third Party—The Declaration of Intent to Enjoy the Benefit

(a) Requirement of a third party's declaration of intent to enjoy the benefit

A declaration of intent by the third party beneficiary to acknowledge and enjoy the benefit of the contract is necessary for the third party to acquire its right (or entitlement to demand performance) against the promisor. The underlying idea is that, in principle, parties are not

[37] Kobe District Court Itami Branch 5 February 1960 (showa 45), Kaminshu (lower court reports) 21-1, 2-236, Hanrei Jiho 592-41.

[38] Sapporo District Court 14 October 1980 (showa 55), Hanrei Jiho 988-37.

empowered directly to affect the third party's legal position even to the extent of giving the benefit to the third party.

As mentioned earlier, there are important exceptions to this principle: insurance contracts for a third party beneficiary (the insured in the case of a general insurance contract, and the recipient in the case of a life insurance contract) and contracts of trust for a third party beneficiary[39] being cases in point. In either situation, the law specifically provides that the third party's declaration of intent is not a prerequisite for the third party's right to receive the benefit (Insurance Act of 2008, Articles 8 and 42;[40] Trust Act of 2006, Article 88[41]).[42]

In the course of the ongoing legislative reform, it was considered and discussed that this should be changed to allow the third party to acquire the right automatically, but ultimately the current rule was retained (see section V), partly because there are already clear rules that admit exceptions in specific areas of practical importance, and also because in other fields concern has been expressed that a third party might acquire a right without knowing anything about it or even wanting it.

(b) Legal effect of the declaration of intent by the third party

A third party is not entitled to acquire a right or entitlement until it declares its intention. The declaration of intent can be express or implicit. The declaration determines the time of acquisition of the right by the third party. As a consequence, in cases where a term is set for the entitlement or enjoyment, the third party has no right if it did not declare its intention to enjoy the benefit within the set term.[43]

[39] An express trust can be created either through a contract, a will or a declaration of trust (Trust Act, Art 2(1), (2), and 3). Categorizing a trust contract for a third party beneficiary, as a contract for the benefit of a third party creates no obstacle, and the right of the beneficiary of a trust is not limited to a claim against the trustee (Trust Act, Art 2(7)) and may arguably be regarded as being a right *in rem*.

[40] Art 42:

> When a recipient of the insurance proceeds is a person other than the parties to the life insurance contract, the recipient of the insurance proceeds shall enjoy the benefit of the life insurance contract, by operation of law.

Art 8:

> When an insured party is a person other than the parties to the general insurance contract, the insured party shall enjoy the benefit of the general insurance contract, by operation of law.

Before the new Insurance Act of 2008 came into force, the rules on insurance contracts were part of the Commercial Code and similar provisions were included, there, too (Commercial Code, Art 675, para 1, before the 2008 revision).

[41] Art 88(1):

> A person designated by the provisions of terms of trust as one who is to be a beneficiary (including a person designated as an initial beneficiary or as a new beneficiary after a change as a result of the exercise of the right to designate or change beneficiaries as prescribed in paragraph (1) of the following Article) shall acquire a beneficial interest by operation of law; provided, however, that if the terms of trust provide otherwise, such provisions shall prevail.

Before the new Trust Act of 2006 came into force, the Trust Act of 1922 had similar provisions (Trust Act of 1922, Art 7).

[42] Although trust contracts and insurance contracts are contracts for the benefit of third parties and exceptions are provided to JCC, Art 537, their relations or legal effects are contemplated in specific acts and there is little room for the provisions of the Code on contracts for the benefit of a third party to play a role.

[43] Supreme Court 29 June 2012, Hanrei Jiho 2160 20. In the case where a moneylending business company A assigned all receivables to B as part of a company restructuring exercise, and the agreement between A and B contained a clause that B should assume A's obligations to its customers to repay the money that customers had paid to A in excess, and a time limit was also set on the clause regulating B's assumption, the court held that there was no effective assumption by B of A's obligation to customer C because C had failed to declare its intention to enjoy the benefit before the clause lapsed.

A somewhat similar situation may be found in respect of prescription (limitation) in Tokyo District Court 28 January 2013 (heisei 25), Kinyu Homu Jijo 1981-125. A company managing Samurai bonds brought an action

The parties to the contract (the promisor and promisee) may not, even by agreement, modify the contract to change or extinguish the right of the third party once the latter has declared its intention to acknowledge the right. Such agreement is void against the third party.

Exceptions to the rule apply in the case of life insurance contracts, where the contracting party may designate or change the recipient until the insured event occurs, unless such power is excluded in the contract (Insurance Contract Act of 2008, Articles 43, 44, and 49).[44]

(c) Hypothetical: selling bread

In a hypothetical scenario in which X leases two adjoining properties to Y and Z, the lease between X and Y bars Y from selling bread because Z is already selling bread from his leased property. X and Y will not be able to have the bar lifted if the contract between X and Y is a contract for the benefit of a third party Z, giving Z a right to demand that Y refrain from selling bread from the property, and if Z has acknowledged the benefit. In the light of the lower court decisions with different outcomes (promise of inaction in the sale of land case, see section IV.2(b) example (8) and section IV.2(d) example (1)), it depends on the factual circumstances of the case whether Z's benefit is only factual or the parties X and Y intend to give Z a right to demand that Y refrain from competing by running a bakery. Consideration will be given to the language of the agreement between X and Y, the details and purpose of the said clause, the negotiations, and the history which led to the inclusion of the clause. Z is likely to be regarded as a third party beneficiary entitled to demand from Y not to sell bread, since the non-competition clause is so specific in its content and purpose—the protection of Z who is already running the bakery.

5. Remedies for Breach by the Promisor

A third party beneficiary may demand performance directly of the promisee. The promisor may bring a defence against the promisee and against the beneficiary (Article 539 of the JCC).

If the promisor does not perform its obligations or duties, resulting in breach, the remedies open to the third party will depend on the type of benefit the third party enjoys. In the basic and typical situation where third party C acquires a claim/obligation right against promisor B, the remedies open to creditors are available to third party C, such as specific enforcement and damages (Articles 414 and 415 of the JCC). On the other hand, promisee A has remedial rights based on its position as a party to the contract, such as an enforcement right (eg, in the case of payment, it can demand that the promisor pay the third party) and the right to terminate the contract (Articles 414, 541, and 543 of the JCC). In sum, the third party has a creditor's right, while the promisee has a right and position as a party to the contract.[45]

As to the specific enforcement right, both A and C have a right to demand performance. Both C and A are entitled to demand that B pay or deliver, etc, to C.

As to damages, C is entitled to seek compensation for losses incurred due to the breach of the obligation in accordance with Articles 415 and 416 of the JCC (or in case of payment,

to interrupt prescription. The court found the contract was a contract for the benefit of a third party, but failing the declaration of intent to enjoy the benefit, the prescription period for the bond holder had expired.

[44] If the event in question is the death of a person, the change of recipient does not produce effect without the consent of the insured party (Art 45, Insurance Act).

[45] It should be noted that questions of breach of contract are dealt with mainly as questions of breach of an obligation under the German-style *Pandekten* system of the JCC.

Article 419 of the JCC). Scholars disagree as to whether A might also seek damages. The answer to this question appears to be mostly in the negative, but there have been strong arguments in favour of it.[46] Those who espouse the latter theory point out that situations might arise where promisee A has a special interest in performance to C, and the question that has to be resolved according to the general rules on scope of damages is whether either C or A can only recover their respective losses.

Only A is entitled to rights such as the right to rescind the contract based on a defect of the declaration of intent to conclude the contract (fraud, duress, etc), or to terminate the contract based on breach of the contractual obligation by the other party to the contract, B, which includes the obligation owed by B to C. Since the exercise of the right to terminate the contract based on B's breach of its obligation to perform to C would extinguish and deprive C of its right, it is argued that C's consent is necessary for A to exercise the right of termination (for the proposed revision, see section V.1).

6. The Promisor's Defence Against a Third Party Beneficiary

A debtor-promisor may raise a defence against the third party beneficiary founded on the contract with the promisee (Article 539 of the JCC).[47]

It is less clear whether the debtor-promisor can defeat the third party's claim for reasons specific to the third party. However, in cases where a third party beneficiary induces the parties to make the contract by misrepresentation to the debtor, the dominant view is that the third party beneficiary should be treated as the third party in applying the relevant provision on fraud (Article 96 of the JCC).[48]

According to Article 96(1) and (2) of the JCC, when a declaration of intent is induced by fraud, the defrauded party may rescind its declaration; however, if a third party has committed the fraud, the defrauded party may rescind the declaration of intent only if the other party was aware of the relevant fact. The question is whether such a case of fraud by a third party beneficiary falls within the category of the party's fraud or a third party's fraud. The dominant view supports the latter, that is to say, the third party beneficiary is treated as a third party and the debtor-promisor may invalidate the contract by rescinding its declaration of intent only if the promisee knew the facts of the fraud. The reasoning is that the effect of the contract is not confined to the acquisition of the right by the third party beneficiary and that the promisee also has rights and duties based on the contract, hence the innocent promisee should be protected under Article 96(2) of the JCC.[49] Incidentally,

[46] 谷口知平・五十嵐清編『新版注釈民法(13)』(補訂版)787頁[中馬義直=新堂明子](有斐閣、2006) (Yoshinao Chuma and Akiko Shindo, 'Article 537' in Tomohei Taniguchi and Kiyoshi Igarashi (eds), *Japanese Civil Code Annotated*, vol 13 (rev edn, Tokyo: Yuhikaku Publishing Co 2006) 787).

[47] Art 539:

> The obligor may raise the defense founded on the contract referred to in Paragraph 1 of Article 537 against a third party who is to enjoy the benefit of the contract.

[48] Art 96:

> (1) Manifestation of intention which is induced by any fraud or duress may be rescinded.
> (2) In cases any third party commits any fraud inducing any person to make a manifestation of intention to the other party, such manifestation of intention may be rescinded only if the other party knew such fact.
> (3) The rescission of the manifestation of intention induced by the fraud pursuant to the provision of the preceding two paragraphs may not be asserted against a third party without knowledge.

[49] Chuma and Shindo (n 46) 785. For other views, see 川島武宜=平井宜雄編『新版注釈民法(3)』498頁〔下森定〕(有斐閣、2003)(Sadamu Shitamori in Takeyoshi Kawashima and Yoshio Hirai (eds), *Japanese Civil Code Annotated*, vol 3 (new edn, Tokyo: Yuhikaku Publishing Co 2003) 498).

the debtor-promisor may seek damages against a third party beneficiary who committed fraud based on tort.

7. The Effect of Contract Clauses on the Third Party

The question of the effect of contract clauses on the third party is illustrated in a hypothetical scenario of an exemption clause for stevedores: X contracts with Y to transport X's goods using Y's ships to a foreign market. The contract between X and Y for the carriage of goods by sea contains an exemption of liability provision which purports to protect Z, the stevedores hired to unload X's goods from Y's ship, upon arrival at the docks. As a result of Z's carelessness, X's goods are damaged while being unloaded and X wishes to sue Z for negligence in order to recover damages for the losses suffered by X. Can Z rely on the exemption of liability provision in the contract between X and Y?

This is not usually conceived of as a question of contracts for the benefit of third parties. In international transport contracts, Article 20-2 of the International Carriage of Commodities by Sea Act of 1957, provides that the legal limitation or exemption of carriers' liability in tort towards senders or recipients extends to the liability in tort of those employed by the carriers against senders or recipients.

Domestically, questions arise as to: (1) whether the limitation or exemption clause extends to liability in tort; (2) whether the limitation or exemption clause extends to the recipient; and (3) whether the limitation or exemption clause extends to those who are under contract to the carriers as employees or independent businesses, in cases where the carriers contract with a sender to transport the sender's goods and the goods are destroyed or damaged during transport, and the agreement contains a limitation or exemption clause in respect of the carrier's liability in the case of negligence (not gross or intentional negligence).

The Supreme Court decision of 30 April 1998 (heisei 10)[50] dealt with question (1), holding that the provision on limitation of liability up to a fixed amount applies not only to liability for breach of an obligation but also to liability based on tort, on the ground that it matches the reasonable intention of the parties and meets the purpose of the limitation clause.

The same Supreme Court decision also addressed question (2) and held that the limitation clause would work in an action for liability in tort brought by the recipient against the carrier, stating that such a limitation clause is reasonable in consideration of the purpose of the clause, the nature of the contract and the convenience and benefits it brings, and that it would be contrary to good faith for the recipient of a relatively low-cost carriage to seek damages beyond that limitation if the recipient approved the carriage of the goods (jewels) to be by ordinary low-cost door-to-door delivery.

In relation to question (3), a Tokyo District Court decision of 25 November 1975 (showa 50) held that the protection afforded by Article 578 of the Commercial Code to the carrier of the high-price goods does not extend to the carrier's employee. Scholarly views are divided. One view is that employees can invoke the limitation or exemption clause between the carrier (employer) and the sender, because it is unreasonable for the employer to be exempt but not its employee, or that the sender may benefit unjustly if the price is determined in consideration of the fact that such a limitation or exemption clause exists. Another view is that it is a matter of interpretation of the contract whether such a clause is also intended not only to determine the allocation of risk between the parties to the contract but also to waive

[50] Hanrei Jiho 1646-162.

compensation rights against employees, harking back to the essence or spirit of contracts for the benefit of a third party.[51]

V. Legislative Developments

1. Deliberations at the Government Level

On October 2009 (heisei 21), the Japanese Minister of Justice launched a consultation requesting the Legislative Council of the Ministry of Justice to present an outline of the revision of the Civil Code in matters related to Obligations, which covers parts of Part 1 (General Provisions) and Part 3 (Obligations) of the Civil Code. A special subcommittee was formed which started deliberations in November 2009. It submitted a draft outline for the revision of the Civil Code (Obligation-related matters) to the general assembly of the Legislative Council in February 2015, which approved and finalized it. The resulting text was submitted to the Minister of Justice in February 2015. A bill to revise the Civil Code, based on the report by the Legislative Council to the Ministry of Justice, was tabled before the Diet in March 2015. The Diet has just concluded its debates on this matter (see section I.3).

The revised Code features two modifications relating to contracts for the benefit of a third party. The first change is an addition to Article 537 stipulating that the fact that the beneficiary of such a contract did not yet exist or had not yet been specified at the time of conclusion of the contract would not render the contract ineffective (new Article 537(2)). This was intended to restate and generalize the current case law.

The second change is an addition to Article 538. According to new Article 538(2), a contracting party (the promisee) may terminate the contract with the consent of the third party if the other contracting party (the promisor) does not perform its obligation to the third party after the right of the third party arises according to Article 537. This was intended to clarify that the intention of the third party, even though not a party to the contract, should be respected.

Other proposals made during the deliberations of the Subcommittee of the Legislative Council to the Ministry of Justice (specifically, some proposals in the interim draft of July 2013) were not taken on board in the final proposal or the bill. One such proposal was to use such concepts as promisor and promisee in this context. Another was to add provisions that the promisee may demand that the promisor perform its obligation to the beneficiary.

The Subcommittee also discussed other issues such as: (1) whether the third party acquires its right to enjoy the benefit automatically, without a declaration of intent, and whether it may waive its right afterwards, at least in some situations; (2) whether several categories of contracts for the benefit of a third party should be established; and (3) whether, if proposal (1) were adopted, new provisions should be added to the effect that the parties to the contract may not revoke or amend the contract to change or extinguish the right of the third party at a certain stage when the third party has a legitimate expectation of its acquisition of the benefit or right.

2. Academic Writings and Draft Proposals

In October 2006, before the consultation by the Minister of Justice and the start of deliberations in the Subcommittee of the Legislative Council of the Ministry of Justice, a group of

[51] 奥田昌道編『新版注釈民法(10-II)』(第2版) 250–255頁(有斐閣、2011) [北川善太郎=潮見佳男(補訂)] (Masamich Okuda (ed), *Japanese Civil Code Annotated*, vol 10-II [Zentaro Kitagawa, supplemented by Yoshio Shiomi] (2nd edn, Tokyo: Yuhikaku Publishing Co 2011) 250–255).

scholars established a working group on the revision of the law of obligations of the Civil Code: 'The Japanese Civil Code (Law of Obligations) Reform Commission'. The Reform Commission consisted of 33 professors with specific expertise (26 in civil law, five in commercial law, and two in civil procedure law) and two officials from the Ministry of Justice, with several supporting staff (young academics and young Ministry of Justice officials). Their draft proposals, the 'Basic Reform Policy (Draft Proposals)' were published in 2009.

The Draft Proposals contain detailed rules on contracts for the benefit of a third party that are worth mentioning since they were referred to during the deliberations of the Legislative Council of the Ministry of Justice, and also, more significantly, because the proposals indicate or reflect current academic thinking relating to contracts for the benefit of a third party. For this reason, it is important to know the Draft Proposals on the subject which the Commission has made available in the English language.[52]

3. Draft Proposals: Book III Obligations—Part Two Specific Contracts—Chapter 16 Supplementary Rules—Division 1 Contracts for the Benefit of Third Parties

[3.2.16.01] (Types of contracts for the benefit of third parties)

The parties to a contract shall be allowed, through the following modes, to agree that one of the parties (promisor) may promise another party (promisee) that it shall grant a certain right or benefit to a third party (beneficiary):

(a) Have the beneficiary acquire a claim vis-a-vis the promisor (claim acquisition type);

(b) Have the beneficiary undertake an incidental encumbrance in the cases of (a) (encumbered claim acquisition type);

(c) Have the beneficiary form a contract assuming an obligation of counter-performance vis-a-vis the acquisition of a claim receiving the transfer of a property right or the provision of services from the promisor (contract formation type);

(d) Have an obligation assumed by the beneficiary vis-a-vis the promisor released (obligation release type); or

(e) Make invocation by the beneficiary of a term relating to limits on or release from the responsibility of the beneficiary vis-a-vis the promisor, agreed upon between the promisee and the promisor, possible (term invocation type).

[3.2.16.02] (Claim acquisition type)

(1) With regard to the agreement of [3.2.16.01], if a promise is made that a claim shall be granted to the beneficiary, the beneficiary shall acquire the claim vis-a-vis the promisor immediately.

(2) In cases of (1), an encumbrance may not be imposed on the beneficiary.

(3) If a beneficiary does not wish to acquire a claim, it may waive the claim through a manifestation of intention made to the promisor and, in such case, the beneficiary shall be treated as not having acquired the claim from the very beginning.

(4) If the beneficiary has manifested either clearly or implicitly to the promisor or the promisee that it approves the acquisition of the claim, the beneficiary may not waive such right.

(5) If an interested party has emerged on the premise that the beneficiary possesses the claim, a waiver by the beneficiary after such may not be asserted against such interested party.

(6) If the beneficiary has made the waiver, it shall be presumed that the promisee stands in the position of the beneficiary as long as this is not contrary to the intent of the contract.

[52] The Draft Proposals are available at <http://wwr7.ucom.ne.jp/sh01/english/draft_en.html> and the provisions cited are available at <http://wwr7.ucom.ne.jp/sh01/english/book3_p2_ch16_en.html> accessed 1 February 2017.

[3.2.16.03] (Encumbered claim acquisition type)

With regard to the agreement of [3.2.16.01], if the beneficiary promises to assume an incidental encumbrance vis-a-vis a claim granted to the beneficiary, the beneficiary shall acquire the claim vis-a-vis the promisor at the time of the beneficiary manifesting an intention of consent to the promisor.

[3.2.16.04] (Contract formation type)

With regard to the agreement of [3.2.16.01], if the beneficiary promises to assume an obligation of counter performance vis-a-vis the acquisition of a claim to receive the transfer of a property right or the provision of services from the promisor, a contract whose contents have been stipulated through an agreement between the promisee and the promisor shall be treated as having been formed between the beneficiary and the promisor at the time of the beneficiary manifesting an intention of consent to the promisor.

[3.2.16.05] (Obligation release type)

With regard to the agreement of [3.2.16.01], if it is promised that the beneficiary shall be released from the obligation assumed vis-a-vis the promisor, the effect of the obligation release shall take effect from the time of the beneficiary manifesting an intention of consent.

[3.2.16.06] (Term invocation type)

With regard to the agreement of [3.2.16.01] , if it is promised that the beneficiary may invoke a term, agreed between the promisee and promisor, relating to limits on or release from responsibility vis-a-vis the promisor, by invoking such term the beneficiary shall be deemed to have received application of the term in the relationship with the promisor from the time of the agreement between the promisee and the promisor.

[3.2.16.07] (Possibility of identification /non-existence of a third party)

(1) It shall not be required that a beneficiary should exist or should be identifiable at the time of an agreement of a contract between the promisee and the promisor made for the benefit of a third party.

(2) If the beneficiary of the contract for the benefit of a third party of [3.2.16.01] (a) does not exist or cannot be identified, the claim of the beneficiary shall accrue from the time of the existence or identification of the beneficiary.

(3) With regard to a contract for the benefit of a third party of [3.2.16.01] (a), if the person who is to be the beneficiary still does not exist or cannot be identified at the time of the performance date of the claim to be acquired by the beneficiary, it shall be treated in the same manner as cases in which the waiver by the beneficiary was made.

(4) With regard to a contract for the benefit of a third party of [3.2.16.01] (b) and (c), if the person who is to be the beneficiary does not exist or cannot be identified at the time when consent by the beneficiary is required, the effect of the agreement between the promisee and the promisor shall be presumed to have been lost.

[3.2.16.08] (Availability of a demand by the promisee for performance vis-a-vis the promisor)

With regard to a contract for the benefit of a third party of [3.2.16.01] (a) and (b), the promisee may demand performance from the promisor to the beneficiary with regard to a claim acquired by the beneficiary.

[3.2.16.09] (Modification/revocation of a right)

(1) With regard to a contract for the benefit of a third party of [3.2.16.01] (a), if the promisee or the promisor has notified the beneficiary of an agreement which does not reserve the right of revocation or the right of modification, or if the beneficiary has manifested an intention approving acquisition of the right to the promisee or the promisor, the promisee and the promisor may not modify the contents of the agreement or revoke it.

(2) With regard to a contract for the benefit of a third party of [3.2.16.01] (b) and (c), if the promisee or the promisor has notified the beneficiary of an agreement which does not reserve the right of revocation or the right of modification, or if the beneficiary has manifested an intention of consent to the promisee or the promisor, the promisee and the promisor may not modify the contents of the agreement or revoke it.

(3) With regard to a contract for the benefit of a third party of [3.2.16.01] (e), the promisee and the promisor may not modify or revoke a term to be invoked by the beneficiary after the beneficiary has come to know of the contents of the agreement without the consent of the beneficiary; provided, however, that this shall not preclude a separate agreement being formed.

[3.2.16.10] (Right of cancellation)

With regard to a contract for the benefit of a third party of [3.2.16.01] (a) and (b), if the promisor does not perform such obligation, the promisee may cancel the contract with the promisor pursuant to the provisions of the Civil Code after acquiring the consent of the beneficiary.

[3.2.16.11] (Defense of the promisor)

The promisor may assert the defense, which can be raised against the promisee based on the contract with the promisee, against the beneficiary.

VI. Conclusions

The JCC started with a negation of the position taken by the Old Civil Code to deny contracts for the benefit of a third party except in very limited situations. The JCC admits that a third party acquires a right or entitlement to demand performance directly of one of the parties to the contract (the promisor). This broad recognition of contracts for the benefit of a third party reflects considerations of practical convenience and the fact that no actual harm is done to the interested parties. The theoretical justification for the acquisition of a right by the third party has not yet been fully developed. In part, this is because there is no systemic obstacle (eg consideration or cause) to render such a contract ineffective. The paucity of arguments is partly mitigated by the requirement of a declaration of intent to enjoy the benefit on the part of the third party.

The concept of contracts for the benefit of a third party is well accepted, widely recognized, and pervasive as a way of thinking, so that an argument can be made and the question put in various situations whether a given case concerns contracts for the benefit of a third party, and the findings will depend on the facts of the case.

It is a question of interpretation of an agreement whether a third party acquires a right against one party to a contract, since such a right arises solely on the basis of the agreement, with the condition, in principle, that the third party declare its intention to enjoy the benefit.

The right or entitlement of third parties extends beyond a simple claim or right to demand performance (personal right) to such rights, entitlements or benefits as property rights, exemptions of obligations, rights with burdens, or contractual position (ability to conclude a contract).

All this does not mean that all matters concerning contracts for the benefit of a third party have now been dealt with.

Under Japanese private law, however, there is no need to fill any gaps or insufficiencies in terms of tort liability, in the case of contracts for the benefit of a third party. Since the Code has a unified general rule on tort liability (Article 709), the coverage of losses/damages is not limited to those incurred by the direct victim.

There is a question as to whether a third party may invoke a contractual clause when that third party is designated in the agreement. There is not much enthusiasm for categorizing this as one of the questions arising in the context of contracts for the benefit of a third party unless the contractual clause gives the third party some rights or entitlements (not exemptions). This is not to say that the third party may not invoke the contractual exemption clause.

Legislative work has been carried out and several issues on contracts for the benefit of a third party have been dealt with, but the actual changes made were minimal.

14

Contract Formation and Third Party Beneficiaries in Korea

*KWON Youngjoon**

I. Introduction

In this chapter, I will present a general overview of contract formation and third party beneficiaries under Korean contract law. Before addressing these issues, I will briefly introduce the background and structure of the Korean Civil Code ('KCC'), which is the most important source of understanding these issues.

Within the dichotomy of civil law and common law traditions, Korean law is classified as civil law. As in many civil law countries, statutory law is the major source of law in Korea.[1] Therefore, the generally recommended way of approaching a given issue in Korean law is to look at the relevant Korean statute and its provisions covering the issue. As for contract formation and third party contracts, the KCC is the governing law. The KCC comprehensively codifies core areas of private law, including contract, property, tort, and family law.[2] The KCC was promulgated in 1958, and came into force in 1960. Since that time, it has functioned as a fundamental norm governing legal relationships among private entities.

In terms of its overall structure, there are close parallels with the *Bürgerliches Gesetzbuch* ('BGB'), the German Civil Code, as well as with the Civil Codes in other jurisdictions of the civil law tradition that have been influenced by the *Pandekten* system.[3] In the manner of the *Pandekten* system, the KCC is divided into five books—general provisions (Book 1), the law of rights *in rem* (Book 2), the law of obligations (Book 3), family law (Book 4), and the law of inheritance (Book 5).[4] The law of contracts is mainly covered in the part on the law of obligations (Book 3) along with the part on general provisions (Book 1). Chapter 2 of Book 3 provides general provisions on contract, dealing with issues such as how a contract is formed, its effect, and how a party can terminate a contract. In Book 1, the KCC addresses legal rules on a 'juridical act'. The notion of juridical act comes from the German notion of *Rechtsgeschäft*, and is shared by other civil law countries such as Austria, Portugal, Poland, and Switzerland as well as Japan and Taiwan. Since a contract is the archetype of a juridical act, the rules on juridical acts in Book 1 are also applicable to contracts.

This resemblance can be traced back to the early history of the KCC. After Japan annexed the Korean peninsula to colonize it, the colonial government promulgated a Decree on Civil Matters on *Joseon* declaring the enforcement of Japanese law in civil matters in the colony.

* Cite as Y Kwon, 'Contract Formation and Third Party Beneficiaries in Korea' in Chen-Wishart, Loke, & Vogenauer, *Studies in the Contract Laws of Asia Vol II: Formation and Third Party Beneficiaries* (Oxford: OUP 2017) ch 14.

[1] Kwon Youngjoon, 'Korea: Bridging the Gap between Korean Substance and Western Form' in EA Black and GF Bell (eds), *Law and Legal Institutions of Asia* (Cambridge: Cambridge University Press 2011) 152–153.

[2] ibid 158. [3] Kwon Youngjoon, 'Civil Law and Civil Procedure Law' in Korean Legislation Institute, *Introduction to Korean Law* (Berlin et al: Springer 2013). 116.

[4] The English version of the KCC is available on the official website of the Korean Legislation Research Institute: <http://elaw.klri.re.kr/kor_service/lawView.do?hseq=29453&lang=ENG> accessed 4 February 2017. The translation of the KCC provisions in this chapter comes from this source.

Contract Formation and Third Party Beneficiaries in Korea. Kwon Youngjoon.

By virtue of this decree, the Japanese Civil Code ('JCC') became the governing norm in Korea in the area of private legal matters. After Japanese colonial rule ended and the Republic of Korea was formally established, the Committee of Law Compilation started work on drafting the first civil code. Western laws, including those of Germany, Switzerland, and France, were studied and examined in the process. However, the influence of the JCC lingered; the German influence on the JCC strongly affected not only the drafting process, but also its later interpretation.

It is worth noting that proposals to amend the KCC have been drafted by the Ministry of Justice in Korea. The KCC first took effect in 1960, and quite a few piecemeal amendments have been made since that time. However, most of these dealt with family law, an area where some of the obsolete traditional values incorporated in the initial Civil Code had to give way to modern ideas of law. There have been very few amendments to the first three books of the KCC. Bowing to incessant calls for an overall revision of the KCC to reflect the tremendous changes in Korean society since it was first adopted, the Ministry of Justice started work on a complete overhaul of the KCC in 2009. This ambitious project was concluded in February 2014. As a result, Korea now has a complete draft for the amendment of the KCC ('Amendment Draft').[5] Interestingly enough, the Ministry has chosen to submit partial drafts in smaller units, more manageable for the National Assembly than reviewing the lengthy Amendment Draft in one go. This should facilitate the legislative process and increase the chances of passage of the drafts. So far, the draft amendments concerning adult guardianship, surety contracts, and travel contracts have passed the National Assembly. The remainder of the Amendment Draft, which is still in the hands of the Ministry, contains some important changes in the area of contract law as well. For example, the draft no longer requires 'fault' for the termination of a contract. The draft also codifies the legal doctrine on change of circumstances, which has already been acknowledged in Supreme Court decisions and scholarly opinion. The draft also presents some changes in the area of contract formation and third party contracts, albeit not drastic ones. Rather, it aims to reflect current academic discourse and case law in the fields of contract formation and third party contracts in a modest way. Where necessary, I will also refer to the Amendment Draft in addition to the KCC as I explain Korean law on relevant issues.

Although the KCC is such an important instrument, its provisions are not sufficiently concrete to offer answers to each and every legal issue arising from diverse cases. Case law, mainly composing of accumulated Supreme Court decisions, fleshes out the legal principles set forth by the KCC, and plays a crucial role in shaping contract law in practice. Korea is not a common law country, and does not employ the principle of *stare decisis*. However, the de facto power of case law is highly significant in practice. In a certain sense, case law is a de facto source of law in Korea. With regard to the topics to be addressed in this chapter, case law bears significant weight. For this reason, I will also cite relevant Supreme Court decisions to highlight the points I make.

II. Contract Formation and Enforceability

1. Basic Principle—Legally Binding Agreement Required

In principle, a contract is formed when there is a legally binding agreement between or among contracting parties. This is a widely accepted notion of contract all over the world,

[5] Part of the Amendment Draft has been published. See Ministry of Justice (ed), *2013 Nyeon Beopmooboo Minbeob Gaejeongsiahn-Jomoonpyeon*-(2013 Civil Code Amendment Draft by Ministry of Justice—Provisions) (Gwacheon: Ministry of Justice 2013).

and Korea is no exception. However, the KCC does not explicitly state this general principle. Indeed, the KCC, in its part on the formation of a contract, spells out detailed legal rules in Articles 527 to 535 without once presenting an abstract and overarching principle of contract formation. Nevertheless, despite the lack of such a provision in the KCC, the aforementioned principle is accepted in Korea, as it can be inferred naturally from the notion of contract itself.

For reference, it should be noted that the Amendment Draft expressly states this general principle in a separate provision. Article 527 of the Amendment Draft stipulates that a contract is formed when the parties reach an agreement that is definite and specific enough to determine its content with the intent to be legally bound by it. The inclusion of this provision does not introduce a novel principle, but rather confirms and codifies the existing conventional understanding of the formation of a contract. It also suggests a slight yet meaningful shift from the 'offer–acceptance model' to the 'agreement model'. I will further articulate the aforementioned principle as it is understood in Korea.

(a) Agreement

First, a contract is formed only where there is agreement between the parties. As I will explain in more detail later, the KCC postulates that a contract is formed by matching an offer and an acceptance. However, a more fundamental and comprehensive justification in respect of the formation of a contract lies in the existence of an agreement in which 'a meeting of the minds' occurs. Since the essence of a contract is an agreement where the intentions of the parties concur, it is quite natural to aver that contract interpretation requires an exploration of the intent of the parties. Accordingly, the Supreme Court of Korea has, in a number of different cases, recognized three categories of contract interpretation to uncover the intent of the parties: (1) natural interpretation, ie the interpretation of a contract based on the actual intention of the parties;[6] (2) normative interpretation, ie interpretation based on the objectively understood intention of the parties;[7] and (3) supplemental interpretation, ie interpretation based on the hypothetical intention of the parties where the parties have failed to make an agreement on a certain issue.[8]

While the explanation that an agreement is a prerequisite to the formation of a contract seems quite clear, there are many cases in which the existence of an agreement is not easy to verify in practice. When there is a written contract, it serves as strong evidence of a certain agreement. However, oral contracts were frequently made in the past when ordinary Koreans were not so accustomed to making contracts in writing. This was partly due to a lack of understanding of the significance of a written contract in terms of evidence, and partly due to baseless optimism that breach of contract would not actually occur. The fact that the KCC has no provisions that render oral contracts unenforceable or disfavour them in any way has strengthened that custom. The abundance of oral contracts in Korea has led to difficulties in adjudicating disputes arising from them. As the existence of a contract and its content were not easy to verify, courts often had to rely on witnesses. The lack of a written contract, which usually provides more reliable information than witnesses, frequently led to the defeat of the plaintiff. Although this is still to some extent true today, the legal culture has changed dramatically. Many parties now clearly recognize the importance of a written contract and actually put their own contracts into writing. The growing use of standard

[6] Supreme Court Decision *93Da2629, 2636* (26 October 1993).
[7] Supreme Court Decision *2008Da90095* (14 May 2009).
[8] Supreme Court Decision *2005Da13288* (23 November 2006).

form contracts in daily transactions has also contributed to a decline in the use of oral contracts.

Furthermore, an implicit agreement is often at issue. One party may claim that an agreement has been made implicitly, while the counter-party rebuts the claim by denying the existence of any such agreement. Such confrontation also causes practical difficulties for the courts. A matrimonial agreement, which is also regarded as a contract, is sometimes the subject of dispute. The Seoul Family Court dealt with one such issue over two decades ago:[9] a man and a woman were in love with each other but did not make an explicit contract or hold an official engagement ceremony. The woman firmly believed that at least an implicit agreement to marry had been formed (under Korean law, such an agreement creates a legal duty not to break off the relationship without just cause). They were in a romantic relationship for two years and had frequent sexual intercourse. Meanwhile, although the man mentioned their future marriage several times, he did not explicitly propose marriage. The woman became pregnant three times. Each time, she had abortions at the request of the man. When the woman became pregnant for the fourth time, she refused to have an abortion and delivered a baby against the wishes of the man. The man subsequently married another woman, thereby breaking off the previous relationship. The first woman sued the man on the ground of emotional distress caused by breach of an implicit agreement to marry. The man argued that no such agreement existed. The Seoul Family Court ruled that a matrimonial agreement had been made implicitly, judging from their relationship, and ordered the man to compensate the non-pecuniary loss.

(b) Voluntariness

Second, a contract is formed by a 'voluntary' agreement of the parties. Freedom of contract is a fundamental principle of contract law. Forcing a party to reach a certain agreement against his or her will infringes this fundamental freedom. Reaching a voluntary agreement does not necessarily mean that the parties should clearly understand every detail of the agreement before they actually conclude a contract. As is often the case with many standard form contracts, some agreements are made in the contract but parties such as consumers do not understand or even perceive what is stated in the lengthy and complicated contract form. Nevertheless, an agreement is deemed to exist when a party agrees to accept all the terms and conditions as set out in the contract form presented by the other party, regardless of actual knowledge and comprehension of these terms and conditions. In any event, this type of agreement threatens contractual fairness. In order to address the potential unfairness of standard form contracts, Korea has a special statute to govern such contracts—the Act on the Regulation of a Standard-Form Contract.[10]

There are some exceptions to the principle of voluntariness. These exceptions are to accommodate compelling public interests. The KCC, for example, stipulates an exception for the purchase of structures or trees on land subject to *superficies*. Article 283 of the KCC entitles a person with the right to *superficies* on a parcel of land to request a settlor of the *superficies* to purchase the structures (mostly buildings) or trees thereon, when the settlor refuses to extend the period of *superficies*. Upon such request, a contract for the purchase of the structure or trees is formed by force of law regardless of the settlor's intent. Such a

[9] Seoul Family Court Decision *94Deu37503* (13 July 1995).

[10] English version of this Act: <http://elaw.klri.re.kr/kor_service/lawView.do?hseq=30151&lang=ENG> accessed 4 February 2017.

provision aims to protect the structure or trees on the land from being destroyed or removed, which might result in reducing its social utility. Similar provisions exist in the KCC, for example Articles 285 (which entitles a settlor of *superficies* to demand purchase), 316 (which entitles a person with *chonsegwon*[11] to request purchase), and 643 to 647 (which entitle a lessee to demand purchase).

(c) Legally binding force of contract

Third, a contract is a 'legally binding' agreement. Therefore, it is important to distinguish a non-binding agreement from a binding one. A contract is enforceable only when the agreement incorporates the mutual intention of the parties to be legally bound by it. A mere social agreement, such as an agreement to treat somebody in return for his or her hospitality or an agreement to help somebody do their homework, cannot constitute a contract, since the parties concerned generally do not intend such an agreement to have any legal consequence. The intention of the parties to be legally bound by the agreement may be inferred from various factors, including the nature of the agreement, the wording of the contract, and the parties' statement or conduct in the course of making the contract. In practice, the line between a legal agreement and a non-legal agreement is not always crystal clear.

The enforceability of a 'best efforts' clause is an intriguing issue in this regard. A best efforts clause is a contractual clause to the effect that a contracting party is required to exert best efforts to fulfil his or her contractual obligation. This clause is often used to reduce the uncertainty of the contractual relationship in circumstances where it is difficult to specify concrete, fixed terms and conditions at the time of making the contract. This clause is sometimes used in long-term contracts, in framework agreements, or in international trade contracts.

A Korean Supreme Court Decision of 1994 explicitly dealt with the legal consequences of a best efforts clause.[12] It concerned an agreement under which the person taking over the management of a company promised to have the company's former president appointed as honorary chairman for a term of six years and to provide him with the same privileges as the president. The person taking over the company promised that he would use his best efforts. The court of lower instance held that the phrase 'use best efforts' showed an intention to provide certain privileges unless the company's financial conditions deteriorated to such an extent that it would be impossible to extend such courtesy. In other words, it showed an intention to lower the threshold for termination of the contract due to a change of circumstances, and therefore the company had a legal obligation to provide privileges. However, the Supreme Court held that it was reasonable to interpret the parties' agreement as imposing not a legally binding obligation but one to be performed only as circumstances allowed, considering the general meaning of 'best efforts' and the reason for inserting such language in the agreement. If the intent had been to legally bind the parties, the words 'use best efforts' would not have been used. While the Supreme Court found that the obligation in this case was not legally enforceable, it does not necessarily follow that the Supreme Court will always deny legal enforceability to a best efforts clause: the reasoning of the 1994 decision was highly fact-specific. However, it does illustrate the court's stance against granting enforceability to best effort clauses too readily.

[11] ie a kind of leasehold right *in rem*.

[12] Supreme Court Decision *93da32668* (25 March 1994).

2. No Consideration or Formality Required

As long as there is a legally binding agreement, a contract is made unless the law establishes further requirements. No specific form is required for the formation of a contract. A contract can be made either orally or in writing.

(a) No consideration required

In common law countries, consideration is generally acknowledged as a requirement for the enforcement of a contract. Consideration is defined as 'something (such as an act, forbearance, or return promise) bargained for and received by a promisor from a promisee'.[13] Even when there is a legally binding agreement, the agreement is not enforceable unless both parties promise to give or do something in exchange. However, this is not the case in Korea, as in most civil law countries. The concept of consideration has no place in Korean contract law. As long as there is a legally binding agreement, lack of consideration does not render a contract unenforceable.[14]

In line with this, a gratuitous contract in which one party gives something to another party but receives nothing in return, can still be enforced under Korean contract law. The lack of consideration in that type of contract does not render the contract unenforceable. The legal consequence of a gratuitous contract, however, is not identical to that of an onerous contract, ie a sales contract. For example, a warranty liability in a sales contract as provided for in Articles 570 to 581 of the KCC is only applicable to other onerous contracts but not to gratuitous contracts. Furthermore, a gratuitous contract generally has weaker binding legal effect than an onerous contract. A gift contract, or donation, is the most typical kind of gratuitous contract. Such a contract is enforceable in Korea, but can easily be terminated. Article 555 of the KCC provides that a gift contract which is not in writing may be terminated by either party even where there is no breach of contract. This is in contrast with an onerous contract, where wilful or negligent breach is required for termination. Articles 556 and 557 of the KCC provide further grounds of termination such as treacherous acts of a donee or a change in the donor's financial state, which are not grounds for the termination of onerous contracts. Such legal grounds weaken the binding effect of a gift contract.

To protect the reliance of the donee, the KCC provides additional provisions. According to Article 558, termination of a gift contract does not have any effect in respect of any portion the performance of which has been completed. In other words, what has already been given to the donee need not be returned.

A distinction should be made between a gratuitous contract and a unilateral promise to give or do something. In the hypothetical case in which a contractor promises a subcontractor to pay extra money to complete the work on time, the unilateral promise does not in itself constitute the contract. Therefore, the subcontractor cannot enforce the additional payment unless it is proved that an additional contract on such payment has been made.

(b) No formality required

Likewise, no formality is required for contract formation or its enforcement in Korea. A contract can be made either orally or in writing. Signature of the contracting parties is not a requirement for the formation or enforcement of a contract either, although it is

[13] BA Garner (ed), *Black's Law Dictionary* (8th edn, Eagan, MN: Thomson/West 2004) 324.
[14] Kwon (n 3) 117.

customary for the parties to stamp a seal or sign their names at the bottom of a contract when it is concluded in writing. The 'no formality rule' is theoretically interconnected with freedom of contract. According to the Constitutional Court of Korea, freedom of contract includes freedom of formality.[15] Thus, contracting parties can freely choose the form of their contract, or choose no form at all.

Consequently, the Statute of Frauds as recognized in the common law does not exist in Korea. The Statute of Frauds refers to the requirement that contracts in certain categories need to be in writing and signed by the parties in order to enforce them. It first appeared in legislative form in England when the Statute of Frauds (1677) was enacted.[16] In the United States, the Statute of Frauds is applied to contracts in consideration of marriage, contracts that cannot be performed within one year, contracts for the transfer of an interest in land, contracts for the sale of goods worth $500 or more,[17] contracts by the executor of a will to pay a debt of the estate with his or her own money, and contracts in which one party becomes a surety for another party's debt or other obligation.[18] There is no similar restriction in Korea. For instance, no matter how high the total amount of a sales contract, it need not be in writing and signed for it to be enforced.

However, there are some statutory exceptions to the 'no formality requirement'. For example, Article 11 of the Act on Contracts to Which the State is a Party ('State Contract Act')[19] stipulates that a contract governed by this Act should be in writing. Similar provisions are found in various statutes, including Article 6 of the Instalment Transactions Act,[20] Article 3 of the Special Act for the Protection of Guarantors,[21] and Article 8 of the Arbitration Act.[22] The legal effect of non-compliance with these regulations varies. Non-compliance with the State Contract Act or the Special Act for the Protection of Guarantors renders the contract invalid. Meanwhile, non-compliance with other consumer-related laws is generally construed not to influence the validity of the contract. The Instalment Transactions Act renders the terms and conditions not included in the written contract void only if such terms and conditions are detrimental to consumers. The Arbitration Act does not give effect to an arbitration agreement that is made orally, but non-compliance with the Act does not affect the validity of a contract at issue.

The 'no formality rule' also has a bearing on the interpretation of contracts. Comparing it with the interpretation of a written contract according to the parol evidence rule in the common law would be helpful in this regard. This rule provides that written contracts that appear to be comprehensive should be interpreted based solely on the wording of the contract, without reference to any extrinsic evidence that might suggest an alternative meaning.[23] Accordingly, in cases where the parol evidence rule is applicable, the content of the contract should not be determined by reference to extrinsic evidence that is contrary to the plain language of the contract, or interpreted in a way that contradicts the plain language of

15 Constitutional Court Decision *89hunma204* (3 June 1991).

16 For text of the statute, see <http://www.legislation.gov.uk/aep/Cha2/29/3/section/IV> accessed 4 February 2017. The statute is still in force.

17 § 2-201, revised Uniform Commercial Code ('UCC') increases the threshold for the Statute of Frauds to $5,000.

18 EA Farnsworth, *Contracts* (4th edn, New York: Aspen 2004) 357–358.

19 English version: <http://elaw.klri.re.kr/kor_service/lawView.do?hseq=33319&lang=ENG> accessed 4 February 2017.

20 English version: <http://elaw.klri.re.kr/kor_service/lawView.do?hseq=27071&lang=ENG> accessed 4 February 2017.

21 English version: <http://elaw.klri.re.kr/kor_service/lawView.do?hseq=24325&lang=ENG> accessed 4 February 2017.

22 English version: <http://elaw.klri.re.kr/kor_service/lawView.do?hseq=18172&lang=ENG> accessed 4 February 2017.

23 Farnsworth (n 18) 414–415.

the contract. Again, Korean contract law has no such rule. It is therefore open to the parties to rely, along with the plain language of the contract, on extrinsic evidence that purports to establish the content of the contract. If the true intention of the contracting parties becomes evident and verifiable, it may override the wording of the written contract.

Let us assume that parties enter into a contract with the intent to conclude an agreement for the sale of property 1, but mistakenly list property 2 as the subject of the sales contract. The written contract cannot thwart the true intention of the parties, which is to sell or purchase property 1. In a Supreme Court case on a similar issue, the court ruled that 'for contractual interpretation one should not, in general, limit oneself to the text of the contract but search for the true intent of both parties'.[24] According to the court, the contract was concluded in respect of property 1 despite a written contract indicating property 2 as the object of sale. This is the basic principle for contract interpretation, but it may also be linked with the 'no formality rule'.

3. Offer and Acceptance

(a) Offer and acceptance as basic model

The typical picture of contract formation is that a contract is composed of an offer and an acceptance.[25] The KCC envisages a contract as such. In the subsection on 'Formation of Contract', nine provisions (Articles 527 to 535) incorporate legal doctrines on contract formation. All nine articles, except for Article 535 on *culpa in contrahendo*, make explicit reference to an offer and an acceptance. Article 527 deals with the binding force of an offer, Article 528 addresses offers specifying a period for acceptance, Article 529 contemplates offers not specifying a period for acceptance, Article 530 deals with the effect of delayed acceptance, Article 531 covers the notice of acceptance in a contract *inter absentes*, Article 532 addresses the formation of a contract without notice of acceptance, Article 533 focuses on the crossed offer, and Article 534 on acceptance with modification.

There are two statutory exceptions to the offer and acceptance model in the KCC: contract formation by realization of intention and crossed offers.

Article 532 stipulates that a contract comes into existence upon the occurrence of an event which may be taken as a declaration of intent to accept, when no notice of acceptance is necessary either by reason of a declaration of intent to that effect by the offeror, or by reason of custom. This exceptional form of contract formation is called 'realization of intention'. While it seems to depart from the traditional offer and acceptance model, a 'realization of intention' actually conforms to it: acceptance has actually been made by way of conduct rather than by oral or written expression. In that respect, it is not a departure from the prototype, but merely a variant. The difference between ordinary contract formation and contract formation by 'realization of intention' is that the latter does not require the declaration of intent subsumed in the conduct to be directed at or dispatched to the offeror. If the offeror made an offer by sending goods and the offeree consumed them without dispatching a notice of acceptance to the offeror, the contract is deemed to have been formed if the offeree's conduct is construed to show its intention to form a contract.

[24] Supreme Court Decision *93Da2629, 2636* (26 October 1993).

[25] An offer or an acceptance is a declaration of intent. When both declarations of intent meet, a contract which is a typical form of a juridical act is formed. A declaration of intent itself is not a juridical act; rather, it is an essential element of a juridical act. A juridical act may take the form of a contract when multiple declarations of intent, eg an offer and an acceptance, are combined. A juridical act may also take the form of a unilateral act, eg a declaration of termination or revocation.

Furthermore, Article 533 stipulates that the contract comes into existence at the time when each of two offers with the same content has reached the counter-party. This is referred to as crossed offers. Let us assume that A sent an offer to sell 100 tons of coal to B, while B, not aware of A's offer, dispatched an offer to buy 100 tons of coal. Although no offer and corresponding acceptance were made, the contract is formed by way of crossed offers. The contract is formed at the time when both offers reach the other party. In essence, crossed offers also represent a meeting of minds except that it does not take place in the exact sequence envisaged by the KCC in the offer and acceptance model.

Although the KCC envisages the contract as a combination of an offer and an acceptance, it is not always easy to pinpoint an actual offer and acceptance in a contract. This is especially true of contracts involving lengthy pre-contractual negotiations. In this regard, the offer–acceptance model does not always reflect actual contract practice. Rather, it is more practical to determine whether or not there is a legally binding agreement, or 'meeting of the minds'.

(b) Offer

(1) Offer in general

The concept of an offer is not explicitly defined in the KCC. Generally, legal scholars define it as a declaration of intent containing sufficient and definite terms that can constitute the contract upon its acceptance.

An offer need not be explicitly labelled as an offer by an offeror, as long as it meets the substantive requirements for an offer. For example, simply sending an invoice may constitute an offer in some cases, even where the invoice does not expressly declare itself as an offer or state its relation to a contract.

An offer generally requires sufficient and definite terms, but it may merely contain a standard by which terms may be determined at a later stage.

In order to qualify as a 'sufficient' offer, an offer should contain essential terms of the contract. What constitutes essential terms of the contract cannot be explained in a few words. It rather depends on the type and nature of the contract, and should be decided on a case-by-case basis. In a sales contract, for example, goods, quantity, price, as well as the identity of the parties constitute essential terms.[26] Without such essential terms, the proposal for a sales contract is not deemed an offer and cannot therefore form the basis of a contract.

In order to qualify as a 'definite' offer, an offer should contain determined or determinable terms. Going back to the sales example, determined terms exist when goods, quantity, and price are expressly specified in the offer.[27] However, a definite offer may still be made by stating the standard by which terms can be fixed in the future. For example, an offer can be made to sell a commodity at a price to be fixed by established market rates at the time of delivery. The Korean Supreme Court has firmly supported a position that a sales contract is formed even without determining the goods and price at the time of the contract if these terms can be determined in the future using a certain standard.[28]

In the end, whether an offer is sufficient and definite is a matter of interpretation. If the recipient can reasonably understand an abstract offer by referring to practice and usage, a sufficient and definite offer is deemed to have been made. For some types of contract, there

[26] Kim Jae Hyung, 'Bebryulhaengwieu hwakjeonggwa gue gijoon' ('Standard of Determining the Meaning of a Juridical Act') (2001) 41(1) Seouldaehakgyo beobhak (Seoul National University Law Journal) 249.

[27] ibid 249.

[28] Supreme Court Decision *84Daka2454* (11 February 1986); Supreme Court Decision *95Da18222* (26 September 1995); Supreme Court Decision *2001Da7940* (12 July 2002).

are legal provisions that supplement the contract when essential terms are missing. For example, Article 656(1) of the KCC stipulates that usages prevail where no agreement has been reached between the parties as to the remuneration in an employment contract. Furthermore, the second paragraph of the same article goes on to stipulate that such usages prevail where no time for paying remuneration has been specified and that, in the absence of any established usage, remuneration is to be paid without delay upon completion of the work agreed upon. In the case of employment contracts, an offer is supplemented by usages and default provisions.

(2) Invitation to make an offer

A mere invitation to make an offer should be distinguished from an offer. An invitation to make an offer does not meet the sufficiency and definiteness criteria required of an offer, or lacks the intent to be bound by its terms upon acceptance. The definiteness of legal intention is to be decided in each individual case, taking case-specific factors into consideration.

In practice, it is not always easy to draw a clear-cut line between an offer and an invitation to make an offer. The Korean Supreme Court interestingly pointed out in a decision made over half a century ago that stopping a public bus at a bus stop constitutes a mere invitation to make an offer, while an offer and acceptance concur when a passenger gets on the bus.[29] However, a prominent civil law scholar objected to this outcome, arguing that stopping a public bus constitutes an offer in itself since public transport cannot refuse to allow a passenger to board.[30] In a bidding procedure, the Supreme Court views a public advertisement to submit bids as an invitation to make an offer, while regarding bidding by a bidder as an offer and the declaration of a successful bid as an acceptance.[31]

The nature of a commercial advertisement is also often disputed in this regard. A commercial advertisement in a newspaper, on radio, television, the internet, or by catalogue is usually deemed an invitation to make an offer. However, it may become an offer if it is sufficient and definite, or if the offeror clearly indicates that it is an offer. In the latter case, the question of the validity of such declaration of intent to constitute an offer without sufficient and definite terms or standards is quite a different matter. If these requirements are not met, such an offer is not valid.

The Supreme Court has addressed the legal nature of a commercial advertisement in several decisions. One case concerned a commercial advertisement for the sale of an office in a building.[32] The seller advertised that the building would be used as a leisure centre with game zones. Based on this optimistic expectation, the seller also advertised that a net profit of at least 1 million won a month was firmly expected to be made once the office space in the building had been commercially leased. The Supreme Court ruled that such an advertisement was a mere invitation to offer and as such did not constitute a contract. The buyer's attempt to seek compensation on the basis of breach of contract was frustrated.

(3) An offer in electronic commerce

Technological progress means that contracts can easily be concluded through electronic means. For instance, consumers frequent online shopping malls where they make instant contracts simply by using online instruments. Sometimes, an offer and an acceptance can easily be exchanged via email. The use of modern technology to make contracts should generally be encouraged. In practice, there are a great number of contracts that are made online.

[29] Supreme Court Decision *4291Minsang906* (18 February 1960).
[30] Kwak Yoon Jik, *Chagwongakron* (*Special Part of Obligation Law*) (6th edn, Seoul: Pakyoungsa 2005) 36.
[31] Supreme Court Decision *74Da402* (22 July 1977).
[32] Supreme Court Decision *99Da55601, 55618* (29 May 2001).

Furthermore, the KCC places no restrictions of form on contract formation, so that there is basically no legal barrier to e-contracts. Classic contract formation rules may also be applied here. The Framework Act on Electronic Documents and Transactions[33] makes this general principle clear where it states, in Article 4(1), that electronic documents are not denied validity merely because they are in electronic form.

Moreover, there are special statutes that expressly state that a declaration of intent by consumers in e-commerce constitutes an offer. The Act on Consumer Protection in Electronic Commerce, etc,[34] specifies in various articles, including Article 8, that an order placed by a consumer in an electronic commerce setting constitutes an offer. Articles to the same effect may be found in other statutes such as the Act on Door-to-Door Sales, etc,[35] and the Instalment Transactions Act. In theory, the act of ordering items advertised on an internet shopping mall may be regarded as an acceptance in certain circumstances. However, the aforementioned statutes uniformly regard an order as an offer. This has an underlying policy rationale. If a public advertisement on an internet shopping mall, which is often specific and sufficiently definite as to its terms and conditions, were to be deemed an offer, then the placement of an order by a consumer would be deemed an acceptance. Upon placing an order, a contract would be formed and thus make the order irrevocable. It would not be possible under this regime for a consumer to change his or her mind and ask for a refund unless there were justifications for revocation or termination of the contract. Therefore, to treat an order as an offer serves to protect consumers by allowing revocation of an offer. All the above Acts provide legal grounds for the revocation of an offer, although an offer is in principle not revocable under the KCC. The same goal may be reached even when an order is deemed an acceptance by allowing a consumer to revoke or terminate the contract during a cooling-off period. However, revoking an offer before completion of the contract seems to be a simpler solution, at least theoretically, than revoking or terminating a completed contract.

(4) When an offer becomes effective

An offer becomes effective when it reaches the offeree (KCC Article 111(1)). The validity of an offer is not affected even if the offeror dies or loses his capacity to act after he or she has dispatched the offer (KCC Article 111(2)). In the case of the death of the offeror, an heir or the heirs inherit(s) the legal status of the offeror unless it is uninheritable by its nature.[36] Legal status is uninheritable where personal identity is critical, such as an employee in an employment contract or a partner in a partnership contract.

As to when an offer is deemed to have reached the offeree, it should be determined by whether the offer has fallen into the domain of the offeree. For example, an offer is deemed to have reached the offeree if the letter containing the offer was placed into the offeree's mailbox. It does not require the actual knowledge of the offeree. However, if the offeree cannot be reasonably expected to find out about an offer, the offer has not reached the offeree. An offer in a memorandum hidden inside a commodity, for example, would not be regarded as having reached the offeree.

[33] English version: <http://elaw.klri.re.kr/kor_service/lawView.do?hseq=28630&lang=ENG> accessed 4 February 2017.

[34] English version: <http://elaw.klri.re.kr/kor_service/lawView.do?hseq=30308&lang=ENG> accessed 4 February 2017.

[35] English version: <http://elaw.klri.re.kr/kor_service/lawView.do?hseq=31937&lang=ENG> accessed 4 February 2017.

[36] Song Deok Soo, *Sinminbeobgangeui* (*New Civil Law Lecture*) (5th edn, Seoul: Pakyoungsa 2012) 1303; Kwak (n 30) 37.

A challenging issue is whether or not an offer has reached the offeree if the offer was made by email. It is quite clear that such an offer is deemed to have reached the offeree if the offeree has actually read it. However, the issue becomes less clear if the email has reached the offeree's electronic mailbox but the offeree has not actually read it. Another circumstance that poses a difficult problem of interpretation is where an email has reached the email server but has not been sent on to the offeree's individual email account due to a full mailbox. Even if it does reach the offeree's individual email account, spam filtering may also prevent the offeree from reading it. The Framework Act on Electronic Documents and Transactions offers a legislative solution for these issues. Article 6(2) of the Act stipulates as follows:

> (2) An electronic document shall be deemed received in any of the following cases:
>
> 1. Where a recipient has designated an information processing system through which he/she will receive the electronic document: When it is entered into the designated information processing system: Provided that where it is entered into an information processing system other than the designated information processing system, referring to the time the recipient prints it out;
> 2. Where a recipient has not designated an information processing system through which he/she will receive the electronic document: When it is entered into the information processing system he/she manages.

Neither provision requires a recipient actually to read the electronic document. As long as it enters into either the designated system or the system managed by the recipient, an electronic document is deemed to have been received.

(5) Revocability of an offer

An offer becomes effective when it reaches the offeree. Article 527 of the KCC states the binding effect of an offer by stipulating that 'an offer of a contract may not be revoked'. In that sense, an offer is binding and not revocable in principle. Under this regime, an offeree's reliance that the contract is concluded as soon as he or she accepts it is better protected. Meanwhile, it may be thought overprotective since it protects the offeree's reliance even before the contract is concluded. This may have a chilling effect on potential offerors who might not be able to retract their offer, thus making the planned transaction less attractive. Some exceptions have therefore been provided to lessen this risk.

It is construed that an offer is deemed revoked if the revocation reaches the offeree before or at least at the same time as the offer reaches the offeree. An offer can also be revoked if the offeror reserved the right to do so and made this known to the offeree. Furthermore, there are several statutes that allow revocation of an offer, mainly in order to protect consumers making an offer.[37] The Supreme Court has also ruled that an employee may revoke his or her offer to terminate an employment contract relationship before it is accepted by the employer.[38] The underlying policy rationale resides in the need to protect the employee. It allows employees to have second thoughts about terminating an employment relationship, a decision that may, after all, have a serious impact on their status.

It should be noted that the Amendment Draft takes a different position on the revocability of an offer. The shift reflects the position of the Supreme Court and legal scholars, which regards an offer as revocable if certain conditions are met. Article 529(1) of the Amendment Draft stipulates that the revocation of an offer is effective if the revocation reaches the

[37] Act on the Consumer Protection in Electronic Commerce, etc; Act on Door-to-Door Sales, etc; and Instalment Transactions Act (see section II.3(b)(3) (An offer in electronic commerce)) have provisions allowing revocation of an offer.

[38] Supreme Court Decision *91Da43138* (10 April 1992).

offeree before the offer reaches the offeree. This significantly alters the concept of an offer as being non-revocable. Article 529(2), meanwhile, lists the exceptions to the revocability of an offer. When an offeror has set a period for acceptance or declared that it will not revoke its offer, or when the other party has appropriately acted in reliance on the fact that an offer will not be revoked, the offer cannot be revoked.

(c) *Acceptance*

(1) **Acceptance in general**

An acceptance is a declaration of intent indicating assent to an offer. Without an acceptance, an offer alone cannot form a contract. An acceptance may be expressed orally or in writing. It may also be construed from conduct such as non-verbal expression.

It is entirely up to the offeree whether or not to accept an offer. In other words, there is no duty to accept an offer on the part of the offeree. Sometimes, the offeror states in the offer itself that a lack of notification of acceptance by the offeree automatically entails acceptance. However, it does not oblige the offeree to respond.[39] Silence is generally regarded as a refusal to accept. Silence is construed as implicit acceptance only in exceptional circumstances, such as when the same transaction has repeatedly taken place so that a practice of regarding silence as acceptance has been established between the parties.[40]

An offer should be accepted without modification. As a consequence, a reply to an offer that purports to be an acceptance but contains additions, limitations, or other modifications is indeed a rejection of the offer, constituting a counter-offer instead (KCC Article 534). Thus, a contract is not formed at the time of the reply, but only when it is met by a counter-acceptance by the original offeror.

An acceptance is valid only if the corresponding offer remains effective at the time of acceptance. The effective period of an offer can be specified by the offeror. In that case, a valid acceptance can only be made during that period (KCC Article 528(1)).

In a case before the Supreme Court where the offeror specified '18:00 August 8th, 1990' as the deadline for an effective offer,[41] the offeree accepted the offer at 18:58 on the specified date, 58 minutes past the designated deadline. The lower court reasoned that '18:00' did not literally refer to an exact time but simply indicated the end of the offeror's working hours.[42] The lower court found no evidence that the offeror's office had stopped work by 18:58, concluding that the offer was still effective at the time of acceptance. However, the lower court's decision was overruled by the Supreme Court, which interpreted '18:00' literally. As such, the acceptance made at 18:58 was not valid since the offer had already expired at 18:00.

Where an offer does not specify an effective period, a valid acceptance can be made within a reasonable period (KCC Article 529). An acceptance after the lapse of a specified or reasonable period is deemed invalid. However, such acceptance may be deemed to constitute a new offer (KCC Article 530). According to the Supreme Court, the term 'reasonable period' refers to the period of time determined objectively by considering the method of offer and acceptance, relevant trade usages, and the significance of the contract to the parties to the contract. The 'reasonable period' generally includes the time required for an offer to reach the offeree, for acceptance of the offer, and for the acceptance to reach the offeror.[43]

[39] Supreme Court Decision *98Da48903* (29 January 1999).

[40] If an offeror and an offeree are both merchants, and they have repeatedly conducted the same type of business transactions, the offeree's silence is deemed an acceptance (Korean Commercial Code, Art 53).

[41] Supreme Court Decision *92Da23537* (12 August 1994).

[42] Seoul High Court Decision *91Na20779* (1 May 1992).

[43] Supreme Court Decision *98Da48903* (29 January 1999).

(2) Late arrival of the notice of acceptance

An acceptance becomes effective when it reaches the offeror, as stated in Article 111 of the KCC. When an acceptance takes effect, a contract is formed. Late acceptance is deemed invalid and cannot form the basis for a contract. For instance, an acceptance is invalid if it reaches the offeror after the offer has expired. However, if the acceptance was dispatched at a time such that, under normal circumstances, it would have reached the offeror within a given period, the offeror has an obligation to dispatch a notice of delayed arrival of the acceptance to the offeree. If that obligation is not fulfilled, the acceptance is deemed not to have been delayed and forms the basis for the contract (KCC Article 528(2)(3)).

(3) Contract *inter absentes*

The KCC contains a special provision on the time of contract formation in the case of a contract *inter absentes*. A contract *inter absentes* refers to a contract between parties who are not in each other's presence, such as a contract concluded via mail. Article 531 of the KCC stipulates that a contract *inter absentes* comes into existence at the time when a notice of acceptance is dispatched.

This provision may be regarded as a reconstruction of the mailbox rule. The mailbox rule states that an acceptance becomes effective and binds the offeror once it has been properly mailed. This rule does not apply, however, if the offer provides that an acceptance is not effective until it has been received. The mailbox rule was first established in the English courts in the nineteenth century, starting with *Adams v Lindsell* (1818),[44] and was soon widely accepted in common law countries. On the contrary, the BGB does not have such a rule. § 130(1) of the BGB provides that a declaration of intent is effective when it reaches the other party, and the BGB allows no exceptions to this principle in terms of a contract *inter absentes*. The question here is how the KCC came to incorporate the mailbox rule when the BGB, by which the KCC was heavily influenced, has no such rule. The answer may be found in Article 526(1) of the JCC which is identical to Article 531 of the KCC, suggesting that this is the origin of the mailbox rule in the KCC. The *travaux préparatoires* of the JCC reveal that the rule comes from English cases such as *Adams v Lindsell*.[45] In short, the mailbox rule, despite its English origin, was adopted in Korea via Japanese law.

The interpretation of Article 531 of the KCC has given rise to controversy. Contract formation and contract effectuation are theoretically differentiated. The wording that a contract 'shall come into existence' refers to contract formation. The general principle is that a contract is formed when an acceptance reaches the offeror. Yet Article 531 of the KCC states that a contract *inter absentes* is formed when an acceptance is dispatched by the offeree. The legislative intention here is to bring forward the time of contract formation which is usually preferred in the transaction.[46] This article has therefore sparked discussion as to the relationship between contract formation and contract effectuation with regard to a contract *inter absentes*.

One position is that a contract is formed at the time of the dispatch of an acceptance but is effectuated retrospectively when it reaches the offeror.[47] Another position is that a contract is formed and effectuated at the time of dispatch of an acceptance unless the

[44] *Adams v Lindsell* (1818) 1 B & Ald 681, 106 ER 250.

[45] Homu daijin kanbo shiho hosei chouchibu, *Houtenchouchikaiminbogijisotkirok (3) (Judicial Chamber Secretariat Official Legislative Research Department, Japan, Statutory Law Research Center Civil Code Stenographic Record)* (Tokyo: Shousihomufenkyukai 1984) 689–692.

[46] Kwak (n 30) 43.

[47] Kim Sang Yong, *Chaegwongakron (Special Part of Obligation Law)* (2nd edn, Seoul: Beopmoonsa 2003) 55; Kim Hyeong Bae, *Chaegwongakron (Special Part of Obligation Law)* (2nd edn, Seoul: Pakyoungsa 2001) 109.

acceptance fails to reach the offeror.[48] Both positions concur that the arrival of the acceptance in the domain of the offeror is a condition for the effectuation of the contract. It harmonizes the general principle for effectuation of the declaration of intent as set forth in Article 111 of the KCC with a special regulation as set forth in Article 531. The difference is in the burden of proof.[49] The former position places the onus of proof of the arrival of an acceptance on the offeree, whereas in the latter position the offeror bears the burden of proof of non-arrival of the acceptance. Another difference concerns the revocability of an acceptance. The former position allows the offeree to revoke acceptance before its arrival, whereas the latter position does not.[50] There is no Supreme Court decision that directly addresses this issue. The second position appears to constitute the majority view among scholars.

Apart from the issue of interpretation, the rule in Article 531 has been criticized for inconsistency with the general principle set out in Article 111 of the KCC, without convincing reason. Progress made in the field of transport and communications has made it unnecessary to regulate the contract *inter absentes* and the contract *inter praesentes*. In order to resolve issues of interpretation and reflect social change, the Amendment Draft deletes Article 531, which provides the legal ground for the mailbox rule, while making it clear in Article 534(1) that a contract comes into existence at the time when a notice of acceptance reaches the offeror. This is in line with the general principle set out in Article 111 of the KCC.

4. Pre-Contractual Issues

(a) Pre-contractual stage and preliminary agreements

Some contracts are formed not discretely, but gradually. This is often the case with long-term or large-scale contracts. In these contracts, parties often go through a lengthy negotiation process in which numerous declarations of intent are exchanged. Preliminary agreements such as a memorandum of understanding ('MOU'), a letter of intent, a comfort letter, or a preliminary contract are often used along the way before a final and complete contract is made. In the pre-contractual stage of such contracts, additional legal issues that are not found in discrete contract formation arise.

The legal effect of preliminary agreements is one such issue. Is an MOU legally binding? Or is it merely a non-binding reciprocal declaration for a binding contract in the future? The same can be said of other forms of preliminary agreement. This issue is highly fact-specific and cannot be answered conclusively. In some cases, the parties explicitly specify that the MOU is legally binding. This is often the case with an MOU drawn up in respect of a large-scale merger and acquisition contract. There, the preliminary agreement is no different from an ordinary contract. By contrast, some preliminary agreements do not purport to be binding contracts. Rather, they present an abstract direction or construct a framework while reserving the detailed determination of rights and obligations to future contracts. Generally, a letter of intent is deemed less binding than an MOU. A preliminary contract is generally binding as well. Article 564 of the KCC presupposes that a preliminary contract for a sales contract is binding and states that a unilateral declaration of intent by an authorized party is sufficient to conclude a contract based on the above preliminary contract.

[48] Kwak (n 30) 43; Kim Joo Soo, *Chagwongakron* (*Special Part of Obligation Law*) (2nd edn, Seoul: Samyoungsa 1997) 89; Lee Yeun Young, *Chaegwongakron* (*Special Part of Obligation Law*) (5th edn, Seoul: Pakyoungsa 2005) 51; Song (n 36) 1308.

[49] Kwak (n 30) 43. [50] Song (n 36) 1309.

(b) Pre-contractual liability

(1) *Culpa in contrahendo*

The KCC offers no comprehensive set of provisions for the issues that arise in the pre-contractual stage. The only provision in the part on contract formation of the KCC that deals with pre-contractual issues is Article 535 on *culpa in contrahendo*. This article stipulates as follows:

Article 535 (*Culpa in Contrahendo*)

(1) In a case where a contract, whose objective is unattainable, is concluded, a party to the contract who was aware of, or should have been aware of such unattainability, shall be liable for damages suffered by the other party who relied upon the contract as valid: Provided that the amount of damages to be recovered may not exceed the profit which would have occurred if the contract was valid.

(2) The provisions of the preceding paragraph shall not apply in a case where the other party was aware of, or should have been aware of such unattainability.

This article may be of significance in theory, but is seldom used in practice. Only a very small number of Supreme Court decisions in Korea have applied it.[51] One such decision concerns the case where the parties' intended objective was unattainable.[52] Company X built a museum near a Unification Observatory run by the local government; company X entrusted the management of the museum to company Y. Company Y promised company X that it would issue combined tickets for the observatory and the museum and pay the ticket price to company X after deducting a management fee. Later, it transpired that such combined tickets could not be issued because of the relevant law. The Supreme Court acknowledged that this was a case where the objective of the contract was unattainable at the time the contract was made, and held that company Y was liable for damages, as it knew or should have known of this circumstance.

The gist of this article is that a party to a contract who knowingly or negligently promises an unattainable object is subject to damages corresponding to the reliance interest as long as it does not exceed the scope of the performance interest, unless the other party knew or could have known of the unattainability. The legal nature of the liability is contractual, since it arises from the contract-making process. However, a contract with an unattainable object at the time the contract was made is null and void. This is in clear contrast with a contract whose object becomes unattainable after the conclusion of the contract. If a house burns down after the conclusion of a sales contract, the contract does not automatically become null and void. However, if the house had already burned down when the contract was concluded, the contract is null and void.

The appropriateness of this dichotomy has been challenged.[53] The Amendment Draft adopted this view, providing in Article 535(1) that unattainability of the object at the time of the contract does not render the contract null and void.

Meanwhile, legal scholars have consistently attempted to broaden the scope of application of Article 535 beyond *culpa in contrahendo*. They have looked for legal grounds for other pre-contractual duties such as the duty to negotiate in good faith, the duty to provide

[51] Supreme Court Decision *73Da775* (27 November 1973); Supreme Court Decision *2010Da1203, 1210* (28 July 2011).

[52] Supreme Court Decision *2010Da1203, 1210* (28 July 2011).

[53] See Choi Heung Seop, 'Wonsijeok Boolneungrongwa Minbeob 535 Jo' ('*Culpa in Contrahendo* and Article 535 of the Civil Code') (1992) 9(1) Jaesanbeob Yeongoo (Studies on Property Law) 106; Yang Chang Soo, 'Wonsijeok Boolneungron (*Culpa in Contrahendo*)' (1995) 5 Minbeob Yeongoo (Studies on the Civil Law) 159 for criticism of the dichotomy.

accurate and timely information, or the duty to protect the interests of the other party. Their arguments have been largely influenced by the legal debate in Germany.[54] However, the Supreme Court does not follow this line of thinking. Of course, if the parties have actually concluded a contract, the injured party can claim damages from the other party on the basis either of contractual liability or of tort liability. If the parties failed to conclude a contract for some reason, however, the injured party can only hold the other party tortiously liable. As such, the Supreme Court derives the aforementioned duties from the general tort provision (KCC Article 750) in cases where contracts have not been formed.

(2) Duty to negotiate in good faith

One oft-disputed issue concerns the case where negotiations are broken off before the contract is concluded. The parties are free to negotiate and are not liable for failure to reach an agreement. This principle flows from the freedom not to make a contract, which is one aspect of the freedom of contract. However, there are some exceptional cases where a party bears liability for breaking off negotiations in a manner contrary to good faith and fair dealing. The following case before the Supreme Court deals with this issue.[55]

The plaintiff was a sculptor. The defendant, the Korean Export Association, extended an invitation to five sculptors, including the plaintiff, to submit a tentative draft for a sculpture to commemorate the fact that Korean exports had reached the 100 billion dollar mark. According to the terms and conditions specified in the published invitation, the defendant was to enter into a contract with the successful applicant. Among the drafts submitted, the plaintiff's draft was chosen by the defendant. However, the defendant did not make any contract with the plaintiff as announced. Nearly three years passed. Surprisingly, the defendant then turned its back on the plaintiff, notifying him that it was revoking its plan to install a sculpture. The plaintiff sued for damages.

The first ground for damages was breach of contract. The plaintiff alleged that the contract was formed when the defendant chose the plaintiff's draft. The underlying logic was that the submission of a draft in response to the defendant's invitation constituted an offer, which was accepted by the defendant at the time when it decided to select the plaintiff's draft. However, this claim was rejected by the court, which ruled that the key elements of the contract such as price, time of performance, and place for the sculpture were lacking.

The second ground for damages was tort. The plaintiff alleged that the defendant's act was a tortious act subject to tortious liability. The court accepted this claim, stating that to 'inflict losses on another party in the negotiation process by refusing to make a contract without proper cause after solid expectation or reliance that a contract would surely be concluded' constitutes an unlawful act. The court further stated that such an unlawful act oversteps the boundary of freedom of contract and is subject to tort liability.

As shown in this decision, a legal ground for liability arising from the breaking-off of negotiations is a tort. In this regard, Korean law differs from the German model which frames pre-contractual liability as an issue of contract law rather than tort law. This has to do with the fact that Korea has an open-ended tort regime. An open-ended tort regime is a tort regime in which a general provision provides a comprehensive set of requirements for tort actions.[56] The KCC governs tort law in Articles 750 to 766. The basic provision is Article 750, which states that anyone who causes losses to or inflicts injuries on another person by

[54] W Krüger and V Emmerich (eds), *Münchener Kommentar zum Bürgerlichen Gesetzbuch* (*Munich Commentary on the Civil Code*) (7th edn, Munich: CH Beck 2016) § 311 Rn 51 et seq.

[55] Supreme Court Decision *2001Da53059* (11 April 2003) (author's translation). The explanation of the case is quoted from Kwon Youngjoon, 'Pure Economic Loss: A Korean Perspective' (2011) 10(2) J Korean L 234–235.

[56] See Kwon Youngjoon, 'Pure Economic Loss: A Korean Perspective' (2011) 10(2) J Korean L 224.

an unlawful act, either intentionally or negligently, is bound to make compensation for damages. Unlike some jurisdictions such as Germany or the UK, where a casuistic approach is taken, Korea does not limit compensability to certain types of tortious act. Rather, it encompasses all types of act as long as they meet the four requirements of torts: unlawfulness, wilfulness or fault, damage, and a causal connection between the act and the damage.[57] Most importantly, it also covers cases of pure economic loss. Since the act of breaking off negotiations takes place before a contract is formed, any liability arising therefrom is deemed to be non-contractual liability. The broad tort regime in Korea also covers this area of liability.

(3) Duty to provide information for purposes of the contract

In order to make an informed decision, accurate and indispensable information needs to be provided to the contracting parties. This is also true when one party has information that the other party needs. In principle, the contracting parties are responsible for gathering their own information and there are no general information duties. In some cases, however, a party may have a duty to provide certain information to the other party. That duty may be statutory or contractual; it may stem from the principle of good faith in accordance with Article 2 of the KCC. Asymmetry of information is a primary triggering factor for the duty to inform. The type of contract, the particularity of the information to be provided, and the nature of the contracting parties are also factors in determining the duty to inform.

There are various approaches and views concerning the nature and extent of information disclosure. These views reflect the philosophical debate on autonomy versus paternalism in the realm of contract law. I will not elaborate on this issue in any detail since it deserves a more extensive discussion. Suffice it to say that the duty to inform, paternalistic though it may seem at first glance, ultimately fortifies the foundation for true party autonomy. When the duty to inform is recognized in any case, failure to fulfil that duty may lead to liability. As I have explained in respect of the duty to negotiate in good faith, a breach of the duty to inform leads to tort liability as opposed to contractual liability.

In Korea, a series of decisions on pre-contractual liability may be found involving misleading or exaggerated commercial advertisements. Most of these concern condominium advertisements.[58] The high number of cases involving condominium transactions is perhaps due to the fact that Koreans overwhelmingly choose to live in condominiums, somewhat inevitably perhaps given that it is a small country with a dense population. In many condominium transactions, the company selling the condominium to individual customers conducts an aggressive campaign using compelling commercial advertisements.

In one case, the buyers of units in a condominium who had acted in reliance on such an advertisement later brought a suit against the sellers on the ground of contractual and tortious liability, claiming that the advertisement was false or excessively overstated.[59] Among the issues in the case was the question of whether tort liability may be established if the seller failed to inform the buyer of important factors that might influence the decision to make a contract. In the case at issue, the defendant did not disclose the fact that a large public cemetery was located near the condominium complex. The plaintiffs discovered this after the contract had been made and invoked the failure to disclose a significant factor in the contract before the contract was concluded as a ground for tort liability. The court ruled that here the defendant had a duty, on the basis of good faith, to disclose the existence of the

[57] Kwon (n 3) 125.

[58] Supreme Court Decision *2005Da5812,5829,5836* (1 June 2007); Supreme Court Decision *2009Da1313* (23 April 2009); Supreme Court Decision *2007Da59066* (22 July 2010).

[59] Supreme Court Decision *2005Da5812,5829,5836* (1 June 2007).

public cemetery, since Koreans generally do not like to live too close to such places. Although this duty is not a contractual one, breach of the duty constitutes a tort.

This case is a typical example of where breach of a pre-contractual duty leads. In exceptional circumstances, it would be deemed a matter of breach of contract. In most cases, however, it would be regarded as a matter of tort liability.

5. Battle of Forms

When the offer and acceptance refer to conflicting standard terms that are provided by each party, and the conflict is not resolved in the contract, a battle of forms occurs. Often, the parties are not even aware that there is any conflict. They innocently believe the contract is formed without any disagreement. This awkward circumstance often arises in commercial transactions where estimates and orders involving pre-printed terms are exchanged between the parties. There are two major issues in respect of the battle of forms. The first is whether or not the contract is formed when such a conflict exists. The second is how the contract should be interpreted. To interpret the contract, the conflicting forms should be examined and a decision taken as to which of them should prevail.

There are several competing theories in this matter. The first-shot rule argues that the terms and conditions of the first form prevail, whereas the last-shot rule argues to the contrary. The best-shot rule or the reasonable-shot rule argues that the best or more reasonable terms and conditions prevail. The predominant view is based on the knock-out rule. According to this rule, neither set of terms and conditions prevails. The court is now entitled to fill the gap in accordance with the applicable law, trade usages, or practices.

So far, the battle of forms has remained an unfamiliar issue to Korean jurists and scholars. As far as I have been able to ascertain, there have been no judicial decisions that explicitly refer to the battle of forms as a legal issue in a case. Little serious scholarly discourse is to be found. This is in clear contrast with the substantial attention paid to this issue at the international level. The Draft Common Frame of Reference ('DCFR'), for example, has a provision on the battle of forms. Article II.-4:209(1) DCFR clarifies that a contract is nonetheless formed despite such conflict and that the standard terms form part of the contract to the extent that they are common in substance. Article II.-4:209(2) DCFR, on the other hand, provides an exception to that principle by stating that no contract is formed if one party indicates, either beforehand or afterwards, its intention not to be bound by the contract if such conflict occurs. Meanwhile, the DCFR does not address the issue of interpretation. To name but a few further examples of international instruments on contract law, Articles 2.1.19, 2.1.20, and 2.1.22 of the UNIDROIT Principles of International Contracts ('PICC') and Article 39 of the Common European Sales Law ('CESL') also provide similar rules on this issue.

The formation of a contract under the battle of forms is an issue closely related to the mirror image rule. The mirror image rule states that the offer and acceptance must correspond exactly to one another in order to constitute contract formation. In other words, the offer must be accepted with no modification. Common law jurisdictions traditionally adhere to this rule,[60] which says that a contract is not formed when standard terms comprising the offer or acceptance collide, unless the contract is formed by subsequent agreements or conduct.[61] Meanwhile, in cases where the mirror image rule is moderated or even

[60] *Hyde v Wrench* [1840] EWHC J90 (Ch), (1840) 49 ER 132.

[61] Subsequent performance of a contract may be deemed an implicit acceptance. See *British Road Services Ltd v Arthur V Crutchley & Co Ltd* [1968] 1 All ER 811 (CA Civ).

abandoned, the battle of forms occurs. For example, § 2-207(1) of the UCC stipulates that 'a definite and seasonable expression of acceptance or a written confirmation which is sent within a reasonable time operates as an acceptance even though it states terms additional to or different from those offered or agreed upon, unless acceptance is expressly made conditional on assent to the additional or different terms'. A similar provision is § 2-19(2) of the UCC, which states that 'a reply to an offer which purports to be an acceptance but contains additional or different terms which do not materially alter the terms of the offer constitutes an acceptance, unless the offeror, without undue delay, objects orally to the discrepancy or dispatches a notice to that effect'. Such provisions open a door to contract formation even when the battle of forms occurs.

What, then, is the approach of Korean contract law to the mirror image rule? There is no unanimous understanding of this issue among Korean scholars. One view holds that Korean law adheres to the mirror image rule. According to this view, a contract is not formed at all when two different sets of terms and conditions collide. If a contract is regarded as having been formed, a last-shot rule is a logically correct formula to resolve the conflict. Another view is that Korean law relaxes the mirror image rule. According to this position, a contract is formed as long as it contains material terms as well as the intention of the parties to be legally bound by it, even where there are conflicting terms. As a consequence, the battle of forms does not arise.

There has been no court decision in Korea so far that expressly addresses this issue. However, there may be circumstances in which the parties intend to form a contract within the scope of the agreed terms and even perform accordingly, while leaving out colliding terms. Under the mirror image rule, the colliding part cannot be regarded as a formed contract. If a dispute arises within the scope of the colliding terms, supplemental interpretation or supplemental application of default provisions or usages will deal with them. In other words, the knock-out rule is likely to prevail in Korea, although it is not widely discussed at present. The last-shot rule favours the party who last referred to its standard terms, and consequently voids preceding standard terms. The knock-out rule, on the other hand, knocks out colliding terms and supplements them with relevant legal provisions.

III. Third Party Beneficiaries

1. Basic Principle

Under a contract for the benefit of a third party, a person who is not a party to the original contract acquires contractual rights by virtue of that contract. Generally, parties to a contract have obligations and enjoy rights arising from the contract. This general rule, often labelled as privity of contract in common law, is the progeny of freedom of contract. Only parties who voluntarily commit themselves to the contract are bound by it. A third party contract is controversial in this regard since it seems to conflict with this principle. For this reason, third party contracts have long been a subject of debate in common law countries. The notion of third party contracts has come to be accepted in common law countries through gradual judicial development by breakthrough decisions or relevant legislative measures. England, for example, reformed the privity doctrine and allowed third party contracts by enacting the Contract (Rights of Third Parties) Act 1999.

By contrast, civil law countries generally have explicit provisions allowing third party contracts in statutory law. Korea is no exception to this. It is true that Korean contract law also acknowledges that, in principle, a contract is only binding on the contracting parties. This is the flip side of freedom of contract, meaning that no one can be forced into contractual responsibility without his or her voluntary commitment. In that sense, Korean contract law also has a privity rule. A third party who is not a party to the contract is not entitled to enforce the contract or to seek compensation for breach of the contract. However, the KCC explicitly acknowledges this exceptional form of contract as follows:

Article 539 (Third Party Contract)

(1) Where a party to a contract has agreed therein to effect an act of performance in favor of a third person, the person may demand such act of performance directly from the obligor.

(2) In the case of the preceding paragraph, the right of the third person shall come into existence from the time when he declares to the obligor his intention to accept the benefit of the contract.

The first paragraph of this article recognizes third party contracts and endows third parties with a right to demand performance by the obligor. To put it differently, a third party can enforce the contract even though he or she is not a party to that contract. The third party here is also referred to as a third party beneficiary.

The second paragraph of the article, however, attaches strings to this right by stating that a declaration of intent by a third party to acquire such a right is required to accept the benefit of the contract. The underlying idea is that even a right, as opposed to an obligation, cannot be forced upon the third party without his or her consent.

A typical scenario for a third party contract is as follows: B (the 'obligor' or 'promisor') makes a loan contract with A (the 'obligee' or 'promisee') to borrow money from A. Instead of paying the money back to A, they agree that B will make direct payment to C (the 'third party' or 'beneficiary') to whom A owes money. This is a simpler way of settling both legal relationships, that between A and B, and that between A and C. Even though C is not a party to the contract, C may acquire a right against B deriving from this contract. I will provide more detailed accounts against this backcloth on the legal relationships arising from third party contracts.

2. Legal Relationships Among Three Parties

(a) Legal relationship between promisee and promisor

(1) Contract with a third party beneficiary clause

The relationship between the promisee and the promisor is not so different from the relationships arising in other ordinary contracts except that it contains an agreement to endow the third party with a contractual right. This agreement is usually called an agreement with a 'third party beneficiary clause'. According to this clause, the promisor is under an obligation to perform for the benefit of the third party instead of the promisee. As a result, the third party is in a position to acquire a contractual right against the promisor. The acquisition of the third party's right is not a prerequisite for the formation or validity of the contract.[62] Thus, a contract is formed and deemed valid even when the third party referred to in the contract refuses to exercise its contractual right.

The existence of such a 'third party beneficiary clause' is not always easy to ascertain. If the contract benefits the third party only indirectly, no third party beneficiary clause is generally acknowledged. The third party who incidentally receives a benefit is not a third party beneficiary, and is not entitled to any contractual rights against the promisor.

[62] Supreme Court Decision *2011Da56033* (13 September 2013).

Let us assume that A directs B, the owner of a flower shop, to deliver a bouquet to C as a gift. A now makes payment to B in accordance with the contract. However, C, who is not a party to the contract and who has not made any payment, is to be enriched by this bouquet. Is there a third party beneficiary clause in the contractual relationship? The answer is likely to be no. B does have a duty to perform to A, but not to C. If B fails to deliver the flowers to C, it is A, not C, who is entitled to contractual relief. In some jurisdictions, such as the United States, the notions of 'intended beneficiaries' and 'incidental beneficiaries' are used, as in § 302 of the Restatement 2nd (Contracts)[63] and relevant literature.[64] The third party as a beneficiary under Korean contract law roughly corresponds to the notion of 'intended beneficiaries'.[65]

Whether or not there is a third party beneficiary clause is a matter of contract interpretation. According to the Korean Supreme Court, 'one should consider various factors including the purpose of a contract, the nature of the parties' conduct in the contractual relationship, gains and losses of the contracting parties or the third party, relevant trade usage, and the social function of the third party contract in interpreting reasonable intention of the contracting parties'.[66]

In some cases, there is an explicit provision to the effect that the contract is a third party contract. In such cases, determining the nature of the contract is relatively easy. Most cases, however, do not include such an explicit provision and it is not obvious whether the parties intended the third party to acquire a contractual right.

A frequent issue in Korea concerns real estate sales contracts. Let us say that A wishes to sell his house to B. When A first bought the house, A took out a loan from bank C. Subsequently, the house was mortgaged by C. When A and B sign the house sales contract, they set a price by deducting the amount corresponding to the mortgage obligation. Furthermore, B agrees to pay back the loan to C on A's behalf. Is this a third party contract? The answer depends on whether C has acquired a right to collect the loan from B.

The Korean Supreme Court does not usually treat such a sales contract as a third party contract.[67] B merely agrees to perform on behalf of A, but not to take over a contractual obligation itself. Therefore, bank C in the above case does not acquire a right against B even if it declares its intention to do so under Article 539 of the KCC. A is still an obligor to C. However, this may add up to a third party contract if A and B make it clear in the contract that they intend to endow C with a contractual right against B. C nevertheless needs to declare its intention to benefit from such a contract.

Discharging A of its obligation is another issue. Even if A and B intended so, such a contract cannot deprive C of its original right against A without C's consent. If A and B intended

[63] § 302 (Intended and Incidental Beneficiaries) states as follows:

(1) Unless otherwise agreed between promisor and promisee, a beneficiary of a promise is an intended beneficiary if recognition of a right to performance in the beneficiary is appropriate to effectuate the intention of the parties and either
 (a) the performance of the promise will satisfy an obligation of the promisee to pay money to the beneficiary; or
 (b) the circumstances indicate that the promisee intends to give the beneficiary the benefit of the promised performance.

(2) An incidental beneficiary is a beneficiary who is not an intended beneficiary.

[64] See eg Farnsworth (n 18) 657–658.

[65] However, for a beneficiary of a promise to be an intended beneficiary, US law requires 'the performance of the promise will satisfy an obligation of the promisee to pay money to the beneficiary; or the circumstances indicate that the promisee intends to give the beneficiary the benefit of the promised performance': see § 302(2) Restatement 2nd (Contracts).

[66] Supreme Court Decision *94Da54481* (26 January 1996).

[67] Supreme Court Decision *2000Da18578* (10 May 2002).

A to remain as an obligor whilst adding B as a co-obligor, such a contract is a typical third party contract. C is a third party beneficiary, and C may exercise its right against B upon its declaration of intent to do so.[68]

(2) Specific performance and damages sought by promisee

Since the third party acquires a contractual right based on the third party contract, it is the third party who is basically entitled to specific performance or damages. Additionally, the promisee can also demand that the promisor make performance to the third party as contracted. A difficult question here is whether the promisee, in addition to the third party, is entitled to relief in the case of default by the promisor. The prevailing view is that the promisee is indeed entitled to such relief, albeit in a restricted form.[69] As to damages, the promisee can only seek damages for harm actually suffered.[70] Damages for harm to the third party can only be claimed by the third party. In terms of specific performance, allowing the promisee to seek performance would frustrate the very goal of the contract, which is for the promisor to render performance to the third party.[71] Therefore, the promisee can only seek specific performance if the third party is not willing to or cannot receive the performance.[72]

(3) Revocation or termination

Since a third party contract is no different from other types of contract except that it has a third party, either of the contracting parties can revoke or terminate the contract as long as he or she has just reason to do so. Under Korean contract law, the revocation of a contract is allowed in the case of contracts involving persons with restricted legal capacity (KCC Articles 5, 10, and 13) or contracts made by fraud, duress, or mistake (KCC Articles 109 and 110). The termination of a contract is allowed when the right of termination is reserved in the contract or if there is breach of contract.

As I will explain later, the third party acquires a contractual right only if it manifests its intention to do so. Until that requirement is met, it is possible to revoke or terminate the contract since the third party has not yet acquired the right. Once the third party acquires the contractual right, however, revocation or termination may alter or even extinguish the right of the third party. Thus, revocation or termination after the acquisition of the third party right is a different matter entirely. According to Article 541 of the KCC, the right of a third party that has come into existence may not be altered or extinguished by the parties. This provision is intended to protect the established right of the third party from arbitrary interference by the contracting parties. For example, the established right of a third party to receive $1,000 may not be reduced to $800 by mere *ex post* agreement of the contracting parties. Likewise, the contracting parties cannot agree to do away with the third party contract after the third party has accepted it. The third party may, of course, consent to any alteration, revocation, or termination of the contract and, in that case, the question of

[68] Supreme Court Decision *97Da28698* (24 October 1997).

[69] Kim Hyeong Bae, *Chaegwongakron* (*Special Part of Obligation Law*) (2nd edn, Seoul: Pakyoungsa 2001) 191–192.

[70] Under Korean contract law, the party can seek expectation damages in principle. The party can also seek reliance damages in lieu of expectation damages when it is easier to prove the amount of reliance damages and the amount does not exceed that of expectation damages. However, reliance damages function merely as a proxy for expectation damages.

[71] Under Korean contract law, a contracting party is entitled to specific performance unless it is not feasible due to the nature of the contract, an agreement, or law to the contrary.

[72] Lee (n 48) 203.

interference with the contractual right of the third party does not arise. However, what happens if the third party does not give its approval? Can the parties still revoke or terminate the contract? An agreement to terminate the contract without contractual or statutory ground might impair the right of the third party, and is thus not allowed.

A more difficult issue arises when there is a proper ground for revocation or termination after the third party has acquired its contractual right. The Supreme Court has posited that no approval by the third party is required[73] since it is contrary to the conventional intent of the contracting parties to deprive the promisor of the right of termination even when there is breach of contract by the promisee, which is deemed a proper ground for the termination of the contract, and that the promisor bears a counter-obligation to the promisee.

Scholarly opinion in this area is divided. The prevailing view among legal scholars concurs with the Supreme Court position.[74] The rationale is that it is consistent with the usual intention of the contracting parties in a third party contract and that the rights of revocation and termination due to the contracting parties need to be protected. The opposite view argues that such an outcome is contrary to Article 541 of the KCC where it states that the right of a third party which has come into existence may not be altered or extinguished by the parties.[75] Proponents of this view point out that the prevailing opinion endangers the stability of the third party's legal status.

(b) Legal relationship between promisor and third party

(1) Acceptance of third party required

The third party is drawn into the contractual framework by a third party contract. This means that the third party may exercise a contractual right against the promisor by virtue of this contract. However, there is one precondition. The third party must declare its intention to benefit from the contract (KCC Article 539(2)). In other words, the acceptance of the third party is a prerequisite for the acquisition of the contractual right.

Comparatively speaking, the Korean position on the requirement of third party acceptance is different from that taken by § 333 of the BGB, where third party acceptance is not considered a requirement for the establishment of the third party right. Rather, the third party may only reject such a right. The position of the KCC in this regard is identical to that of the JCC, Article 537(2), where the acceptance of the third party is a prerequisite for the accrual of the third party right.

The declaration of acceptance should be made to the promisor (KCC Article 539(2)). It can be made either explicitly or implicitly. If the third party demands performance or files a lawsuit against the promisor, the declaration of acceptance is deemed to have been made.[76] This is in fact the most common way of making a declaration.

Controversy arises if the contracting parties can opt out of the requirement of acceptance so that they can grant a right to a third party regardless of the latter's acceptance. All depends on how the nature of KCC Article 539(2), which provides the statutory ground for the requirement of acceptance, is understood. If it is understood as a mandatory provision, the contracting parties cannot do away with this requirement by contractual means. If, on

[73] Supreme Court Decision *69Da1410,1411* (24 February 1970).

[74] Kwak (n 30) 131–132; Kim Jeung Han, *Chaegwongakron* (*Special Part of the Obligation Law*) (Seoul: Pakyoungsa 1988) 76; Kim Joo Soo, *Chaegwongakron* (*Special Part of Obligation Law*) (2nd edn, Seoul: Samyoungsa 1997) 106.

[75] Lee (n 48) 205; Kim Hyeong Bae, *Chaegwongakron* (*Special Part of Obligation Law*) (2nd edn, Seoul: Pakyoungsa 2001) 193; Song (n 36) 1352.

[76] Supreme Court Decision *72Da1208* (29 August 1972).

the other hand, it is understood as a default provision, they may contract out of it. There is no judicial precedent that directly addresses this issue, and opinions on the matter differ. Since the rationale of the provision is not to force the third party to acquire the right, it would be appropriate to regard it as a mandatory provision to protect that interest. It is true that the third party can still waive its right once it has automatically acquired the right under the contract, thereby reserving its choice. However, that is not what the legislator had in mind, judging from the relevant provisions.

While acceptance is up to the third party to decide, the obligor may demand of the third party that it clarifies its intention, as the following provision shows, so that the legal relationship can be put on a stable footing. Silence of the third party is deemed a refusal.

> **Article 540 (Obligor's Right to Demand Third Person's Answer)**
> In the case of the preceding Article the obligor may, with a reasonable period fixed, demand the third person to answer whether or not he will receive and enjoy the benefit stipulated in the contract. If the obligor has not received a definite answer from the third person within such period, it shall be deemed that the third person has refused to receive the benefit stipulated in the contract.

It should be noted that there are statutory exceptions to this precondition of acceptance. For instance, an insurance contract for the third party is a third party contract by its nature. However, Article 639(2) of the Korean Commercial Code makes it clear that the acceptance of the third party benefiting from the insurance contract is not necessary. The situation is very much the same with trust. Article 56(1) of the Korean Trust Act[77] stipulates that the beneficiary designated in the deed of trust obtains the right to benefit without a separate declaration of intent.

(2) Legal effect of acceptance

Once the third party accepts the benefit from the contract, the third party acquires a contractual right. This is to be distinguished from the assignment of a right by the promisor. Rather, it is a direct acquisition arising from the contract itself.

Acquiring a contractual right as a third party does not mean that he or she becomes a party to the contract. Therefore, the third party does not assume any contractual obligation in return. The third party does not have the right of revocation or termination enjoyed by the contracting parties. If the promisor refuses to fulfil its promise, the third party may resort to legal relief such as specific performance or damages.

Defences arising from the contract are available to the promisor against the third party. Article 542 of the KCC stipulates that the promisor may raise defences incidental to the third party contract. The third party's right is based on the contract between the promisor and the promisee. Therefore, the third party is subject to defences of the promisor against the promisee. These defences include invalidity of the contract due to a violation of public policy (KCC Article 103), an unfair juristic act (KCC Article 104), a declaration of untrue intention (KCC Article 107), a sham transaction (KCC Article 108), a violation of mandatory provisions, as well as the voidability of the contract due to incapacity (KCC Articles 5, 10, and 13), mistake (KCC Article 109), fraud or duress (KCC Article 110), or termination of the contract (KCC Article 544). The third party is also subject to conditions of the third

[77] Korea enacted the Trust Act in 1961. Although trust law originated in the common law countries, it is now not rare for civil law countries to have their own versions of trust law, as is seen in Japan, Korea, Taiwan, and France. The Korean Trust Act was revised in 2012, in order to introduce further types of trust. English version: <http://elaw.klri.re.kr/kor_service/lawView.do?hseq=29457&lang=ENG> accessed 4 February 2017.

party contract. The promisor may refuse performance to the third party until the promisee tenders performance in the bilateral contract (KCC Article 536).

(c) Legal relationship between promisee and third party

A third party contract covers the relationship between the promisee and the promisor, and the relationship between the promisor and the third party. The legal relationship between the promisee and the third party falls outside the scope of a third party contract. Even where there is no legal relationship between the promisee and the third party, the validity of the third party contract is not affected. For example, the promisee might merely desire to make a present to the third party by using the promisor as an intermediary.

However, it is quite common for the promisee to make a third party contract with the promisor because of the relationship between the promisee and the third party. The promisee may owe the third party something, and then have the promisor pay the third party on his or her behalf. Even if the relationship between the promisee and the third party becomes the cause of a third party contract, the validity of that relationship will not affect the validity of the third party contract. In that sense, the two relationships are independent of one another.

A sophisticated issue arises when unjust enrichment steps into this picture. Let us say that A and B made a contract designating C as a third party beneficiary. A sold an item to B and B made payment to C accordingly. Later, A was unable to transfer the ownership of the item bought by B. B terminated the contract. Can B require C to return the money he has received? Or should B turn to A for reimbursement?

The Supreme Court of Korea has ruled as follows:[78]

> When a third party contract governing the relationship between a promisor and a promisee is terminated, the contractual relationship should be settled between the promisor and the promisee. Therefore, the promisee cannot seek the return of what he performed to the third party based on the claim for restoration or unjust enrichment in principle.

The court of second instance, which ruled likewise, elaborated on the underlying legal doctrine as follows.[79]

(1) The entire performance made by the promisee is based on the contract between the promisor and the promisee. The third party has no direct relationship with this contract. Therefore, the return of unjust enrichment is also a matter to be resolved between the promisor and the promisee.

(2) The third party received payment because of his or her right towards the promisor. Therefore, regardless of the validity of the contract between the promisor and the promisee, the third party has a justified ground for receiving such payment. The promisee should request the return of unjust enrichment against the promisor who cleared off his or her debt by the performance of the promisee.

(3) If the promisee is entitled to the return of payment against the third party, this will run counter to the spirit of contract law since the promisee can inappropriately shift the risk arising from the contract to the third party.

In a nutshell, the Supreme Court ruled that the promisee should resolve any unjust enrichment issue with the promisor, not with the third party.

[78] Supreme Court Decision *2005Da7566,7573* (22 July 2005).
[79] Gwangju District Court Decision *2002Na2443* (31 December 2004).

3. Other Cases

(a) *Supreme Court cases*

(1) Identity of third party

One case worthy of note is a case regarding the identity of the third party.[80] The matter revolved around a security contract. The defendant was a security company and made a security contract with company A, using the pre-printed standard form provided by the defendant. The purpose of the contract was to protect the security and safety of the house owned and lived in by B, the finance manager of company A. B's wife, who also lived in the house, invited some friends to stay. While they were in the house, a burglar broke in and robbed them of their belongings. B's wife and her friends sued the defendant, alleging that the defendant breached the contract by not safeguarding the house appropriately.

The lower court ruled that the defendant was not liable to the plaintiffs under the security contract since the plaintiffs were not parties to the contract.[81] The contract indeed included a provision stating that the purpose of the contract was to protect the life and property of the 'user' through a security service rendered by the defendant. However, the lower court held that the 'user' in the above provision only referred to company A, a contracting party, but not to B, B's family, or visitors to the house. The lower court found no other explicit provisions in the contract to the effect that contractual liability extended to any third parties. In brief, the lower court understood the contract as an ordinary contract, not as a third party contract.

The Supreme Court reversed the ruling by the lower court. The Supreme Court held that the term 'user' in the above context should be construed to mean residents living in the building, not company A. The court pointed out that the reasonable interpretation of 'life and property' to be protected by the security service naturally led to the conclusion that the word 'user' actually refers to a person, not a company. In that regard, the Supreme Court viewed the security contract as a third party contract with company A as the promisee, the defendant as the promisor, and B and his family as the third party beneficiary. However, the Supreme Court ruled that the visitors were not within the scope of 'user' in the contract. Since B's wife, as a third party beneficiary, declared her intention to acquire a contractual right by filing a suit against the defendant, the Supreme Court ruled that B's wife at least should be entitled to contractual damages against the defendant.

In the contract at issue, the third party was not specified by name, address, or other factors. The contract, which was a boilerplate, merely referred to the 'user'. However, this did not prevent the contract from being labelled a third party contract.

(2) Identifiability of third party

Another case involving the determination of a third party concerned a child delivery contract. The factual background was as follows: a mother A delivered baby B in hospital C. Due to the negligence of a doctor during delivery, B was born with a disability. A and B sued C, claiming that C negligently breached the child delivery contract.[82] At issue was whether the contract between A and C was a third party contract with B as the third party. Since B was not and could not be a party to the contract as B had not even been born at the time of the contract, B was able to claim damages based on breach of contract only if B was deemed a third party. The decision in the case was handed down by the Seoul High Court.[83]

[80] Supreme Court Decision *92Da23339* (27 August 1993).

[81] Busan High Court Decision *91Na32* (1 May 1992).

[82] A and B also sought damages based on tortious liability. However, that claim was unfounded since the prescription period for tortious liability had expired. The remaining claim was therefore based on the contract.

[83] Seoul High Court Decision *2006Na14693* (26 October 2006).

The first issue was the validity of the third party contract which designated a third party who did not exist as a natural person at the time of the contract. When A and C initially made the child delivery contract, B had not yet been born. Under Korean law, a foetus does not have the capacity to enjoy a right unless the law expressly provides otherwise.[84] Therefore, B as a foetus could not enjoy a right as a third party at the time of the contract. According to the Korean Supreme Court, however, the third party beneficiary in a third party contract need not actually exist at the time of the contract as long as the beneficiary can be determined at the time of the acquisition of the right. For example, the Supreme Court ruled that a corporation that has not yet been established can become a third party beneficiary.[85] The Supreme Court also ruled that the future purchaser of a condominium unit is a third party in the guarantee contract between the condominium developer and a statutory guarantor for the development.[86]

Based on this assumption, the Seoul High Court acknowledged the child delivery contract as a form of third party contract, and allowed B, who was merely a foetus at the time of the contract, to seek damages based on the breach of contract claim against C. The following is an excerpt from the ruling:[87]

> Ordinarily, medical treatment is a one-on-one contract between a doctor (or a hospital) and a patient that is formed by the offer of a patient requesting treatment and its acceptance by a doctor. When it comes to a child delivery contract, however, not only the contractual relationship between the doctor and the mother comes into question but also the contractual relationship between the doctor and the foetus. Unlike other ordinary medical contracts, a child delivery contract concerns the delivery of a person through a proper delivery process in addition to safe treatment of the life and body of the mother during the process. Therefore, proper performance of the contract is of significance to the foetus. There is no explicit provision that entitles the foetus to exercise a right except for Article 762 which gives a foetus an exceptional right to seek damages for tortious acts. However, a child born through the delivery process can acquire a contractual right as a third party beneficiary by declaring its intention to do so through a legal representative. This conclusion is also in line with the intent of the doctor and the mother, the contracting parties of the child delivery contract.

(b) Hypothetical cases

The following cases are discussed for the purpose of making a comparison with other jurisdictions, and they help us to better understand the position of Korean law on third party contracts.

(1) Exemption clauses for stevedores

The first hypothetical case concerns exemption of liability for a third party.

X contracts with Y to transport X's goods using Y's ship to a foreign market. The contract for the carriage of goods by sea between X and Y contains an exemption of liability provision which purports to protect Z, the stevedores hired to unload X's goods from Y's ship once it arrives at the docks. As a result of Z's carelessness, X's goods are damaged while they are being unloaded from the ship and X wants to sue Z for negligence to recover damages

[84] The KCC provides the following exceptions whereby a foetus can exceptionally exercise a right: gift effective upon death of the donor (Art 562); damages for tortious acts (Art 762); inheritance (Art 1000); inheritance by representation (Art 1001); and bequest (Art 1064).

[85] Supreme Court Decision *4292Minsang773* (21 July 1960).

[86] Supreme Court Decision *96Da6592, 6608, 6615, 6622, 6639* (28 May 1996).

[87] Author's translation.

for the losses suffered by X. Can Z rely on the exemption of liability provision in the contract between X and Y?

The KCC does not address the issue of exemption. Rather, Article 539 of the KCC only mentions 'an act of performance in favour of a third person'. The general interpretation of this article among Korean scholars is that the third party acquires a 'right' through the third party contract. Exemption from liability does not fit the notion of a right. Therefore, Article 539 does not directly apply to this case.

However, the Supreme Court also acknowledges the validity of such contracts.[88] Scholars also recognize them as a modified form of third party contract and treat them as such.[89]

An underlying rationale for the recognition of such contracts may be found in an analogical application of Article 539. Although exemption of liability is not a 'right' per se, it is analogous to a right in that it confers a benefit on a third party. Therefore, Article 539 may, by analogy, albeit not directly, apply to such contracts as well. Thus, Z in the hypothetical case can rely on the exemption of liability provision in the contract between X and Y, by manifesting its intention to benefit from that provision.

(2) Selling bread

The second hypothetical case concerns the conferral of a benefit on one of the lessees by barring another lessee from running the same type of business.

X leases two adjoining properties to Y and Z. The lease between X and Y barred Y from selling bread because Z sold bread from his leased property. Can X and Y agree to lift the bar?

In this case, Z benefits from the lease contract between X and Y. If Y sells bread from the adjoining property, Z's revenue from the sale of bread is likely to decrease due to the competition compared to the situation where Z enjoys a monopoly on the bread market in the vicinity of X's properties. The question that arises is, is the restrictive covenant between X and Y barring Y from selling bread a third party beneficiary clause in the contract between X and Y?

If so, Z may acquire a third party right by declaring its intention to accept the right. According to Article 541 of the KCC, the right of a third person which has come into existence may not be altered or extinguished by the parties. As I have explained in the general account, this provision is intended to protect the established right of the third party from arbitrary interference by the contracting parties. As a consequence, X and Y, who are parties to the third party contract, are not allowed to lift the bar without the consent of Z.

However, this may not be an issue if the restrictive covenant between X and Y does not constitute a third party beneficiary clause. In that case, what Z obtains from the contract is a mere de facto interest, not a legitimate third party right. Therefore, X and Y may freely agree to lift the bar, against which Z has no remedies.

Whether or not the bar on Y constitutes a third party beneficiary clause is a matter of contract interpretation, thus highly dependent on the facts of the case. The key issue in the interpretation is whether X and Y intended to confer a given legal right enforceable against Y not to run a bakery. In this hypothetical case, this is not likely.

For reference, there are many Supreme Court cases in which a lessee is entitled to obtain an injunction against another lessee on the ground that he or she breached the restrictive

[88] Supreme Court Decision *78Da709* (24 September 1980).

[89] Park Joon Seo (ed), *Minbeob Jooseok* (*Annotated Civil Law*) (3rd edn, Seoul: Hankooksabeobhaengjeonghakhoe 1999) 434; Lee (n 48) 199.

covenant on a particular type of business.[90] These cases may seem similar to our hypothetical case in that they deal with a business restriction, yet they concern a situation where the owner of a commercial building designates the type of business for each unit in the building in advance and leases them to different lessees demanding a commitment to abide by the restriction, so as to maximize profit. The Supreme Court reasons that there are implicit contracts among the lessees to abide by these restrictive covenants, thereby entitling each lessee to exercise a right against the others on the basis of the above contracts.

(3) The stolen shop takings

The third hypothetical case concerns the nature of a security contract which benefits a third party.

X bank makes a contract for Y security company to collect Z store's taking. The contract requires Y to use armoured vehicles and take out insurance. Y failed to do these and the takings were stolen while being collected in an ordinary car. Can Z sue?

This case also concerns the existence of a third party beneficiary clause. Although the security contract was made between bank X and security company Y, Z may sue if the contract is deemed to be a third party contract, that is to say, a contract with a third party beneficiary clause. It is a matter of contract interpretation whether bank X and security company Y intended to confer a third party right on Z. A comparable case was cited earlier in this chapter.[91] That latter case was about a security company which failed to take the necessary measures required by a contract made with another company, thereby inflicting loss on the residents and visitors of the property. The Supreme Court held that the contract was a third party contract intended to protect residents, including their families, thereby conferring upon them a right to sue the security company. If the contract in the hypothetical case was intended to protect Z's legitimate interests, Z is likely to be regarded as the third party and as such be entitled to sue. By suing Y, Z may also be deemed to have declared its intention to accept the benefit of the third party contract. If the contract in the hypothetical case was intended to protect X's legitimate interests (this may be the case where Z, at the time of handing over the shop's takings to the company collecting them, is deemed to have deposited money with bank X, so that the loss of the theft falls wholly on bank X), Z may not be regarded as a third party beneficiary. Once again, the answer to this question is highly fact-specific and should be determined on a case-by-case basis.

[90] Supreme Court Decision *2004Da20081* (24 September 2004); Supreme Court Decision *2011Da79258* (29 November 2012).

[91] Supreme Court Decision *92Da23339* (27 August 1993).

15

Contract Formation in Taiwan

*WU Ying-Chieh**

I. Introduction: Setting the Scene

The chapter aims to explore the issues of formation of contracts and the doctrine of *culpa in contrahendo* (ie pre-contractual liability) under the Taiwanese law of contract. Taiwanese contract law constitutes part of the Taiwan Civil Code. The Taiwan Civil Code (also known as the Civil Code of the Republic of China) was promulgated in 1929 in mainland China. However, the Code was repealed in mainland China in 1949 following the establishment of the People's Republic of China, while it has survived in Taiwan since the Chinese National Party, retreating from mainland China in 1945, continued to apply the Code. Prior to that, Taiwan was a colony of Japan from 1895 to 1945. The Code has thus been enforced in Taiwan for over 70 years, and if we add those periods in which the Code was applied in mainland China, the Civil Code of Taiwan (or the Republic of China) is nearly 90 years old.

The Taiwan Civil Code contains five books: (1) General Rules of the Code; (2) Obligations; (3) Property; (4) Family; and (5) Succession. This format is derived from the German Civil Code, the *Bürgerliches Gesetzbuch* ('BGB'), and is commonly called the *Pandekten* style. The law of contract forms part of the law of obligations, which, along with the law of torts, unjust enrichment, and *negotiorum gestio*, is one of the four areas treated as causative events for triggering rights *in personam* (ie personal rights). The rules on contract law are mostly embedded in the articles contained in the first book (on the general rules of the Civil Code) and second book (obligations) of the Code. Over the past eighty or so years, only a few reforms have been carried out, apart from the major reform carried out in 1999, in which many interpretations and doctrines presented by academics and judges were absorbed into the Code; the law of obligation was also part of that reform project. This shows that academics and judges have been playing important roles in developing and shaping Taiwanese civil law. Being a sub-area of the law of obligation, the law of contract that will be dealt with in this work is also based on the revised version of the Taiwan Civil Code.

Contract is one of the instruments by which people can meet their goals or needs in modern capitalist economic markets. Markets cannot survive without contract mechanisms and vice versa. Thus, contract and market, as two sides of the same coin, are closely connected. However, there is another element worth noting: trust regarding the other contracting party. It must be stressed at the outset that the term 'trust' used in this context does not denote any 'personal or moral trust' in the other party, but an 'economic or commercial trust' that the other party will 'cooperate', thus making both parties' positions better if the contract is formed and realized. In consequence, the trinity of the market, contract, and trust can be regarded as core features of modern economies. As a corollary of this, the laws governing private wealth in most capitalist countries, though with different forms, tend to

* Cite as Y-C Wu, 'Contract Formation in Taiwan' in Chen-Wishart, Loke, & Vogenauer, *Studies in the Contract Laws of Asia Vol II: Formation and Third Party Beneficiaries* (Oxford: OUP 2017) ch 15.

Contract Formation in Taiwan. Wu Ying-Chieh.

be developed on these assumptions. Taiwan is no exception to this tendency since its Civil Code was promulgated in 1929.

Markets are places for making contracts, and contracts are instruments for achieving needs by facilitating trust and cooperation. A question then arises as to the function of *trust* under this trinity of market, contract, and trust. The trust component of a contract has two dimensions: the trust before the contract and that after it. The former is concerned with the trust in the negotiation of the contract; the latter in the performance of it. In the rubric of the contractual regime, the former trust is called 'reliance' and the latter 'expectation'. If they are broken, and the law remains silent, then the innocent party to a contract would be left unprotected, which would accordingly cause the market to lose its order and security. Put differently, the fulfilment of a contract is very much dependent on protecting the aforementioned trusts of reliance and expectation. It is to the protection of these trusts that the law of contract is mostly devoted, though each jurisdiction might adopt different approaches or levels of protection. To sum up, these trusts function as a compass that points in the direction of where legal remedies (ie reliance and expectation damages) should rest.

Reliance and expectation damages both have preventative as well as corrective functions. They direct people to negotiate and perform contracts properly. Otherwise, the law would assist the wronged party to recover his original position, though the recovery has different implications. If reliance is betrayed in the process of negotiation, the law helps the injured party to 'return' to the position he would have been in but for negotiation (ie without the contract). If expectation is contravened, and the contract is not properly performed, the law helps him to 'reach' the position he would have enjoyed if the contract had been completely realized (ie if the contract had been properly performed). Negotiation takes place before the contract, performance presupposes an effective contract, and between the spectrum of negotiation and performance is the issue of formation of contract. In other words, formation of a contract demarcates the nature of the liability (ie reliance or performance damages) owed by a breaching party.

Thus, there are three theoretical and practical stages in the chronological life of a normal contract: (1) the pre-contractual stage; (2) the formation stage; and (3) the performance stage. The present work only deals with the pre-contractual and part of the formation stages since debates surrounding defects in the formation stage and those of the performance stage will be discussed in the fourth volume of this series. This section explores the formation stage prior to the discussion of the pre-contractual stage, pointing out the boundaries where the pre-contractual stage ends, thus providing us with a clear idea of when *culpa in contrahendo* (fault in negotiation) can be established. We turn now to the first issue, formation of contract, from which the story of the life of a contract begins by virtue of offer and acceptance.

II. Formation of Contract: The Rules of Offer and Acceptance

1. Introduction

'When the parties have reciprocally declared their concordant intent, either expressly or impliedly, a contract shall be constituted' (article 153(1) of the Taiwan Civil Code).[1] As this provision shows, the parties' intentions to create a legal relationship are sufficient to create a binding contract, and whether or not there is a promise of counter-performance or deed

[1] The official English translation of the TCC is available on the Ministry of Justice website <http://law.moj.gov.tw/Eng/LawClass/LawContent.aspx?PCODE=B0000001>; the present work in principle adopts this official version, but some modifications are made where necessary to convey a more precise meaning of the text.

is not relevant.[2] The expression 'concordant intent' involves the parties' offer and acceptance. Thus, offer and acceptance are preconditions for a contract to be created under the Taiwan CC. The Taiwan CC provides for the rules pertaining to offer and acceptance mainly from articles 153 to 163. Both offer and acceptance are of the nature of manifestation of intent; therefore, some other articles of the Taiwan CC concerning the rules of manifestation of intent will also be relevant. This section will provide an overview of how those articles (and rules embedded in them) are applied and interpreted by local academics and judges. I will use a very simple hypothetical illustration: A and B intend to conclude a contract, A is the party who makes an offer (the offeror) and B is the counterparty who accepts the offer (the offeree).

2. The Offer

(a) Creation and effectuation

In the illustration above, A as the offeror surely needs to convey his will to B, the offeree, in order to enter into a contract with B; the law will not support A if he keeps his willingness in his mind only. Moreover, A's intention must be conveyed to B and it is not enough that B accidentally became aware of A's thinking. The process of A conveying his will to B is commonly referred to as the manifestation of intent. Therefore, the offer is created at the moment the manifestation of intent is made. When does the law regard that to have happened?

The Taiwan CC gives different answers depending on the situation in which the offer is made. According to article 94 of the Taiwan CC, 'an expression of intent *inter praesentes* [made directly] becomes effective at the moment when the person to whom it is made understands it'. Thus, if A and B communicate with each other by means of instantaneous methods, such as direct dialogue or by telephone, the moment A's intention is addressed to B and B understands it,[3] A's offer is created and becomes effective. Thus, not only does B need to receive the offer but he also needs to know that the offer is made to him. This is relatively straightforward compared to a case where both parties are not in direct communication.

For communications made at a distance (eg by post), article 95(1) of the Taiwan CC prescribes that 'an expression of intent *inter absentes* [between those absent] becomes effective at the moment when it reaches the other party'. The verbal expression 'reach' gives rise to ambiguity: does it mean the other party must receive and *know* of the offer as in the case of instantaneous communication, or would simply receiving the offer suffice? The Code remains silent, and an interpretation is required. The Supreme Court of Taiwan ruled that, 'the expression "reach" denotes that the manifestation of intent arrives at a place that is under the other party's control, which creates an objective circumstance in which the other party can understand the contents of the offer'.[4] This implies that the other party does not need to actually know that the offer is made to him; the possibility of knowing it satisfies the requirement for the offer to become existent and valid. Thus, if A sends his manifestation of intent to B by post to make an offer for a contract, the offer is created and effectuated once the post *arrives* at B's home or business addresses, provided they are under B's control. A's

[2] However, we do see some deviation from this norm in the case of gratuitous contracts: see section II.6.

[3] eg if A intentionally addresses his intention to B in English which B does not understand at all, B is not considered to have understood A's intention.

[4] Taiwan Supreme Court decision 58 TaiShang No 715 (1969) (The number '58' here denotes the 58th year after the Republic of China was established in 1911. Therefore it also means the year 1969. The expression 'TaiShang' tells us that it is an appeal case, and the number '715' is the case number).

actual notice of the post (ie the offer) is irrelevant. Japan and Korea adopt the same rule.[5] After the successful creation and effectuation of an offer, a series of legal consequences follows to which we now turn.

(b) Binding effect

Once an offer is created and effectuated, the offeror is bound by the offer he makes. Article 154(1) of the Taiwan CC states: 'A person who offers to make a contract shall be bound by his offer'. This means: first, the offeror is not allowed to change his mind before the offeree's response; and, second, the offeree obtains a legal position or capacity to accept the offer.

The first point implies that the offeror cannot expand, limit, alter, or withdraw his offer.[6] The rationale is to protect the offeree's reliance on the offer and to promote the efficiency of the transaction. This rule is imported from § 145 of the German Civil Code (*Bürgerliches Gesetzbuch*, 'BGB'). In contrast, French law[7] and English law[8] deny the offer's binding effect. Thus, the offeror is free to withdraw his offer before the offeree's acceptance.

However, the Taiwan CC also gives the offeror an opportunity to retreat from his offer, for otherwise the law would be far too draconian to the offeror, and would result in an extreme imbalance between the offeror and the offeree. The Taiwan CC offers three exits. The offer binds the offeror unless: (1) 'at the time of offer he has excluded its binding effect';[9] (2) 'the withdrawal of it reaches the other party in advance or simultaneously';[10] and (3) if the offeree does not respond to it within a reasonable time.[11] Thus, A in our case is bound by his offer; A is not allowed to withdraw his offer until B's decision. However, A can withdraw his offer (or manifestation of intent) if he expresses his will not to be bound by it. A can also immediately send a notice to withdraw his offer so that it reaches B before or along with his offer. Lastly, A's offer will lose its efficacy if B does not reply to A's offer within a reasonable time. Japanese law (Article 521(2) of the Japanese Civil Code ('JCC')) and Korean law (Article 529 of the Korean Civil Code ('KCC')) take the same approach in that an offer loses its binding effect once the time for acceptance has lapsed. However, they are different from Taiwanese law where an offeror's express intent to withdraw his offer is concerned. Under Taiwanese law, an offer does not have binding effect if the offeror's intention to withdraw reaches the offeree before or along with the offer. But under Japanese law[12] and Korean law[13] offerors are *still* bound by their offer until a reasonable time to consider the offer has passed.[14]

The other main issue centres on the assignability and succession of the offeree's legal position or capacity to accept the offer. The general view regarding assignability is that the offeree can transfer his position as offeree to a third party subject to the offeror's consent.[15] However, it would be more reasonable to consider that the offer loses its efficacy upon the offeree's rejection, and regard the offeror's consent as a fresh offer to the person to whom the original offeree tries to transfer his position as offeree.

The next problem is whether the position as offeree can be succeeded by the offeree's successor should the offeree die before making an acceptance. In other words, is the offeree's successor entitled to accept the offer? One scholar argues that he is, unless the nature of the

[5] Decision of 20 April 1961 of the Supreme Court of Japan (published in *Minshu* vol 15, no 4, p 774); Judgment of the Supreme Court of the Republic of Korea *97da31281* (25 November 1997).

[6] Taiwan Supreme Court decision 81 TaiShang No 565 (1992).

[7] B Nicolas, *French Law of Contract* (2nd edn, Oxford: OUP 1991) 63.

[8] *Routledge v Grant* (1828) 4 Bing 653, 130 ER 920 (Ct of CP).

[9] Taiwan CC, proviso to art 154(1).

[10] ibid proviso to art 95(1).

[11] ibid art 157.

[12] ibid art 524.

[13] KCC, arts 527 and 529.

[14] U Takashi, *Special Provisions of Obligations* (3rd edn, Tokyo: Tokyo University Press 2011) 36.

[15] T-C Wang, *Principles of the Law of Obligation I* (Taipei: Wang Mu Hua 2009) 186.

offer presupposes the deceased offeree's personal character.[16] Another jurist argues that the position to accept is not a conventional 'right' corresponding to that employed in the law of property or obligation, and thus it cannot be passed on to a successor. However, if an offer were to involve no personal dimension (eg an offer to buy a book), it could be deemed as an offer addressed to an uncertain public. Thus, the offeree's successor could become the offeree himself and accept the offer.[17] With respect, I believe both views are flawed, for both views force the offeror to conclude a contract with someone to whom the offer was not made, which violates the positive freedom or formative freedom to select his counterparty to a contract. A more balanced approach would be to regard it as an invitation to make an offer (ie an 'invitation to treat' in English law). It should then be up to the offeree's successor to decide whether or not to make an offer.

(c) Extinction

The extinction of an offer means the offer loses its binding effect. The offeror would thus no longer be bound by an offer he made. Two grounds are provided in the Taiwan CC to extinguish an offer: (1) the offeree's rejection of the offer;[18] and (2) the offeree's failure to accept the offer within a certain period. However, the death or incapacity of the offeror is irrelevant to the effect of an offer.

Since an offer binds the offeror, the existence of a time limit can maintain an equilibrium between the parties, otherwise the offeror would be bound by his offer forever, which would seriously harm the offeror's interests. The main problem here is how to decide the scope of the time limit. The Taiwan CC offers some guidance. If the offer itself does not contain any time limit fixing the period in which the offer stands, 'an offer made *inter praesentes* ceases to be binding if it is not accepted immediately'[19] and 'an offer made *inter absentes* ceases to be binding if it is not accepted by the other party within the time during which the acceptance may be expected to arrive under the ordinary circumstances'.[20]

The requirement 'immediately' in the former case does not necessarily mean that the other party should respond immediately after the offer is made. As long as the response is made within a reasonable time, it is sufficient for an agreement to be established. For example, A makes an offer to B over the telephone or during an online chat, but B says he will give an answer before they end their conversation. If B accepts A's offer before their communication is over, it would meet the requirement of 'immediately'. In the case of an offer made *inter absentes*, the general approach is to decide the effective period of an offer according to the type of contract, business practices, and the nature of the parties (eg individual, association, or company).

Unlike the rules dealt with above, the effect of an offer is not influenced by the death or the loss of capacity of the offeror. Article 95(2) of the Taiwan CC states that 'even if the person who expresses his intention dies or loses his mental capacity…his manifestation of intention does not lose its effect'. The rule is designed to protect the reliance of the other party. Therefore, even if A dies or becomes incapacitated after sending the offer to B, the contract still takes effect if B accepts. The person who inherits the rights and obligations of A (on A's death) or A's guardian (in the case of A's loss of mental capacity) is obliged to perform the contract. The rule is, however, only a principle; exceptions are generally admitted in those

[16] YP Cheng, *General Principles of the Law of Obligation* (2nd edn, Taipei: Sanmin Publishing) 51.
[17] SY Sun, *General Principles of the Law of Obligation* (rev edn, Taipei: Sun Sen Yen 2013) 58.
[18] Taiwan CC, art 155. [19] ibid art 156. [20] ibid art 157.

cases in which the obligation embodied in the offer is of a personal character and thus could only be performed by the offeror himself (eg an offer to give a lecture or to cook).

3. Acceptance

(a) *Effectuation and withdrawal*

Acceptance is a manifestation of intention expressing the offeree's willingness to accept the offer. Thus, articles 94 and 95 regarding manifestation of intention also apply to acceptance. In brief, an acceptance addressed *inter praesentes* becomes effective at the moment the offeror is aware of it.[21] An acceptance sent *inter absentes* becomes effective at the moment it *reaches* a place under the offeror's control,[22] unless the withdrawal of the acceptance reaches the offeror before or simultaneously with the acceptance.[23] The offeree's acceptance remains valid in spite of the offeree's death or incapacitation after the acceptance is sent,[24] unless the obligation owed by the offeree belongs to him personally. It should be stressed that an acceptance takes effect when it actually reaches the offeror under Taiwanese law. The postal rule[25] under English law is not adopted in Taiwan. However, the rule is accepted in Japan[26] and Korea,[27] and thus an agreement or contract will take effect in these jurisdictions when acceptance to the offeror is sent.

(b) *Acceptance delayed, new offer, and counter-offer*

If the acceptance is delayed (ie it exceeds the fixed period set by the offer, or arrives later than the normally expected period), the acceptance does not give rise to any effect. The offeror is not bound and the contractual relationship is not formed. However, if the offeror wants to enter into a contract with an offeree whose acceptance arrives late, he can treat the late acceptance as a new offer, which he can accept.[28] Thus, if B's acceptance arrives late, A can take it as a new offer and send his acceptance to B to form the contract. This is also the case under Japanese law[29] and Korean law.[30]

Where the offeree's acceptance is delayed, but the delay is not caused by the offeree's fault (but rather, eg, by postal strikes or natural disasters), the law imposes upon the offeror a duty to inform the offeree of the delay immediately: 'if an acceptance arrives late though it should usually arrive within a reasonable time according to its manner of transmission, and when the offeror should have known of it, the offeror is under a duty to immediately notify the offeree of such delay'.[31] If the offeror gives due notice, there is no contract. Otherwise, 'the acceptance shall be deemed to have arrived on time.'[32] Thus, if B's acceptance in our illustration arrives late due to a national strike by postal workers, A is required to inform B of the delay within a reasonable time, otherwise B's acceptance is deemed to have arrived on time and a contract between them is successfully formed.[33]

Finally, 'an acceptance that extends, limit, or alters the contents of the offer shall be deemed to be a refusal of the original offer and the making of a new offer.'[34] Thus, if B accepts the offer with any modifications to the terms offered by A, it does not amount to a valid acceptance, but becomes a new offer. A must then decide if he will accept it.[35]

21 ibid art 94. 22 ibid art 95(1). 23 ibid art 95(1). 24 ibid art 95(2).
25 *Adams v Lindsell* (1818) 1 B & Ald 681, (1818) 106 ER 250 (KB). 26 JCC, Art 526(1).
27 KCC, Art 431. 28 Taiwan CC, art 160(1). 29 JCC, Art 523. 30 KCC, Art 530.
31 Taiwan CC, art 159(1). 32 ibid art 159(2).
33 KCC, Art 528(2) and (3), and JCC, Art 522(1) and (2), provide for the same rules.
34 Taiwan CC, art 160(2).
35 KCC, Art 534 and JCC, Art 538 show that this is also the case in South Korea and Japan.

Therefore, when A makes an offer on one set of terms, and B purports to accept on a different set of terms *and performance begins* (typically known as the 'battle of forms' in English law[36]), there is no contract between A and B. Courts in Taiwan have rarely regarded a contract as formed or valid by considering other values than the parties' contractual intention (eg business efficacy).

Nevertheless, this result is subject to two exceptions. First, since B's acceptance with different terms becomes a new offer,[37] A can accept it either by expressing his intention to B, or actually receiving the performance (ie subsequent conduct) made by B.[38] Second, even if the terms contained in B's acceptance do not correspond with A's offer, the contract can be effectuated if the terms not agreed upon are not related to the core duties of the contract (eg the price for the item) but to ancillary duties (eg whether to use a bag or box when delivering the item), the court will determine as a matter of interpretation or implication of term, viz, the court will choose the one (ie bag or box) that can be supported by some other objective and extrinsic resources available to the court such as the context and purpose of the contract, the parties' words exchanged during negotiations, the relevant commercial practice, the good faith principle and so on. However, ancillary duties can be transformed into core duties depending on the parties' intentions or agreement, though the parties' intentions would be left open to interpretation should they be ambiguous.

4. The Interpretation of Intentions: The Subjective Test?

Offer and acceptance, when combined with agreed terms, generate a binding contract. The law will recognize parties' intentions expressed in the contract. However, disputes may arise over whether the parties' conduct or words amount to an offer or an acceptance. For example, A promises to give private English lessons to B for three weeks and B agrees to it; does the expression 'three weeks' mean 21 days or 15 days? The question calls for interpreting the parties' manifestations of intent. The reasons for requiring interpretation may vary. They could spring from the lack of detailed explanations for the terms agreed or be triggered by the vagueness of the language itself. The question is how to decide the meaning of the words expressed in the contract, objectively or subjectively? In other words, should we put emphasis on the objective meaning of the words used or the subjective meaning intended by the parties?

According to article 98 of the Taiwan CC, 'in the interpretation of a manifestation of intent, the real intention of the parties must be sought rather than the literal meaning of the words'. The rule adopted is the subjective test. However, the expression 'real intention' causes some trouble because it is impossible to verify what is really in the parties' minds when the contract was made. How, then, can courts discern the true intentions of the parties? According to the Taiwan Supreme Court,[39] the subject matter of the interpretation is not the intention kept in the parties' minds, but that expressed *outwardly*. And in interpreting the intention expressed in a contract, the following elements (ie background information) are considered: (1) the purpose(s) of the contract; (2) the conventions or customs of the market; (3) the provisions involving default rules; and (4) the good faith principle. In other words, the 'real intention' is found through objective materials before the courts and the final element gives the courts discretionary power to decide the contents of the intentions

[36] *Butler Machine Tool Co v Ex-Cell-O Corp (England) Ltd* [1979] 1 WLR 401 (CA); for more details, see M Chen-Wishart, *Contract Law* (Oxford: OUP 2012) 62.

[37] Taiwan CC, art 160(2).

[38] This would count as the so-called constructive acceptance, a concept that will be discussed in section II.7(c).

[39] Taiwan Supreme Court decision 88 TaiShang No 1671 (1999).

in question. If the terms of the contract are still vague after considering the aforementioned information, the contract will be considered void for lack of agreement.

The method adopted has blurred the line between the subjective and objective tests since the intentions discerned from objective materials may be regarded as contrary to the parties' true intentions. However, both academics and the courts seem to unequivocally insist that the intentions obtained through the above process are the parties' true intentions. Thus, it is a subjective test, although it is virtually tantamount to an objective test.

It is also the general view that the true intention of the parties is searched for and reflected subjectively, and thus can be taken as a case where the subjective test applies, if the case involves the rule of *falsa demonstrio non nocet*. Thus, the rule applies where the parties' intentions are miswritten on the contract. For example, A and B agree to make a contract to sell A's BMW car to B, but writes down 'Mercedes' by mistake; provided both A and B accept the mistake and do not argue about it; the subject matter of the contract is then the BMW rather than the one that was objectively written, ie the Mercedes. The result is that the contract, though mistakenly written, remains good. However, the present author argues that this view is also flawed, for we still need to resort to some external evidence to prove that the BMW is the subject matter of the contract.[40]

5. Formalities

(a) Introduction

The basic approach adopted by the Taiwan CC adheres to the principle that as long as offer and acceptance are construed as existing, an enforceable contract arises without any requirement of formality. Article 153(1) of the Taiwan CC states, 'when the parties have reciprocally declared their concordant intent, either expressly or impliedly, a contract shall be constituted'. However, Taiwanese private law in various special cases makes some use of formalities in the creation of certain contracts. Formality requirements in these cases, in some sense, curtail the parties' formative freedom, but, as we shall see, each formality is grounded upon rather sound justifications and, indeed, the circumscription of the freedom is made for the parties' benefit. For reasons of space, the section only deals with some of the main areas under the Taiwan CC where formality must exist to validate a contract.

(b) Agreement to use a specific formality

The first example where the parties to a contract are subject to using a formality is where they *agree* to levy a formality requirement as a condition of the validity of their contract. In this case, both parties are obliged to perform the formality they promised to adopt (eg writing or attestation by witnesses). The type of formality is at the parties' will. Here we see a contradiction: imposition of a formality itself is a restriction, but the restriction is created by the parties' agreement. The policy grounding for this formality requirement is rooted in the parties' autonomous will. The law has no reason to object to it.

However, the Taiwan CC states,[41] 'if it is agreed between the parties that a contract shall be made in a certain form, the contract is presumed to be not constituted before the completion of such form'. Since the rule is presumptive, the party seeking to enforce the contract

[40] This issue will be further elaborated in Y-C Wu, 'Ascertaining Contractual Terms in Taiwan' in Mindy Chen-Wishart et al (eds), *Studies in the Contract Laws of Asia Vol III: Contents of Contracts and Unfair Terms* (Oxford: OUP forthcoming).

[41] Taiwan CC, art 166.

has the burden of rebutting the presumption in order to argue that the formality requirement merely plays an evidentiary role concerning the existence of the contract. Of course, whether it is an evidential or a constituent element is a matter of the construction of their intentions, but the default rule enshrined in the provision (by means of the presumption) favours the party who argues that the contract is not constituted. Thus, if A and B agree to conclude a contract in writing but fail to satisfy it, the contract between them is presumed not to have been formed; if either party wants to deny the constituent nature of the formality in their contract, he must prove that the agreed formality requirement only performs an evidentiary function.

(c) *The requirement of writing*

We began from 'freedom not to use any formality' and moved to 'freedom to be bound by a formality'. Now we move to scenarios in which the use of a formality is *mandatory*. For example:

- 'lease of land[42] for a period exceeding one year shall be executed in writing. If it is not so executed in writing, it is deemed to have been made for an indefinite period';[43]
- 'the contract of annuity[44] for a lifetime shall be made in writing';[45]
- 'the contract of employment guarantee[46] shall be made in writing'.[47]

The legal policies underlying each of the above share a common feature: they affect the promisor's interests so severely that the law is determined to strike a balance by imposing upon him a requirement of writing so that the promisor can have an opportunity to seriously consider the agreement and the parties to the contracts can avoid disputes arising from the lack of certainty as to the promisor's intention.[48]

(d) *Land transactions: towards a notarization regime?*

The picture gets rather complicated in transactions regarding land. The mode that needs to be followed in respect of land transactions is imported from Germany.[49] If A sells his land X to B, the basic structure under the Taiwanese civil law takes the following three steps.

- First, A and B conclude a sale contract in respect of X, and A is obliged to transfer the title to X to B, while B is under an obligation to pay the price. This is the contractual stage.
- Second, the law also imposes upon A and B a duty to make a written agreement that shows the fact that A thereby transfers the title to B, and B agrees to receive it. Unlike

[42] Though lease of land belongs to the law of property in the common law world, it falls within the law of contract in Taiwan, although the lease of land may bind third parties if the lessee takes possession of the land. Since the contract (plus possession) can be used against non-parties to the contract, the lease contract is normally addressed as an 'obligation towards proprietary nature'. A loose parallel may be made with the English expression of 'chattel real'.

[43] Taiwan CC, art 422.

[44] 'A contract of annuity for lifetime is a contract whereby the parties agree that one of them shall make periodic payments in money to the other party, or to a third party during the lifetime of one or the other parties, or of a third party' (ibid art 729).

[45] ibid art 730.

[46] 'An employment guarantee is a contract whereby the parties agree that one of them shall be bound to make compensation while the other party shall be liable to compensate the other party for the performance of his duties in the future' (ibid art 756-1(1)).

[47] ibid art 756-1(2).

[48] CW Chen (ed), *Civil Code* (12th edn, Taipei: New Sharing Publishing 2013) B-644, B-896, B-931.

[49] For more details, see T-C Wang, *Property Law* (2nd edn, Taipei: Wang Mu Hua 2011) 66–97.

the first step, this written agreement does not produce any obligations between the parties; this step is the transfer stage.

- Third, after the written agreement made in the second step is accompanied by registration, the land transaction between A and B is perfected, and B acquires the title to X.

Lawyers from common law jurisdictions may be puzzled by the threefold structure. This highly conceptual (or extremely artificial) structure dissects the land transaction into the aforementioned three stages, each of which has its own purpose.

- The first step relates to the *intention* to owe certain obligations to each other. Thus, A and B are obliged to perform their obligations.
- The written agreement executed in the second step relates to the intention to transfer the title itself. It has nothing to do with any intention to owe any obligations.
- The third step that requires X to be registered (thus publicizing X) is aimed at protecting third parties in the market from unexpected damage caused by the uncertainty of vesting the title to X.

Thus, the second and third steps are expressly enunciated by the Taiwan CC. Article 758(1) provides that 'the acquisition, creation, loss or alternation of rights in rem in land through the juridical act will not be valid if it is not registered'. Article 758(2) provides that 'the acts specified in the preceding paragraph shall be made in writing'. The transfer of X between A and B involves A's loss of X and B's acquisition, which represents an acquisition of, as well as a loss of, a right *in rem* over land X. Therefore, the provisions of article 758(1) and (2) are applied: the transfer must be carried out by both registration and a written agreement in respect of the transfer itself.

The question is whether there is any formality requirement imposed upon the first step; that is, the contractual step. The Civil Code was silent on this issue, and the Supreme Court had continuously maintained that oral agreement alone would suffice to form a contract involving proprietary interests in land.[50] However, a radical reform was carried out in 1999 imposing a requirement that contracts involving the acquisition, transfer, or alteration of rights *in rem* over land be notarized.[51] Again, this requirement comes from Germany[52] and the policy basis for this change is no different from those mentioned earlier regarding the writing requirements. However, considering that land is of relatively higher economic value, the law goes further than asking for mere writing and demands that the contract must be notarized.[53]

As shown earlier, the law changed the legal tradition in contracts from a formality-free model to a notary system: a reform which was truly drastic and abrupt. Enforcement would have certainly caused much confusion in the short term, therefore in order to alleviate the inconvenience, the law-makers decided not to enforce it immediately. The reform (ie article 166-1) will be applied on a date co-decided by the Executive Department and the Ministry of Justice.[54] Nearly 20 years have passed since the reform was carried out, yet the specific date is still undecided. It is extremely doubtful whether the reform will be put into practice; people living in Taiwan do not want to incur the expense of public notaries for formalities and the government will be reluctant to enforce it. As a result, the new article involving the notary system is very likely to be a dead letter. To sum up, as far as the contractual stage (ie the first step) in relation to the transfer, creation, or alteration of rights *in rem* over land is

[50] Taiwan Supreme Court decision 57 TaiShangZi 1436 (1968); Taiwan Supreme Court decision 70 TaiShangZi 453 (1981).

[51] Taiwan CC, art 166-1.

[52] See § 311b(1) BGB.

[53] Chen (n 48) B-245.

[54] Law of Obligation Enforcement Act, art 36.

concerned, oral agreement is sufficient to produce a valid contract. Each party can then force the other to perform the second and third stages. Neither Japan nor South Korea require a contract concerning land transactions to be made in writing, and oral agreement is sufficient for the contract to take effect.

6. Gratuitous Promises: Contracts for Gratuitous Loans and the Case of Gifts

Contrary to the common law position, the civil law tradition admits that gratuitous promises are enforceable even if they are not supported by any consideration. What matters is the parties' intention. This requires a construction of the parties' intention to determine whether there was a willingness to be bound by the promises they made. However, the law in some cases requires parties to gratuitous promises to satisfy certain requirements in order to make the contract effective.

For instance, in the case of a gratuitous contract of loan for the use of a thing (either a chattel or land), it is not until the thing itself is *delivered* to or *possessed* by the promisee that the contract becomes effectuated.[55] This is also true of gratuitous contracts for deposits; the contract is only validly constituted once the subject matter of the deposit is delivered and possessed by the custodian.[56] Another instance can be found in the case of a gratuitous contract of loan for consumption. In this case, ownership of the fungible thing must be *transferred* to the other party for the gratuitous contract to take effect. Thus, if A promises to lend money to B gratuitously, the title to the money must be vested in B in order for the gratuitous contract to be effective.[57] Each of these three cases is derived from the Roman *commdatum*, *mutum*, and *depositum* respectively. The rationale behind these three cases is to accord the promisor an opportunity to reconsider the gratuitous promise before delivering the possession or transferring title to the promisee.[58]

Unlike the aforementioned three cases, a contract for a gift, though gratuitous, can be established by mere *agreement*.[59] The promisor does not need to deliver the possession or transfer the title to the promisee. Once a promisor promises to offer a thing, and the promisee accepts it, the gift contract is successfully concluded.[60] However, the law here also affords the promisor a right to revoke his promise before he performs his gift contract,[61] unless it is notarized.[62] Moreover, a donor may refuse performance of a gift if, after the gift has been agreed upon, his economic conditions have changed to such an extent that the performance of the gift would seriously affect his means of livelihood or hinder his duty to furnish maintenance to others.[63] The result is identical to the previous three cases: the promisor has a chance to retreat from the gratuitous promise before performing the obligation. The difference is that 'revocation' and a 'right to refusal' are used since the contract has already been effectuated by mutual agreement. This contradicts the rule of *pacta sunt servanda* (ie promises must be observed). It would be more consistent if the law said a gift contract is only valid once the title to the subject matter of a promise is transferred to the promisee.

Apart from the difference that a gift can be revoked at any time before the donor performs his obligation, gift contracts also show different features compared to general contracts in relation to the remedies available for the donees:

[55] Taiwan CC, art 464. [56] ibid art 589. [57] ibid art 464.

[58] R Zimmerman, *Law of Obligation: Roman Foundations of the Civilian Tradition* (Oxford: OUP 1996) 163.

[59] Taiwan CC, art 406.

[60] However, the remedies for breach of a gift contract differ from general sale contracts, for reasons of space the issue will be dealt with in another volume of the series on remedies.

[61] Taiwan CC, art 408(1). [62] ibid art 408(2). [63] ibid art 418.

- first, when performance is delayed, the donee is only entitled to urge the donor to perform his obligation; the donee cannot claim any damages for delayed performance;[64]
- second, if the donor becomes unable to perform his obligation, the donee is entitled to claim the value of the obligation not performed, only if the non-performance is caused purposely or recklessly; moreover, he cannot claim for any other damages arising from the non-performance;[65]
- third, in the case of defective performance, the donor is not liable for the defect unless he has not informed the donee of the defect purposely or he guaranteed there would be no defect.[66]

As for contract modifications, promising to pay a higher price for the performance of an existing contract is perfectly valid and enforceable even if nothing extra is received in exchange (ie want of any consideration). This is merely a case of a contract modification by the agreement of the parties to the contract, and no further counter-promise or performance is required for the modified terms to take effect. An agreement on the new term is sufficient.

For example, a contract takes full effect in a delayed building project as follows: X contracts for Y to refurbish 27 flats for £20,000. However, Y runs into difficulties. X is concerned about having to pay a penalty under the head contract, and promises to pay Y an extra £10,300 to complete the work on time. Y in this case can enforce the delivery of the additional £10,300 simply through the agreement between X and Y even though Y was already under an obligation to finish the building project and the additional amount is promised by X without Y acquiring any new obligation. In English law, an act done, or a promise made by one party when he is already under a contractual obligation to perform it, cannot be good consideration. Thus, the promise made has no binding effect[67] unless there is some additional benefit involved. In the case of *Williams v Roffey Bros & Nicholls (Contractors) Ltd*,[68] the facts of which are identical to those above, the English Court of Appeal held that X did obtain a 'practical benefit' since it would promote the timely completion of X's building work, and thus avoid the need for X to pay the penalty and save X the cost of acquiring another subcontractor. It is interesting to find that, although the basic rule is not identical, the final results are the same in both jurisdictions. While the promise of the additional payment by X is valid in Taiwanese law because no further counter-promise or performance is required for that promise to be enforceable, English law found that there was a 'practical benefit' for X's promise, and thus valid consideration for Y to enforce X's promise.

The upshot is that, though gratuitous contracts do not need to be supported by consideration or deed under the Taiwan CC, the reality is that the promisor is in principle apt to escape from gratuitous promises he makes. Thus, it seems to the present author that the ultimate results are not distinct from those drawn from the common law system, though the legal techniques adopted by each tradition are dissimilar.

7. Miscellaneous Cases

(a) Introduction

In the next three subsections, we will look at examples where contracts are formed through rather different processes compared to the cases dealt with previously, although offer and acceptance still comprise the core elements in forming these types of contracts. These cases

[64] ibid art 409(1) and (2). [65] ibid arts 409(1) and (2) and 410. [66] ibid art 411.
[67] *Stilk v Myrick* (1809) 2 Camp 317 (NP). [68] [1991] 1 QB 1 (CA).

are: (1) invitation to treat; (2) constructive acceptance; and (3) agreements by means of electronic devices.

(b) Invitation to treat

An offer must be distinguished from an invitation to offer. While an offer anticipates an acceptance, an invitation to treat anticipates an offer. Thus, an invitation to treat is a preliminary proposal to attract a person to make an offer. A good example is newspaper advertisements.[69] However, in contrast to English law,[70] displays in shop windows with prices on the products are treated as offers in Taiwanese law. Article 154(2) of the Taiwan CC states: 'displaying goods for sale with their selling price shall be deemed to be an offer'. This would also apply to displays on supermarket shelves.[71]

However, the proviso of article 154(2) states that the transmission of a price list does not amount to an offer; it only constitutes an invitation to offer. An announcement of items for sale at an auction is also regarded as an invitation to treat only;[72] the owner of an item is entitled to refuse to sell. Here lies the benefit of a notice being interpreted as an invitation to treat, for, unlike offers, invitations to treat are not burdened with binding force. A case may be interpreted as an offer or that of invitation to treat depending on the following factors:[73]

- whether the offer is made to a specific person or to the public (an offer made to a specific person is interpreted as an offer, while that made by an advertisement is regarded as an invitation to treat);
- conventions normally conducted in the market (eg waving a hand for a taxi is interpreted as an invitation to treat; the person waving their hand can refuse to get in the taxi).

(c) Constructive acceptance

Technically speaking, contracts cannot be established without an expressed acceptance of an offer. Unfortunately, reality is not always as straightforward as we would like. There may be circumstances where acceptance is construed as existent, yet it is not expressed. Article 161(1) and (2) of the Taiwan CC states: 'in cases where according to customs or owing to the nature of the affair, a manifestation of acceptance is not necessary, the contract shall be constituted when there is an act which may be considered as an acceptance to the offer'. Moreover, 'the provision of the preceding paragraph shall be *mutatis mutandis* applied when at the time of offer the offeror has waived manifestation of acceptance'.

Thus, custom may waive the manifestation of acceptance. For example, A wants to buy books from B (a book retailer) and send him a book list with a postal money order or credit card number. Once B sends the books and they reach A's location, the contract for the sale is concluded even though B has not manifested his intention of acceptance to A at all. This is so because the sending and receiving of the books to A are customarily sufficient to form facts that waive express acceptances. Furthermore, the nature of affairs may also exempt offerees from the need to express acceptance to the offeror. For example, A inserts coins into

[69] Taiwan Supreme Court decision 73 TaiShangZi 2540 (1984).

[70] In English law, displays in shop windows (*Timothy v Simpson* (1834) 6 C & P 499, 172 ER 1337 (Ct Exch)) and on supermarket shelves (*Pharmaceutical Society of Great Britain v Boots Cash Chemists (Southern) Ltd* [1953] 1 QB 401 (CA)) are usually treated as invitations to treat.

[71] Wang, *Principles of the Law of Obligation I* (n 15) 175.

[72] Taiwan Supreme Court decision 82 TaiShangZi 1850 (1993); English law also adopts the same approach (*British Car Auctions Ltd v Wright* [1972] 1 WLR 1519 (QBD)).

[73] Wang, *Principles of the Law of Obligation I* (n 15) 175.

a vending machine that is run and owned by B to buy a bottle of water—B is the offeror and A is the offeree. The nature of the affair shows us that the fact that the bottle has automatically come out means that the contract is validly formed and performed. There is no reason why A, the owner of the coins, should manifest his acceptance to B's (the owner of the machine) offer. Finally, another case highlights the positive freedom to contract, because a waiver of acceptance can be created by parties to a contract. For instance, if A says to B, 'You can borrow my car anytime you want, just get the keys from my secretary, and you do not need to contact me to get my approval (ie acceptance) every time.' A's acceptance is waived based on his own will, and all B has to do is get the keys from A's secretary; the contract of loan for use is therefore created between them.

Though acceptances are not required to be enunciated in the cases mentioned above, the truth is that they are all predicated on acts that carry with them the offeree's acceptance. In other words, acceptance was not given verbally, but through the acts themselves. Acceptances may be realized by acts. The philosophical basis for these three cases is essentially to enhance the efficiency of the creation of contracts.[74]

(d) Agreements made through electronic devices

Agreements made through electronic devices are one of the most important means of concluding transactions in the modern world. The central problem is when can contracts made through electronic devices (eg computers) be regarded as formed? If a contract is entered into through emails between A and B, when is it formed? Section 4(2) of the Electronic Signature Act gives us the answer to this question. An 'electronic document', such as an email, is considered to be received: (1) at the moment the document has arrived at the other party's electronic system, if the person who accepts the document has required it to be sent to that specific information system;[75] or (2) at the moment the other party notices the document, if the information system to which it has been sent is not the one specified by the other party. Therefore, A (the offeror) and B's (the offeree) contract will be formed when B's acceptance arrives at A's email inbox (ie information system) if that email address is the one specifically designated by A; but if B's acceptance arrives at A's email inbox which is not previously designated by A, then the acceptance takes effect when A notices B's email.

As regards online purchases, a statutory rule regulating this field has yet to be created. However, section 15 of the guidelines[76] issued by the Consumer Protection Committee, provides that, 'business sectors must send a re-confirmation response to the consumer if the purchase is made through internet…and the transaction is formed once the consumer confirms it'. Thus, if B tries to purchase an item on an internet website run by A, A's online system must have a mechanism that automatically sends a re-confirmation response to B, and the online contract between them goes through only when B confirms it on his computer.

III. Pre-Contractual Liability (*Culpa in Contrahendo*)

1. Introduction

It is time for us to rewind the story back to the pre-contractual stage. Clearly, no binding contract has been concluded, and so no liability has arisen. Any protection for the negotiating

[74] ibid 201. [75] eg hotmail, gmail, or email systems provided by workplaces.

[76] The full name of this guide is: Guiding Principles on the must-have and must-not-have information for the Online Standard Form Contract [The Consumer Protection Guideline No. 0940003165 (31 March 2005)]. The guidelines are only available in Mandarin at the following website: <http://www.lia-roc.org.tw/index06/regulation_old/94regu60.htm> accessed 25 August 2017.

parties is outside the scope of the law of contract. However, as early as the nineteenth century, doubts were expressed about this proposition by one of the great lawyers in German legal history. Rudolf von Jhering argued that this issue needed to be revisited. His basic arguments were, briefly, as follows: the process of negotiation should be brought into the sphere of the law of contract, otherwise one party would be able to manipulate the negotiation process and damage the interests of the other party. He further argued that negotiations must be carried out in good faith as trust may grow between the parties during the negotiations, and trust placed by one party in the other during the negotiations must be protected.[77] Jhering believed that when a breach of trust through conduct that contravenes the good faith duty occurs, reliance damages ought to be paid by the blameworthy party. This pre-contractual liability is called '*culpa in contrahendo*'. The gist of the theory is that the embryo of a contract is also worth protecting despite the fact that the parties to the contract are normally adversarial.

The doctrine of *culpa in contrahendo*, though not prescribed in the BGB, has heavily influenced both German scholarship and judicial cases. France and England, on the other hand, have not particularly characterized negotiation as constituting a legally protected relationship, and thus there is no general rule of pre-contractual liability in those jurisdictions.[78] English law seems reluctant even to recognize any liabilities between negotiating parties.[79] The Civil Code of Taiwan along with that of South Korea, being influenced by German law, imported Jhering's theory. But, unlike their source law and the Japanese law that accepted the theory without any provision in the Civil Code, the doctrine is manifested by an express provision in the Taiwanese and South Korean Civil Codes. The relevant provisions are article 245-1 of the Taiwan CC and Article 535 of the KCC. But, unlike South Korea's rather general provision, the Taiwan CC deals with some specific situations that give rise to pre-contractual liability.

2. Article 245-1: *Culpa in Contrahendo*

(a) *Causes triggering liability*

Pre-contractual liability is only established by events *prior to* the contract's creation; causes found after the contract is made form the basis of non-performance liability. Therefore, the Supreme Court declared that 'the pre-contractual liability prescribed in article 245-1 only applies when contracts are not concluded. Thus if contracts are successfully formed, no pre-contractual liability can arise and the provision does not apply.'[80] In other words, if a contract between A and B is made but A made a dishonest or fraudulent misrepresentation, the aggrieved party (ie B) can only sue A for either A's fraud and rescind the contract,[81] or the tort of deceit[82] and claim for the damages suffered.

Article 245-1 of the Taiwan CC provides not only for a general duty requiring that the parties to the contract should negotiate in good faith, but also offers some specific duties in the negotiations:

[77] R von Jhering, '*Culpa in contrahendo* oder Schadensersatz bei nichtigen oder nicht zur Perfektion gelangten' [1861] 4 Jhering Jahrbücher 1–113.

[78] For a comparative analysis of French and English law, see P Giliker, *Pre-Contractual Liability in English and French Law* (The Hague: Kluwer Law International 2002). For more information on pre-contractual liability in Europe, see J Cartwright and M Hesselink (eds), *Precontractual Liability in European Private Law* (Cambridge: Cambridge University Press 2009).

[79] *Courtney & Fairbairn Ltd v Tolaini Brothers (Hotels) Ltd* [1975] 1 WLR 297 (CA) 301 (Lord Denning MR).

[80] Taiwan Supreme Court decision 100 TaiShang 1906 (2011).

[81] Taiwan CC, art 92(1).

[82] ibid art 184(1).

> [W]hile the contract is not yet concluded and the parties to the contract are in the process of negotiations, one of the parties is entitled to claim damages against the other if any of the following criteria exists and the former believed the contract shall be concluded:
>
> 1) Concealing in bad faith or dishonestly explaining a gravely relevant matter to the contract when the other party has inquired into it.
> 2) Intentionally or recklessly divulging the other party's secrets known or held by himself which the other party has explicitly requested be kept secret.
> 3) Any other matter obviously in breach of good faith.

Subsections (1) and (2) are somehow unique in terms of their legislative form, since we can seldom find any civil code in East Asian civil law jurisdictions that lists specific examples of acts against good faith that generate pre-contractual liability. It is unclear why the lawmakers decided to extract these two types of breach of good faith from the general duty of good faith set out in subsection (3). But the purpose of doing so might have been to set distinctive requirements according to the types of breach during negotiations. We shall explore them in more detail.

According to the first subsection, pre-contractual liability can arise where one of the parties hides in bad faith, or dishonestly explains, a gravely relevant matter to the contract when the other party asked about it. The provision imposes upon the parties the duty to inform, which seemingly goes against the adversarial character of the negotiation of contracts. People generally conclude contracts for their own benefit, and there is no compelling reason why the other party has to disclose all its information. It is the opposite party that should bear the responsibility for obtaining the information he needs. Inequality of information is a natural phenomenon and an inevitable reality in the market, and so each party should bear the disadvantage flowing from it. Therefore, the fundamental rule must be that each party to the contract is not obliged to provide the other with all information during the negotiations.

However, the story dramatically changes if the other party makes an inquiry in the process of negotiations, for any silence or untrue response would damage the reliance built in the negotiations. Once an inquiry has been made, the relevant information must be provided unless the other party clearly informs the inquirer that the information is not available since it is a business secret or that the information required has nothing to do with the contract in question (eg an inquiry about how many children the other party has in a car-sale contract). Otherwise, the party cannot hide or misrepresent the relevant information. This reflects the value judgment made by the legislature based on local culture. Therefore, the imposition of a duty to inform is justified by the fact that the provision requires a further condition for it to be met in order for the duty to be established (ie the other party's inquiry). This strikes a balance between the protection of the parties to contracts and the preservation of the adversarial nature of contracts.

Moreover, facts that may inflict mental or physical harm on the other party should be disclosed. For example, information such as whether the house under negotiation is built using toxic cement or whether someone once committed suicide[83] in that property.

According to the second subsection, when one of the parties to a contract intentionally or recklessly discloses the other party's secrets, which the other party has explicitly said

[83] This is regarded as a very important matter in Taiwanese society since the Taiwanese (as are the Koreans and Chinese) are reluctant to live in a place where people are killed or have committed suicide. Therefore, what happens in practice in Taiwan is that if you buy a house through an agent, the agent will prepare a form that requires the seller to tick a box that asks if anyone has committed suicide or was killed prior to the sale.

should be kept secret, that party will be liable for breach of pre-contractual duty. This also aims at protecting the reliance of one party on the other in the process of negotiations. It is sometimes inevitable that novel ideas about a business project are shared when negotiating a contract with investors. If no sanction is given even if the other party uses or discloses certain secret ideas procured through the process of negotiations, the party sharing the secret information would confront a dilemma: either take the risk of sharing business secrets or abandon the chance of entering into a contract. The Taiwan CC's position is to stop the misuse of the other party's secrets obtained through negotiations, but with one qualification: there must be a request by the party sharing the information not to divulge it. The purpose of this condition is again to maintain the balance between the negotiating parties.

The third basis for pre-contractual liability is a breach of good faith. However, the subsection is a general provision. The types of cases falling within the ambit of this provision cannot be exhaustively listed. However, two cases merit special attention: the untimely breaking off of negotiations and harm caused in the process of negotiation.

Freedom of contract includes the freedom not to conclude contracts. So the parties to a contract are free to abandon their negotiations. Otherwise, the beginning of negotiations itself would have binding force and thus compel parties to enter into the contract. However, if we adhere strictly to this norm, harm would be inflicted on the party whose reliance concerning the conclusion of the contract is *worth* protecting. Therefore, it is preferable not to permit the abrupt breaking off of negotiations that results in damage to the other party. The question is when his reliance on the successful conclusion of the contract deserves the law's protection. Of course, the test should consider the type of contract, commercial practices, the relationship between the parties, and the degree of reliance accumulated during the negotiations. Since the provision, unlike the previous two subsections, does not contain any qualifications, the courts will have considerable discretion in deciding whether the relevant break-off in particular cases is untimely and thus against the good faith principle.

Another example typically discussed under this category is the case where one of the parties' body or property is harmed negligently by the other party during the negotiations. For example, A visits B's bookshop to buy a medical textbook, but suffers a fall due to some water spilt on the floor. Or, A visits B's restaurant for lunch, but A's coat is damaged when B negligently spills hot soup over it. The pre-contractual liability is imposed according to whether the harm was caused in a place under B's control. In other words, the location of the negotiations matters in addition to the negligently inflicted harm. Therefore, failure to prevent harm to the other party's body or property during negotiations in a place which the defendant controls defines the content of the breach of the good faith principle. However, it must be noted that this 'place-control' formula, though academically introduced and discussed, has rarely been applied in Taiwan. This is because article 188(1) of the Taiwan CC, which provides for business owners' tortious liability, prescribes that business owners should prove that they are not negligent in choosing and supervising their employees' acts that damage their clients in their place of business.[84] The upshot is that claimants (ie the harmed party during negotiations in the defendant's place) are normally motivated to raise a claim through tortious liability rather than pre-contractual liability.

[84] Taiwan CC, art 188(1):

> The employer shall be jointly liable to make compensation for any injury which the employee has wrongfully caused to the rights of another in the performance of his duties. However, the employer is not liable for the injury if he has exercised reasonable care in the selection of the employee and in the supervision of the performance of this duties, or if the injury would have been occasioned notwithstanding the exercise of such reasonable care.

(b) Damages and the nature of the liability

The law protects reliance in the process of negotiation, by 'returning' the relying party to the position that he would have been in but for the negotiations. Therefore, once one of the parties to a contract has a pre-contractual liability, he is under an obligation to make up for the loss that the other suffered from believing that the contract would be successfully concluded. For example, A is negotiating with B to rent B's land for five years in order to operate a restaurant on it, and B in the process of the negotiation convinces A that B will lease his property to A. They decide to make a written contract since a lease for a period exceeding one year must be made in written document.[85] If B terminates the negotiations and refuses to lease the property to A abruptly before the promised date on which the written contract was to be made, B is liable to compensate A for the costs he incurred (eg wasted lawyer's fees). Since A's expenses were incurred by relying on B's acts and words during the negotiations before the break-off, B is obliged to make up for them as reliance damages.

Although the defendant is under an obligation to compensate the injured party with reliance damages for his actions during the negotiations for a contract, and the issue of the pre-contractual liability is usually dealt with as part of the contents of contract law courses, the nature of the liability is not contractual: it is a liability arising by operation of law. This is easy to understand since the pre-contractual liability is constituted before the contract is formed, and so it can hardly be imagined that the liability can be contractual. Contractual liability and pre-contractual liability are mutually exclusive. Therefore, the nature of pre-contractual liability belongs to a third type of civil liability distinct from both contractual and tortious liabilities, yet it can occur concurrently with the latter.

(c) Burden of proof and concurrent liabilities

Let us briefly revisit the specific cases discussed so far where pre-contractual liability may arise in Taiwan: concealment of important information in bad faith, dishonest misrepresentation of important information, intentional or reckless release of the other party's secret information, and the untimely break-off of negotiations. If any of these are found, it is normally the case that pure economic loss is caused, which may also amount to tortious liability.[86] Pre-contractual liability and tortious liability can be generated concurrently. However, the burden of proof concerning subjective elements (ie bad faith, dishonesty, and intentions) varies between the two claims: the burden of proof is on the claimant in a tort claim, but shifts to the defendant in a pre-contractual claim. It is up to the party breaking off the negotiations to show that he acted in good faith. Thus, if A breaks off the negotiations with B after convincing B that A would not do so and B sues A for pre-contractual liability, A has the burden of proving that he did not act in breach of good faith. On the other hand, if B sues A for tortious liability, it is B who needs to prove that A broke off the negotiation intentionally or negligently. The reason for the shift is to protect the aggrieved party who has entered the negotiation stage of a contract:[87] here lies the benefit of asserting pre-contractual liability. The rule on the allocation of the burden of proof in the case of pre-contractual liability is borrowed from the breach of contract case, where the only thing the wronged party needs to prove is the fact of breach itself (ie an objective element), while the

[85] ibid art 422.

[86] It must be noted that tortious liability for causing pure economic loss can only be established when the tortfeasor has intentionally (dishonestly or in bad faith) caused it. For more details on the issue, see TC Wang, *The Law of Torts* (Taipei: Wang Mu Hua 2011).

[87] Wang, *Principles of the Law of Obligation I* (n 15) 282.

breaching party has to prove that the breach is not caused by his fault (ie a subjective element). Since a subjective element is normally hard for the claimant to prove, the defendant's fault is presumed once the claimant proves the objective element, leaving the defendant to rebut the presumption. This same balance of the burden of proof is also true in cases of pre-contractual liability. Therefore, claimants are in a more favourable position in cases of pre-contractual liability and breach of contract. That being said, it seems that the law regards the life of a contract as beginning from the moment negotiations begin: the negotiation process is treated as something like an embryo of a fully fledged contract that deserves protection.

IV. Conclusion

This chapter has introduced and discussed various rules on the formation of contracts under the Taiwanese law of contract. Some rules mirror their source law (ie German law), and some do not. Some rules have also been compared with those of other East Asian civil jurisdictions (eg South Korea and Japan).

Regarding offers, the rules can be summarized as follows:

(1) the moment the offeror's intention to make an offer is conveyed to the offeree and the latter understands it is the time that the offer is created and becomes effective;
(2) if the offeror sends his offer to the offeree by post, it is created and effectuated once the post arrives at the offeree's home or business address provided they are under the offeree's control;
(3) the default rule is that the offeror is bound by his offer after the offer takes effect;
(4) however, the binding effect of an offer loses its efficacy if it is rejected by the offeree or fails to be accepted by the offeree within certain periods.

As for acceptance, the relevant rules can be outlined as follows:

(1) an acceptance conveyed instantaneously becomes effective at the moment the offeror understands it;
(2) an acceptance sent by post also becomes effective the moment it reaches the place under the offeror's control. The so-called postal rule adopted in England is not the law in Taiwan. However, it is interesting to find that the postal rule is adopted in South Korea and Japan;
(3) an acceptance which is delayed is deemed to be a new offer.

Furthermore:

(1) regarding the test used to construct the parties' intentions, the subjective test is considered to be the basic rule of Taiwan, although the practical consequence are not so different from the objective test, unless the rule of *falsa demonstrio non nocet* applied; and
(2) no formality is needed to form a contractual relationship unless otherwise required by law.

Pre-contractual liability was dealt with in the final section of the chapter, and the following four elements merit recalling.

(1) The legislative form of the article (ie article 245-1 of the Taiwan CC) providing for pre-contractual liability is unique in that it lists two particular grounds triggering the liability, rather than simply prescribing breach of the good faith principle.

(2) Pre-contractual liability may arise when one party: (a) conceals in bad faith or dishonestly explains material information involving the contract when the other party asks about it; (b) intentionally or recklessly divulges the other party's secrets when the other party has explicitly requested that they be kept secret; or (c) breaches the good faith duty by, for example, abruptly breaking off negotiations or inflicting harm in the process of negotiation.

(3) Once liability is established, the defendant is liable for the payment of reliance damages suffered by the claimant.

(4) Pre-contractual liability is classified as a third type of civil liability arising by operation of law distinct from both contractual and tortious liabilities.

16

Contracts for the Benefit of Third Parties Under the Taiwan Civil Code

*Sheng-Lin JAN**

I. The Principle of Relativity of the Relationship of Obligation

As a general principle, the doctrine of privity of contract is fundamental in Taiwanese contract law. Under this doctrine, a contract can generate rights and duties only for and against the parties to the contract. The privity rule of contract can be easily justified by the reason that contractual rights and duties are personal to those who create them.[1]

Article 199 paragraph 1 of the Taiwan Civil Code ('Taiwan CC') provides that by virtue of the relationship of obligation the creditor is entitled to claim performance from the debtor. Based on this provision, the Taiwan Supreme Court ruled that a right to claim is a right against a specific person and that the creditor is only entitled to demand performance from the debtor; the creditor is not entitled to demand performance from any person other than the debtor.[2] Furthermore, the Taiwan Supreme Court has ruled that a sale contract does not have any effect against a third person who is not a party to the contract.[3] The precedents of the Supreme Court demonstrate that under the privity rule those who are not parties to the contract can neither be conferred an enforceable right to claim contractual performance nor shall they be obligated under the contract.

It is worth emphasizing that, as in German law,[4] Taiwanese law recognizes not only the principle of 'privity of contract', but also the principle of 'privity of all relationships of obligations'. In addition to contract, a relationship of obligation can also arise from *negotiorum gestio* (management of the affairs of others), unjust enrichment, and torts. Accordingly, if any claim arises from a tortious act, the victim is entitled to demand compensation for damage only from the specific tortfeasor or other persons who are, specified by law, liable for the damage. As a result, the general concept in Taiwanese law is the 'relativity of the relationship of obligation'[5] rather than the privity of contract.

* Cite as S Jan, 'Contracts for the Benefit of Third Parties under the Taiwan Civil Code' in Chen-Wishart, Loke, & Vogenauer, *Studies in the Contract Laws of Asia Vol II: Formation and Third Party Beneficiaries* (Oxford: OUP 2017) ch 16.

[1] M Chen-Wishart, *Contract Law* (4th edn, Oxford: OUP 2012) 17.

[2] Taiwan Supreme Court Precedent 18 Shang No 1953 (1929).

[3] Taiwan Supreme Court Precedent 20 Shang No 2405 (1931).

[4] S Vogenauer, 'The Effects of Contracts on Third Parties: The *Avant-projet de réforme* in a Comparative Perspective' in J Cartwright, S Vogenauer, and S Whittaker (eds), *Reforming the French Law of Obligations* (Oxford: Hart Publishing 2009) 236.

[5] TC Wang, *Principles of the Law of Obligations I* (Taipei: Wang Mu Hua 2012) 10.

Contracts for the Benefit of Third Parties Under the Taiwan Civil Code. Sheng-Lin Jan.

II. Statutory Provisions Relating to the Contract for the Benefit of Third Parties

Since the enactment of Book 2 (Law of Obligations) of the Taiwan CC in 1930, the legal institution of the contract for the benefit of third parties has been codified in articles 269 and 270 and is therefore acknowledged as a matter of general principle.

Article 269 of the Taiwan CC provides:

(1) When by way of a contract performance shall be rendered to a third party, the offeror[6] may demand the debtor to render the performance to the third party, and such third party is also entitled to demand performance directly from the debtor.

(2) So long as the third party has not expressed his intent to take the benefit of the contract specified in the preceding paragraph, the parties may modify the contract or revoke it.

(3) If the third party expresses to either of the parties his intent not to take benefit of the contract, he is deemed to never have acquired any right under the contract.

In addition, article 270 of the Taiwan CC provides: 'The debtor specified in the preceding article may raise all the defenses arising out of the contract against the third party beneficiary'.

Paragraphs 1 and 2 of article 269 of the Taiwan CC adopted articles 537 and 538 of the 1896 Japanese Civil Code,[7] and paragraph 3 of that same article is derived from § 333 of the 1900 German Civil Code (*Bürgerliches Gesetzbuch*, 'BGB').[8]

Models for article 270 of the Taiwan CC are Article 539 of the 1896 Japanese Civil Code[9] and § 334 of the BGB.[10]

III. Right of the Third Party to Claim Performance Directly From the Debtor

Pursuant to article 269 of the Taiwan CC, the parties are free to conclude a contract for the benefit of a third party, for example when parents buy houses, apartments, or valuable movables for their children as gifts.[11] The parents would then make the owner of the object an

[6] The term 'offeror' is used here because the third part beneficiary is also a 'creditor' of the debtor. In order to differentiate these two 'creditors', the person who concludes the third party beneficiary contract with the debtor is referred to as the 'offeror'.

[7] Art 537 of the Japanese Civil Code provides:

> If a party by a contract has agreed to make a presentation to a third person, the latter has a right to claim such presentation directly from the debtor. In the cases set forth in the preceding paragraph, rights of the third person comes into existence at the time when he expresses to the debtor his intention to enjoy the benefit of the contract.

Article 538 of the same Code provides:

> After rights of the third person have come into existence in accordance with the provisions of the preceding Article, the parties may not modify or extinguish those rights.

See <https://archive.org/stream/cu31924069576704#page/n161/mode/2up> accessed 5 December 2016.

[8] § 333 BGB provides:

> If the third party rejects the right under the contract towards the promisor, the right is deemed to not have been acquired.

[9] Art 539 of the Japanese Civil Code provides:

> The debtor may raise the defense founded on the contract referred to in paragraph (1) of Article 537 against a third person in whose favor the contract is made.

[10] § 334 BGB:

> Defences arising from the contract are available to the promisor even as against the third party.

[11] This occurs in Taiwan quite often among wealthy families when the children become adults or are about to marry.

offer to buy and, either at the same time or later, ask the owner to give an extra promise that not only the buyer (ie the parents), but also the benefited child(ren) should have the right to demand the transfer of the ownership and the possession of the object. If the owner not only agrees to sell but also agrees on the extra request of the buyer, then, so said the Taiwan Supreme Court, they conclude a sale contract with an adhered 'clause for benefit of third parties'. This does not need to be express. What must be proved is that the debtor and the offeror agreed on a third party's direct right to claim against the debtor. The sale contract described in this case is the 'causal contract', and the extra agreement of the parties to confer the right to claim on the third party a 'clause for the benefit of third parties'.[12] Another example is as follows: A concludes a contract with B under which B is obliged to take care of C who is A's parent. A and B agree that it is A who has to pay B but it is not only A but also C who has the right to ask for contractual performance from B. In this case, the 'causal contract' is the contract between A and B and the main content of which is that B is obliged to take care of C. The 'clause for the benefit of third parties' in this case is that C is entitled to claim directly against B.

A contract for the benefit of third parties is in addition often concluded when married couples plan to divorce through mutual content.[13] A couple, especially if they have minor children, would normally agree that one of the parents is obliged to transfer real estate to the minor children or make periodical payments to them until they become adults. In such a case, a contract for the benefit of the minor children is deemed to have been concluded if the couple make clear in their divorce agreement that the minor children shall be entitled to demand the transfer of the ownership or the payments of the money.[14]

The feature of a contract for the benefit of third parties is that the third party beneficiary shall be entitled to demand performance directly from the debtor. Only with such direct right of the third party to demand performance is a contract a genuine 'contract for the benefit of third parties' under article 269 of the Taiwan CC. This should be distinguished from the so-called 'spurious contract in favour of a third party'.[15] In such a contract, one of the parties enters into the contract with the intention of benefiting a third party by performance of the other party, but does not agree with the other party to confer on the third party the right to demand the contractual performance.[16] For example, A buys a house from B and the contract of sale only lays down that the ownership of the house shall be transferred to C, without stipulating in the contract (expressly or impliedly) that C is entitled to claim the transfer directly from B. In this kind of case, the Taiwanese courts are inclined to conclude that due to the lack of an explicit agreement of the parties on C's right to claim, the contract is not a contract for the benefit of third parties in the sense of article 269 of the Taiwan CC. As a result, C, in spite of his undisputed character as the third party beneficiary of the contract, is not entitled to sue the seller B for performance or damages for breach.[17] The same applies when A buys a house from B and the contract stipulates that A is free to designate the name of the person to whom the title shall be transferred and that B may not intervene with the designation. According to the Taiwan Supreme Court, since the

[12] Taiwan Supreme Court Decision 95 Tai-Shang No 1691 (2006), Taiwan Supreme Court Decision 98 Tai-Shang No 1450 (2009) etc.

[13] According to the Taiwan CC, there are two types of divorce: divorce by mutual content (Taiwan CC, arts 1049 and 1050) and divorce by judicial decree (Taiwan CC, art 1052).

[14] See Taiwan Supreme Court Decision 69 Tai-Shang No 244 (1980), Taiwan Supreme Court Decision 83 Tai-Shang No 2945 (1994).

[15] S Vogenauer, 'Contract in Favour of a Third Party' in J Basedow et al (eds), *The Max Planck Encyclopedia of European Private Law*, vol 1 (Oxford: OUP 2012) 386.

[16] Taiwan Supreme Court Decision 98 Tai-Shang No 81 (2009).

[17] Taiwan Supreme Court Decision 98 Tai-Shang No 1450 (2009).

contract does not specify that B is obliged to transfer the title to a third party, the contract concluded by A and B is not a contract for the benefit of third parties under article 269 of the Taiwan CC.[18] In short, according to the Taiwan Supreme Court, in order to constitute a genuine contract for the benefit of third parties it is not enough that the debtor is made aware by the offeror that the interest of a third party is involved in the contractual performance. It must be agreed (expressly or impliedly) by the debtor that he is obliged to render performance to a specified third party upon either the request of the offeror or that of the third party.

It should be noted that pursuant to paragraph 1 of article 269 of the Taiwan CC, both the offeror and the third party beneficiary are entitled to demand the debtor to perform. The enforceability of the right to claim conferred on the third party is as good as the offeror's right to claim. However, both of the rights may only be exercised when it is claimed that the contractual performance shall be rendered to the third party beneficiary. In other words, in the case of a contract for the benefit of a third party the offeror's right to claim is limited insofar as he is only entitled to demand that the debtor render specific performance to the beneficiary specified in the contract; a claim that the debtor renders performance to the offeror is excluded and shall be dismissed.[19]

IV. Breach of the Contract for the Benefit of Third Parties

Since the beneficiary of the contract for the benefit of third parties has a personal right to claim performance, in the case of non-performance for which the debtor is liable, the third party beneficiary is entitled to sue for breach. In such a case, specific performance and damages are available remedies that the beneficiary may enjoy. However, since the beneficiary is not a party to the contract he may not resort to termination of the contract. In the case of impossibility of performance, the beneficiary's recoverable damages include compensation for expectation loss as the remedy of damages in lieu of contractual performance.

Although the contract for the benefit of third parties purports mainly to confer the contractual performance on the third party beneficiary, the promisee might have his own personal interest that the contract shall be performed properly. Accordingly, all European legal jurisdictions recognizing a contract for the benefit of third parties permit the promisee not only to enforce the debtor's actual performance but also to claim damages against the debtor for breach of non-performance.[20]

The same is the case in Taiwanese contract law. According to the Taiwan Supreme Court, as both the beneficiary and the offeror are entitled to claim against the debtor, this may result in compensation for damage caused not only to the beneficiary but also to the promisee. For example, A makes a contract with C to sell B's house to C and the contract contains a penalty clause to deal with the situation where A fails to enable C to acquire ownership. The contract also states that C has a right to claim the transfer of ownership directly from B. A also makes a contract with B for B to transfer the property to C. Where B breaches the contract and transfers the title of the subject house to D, the Taiwan Supreme Court ruled that both C and A are entitled to sue for damages. C may claim compensation for the loss of expectation, for example the market value of the disputed house, and A may demand that B compensate for A's loss resulting from the penalty clause between A and C.[21]

[18] Taiwan Supreme Court Decision 93 Tai-Shang No 2537 (2004).

[19] See the opinion of the High Court in the decision of the Taiwan Supreme Court 93 Tai-Shang No 2537 (2004).

[20] H Beale et al (eds), *Cases, Materials and Text on Contract Law* (Oxford: Hart Publishing 2002) 911.

[21] Taiwan Supreme Court Precedent 66 Tai-Shang No 1204 (1977).

Based on the opinion of the Taiwan Supreme Court as described above, no hierarchy between the claims of the promisee (offeror) and any claims enjoyed by the third party exists. The Taiwan Supreme Court only opines that although the promisee (offeror) is also entitled to demand the debtor to specifically perform, he is bound to request that performance be rendered to the beneficiary. The question of whether in the case of breach by the debtor, the promisee (offeror) or the third party shall have the privilege priority to enjoy the remedies, has yet to be decided by the courts. Instead, the Taiwan Supreme Court emphasized that the promisee (offeror) and the third party beneficiary are free to avail themselves of all possible remedies. As far as damages are concerned, both of them may only claim compensation for their own damage loss resulting from the debtor's failure to render performance to the third party.[22]

V. Defences Available to the Debtor

Where the third party beneficiary brings an action against the debtor, the debtor may rely on all defences which would have been available to him as if in an action brought by the offeror. This is explicitly laid down in article 270 of the Taiwan CC. According to the Taiwan Supreme Court, since the basis of the third party's personal right to claim performance is the causal contract entered into by the offeror and the debtor, the debtor may raise against the third party all types of defences available to him under the causal contract.[23]

Thus, in the normal case where the causal contract between the offeror and the debtor is a bilateral one,[24] the debtor may withhold performance until the offeror himself has performed.[25] Of course, the debtor may not demand counter-performance from the third party because the third party is not a party to the causal contract.[26]

Can the third party sue the offeror on the basis that the offeror's non-performance in effect varies or extinguishes the third party's right? The answer depends on the nature of the legal relationship between the offeror and the third party. In the example where parents buy a house for their child and the seller is obliged to transfer ownership to the child, the child is normally not entitled to sue the parents to perform. Therefore, if the seller withholds performance because the parents do not pay, the child cannot sue his parents. However, if the legal relationship between the offeror and the third party entitles the third party to claim specific performance against the offeror and the content of such specific performance is exactly the subject of performance by the debtor, the third party can sue the offeror if the debtor withholds performance due to the offeror's non-performance. For example, A buys B's car and sells it to C before B delivers. A tells B that the price will be paid by A and asks B to deliver to C as required by C. B agrees. When C requires B to deliver, B refuses on the ground that the price has not been paid. In this case, under the contract between A and C, A is obliged to make C the owner of the car and B's legitimate refusal to deliver the car constitutes A's breach of his contract with C. As a result, C can sue A for breach of contract.

The debtor is furthermore entitled to refuse to render performance to the third party if the causal contract is void (eg because it contradicts prohibitory law) or has been avoided

[22] Taiwan Supreme Court Precedent 83 Tai-Shang No 836 (1994).

[23] Taiwan Supreme Court Decision 97 Tai-Shang No 266 (2008).

[24] Since the debtor is obliged to render performance to the third party but not entitled to claim counter-performance against the third party, the debtor will, in general, only promise to do so when he will be entitled to claim counter-performance against the promisee based on the 'causal contract' between him and the promisee. Hence, the 'causal contract' is usually a bilateral one.

[25] Taiwan Supreme Court Decision 100 Tai-Shang No 1679 (2011).

[26] Taiwan Supreme Court Precedent 71 Tai-Shang No 1498 (1982), Taiwan Supreme Court Decision 89 Tai-Shang No 2048 (2000).

(eg due to non-performance) or withdrawn (eg due to fraud, article 92 of the Taiwan CC).[27] However, if the causal contract has been avoided or terminated after the debtor has performed, only the offeror has the duty to restore the contract; the third party, being not a party to the causal contract, is not liable for the restoration.[28] For example, X sells a car to Y, which Y intends to give to Z as a gift. X also agrees that Z may demand the delivery. X has delivered but then terminates the sale contract because Y has not paid the (total) price. According to the above stated opinion of the Taiwan Supreme Court, X may only sue Y for non-performance and cannot sue Z for return of the car.

Where the third party has coerced the offeror to contract with the debtor, the offeror can raise the defence of coercion to avoid the contract with the debtor. However, if the third party misrepresented to the offeror to contract with the debtor, the offeror may raise the defence of misrepresentation/fraud only if the debtor is aware or ought to have been aware of the misrepresentation/fraud.[29]

Defences provided for in article 270 and available to the debtor must arise from the causal contract between the debtor and the offeror. Any defect in the legal relationship between the offeror and the third party beneficiary does not give rise to any defences that the debtor can raise against the claim of the third party. If the third party induced the 'causal contract' between the debtor and the offeror by misrepresentation to the debtor, only the debtor who contracted with the offeror may rescind the 'causal contract' and only if the offeror is aware or ought to have been aware of the misrepresentation.[30]

Finally, as a general rule, the third party's claim is subject to set-off if the counterclaim to be set off is based on the legal relationship between the debtor and the third party.[31] However, article 341 of the Taiwan CC provides that the debtor who is bound by an agreement to render performance to a third party may not set off his obligation to render such performance against the obligation owed to him by the other party to such agreement.[32] As a consequence, the third party's claim is not subject to the defence of set-off raised by the debtor if the counterclaim to be set off arises from the legal relationship between the debtor and the offeror.[33]

VI. Variation and Revocation of the Contract for the Benefit of Third Parties

According to paragraph 2 of article 269 of the Taiwan CC, as long as the third party beneficiary has not expressed his intent to enjoy the benefit of the contract, the contract is subject to any modification made or revocation declared by the parties to the contract.

The Taiwan Supreme Court infers from the wording of this provision and rules that once the third party declares his intent to enjoy the benefit, the parties to the contract are no longer permitted to modify or revoke the contract.[34]

[27] Taiwan Supreme Court Decision 87 Tai-Shang No 180 (1998).

[28] Taiwan Supreme Court Decision 89 Tai-Shang No 1769 (2000).

[29] Taiwan CC, s 1, art 92. [30] ibid.

[31] Taiwan CC, art 334 provides:

> If two persons owe each other obligations the object of which is of the same kind and the performances of the obligations are both due, each party may set off his claim against the claim of the other party, except that set-off is not possible due to the nature of the obligations or is not permissible in accordance with the agreement of the parties. The agreement provided in the preceding paragraph may not be asserted against any bona fide third party.

[32] Taiwan CC, art 341 adopted the Swiss Code of Obligations, Art 122.

[33] UP Cheng, *General Principles of the Law of Obligations* (Taipei: Sanmin Publishing 1963) 394; SY Sun, *General Principles of the Law of Obligations* (Taipei: Sun Sen Yen 2012) 848.

[34] Taiwan Supreme Court Precedent 18 Shang No 298 (1929), Taiwan Supreme Court Decision 72 Tai-Shang No 3887 (1983).

The intent of the third party to enjoy the benefit can be expressed explicitly or implicitly, and the expression can be made either to the offeror or to the debtor. In a Taiwan Supreme Court case, X and Y lived together for a long period of time and Y gave birth to their daughter Z. X and Y agreed to terminate their relationship and X also agreed to give Z a lump sum of two million New Taiwan Dollars as alimony. Pursuant to this agreement, X concluded with a bank a three-year time deposit contract in Z's name and gave the certificate issued by the bank to Y, since Z was a minor. The Taiwan Supreme Court upheld the opinion of the Court of Appeal and ruled that there was a legal relationship of third party beneficiary between X and Z by X agreeing with Y to conclude the three-year time deposit contract for Z. Z expressed her intention to enjoy the benefit since Z provided X with her registered stamp (ie a stamp registered in the public office to verify a person's identity on a formal document). Therefore, X may not rescind the third party beneficiary contract in favour of Z.[35]

It should be noted that 'revocation' in the sense of paragraph 2 of article 269 of the Taiwan CC means that the parties terminate the contract *by agreement*.[36] The Taiwan Supreme Court emphasizes that this provision does not deprive the parties of the right to terminate the contract where the right of termination is based on legal grounds specified by laws and regulations.[37] Consequently, if the offeror breaches his obligation of counter-performance and as a result the debtor terminates the contract in accordance with the provisions of article 254, 255, or 256 of the Taiwan CC,[38] the third party beneficiary cannot sue the debtor for performance although he has evinced his intention to enjoy the benefit before the termination of the contract.[39] In addition, even if the debtor, following the expressed intention of the third party to enjoy the benefit, has rendered the contractual performance to the third party, the debtor may still terminate the contract based on the statutory provisions. In such a case, according to the Taiwan Supreme Court, the debtor is entitled to sue the third party for restitution on the basis of unjust enrichment.[40] On the other hand, under the general principle of specific performance based on article 199 of the Taiwan CC, the third party may sue the offeror to render counter-performance.

VII. The Rules of the Contract for the Benefit of Third Parties as a Mechanism to Fill Gaps in the Law of Tort?

1. Introduction of German Law

In some jurisdictions, the provisions governing contracts for the benefit of third parties play an important role in filling gaps in the law of tort. This is particularly true in Germany.[41] The starting point is a decision of the German Imperial Court (*Reichsgericht*) in 1930. There, a maid employed by a widow, Mrs M, was entitled to sue for compensation for damage resulting from an explosion on the basis of contract against a repairman and his employee, who contracted with the widow to repair a gas stove for her and who caused the

[35] Taiwan Supreme Court Decision 85 Tai-Shang No 857 (1996).

[36] Sun (n 33) 844

[37] Taiwan Supreme Court Decision 82 Tai-Shang No 150 (1993).

[38] Taiwan CC, arts 254–256 deal with the creditor's right of termination in cases where the performance of the debtor is impossible, in default, or incomplete.

[39] Taiwan Supreme Court Decision 83 Tai-Shang No 2599 (1994). Cf TC Wang, 'The Termination of a Contract for Third Party and its Effects' (1992) 43(3) Falingyuekan (The Law Monthly) 8.

[40] Taiwan Supreme Court Decision 92 Tai-Shang No 1189 (2003), Taiwan Supreme Court Decision 95 Tai-Shang No 2670 (2006), Taiwan Supreme Court Decision 97 Tai-Shang No 1614 (2008). The Taiwan Supreme Court used to hold the opinion that where a contract for the benefit of third parties was terminated, the debtor was only entitled to sue the promisee for restitution; the enriched third party was not subject to a claim of unjust enrichment brought by the debtor. See Taiwan Supreme Court Decision 87 Tai-Shang No 61 (1998), Taiwan Supreme Court Decision 88 Tai-Shang No 657 (1999).

[41] H Kötz and A Flessner, *Europäisches Vertragsrecht I* (*European Private Law*) (Tübingen: Mohr 1992) 252.

explosion of the stove due to gross negligence. The *Reichsgericht* pointed out that the contract concluded by the repairman and the widow bound the defendants to take the care normally required in carrying out the work. Not only was Mrs M entitled as a contracting party to have that care taken, and to be compensated for the damage caused by the neglect of it, but the plaintiff was also entitled insofar as the contract must be taken to have been a contract for the benefit of third parties.[42]

The outcome of the case was welcomed but the reasoning of the decision was criticized by German legal scholars. The fundamental criticism was that if the contract between the widow and the repairman had been a genuine contract for the benefit of a third party, as held by the *Reichsgericht*, the injured plaintiff would have been able to claim performance of the necessary works for the repair of the stove, which, however, would definitely have been against the intention of the contracting widow and repairman.[43]

What lay behind the German approach of making use of the beneficiary third party contract to allow an injured non-party to claim, was the unsatisfactory possibility of exculpation regarding a master's liability for his servants in tort law (§ 831 of the BGB). However, if the injured person bases his claim on *contract*, the master who has a contractual relationship with the injured person can be held strictly liable for his servant's performance that caused the injury. In addition, the German preference for the *contractual* approach can be explained by the desire to avoid the hotly disputed issue of claims for pure economic loss where there has been no infringement of life, body, health, freedom, ownership, or any other absolute right enumerated in § 831(1) of the BGB.[44]

Nowadays, German courts resolve these problems by using the doctrine of '*Vertrag mit Schutzwirkung für Dritte*' (contract with protective effects for third parties). Under this doctrine, a contract may contain protective effect in favour of third parties if the debtor should be aware that his contractual performance may come into contact with and thus cause damage to third parties who have a close legal relationship with the creditor, and the creditor has a special interest in their protection. When third parties sustain personal injury or property damage due to the defective performance of the debtor, they are entitled to sue the debtor on the basis of breach of contract together with a concurrent right to sue in tort. German courts have even extended the availability of this doctrine to cases where third parties attempt to claim compensation for pure economic loss when they would usually have no claim in tort.[45]

2. The Situation in Taiwanese Law

Taiwan's tort law contains similar provisions that forced the German courts to circumvent the unsatisfactory tortious liability and take the contractual approach as described above. Article 188 paragraph 1 of the Taiwan CC also permits the debtor master to escape tortious liability if he is able to prove that he exercised all due care in selecting, training, and supervising his servant who actually caused the loss or damage in the execution of the business assigned to him. Furthermore, predominant academic opinion[46] and recent decisions of

[42] RGZ 127, 218, 221. Refer to the English translation by FH Lawson and BS Markesinis in BS Markesinis and H Unberath (eds), *The German Law of Torts: A Comparative Treatise* (4th edn, Portland, OR: Hart Publishing 2002) 798.

[43] K Larenz, *Lehrbuch des Schuldrechts*, Bd I (14th edn, Munich: CH Beck Verlag 1987) paras 225f.

[44] Kötz and Flessner (n 41) 253–254; E du Perron, 'Contract and Third Parties' in AS Hartkamp et al (eds), *Towards a European Civil Code* (2nd edn, Nijmegen: Kluwer 1998) 323–324; Markesinis and Unberath (n 42) 701–705.

[45] Larenz (n 43) para 229; K Zweigert and H Kötz, *An Introduction to Comparative Law* (Tony Weir trans, 3rd edn, New York: OUP 1998) 461–462.

[46] TC Wang, *Tort Law* (Taipei: Wang Mu Hua 2011) 85; Sun (n 33) 210.

the Supreme Court[47] infer from the basic tortious provision of article 184 of the Taiwan CC[48] that the protected interests in tort law are in principle confined to absolute rights (eg life, body, health, freedom, reputation, tangible and intangible property), and that an infringement of pure economic interest will result in tortious liability only when either the wrongful act is intentionally committed and in a manner contrary to good morals, or that a statute intending to protect the interest of others is violated.

However, the Taiwanese courts have neither applied the rules of the contract for the benefit of third parties (ie articles 269 and 270 discussed earlier), nor adopted the German doctrine of contract with protective effects for third parties, in order to enable an injured third party to claim damages in contract. This could possibly be explained, first, by the fact that, in practice, Taiwanese courts very rarely allow a master to exculpate himself from tortious liability by adducing proof that his servant whose conduct inflicts damage on a third party was properly selected, instructed, and supervised. Hence, the result is practically the same as under German law. Second, a restricted protection of pure economic interest is acceptable not only to most Taiwanese courts but also to legal academics; wider protection, at least in the cases dealt with by the courts, has not been considered necessary. Difficult cases in which German courts conferred remedies in contract on a person who was not a party to a contract but suffered pure economic loss due to negligent contractual performance (such as BGH NJW 1977, 2073[49]) have not yet been dealt with by the Taiwan Supreme Court.

VIII. Case Analysis

1. Exemption Clauses for Stevedores

X contracts with Y to transport X's goods using Y's ship to a foreign market. The contract for the carriage of goods by sea between X and Y contains an exemption of liability provision which purports to protect Z, the stevedores hired to unload X's goods from Y's ship once it arrives at the docks. As a result of Z's carelessness, X's goods are damaged while they are being unloaded from the ship and X wants to sue Z for negligence to recover damages for the losses suffered by X. Can Z rely on the exemption of liability provision in the contract between X and Y?

The issue is whether a person is entitled to raise defences contained in a contract to which he is not a party.

German law would answer the question in accordance with the doctrine of '*vertragliche Haftungsausschluß mit Wirkung für Dritte*' (contractual exemption of liability with effect

[47] Taiwan Supreme Court Decision 98 Tai-Shang No 1961 (2009), Taiwan Supreme Court Decision 100 Tai-Shang No 2092 (2011), Taiwan Supreme Court Decision 102 Tai-Shang No 1458 (2013).

[48] Taiwan CC, art 184 provides:

(1) Any person who, intentionally or negligently, unlawfully infringes rights of others shall be liable for compensation for damage. The same applies if a person intentionally inflicts damage on another person in a manner contrary to good morals.
(2) A person, who violates a statutory provision enacted for the protection of others and therefore causes damages to others, is liable for compensation, except no negligence in his act can be proved.

[49] In the case of BGH NJW 1977, 2073, the defendant was an attorney who represented the plaintiff's father in divorce proceedings and drew up a divorce agreement for the plaintiff's father and mother. Due to negligence, the defendant failed to inform the plaintiff's father of the need to implement a clause contained in the divorce agreement and thereby inflicted pure economic loss on the plaintiff. The German Federal Supreme Court (*Bundesgerichtshof*, 'BGH') pointed out that the very words of the clause showed that the children, including the plaintiff, were its sole beneficiaries. As a consequence, the BGH upheld the opinion of the Court of Appeal that although the plaintiff was not a party to the contract concluded between his father and the defendant, the plaintiff was entitled to sue the defendant for damages for breach of contract.

for third parties).[50] In a case decided by the BGH in 1961,[51] a surveillance service company was obliged under a contract with the owner of two vehicles to take care of the vehicles. The contract laid down, inter alia, that 'harm which arises in the operation and guarding of machines, heaters, boilers and heating devices . . . is excluded from liability'. The 71-year-old defendant, an employee of the surveillance service company, was on duty to guard the vehicles. Due to the defendant's negligence, a vehicle caught fire and was destroyed with all its contents. The claimant, an insurance company, paid for the damage based on an insurance policy and sued the defendant for the payment. The Court of Appeal quashed the decision of the District Court and dismissed the claim on the ground that the exemption clause contained in the contract between the owner of the vehicles and the surveillance service company was also available to the defendant. The BGH agreed with the Court of Appeal:

> The assumption that the Surveillance Service Company wanted to extend the protection of the clause to its employees seems appropriate for the simple reason that the Surveillance Service Company could be held to this on the basis of duty of care which it owed. It undertook the task of protecting from harm the objects which it guarded. It regarded the risk here as so significant that it sought to limit its liability in relation to the guarding and operation of heaters, so that it did not have to take responsibility for gross negligence by its employees. To have shifted this risk which it recognized from its own shoulders and yet to have wished to burden its employees with it would be incomprehensible. They were weaker economically and still less in a state than their employers to bear the consequences of their failings resulting from general human weakness. In these circumstances, simply the duty of care which the Surveillance Service owed required it to include its employees in the protection which it considered necessary. It is to be assumed, in the absence of grounds indicating the contrary, that it wanted to fulfil this duty by the exemption from liability clause.[52]

It is hard to anticipate whether Taiwanese courts would adopt the German doctrine of *vertragliche Haftungsausschluß mit Wirkung für Dritte*, since no such cases have ever been decided by the courts.

Coming back to the present case study, it is clear that, under Taiwanese law, Z may rely on the exemption of liability provision in the contract between X and Y. Since the exemption clause contained in the contract between X and Y purports to protect Z, it is apparent that Z is within the scope of the protective effect of the contract. X is aware that it is not Y but Z who will actually unload X's goods from Y's ship. As a consequence, X should be prevented from asserting that the clause in dispute only enables Y, and not Z, to be exempted from liability.

In addition, article 76 of the Taiwan Maritime Act, the so-called '*Himalaya*' clause,[53] provides that:

> (1) The agent or servant of the carrier is entitled to avail himself of the defense and the limitation of liability, as entitled by the carrier under this Section, against the shipper or other third party for the loss of or damage to the cargo; except that it is proven that the delay for delivery, loss of or damage to the cargo is due to an intended act or gross negligence on the part of the agent or servant.
>
> (2) The provisions of the preceding paragraph shall be applicable to any parties who are performing their duties within the commercial harbor area for the loading, unloading, handling, carriage, custody, keep, care, stowage, tally, lashing and dunnage.

[50] Larenz (n 43) para 230. [51] BGH JZ 1962, 570.
[52] The English translation of the decision is referred to in Markesinis and Unberath (n 42) 541.
[53] *Adler v Dickson (The Himalaya)* [1954] 2 Lloyd's Rep 267, [1955] 1 QB 158 (QBD).

A decision rendered by a Taiwanese District Court in 2003 justified this provision by referring to Article IVbis of the 1968 Hague–Visby Rules,[54] and pointed out that it is evidently unfair if the servants of the carriers are held liable in tort while the carriers may avail themselves of the exemption clause; consequently, where the carriers are exonerated from liability on the grounds specified in the exemption clause, unless the claimant is able to prove that the servants of the carriers inflicted the damage to the goods intentionally or with gross negligence, the servants will also be entitled to enjoy the benefit of being exempt from liability.[55]

2. Package Holidays for Family Members

X purchases a package holiday for X and her family, which includes Z, from Y's travel agency. The holiday turns out to be an absolute disaster, with poor-quality accommodation, unacceptable food, uncomfortable travel, and numerous delays attributable to Y's poor planning. Can Z sue Y for breach of contract? If X were to sue Y for breach of contract, can X's claim for damages include Z's loss, whether pecuniary or non-pecuniary losses (loss of pleasure, amenity, and enjoyment)?

Article 514-6 of the Taiwan CC stipulates that the travel organizer is obliged to provide travel services in such a way that it has the ordinary value and agreed qualities. Article 514-7 provides that if the travel service does not have the value or qualities required by the preceding article the traveller may request the travel organizer to cure. If the travel organizer does not, or is unable to, cure, the traveller may demand reduction of the price. If the expected purpose of the travel is difficult to achieve, the traveller may terminate the contract. If owing to circumstances for which the travel organizer is responsible, the travel service does not have the value or quality specified in article 514-6, the traveller may, in addition to demanding reduction of the price or terminating the contract, demand compensation for damages. Where the traveller terminates the contract, the travel organizer shall transport the traveller to the original place of departure at the cost of the travel organizer. Furthermore, article 514-8 provides that if owing to circumstances for which the travel organizer is responsible the travel does not proceed according to the agreed itinerary, the traveller may, in respect of the waste of his time, demand compensation for an appropriate sum of money which is counted by the day. However, the sum of the compensation for each day shall not exceed the average sum of each day which the travel organizer has received from the contract price.

In this hypothetical case, the defective travel service provided by Y violates the requirement of article 514-6 of the Taiwan CC and thus constitutes a breach of contract. The question is: who can sue Y?

[54] This provides:

1. The defences and limits of liability provided for in these Rules shall apply in any action against the carrier in respect of loss or damage to goods covered by a contract of carriage whether the action be founded in contract or in tort.
2. If such an action is brought against a servant or agent of the carrier (such servant or agent not being an independent contractor), such servant or agent shall be entitled to avail himself of the defences and limits of liability which the carrier is entitled to invoke under these Rules.
3. The aggregate of the amounts recoverable from the carrier, and such servants and agents, shall in no case exceed the limit provided for in these Rules.
4. Nevertheless, a servant or agent of the carrier shall not be entitled to avail himself of the provisions of this article, if it is proved that the damage resulted from an act or omission of the servant or agent done with intent to cause damage or recklessly and with knowledge that damage would probably result.

[55] Taiwan Keelung District Court Decision 89 Insurance No 2 (2003).

Since Z is not a party to the travel contract between X and Y, Z seems to be precluded from suing Y for breach of contract under the privity rule. However, when Y was concluding the contract he was aware that not only X but also X's family, including Z, would travel under the contract. Y was also aware that the services involved in the package travel (transportations, meals, accommodations, entertainment, etc) were going to be rendered not only to X but also to Z, and any defect in the services would affect both X and Z. Hence, it should be implied that X and Y concluded the contract with the intention that Z also had the right to demand that Y provide the agreed travel services to him, Z. In other words, in relation to the services which were to be provided to Z, X and Y concluded the travel contract for the benefit of Z. Consequently, Z, being a third party beneficiary, is also entitled to sue Y for breach of contract.

It was explained in section IV above that the Taiwan Supreme Court permits, in the case of a contract for the benefit of third parties, both the offeror and the third party beneficiary to enforce performance and sue for non-performance. As far as the remedy of damages is concerned, the offeror is entitled to claim compensation for his own damage resulting from the debtor's failure to render performance to the third party.[56] As a result, if X were to sue Y for breach of contract, X, being offeror of the contract for the benefit of the third party, may only claim for her own pecuniary and non-pecuniary losses in accordance with the provisions of articles 514-7 and 514-8 of the Taiwan CC. Z's personal losses sustained due to the defective travel services provided to Z, in particular Z's non-pecuniary loss, cannot be claimed in the suit brought by X unless Z, the third beneficiary, has legitimately assigned their claim to X. However, under article 195 paragraph 3 of the Taiwan CC, X may be able to sue for the non-pecuniary loss of distress from seeing their family suffer if the suffering constituted severe damage to the relationship between X and her parents, children, and spouse. Taiwanese courts would recognize such severe damage usually only when the parents, children, or spouse sustain serious injury to body or health.

3. Selling Bread

X leases two adjoining properties to Y and Z. The lease between X and Y barred Y from selling bread because Z sold bread from his leased property. Can X and Y agree to lift the bar?

If it can be inferred from the agreement in the lease contract that prohibits Y from selling bread, that Z has a right to claim against Y—which is question of interpretation of the lease contract—the lease agreement is a third party beneficiary contract under article 269 of the Taiwan CC. Under this circumstance, X and Y can lift the bar if Z has yet to express his intent to enjoy the advantage of the contract.

4. The Stolen Shop Takings

X bank makes a contract for Y, a security company, to collect Z store's takings. The contract requires Y to use armoured vehicles and take out insurance. Y failed to do these and the takings were stolen while being collected in an ordinary car. Can Z sue?

Again, if Z in the case described above acquires a right to claim against Y to use armoured vehicles while collecting the store's taking from Z, the contract between X and Y constitutes a third party beneficiary contract and consequently Z is entitled to sue Y for damage due to Y's failure to use armoured vehicles.

[56] Taiwan Supreme Court Precedent 83 Tai-Shang No 836 (1994).

IX. Conclusions

Like other jurisdictions, Taiwan contract law also adopts the principle of privity of contract. Nevertheless, this does not make it difficult for the draftsmen of the Taiwan CC to recognize the legal institution of the contract for the benefit of third parties. The contracting parties are free to attach a 'clause for the benefit of third parties' to their 'causal contract'.

A feature of the Taiwanese doctrine of third party beneficiaries is that the third party acquires the right to claim contractual performance directly against the promisor. Whether the third party acquires this direct right to claim from the parties' 'casual contract', is, if not explicitly agreed upon by the parties, usually a question of interpretation in concrete cases.

In the normal case that the 'causal contract' is bilateral, the promisor may raise defences arising from this contract against the third party, including: withholding performance until the promisee has rendered counter-performance, revocation, avoidance or termination of the causal contract, and limits of prescription, and so on. However, the promisor may not rely on defences based on the legal relationship between the other contracting party and the third party.

The promisor's breach of performance can result in the remedies available both to the promisee and the third party beneficiary. If the breach is a simple refusal to perform, both the third party beneficiary and the promisee may force the promisor to render performance to the third party beneficiary. Where performance has become impossible or is defective due to circumstances for which the promisor is accountable, the promisee and the third party beneficiary can claim for their own loss arising from breach. The losses sustained by the promisee and the third party beneficiary are usually not identical. As a result, there is no hierarchy between these two claims.

17

Formation of Contract and Third Parties in Cambodia

*LY Tayseng**

I. Historical Development of Contract Law

The general development of law in Cambodia can be divided into two main phases. The first phase is made up of ancient legal rules, the second consists of a body of modern legal rules.[1] The ancient rules are largely based on customary rules rooted in religious precepts borrowed from Hinduism and Buddhism in India. The king made laws; disputes were decided by the king in accordance with customary rules or religious principles.

The codification of laws in Cambodia was probably started in 1620 by King Chey Chettha II,[2] who wrote the *Khmer Kram* (Khmer Code) during his reign (1618–28). However, the Code was published only after France took over control of Cambodia (1863–1954). The French administration brought its own legal and judicial systems with it to Cambodia. Further legislation and codification of Cambodian laws then resumed from 1910 onwards. On 20 November 1911, Cambodia adopted a Criminal Code and a Code of Criminal Procedure and Court Organization. These codes were implemented from 1 July 1912, the date on which Cambodia officially adopted the civil law tradition based on the Romano-Germanic system. On 26 July 1915, Cambodia adopted a Civil Code (the 'Old Civil Code') and implemented it from 25 February 1920, by the Royal Ordinance of King Sisowat. This Old Civil Code was mainly influenced by the Napoleonic Civil Code of France. It was amended in 1967 and its amended version remained in force until 17 April 1975.

On 25 April 1975, the Democratic Kampuchea regime took power and remained in place for nearly four years.[3] The Democratic Kampuchea (known as the Khmer Rouge) led the country on the basis of Maoist ideologies and applied a socialist/communist economy. During that time, no law was even needed; all pre-existent laws and the judiciary were abolished outright. The Khmer Rouge regime collapsed on 7 January 1979 with the Kampuchean National United Front for National Salvation declaring victory over the Khmer Rouge and taking control of Phnom Penh and most parts of Cambodia. A new Constitution was promulgated on 9 July 1981 establishing the People's Republic of Kampuchea. The Cambodian economy became a Soviet-style socialist/communist one, adopting collectivism following Marxist–Leninist doctrine. This lasted until 1989, when the changing international political

* Cite as T Ly, 'Formation of Contract and Third Parties in Cambodia' in Chen-Wishart, Loke, & Vogenauer, *Studies in the Contract Laws of Asia Vol II: Formation and Third Party Beneficiaries* (Oxford: OUP 2017) ch 17.

[1] See a further description of the history of Khmer law in Part 1: Legal Status, ch 1, 'Khmer Law and its Historical Development' in L Avillaneda et al, *Introduction au droit cambodgien* (Phnom Penh: Royal University of Law and Economics 2003) 6–25.

[2] ibid 18.

[3] The Revolutionary Army (also referred to as the Khmer Rouge Troops) proclaimed victory on 17 April 1975 and declared the establishment of the Democratic Kampuchea by adopting the third Constitution of Cambodia on 5 January 1976. The Constitution provided no legal guarantee for civil and political rights and due process of law, abolished all private ownership, and created a collective society called Angkar. The country was led by Angkar.

Formation of Contract and Third Parties. Ly Tayseng.

climate at the end of the Cold War and the need for national reconciliation between the pro-socialist and pro-capitalist factions led to a fundamental overhaul of Cambodia's economic system, moving from a planned economy to a free market system. The People's Republic of Kampuchea (1979–89) became the State of Cambodia (1989–93). A number of laws and regulations were adopted as part of that economic liberalization process. Notably, on 28 October 1988, the State Council of the People's Republic of Kampuchea adopted Decree No 38 on Contract and other Liabilities ('Decree No 38'), containing 138 articles organized into three chapters—Chapter I on 'Contracts', Chapter II on 'Some Frequently Used Contracts', and Chapter III on 'Other Liabilities'. Although the Decree only provided for some basic rules on formation, interpretation, validity, performance, and termination of contract, and for some types of contract such as sale, lease, independent contractor agreements, loan, suretyship, and carriage, it was used as the main legal text on contract law in Cambodia until a new Civil Code was ready to enter into force. It is worth noting that Decree No 38 did not expressly abrogate the Old Civil Code, but the Old Civil Code had already fallen into disuse and was no longer applied by the competent courts in making their decisions.

The Royal Government of Cambodia established a drafting group led by officers of the Cambodian Ministry of Justice and tasked it with drafting a Civil Code and a Code of Civil Procedure, with the help of professors and legal experts from Japan and financial support from the Japanese Government. Some of the legal concepts and principles enshrined in the resulting new Civil Code are similar or identical to those in the Japanese Civil Code. Like the latter, the Cambodian Civil Code is structured following the German *Pandekten* system of the nineteenth century which is different from the French institutional system.[4] In drafting the new Civil Code, its authors appear to have considered Cambodian legal traditions and customs, the lessons learned from the application of the Civil Code in Japan, and taken account of the modernization and harmonization of civil law in Europe and Asia, also paying heed to calls on the Japanese Government to update the Japanese Civil Code. Therefore, the Cambodian Civil Code is believed to contain more modern legal concepts and principles than its Japanese model.

The new Cambodian Civil Code was promulgated by Royal Kram No 12007/030 of 8 December 2007 and entered into force on 21 December 2011 in accordance with Royal Kram No 0511/07 of 31 May 2011. The 1305 articles of the new Civil Code are quite comprehensive and embody a large number of modern civil law concepts as enshrined in European and other Asian legal systems. Book IV and Book V of the Civil Code are the main texts for the law of obligations and the law of contract. The Civil Code abrogated most of the provisions of Decree No 38,[5] except for Articles 83 to 88 dealing with transport

[4] The Civil Code of Cambodia is divided into nine books: Book I—General Provisions, Book II—Persons, Book III—Real Rights, Book IV—Obligations, Book V—Specific Contracts and Tort, Book VI—Security, Book VII—Relatives, Book VIII—Successions, and Book IX—Final Provisions. The German *Pandekten* system is different from the French institutional system which originated in the Roman *Gai Instititutiones* or *Justiniani Institutiones*, such that the French Civil Code is divided into three Books: Book I—Persons, Book II—Property and Different Types of Ownership, and Book III—Different Modes of Acquiring Property.

[5] It should also be noted that Art 82 of the Law on Implementation of the Civil Code states that the 1920 Civil Code and its amendment have no effect. In fact, for historical reasons, as explained in this chapter, the 1920 Civil Code had not been enforced in Cambodia since 17 April 1975. However, Art 139 of the 1993 Constitution stipulates that laws and standard documents in Cambodia that safeguard state property, rights, freedoms, and private property in conformity with the national interest, will continue in force until amended or abrogated, with the exception of provisions that are contrary to the spirit of the Constitution. Since the adoption of the 1993 Constitution, there has been no law that abrogates the 1920 Civil Code but nevertheless Cambodian courts have not applied any of that Code's provisions. With respect to contract law, only Decree No 38 has been used by the courts as a basis for their decisions.

contracts, which would remain in force. Legal relationships under contracts concluded prior to the entry into force of the new Civil Code would be governed by the new Code, with the exception of issues expressly exempted in the 'Law on the Application' of the Civil Code promulgated by Royal Kram No 0511/07 of 31 May 2011.

Since the new Civil Code has not been in existence for very long, there are not as yet enough academic studies, doctrines, and judicial decisions to serve as guidance for the Cambodian courts and practitioners in interpreting and enforcing certain principles of contract law. The Cambodian Ministry of Justice, with technical support and cooperation from the Japanese International Cooperation Agency (JICA) has produced commentaries on individual articles of the Civil Code and published a number of textbooks for training judges and other court officers to help them to implement the Code. These commentaries and textbooks are key references and educational materials for Cambodian judges and court officers. However, there are still undecided issues in need of judicial interpretation by the courts of Cambodia in accordance with the country's social and legal context.

II. Sources and Application of Contract Law

The sources of contract law may be found in the legislative acts (passed by Parliament) and executive regulations (issued by the government, ministries, and other public institutions) which flow from the Constitution, the supreme law of the country, as well as in trade practices and customs.

Cambodia has opted for the civil law tradition. It does not have a binding precedent system and the courts of first instance are not bound to follow nor are they required to refer to the decisions of the Appeal Court and the Supreme Court, other than the codified laws. In the absence of written laws, the courts may refer to the principle of fairness, 'good conscience', and trade customs in rendering their decisions.

So far, court decisions, in particular those of the Supreme Court, have not been widely published. They are not compiled or classified in a manner that would allow scholars and researchers ready access to study and comment on those decisions. It is quite difficult, therefore, to predict how the courts will apply certain provisions of the Civil Code. Much work will need to be done by the Cambodian Ministry of Justice and the Supreme Court to harmonize the interpretation and application of the Civil Code by the courts throughout the country, so as to ensure consistency in the application of laws and provide legal certainty and stability for commercial transactions and contractual relationships. To achieve these aims, it is essential that the Supreme Court compile and publish its decisions.

The Civil Code governs general civil relationships and some types of special contracts, such as contracts of sale, exchange, donation, loans for consumption, lease, borrowing, agency, independent contractor agreements, employment contracts, bailment, enterprise contracts, annuities contracts, set-off, and other types of security agreement. If there are exceptions stated in other special laws or if the provisions of the Civil Code contradict the provisions of a given special law, the general rules of the Civil Code do not apply. For example, the setting of interest rates in consumer loan agreements according to the implementing regulation of the Civil Code is different from the interest rate allowed by the National Bank of Cambodia; security agreements created pursuant to the Law on Secured Transactions are different from those created according to the Civil Code. It is also not uncommon to find contracts that are subject to both the general rules of the Civil Code and the special law, for example employment contracts,[6] insurance contracts,[7] and concession contracts. It should be noted that the Cambodian Government is preparing a draft law on commercial contracts, aimed at regulating commercial relationships between merchants. If that draft bill is adopted, there will be a separate law governing commercial contracts.

III. Some Basic Principles

Like the German, French, and Japanese Civil Codes and other civil law systems, the Cambodian Civil Code recognizes overriding modern principles of contract, such as freedom to contract, party autonomy, good faith and fair dealing, equality of bargaining power, and the notion of reasonableness. Such concepts form basic common rules for all types of contract stipulated in the Cambodian Civil Code.

1. Freedom of Contract and Party Autonomy

The Constitution of Cambodia promulgated in 1993 adopted modern political, economic, and legal principles. It enshrines the principles of a free market economy, guarantees private ownership, and protects the civil and political rights of the individual, etc. The Civil Code recognizes freedom to contract and the autonomy of a person to enter into a contract. It upholds, to the greatest extent possible, the principle of freedom of contract as developed in the seventeenth and eighteenth centuries and as recognized by most modern contract laws of many countries belonging to either the civil law or the common law tradition. Article 2 of the Civil Code stipulates the principle of human dignity, equality between men and women, and property rights as set forth in the Constitution.

Freedom of contract and party autonomy are reflected in the concept of free will. Article 3 of the Civil Code provides for respect of the free will of the parties in private transactions. The application of free will may be understood to include the following contexts.

(1) Freedom to enter or not to enter into a contract and freedom to choose a contracting partner. No one is obliged to conclude a contract against his will, unless special legal provision so requires.

(2) Freedom to decide the contents of contract terms. The parties to a contract are free to choose the type, form, terms, and mechanisms of the contract that they can agree upon within the domain of the contract. They may also choose the scope of obligations, remedies in the case of non-performance, modes of termination, exoneration of liability, or waiver of their own rights recognized by law.

(3) Freedom to depart from the established types of contract. The Civil Code provides for several types of contract, such as sale, consumer loans, agency, etc. The parties are free to agree differently on certain terms and conditions, except on those provisions that are regarded as mandatory rules. The Civil Code provides for default provisions which the contracting parties may follow. Otherwise, they are free to vary the provisions, except in the case of mandatory provisions in the Code.

[6] Art 668 of the Civil Code provides that employment contracts follow the provisions of the Labour Code, except where the Civil Code stipulates otherwise. Art 65 of the Labour Code stipulates that an employment contract is subject to the general law and can be concluded in whatever form agreed by both parties.

[7] Insurance contracts were governed by the Law on Insurance promulgated by Royal Kram NS/RKM/0700/02 of 20 July 2000, later replaced by a new Law on Insurance promulgated by Royal Kram NS/RKM/0814/021 of 4 August 2014.

As a general rule, freedom of contract may also be viewed from the perspective of positive or negative freedom. Positive freedom of contract means that the parties are free to create a binding contract reflecting their free will, whereas negative freedom of contract means that the parties are free from obligations as long as no binding contract has been concluded.[8]

The legislator and the courts may not interfere unreasonably or adopt restrictive measures against the exercise of such freedoms. In private relationships or private transactions, freedom of contract requires that an agreement freely entered into by the parties be enforced by the courts. Article 182 of the Cambodian Code of Civil Procedure provides for the courts to adjudicate all claims raised by the disputing parties, but the courts are not to adjudicate any matters not raised by the parties themselves. The courts may not attempt to rewrite or adjust the terms of any agreement thus freely entered into. The courts must respect the parties' autonomy, in other words, the rights and legal relationships that are the subject of the proceedings must be decided according to the free will of the parties. Article 13 of the Code of Civil Procedure also recognizes the right of the parties to choose the competent courts to resolve their conflicts.

Similarly, in other legal systems, the respect for freedom of contract involves two related forms of legislative and judicial restraint. First, freedom of contract entails that the parties shall have 'the utmost liberty of contracting'. This means that the parties are left free to set their own terms, and the legislature and courts should be slow to limit the kinds of transaction, or kinds of terms, that the parties can agree upon within the domain of contract. Second, freedom of contract entails that the parties' freely-made agreements shall be enforced by the courts. The courts might be tempted to release the parties from hard bargains, but where agreements have been freely made such a temptation must be resisted. To mark these two aspects of freedom of contract, we can call the first restraint, the ideal of 'term freedom' (ie freedom of contract in the narrow sense) and the other ideal as 'sanctity of contract'.[9] More specifically, term freedom sets a presumption that there should not be any unnecessary restrictions on the kinds of agreement that the parties can make; sanctity of contract emphasizes that parties are to be held to the agreements that they have freely agreed. Term freedom implies a licence to write contracts with whatever content the parties see fit to include. There are some limitations to such licence, however. The court may only invalidate such contracts which violate the mandatory rules, public order, and good custom. The mandatory rules, public order, and good custom provisions are aimed at protecting the public interest, the public policy of the state and are regarded as transcending the individual's rights or interest. The courts may also take steps to limit the licence to contract but only if they have good reason. However, views on what constitutes good reason for limiting the freedom of contract may, of course, differ, as may the arguments brought forward to justify it. These latter might be based on one or more of the following grounds:[10] (1) that the terms or general purpose of the contract are harmful to the interest of third parties (eg where the purpose of agreement is to commit a criminal offence against property or a person); (2) that the terms or general purpose of the contract are harmful to public interest (eg an agreement to evade government tax or to bribe a public officer); (3) that the transaction is harmful to the interests of one of the contracting parties (eg a sale of undervalued property or a loan with interest in excess of the legal threshold); and (4) that the transaction is harmful to the interests of both contracting parties (eg gambling contracts or contracts for sexual favours). Article 4

[8] N Cohen, 'Pre-Contractual Duties: Two Freedoms and the Contract to Negotiate' in J Beatson and D Friedmann (eds), *Good Faith and Fault in Contract Law* (Oxford: OUP 1995) 25–26.

[9] M Furmston, *The Law of Contracts* (London: Butterworths Common Law Series 1999) para 1.40, p 26.

[10] ibid.

of the Civil Code prohibits the abuse of the rights of other persons. Any action in exercise of a right that exceeds the scope of the protection afforded is without legal effect.

2. Equal Protection of Rights and Equality of Bargaining Power

Article 3 of the Civil Code also recognizes the principle of equal protection of rights between private parties. In a private transaction, the state as a legal entity is also considered a private party and enjoys the same rights and protection as a private contracting party. The parties to a contract, regardless of their social or political status, enjoy equal protection under the law.[11] Their private property enjoys no immunity from the application of laws or claims by the other party in the event of a dispute.

Cambodian law explicitly recognizes the doctrine of equality of bargaining power. The courts may investigate whether the transaction is a fair one or whether one of the parties has taken undue advantage of the other party. Article 11 of Decree No 38 allowed a party to rescind a contract if, upon entering into the contract, the other party took advantage of the aggrieved party with undue profit. This principle is also recognized by Article 351 of the Civil Code, which allows a party to rescind the contract if it was concluded by taking advantage of another party's economic difficulty, ignorance, inexperience, and if excessive profit is made from the contract. The court may intervene if the contract was formed as a result of an inequality of bargaining power between the parties. Article 13 of the Labour Code also allows the court to invalidate any contract or agreement between an employee and an employer if the benefit to the employee is less than that stipulated in the Labour Code.

Classical theory has it that the courts should refrain from querying the bargaining power of the contracting parties. The court's role is to ensure procedural fair play; it is not the court's business to ensure that the bargain is fair, or to see that one party does not take undue advantage of another, or impose unreasonable terms by virtue of a superior bargaining position. Any superior bargaining power itself is a matter for the market to rectify. However, contemporary society takes a rather different view. The Civil Code allows the courts to invalidate a contract which is made in violation of good morals and custom in Cambodia. A compromise contract which is made in violation of good morals can also be invalidated by the court, in accordance with Article 725(2) of the Civil Code.

Cambodian judges and practitioners are also increasingly concerned about the use of contracts in standard form and the inclusion of exemption clauses in certain contracts, especially in consumer contracts, standard warranties, consumer loans granted by banks, standard contracts for the sale of apartments or condominium units, and so forth. In general, ordinary clients do not diligently read the provisions or the standard terms in such contracts and they are not given sufficient opportunity to read the lengthy contracts prepared by banks or developers or, if they do read them, they may not understand their complex terms or structures. The sellers or bank credit officers may not have properly advised them or, if the buyer or borrower does raise objections, he may simply be told that these are standard terms or even to take the contract as it is or leave it. Clients will often not have sought any legal advice or been given sufficient time to understand complex standard terms. In such a situation, there is no true bargain and the operation of free will is severely limited. Overall, it should be noted that Cambodian courts will tend to uphold the contracts as an expression of free and informed consent by the parties without rejecting the validity of written terms signed and agreed by them. Nevertheless, Cambodian courts may also seek to

[11] Cambodia does not yet have any consumer protection laws or rules to protect consumers, which are deemed to be the weaker party in commercial transactions.

delimit the application of principles of equality of bargaining power, since there are many circumstances where that equality is quite relative, rather than absolute. This is a matter where the courts will need to develop precedents.

3. Good Faith

In many civil law systems,[12] the law of obligations recognizes and enforces the overriding principle of good faith. The principle has also long been recognized in Cambodian contract law principles and is enshrined in Article 5 of the Civil Code. Lawyers and judges are familiar with the concept of subjective good faith, which is generally referred to as a sense of honesty, trust, and a clear conscience. However, the concept of good faith has rarely been defined in any judicial decisions, nor has it been a subject of academic study in Cambodia.

It is nevertheless quite difficult for the courts and lawyers to determine the objective requirements of the doctrine of good faith in litigation. Sometimes, it might imply an ethical standard, such as fair play. The Civil Code provides no guidance on how to determine and apply the concept. Prior to the Civil Code, Decree No 38 contained references to an 'atmosphere of trust and honesty', respect of social ethics, targeting in particular the concept of exploitation of one party by the other. In practice, this means that the courts will generally take these factors in account: (1) the social ethical standard; (2) the private interest of a party; (3) human dignity; and (4) good trade practice. Applying the principle of good faith is complicated by the fact that no one really knows what the scope and requirements of socio-ethical standards might be; without clear moral reference points, there is endless uncertainty in the determination of good faith. For example, in deciding whether the legitimate private interest of the other contractual party is being exploited, the pursuit of self-interest by the 'exploiting' party is hardly a valid argument, since parties will naturally have their own interests at heart when entering into negotiations. The doctrine of good faith may also contravene the principle of party autonomy if it were to regulate the contractual negotiation process to ensure that the agreement is genuine; likewise, good faith impinges on the fundamental philosophy of freedom of contract if it promotes the idea that contract law should set a quantifiable framework for self-regulation of interests by the parties.

Article 384 of the Civil Code requires the parties to perform their contractual obligations in accordance with the purpose of the contract and with the principle of good faith and fair dealing. In much the same way, Article 440 of the Civil Code requires an obligor to perform its obligation in accordance with the terms of the obligation and in good faith. On the basis of these articles, the courts should refrain from bringing the principle of good faith into play prior to the conclusion of the contract. In other words, there is no requirement for the negotiating parties to negotiate in good faith during the negotiation stage itself. However, if the bad faith of one party were to result in excessive profit or abuse of the interests of the other party, the aggrieved party would not be required to perform its obligations. This means that the courts can invalidate the contract if it was not made in good faith.

4. Reasonableness

The Civil Code also recognizes the notion of reasonableness. In classic contract law theory, it has been argued that an intention-based model of contract has no need for the concept of reasonableness. The intention of the parties (according to the 'meeting of minds' or 'will'

[12] See eg the Lando Commission's Principles of European Contract Law, Art 1:106, the German Civil Code, § 242, the old French Civil Code, Art 1134(3), and the Japanese Civil Code, Art 1.

theory) will determine whether there is a contract or not. If there is a contract, it will determine how it is to be interpreted and enforced. The cornerstones of law, free agreement, and sovereign intention serve to exclude questions as to the reasonableness of the transaction or its enforcement.

The idea of reasonableness that permeates the Cambodian Civil Code is, overall, used either as a supplementary principle or a limiting principle. It is supplementary when the court is at liberty to inquire into the parties' intention on the assumption that the express terms of the contract fail to offer clear guidance. For example, according to Article 40 of the Civil Code, the court may grant reasonable fees to the administrator; Article 158(2) of the Civil Code allows the court to grant a grace period 'of reasonable length' to the owner; Article 403(3) of the Civil Code stipulates that the court can decide to increase or reduce the liquidated damages agreed by the parties before damage occurred if it finds that the amount agreed is either too large or too small in relation of the actual damage. Reasonableness is used as a limiting principle when, for example, the terms of a contract are to be incorporated by notice, in which case the notice must be reasonable. A party pleading economic duress must show that there was no reasonable alternative other than to accede to the demand made by the other party, and steps in view of avoiding the contract must be taken within a reasonable time.

IV. Formation of Contract

1. Reaching an Agreement

A basic question of contract law is whether two or more parties arrived at an agreement or not. In a free market economy, people transact with each other very often; a party commits itself to do or refrain from doing something, and then another party takes a counter-commitment. Such commitments are made by way of manifestation of intent. Therefore, it is central to the formation of a contract that the intention of the parties matches.

The Civil Code, in its Article 310(1), adopts the principle that a contract is formed by a *declaration* of intent to create a legal effect by a party. This means that the declaration of intent is the key element in forming a contract and establishing the existence of a contract. This principle is also found in Article 91 of the Japanese Civil Code and Article 2:102 of the Principles of European Contract Law ('PECL'). Cambodian law deals with the declaration of intent separately from the exchange of consent by the parties in concluding a contract. Furthermore, it also provides one set of rules for making an offer and another for acceptance of an offer. These rules differ from those adopted by the French Civil Code before its recent revision, which merely required consent. French contract law focuses more on real intention (*volonté réelle*) than declared intention (*volonté exprimée*).[13] This condition is similar to the conditions required by Cambodian Decree No 38. Under Article 1 of Decree No 38, a contract was defined as an agreement of two or more persons to create, change, or extinguish one or more obligations binding them. According to Articles 3 and 6 of Decree No 38, a contract was not valid if it was not made by real or free agreement. In this regard, the courts were required to confirm the existence of real and free agreement in order to determine the validity of the contract. With the current Civil Code, the court may no longer need to do so.

The Civil Code provides no guidance as to how the court should determine the declaration of intent. However, the Code of Civil Procedure allows the court to consider both the evidence and circumstances that were raised during the proceedings. It may determine the

[13] J-M Lacquet, 'Le droit français des contrats et les Principes d'UNIDROIT' [2008] Uniform L Rev 108.

facts on the basis of proven admissions as well as facts it has discovered for itself.[14] Hence, in this regard, the court can take a pragmatic view by applying both objective and subjective tests to determine the existence of the intent of the parties. The objective test seeks to assess the intention of the parties objectively, or to confirm their intention if it was openly manifested, whereas the subjective test aims to assess the subjective (actual) intention of the parties or what was in the parties' minds but not made manifest.

2. Essential Elements for Contract Formation: Offer and Acceptance

Article 336 of the Civil Code provides that a contract comes into effect when an offer and the acceptance thereof coincide. This Civil Code provision is similar to the mirror image rule of contractual formation which is adopted by the courts in common law countries. That is to say, they must find a clear and unequivocal offer which is matched by an equally clear and unequivocal acceptance. The formula that the contract is formed by offer and acceptance is widely used in modern contract law.

(a) Making an offer

An offer is defined as a proposal to enter into a contract by expressing an intention to be bound by the acceptance thereof of another party (Article 337(1) of the Civil Code). Theoretically, the offer should include all the necessary elements of the intended contract, so that the offeree need only say 'yes' or 'agreed' or 'no' to the offer. This is the most basic way of forming a valid contract.

The Cambodian Civil Code provides a general definition of an offer and for specific legal regimes for offer and acceptance. However, it does not provide any criteria for what constitutes a valid offer. It simply states that an offer is effective when notice thereof reaches the addressee. The Civil Code does not set any other criteria or list essential elements for a proposal to be considered as an offer. An offer may be made orally or in writing.

Nonetheless, theoretically one such essential element would be the proposal to make a contract if the other party accepts the offer: in other words, the offer must indicate the offeror's intention to be bound in the case of acceptance.

(b) Intention to create a legally binding obligation

A valid offer must evidence the offeror's intention to create a legally binding obligation. In other words, the intention must be a serious one: a contract is formed by the mere acceptance of the offer by the offeree—the offeree is not required to ascertain the offeror's intention. The offeror gives the offeree the power to conclude the contract by its acceptance. If the offer does not evidence the offeror's serious intention, it is not valid and cannot result in a contract.

This constituent element of the offer is very important when it comes to distinguishing between a contract to negotiate or a gentlemen's agreement or non-binding memorandum

[14] Art 123 of the Code of Civil Procedure provides that:

1. The court shall recognize facts based on evidence. However, the court may consider all matters and circumstances that are raised in the trial.
2. Facts admitted to by a party in court, and facts the existence of which is obvious to the court, need not be proven by evidence.
3. A party may retract an admission in the following circumstances:
   (a) where the adversary party does not object;
   (b) where the admission is false and made based on a mistake; or
   (c) where the admission was made due to the criminal act committed by another.

of understanding, which are often used in commercial practice and are recognized predominantly in the common law. Based on this requirement, it is understood that the display of prices in a shop or advertising prices in a newspaper may not constitute a valid offer unless the offeror clearly expresses its intention to create a legally binding contract.

As stated in Article 310(1) of the Civil Code, the declaration of intent is the expression of a party's intention to create a legal effect. In other words, even if all the other essential elements of a contract are present, there is no contract unless the parties also intend their agreement to be legally binding. This article raises a number of practical issues since parties to a contract generally may not understand the legal consequences of their intention or fail to consider them at the time of making their contract. In pondering the requirement to create a legal consequence, theoretically the following difficult situations might arise for the courts, as addressed by Professor John Edward Murray, Jr.[15]

(1) *The parties express their intention to be legally bound.* Should the intention of binding effect be stated in the contract or not? It is apparently quite rare in Cambodia for the parties to a contract to carefully consider the legal consequences of their agreements. Another issue is that the parties may consciously state their intention to be legally bound by a contract which is illegal or unenforceable for public policy reasons.

(2) *The parties express their intention not to be legally bound.* This would seem to indicate that the parties are free from any obligations in the contract by which they did not intend to be legally bound. For example, in the case of a gentlemen's agreement, a letter of intent, etc, the courts will enforce the manifest intention of the parties. Problems may arise, however, in complex transactions such as mergers, acquisitions, consecutive long-term transactions, project financing, where parties may sign letters of intent or agreements in principle to avoid any obligations or liabilities but the records of which might eventually be used as evidence of contract.

(3) *The parties' expressions of intention are interpreted as intending or not intending to produce legal consequence.* Where the parties have not clearly expressed their intention as to the legal consequences, the courts must interpret the manifestations of intent by having regard to all the circumstances of the case, to establish whether the parties intended to be legally bound. In this regard, two difficult situations might arise. One is where one of the parties intended the offer to have legal consequences whereas the other party did not, perhaps (mis)interpreting the offer as joking or bragging. Another situation is where a physician, for example, suggests a surgical procedure coupled with an assurance of that the recovery period will not exceed a certain time. The question here is whether such assurance by a physician can be considered as an intention to create legal consequences in the same manner as the manifestation of such intention in a commercial transaction. In general, courts will tend to be reluctant to impose such contractual liability on physicians.

(4) *The parties manifest no intention as to legal consequences.* Where the parties have not manifested any intention as to legal consequences, the courts may not establish such intention by interpreting the parties' expressions. Such a situation may arise in social agreements or agreements between married persons or other domestic arrangements. If the parties enter into a social agreement, no legal obligation attaches. It is generally understood that agreements between spouses are ordinarily not intended to be legally binding.

[15] JE Murray, Jr, *Murray on Contract* (4th edn, Newark, NJ: Matthew Bender & Co Inc 2001) 64–70.

(5) *Final writing contemplated by the parties.* In general, where the parties have reached an agreement but contemplate a final writing, the contract is formed at the time of writing. By the same token, if the parties have manifested their intention as to when their agreement is to become legally binding, there is no problem either. However, if the parties' expression of agreement and other circumstances indicate that they themselves understood the agreement to have been made before the final writing, the contract came into being as soon as they reached an agreement even though no final writing was created. In such cases, the final writing is intended as nothing more than confirmation of an existing contract.

(c) Communication of offer

Article 310(2) of the Civil Code determines the point at which the declaration of intent becomes effective. Notice of such intent must be given to the other party. The starting point for reaching an agreement is the moment at which the declaration of intent reaches the other party. This implies that the recipient must be in a position to receive the notice. It is not necessary for the addressee physically to have read the notice of intent. Furthermore, if notice is given by mail, the time of notice is the time at which the notice is placed in the recipient's mailbox.

An additional requirement for an offer to be valid (to take effect) is that it be communicated to the offeree. It is hard to imagine a scenario in which an offeror really wished to make a contract with another party yet never communicated its offer to that party. But when an offeror does communicate its offer to the offeree, it is strong evidence that the offeror did wish to make a contract with that offeree. So it is a key rule of contract law that an offer is not valid, and a contract cannot be formed, until the offeror has communicated its offer to the offeree. In other words, it is crucial for an offeror to communicate its offer to the offeree and make sure that it reaches the offeree so that the latter can make the contract by accepting the offer.

This rule affords some protection for the offeror, who is free to choose with whom it wishes to make a contract as well as the time and manner in which it will communicate the offer to the other party. As an old contract law saying goes, 'the offeror is the master of his (her) offer'.

(d) Withdrawal of offer

An offer can be withdrawn before notice of the offer reaches the addressee or the notice of revocation reaches the addressee at the same time as the notice of offer. The concept of withdrawal of offer in the Civil Code is similar to the concepts set out in Article 1:303(5) of the PECL. It is a useful concept in that it gives the offeror a chance to change its mind if the offer was hastily made and does not reflect the offeror's real intention. The Civil Code does not distinguish between withdrawal of offer and revocation of offer. In general, withdrawal of offer is understood to occur if it is made before the offer reaches the addressee. This principle is recognized in Article 337(2) of the Civil Code. In practice, this could happen if the withdrawal of the offer is sent by courier or delivered by hand.

(e) Revocation of offer

Articles 338 and 339 of the Civil Code provide for revocation depending on the kind of offer involved. The offeror can make an offer with or without a stipulated period for its acceptance.

(1) Revocation of an offer with an acceptance period

Article 338 of the Civil Code does not allow the offeror to revoke an offer that specifies an acceptance period, before that period has expired. It is reasonable and fair not to allow the offeror to revoke an offer that is seriously intended and duly communicated to the offeree, during the period where the offeree is free to accept the offer. In this case, the offeree has the final say on the conclusion of the proposed contract.

An offer with an acceptance period lapses in the following cases: (1) where there is no acceptance upon expiry of acceptance period; and (2) where a notice of rejection from the other party reaches the offeror within the acceptance period.

It should be noted that, as a general rule, an offer with a fixed time for its acceptance is considered irrevocable even if it does not expressly state so. The Civil Code appears to follow the approach taken by the PECL as well as that of the German Civil Code. It is different from the principle of irrevocability laid out in the UN Convention on Contracts for the International Sale of Goods ('CISG'), where a fixed time for acceptance does not presume the irrevocability of the offer.

(2) Revocation of an offer without an acceptance period

Under Article 339 of the Civil Code, an offer that states no acceptance period and is made *inter absentes* cannot be revoked by the offeror until a reasonable period of time has elapsed. This rule offers more protection to the offeree. In doing so, the Civil Code follows civil law traditions such as those of France and Germany, where an offeror generally cannot revoke its offer before a reasonable time has lapsed, unless the offer itself stipulates otherwise. 'Reasonable time' refers to the period of time needed by the offeree to consider whether to accept the offer or not. The length of the period depends on the terms and type of contract and is determined by the courts if there is a dispute. For example, if the offer involves a large amount of money or if the subject matter of the contract has high economic value or relates to immovable property, the reasonable time period might be a long one, whereas it will be relatively short for a simple contract.

However, an offer without an acceptance period may be revoked after reasonable time has passed. This takes effect only after the notice of revocation reaches the offeree, and prior to the offeree's dispatch of a notice of acceptance.

An offer that states no acceptance period and is made *inter praesentes*, where the offeree can respond at once, lapses unless it is accepted forthwith by the offeree (Article 339(1) of the Civil Code). Since the offeree is in a position to respond to the offer immediately, it is reasonable to provide that the offer lapses if it does not do so.

Article 344 of the Civil Code provides that an offer made to unspecified parties by means of public advertisement or other method can be revoked only by using the same method employed to make the offer.

(f) The concept of acceptance

Under Article 337(3) of the Civil Code, an acceptance is defined as an expression of intention by the offeree to accept the offer. By accepting the offer, the offeree agrees to make the proposed contract. An acceptance is effective as soon as it reaches the offeror unless it is withdrawn before that by the offeree. The time when the acceptance reaches the offeror marks the birth of the contract. The Civil Code follows the receipt or reception theory enshrined in the German Civil Code and the PECL.

An acceptance can be made by any means—expressly (using language, either orally or in writing, eg in a document such as a letter, or by telephone) or impliedly (using conduct, eg conduct that clearly indicates to the offeror that the offeree has accepted the offer). Under Article 343 of the Civil Code, a contract can be made even when there is no acceptance notice, if the offeror has expressed its intention not to require a notice of acceptance or if there is an act that is deemed tantamount to acceptance in accordance with the customary rules of trade practices. In this situation, a contract is deemed to be formed upon the occurrence of such an act. For example, if a customer requests a haircut and the barber cuts the customer's hair without comment, the barber's performance of the specific act requested by the customer may be deemed an acceptance of the customer's offer.

The Cambodian Civil Code, unlike common law jurisdictions, makes no distinction between unilateral and bilateral contracts in terms of acceptance. Furthermore, the Civil Code also recognizes the formation of a contract without acceptance if it is so intended by the offeror; a contract can also be formed by an act that could be deemed to constitute acceptance in accordance with the customary rules of trade practices even though the addressee has not given express notice of acceptance.

(g) Effectiveness of acceptance

As discussed earlier, for an acceptance to be valid it must be identical to the offer (mirror image rule). A notice of acceptance is effective and a contract is formed when appropriate notice is received by the offeror (Article 340 of the Civil Code). However, a notice of acceptance is not required if, in accordance with the offeror's intention or the applicable trade customs, the contract is deemed formed when the act that is recognized as an acceptance is performed (Article 343 of the Civil Code). Thus, a notice of offer or acceptance can be made in writing or by telephone or any other electronic means, provided there is proof of the other party's receipt of such.

The Civil Code also regulates late acceptance. As a general rule, acceptance must be notified to the offeror on time. If acceptance arrives late, but the offeror is aware that a notice of acceptance has been sent, the offeror must notify the offeree without undue delay. If it fails to do so, such delayed acceptance would also be valid. This situation may occur if the offeree has made a mistake in dispatching the notice of acceptance or if there are irregularities in the means of communication or dispatch. The Civil Code seems to follow the approaches taken by Article 2:207 of the PECL, Article 21 of the CISG, and Article 2.1.9 of the UNIDROIT Principles of International Commercial Contracts ('PICC'). In the event of late acceptance, the offeror may also regard the offer as a new offer and inform the offeree orally about the late acceptance; in that case, no contract is formed, unless the original offeror accepts the new offer by notice of acceptance or by its conduct.

(h) Conditional acceptance or acceptance with modified terms

As a general rule, and as in common law jurisdictions, a valid acceptance must be identical to the offer, like a reflection in a mirror (mirror image rule). It is not, as a rule, proper acceptance if the offeree attempts to accept the offer with new or different terms or conditions. Such acceptance cannot create a contract. On the contrary, such acceptance terminates the offer made by the offeror and constitutes a new or counter-offer. A contract is formed only where the original offeror accepts the new offer.

However, if the condition or modification attached to the acceptance does not substantially change the original offer, unless the offeror raises an objection forthwith, the acceptance is deemed valid. In that case, the contents of the contract incorporate the condition or modification contained in the intended acceptance unless the offeror raises an objection forthwith.

It should also be noted that some countries have a rule for the letter of confirmation issued or exchanged subsequent to the parties' agreement on the formation of the contract. Where the letter of confirmation merely repeats or reconfirms exactly what has been agreed upon, there is no problem. However, a difficulty may arise if the points confirmed or the letter itself refer to different terms. The Civil Code follows the approach taken in the PECL, namely that with regard to the letter of confirmation, the rules for offer and acceptance with modified terms apply. This approach differs from that of the common law jurisdictions, which uses the 'battle of forms' or 'last-shot rule'.

3. Consideration Not Required

The doctrine of consideration, bargain for exchange in the common law countries and the former doctrine of '*cause*' in French law,[16] have not been taken on board by the Cambodian Civil Code. The Civil Code recognizes both the unilateral act and the bilateral contract. It enforces gratuitous contracts as well as onerous contracts. The key benchmark for validity of a contract is that there be an intention to create a legal effect. Thus, a contract would be binding even if there is no ground for assuming such contractual obligation. A party may willingly create a unilateral contractual obligation in favour of another party without any consideration. For example, it may waive its right to demand compensation, agree to extend the time limit for performance of a certain act, or change the contractual terms to the exclusive benefit of the other party.

Case study: delayed building work: X contracts for Y to refurbish 27 flats for £20,000. However, Y ran into difficulties. X was concerned about having to pay a penalty under the head contract, and promised to pay Y an extra £10,300 to complete the work on time. Can Y enforce the additional £10,300?

In this situation, X's promise to pay Y an additional sum would be deemed a valid offer and Y can enforce such right on the ground that the Civil Code requires an offer to be valid if the offeror intends to create a legally binding obligation and the offeree simply accepts it. The Cambodian courts would not be required to investigate whether there is any consideration or valid cause for enforcing the offeror's promise.

4. Rules for the Interpretation of a Contract

The rules for the interpretation of contracts were set out in Article 23 of Decree No 38. If a contract is unclear as to its meaning, it must be interpreted and performed in accordance with good custom or practice at the place where the contract was made.[17] However, the Civil Code does not provide for rules on the interpretation of contracts in the case of uncertainty.

[16] Art 1131 of the old French Civil Code provided that an obligation without *cause*, or with a false *cause*, or with an illicit *cause* cannot have any effect. Art 1132 of the same Code provided that an agreement is nonetheless valid even though the *cause* is not expressed.

[17] Art 23 of Decree No 38:

> If the contract is not clear in its meaning, that contract shall be interpreted according to the common practices or customs of the place where the contract has been made, but the interpretation shall not conflict with the provisions of this law. If there is any ambiguity, the contract shall be interpreted in favour of the obligor.

5. No Requirements as to Form

As a general rule, there are no requirements as to form for a contract to be valid. A contract may be concluded orally or in writing. No formality is required other than the declaration of intent to create a legal effect to the contract. Similar to the principles set out in the Japanese Civil Code and the PECL, Cambodian law requires that the intentions to be legally bound by a contract match and that the acceptance conforms to the offer. Contrary to the rules adopted in the common law countries (the Statute of Frauds, the doctrine of 'bargained-for exchange', or parol evidence rule, which set additional requirements for the valid formation of a contract and its enforceability), and the old French Civil Code[18] (which imposes certain requirements as to form in respect of the execution of an instrument or contract involving certain monetary values), Cambodian law adopts the same rules as the Japanese Civil Code and the PECL, which do not have formality requirements. The existence of a contract may be proven by any available means, including electronic correspondence. According to Article 126 of the Code of Civil Procedure, the court must examine all evidence adduced by the parties.

There are some exceptions to these general rules under the Civil Code, in respect of certain matters requiring written instruments or registration of such instruments with a government registry in order for them to be legally irrevocable or indefeasible by a third party.

(1) The Civil Code prescribes that a contract which has the effect of acquiring or transferring ownership of an immovable property must be made by notarial act (Article 336(2)). A notarial act is a type of contract authenticated by a notary public or an officer authorized to carry out the notarial mission. In such cases, therefore, it is not enough for the offer and acceptance to match for the contract to acquire legal effect. Furthermore, the transfer of ownership over an immovable property is effective only upon registration with the cadastral authorities (Article 135), which require the parties to execute an additional document, namely a Deed of Final Sale ('*vente définitive*'), which replaces or is supplemental to the contract of sale signed between the parties.

(2) The Civil Code also requires a written document for a guarantee to be irrevocable. An oral guarantee can be revoked by the guarantor at any time. Furthermore, the written letter of guarantee must specify the contents of the guaranteed obligation; the guaranteed sum must be written out by hand in order to guarantee any obligation having as its objective the payment of money (Article 901). Similarly, in respect of gifts, the promise of a gift can be revoked at any time before implementation of the gift if it has not been made in writing (Article 570).

(3) The Law on Secured Transactions requires a security agreement to be made in writing and the debtor is required to authenticate the agreement describing the collateral (Articles 7 and 9). This means that the formation of security agreements must contain written descriptions and be signed by the parties. To perfect the security agreement so as to provide priority rights to the secured creditor, the security agreement must be filed with the Secured Transactions Filing Office.

[18] Art 1341 of the old French Civil Code provided that an instrument must be executed before notaries or under private signatures 'in all matters exceeding the sum or values fixed by decree, even for voluntary deposits, and no proof by witness is allowed against or beyond the contents of instruments, or as to what is alleged to have been said before, at the time of, or after the instruments, although it is a question of a lesser sum or value'. In a similar vein, Cambodia's Decree No 38 imposed formal requirements on the formation of contracts: a contract made for a monetary value of 5000 Riel (approximately US$1.25) could only be evidenced if made in writing.

The main reasons why written documents or registration of executed instruments are required, are the need to protect the interests of a party, particularly the weaker party, and the need to ensure that the party who has signed the documents did so in accordance with its real intention and understanding of the content of these documents and the requirements stipulated therein. It is generally acknowledged that the lack of knowledge and caution of certain parties, especially in rural areas, will require certain rules to be in place in order to protect them. Furthermore, written or notarial instruments can also be used as hard evidence in court proceedings and they protect a party's rights against any third party claims asserting the same rights. Without notarial deeds, disputes as to the real intentions of the parties to an agreement may not be easily settled.

Cambodian law does not yet have any specific rules for electronic communication. Laws on e-commerce and cyber-law are in the making that will lay down more rules for electronic transmission and communications. At present, the courts may examine evidence produced by electronic means in the same way as other written evidence. A contract signed by electronic signature or an exchange of emails or facsimile is likewise valid. However, in practice, the Cambodian authorities often require original contracts to be signed by the parties if such contracts are required to be registered with a land registry, as a protection against fake or forged instruments. It should also be noted that, although signatures are generally accepted in practice, parties may also be required to affix their respective thumbprints or seals in order to confirm their consent to a contract. Cambodian courts would accept as evidence contracts both with a signature or a thumbprint.

The Cambodian authorities are seemingly quite concerned about the originality and authenticity of instruments. It has been quite hard for them to differentiate between real and fake documents since the advent of modern technologies. That is why they still require parties to affix their original signature or thumbprint, or the company seal, to the contract. It is also quite common for the parties to a business transaction to seek confirmation, certification, or witness from a lawyer or a notary public to guarantee the originality of documents.

V. Third Parties

1. Introduction

Decree No 38 did not have specific provisions concerning contracts for the benefit of a third party. It followed the principle that a contract is 'a legally binding agreement between the parties', and 'binds only the parties to the contract'.[19] Under Decree No 38, only the parties to a contract were entitled to ask another party to perform the promise, and a third party—not party to the formation of the contract—would not generally be entitled to enforce the contract.[20] This position of Cambodian law was similar to the doctrine of 'privity of contract' adopted in the common law countries.[21]

The new Civil Code does include rules on third party contracts in Section 5 of Book IV. As in most civil law countries such as Japan and continental European countries, Cambodian

[19] Decree No 38, Art 22 stated that:

A contract is a legally binding agreement between the parties. Amendments to the contract can only be made with the consent of both contracting party.

A contract shall be executed honestly and according to the will of the parties.

A contract binds only the parties to the contract.

[20] Under Decree No 38, any person was entitled to sue to rescind a void contract (arts 5 and 18).

[21] The doctrine of privity of contract describes an ambit of persons who are interested in a contract. As a general rule, none other than a party to the contract is entitled to enforce or be bound by the terms of the contract.

law now recognizes several modern contract law principles. It allows the parties to a contract to confer rights or benefits on a third party and allows that third party to enforce those rights, even though it is not a direct party to the contract. This is essential in social and economic terms, since it helps daily life and commercial transactions to run smoothly. Third party contracts can be found in both civil and commercial matters. Examples include insurance contracts, life annuity contracts, assignment agreements, sale of goods agreements, bills of exchange, letters of credit, and so forth.

In the context of privity and the matter of third party benefits, two questions must be answered: (1) can a party sue on a contract made for its benefit but to which it is not a party; and (2) can a party be prejudiced by a contract to which it is not a party? The answer to the first question has long been controversial in both common law and civil law countries. The common law countries for a long time adhered strictly to the doctrine of privity of contract and the civil law countries stuck to equivalent principles but often came to different conclusions on this issue. However, the answer to the second question always appears to have been in the negative in both common and civil law jurisdictions, right up until modern times.

More specifically, answers need to be found to the following questions in order to determine the rights and obligations of third parties.

(1) Can a party enforce a term of a contract to which it is not a party?

(2) Can a party set up a defence based on the terms of a contract to which he is not a party in order to answer a claim brought by a person who is a party to the relevant contract?

(3) Can a contracting party set up a defence based on the terms of his own contract in order to answer a claim brought by a person who is not a party to the relevant contract?

(4) Can a contracting party enforce the terms of its own contract against a person who is not a party to the relevant contract?[22]

The classic position taken by Decree No 38 would be to answer all four of these questions in the negative. However, the same is not necessarily true in modern contract law. The position of the Civil Code and some other substantive laws such as the labour code, the law on commercial enterprises, and the law on negotiable instruments and payment transactions, would provide affirmative responses to some of those questions. The courts would be entitled to take into account specific circumstances that might allow the defence as well as the claim made by relevant party even though such party is not a party to the contract. Article 2(2) of the Code of Civil Procedure provides that no person shall be denied the right of access to the courts. Article 32(1) of the same Code also stipulates that any person who has rights and obligations according to the Civil Code and other laws may act as plaintiff or defendant in a civil action. Therefore, the courts shall take into consideration the valid existence of rights and obligations of the parties.

2. Definition of a Third Party Contract

A third party contract is a contract in which the parties to the contract agree to confer a right or benefit arising under the contract upon a third party (Article 379 of the Civil Code). The third party beneficiary is entitled to demand performance from the contract donor directly. The person who promises to perform obligations to a third party is called the

[22] Furmston (n 9) 904.

'contract donor'; the other party to the contract is called the 'contract donee'; and the third party is called the 'beneficiary'. Below are classic examples of a third party contract.

(1) Seller A and buyer B enter into a sale of property contract. Seller A wishes to transfer the right to receive payment from buyer B to his creditor C. In this case, creditor C is a third party beneficiary of the contract between seller A and buyer B. Creditor C has the right to be paid directly by buyer B for debts owed to him by seller A. Creditor C is a credit beneficiary.

(2) A father purchases a life insurance policy from an insurance company and wishes to bequeath any premium due in the event of his death to his son. The son's name is stated in the beneficiary section of the policy. In this case, the son receives the benefit of the life insurance policy. He is a donee beneficiary.

(3) A factory owner engages the services of a security company to protect the factory and the property and safety of the employees working there and staying at the factory warehouse. The factory employees could be considered the beneficiaries of the security service agreement between the factory owner and the security company. The employees are donee beneficiaries.

3. Formation of a Third Party Contract

The formation of a third party contract is governed by the general rules on the formation of other types of contract except that acceptance by the beneficiary is not required in order for the contract donor's promise to perform to be effective and binding on the donor. The validity of the third party contract may be affected by certain elements such as: (1) the agreement of the parties to confer the right or benefit on the third party; (2) the third party's declaration of intent to receive the benefit; and (3) the requirement that the third party be identified at the time of conclusion of the contract.

(a) Valid agreement of the parties

One of the requirements for the validity of a third party contract is the existence of a valid agreement between the parties to contract on the conferral of a right on a third party. If the agreement is not valid because of flawed consent or other issues such as impossibility to perform, illegality, public order, and good custom, the third party contract would likewise be affected. Therefore, the validity of the conferral of a right should be determined in conjunction with the validity of the agreement between the parties. In general, the rights of the parties would rank higher in terms of priority for protection than the rights of the beneficiary, since the parties are direct parties to the contract. Under Article 382 of the Civil Code, the contract donor may raise any defences arising from the contract against the contract beneficiary, such as breach of contract by the contract donee. For example, if seller A fails to comply with its obligation to transfer ownership of a house to buyer B. Buyer B may raise this as a defence for non-performance of its promise to pay creditor C.

(b) Declaration of intent by the third party beneficiary

It is important to establish whether the third party beneficiary is automatically entitled to benefit from the promise of performance or whether he is required to declare his intention to accept such performance. In Cambodia, the right to demand performance is automatic. If the beneficiary exists and is aware of the promise to confer a right or benefit on him, he can declare his intention to accept or reject the conferred right or benefit by any means at his disposal.

(c) Existence of the third party beneficiary

The third party beneficiary need not actually exist at the time of formation of the contact (Article 380 of the Civil Code), provided there are clear indications or standards that make it possible to identify the third party beneficiary. However, if the third party beneficiary still does not exist at the time of performance by the donor, the donor is discharged from performing its obligation or the promise to perform lapses.

For example, in the case of an insurance contract, if the father dies before the birth of his son, the insurer may not be required to pay the premium under the life insurance policy.[23] It is reasonable to stipulate that a foetus due to be born within the next three to four months is the beneficiary of an insurance contract, but if the child has not been born when the premium is due to be paid there can be little question of damage suffered by the foetus. The situation may be different in other countries subject to trust law. A donor may hold the benefit in trust for the child until it has been born. Cambodia does not yet have trust law, hence the insurer may not be required by law to hold the benefits for the unborn foetus.[24]

When it comes to establishing the right or benefit of the third party, the question may also arise as to who are the parties to the contract and who is the beneficiary. Take, for example, a husband and wife going to lunch at a restaurant. The husband orders and pays for the meal, but the wife later develops food poisoning. Assuming there was no negligence on the part of the restaurant owner, the wife would only be entitled to compensation for damage on the contract, not tort. Can she sue? The Civil Code does not seem to provide any clear definition of the term 'third party'. Can the wife be considered a third party?

4. Withdrawal and Alteration of the Promise to Perform

The contract donor may withdraw its promise to perform prior to the declaration of intent to accept by the third party beneficiary.[25] This principle was also adopted in the old French Civil Code,[26] the Japanese Civil Code,[27] the Civil Code of Quebec, and the Article 6:110 of

[23] The Law on Insurance, Art 32, provides that a life insurance policy must indicate the following, besides the necessary terms and conditions specified in the insurance contract: (1) the full name and date of birth of the applicant; (2) the full name of the beneficiary, if any; in the case of an insurance policy, the beneficiary cannot be a foetus.

[24] The exercise of rights under a third party contract can differ from the exercise of rights in the case of tort or succession. The Civil Code, Art 9, provides that:

> (1) A foetus in existence at the time when a tortious act is committed shall be entitled to seek damages for the harm arising from such act after it is born.
> (2) A foetus in existence at the time of death of a decedent who dies intestate shall be entitled to inherit from the decedent after it is born.
> (3) A foetus in existence at the time of death of a testator is entitled to receive the effect of the testament.

[25] Civil Code, Art 381(1), stipulates that a contract donee may, at any time prior to the time when an intended third party beneficiary declares its intention to accept the rights or benefit, extinguish the third party beneficiary's right to receive the right or benefit via notification to the contract donor or the third party beneficiary.

[26] The old French Civil Code, Art 1121, provided that one 'may stipulate for the benefit of a third party when it is the condition of a stipulation made on one's own account or of a gift that one makes to another'. He who makes such stipulation may no longer revoke it if the third party had declared that he wishes to benefit thereby.

[27] Japanese Civil Code, Art 537:

> Article 537(1): If one of the parties promises in a contract that he/she will tender a certain performance to any third party, the third party shall have the right to claim that performance directly from the obligor. (2) In the cases set forth in the preceding paragraph, rights of the third party shall accrue when the third party has expressed his/her intention to the obligor to enjoy the benefit of the contract under that paragraph.

the PECL. The rationale behind this principle is to provide a balance of rights or benefits between the contract donor and the contract donee. In general, the conferral of rights or benefits by the contract donor on the beneficiary could be in the form of a gratuitous act such as gift, which does not have a strong binding effect. Furthermore, the third party contract is a contract between the contract donor and the contract donee; it is not a contract between the contract donor and the third party beneficiary. As a consequence, it is generally acceptable for the contract donor to be allowed to withdraw its promise to perform.[28]

The conferral of rights or benefits on a third party beneficiary cannot be altered or extinguished after the third party beneficiary has expressed its intention to receive those rights or benefits. However, the contract donor may rescind the contract if the contract donee fails to perform its obligations (Article 382 of the Civil Code). This principle is also found in Article 6:110 of the PECL.

5. Annulment, Rescission, and Termination of a Third Party Contract

If there is any ground for annulment or rescission of the contract between the donor and the donee, either party may nullify or rescind the contract in accordance with the provisions on annulment or rescission of contract, even if there is a third party beneficiary. The annulment or rescission of a contract does not require the consent of the third party beneficiary. There might be some discussion as to the ranking of the rights of the parties and those of the beneficiary. In general, it is recognized that the rights of the contract parties have priority over those of the beneficiary, and it might be inappropriate to protect the rights and benefits of a third party beneficiary if they were granted on the basis of a void or voidable contract.

As to termination of the contract, the donor may terminate the contract on the ground that the contract donee breaches the contract. In that case, the consent of the third party beneficiary is not required. By contrast, the beneficiary's consent is required if the donee wishes to terminate the contract on the ground of breach by the donor (Article 383 of the Civil Code). What is the reason for this difference? The general rule for termination of contract for breach by the obligee (donee) would apply in the former case, and there is no cause for concern here. However, if termination is demanded by the donee, the beneficiary's consent is required because the right or benefit has already been granted. Yet the beneficiary is not entitled to terminate the contract because it is not a party to the contract. Hence, it is appropriate to allow the donee to terminate the contract but with the beneficiary's consent.[29]

6. Enforcement and Recovery of Damages under the Third Party Contract

Article 379(2) of the Civil Code provides that a third party beneficiary is entitled to demand performance from the promisor directly. This sets the third party contract apart from other kinds of contract. For example, borrower X and lender Y conclude a consumer loan agreement for the purpose of purchasing a flat from developer Z. Under the agreement, X and Y provide for Y to disburse the loan directly to Z according to the terms stated in the contract of sale. This entitles Z to demand payment of the purchase price from Y directly under the terms of the sale contract even though Z is not a party to the consumer loan agreement.

[28] See also the explanatory note to Art 382 of the Civil Code in the Explanatory Notes for each article of the Civil Code, Vol II, for Book IV (Ministry of Justice 2010) 55–56.

[29] See the explanatory note to Art 383 in the Explanatory Note of each article of the Civil Code, Vol II on Book V (Ministry of Justice 2010) 97–98.

The Civil Code does not stipulate specific requirements for remedy or damages caused to the contract donor by the beneficiary or vice versa. In this regard, the donor or the third party beneficiary may seek to enforce the obligations in accordance with the provisions on performance of obligations under the general principles of contract. Under Article 390 of the Civil Code, in the case of non-performance of its obligations by the obligor, the obligee is entitled to: (1) demand specific performance; (2) claim compensation for damages; or (3) demand rescission of the contract. Problems may arise in cases of damage caused by the beneficiary to the donor, since the beneficiary is not a direct party to the contract. Therefore, the first question is whether the donor is entitled to seek remedy from the beneficiary. The Civil Code does not seem to provide a clear solution in this regard. It would be reasonable to argue that the donor is entitled to seek compensation for damages from the beneficiary for tort rather than specific performance or rescission, since the beneficiary is not the obligor vis-à-vis the donor.

By contrast, the beneficiary would be entitled to seek specific performance or compensation for damages if the damage was caused by a breach of contractual obligations by the donor, since the beneficiary is entitled to demand performance of the donor directly. As a general rule, the beneficiary is entitled to any remedy available in the case of breach of contract by the donor.

7. Case Studies

Below are further considerations on the enforcement of rights and recovery of damages in the case studies.

(a) Exemption clauses for stevedores

X contracts with Y to transport X's goods using Y's ship to a foreign market. The contract for the carriage of goods by sea between X and Y contains an exemption of liability provision which purports to protect Z, the stevedores hired to unload X's goods from Y's ship once it arrives at the docks. As a result of Z's carelessness, X's goods are damaged while they are being unloaded from the ship and X wants to sue Z for negligence to recover damages for the losses suffered by X. Can Z rely on the exemption of liability provision in the contract between X and Y?

The contract for carriage of goods is governed by Decree No 38.[30] Article 86 of this Decree makes the carrier liable for loss or damage to the transported goods. Neither Decree No 38 nor the Civil Code provide clear guidance as to the enforceability of exemption or limitation clauses. As a general response to the above case study, it is believed that Z can rely on the exemption of liability clause so long as it passes the enforceability test. Under Article 379 of the Civil Code, the contract will only confer a right or benefit on the third party; it cannot lay a burden on that party. Therefore, it is reasonable to hold that Z is not liable for the damage to the transported goods.

(b) Selling bread

X leases two adjoining properties to Y and Z. The lease between X and Y barred Y from selling bread because Z sold bread from his leased property. Can X and Y agree to lift the bar?

[30] According to Art 79 of the Law on Application of the Civil Code, all provisions of Decree No 38 were to be abrogated after the entry into force of the Civil Code, except for Arts 83–88 (on the contract of carriage).

The answer in this case would be no: X and Y cannot lift the bar if Z has already declared its intention to receive the benefit of the contract between X and Y, according to Article 381 of the Civil Code.

(c) The stolen shop takings

X bank makes a contract for Y security company to collect Z store's takings. The contract requires Y to use armoured vehicles and take out insurance. Y failed to do these and the takings were stolen while being collected in an ordinary car. Can Z sue?

The answer in this case is yes. Z may rely on the security service contract between X bank and Y security company because the provision of security for the store's takings would be to Z's benefit.

18

Formation of Contract and Stipulations for Third Parties in Indonesia

*Gary F BELL**

I. Introduction: Contract Laws in Indonesia

Before discussing the topics below (formation of contract and benefits for third parties), I must first explain which Indonesian law I will be describing—the Indonesian 'European' civil law of contract as opposed to Indonesia's Islamic or adat laws of contracts. Second, I must also explain when that law (as opposed to the adat laws or the Islamic law of contract) applies in Indonesia. Third, I must also say a few words about the (sorry) state of the Indonesian civil law of contract in order to explain why one cannot find the kind of certainty and precision one would expect from a civil law jurisdiction on such basic topics as formation of contract and benefits for third parties.

1. The Three Indonesian Laws of Contract

As I have written elsewhere:

> Indonesia's national motto, '*Bhinneka Tunggal Ika*', is often translated as 'Unity in Diversity'.[1] When it comes to law, Indonesia truly abides by this motto—it is one of the most legally diverse, and consequentially legally complex, countries in the world. And it is also the largest country [by population] in the world to have a civil code and a commercial code in the French tradition (through the Dutch).[2]

This chapter will focus on the contract law normally used in Indonesia for commercial transactions—that is, the civil law as found in the Civil Code of Indonesia.

However, one must first make clear that Indonesia practises legal pluralism, which means that different laws apply to different people depending on their ethnicity, their religion, or

* Cite as Gary F Bell, 'Formation of Contract and Stipulations for Third Parties in Indonesia' in Chen-Wishart, Loke, & Vogenauer, *Studies in the Contract Laws of Asia Vol II: Formation and Third Party Beneficiaries* (Oxford: OUP 2017) ch 18. I want to thank Mr Ibrahim Sjarief Assegaf of Assegaf Hamzah & Partner, Jakarta, for his detailed and extremely helpful comments on a previous draft of this chapter. All shortcomings are mine. Translation of the doctrine from Indonesian to English or from French to English are mine unless otherwise stated.

[1] Literally in old Javanese: 'in pieces, yet one'. The motto is uncharacteristically in old Javanese rather than in the Indonesian national language as it is taken from a poem written in the fourteenth century during the glorious Majapahit era. Interestingly, that poem was advocating religious tolerance between Buddhists and Hindus (this was before the Islamization of Java). It states that although the truth of the Buddha and the truth of Shiva are indeed different they are one. This tolerance and multivalence explains in part the success of the Majapahit Empire. For a translation, see MC Ricklefs, 'Unity and Disunity in Javanese Political and Religious Thought of the Eighteenth Century' (1992) 26 Modern Asian Studies 663–678, quoting the translation by S Santoso, *Sutasoma: A Study in Old Javanese Wajrayana* (New Delhi: International Academy of Indian Culture 1975).

[2] GF Bell, 'Codification and Decodification: The State of the Civil and Commercial Codes in Indonesia' in W-Y Wang (ed), *Codification in East Asia—Selected Papers from the 2nd IACL Thematic Conference* (Switzerland: Springer International Publishing 2014) 39–40.

Formation of Contract and Stipulations for Third Parties in Indonesia. Gary F Bell.

the choice of law they have made. There are three types of contract law in force in Indonesia: the adat contract laws, the Islamic contract laws, and the European civil law of contract.[3]

Historically, the adat laws are the oldest as they are the indigenous laws of Indonesia. They were later influenced by the arrival of Hinduism and Buddhism which were the main religions of the western parts of what is today Indonesia before the arrival of Islam. Islam came to Indonesia in the thirteenth century but its spread was not sudden and it is only by the end of the sixteenth century that Islam overtook the Hinduism and Buddhism in Sumatra and Java. Islamic law played an increasing role though not necessarily a predominant one—the adat laws survived. Then came the Dutch from the late sixteenth century. The Dutch brought their law but made it applicable only to Europeans and to commerce, letting both adat and Islamic law survive. Eventually in 1847, a Civil Code and Commercial Codes were adopted in Dutch for Indonesia and to this day, this Civil Code, still in Dutch, is the main law for commercial contracts in Indonesia.

This legal pluralism could mean, for example, that a Muslim couple would have Islamic marriage law apply to them, but Javanese adat law might govern some matters of succession if they are Javanese (whether they reside in Java or not)[4] and when one of them writes a cheque, he or she would have been deemed to have voluntarily submitted to the Civil and Commercial Codes (European civil law) including European contract law, unless of course they are the clients of an Islamic bank in which case they would be deemed to have voluntarily chosen Islamic law. One cannot therefore talk of one Indonesian contract law, one must instead always first ask which contract law applies to whom and to which transactions. I will briefly describe the adat and Islamic contract laws, but should right away state that legal pluralism is usually not an issue in commercial settings—the civil law of contract is almost always presumed to be the law chosen by the parties.

(a) Contract law in adat laws

The adat laws are the indigenous laws of each ethnic group. They are themselves plural: there is not one adat law for all of Indonesia but many adat distinct laws—based on ethnicity rather than territory—the adat of the Minangkabau in Sumatra will be very different from the adat of the Balinese. The Dutch scholar Van Vollenhoven who documented adat law, was of the view that there were 17 adat law regions in Indonesia—each region having adat laws that, in his view, had a certain degree of similarity. There would also be some diversity within each region.[5]

Adat contract law deals primarily with exchanges in rural settings mainly about land and its produces, although land itself is today meant to be governed by the Basic Agrarian Law[6] which is said to be a codification of adat law. Adat law principles are different from European civil law. It is a customary, communal law, which until the arrival of the Dutch was largely unwritten.

Adat contracts are, for example, 'real contracts', to use a Roman law category—they were generally not formed by consent alone but by the physical transmission or delivery (*traditio*) of the thing that is the object of the contract. One could also sometimes form (seal) the

[3] For a more detailed discussion of the different sources of law in Indonesia, see GF Bell, 'Indonesia: The Challenges of Legal Diversity and Law Reform' in EA Black and GF Bell (eds), *Law and Legal Institutions of Asia—Traditions, Adaptations and Innovations* (New York: Cambridge University Press 2011) 262–298.

[4] Although it now seems that, for Muslims, Islamic law will prevail in most matters of succession.

[5] Though the Dutch judges applying adat law in Indonesia before Independence may not have been aware of this further diversity.

[6] Law No 5 of 1960. It is known in English as the Basic Agrarian Law but its full Indonesian title is *Undang Undang No. 5 Tahun 1960 Tentang Peraturan Dasar Pokok-pokok Agraria.*

contract by delivering a small amount of money or token object (*panjer* in Javanese) which is different from the main object of the contract. If the party who gave the *panjer* does not perform, he will lose it. If the party who received the *panjer* does not perform, he will have to return it, and in some cases would have to return double the *panjer*. This is similar to the concept of *arrhes* in the French Civil Code[7] or *earnest* in the common law. There are many kinds of specific contracts in adat (in some adat laws, one can sell a tree without the land under it, one can sell parts of an animal not yet slaughtered) and it includes some credit transactions similar to pledges and loans.[8]

Adat law is a very collectivist and communal kind of law and therefore one can assume that some contracts have effect on third parties. For example, in some regions, contracts of loan would bind not only the individual debtor but would entail a kind of joint and several liability of the entire adat community to which the debtor belongs—a case of a party creating an obligation for third parties.[9]

Because most contracts in modern Indonesia are not governed by adat law and almost no commercial contract is governed by adat law, but also because this author would not be competent to discuss adat law,[10] this chapter will not further mention adat law and will concentrate on European civil law.

(b) Islamic contract law

The other contract law applicable in Indonesia is the Islamic contract law. Although, in the past, it mainly applied to marriage contracts, the development of Islamic banking and financing has led to a resurgence of Islamic contract law in Indonesia. Islamic law is itself pluralistic. Almost all Indonesian Muslims belong to the Shafi'i School of Islamic Jurisprudence (*madh'hab* in Arabic),[11] one of the four main schools in Sunni Islam (Shia Islam has its own schools).[12] Although the general principles of contract law would be the same across the schools, these schools do not agree on the contours of the law and this is true with respect to contract law—there are in the details many differences between the different schools of law. For example, the Shafi'i School is more permissive than some other schools when it comes to Islamic financing.

One can belong to whatever School of Jurisprudence one chooses to belong—in a sense, the law applicable is a matter of choice and one can change school simply by declaring it, at

[7] French Civil Code, art 1590: 'Si la promesse de vendre a été faite avec des arrhes chacun des contractants est maître de s'en départir, celui qui les a données, en les perdant et celui qui les a reçues, en restituant le double.' Translation: 'Where a promise to sell was made with an earnest, each contracting party is at liberty to withdraw. The one who has given it, by losing it. And the one who has received it, by returning twice the amount.' In this chapter I use the versions of the French code available at https://www.legifrance.gouv.fr

[8] For more details in English on adat law, see S Gautama, *Indonesian Business Law* (3rd edn, Bandung: Citra Aditya Bakti 2006) 68–75. See also MB Hooker, *Adat Law in Modern Indonesia* (Kuala Lumpur: Oxford University Press 1978), S Soekanto and S b Taneko, *Hukum Adat Indonesia* (3rd edn, Jakarta: CV Rajawali 1986).

[9] Gautama (n 8) 74.

[10] One would in fact need to speak Javanese or Balinese to study Javanese or Balinese adat, eg, and I only speak Indonesian—I do not speak any local language.

[11] In principle, each individual is free to choose his or her *madh'hab* or school of law, and some countries have great diversity of schools in their population. However, a vast majority of Malays and Indonesians follow the Shafi'i school of law.

[12] For more detail on Islamic law as a source of law in Indonesia, see Bell (n 3) 269–270. See also RM Feener, *Muslim Legal Thought in Modern Indonesia* (Cambridge: Cambridge University Press 2007) ch 2; RM Feener and ME Cammack (eds), *Islamic Law in Contemporary Indonesia—Ideas and Institutions* (Cambridge: Harvard University Press 2007); MB Hooker, *Indonesian Islam—Social Change through Contemporary Fatawa* (Honolulu: University of Hawai'i Press 2003); MB Hooker, Indonesian Syariah—Defining a National School of Islamic Law (Singapore: Institute of Southeast Asian Studies 2008); MB Hooker and Tim Lindsey, 'Public Faces of Syariah in Contemporary Indonesia: Towards a National Mazhab?' (2002) 4 Australian J Asian L 259.

least in principle.[13] In principle, the schools are not territorial and a judge should therefore ask Muslim parties which school they belong to before applying the appropriate law, though most Indonesians are presumed to belong to the Shafi'i School.

With respect to stipulations for the benefit of third parties for example, the Hanafi School of Jurisprudence does not allow them whereas the Hambali School recognizes them.[14]

This chapter will not look into the Islamic law of contract applied in Indonesia as the author is not qualified in Islamic law (I do not even speak Arabic) and that law is, at this point, used mainly for specialized purposes (Islamic banking and finance, marriage contracts)—it is not widely used in commercial matters.

(c) The civil law

The third contract law found in Indonesia is the European contract law brought to Indonesia by the Dutch colonizers and which is part of the French civil law tradition. As I have written elsewhere:

> The *Burgerlijk Wetboek* (the civil code known in Indonesian as the *Kitab Undang-Undang Hukum Perdata* or KUHPer) is a statute proclaimed for Indonesia by the Dutch authority in 1847.[15] So is the *Wetboek van Koophandel* (the commercial code known in Indonesian as the *Kitab Undang-Undang Hukum Dagang* or KUHD).[16]... These codes were based on the Dutch codes. The Dutch had slightly adapted and modified the French codes (and I would argue, had given to the provisions of the civil code a clearer organization than the one found in the original French code). To this day, the text of the civil code on contract law for example is, most of the time, a word for word translation into Dutch of the French civil code.[17]

The Civil Code—where the principles of contract law are found—is a colonial law which made no attempt to adapt to local circumstances, cultures, and needs. In any event, under the Dutch, the Code would in principle only apply to Europeans (mainly the Dutch) and the locals would continue to be governed by their adat and Islamic laws which the Dutch continued to enforce. The Code, to this day, is in force only in its Dutch version—no Indonesian version was ever adopted by Parliament. Adopting a new Civil Code has been part of the National Legislative Programme for some time.[18] There has been a draft of a new bill on the Code of Civil Procedure (though it has not yet been adopted) but to my knowledge there is no official draft of a new Civil Code yet. There have been recent academic efforts under the National Law Reform Commission (*Badan Pembinaan Hukum Nasional*, 'BPHN') towards a reformed contract law (short of a new Civil Code) but thus far this has not led to new legislation and is unlikely to lead to legislation any time soon.[19] This follows other academic efforts in 1994 for a reform of the law of obligations, which also were not followed by any legislative action.[20]

[13] It is difficult to do so when one lives in an area where everyone is of the same school and there are no jurists knowledgeable of the other school in the area, but it is in principle a matter of personal choice. There are minority Muslims in Indonesia including some Shia Muslims, but the vast majority of Indonesian belong to the Shafi'i School.

[14] A Khorshid, *Islamic Insurance: A Modern Approach to Islamic Banking* (London/New York: RoutledgeCurzon 2004) 65.

[15] S 1947 No 23. [16] Also S 1947 No 23. [17] Bell (n 2) 41.

[18] It was mentioned in the 2009–2014 Prolegnas (Program Legislasi Nasional) but no law was adopted during this period.

[19] *Naskah Akademik Rancangan Undang Undang Hukum Kontrak* (Academic Paper for a Draft Legislation on the Law of Contract) written by a group of academics headed by Dr Bayu Seto Hardjowahono, SH, LLM, published by the National Law Reform Commission of the Ministry of Law and Human Rights in 2013.

[20] *Naskah Akademik Peraturan Perundang-Undangan Tentang Hukum Perikatan* (Academic Paper on the Legislative Regulation on the Law of Obligations), also published by the National Law Reform Commission of the then Ministry of Justice in 1994. That project actually included a proposed legislative text for adoption to replace the law of obligations (including contract law) of the Civil Code.

The Codes were continued after Independence.[21] Some parts of the Civil Code were replaced by legislation (eg the law of immovable property and hypothecs relating to them, the law of marriage), but the law of contract is still governed by the Civil Code.

This chapter will only address the civil law of contract governed by the KUHPer (Civil Code). I will refer to that law as the civil law of contract, by which I mean the law of contract in the European civil law tradition.

2. When Does the Civil Law of Contract Apply?

As mentioned above, the Civil Code was initially intended to apply only to Europeans. The contract law applicable under the Dutch depended on the ethnic group to which one belonged. The Dutch, other Europeans, and all companies were governed by the Civil and Commercial Codes. Locals were governed by local law (adat and/or Islamic law). At first it was simple but it became more complicated. For example, the Japanese were considered Europeans after Japan adopted a European-inspired Civil Code though the same treatment was not given to the Chinese when China adopted a Civil Code. Chinese merchants were, however, bound by European law when dealing commercially with the Dutch.

Although in principle the law applicable depends on one's law group (European law for companies and Europeans, local law for locals), one important principle can alter this and often does: the parties were and are still free to choose the law applicable to the contract whether implicitly or explicitly. In commercial contracts, parties sometimes explicitly state that the contract is governed by the Indonesian Civil and Commercial Codes (stating that it is governed by Indonesian law might not be sufficiently specific). Even when the parties do not explicitly select the Codes as the governing law, they are often deemed to have done so implicitly. I have already given the example of the person who writes a cheque to be drawn on a non-Islamic bank—obviously the person makes an implicit choice of European law: the Civil and Commercial Codes will apply since cheques are not known in local law. But this is true of many other transactions. Any contract that seems to be drafted with reference to categories only found in the Civil Code will be interpreted as being governed by that Code.

Effectively, all commercial contractual transactions (excluding land transactions and certain security rights) are usually governed by the Civil and Commercial Codes. The Civil Code is by far the most important source of contract law in Indonesia in all matters commercial.

3. The State of the Indonesian Civil Law of Contract

Imagine a country applying a law of contract written in a foreign language that probably close to 98 per cent of lawyers and judges do not understand. That is Indonesia.

In addition, in the past one could look at the Netherlands for doctrine and jurisprudence but that country now has a new Civil Code, which is quite different from the Indonesian Civil Code and therefore, even if one could read Dutch, recent doctrine and jurisprudence would now be of limited use since they apply a very different Code. French doctrine and jurisprudence could help, but Indonesian jurists understandably do not speak French. In any event, the French reform of contract law came into force on 1 October 2016 and, therefore, the French Code will no longer be similar to the Indonesian Code.

This insularity from Dutch and French sources has affected the state of the doctrine and jurisprudence on contract law.

[21] The Transitional Provisions of the original *Constitution of 1945* (*Undang-Undang Dasar 1945*) art II is now renumbered art I.

(a) The state of the doctrine

As I have written elsewhere:

> Unfortunately, generally, . . . the production of local doctrine is not what it should be in Indonesia. Short of the treatises written by Satrio[22] and some articles written by Gautama[23] there are only a few books on contract and commercial law, most of them 200- or 300-page long, meant only as introductions. There are very few specialized books for example on the law of sale, of lease etc. And there are very few debates about where the law should go and what reforms should be envisaged—the doctrine is mainly descriptive. [There are also very few law review articles and dissertations on the subject.]
>
> The main reason for this situation in my view is that the codes are still in Dutch, all pre-independence jurisprudence and doctrine are also in Dutch and the best source of non-binding comparison until recently was Dutch law. The two academics I mentioned above as having greatly contributed to the doctrine have had the advantage of being fluent in Dutch. The young academics, who are most of the time fluent in English but almost never speak any Dutch, choose to specialize in other fields where the law is in Indonesian and if foreign law is useful in those other fields it is likely to be largely available in English.[24]

More recent publications by younger writers, not fluent in Dutch and sometimes with graduate degrees from Australia, England, or the United States, sometimes rely too heavily on common law materials leading to confusion and uncertainty in the doctrine.

(b) The state of the jurisprudence

'[The Indonesian] courts should produce much needed jurisprudence, but for all kinds of reasons, the jurisprudence has either not come (not published) or has not come to much.'[25] The civil courts in Indonesia are not held in high esteem and the two main problems are the lack of competence of many judges, especially in contract and commercial law, and the corruption of the system. What I am writing is common knowledge in Indonesia. In fact, even the former President of Indonesia, Susilo Bambang Yudhoyono, promised to fight what he himself referred to as 'the judicial mafia'.[26]

The reasoning of the judgments of the courts is often not extremely useful, or illuminating. With respect to the Supreme Court what I have stated earlier remains true:

> However, to be fair to the judges, their workload is unreasonable and the resources available to them are completely inadequate. Even a fair, honest, and competent judge could not possibly produce well-reasoned judgments given the unreasonable number of cases he or she has to handle and the lack of access to legal research tools (lack of library, of books, of access to databases etc.).
>
> In any event, until recently, very few decisions were published. This has improved recently with the publications of decisions of the Supreme Court but much more needs to be done. It is still very difficult to find any helpful case from the Supreme Court on any detailed issue of commercial law. I sit as an arbitrator in many cases where the governing law is Indonesian law, and the parties and their Indonesian legal experts are almost always unable to cite any case because, on complex commercial issues, there almost never is any case to be found in Indonesia. It does

[22] J Satrio, *Hukum Perikatan—Perikatan Yang Lahir Dari Perjanjian—Buku I* [*The Law of Obligations—Obligations Arising from Agreements—Book I*] (Bandung: Penerbit PT Citra Aditya Bakti 1995).

[23] Gautama (n 8). [24] Bell (n 2) 46–47. [25] ibid 47.

[26] J Latul, 'Yudhoyono Vows to Eradicate Indonesia's "Judicial Mafia" in 100 Days' *Jakarta Globe* (Jakarta, 6 November 2009) < http://jakartaglobe.beritasatu.com/archive/yudhoyono-vows-to-eradicate-indonesias-judicial-mafia-in-100-days/> accessed 28 October 2016.

not help of course that given the state of the courts, business people avoid them and choose arbitration instead, thus reducing the possibility that there could be decisions by the courts in such commercial matters in the future.[27]

There is, therefore, a great paucity of doctrine and jurisprudence on contract law in Indonesia.

II. The Formation of Contract

It should first be noted that formation of contracts is an issue of fact in Indonesia as it is in France.[28] Therefore the Supreme Court (*Mahkamah Agung*) rarely intervenes, which means that there is little guidance from the top court on issues of formation of contract.

There is only one provision of the Indonesian Civil Code (KUHPer) on the formation of contract and its does not help much.

Original Dutch (in force) **Artikel 1313**	**Indonesian translation** **Pasal 1313**	**English translation** **Article 1313**
Eene overeenkomst is eene handeling waarbij een of meer personen zich jegens een of meer andere verbinden. (Bw. 1233v.; Civ. 1101).	Suatu perjanjian adalah suatu perbuatan dimana satu orang atau lebih mengikatkan diri terhadap satu orang lain atau lebih.	An agreement is an act pursuant to which one or more individuals bind themselves to one or several others. (Bw. 1233v.; Civ. 1101)

This is in part a translation in Dutch of the former article 1101 of the French Civil Code:

Original French **Code civil des Français article 1101**	**English translation** **French Civil Code article 1101**
Le contrat est une convention par laquelle une ou plusieurs personnes s'obligent, envers une ou plusieurs autres, à donner, à faire ou à ne pas faire quelque chose.	A contract is an agreement by which one or several persons bind themselves, towards one or several others, to transfer, to do or not to do something.

The only other article of some relevance in the Code is article 1320(1) which is not particularly helpful either—it just states that one of the four things required for a contract to be validly formed is consent (the others being capacity, object, and cause).[29] We therefore have to turn to the doctrine and the jurisprudence to help determine the law on this matter, but neither are voluminous in Indonesia.

The main, and often the only, source on the issue of formation of contract are Professor Satrio's publications on contract law.[30] He is the only one to discuss the matter at some length. He, however, mainly refers to old jurisprudence by Dutch courts under the old Dutch Civil Code which was essentially the same as the Indonesian Civil Code. This is because there is in fact so little guidance from Indonesian jurisprudence and doctrine. On

[27] Bell (n 2) 49.

[28] In France the jurisprudence acknowledges the principle of the 'pouvoir souverain des juges du fond pour interpréter la volonté des parties' ('the sovereign power of the judges of facts to interpret the will of the parties')—ie whether there is a contract is an issue of fact. See Civ 1re 21 déc 1960: D 1961.417. Note Malaurie (revocation of the offer is possible until the reception of the acceptance).

[29] Art 1320(1) read, in Dutch 'Tot de bestaanbaarheid der overeenkomsten worden vier voorwaarden vereischt: 1o. de toestemming van degenen die zich verbinden (Bw. 28, 1321v);'; Indonesian translation: 'Supaya terjadi perjanjian yang sah, perlu dipenuhi empat syarat; 1. kesepakatan mereka yang mengikatkan dirinya'; English translation: 'In order to be valid, an agreement must satisfy the following four conditions: 1. there must be consent of the individuals who are bound thereby; (Bw.28, 1321v.)'. In this chapter I normally use this translation of the code: http://www.kuhper.com/Trilingual%20Indonesian%20Civil%20Code.pdf

[30] For our topics, the relevant book is his first one on contracts: Satrio (n 22).

many occasions, Satrio also refers to the then Draft Civil Code of the Netherlands (now the new Dutch Civil Code) since it has more detailed provisions on offer and acceptance and formation of contracts. I will, however, not refer to these provisions as they are not part of Indonesian law—Indonesia still has the old Code and has no serious plan yet to adopt a new one.

Another more limited source is Professor Subekti who in his very short book on contract law (exactly 100 pages for all of contract law) briefly addresses some of the issues, but he rarely goes into much detail.[31] Professor Gautama sometimes addresses the issues very briefly.[32]

I have consulted close to 20 other doctrinal works and they rarely ever go beyond repeating the content of article 1313 of the Code. Whenever they do say more, I make reference to them.

As to the jurisprudence it is thin. Again, the Supreme Court rarely pronounces on issues of fact, of which the formation of contract is one. The decisions of the courts below have only recently started to be published but without any systematic indexing. The main doctrinal authors (Satrio and Gautama) rarely refer to decisions of Indonesian courts and refer more generously to decisions of Dutch courts under the old Dutch Civil Code which is no longer in force in the Netherlands.

Therefore, on the issue of the formation of the contract, there is a great paucity of legislation (only one article of the Code), a paucity of doctrine (Satrio being the only exception though he too does not go into sufficient detail to address all the issues) and a great paucity of indigenous jurisprudence. We will make do with what is available and will rely mainly on Professor Satrio.

1. The Four Required Elements for the Formation of a Contract

Article 1320 of the Code reads as follows:

Original Dutch (in force) Artikel 1320	Indonesian translation Pasal 1320	English translation Article 1320
Tot de bestaanbaarheid der overeenkomsten worden vier voorwaarden vereischt:	Supaya terjadi perjanjian yang sah, perlu dipenuhi empat syarat;	In order to be valid, an agreement must satisfy the following four conditions:
1o. de toestemming van degenen die zich verbinden (Bw. 28, 1321v); 2o. de bekwaamheid om eene verbindtenis aan te gaan (Bw. 1329v); 3o. een bepaald onderwerp (Bw. 1332v); 4o. eene geoorloofde oorzaak (Bw. 1335v.; Civ. 1108).	1. kesepakatan mereka yang mengikatkan dirinya; 2. kecakapan untuk membuat suatu perikatan; 3. suatu pokok persoalan tertentu; 4. suatu sebab yang tidak terlarang.	1. there must be consent of the individuals who are bound thereby; (Bw.28, 1321v.) 2. there must be capacity to enter into an obligation; (Bw. 1329v.) 3. there must be a specific object; (Bw. 1332v.) 4. there must be a licit cause. (Bw.1335v.; Civ. 1108)

This is an approximate translation of the old article 1108 of the French Civil Code and clearly states that for a contract to be valid, it needs four elements: consent, capacity, object, and cause—this is an issue of validity.

[31] Subekti, *Hukum Perjanjian* (Jakarta: Penerbit Intermasa 2001).

[32] Gautama (n 8).

What follows article 1320 in the Indonesia Code on the four requirements for a valid contract, is the law relating to the invalidity of contract. For example, the very next article, article 1321, states how consent may be invalid and thus the contract invalid: 'No consent is valid if it is granted based on error [mistake in common law] or obtained by force [duress] or fraud [misrepresentation].'[33] Article 1322 talks of how error makes the contract invalid, articles 1323 to 1327 do the same with respect to force, and 1328, with respect to fraud. These are all articles on the invalidity of contract due to a lack of consent.

In a civil law treatise on contract formation, these defects of consent would be discussed here, but in this series of books, the invalidities of contracts in law will be discussed separately in the fourth volume on invalidities. I will therefore limit my comments on consent to the issue of whether the test of intention is objective or subjective (which is more an issue for interpretation of contract than of formation) and will then discuss the invalidities of the contract due to defects of form (formalities). This is not how it would be done in civil law, but in comparative law one has to adopt a way of organizing materials which cannot follow both the civil law and the common law structures.

Similarly, this is where in civil law I would discuss the issue of capacity to contract and which contracts are invalid due to incapacity but this will also have to wait for the fourth volume of the series which will be concerned with invalidities.

Likewise, for the object and the licit cause—the lack of which will cause the invalidity of the contract—it will have to wait for the sixth volume of the series on illegality and public policy. However, because the common law reader may not be familiar with the concepts of object and cause in the civil law, let me very briefly explain what they are.[34]

The *object* of the contract (as opposed to the object of a specific obligation under the contract—the prestation—owed by a party), is the juridical operation the parties have envisaged. The object of the contract must be licit or the contract would be invalid. For example, in many jurisdictions the sale of one's blood (the object of the contract) would be illegal and therefore the object invalid and the contract also invalid.

The *cause* of the contract (as opposed to the cause of the obligation) is the reason, the purpose of the contract: why the parties entered into the contract. This cause must be licit or the contract is invalid. The requirement of a cause has been the object of very long and elaborate debates in the French civil law tradition—too long to discuss in detail here. Many have argued that it is a useless notion and in fact the new French law of contract (amendments to the Civil Code that came into force on 1 October 2016) abandons the concept of cause. Not much can be found on the concept of cause in Indonesian doctrine and jurisprudence, except the general statement that there must be one and it must be licit.

2. The Test of Intention

As is to be expected in a civil law jurisdiction of French tradition, the test of intention is more subjective than it would be in common law jurisdictions. The actual intention of the parties to be bound determines whether a contract is formed. Satrio repeats this when he discusses gratuitous contracts which rely entirely on the intention of the person making the promise.[35]

[33] Words in square brackets added by author.

[34] For more on consent, capacity, object, and cause, please refer to the fourth volume on invalidities in this series.

[35] Satrio (n 22) 20: 'Once again we see that the intent/purpose of the parties is an important factor for the existence of the agreement.' All translations of Satrio, Subekti, and others are my own.

That the actual subjective intention of the parties is more important than the objective statements they have made is illustrated by the main provision on the interpretation of contracts found in the KUHPer:

Artikel 1343	**Pasal 1343**	**Article 1343**
Indien de bewoordingen eener overeenkomst voor onderscheiden uitleggingen vatbaar zijn, moet men veeler nagaan welke de bedoeling der Indonesie partijen geweest zij, dan zich aan den letterlijken zin der woorden binden (Bw. 886, 1257, 1473, 1855; Civ. 1156).	Jika kata-kata suatu perjanjian dapat diberi berbagai penafsiran, maka lebih baik diselidiki maksud kedua belah pihak yang membuat perjanjian itu, daripada dipegang teguh arti kata menurut huruf.	If the wording of an agreement is open to several interpretations, one should ascertain the common intent of the parties rather than be bound by the literal meaning of the words. (Bw. 886, 1257, 1473, 1855; Civ. 1156)

It should, however, be kept in mind that in the interpretation of the contract, the KUHPer takes a more objective approach than the French Code does: Article 1342, which precedes the article just quoted, states that 'If the wording of an agreement is clear, deviation from it by way of interpretation is not permitted (Bw. 855)', which suggests a prima facie objective approach to interpretation. This article was added by the Dutch and had no equivalent in the French Civil Code. However, it seems that the courts are quick to find an ambiguity and then look for the subjective intention of the parties (article 1343). It should be noted that article 1342 ('clear meaning') is concerned with the interpretation of the contract rather than its formation which might also explain why the judges seem not to apply an objective approach in deciding whether a contract was formed.

Although this chapter will not look at factors vitiating consent (error/mistake, fraud/misrepresentation, etc), a quick look at error (*kesesatan/kekeliruan* in Indonesian, *dwaling* in Dutch, *erreur* in French) as a vitiating factor would confirm the extent to which the Indonesian civil law is concerned with the subjective intention of the parties (see article 1322 KUHPer). Satrio states that, in determining whether the unilateral error of a party is sufficient to make a contract invalid, the subjective theory of intent is preferable as it is fairer or more just (*lebih adil*).[36]

Satrio gives the example of a Dutch case of sale of equipment which was to be set to certain specifications by the seller. The specifications and the particular use could not be determined by a reading of the written contract and therefore the Supreme Court in the Netherlands had recourse to the subjective intention of the parties rather than the letter of the contract. It was noted that the buyer had informed the seller of the specifications and that, although this was not part of the written contract, the subjective intention of the parties prevailed.[37]

Satrio also mentioned a case from the highest court in Indonesia before the Second World War. A buyer had stated to the seller his intention to buy a car to travel frequently by a certain road from Jakarta to Bandung. Jakarta is at sea level but Bandung is high up in the mountains and a powerful engine would be required. The seller sold him a car which had

[36] Satrio (n 22) 283.

[37] Case of 'A.B. Haldataxameter – Groenewegen', HR 5 November 1936, reproduced in HR Hoetink, *Arresten Over Burgelijk Recht* (8th edn, Haarlem: Tjeen-Willink & Zoon 1951) 226; mentioned and translated in part in Satrio (n 22) 284–287.

too weak an engine. The court held that the subjective intention of the buyer would prevail over the written contract as this was the subjective intention of the parties.[38]

Indonesia has no parol evidence rule and therefore the judge is free to look at any evidence of the intention of the parties including, for example, the negotiations of the contract and conduct subsequent to the contract.

3. Formality Requirements

In principle, there is no formal requirement to make a contract unless the law provides otherwise. Contracts can be informal and oral.[39]

(a) When must enforceable contracts satisfy formality requirements?

There is no clear provision in the law and no mention that I could find in the doctrine, but it would seem logical that, if there is a formality requirement for validity, it must be met at the time of formation of contract.

(b) What are the formality requirements?

(1) Language

Law No 24 of 2009 Concerning the National Flag, Language, Emblem, and Anthem came into force on 9 July 2009. It has obvious nationalistic goals. Article 31 of the law reads as follows:

Pasal 31	**Article 31**
(1) Bahasa Indonesia wajib digunakan dalam nota kesepahaman atau perjanjian yang melibatkan lembaga negara, instansi pemerintah Republik Indonesia, lembaga swasta Indonesia atau perseorangan warga negara Indonesia.	(1) Indonesian must be used in memoranda of understanding or agreements that involve state organs, government institutions of the Republic of Indonesia, private Indonesian institutions or individuals who are citizens of the Republic of Indonesia.
(2) Nota kesepahaman atau perjanjian sebagaimana dimaksud pada ayat (1) yang melibatkan pihak asing ditulis juga dalam bahasa nasional pihak asing tersebut dan/atau bahasa Inggris.	(2) Memoranda of understanding or agreements as specified in paragraph (1) that involve foreign parties may also be written in the national language of the foreign parties and/or English.

Article 40 of the law also provides that further regulations on the use of the Indonesian language may be adopted by presidential regulation, but none were adopted.[40]

Article 31 has raised a lot of concerns among the international business community in Jakarta and among Indonesians who have business relationships with foreign parties. One key issue of concern has been the effect of this article on contracts written only in a language other than Indonesian. Would such contract be invalid?

[38] Case of 'Mobil Benz' (Benz Car), HgH 23 December 1926, cited in the *Indisch Tijdschrif van het Recht* (Law Report of the Dutch East Indies) T.125:90, mentioned and translated in part in Satrio (n 22) 287–289.

[39] Gautama (n 8) 82.

[40] 'Pasal 40: Ketentuan lebih lanjut mengenai penggunaan Bahasa Indonesia sebagaimana dimaksud dalam Pasal 26 sampai dengan Pasal 39 diatur dalam Peraturan Presiden.' ('Further provisions on the use of Indonesian as mentioned in Article 26 through Article 39 are to be regulated by a Presidential Decree.')

There has been a lot of debate on this issue among scholars and lawyers. Before there were any court decisions on article 31, the majority view among Indonesian lawyers seems to have been that, without further regulations implementing and clarifying the law, the law would not render invalid contracts involving an Indonesian party drafted in a language other than Indonesian.

The law itself does not declare that contracts not written in Indonesian are invalid—it does not provide for invalidity as a sanction. In fact, the law provides no sanction or penalty for not respecting the requirement of article 31 whereas it does provide for penalties and prison terms for the violation of other articles of the law. There is therefore no clear intention on the part of the legislator to provide any specific sanction. In addition, the law in article 73 (which is part of the closing provisions of the law) provides that regulations for the implementation of the law shall be adopted within two years. As mentioned, such regulations have not been adopted. Without such regulations clarifying the sanction for not conforming with article 31, contracts written in a language other than Indonesian should remain valid in my view.

Many lawyers had written to the Ministry of Law and Human Rights for a clarification or interpretation of this article. In December 2009, the ministry issued a letter, which, even though not legally binding, gave what should have been a reliable interpretation of the law.[41]

The ministry's letter stated that, in its opinion, until the adoption of implementing regulations, contracts drafted exclusively in a foreign language would continue to be valid and that the regulations, when adopted, would not be retroactive. The letter also stated that when contracts are bilingual, the contracting parties are free to designate a prevailing language in the event of inconsistencies between the different versions.

Although a letter from the ministry is not legally binding on the courts, it was hoped that it would be very influential as the ministry is likely to be the one drafting the implementing regulations.

Unfortunately, however, a trial court (District Court) has held that contracts not drafted in Indonesian were invalid. In that case, *PT Bangun Karya Pratama Lestari v Nine AM Ltd*,[42] a US$4,000,000 contract of loan was held invalid *ab initio* because it was drafted only in English and one of the parties was an Indonesian company. This decision was upheld by the High Court (ie Court of Appeal) of Jakarta.[43] On 31 August 2015, the Supreme Court (*Mahkamah Agung*) announced that it would uphold the decision of the High Court.

The decision of the Supreme Court was published more than a year later. In its reasons, the court explained that the appellant had argued that in the absence of a clear sanction in the legislation, the presumption should be that a contract drafted in another language remains valid. The court, however, rejected that argument and held that such a contract violated the law and was void because it has an invalid cause. It held:

> The fact that the Loan Agreement is not drafted in the Indonesian language proves that the contract between the parties violates the provision of article 31 paragraph (1) of Law Number 24 Year 2009, therefore the Loan Agreement is a contract that has a cause which is illicit, therefore in accordance with article 1335, read in conjunction with article 1337 of the Civil Code, the contract is invalid.[44]

[41] See *Surat Menteri Hukum Dan Hak Asasi Manusia Nomor M.HH.UM.01.01-35 Tahun 2009* (Letter of the Minister of Law and Human Rights Number M.HH.UM.01.01-35 Year 2009).
[42] Decision No 451/Pdt.G/2012/PN.Jkt Bar. dated 20 June 2013.
[43] Decision No 48/PDT/2014/PT.DKI dated 12 February 2014.
[44] Supreme Court, Decision No 1572 K/Pdt/2015 at p 79.

Article 1335 of the Civil Code provides that a contract without a cause, or concluded pursuant to a fraudulent or an illicit cause, is invalid. Article 1337 provides that a cause is illicit if it is prohibited by law or if it violates morality or public order.

The court therefore decided that all contracts 'that involve state organs, government institutions of the Republic of Indonesia, private Indonesian institutions or individuals who are citizens of the Republic of Indonesia'[45] are invalid unless they are drafted in Indonesian. It should, however, be noted that in Indonesia, a civil law country, there is no strict doctrine of *stare decisis*, although decisions of the Supreme Court do carry a lot of weight.

It should also be noted that even though article 31 seems to be concerned only with written contracts, both paragraphs of that article mention 'memoranda of understanding and agreements', and agreements could include oral agreements. However, the second paragraph states that 'Memoranda of understanding or agreements...that involve foreign parties may *also* be *written* in the national language of the foreign parties and/or English' which seems to suggest that only written agreements are considered by article 31—'may also be written' (in Indonesian: *ditulis juga*) assumes that all the agreements governed by article 31 are in writing.

Some other specific statutes also require that some specific kinds of contracts be in the Indonesian language.[46]

(2) Contracts which must be in writing

The general rule is that there is no requirement of form for contracts, unless the law specifically provides otherwise.

Many contracts are required by law to be in writing. For example, the settlement out of court of a litigation or potential litigation must be in writing.[47] It seems that the justification is to promote certainty.

When a contract is required by law to be in writing, an oral contract would be invalid.

Surprisingly, however, the Consumer Protection Act[48] does not impose any writing requirement for any category of consumer contracts.

(3) Contracts which must be in the form of an authentic deed

In addition to being in writing, some contracts must also be executed in the form of an authentic deed (also called notarial deed—*akta notaris* in Indonesian)[49] drawn by a notary or other authorized public official.[50] The Civil Code itself requires a few contracts to be in the form of an authentic deed—for example, the contracts of gift,[51] and of subrogation by the will of the debtor[52] must be done through an authentic deed.

[45] Law No 24 of 2009 Concerning the National Flag, Language, Emblem, and Anthem, art 31.

[46] eg Regulation No 1/POJK.07/2013 of the Financial Services Authority (Otoritas Jasa Keuangan) art 7, on Consumer Protection in the Financial Sector requires that contacts be in Indonesian.

[47] KUHPer, art 1851: [Translation:] 'A settlement is an agreement in which parties, by handing over, agreeing, or retaining a matter, resolve a matter which is pending lawsuit, or prevent a lawsuit. (Amended S.25-525) This agreement shall be valid only if it is concluded in writing.'

[48] Law No 8 of 1999. [49] Also referred to as '*akta otentik*' by some authors. [50] Gautama (n 8) 82.

[51] KUHPer, art 1682 [Translation:] 'Any gifts, with the exception of those stipulated in article 1687, may only take effect by notarial deed, and the original document of such gift is to remain with the notary.' The exception at article 1687 is for what is called a manual gift, that is the gift of movable property with actual physical delivery of the thing given. KUHPer, art 1687 [Translation:] 'Gifts of movable, tangible objects, or debt claims to be paid to bearer, do not require any deeds, and shall be valid by a single delivery to the donee, or to a third party, who accepts the gift on his behalf.'

[52] KUHPer, art 1401(2) [Translation:] 'The subrogation arises by agreement:...2. Where the debtor borrows a sum of money for the purpose of payment of his debt and the debtor stipulates that the lender will assume the rights of the creditor, in order to validate this subrogation, both the loan agreement and the note of debt discharge must be documented in an authentic deed, and the loan document must stipulate that the loan was made to satisfy

Other laws also require that some contracts or acts be by authentic deed, for example (among others) the articles of association of a limited liability company,[53] as well as any contract or agreement that transfers any rights over land, creates new rights over land, or uses land as lien.[54]

An authentic deed 'is one which has been drawn up in a legal format, by or before public officials who are authorized to do so at the location where this takes place'.[55] 'An authentic deed provides conclusive evidence regarding the contents stipulated therein for the parties, their heirs or parties having rights therein.'[56] An authentic deed therefore has a special evidentiary status in court—it proves its content conclusively and it is extremely difficult to contest its content—only by a special and difficult procedure can one contest the validity of the authentic deed. The increased evidentiary weight also extends to the capacity of the parties and the necessary formalities as the notaries are required to ascertain these as well.

Notwithstanding the fact that the authentic deed is conferred a special and privileged evidentiary status, when the law requires that a contract be in an authentic deed it does so as a condition of its validity, and not simply for evidentiary purposes. For example, a gift that is not in an authentic deed is simply invalid.

In some instances, the justification for the law requiring a notarial deed is because the operation is complex (eg articles of associations) or affects third parties (subrogation by the will of the debtor). It is also a way to make sure the parties have received legal advice as the notary must read the contract and explain its legal effects to both parties

It should be noted that any contract may be in the form of an authentic deed even if the law does not require that it be so—parties may want the contract to be in that form in order for it to be officially registered and because of its additional evidentiary value.

(4) Real contracts formed by delivery

A contract of loan for consumption[57] and a contract of deposit[58] are real contracts. The meeting of minds (offer and acceptance) is not sufficient to create a contract (or as is sometimes said 'to make the contract perfect')—the contract is formed only when the movable thing loaned or deposited is in fact physically delivered—hence the term *real* contract (*res, rei*, Latin for 'thing'). The delivery of the thing is therefore a required formality for the formation of these two contracts.

Although mutual promises from a bank to make a loan and from the borrower to take the loan and pay it back with interest would not form a contract until the bank actually gives the money, the jurisprudence and doctrine in France have found ways to hold the parties to their promises but without stating that the promises formed a contract of loan. If the bank refuses to give the money, the courts will entertain an action for damages, but not one for specific performance (which would be a right, if a contract had been formed).[59] It is not clear whether Indonesian courts will adopt this position.

such debt; while the note of debt discharge must stipulate that the payment was made with money lent by the new creditor.

Such subrogation is arranged without the assistance of the creditor. (Bw. 400, 613, 1382, 1403, 1848; Civ. 1250).'

[53] Law No 40/2007 on Limited Liability Company, art 7(1).

[54] eg Government Regulation No 10/1961.

[55] KUHPer, art 1868.

[56] ibid 1870.

[57] ibid art 1754 [Translation:] 'A loan for consumption is an agreement, in which one party delivers another with a specific amount of consumable items, subject to the condition that the latter mentioned is return similar types of items of the same amount and quality. (Bw. 505, 1392, 1740, 1763; Civ. 1892).' This provision is interpreted so that there is no contract until the thing loaned is actually physically transferred to the borrower.

[58] KHUPer, art 1697: [Translation:] 'The agreement [of deposit] is not deemed to have been consummated other than by actual or presumed delivery of the objects.'

[59] *Cour de Cassation*, Civ 1re, 20 juillet 1981. Fr Terré et al, *Droit civil—Les obligations* (11th edn, Paris: Dalloz 2013) para 148.

(5) Stamp duty

If you ask most Indonesian laymen, they will tell you that written contracts must be stamped. These stamps are available in any post office and must be affixed to each copy of a contract (and to many other documents). The maximum duty is Rp 6,000 per document or copy of document (about US$0.50). The practice is that the stamp is put on the signing page of the contract and the document is signed in part over the stamp. It is essentially a tax collected by the state on any contract entered into—literally a stamp duty.

In Indonesia, many lay people think that a contract is invalid unless it is stamped, but it is not so. What is the sanction? Article 7(9) of the Law on Stamp Duties[60] provides that a contract or document which is not stamped is indeed '*dianggap tidak bermeterai*'—'deemed not stamped'! The consequence, however, is not the invalidity of the contract but the impossibility of using the written contract as evidence in court or to use it for any official purpose. Article 11(1) of the Law provides that if the stamp duty is not duly paid, government authorities, judges, registrars, bailiffs, notaries public, and other public officials are prohibited in the exercise of their duties from receiving, considering, keeping, or making copies or summaries of the relevant document. Basically, the document cannot be entered into evidence unless it has been stamped. The contract is nonetheless valid, but basically unenforceable. However, it is possible to stamp any document even after it has been signed simply by paying a penalty of twice the amount of stamp duty owed. Therefore, rather than pay the maximum stamp duty of Rp 6,000, one must put stamps for a total of Rp 12,000 (or about US$1).

Indonesia adopted the Law on Electronic Information and Transactions[61] in 2008, which states: 'Electronic Transactions that are stated in Electronic Contracts shall bind parties'.[62] I am not quite sure where one is supposed to fix the stamp on an electronic contract and how an electronic signature can be done over a stamp! The stamp duty law does not address these issues. However, I understand that in practice, lawyers submit a print-out of the electronic document and affix a stamp to it.

(c) What are the consequences of non-compliance? Are parties' reliance protected?

I have discussed above the consequences of non-compliance with respect to each type of formal requirement.

There is no special rule or principle on reliance in such context. One could, I guess, sue in delict (tort) under the general principle of delictual liability if the other party is at fault,[63] however, I am not aware of any case to that effect.

4. Are Offers Binding?

Whether an offer is binding depends on the nature of the offer. If an offer comes with a determined time period for acceptance, then the offer is binding and cannot be revoked before the expiry of that time period, unless of course it is rejected by the offeree at which point the offer would lapse (even before the end of the time period). However, if the offer does not fix a time period for acceptance it can be revoked before the contract is formed (which as we will see is when the acceptance reaches the offeror). It also cannot be accepted after the passing of what would be a reasonable period of time for acceptance under the circumstances (no offer is valid forever).[64]

[60] Law No 13 of 1985. [61] Law No 11 of 2008. [62] ibid art 18(1). [63] KUHPer, art 1365.
[64] Gautama (n 8) 81.

Satrio mentions that an offer that includes a specific time period for acceptance cannot be revoked before the end of that time period. The offer is said to be a unilateral act by which the offeror waives his right to withdraw the offer.[65] He gives the example of advertisements in newspapers for a sale on certain days or during a certain period of time. The seller will be bound by that offer only during that period of time.[66] Gautama agrees.[67] Presumably, as is the case in France, such offers by advertisement are assumed to be while stocks last.

It should be noted that offers to the public in general are binding—Satrio says that a rickshaw driver on the street is making an offer to anyone to ride in his rickshaw.[68] I am not sure I agree with this analysis. There is normally no fixed price for rickshaw rides in Indonesia nor (of course) is there a meter on rickshaws. The price must be negotiated in advance and, therefore, the rickshaw driver is not making an offer as the acceptance could not create a contract—all essential elements (including the price or a way of determining the price) are required for an offer to be valid. A contract should be formed when an offer is accepted but here, no contract is formed and there must be further negotiations. However, if we replace the rickshaw with a taxi (in Jakarta at least, where meters are the norm) then the taxi driver waiting for a passenger is making an offer which, if accepted, will form a valid contract. Note that Indonesian civil law does not have or need the common law concept of an 'invitation to treat'.

There may, however, be an exception to the offer to the public. It was held by a court that a merchant who puts its merchandise on display with prices is making a binding offer to the public. However, when the merchant refused to sell the goods to a competitor who came into his store, the court held that the valid offer to the public in general should be interpreted as not including the merchant's competitors.[69]

An offer which does not grant a specific period for acceptance can be revoked before the acceptance is received.[70]

It should be noted that in order to be binding, an offer must include all the *essential elements* of the contract. This is a much more stringent requirement than is the case in common law. In particular, a specific provision of the Civil Code provides that the contract of sale cannot be formed unless the parties had agreed on the price or a third party who will determine the price. Article 1465 KUHPer states: 'The sale price must be determined by the parties. The valuation, however, may be delegated to a third party. If the third party is unwilling or unable to do so, then no sale takes place.' The court will not be able to fix a reasonable price to save the contract.

For an offer to be binding, it must first be an offer, and it will be an offer only if a contract can be formed by a simple 'yes' as an acceptance. Therefore, for an offer to be binding it must have all the essential elements of the contract pursuant to the Code.

An attempted revocation during the time period granted for acceptance by the offeror will not be effective and the offeree will be able to accept the offer and form a contract. Similarly, an attempted revocation after the acceptance is received will be of no effect.

5. Good Faith in Contract Negotiation

It is quite clear that contracts must be performed in good faith:

[65] Satrio (n 22) 246. [66] ibid 246–247. [67] Gautama (n 8) 81. [68] Satrio (n 22) 249.
[69] ibid 250. [70] ibid 248.

Artikel 1338	**Pasal 1338**	**Article 1338**
Alle wettiglijk gemaakte overeenkomsten strekken dengenen die dezelve hebben aangegaan tot wet.	Semua perjanjian yang dibuat dengan sah berlaku sebagai undang-undang bagi mereka yang membuatnya.	All valid agreements apply to the individuals who have concluded them as law.
Zij kunnen niet berroepen wrden, dan met wederzijdsche toestemming, of uit hoofde der redenen welke de wet daartoe voldoende verklaart.	Perjanjian itu tidak dapat ditarik kembali selain dengan kesepakatan kedua belah pihak, atau karena alasan-alasan yang ditentukan oleh undang-undang.	Such agreements are irrevocable other than by mutual consent, or pursuant to reasons stipulated by the law.
Zij moeten te goeder trouw worden ten uitvoer gebragt	Perjanjian harus dilaksanakan dengan itikad baik.	They must be performed in good faith.
(Bw. 751, 1066, 1243v., 1266v., 1335v., 1363, 1603, 1611, 1646-3o, 1688, 1813; Civ. 1134).		(Bw. 751, 1066, 1243v., 1266v., 1335v., 1363, 1603, 1611, 1646-3, 1688, 1813; Civ. 1134)

This article is identical to the corresponding old article 1134 of the French Code and of the old Dutch Code. As was the case in France before the code was amended and was the case in the Netherlands before the adoption of the new Dutch Civil Code, the Indonesian Code does not have a general explicit obligation to act in good faith, but only has an obligation to perform contractual obligations in good faith.

In France, the courts have held that there is a general obligation to act in good faith even in the absence of a contract, including in the negotiation of a contract.[71] The courts have even developed a doctrine of abuse of right which applies in all contexts, including negotiations and the withdrawal of offers.

I should add, however, that Indonesian law does not seem to have a fully developed doctrine of abuse of right (French: *abus de droit*, Dutch: *Misbruik van Recht*, Indonesian: *penyalahgunaan hak*). Nonetheless, the concept is discussed by Satrio who refers to Dutch doctrine and also refers to the famous French case of *Doerr v Keller*,[72] decided in Colmar, France in 1856. In that case, the court condemned a property owner to damages for building a false chimney with the sole purpose of removing almost all the daylight left in his neighbour's window. This was held to be an abuse of right—a breach of a general obligation to act in good faith, not only in the performance of a contract but in all fields of law (this was an abuse of a property right).[73]

This doctrine is not well developed in Indonesia and Satrio devotes a few pages to it, referring to many old cases under the Dutch administration but none from Indonesian courts after independence in 1945.[74] However, interpreting the obligation of good faith to apply to the negotiation of the contract would be consistent with the French and Dutch civil law traditions and seem like a small step for an Indonesian court to take. In fact, there has been one Indonesian book entirely devoted to the abuse of circumstances (*penyalahgunaan keadaan* in Indonesian, *misbruik van omstandigheden* in Dutch) as a new source of nullity of contract following developments in the Netherlands.[75]

[71] Now codified in the new art 1112 of the French Civil Code.

[72] Colmar, 2 May 1855, DP 1856.2.9 (*Doerr v Keller*).

[73] J Satrio, *Hukum Perikatan—Perikatan yang Lahir dari Undang-Undang—Bagian Pertama* [*The Law of Obligations—Obligations Arising from the Law—Part One*] (2nd edn, Bandung: Citra Aditya Bakti 2001) 207.

[74] ibid 206–221.

[75] HP Panggabean, SH, *Penyalahgunaan Keadaan (Misbruik Van Omstandigheden) Sebagai Alasan (Baru) Untuk Pembatalan Perjanjian (Berbagai Perkembangan Hukum Di Belanda)* [*The Abuse of Circumstances (Misbruik van Omstandigheden) as a (New Ground) for the Nullity of Contracts (Different Legal Developments in the Netherlands)*] (Yogyakarta: Liberty 1992).

Another author, Madjedi Hasan, is of the view that the obligation to act in good faith applies not only to the performance of the contract but to its formation (negotiations):

> The principle of good faith laid down in Article 1338 is applicable both at the time of performance of this agreement and at the time the agreement was made. That is, an agreement is not valid if made based on bad faith, such as fraud and therefore the principle of good faith implies that the freedom of the parties to make an agreement is limited by good faith.[76]

The content of the obligation and the consequences of its breach are, however, unclear in Indonesian law. There is to my knowledge no jurisprudence or elaborate doctrine on the topic.

6. The Requirements for Acceptance and Delay in Acceptance

Professor Satrio goes into some detail as to when the contract is formed and explains which theory of contract formation Indonesian law accepts. He raises the issue of when the contract is formed by asking this question: 'if after there is an acceptance, but before the acceptance reaches the offeror, the offeror sends a message, for instance by telegram, stating that he withdraws the offer—was the contract formed?'[77]

He explains that the time at which the contract is formed is important to determine the transfer of risks, whether one can withdraw an offer, when the prescription (limitation period) starts, and where the contract is formed (at the place of the offeree or the offeror).[78]

Professor Satrio rejects the statement theory by which a contract would be formed when the offeree expressed his acceptance on paper and before he even attempts to send the acceptance. He also rejects the expedition or dispatch theory—which he mentions is the position in England—the postbox rule. He views that rule as unfair to the offeror who would be bound by contract without notice. He also rejects the knowledge theory (contract formed when the offeror learns of the acceptance—after actually opening the letter containing the acceptance and reading it, for example) and rejects as well the deemed knowledge theory (contract formed a reasonable time after the acceptance has been received).[79]

He states that the theory accepted by many scholars and by many court decisions is the reception theory—the contract is formed when the acceptance is received by the offeror.[80] He gives the example of a Dutch case in which the court held that the withdrawal of an offer received by the offeree after he had sent his acceptance but before the acceptance was received by the offeror, was a valid withdrawal of the offer. The contract was not formed.[81]

Subekti is of the same view: the contract is formed only when the acceptance is received. He states that, 'According to the teachings commonly adopted today, the agreement shall be deemed to be born at the time the offeror receives a response contained in a letter, because that precise time is what can be considered as the time of birth of the contract.'[82] Gautama also agrees: 'A written acceptance is effective upon receipt.'[83]

[76] 'Berlakunya asas itikad baik yang ditetapkan dalam Pasal 1338 tersebut mempunyai daya kerja baik pada waktu perjanjian dilaksanakan maupun pada waktu perjanjian itu dibuat. Artinya, suatu perjanjian tidak sah apabila dibuat berlandaskan itikad buruk, seperti penipuan dan karenanya asas itikad baik mengandung pengertian bahwa kebebasan suatu pihak dalam membuat perjanjian dibatasi oleh itikad baiknya.' M Hasan, *Kontrak Minyak dan Gas Bumi Berazas Keadilan dan Kepastian Hukum* (Jakarta: Fikahati Aneska 2009) 121–122.

[77] Satrio (n 22) 255. [78] ibid 256. [79] ibid 257–261. [80] ibid 261–262.

[81] Case of 'T. Bosch-V. Maren', HR 21 December 1933, reproduced in HR Hoetink, *Arresten Over Burgelijk Recht* (8th edn, Haarlem: Tjeen-Willink & Zoon 1951) 225; mentioned and translated in part in Satrio (n 22) 262–264.

[82] 'Menurut ajaran yang lazim dianut sekarang, perjanjian harus dianggap lahir pada saat pihak yang melakukan penawaran (*offerte*) menerima jawaban yang termaktub dalam surat tersebut, sebab detik itulah yang dapat dianggap sebagai detik lahirnya kesepakatan.' Subekti (n 31) 28.

[83] Gautama (n 8) 81.

It follows that the risk of loss of the acceptance in transit falls on the offeree. Concretely, in order to prove that he has a contract the offeree will have to prove, not that he has sent his acceptance but that it has been received. In practice, if acceptance is made in writing, the offeree will need to seek evidence of receipt from the mail or courier service he uses.

7. 'Battle of Forms'

As to formation of the contract, Indonesian law seems to take the classical position that the acceptance must be the mirror image of the offer, otherwise it is not an acceptance but a counter-offer.[84] The doctrine and the jurisprudence do not seem to have considered the situation where the offer and the acceptance do not correspond to one another and the parties nonetheless start the performance. Maybe the courts would simply decide that there was no contract, which is not necessarily the most practical or efficient solution. This is what Satrio suggests when he says that a conditional acceptance is not an acceptance but a counter-offer.[85] Indonesian jurisprudence and doctrine therefore do not use the concept of 'battle of forms' of the common law.

8. Vague or Uncertain Terms: Are Gaps in the Contract Filled?

As mentioned above, the offer must contain all the essential elements of the contract or it is not an offer. As was explained earlier, in the case of the contract of sale, unless the parties have agreed on a price or a person to fix the price, there will be no contract of sale: the judge cannot fill the gap. Therefore, some gaps cannot be filled.

It is therefore not perceived to be the role of the judges to fill in the gaps in the contract when the parties have not agreed on essential stipulations.

However (and this may seem contradictory), through interpretation the judge may often conclude that the intent of the parties in fact is clear and that there is no actual gap, notwithstanding the fact that the written contract seems to have a gap. As mentioned above, the judge may look at all and any evidence before and after the conclusion of the contract to find the true intention of the parties. As we saw earlier, article 1343 of the Civil Codes states, 'If the wording of an agreement is open to several interpretations, one should ascertain the common intent of the parties rather than be bound by the literal meaning of the words'. The ambiguity or gap may be filled in this manner.

If this is not sufficient to fill in a gap, the judge could use article 1339 of the Code (the translation in Dutch of old article 1135 of the French Civil Code):

Artikel 1339	**Pasal 1339**	**Article 1339**
Overeenkomsten verbinden niet alleen tot datgene hetwelk uitdrukkelijk bij dezelve bepaald is, maar ok tot al hetgeen dat, naar den aar van dezelve overeenkomsten, door de billijkheid, het gebruik of de wet, wordt gevorderd (AB. 15; Bw; 1347, 1482, 1492, 1800v., 1817, 1819; Civ. 1135).	Perjanjian tidak hanya mengikat apa yang dengan tegas ditentukan di dalamnya, melainkan juga segala sesuatu yang menurut sifatnya perjanjian dituntut berdasarkan keadilan, kebiasaan, atau undang-undang.	Agreements bind not only as to what is therein expressed, but also as to all the consequences that equity, usage, or law impose upon the obligation according to its nature. (AB.15; Bw. 1347v., 1482, 1492, 1800v., 1817, 1819; civ. 1135)

Therefore, the judge could fill the gap with usage or what is required by equity and fairness.

[84] Satrio (n 22) 237. [85] ibid 242.

9. Contracts Concluded Through Electronic Means

Law No 11/2008 concerning Electronic Information and Transactions governs any kinds of transactions concluded via computer, computer network, or other electronic media. It specifically provides that electronic information is considered to be received once such information enters the electronic system of the intended receiver (article 8 of Law 11/2008). Thus, in the case of contract formation, an acceptance of an offer is considered to have reached the offeror once the notice of acceptance enters the offeror's electronic system.

The Consumer Protection Act[86] does not impose any particular requirement as to form. There is no mention in the Civil Code of standard form contracts or, as we would say in civil law, of contract of adhesion.

10. Intention to Create Legal Relations

There is no specific test of intention to create legal relations and this is not a separate topic of study in civil law the way it is in common law.

It should, however, be repeated that the subjective intention of the parties is what is important in determining whether a contract has been formed and whether or not a contract is formed is an issue of fact. Therefore, the court would entertain arguments to the effect that there was no subjective intention to be bound by contract in the circumstances of the case.

For example, a newspaper advertisement of wares for sale at an erroneously low price would not be binding as a court would readily believe that, subjectively, the offeror had no intention of being bound at that price (normally newspaper advertisements are binding in Indonesia).[87] Similarly, a gentlemen's agreement would not be a binding contract if the parties did not so intend. It all goes to the subjective intent of the parties, taking into account all the circumstances (no parol evidence rule in Indonesia).

11. Gratuitous Promises

As mentioned earlier, in Indonesia, as in most jurisdictions following the French model, loans for consumption and deposits are unilateral real contracts. They are real contracts because they cannot be fully formed by consent alone—a loan for consumption is formed not when the parties agree on all the terms of the loan (offer and acceptance), but later, when the loaning party actually loans the thing or the money.[88] The same with the deposit: the contract is formed only when the thing is deposited.[89] Therefore, the contract is formed by the delivery of the thing. Why are loans and deposits not consensual or 'good faith contracts' in the French civil law tradition? Because it was like that in Rome—that is the best explanation I can provide.

Because the loan and deposit are formed only when the thing loaned or deposited is delivered, at the time the contract is formed, only one party has an obligation. If a bank agrees to lend me $1,000, the contract will be formed only when I am in possession of the $1,000. At that point, I will have an obligation to repay the bank with interest but the bank is likely not to have or ever have had any contractual obligation towards me—the bank was

[86] Law No 8 of 1999. [87] Gautama (n 8) 82.

[88] KUHPer, art 1754 (n 57). This provision is interpreted so that there is no contract until the thing loaned is actually physically transferred to the borrower.

[89] KHUPer, art 1697: [Translation:] 'The agreement [of deposit] is not deemed to have been consummated other than by actual or presumed delivery of the objects.'

never contractually obligated to give me the $1,000 since the contract was created only once it had already given it to me.[90] For that reason, that contract is unilateral—only one party has an obligation at the time the contract is formed. However, it is not gratuitous as the bank lends me the money in order to collect interest.

But, indeed, most unilateral contracts are also gratuitous: the contract of gift is the best example of a contract that is both unilateral and gratuitous.

Article 1314 KUHPer on gratuitous contracts states:

1314. Eene overeenkomst wordt aangegaan om niet, of onder eenen bezwaarden titel.	**1314.** Suatu perjanjian diadakan dengan cuma-cuma atau dengan memberatkan.	**1314.** An agreement is concluded gratuitously or onerously.
De overeenkomst om niet is de zoodanige waarbij de eene partij aan de andere, zonder eenige baat, een voordeel toekent.	Suatu perjanjian cuma-cuma adalah suatu perjanjian, bahwa pihak yang satu akan memberikan suatu keuntungan kepada pihak yang lain tanpa menerima imbalan.	The gratuitous agreement, is an agreement in which one party grants a benefit to the other party without any benefit in return.
Eene overeenkomst onder eenen bezwarende titel is zoodanig eene welke ieder der partijen in de verpligting brengt om iets te geven, te doen, of niet te doen (Bw. 1234, 1666; Civ. 1105v).	Suatu perjanjian memberatkan adalah suatu perjanjian yang mewajibkan tiap pihak untuk memberikan sesuatu, melakukan sesuatu atau tidak melakukan sesuatu.	An onerous agreement is an agreement in which each party is obligated to provide something, to do or not to do something. (Bw. 1234, 1666; Civ. 1105v.)

The civil law does not know the concept of consideration and therefore there is no objection to unilateral and gratuitous contracts being valid and enforceable. It reflects the greater moral emphasis of the civil law on the importance of performing one's promises once they are accepted.

As mentioned earlier, one of the formality required for a contract of gift is that it be in notarial form (unless it is a manual gift).[91] That requirement, however, does not apply to services offered for free. For example, if I offer to wash your car for free and you accept the offer, there is no need for a notarial deed as this is not a contract of gift (no ownership is transferred).

The remedies for non-performance and grounds of invalidity (or vitiation) are essentially the same as for onerous (or 'bilateral') contracts. However, in the case of a gift, article 1688 KUHPer (the exact equivalent of article 955 of the French Civil Code) provides that a gift can be revoked if the donee murders the donor or commits another crime against him, or if he refuses to support the donor after he has fallen into circumstances of poverty.

12. 'Bilateral' Contracts ('Consideration' at Common Law)

As mentioned earlier, under Indonesian law, consideration is not needed to form a contract. You can enforce a gratuitous contract as long as the party being granted the benefit has accepted that offer. This is no different from bilateral contracts.

As mentioned above, it is not the case that all gratuitous contracts need to be in writing. The contract of gift must be in notarial form but not if it is a manual gift. The contract by which I bind myself to wash your car for free is not a gift and need not be in writing.

[90] I will not discuss in this chapter the pre-contractual obligation of the bank to loan the money, save that a breach of this pre-contractual obligation would not give rise to the usual full contractual remedies.

[91] n 51.

As mentioned, there is normally no requirement of form for bilateral contracts, but again there are many exceptions (articles of associations, etc).

13. Case Study

The authors of the different chapters have been asked to consider the case study of 'the delayed building work': X contracts for Y to refurbish 27 flats for £20,000. However, Y ran into difficulties. X was concerned about having to pay a penalty under the head contract, and promised to pay Y an extra £10,300 to complete the work on time. Can Y enforce the additional £10,300?

The additional contact modifying the original contract would be enforceable. Consideration does not exist in Indonesian law and the concept of cause, which does exist, is different from consideration and does not prevent the formation of unilateral contracts, that is the unilateral modification of a contract without consideration.

III. Stipulations for the Benefit of Third Parties

There are no current doctrinal and theoretical debates concerning the contractual rights of third parties in Indonesia. There are hardly any writings on the topic. I have looked at about 20 books on contract law and could rarely find any mention of stipulations for third parties in them. When they do mention article 1317 KUHPer, they usually do not add much to the text of the article.

Only one author, Professor Satrio, spends 25 pages on the topic and what follows is in large part an account of Professor Satrio's work. Professor Satrio mentions mainly Dutch doctrine and cases on the matter. Although there are many Supreme Court cases that mention article 1317 KUHPer, I was unable to find seminal cases which would elaborate on the principles relating to stipulation for third parties.

1. Privity of Contract

The Civil Code has provisions that specifically state the principle of relativity of contracts (which is the terminology used in French civil law to describe what the common law calls privity of contract). Contracts, in principle, only have relative effects (ie effects between the parties to the contract). The general principle is stated in article 1315 KUHPer:

Artikel 1315	**Pasal 1315**	**Article 1315**
In het algemeen, kan niemand zich op zijnen eigen naam verbinden of iets bedingen, dan voor zich zelven (Bw. 1316, 1340, 1357, 1382v., 1645, 1655, 1792, 1820; Civ. 1119).	Pada umumnya seseorang tidak dapat mengadakan pengikatan atau perjanjian selain untuk dirinya sendiri (Bw. 1316, 1340, 1357,1382v., 1645, 1655, 1792, 1820; Civ. 1119).	In general, an individual may only commit to or agree to something for and on behalf of himself. (Bw. 1316, 1340, 1357, 1382v., 1645, 1655, 1792, 1820; Civ. 1119)

Article 1315 KUHPer is a translation of the French Civil Code:

Code civil des Français, article 1119	**French Civil Code, old article 1119**
On ne peut, en général, s'engager, ni stipuler en son propre nom, que pour soi-même.	As a rule, one may bind oneself and stipulate in his own name, only for oneself.

This principle is repeated in article 1340 KUHPer:

Artikel 1340	**Pasal 1340**	**Article 1340**
Overeenkomsten zijn alleen van kracht tusschen de handelende partijen. Dezelve kunnen aan derden niet ten nadeele verstrekken; zij kunnen aan derden geen voordee aambrengen, da alleen in het geval voorzien bij artikel 1317 (Bw. 1178, 1523, 1815, 1818, 1857; F. 152; Civ. 1165).	Perjanjian hanya berlaku antara pihak-pihak yang membuatnya. Perjanjian tidak dapat merugikan pihak ketiga; perjanjian tidak dapat memberi keuntungan kepada pihak ketiga selain dalam hal yang ditentukan dalam pasal 1317.	An agreement applies only to the parties thereto. An agreement cannot be detrimental to third parties; third parties cannot benefit from them, except for the case stipulated under Article 1317. (Bw. 1178, 1523, 1815, 1818, 1857; F.152; Civ. 1165)

This is again a translation of the French Civil Code:

Code civil des Français, article 1165	**French Civil Code, old article 1165**
Les conventions n'ont d'effet qu'entre les parties contractantes; elles ne nuisent point au tiers, et elles ne lui profitent que dans le cas prévu par l'article 1121.	Agreements produce effect only between the contracting parties; they do not harm a third party, and they benefit him only in the case provided for in Article 1121.

The Code recognizes the possibility of someone promising that a third party will do something: for example, A promises B that C will give a car to B, but in such a case only A is liable to B if C does not deliver—C cannot be bound by a contract he did not consent to. Therefore, a contract can never create obligations for third parties. Here is the relevant provision of the Code:

Artikel 1316	**Pasal 1316**	**Article 1316**
Niettemin kan men zich voor eenen derde sterk maken of instaan, door te beloven dat dezelve iets doen zal, behoudens de vordering tot schadevergoeding tegen dengene die voor eenen derde ingestaan of beloofd heeft denzelven iets te doen bekrachtigen, indien deze derde weigert om de verbindtenis na te komen (Bw. 1338, 1645, 1823, 1873; Civ. 1120).	Meskipun demikian adalah diperbolehkan untuk menanggung atau menjamin seorang pihak ketiga, dengan menjanjikan bahwa orang ini akan berbuat sesuatu, dengan tidak mengurangi tuntutan pembayaran ganti rugi terhadap siapa yang telah menanggung pihak ketiga itu atau yang telah berjanji, untuk menyuruh pihak ketiga tersebut menguatkan sesuatu, jika pihak ini menolak memenuhi perikatannya.	Notwithstanding this, an individual may guarantee the fulfilment of a third party's commitments, without prejudice to the claim for compensation of damages against the individual who has guaranteed the third party or has agreed to secure the third party, if such third party refuses to fulfil the contract. (Bw. 1338, 1645, 1823, 1873; Civ. 1120)

However, a contract may create rights or benefits for a third party, which is what the next article of the Code provides and which we will discuss in the next section. As we will see, 'Article 1317 KUHPer provides an exception that is so deep that the principle [of relativity of contract] has been undermined from within, so that it is almost empty'.[92]

After mentioning the two exceptions to the principle of relativity of contract—promise for another (article 1316) and benefits for third parties (article 1317)—the next article,

[92] Satrio (n 22) 107.

1318, restates the general principle of relativity in the form of a presumption against the creation of obligations or benefits for third parties:

Artikel 1318	**Pasal 1318**	**Article 1318**
Men wordt verondersteld bedongen te hebben voor zich zelven, en voor zijne erfgenamen en regtverkrijgenden, ten ware het tegendeel uitdrukkelijk bepaald zij, of uit den aard der overeenkomst mogt voortvloeijen (Bw. 175, 178, 807-1o, 833, 955, 1575, 1612, 1743, 1784, 1813, 1826; Civ. 1122).	Orang dianggap memperoleh sesuatu dengan perjanjian untuk diri sendiri dan untuk ahli warisnya dan orang yang memperoleh hak daripadanya, kecuali jika dengan tegas ditetapkan atau telah nyata dan sifat perjanjian itu bahwa bukan itu maksudnya (Bw. 175, 178, 807-1, 833, 955, 1575, 1612, 1743, 1784, 1813, 1826; Civ. 1122).	An individual shall be presumed to have entered into an agreement for his own benefit, and for the benefits of his successors and individuals having rights thereto, unless the contrary is expressly stipulated or is apparent from the nature of the agreement (Bw. 175, 178, 807-1, 833, 955, 1575, 1612, 1743, 1784, 1813, 1826; Civ. 1122).

2. Contracts for the Benefit of a Third Party

The Civil Code provides for the enforcement by third parties of the stipulations made for their benefit in a contract to which they are not parties.

The Code has only one article on stipulations for the benefit for a third party:

Artikel 1317	**Pasal 1317**	**Article 1317**
Men kan ook ten behoeve van eenen derde iets bedingen, wanneer een beding, hetwelk men voor zich zelven maakt, of eene gift die men aan een ander doet, zulk eene voorwaarde bevat.	Dapat pula diadakan perjanjian untuk kepentingan orang ketiga, bila suatu perjanjian yang dibuat untuk diri sendiri, atau suatu pemberian kepada orang lain, mengandung syarat semacam itu.	An individual may also enter into an agreement for the benefit of a third party, if such agreement, which the individual concludes on his own behalf, or gift granted by him to another party, contains a stipulation to this effect.
Die zoodanig een derde verklaard heeft, kan hetzelve niet meer herrroepen, indien die derde verklaard heeft daarvan te willen gebruik maken.	Siapa pun yang telah menentukan suatu syarat, tidak boleh menariknya kembali, jika pihak ketiga telah menyatakan akan mempergunakan syarat itu.	An individual, who has concluded such an agreement may not revoke it, if the third party has declared his intent to rely on it.
(Bw. 1323, 1338, 1669v., 1688, 1778, 1823; Civ. 1121).	(Bw. 1323, 1338, 1669v., 1688, 1778, 1823; Civ. 1121).	(Bw. 1323, 1338, 1669v., 1688, 1778, 1823; Civ. 1121).

This again is a translation in Dutch of the French Code (please note, however, the better English translation of that provision):

Code civil des Français, article 1121	**French Civil Code, old article 1121**
On peut pareillement stipuler au profit d'un tiers lorsque telle est la condition d'une stipulation que l'on fait pour soi-même ou d'une donation que l'on fait à un autre. Celui qui a fait cette stipulation ne peut plus la révoquer si le tiers a déclaré vouloir en profiter.	One may likewise stipulate for the benefit of a third party, where it is the condition of a stipulation which one makes for oneself or of a gift which one makes to another. He who made that stipulation may no longer revoke it, where the third party declares that he wishes to take advantage of it.

Let us first establish the terminology. Following the French terminology, which Satrio adopts, if A gives money to B in exchange for B's promise to give a car to C, A is the stipulator, B is the promisor of the benefit, and C is third party beneficiary.[93]

It is important to note that, notwithstanding the wording of the Indonesian and English translations of article 1317, it is not necessarily the whole contract which is for the benefit of the third party, it could be that only one of the stipulations of the contract is made for the benefit of a third party, the others being for the benefit of the stipulator (A). In French, we therefore speak of 'stipulation for a third party' (*stipulation pour autrui*) rather than contract for the benefit of a third party.

How should one interpret article 1317? If we were to interpret it literally, as Satrio explains, a stipulation for third parties would be allowed only if it meets either of two conditions or requirements (they are alternative, not cumulative conditions).

First, there could be a benefit for a third party if that benefit is a condition for a stipulation for the benefit of the stipulator (A). Basically, there could be a benefit for a third party only if the stipulator (A) also gets a different benefit from the promisor (B). A purely gratuitous contract would not be valid—for example, the following contractual benefit for the third party would be invalid: A to give money to B and B to give a car to C, but B would not give anything to A. Because A gets no benefit, it could not fit under the first condition.[94]

Second, and alternatively, the benefit could be valid if it is a condition of a gift to B. For example, the following benefit would be valid: A gives a million dollars to B on the condition that B gives a bicycle to C when he turns 21. There is clearly a gift to B and therefore the stipulation for a third party is valid.[95]

These alternate requirements overly limit the possibility of stipulating benefits for third parties: most of the time, when one wants to create a benefit for a third party, one does not want to get a benefit in return and one does not want to make a gift to the promisor. For instance, when the stipulator buys a life insurance for the benefit of her spouse and children, she does not want the insurance company to give her anything in return and she certainly does not want to make a gift to the insurance company in addition to the premiums she has to pay!

Beale describes how, in France, notwithstanding the same two requirements in the French Civil Code, the courts have effectively completely done away with them and now recognize stipulations for the benefit of third parties in all circumstances, almost *contra legem*:

> If the requirement of article 1121 C.civ. [ie the French Civil Code equivalent of article 1317 KUHPer] were taken seriously, a beneficiary of the life insurance policy would acquire an enforceable right against the insurer (promisor) only if either the insured (promisee) [or stipulator] were himself the beneficiary of a stipulation made for his benefit by the insurer or if the insurer had received something from the insured as a gift. The courts under pressure to recognize and enforce third parties' rights under insurance contracts, dismantled these restrictions. They held that the performance that a promisee [stipulator] must make to the promisor under article 1121 need not be a 'gift' in the technical sense; *any* performance, such as the payment of the premium will suffice. The alternative requirement of article 1121, that the promisee [stipulator] must at the time of the contract always stipulate something for himself, has been understood by the courts as being satisfied if any 'moral benefit' accrues to him as a result of the transaction. In the case of insurance such a *profit moral* exists in the insured's certainty that the insured sum will be paid to the third party on the occurrence of the insured event. Thus, the limiting requirements of article 1121 have been effectively struck out by the courts, since it is hardly conceivable that a promisee [stipulator] who intends to benefit a third party, by way of an insurance contract

[93] ibid 108–109. [94] ibid 109–112. [95] ibid 112.

> or any other agreement, does not derive at least a *profit moral* from the assurance that his intentions will eventually be implemented.
>
> The reinterpretation of Article 1121 C.civ. is part of a shift of attitude vis-à-vis contracts for the benefit of third parties that occurred in most continental jurisdictions toward the end of the nineteenth century. More modern codifications reflect this position.[96]

Dutch law evolved in the same direction as French law, and Indonesian law followed. After describing the two limiting requirements mentioned above, Satrio goes over a few Dutch cases in which the courts effectively refused to implement these alternative requirements and effectively allowed benefits for third parties to stand even if they did not strictly meet the requirements set in the Dutch equivalent of article 1317 KUHPer.

For example, Satrio mentions the Paul Kruger case in the Netherlands decided in 1914. In that case a man (A) made a loan to a museum (B) and stipulated that at the end of the loan either A or a third party (C) could claim back the artefacts that had been loaned. One of the problems with this arrangement was that if C claimed the artefacts, then A received no benefit and therefore the first requirement was not met (A did not get a benefit for himself while at the same time creating a benefit for C). The alternate requirement that A make a gift to B was not met either (a loan is not a gift). So, under a strict reading of the Dutch equivalent of article 1317 KUHPer, the benefit should have been held to be invalid.

The court noted the differences of opinion on how to interpret this article. It went on to decide that even though A could technically be said not to get a benefit from B if C claimed the benefit, the benefit for third party C was nonetheless valid. It was therefore sufficient that there be a potential rather than an actual benefit going to A. The court started to chip away at the requirement of article 1317![97]

Satrio then mentions a 1920 Dutch case in which the court enforced the following contract: A sells to B but B does not pay A, but instead pays C who are A's creditors. A does not get a benefit from B and A makes no gift to B, and therefore technically neither of the requirements of article 1317 are met. Nonetheless, the court recognized the benefit for the third party.[98]

In a 1924 case, the stipulator (A) argued that the promisor (B) owed him a benefit and tried to claim it arguing, on the basis of the equivalent of article 1317 KUHPer, that if he did not get a benefit from B, the benefit for the third party (C) would be invalid. The court stated that the intention of the parties (A and B) was to provide a benefit for the third party (C) and no benefit for A, and the court upheld the benefit for the third party as valid even though there was no benefit for A and even though there certainly was no gift to B. Basically, the court clearly ignored the two requirements—as long as the intent of the parties is to give a benefit to third parties, the fact that the requirements of article 1317 are not met lacks any consequence.[99]

This led Satrio to conclude that with these decisions, 'the terms of Article 1317 has been somewhat watered down', and to report that Dutch scholar Scholten has concluded that the benefit for a third party is always allowed, as long as it is not the only matter found in the agreement.[100] I should add that if the benefit for a third party was the only matter found in the contract (ie if A had no obligation and B had no other obligation than giving the benefit to C), then when the benefit is to give something to C, this would effectively be a gift

[96] H Beale et al, *Cases, Materials and Text on Contract Law* (2nd edn, Oxford: Hart Publishing 2010) 1174–1175. Text in square brackets added by this author.
[97] See *The Paul Kruger Case*, HR 26 June 1914, NJ 1914, 1028, as summarized in Satrio (n 22) 113–116.
[98] See *Wamerdam - Damen case*, HR 29 January 1920, summarized in Satrio (n 22) 116–117.
[99] See *Daalhuijsen - Goeting case*, HR 8 February 1924, summarized in Satrio (n 22) 118–121.
[100] Satrio (n 22) 120.

disguised as a benefit for a third party, probably for the purpose of avoiding the requirement that gifts be made by authentic deeds.[101] One can therefore understand the reluctance of the doctrine to allow benefits for third parties if the contract does not have any other obligation in it. The vast majority of contracts with a stipulation for a third party, however, are not disguised gifts. When A promises money to B and B promises to deliver a car to C, this is not a gift but a contract of sale with a benefit for a third party. It would be a disguised gift, however, if A made no promise to B (A has no obligation) and B unilaterally promised A that he would give a car to C—the only obligation is the giving of the car to C and it is therefore a gift disguised as a contract with a stipulation for a third party.

In the end, Satrio concludes that all that is required for the contract with a stipulation for a third party to be valid is that the stipulation for the third party be part of a valid agreement.[102]

Therefore, contracts with a benefit for third parties are valid in Indonesian law even if they do not strictly meet the two requirements found in article 1317 KUHPer.

I should add, however, that in order for the stipulation for the benefit of a third party to be binding, that is, for the stipulator to not be able to revoke it, the third party must 'declare his intent to rely on it' (article 1317 paragraph 2 KUHPer).[103]

Some would see this as a kind of acceptance of an offer: the contract offers a benefit to the third party, which becomes binding when it is accepted. This seems to be how a court in the Netherlands justified the binding nature of the benefit on the stipulator.[104]

However, Gautama hesitates to use the words 'offer' and 'acceptance' and reminds us that article 1317 KUHPer does not talk of an acceptance by the third party but of a 'declaration' of his intent to rely on it.[105] There is no indication in the Code as to the form which this declaration of intent should take.

Therefore, all that is required is a declaration and it does not say to whom the declaration should be made. In some jurisdictions, it has been held that even if the third party declares his intention to the promisor rather than stipulator, the benefit becomes binding—if the stipulator tries to revoke it, the promisor will simply inform him that he cannot because the third party has declared his intention to use it.[106] The position in Indonesia is not clear—no mention in the jurisprudence or doctrine—but the text of article 1317 ('declaration' instead of 'acceptance') would support such an interpretation.

Until the third party has declared his intention to take the benefit, the stipulator may revoke the benefit. That would not release the promisor from his promise, however. The stipulator would then simply become the beneficiary. If A promises money to B and B promises to give a car to C, until C has declared that he will take the benefit, A may revoke the stipulation for a third party. B would still have to deliver a car but to A rather than C.[107] The Code provides that A can revoke the benefit, not terminate the contract. The benefit therefore then goes to the stipulator (A) or to another person designated by him with compensation for any additional costs incurred by B.[108]

[101] n 51. [102] Satrio (n 22) 121. [103] See also ibid 124.

[104] See *Gouda—Government of the Netherlands case*, HR 13 February 1924, NJ 1924, 711, summarized in Satrio (n 22) 128.

[105] Gautama (n 8) 87.

[106] eg Quebec has codified decades of jurisprudence by adopting art 1446 in the Civil Code of Quebec: 'The stipulation may be revoked as long as the third person beneficiary has not advised the stipulator or the promisor of his will to accept it.'

[107] Satrio (n 22) 128.

[108] This is the case in French law: 'The stipulator may revoke the stipulation he made for the benefit of the third party and may transfer the benefit to another person or allocate it to himself personally.' F Terré et al, *Droit civil—Les obligations* (10th edn, Paris: Dalloz 2009) para 538.

(a) *Third party action in contract cannot be regarded as filling a gap in the law of tort in Indonesia*

As mentioned, the Indonesian civil law is part of the French tradition. Unlike the German tradition, the French tradition grants damages for pure economic losses in delict (the civil law equivalent of tort). Since French law is not 'defective' in that respect, there is no need to compensate for the defects of tort law by overly extending contract law as the German law does with the concept of *culpa in contrahendo*.

(b) *The third party's remedies*

There is not much said about this in Indonesian doctrine or jurisprudence. The third party can indeed enforce his benefit directly against the promisor.[109] The remedies would be the same remedy the stipulator could exercise, although again this is not mentioned in the doctrine or jurisprudence.

(c) *The promisor's defences*

The promisor would be entitled to use against the third party all the defences that he could raise against the stipulator. For example, Satrio mentions that, even after the third party has accepted the benefit, the stipulator may be entitled to demand that the contract be resolved (avoided) if the promisor is not performing his part of the bargain.[110] In such a case, effectively, the benefit would also become void and the promisor could raise against the third party the avoidance of the contract as his defence for not performing on the benefit. Can the debtor-promisor defeat the third party's claim for reasons specific to the third party (eg if the third party had induced the contract by misrepresentation to the debtor)? This question has not been addressed in Indonesian law, as far as I know. Whether the third party's misrepresentations could lead to a nullity of the contract would probably depend on whether his fraud (the civil law term for misrepresentation) could be considered a fraud 'by one of the parties' to the contract under article 1328 of the Code which reads as follows:

Artikel 1328	**Pasal 1328**	**Article 1328**
Bedrog levert eenen grond op tot vernietiging der overeenkomst, wanneer de kunstgrepen, door eene der partijen gebezigd, van dien aard zijn dat het klaarblijkelijk is dat de andere partij zonder die kunstgrepen de verbindtenis niet zoude hebbe aangegaan.	Penipuan merupakan suatu alasan untuk membatalkan suatu perjanjian, bila penipuan yang dipakai oleh salah satu pihak adalah sedemikian rupa, sehingga nyata bahwa pihak yang lain tidak akan mengadakan perjanjian itu tanpa adanya tipu muslihat.	Fraud is a cause of nullity of an agreement when the schemes and devices used by one of the parties are such that it is clear that without them the other party would not have contracted.
Bedrog wordt niet verondersteld, maar moet bewezen worden (Bw. 1053, 1065, 1449, 1865, 1922; Civ. 1116).	Penipuan tidak dapat hanya dikira-kira, melainkan harus dibuktikan.	Fraud is not presumed and must be proven. (Bw. 1053, 1065, 1449, 1865, 1922; Civ. 1116)

[109] Satrio (n 22) 127–129. [110] ibid 129.

(d) Variation or rescission of the benefit to the third party

We have discussed above that it is possible to revoke the stipulation before the third party has declared his intention to use it—the stipulation for a third party becomes binding only when the third party makes a declaration that he will take it.

After the third party has made such a declaration, article 1317 paragraph 2 KUHPer specifically states that the stipulation for the third party cannot be revoked. Presumably it could be modified or revoked with the consent of the third party and the promisor, but the doctrine and jurisprudence are silent on this.

3. Indirect Enforceability by Third Party Beneficiaries

This is not really an issue in Indonesia: since the contract can be directly enforced by the third party, there is no need to indirectly enforce it.

4. Enforceability by the Promisee-Contract Party

Indonesian law and doctrine are silent on this. Of course, the stipulator (promisee) can enforce the contract since he is a party, and as mentioned above, the third party can enforce the benefit, but the doctrine and jurisprudence in Indonesia do not go beyond that.

(a) Can performance remedies be ordered against the promisor, or damages for losses suffered by the promisee, or damages for the losses suffered by the third party (if so, does the promisee owe a duty to hand over the damages awarded), or any other judicial remedy?

No information was found in the Indonesian doctrine and jurisprudence available to me, but as would be the case for any other contract, the promisee (stipulator) and the beneficiary are entitled to the normal remedies available in Indonesian contract law.

(b) Is there a hierarchy between the claims of the promisee and any claims available to the third party (ie is the loss regarded as more properly belonging to one party)?

No information was found in the Indonesian doctrine and jurisprudence available to me.

(c) How is the promisor's potential risk of double liability dealt with?

Certainly, the promisor should not be doubly liable, however I could find no information in the Indonesian doctrine and jurisprudence available to me.

5. Case Studies

(a) Exemption clauses for stevedores

X contracts with Y to transport X's goods using Y's ship to a foreign market. The contract for the carriage of goods by sea between X and Y contains an exemption of liability provision which purports to protect Z, the stevedores hired to unload X's goods from Y's ship once it arrives at the docks. As a result of Z's carelessness, X's goods are damaged while they are being unloaded from the ship and X wants to sue Z for negligence to recover damages for the losses suffered by X. Can Z rely on the exemption of liability provision in the contract between X and Y?

There is to my knowledge no case in Indonesia where the benefit for a third party was a clause exempting the third party from liability. However, arguing from first principles, the clause would not be binding (ie could be revoked) until Z accepts it. Who is promising the benefit here (promisor) and who is the stipulator? It seems to me that it is X who is the promisor since the exemption clause is to its detriment and therefore Y is the stipulator (promisee). Y would not be likely to want to revoke the benefit.

There is, however, no case and no doctrine on this point in Indonesia.

(b) Selling bread

X leases two adjoining properties to Y and Z. The lease between X and Y barred Y from selling bread because Z sold bread from his leased property. Can X and Y agree to lift the bar?

Again, from first principles and assuming that the lease between X and Y mentioned Z, if Z accepted the benefit, then the benefit could not be revoked. To modify the benefit to Z, his consent would be required. But if the contract between X and Y does not specifically attribute the benefit to Z, then Z would have no right as the prohibition against selling bread would not be a stipulation for him as a third party.

(c) The stolen shop takings

X bank makes a contract for Y security company to collect Z store's takings. The contract requires Y to use armoured vehicles and take out insurance. Y failed to do these and the takings were stolen while being collected in an ordinary car. Can Z sue?

These facts are taken from a French case.[111] The main point of interest in that case is that the third party was not named in the contract and in fact there was no clause that made clear that the use of armoured vehicle was meant for the benefit of third parties—the court was of the view that the promisor should have understood that the compulsory use of armoured vehicles was for the benefit of unnamed third parties. But it should be noted that the *Cour de Cassation* (Supreme Court) only repeated the reasons of the *Cour d'appel* as the *Cour de Cassation* does not have jurisdiction on issues of fact and whether there is a stipulation for a third party is an issue of fact.

There is, to my knowledge in Indonesia, no instance where article 1317 has been extended to situations where there is no mention of third parties in the contract. Arguing from first principles, the beneficiary would be Z and the stipulator X. Therefore, Y could not revoke the benefit, only X could. If Z declares its intent to take the benefit before it is revoked it could no longer be revoked and presumably Z could sue. The fact that Z did not declare its intent before the events should not be relevant—the benefit existed all along, the declaration is not an acceptance but simply prevents the revocation of the benefit. But this answer is highly speculative and tentative as I am unaware of any doctrine or case precisely on point.

IV. Conclusion

Indonesian contract law does not provide all the answers to the questions raised. For all kinds of reasons, the jurisprudence is not as developed and as reliable as it is in many other

[111] Cass civ, 1er ch civ, 21 novembre 1978, JCP 1980.I.19315, note P Rodière.

civil law jurisdictions. One of the reasons might be that large commercial disputes are often settled by arbitration as the courts in Indonesia do not have the best of reputations.

The doctrine—the writing mainly of law professors—so essential in a civil law system, is also not as developed as it is in other jurisdictions. The fact that the Code is still in Dutch does not make it very attractive for young scholars. In Indonesia, we have seen a much more prolific development of doctrine in public law (which is in Indonesian) than in private law (which is still in large part in Dutch).

Notwithstanding the shortcomings of Indonesian civil law in terms of doctrine and jurisprudence, it clearly stands well within the French model of the civil law tradition as opposed to the German model followed in East Asia. On both topics—formation of contracts and stipulations for third parties—Indonesian civil law is very close to still recent French law and to former Dutch law, as is to be expected given they shared essentially the same Code.

That tradition stands in contrast to the common law in its willingness to bind people on the basis of their promises alone (no consideration) hence an offer can be binding and so can a benefit for a third party.

19

Formation of Contract, Enforceability, and Pre-Contractual Liability in Thailand

*Pattarapas TUDSRI & Angkanawadee PINKAEW**

I. Introduction

1. Brief History of the Civil and Commercial Code of Thailand

The modern scheme of Thai contract law is a legacy of the major reform of the Siamese[1] justice system during the reigns of Kings Rama V and VI, which ultimately produced the codifications of the Penal Code of 1908 as well as the Civil and Commercial Code of 1925 ('Thai CCC').[2] Prior to the codification, the provisions governing contract law were drawn primarily from two sources. The first was the written law on nominate contracts as prescribed in the ancient Law of the Three Seals[3] and subsequent legislation.[4] By the late nineteenth century, these laws were immensely outdated; they had no general applications and primarily governed the few particular types of contracts they were designed to address.[5]

The second source was the common law of England that was taught in Thai universities and alluded to by Thai judges. The relevance of English law in the Thai justice system can be traced back to the second half of the nineteenth century, the era in which Siam witnessed a rapid expansion in international commerce, an unprecedented level of contact with Western tradesmen, and a threat from the colonial ambitions of the foreign sovereigns.[6] With trade disputes often having unfavourable outcomes for foreign subjects, the European colonial powers criticized the local law for anachronism and pressured Siam for treaties granting extraterritorial rights to their consular courts. To appease the demands of the foreign sovereigns as well as to compensate for deficiencies of the local law, the Siamese Government contemplated a major overhaul of the existing legal system. However, in the beginning, a complete codification of law was thought to take considerable time. To respond to the more immediate need, the

* Cite as P Tudsri & A Pinkaew, 'Formation of Contract, Enforceability, and Pre-Contractual Liability in Thailand' in Chen-Wishart, Loke, & Vogenauer, *Studies in the Contract Laws of Asia Vol II: Formation and Third Party Beneficiaries* (Oxford: OUP 2017) ch 19. The authors are indebted to Dr Alexander Loke, Professor of Law at City University of Hong Kong, for constructive comments on the drafts of this chapter, as well as to the participants at the conference which resulted in the publication of chapters in this volume. Much is also owed to the enthusiastic assistance of teaching assistants at Chulalongkorn University.

[1] Siam officially adopted the name 'Thailand' for the first time in 1939. However, the adjective 'Thai' may also refer to the Thai people who comprised the majority of the Siamese population. This chapter only uses 'Siam' or 'Siamese' to refer to matters pertaining to the pre-1939 kingdom or government.

[2] Rama V (1868–1910); Rama VI (1910–25). The first drafting committee was formed immediately after the conclusion of the drafting of the Penal Code in 1908, which eventually led to the first enactment of the Code in 1925.

[3] The Law of the Three Seals is a collection of ancient law texts compiled in 1805 after the collapse of Ayutthaya (1351–1767), Siam's predecessor kingdom.

[4] S Boonchalermvipas, *The Thai Legal History* (8th edn, Bangkok: Winyuchon Publication 2009) 204.

[5] R Lingat, *The Thai Legal History, Vol II* (Bangkok: Thai Watana Panich Press 1983) 281.

[6] P Kasemsup, *Introduction to Jurisprudence for First Year Undergraduates I* (Bangkok: Jaroenpol Press 1983) 31–33; R Guyon, 'Revision and Drafting of the Thai Codes (Part II)' translated by P Punyapan and C Kemacharu (1959) 6(5) Dulapaha 255–256.

Formation of Contract, Enforceability, and Pre-contractual Liability in Thailand. Pattarapas Tudsri and Angkanawadee Pinkaew.

adoption of English common law was seen as an optimal solution. While the local law retained its primary applicability, English rules were routinely applied in a piecemeal fashion where there were deficits in the local law.[7] English law never formally carried the force of law in Siam, yet the Thai legal academics and judges in the late nineteenth and early twentieth centuries, often graduates from English universities, were well acquainted with it.

The significance of the English common law in Siam, however, diminished following the codification of the Thai CCC. The codification committee drafted the Code, employing the German Civil Code of (*Bürgerliches Gesetzbuch*, 'BGB') and the Japanese Civil Code of 1898 (民法: 'Minpō') as primary models. The French Civil Code of 1804 and the Swiss Civil Code of 1907 were also consulted as secondary models along with the customary law of Siam.[8] This culminated in the Thai CCC of 1925, which has remained in force until today.

Two important remarks should be made on the history of codification; first, the drafts of the contract law provisions in the Thai CCC were heavily influenced by French law. The reason is that the original drafts of Books I and II of the Code that were finished in 1923 were modelled primarily on the French Civil Code.[9] Notably, the drafts contained no references to the notion of 'juristic act'—the very notion that characterizes the modern version of Book I as well as the modern thinking on the Thai law of obligations. The drafts of 1923, however, faced heavy criticism by judges for their unintelligibility, and they never came into force. The codification committee went on to revise the drafts, this time using the BGB and Minpō as primary models.[10] The subsequent drafts produced by this committee led to the promulgation of the revised version of the Thai CCC in 1925. As a result, the modern provisions of Thai contract law exhibit traits of German, Japanese, and French law.

Second, the complete redrafting based on the models of the BGB and Minpō was done within a short span of time from 1923 to 1925. The Western powers and their colonial governments in Indochina had been pressuring Siam, conditioning the cancellation of the Extra-Territorial Jurisdiction Treaties on Siam's adoption of a civil code. The result was the swiftly drafted Code that lacked the intricacies and depths of its models. Yet, judges became strictly bound by the language of this Code; they felt increasingly reluctant to exercise the interpretative and scrutinizing powers at the level that they once had. A return to judge-made law risked establishing judicial imperialism, usurping the role of the Code and doing disservice to the country's newly reformed civil justice system. The court's perception of its role as a defender of the Code is long-lasting. Judges—and, indeed, many academics—today seem to adhere to a strict interpretation and literal reading of the Code. The stringency of the Code's interpretation represents the general trend that emerges from an examination of the academic debates and the Supreme Court's judgments presented in this chapter.

2. Contract Law in the Modern Civil and Commercial Code

The modern Thai CCC arranges the rules applicable to contract within Books I to III. The first Book, entitled 'General Provisions' (sections 1–193), provides, inter alia, for the general rules on 'juristic acts'. The rules concerning capacity to contract, declaration of intention, formality, and validity of juristic acts (voidness and voidability) are prescribed in this book.

[7] P Kasemsup, 'Reception of Law in Thailand, A Buddhist Society' in M Chiba (ed), *Asian Indigenous Law* (London: KPI Ltd 1986) 267, 292–293.

[8] C Sawaengsak, *Influence of France on the Reformation of Thai Law* (Bangkok: Nititham Publishing 1996) 68.

[9] ibid 50–51.

[10] *Report of the Drafting Committee Meeting on 25th May 1925* (Library of the Office of the Council of State 1925); *Transcription of the Interview with Phraya Manawaratchasewi* (Division of Social, Historical and Philosophical Law Study, Faculty of Law, Thammasat University 1982) 4, 44.

Book II, 'Obligations' (sections 194–452), deals with formation, effects, and termination of contract. The provisions in these two books comprise the general rules of contract law—the default rules applicable to all contracts. Further rules that set out the particularities of certain nominate contracts are found in Book III, 'Specific Contracts', which encompasses, for instance, the contract of sale, hire of things, and hire of labour.

This chapter divides the discussion on formation and enforceability of contract into three sections. Section II.1 concerns the provisions of Book I; namely, the general rules on 'juristic acts'. 'Juristic act' is a preliminary concept, yet it is essential to understanding the constituent elements of a contract as well as the validity of the declaration of intention. The rules identified in this section ('fictitious intention' and 'concealed juristic act') relevantly point, first, to whether a contract is validly declared and, second, to its juridical nature. The discussion on formalities is also placed in this section because it is concerned with the question of whether the declaration of intention is legally effective. Furthermore, the segment on formalities implicates two important issues. The first is the re-characterization exercise engaged in by the Thai courts, whereby a particular kind of contract which fails for lack of formality can be 'rescued' through reinterpretation as a valid agreement of another kind ('transforming a void act'). The second is the view in academia which advocates permission for contracting parties to circumvent certain formality requirements by setting up an informal, yet legally effective, preliminary agreement to formally conclude a contract on a later date ('preliminary agreement'). In addition, as the discussion on the effectiveness of a declaration of intention intersects both synallagmatic (or reciprocal) contracts as well as gifts (which some civilian jurisdictions including Thailand regard as a nominate contract), a section on the creation of gifts will also be included in this section.

Section II.2 deals with the provisions of Book II which primarily engage the rules on offer and acceptance. Finally, section III discusses the suggestions as to how the Thai CCC may impose pre-contractual liability for breaking off from contractual negotiations without good reasons.

II. Formation and Enforceability of Contract

1. General Rules on Juristic Acts

Juristic acts, which include (but are not limited to) all contracts, are defined in section 149 as:

> voluntary lawful acts, the immediate purpose of which is to establish between persons relations, to create, modify, transfer, preserve or extinguish rights.

Book I lays down the four composite elements of juristic acts: a person's capacity (section 153), object (sections 150 and 151), intention (sections 154 and 155), and formality (section 152). In this chapter, only the last three elements will be discussed.

(a) Object

Thai law requires that every juristic act has an object—an ultimate purpose of the person making the declaration of intention to do a juristic act; a purpose that can be achieved through that juristic act.[11] A contract, itself a category of juristic acts, must also bear an object. The object of a contract must be legal, determined, or determinable; the court which is asked to enforce the contract must be able to know what it is that is to be enforced. 'Object' is thus used

[11] eg Supreme Court Decision No 521/2489, considering whether a lease of property 'as a place of business of a co-operative as well as residence' had as its object a commercial lease or residential lease; only the latter would fall within the scope of certain rent-controlling legislation enacted in the aftermath of the Second World War.

to prevent one party from being able to arbitrarily fix the content of the contract. Its absence in the Germanic system suggests that the object requirement in the Thai CCC was derived from the Franco-Romanistic systems.[12] In the contract of sale, for instance, the object of the contract on the part of the purchaser is to acquire ownership of property; the vendor's object is to obtain price payment. Interestingly, Thai law does not make a meaningful distinction between what French lawyers consider as an *objet*—the subject matter of the contract—and a *cause*—the particular purpose for which the contract is entered into.[13] In Thai law, the understanding of 'object' is wide enough to subsume both the French notions of *objet* and *cause*.

Prior to the enactment of the Thai CCC, the English rule of consideration was applied by the Thai courts,[14] and the agreement in which only one party was obliged to act was not regarded as a binding contract.[15] This requirement of consideration was, however, abrogated with the introduction of the Thai CCC. It is on this note that early writings on Thai contract law contrasted the Code's notion of object with the rule of consideration.[16] Both concepts served to distinguish an actionable contract from a bare agreement; yet, unlike consideration, the post-codification rule that a contract must carry an object did not require that there be any objective value. Under the Thai CCC, a unilateral promise is an enforceable juristic act under the general provisions on obligations.[17] Gifts of property also compose a category of specific contracts regulated in Book III[18] and are enforceable as contracts provided that the formality requirement is met.[19]

Though object retains its distinct status as one of the four essential elements of contract in standard Thai contract law textbooks, the explanation of it rarely lasts beyond a few paragraphs. This is understandable since modern contract disputes turn on detailed arrangements between the parties, often concluded in writing or other forms which clearly spell out the scope of each party's obligations. Nonetheless, the requirement of object remains relevant for one practical reason: the prohibition in section 150 of a contract with an illicit object entitles the courts to discern the parties' motives in reaching an agreement. This is perhaps a major qualification to the conception of motive as internal in the mind of one party which is generally not of concern to his contracting partner. The internal motivation of a purchaser of a car as a vehicle for his illegal activities such as drug dealing would not normally invalidate the sale. Nonetheless, if an illicit motive is known to the other party, the motive would form part of the object of the contract.[20] Such a contract is void.

(b) Intention

Another important aspect of a juristic act is that it must be intended to have legal effect, or to create legal relations. The intention to render mere acts of kindness or generosity or arrangements relating to social or domestic occasions, such as a promise to invite a friend for a treat or a promise to attend a friend's wedding, would be insufficient to support a contract.

[12] arts 1126–1130, French Civil Code. See O Lando and H Beale (eds), *Principles of European Contract Law* (The Hague: Kluwer International 2000) 148.

[13] There is also a debate in French law whether the notion of cause retains a distinct practical utility. For an argument that it does, see E Steiner, *French Law: A Comparative Approach* (Oxford: OUP 2010) 331–333.

[14] Supreme Court Decision No 478/2464.

[15] Supreme Court Decision No 343/2465.

[16] S Pramoj, *Civil and Commercial Code: Juristic Acts and Obligations (Parts I–II), Vol II* (Bangkok: Sawaengsutthikanphim Painting 1978) 340.

[17] s 213. [18] s 521. [19] ss 524–526.

[20] See the dictum in Supreme Court Decision No 1124/2512 (banking contract valid despite banker having no banking licence; client unknowing of lack of licence).

In assessing whether a juristic act is formed, and if so, the nature of the juristic act, the touchstone in the Thai CCC is the subjective intention of the parties. Section 171 provides:

> [I]n the interpretation of a declaration of intention, the true intention is to be sought rather than the literal meaning of the words or expressions.

Formation thus essentially depends on the parties' subjective intention. Where the declaration of intention does not accurately reflect the subjective intention to form a particular kind of contract, the Thai CCC provides three rules to determine whether the contract has been formed. Section 154 deals with a situation where one party's intention is 'hidden' from the other. Section 155 covers two varieties of untruthful manifestation of intention that is mutual to both parties: section 155(1) concerns the rule of 'fictitious intention' while section 155(2) deals with a 'concealed juristic act'.

(1) Hidden intention

The rule in section 154 is relatively straightforward. It provides that a hidden intention of one party has no bearing on the validity and the objective meaning of the contract—unless the hidden intention is known to the other party. Where the hidden intention is known, there cannot be serious intention to contract, and the purported agreement would be a nullity.

(2) Fictitious intention

In the second rule, section 155 reads:

> (1) A declaration of intention made with the connivance of the other party which is fictitious is void; but its invalidity cannot be set up against third persons injured by the fictitious declaration of intention and acting in good faith.
>
> (2) If a declaration of fictitious intention under paragraph one is made to conceal another juristic act, the provisions of law relating to the concealed act shall apply.

In the inquiry into the alleged fictitiousness under section 155(1), the court will consider the nature and effect of the contractual arrangements, the attendant circumstances, and the parties' motives in structuring the contract as it appears. For example, a registered contract for sale of land was held to be void where there was no price payment and the conveyance was designed purely to frustrate a prior (unregistered but valid) agreement to buy and to sell.[21]

It is possible that the inquiry may reveal some parts of the agreement to be fictitious and the other parts to be a genuine declaration of intention. Only the latter will have a binding effect. For example, in Supreme Court Decision No 2952/2554, the defendant defaulted on a loan and faced a foreclosure threat to her dwelling. As the defendant had no credit standing, her applications for new loans were rejected. The plaintiff's sister, Suporn, offered to help. She devised a plan in which the defendant would obtain financing by having the plaintiff purchase the land and obtain a mortgage using the plaintiff's credit. The defendant was permitted to continue living on the land as a tenant in a lease agreed with the plaintiff as part of the sale agreement, which included a condition that the rent would be forwarded to the bank as mortgage repayment instalments. Suporn also asked to occupy half of the land, agreeing that she and the defendant would each be responsible for half of the mortgage loan, and at the end of the mortgage term Suporn and the defendant would each be entitled to half of the property. One and a half years into the lease, the defendant defaulted on the rent payments and the plaintiff sought to evict the defendant.

[21] Supreme Court Decision No 2041/2547.

The court investigated the surrounding circumstances and stated that it would not honour the sale and lease arrangements as they were fictitious. It was never the intention of the parties that the plaintiff would be the sole proprietor of the land. However, the court found that the collateral agreement which would grant half an interest in the property to both the defendant and Suporn accurately reflected the parties' mutual intention. They had demarcated the precise plots of land on which each would build a house to inhabit. Consequently, the court concluded that the parties intended the defendant to be an owner in common upon commencement of a payment on the mortgage instalments, and accordingly the court refused to grant an order for eviction. Through the use of its explorative and interpretative powers, the court was able to discover the parties' true intention and sanctify the declaration of that intention. Though the main contract was void for lack of serious intention, the collateral agreement was effective to grant Suporn and the defendant specific shares in the property.

Section 155(1) also lays down the rule that the fictitious intention cannot be set up against a third party who acts in good faith and whose right is jeopardized by the invalidity resulting from the fictitious intention. For instance, the defendant purchaser of shares could not invoke the invalidity of a transfer of unpaid shares when the company made a call for the unpaid amount on the defendant, whose name still remained as shareholder in the company's share register.[22]

This provision seems to safeguard against asymmetry that may otherwise result from the invalidity due to fictitious intention. Take, for example, Decision No 2952/2554 mentioned earlier; if the plaintiff-mortgagor was ordered to re-convey the land, thus having no title or ownership rights, what would become of the mortgage between her and the lending bank? Asymmetry could result as regards the bank's position if the court's re-conveyance order were to defeat the security of the loan made to the mortgagor. However, if the invalidity could not be invoked against the bank, the ownership rights of the new owners (the defendant and Suporn) must be subject to the same encumbrances affecting the land before it was re-conveyed. The end result could be that the bank still had a valid claim under a contract of loan with the plaintiff secured by a mortgage on the land now held in the defendant and Suporn's names; and the defendant and Suporn would still be required to keep up with the instalments under a valid collateral agreement with the plaintiff. From the bank's perspective, there were no material changes in the financing arrangements: the debt was still personally owed by the plaintiff and secured by a mortgage on the very same piece of property.

(3) Concealed juristic act

The third rule, contained in section 155(2), governs situations where the declaration of fictitious intention is made in order to conceal another juristic act. In such cases, while the juristic act as expressed is void, the concealed juristic act which reflects the true mutual intention will be enforced if the formality or evidentiary requirements of the concealed act are duly met in the contract document. Here, the formality requirements of the concealed act may be satisfied by the express act if both transactions have analogous purposes. Hence, while the concealed sale of property may not be enforced when expressed and registered as a lease, a gift of property may be valid notwithstanding that the written contract is expressed and registered as a sale. Thai courts have held that a sale and a gift carry an analogous purpose; namely, the disposition of property.[23] The fact that one is a gratuitous contract while the other is reciprocal does not prevent the court from enforcing the parties' real intention,

[22] Supreme Court Decision No 848/2534.
[23] Supreme Court Decisions No 1871/2549; No 6342/2552.

which is to grant title to the disponee. In other cases, a sale arrangement may be found to conceal a contract of loan of money; a written contract of sale may also satisfy the evidentiary requirements of a loan agreement.[24]

The court will investigate the circumstances in order to reach a conclusion on the parties' actual intention. Interestingly, in determining that the parties do *not* intend to conceal a juristic act, the courts have frequently referred to the parties' knowledge of the differences in the nature of the express transaction and the transaction that is alleged to be concealed.[25] For instance, a contract of loan made by a banker was held not to conceal a contract of agency for loans since the banker must have been fully aware of the difference between the two transactions.[26] These judgments have been criticized for the reason that a party's knowledge should be irrelevant;[27] if anything, existence of the knowledge is indicative of the possibility that there might be a concealed juristic act. This argument does carry some weight. However, there may as well be an underlying, albeit unstated, judicial presumption that a knowledgeable person would, acting in good faith, intend a juristic act as it is expressed. The cases perhaps reveal a general reluctance of the court to intervene where evidence of a concealed juristic act or a fictitious intention is at best equivocal.

Whether there is a concealed juristic act for the courts to enforce is fact-sensitive. For example, the courts, in deciding that a gift is concealed within a document expressed as a sale, have been persuaded by evidence showing that the donor did not wish to reveal to the claimant (usually the donor's heir/estate) that the gift was made to the defendant-donee,[28] or that the property had earlier been given to the donor as a gift that was also expressed as a sale.[29] Furthermore, the court may hold that a particular transaction is designed to conceal another juristic act where the parties' choice of transaction indicates an attempt to evade the mandatory rules of some legislation that would otherwise be applicable. In Supreme Court Decision No 6532/2544, a mortgage contract coupled with a contract to create right of superficies over the land was held to be an arrangement that concealed an agreement to buy and to sell land, the sale of which was prohibited for a period of ten years by certain legislation. The concealed sale was therefore void for illegality.[30]

A number of reported judgments concern a contract of loan which was expressed as a sale, or a sale with the right of redemption. For example, in Supreme Court Decision No 1050/2536 the court examined a transaction between Muslim relatives. As lending money with interest contravened Muslim beliefs, the parties chose to document the transaction as a sale. In exchange for the funds, the vendor agreed to sell a rubber estate to the purchaser; such a sale would result in the purchaser having usufruct over the plantation, which was intended as an alternative to an interest payment in cash. The apparent sale would also prevent foreclosure by the vendor's creditors. The evidence led the court to conclude that the parties had intended the transaction to be a loan, and the court accordingly rejected the purchaser's motion for conveyance registration. Similarly, in Supreme Court Decision No 1441/2545, a concealed loan was found where the transaction registered as a sale of land with the right of redemption was done at a very low price; the purchaser accepted deposit of the title deed only as security and not for the purpose of effecting conveyance;[31] and the parties simultaneously agreed on a separate unsecured loan of a much higher figure which

[24] Supreme Court Decisions No 1050/2536; No 4696/2536; No 3946/2533.

[25] Supreme Court Decisions No 4007/2552; No 2405/2551.

[26] Supreme Court Decision No 4007/2552.

[27] S Sotthibandhu, *Juristic Acts—Contracts* (18th edn, Bangkok: Winyuchon Publication 2014) 116, fn 13.

[28] Supreme Court Decision No 1871/2549.

[29] Supreme Court Decision No 6342/2552.

[30] See also Supreme Court Decision No 1136/2540.

[31] See also Supreme Court Decision No 4696/2536 (delivery by the vendor to the purchaser 'to simply keep' and 'not to use' a car was indicative of a concealed loan with the car pledged as security).

also included the payment already made under the sale. As a result, the court found the sale with the right of redemption to be void and declined the purchaser's motion for eviction. The agreement was enforced as a loan, with the title deed pledged as security.

While Thai judges possess extensive interpretative powers to work out the intention of contracting parties, one should be wary of overestimating the boundaries of those powers. The test of subjective intention under section 171 may arguably permit judges a potentially wide margin of discretion but, as the Supreme Court's judgments demonstrate, unless it is clear from the circumstances that an express juristic act is not the transaction intended, the judges are unlikely to intervene. Therefore, where the contracting parties have a choice of legal forms, such as between the permissible forms of secured transactions,[32] the court will regard their choice as legitimate; and hence not involving a concealed act. The court thus rejected the 'borrower's' argument that a simple loan had been intended when the 'borrower' made an application for the 'lender' to obtain a car for the purpose of reselling to the 'borrower' on a hire-purchase agreement.[33] Similarly, a hire purchase was upheld when the financing company, the 'lender', promised to sell to the 'borrower' a car the title to which it had yet to obtain.[34] These arrangements were legitimate businesses falling within the objectives of the financing companies and hence were not designed to conceal an unsecured loan. In other cases, a sale of land with the right of redemption was held not to be a concealed mortgage where it was not shown that instalment repayments of interest were made periodically,[35] or where the vendor openly contemplated the choices before the registration officer.[36]

(c) Formality and evidentiary requirements

In Thai law, as in other systems, formality and evidentiary requirements generally serve three functions. First, specific forms may be required to ensure that there is serious intention, and thus also protect a party from the risk of abuse. These include, for example, writing and registration requirements for dispositions—whether in the form of a sale, an exchange, or a gift—of assets that the law deems substantial.[37] Second, some formalities are compulsory in order to give notice to third parties whose rights may potentially be affected by the contract. These include registration for contracts that alter rights in or over land and certain other kinds of property,[38] a lease with the duration of three years or over or with the duration of the lifetime of the lessor or lessee,[39] and a contract of mortgage;[40] and a requirement that an assignment of debts needs to be made in writing.[41] Third, written evidence may have some probative value: surety contracts,[42] short-term leases,[43] and a loan of an amount of 2,000 baht and over are required to be evidenced in writing.[44] In the absence of written evidence, for some juristic acts the existence of a contract may also be attested by the giving of earnest money or part performance. This latter rule applies to an agreement or

[32] The range of transactions secured by property permitted by the Thai CCC is rather limited; viz pledge, mortgage, hire purchase, and sale with the right of redemption. Other permissible forms of security were few and governed by specific legislation until a recent major reform which culminated in the enactment in 2015 of the Business Collateral Act BE 2558 (2015). See also Cars (15th Instalment) Act BE 2551 (2008), permitting the creation of charges over cars.

[33] Supreme Court Decision No 2899/2545.

[34] Supreme Court Decision No 7308/2545.

[35] Supreme Court Decision No 2405/2551.

[36] Supreme Court Decision No 391/2534.

[37] ss 456 (sale); 519 (exchange); 525 (gift). The prescribed categories of property include ships or vessels of 6 tons and over, steam launches or motor boats of 5 tons and over.

[38] ss 456 (sale); 525 (gift); 1299 (acquisition of immovables and real rights).

[39] s 538.

[40] s 714.

[41] s 306.

[42] s 680(2).

[43] s 538.

[44] s 653.

a promise to sell and to buy assets that normally requires registration[45] and to a sale of movables at a price of 20,000 baht or over.[46]

(1) Defect of form

The Thai CCC distinguishes between two kinds of defects of form. First, some provisions may require that a contract simply 'be evidenced in writing'. No formality is required here for a valid formation of contract; a failure to conclude the contract in written form will not be fatal. A written document procured after an oral agreement has been made is admissible evidence of a contract.[47] Absent written evidence signed by the debtor, the contract is treated as unenforceable, meaning that an obligation may still be validly discharged upon performance. Of special note in relation to this type of defect are the techniques employed by the Thai draftsmen, which permit the court to achieve an outcome essentially similar to the one reached by the German system but through a different process. The BGB seems to adopt the more direct approach, stating that non-compliance will render the contract *invalid*, though performance may cure the defect of form.[48] The Thai CCC, on the other hand, refrains from the language of 'invalidity' and resorts to the notion of enforceability, holding that lack of writing simply results in the contract being unenforceable.

Second, where the defect is a failure to conclude the contract in a specific form required by law, the rule of nullity applies.[49] A contract of hire purchase, for example, has to be made in writing;[50] a contract for sale of land and of prescribed types of property has to be made in writing as well as registered. Generally, a failure to register will render the contract void, and therefore completely frustrate the parties' intention. One apparent exception is a lease of a duration exceeding three years. Here, the failure to register will render the contract simply unenforceable; but, if evidenced in writing, it will be enforceable for three years.[51] The reason perhaps lies in the peculiar need for lessee protection. It has little to do with the court's desire to uphold the parties' declaration of intention, and it shall not be pursued further.

There are, nonetheless, techniques that the court may employ to give effect to the parties' intention notwithstanding the non-compliance with the formality requirement. These will be treated in turn in the following sections.

(2) 'Transforming a void act'

A large scope for derogation from the rule of nullity is introduced by the court's exercise of its interpretative power under section 174:

> If a void act complies with the requirements of another act which is not void, it is valid as the other act, if it may be assumed that such validity would have been intended by the parties, had they known of the invalidity of the intended act.

The wording of section 174 opens up the possibility that the court may employ this power in a proactive and potentially aggressive manner: the valid juristic act may be implied if 'it may be assumed' that the parties would have intended such a result. For instance, where the intended donor writes up a deed for a gift of land but fails to register it on the land register, the intended gift will be void for failure to comply with the formality requirement. However, provided that the document is done entirely in handwriting and completed with a date and

[45] s 456(2). [46] s 456(3); see Supreme Court Decision No 5522/2550.

[47] Supreme Court Decisions No 3464/2528 (permitting the plaintiff to use a contract of mortgage as evidence of loans); No 2161/2542 (using a spouse's ratification of loan as evidence of the contract of loan taken out by the other spouse).

[48] § 766 sentence 3 BGB (surety); § 518 II BGB (gift); § 311b I BGB (obligation to transfer title to land).

[49] s 152. [50] s 572(2). [51] s 538.

a signature,[52] the court may treat the document as a valid testamentary gift, which is to take effect after the donor's death. This is notwithstanding the fact that the donor, both subjectively and as it appears on the surface of the document, intends an *inter vivos* gift. Section 174 permits the court to make an assumption of the parties' intention.[53]

The power to 'transform a void act', as it is called in Thai legal theory, has a broad application to the transfer of land for which a title deed has not been issued. These are usually pieces of land in remote, sparsely populated areas where access to justice or government officials is relatively scarce. Strict compliance with the registration requirement for a contract of sale of land may not be feasible. Thus, the court has found that an unregistered contract for the sale of land without a title deed could be interpreted as a contract for the delivery of possession of that land when a contractual clause specifies a duty to deliver possession on the date of the contract.[54] Similarly, a 'sale' coupled with delivery of possession was treated as a valid consensual transfer of the right of possession despite the invalidity of the sale contract. This entitled the 'purchaser'-possessor, and not the 'vendor', to be issued a title deed.[55]

(3) Preliminary contracts I: 'agreement to buy and to sell' land and prescribed types of movable property

The second possible derogation from the strictness of the registration requirement is found in the provision governing sales of land and other prescribed types of property. Section 456 prescribes:

> (1) A *sale* of immovable property is void unless it is made in writing and registered by the competent official. The same rule applies to ships or vessels of six tons and over, to steam launches or motor boats of five tons and over, to floating houses and to beasts of burden.
> (2) An *agreement to buy and to sell* any of the aforesaid property, or a *promise of sale* of such property is not enforceable by action unless there is some written evidence signed by the party liable or unless earnest is given, or there is part performance.
> (3) The provisions of the foregoing paragraph shall apply to a *contract of sale* of movable property where the agreed price is twenty thousand baht or upwards.

While registration is strictly required for the 'sale' of certain property under section 456(1), section 456(2) lays down a simple 'evidence in writing' requirement for a *preliminary contract* in the form of 'an agreement to buy and to sell' and 'a promise of sale', that is an offer. When armed with an appropriate written preliminary contract, an intended purchaser may seek the court's declaratory judgment to make alterations to the land register in the event that the vendor refuses to proceed with the sale. Furthermore, an earnest or part performance such as payment instalments can also be used to evidence an oral agreement to buy and to sell land; this is much like the equitable principle of part performance in English law.[56] Effectively, the formality requirement for the contract of sale of land is circumvented.

How does the Thai position compare with the German counterpart? In the German system, a contract for the sale of land is valid upon being recorded by a public notary.[57] The German notarial requirement is used as a means to ensure that the contracting parties are given basic legal advice by a public official and that they have a serious intention to

[52] So as to comply with the formality requirement of a will written as a holograph document: s 1657.
[53] Sotthibandhu (n 27) 175–176.
[54] Supreme Court Decision No 378/2525.
[55] Supreme Court Decision No 6597/2542.
[56] *Steadman v Steadman* [1976] AC 536.
[57] A contract that has not been recorded by a notary may, however, become valid when the defect of form is cured by registration: § 311b I BGB.

contract.[58] After a valid contract is concluded, changes to title registration would then be made when an application is lodged with the competent officials at the land registry. The German system is fundamentally premised upon the coexistence of the offices of the notary public and the land register. By contrast, in Thailand there is no public notary; the registration of both the contract of sale and the title is done by the competent official at the land registry. It is, hence, impractical to register solely the contract of sale of land without simultaneously effecting the passing of property by making the necessary registration in the land register. Any sale arrangement set to be registered on a future date is thus made in the form of an 'agreement to buy and to sell'.

Because section 456(2) envisions a preliminary contract that is not subject to the registration requirement of the principal contract in section 456(1), Thai lawyers widely accept that an *agreement to buy and to sell* may be considered a relaxation of the formality requirement of a *contract of sale*. This assertion may be accurate in relation to a sale within the context of section 456(1), but it also raises the question of whether preliminary contracts may have a broader application generally in Thai contract law. There are two classic debates about this issue. The first is whether an *agreement to buy and to sell* may also apply to a sale of non-prescribed movable property. The significance of recognizing an agreement to buy and to sell in that context lies with the ability of the parties to circumvent the requirements of section 456(3), which exclusively applies to a *contract of sale*, but not an *agreement to buy and to sell*.

The second debate is concerned with the conceptual extension of an *agreement to buy and to sell* into the more general realm of contract law. The question is whether and to what extent a generic *preliminary agreement* may be recognized in relation to nominate contracts other than sale, and how Thai contract law may address its interaction as well as potential conflicts with the formality rules that apply to the principal agreement. This chapter will offer a tentative answer to the two important debates. Suffice it to say that the Code is silent on both issues, so any legitimate answer must be drawn from first principles.

(4) Preliminary contracts II: 'agreement to buy and to sell' non-prescribed movables exceeding 20,000 baht

As section 456(3) requires a *contract of sale* of movables of value exceeding 20,000 baht to be evidenced in writing or the giving of earnest, a party who cannot point to the required evidence may seek to enforce the agreement by arguing that it was agreed not as a *contract of sale*, but as an *agreement to buy and to sell*. The question for Thai lawyers is whether for movables these two forms of agreement are conceptually distinguishable. On one view, an agreement to buy and to sell movables would be little different from a simple contract of sale with a term for passing of property on a future date. Unlike section 456(2) in which an agreement to buy and to sell is specifically recognized, section 456(3) makes no reference to an agreement to buy and to sell, which on this view would be redundant altogether because it is considered a variation of a *contract of sale*. Hence, the requirements of section 456(3) would be equally applicable to any arrangement which purports to be an agreement to buy and to sell. The opposite view holds that a general preliminary agreement to buy and to sell would be enforceable as an 'innominate contract', unencumbered by the requirements that section 456(3) imposes specifically on a contract of sale. Which view is right?[59]

[58] B Markesinis, H Unberath, and A Johnston, *The German Law of Contract: A Comparative Treatise* (2nd edn, Oxford: Hart Publishing 2006) 84.

[59] See generally S Sotthibandhu, *Sale, Exchange, Gift* (6th edn, Bangkok: Winyuchon Publication 2013) 93–94 and literature cited therein.

To answer this question, one needs to correctly appreciate the significance of the choice of words used by the draftsmen of the Code in section 456. This section was primarily designed to lay down the formality and evidentiary requirements for sales, but the expression 'an agreement to buy and to sell' also seems to have some important doctrinal implications. To a large extent, it transplants into Thai law the German conception of *Vorvertrag*, a pre-contract pursuant to which both parties agree to enter into the principal contract on a later date, usually because of some technical or legal reasons.[60] What is created by a *Vorvertrag* is an obligation to enter into the principal contract. The obligation arising from a *Vorvertrag* is a fully binding obligation the breach of which will attract judicial remedies in damages or specific performance. In Germany, a *Vorvertrag* is subject to the same formality and evidentiary requirement as the principal contract particularly where the requirement aims at preventing a party from precipitous actions. Thus, in the context of a sale of land, a *Vorvertrag* is invalid if it is designed to circumvent the notarial authentication requirement.[61]

In relation to section 456, some commentators have written that the three paragraphs rank the types of sale agreement in order of their seriousness.[62] Section 456(1), dealing with *sales* of land and the prescribed types of property which the law regarded as being of highest importance, imposes both writing and registration requirements. Section 456(2) introduces a lesser evidentiary requirement for the preliminary *agreement to buy and to sell* land; and then section 456(3) imposes the same requirement on a *contract of sale* of movables that exceeds a certain price. On this view, section 456's silence on the *preliminary contract for sale* of movables implies its complete negligibility. A relative insignificance means, as the argument goes, there must be no formality or evidentiary requirement.

However, this reasoning seems to be a mere conjecture from the way that section 456 is structured. A better analysis must rest on the rationale of the institution of the *Vorvertrag* itself. A *Vorvertrag* is agreed prior to the principal contract because of some present technical impediments. As already explained, a *Vorvertrag* may not be employed to circumvent a formality requirement that exists to ensure a serious intention to contract. Where the evidentiary requirement is concerned, it would be odd if a party were permitted to sidestep the evidentiary requirement of the principal sale contract by simply alleging that there was an oral, executory agreement for a preliminary contract rather than a principal contract of sale. Accordingly, readers of Thai contract law should be extremely cautious of the commentators' tendency to overstate the reach of a preliminary contract in the context of the evidentiary requirement of section 456(3). An agreement to buy and to sell movables referred to in section 456(3) should be subject to the same evidentiary requirement as that imposed on a contract of sale. Non-compliance with section 456(3) will result in the unenforceability of the agreement.

(5) Generic preliminary contracts

As we have seen, *Vorverträge* as set out in section 456(2) are specifically recognized in the context of sale of land and prescribed movables, and (unlike German law) are not subject to the formality requirement of the principal sale. However, the parties should not be permitted to use a *Vorvertrag* to circumvent the evidentiary rules of the principal contract; this is seen in relation to the sale of non-prescribed movables the value of which exceeds 20,000 baht.

This brings us to the additional question of whether Thai law theorizes a general principle analogous to the notion of *Vorvertrag* that has applications beyond the context of sale.

[60] Markesinis, Unberath, and Johnston (n 58) 78. eg a *Vorvertrag* is used where the market price is fluctuating, the place of delivery is undecided, or a necessary licence has not yet been granted.

[61] § 125 BGB.

[62] Sotthibandhu (n 59) 93–94.

For example, can an intended donee who can prove the existence of an unregistered preliminary agreement or a promise to make a gift of land enforce the preliminary agreement to obtain a declaratory judgment to unilaterally effect land disposition? The analysis turns on the question whether, and to what extent, a preliminary contract may legitimately be used without running the risk of contravening the formality requirements of the principal contract.

One approach is to hold that the court may use its interpretative technique to reach an answer that is most consistent with the objective of the formality requirement in each context. Though this approach is not free from difficulties and ambiguities, arguably it may permit the court to strike a balance between the need for commercial certainty—namely, the need to comply with the formality required by law—and the need to hold a party strictly to his promise and to protect an innocent party from the harsh consequences of the failure to comply with the formality. In the context of a gift of land, the court has declined to recognize a written but unregistered preliminary agreement to make a gift as this would defeat the protective purpose of section 525.[63] One judgment specifically explains that section 456(2), which permits an agreement to buy and to sell land, does not apply *mutatis mutandis* to the gift regime of section 525 which strictly requires registration.[64]

More controversial is the preliminary agreement for a lease. While section 538 imposes writing and registration requirements on a contract of lease for a duration exceeding three years,[65] an unregistered but written three-year lease with a preliminary agreement to lease for an additional three years was held to be enforceable for up to three years only.[66] The justification for this result is not obvious: if under section 456(2) a promisee of land disposition can avail himself of a written agreement to buy and to sell by simply presenting the written evidence in order to obtain the court's declaratory judgment, there is no clear reason why a promisee of a preliminary agreement for a lease—a lesser interest than an ownership interest—should not be able to do the same.[67]

As for a mortgage,[68] there were traces of recognition of a preliminary mortgage contract in old judgments but this was quickly abandoned. In an older judgment, the defendant handed over a land title deed and other necessary documents to the plaintiff in a promise to effect a mortgage to secure the debt owed by the defendant's son, but the arrangement was not registered.[69] The Supreme Court held that the agreement was invalid as a mortgage because it was made to secure a pre-existing debt. This left unanswered the question whether the arrangement could have been valid despite the lack of registration had it been used as a security for a fresh debt. The suggestion that a party may enforce a preliminary unregistered agreement for a mortgage was, however, put to rest definitively in a subsequent judgment.[70]

[63] s 525:

> The gift of a property the sale of which must be made in writing and registered by such competent official is complete only when so made and registered by the competent official.

[64] Supreme Court Decision No 4193/2536. See also Supreme Court Decisions No 1931/2537; No 586/2538.

[65] s 538:

> A hire of immovable property is not enforceable by action unless there is some written evidence signed by the party liable. If the hire is for more than three years or for the life of the latter or hirer, it is enforceable only for three years unless it is made in writing and registered by the competent official.

[66] Supreme Court Decision No 146/2495. See Supreme Court Decision No 563/2540 (a written promise to lease for 15 years after the end of the original lease was unenforceable).

[67] For a view that a formality requirement is not applicable to a preliminary agreement for lease, see S Sotthibandhu, *Hire—Hire-Purchase* (5th edn, Bangkok: Winyuchon 2011) 55.

[68] P Thanomrod, *Loan, Surety, Mortgage, Pawn* (9th edn, Bangkok: Krung Siam 2013) 210–211.

[69] Supreme Court Decision No 1183/2521.

[70] Supreme Court Decision No 2286/2538 (an agreement to register a mortgage if a cheque was to be dishonoured was void).

The principle of *Vorvertrag* that has its origin in the language of section 456(2) has engendered a ferocious academic debate in Thailand. It is only regrettable that this debate is not taken seriously by the judges, whose concern seems to be limited to the restrictive, literal reading of the Code's provisions on specific contracts. Apart from the contract of sale, *Vorverträge* are always made subject to the formality requirements of their principal contracts.[71] An alternative approach is to utilize the potential of the general provisions on the binding nature of a declaration of intention to give effect to the wider varieties of preliminary agreements.

How is it the case that the broader recognition of the preliminary contracts will not necessarily upset the requirements of the principal contracts? This chapter proposes that we distinguish between the formality and the evidentiary requirements. First, as indicated in the discussion on section 456(3), a party should never be permitted to sidestep the evidentiary requirements of the principal contracts. Second, where a preliminary agreement is made without regard to the formality requirement of the principal contract, the court may as a general rule award damages for failure to enter into the principal contract, rather than enforce specific performance.[72] Thus, in the context of lease, while the lease itself is unenforceable because of defect in form, at least a preliminary agreement for lease could entitle the promisee to damages. In a more problematic area where, for example, the principal contract is a mortgage, damages may have to be calculated on the basis of the loan that would have been made by the lender had there been no security. While the assessment may be based on a hypothetical case and susceptible to the accusation of artificiality (the lender may never want to give unsecured loans), the court is not so unfamiliar with such exercises.[73]

The alternative approach advocated here would result in a compromise, though it is not entirely free from doctrinal inconsistencies. For instance, it still does not explain why an unregistered preliminary agreement for lease cannot entitle the promisee to specific performance while the preliminary agreement for sale of land does. Perhaps the conundrum is an inevitable result of the agreement to buy and to sell land, unlike most other forms of preliminary agreements, being explicitly recognized in the Code. More fundamentally, it highlights one underlying problem: the Thai CCC often lacks the elegance of its model codes;[74] and the rationale for the particular rules was lost in the process of transplant. Just as exemplified by the problem of a preliminary agreement for lease, where shortcomings or inconsistencies exist, the judicial tendency is usually one of strict interpretation.

(6) Gifts

The Thai provisions on gifts are closely analogous to the BGB, though they differ in one important respect. Whereas the BGB prescribes that a promise to make a gift of *any kind* is not valid unless it is authenticated by a notary,[75] under section 525 of the Thai CCC the formality requirement is imposed only on a promise of a gift of land and other prescribed categories of property.[76] Such gifts have to be made in writing and registered by a competent official in order to be valid. The departure from the BGB here seems to have two reasons.

[71] Except s 456(2), which is the only instance in the Code where a preliminary contract is explicitly recognized.

[72] See eg Sotthibandhu (n 67) 55.

[73] For an analogy in English law, see *Wrotham Park Estate Co Ltd v Parkside Homes Ltd* [1974] 1 WLR 798.

[74] eg § 550 BGB recognizes a need to protect lessees from non-compliance with formality: the lease will be valid as a lease for an indeterminate time, the BGB treating lessees in such leases favourably. Markesinis, Unberath, and Johnston (n 58) 84.

[75] § 518 I BGB.

[76] Ships or vessels of 6 tons and over, steam launches or motor boats of 5 tons and over, floating houses, and beasts of burden.

First, at the time of the enactment of the Code, Siam had neither a notarial system nor resources for it. Basic legal advice of the kind given by a German notary public to the intended donor of *all* kinds of property was an unaffordable luxury in Siam.[77] The formality requirement was thus imposed, under section 525, only on the kinds of property that the Code presumes to represent a substantial asset, particularly land. For other 'lesser' types of property, there is no requirement of formality. However, as section 523 provides that gifts become 'complete' only upon delivery,[78] there is a debate in Thai law whether a simple promise to make a gift, which is essentially 'incomplete' because of lack of delivery, is ever enforceable.[79] The consensus seems to be that the promisee may enforce a promise to make a gift; such a promise is considered a binding juristic act that engages the enforcement procedure under the general provision of section 213: 'If a debtor fails to perform his obligation, the creditor may make a demand to the Court for compulsory performance.' The 'incompleteness' of the gift only means that property does not pass until delivery and that the promise of a gift does not have effect on a third party who may, subsequent to the promise, obtain a right in relation to that property.

Second, there is a doctrinal reason: the strength of the declaration of intention or its binding effect varies in the Thai and the German systems. In the German system, the sanctity of a declaration of intention rigorously characterizes its law of obligations. The German courts have made extensive use of the duty of good faith and the peculiar concept of *culpa in contrahendo* to impose liability on a party who has led the other party to rely on his promise which he later retracts.[80] Indeed, the German courts have gone so far as to protect not just the reliance interest, but the expectation interest.[81] The notion of good faith was even employed to create a full legal obligation which would otherwise fail, including a non-notarized promise to transfer land. Though these decisions are not without controversy, they take very little away from the more general point that German law treats a person's promise with exceptional rigour. But holding a person strictly and extensively accountable for a promise which is made gratuitously can only be justified when there is a mechanism to ensure that the promisor appreciates the gravity of his promise. The German notary system fittingly serves this purpose.

In contrast, in Thai law, the courts have not employed such a stringent standard of good faith. An unregistered promise to make a gift of land is completely invalid. Gifts of other property are only 'complete' upon delivery.[82] The corollary of this provision seems to be that prior to delivery the underlying promise is regarded by law as imperfect. Given this imperfection, the court would naturally be cautious in affording extensive protection to a disappointed party when the promise is withdrawn. In cases of an enforceable promise of a gift of land that is completed by registration, the Thai CCC clearly provides that the intended donee is only entitled to the delivery up of the property promised or an equivalent value; no damages can be awarded to compensate other losses.[83] A fortiori, there is no reason why the protection afforded to a promisee who relies on a promise of other types of gift, which need neither be in writing nor registered, should be more extensive. Unlike in cases of synallagmatic contracts, consequential losses suffered by a promisee of a gift are irrecoverable. It is therefore safe to conclude on the weaker nature of a promise of a gift in Thai law.

As regards the quality of the donative intention, the Thai CCC does not prescribe a separate regime for its evaluation. The question whether gifts are vitiated by reasons such as mistake

[77] Sotthibandhu (n 59) 391.
[78] For an analogous rule in German law, see § 518 II BGB.
[79] Sotthibandhu (n 59) 390.
[80] Markesinis, Unberath, and Johnston (n 58) 85–86, 100.
[81] BGHZ 48, 396 (27 October 1967); Markesinis, Unberath, and Johnston, ibid 100–101.
[82] s 523.
[83] s 526.

or duress is governed by the general provisions of sections 154 to 171 that also apply to synallagmatic contracts.[84] The Thai approach approximates the German perception of gifts as a kind of contractual obligation to be similarly governed by the same set of general rules that also apply to contracts for value. This leads to one possible tension. While the constitution of a gift in German law needs quite a clear manifestation of intention buttressed by either a notarial record or delivery, in Thai law the outward communication of a donative intention suffices. Hence, it is doubtful whether the German restrictive conception of mistake, which means it is relatively difficult to unwind a gift,[85] should be transplanted into a code which more readily enforces a promise of a gift. Perhaps in order to compensate for the relative ease of enforceability of gifts, Thai law needs to recognize a wider category of actionable mistakes and additional grounds for undoing the gifts (eg ingratitude).[86] Such a difference in the conception of gifts between the Thai CCC and the BGB would not be wholly unfamiliar: for example, unlike German law the Thai CCC does not prescribe compensation for loss suffered by a recipient who acted in reliance of a gift that was rescinded for mistake.[87]

2. General Rules of Contracts

The rules governing formation of contract are prescribed in the general provisions of obligations in Book II, under the chapter 'Contract'. The contents include the rules on offer, acceptance, and promise. To reflect the reality in negotiations of modern contracts, it is also necessary to consider the rules set out in the Electronic Transactions Act BE 2544 (2001).[88]

(a) Offer

(1) Definiteness and completeness

The general rule is that an offer must be complete and definite. 'Definiteness' is shown by an express intention to be bound, which substantially depends on the facts.[89] 'Completeness' requires that an offer be precise on all essential terms of the intended contract; what amounts to an essential term is determined by reference to Book III's provisions that define each form of specific contract. This is usually the contents of the first section of the Code's rules governing each specific contract. The basic test advocated by academics is that the offer must be so precise that a simple affirmative reply from the offeree will result in the creation of a contract.[90]

The tests for 'definiteness' and 'completeness' may be overlapping in practice. For instance, an offer for sale is complete when the goods to be sold are specified. The Code does not require the price to be fixed; parties need only agree on how the price is to be determined,

[84] Sotthibandhu (n 59) 394.

[85] eg a mere motivational mistake cannot be a ground for rescission of gifts or contracts for value.

[86] s 531. The current scope of 'ingratitude' is quite limited; hence there is a call for it to be widened. Note that ingratitude may be shown by serious defamatory remarks, and the court takes a very restrictive approach when determining whether a remark is sufficiently serious. The standard seems, however, more relaxed where parents seek to revoke a gift made to children who later defame them. Sotthibandhu (n 59) 395–396, 401–402. cf Supreme Court Decisions No 8306/2548 (pejoratives made to distant relatives); No 123/2541 (defamation to adoptive mother); No 728/2536; and No 3502/2535 (defamation to parents).

[87] § 122 BGB. For a comparative remark on German law on this point, see B Häcker, 'Mistaken Gifts after *Pitt v Holt*' (2014) 67 CLP 333, 354–359.

[88] BE or Buddhist Era is the official year-numbering system used in Thailand. It is 543 years ahead of the AD system; thus the year BE 2544 is the year 2001 in the Gregorian calendar.

[89] eg advertisement leaflets are simply an invitation to treat, not an offer: Supreme Court Decision No 748/2544.

[90] See Pramoj (n 16) *Vol II* 342; Sotthibandhu (n 27) 311; C Hemaratchata, *The Law of Contract* (2nd edn, Bangkok: Chulalongkorn University Press 1996) 119.

or failing that the court may impose a reasonable price.[91] It follows that an offer can be complete without a price being determined or determinable. Nonetheless, in Supreme Court Decision No 927/2498, an offer to buy 1,350 timbers of teakwood at a price that the offeree considers reasonable was held to be 'incomplete' and, as a result, did not bind the offeror. This reasoning perhaps needs clarification; an offer can be complete even if silent on price. The better reading of this case is that the court was particularly cautious about the purported offer that put an offeror at the mercy of an offeree; as such, it preferred to read such an offer as indicative of the insufficient definiteness of an intention to offer.

(2) Strong binding effect and irrevocability

The rules *against* revocation of offers are set out in the Code: for contracts to be concluded at a distance, the offer is not revocable during the period for acceptance specified by the offeror;[92] and if such period is not specified, the offer cannot be withdrawn during the reasonable period that a notice of acceptance may normally be expected.[93] The withdrawal of an offer, even if successfully communicated before acceptance takes place, is wholly ineffective.[94] There are two important points to be made. First, the reason for this rule lies possibly in the difficulties in the communication process during the early twentieth century when the Code was drafted. It was thought that offerees should be afforded some protection for their actions made in reliance of the offer during the period in which the notice of acceptance was being communicated. Second, the rule reflects the general conception of individual freedom in Thai private law as well as its stringent demand for certainty. Once an offer is made, the offeror effectively puts a restraint upon his own autonomy; he is strictly bound by the offer and is therefore barred from resorting again to the right of autonomy to withdraw himself from the offer.[95] The balance of rights is then shifted towards protecting the offeree's autonomy: Thai contract law thus confers extensive protection to the offeree's act made in reliance of the offer, even if that act takes place before a notice of acceptance is communicated.

The extensive offeree protection afforded in the sphere of contract law perhaps helps explain the general indifference towards a call to introduce a pre-contractual liability regime analogous to the German conception of *culpa in contrahendo*.[96] An offeror who wishes to withdraw from the offer may still be liable in contract to the offeree who accepts the offer. This liability is extensive, as the existence of a contract means the offeree's expectation interests are protected. Liability seems not to be limited to the reliance measure. The scope of the offeree's protection in the Thai CCC will be revisited in section III (pre-contractual liability) of this chapter.

(b) Promise

Apart from offers, the Thai CCC explicitly recognizes promises as a distinct class of unilateral juristic acts that bind the person making a declaration. Promises within the meaning of the Code can either take the form of a promise addressed to a specific individual or a promise made to the general public. The former category includes, for example, a promise to buy,

[91] s 487. [92] s 354. [93] s 355. See § 147 BGB.

[94] Sotthibandhu (n 27) 315; Pramoj (n 16) *Vol I* 457; J Sethabutr, *The Law of Juristic Acts and Obligations* (2nd edn, Bangkok: Faculty of Law, Thammasat University 1979) 263; C Tingsabadh, *The Civil and Commercial Code Book II: Sections 354 to 452 on the Sources of Obligations* (5th edn, Bangkok: Faculty of Law, Thammasat University 1983) 13.

[95] S Sotthibandhu, *Pre-Contractual Liability* (3rd edn, Bangkok: Winyuchon 2005) 151.

[96] A notable exception to this is found in Sotthibandhu, ibid.

a promise to sell, and a promise to make a gift. These are subject to the same formality and evidentiary requirements as a preliminary agreement of sale and gift.[97] The latter category comprises promises of rewards, either for completion of an act as specified by the promisor or of a prize in a competition. These are governed by the special rules of sections 362 to 365, which constitute an equivalent regime to §§ 657 to 661 of the BGB.

Given, as we have seen, the strength that Thai law gives to the binding effect of an offer, it is a point of debate whether, and how, promises and offers are substantively different. The general consensus is that promises indicate a stronger intention to contract than offers;[98] as a consequence, the 'reasonable time' lapse of offers does not apply to promises. The general rule is, therefore, that unless a period for acceptance is indicated in the original promise, or the promisor has since notified the promisee of a reasonable period, the promise will not expire.[99] The Supreme Court once remarked, 'the promise is binding indefinitely; even after dozens of years have lapsed, a promise is still binding upon the promisor'.[100]

There are, however, two exceptions to this perpetuity rule. First, a promise of reward which is made by advertisement to the general public may be withdrawn by the same advertisement channel used for the announcement of the promise.[101] Second, a promise made as part of a contract—such as a promise to lease for an additional, fixed length of time after the original lease expires—will cease to be binding when the principal contract terminates.[102]

Two further points merit special mention in relation to a promise made as part of a contract. First, the court has been stringent with the requirements: (1) that there be a clear intention to be bound; and (2) that a promise be precise on all its essential terms. Thus, 'a promise to consider renewing the lease should the lessee complete the lease with no breach of any terms of the lease' has been treated as a contract term that gives the lessor a discretion whether to renew the contract; it is not an enforceable promise to renew the lease.[103] Similarly, a promise to renew the lease with rent and lease duration 'fairly adjusted in accordance with a customary practice' has been held to be insufficiently precise as to the essential terms of a lease—rent and length—and thus failed to constitute a valid promise.[104]

Second, a promise is a unilateral juristic act that is no more a source of obligations than an offer. Thus, it cannot be enforced unless it has assumed the form of a contract or a promise of a gift acceptance of which the addressee has successfully communicated. Thus, where a lessee fails to explicitly accept a promise of a new lease before the existing lease expires,[105] the fact that the lessee continues to remain on the premises and to pay rent only indicates that the lease is renewed as a statutory lease for an indefinite period, determinable at will,[106] and is not a lease for a promised term.[107] Also, a lessee cannot accept the promise to renew the lease after he learns of the promisor's death; an unaccepted promise cannot be enforced against the promisor's estate.[108]

[97] ss 456 (sale); 526 (gift). [98] Pramoj (n 16) *Vol II* 361; Sotthibandhu (n 27) 327.

[99] s 454(2) (promise of sale).

[100] Supreme Court Decision No 1004/2485 (contract of sale of land with a promise to resell to the purchaser; the purchaser only accepted the promise after ten years).

[101] s 363(1). [102] Supreme Court Decision No 1170/2506.

[103] Supreme Court Decision No 3263/2535. However, though this point is not contended, it is arguable that such a promise should be enforceable to the extent that the promisor will exercise a discretion in good faith (s 5), and, as such, the discretion is reviewable by the court.

[104] Supreme Court Decision No 3801/2555. [105] Supreme Court Decisions No 1170/2506; No 876/2537.

[106] s 570. The lease is determinable at will, subject to the notice requirement of s 566.

[107] Supreme Court Decision No 876/2537.

[108] s 360. See Supreme Court Decisions No 1213/2517 (General Assembly); No 1602/2548 (first lease renewal was valid since lessee accepted promise to renew before learning of lessor's death, second renewal was invalid).

(c) Acceptance

(1) Strict correspondence with an offer

Thai courts require a strict correspondence between an offer and an acceptance; section 359(2), a direct translation of § 150 II of the BGB, states:

> [A]n acceptance with additions, restrictions or other modifications is deemed to be a refusal coupled with an offer.

Thus, the contract is taken to be concluded on terms identified in the final offer (or counter-offer) before acceptance. The contents of the contract are essentially determined by the party making the 'last shot' at the negotiation table.

(2) Statutory presumptions

There are two code presumptions that play a significant role in the determination of whether certain discordance between offer and acceptance would prevent the conclusion of a contract. These two presumptions are employed to refine the application of section 359 ('last-shot' doctrine) and to assist the court in determining whether a contract exists in the 'battle of forms' between the contracting parties; and if so, on what terms. Section 366, essentially a translation of § 154 of the BGB, lays down a strong presumption of no contract being formed first, when there is dissent over a term that either party has declared to be essential or, second, when the parties agree that the contract should be in writing and no written contract has yet been executed. Section 366 provides:

> (1) So long as the parties have not agreed upon all points of a contract upon which, according to the declaration of even one party, agreement is essential, the contract is, in case of doubt, not concluded. An understanding concerning particular points is not binding, even if they have been noted down.
>
> (2) If it is agreed that the contemplated contract shall be put into writing, in case of doubt, the contract is not concluded until it is put in writing.

In Germany, the stringency of this presumption is arguably compromised by the present tendency of the court to impute the intention of the parties by analogy with § 315 of the BGB,[109] which permits the court to assume that a party who is given a discretion to specify a contract performance would exercise it reasonably; and to supplant the exercise of such discretion with the court's own discretion if it is not made equitably. The presumption of § 154 of the BGB may be rebutted, for example, by the finding that the parties have started performance, and a particular contested clause may be assumed to have been agreed upon on terms that the court, using its investigative and interpretative powers, considers reflective of the parties' mutual intention.[110]

Whether Thai courts would similarly sanction the application of a section 366 presumption is, however, questionable. There is no equivalent of § 315 of the BGB in the Thai CCC, and the courts may well be very unfamiliar with overriding a party's express preference in favour of an assumed or imputed intention. In Supreme Court Decision No 3827/2552, for

[109] § 315: Specification of performance by one party

> (1) Where performance is to be specified by one of the parties to the contract, then in case of doubt it is to be assumed that the specification is to be made at the reasonably exercised discretion of the party making it.
>
> ...
>
> (3) Where the specification is to be made at the reasonably exercised discretion of a party, the specification made is binding on the other party only if it is equitable. If it is not equitable, the specification is made by judicial decision; the same applies if the specification is delayed.

[110] Markesinis, Unberath, and Johnston (n 58) 72.

example, a written agreement entitled a 'sales contract' was treated as not having been formed as a valid contract because the substantial disagreement as to price during the course of negotiations revealed that price was intended to be an essential term of the contract, and this had not been agreed upon. The court found that no contract had been formed notwithstanding the fact that the defendant, through its marketing manager, later sent the notice of termination of contract in accordance with a clause permitting it to do so in the event of fluctuations in exchange rate. A strong argument could have been made that the defendant had subsequently treated the contract as valid; by sending the notice of termination the defendant had implicitly renounced its holding that price comprised an essential term. As such, the price could arguably have been fixed by the court's exercise of its statutory power to set a reasonable price for a contract of sale.[111] The fact that the court did not uphold the contract in this case demonstrates not only the general reluctance of the court to rebut the presumption of section 366, but also the weight that the court has given to the parties' conduct during negotiations when determining what terms they regard as essential.[112]

In contrast, the court will not entertain the argument that the contract has not been concluded just because some forms that have previously been used by the parties have not been signed. Section 366(2) will not be engaged if a party fails to make explicit the fundamentality of the written contract. In Supreme Court Decision No 5343/2542, the defendant rice seller wished to change the price and certain other conditions of an existing written contract. The plaintiff accepted the offer and sent a notice to the defendant to start delivery, to which the defendant responded with a request for delay. It was not open to the defendant to later challenge the validity of the contract on the basis that a contract had not been signed, and that the terms as to liquidated damages, performance bonds, and delivery had not been agreed upon. In reaching its conclusion, the court took notice of the defendant's previous dealings with other traders, in which the defendant simply started delivery upon receiving the buyers' demands for rice. The conduct of both sides sufficed to take the case outside section 366, and the contract was held to have been concluded on the terms of the defendant's offer and the plaintiff's acceptance. Similarly, an employment agreement 'subject to contract to be made in writing' was treated as a valid unwritten contract when the employer let the employee in to start working, thus conclusively waiving its intention to have the contract made in writing.[113]

In most other cases, the stringency of a section 366 presumption is evident. This may be demonstrated by the Thai court's tendency to find an absence of contract when one contracting party expresses its disagreement with the terms drafted by the other party and specifically identifies those terms. Additionally, the court has held that a deposit already given may be indicative of the existence of a contract, but this may be rebutted by an express disagreement as to terms.[114] The deposit can then be recovered through an action for undue enrichment. By parity of reasoning, the commencement of performance is not normally conclusive of the existence of the contract.

Cases reveal that in considering what the parties hold as essential within the meaning of section 366, the court may also take into account the customary industry practice. Thus, in Decision No 5343/2542, the rice traders' normal practice in delivering the products

[111] s 487.

[112] However, the court also rejected the contract on the basis that it was not signed by the authorized person, viz the defendant's managing director, as originally agreed. Thus, even if the court could have rebutted the presumption of s 366 on the point concerning price, the contract would still have failed for lack of authority.

[113] See Supreme Court Decision No 2036/2542.

[114] See Supreme Court Decisions No 811/2492; No 154/2509; No 3942/2545. In the final case, the plaintiff underlined the disagreed terms with red ink before returning the document to the defendant.

immediately following the customers' demands did influence the court's finding of a contract despite no formal arrangements having been signed. No formal contract was treated as essential in the industry practice of rice traders. Similarly, in Supreme Court Decision No 3942/2545, the court remarked that the plaintiff's request to change the particular terms regarding the deadline for house construction and the date for the division of title deeds was customary in the purchasers' contracts with a housing developer. This was held to reveal the purchaser's intention to contract only after the necessary changes; no contract could have been concluded before that moment despite the purchaser having paid two deposit instalments.

The second relevant presumption is found in section 367 (§ 155 of the BGB), which presumes the contract to be valid when there is a hidden dissent on a minor or trivial point:

> If the parties to a contract, which they regarded as concluded, have in fact not agreed as to one point upon which an agreement was to be settled, those parts which were agreed upon are valid in so far as it may be inferred that the contract would have been concluded even without a settlement of this point.

Under this section, if the parties treat the contract as having been concluded, the actual disagreement as to trivial terms, which the parties may not be aware of until the dispute arises, will not affect the validity of the terms agreed. In considering which *dissens* is trivial, the courts ask whether it may still be assumed that the contract would have been concluded despite the disagreement on that particular point. Without the actual agreement between the parties, it is the court's function to determine the 'presumed intention' of the parties as to the contents of those trivial terms.[115] Here, section 367 only presumes the existence of a contract; it is silent on how the problem of the contested (trivial) terms is to be resolved. Hence, the basic rule is still that of the last-shot doctrine of section 359. It is nonetheless open to the courts to take into account all surrounding circumstances, including the intention of the parties as evidenced from the correspondence, good faith, and custom of the particular trade for guidance on how the contested terms fit the contract in question. The test is not significantly different from the normal rule of a good faith interpretation of section 368.[116] Thus, in Supreme Court Decision No 596/2538, the contract for the services of a barrister was found to exist despite no explicit arrangements as to remuneration. The court applied sections 367 and 368 and calculated the remuneration on the basis of a good faith interpretation, taking into account customary practices.

So how do the presumptions of sections 366 and 367 interact in relation to the 'battle of forms'? Recall the basic 'last-shot' doctrine under section 359: the contract is agreed on the terms given by the party who sent out the final form. However, the precise question of who has the 'last shot' in the battle is rarely considered by the courts. The exceptional strength of a section 366 presumption of no contract may be the reason. Where the offeree responds to an offer with the offeree's own form, it would normally be a case of open *dissens*; there would be no contract even if the parties have started to perform while still exchanging the forms. Section 359 then dictates that the offeree's response is treated at best as a counter-offer. The 'last shot' will not be secured by the simple fact that the counter-party has commenced performance; the courts do not readily find acceptance merely from performance. The strength of section 366 means that no contract has been concluded; reliance on the

[115] Markesinis, Unberath, and Johnston (n 58) 73.

[116] s 368:

> Contracts shall be interpreted according to the requirements of good faith, ordinary usage being taken into consideration.

purported contract would not be protected by contract law. Without a contract, remedies must be sought through other avenues such as the recovery of a benefit conferred in accordance with the principle of undue enrichment.

Can there be room for an argument that if the modifications made in the counter-offer are related to trivial terms, the performance of the principal obligations may indicate that the contract is regarded by the parties as having been concluded and thus triggers the presumption of section 367? While the language of section 367 is broad enough to cover this possibility, its actual scope of application seems extraordinarily narrow. The operation of section 367 has not been examined at length either by the courts or in academia; it is suggested that it should be applicable to very minor points such as fees associated with the contract,[117] or where, as in Decision No 596/2538 (Barrister Case), the performance was 'substantially completed' despite the hidden *dissens*.[118] However, where each party is insistent on the exclusive use of its own form, it can be inferred that the points of dissent are non-trivial; this would trigger the presumption of section 366, rather than section 367.

The strength of section 366 and the narrowness of section 367 seem to concur with Thai cultures—both legal and beyond. Holding a contract valid despite disagreements would breed hostility—an undesirable outcome especially in a system in which specific enforcement is mostly considered the primary remedy for non-performance.[119] Moreover, the feeling of hostility between business partners is antithetical to the non-confrontational culture of Thai businesses.[120] In the context of consumer contracts, invalidating the contract would also provide a measure of consumer protection since it is often the big conglomerate provider who would otherwise have the 'last shot' in contractual negotiations.[121]

(d) Communication

(1) General rules

The Thai rules on the communication of offer and acceptance are governed by the general provisions of Book I on the declaration of intention under sections 168 and 169. If a declaration is made in the addressee's presence, whether in person or on the telephone or other similar devices, the 'theory of perception' applies; namely, that the communication becomes effective once it is known and understood by the addressee.[122] In comparison, as in the BGB, the 'theory of reception' applies where the communication is non-instantaneous and the addressee is not present to immediately perceive the message; the declaration of intention becomes effective when it reaches the addressee's sphere of influence. The general consensus is that 'receipt' takes place when the addressee has a possibility to take notice of the declaration and can reasonably be expected to do so. Risk of postponement or destruction prior to the declaration's entry into the addressee's sphere of influence is borne by the person making the declaration.[123]

[117] Sotthibandhu (n 27) 333.

[118] Supreme Court Decisions No 596/2538 (barrister redrafted the complaint that already resulted in a favourable judgment in the Supreme Court); No 3657/2538 (lessee was permitted to occupy the building immediately after a reservation was made for a 20-year lease. The court rejected lessor's action for eviction ten years later, and ordered registration as a lease with the period counting from the date of reservation).

[119] cf discussion in M Pongsapan, 'Remedies for Breach of Contract in Thai Law' in Chen-Wishart, Loke, & Ong, *Studies in the Contract Laws of Asia: Remedies for Breach of Contract* (Oxford: OUP 2016) ch 16.

[120] See generally G Hofstede, *Culture's Consequences: Comparing Values, Behaviors, Institutions and Organizations Across Nations* (2nd edn, Thousand Oaks, CA: Sage Publications 2001).

[121] See eg Supreme Court Decision No 3942/2545 (contract between purchaser and housing developer).

[122] s 168; this rule is not expressly provided in the BGB, though the position in German law seems similar: Markesinis, Unberath, and Johnston (n 58) 70.

[123] A similar position in German law, see § 130 BGB. Markesinis, Unberath, and Johnston, ibid 69.

There are, however, at least two significant deviations from these general rules. First, if the notice of acceptance is delayed but it was sent in such manner that it would ordinarily have arrived in time, the offeror must, upon receiving the notice of acceptance, immediately notify the offeree of the delay; otherwise, the acceptance would be deemed to be made in due time.[124] The risk of postponement is shifted to the offeror unless he gives notice of delay to the offeree. Second, no notice of acceptance is necessary if such is the declared intention of the offeror or the ordinary usage.[125] What can be waived here is the notification of acceptance, but the intention to accept must still be externalized in some way. Usually, this will be by the offeree's conduct in complying with the offeror's request.[126]

(2) Electronic communication

The Electronic Transactions Act BE 2544 (2001) confirms the usage of electronic exchanges as an effective method for communication of declaration of intention. Communication of offer and acceptance may be done electronically, and the validity of a contract concluded thereby cannot be challenged on the basis that it is made in electronic form.[127] The Act defines the moment of information being sent as the time at which the information is placed outside the sender's control,[128] and the moment of receipt as the moment when the information is registered in the receiver's information system.[129]

One flexible meaning of 'receipt' is introduced by the Act. Under section 23(2), if the recipient has provided a specified destination for the communication, communication takes effect once it has reached the recipient's designated information system; if not, then a communication that is sent to the recipient's alternative system is effective once it is downloaded from that alternative address. This rule is thought to apply specifically to emails to safeguard a sender from the possibility of mixing up the recipient's valid addresses, barring an argument that the communication is inconsequential when it is shown to have already been downloaded by the recipient.

Otherwise than the aforementioned, the Act seems to carry no doctrinal implications on the way in which Thai law perceives formation of contract. Regardless of the means of communication, it still needs to be determined whether the communication is made in the presence of the addressee or made in his absence; the rules of perception and reception apply respectively. More problematically, communication that immediately reaches the addressee after being sent, such as information sent through text messaging, email, and facsimile, may fall into either category. This depends on whether the sender and the recipient can establish live correspondence, usually by the recipient immediately communicating his notification of receipt.

III. Pre-Contractual Liability

As already mentioned in the introduction to this chapter, the general trend that emerges from an investigation into the Supreme Court's judgments is the demand for certainty. Extensive judicial creations are not merited on the matters already specifically governed by the Code. The refusal to recognize a separate liability regime for reprehensible conduct during the pre-contractual stages, where none exists in the Code, reinforces the predisposition of the court to give a literal reading to Code provisions and its antipathy towards judicial activism in the sphere of civil law.

[124] s 358. See § 149 BGB.

[125] s 361(2). See § 151 BGB.

[126] Supreme Court Decision No 657/2549; an application for a telephone service is an offer made by the customer at a branch of a telephone company. The acceptance takes place when the main branch approves the application and provides the service as requested; there is no need for a separate notification of acceptance.

[127] s 13, Electronic Transactions Act BE 2544 (2001).

[128] ibid s 22.

[129] ibid s 23.

It is well established in Thai law that no rights or duties may arise prior to the conclusion of a contract. A few exceptions may exist within the rules that are designed to ensure the quality of the parties' consent, such as a duty to avoid misrepresentation or exerting undue pressure on the contracting party. But these have no bearing on the rule that parties are free to break off from contract negotiations without having to give any reasons for doing so. Thai law has taken a firm position that during negotiations parties only concern themselves with their own interests; a duty of good faith is inconsistent with the nature of negotiation where each party essentially pursues his own interest. This is why a duty to negotiate in good faith is not conceived of as a separate ground for liability in the Thai CCC, and the court has never entertained academic suggestions in its favour.

Hence, protections for the parties in the pre-contractual stages, if any, would have to be found in either the Code's conventional regimes for contractual or extra-contractual liability, which are to be considered in this section.

1. Contractual Regime

In this introduction, it should be briefly pointed out that the imposition of pre-contractual liability is addressed quite differently in the laws of Thailand and Germany. In Germany, the contractual regime of the BGB adopts a wide conception of contractual obligations that extends to the stages of negotiations prior to the conclusion of the contract. German courts use the duty of good faith under § 242 to refine an obligation to take into account the interest of a contracting party (§ 241(2)) right from the commencement of negotiation (§ 311(2)). In other words, the ubiquitous duty of good faith is used to qualify the pre-contractual obligations that are already well entrenched within the BGB.

In contrast, the Thai CCC does not directly conceive of any pre-contractual obligations. Hence, during negotiations each party generally owes no obligations at all which can methodically be refined by the equivalent generic 'good faith' provision (section 5).[130] As a result, losses occasioned by a party breaking off from negotiations can be remedied only through the conventional regime of contractual liability, namely, a holding that the party is liable in breach of contract, following either a finding that a contract has been concluded or that there is a tender contract.

(a) Contract

One hypothetical case best illustrates the extent of protection that Thai law gives to the innocent party when the other party breaks off, especially during the later stages of negotiations. Consider a case of a person successfully communicating his offer for sale of a specific property to a prospective purchaser but, prior to an agreement being concluded, swiftly selling the property to a third party. What is the legal protection for the offeree who might already have acted in reliance on the offer? Some commentators advocate the introduction of a pre-contractual liability regime based purely on the requirement of good faith under section 5, similar to the German concept of *culpa in contrahendo*.[131] According to this argument, once the property is sold to a third party, any contract of sale set to be concluded with

[130] s 5 reads:

> Every person must, in the exercise of his rights and in the performance of his obligations, act in good faith.

[131] Sotthibandhu (n 95) 151–153.

the plaintiff would be void for impossibility of performance.[132] Therefore, the only possible avenue for recovery would be non-contractual.

However, this suggestion has not been taken up seriously by the courts; unlike the BGB, the Thai CCC does not explicitly take cognizance of a pre-contractual duty to take into account the interests of the other party. There are no pre-contractual obligations to be performed; and hence nothing to be performed in good faith. Saying that negotiating parties owe each other a duty of pre-contractual good faith would be to expand the contents of the 'good faith' provision and to establish a separate *sui generis* duty and ground of liability where none otherwise exists. This expansion would be an unwelcome innovation that directly runs contrary to the courts' concern for certainty. The better view is that, as explained in connection with the strong binding effect of an offer, Thai law may protect the innocent party by holding that the party breaking off has already made an offer which is sufficiently complete and definite. This constitutes an irrevocable offer that may be accepted by the offeree.

The problem encountered in this technique is whether the offeror's sale to the third party may amount to an implied withdrawal, especially if it is known to the offeree before he makes a decision to accept. Arguably, the answer is found in the rule laid down by section 355 that unless a reasonable period of time has lapsed, an offeror who has not specified a period for acceptance cannot withdraw his offer. There is no reason why this preclusion of an express withdrawal should not a fortiori apply to an implied withdrawal. An offeror should not be allowed to escape from his offer when he is responsible for the factual impossibility of his offer. Finding that there is a contract, the court may then award damages that reflect the expectation interests of the offeree.

To assess the logic of this approach, first, one may draw a useful analogy with a debtor's obligation under section 218 to make compensation when impossibility of performance is attributable to him.[133] Section 218 may, however, have no direct application to the offeror, who strictly speaking owes no 'debt' since it is only when the offer is accepted that a contract, and thus a 'debt', arises. Second, consider a case where the offeree makes out an acceptance *before* the seller sells the property to a third party. In such case, the contract would be validly formed, resulting in the offeree's full entitlement to contractual damages. It would then beg the question as to why the remedy for an offeree whose acceptance reaches the seller *after* he concludes a sale with a third party should be any different. As exclusively between the offeror and the offeree, whether an acceptance reaches the offeror *before* or *after* he concludes a sale with a third party should be inconsequential. The ground and extent of liability, insofar as the law of obligations is concerned, should not depend on the mere accident of timing.[134]

There are, however, two caveats to this contractual technique. First, good faith is required of the innocent party. Thus, an offeree who has not seriously contemplated accepting the offer will not be permitted to take advantage of the offer to claim expectation damages. This requirement of good faith, unlike the one suggested by the school of thought advocating the *sui generis* duty of good faith, is not a free-standing principle; it is grounded in the exercise of rights created by the contract. It reflects a conventional understanding of good faith,

[132] ibid 150. Thai CCC, s 150.

[133] s 218(1):

> When the performance becomes impossible in consequence of a circumstance for which the debtor is responsible, the debtor shall compensate the creditor for any damage arising from the non-performance.

[134] However, as under Thai law property passes at the time of the contract being concluded, timing may still be essential in the question of whether the offeree or a third party has acquired title. That the accident of timing can be relevant may well be a peculiar feature of property law which, unlike the law of obligations, has a broader concern than regulating the exclusive relationship between parties.

which provides a standard against which the performance of an existing obligation or the exercise of rights is to be assessed. Hence, the offeree, having accepted the offer and concluded the contract, is only permitted to exercise the right to claim damages in so far as it does not amount to an abuse of right. The principle may then reduce the claim of an honest but hesitating offeree to reliance damages only.

Second, for the court to find that the offeree may accept an offer, the offer must have been sufficiently complete in all its essential terms. The threshold for completeness may on occasions be relaxed; agreements as to price or other forms of remuneration may not be essential.[135] Also, the requirement of completeness seems to be relaxed in the context of section 576 which permits the court to imply a contract for hire of services if under the circumstances it cannot be expected that the services are given gratuitously. However, this technique may still not afford remedies in the wide range of situations where parties start performance during negotiations which are made 'subject to contract', or when they are in the middle of a 'battle of forms'. Subject to the presumptions in sections 366 and 367 as discussed earlier, these parties generally perform at their own risk.

(b) Tender contract

The tender process raises important questions concerning the basis of liability of the interested parties in the following scenarios. First, the successful bidder may refuse to proceed to contract with the caller. Second, the caller may similarly refuse to contract after sending the notification of a successful bid to the bidder, allegedly exercising the caller's reserved right of withdrawal. Third, the caller may have no serious intention to contract; the tender announcement is made simply to collect free information from the bidders who may have to invest substantially in preparing for the bid submission. Fourth, the caller may without good reasons exclude the bid of a particular bidder.

The outcome of these scenarios ultimately depends on the juristic analysis of a call for tender, a bid, and a 'tender contract'. Case authorities indicate that a call for a bid is considered an invitation to tender; the bid is an offer, and a notification sent to a successful bidder constitutes an acceptance for a 'tender contract'—a kind of collateral contract agreed upon prior to and separate from the principal contract.[136] This collateral contract obliges each party only to 'negotiate'.[137] There is, however, no duty to conclude the principal contract. Thus, unlike the true kind of preliminary contract, the *Vorvertrag*, a tender contract will not entitle a disappointed party to a remedy of specific performance where the principal contract is not agreed upon for whatever reason. In addition, the contractual remedies based on the tender contract are rather limited. The disappointed caller is entitled to confiscate the deposits but other consequential damages such as the costs involved in obtaining performance elsewhere are considered part and parcel of the principal contract and are thus normally irrecoverable.[138] Exceptionally, the caller may, as part of the original call, impose a condition on the successful bidder, requiring him to make compensation for failure to

[135] s 487; the court may impose a reasonable price in the contract of sale if it has not been agreed. While there is no analogous provision in other forms of contracts, the court could make use of a duty to perform in good faith to permit a reasonable remuneration. cf analogous provisions in the BGB: §§ 612 (contract for services); 632 (contract for work); 653 (brokerage contract).

[136] Supreme Court Decision No 931/2480 is the seminal case that is followed by subsequent judgments; see eg Supreme Court Decisions No 1131/2520; No 1825/2522; No 3550/2526; No 2811/2529.

[137] This 'negotiation' takes place with the scales tipping heavily in favour of the caller, because the bidder is usually strictly bound by the terms of the bid.

[138] Supreme Court Decisions No 931/2480 (new bidding process resulting in higher price); No 1825/2522 (higher price charged by alternative supplier).

sign the principal contract.[139] Even so, the courts have limited the amount of compensation to the difference between the price offered by the successful bidder and that offered by the second best bidder in the same bidding process,[140] and rejected the clause obliging the bidder to make up the difference between the successful bidder's price and the price charged by any alternative performer.[141]

As for the bidders, the court's holding that a tender contract is created only at the caller's announcement of a successful bid may have some harsh consequences. According to this rule, the caller would have an unfettered discretion to cancel the bid before the notification of a winning bid is given; there is no contractual obligation on the part of the caller to carry through the bidding process, or even to consider any given bid. Furthermore, in practice the caller inviting bids would invariably make an express reservation on the right whether or not to contract with the best bid. This reservation has proved to be an obstacle to the disappointed bidder who is refused the contract even after the successful bid has been announced.[142]

In view of the inadequate protection afforded to the bidders, the alternative position advocated in this chapter is to hold that the caller's announcement for bidding performs dual functions. This announcement may simultaneously amount to both an invitation for a tender in relation to the principal contract, and an offer in relation to the collateral tender contract.[143] Each qualifying bid may then function as an acceptance of the collateral contract. As a consequence, the tender contract arises not at the moment of the announcement of a successful bid, but at the moment of submission of a valid bid. The caller will accordingly owe a contractual duty under this collateral contract to each and every bidder. The principle of good faith under section 5 then dictates that the performance of a contractual obligation— here the duty to carry out the entire bidding process—be done in good faith. In this way, the tender contract can then be used as a basis for awarding remedies to the bidders whose bids are unfairly rejected. Bidders are also protected where the caller cancels the entire bidding process without good reason. The same reasoning applies to the successful bidder who is disappointed by the caller's exercise of the reserved right to refuse to contract.

However, the contractual approach advocated here has not been adopted by the courts. As will be discussed in the next section, the courts seem to have taken a very restrictive stance on the use of a tender contract and repeatedly suggested that the proper route for recovery for the disappointed bidders, if any, must lie in an action based on delict rather than contract.

It is interesting to note the minority view which disagrees with the use of a 'tender contract' altogether.[144] On this view, the objection to the tender contract lies with the strength of the presumption under section 366. If the caller had made clear that the principal contract would be subject to further negotiations or would have to be made in writing after the end of the bidding process, section 366 raises a strong presumption that the parties are not bound by any contract prior to further negotiations being concluded. Holding the caller

[139] Supreme Court Decision No 1131/2520 (permitting recovery of difference between successful bidder's price and price charged by second best bidder).

[140] ibid.

[141] Supreme Court Decision No 1418/2529 (term for successful bidder to compensate for difference between successful bidder's price and price charged by alternative supplier considered an object of principal contract of sale, not of tender contract).

[142] See eg Supreme Court Decision No 8898/2544. Cancellation in accordance with the caller's reserved right to abandon the successful bid did not lead to liability even in the case of the caller's five-year delay.

[143] Sotthibandhu (n 95) 151, 159–161.

[144] C Tingsabadh, *Supreme Court Decision No 320/2522 (Case Commentary)* 341; criticized in Sotthibandhu (n 95) 151, 158.

and the bidder to a separate contract (a tender contract) would run contrary to the parties' intention that there be no contract at all. On this view, the absence of a tender contract would have one important consequence. The 'deposit' given along with the bid cannot be confiscated as an earnest given in connection with a tender contract.[145] Instead, the 'deposit' must be considered as a penalty, which under Thai law can be freely promised for a person's doing or forbearing to do some act, apart from any contractual relationship.[146] Thus, this 'deposit' would be subject to the Code's rule for assessment of fairness of penalty. However, these findings are not supported by case law, and the courts have not considered bid deposits as a penalty.

2. Extra-Contractual Regime

The explanation on pre-contractual right, duty, and liability cannot be complete without at least briefly considering the possibility of employing the extra-contractual regimes set out in the Code. The first possibility, which has not been entertained by the court, is to resort to the more generous reading of section 5 on good faith. Failing this technique, there are also attempts to invoke the delict provision of section 420, which reproduces the German delictual regime of § 823 of the BGB. Section 420 provides:

> A person who, wilfully or negligently, unlawfully injures the life, body, health, liberty, property or any right of another person, is said to commit a wrongful act and is bound to make compensation therefore.

The equivalent problems encountered by the German jurists thus surface in the Thai context: there are uncertainties about the meaning of 'unlawfulness' of the defendant's conduct and whether the financial loss, 'pure economic loss', inflicted upon the claimant would fall under the list of protected interests. The general consensus is that by breaking off from negotiations, the defendant simply exercises his freedom to contract and can hardly be said to act unlawfully. As for 'pure economic loss', the protected interests enlisted in section 420 may encompass the claimant's pure economic interests; but there might be difficulties in proving causation.[147]

The suggestion that one party breaking off from negotiations may attract delictual liability has been noted by the Supreme Court on several occasions.[148] However, since in all these cases remedies were ultimately denied on the facts, one remains unsure of precisely how the delict regime may establish pre-contractual liability. For instance, in Supreme Court Decision No 8898/2544, the plaintiff sued in delict for loss caused by the five-year delay in the defendant government authority's exercise of its reserved right to abandon the successful bid on the basis of the protection of public interest. The court rejected the claim and, hence, aligned this case with the general rule that no claim is possible where the caller reserves its right of cancellation. However, the court's reasoning may have opened up the possibility that a substantial delay caused by bad faith or negligence could have founded a delictual claim. It would have been sufficient for the court to conclude that the

[145] ss 377 and 378.

[146] s 383(2): the rule for the assessment of contractual penalty 'applies also … if a person promises a penalty to the case of his doing or forbearing to do some act'.

[147] For a minority suggestion that pure economic loss is not a cognizable item of damages under s 420, see Supreme Administrative Court Decision No อ.80/2548 at 23 (dissenting opinion).

[148] For judgments considering the possibility of a delictual claim despite no tender contract, see Supreme Court Decisions No 2811/2529 (loss not pleaded); No 3550/2526 (no wrongs). For judgments considering the possibility of a delictual claim in tandem with breach of tender contract, see Supreme Court Decisions No 8898/2544 (no breach); No 1599/2522 (no breach); Opinion of Attorney-General Case No 125/2533 (recommending damages).

delay—a product of extensive studies on the environmental impact of the proposed rubbish-disposal project—was a good faith exercise of the defendant's reserved right pursuant to a tender contract; but the judges chose to engage openly with the notions of 'delict', 'negligence', and 'intentional tort', eventually dismissing the claim on the basis that, despite the five-year delay, the government's act did not amount to a delict under the regime of section 420. This reasoning could thus be read as giving support to the proposition that the delict regime directly applies to the establishment of liability for breaking off. Alternatively, the interpretation of this judgment may be that the court did not really discuss the possibility of a direct delictual liability, but that the existence of delict could have informed the assessment of the good faith exercise of a contractual right pursuant to the tender contract.

While the extent to which the delict regime of section 420 of the Thai CCC may impose pre-contractual liability remains unclear, many of the existing Supreme Court's judgments involved a caller that was a government office or state agency and would now be governed by a separate liability regime under section 9(3) of the Act on Establishment of Administrative Courts and Administrative Court Procedure BE 2542 (1999).[149] It is well established in the Administrative Court that this Act permits the disappointed bidder to bring a delictual claim against the wrongful caller, notwithstanding the caller's reservation of the right to cancel the bidding process.[150] The Supreme Administrative Court considered that the caller's wrongful act fell squarely within section 420 of the Thai CCC; hence, it applied section 438 in determining the measure of damages, which the court held was to cover reliance expenses made in connection with submitting the bid as well as any works done in anticipation of the principal contract.[151] Further, the Supreme Administrative Court in one case, by majority, decided that recovery was not confined to reliance expenses; holding that lost profits were also actionable.[152] Nonetheless, the Administrative Court's delictual characterization of the claim for breaking off remains peculiar to the regime of liability under the Act; it has not been shown convincingly that the Supreme Court has embraced this conception of pre-contractual liability within the delictual regime of section 420.

Furthermore, the Thai CCC does not contain a provision analogous to § 826 of the BGB that provides a more extensive scope of protection covering economic loss where such loss is caused intentionally and in a manner that is *contra bonos mores*. Thus, unless section 420 applies, there is no supplementary delictual liability regime to catch a party who engages in a lengthy but unproductive negotiation with a covert intention to prejudice the other party's business or to gain certain information.

[149] s 9:

> Administrative Court has the competence to try and adjudicate or give orders over the following matters:
>
> ...
>
> (3) the case involving a dispute in relation to a wrongful act or other liabilities of an administrative agency or State official arising from the exercise of power under the law or from a law, administrative order or other orders, or from the neglect of official duties required by the law to be performed or the performance of such duties with unreasonable delay.

[150] Central Administrative Court Decisions No 426/2547 (wrongful exclusion of bidder); No 1543/2547 (irregularities in the bidding process); No 1618/2547 (delay in returning deposits); Supreme Administrative Court Decision No อ.63/2546 (delay in contracting with successful bidder).

[151] See eg Supreme Administrative Court Decisions No อ.80/2548 at 14; No อ.154/2547 at 8, 19.

[152] Supreme Administrative Court Decision No อ.80/2548 at 18 (lost profits recoverable by person submitting best quotation in a call for price inquiry; dissenting opinions at 23, 28). cf Supreme Administrative Court Decision No อ.154/2547 at 19 (no recovery of consequential loss for best tenderer in a call for competitive bidding). 'Price inquiry' and 'competitive bidding' are two separate tender procedures governed by Regulations of the Office of the Prime Minister on Procurement BE 2535 (1992).

Finally, to a certain extent, a party's reliance on a contract that fails to materialize may also be protected by an action in undue enrichment.[153] Information given to the other party during the negotiation or bidding process may be recoverable. However, recovery is only limited to property or other benefits conferred on the other party. It does not extend to other reliance losses such as an outlay made in preparation for the contractual performance.

IV. Conclusion

Large parts of the fundamentals of the Thai law of contract are products of legal transplantation and cross-pollination of foreign laws, particularly the Romano-Germanic systems adopted in Germany and Japan. The extraterritorial exercise of jurisdiction by the Western powerhouses during the height of European colonization in Indochina put pressure on the Siamese Government to adopt a legal system that would be well regarded by imperial powers. The drafts which culminated in the Book on Obligations were hastily done; and the rules largely reflected precisely the language of the codes on which they were modelled. However, during the rush to complete the drafts, on several occasions some convoluted details of the model laws were lost. On others, rules were modified to accommodate the contemporary legal and administrative reality of Siam.

Early post-codification academic writings became the main sources of reference; yet, in many instances, the rules as stated in the Code were not entirely comprehensible.[154] The bureaucratic obstacles to accessing the Supreme Court's full judgments seemed to be of little help in clarifying the law.[155] Thai commentators sought assistance from foreign laws, and it has become entrenched practice for commentators to explain Thai law by way of juxtaposition with foreign rules—in particular the English, French, and German. From within the domestic jurisdiction, the court's judgments often fail to offer adequate explanations. On the few occasions that an explanation is offered, the attitude of the judges frequently appears to favour a highly restrictive and literal approach to the reading of the Code. The commentators' recommendation for an extensive interpretation of some unclear rules thus remains largely speculative. We have seen this in relation to the notion of *Vorvertrag*—though academics advocate the incorporation of *Vorvertrag* besides section 456(2), there is to date no conclusive judicial comment on this. Another example would be the use of good faith under section 5 as a *sui generis* basis of liability to remedy shortcomings in Thai law in the protection of negotiating parties during the pre-contractual stage.

[153] s 406:

(1) Any person who, through an act of performance made by another person or in any other manner, obtains something to the prejudice of such other person without legal ground, must return it to the latter. The acknowledgment of the existence or non-existence of a debt is deemed to be an act of performance.

(2) The same provision shall apply if something has been obtained on account of a cause which has not been realized or has ceased to exist.

[154] eg s 456(2) (whether a general agreement to buy and to sell should be recognized); s 5 (whether lack of good faith can be a *sui generis* basis of liability); s 523 (whether an imperfect gift is enforceable, and if so, how; measure of damages for breaking off a promise of gift).

[155] The Supreme Court's full judgments in Thailand are not readily available to the public: s 54, Code of Civil Procedure. A 'short' and 'long' summary of judgments may be accessed online at the Supreme Court's database deka.supremecourt.co.th; but the full judgments can only be obtained in person at the Office of Excellence Legal Centre at the Supreme Court. Applicants are required to provide a government-issued ID card as well as supporting documents which state reasons for the request, and pay the associated fees.

It is against the backdrop of legal history that the Thai CCC should be read. In the proximate future, Thai law will continue to learn a great deal from foreign experience. Yet, this should not result in a general reluctance to step out of the shadow cast by foreign laws. As this chapter attempts to demonstrate, an understanding of the Thai CCC can be obtained from within as much as from without, with explanations equally drawn from both the reported Supreme Court's judgments and the principles discussed overseas.

20

Third Party Beneficiaries in Thai Contract Law

*Pattarapas TUDSRI & Angkanawadee PINKAEW**

I. Introduction: A General Comparative Remark

The starting point under Thai law, with regard to the entitlement of a third party to enforce benefits conferred by a contract to which it is not a party, is section 374(1) of the Thai Civil and Commercial Code 1925 ('Thai CCC'). As in other parts of the Thai CCC, this is a direct translation of the equivalent provision in the German Civil Code 1900 (*Bürgerliches Gesetzbuch*, 'BGB').[1] The related provisions read:

> **Section 374**
> (1) If a party by a contract agrees to make a performance to a third person, the latter has a right to claim such performance directly from the debtor.
> (2) In the case of the foregoing paragraph the right of the third person comes into existence at the time when he declares to the debtor his intention to take the benefit of the contract.
>
> **Section 375**
> After the right of the third person has come into existence in accordance with the provisions of the foregoing section, it cannot be charged or extinguished by the parties to the contract.
>
> **Section 376**
> Defences arising from the contract mentioned in section 374 can be set up by the debtor against the third person who receives the benefit of the contract.

The Thai CCC, like other civilian systems, affords some protection for third party beneficiaries in a contract between two others. Nonetheless, the outward appearance of section 374 as a direct translation of a BGB provision should not belie the specificities of particular rules that may differ significantly from the ones adopted in the German system. Two important observations must be made on the context of Thai law that may have helped shape Thai lawyers' understanding of the section 374 regime.

First, section 374 is, just as § 328 of the BGB, an exception to the general rule of privity or, to use a German term, 'relativity of contract' which dictates that a third party may not derive rights from a contract. As an exception, the scope of application of the section must be narrow.[2] The exception is neither designed for, nor does it have the effect of, displacing the broader rule that prevents outsiders from enforcing a contract. Thus, a stranger can seek enforcement only where it is unequivocally the intention of the original parties that such should be the case. The test for what amounts to such an unequivocal intention may,

* Cite as P Tudsri & A Pinkaew, 'Third Party Beneficiaries in Thai Contract Law' in Chen-Wishart, Loke, & Vogenauer, *Studies in the Contract Laws of Asia Vol II: Formation and Third Party Beneficiaries* (Oxford: OUP 2017) ch 20.

[1] § 328(1) BGB.

[2] See eg A Sumawong, *Explaining the Civil and Commercial Code: Juristic Acts—Contracts* (Bangkok: Institute of Legal Education of the Thai Bar 2012) 291; S Sotthibandhu, *Juristic Acts—Contracts* (18th edn, Bangkok: Winyuchon Publication 2014) 344; D Thirawat (ed), *Sethabutr on the Law of Juristic Acts and Obligations* (7th edn, Bangkok: Faculty of Law, Thammasat University 2013) 259.

however, differ from one jurisdiction to another. The following questions may be asked: is there a need for an express clause stipulating that a third party may acquire a right? If not, to what extent may such a third party's entitlement be inferred from the circumstances? Unlike the BGB or the equivalent statutory regime in English law,[3] the Thai CCC is completely silent on the issue, and what amounts to 'an agreement to make a performance to a third person' within the meaning of section 374 has become a subject of debate.[4] As will be demonstrated, Thai courts have shown reluctance to apply section 374 and generally require compelling evidence to show that the contract is designed specifically to confer a right on a third party. Some merely incidental benefits accruing to a third party in the performance of the contract that is primarily in the promisee's interests would not typically qualify as a contract for the benefit of a third party which confers on the third party the right of enforcement. The approach favoured by the Thai court in the interpretation of section 374 seems to be a very restrictive one.

The second observation is related to another technique adopted by German lawyers to relax the rule of relativity of contract alongside the regime of § 328 of the BGB. The concept of *Vertrag mit Schutzwirkung für Dritte* or 'contract with protective effects towards third parties' was judicially developed in German law to remedy the lack of breadth in the German tort regime; particularly the failure to recognize pure economic loss as an amenable loss within the prescribed list of 'protected interests' under § 823(1) of the BGB.[5] Recovery of a negligently inflicted pure economic loss is generally precluded in the German law of tort. Because of the structural deficiencies in tort law, German jurists push what is essentially a tort issue over into the territory of contract, and permit a third party to recover the loss on the premise of a contract entered into by the original contracting parties. Hence, an intended beneficiary of a will could recover against the solicitors who under the service contract with the testator negligently excluded the claimant from the testament. A valuer may also be liable on the basis of a service contract with the vendor for loss caused to a third party mortgagee who provided loans in reliance on negligently prepared reports of valuation.[6] In contrast, section 420 of the Thai CCC, despite being a direct translation of § 823(1) of the BGB, embraces pure economic loss within the meaning of 'any other right' in the prescribed list of protected interests. Therefore, unlike German law, there is generally no immediate need to adopt the concept of 'contract with protective effects' as a regime supplemental to the traditional 'contract for the benefit of a third party'.

Suffice it to say that the appearance of translation or legal transplant should not lead legal comparatists to a presumption of equivalence. This chapter will demonstrate how the technique adopted by Thai jurists to relax the general rule of privity may exemplify a situation in which the particular rules of one code may be substantially at variance with the rules adopted in the codes it is modelled after. Hence, in addition to working out the substantive rules of Thai law, this chapter will, where appropriate, make comparative references to foreign rules in equivalent scenarios.

To examine the issues raised in Thai law as well as the answers given by it either conclusively or tentatively, this chapter is divided into three further sections. Section II investigates

[3] § 328(2) BGB. For English law, see s 1(1)(b) Contracts (Rights of Third Parties) Act 1999.

[4] See eg K Chunchaemsai, 'Contracts in Favour of Third Parties: The UNIDROIT Principles of International Commercial Contracts 2004 and Thai Laws' (2010) 39 Thammasat LJ 339.

[5] B Markesinis, H Unberath, and A Johnston, *The German Law of Contract: A Comparative Treatise* (2nd edn, Oxford: Hart Publishing 2006) 204. Another rule that the concept of protective effects is developed to remedy is the weak rule of vicarious liability under § 831 that permits an employer to escape liability by proving care in the selection and supervision of employees. In contrast, under s 425, Thai law embraces a broader version of vicarious liability and, hence, the German concept of protective effects is not needed.

[6] ibid 210–211.

the court's restrictive interpretation of section 374 in answering the question of whether a contract qualifies as a 'contract for the benefit of a third party'. Controversies in Thai law revolve around two important issues—namely, an intention to benefit an outsider and the meaning of benefits. Another controversial area is the discussion in section III which deals with crystallization of the third party's right and its effect in barring revocation and modification by the original contracting parties. Section IV raises issues pertaining to enforcement by the beneficiary as well as the promisee.

II. Creating Contract for Third Party's Benefit

1. Need for Unequivocal Intention Before Outsider May Acquire Right

Most critical to the understanding of section 374's scope of application is the correct interpretation of the section. The unfortunate part is that section 374 is a simple statement of principle which merely states that a 'contract to make a performance to a third party' may be enforced by that third party. It does not provide any guidance on whether a particular agreement may be regarded as falling within its scope. At least three solutions may be suggested. First, given that section 374 is a direct translation of § 328(1), one might wish to align the Thai contract for the benefit of a third party with the equivalent German regime. There, the general statement of § 328(1) of the BGB is immediately followed by § 328(2) that states whether a third party may acquire a right may be express or 'inferred from the circumstances, in particular from the purpose of the contract'. Hence, it can be suggested that the Thai CCC similarly permits the court to make an inferential finding of an intention that a third party may acquire a right. This may result in a wide application of section 374.[7]

Second, section 374 is open to the possibility that the court may adopt a test involving a presumption and a displacement favoured by the English rules prescribed in sections 1(1)(b) and 1(2) of Contracts (Rights of Third Parties) Act 1999.[8] Here, a contract which purports to confer a benefit on a third party may presumptively trigger the regime of contract for the benefit of a third party; the presumption is only rebutted if on a proper construction of the contract the parties have evinced an intention to the contrary.[9] In other words, where the contract is neutral on the question whether a third party may enforce it, the conferment of a benefit on the third party raises a presumption in favour of enforceability by the third party. Whether this method is significantly different from the German test may be a matter of debate; ultimately, what amounts to a 'conferment of benefit' that will raise the presumption largely depends on whether the benefit is specifically intended for a third party or whether it is merely incidental that the benefit accrued to the third party.[10] The upshot is that a test involving a presumption is likely to have a relatively low threshold; the court may readily discover the requisite intention to benefit particularly when the class of potential beneficiaries is tightly circumscribed.[11]

The third approach involves a much narrower test than both the German and the English tests. It strictly confines the contract for the benefit of a third party to scenarios where the parties have unequivocally manifested an intention that a third party may acquire a right of

[7] See ibid 187, for a list of scenarios recognized as involving a contract for the benefit of a third party under § 328. Many in the list would, however, not be considered by Thai courts as falling within the scope of s 374.

[8] Transplants of the UK Act can be found in Singapore and Hong Kong: see B Ong, 'Contracts for the Benefit of Third Parties: The Singapore Law Perspectives', ch 9; and L Mason, 'Contracts for the Benefit of Third Parties: Hong Kong', ch 11.

[9] *Nisshin Shipping Co Ltd v Cleaves & Co Ltd & Ors* [2004] 1 All ER (Comm) 481 [23]–[24].

[10] Markesinis, Unberath, and Johnston (n 5) 184.

[11] The test would still fail to catch a contract for valuation services; the benefit to third parties who may rely on the valuation report is merely incidental: *Hedley-Byrne & Co v Heller & Partners* [1964] AC 465.

enforcement. Such an intention may either be express or is a necessary implication of the particular contract. Under this approach, the court's exercise of an inferential finding similar to § 328(2) of the BGB is to be either avoided entirely or at least significantly curtailed; and there can be no presumption of enforceability by an outsider on whom the contract purports to confer a benefit. Given the fundamental nature of section 374 as an exception to the general rule of privity, much can be argued in favour of the view that section 374 must receive a restrictive interpretation.[12] An inquiry into the courts' judgments discloses four strands of cases where the Thai courts have traditionally found an unequivocal intention that a third party may acquire a right of enforcement: insurance contracts, contracts of compromise, contracts pursuant to which the benefit conferred is the discharge of a debt separately owed to the third party beneficiary, and contracts giving an option to a third party. It is arguable that the dearth of cases beyond these four traditional categories indicates that Thai courts envisage a much narrower conception of contract for the benefit of a third party than that embraced by German or English law.

(a) Insurance and annuity contracts

In the first category, insurance and annuity contracts are nominate contracts which have a separate treatment in Book III of the Code.[13] While the Thai CCC does not specifically state whether a third party beneficiary under an insurance contract may acquire a right of direct enforcement, it would be extremely odd if the beneficiary's direct enforcement is not possible. After all, the driving force behind the relaxation of the rules of relativity was precisely the need to give effect to insurance and annuity contracts.[14] Enforceability by the beneficiary is thus presumed in the specific provisions regulating insurance and annuity contracts. Section 881, for example, obliges the beneficiary to inform the insurer upon learning that the insured risk has materialized. Similarly, section 891 prevents the insured from reassigning the proceeds of a life insurance policy to a new beneficiary, provided that the named beneficiary has acquired possession of the insurance policy document and has submitted a written notice of assent to the insurer. Judicial decisions have also pronounced on the right of a beneficiary to enforce insurance contracts.[15]

An interesting comparison may be drawn between the location within the Thai and German Codes of the reference made to life insurance contracts. Whereas sections 374 to 376 of the Thai Code purport to lay down only a general rule and are silent on the contracts regarded as contracts for the benefit of a third party, in German law § 328 of the BGB is followed almost immediately by a reference to life insurance. § 330 prescribes that in case of doubt, the third party in a life insurance contract is presumed to acquire a direct right of enforcement. This is supplemented by § 331(1) which clarifies that the right is acquired upon the death of the insured-promisee. German courts have then interpreted the provisions to exclude the life insurance proceeds from the estate of the insured; the right to performance is the beneficiary's 'direct' right which arises by reason of the contract between the insurer and the policyholder and comes into existence upon the policyholder's death.[16] Hence, the beneficiary is protected if the policyholder dies insolvent. Notably, Thai courts have reached the same outcome, but since there are no provisions equivalent to §§ 330 and 331,

[12] Chunchaemsai (n 4) 355. [13] ss 861–888 (insurance); ss 889–897 (life insurance and annuity).

[14] Markesinis, Unberath, and Johnston (n 5) 187.

[15] See eg Supreme Court Decisions No 775/2522; No 1752/2543 (termination of hire purchase of car has no effect on validity of insurance; vendor-lender is capable of enforcing as beneficiary).

[16] Markesinis, Unberath, and Johnston (n 5) 194–195.

the technique used is by reference to Book VI on Succession.[17] The general wording of section 1600 which refers to the deceased's estate as all assets and liabilities is interpreted as all assets and liabilities which exist at the moment of death. This excludes benefits payable under life insurance, which do not come into existence until death.

(b) Contract of compromise

The second category of cases in which the courts have traditionally found the parties' mutual intention that a third party may acquire a right of enforcement involves a dispute compromise under section 850. A compromise contract is a mutual concession through which parties formally agree to settle a dispute according to the terms of their contract. Where a compromise stipulates a performance in favour of a third person, the courts have consistently held that the third person acquires the right of enforcement. The rationale for this outcome probably lies in the unique nature of a compromise—it is a formal settlement of dispute pending litigation, usually finalized in the presence of a court official. This indicates the promisor's intention to be strictly bound by its terms. Further, as a compromise results in the promisee's existing right of action being extinguished, it is in the promisee's interest that the promisor be strictly bound. Where a compromise has a third party beneficiary, enforceability by the beneficiary is a ready implication of the exceptional strength of the parties' intention. It would provide additional teeth that keep the promisor to the terms of the compromise.

In Thailand, the fact that a compromise is enforceable by the beneficiary is of practical use in settlements of dispute concerning division of matrimonial property following divorce and distributions of estate of deceased persons; the courts' judgments on section 374 typically concern these two areas. In the first strand of cases, children named as beneficiaries of a divorce settlement are permitted to recover a property transferred by the divorcé(e) in breach of the terms of the settlement.[18] As Thai law does not recognize a separation of title into legal and equitable or beneficial title, the courts' reasoning does not take on a proprietary dimension. The right asserted by the children is an entitlement to a specific court order, given purely on the basis of the section 374 right to enforce a contract between the divorcing parties. Accordingly, an order for cancellation of title transfer was granted against the volunteer transferee, together with an order for a new transfer in favour of the children-beneficiaries.

The second strand of cases sees unpaid creditors of a deceased person successfully bringing a suit against a promisor—usually an heir of the deceased or a legatee named in the deceased's will.[19] In these cases, a compromise agreement is made between the heirs to settle a dispute concerning estate distribution. To avoid having to realize assets of the deceased to satisfy all outstanding debts prior to distribution, a particular heir, in exchange for a larger share in the estate, may undertake to pay the debts. It has been decided that such a compromise between heirs is enforceable by the creditor. There is merit in the result, which is ultimately instrumental in facilitating asset distribution. If the beneficiary-creditor cannot enforce the compromise against a particular heir or legatee who is required to pay the debt owed by the deceased, the estate may have to wait until all debts are paid before distribution

[17] Supreme Court Decision No 4714/2542.

[18] Supreme Court Decisions No 2435/2536; No 2675/2551. Note, however, that under s 1562, children do not have standing to sue parents. In both cases, the defendant was a subsequent partner of the promisor. If property is still held by the promisor, then recourse would have to be sought by the promise. See also, Supreme Court Decision No 1432/2522.

[19] See eg Supreme Court Decision No 7355/2553.

can commence. Such a delay is unlikely to have been intended by the heirs in agreeing to the contract of compromise.

There may also be another exception to the rule of privity in cases concerning a compromise reached in court following a judgment. This particular kind of compromise is regarded as part of the enforcement of a judgment. The Supreme Court has held that the right of enforcement is reserved for the parties to the dispute,[20] although it has been suggested that the third party beneficiary may apply to become an interpleader with a vested interest in the dispute.[21] However, this avenue does not dispense with the need to have the promisee present; it should thus be regarded at best as a pseudo exception to the privity rule.

(c) Contract discharging debt separately owed to third party

The more generic types of contracts which have been recognized as granting an enforceable right to a third party typically involve an arrangement for the promisor to make a performance which would discharge a debt or other binding promises—whether present or future—separately owed by the promisee to the third party. In these instances, Thai courts have held that there is an intention for the third party to be given a right of enforcement. An example frequently cited is an agreement between a landowner and a developer pursuant to which the landowner agrees, in exchange for ownership of the building, to register a long lease in favour of any contributors to the building construction costs. The contributors would only be in a direct contractual relationship with the developer, but they would be the beneficiaries under the contract between the landowner and the developer.[22]

In the reported judgments in this category, it seems that the promisor intended to conclude the contract on the precise premise that only the performance by the promisor could discharge the debt owed separately to the beneficiary. As explained earlier, in Thai law the mere fact that a benefit is given to a third party does not carry the inference or raise any presumptions as to the third party's right of enforcement. Something more is required. Typically, the beneficiary's right of enforcement against the promisor would be a necessary implication of the contract where the debt owed to the beneficiary cannot be performed by anyone other than the promisor, and the promisor is aware of that fact. Hence, cases often involve enforcement against the promisor-owner of land who promises to grant certain interests in the land to the beneficiary.[23]

This category of contracts may also be broad enough to cover cases where the beneficiary has specifically nominated the promisor to render performance, and the promisor enters into the contract with the promisee precisely on this understanding. Consider a hypothetical case where Y security company contracts with X bank to collect takings from Z store and agrees to deploy a specially armoured vehicle and to take out insurance. Such an

[20] Supreme Court Decision No 269/2508.

[21] s 57(1) Code of Civil Procedure; S Sotthibandhu, *An Explanation on the Civil and Commercial Code in Order of Sections: Contracts* (Bangkok: Professor Sethabutr Fund, Faculty of Law, Thammasat University 2008) 127.

[22] Supreme Court Decisions No 175/2512; No 2530/2517; No 987/2549.

[23] See eg Supreme Court Decisions No 2732/2519 (vendor in a hire purchase of land transferred the land to mortgagee bank on condition that the land would be reconveyed to purchaser); No 2873/2519 (promisees sold land to promisors on condition that promisors would respect an agreement to buy and to sell previously concluded between promisees and third parties). cf Supreme Court Decision No 7894/2553 (lessor and lessee arranged a special type of lease, where the lessee agreed to make a substantial contribution to the building construction costs. In Thai law, this is a special kind of lease which has no formality requirements for it to be enforceable against the lessor. However, here the lessor sold the land to the purchaser. It was held that the lease was unenforceable against the purchaser; the lessee failed to show that the purchaser agreed to benefit him even though she was aware of the special lease arrangement. The court noted that even a mere oral agreement by the purchaser would have amounted to a contract under s 374 which would result in the special lease being enforceable against the purchaser. See also Supreme Court Decision No 1002/2509).

arrangement would not typically grant Z a direct right of enforcement. If Y uses an ordinary car and the takings are stolen, Z may only seek damages in the contract with X who may in turn have recourse in a contractual action against Y. The usual rule of privity applies. However, this does not rule out the narrow possibility that Z may have specifically nominated Y to perform and the contractual setting was such that Y clearly intended Z as the enforcing beneficiary. Z might have been heavily involved in the contractual negotiations between X and Y such that there was an implicit understanding among the parties that Z should have a direct right of enforcement. In such cases, the exception to the rule of privity might apply.

One qualification is widely observed in relation to this category of contracts. It must be shown that the promisor clearly obliges himself to confer the benefit on the third party. Here the wording in the contract may be crucial; it is apparently not sufficient if the purported promisor retains a discretion whether to confer the benefit on an outsider. In Supreme Court Decision No 639/2530, a term of the building contract permitted the employer to deduct the amount owed to the builder and pay the labourers directly should the builder fail to pay the labourers' wages in a timely manner. The court construed the term as having the goal of ensuring that the labourers would continue with the work until completion; it created the right on the part of the employer to choose the method of payment, not the right to obtain payment on the part of the labourers. Similarly, in Supreme Court Decision No 3467/2535, a term in a lease prohibiting a lease-transfer unless written permission was obtained from Crown Property was held to grant Crown Property the right to refuse a lease-transfer application. It did not give any right to the prospective lease transferees.

(d) Contract giving option to third party

The courts recognize as falling within the ambit of section 374 agreements which give to a third party the option to enter into a contract with the promisor. For instance, the right given to the beneficiary to adopt the hire purchase of a car after the purchaser's death was directly enforceable against the vendor.[24] This type of arrangement may be particularly useful in permitting the promisee to pass on a contractual entitlement which would otherwise be considered a personal right incapable of being passed on to the promisee's estate. For example, in Thai law, a lease contract is considered strictly personal; a term permitting the lessee to transfer the lease upon paying a fixed fee to the landlord could not be relied upon by the lessee's heir who attempted to adopt the lease after the lessee's death.[25] Nonetheless, a term in a lease which permits the lessee's heir to continue the lease should be enforceable against the lessor.

(e) Other contracts

Few cases involving section 374 exist beyond the categories listed earlier. The simple fact that a contractual performance is to be rendered to a third party is not of itself sufficiently indicative of an intention that the named third party is given the right of enforcement. In contrast with the German approach, a contract between the parents of a child and a hospital for treatment of the child would not entitle the child to enforcement and any contractual damages if the treatment is carried out negligently.[26] It is also unlikely that a family package

[24] Supreme Court Decision No 1366/2516. [25] Supreme Court Decision No 383/2540.
[26] Markesinis, Unberath, and Johnston (n 5) 189.

holiday agreed between a customer and a travel agency would be considered a section 374 contract which is enforceable by the customer's family members. In contrast, an agreement between a groom's father and the bride's parents that the father would have a 'newly-wed family home' built for the newly-weds was considered a contract for the benefit of a third party.[27] What supports the finding is perhaps a cultural value underlying the typical Thai marriage, which considers the wife as belonging to her husband's family. The 'price'—known as *Sinsod* and *Khongman*—is to be paid to the bride and her parents respectively.[28] The groom and his parents are culturally expected to strictly honour the prenuptial promises.

There are uncertainties as to the status of the consignee in a contract of carriage. In a contract of carriage in which a bill of lading is issued, the consignee is given a statutory assignment of the consignor's contractual right.[29] Where a bill of lading is not used, such as in the case of a retailer's domestic sale agreed at a distance, the recipient would normally be protected as the owner of the goods. Any damage to the goods would then be recoverable in a delictual action.[30] The position of the non-owner recipient remains unclear: in very narrow circumstances it may be arguable that at least in the commercial context the contract of carriage may be considered a contract that discharges a debt owed to the third party (the consignee); and may accordingly be enforced by him.[31]

2. Meaning of Benefits

The previous section explains one requirement for an agreement to be characterized as a contract for the benefit of a third party: the contracting parties must clearly intend, whether expressly or as a necessary implication of the contract, that the third party beneficiary may enforce it. There is, however, one further important qualification: the beneficiary's enforcement is only possible in relation to the 'benefit' bestowed upon him. This raises the question of what counts as the requisite benefit.

Section 374, following the model of § 328(1) of the BGB, simply describes the contract for the benefit of a third party as a contract pursuant to which a promisor agrees to 'make a performance to a third person'. The section thus requires that there is a benefit in the form of a performance. Two issues emerge here. The first is whether a burden imposed on the third party as a condition precedent for the receipt of the stipulated benefit would preclude the agreement from being a contract for the benefit of a third person. The second issue deals with benefits which assume the form of an entitlement other than a performance.

(a) Burden imposed as condition for receiving benefit

That a burden may be imposed upon a third party as a condition for receiving a benefit is affirmed in Supreme Court Decision No 2733/2517.[32] There, a compromise of a dispute concerning the distribution of estate obliged the promisor, upon payment of 2,000 baht by the promisee's children, to convey a piece of land to the promisee, who agreed to transfer

[27] Supreme Court Decision No 173/2477. However, on the facts of the case, the holding that the agreement qualifies as a s 374 contract was an obiter dictum; the groom and the bride were not parties to the litigation, which was entirely between the parents.

[28] s 1437. [29] s 627. See also Supreme Court Decision No 1556/2509.

[30] Contrast with the equivalent scenario in Germany, where the peculiar German rules on the passage of risk and title results in the doctrine of *Drittschadensliquidation*: Markesinis, Unberath, and Johnston (n 5) 220. A loss suffered by the consignee is treated as having been 'transferred' to the consignor, leading to a possible contractual claim by the consignor against the carrier. The consignee can then bring an action as an assignee of this contractual claim.

[31] Sotthibandhu (n 2) 350. [32] See generally Chunchaemsai (n 4) 339, 355.

half of the land to the children. The children were held to be beneficiaries of the compromise, and could therefore enforce the disposition of the part of land that had been designated as theirs.

A remarkable aspect of section 374's coverage of the scenario just described is that it may help to clarify the Thai understanding of an 'assignment of contract' particularly where the promisor, as a business successor of the promisee, wishes to continue the promisee's contract with the third party. Traditionally, the assignment of a contract is understood to be a novation involving the substitution of a new debtor. This requires that a new contract is concluded between the creditor and the new debtor.[33] Thus, if a land developer ceases trading and sells all its businesses including the residential allotments it is currently developing to another developer, the terms of the agreement to buy and to sell or any reservations that the first developer has earlier made with its customers cannot automatically bind the new developer. Further, absent a fresh contract, the customers may not owe any obligations to the new developer.

Once it is appreciated that the contract for the benefit of a third party may lay a burdensome condition for the receipt of the benefit, an 'assignment of contract' may have to be re-conceptualized. The assignment, in the land developer's example, is part of the sale of a business between the developers; and typically the new developer undertakes the obligations owed under the contract with the customers. The arrangement between the developers would thus be a contract for the benefit of a third party (the customers); the relevant benefit is the performance owed by the developer, given on the onerous condition that the customers continue to perform their part of the contract (by paying the price).

This is precisely the result reached in Supreme Court Decision No 2468/2549. In this case, there was an assignment, by the first defendant (land developer) to the second defendant (bank), of contracts that the first defendant had concluded with its customers. A written notice was duly given to the customers. When the second defendant failed to complete the house construction and make conveyance in a timely manner, the claimant-customer terminated the contract and brought an action to recover the amount he had paid to the first defendant. The Supreme Court upheld the claim, explaining that the assignment of contract was itself a contract for the benefit of a third party. Here, the claimant as the third party beneficiary in the arrangement between the defendants was entitled to enforce the benefit (which is the bank's assumption of the obligation to perform the duty owed by the developer) against the second defendant, the bank. This decision is, however, roundly criticized.[34] The gist of the criticism is that the contract for the benefit of a third party cannot impose any obligation on the beneficiary. The arrangement between the first and second defendants had the effect of imposing a new onerous relationship between the second defendant and the claimant, which replaced the relationship between the first defendant and the claimant. Such a result could only be obtained by the doctrine of novation, which would have required a new contract. And since the relevant contract was an agreement to buy and to sell an immovable property, the new contract would have to be evidenced in writing; a mere written notice to the claimant and the claimant's consent to the assignment did not suffice. The critics contend that the Supreme Court's decision distorted the logic of the principle of privity which prohibits the contracting parties from imposing an obligation on an outsider; and that the reasoning overstepped the territory traditionally covered by the principle of novation.

Arguably, these arguments are misconceived and the Supreme Court's reasoning is ultimately defensible. There was no new obligation imposed on the beneficiary; and it was

[33] s 350. [34] Sotthibandhu (n 2) 344–445 fn 2.

not a case of novation. What must first be appreciated is that the language used by the parties to the litigation, the 'assignment of contract',[35] may be somewhat misleading. It results in a misconception that the first defendant ('the assignor') would drop out of the picture once the contract was 'assigned' to the second defendant ('the assignee'). The claimant would, the argument goes, be made subject to a fresh onerous contract with the second defendant. However, this was arguably never the result intended by the Supreme Court. The arrangement between the first and second defendants consisted of two parts. First, it was a valid assignment of debt (of price payment, owed by the claimant) from the first to the second defendant. There was no fresh obligation imposed on the claimant as third party. Second, the arrangement that the second defendant would make a performance owed by the first defendant was a contract for the benefit of the claimant. This was not a case of novation; the first defendant still owed an obligation under the original contract. On the failure of performance, the claimant could have pursued a claim either against the first defendant on the basis of the original contract, or the second defendant pursuant to a contract for the benefit of a third party.[36]

(b) Benefit in the form of entitlement other than performance

The second issue lies in the meaning of performance for the purpose of section 374. Defining 'benefit' in terms of 'performance' seems to have systematically constrained the potential reach of section 374—'performance' is, by the plain meaning of the word, narrower in scope than 'benefit'. Performance necessarily implies a positive act or restraining from committing a certain act; and in the context of section 374, the word has been interpreted as such.[37] A benefit may, however, assume the form of an entitlement other than a performance. This may include, for example, a warranty, an exemption of liability, and a limitation clause. In these cases, the relatively narrow meaning of benefit defined by reference to 'performance' may preclude the operation of section 374; Thai law must resort to alternative avenues in order for a third party to benefit from these arrangements.

A quick glance at comparative law may assist. In English law, section 1(6) of Contracts (Rights of Third Parties) Act 1999 explicitly refers to exclusion and limitation of liability clauses as a term enforceable by a third party. The meaning of 'benefit' is also wide enough to cover warranties, though in some industries such as construction the standard practice is to have a collateral warranty in the form of a separate written agreement between the remote parties. In Germany, the courts have no linguistic difficulties in accommodating the exclusion and limitation clauses within the language of § 328 of the BGB which defines a benefit in terms of the promisor's performance.[38] A similar analysis also applies to a manufacturer's warranty which runs with the goods.[39]

The problem encountered by Thai courts is that the benefit conferred on a third party in the form of an entitlement other than performance is not caught by the literal reading of section 374. Take, for example, a situation where a consignor and a carrier conclude a contract of carriage with a clause purporting to exempt liability for damage negligently caused by loading and unloading by the stevedores. The following may be suggested.

[35] The actual wording is the 'assignment of debts and duties pursuant to the agreement to buy and to sell'.

[36] In the actual case, the first defendant went into administration and the claim against it was suspended.

[37] C Hemaratchata, *The Law of Contract* (3rd edn, Bangkok: Chulalongkorn University Press 2004) 307–309; S Sanongchart, *The Civil And Commercial Code: Juristic Acts—Contracts* (11th edn, Bangkok: Nitibannakarn 2014) 444–449.

[38] For German case law on the admissibility of the *Himalaya* clause, see M Sturley, 'International Uniform Law in National Courts: The Influence of Domestic Law in Conflicts of Interpretation' (1987) 27 Virginia J Int'l L 729.

[39] Markesinis, Unberath, and Johnston (n 5) 187.

First, the exclusion and limitation of liability expressed in a contract may operate as a duty-refining clause which delimits the duty of care owed in tort. While it is possible to refine the duty of care through a contract that exists between the tortfeasor and the victim,[40] the question here is whether the law permits a contract to adjust the scope of duty of care owed by outsiders. One may conceive of an argument that it is permissible: the stevedores' performance discharges part of the obligation owed by the carrier under the contract of carriage; it is a performance in lieu of the original debtor's;[41] hence, the duty assumed by the stevedores in handling the goods is akin to a contractual duty and should not be more extensive than the duty contractually owed by the original debtor (the carrier). However, whether this proposition will prevail may be controversial, for again we encounter the stringency of the rule of privity: a contract only takes effect between the contracting parties and it should not be able to supplant the duty owed separately by non-parties.

The alternative approach is to outwardly accept that there is a contract between the consignor and the stevedores. On this view, the exclusion or limitation of a liability clause in the original contract of carriage may be treated as a collateral promise made to the stevedores, which is accepted upon the stevedores' loading and unloading of the consignment. The third party (stevedores) may then raise this collateral contract in a defence against a tortious action brought by the consignor. Here, the analysis is based on a contract to which the consignor and the stevedores are immediate parties. The finding of this direct contractual relationship effectively circumvents the problem encountered in the previous approach. The reasoning may also be defensible as it is analogous to the conventional explanation in Thai law of a manufacturer's warranty given to ultimate purchasers.[42] It is therefore a preferable solution.

The Thai courts' restrictive, literal reading of benefit as 'performance' under section 374 perhaps echoes the general perception of the nature of section 374 as an exception to the general rule of privity. As suggested recently, a more flexible reading may be established if the basis of section 374 is re-conceptualized as reflecting the general principle of freedom of contract—the promisor's expression of an intention to be bound by the benefits enforceable by the beneficiaries.[43] The current approach is, however, deeply rooted in conventional judicial and academic reasoning. Where the conferred benefits do not fit within the narrow description of a 'performance', third party beneficiaries may have to find relief, if any, in a collateral promise that ties them in a direct contractual relationship with the promisor.

3. Identification of Beneficiary

For a contract to be enforceable by a third party, the courts have required the identity of the third party beneficiary to be sufficiently determinable. The beneficiary need not be in existence at the time of the conclusion of the contract;[44] but the contract must at least describe a character or quality that the intended beneficiary must possess. For example, in Supreme Court Decision No 175/2512, an agreement between a landowner and a builder contained

[40] However, the law imposes a restriction on the use of contract to refine a duty of care owed in tort: see s 8, Unfair Contract Terms Act BE 2540 (1997) (prohibiting the exemption and limitation of liability for personal injury. For other losses, the clause is subject to the test of fairness): see ss 58 and 60(1), Carriage of Goods by Sea Act BE 2534 (1991) (setting a minimum amount for limitation of liability clause; and prohibiting limitation of liability for damage intentionally or recklessly caused).

[41] s 314.

[42] S Sotthibandhu, *Sale, Exchange, Gift* (6th edn, Bangkok: Winyuchon Publication 2013) 196.

[43] Chunchaemsai (n 4) 349, 355.

[44] The beneficiary may be described as a child who is unborn, or a corporation that has yet to be founded: Supreme Court Decision No 277/2551. See also Thirawat (n 2) 260; S Pramoj, *Civil and Commercial Code: Juristic Acts and Obligations (Parts I–II), Vol I* (2nd edn, Bangkok: Nitibannakarn 1965) 517; Sotthibandhu (n 21) 123.

a clause obliging the owner to register a ten-year lease in the name of any prospective lessee who would make financial contributions to the construction of the commercial buildings on the land. The description was held to be sufficiently precise for the purpose of section 374.

III. Crystallization of Third Party's Right: Modification and Revocation

Section 375 prohibits the contracting parties from modifying or revoking the right of a beneficiary without his consent, provided that the right has already 'come into existence'. Under section 374(2), the right comes into existence:

> ...when he [the third person] declares to the debtor his intention to take the benefit of the contract.

The usual rules relating to declaration of intention under sections 168 and 169 apply. The third party's assent may also be implied by the beneficiary's conduct which is known to the promisor.[45] Hence, where X leases two adjoining properties to Y and Z, and the lease prohibits Y from selling bread in order to protect Z's interests in Z's adjoining bakery, Z's continuing operation of the bakery may amount to an assent that bars X and Y from lifting that particular condition stipulated in the lease.

The draftsmen of the Thai CCC recorded that section 375 is modelled after section 538 of the Japanese Civil Code 1898 and § 328 of the BGB 1900.[46] Yet, the wording in the section is much closer to the Japanese Code (in fact a direct translation of it) than the current version of the BGB (2002). The BGB appears to introduce a more flexible approach which permits the courts to construe the actual agreement and to draw inferences on whether, when, and on what conditions the parties intend the beneficiaries' right to be modifiable or revocable. In contrast, the traditional focus of the Thai courts and academics continues to be on the two rules of thumb: first, that no revocation or modification is possible after assent and, second, that revocation or modification must be agreed to by all the contracting parties. As will be shown later, the strict application of these rules is unsatisfactory. It is at least arguable that section 375 should not preclude the courts from applying the rules of construction in order to work out the intention of the parties in relation to the question whether the contract is revocable, and on what conditions. The general attitude, however, remains faithful to the rules of thumb and the courts remain reluctant to take a flexible stance on section 375.

1. Relevance of Beneficiary's Assent

Thai law's disproportionate emphasis on irrevocability being contingent on the beneficiary's giving of assent means that little is discussed on the ability of the original contracting parties to set a condition for revocation that is independent of assent. This leads to uncertainties on two important issues. The first is whether the parties may agree to make a contract absolutely irrevocable regardless of the giving of assent by the intended beneficiary. Whereas in German law the wording of § 328 of the BGB makes clear that setting such a condition is possible,[47] the Thai CCC is silent on this issue. However, it may be suggested that the

[45] Supreme Court Decision No 4278/2530 (promisor was obliged to let beneficiary use a path over promisor's land; beneficiary's continued use of the path amounted to an assent).
[46] Sotthibandhu (n 21) 133.
[47] On the issue whether the parties may create an irrevocable contract in favour of a third party, the position taken by the BGB is not exceptional. For another example, see the Dutch Civil Code, Art 6:253(4); J Hallebeek and H Dondorp (eds), *Contracts for a Third Party Beneficiary: A Historical and Comparative Account* (Leiden: Martinus Nijhoff Publishers 2008) 152.

position taken by Thai law is quite different from the BGB. In Thai law, the beneficiary's right under section 374 is strictly considered an *exception* to the general rule of privity; and by virtue of its nature as an exception, it must be narrow in scope. Hence, augmenting the third party's right by declaring that it may be made absolutely irrevocable even before an assent is given should be impermissible.

The second issue concerns the contracting parties' reservation of a right to revoke a third party's benefit.[48] It is relatively clear that the parties may reserve the right of revocation, but the contention here is rather on the degree of clarity or explicitness that the contracting parties need for the constitution of this reservation. It has, for example, been observed that section 375, just as section 374, must have a strict interpretation.[49] Thus, unless the parties expressly reserve the right to revoke, the courts should be extremely cautious in finding that reservation of the right to revoke was intended.

The requirement that the reservation must be expressed may have significant ramifications on contracts in which the promisor's obligation will potentially not fall due for a long period of time. For example, in a death benefit policy the beneficiary could, by giving assent, effectively prevent a policyholder from changing his mind later in life. In Supreme Court Decision No 2401/2515, the court upheld a claim brought by the wife and son of the policyholder, a Mr Wittaya, in respect of the proceeds of the death benefit policy arranged with Mr Wittaya's employer, for which Mr Wittaya had named his father as a beneficiary. The father, however, died before Mr Wittaya. It was held that by the time of the father's death, his right as beneficiary had not crystallized because he had not communicated his assent to the employer. Hence, the benefit was payable to the estate of Mr Wittaya, rather than that of the father.

The Supreme Court's reasoning has a striking implication: had the father assented to the policy, the benefits would have been payable to the father's estate. However, in reality the policyholder may have wished to change the beneficiary after he learnt of the beneficiary's death. Or else, his personal preferences may have changed over time and he may subsequently have wished to exclude the original beneficiary for purely subjective reasons. There is nothing inherent in the death benefit policy, often a gratuitous arrangement, to indicate that the policyholder should strictly be bound by his original choice of beneficiary. Yet, the courts' narrow approach to the reservation of the right of revocation seems to tie the policyholder to that original choice. The policyholder seems to be absolutely barred from denying the beneficiary his entitlement to the benefit after the beneficiary has given assent.

The better approach is to move away from the strict 'assent-crystallization' analysis, and to have the courts explicitly address the construction of the particular contracts. In relation to a death benefit policy, it would normally be the intention of the policyholder that the beneficiary's right only crystallizes upon death of the policyholder and that the policyholder reserves the right of revocation.[50] An analogous situation in German law would be governed by § 332 of the BGB; with the beneficiary's mere chance of getting the benefit being considered no right at all, but only *nur eine Hoffnung* (mere hope).[51] In comparison, for instance, where the vendor is named as the beneficiary of an insurance policy taken as security for the hire purchase of a car, it is likely that the policyholder (purchaser) intends it also to be irrevocable at least until the purchase price is fully paid.[52]

[48] Supreme Court Decision No 3057/2527. [49] Sotthibandhu (n 21) 132–133 fn 104.

[50] Private life insurance policies normally expressly reserve the right of revocation or modification. However, the Thai CCC also provides a separate rule for giving of assent: s 891 subjects irrevocability to two conditions, viz: (1) that the beneficiary must have possession of the insurance policy documents; and (2) that the beneficiary has given a written notice of assent to the insurer.

[51] Markesinis, Unberath, and Johnston (n 5) 196. [52] cf Supreme Court Decision 489/2524.

2. Revocation or Modification Not to be Done Unilaterally

The next important question is related to the mode in which revocation or modification can be made prior to the giving of assent by the beneficiary. The traditional focus is on the need for the alteration to be made only by a subsequent agreement between all the original contracting parties. In Supreme Court Decision No 6104/2534, a compromise agreement was reached for the dissolution of a limited partnership—the first defendant. Two of the three partners—the second and third defendants—undertook to pay tax owed to the Inland Revenue (the claimant-beneficiary) in exchange for the remaining assets of the partnership. This compromise was purported to be cancelled by the partnership's subsequent tax undertaking, which was made pursuant to an agreement between the partnership, through the second defendant acting as the managing partner, and the third defendant. The subsequent agreement was held to be ineffective as it did not involve all the parties to the original compromise—it was lacking the second defendant acting in his personal capacity, and the third partner. The Inland Revenue's claim thus succeeded on the basis of the original compromise.

This rule is understandable; the promisor and the promisee may each have a legitimate interest in not having the benefit to the third party revoked or modified. However, this raises an important question in the insurance context where the insurer (promisor) is typically neutral as to whether the policyholder (promisee) may revoke the benefit granted to a particular beneficiary. In Supreme Court Decision No 489/2524, a car insurer resisted making a payment to the policyholder—the purchaser of a car subject to hire purchase, alleging that the proceeds were payable only to the beneficiary named in the policy, namely, the vendor of the car. This argument was favoured at first instance and in the Court of Appeal. The Supreme Court reversed the decision on the basis that the policyholder was in principle entitled to change the beneficiary until the assent is given. Here, the vendor had not assented to the benefit, and the court ordered a retrial for further evidence.

The Supreme Court's decision, clearly led by the emphatic 'assent-crystallization' analysis, was somewhat missing the point. It was not the parties' contention that the named beneficiary had or had not given assent—for there was clearly no such assent. The dispute was rather simply whether the policy documentation allowed the policyholder to unilaterally change the name of the beneficiary. It is at least arguable from the order for a retrial that the court did perceive the possibility that on a proper construction of the contract, the benefit to a third party may be subject to revocation or modification at the behest of one party. Further evidence was therefore needed to establish whether the insurer had a positive interest in holding the benefit of the insurance contract open for this particular beneficiary. But this conclusion, for the time being, remains a matter of speculation. A unilateral alteration as to the identity of the beneficiary is clearly permitted in relation to life insurance contracts,[53] but it remains unclear whether the courts would explicitly embrace a wide power of construction and permit a unilateral alteration in other contexts.

IV. Enforcement

Once it is established that a given contract fits within the narrow definition of contract for the benefit of a third party, the application of section 374 means that the third party may directly enforce performance from the promisor. What the beneficiary acquires is a right of enforcement. The promisor's failure to perform or his defective performance amounts to breach of contract which entitles the beneficiary to a primary remedy of specific performance

[53] s 891 (see section II.1(a)).

and a secondary right to payment of damages. The beneficiary, however, does not become privy to the contract. Consequently, he may not acquire other personal rights which belong to the original contracting party (the promisee) such as the rights of avoidance or termination of the contract.[54] This much is clear. There are, however, three points of obscurity, which characterize the apparent deficits in Thai law. Given the absence of clear authority on point, the position taken in this chapter on each of the issues is at best tentative. Nonetheless, it shall be defended with arguments drawn from principle.

As an introductory remark, it should be noted that each of these issues revolves around the questions of what exactly the beneficiary's 'direct right of enforcement' entails, and to what extent the contents of this right are different from the promisee's right. To examine these two questions, we must clearly understand what the beneficiary's direct right of enforcement is *not*. The first fundamental point is that the beneficiary's right is not an assigned right of the promisee. It is unfortunate that the Thai courts have failed to mark a clear line between assignments of debt and contracts for the benefit of a third party. Arguably, the identification of a given juristic act as an assignment or a section 374 contract is of critical importance, for it carries crucial implications on the rights of the intended assignee or beneficiary.

The second point is that the beneficiary's direct right and the promisee's right are not duplicative of each other. Of course, both the promisee and the beneficiary may exercise a right of enforcement in seeking specific performance of the promisor's obligation; the explanation in Thai academic literature often stops at observing this apparent similarity. As an alternative to the beneficiary, the elusive, more controversial question is whether the law permits the promisee to seek compensation for the loss suffered by the beneficiary. The law remains silent on this precise issue. However, once the beneficiary's right is conceived of as a 'direct right', we begin to understand that it is a separate right which may vary in scope and content from the right of the promisee.

Following from the previous point that the third party right is direct and distinct from the promisee's right, the third point is that the defences that the promisor has against the promisee may sometimes differ from the ones that can be set up against the beneficiary. This conclusion may appear contradictory with the general statement of section 376, but we may be able to conceive of a scenario in which it may be inferred that the parties intend to exempt the beneficiary from defences that the promisor may have against the promisee. Conversely, there might as well be defences which only apply personally against the beneficiary: the beneficiary will here be barred from enforcing the contract which remains perfectly enforceable by the promisee. As the promisee's and the beneficiary's rights are distinct, the extent of the beneficiary's right may not always correspond to that of the promisee's.

1. Potential Overlap with Assignment of Debt

First, there is an issue of potential overlap between a contract for the benefit of a third person and an assignment of debt. A creditor may wish to assign a debt to another person, thus making the position of the assignor/creditor factually analogous to that of the promisee; the debtor to the promisor; and the assignee to the beneficiary. The correct appreciation of each matrix may be crucial as it raises important questions of who may enforce the debt, and of when the right of the assignee-beneficiary crystallizes. In the case of assignment, by assigning a debt to a new creditor, the assignor gives up his status as a creditor and any right of enforcement. The right of the assignee crystallizes immediately upon assignment, when it is

[54] See generally Sotthibandhu (n 21) 124; Thirawat (n 2) 263.

made in writing.[55] But because the debtor may continue to obtain a good discharge from the assignor until a written notice of assignment has been given, in such cases the remedy for the unpaid assignee lies in an action against the assignor for breach of contract or for undue enrichment.

This posits an assignment of debt in direct contrast with the contract in favour of a third person on at least four counts. First, in the latter arrangement, the promisee as a contracting party fully retains the right to enforce the debt due by the promisor to the beneficiary. Second, there is no requirement that a contract for the beneficiary be made in writing. The beneficiary may prove existence of an agreement through the parties' conduct and does not need to adduce any evidence of a written assignment.[56] Third, whereas the assignee's right crystallizes immediately, the beneficiary's right may be revoked or modified until a notice of assent is given to the debtor-promisor. Hence, if performance is made to and duly accepted by the promisee prior to the giving of notice by the beneficiary, no recourse would lie against the promisor or the promisee.[57] Fourth, the uncrystallized right of the beneficiary may not form part of the beneficiary's estate.[58] If the beneficiary dies prior to communicating his assent to the benefit, the benefit stipulated may not be payable to the beneficiary's estate. The estate of an unknowing beneficiary may thus run a serious risk of losing out on the benefit, whereas the estate of an unknowing assignee will not.

Given the conceptual distinction between an assignment and a contract for a third party beneficiary and the practical differences that it entails, it is unfortunate that the Supreme Court has recently conflated the two techniques, holding that a single set of facts can equally be decided on the basis of there being simultaneously both a section 374 contract and an assignment.[59] In Supreme Court Decision No 12616/2555, to arrange for payment of a debt owed to the creditors (beneficiaries) of the builders (promisees), it was agreed that the instalments due from the builders' employers (promisors) under the building contract would be paid directly to the creditors. The creditors then sent a written notice to the employers to pay instalments directly to them by way of cheques. When the creditors were ordered to cease trading, the builders asked the employers to withhold payment of all the remaining cheques and pay the outstanding amount to the builders. The employers complied with the request. The question asked of the Supreme Court was whether the employers validly discharged the debt owed under the building contract. The Supreme Court held that they had not done so. This result is unimpeachable, but the court's reasoning is far from satisfactory. The Supreme Court considered that the arrangement for the employers to make a payment directly to the creditors (beneficiaries) amounted to a valid assignment of debt pursuant to section 306, as well as a contract for the benefit of a third party under section 374. Accordingly, the court applied section 375, with the result that the written notice given by the creditors prevented the promisee-builders from revoking the creditors' right.

[55] According to s 306, the assignment is valid only if made in writing. Yet, the assignment can be set up against the debtor only after a written notice has been given to him.

[56] Supreme Court Decision No 3702/2545 (purchaser (promisor) agreed with property developer (promisee) to pay outstanding debt directly to developer's creditor, the decorator (beneficiary). The arrangement was held to be a contract for the benefit of a third party, proved by offer and acceptance. The offer was found in the property developer's written order made to the purchaser to inspect the decorator' work and, upon approval of the work, to pay the decorator. Evidence of the acceptance consisted of: (1) the entry in the purchaser's internal account of the debt owed directly to the decorator; (2) the purchaser's approval of the work done by the decorators; and (3) the purchaser having directly made some payment to the decorators).

[57] Supreme Court Decision No 475/2522 (insurance policyholder's acceptance of payment of insurance proceeds from insurer was held to be a revocation; the named beneficiary had not communicated his assent to the benefit).

[58] Supreme Court Decision No 2401/2515.

[59] Sotthibandhu (n 2) 344 fn 2; 347–348 fn 6.

Arguably, this dual rationale is unnecessary. If the arrangement is already an assignment of a debt duly completed in writing, it would be irrevocable from the moment of the original assignment; the builders simply having fallen out of the picture. The reasoning through assent to the benefit under section 375 is thus entirely superfluous and, for the distinctions set out above, inappropriate.[60]

2. Enforcement by Promisee

What section 374 does is to grant the right of enforcement to the beneficiary; it does not disentitle the promisee from the right associated with his status as a party to the contract. Hence, the promisee retains the full right of enforcement;[61] he may demand that the promisor specifically perform the obligation as agreed, and compensate the promisee for any losses the latter personally incurred due to the promisor's failure to perform. The promisee could therefore have contractual recourse against the promisor where the promisee is himself liable to the beneficiary on the basis of a separate contract with the beneficiary. Less clear is an answer to the question whether the promisee who has not suffered any direct loss as a consequence of the promisor's failure to perform may nevertheless recover losses suffered personally by the beneficiary. This is important particularly where there is no direct contractual relationship between the promisee and the beneficiary so that the promisee is not contractually liable, or where the beneficiary for some reason refuses to pursue a claim against the promisor, or where the loss of the beneficiary is idiosyncratic, ie exceeds that of the promisee.[62]

Take, for example, a case where the promisee company, X, contracts with the promisor builders, Y, to build on land belonging to Z, a wholly owned subsidiary of X.[63] Losses incurred by Z as a result of numerous serious defects found in the building would be recoverable by Z on the basis of section 374; Z's entitlement to specific enforcement as the beneficiary in the contract between X and Y extends to a claim for recovery of costs of cure and damages for other consequential losses.[64] Enforcement by X, however, is more controversial. Beyond the basic premise that X may seek specific performance, Thai law is generally silent on X's entitlement to damages. The relevant questions are arguably twofold. First, can X seek damages in respect of Z's loss? Second, does Y's failure to perform count as a loss to X in the sense that X does not receive the performance he has bargained for, despite having suffered no apparent financial losses?

Thai courts have not been asked these specific questions. Understandably, this is because of the limited range of situations where the contract enforceable by a third party is recognized. In many of these situations, the benefits conferred on the third party are owed under a separate contract between the promisee and the beneficiary; and the promisee may recover damages for a personal loss, namely, a compensation earlier made by the promisee to the beneficiary. In other cases, the contract of compromise in particular, the promisee is only interested in pursuing specific performance. The question whether the promisee may directly recover compensation for the loss incurred by the beneficiary does not surface in

[60] ibid 347–348 fn 6.

[61] eg Supreme Court Decision No 5925/2538 (policyholder demanding payment of insurance proceeds to beneficiary).

[62] For a parallel discussion in German law, see Markesinis, Unberath, and Johnston (n 5) 220–225.

[63] The scenario is adapted from the facts in the English case of *Alfred McAlpine Construction Ltd v Panatown Ltd* [2001] 1 AC 518.

[64] For a claim in damages, Thai courts have awarded a contractual measure of damages under s 391 for the beneficiary's compensation: see eg Supreme Court Decisions No 987/2549; No 2530/2517.

the academic literature or judicial decisions. Nonetheless, should it do so, we may be able to draw some useful inferences from the following observations.

Thai courts have consistently held that entitlement to the benefit is vested with the beneficiary. Here we must distinguish between *the entitlement to the benefit*, and *the right of enforcement*. The right of enforcement may be exercised by either the promisee or the beneficiary, but the benefit belongs solely to the latter. However, where the beneficiary has declined to accept the benefit, the courts hold that the promisee may obtain the residual benefit for himself according to the general principle that parties to a synallagmatic contract may benefit from each other. For example, the insurance proceeds under a policy which named the financing company as the beneficiary were payable to the insured when the beneficiary declined the benefit by commencing litigation to recover the amount due under the hire purchase.[65] On the other hand, where it is only *legally possible* to give the benefit directly to the beneficiary, the promisee cannot obtain any residual benefit. Thus, the plaintiff who was the ex-owner of the dominant land did not have standing to pursue a claim against the owner of the subservient land where the agreement was to create an easement in favour of the plaintiff or any subsequent owners.[66] The agreement to create an easement was held to be enforceable only by the present owner of the dominant land. In such cases, the promisee does not have any entitlement to the residual benefit. Further, as an exception to the general rule that the promisee may enforce the contract, enforcement here seems to be available only at the suit of the beneficiary.

From the foregoing paragraph, we may derive the proposition that the benefit is vested with the beneficiary and that the promisee may personally obtain a residual interest on two conditions. First, the beneficiary must already have declined the benefit. Second, the benefit must be generic in character such as a payment of debt; it cannot be a benefit that is legally tied to the beneficiary. Returning to our example of a contract for building on land belonging to the subsidiary, the promisee's (X's) claim for compensation may probably fail at both hurdles. First, by permitting Y to build on the land, Z could be treated as having by conduct agreed to accept the benefit. There is no residual benefit for X to obtain. It would be conceptually inconsistent to argue that Z accepted the benefit of a specific performance (erection of a building) yet declined the benefit in respect of entitlement to any consequential damages (caused by defects). Second, compensation is legally tied to the person suffering the loss; no compensation is possible where the promisee suffers no actual losses. Hence, it is unlikely that the promisee can seek compensation with respect to the beneficiary's loss. Neither does he have standing to sue the promisor to have the latter pay damages to the beneficiary. Analogous to the easement example, compensation in the form of damages can only be sought and enforced by the person who is entitled to it.

This, however, leaves open the possibility that X may recover the theoretical loss measurable by the difference in value between what it actually obtains (a seriously defective building) and what it bargained for (a building built to construction specifications). Yet, permitting this action may potentially subject Y to double liability. The courts may, of course, respond by adopting the rule that excludes X from recovery where Z has already recovered,[67] or that X must hold the benefit on behalf of Z.[68] However, such an approach would run contrary to the fundamental rule in Thai law that Z, rather than X, has an absolute interest in the benefit conferred on it. Permitting X to sue may also lead to a race to litigation between X and Z, as well as a potential conflict between Z and the general creditors

[65] Supreme Court Decision No 1950/2543. [66] Supreme Court Decision No 778/2541.
[67] See eg the English rule in s 5 Contracts (Rights of Third Parties) Act 1999.
[68] See eg *Alfred McAlpine Construction Ltd v Panatown Ltd* [2001] 1 AC 518, 533.

of X (particularly where X's insolvency is looming). The better view is therefore that where Z has a direct recourse against Y, the damages recoverable by X should be nominal only.

A brief comparative remark should be made on this point with respect to German law. In a limited range of circumstances, particularly 'where all the damage due to the harmful conduct of the obligor is suffered by a third party rather than by the person with title to sue',[69] a contracting party may recover loss suffered by the third party. This is known as the doctrine of *Drittschadensliquidation*. The loss is treated as having been suffered by the contracting party; and the third party may seek a statutory assignment of the contractual action available to the contracting party.[70] While *Drittschadensliquidation* is a separate doctrine from a contract for the benefit of a third party under § 328 and has an independent area of application, it perhaps reflects the German generosity in allowing recovery in respect of loss suffered by another person. This attitude has, however, never been adopted by the Thai courts. Neither has the doctrine of *Drittschadensliquidation*.

3. Set Up of Contractual Defences Against Beneficiary's Claim

Under section 376:

> Defences arising from the contract mentioned in section 374 can be set up by the debtor against the third person who receives the benefit of the contract...

The relevant discussion in Thai academic literature emphasizes two points. The first is concerned with the meaning of 'defences', which have been interpreted to include claims that the contract is void, voidable, illegal, or contrary to public morals, as well as defences which arise only after the conclusion of the contract, such as failure of the promisee to perform his part of the contract. The second point of focus is the requirement that the defence must be one which pertains to the contract between the promisee and the promisor. Hence, where the promisor was obliged to pay up a debt owed by the promisee to the beneficiary in a separate contract, the court held that the promisor could not set up as a defence the fact that the debt owed by the promisee to the beneficiary had expired.[71] This corresponds exactly to German law's distinction between defences stemming from the *Deckungsverhältnis* (promisor–promisee) relationship and the *Zuwendungsverhältnis* (promisee–third party) relationship; only the former may be set up by the promisor against the third party beneficiary (§ 334 of the BGB).[72]

More significant for our purpose is the absence in Thai academic literature of an explicit recognition that the contractual defences which are available against the promisee may in certain contexts differ from the ones that lie against the beneficiary. This is perhaps attributable to a failure to clearly grasp the beneficiary's right as a direct and distinct right, not contingent on the right of the promisee. Here a clear contrast with an assignment of debt is useful. In an assignment, any defences, set-offs, or counterclaims that the debtor may have against the assignor can be set up against the assignee.[73] This rule is a logical extension of the fact that the assignee's right is derivative of the assignor's; the derivative nature of the right means that the quantum of the derivative right cannot exceed that of the original right. The only apparent exception to this rule is that when the debtor has given a written notice of consent without reservation to the assignment, the defences cannot be raised against the assignee.[74] But this is not to say that the assignee's right exceeds the assignor's.

[69] Markesinis, Unberath, and Johnston (n 5) 219.
[70] ibid 220; § 285 BGB.
[71] Supreme Court Decision No 3702/2545.
[72] Markesinis, Unberath, and Johnston (n 5) 202.
[73] s 308(2).
[74] s 308(1).

It is simply a consequence of the debtor being estopped from denying the effect of his written consent.

In comparison, a contract for the benefit of a third party creates a direct right in favour of the beneficiary. The quantum of the third party's right is determined directly by the agreement. Section 376 limits that right by permitting the promisor to invoke a contractual defence that he may have against the promisee. This should not, however, be understood as an indication that the third party's right is derivative of the promisee's: the rule of section 376 only reflects the fact that the third party's right is based on the contract. Further, because the third party's right is created directly by the contract, it may be possible that on a proper construction of the particular contract the third party's right is not to be subject to a contractual defence. For example, German courts have held that an agreement between an airline and a travel agency—a charter for a fixed number of seats on a certain flight—is a contract for the benefit of a traveller which contains an implied term that the airline cannot plead default of payment by the travel agency to refuse service to the traveller who has obtained a validly issued ticket.[75] There is a mutual assumption that travellers cannot be expected to understand the complex arrangements between the airline and the travel agency as well as the ticketing process. In comparison, the fate of the travellers in an analogous situation in Thai law is unclear. That section 376 may be treated as mandatory and may not be overridden by way of construction of the contract may indicate that the travellers are left in a rather precarious position. The Supreme Court's conflated treatment of an assignment and a contract in favour of third party beneficiaries helps little to clarify this point.

In other contexts, it may also be possible that enforcement by the third party beneficiary may be barred by a separate reason such as bad faith while the contract remains afoot as against the promisee. For instance, a promisor who is induced to enter into a contract by a third party's fraudulent misrepresentation may not rescind the contract unless the promisee has notice or can reasonably be expected to have notice of the misrepresentation.[76] The promisee remains perfectly entitled to enforce the contract, but direct enforcement by the third party may arguably be barred for bad faith. By using the notion of bad faith as a touchstone, it is possible that Thai courts may treat a negligent inducer more leniently.

V. Conclusion

It is the authors' intention to restate in detail the Thai rules on a third party beneficiary's right, a subject on which leading Thai legal materials have spilt little ink, and to highlight some tensions and uncertainties that have surfaced in relation to these rules. The general perception by Thai courts is that the regime for contracts in favour of a third person, which encompasses sections 374 to 376 of the Code, is at its foundation an exception to the principle of privity of contract. Because of its fundamental character as an exception, the regime has a restrictive application. Further, within this narrow sphere of application, the regime seems to demand a literal interpretation, leaving little room for the courts to engage the rules of construction in order to determine the actual intention of the parties. As demonstrated earlier, the courts are reluctant to infer an intention to grant a right of enforcement to a third party when the contract does not fall within one of the four established categories that the courts have taken cognizance of as section 374 contracts. The law currently does

[75] Markesinis, Unberath, and Johnston (n 5) 194.

[76] s 159(3):

> When a party has made a declaration of intention owing to a fraud committed by a third person, the act is voidable only if the other party knew or ought to have known of the fraud.

not permit the inference of an intention that the revocation of a third party's right may be conditioned on events other than the giving of assent by the beneficiary, or that certain contractual defences, such as failure of performance by the promisee, may be barred in an action brought by the beneficiary.

On the issue of 'legal transplant' which is the theme underlying the chapters in this volume, this chapter offers an example of a jurisdiction which, following the original drafting done primarily through a direct translation of the foreign codes, seems to have developed its own principles and jurisprudence uninfluenced by the directions which foreign laws have since taken. In deciding cases, Thai courts analyse the provisions in the Thai CCC from first principles. Drawing assistance from foreign law is not a traditional practice of Thai judges.[77]

By contrast, referring to foreign law is a common occurrence among Thai academic writings; yet, the comparative remarks are not confined to the foreign codes after which the relevant Thai provisions were modelled. English law and cases are often used as points of references. However, solving uncertainties concerning the scope of third party beneficiaries' rights largely remains an exercise of academic speculation. Some writings have offered detailed accounts of foreign law, but the authors of this chapter have not seen a sustained attempt to reconcile a proposed foreign position with the principles elaborated in the judgments rendered by the Supreme Court of Thailand. Such an approach might arguably be unnecessary because the judicial pronouncements in Thailand are not strictly binding. Nevertheless, given the central role of judgments in Thai legal education and their treatment as persuasive in subsequent cases, the most useful dimension of this chapter is its giving of tentative answers supported by the ratio of the judgments of the highest appellate court of the jurisdiction.

[77] This may be contrasted with the approach taken in some civilian jurisdictions such as the Netherlands: see E Mak, 'Why Do Dutch and UK Judges Cite Foreign Law?' (2011) 70 Cambridge LJ 420.

21

Contract Formation and Contracts for the Benefit of a Third Party in Vietnam

*LE Net**

I. Introduction

The general principles relating to contract formation and contracts to confer a benefit on a third party in Vietnam are found in the Vietnamese Civil Code ('VCC'). The current version of the Vietnamese Civil Code was adopted in November 2015 and effective from 1 January 2017 ('VCC 2015'). The VCC 2015 revises substantially the Vietnamese Civil Code 2005 ('VCC 2005') which, in turn, revised the Vietnamese Civil Code 1995 ('VCC 1995'). The VCC 1995 is one of the signature pieces of legislation that emerged from the market-oriented reforms of the early 1990s (the '*Grand Change*') that traced their inspiration to *Doi Moi* (the 'Renovation') in 1986. The move from a planned economy to a socialist-oriented market economy required legal infrastructure which supported these changes; along with the Law on Private Enterprises (1990–2000) and the Company Law (1990–2000), the VCC 1995 provided the basic ground rules by which the private sector was to function.

Scholars and legal practitioners from capitalist economies will find in the Vietnamese Civil Codes many familiar themes. These include freedom of contract, *pacta sunt servanda* (agreements must be kept), rules on effective communication, and rules on silence. A number of these themes, it will be argued, can be traced back to the pre-colonial Vietnamese codes and should not be seen merely as Western imports. Importantly, amidst the familiar, it is easy to lose sight of the thick layer of state regulations that apply to diverse specific transactions. In other words, the rules which this chapter is concerned with deal only with the foundational rules for creating contractual obligations. The further requirements for validity—whether in the nature of precise formal requirements for specific contracts, further public policy concerns, or regulatory approvals—need to be investigated, especially given that the market transactions are to take place within a socialist state. As such, actual operation of the rules may take on special Vietnamese characteristics, whether by reason of the way in which Vietnamese culture regards fair dealing, or by reason of the socialist political system in which the Code is to be applied.

Section II sets out the historical background of the law on civil obligations. The *Hong Duc Code* (1483) was impressive in its sophistication; in the field of private law, the subjects it dealt with ranged from guarantees, protection against devaluation of money, to what would be considered force majeure today. The *Hong Duc Code* and the French Napoleonic Code introduced during the colonial era are starting points for understanding the VCC, but they are no more than starting points. Importantly, though there was input from Japanese,

* Cite as N Le, 'Contract Formation and Contracts for the Benefit of a Third Party in Vietnam' in Chen-Wishart, Loke, & Vogenauer, *Studies in the Contract Laws of Asia Vol II: Formation and Third Party Beneficiaries* (Oxford: OUP 2017) ch 21.

Contract Formation and Contract for the Benefit of a Third Party in Vietnam. Le Net.

French, and English trained scholars, the drafters of the VCC were trained in the socialist legal tradition and socialist ideology pervaded the laws they drafted. In land law, this is evident in the notion that all land belongs to the state. In contract law, the concept of public interest which qualifies freedom of contract can only be properly appreciated when one is mindful of what Vietnamese socialism entails.

Section III deals with the formation of contracts. Under the VCC, a contract is a juridical act (*giao dịch dân sự*). Chapter VIII of Part I (Articles 116 to 133) of the VCC 2015 contains general provisions on juridical acts, such as conditions for substantive validity of juridical acts, formal and material requirements of juridical acts, grounds of invalidity of juridical acts, interpretation of juridical acts, together with remedies available for non-performance. As these matters apply equally to contracts, they are not repeated again in Part III of the VCC on Contracts and Obligations. Part III of the VCC deals with general provisions on obligations and contracts, formation, performance, security, assignment, and termination, as well as different types of contracts. Moreover, some contracts are subject to specific regimes. These include the Law on Housing which governs house rental and sale contracts of houses,[1] the Law on Land and its implementing Circulars which govern land transfers, rent, or mortgage contracts,[2] and the Commercial Law which governs commercial sales contracts, logistics contracts, and agency matters, etc.[3]

As in many other former socialist and civil law countries, Vietnamese law prescribes standard contents for certain types of contracts. Such prescribed standard terms serve a variety of purposes. They may address the unequal bargaining power of contracting parties; they also serve to protect public or state interests when state interests or state investments are involved. Such regulated contracts include the following:

(1) commercial contracts (eg exhibition or distribution contracts) under the Commercial Law);
(2) product-sharing contracts under the Petroleum Law;
(3) construction contracts under the Construction Law;
(4) build-operate-transfer contracts, build-transfer contracts, or build-operate-own contracts under the Public-Private Partnership Regulations ('PPP'); and
(5) technology transfer contracts.[4]

While there remains room for freedom to negotiate certain terms, these contracts highlight the premium given to the protection of domestic enterprises and state interests. The requirement to register the royalty fee in a technology transfer contract at the local department of science and technology as a means for it to be considered to have been agreed at arm's length and to be tax deductible, facilitates tax collection; while the ceiling on the interest rate that can be charged in loans related to a PPP contract seeks to circumscribe the permissible cost of lending. As the Vietnamese economy evolves, the present restrictions are likely to change as the regulatory approach is reconsidered and revised.

Section IV deals with pre-contractual liability, and section V examines the concept of contracts for the benefit of third parties in Vietnam.

[1] Law on Housing No 65/2014/QH13 dated 25 November 2014.

[2] Law on Land No 45/2013/QH13 dated 29 November 2013.

[3] Commercial Law No 36/2005/QH11 dated 14 June 2005.

[4] See Government Decree 37/2015/ND-CP dated 22 April 2015 on construction contracts; Government Decree 15/2015/ND-CP dated 14 February 2015 on public-private partnership contracts; Government Decree 33/2013/ND-CP dated 22 April 2013 on petroleum-product-sharing contracts; Circular 14/2014/TT-BCT of the Ministry of Industry and Trade dated 24 June 2014 on power-purchase agreements.

II. Historical Background of the Law of Contract

1. The *Hong Duc Code*

Prior to the commencement of the process of French colonization in 1862, the area now known as Vietnam was a single state administered by a monarch and his royal court. At first, civil relations were governed by usages and practice. Although Vietnam was said to have thousands of years of history, during almost a thousand years from 42 BC to AD 935, Vietnam was occupied by China. Nearly one thousand years of Chinese domination have definitively drawn Vietnam into the Chinese cultural sphere of influence. Yet old customs, remnants of the previous way of life prior to the Chinese conquest, still survive. During the first centuries of independence, Vietnamese kings stressed many times that 'each of the Northern and Southern countries (China and Vietnam) is sovereign within its sphere and does not need to follow each other's laws'.[5] In 1483, King Le Thanh Tong ordered the mandarins to rewrite usages and previous edicts into a code and thereafter promulgated the *Hong Duc Code*. It comprised 722 articles set out in six volumes and, as amended from time to time, it remained in force throughout Vietnam until the end of the eighteenth century. The *Hong Duc Code* was inspired by the *Tang Code* in China. However, it dealt with the same topic with slightly similar or totally different solutions. Among the 722 *Hong Duc* articles, 342 had no corresponding provisions in the Chinese *Tang* and *Ming Codes*. As for the other articles, where the three Codes dealt with the same topic, only 200 articles of the *Hong Duc Code* were influenced in varying degrees by the *Tang Code*, and 14 were directly borrowed from the *Ming Code*.

The *Hong Duc Code* contained civil and criminal laws, and rules of procedure. It was a product of mostly Vietnamese customary law with little Chinese and no Western influence. For a document of that period, it may be considered relatively enlightened since it is referred to as the dawn of the law-governed state of Vietnam.[6] To begin with, the Code safeguarded what we would today regard as fundamental civil liberties; these include the requirement for an arrest warrant, the right to release on bail, the right to a speedy and public trial, and the right to confront witnesses.[7] Furthermore, the *Hong Duc Code* contains many features found in modern legal systems, which find no counterpart elsewhere in Asia, not even in the Chinese *Tang Code*. Amongst these are the rectification of mistakes and the composition of debts; the institution of the guarantee; an institution akin to leasing; the acquisition of land *solo animus*; protection against monetary devaluation; and a concept similar to force majeure. Significantly, the system of land recording antedated those in Europe.[8] Many concepts governing contracts will be familiar to the modern contract lawyer, such as freedom of contract, written form for contract, obligation to perform contract, and damages for breach of contract.[9] Indeed, the notion of 'human rights' has been found recorded in the *Hong Duc Code*. In short, the *Hong Duc Code* was protective of private ownership and private autonomy in ways which resonate with the Western legal tradition. As the *Hong Duc*

[5] Nguyen Trai (1481), 'Proclamation of Victory', lines 2 and 3: 'As to Dai Viet, a country of great culture with a long tradition, its mountains and rivers are lawfully delineated. In addition, our customs are different from those in the North.' See <http://www.thewriterspost.net/V12I2_ff2_vudunhdinh.pdf> accessed 6 December 2016.

[6] JS Gillespie, *Transplanting Commercial Law Reform: Developing a 'Rule of Law' in Vietnam* (Farnham: Ashgate 2006) 44. See also 'Hong Duc Code: Vietnamese History' <http://www.britannica.com/topic/Hong-Duc-code> accessed 6 December 2016.

[7] Lan Quoc Nguyen, 'Traditional Vietnamese Law—The Le Code and Modern US Law' (1989) 13 Hastings Int'l & Comp L Rev 6.

[8] MB Hooker (ed), *Laws of South-East Asia* (Singapore: Butterworth 1986) 493.

[9] Nghia Duy Pham, *Chuyên khảo luật kinh tế* [*Treaty of Economic Law*] (Hanoi: Publisher of Hanoi National University 2004) 391–397.

Code is rooted in the social and religious conditions of Vietnam, a French scholar Briffault has said: 'In order to understand [the] Vietnamese legal system, one should read the Hong Duc code.'[10]

2. The *Gia Long Code*

In 1803, the *Gia Long Code* promulgated by King Gia Long repealed the *Hong Duc Code* which had been applied for more than 300 years. Gia Long was the first king of the Nguyen Dynasty which came into power after the collapse of the Le Dynasty. There were two reasons for the repeal of the *Hong Duc Code.* First, the *Hong Duc Code* was considered the law of the Le Dynasty, applicable to essentially the Northern part of Vietnam, whereas the territory of the Nguyen Dynasty was more than twice as large, including the territory conquered from Champa and a part of Cambodia, where the *Hong Duc Code* had no influence. Second, King Gia Long was impressed by the might of the Qing Dynasty and wanted to develop a large country comparable to the country in the North, that is China.

The *Gia Long Code* was essentially a copy of the *Qing Code* of China. The *Gia Long Code* applied at province, city, town, and township level. Cases at the village level were determined by applying the customary law of the village. In the feudal periods (up to the end of the nineteenth century) there was no clear distinction between the executive and the judiciary. Also, no legal profession or representation of plaintiffs or defendants was created. Trials were conducted before the mandarins when the *Gia Long Code* applied or before the village council (*Hoi Dong Ky Muc*) when customary law applied. Parties represented themselves without the assistance of lawyers. Prosecution was mostly by military personnel who carried out the arrests. Since customary laws were more practical and directly governed Vietnamese daily life, rather than the *Gia Long Code*, it was said that 'the law of the King must give way to the custom of the village'. History shows that Vietnam had some tradition of contract law under the Le Code (ie the *Hong Duc Code*), but either it was disrupted by the introduction of the *Gia Long Code*, or because it was ignored and replaced by village customs, it did not develop to become provisions of the law. Contract laws develop gradually with trade, and as the Vietnamese people are largely farmers, it is not hard to understand why the tradition of contract law has no deep roots in the lives of the Vietnamese people until recently.

3. The Napoleonic Code and the Three Civil Codes under French Colonial Rule

The process of French colonization began in 1874 with the annexation of six provinces in Southern Vietnam which was then known as Cochin-china.[11] From that time, the French Napoleonic Code of 1853 was applied to Cochin-china and a court system duplicating that of France's was established. Cochin-china remained a French colony and the remainder of Vietnam was divided by France into two territories, Tonkin (northern Vietnam) and Annam (central Vietnam). After the occupation of Cambodia and Laos, France renamed the entire region under its occupation 'French Indochina'. It was a federation under the control of a French governor. Annam, Laos, and Cambodia were autonomous kingdoms,

[10] See Duc Lang, *Le Franxais et la Culture Vietnamienne* [*French and Vietnamese Culture*] (Saigon: Imprimerie Franiaise d'Outre-Mer 1952) 15.

[11] Vu Hong Lien and P Sharrock, *Descending Dragon, Rising Tiger: A History of Vietnam* (London: Reaktion Books 2014) 128.

whose respective kings formally ruled their countries. Tonkin became a protectorate and Cochin-china a colony.

Each territory in Vietnam had its own civil code. The French introduced a Basic Code for Civil Laws in Cochin-china (1883), a Civil Code in Tonkin (1931), and a Civil Code in Annam (1939). These three codes took as their model the Napoleonic Code. The drafting style of these codes is called the French style, which was not followed in the first postwar Civil Code. Vietnam's legal professionalism started to develop under eminent lawyers such as Nguyen An Ninh, Nguyen Manh Tuong, and Vu Van Mau who contributed to the French legal transplantation in Vietnam until 1954 in the North and 1975 in the South, but after the country was dominated by communists, French laws were largely considered capitalist ideology and ignored.[12]

4. Contract Law During the Two Indochina Wars

In August 1945, the Viet Minh uprising under the command of Ho Chi Minh entered Hanoi and on 2 September 1945 an independent Democratic Republic of Vietnam was declared. Shortly afterwards, the French attempted to reimpose colonial rule. The first Indochina war (1946–54) between Viet Minh and France and the second Indochina war (1955–75) between Vietnam and the United States came one after the other—a total of almost 30 years of war.

The legal systems varied according to territories:

(1) areas under Viet Minh control between 1945 and 1954;
(2) North Vietnam being the area north of the 17th parallel from 20 July 1954;
(3) South Vietnam being the area south of the 17th parallel from 20 July 1954; and
(4) areas occupied by French forces between 1945 and 1954.

The laws applicable to the areas under Viet Minh control and later to North Vietnam were the laws and decrees passed by the National Assembly which first met in October 1945. However, under Order 90/SL dated 10 October 1945, the Napoleonic Code was still applicable if 'its provisions are not contrary to the independent principles of Vietnam and the democratic regime'. These principles somewhat modified the Napoleonic Code, making it fit for a socialist society; the Napoleonic Code continued to apply until the enactment of the VCC 1995.

In French occupied areas (1945–54), the Napoleonic Code still applied. South Vietnam under the Saigon regime continued from 1954 to apply the Vietnamese version of the Napoleonic Code, together with the last amendment—the Civil Code 1973 (*Bộ Dân Luật 1973*). Legal professionalism continued to develop under scholars such as Vu Van Mau, Nguyen Van Bong, and Nguyen Huu Tho (who later became President of the National Front of Liberation, ie the Viet Cong).

5. Contract Law from End of the War with the United States to Introduction of the VCC 1995

After 30 years of war, Vietnam was unified again on 30 April 1975 and named the Socialist Republic of Vietnam. Until 1986, the country followed a Soviet-style economic and political

[12] M Sidel, *Law and Society of Vietnam: The Transition from Socialism in Comparative Perspective* (New York: Cambridge University Press 2008) 6.

system. Many principles of the free market economy, such as freedom of contract, private autonomy of contractors, duty of good faith, and even the principle of *pacta sunt servanda* were undermined. When a 'contract' was signed by two state-owned enterprises, its terms and conditions were not decided by the parties, but determined according to the state plan. In these circumstances, contracts were not the means by which private transactions could be effected or carried out; rather, they were the means by which the state plan was to be realized. Economic disputes were settled by economic arbitrators, following a procedure similar to the civil judicial procedure. As the contracts represented arrangements to implement the state plan rather than bargains struck between parties, the role of economic arbitrators was necessarily different from that of a court determining the rights and remedies of contracting parties. Laws and regulations, together with the contracts made during that period, reflect their administrative function under the state plan rather than the civil rights and obligations of parties.

In the early 1990s (the period of the '*Grand Change*'), Vietnam moved towards a 'market economy with a socialist orientation'. Such a market economy required a legal infrastructure which has at its heart the fundamental principles of civil law. In 1994, economic courts were created to handle economic litigation.[13] State arbitrators became economic judges. A civil procedural code providing comprehensive procedural provisions to enable the enforcement of private rights was adopted in 1998 and amended in 2008 and 2016.

The biggest legal achievement in the *Grand Change* was the introduction of the VCC 1995. From the outset, the VCC 1995 may be seen as a continuation of the Vietnamese legal 'tradition' dating back to the *Hong Duc Code*, for example in the principle of voluntariness and equality in the formation of contract (Article 395.2); the contract being deemed null and void if one or both parties were forced to enter into it (Article 136); and in the principle of freedom of contract (Article 7). Even the principle of goodwill and honesty (Article 9) could find its antecedent in the *Hong Duc Code*.[14] In reality, however, those who drafted the VCC 1995 did not have the *Hong Duc Code* in mind as they were trained in the Soviet Union, East Germany, and Poland. This meant that the influence of the German Civil Code (*Bürgerliches Gesetzbuch*, 'BGB') was moderated by socialist legal education and socialist codes. The preparation of the VCC started in the early 1980s.[15] The drafting committee under the Ministry of Justice translated and consulted the civil codes of the German Democratic Republic (East Germany ('GDR')), the Russian Federation, Poland, Czechoslovakia, Hungary, China, France, Germany, Canada, Japan, and Thailand.[16] Experts from the GDR, Russia, France, and Japan were invited to provide suggestions on the drafting of the VCC. Vietnamese draftsmen were also sent to Germany, France, and Japan to study the Civil Codes of these countries. Apart from the VCC, Vietnam was also active in enacting other laws on civil issues. These included the Ordinance on Transfer of Technology from Abroad (1988), the Ordinance on Protection of Industrial Property Rights (1988), the Ordinance on Succession (1990), the Ordinance on Housing (1991), the Ordinance on Civil Contracts (1991), the Law on Marriage and Family (1986), the Ordinance on Emigration (1992), Land Law (1993), and the Ordinance on Copyrights (1994).

After its completion, the first draft of the VCC provoked a prolonged debate in the National Assembly and all citizens were invited to comment on the draft. When the ninth

[13] A Harding and P Nicholson (eds), *New Courts in Asia* (London/New York: Routledge 2010) 32.

[14] *Hong Duc Civil Code*—Vietnamese version by Vietnam Institute of History (Ha Noi: Judicial Publishing House 1991).

[15] C Rohwer (1997), 'Progress and Problems in Vietnam's Development of Commercial Law' (1997) 15 Berkeley J Int'l L 275, 285.

[16] ibid 286.

draft was presented to the National Assembly, the Assembly appointed the Ministry of Justice, the Law Committee of the National Assembly, the Supreme Court, and the Supreme Procuracy to coordinate the drafting process of the code. The 12th draft was completed at the end of 1994. This draft was the subject of extensive discussion throughout Vietnam. Further amendments were introduced. It was the 14th draft that was finally adopted by the National Assembly. The VCC was promulgated by the President on 28 October 1995, and it came into effect on 1 July 1996. The VCC 1995 was subsequently amended on two occasions—in 2005, with the strong influence of Japanese experts and support from the Japan Investment Cooperation Agency ('JICA'), and in 2015, by young jurists trained in France, Japan, or England and amending the VCC 1995 with the aim of modernizing the country in a free market economy.

The 20-year development of the VCC witnessed the decline of socialist norms. But any notion that Vietnamese law is heavily influenced by French law is a mistaken one. The reality is that the drafters of laws passed during the *Grand Change* studied in the Soviet bloc; a contract is thus seen not purely as a private matter between parties but one in which the state is expected to have a role in structuring and regulating. While it is true that Japanese experts and legal scholars who studied in France and England had some influence, the hold that the socialist legal tradition exerts over the Civil Code is only beginning to diminish as the original drafters of the VCC retire. Nonetheless, the VCC must be interpreted within the framework of its constitution, which determines that Vietnam is a market economy with a socialist orientation. As such, the legal concepts employed must be explained in such a way that it is understood by socialist philosophers; a recurring theme will be the overarching nature of state interest, which necessarily prevails over private interests. The mode of legal inquiry would track the way socialist legal scholars approached a legal problem. As such, beyond the general principles of contract law, one must necessarily inquire whether the contract in question is of a type that is governed by specific legislation prescribing more detailed requirements. A contract dealing with land, for example, implicates the *Grundnorm* (basic norm) that all land belongs to the state and that land use must be consistent with the state interest, one manifestation of which is compliance with the zoning plan. While planning regulation is today also a common feature in non-socialist jurisdictions, what is striking is how socialist legal thinking necessarily incorporates state interest as an integral step in the legal analysis. Therefore, even as freedom of contract underpins the VCC, contractual freedom is very often further circumscribed in the regimes affecting specific contracts. The concept of public interest, whether in general or specific form, pervades Vietnamese legal thought and potentially undercuts freedom of contract. This carries theoretical implications.

For one, an integral step in dealing with contractual issues involves how the general law represented by the VCC interacts with the special regimes.

6. Contract Law After Introduction of the VCC and Commercial Law in 2005 and 2015

In 2005, a new VCC replaced the VCC 1995. The VCC 2005 relaxed a number of formality requirements for contract validity. For example, whereas the VCC 1995 required the authority to sign a contract on behalf of a principal to be in written form, Article 146 of the VCC 2005 recognized the concept of apparent authority, and permitted the principal's silence to be considered as acceptance of the agent who purported to act on his behalf. This regulation is also retained in Article 143 of the VCC 2015.

The new constitution, adopted in 2013, formally accepts the principle of freedom of contract and the right of citizens to engage in private businesses.[17] Consistent with the direction set by the new constitution, the VCC 2015 incorporates many changes which are underpinned by the principle that the law should facilitate and support private ordering desired by individuals and business entities. Under the VCC 1995 and 2005, civil rights were exercised 'in accordance with laws'; under the VCC 2015, people are free to agree upon their rights unless specific laws prohibit them from doing so. The shift in orientation towards greater liberality is subtle but significant. The introduction of the concept of usufruct (similar to trust) and the provision for a third party to enforce rights conferred upon him by a contract point to a more law-enabling approach. Similarly, the 2015 recognition of apparent authority, which extends the hitherto strict notion of agency based on actual authority, facilitates the manner in which parties transact and decreases the transaction costs exacted by the strict notion of agency. The introduction of the concept of hardship in Article 420 of the VCC 2015, modelled on the UNIDROIT Principles of International Commercial Contracts ('PICC'), brings Vietnamese contract law closer to many modern contract law regimes' modes of dealing with supervening events.

Vietnamese contract law receives a major revision approximately every ten years. The preparatory work for the draft amendments culminating in the VCC 2015 was carried out by the Ministry of Justice and the Civil-Economic Law Department; the draft proposals were then reviewed by the National Assembly Office under Ngo Van Minh, Tran Dinh Long, and Nguyen Tu Long. Many experts were asked to comment on the drafts, including those from the Vietnam Bar Federation, law schools, the Supreme Court, the Supreme Procuracy, and the Public Notary Office.[18] Some 50 per cent of the VCC 2005—or over 300 articles—were repealed or amended. Two of the most notable changes are the introduction of legal precedents and the concept of fair dealing. Legal precedents will consist of rulings by appellate courts and the Supreme Court which are useful for judges in future cases. Fair dealing, on the other hand, is a general principle that allows judges to determine a case on fair terms in the absence of legislative provisions or contractual agreement.

Whether deeply ingrained legal attitudes and approaches will allow these changes to develop and flourish is an open question. These new principles and norms necessarily interact with the existing principles and norms. Vietnam does not collate judicial decisions for reference or future guidance. Without a system of precedents which tracks how principles are being developed and how conflicting norms receive resolution, it will be difficult to study whether the new thinking is taking root. When the Supreme Court introduced the first 30 'legal precedents' in 2015, legal scholars were surprised to find that they were not decisions applying the law to disputes; rather, they consisted of broad statements of principles. For example, one of these states: 'under a claim of restitution of a thing, the court need to consider the contribution of the good faith possessor to the value of such thing'.[19]

The collation and public availability of judgments would greatly assist the development of a more sophisticated legal system. Except for certain cassation judgments from the Supreme Court, judicial decisions are not publicly disclosed. As such, professors, scholars, and lawyers apply laws from the books without knowing how the court applies the law.

[17] Art 33, Constitution of Vietnam dated 28 November 2013, effective from 1 January 2014.

[18] Experts included Do Van Dai (Ho Chi Minh City Law University), Tuong Duy Luong (Supreme Court), Le Net (Vietnam Bar Federation), Nguyen Ngoc Dien (Ho Chi Minh City National University), Nguyen Thi Hang (Hanoi National University), Nguyen Minh Hang (Foreign Trade University), and Phung Trung Tap (Hanoi Law University).

[19] See Supreme Court Resolution No 03/2015/NQ-HDTP dated 28 October 2015 on collection and announcement of legal precedents.

Since judicial decisions are not available for study and critique, an essential condition for deep analysis and jurisprudential development is lacking. While some scholars collect cases and make comments on them, the availability of a reliable source of authoritative judicial decisions will greatly assist in the development of a 'thick' jurisprudence.[20]

The second issue which impacts whether and how new principles and norms take root is custom and the hold of the existing legal culture. The clash between Code principles and custom affects how Code principles find effect. In contract interpretation, for example, custom follows the maxim *bút sa gà chết* (what is written binds the writer). At the same time, the VCC follows the principle that contract interpretation should be based on the common intention of the parties; if there is a discrepancy between the words uttered and the intention, the intention prevails.[21] This discrepancy creates a reluctance on the part of the court to apply the VCC where the legal provisions are at odds with conventional thinking. Similarly, traditional notions of agency and the absence of a system of decision reporting have prevented the concept of apparent authority from developing. Without a system for reporting decided cases, it will be challenging to study how new legal concepts interact with custom and whether they are taking root as intended by the legislature.

It is hoped that the introduction of the fairness concept and legal precedents will change the way Vietnamese law develops. It is expected that they will promote equality and objectivity in decision making, as well as eliminate subjectivity of the competent authority in the event that there is no legal provision governing the case.

The development of the civil law in Vietnam demonstrates that considerable effort has been put into adapting the legal system to reflect its needs, unique values, and tradition. It is erroneous to think that Vietnamese civil law is merely a replica of French law or Soviet law. Nonetheless, the desire to develop an autochthonous legal system—and more specifically a civil law—will also require supporting institutions that help reforms take root and develop. An initiative to provide public access to the judgments that apply the law will first give a grounded feel of how the law has effect. By exposing the way judges engage in legal reasoning, the legal process is rendered more transparent and accountable; such exposure also promises to develop a thicker jurisprudence as jurists and lawyers work out the more nuanced aspects of how the rules and principles interact and how tensions are resolved.

III. Formation of Contract

Under Article 385 of the VCC 2015, as in most legal systems, a contract is formed by a meeting of the minds of the parties when an offer made by one party is accepted by the other party. Moreover, a contract is a civil transaction; to be effective, the conditions in Article 117 of the VCC 2015 must be met: (1) the participating persons are competent and voluntarily enter into the contract; (2) the purpose and content of the contract are not immoral or illegal; and (3) the form of the transaction is in conformity with the relevant legal documents. In a nutshell, there are no further specific criteria for creation of a contract. Thus, a short summary of the elements which must be satisfied for the creation of a legally binding contract are: (1) offer; (2) acceptance; (3) compliance as to form of contract; (4) legal capacity; and (5) content of contract is not illegal, immoral, or distorted by mistake, fraud, or duress.

[20] See eg Do Van Dai, *Vietnam Contract Law—Cases and Comments* (Ho Chi Minh City: National Political Publishing House 2009).

[21] Arts 121 and 404, VCC 2015.

1. Offer and Acceptance

Just as in other legal systems, formation of a contract founded upon a meeting of offer and acceptance is the way of contract formation in Vietnamese law. Generally, no contractual obligation is created unless and until an offer is accepted.

(a) Offer

(1) Definition

An offer is defined in Article 386 of the VCC 2015 as an expression of will made by one party, addressed to another specific party or to the public, about the first party's intention to enter into a contractual relationship with the latter.

The VCC 2015 does not clarify the following questions relating to an offer: (1) how does one contribute to and what contributes to the expression of will; (2) does 'specific party' refer to one or more than one person; and (3) what is the meaning of intention to enter into contractual relationship? It is worth noting that an 'invitation to treat' is not codified separately from an offer in the VCC. Having said that, these elements can be explained as follows.

First, the concept of an 'expression of will' stems from the Hegelian dichotomy between 'freedom of will' and 'expression of will' under the BGB.[22] If an 'expression of will' is consistent with one's 'will', then there is consent and freedom of will. If an expression of will is not consistent with one's 'will', then there is no consent and thus no freedom of will, therefore the contract is void. This expression of will has to be from an offeror or his authorized agent. The offeror or the agent must be fully conscious of what he is doing, what his intention is, and what the legal consequences of his offer are.

Unlike the position under the VCC 1995, to amount to an offer it is necessary that an expression of will states the essential content of the contract. For example, an expression of will by a person stating 'I would like to sell a car' may not be an offer, because it is not specific or not ascertainable. On the contrary, if he says, 'I want to sell *my* car' this would amount to an offer. He may also say, 'this year I will provide you with a certain number of oranges and appoint you as my distributor'. This is also an offer, because the subject matter of his offer is specific enough—a distributorship contract rather than a sales contract. Thus, the subject matter of the contract is always an essential element. The price of goods or the tariffs for provision of services are not always essential elements of an offer. In a sales contract, if the price is not established, the price of similar goods of the same quality shall be deemed the reasonable price of the goods. For example, the rent is not an essential term of a lease contract but the term of the lease is an essential term. In short, the minimum required elements that will enable the promisor to perform the contract will be considered the essential contents of the contract. These elements must be clear and specific so that the counterparty understands how he is to perform the contract after it is concluded.

Second, under the VCC 2015, an offer is no longer required to be addressed to a specific party; it can be addressed to the public. This is a positive legal change, which makes the VCC 2015 cover more situations in real life. To illustrate, when a party offers a reward to whoever finds his lost item, this would not be considered an offer under the VCC 2005 because there was no specific party receiving such offer. Therefore, the offeror in that case could withdraw his offer, which used to happen frequently, without any sanction under the VCC. However, under the VCC 2015, which came into effect on 1 January 2017, such an offer is valid.

[22] See C Yeomans, *Freedom and Reflection: Hegel and the Logic of Agency* (Oxford/New York: OUP 2011).

Hence, an offer can be addressed to the world at large. In the famous case of *Carlill v Carbolic Smoke Ball Co*,[23] the English Court of Appeal saw no conceptual problem with an offer made to the world at large. If an offeror chooses to frame his words such that he evinces an intention to contract with the members of the general public who accept his offer, he should be held accountable to his offer should it be accepted. A person who advertises to the world must therefore be careful in the statements made so that contractual liability is created when it is intended. If he does not intend to assume contractual liability, appropriate words should be inserted to signify that that there is no intention as yet to assume contractual responsibility. Thus, a person who runs an e-commerce website should appreciate the difference between 'We accept your order' (an acceptance) and 'We acknowledge your order. A confirmation email will be sent once we confirm the availability of the product ordered.' (This is a mere acknowledgement postponing the moment of acceptance.)

The third element of an offer is intention to enter into a contractual relationship—this posits that the person is on the brink of entering a legal relationship. The mere indication of the price of an item is unlikely to amount to an offer because the vendor may be regarded as not yet ready to assume contractual responsibility. It is likely to be construed as indicating the cost of the item if it is provided. Failure to satisfy the element of an intention to enter into contractual relationship renders it legally insignificant from the perspective of contractual formation; it would be characterized as an invitation to treat in common law. The expression 'contractual relationship' indicates serious legal consequences are expected between the parties. It seems consistent with the definition of a contract, which is 'an agreement of [two or more] parties directed towards the creation, modification, or termination of civil rights and obligations'.[24] Clearly, the offeror must present to the offeree at least the essential terms so that the offeree can perform accordingly. For example, members (shareholders) of a limited liability company have first right of refusal if one member intends to sell shares in the company to a third party. Before such sale, the member being the seller needs to send an offer to sell to another member, who must either accept all, or reject all, terms and conditions in the offer. If the other member accepts the offer, the contract is considered formed and the seller may no longer sell to a third party. The seller is bound by his offer.

The VCC 2015 does not expressly stipulate the difference between an offer and an invitation to make an offer. Such distinction can be made from *a contrario* interpretation of item 1 of Article 386 of the VCC 2015: 'An offer means a clear intention to enter into a contract and to be bound by such offer to the other specific party or the public'. As mentioned earlier, a proposal which does not have the intention of entering into the contract or does not set out obligations and rights of the parties would not be an offer; it is an invitation to make an offer. A typical invitation to make an offer is one which leaves out the object of the contract such that the parties cannot identify their obligations. The clarity with which the obligations are defined is indicative of whether a party is ready to assume contractual responsibility. Nonetheless, even when obligations have been clearly set out, a further question is whether the parties have concluded their negotiations and whether there remain further obligations to be finalized before they are prepared to assume contractual responsibility.

(2) Effective offers

The VCC 2015 provides protection for the offeree and obliges the offeror to be responsible for the offer he has made. Article 386 of the VCC 2015 further stipulates that if an offer fixes a period of time for the offeree to respond, the offeror is bound by the offer. Coming back

[23] [1893] 1 QB 256 (CA). [24] Art 385, VCC 2015.

to the example mentioned earlier of an offer to sell shares to another member who has the right of first refusal, if the seller sets a 30-day period for the current member of a limited liability company to exercise the right of first refusal, the seller cannot withdraw the offer and sell the shares to a third party before such time. In addition, the charter of a limited liability company may state that after the expiry of such right, the seller may sell his shares to a third party with a condition not more favourable than that which was offered to the current member. This poses a question whether the condition would apply if the offeree did not exercise the right of first refusal effectively. For example, if the seller stated in his offer, 'if you decide to buy my shares, you must pay me before 10 August 2016'. On 8 August 2016 the offeree replied that he would buy the shares but payment would be on 11 September 2016. The offer expired and the seller signed a contract with a third party on 10 August 2016. The payment was actually made on 11 August 2016. Would that be considered a breach of the right of first refusal? In this commentator's opinion it would not, because the current member could not pay even on 11 August 2016. And by offering payment on 11 September 2016, the current member had already set a new term that replaced the original term of 'payment by 10 August 2016'.

In the VCC 2005, as an offer represented the offeror's intention to enter into a contract with the offeree, he was required to indemnify the offeree if he changed his intention and concluded a contract with a third party within the offer period, provided that such action caused damage to the offeree. This provision has been deleted by the VCC 2015; hence, if the offeror offers to sell a car to the offeree and the offeree says that he will answer within three days, the offeror's acceptance to wait will not be considered an agreement fixing a period by the offeror for the offeree to reply, and the offeror will be bound by the offer.

Article 388 of the VCC 2015 stipulates that an offer to enter into a civil contract takes effect: (1) at the time fixed by the offeror; or (2) when the offeree receives the offer, if the time is unfixed. Article 388 also specifies that an offer is deemed received by the offeree when: (1) the offer is sent to the offeree's place of residence or headquarters; (2) the offer is introduced into the official information system of the offeree; or (3) the offeree knows of the offer by other means.

(3) Withdrawal and revocation of offers

From the time the offeree receives the offer, the offer is considered to be irrevocable.[25] However, according to Article 389 of the VCC 2015, the offeror is still entitled to withdraw or revoke his offer if the offer contains a provision stating that the offer can be withdrawn. If the offer stipulates the right of revocation, the offeror shall notify the offeree of such right and such notice shall be effective if the offeree receives the notice before the offeree accepts the offer.

(b) Acceptance

(1) Definition

The offeree's acceptance is an expression of his consent to all the terms of the offer. This definition remains in Article 393.1 of the VCC 2015. An acceptance that changes the offer's terms is considered a counter-offer (a new offer). In this case, the former offeree becomes the new offeror and the old offer becomes ineffective. An acceptance is more than consent to the offer; it is a consent that creates rights and obligations between the parties. Therefore, it must be clear and not ambiguous. The meeting of minds is made at the time the offeror

[25] Art 389, VCC 2015.

receives the acceptance, except when the law provides otherwise.[26] According to Article 400, a contract is concluded when: (1) the offeror receives the acceptance of the offeree; or (2) the time limit has expired, if the parties agree that silence constitutes acceptance after expiry of a specific time limit; or (3) the parties have reached an oral agreement on the content of the contract; or (4) the last party signs the written documents or written acceptance, if the contract is signed in writing. If the offeree sends his acceptance by courier on 6 January and the acceptance document reaches the offeror on 7 January, the time for the conclusion of the contract is 7 January.

The offeror is deemed to have received the acceptance when it reaches the offeror's place of residence or place of business, or when it reaches the offeror's server or telefax machine (if sent by email or telefax), or when the offeror should have known of the acceptance (eg by email on the computer or on the smartphone, or by text messaging service).[27]

However, if the contract is in writing, then the time of contract conclusion is when the last party (the offeror or offeree) signs the contract (manually on paper or electronically on an e-document).[28] The case of *SEECOM v LOTECO* illustrates the perspective of the courts on acceptance. Although the Court of Appeal in denying the effect of a transaction accepted and concluded via telefax, reversed the judgment of the First Instance Court, the Cassation Court shared the view of the First Instance Court that the transaction was valid and annulled the decision of the Court of Appeal accordingly.[29]

(2) Silence, inactivity, or forbearance

Acceptance must be clear and unambiguous; therefore silence, inactivity, or forbearance in itself, which generally does not satisfy this criterion, is not considered acceptance. Under Article 393.2 of the VCC 2015, the offeree's silence cannot be deemed acceptance—unless otherwise agreed between the parties or there is an established custom between the parties to the same effect. There must therefore be a context which is capable of rendering such silence unambiguous. Thus, if the customary manner of dealing regards silence as consent, the context acts to give a presumptive meaning to the silence. Similarly, if the parties agree in a contract that subsequent silence is to be given a certain meaning, that agreement should govern. For example, in a case handled by the People's Court of Go Vap District, Ho Chi Minh City, Mr Tuan was a contractor who built a house for Mr Truyen and his wife Mrs Bach. After the house was finished, Mr Tuan who was supposed to marry the daughter of Mr Truyen and Mrs Bach wrote and signed a document waiving his right to demand the construction contract price, then he gave such document to Mr Truyen and Mrs Bach. Later, Mr Tuan sued Mr Truyen and Mrs Bach for the contract price and Mr Tuan contended that the document he gave to Mr Truyen and Mrs Bach was not an effective contract due to the fact that it was not signed by both parties. The Court of First Instance held that Mr Tuan by giving the document to Mr Truyen and Mrs Bach had tendered an offer and Mr Truyen and Mrs Bach by taking the document had accepted the offer. Note that Mr Truyen and Mrs Bach after receiving the document did not expressly accept the so-called offer.

[26] Art 400.1, VCC 2015. [27] Art 388.2, VCC 2015. [28] Art 400.4, VCC 2015.

[29] See Decision No 08/KDTM-GDT dated 8 December 2005 of the Cassation Court of the Supreme People's Court (*SEECOM v LOTECO*): the claimant made an offer by telefax to the defendant, which was subsequently accepted and signed before it was sent back to the claimant by the defendant. The defendant later announced that the offered goods did not meet the defendant's requirements and that the formation of the transaction was not legally acceptable. Accordingly, the defendant refused to pay the remaining amount and requested the claimant to take back the goods. The claimant brought the case to the First Instance Court, where the validity of the transaction was recognized. The same view was maintained by the Cassation Court though the Court of Appeal did not agree with the judgment of the Court of First Instance.

Rather, they were silent about it because their obligations under the construction contract had ended, the Court explained.[30]

(3) Time limit for acceptance

When the offeree rejects, modifies, remains silent, or the time for responding to the offer has expired without any reply from the offeree, the offer will be considered terminated.[31]

The postal rule still exists under Article 394 of the VCC 2015; if the acceptance is sent by post, and the acceptance arrives late for reasons not due to the offeree's fault and the offeror knows or should have known of the reasons, such acceptance remains effective. The VCC 2015 further stipulates that when the offer does not specify the deadline for acceptance, the acceptance shall be effective only if it is received within a reasonable time. Given today's sophisticated means of communication (eg email, text messaging service, telefax, etc), the offeree should check whether his acceptance has been received. Therefore, this situation applies only when the parties contemplate acceptance by post. After all, if the parties negotiated by telephone or email, they would not expect acceptance by post unless a disclaimer is stated in an email or communicated by telephone.

(4) Rejection

If the offeree does not agree with the content of the offer, the offeree may reject the offer at any time. The offeror shall not be bound by his offer after the offeree gives notice of his rejection to the offeror. According to Article 391 of the VCC 2015, upon receipt of the offeree's rejection, the offer shall be terminated.

(5) Delayed acceptance

Under Articles 397 and 394 of the VCC 2015, it should be noted that if an offer expressly sets a time limit for acceptance, an acceptance made after such time limit is considered a new offer. The former offeror may decide whether to accept or reject this 'late acceptance'. When the former offeror accepts the 'late acceptance', a contract is formed.[32]

(6) Discrepancies between offer and acceptance

Sometimes there are discrepancies between the acceptance and the original offer. As mentioned earlier, such acceptance will be considered a new offer.[33] As long as the contract is not concluded, the parties are free to alter the terms and conditions of the offer from their counterparties. Only when an offer is accepted without any alteration, then the contract is concluded. During the course of the drafting of the VCC 2015, a proposal had been made to adopt the approach of Lord Denning in *Butler Machine Tool Co Ltd v Ex-Cell-O Corp (England) Ltd*.[34] That is, an acceptance with a minor alteration that is not objected to by the offeror is still considered an acceptance and not a counter-offer. Otherwise, the offeror can walk away from his offer due to a small deviation from the offer. However, the proposal was not adopted.

(7) Gratuitous contracts and onerous contracts

The concept of gratuitous contracts and onerous contracts is not mentioned in Vietnamese civil law. Parties are entitled to freedom of contract and may choose on which terms to contract, provided that such terms are not illegal or immoral (Article 3(2) of the VCC

[30] Judgment No 425/2006/DS-ST dated 15 September 2006 of the People's Court of Go Vap District.
[31] Art 391, VCC 2015. [32] Art 394.1, VCC 2015. [33] Art 392, VCC 2015.
[34] [1977] EWCA Civ 9, [1979] WLR 401 (CA).

2015). Under Vietnamese contract law, the concept of a gift with condition is somewhat similar to the concept of a gratuitous contract and an onerous contract.

Generally, in a gratuitous contract the donor confers an advantage with no intention of receiving something in return (*do ut des*) from the beneficiary. The cause is rooted in the intention of giving—the *animus donandi*.[35] Most gratuitous contracts are unilateral contracts, and effective upon delivery of the gifts, and not upon the making of the promise to provide the gifts, or upon acceptance of the gifts, except otherwise agreed on. This means that a promise to give a gift is not binding and cannot be enforced until the promise is effected. However, some contracts which are gratuitous by nature may become onerous, for example if the donor requires any condition to be fulfilled by the beneficiary, such contract is no longer gratuitous. Therefore, the donor is liable for damages if the proposed recipient has fulfilled the condition but the donor refuses to provide the gift to the latter. Indeed, giving a gift or donation with condition, in Vietnam, shares the same nature of an onerous contract. However, to the extent that the VCC favours the protection of patrimony, transfers of goods are more likely to be interpreted as sale rather than as donations or gifts. An additional point is that under Vietnamese law, in a conditional gift contract, if the beneficiary does not fulfil the condition, the donor is entitled to reclaim the gift and even claim compensation for damage suffered.[36] This position is different from that in other civil law countries, such as France, where the donor's obligation is not changed in a conditional gift contract even when the beneficiary fails to fulfil the condition.[37] Although there is no concept of onerous contracts or gratuitous contracts in the VCC, there is the concept of unilateral and bilateral contracts. If we treat unilateral and gratuitous contracts as similar, the effective date of the making of a unilateral contract/gratuitous contract is the date of delivery of the subject matter of the contract.

2. Formality Requirements

(a) Contracts required to be written and notarized

Like other legal systems, the VCC in general does not specify any formality requirements for enforceability of contracts. A contract, like any other juridical act, may be concluded in oral, written, or any other specific form if the law does not otherwise specify (Article 401 of the VCC 2005; Article 683.7 of the VCC 2015).

The requirement for a contract to be in written form does not pose any argument between legal libertarianism and paternalism. Unlike the argument of German paternalism: 'The German law rules about formality are meant to protect the parties by ensuring that they enter legal transactions only after serious consideration of the consequences of their acts',[38] Vietnamese law seems to be influenced by its tradition of 'form over substance' for no reason. For example, a loan contract with a bank, an insurance contract, or a construction contract must be in writing under specific laws and regulations. In theory, it does not mean that a lack of written form would make the contract invalid. When a contract is not in the necessary form, the court will give the parties one month to validate the form. In practice, however, problems arise if one of the parties refuses to correct the form, in which case the

[35] N Le, 'Vietnam's Contract Monograph' in J Herbots (vol ed), *International Encyclopaedia of Laws* (Alphen aan den Rijn: Kluwer Law International 1999) 49.

[36] Art 470, VCC 2015; Art 462, VCC 2015.

[37] N Le, 'Vietnam' (contract monograph) in J Herbots (vol ed), *International Encyclopaedia of Laws* (Alphen aan den Rijn: Wolters Kluwer Law & Business 2012) 49.

[38] M Hogg, *Promises and Contract Law: Comparative Perspectives* (Cambridge: Cambridge University Press 2011) 281.

contract may be held invalid. This rule, imposed by the VCC 1995, has not been corrected by the VCC 2015. The rigidity of the requirement as to form could only be explained by the lack of trust in true intention, and the Vietnamese mindset for 'form over substance' instead of 'substance over form'.

As discussed earlier, a unilateral contract is valid upon delivery of a thing, and not at the time of consent to the contract. Contracts which do not have effect until certain acts are performed are called 'solemn' or 'real' contracts. Many types of contracts, such as those relating to sale of cars or sale of houses, are required to be executed in written form, notarized by a public notary, or approved by a competent state authority.

Contracts that must be concluded in written form are, inter alia, economic contracts, house rental contracts (with a term of more than six months), contracts for the transfer of obligations, contracts of agency, contracts for sale of real estate, contracts for holding security (pledges, mortgages), guarantee contracts, and other specific contracts, such as transfer of technology contracts or licensing contracts. When the written form requirement is an essential condition to the conclusion of a contract, non-conformity may make the contract void *ab initio*.

Some contracts must be notarized. Land mortgage contracts for transfers of land-use rights will be null and void if they are not concluded in written form and not subsequently registered before a public notary. In Vietnam, a public notary not only certifies the signatures of the parties signing the contract, he also reviews the contract for compliance with the law relating to contracts, and keeps a copy of the contract for security purposes. As such, the importance of a public notary in Vietnam may be different from that of a notary public in common law countries.

The current VCC 2015 once again accepts 'form over substance', as if to prove the truth of the adage that old habits die hard. Article 129 of the VCC 2015 stipulates:

> If the form of a civil transaction, required to be established in writing, does not comply with regulations of law, but a party or the parties has/have fulfilled at least two-thirds of the obligations in the transaction, a court, at his/her/their request(s), shall issue a decision on recognition of the validity of such transaction.

Accordingly, if the transaction was in written form or notarized as required but such written form or notarization is not in compliance with the law and one party has performed at least 'two-thirds of the obligations in the transaction', then as he so requests of the court, the court will recognize the transaction's validity, and notarization is no longer necessary. This regulation is odd because no one can define what constitutes 'two-thirds of the obligations'. During the course of drafting the VCC 2015, a proposal was made to replace 'two-thirds' by 'partially'—as an indication that the parties are serious about performance of the contract. Suppose two parties sign a contract for the sale of a house. If the buyer has paid 50 per cent of the sale price but the contract has not been notarized, can the seller void the contract? The reasons for keeping the two-thirds rule and not replacing it are hard to identify. One possible explanation is that common intention is not important for this type of contract, but in the case of a land transfer contract that is not notarized many risks could arise, as many other assets can be built and developed on land.

When parties execute a written contract with a four-corner clause, ie terms and conditions provided in such a contract constitute an entire agreement and extrinsic evidence such as an oral agreement cannot be evaluated, the court may, however, refer to the communications leading to such contract to ascertain the common intention of the parties when interpreting the meaning of the written agreement.[39]

[39] See *Dat Thinh v Giao Thong Van Tai Hai Phong* (1995).

(b) Electronic contracts

Vietnamese law recognizes the legality of e-contracts. Article 34 of the Law on Electronic Transactions 2005 ('LET') provides that 'the legal validity of an e-contract cannot be disclaimed for the sole reason that it is expressed as a data message'. A contract that is concluded between an automatic information system and a person or between automatic information systems cannot be denied legal validity on the ground that there is no one checking or intervening in each specific action performed by the automatic information system or in the conclusion of the contract. In the process of entering into and executing an e-contract, a notice in the form of a data message shall be as legally valid as a notice in the traditional form. Besides, Article 119.1 of the VCC 2015 states that civil transactions effected through electronic means in the form of data messages as stipulated by the LET are considered transactions in writing.

According to the LET, e-contracts are contracts established in the form of data messages provided for in this Law; a data message is data created, transmitted, received, and stored by electronic means. An electronic means is a means that utilizes electrical, electronic, digital, magnetic, wireless, optical, electromagnetic technology, or other similar technology.

The principles of entering into and execution of e-contracts are as follows:

(1) Parties shall have the right to use electronic means to enter into and execute contracts.
(2) Entry into and execution of e-contracts shall comply with the provisions of the LET and the law on contracts.
(3) When entering into and executing e-contracts, parties shall have the right to agree on technical requirements, certification, and conditions ensuring the integrity and confidentiality of such e-contracts.

E-documents generated by customers and sent using an online ordering function are regarded as customers' offers for conclusion of contracts for the goods or services associated with that online ordering function. The time of conclusion of a contract formed through using the online ordering function on an e-commerce website is the time the customer receives the acceptance from the trader, organization, or individual selling the goods online.

3. Capacity of Parties

To enter into a contract, the parties must have suitable mental capacity to be aware of the legal consequences of their acts. To have full capacity, a party who is an individual must be at least 18 years old and of sound mind; if he is over six years old and of sound mind, he has sufficient capacity for minor transactions; if he is over 15 years old and of sound mind, he can engage in manual work.

If a party is a legal entity, the contract must be compatible with its business activities or business functions as stated or described in its incorporation certificate, and also it must be duly entered into by its authorized representative. In general, a representative establishes and performs a civil transaction in the name and for the interest of another person (the represented person) within the scope of representation (Article 134 of the VCC 2015).

There are two types of representative.

(1) Legal representative: a legal representative is a person whom the law states or a competent state agency decides can be appointed as such. For example, if a legal person is a company, then its legal representative is either the general director or the

chairman of the members' council or of the management board. The New Law on Enterprises which was promulgated in 2014 allows a joint stock company ('JSC') or a limited liability company ('LLC') to have more than one legal representative, one of whom is required to reside in Vietnam. If a JSC has more than one legal representative, the chairman of the management board and the general director must both be the legal representatives.

(2) Authorized representative: an authorized representative is a person who is given the authority to act by and for the represented person. The form of the authorization shall be agreed by the parties, except where the law has provided that the authorization must be in writing.

Vietnamese law provides that persons from age 15 to under 18 may act as authorized representatives, except for civil transactions that the law requires must be established and/or performed by persons aged at least 18 or over.

An authorized representative has to act strictly on behalf of the represented person within the contractually specified scope of authorization. If he does not do so, the authorization may be invalid and the contract may be avoided.

Under the VCC 2015, the concept of apparent authority is recognized. Under Article 142, when an agent acts on behalf of a principal without proper authorization, his act may bind the principal if:

(1) the principal ratifies the act;
(2) the principal knows of the act but does not object to it within a reasonable time;
(3) the principal is at fault in leading the third party to enter into contract with the agent in the belief that the agent has authority when there is actually no proper authorization.

For example, if an agent of a car dealer uses the dealer's office to accept deposits from customers, the car dealer may not later deny that the agent is authorized to receive deposits, if the car dealer in allowing the agent (or so he calls himself) to use his office gives customers the impression that the agent is properly authorized. This reform is a major success in Vietnam, if we do not forget that not long ago Vietnam still voided contracts for trivial reasons.

4. Content of Contract

(a) Consistency between expression of will and the will itself

Formation of a contract can be interpreted as a process of expressing and unifying the will of the parties under the forms, contents, principles, and sequences prescribed by the law, in order to establish civil rights and obligations. Article 385 of the VCC 2015 defines a contract as 'an agreement of [two or more] parties directed towards the creation, modification, or termination of civil rights and obligations'. Broadly speaking, the notion of contract is extended to the transfer of legal consequences among the parties involved through mutual consent. The content of the contract, therefore, must be sufficiently clear to enable the parties to understand what is required of them. Moreover, it must not be illegal or immoral. The content of the contract may be interpreted and performed in good faith, as explained below.

(1) The delayed building work

X contracts for Y to refurbish 27 flats for £20,000. However, Y ran into difficulties. X was concerned about having to pay a penalty under the head contract, and promised to pay Y an extra £10,300 to complete the work on time. Can Y enforce the additional £10,300?

Y can enforce the additional £10,300 as there is no concept of consideration under Vietnamese law, and every contractual term is subject to consent between the parties.

By using 'agreement' in Article 385, the VCC 2015 intends to refer to the common will ('mutual consent') and expression of intention of at least two parties to the contract. Without a meeting of the minds there is no contract, ie the contract might be voidable for mistake, fraud, or deceit. When a will is defective, it is not a voluntary will (ie there is no true freedom of will) and therefore there is no consent. Where fraud/deceit exists, the will is defective, it having been induced by an illegitimate representation. Although the will of each party does exist, there is no consent. For example, if A intends to buy a car produced in 2015, and B represents that the car is made in 2015, but in fact it is not, A may avoid the contract because it is not his intention to buy this particular car.[40] A mistake may be an induced mistake (by the counterparty) or not induced by the counterparty (self-induced), but in both cases the contract is voidable unless the other party agrees that there is a mistake and agrees to amend the contract according to the correct understanding.[41] For example, a buyer who mistakenly understood a printing machine to be made in Japan could void the contract because he later found out that the machine was made in China. However, instead of voiding the contract, he could request the seller to amend the contract to state that the machine was made in China and claim for a price reduction. Should the seller agree with the buyer's request, the contract would not be voided.

Another question on consent to contract is that relating to a memorandum of understanding ('MOU'). Although MOUs may often be regarded as pre-contractual documents (presumably without assumption of responsibility), the will of the parties as expressed in the MOU can amount to a legally binding contract. The MOU can be binding and legally operative provided that it: (1) identifies the contracting parties; (2) spells out the subject matter of the agreement and its objectives; (3) summarizes the essential terms of the agreement; (4) is signed by the contracting parties; and (5) fulfils all the formality requirements.[42] As explained earlier, the common will and mutual consent are fundamental to the establishment of a contract. However, even with the will and consent of the parties, the contract can still be voidable for mistake, fraud, or deceit. For example, in a case between buyers and a seller, there was intention and mutual consent was given but the contract was still voidable due to deceit.[43]

[40] Art 127, VCC 2015. [41] Art 126, VCC 2015.

[42] See Judgment No 173/2009/DS-GDT dated 18 May 2009 of the Civil Court of the Supreme People's Court (*Tran Thi Tuyet Nhung v Nguyen Thien Dan*): with the help of Mr Dan, Ms Nhung owned two land lots totalling 24,168 sq m and she later built a house on her land. Mr Dan also owned an area of 8,468 sq m. Five years later, Mr Dan filed a lawsuit demanding that Ms Nhung return to him 7,850 sq m with attached assets due to an 'MOU on cooperation in an ecotourism project' signed between them. In this MOU, the two parties agreed that Ms Nhung would contribute 16,318 sq m of land, and Mr Dan 8,468 sq m as an investment in the ecotourism project. The project was not carried out as planned; Mr Dan requested the court to force Ms Nhung to return 7,850 sq m of land with attached assets to him. The Civil Chamber of the Supreme People's Court, in Cassation Judgment, ruled that an MOU was binding and created a valid agreement to commit a capital contribution by each party, regardless of whether the ecotourism project was later implemented or not. The court's reasoning was as follows: (1) Ms Nhung and Mr Dan were identified as the two parties to the contract; (2) the subject of the MOU was the cooperation contract and the objective of the contract was ecotourism; (3) both parties agreed to contribute land; (4) the MOU was signed by Ms Nhung and Mr Dan; and (5) all the formality requirements were fulfilled.

[43] See Judgment No 112/2009/DS-GDT dated 24 March 2009 of the Civil Court of the Supreme People's Court (*Thoi and Loan v Bay*): Mr Thoi and Mrs Loan (the buyers) bought 44 sheep from Mr Bay (the seller). The seller guaranteed that the sheep were female, short-tailed, of good quality, and reproduced twice a year. Later, the buyers filed a lawsuit demanding reimbursement because 38 of the 44 sheep were long-tailed (their tails were cut short when they were delivered to the buyers). The Civil Chamber of the Supreme People's Court ruled that the seller deceived the buyers by providing 'unqualified' sheep. The common will and consent did exist but it was based on deception. The buyers consented on the basis of conditions that did not exist in the sheep and which could not be cured by the seller. Therefore, under Art 132 of the VCC 2005, the contract was voidable due to deceit. The contract was also void under Art 127 of the VCC 2015.

(b) Goodwill, honesty, and good faith

There are two fundamental principles of Vietnamese civil law on which formation of contract is based (Article 3 of the VCC 2015), the first of which is freedom of formation of contract, ie a party is free to enter into a contract and to draft the contract in whatever form and with whatever content he has agreed with the other party, provided that such form or content is not immoral or illegal.

The second fundamental principle is goodwill and honesty. As a general principle of civil law (Article 3 of the VCC 2015), goodwill and honesty apply not only to contracts, but also to all civil juridical acts. When Vietnam was a French colony, the principle was enlarged to become the super control norm that the modern trend now seems to suggest it to be.[44] However, the difference between approaches should not be exaggerated. The importance of this principle does not lie in how wide the scope of goodwill and honesty is, but in how the courts interpret and apply this principle. Since the meaning of goodwill and honesty is unclear, imposition of such a principle could risk freedom of interpretation. So far, practice has shown very few attempts by the courts to decode a case based on the principle of goodwill and honesty. It is also partly because Vietnamese judges are not allowed to make law, that they normally follow the same source taken or accepted by other judges.

The general words 'goodwill and honesty' can be summarized by a term which is commonly used in other countries—good faith (in an objective sense). Another meaning of good faith (in a subjective sense) describes the situation where a person keeps a thing without knowing that he has violated the rights of another. This chapter deals with good faith in the objective sense. One may argue that the concept of 'goodwill and honesty' is congruent with good faith in civil law. This principle is one of the five fundamental principles of the VCC. The other four principles are: (1) equality among parties; (2) freedom of contract; (3) respect of public interests; and (4) self-responsibility for non-performance.[45] However, no analysis has been made of how the two concepts (good faith vs goodwill and honesty) could be compared. One might argue that good faith is more of a Christian concept than a Taoist or Buddhist concept, and as such is difficult for Vietnamese scholars to understand. One should also remember that the Vietnamese legal tradition was a socialist one, and therefore such a Christian concept was categorically replaced by Soviet scholars. Without a comparison of the two concepts, plus the Vietnamese mindset of 'form over substance' elaborated on earlier, a contract once adopted could not be changed and the parties have to follow it strictly. Any change, even one that does not affect the economic situation of the counterparty, could be rejected, let alone a renegotiation proposal based on hardship.

So far, not much has been written in Vietnam about what goodwill and honesty, vis-à-vis the concept of good faith, is. It is also challenging to view these two concepts from a comparative perspective. The term 'good faith' in the VCC is used in a subjective sense to refer to a person who possesses a thing without knowing (and cannot know whether) he has violated others' property rights (*ngay tình*). For example, Articles 131 and 133 of the VCC 2015 state that even when a contract is void, the rights of a third party in possession of a thing in good faith will be protected, and he does not have to return the item to the original owner (even though as a result, the contract becomes void). Articles 167 and 168 of the VCC 2015 state that a claim to repossess an item by its owner is ineffective against a third party possessor in good faith. For the protection of a possessor in good faith, if the item is not subject to registration, then the possessor in good faith must acquire such item through a contract with the person who has no right to dispose of the item, and the acquisition must

[44] See § 204 BGB; Art 6:248 of the new Dutch Civil Code; Art 1.7 PICC.

[45] Art 3, VCC 2015.

be paid for.[46] For example, if A gives B his computer, and B sells it to C and C acquires it in good faith, A cannot reclaim the computer, because C's acquisition of the computer is in good faith and paid for. But if B gives the computer to C, then A can reclaim the computer because no payment was given to B by C. On the other hand, if the item is subject to registration, then the possessor must duly register the item in order to be protected against the original owner.[47] For example, if A gives B his car and B sells it to C, who successfully registers it under his name, then C obtains a good title to the car and A cannot reclaim it.

However, drafters do not know 'good faith' in the objective sense—that is, a general duty that parties in a contract will take care of each other's interests. The reason for drafters not using the 'good faith' concept in the VCC is their not wanting readers to confuse subjective good faith with objective good faith. Instead, the VCC introduces a concept of 'goodwill and honesty'. This concept contained in Article 3 of the VCC 2015, is a general principle that guides parties to create, perform, or terminate a contract. It is unfortunate that although 20 years have passed since Vietnam adopted its civil code in 1995, the concept of goodwill and honesty has not been developed by the courts into a legal doctrine. Therefore, it is unclear whether goodwill and honesty is an improvement on 'good faith'. To a Vietnamese who has studied in Western countries, goodwill and honesty can be seen as synonymous with good faith. To a foreign scholar, goodwill connotes a greater degree of care for the interest of the counterparty, whereas good faith can arguably be seen as connoting a lesser degree of care for the interests of the counterparty.

It is interesting to note that the goodwill and honesty concept appeared many times in the VCC 1995 and the VCC 2005; the wording in Article 389 of the VCC 2005 and Article 412 of the VCC 2005 can be summed up by a term which is common in other countries—good faith. Article 389 of the VCC 2005 stated that the principles in formation of contract were voluntariness, equality, goodwill, cooperation, and honesty and fair dealing. In addition, Article 412 of the VCC 2005 provided that 'a contract must be performed honestly, in a spirit of cooperation so that it brings the best benefits for the parties and protects their mutual trust'.

Let us compare the above wording with the definition of good faith in other nations' laws. The Court of Justice of the European Union has referred to good faith as a 'principle of civil law'[48] and the proposed Common European Sales Law includes a definition of 'good faith and fair dealing' as 'a standard of conduct characterised by honesty, openness and consideration for the interests of the other party to the transaction or relationship in question'.[49] In Japan, one of the fundamental principles in its Civil Code is also 'the exercise of rights and performance of duties... in good faith'. In common law countries, even though courts often refer to and emphasize good faith, there is no commonly accepted definition and it all depends on the facts of each case. In an attempt to define the term, the court in *CPC Group Ltd v Qatari Diar Real Estate Inv Co*,[50] concluded that to act in 'utmost good faith' did not require one party to subordinate his interests to those of the other party, but was likely to require it to: (1) avoid a cynical resort to black letter law; (2) observe reasonable commercial standards of fair dealing; (3) be faithful to the agreed purpose of the agreement; and (4) act consistently with the justified expectations of the other party.

[46] Art 167, VCC 2015. [47] Art 168, VCC 2015.

[48] C-489/07 [2009] ECR-7315, last para. <http://curia.europa.eu/juris/document/document.jsf?text=&docid=73082&pageIndex=0&doclang=en&mode=lst&dir=&occ=first&part=1&cid=497156> accessed 1 November 2016.

[49] Art 2 of the Proposal for a Regulation of the European Parliament and of the Council on a Common European Sales Law, Com/2011/0635final-2011/0284.

[50] [2010] EWHC 1535 (Ch).

Accordingly, the wording may vary, but the spirit of the words is apparently similar. In the most general understanding, good faith is to act honestly, fairly, equitably, reasonably, and in a cooperative spirit. Hence, Articles 389 and 412 of the VCC 2005 did cover the concept.

Another approach to good faith in Vietnamese law is that there is a concept similar to good faith which is deeply entrenched in Vietnamese legal tradition—morality and respect of traditional values—as taught by Buddhism, Christianity, Confucianism, or Taoism. When the current VCC was drafted, the drafters refused to use the Western expression 'good faith' and chose instead to return to the Vietnamese traditional concept of mutual trust by naming it the principle of 'goodwill and honesty'. This principle underlines a number of other provisions contained in the Civil Code and other laws and regulations related to contracts. By stating 'the parties must follow the principle of goodwill and honesty', Article 3 of the VCC 2015 clearly indicates that the parties' behaviour must conform to goodwill and honesty throughout the life of the contract, and perhaps also in the negotiation process.

In principle, goodwill and honesty has two supplemental functions in contract law: (1) to fill the gap in the law, the court may use *analogia iuris* (legal analogy) and decide how the gap in the law can be filled if there is nothing agreed by the parties in the contract, in accordance with the principle of good faith; and (2) to restrict or read down provisions which may lead to performance contrary to goodwill and honesty. So far, however, good faith has rarely been enforced by the courts, and judges have tried to use other terms with the same function, such as 'due consideration' and 'encouragement of ethical conduct of the parties'. In short, good faith in Vietnamese law is viewed not only at the time the contract is made but also at the time it is performed.

Ultimately, good faith is nothing but a basis for both parties to strike a balance in arriving at a 'fair' solution. But what is fair is a matter of perspective and presentation. From Vietnam's perspective, the 'richer' party has a moral obligation to share risks with the 'poorer' party. That said, each judge while deciding a case and each person while considering signing a contract, makes a decision based on his knowledge and cultural background.

The principle of good faith also supplements the principle of freedom of contract. Just like freedom of enterprise is the fundamental principle of economics, freedom of contract is the fundamental principle of law, because the contract is an agreement between the parties. An agreement loses its meaning if it does not spring from the freedom of mind of the parties. A contract which does not respect this principle would be held void for lack of voluntariness (Article 122 of the VCC 2015). Obviously, freedom of contract can be abused by the stronger party to a contract in the imposition of unreasonable conditions on the weaker party. Of course, the principle of good faith cannot correct the disadvantages of the principle of freedom of contract; but in referring to good faith, the legislators of the VCC expect the stronger party not to exploit the weaker party without considering his interest. In reality, it is difficult to know how fair a contract is for two parties but, at least, if both parties act in good faith, both will gain what they expect to gain when entering the contract.

There are many urgent areas where the principle of goodwill and honesty can play an important role. These are gross disparity, excessive risk, and hardship, which are discussed in section III.5.

5. Modification of Contract

(a) Modification by parties

A contract validly concluded may be modified or even terminated by mutual agreement between the parties without further requirement such as *causa* or consideration. It is unclear under Vietnamese jurisprudence whether such a contract as modified is a new contract. In any case, the only contract still in force is the old contract with the relevant modification. When the contract is concluded in a specific form (eg in writing, notarized, certified, registered, or approved), the modification must also follow such form in order to be effective (Article 421 of the VCC 2015).

(b) Modification by the judge for unforeseen circumstances

The clause under which contract modification or adjustment can be effected for unforeseen circumstances that alter materially the equilibrium between the parties is called *clausula rebus sic stantibus* or 'hardship clause'. The clause is well known in foreign laws and international jurisprudence. Perhaps the most complex regulations on hardship are provided in Section 2, Chapter 6 of the PICC, which later inspired the legislators to amend the VCC in 2015. The new VCC 2015 introduces the concept of hardship which enables the court, based on the principle of good faith, to set aside or, upon request of one party, to modify the contract if unforeseen circumstances arise and create major difficulties in performance of the contract. Article 420 stipulates that a hardship situation occurs when: (1) it is unforeseeable by the parties at the time of contract conclusion, and had the affected party known of it, he would not have entered into the contract; (2) the situation which occurred is beyond the control of the parties after the conclusion of the contract; (3) the affected party has used his best efforts but is still unable to remedy the situation or minimize the damage; and (4) the continuance of the contract will cause severe damage to one of the parties. In this event, the affected party may request the other party to restore a balance between the parties within a reasonable time. If the parties fail to reach an agreement, one of the parties may request the court to terminate the contract or modify it so as to balance the rights and obligations of the parties. The modification is only allowed if it costs more to the parties to terminate the contract than to modify it.

Since the hardship clause is considered an exception to the principle of *pacta sunt servanda*, and the habit of Vietnam is to stick to the agreement, the hardship clause was objected to by many scholars during the course of drafting the VCC 2015. Finally, the drafters compromised by imposing many severe conditions that make the hardship clause almost impossible to implement. It remains to be seen how Vietnamese judges will develop the hardship clause in the VCC into a legal doctrine. Before the adoption of the VCC 2015, the concept of hardship was often criticized by judges and legislators, who believed that the clause would create a loophole for contracts to be dishonoured. The intention of the VCC's drafters was that should hardship occur and parties might not be agreeable to renegotiation of the contract, then the court would rather terminate the contract than amend the contract without the parties' consent. The court could only amend the contract if the costs to the parties of terminating the contract would be greater than the benefit to the parties of amending the contract.

The introduction of the hardship concept may not cause concern to the parties in the near future, because Article 420.4 of the VCC 2015 states that during renegotiation between the parties or settlement by the court, the parties must perform the contract in accordance with the agreement. That means, unless the court decides to terminate or amend the contract, the party taking advantage of the hardship has no incentive to renegotiate.

No matter how meaningful a hardship clause is, it is still a general clause and will ultimately be subject to judgment. On the other hand, the judgment of the party or the judge depends mostly on his background and knowledge.

(c) Modification by the judge for error

When a party concluded a contract because of an error or a mistake caused by the other party's unintentional fault regarding the subject matter, nature of the object (eg its quality, colour, etc), or content of the contract, the innocent party was entitled to request the other party to change the contract as he understood it to be, if the other party knew that there was a mistake (Article 131 of the VCC 2005). If the other party refused to change the contract, the mistaken party was entitled to request the court to invalidate the contract. Hence, at first, the mistaken party only had the right to ask for rectification (from the other party); if rectification was rejected by the other party, then he could ask the court to declare the contract invalid. Unlike some civil law countries, in this instance, Vietnamese judges could not modify the contract, as modification could violate the parties' voluntariness.

Article 131 of the VCC 2005 has been amended by Article 126 of the VCC 2015. In the VCC 2015, only when a mistake causes one or both parties to be unable to achieve the purpose of the contract, can the mistaken party request the court to declare the contract void. Otherwise it is still valid. For example, any mistake as to the price or the value of the contract's subject matter shall not be considered. Only mistakes as to the nature of the subject matter can be accepted. For example, if a buyer bought a printing machine for 3 billion VND (about US$150,000) because the seller said the machine was subject to a 20 per cent discount; he could not avoid the contract just because after he bought the machine, he discovered that another shop sold it at half price. There is no fraud or mistake in this case. The seller has the right to value his machine as he sees fit.

6. Purpose of Contract

Loyal to the civil law tradition, Vietnamese contract law emphasizes the purpose of the contract which is similar to the reason why the contract is concluded. The purpose of the contract, a juridical act, is defined as the rights and interests that the parties wish to obtain by concluding the contract (Article 118 of the VCC 2015).[51] To this commentator, the purpose or the reason of a juridical act is similar to the concept of consideration. However, unlike common law, the purpose of a contract is not a condition for the validity of the contract. As a contract is a juridical act, the purpose of a contract is required to be not contrary to the law or immoral; if the purpose is contrary to the law or immoral, the contract will be void.

Similar to other legal systems, the notion of purpose of contract in Vietnam has created great uncertainty and more problems than it has solved. Vietnamese legal science uses the term *khach the*, which is more useful as a philosophical notion than a legal notion, to refer to the purpose of contract. Until now, there is still a discussion among theorists as to whether *khach the* is what the parties participating in the juridical act focus on; or *khach the* is the reason for which the parties establish a contractual relationship. If the first definition prevails, then the notion of *khach the* will be equivalent to the notion of *causa* in some civil law countries.

IV. Pre-Contractual Liability

The conduct or representation of a party in the pre-contractual phase can influence the juridical relationship of the parties in the following ways.

[51] Art 124, VCC 2015 (similar to Art 129, VCC 2005) stipulates that a transaction established to conceal another transaction is invalid.

(1) First, it may mislead the other party as to the subject matter, nature of the object, or content of the transaction with an intention to guide such other party to conclude a contract with the first party.

(2) Second, it may mislead the other party as to the possibility of contract conclusion but no contract is entered into because of the first party's refusal to do so, therefore causing the other party to incur expenses and to start to perform other works in view of the probability of conclusion of the contract.

In the first case, we have a situation of fraud or misrepresentation, which is regulated by Article 127 of the VCC 2015. The second case would lead to controversy as to whether the defaulting party is liable for damage caused to the innocent party, since no contract has been concluded, and the aggrieved party could not have any contractual basis to claim damages. This situation was mentioned and analysed more than a hundred years ago by the German jurist, R Ihering.[52] Since then, German law has imposed pre-contractual liability to help the innocent party (liability for *culpa in contrahendo* (fault in contracting)).[53]

For the moment, the concept of pre-contractual liability does not exist in Vietnamese law. Until the contract is formed, the parties are free to break off negotiations without any obligation to compensate the other party. The only recourse for the aggrieved party is to claim damages in tort (extra-contractual liability). Nevertheless, it is difficult to prove, under the current legislation, that the act of the party in the pre-contractual phase is an unlawful act; so far no judgment on this matter has been recorded.

V. Contracts for the Benefit of Third Parties

1. Third Party's Standing and Involvement in a Contract

As in other legal systems, contracts in Vietnam are normally effective only between the parties to the contract. The rights obtained under a contract are rights *in personam*. The parties to a contract may agree on performance for the benefit of a third party. By the same token, one of the parties may promise that a third party will perform the contract. Obviously, obligations may not be imposed on third parties without their consent. Otherwise the principle of voluntariness would be contravened. The VCC is silent on the position of a third party who consents to take the rights and obligations under the contract, whether or not he becomes a party to the contract. In principle, since the third party does not have the right to negotiate the terms and conditions of the contract, he cannot be a party to the contract.

However, exceptions can be found in contracts which an unauthorized agent has signed, with the knowledge of the principal,[54] or in a collective labour agreement within an enterprise where, from the date the agreement is registered at the local agency of labour, war invalids, and social affairs, its terms and conditions are binding on employers and employees entering the enterprise.

[52] F Kessler and E Fine, '*Culpa in Contrahendo*, Bargaining in Good Faith, and Freedom of Contract: A Comparative Study' (1964) 77 Harv L Rev 401, 439.

[53] § 311(3) BGB. Under this provision, a pre-contractual obligation may:

> come into existence in relation to persons who are not themselves intended to be parties to the contract. Such an obligation comes into existence in particular if the third party, by laying claim to being given a particularly high degree of trust, substantially influences the pre-contract negotiations or the entering into of the contract.

[54] According to Art 562, VCC 2015 (and Art 581, VCC 2005), an agency contract is an agreement between the parties pursuant to which the agent is obliged to perform a task in the name of the principal, and the principal must remunerate the agent, if so agreed by the parties or provided by law.

The two most common situations where a third party may be involved in a contract is a contract for the benefit of the third party, or a contract burdening a third party. Also, a three-party relationship may arise in certain cases, for example when a transfer of property is made to swindle, hinder, or harm a creditor, ie *actio pauliana* can be invoked—in which case the creditor may avoid the contract. Under Article 59 of the Law on Bankruptcy 2014, a transaction executed within six months of the bankruptcy declaration of an enterprise could be voided if such transaction is aimed at: (1) giving or transferring assets not on arm's length terms; (2) further encumbering assets in the form of security interests; (3) setting off or repaying loans in favour of one unsecured creditor to the detriment of the other creditors. In addition, a transaction executed within 18 months of the bankruptcy of an enterprise would be voidable if it is a related party transaction unless proven to be transacted on an arm's length basis.

Another example of a situation that may influence the position of a third party is the situation where a third party acquires legitimate interests in good faith. For example, if a third party obtains a right of superficies or a right to the usufruct of an asset, the transfer of the right of ownership of such asset must not affect the right of superficies or right of usufruct.

2. Definition of Contract for Third Party's Benefit

Article 402.5 of the VCC 2015 explicitly recognizes that a third party who is conferred a right under a contract to which he is not a party may be entitled to enforce such a right. The article states:

> Contract for the benefit of a third party is a contract whereby both parties to the contract have to perform their obligations and a third party is entitled to receive the benefit raised from such performance of obligations.

Hence, to effectively confer a benefit on a third party, two elements must be satisfied. First, there must be a promise between the promisor and the promisee that the promisor will convey a benefit to a third party, the beneficiary.[55] Second, the effect of the term or condition of the contract is such that a benefit will be conveyed to a third party. If the beneficiary announces his acceptance of the benefit, the parties to the contract may not change the contract or terminate it, unless the beneficiary agrees to the change or termination.[56] If the beneficiary rejects the benefit (which has yet to be given to him), the contract is terminated or modified by agreement between the parties.[57]

(a) Exemption clauses for stevedores

X contracts with Y to transport X's goods using Y's ship to a foreign market. The contract for the carriage of goods by sea between X and Y contains an exemption of liability provision which purports to protect Z, the stevedores hired to unload X's goods from Y's ship once it arrives at the docks. As a result of Z's carelessness, X's goods are damaged while they are being unloaded from the ship and X wants to sue Z for negligence to recover damages for the losses suffered by X. Can Z rely on the exemption of liability provision in the contract between X and Y?

Vietnamese civil law does recognize third party benefits in the form of exemptions from liability. The VCC does not have a separate provision on exemption clauses, except for exemption clauses in standard form contracts. As Article 405.3 of the VCC 2015 voids only

[55] Art 415, VCC 2015. [56] Art 417, VCC 2015. [57] Art 416, VCC 2015.

an exemption clause inserted in a standard form contract, for Z to rely on the exemption clause, the contract between X and Y *must not* be a standard form contract—this is one means of relying on the clause by Z. Besides, if the exemption clause is in a non-standard form contract that is freely agreed on by X and Y, such exemption clause is valid. The principle *pacta sunt servanda* is still paramount.

It should be noted that the third's party enforceable right depends on there being no dispute between the contracting parties. In the event of a dispute between the contracting parties, the third party has no right to seek performance.[58]

3. Conditions for Validity of Contract for Third Party's Benefit

From the definition, it is evident that the third party's acceptance of the benefit is not a prerequisite for contractual validity. Thus, a contract for the benefit of a third party takes effect from the date both parties agree to conclude it. However, the third party acquires his right by accepting the benefit, but the obligation between the parties is created earlier, that is when the contract is concluded.

The right to revoke the term of the contract which confers the benefit on the third party stems not from the ineffective character of the contract, but from the principle of freedom of contract. As mentioned earlier, parties to the contract may at any time modify or terminate contractual terms and conditions by mutual agreement. However, the VCC 2015 also restricts the right to revoke or modify when the third party has accepted the benefit (albeit not yet performed). Article 417 of the VCC 2015 provides that when the third party has accepted the benefit, the parties can no longer revoke or even modify the terms of the contract without the consent of the third party. Acceptance does not mean accepting the performance; it means accepting the benefit that stems from the obligations to be performed. The phrase 'accepting the benefit of the contract' therefore indicates a willingness to accept the benefit, orally or in writing. Acceptance can also be expressed by conduct, ie when a third party proves that he has relied on the term of the contract and the promisor is aware or should be aware of such reliance.

Hence, once the third party has accepted the contractual term of the parties, he is deemed to have become a party to the contract. There has been no in-depth study on the subject of third party rights in Vietnamese law, nor has any foreign legal doctrine on the same subject been adopted. The VCC 2015 makes no change to contracts for the benefit of third parties—in comparison with the VCC 2005. This area of the law awaits further development in Vietnam. There are a number of unresolved issues arising from the terse provisions on third party rights.

First, it is not clear whether the parties' intentions feature in the third party's acquisition of an enforceable right. Freedom of contract should mean that if the contracting parties provide explicitly that they do not intend the third party to acquire an enforceable right, that intention should prevail. The VCC 2015 is silent on this point.

Second, what qualifies as a benefit enforceable by a third party within the ambit of Articles 402.5 and 415 of the VCC 2015? The dichotomy between direct benefit and incidental benefit is presumably embedded in what qualifies as an enforceable benefit.

(a) Selling bread

X leases two adjoining properties to Y and Z. The lease between X and Y barred Y from selling bread because Z sold bread from his leased property. Can X and Y agree to lift the bar?

[58] Art 415, VCC 2015.

It is permissible under Vietnamese civil law for lessors to restrict tenants from doing certain businesses, as it is up to the parties to choose the terms on which to contract. Hence, in the above case, if X and Y agree to lift the bar, X would be in breach of his contract with Z. Z then can sue X, but cannot sue Y because between Z and Y there is no contractual relationship.

(b) The stolen shop takings

X bank makes a contract for Y security company to collect Z store's takings. The contract requires Y to use armoured vehicles and take out insurance. Y failed to do these and the takings were stolen while being collected in an ordinary car. Can Z sue?

In this case, Z does not have a contract with X or Y. There is no agreement between Z and X about the type of vehicles to be used to collect Z store's takings. Risks are normally transferred to Y upon its undertaking an obligation to protect X's property according to the contract (Article 162 of the VCC 2015). Because Y has taken on the responsibility to protect Z store's takings at the time they were lost, the risk is on Y, so that Z can sue Y under tort law for breach of the duty of protection (Article 584 of the VCC 2015). And X can sue Y for breach of their contract under Article 351 of the VCC 2015.[59] But under Article 415 of the VCC 2015, Z cannot sue Y under the contract.

Third, while Article 416 of the VCC 2015 provides that the contract is terminated if the third party rejects or waives his right to receive the benefit, the VCC does not deal with the scenario where the obligation to benefit the third party is only one of many obligations between the contracting parties in a more complex contractual agreement.

Fourth, there is no provision on the promisor's defences against the third party. Besides Articles 402.5 and 415 that recognize rights of enforcement of benefits conferred on him, a third party is also able to enforce a contract if the contract is made on his behalf. A principal who is not disclosed by the agent to the third party at the time of contracting, may not step in to ratify acts done by the agent in excess of what had previously been authorized. The VCC recognizes the notion of the principal under Article 141, on scope of representative.

Another issue is that there is no provision in the VCC 2015 which stipulates whether third parties have to be in existence before contracts can be made in their favour. For example, the VCC does not anticipate what would happen if at the time of contract formation, the third parties are not yet in existence. Such third parties could be future employees, subcontractors, or unborn babies. Having said that, the general principle under contract law is that if anything is not expressly prohibited, it is allowed. The parties could provide benefits for unspecified third parties, and they are free to modify the terms of the contracts until such third parties come into existence and express willingness to accept the benefits.

Beyond what is written in the law, it is hard to say what the parties—the promisee, the promisor—need to do, and how the definition of a contract for the benefit of a third party in Article 402.5 of the VCC 2015 impacts the contours of the law on the subject. By saying 'benefit to a third party', the law envisages a direct benefit. An incidental benefit is one that is either not stipulated or one that refers to a situation of unjust enrichment where a third party to a contract receives incidental benefits from a promisee who has never committed himself to render the benefit. In this case, the third party needs to return the benefit to the promisor.

The wording of Article 402.5 does not necessarily mean that both parties have to perform their obligations to a third party. In the case of a unilateral contract, the contract creates

[59] See section V.4 (Rights and Duties of Promisor, Promisee, and Third Party), last para.

only rights in one party and only obligations in the other, the creditor may request the promisor to perform his obligation to a third party. In the case of a bilateral contract, one party may perform his obligation to the other party, in exchange for the performance by the other party to a third party whom he may appoint. This is usually a situation where there is a particular relationship between such party and the third party, for example parent company and subsidiary company. These contracts also qualify as contracts for third parties' benefit. Article 415 states that 'the third party may also request the promisor to perform the contract for the benefit of the third party'.

4. Rights and Duties of Promisor, Promisee, and Third Party

The promisor is under a general duty to perform the contract for the benefit of the third party. He is directly liable to the promisee for the performance (Article 415 of the VCC 2015).

As mentioned earlier, the third party (beneficiary) may accept the benefit and become a party to the contract. He may also reject the benefit. Article 416 regulates this situation.

If the third party rejects the benefit before the promisor performs his obligation, the promisor is released from performance. However, the promisor must notify the promisee of the effect of the third party's rejection. In such a case, the contract is deemed null and void. The promisor has to restore the promisee to his pre-contractual position by giving back what he has received from the promisee and vice versa.

If the promise to confer a benefit on a third party is one amongst many obligations contracted between the parties, for example the promisor promises to pay: (1) 30 per cent to X; (2) 20 per cent to Y; and (3) 50 per cent to the promisee; the promisor also promises to procure W to mow the promisee's garden, then the situation must be looked at obligation by obligation. The whole deal would not be unravelled because X rejects the payment, but only as far as the obligation to X is concerned—in this case, the promisor does not have to perform 30 per cent of his obligations to X and the contract shall be deemed amended to the effect that the promisor does not have to pay 30 per cent of the payment obligations and the amount that the promisor has to pay now is reduced to 70 per cent of the original amount.

If the third party rejects the benefit after the promisor has performed his obligation, the promisor is discharged from his obligation upon performance. However, in a bilateral contract, the promisee still has to fulfil his counter-promise to the promisor. Nevertheless, the VCC 2005 did not resolve the question of whether the third party was entitled to benefit from the performance of the promisor. Under Article 416 of the VCC 2015, benefits arising from such a contract belong to the party who should have been the beneficiary if the contract is not performed for the benefit of the third party, unless otherwise agreed between the parties.

If the promisee does not fulfil his obligation, the promisor is entitled to remedies for non-performance (ie order to perform, order for termination, and/or damages). Basically, the third party only has benefits under the contract, therefore the promisor cannot claim against the third party. However, if the third party is required to perform an obligation, for example, present certain original documents in order to receive payment, presentation of a copy of the documents would not be considered sufficient and the promisor may refuse to perform. Furthermore, if the promisor has a dispute with the promisee, he need not perform to the third party until after the dispute is resolved.[60]

[60] Art 415, VCC 2015.

As a general principle, a person who does not perform or improperly performs a civil obligation must bear civil liability if he is intentionally or unintentionally at fault, except where the parties agree otherwise or the law provides otherwise (Article 351 of the VCC 2015). However, in a breach of contract the fault of the non-performing party is presumed.

5. Right of Direct Action

The creditor of an obligation has a right of direct action against a third party if such a third party is the promisor of the promisor of the creditor (ie the sub-promisor, or subcontractor).[61] From the fact that the contract only creates a bipartite relationship, the creditor may not bring a claim against the third party. The one who is directly responsible for performance is the promisor and the creditor may only bring a claim against the promisor. However, if the parties sign a direct contract with the third party, then the creditor may have such rights. In a construction contract, if the employer pays the main contractor but the latter fails to pay the subcontractor, the employer may subsequently stop payment to the main contractor and instead pay the subcontractor directly so that the latter can complete the outstanding works. However, this stipulation is rather rare and requires an agreement on direct payment to the subcontractor to be made between the employer and the main contractor. In addition, Vietnamese law does not pay attention to the difference between direct benefit and incidental benefit as a means to keep in check the breadth of such allowance for conferment of rights on third parties.

If there is a dispute on contractual performance, the third party may not request the promisor to perform his promise until the dispute is settled. Also, he is not entitled to rescind the contract, unless it is so provided in the contract between the first two parties (Article 415 of the VCC 2015). Obviously, apart from the third party, the promisee is also entitled to request the promisor to perform the contract for the benefit of the third party.

An example of the right of direct action is third party liability insurance for motor vehicles. In this case, the injured third party has a right of direct action against the insurance company (the promisor to the insured) for an indemnity against loss suffered by the injured third party as a result of the insured-promisee's act.

In an action against the promisor, the third party's rights and obligations are the same as the promisee's in an action between the promisee and the promisor. Therefore, the promisor may use the same defences it would have against the promisee, for example force majeure, fault of the promisee, or even fault of the third party beneficiary.[62] These defences are applicable because the promisor is party to a contract. The promisor need not pay damages to the third party beneficiary as long as he can prove that non-performance is not caused by his fault.

6. Contracts Burdening a Third Party

Under the general law governing contracts, contracting parties cannot by their contract impose a burden on a third party. As noted, a contract is effective only *in personam* between parties to the contract.

However, there is an exception where a contract burdening a third party may be effective between the two parties, in the sense that one of them undertakes to make a third party perform an obligation (by free will). In this sense, if the third party fails to perform, he is

[61] Art 415, VCC 2015.

[62] Art 415, VCC 2015.

responsible as a guarantor. But the third party is not liable for non-performance, except as explained in section V.5.

VI. Conclusion

Formation of a contract under the VCC is similar to that in many other countries. Vietnamese contract law has also adopted modern rules of contract law—allowing offers to be made to the public, minimizing the role of the postal rule, and applying legal precedents and equity to contract law. It is hoped that these reforms will bring dynamism to contract law. Another reform made to contract law is the acceptance of the concept of apparent authority regarding contractual capacity, which reduces avoidance of contracts. And last but not least, the hardship concept is introduced. But, at the same time, Vietnamese law is still loyal to the battle of forms in offers vis-à-vis acceptances and, as such, there may be risks of contracts being avoided or risks of claims of no contract from offerors acting in bad faith.

As for third party benefits, there has been no reform of the VCC 2005. The language of the laws is still vague and sometimes misleading. Therefore, it is hoped that the Supreme Court will, based on its collection of legal precedents, clarify or interpret issues concerning third party rights.

22

Formation and Third Party Rights in the Myanmar Law of Contract

*Adrian BRIGGS & Andrew BURROWS**

I. The Sources of Myanmar Law

The source material from which this chapter is drawn is almost exclusively local to Burma or Myanmar (according to the date of its creation). The obvious point of departure is the Contract Act 1872, which even as it approaches its 150th anniversary, is a remarkably robust and lucid statement of the law. It is not perfect, of course. It probably was not perfect when it was made, and the way people make contracts today is not exactly the same as it was in 1872. It is perhaps unsurprising that there are some points on which law reform bodies could make useful improvements, but the marvel is that there are rather few of them. It is true that the advance of technology, the changing ways in which business is done, and the things that people contract about, all prompt the question whether, if it were to be drafted today, a Contract Act 2022 would look like the one made in 1872: the answer to that question is not easy to give. But for now, and for the foreseeable future, the 1872 Act is and will remain the foundation of Myanmar contract law.

It is important to appreciate that, with the exception of a few minor factual changes in its Illustrations (such as replacing Bombay by Rangoon), the Myanmar Contract Act 1872 is identical to the Indian Contract Act 1872.[1] Its enactment in Burma represented the application of the law in India to that part of India which, from 1897, included the province of Burma. India, including Burma, was at that time ruled by the British. The Indian Contract Act 1872 largely represented an attempt by the British to codify in statute the judge-made English law of contract for use in India and hence also, from 1897–8, in Burma. The main draftsman was Sir James Fitzjames Stephen and the general law of contract is set out in 75 sections. After the 1872 Act itself, and some more specific Acts, such as the Specific Relief Act 1877, the next most important source is the decisions of courts in Burma, and then in Myanmar. There is, in fact, a rich case law comprising the decisions of the Burmese-Myanmar courts in interpreting the 1872 Act or, occasionally, in dealing with issues that fall outside that Act.

What the authors were able to read ran out in 1969. Up until that time, the law reports were in English. After that time law reporting became sporadic and in any event was in Burmese only. The authors have managed to locate two or three helpful contract cases since 1969 and they have asked Burmese lawyers and members of the university law faculties in Yangon, to let them know of any other important cases on contract since that date. But what

* This chapter is largely extracted from A Briggs & A Burrows, *The Law of Contract in Myanmar* (Oxford University Law Faculty 2017) chs 1.1, 2, 3, and 5.9; cite as A Briggs & A Burrows, 'Formation and Third Party Rights in the Myanmar Law of Contract' in Chen-Wishart, Loke, & Vogenauer, *Studies in the Contract Laws of Asia Vol II: Formation and Third Party Beneficiaries* (Oxford: OUP 2017) ch 22.

[1] Act IX of 1872 (India). The Contract Act 1872 has also been adopted in, for example, Bangladesh, Brunei, Malaysia, Pakistan, and Tanzania.

Formation and Third Party Rights in the Myanmar Law of Contract. Adrian Briggs and Andrew Burrows.

the authors have been told is that there are unlikely to be many general contract cases that they have missed because, under the military socialist regime, the Supreme Court from the mid-1960s onwards did not tend to hear contract cases.

The authors derived considerable help in understanding the Myanmar law of contract and how it works in practice from meetings with lawyers working in Myanmar whether local or government lawyers or international lawyers. And the authors sent round a questionnaire which helped in pinpointing some of the important points in practice.

In 2016 the principal series of law reports, along with the Burma Code, and certain other materials, were copied and made freely available in electronic form on the AsianLII website (<http://www.asianlii.org>). As the most recent judgments, in the Myanmar language, are published on the website of the Union Supreme Court, this means that, if one knows how to look for it, the judicial authorities on the law of contract in Myanmar are accessible, in their original form, to anyone with an internet connection.

From time to time it has been asked whether these authorities, in which the judgments of the courts of colonial Burma play a significant part, are reliable as a source of current law. From within the country there have been occasional suggestions that the decisions of courts from an earlier time are not necessarily helpful in a country whose government was seeking to steer or drive society in a new direction.[2] From outside the country there have been other suggestions, that the post-independence history of Burma, then of Myanmar, has transformed the law and legal culture, several times over, and that unless all this is properly understood one cannot hope to understand the law of Myanmar.[3] There is certainly also a view, heard inside the country and not rarely, that it does not matter what a contract, or the law, actually says, because power is more important than law. And there have certainly been problems in the administration of justice, not least because of the shortage of resources allocated to the adjudication of disputes in accordance with the law.

And yet if one asks lawyers in Myanmar whether their contract law is contained in the Contract Act, the answer one always receives is that it is; and if one asks those same lawyers whether the law is expounded by the judges, the answer is just the same: the law is what the judges have said it is. It is unrealistic to suppose that the only authentic decisions on the contract law of Myanmar are those handed down by the courts in the years since 2008, or whichever date is chosen: that would simply mean that a book of the law of contract would be mostly blank where business and ordinary people alike need information and guidance. The basis on which the authors have proceeded is that the decisions of the courts of Myanmar on the interpretation of the Contract Act (or more rarely, where there is no statutory provision) are the best evidence of what the law of contract in Myanmar actually is. The decisions of judges, especially those given in the years after independence, are a remarkable treasury of legal analysis. They show that the courts of Myanmar were capable of powerful analysis and effective reasoning.

Among Myanmar lawyers there appears to be a hesitation about placing reliance on textbooks, even those compiled in earlier times by those who were masters of the subject. However, it is a challenging task to understand the law without the aid of a book to explain

[2] Dr Maung Maung, then Minister for Judicial Affairs, wrote that 'since the circumstances vary from case to case depending on social and historical factors reliance on previous rulings which were from different times should not be made. Foreign rulings should not be cited at all' (Foreword to the *Courts Manual* (Rangoon: Chief Court Press 1973)).

[3] For an interesting analysis of whether Myanmar in 2006 could still be considered as a common law system, see J Southalan, 'Burma and the Common Law? An Uncommon Question' (2006) 25 Legal Journal on Burma 4, also available at <http://www.thailawforum.com/articles/john-southalan.html>. The irony, given that in 2006 one might have taken the view that Myanmar had decided to depart in several respects from key tenets of the common law, is that over ten years later the very opposite appears to be true.

where it is to be found and what it means; and even if the writings of those who have read and thought about this material are not a formal source of law in Myanmar, their work in helping Myanmar lawyers discover or rediscover their law makes its own contribution.

The Contract Act may, in certain cases, be displaced or overridden by special legislation,[4] for special provisions in statutes override general ones.[5] For example, the Contract Act allows the parties to a contract to agree on the terms which they wish. But in certain cases, other legislation may supervene to give a different answer. Suppose, for example, in a contract of employment the employer and employee agree upon a daily wage at a rather low level. If the government legislates to fix the minimum wage above this figure, the new legislation will override the figure which had been agreed, and on this point the Contract Act will not provide the answer to the question of what the employee is entitled to be paid under the contract of employment. This happened in 2013,[6] and was followed by a decision to impose a minimum wage in certain sectors of the economy in 2015. It is obvious that this prevails over the terms of the contract, and to this extent the Contract Act 1872 is partially set aside by a provision from another statute.

Where the Contract Act appears to be incomplete, it should be remembered that it says, at the beginning, that it is expedient 'to define and amend certain parts of the law relating to contracts'.[7] The Act does not set out to provide a complete and comprehensive statement of the law of contract. It is on occasion supplemented by rules taken from other statutes,[8] and may on other occasions be supplemented by well-established principles from other common law jurisdictions.[9] And where the Act appears unable to answer a particular question, the Burma Laws Act 1898, section 13(3), may assist the court:

> **13(3).** In cases not provided for by…any other enactment for the time being in force, the decision shall be according to justice, equity and good conscience.

The significance of this provision is underlined by an important judgment of the Chief Court[10] in which the court had been pressed with the argument that, where the written laws of Myanmar did not make express provision for the relief applied for, there was nothing the court could do. The court disagreed, saying: 'where there is neither provision nor prohibition [the court] has to be guided by ordinary principles of common sense, justice, equity and good conscience'.[11] Following the guidance of the Chief Court it is always necessary to explore how section 13(3) may be available to help a court to arrive at a decision which could not otherwise be reached.[12] The availability of section 13(3) means that, if the judges are confident in the exercise of this power, there is considerable scope for the law of contract to be adapted or modernized without the need to wait for legislation.[13] That is not to deny,

[4] eg a claim against a common carrier sued as such is not governed by the Contract Act 1872 but by the Carriers Act 1865: see eg *The State Agricultural Marketing Board, Aykab v The Arakan Carriers' Syndicate, Aykab* (1958) BLR 138 (HC).

[5] *Daw Mya Swe v The Union of Burma Airways* (1964) BLR 279 (CC) 291. See for illustration the way in which the Urban Rent Control Act 1948 overrode the normal rights and incidents of a lease: *Mrs Constance Minoo Writer v AM Khan* (1951) BLR 169 (SC).

[6] Minimum Wage Law 2013.

[7] Contact Act 1872, Preamble.

[8] For an obvious example, the Evidence Act 1872.

[9] eg *Hollandia Pinmen v H Oppenheimer* AIR 1924 Ran 356; *Daw Mya Swe* (n 5).

[10] *Steel Bros & Co Ltd v YA Ganny Sons* (1965) BLR 449 (CC).

[11] ibid 463.

[12] Of course, Burma Laws Act 1898, s 13(3) cannot be used to prevent the application of a statutory rule which does govern the issue before the court: *Mohamed Farooq v Sahib Jan* (1960) BLR 51 (HC) (specific provision of Transfer of Property Act preventing application, by general reference to s 13(3), of a principle of Mohamedan law as to mode of making gifts).

[13] eg in *The Government of the Union of Burma v GC Mangapathy* (1949) BLR 234 (HC) the court applied Contract Act 1872, s 152 as a rule of justice, equity, and good conscience to a case (duty of care of government which had requisitioned goods) to which it did not apply, because no rule otherwise would have applied. In

however, that the application of the principles of 'justice, equity, and good conscience' may be thought to produce considerable uncertainty compared to the law set out in statute. It may, therefore, be powerfully argued that any gaps in the 1872 Act would be best dealt with by statutory reform of the Act rather than relying on the judicial application of those vague principles.

There is a separate question, which has arisen in some cases, on whether section 13(3) is really an instruction to the court to apply English common law.[14] However, even if this is how it was once understood, the persuasive force of this reasoning must now be much diminished, not only in those areas in which the law of Myanmar appears to have diverged from English law and in which recourse to English law would be to look for a rule which will no longer fit the gap, but also more generally because familiarity with English law on the part of Myanmar judges, advocates, and clients appears to be weaker than it once was. The result is that the pragmatic case for using the English common law in a supplementary role is perhaps less strong than in former times. It may also be argued that the common law of England has not had to face up to the acute difficulty facing a populace living under enemy occupation,[15] with the further consequence that it is not always best suited to fill in some of the gaps in Myanmar law.

Given the paucity of modern case reports and books on contract law, this book will not contain a bibliography on Myanmar law.

II. Formation of Contracts

In this section we start at the beginning, with the rules which establish whether an agreement has been formed, and if it has been formed, with whether it will, in principle, take effect in law as a contract. The purpose of this section is to examine and think about the way in which the law looks at the formation of contracts. We will organize the material under ten points, which are as follows:

(1) the elements which make a contract according to the Contract Act;
(2) proposals;
(3) acceptance of proposals;
(4) consideration;
(5) what converts an agreement into a contract;
(6) the intention to create legal relations;
(7) practical problems with the formation of agreements: informality, incompleteness, imprecision, and incoherence;
(8) problems of formation with more complex contracts;
(9) agreements to negotiate and agreements not to negotiate; and
(10) formation of agreements contrasted with variation of contracts already made.

China-Siam Line v Nay Yi Yi Stores (1954) BLR 270 (HC) the court applied the Carriage of Goods by Sea Act 1925 via Burma Laws Act 1898, s 13(3) to a factual situation to which it did not apply, namely carriage from a port outside Myanmar, as there was no other basis to find a sensible law to apply to determine the issues arising on the claim alleging short delivery. As the legislators had decided not to apply the 1925 Act to shipments from Hong Kong, it was a strikingly bold decision of the court to do so.

[14] See *Daw Mya Swe* (n 5). One may also see *U Ba Yi v Mahant Singh* AIR 1937 Ran 303; *The Tajmahal Stationery Mart v KE Mohamed Ebrahim VS Aliyar & Co* (1950) BLR 41 (HC); *The Union of Burma v U Htoon Pe* (1958) BLR 50 (HC); *Ko Maung Gale v Ma On Nyunt* (1963) BLR 515 (CC), each of which approve recourse to the English common law to fill gaps in the written laws.

[15] *VERM Krishna Chettiar v MMK Subbiya Chettiar* (1948) BLR 278 (HC) 295–303 (whether outbreak of war terminates agency).

Some of these points will be restricted to examination of the provisions of Chapter I of the Contract Act, but the later ones will test the extent to which the Contract Act is able to deal properly with some of the problems which arise in connection with the formation of contracts in a world in which methods of communication, and methods of contracting, can be very different from those which were known in 1872, and in which the expectations of modern commerce may call for solutions which would not have been known about in 1872, or even in 1972. It is always important to remember this when dealing with the Contract Act: it was enacted to assist the development of commerce, not to hold it back. We should always keep this in mind when questions of its interpretation arise.

In section II.11 we shall also look at two sections of the 1872 Act on void agreements that are relevant to formation.

1. The Elements Which Make a Contract According to the Contract Act

We start with section 2 of the Contract Act, and although we are initially concerned only with section 2(e), it is convenient to set out a large part of the section, in order to show the manner in which the Contract Act sets out the elements which lead to an agreement, and then to a contract:

> 2. **Interpretation clause**. In this Act, the following words and expressions are used in the following senses, unless a contrary intention appears from the context:
> (a) When one person signifies to another his willingness to do or to abstain from doing anything, with a view to obtaining the assent of that other to such act or abstinence, he is said to make a proposal;
> (b) When the person to whom the proposal is made signifies his assent thereto, the proposal is said to be accepted. A proposal, when accepted, becomes a promise;
> (c) The person making the proposal is called the 'promisor', and the person accepting the proposal is called the 'promisee';
> (d) When, at the desire of the promisor, the promisee or any other person has done or abstained from doing, or does or abstains from doing, or promises to do or abstains from doing, something, such act or abstinence or promise is called a consideration for the promise;
> (e) Every promise and every set of promises, forming the consideration for each other, is an agreement;
> (f) Promises which form the consideration or part of the consideration for each other are called reciprocal promises;
> (g) an agreement not enforceable by law is said to be void;
> (h) an agreement enforceable by law is a contract...

In other words, we first look for a *proposal* (section 2(a)), and then for its *acceptance* (section 2(b)), which creates a *promise*. If there is *consideration* for the promise or promises, there is an *agreement* (section 2(d), (e), and (f)). If the agreement is not made void by the Act, the agreement is enforceable by law and is therefore a *contract* (section 2(g) and (h)). This suggests that the law takes a very organized, step-by-step, approach to the formation of contracts, and that the formation of contracts requires each element to be separately identified and separately satisfied. There are, in principle, six elements in the analysis: proposal-acceptance-promise-consideration-agreement-contract: P-A-P-C-A-C.

Before we go any further there are two preliminary points to make. The first is that this structure, set out by the Contract Act for the formation of contracts, is elaborate. In many other common law jurisdictions, the equivalent would be proposal (or offer), plus acceptance equals an agreement which, provided there is consideration, constitutes a contract.

In particular, there would be no distinction between proposal (or offer) and promise, for the proposal would be seen as a promise which would become an agreement on acceptance. In other words, there would be five not six steps (proposal, acceptance, agreement, consideration, contract). To point out this difference is not to suggest that one approach is better than the other, but it shows that the Contract Act analysis, which this chapter will follow, is more elaborate than one might expect it to be.

The second general point is that the lives of ordinary people are not as tidy as those who draft the law might wish them to be. And when this is appreciated, it is the law which has to bend to accommodate real life, not real life which has to bend to fit the law. A very senior English judge, in a case before the Privy Council on appeal from the courts of New Zealand,[16] said something of real significance, which is worth quoting here. It contains important guidance for anyone dealing with the common law system of contract and contract formation:

> It is only the precise analysis of this complex of relations into the classical [proposal][17] and acceptance, with identifiable consideration, that seems to present difficulty, but this same difficulty exists in many situations of daily life, e.g., sales at auction; supermarket purchases; boarding an omnibus; purchasing a train ticket; tenders for the supply of goods; offers of rewards; acceptance by post; warranties of authority by agents; manufacturers' guarantees; gratuitous bailments; bankers' commercial credits. These are all examples which show that English law, having committed itself to a rather technical and schematic doctrine of contract, in application takes a practical approach, often at the cost of forcing the facts to fit uneasily into the marked slots of [proposal], acceptance and consideration.[18]

The reason this is important is because it acknowledges that there are many kinds of contract, from the everyday case of the person who gets onto a bus to the fantastically complicated contracts which are used in international commerce, which do not naturally seem to follow the clear and separate steps of the kind set out in the Contract Act. Yet we are required by our law—by the common law of which family of law Myanmar is a part, and by the Contract Act 1872 which lays down this part of the common law in Myanmar—to demonstrate how these real and everyday contracts fit into this formal structure. In this section, once we have understood the basic framework put in place by Chapter I of the Act, we will do some of this fitting in of contracts. We will always bear in mind that, although the Contract Act is precise, real life is untidy; that businessmen do not check their copies of the Contract Act before they make or respond to a message from those they are negotiating with; and that ordinary people are far too busy just trying to cope with the stress and strain of daily life to care about any of this analysis. But it is the law of Myanmar, and it is the duty of contract lawyers in Myanmar to explain how it works for ordinary people making domestic contracts, as well as for companies and commercial organizations making complex commercial deals. The Contract Act applies to them all.

Is it possible to have an agreement, or a contract, which does not fit, and which simply cannot be made to fit, within this framework, or this sequence of events? The answer to that is yes: there are certainly contracts which do not quite fit this sequence of creation.[19] Contracts are now made in circumstances which are much more challenging than anything found in the Illustrations in Chapter I of the Act, and it would be damaging to Myanmar law

[16] *The Eurymedon* [1974] UKPC 1, [1975] AC 154.

[17] We have replaced 'offer' in the English original with 'proposal', which means much the same thing, and which is the term used in the Contract Act 1872.

[18] *The Eurymedon* (n 16) 167.

[19] In *Maung Po Naing v Ma On Gaing* AIR 1917 PC 214, the Privy Council accepted that the rigour of the common law analysis, which may make sense if applied strictly in England, may need a greater measure of flexibility in Myanmar where the manner in which business is done may be rather different.

if it were to be held that the Contract Act was not capable of dealing in a business-like way with such contracts. How, therefore, is this to be done?

In some cases section 13(3) of the Burma Laws Act 1898 will provide a solution, allowing or requiring a court to fill in gaps in the written laws by the application of the principles of justice, equity, and good conscience:[20] in this context, perhaps, it should be taken to mean that the court will apply good commercial sense. We remember, second, that the Act is a code, but not, according to the preamble, a complete code. And we need always to remind ourselves that the Contract Act was made to facilitate the process of contracting, not to impede or to complicate it or tie it up in red tape. Our task is to approach the Act with this in mind.

We should also acknowledge that there may well be several perfectly sensible answers to a question, and it is not always necessary to select between them. For example, as we shall see later, the analysis of how a contract is made in a shop is not always clear: it could be the customer who makes a proposal to buy, which the shopkeeper accepts or rejects as he chooses; it may be the shopkeeper who makes the proposal to sell, which the customer accepts or rejects as he chooses. Each analysis will lead to the conclusion that there is a contract of sale, and in those many cases in which each side is happy with that answer, the details of the legal analysis are not that important. But in those rare cases in which it does matter—where the law asks when, precisely, a contract came into existence—we may need to be more careful about our analysis, and will need to deal with the rules which we are about to examine.

Are there any other requirements, not expressly stated in section 2 of the Contract Act, which must be satisfied before an agreement, or a contract, is formed? We will deal with some specific points in section II.11 which mean that the agreement is void, or that the supposed agreement is void. One point, however, is not mentioned anywhere, and that is the intention of the parties to create legal relations. We will think in greater detail about that in section II.6 of this chapter, but it is sensible to say something about it now. The Contract Act deals with contracts which are subject to the enforcement processes of a court. The effect of making a contract to which the Act applies is that it is potentially subject to judicial supervision and enforcement if anything should go wrong. Yet we all make agreements in our daily lives which we would never imagine had anything to do with the courts or with the legal system. The husband who promises to buy his wife a new dress if she will accompany him to his company's annual dinner does not expect the agreement to land him in court if he forgets or changes his mind. The intention to create legal relations may not be specifically mentioned in the Act as one of the requirements for the formation of a contract, but we must accept that it is there, written in invisible letters.

Let us therefore begin with proposals, and how they are made.

2. Proposals

A proposal—what some other common law systems refer to as an offer—is the label we use 'when one person signifies to another his willingness to do or to abstain from doing anything, with a view to obtaining the assent of that other to such act or abstinence'.[21] Sometimes a person will say to another: I will do this if you agree to do that, and if this is followed by what the law regards as an acceptance, the proposal becomes binding and, according to the Act, is turned into a promise.[22] What we have to consider here is what a proposal is, how it

[20] See above, text to n 9. [21] Contract Act 1872, s 2(a).

[22] An alternative analysis, but which is not that used by the Contract Act 1872, would be that the proposal is itself a promise which becomes binding on the proposer when it is accepted. This analysis uses two stages to reach the point which, under the Contract Act 1872, takes three.

is communicated to someone else, how long it exists as a proposal which is open for the other party to accept, and how revocation of a proposal may be prevented.

(a) What is a proposal?

Section 2 of the Act is drafted on the basis that a proposal can be accepted, and that when it is accepted the first step towards the making of a contract—the making of an agreement—has been taken. It follows that a proposal should be a statement that lends itself to acceptance. It should be something which the party to whom it is addressed could accept with a simple 'I agree'. In a few words, it cannot be a proposal unless it can be accepted; and we therefore have to know a little about acceptance in order to decide whether we are dealing with a proposal. In slightly more words, we need to be able to see that what the person who made the suggested 'proposal' said or communicated was a statement that he was willing to be bound, and to have his proposal turned into a promise, by the simple acceptance of the other party and without further involvement of his own part. In other words, he had given the other party an option to say yes or no.

It follows that something is not a proposal if it is really just an invitation to another party to enter into negotiations.[23] It is not a proposal if it is an invitation to another to make a proposal. For example, if I have a car for sale and I advertise it, saying 'offers above $5,000', I do not make a proposal. I am asking or inviting other people to make proposals to me, telling them what sort of proposal would be likely to interest me. English lawyers would call such a statement an invitation to treat, or an invitation to offer; but it does not really need a name. By contrast, if I say 'car for sale to the first person to offer $5,000', I make a proposal, for all that is required to produce full and complete agreement is for another person to tell me that she agrees to pay $5,000. Notice that although I may appear to say that the buyer is invited to offer, the law will say that I made the proposal, and that the would-be buyer accepted it.

If I say 'car for sale to highest bidder; all bids to be received by 5 pm', this too will look like a proposal. I am not inviting people to negotiate with me; I am telling the world that whoever is the person who makes the highest bid is the person to whom I will be bound to sell the car, with no further question asked. A slight difficulty may arise if a person responds to such a proposal by saying that she makes a bid of '$50 higher than the next highest bid', claiming that by doing so she has submitted the highest bid, but we will deal with this case below, for the issue it raises is better analysed within the law on the acceptance of proposals.[24]

If I announce that my car is for sale for a price above $5,000, and you say: 'Agreed', there is no agreement, because my statement was not a proposal. There is no agreement, for if one were to ask a judge what price was agreed to, the judge will say that no price has been agreed; no price, no contract. The reason for this is that I invited you and the rest of the world to make a proposal. You made one (even if you thought it was an acceptance), and it was then up to me to decide whether to accept it.

Suppose in this last example you had said: 'I will buy it for $6,000'. Does this change things, and mean that you have accepted my proposal? Again, the answer is no, because I did not offer or propose the sale of my car for sale for $6,000; and you cannot accept a proposal which I did not make.[25]

[23] For an excellent illustration see *Hardandass v Rani Mohori Bibi* (1913–14) LBR 343 (telegraphic communications concerning a possible sale, but even if there was a clear proposal, it was not followed by an unconditional acceptance).

[24] See section II.3(f) below.

[25] *Hardandass* (n 23).

This set of simple cases teaches us a number of things. One is that people may make proposals without realizing that this is what they have done. Another is that people may not have made proposals even though they think they have, and may have made acceptances even though they were asked to offer something. And a third is that we can sometimes only decide if something is a proposal by inquiring into whether it would be possible to accept it. The question is whether the communication from one side was, in effect, a statement of unconditional willingness to be bound, to have the proposal converted into a promise, by a simple conforming acceptance. It may require us to think for a moment before we leap to the conclusion that there was an acceptable proposal and an acceptance of it.

What, then, do we say about the person who advertises his bicycle for sale for 20,000 kyats, or a shopkeeper who puts goods on a shelf in his shop with a price label attached? It might be thought to be obvious that in these cases the seller is proposing to sell, and that the proposal can be converted into a promise to sell by a simple and straightforward acceptance by the customer. If you think so, many people would agree with you. But it may not be quite so easy: think about it this way. Suppose ten people respond to the owner of the bicycle, saying that they agree to buy it for 20,000 kyats: have they all accepted the proposal? Does the owner now face being sued by at least nine of them if he fails to deliver the bicycle to them? Questions like this lead some people to think that the advertisement cannot really be a proposal, even if it looks like one.

And what of the shopkeeper: is he bound to sell to the customer who picks up the item and brings it to the till? What if the price label stuck to the item was wrong: does the shopkeeper have to sell it at the price marked? What if the shopkeeper takes the responsible view that he should not sell the thing (say a knife, or a hammer) to this particular customer: is he bound to do so? Questions like this lead some people to think that the display of goods cannot be seen as a proposal to sell them, but is in fact an invitation to a customer to make a proposal to the shopkeeper. It may be that in Myanmar it may be easier to understand that the customer proposes to the shopkeeper, and not the other way around, because few goods or services available for purchase or acquisition come with a price label fixed to them; it is easier in Myanmar than in, for example, England to understand that it is the customer who makes a proposal to buy, and that it is not the shopkeeper who proposes a sale. The shopkeeper, the taxi driver, and so on, invite customers to make proposals, at least in the usual case. Of course, if the advertisement says 'for sale to the first person to offer 20,000 kyats', it is much easier to see that this is a proposal, for only one person can meet the terms, and there is no problem in treating this as a proposal. The answer in all these cases will depend on interpretation of the words and deeds, but also upon the commercial common sense of the relationship between the parties.

(b) How is a proposal communicated?

According to section 4 of the Contract Act, and as a matter of common sense, a proposal has to be communicated:

> **4. Communication when complete**. The communication of a proposal is complete when it comes to the knowledge of the person to whom it is made...

It is hard to know why the Act deals with the communication of proposals, for the real issues arise in relation to acceptances and revocations. A proposal cannot be accepted unless, and until, the other party knows of it, and so an un-communicated proposal cannot be accepted. The reason for the statutory rule is a bit of a mystery.

(c) *For how long is a proposal open for acceptance?*

In principle, a person who makes a proposal is treated as making it continuously until he has brought to the attention of the other that it has been withdrawn and is no longer open, that is, that it has been revoked. It follows that a proposal can be accepted unless it has expired or has been revoked. The question of how it may be accepted (and converted into a promise) is considered later, but a proposal which says that it is open for acceptance until the last day of the month obviously cannot be accepted on the first day of the following month, for that would be to accept a proposal which had not been made.

It is always possible, of course, that a proposal will not be accepted: if not accepted, it does not have any effect in law. But as said, a proposal which has been made may be revoked by the proposer, with the consequence that a person who might otherwise have accepted it is no longer able to do so. Section 5 of the Contract Act explains *when* this may be done:

> **5. Revocation of proposals and acceptances.** A proposal may be revoked at any time before the communication of its acceptance is complete as against the proposer, but not afterwards…

It follows that if I have offered my car for sale to the first person to agree to pay a certain sum for it, I may revoke this proposal if the communication of its acceptance by another is not yet complete: we will deal with what this means later. It is obvious that if there has been no acceptance, no harm is done to anyone if I withdraw the proposal. For this reason, the Contract Act[26] allows unaccepted proposals to be revoked.

And section 6 of the Contract Act explains *how* the revocation is done:

> **6. Revocation how made.** A proposal is revoked—
> (1) by the communication of notice of revocation by the proposer to the other party;
> (2) by the lapse of the time prescribed in such proposal for its acceptance, or, if no time is so prescribed, by the lapse of a reasonable time, without communication of the acceptance;
> (3) by the failure of the acceptor to fulfil a condition precedent to the acceptance; or
> (4) by the death or insanity of the proposer, if the fact of his death or insanity comes to the knowledge of the acceptor before acceptance.

We do not need to say much about section 6(2), (3), and (4) which largely speak for themselves. As to section 6(2) there will, no doubt, be cases in which there is an argument about whether the time which has elapsed without communication of acceptance is a reasonable time, but there can be no hard-and-fast rules: it will depend on the nature of the contract or on the nature of the goods or on any previous dealings between the parties. Section 6(3) is also easy enough: if I say that you must do a specific thing in order to accept the proposal—say, pay a certain sum of money by a certain date—and you do not, then the offer is revoked. The Act might have said that in such a case the proposal is not accepted, but it goes further and treats the proposal as though it had said that 'unless a specific thing is done by a specific day, the proposal lapses'. It will follow that it will not be possible for it to be accepted later because it has already been revoked. The situation described by section 6(4) is not one which comes up very often.

[26] However, in *Municipal Corporation of Rangoon v Saw Willie* (1941) RLR 724, AIR 1942 Ran 70 it was held that where specific legislation (in that case, the Rangoon Municipal Act, and rules made by the corporation under the legislative authority of the Act) overrode Contract Law 1872, s 5 and provided that a tender submitted to the corporation was irrevocable, s 5 did not apply.

Revocation by communication of notice of revocation raises delicate questions. What does a person actually have to do if she is to be able to say that she revoked the proposal by communicating notice of her revocation? The answer comes from section 4 of the Contract Act, the third (unnumbered) point of which says:

> **4. Communication when complete.** The communication of a revocation is complete:
> - as against the person who makes it, when it is put into a course of transmission to the person to whom it is made, so as to be out of the power of the person who makes it;
> - as against the person to whom it is made, when it comes to his knowledge.

This means that you can no longer accept my proposal if the fact that I had revoked it had come to your knowledge. That is easy enough, but what of the case in which perhaps you should have known, but did not actually know, that I had revoked the offer? Suppose I revoke by letter, which is delivered to you but which you do not open, or I revoke by sending a telephone message to your voicemail, or a text message to your mobile telephone, or an email to your email address, but for some reason you do not open the letter, play back the message, read your text or email at the time when I would have expected you to have done so? If section 4 means what it says, there is no revocation by the communication of notice of revocation if the notice has not come to the knowledge of the other party. However, a court may consider that if a proposer has done all that he reasonably could to communicate his notice of revocation, and that the reason it did not come to the knowledge of the other party was because he behaved unreasonably in not checking for messages in a timely fashion, the proposer has done enough to revoke the proposal. This would involve interpreting 'knowledge' in a particular way or reading words into section 4 which are not there (such as 'or would have come to his knowledge but for his own fault') and, in line with the general common law idea of constructive knowledge, there is good reason to think that that is what would be done.

Something similar may be needed for the case in which I advertise a reward for the person who finds my lost bicycle. If I decide to revoke this proposal, perhaps because I no longer want the bicycle, and do not wish to pay the reward to the finder, it cannot really be necessary for me to communicate notice of revocation to the person or persons who may be looking for the bicycle: I do not know who they are, after all. A sensible solution would be for the law to be that, as long as I publish the revocation in the same way that I published the original proposal, that would be sufficient to revoke the proposal. However, it may be just too difficult to stretch the words of the Act to allow for this; it may be that the Contract Act means that there are some proposals which, once made, cannot be revoked by the communication of notice and for which revocation by the other paragraphs of section 6 of the Contract Act is all that is allowed.

(d) Can the revocation of a proposal be prevented in advance?

The only way to prevent the revocation of a proposal which has not been accepted is to show that there was a (separate) agreement not to revoke it. Suppose you propose to sell me your car for $5,000, but I realize that I will need time to find out whether I can raise the money. The problem for me is that if I have not yet communicated my acceptance, you may communicate notice of revocation at any time before that.[27] The only way to prevent this is for me to enter into a separate agreement, which takes effect as a separate contract,

[27] *Ma Thin v HM Yassim* AIR 1916 LB 18.

with you that the offer will be kept open for a certain period, and will not be revoked before then. Like all other agreements which are intended to operate as contracts, there will need to be consideration for your promise to keep the proposal open for my acceptance. But if I pay or otherwise provide consideration for your promise to keep the proposal open and to not revoke it, I have purchased an 'option' to accept the proposal within the stipulated period.

(e) Can a proposal be revoked when the other party has started to perform the acts specified as acceptance?

The Act says that a proposal may be revoked at any time before the communication of acceptance is complete. This makes sense where the other party has not yet decided, or has not yet acted upon his decision, to accept. But it is much less satisfactory if the other party has started to perform the acts required by way of acceptance, but has not yet completed them. As we shall see later, in relation to section 8 of the Contract Act, performance of the conditions of a proposal will be an acceptance; it appears to follow that partial or incomplete performance will not. If that is so, the proposer would be free to revoke a proposal—assuming that the revocation is communicated—at the point at which the other party has almost, but not quite, completed the acts specified as required for acceptance. So, for example, if a person offers a prize to the student whose performance is the best in the year, but just before the end of the year notifies the students that he has revoked the offer, it would be unsatisfactory if those who had worked hard in an attempt to satisfy the conditions were deprived of the opportunity to meet the condition, accept the offer, and claim the prize. Again, if I promise to make a payment to a person who walks from Pegu to Yangon to raise money for a charitable cause, but then revoke the offer as he approaches Yangon, section 5 of the Contract Act would suggest that I am free to do so, because acceptance has not yet taken place. This would not be satisfactory.

One possibility would be to argue that there is a distinction between (on the one hand) acceptance of the proposal for the purpose of claiming the payment or the reward, for which full performance of the conditions would be required, as section 8 of the Contract Act says, and (on the other hand) acceptance of the proposal for the limited purpose of preventing its revocation. In effect there would be a distinction between full acceptance for the purpose of enforcing the offer, and limited acceptance for the purpose of preventing revocation. So, for example, if I advertise a reward for the person who finds evidence that a rare animal is not yet extinct, and an explorer spends a lot of money in mounting an expedition into the remote jungle to look for it, I would not be permitted to revoke the proposal if the explorer had embarked on doing what I had specified, though I would not be bound to pay the reward unless a conforming discovery were made. Although the law is not yet clear on this point, the analysis put forward here appears to be consistent with the requirements of 'justice, equity, and good conscience' as laid down in section 13(3) of the Burma Laws Act 1898.

If there has been a proposal, and there has been no effective revocation of it, we next need to consider how a proposal is accepted.

3. Acceptance of Proposals

We need to examine the definition of an acceptance to be able to decide whether there has been an acceptance, and to identify the date on which an acceptance is effective to convert the proposal into a promise.

(a) The definition of acceptance

According to sections 7 and 8 of the Contract Act:

7. **Acceptance must be absolute**. In order to convert a proposal into a promise, the acceptance must—
   (1) be absolute and unqualified;
   (2) be expressed in some usual and reasonable manner, unless the proposal prescribes the manner in which it is to be accepted. If the proposal prescribes a manner in which it is to be accepted, and the acceptance is not made in such manner, the proposer may, within a reasonable time after the acceptance is communicated to him, insist that his proposal shall be accepted in the prescribed manner, and not otherwise; but if he fails to do so, he accepts the acceptance.
8. **Acceptance by performing conditions or receiving consideration**. Performance of the conditions of a proposal, or the acceptance of any consideration for a reciprocal promise which may be offered with a proposal, is an acceptance of the proposal.

In other words, there is acceptance by expression of agreement, and acceptance by the performance of a condition specified by the proposer; and each of these is capable of being interpreted flexibly. Once an acceptance, which conforms to the proposal, has been effectively made by the person to whom the proposal is made, the proposal becomes a promise.[28]

(b) Who may accept a proposal?

It is obvious—the Act does not say so, but that does not matter—that the acceptance must be by the person (if it was specifically addressed to one person only), or by a person who falls within the class (if it was directed to a class of persons) to whom the proposal was addressed. Where this does not happen, and a proposal is 'accepted' by someone to whom it was not addressed, or was not open for acceptance, there is no acceptance and therefore there can be no promise, no agreement, and no contract. In a case like this it is likely that there has been some form of mistake, and for this reason we will not explore the case here.

(c) Acceptance by expression of agreement

If you offer to sell me your bicycle for 20,000 kyats, and I say 'I agree', or 'I accept', or use words which convey the same meaning, your proposal is converted into a promise by my acceptance. I have expressed unqualified and unconditional agreement to your terms, and this will comply with the definition in section 7(1) of the Contract Act. However, if I say 'Give me time to think it over', or 'Would you accept 15,000?', this is not an acceptance of the proposal. The position is the same if I should say 'I agree if you will arrange for the delivery to my house': in this case the agreement which I express is qualified with further conditions or requests. None of these will be an acceptance, and in accordance with general principles, the proposer is not bound. He may therefore sell the bicycle to another person, or decide not to sell at all, by revoking the proposal which has not been accepted. If he does this, and the other party then changes his mind and decides to accept, he will be responding to a proposal which is no longer open for acceptance, and there will be nothing for him to accept.

[28] *SM Bholat v Yokohama Specie Bank Ltd* AIR 1941 Ran 270 explains that the acceptance must, if not made by the person to whom the offer is made in person, be made by a person with authority to act on his behalf, and not by an unauthorized employee. For what counts as authority, see further below.

It is for this reason that a person to whom a proposal is made, but who needs time to consider her position, to see whether she can raise the necessary finance, and so forth, is at risk of the proposal being revoked in the meantime. To avoid this, as we have seen earlier, she will need to make a separate agreement, supported by consideration, for the proposal to be kept open and not to be revoked. This constitutes an 'option' to accept the proposal, and is a common feature of many forms of pre-contractual negotiation in which an instant response is likely to be difficult to give.

The straightforward case of acceptance by expression of agreement is seen when parties deal face to face, and the acceptance is communicated from mouth to ear. But many contracts are not negotiated and agreed to in this way, and the expression of acceptance must take some other form. Section 7(2) of the Contract Act is flexible in the manner in which it allows the acceptance to be communicated to the proposer: any reasonable means will do. However, if the proposer specifies the mode or manner of acceptance, this is binding on the acceptor. In principle, a proposer is entitled to say that his proposal must be accepted in the way he specifies, and it is not open to the acceptor to say that some other means of expression of the agreement was just as good, or just as effective. If I say to the other party 'I must have your acceptance in writing by 4 pm on Friday', and you purport to accept by telephone, or by sending an employee to say that you are accepting the offer, before then, I am entitled to say that this is not the acceptance I asked for. Likewise, if you deliver your acceptance in writing, but only on Sunday, but also say that as the offices were closed for the weekend, this makes no difference to the proposer, the proposer is entitled to say that this is not an acceptance which conforms to his proposal, and that it is not effective to convert the proposal into a promise. Section 7(2) of the Contract Act does, however, provide for this irregular attempt at acceptance to be treated as effective if the proposer, who has received the irregular communication, has not done anything to show that he objects to the manner or form of the acceptance. His lack of objection may have the effect of converting an irregular acceptance into one which is legally effective.

(d) Date of acceptance

The application of the rule in section 7(2) of the Contract Act does require us to pinpoint the date of acceptance. That is done by section 4 of the Act, which says, in material part, that:

> **4. Communication when complete**. The communication of an acceptance is complete
> - as against the proposer, when it is put in a course of transmission to him, so as to be out of the power of the acceptor;
> - as against the acceptor, when it comes to the knowledge of the proposer.

If acceptance is by posting a letter, the acceptance takes effect as against the proposer when the letter is posted; as against the acceptor it takes effect when it arrives. The uncertainty which this rule can produce when communications are delayed in transit provides a powerful reason for a proposer to make it clear that he requires the acceptor to communicate his acceptance in a particular way.

The question of where a contract is made rarely arises in ordinary contract litigation, but it may be decisive for some purposes (eg tax liability) and when it does arise, an answer of the kind given in section 4 would not be satisfactory. The court will therefore ask, instead, where the acceptance was made. If acceptance is by sending a telegram, the place where the acceptance is made, and therefore where the contract is made, is the place from which the telegram is sent.[29]

[29] *Messrs WW Wood & Sons v The Commissioner of Income-Tax Burma* (1963) BLR 45 (CC). A similar, but different, question arises if it is necessary to say where a cause of action in contract arose for the purpose of

(e) Acceptance by performance of conditions

If I say to you that I will pay you a sum of money if you find my lost ring, and you complete that performance, you have accepted my proposal and I am now treated as having made a promise to pay the sum which you are now entitled to demand. In such a case there is no need to express or communicate an acceptance, for the proposer has expressly provided that acceptance shall be complete on the performance of a condition which does not require notification by the acceptor that she is going to perform that condition. Suppose I advertise a new medicine which will prevent the person who takes it catching the flu and I say that, if anyone who uses the medicine in accordance with the instructions for a month catches the flu, I will pay them a sum of money. A person who uses the medicine for a month satisfies the condition which I specified; and if they nevertheless catch the flu, I am bound to make the payment, as my proposal, which was accepted by performing the acts specified, has become a promise.

Suppose I make the proposal, and you have started to use the medicine, but before completion of the course I revoke the proposal. It might be thought that as you have not yet accepted the proposal, because you have not yet fulfilled the condition which I specified for acceptance I am free to revoke the proposal. We dealt with this question in the context of revocation of proposals,[30] but return to it here as it is equally an aspect of the law on acceptance. It may be contended that a person who intends to accept by the performance of conditions runs the risk that the proposer will revoke the offer so that the acceptor has acted in vain. But the better view is that once the acceptor has embarked on the acts which will constitute acceptance if they are all performed, the proposer loses the power to revoke the proposal, even though authority for this analysis is hard to find. If the answer were to be that the proposal could be revoked just as the other party is finishing the performance stipulated as amounting to acceptance, it would be contrary to 'justice, equity, and good conscience', with the result that section 13(3) of the Burma Laws Act 1898 provides the solution.

In other common law jurisdictions, the difference between a contract formed by the exchange of promises, and a contract formed by a promise followed by the performance of stipulated conditions, is indicated by calling the first kind of contract a 'bilateral' contract, and the second type a 'unilateral' contract. In a bilateral contract both parties are bound, whereas in a unilateral contract only one party is bound (because only one party is making a promise). These terms do not appear in the Contract Act, but section 8 of the Act, in particular, is a clear indication that Myanmar law reflects this natural distinction between types of contract.

(f) The acceptance must conform to the proposal

We should return to the seller who makes a proposal to sell his car to the highest bidder. If a calculating buyer responds to the proposal by making a bid of '$50 above the next highest bid', and claims by doing so that she has submitted the highest bid, she will probably fail. The law will say that the seller's proposal only invited bids expressed in absolute terms, in real numbers, and could therefore be accepted only by a bid which conformed to this description.[31] The 'referential' bid did not conform to the terms of the proposal and will be ineffective as an acceptance.

ascertaining whether a court has jurisdiction under the Civil Procedure Code, s 20, for it is perfectly feasible to say that a cause of action arose in more places than one, and that this is sufficient to establish the jurisdiction of the court: see *Shantilal Surajmal Mehta v Mariam Bibi* (1960) BLR 359 (HC).

[30] See section II.2(c)–(e).

[31] A justification for this conclusion is that, if a referential bid were effective as an acceptance of such a proposal, a real problem arises if there are two such bids. What seems to be a perfectly sensible way of selling a car would become unworkable.

(g) Acceptance by silence?

Is it possible to accept by simply remaining silent? In principle, the answer must be no. If a person who wishes to acquire land approaches a small farmer and says 'I am willing to buy your land for $1,000, and unless I hear from you by Friday we will have a contract', then if the farmer does not respond, one could not say that this formed a contract which required the farmer to part with his land for $1,000. In principle, a person is entitled to ignore a proposal made to him.[32]

But suppose we have been negotiating for the sale (by me) and purchase (by you) of a horse, and we have settled on a price; and suppose I say to you that unless I hear from you to the contrary, I shall assume that you are buying it. You say nothing more: does that allow me to say that acceptance has taken place? It seems unreasonable that a party who does not respond to a proposal can be considered to have accepted it but, on the other hand, if you were to argue that you had bought the horse and were entitled to demand it, and that you had no need to express or communicate your acceptance because I had said that you did not need to, it seems that you would be right and that you would have converted my proposal into a promise. In other words, the law does not require me to speak out to prevent a proposal turning into a promise, but if the proposer says that he does not need to have acceptance expressed to him, he can be held to what he has said; and if the other party wishes to accept the proposal, he is free to do so, by silence if that is what the proposer has stipulated. In short, the proposer can waive the need for communication of acceptance so that silence can constitute acceptance but, in contrast, the proposer cannot insist, if the other party is unwilling, that silence shall constitute acceptance.

(h) Acceptance without knowledge of the terms

It is generally accepted that a person cannot accept a proposal of which he had no knowledge, even if he acts in conformity with the terms of the proposal. For example, if you have lost your wallet or your ring and I find it and return it to you, but when I did this I was unaware that you had advertised a reward for finding it, I cannot claim the reward (even though you would be acting without honour in taking that technical point against me).[33] On the other hand, when I do accept a proposal, it is not necessary that I know or understand the terms contained in it. For example, when I make a contract with an airline, I accept a proposal but have no, or almost no, knowledge of the terms on which the airline proposes to deal with me: I neither know nor care about this. This goes to show that it is not necessary for me to know or understand the terms of the proposal, though as said, my acceptance must be based, or considered to be based, on knowledge of the existence of the proposal. The question whether all of the terms of the proposal thus accepted are binding on me, especially where they are harsh or unkind terms, is better understood as an issue regarding the terms of the contract.

(i) Acceptance converts the proposal into a promise

When an acceptance takes place, the proposal is converted into a promise by which the proposer—now the promisor—is liable to be legally bound. She can no longer withdraw the

[32] *SM Bholat* (n 28), following and applying the English authority of *Felthouse v Bindley* (1862) 11 CBNS 869.

[33] See *Lalman Shukla v Gauri Datt* (1913) Allahabad LJ 489 (no reward for a person finding son who had absconded if the son was found and returned before finder knew of the reward, though in this case the finder did know of the reward). For the real reason there was no contract, see the discussion of consideration, at section II.4 below.

proposal, because it is no longer a mere proposal. It now has the status and effect of a promise, of something from which an agreement, and then a contract, may be formed.

4. Consideration

The factor which converts the promise or promises into an agreement is consideration, as is shown by section 2(d) of the Contract Act which has been set out above. A promise, standing alone, is not by itself enforceable; the common law, and the Contract Act, requires the promise to be supported by consideration before it may become a contract.[34]

What is consideration? In summary, it is what the promisee (the person to whom the promise is made) or what another person does in return for the promise which the promisor has made. As section 2(d) makes clear, this something may take the form of doing an act, such as making a payment of money; or it may take the form of an abstaining from doing something which one would otherwise have been free to do, such as giving up a claim. Consideration may also be found in the promise to do, or to abstain from doing, something. It is reiterated in section 2(e) of the Contract Act that mutual promises are good consideration for each other. This is the reason why we have an agreement if I promise to pay 10,000 kyats for your book which you promise to deliver to me: the paying or the promise of paying is capable of amounting to consideration.

So, for example, if A agrees to sell his house to B for $50,000, the promise of B to pay $50,000 is the consideration for A's promise to sell the house; A's promise to sell the house is the consideration for B's promise to pay $50,000.[35] If C promises, for a certain sum paid to him by D, to make good to D the value of D's cargo if it should be lost at sea, C's promise is the consideration for D's payment, and D's payment is the consideration for C's promise.[36] If E promises to maintain F's child, and F promises to pay E 50,000 kyat per month for the purpose, the promise of each party is the consideration for the promise of the other party.[37]

If a person—and it does not need to be the promisee[38]—promises, or does, something which the law regards as having value, at the desire of the promisor (eg in return for the promise) there will be consideration for the promise. There are therefore only two requirements. The first requirement that the promise, act, or abstinence is of value is implicit in section 2(d) of the Contract Act. The second explicit requirement is that the promise, act, or abstinence is 'at the desire of the promisor'. If there is consideration, the agreement may be a contract; however, it does not necessarily follow that if there is no consideration the agreement is not a contract because, as we shall see, section 25 of the Act makes clear that, while an agreement without consideration is normally void, in certain defined circumstances the absence of consideration does not render the agreement void.

We now turn to consider the two requirements.

(a) Something of value

Promising or paying money will generally be seen to be of value for the purpose of the law on consideration, as will promising or performing a service, as will forbearing to pursue,

[34] *Ma Mo v Ma Set* AIR 1926 Ran 71 (no consideration meant deed of sale was void; there was no requirement to apply under Specific Relief Act 1877, s 42 for cancellation of an instrument which was void); *Maung Par v U Tun Hlaing* (1952) BLR 32 (HC) (no consideration for a document by debtor in which the creditor did not appear to give up, or promise to give anything up).

[35] Contract Act 1872, s 23 Illustration (a).

[36] Contract Act 1872, s 23 Illustration (c).

[37] Contract Act 1872, s 23 Illustration (d).

[38] In other words, 'consideration need not move from the promisee'. The importance of this, which is linked to the question of whether there is a 'privity of contract' doctrine in Myanmar, is discussed below, see section III.3.

or otherwise giving up, a legal claim.[39] It is no part of the law (and this is made clear by the second Explanation to section 25 of the Contract Act) that the consideration must be proportionate in value to the promise for which it is given, for it would make the law very uncertain (and the making of profitable bargains would be hampered) if consideration had to be in some sense 'adequate' or 'proportionate' to the advantage which the promise will give.[40] This also means that the law allows agreements to take effect as contracts by the provision of a token payment, or a token act: the ability to give and take 'nominal consideration', as it is sometimes called, is important for the way in which it allows parties to give contractual force to an agreement which they wish to make legally binding. So, for example, an agreement to sell a bicycle for 100 kyats may be a contract; an agreement to sell a horse for a sum representing 1 per cent of its probable value may be a contract;[41] an agreement to pay 1,000 kyats for the transfer of a parcel of much more valuable shares in a company may be a contract. So also is a promise to pay 100,000 kyats for a caged bird: the law of contract does not ask whether the consideration is too much or too little. So long as their consent was free, the size or nature of consideration which supports the agreement is a matter for the parties to decide for themselves; and because this point is dealt with explicitly in the second Explanation to section 25 of the Contract Act, we will return to it in due course.

By contrast, if the so-called consideration has *no* value, it is not consideration after all. A promise to pay a sum of money in return for a smile, or in return for love and affection, is almost certainly not supported by consideration: these things, even if they are desired by the promisor, have no economic value, even if they were capable of definition and measurement, which they are not. And a promise to pay 100 kyats in return for the payment of 100,000 kyats is not good consideration, either: simple arithmetic is all one needs to show that this is not an exchange of things which have value, but a gift pretending to be a contract.[42] It is for this reason that if A promises for no consideration to give a sum of money to B, the agreement is void. If A makes the payment it may be effective as a gift, but the law of gifts regulates the legal consequences of gifts.[43] The law of contract looks after contracts, and this is why we need to be able to distinguish between contracts and gifts.

It has also been said that if I promise to pay you a sum of money if you return my watch, which you have stolen from me, there is no consideration for my promise, for what you do has no value in the eye of the law. The explanation is that you were already duty-bound to me, in law, to return my property, immediately; and to do what you are already bound to me to do is not to furnish me with any benefit; the value of the return of a thing stolen by a thief to its owner is zero, for though I am happy to have the watch back, I was always entitled to it.[44]

Similarly, if you are my employee and you perform the duties of your employment, you do only what you were bound to me to do; the performance of these duties could not, in principle at least, be seen to be consideration for a fresh promise by me to increase your wages.[45] However, as the consensual variation of the terms of the contract may not, in Myanmar, require consideration to make it legally binding, the fact that there is no consideration where one party merely performs what she was already bound to do under the

[39] *Maung Par* (n 34).

[40] *Kalimuthu v Maung Tha Din* AIR 1936 Ran 49 (consideration small, but adequacy not an issue for the court).

[41] Contract Act 1872, s 25 Illustration (f).

[42] It may be different, though, if I pay you a sum of money today in exchange for your promise to pay me (or to pay someone else) a larger sum of money in ten years' time.

[43] Dealt with in the Transfer of Property Act 1882, ss 122–129.

[44] *Ma Shwe Khan v Maung Khan* (1902–3) UBR 8. It is obviously different if the promise is to pay a reward to the finder of my watch, for although the handing over of the watch, when found, is required by law, the searching for another's lost property was not, and therefore has value: see Contract Act 1872, s 25 Illustration (c).

[45] *Lalman Shukla* (n 33).

contract, may, in contrast to many other common law systems, not be a problem.[46] The variation may be effective despite the lack of consideration.

(b) At the desire of the promisor

Consideration, whether it takes the form of doing or promising to do (or abstaining or promising to abstain), must be 'at the desire of the promisor' if it is to satisfy the definition in section 2(d) of the Contract Act. If I ask you to do something, such as to dig my garden, for which I promise to make you a payment, the digging or the promise to dig is plainly something which is done 'at my desire': if I asked for it, it is obviously done at my desire: the first four Illustrations given under section 23 of the Act make the point.

But suppose you do something for which I am grateful, but which it cannot be said that I asked for: can it then be said that the doing was 'at my desire'? Suppose our marriage has broken down and we are planning to separate, but that I promise to pay you a sum of money each year. As a result of the promise, you do not take me to court to ask for a divorce, or for financial maintenance or other support: in short, you abstain from doing something which you might otherwise have done: is there, in your forbearance, consideration for my promise to pay you money? The answer is not clear. It may well be correct to say that your conduct, in abstaining from legal proceedings, is something which I welcomed, or even hoped for; but I did not ask for it. If that is an accurate statement of what was or appeared to be in my mind, does that lead to the conclusion that the abstaining was or was not 'at my desire'? Some common law systems interpret this aspect of the law of consideration as meaning that the consideration has to be something which was asked for, either expressly or by implication.

It may however be that the Contract Act sees that consideration is present when I encourage you to act in a particular way, which I welcome, even though I do not actually ask you to act in that way. To give another example, which is similar to the example of the marriage breakdown above, suppose that I promise to make a financial contribution to a charitable organization which is undertaking a building project and which is to be funded by contributions from its supporters. If I then refuse to pay, is the fact that the work was done in accordance with my wishes, and was what I intended to happen, sufficient to say that it was done 'at my desire'?

This is a difficult question. But it can be powerfully argued that the stress given in section 2(d) of the Contract Act to a promisee doing or abstaining from something desired by the promisor naturally embraces where the promisee has relied on the promise even if the reliance was not asked for by the promisor. 'At the desire of' is not the same as 'at the request of'. What it would plainly not cover would be reliance by the promisee that was not desired by the promisor.

(c) Agreement enforceable as a contract though consideration is inadequate

As we have shown, the Act draws a distinction between agreements supported by consideration and those not so supported. In the case in which there is consideration—in the sense that there is something of value, whether a small sum of money or other thing—but this consideration appears to be wholly out of proportion with the promise which it is sought to enforce, the Second Explanation to section 25 of the Contract Act, which is set out

[46] See discussion in section II.10.

below,[47] states that there is consideration, but that the very small size of it may be a reason to check that consent was freely given.[48] This makes sense, but one must be careful of reading too much into it. If I agree to sell a horse for a sum which is one-tenth, or one-hundredth of its value, one possible explanation for my actions may be that I have been the victim of undue influence or other vitiating factor. But another explanation may be that because we knew perfectly well that a promise unsupported by consideration would not be enforceable as a contract, we agreed upon the payment of a token sum to ensure that consideration was present and that the promise was contractually binding. 'Inadequate' consideration, which means consideration which is present but very small indeed, may be a symptom of unfree consent, but may also be a sign that the parties used the law intelligently, to make a binding agreement where this would not otherwise have been possible.[49]

5. The Distinction Between an Agreement and a Contract

If a proposal has been accepted and is converted into a promise, and if there is consideration for the promise or promises so that there is an agreement, the agreement is a contract unless it is a void agreement. As we have seen,[50] that is all made clear by section 2 of the Contract Act with section 2(g) laying down that 'an agreement not enforceable by law is said to be void' and section 2(h) saying that 'an agreement enforceable by law is a contract'.

It appears, therefore, that in addition to what we have so far looked at in this chapter, the only additional factor relevant to converting an agreement into a contract is that the agreement must be enforceable rather than void. The grounds on which the Contract Act lays down that an agreement is void (and they include whether the consideration or object of the agreement is lawful or not) are not examined in this chapter. In that regard, it should be noted that, although the Act does not say in express terms that an agreement is void where one or both of the parties are incompetent to contract, that interpretation of the Act has been established in the case law.

However, there is one confusing complication. This is because the Contract Act makes an additional observation as to which agreements are contracts, in section 10:

> **10. What agreements are contracts.** All agreements are contracts if they are made by the free consent of parties competent to contract, for a lawful consideration and with a lawful object, and are not hereby expressly declared to be void.

Apart from four words, section 10 confirms what we have just said. If the agreement is made by parties competent to contract, and the consideration is lawful, and the object of the agreement is lawful, and the agreement is not expressly declared by the Act to be void, the agreement is a contract.

However, the insertion into section 10 of the four words 'the free consent of' is problematic. The question of whether the parties consented freely, or gave consent which was free, is a different issue. If the consent of a party was not free, the contract may be voidable at the option of the party whose consent was not free, which means that the contract may be undone, unmade; but if she does not exercise this option, the agreement continues to be a contract. In other words, the contract is not void. It is therefore *not* correct to say that the free consent of the parties is required for there to be a contract. It follows that section 10 must be

[47] Below, section II.11(b).

[48] *Kalimuthu* (n 40) (consideration small, but adequacy not an issue for the court; no evidence that it was an extortionate and unconscionable bargain which could be set aside as contrary to public policy).

[49] See the Contract Act 1872, s 25 Illustration 2, which is set out below, section II.11(b).

[50] See above, section II.1.

interpreted in accordance with the overall scheme of the Act; and as a result, the words 'the free consent of' in section 10 should be regarded as an oversight on the part of the draftsman, and disregarded for the purposes of understanding what constitutes a contract.

At this point we have examined the main stages in the process of formation of a contract, as this is set out in and regulated by the Contract Act. It is now necessary to deal with a small number of related points, not specifically mentioned by the Act.

6. The Intention to Create Legal Relations

Is every agreement in which there is consideration one over which the courts have jurisdiction? Is every agreement which I make one which carries the threat of legal proceedings if I fail to perform?

The answer is plainly no: there are plenty of agreements which are binding in honour only, but not binding as a matter of law. It could hardly be otherwise. In some legal systems, a promise made by a husband to his wife, to pay her a modest sum of money if she keeps the house tidy, may involve a proposal, acceptance, promise, consideration, and agreement, but it will not be a contract. The reason is that the parties did not expect or intend their agreement to be one which a court had power to enforce; the law will not suppose that they intended to make an agreement which the law would enforce against a defaulting party. The technical justification for this reason is that there is no intention to create legal relations, or, perhaps more precisely, the law will not conclude that there was an intention to create legal relations unless the circumstances of the case suggest that it should. Agreements made within the four corners of a matrimonial relationship, or in other domestic circumstances, will not generally be seen to have this characteristic.

It does not mean, however, that all agreements made within the family are outside the jurisdiction of the courts. Agreements by spouses to pay maintenance are obviously capable of giving rise to legal relations, at least in the sense that legal proceedings can be brought to enforce the obligation. And in Myanmar, it has been held that in a Buddhist marriage, a husband owes his wife a legal duty to maintain her, and that this duty can be enforced by judicial proceedings.[51] It may be better, however, to explain this result not as one which rests on an agreement which is intended to be legally enforceable, but on the law of status which is imposed on spouses regardless of any agreement.

Illustration (d) to section 23 of the Contract Act, which we will examine later, suggests that a promise to pay a person for looking after the promisor's child is enforceable as each promise is lawful consideration. But the Illustration does not suggest the existence or absence of a relationship between the parties. If a mother promises the father to look after the child, it seems unlikely that this was intended as an agreement which would land the parties in court if it were not performed; but if the promise was made to a stranger, the position is likely to be very different. A contract by which a father agrees to sell part of his land to his son will be likely to be one which the courts may enforce: the fact that it is between father and son does not necessarily mean that it is not subject to judicial enforcement.

The common law refers to this idea, and this requirement, as the intention to create legal relations. The reasons for its use as part of the common law are practical as well as theoretical. As a practical matter, the majority of domestic and social agreements and disagreements are not easy for a court to investigate, even if they could do it: the evidence, at least, is likely to

[51] *Ma Saw Nwe v U Aung Soe* (1939) RLR 527. It appears that marriage is considered to constitute an express or implied contract that the husband shall maintain the wife: *Ardaseer Curtetjee v Perozeboye* (1856) 6 Moo IA 348 (referred to and relied on in *Ma Saw Nwe v U Aung Soe*).

be very messy. At the theoretical level, if the basic premise of the common law is there is freedom of contract, that parties may make the agreements they wish to make so long as they do not violate the law of the land, there is no reason why parties should not be able to make an agreement which is not for judicial determination, but which will instead be binding on them only as a matter of honour: the freedom not to subject one's agreements to legal proceedings is a small part of the larger freedom to make or to not make agreements which are binding in law.

The same principle must apply where parties make an agreement which is 'subject to contract': this is a way of saying that the parties do not wish to be committed to each other, and do not wish the courts to be involved, until they have made a formal contract.[52] An 'agreement subject to contract' is, therefore, an agreement which is not supposed to be referred to the courts, even if it is departed from. The same would be true if the parties had agreed that they were not to be legally bound until a written contract had been drawn up.[53]

Where in the Contract Act is this requirement to be found? The answer is that it is not: there is no mention of a requirement that an agreement be one which was intended to give rise to, or to create, legal obligations. This is surprising. For it cannot be the case that in Myanmar wives can sue their husbands, or sons sue their fathers, whenever it is said that an agreement made between them was not carried into effect. Families and friends, as well as parties in negotiation, must have the power to create an environment which is regulated by honour and decency, but without recourse to the law of contract if anything goes wrong. This must be taken to be the law, even if the Act does not explicitly say so. This is best rationalized by saying that, in line with all other common law systems, 'justice, equity, and good conscience' under section 13(3) of the Burma Laws Act 1898 entails the recognition of a requirement of 'an intention to create legal relations'.

7. Practical Problems with the Formation of Agreements: Informality, Incompleteness, Imprecision, and Incoherence

We should say a little more about one aspect of the formation of contracts, by returning to a point made earlier. We have seen how the Act identifies the stages of proposal, acceptance, promise, consideration, agreement, and contract. If the world really were as tidy as that, the formation of contracts would be clear and straightforward. But, in fact, life is not like that: in the course of a day a person will make several contracts, without giving a moment's thought to any of this. A professor may go to a neighbourhood stall for a bowl of noodle soup for breakfast, buy some fruit for her lunch, and then take a taxi to the university. She may buy a magazine on the way home, and go out for dinner. She will have made many contracts. The problems which we are about to deal with concern those agreements, just like these agreements, which are casual, informal, or incomplete, as well as those in which the meaning of language actually used by the parties is rather problematic.

(a) Casual, informal, and incomplete agreements

We make contracts, even in circumstances in which we do not really know what we are doing, with people who do not speak our language and whose language we do not speak,

[52] For a similar argument, where the documents plainly showed that there would be no contract until a more formal document was generated, see *Burma Timber Co v American International Underwriters (Burma) Ltd* (1962) BLR 18 (HC); *The State Agricultural Marketing Board* (n 4).

[53] See *DK Parekh v The Burma Sugar Co Ltd* (1948) BLR 257 (HC). But on a true construction of the agreement in that case, the drawing up of a written contract was an expectation, but not a precondition to being legally bound.

and on terms which may very well be rather imprecise (the negotiations and terms of a journey by taxi being more mysterious than most). Yet all these are contracts; in principle, at least any of them could be brought before a court for adjudication, and if the court was called upon to do it, it would decide whether there was a contract, and what its basic terms were, by the analysis which we have just described.

What this shows is that the Contract Act, and the common law of contract more generally, provides a set of rules by which to analyse the relationship between the parties when something has gone wrong. We do not need to understand the Contract Act before we can buy our breakfast; we just do what we do. If there is a problem, if there is a disagreement about the price, or about the quality of the food, a court may start its analysis with the Contract Act: even though we did not do so, the court will.

And what will happen when it does? Take the example of an English visitor to Yangon who goes into a teashop for something to eat. The boy who fetches the tea and the snacks speaks no English, and the visitor speaks no Burmese. If the visitor is lucky, there may be a menu: an invitation to treat;[54] if there is not, the fact that the shop is open is invitation enough. The visitor, now a customer, tries to say what she wants by sign language and smiling: a proposal to buy. The boy goes off to fetch it: acceptance of the proposal, which means that the teashop has made a promise to sell the tea and snacks which the customer has ordered. The customer promises to pay, which is consideration for the tea and snacks, and there is therefore a contract, made between two people who did not speak the same language, and who will not really have understood what the other was saying. And, in fact, although the contract will be between the customer and the owner of the teashop, it was not made with the owner directly, but through his employee or agent.

How, then, did the law arrive at the conclusion that there was a contract between the parties? The answer is that there just has to be a contract in a case like this, and if necessary the facts can be fitted into the slots which go to show that a contract was made. Insofar as there was communication, it was done not so much by words but by body language—so there was a common language after all, even though it was not a sophisticated language—and by this means the agreement was made. It was true that there was no discussion of the actual price, but the court will say that there was an agreement on price: although the parties did not negotiate the numbers, and although the customer may have had no idea what the right numbers were, it was obvious that the customer agreed to pay the usual price, and that no words were needed to communicate this: in some circumstances, actions speak louder than words.

This teaches us two things, in particular, which we should remember. The first is that the making of contracts does not require any knowledge of the Contract Act, and does not require clear and precise words, or anything like that. Neither does it require any formality, such as writing or signature. The question for the court will be whether it appeared that there was enough of an agreement between the parties, or enough of an agreement for the court to explain what was said without words and to find a contract as a result. The questions are, 'does there appear to have been enough of a proposal?', 'does there appear to have been enough of an acceptance?', and so on. The law is not so concerned with what one party privately thought but what that party appeared to be communicating, saying, to the other.

Suppose there were to have been a disagreement as to the price, and that the customer were to say, perfectly correctly, that there was no mention of the price (or that the prices were written in Burmese script, which she did not understand and could not have agreed

[54] Not a proposal to sell, for the teashop may not have everything on its menu available for sale at all times of the day.

to), and that there was therefore no contract. The court will say that there was a contract, and if the price is disputed, it will be (or will have been) the usual price for what the customer ordered, whether the customer knew what that was or not. She is bound to pay, and this will be the figure. Suppose, to put things the other way around, the teashop owner says that the customer was told, in Burmese, that the price would not be 1,000 kyats, but 10,000 kyats, and that the customer did not object. This will not lead to the conclusion that there was a contract to pay 10,000 kyats for tea and snacks. One possible reason will be that the owner caused, and knew that he had caused, the customer to be mistaken as to the price. As we shall see, section 18(3) of the Contract Act will mean that if there is a contract it is a voidable contract: a possible but inconvenient answer after the tea has been drunk and food eaten. A better reason will be that the offer will be interpreted as an offer to sell at the usual price unless the seller has made it clear to the customer that the price is not the usual one and the customer has equally clearly agreed to it. In short, courts decide whether a contract was formed, and determine the terms of that contract, from the perspective of the reasonable bystander, adopting an objective point of view in relation to the dealing of the parties.

So for another example; if I attend an auction, and bid for Lot 1 when I had become muddled and had thought that the auctioneer was selling Lot 2, I will be bound to complete the purchase of Lot 1 if the auctioneer accepts my bid as the winning bid. The fact that I actually and genuinely intended to bid for another lot, and can show evidence which suggests that this is really true, will be irrelevant.[55] The auctioneer invited bids for Lot 1; I made a bid in response to this invitation, and this bid was accepted. The auctioneer's promise to sell to the highest bidder, and my promise to pay, are good consideration for each other and, as any reasonable observer of the event would confirm, we have concluded a contract.

The second general point, which will now be obvious, is that there will often be gaps in the parties' negotiations which the court will need to fill, and will fill. The task of the court is, in practice, to try to satisfy itself that there was a contract which it can enforce; it may come to the opposite answer, but when the parties have performed what they evidently assumed was a contract, it will be very inconvenient if the court says that they were wrong. If it is clear that the parties intended to make a contract, and considered themselves to be contractually bound to each other, the law will go as far as it properly can to fill in the detail which can properly be filled. Only where there is a gap which cannot be filled by these means will the answer be that there is no agreement or no contract. For example, if we appear to have agreed that you will do some work for me, but have not agreed a fee, the court will not be able to fill the gap and enforce the contract: the gap will be one which simply means that the parties had not agreed, and would not be thought by an observer to have settled on, a fee for the work. It is different from the case of the teashop where the court will be able to see an agreement to pay 'the usual price', even if this was not said, and even though the customer had no idea what the usual price may have been. It all depends on whether the term or details not precisely specified are of importance in the context of the agreement made.[56]

(b) Interpretation of what the parties did agree

The parties may have used words which seem clear enough, but which, on closer inspection, may not make quite as much sense as was supposed. The question which may arise is how

[55] And see, for comparison, Evidence Act 1872, s 95 (which deals with written contracts).

[56] See *DK Parekh* (n 53) (contract can be complete even if details of time and mode of delivery not specified if the parties had whole season before them and delivery could be made according to their convenience).

to interpret the terms used by the parties. In some parts of the common law world an astonishing amount of ink has been spilled on this topic; yet there is no space to examine it in detail in this chapter. But it is convenient to make a couple of points about it at this stage as it is concerned with the precision or imprecision of communications, and its effect on the formation of contracts.

The first is that, applying the approach in other common law systems, the courts interpret what people say by asking what a reasonable person, in the position of listener, would take the speaker to mean. We are not really concerned to find out what the speaker did intend, but ask what a reasonable person would understand him to have meant.[57] This is one aspect of the principle of 'objectivity' which underpins much of the common law of contract.

The second is that the same objective approach applies where a contract is reduced to writing. It follows that the courts assume that the parties meant to be bound by the words interpreted according to their natural meaning given the context and purpose of the contract. When confronted by a term in a contract which suggests that 'something has gone wrong with the language', a court should put the language right. If the written contract says 'buyer' where it is obvious that it should have said 'seller', the court should correct the typographical error, even if the error was no more than a slip of the typist's fingers. However, it is sometimes more difficult. Suppose the contract says that 'the buyer shall deliver' the goods which are being bought and sold. Something has clearly gone wrong with the language, for a buyer does not deliver. But what did the parties mean? Did they mean to say that the seller shall deliver? Or did they mean that the buyer should arrange for delivery? Applying the objective approach, a court may look to see whether it can work out what the parties really intended to say by reading the other terms of the contract and taking into account the context in which the contract was made which may include any usage or custom of the trade.[58] It is also conceivable that some help may be given by considering the law on implied terms.

8. Problems of Formation with More Complex Contracts

We must mention some circumstances in which the usual analysis has to be set aside in order to make sense of the relationship between the parties.

One possible example is the very common business situation where parties each sign a written agreement. Although one may say that the first party who signs is making a proposal to the other which is then accepted when that party signs, this is somewhat unrealistic and the better view is that, because there is plainly an agreement, supported by consideration, there is no need to go through the proposal, acceptance, promise, consideration, and agreement analysis. The signatures to the written document suffice to establish the contract.

As another example, suppose a sailing race is organized, and that the terms on which every participant enters the race are set out in a document issued by the organizer, intended to operate as a contract providing, for example, that each participant is freed from any liability to any other participant which would otherwise arise for causing property damage. It is easy to see that each participant enters into a contractual relationship with the organizer,[59] but less easy to see that such a relationship is created between the individual participants:

[57] *Mg Shwe The v Ma E Bon* AIR 1923 Ran 128.

[58] Contract Act 1872, s 1 expressly preserves 'any usage or custom of trade' that is not inconsistent with the provisions of the Act. Whether custom can be used to override the clear terms of a contract reduced to writing is unclear: see *Steel Bros & Co Ltd v Tokersee Mooljee* AIR 1932 Ran 162, (1932) ILR 10 Ran 372.

[59] However, there was held to be no contract between the Rangoon Turf Club and the owners of horses in Myanmar which allowed owners to require the club to classify their horses according to its rules: *J Chan Toon v The Stewards of the Rangoon Turf Club* (1949) BLR 327 (HC).

they do not know the name or identity of the others. Yet there must be a contract between all the participants, for otherwise every participant would be at risk of being sued by another participant whose yacht he had damaged outside the terms of the contract which may intend to place mutually beneficial limits on the liability of the participants to each other.

The practical answer has to be that the law can find a contract here. One way of doing it is to say that every participant, in entering the race, makes a proposal to every other participant to excuse them from liability for accidental damage, and that these other participants accept that proposal either by entering the race or (if they have already entered) by continuing to participate. If this looks as though it stretches the law to the point where it may break, the only answer one may give is that which was given by the Privy Council in the case we mentioned, and from which a quotation was given, at the start of this chapter. Multi-partite contracts are one of many examples in which we all know that there has to be a contract, but where we realize that we may have to work quite hard to show a court how to arrive at this conclusion.

And we should perhaps say something about the case from which that quotation was taken. It concerned a case of carriage of goods—a very expensive piece of drilling equipment—by sea from Liverpool, England, to a port in New Zealand. Contained in the contract, which was made between the owner of the equipment and the sea carrier when the equipment was put on board the ship *The Eurymedon*, was a promise, made by the owner and given to the sea carrier, that the owner would not more than a year after delivery of the goods sue the sea carrier, or anyone whom the sea carrier engaged to do the unloading of the goods, for any damage done to the goods by negligence in their carriage or their unloading. Although this may seem a slightly strange thing for the owner of goods to agree to, it made commercial sense, as it allowed the sea carrier to transport the goods for a lower price than he would have had to if he faced unlimited liability.

The stevedore damaged the goods by unloading them negligently, and the unhappy owner sued the stevedore more than a year afterwards. The stevedore defended itself by pointing to the contract between the owner and the sea carrier, and the term in it which provided that the owner would not sue the stevedore after a year. The owner objected that as a matter of English law, the stevedore was not party to the contract between the owner and the sea carrier, and that the doctrine of privity of contract, which we will cover below,[60] and which may be seen *not* to be part of Myanmar law, meant that the stevedore could not take advantage of a term contained in a contract to which he was not party. The stevedore therefore sought to show that there was another contract, this time between the stevedore and the owner of the goods, and that this contract contained the same provision. The problem was that the owner had had no dealings with the stevedore, did not know who the stevedore was (and really did not care), and did not ask for anything from the stevedore; and the stevedore did not know who the owner was (and really did not care) and, in any case, provided no consideration because all the stevedore did was unload the ship, which it had already agreed with the sea carrier to do.

The court held that there was a contract formed between two parties who neither knew nor much cared who the other was, and that the unloading of the cargo, which the stevedore was already bound by his contract with the sea carrier to perform, was capable of being good consideration for the owner's promise to the stevedore (even though the owner maintained that he had made no promise to anyone other than the sea carrier, and even though the stevedore had no conscious awareness that an offer had been made to it by the owner).

[60] Below, section III.

The detailed reasoning in the case is not our particular concern, but what shines through the judgment is a clear perception by the court that all the participants in the industry had a clear interest in its coming to the conclusion that there was a contract, and a clear message that the court would go to the limits of its proper powers to find it.

It remains, however, a striking lesson: that a contract can be formed between persons who really had no intention of dealing with each other, who did not wish to deal with each other, who did not realize that they were dealing with each other; and in circumstances in which consideration appeared to have been manufactured out of thin air. As the court said: 'English law, having committed itself to a rather technical and schematic doctrine of contract, in application takes a practical approach, often at the cost of forcing the facts to fit uneasily into the marked slots of [proposal], acceptance and consideration.'[61] It is not surprising to discover that we have to take the same approach to the common law of contract, as set out in Myanmar in the Contract Act nearly 150 years ago. Not all contracts are simple and straightforward, and for those that are not, the creative use of the Contract Act to produce a commercially sensible, and modern, solution, is the path to progress and the best way to refresh and upgrade the contract law of Myanmar.

9. Agreements to Negotiate and Agreements Not to Negotiate

A modern phenomenon of contract law, which is all the more important in the context of large commercial agreements, is that parties who realize that their negotiations will take a long time to conclude may be uncomfortable with the rule of the common law that unless and until there is an acceptance which takes the form of an unqualified assent to the proposal, either side may walk away from the negotiating table. That may mean that lengthy negotiations produce no contract, but it may result in something worse: that a party who learns in negotiation much—and much that may be confidential or sensitive—about the other may be able to exploit it. Indeed, the fact that A is negotiating with B does not mean that A may not also be negotiating with C, and using information gathered from one set of negotiations to help him in the other.

If the common law could do nothing to regulate, or to prevent, the difficulties liable to result from such behaviour, it would be a stain on the reputation of the common law. Fortunately, the Contract Act can be used to give effect to a number of agreements which might be helpful in these circumstances.

(a) An agreement to negotiate an agreement in good faith

The parties to a negotiation may consider making an agreement to negotiate an agreement in good faith, or to use their best endeavours to conclude an agreement. By doing so, each may seek to bind the other to negotiate in a constructive way, and to bind the other to do his best to bring the negotiations to a satisfactory conclusion. The question is whether such an agreement is capable of constituting an agreement, and if consideration is found, as it will presumably be found in the mutual promises, being enforced as a contract.

The answer to the question is not completely clear. The traditional approach of common law courts was to reject the idea that this could be seen as an agreement with contractual effect. The immediate objection is that the terms which define the obligation are vague and imprecise,[62] and are in any event contrary to the basic approach of the common law which

[61] *The Eurymedon* (n 16) 167. See also discussion in section II.1 above.
[62] Contract Act 1872, s 29, set out below, section II.11(a).

has been to see parties in negotiation almost as though they were in a hostile relationship, each acting, and entitled to act, entirely in its own interests. How, one may ask, can there be an agreement to act in a way which is not entirely self-interested? How can parties in negotiation really promise each other that the negotiations will end in a particular, preordained, outcome? How can a court be expected to assess and adjudge whether the negotiating behaviour of one of the parties amounted to good faith, or manifested an absence of good faith? Does good faith mean that a party must sometimes act against its own interests? How can a court be expected to assess what the consequences would have been if a breach of the obligation had not taken place? The questions could be multiplied, and those who consider that the common law of contract cannot tolerate such agreements do tend to multiply them; and they do have a considerable weight.

Yet there are mature legal systems which regard the principle that one must act in good faith as underpinning the whole of private law, and these systems do not appear to find difficulty in assessing whether a person has complied with the requirements of the doctrine of good faith. Most countries of the civil law family recognize a principle of this approximate kind. To ask a judge to decide whether a party had exercised good faith would not be to set him an impossible task. It may be that the standards are hard to define with mathematical precision, but that is true of many concepts used in the common law, of which 'reasonableness' is perhaps the most obvious. The problem of definition should not be seen as fatal.

There is still very little support among common lawyers for the idea that there should be a general duty of good faith required to be observed by all parties in a contractual bargaining relationship. But the present case is very different. If the parties make an agreement in express terms along the lines which we have been considering, there is no question of the law imposing on them a duty of which one or both may have been unaware; rather, the duty is freely assumed and, if it is of imprecise definition, it is the parties who made it so, and they can hardly complain. No doubt there will be cases in which it is hard to be sure whether the agreement has been performed or breached, and no doubt there will be problems in assessing any compensation due if the agreement is said to have been breached, but these all result from the law seeking to give contractual effect to an agreement which the parties chose to make and freely consented to. In those circumstances a court should take a constructive view of its role in assisting commercial relationships, and do what it thinks it may to enforce the agreement.

(b) An agreement not to negotiate with anyone else: a 'lock-out' agreement

It is possible—it is not controversial—for parties to make an agreement, with contractual effect, that neither party will negotiate or communicate with anyone else for a defined period of time. If negotiations are expected to be lengthy, and if there is felt to be a risk that others may also be keen to put themselves forward as potential counterparties, the parties to the negotiation may make a lock-out agreement, the legal effect of which is that neither will negotiate with anyone else for a defined period of time. No doubt it will be necessary for the terms of the agreement to be defined with reasonable precision.

However, an agreement not to negotiate with anyone else does not, in and of itself, mean that the negotiation with the other party must succeed, or must be conducted in good faith, or with the best endeavours of each side, and so on. In practice, then, a lock-out agreement will be more effective if accompanied by an agreement requiring the other party to negotiate in good faith; and as indicated earlier, as the law currently stands it is not clear whether such an agreement would be given effect by a Myanmar court.

10. Formation of Agreements Contrasted with Variation of Contracts Already Made

In this section we have set out and examined the rules by which the Contract Act explains how and when a contract is formed or made, as well as some supplementary principles of common law which may also contribute to the law on formation of contracts. We should say something about the case in which the parties to a contract agree to vary the terms of their agreement and, from one point of view at least, make a new contract.

It follows from what has been said earlier about consideration, and in particular from the example of the person who returns a stolen ring who does not, when he does what he was already under a legal obligation to do, provide anything of value to the other party, that if I promise to you that I will do something which I am already obliged to you to do, this has no value so far as the law is concerned, and it will not be capable of being consideration for a separate promise made by you. The analysis would, of course, be different if I were to make you a promise that I would perform a duty which I already owed to someone else: the law would accept that you obtain something which you did not have before (ie the right to sue me for breach of contract if I fail to perform), and I assume a burden or liability by which I was previously bound (ie the liability to be sued by you if I fail to perform). But a promise to do something which I am already bound to you to do appears to have no value.

It might be thought to follow from this that if A and B have made a contract by which B is obliged to A, then if A promises something additional to B if B performs his existing promise, B provides no consideration for A's promise of extra, and A cannot be required to perform it. Likewise, if B is indebted to A and A, realizing that B cannot meet the terms of the original obligation, agrees to let him off a fraction of the obligation, B provides no consideration for A's promise to let him off; and in neither case would A be required to act in accordance with what has been promised. In each case, if one were to focus on the 'new' agreement and compare it with the old, it would fail to take effect as a contract for want of consideration. That would be the analysis in a number of common law jurisdictions; but, at least as regards a promise to accept a lesser performance than is owed, it is not the law in Myanmar. This will be explored and explained in a subsequent volume (Volume V) in this series.

11. Two Sections of the 1872 Act on Void Agreements That Are Relevant to Formation

(a) Agreement void because the meaning of the agreement is too uncertain

The law can only give legal force to an agreement, and regard it as a contract, if it can be sufficiently certain that the parties agreed, and sufficiently certain what the parties actually agreed to. The law is laid down in section 29 of the Contract Act, which provides as follows:

> **29. Agreements void for uncertainty**. Agreements, the meaning of which is not certain, or capable of being made certain, are void.

The only real question is whether a court, when the point is raised, would be able to say that, although the words used by the parties may appear at first sight to be uncertain, they can in fact be understood as being sufficiently certain for the agreement to have contractual effect, or (on the other hand) that although the words appear at first sight to be certain, in truth one cannot tell whether they bear one or another meaning. The ultimate question is whether the words used in the agreement are, or can be made, sufficiently certain for a court to be able to enforce the agreement.[63] Section 29 of the Contract Act is principally concerned with words which may not be certain; it is not so directly concerned with cases in which the agreement has not been spelled out in great detail. Some illustrations may make the point.

(1) Agreements in which the words actually used may not be sufficiently certain

Let us start with an easy example. Suppose I agree to sell to a buyer '100 tons of oil', and that there is nothing to explain (or nothing which would help the reasonable bystander understand) what kind of oil was intended. Illustration (a) to section 29 of the Contract Act says that the agreement is void for uncertainty.

Next, let us take a slightly more difficult version of the same problem. Suppose I make an agreement to undertake some legal work on behalf of a Singapore company which requires advice on Myanmar law, and I agree with the company that my hourly rate for the work will be 'four hundred dollars per hour'. Suppose I do 50 hours of work for the company, and inform the company that I have done so. Suppose the Singapore company sends payment in the sum of 200,000 Singapore dollars; but I protest, saying that I meant four hundred US dollars per hour, and that 200,000 US dollars is a rather larger figure. We 'agreed' that the price will be 200,000 dollars, but now disagree as to what this means in actual money terms. What is the court to do? The answer must be this: that if the court concludes that it is clear enough what each party meant, but that they meant different things, the agreement which they made is void because it is no agreement at all. The consequence of this for the parties—after all, if the legal services have been provided, one would expect the Act to provide some mechanism for payment—will not be covered in this chapter.

However, it may be possible to see beyond the immediate lack of certainty and conclude that there was agreement after all. Suppose that I make an agreement to sell you my bicycle for 20,000 kyats, but that I actually own two bicycles, and that when I hand the bicycle over to you, you object and say it is not this one, but the other one, that you agreed to buy. The starting point may be that although the words 'my bicycle' are clear enough, in a case in which the seller has two bicycles they may not be, and if there were no more to be said about it, the agreement would be void. But suppose the court is told that you had taken one of the bicycles, but not the other bicycle, for a test ride, and that you had found the bicycle to be satisfactory, and that this piece of evidence shows which bicycle we were really making an agreement about. It is very likely, in these circumstances, that a court would say that the language of our agreement, which at first sight is not certain enough to be clear, can be made certain by this other information, and that as a result the parties' agreement is sufficiently certain for a court to be able to enforce it.[64]

What this shows is that an agreement which appears to be uncertain may, in the language of section 29 of the Contract Act, be 'capable of being made certain'.[65] Let us take another example in which a Myanmar company which sells rice agrees to sell to a Singapore company a specific quantity of rice at a price of 'five hundred dollars per ton'. Let us suppose that the Myanmar company meant US dollars, but that the Singapore buyer meant Singapore dollars, which are worth only 75 US cents. If the Singapore buyer genuinely meant Singapore dollars, and the Myanmar seller meant US dollars, the court may be forced to conclude that the agreement is uncertain—the price has not, after all, been agreed—and is therefore void.

[63] For illustration, *Swee Chwan Bee Rice Mill Co v Sukru Nahag* (1955) BLR 291 (HC) (price for provision of coolie labour implicitly agreed as the 'old rates', which were then paid without objection: agreement on price sufficiently certain).

[64] This would still be the case if the contract had been reduced to writing: Evidence Act 1872, s 96 (and Contract Act 1872, s 29 Illustration (a)).

[65] *Swee Chwan Bee Rice Mill Co* (n 63).

But suppose the court is given evidence that dealings on the international market in rice are always conducted in US dollars, and that whether the parties are in Australia or Singapore, where the currency is called dollars, or in India or the UK, where the currency is not called dollars, contracts for import and export of rice are always priced in US dollars, and that everyone would make that assumption. The court will be able to decide that the language of 'five hundred dollars per ton', which *may* be uncertain, means 'five hundred US dollars per ton', and that the agreement is capable of being made certain.

And if we now go back to the '100 tons of oil' example which we mentioned earlier, if the seller is a merchant who deals only in coconut oil, the court will be able to conclude that the agreement is not void for uncertainty, for in the circumstances, 'oil' can only have meant 'coconut oil'.[66]

Now suppose the parties agree that the one will provide services to the other 'at a price to be determined by X' (a named person, or the holder of a specific office) if not agreed by the parties; the agreement is capable of being made certain, for the agreement itself contains the mechanism for its clarification.[67] Likewise, if a fisherman makes an oral agreement to supply a quantity of fish to a restaurant on a particular day 'at market price', the court may receive evidence of the market price for that fish on that day, and treat the price as one which is capable of being made certain.[68]

In all these cases, therefore, the guiding principle is that an agreement can be considered certain if it is capable of being made certain.

A particular problem arises when parties make an agreement that they will use their best endeavours to conclude a contract in the future, or by a particular date. If they do not succeed in coming to such an agreement, the question may arise whether there was a contract to 'use best endeavours', and if there was, whether it was broken. As was suggested further above,[69] it is hard to say what a court should do. On the one hand, it may say that the precise content of an obligation to 'use best endeavours' or 'to negotiate in good faith' is impossible to define; that the language is just too imprecise for a court to be able to give a legal meaning to it, and that it is neither certain nor capable of being made certain. On the other hand, a court may say that although it could not give a full, complete, and detailed definition of what 'best endeavours' or 'in good faith' means it can still be sure that the way in which one party behaved would not satisfy the meaning of the term, whatever it actually meant. It may therefore find that the agreement is capable of being made certain, because 'certain' in this context means 'certain enough for the court to enforce it in this case'.

(2) Agreements in which the parties do not specify all the terms or details

Of course, parties who make a contract do not usually agree and spell out all the terms of their agreement. If they agree to sell and buy goods, they will usually specify the goods and the price, will often specify the date and place of delivery, and will sometimes specify the place of payment. If a contract is made in a shop or in the market, it is likely to be very short of detail. By comparison with contracts in many other countries of the common law world, contracts made in Myanmar are very short, and many of the issues which would be spelled out in writing in a contract made in England—for example, an English contract of employment is often in a very lengthy document, but in Myanmar the document is usually rather short—are not specified in the contract in Myanmar.

[66] Contract Act 1872, s 29 Illustration (c). [67] Contract Act 1872, s 29 Illustration (e).

[68] It is debatable whether the same would be true if the contract had been reduced to writing: see Evidence Act 1872, s 93.

[69] Above, section II.9.

This shortness in drafting or expression, however, does not mean that the agreements are void because their (full) meaning is not certain, even though the details which a court will need are not spelled out in their entirely by the parties. In some contexts—the sale of goods is the best known example—the law provides a set of supplementary terms which will be included in (or imposed onto) the contract if it is otherwise silent: the result is that many of the terms of the contract are imposed by law by statutes, such as the Sale of Goods Act 1930, and as a result there is no problem of uncertainty. In other contexts, the answer to a question may not be found in the express words of the contract, but in the 'usage or custom of trade' which section 1 of the Contract Act preserves. The question of the precise nature of the duties owed by an employee to his employer, or by the employer to the employee, may be found in unwritten law to which the court is permitted under the Act to turn. After all, the main purpose of section 29 of the Act is to deal with the case in which the words used by the parties are not certain enough to be enforced by a court, and not capable of being made certain enough. It is not so obviously intended to apply to a case in which the contract appears to contain gaps or silences between words which are clear enough to be enforced.

In most other systems of the common law world, the problems of contracts which do not appear to contain all the detail which may be needed by a court are solved by a general rule that terms may be 'implied' into a contract: not only by statute (the Sale of Goods Act 1930 implies terms into a contract, and these terms may then answer questions which may arise), but also by reference to general principles of common law. The law on the implication of terms into contracts is a part of the exercise of identifying the terms and meaning of a contract.

(b) Agreement void because made without consideration

The next issue to consider is whether there was consideration which is, in general, necessary to convert the agreement into a contract. The meaning of consideration was considered above,[70] but for convenience of reference the general definition from section 2(d) of the Contract Act is repeated here:

> **2. Interpretation clause.** In this Act the following words and expressions are used in the following senses, unless a contrary intention appears from the context...
>
> (d) When, at the desire of the promisor, the promisee or any other person has done or abstained from doing, or does or abstains from doing, or promises to do or to abstain from doing, something, such act or abstinence or promise is called a consideration for the promise;

The general requirement that there be consideration is qualified by section 25 of the Act.

> **25. Agreement without consideration void, unless it is in writing and registered, or is a promise to compensate for something done, or is a promise to pay a debt barred by limitation law.** An agreement made without consideration is void, unless
>
> (1) it is expressed in writing and registered under the law for the time being in force for the registration of documents, and is made on account of natural love and affection between parties standing in a near relation to each other; or unless
>
> (2) it is a promise to compensate, wholly or in part, a person who has already voluntarily done something for the promisor, or something which the promisor was legally compellable to do, or unless

[70] Above, section II.4.

(3) it is a promise, made in writing and signed by the person to be charged therewith, or by his agent generally or specially authorized in that behalf, to pay wholly or in part a debt of which the creditor might have enforced payment but for the law for the limitation of suits.

In any of these cases, such an agreement is a contract.

Explanation 1—Nothing in this section shall affect the validity, as between the donor and donee, of any gift actually made.[71]

Explanation 2—An agreement to which the consent of the promisor is freely given is not void merely because the consideration is inadequate; but the inadequacy of the consideration may be taken into account by the Court in determining the question whether the consent of the promisor was freely given.

The point of departure is that an agreement without consideration is void and not legally enforceable unless the Act says otherwise;[72] and section 25 of the Act says otherwise in three cases. What these three cases have in common is that the legislator took the view that, although there was no consideration, there was a sufficient alternative reason to treat the agreement as being legally binding, and therefore as being a contract. After all, if the principal function of the requirement of consideration is to separate agreements which should be subject to judicial enforcement from those which are not so subject, it is unsurprising that there may be a small number of cases in which the law may say that, although there is no consideration, there is an alternative, and sufficient, reason to enforce the agreement as a contract.

In the first case, an agreement is made in writing between parties who are in a close relationship, is made for reasons of natural love and affection, and is registered under the Registration Act 1909 or other legislation providing for the registration of documents. If A promises B $10,000 because B is A's nephew and does so out of 'natural love and affection' there is no consideration for A's promise. However, if the conditions of section 25(1) are met, which mean in effect that it is committed to writing and registered, it may be enforced by B against A.[73] If it is argued that the agreement is not enforceable for additional reasons, such as that there is no intention to create legal relations in a familial relationship like this, the response is that the Contract Act does not expressly contain such a requirement, and if it did, the registration formalities referred to in section 25(1) are more than enough to show that the parties to the agreement intended it to be enforceable by the courts.

In the second case, it is supposed that a person has done something for the promisor, who then promises to compensate that person for doing it: suppose you have dug my garden, or painted my portrait, or found my lost property and returned it to me, and I then promise to pay you for the work. Or as in Illustrations (c) and (d) to section 25: A finds B's purse and B then promises to give A 5,000 kyat; or A supports B's infant son and B then promises to pay A's expenses for having done so: the agreement is a contract. These promises could not be seen as supported by consideration, for the supporting acts were finished and done before the promise to pay was made. As it is said in some systems, 'Past consideration is not good consideration'. So in some systems of the common law, such a case would be treated as one in which there was no consideration and hence no legally binding promise unless there was a silent promise to pay for the performance before the work was done, with the later promise to pay being no more than an express articulation of that earlier, silent, promise. The Contract Act takes a much more sensible view: that if in these

[71] On this: *Lal Mohamed v Mra Tha Aung* AIR 1915 LB 86.
[72] *Ma Mo* (n 34).
[73] See Contract Act 1872, s 25 Illustration (b).

circumstances the work has been done and the promisor, who need not do so, then promises to pay for it, there is no good reason why his promise should not be just as enforceable as one which is supported by consideration. After all, if the promisor were to be unhappy, he could have refrained from promising to pay; any claim by the promisee would then be dealt with under section 70 of the Act.

The third case arises when a written and signed promise is made to pay a debt which would otherwise be irrecoverable by reason of the Limitation Act 1909 or other statutory provision.[74] The reason for this is that limitation is a defence to a claim to enforce a contract which the debtor may, but need not, take. It is clear that if a suit is brought on a debt which could be defeated by a plea of limitation, but the debtor elects not to plead limitation, the creditor may proceed.[75] The result of this is that if a promise is made to pay a time-barred debt which is unequivocal[76] and in a form which complies with section 25(3) of the Contract Act, the promise may be accepted by words or by conduct and when this happens the result is a fresh agreement—it is not a revival of the old agreement, but the creation of a new one[77]—by which both sides are bound and which may thereafter be enforced despite the lack of consideration.[78]

It is sometimes said that the flexibility of the doctrine of consideration means that a court can almost always discover consideration for the promise; and this seems to be a justifiable observation. Only in those few cases in which a court cannot find consideration will it be necessary to ask whether a promise may be enforceable without it; but in the final analysis, if there is no consideration, and if the promise not supported by consideration is not within any of the three subsections to section 25 of the Act, the agreement is not enforceable as a contract, and any effect it may have in law must be found outside the law of contract.

III. Third Parties and Privity

1. Parties and Non-Parties to the Contract: The Concept of Privity

In all the cases considered so far we have assumed that the persons who created the contract, and the persons who are involved in litigation to enforce the contract, are the same. But there may be cases in which contracting parties A and B intend to confer a benefit on C (and C wishes to claim that benefit) or to impose a burden or restriction on C. The common law treats this broad issue of who, apart from the contracting parties themselves, can be affected by the obligations created by the contract, as depending on the doctrine of privity. We will examine its place in the contract law of Myanmar by starting with the easier case in which contracting parties seek to create and impose burdens on another.

Myanmar contract law does not contain a doctrine of privity of contract of the kind historically found in[79] other common law[80] systems. How it happened that this restrictive (and frequently unwelcome) principle of the common law was not mentioned in the Contract

[74] *Abdullakin v Maung Ne Dun* AIR 1929 Ran 240, (1929) ILR 7 Ran 292 (which also discusses whether Evidence Act 1872, s 92 prevented the party showing the real character of the consideration fixed between the parties).

[75] It also follows that if an agreement is made not to plead limitation, this agreement may be enforced as a contract if its object is lawful (and there is nothing unlawful about not taking a defence of limitation) and is supported by consideration.

[76] This will involve the interpretation of the document to ascertain whether it is a mere acknowledgement of old indebtedness of a promise to pay that debt: *The Bank of Communication v Khyn Co* (1966) BLR 255 (CC). It is not necessary that the agreement should refer in express terms to the old debt: *Smith v Heptonstall* (1938) RLR 6.

[77] *State Commercial Bank v U Ba Thin* (1963) BLR 375 (CC).

[78] *George Newnes Book Co (India) Ltd v KVS Iyer* (1940) RLR 377, AIR 1940 Ran 159.

[79] And in those systems, frequently legislated out of.

[80] It is, however, reflected in civil law systems as well.

Act is not known, but this fact allowed the courts of Myanmar to develop the contract law of Myanmar free from the unwelcome elements of the doctrine. The question, therefore, of who is bound by, and who entitled by, a contract is most conveniently considered as an aspect of the construction of the terms of the contract.

2. Burdens created by a contract

The first half of the common law rule of privity is that only those who are party to the contract can be bound or burdened by it: it is not possible for A to promise B that C will perform an act or a service, with the consequence that B can sue C to require C to perform an act which C did not promise to perform, unless A is C's agent, authorized to make promises on C's behalf (eg as when B, who wishes to secure C's services, deals with A, the agent of C and who is authorized to give promises on C's behalf). Generally speaking, the common law elsewhere takes the clear position that burdens of contracts cannot be imposed on those who are strangers to the contract; and there is absolutely nothing in the Contract Act to suggest that Myanmar law takes a different view.[81]

Suppose that A manufactures an industrial product which A sells to B, and in the contract with A, B promises that neither B nor any person to whom B may sell the product, will sell it at a price lower than that specified in the contract between A and B. If C buys the thing from B, and then sells it at a price lower than that specified in the contract between A and B, C is free to do so: C was not party to the contract; B did not contract with A as C's agent; and the idea that A and B can create and impose burdens on C is not tenable.

Precisely the same reasoning applies if C knows that A, who sells property to C, had contracted with B to allow B to use that property for a period of time which has not yet expired: C is not affected or bound by the contract between A and B. If A agrees to let A's car[82] to B for a period of 12 months, but then sells it to C, then even if C knew of the contract of letting and hiring between A and B, B cannot enforce his rights against C, for C was not party to the contract of letting and hiring; the parties to the contract of letting and hiring cannot place burdens on C, and C has no obligations under the contract between A and B. If A agrees to sell a car to B, but before the sale is performed and title passed, A sells and delivers it to C, C cannot be sued by B. C is not party to the contract under which B derived rights to the car; and the fact that A is now liable to be sued by B for breach of contract is of no concern to C.

3. Rights created by the contract

Traditionally, much of the common law world drew a similar conclusion about the rights created by the contract: the second half of the doctrine of privity is that only the parties to the contract can enforce the promises contained in the contract. According to this, if A promises to B that A will pay a sum of money to C, or do some other act which would be for

[81] *Mahanth Singh v U Aye* AIR 1936 Ran 514, (1936) ILR 14 Ran 336 (the fact that A, who has contracted with B, happens to be a trustee of a religious institution does not make the other trustees party to the contract unless A was authorized to contract on their behalf and did so. The other trustees are not liable as they are not parties; the claim lies simply against A in his personal capacity, whether or not the trust decides to help him out if he incurs liability). The further appeal to the Privy Council, *Mahanth Singh v U Ba Yi* (1939) RLR 358, AIR 1939 PC 110, (1939) 66 Ind App 196, dealt with the liability of sureties, and not with this point. It is the same if a person contracts with another who is a receiver: the receiver, as contracting party, is personally liable, though he may have a right of indemnity from the estate: *Rev Brother Patrick v Lyan Hong & Co* (1938) RLR 611.

[82] It is possible that the analysis is different if the property in question is land (see Specific Relief Act 1877, s 27(b) Illustrations), but questions concerning rights and duties in relation to land are not within the scope of this chapter.

C's benefit, C cannot enforce the promise of A, as C was not party to the contract between A and B.

It is, however, clear that Myanmar law does not adopt this view. Although there are references in the 1872 Act to the parties to the contract, there is nothing explicitly in the Act that prevents a third party, who is intended to be the beneficiary of the promise, from enforcing the contract. Nor is the rule, which is somewhat similar to that of privity—that consideration must move from the promisee or plaintiff—set out anywhere in the 1872 Act. On the contrary, the definition of consideration in section 2(d) of the Contract Act explicitly includes consideration that moves from a third party rather than from the promisee.

On three occasions on which the issue arose directly[83] before it, the High Court refused to apply this aspect of the doctrine of privity, holding that a non-party in the position of C could herself directly enforce the promise contained in the contract between A and B which was for her apparent benefit.[84] The judgments in these cases are plainly based on the view that the doctrine of privity was a restriction on the enforcement of promises which was unnecessary in Myanmar; it is less clear whether the judges thought that their decisions were consistent with the English common law.[85] There is high authority, though from outside Myanmar, to contrary effect;[86] but the view taken by the Myanmar courts is attractive and sensible. Most countries of the common law have legislated to get rid of this element of the doctrine of privity which would prevent a third party from taking advantage of a promise made for his benefit. Myanmar law does not suffer from this problem, so that there is not the same need for reform.

As the High Court observed in 1953,[87] section 37 of the Contract Act obliges the parties to a contract 'to perform or offer to perform their respective promises'. Nothing is more natural than to allow the person to whom performance must be delivered or offered to enforce the promise if this does not happen.

Once the contract has been properly formed in accordance with Chapter I of the Act, the subsequent, or consequential, question 'who may enforce it?' does not have to be answered by asking 'who created it?', for creation and enforcement are distinct processes. After all, there is no rule that a car can be driven only by the person who made it, or that food can be eaten only by the person who cooked it. Creation of a thing, and dealing with the thing which has been created, are separate events which may properly be governed by separate rules.

The fact that the doctrine of privity does not bar the claim when brought by C, however, only marks the starting point of another series of questions. For example: is it necessary that the contract state that C is intended to be able to enforce it in C's own name, or is it sufficient that C is someone who would benefit from the performance of the promise made by A?

[83] It arose indirectly in *AKACTAL Chettyar v AKRMMK Firm* (1938) RLR 660, AIR 1939 Ran 84, which though it dealt with Contract Act 1872, s 63, which is not concerned with the formation of contracts but with their discharge, refused to allow the doctrine of privity to prevent a stranger to a concession by a creditor, in an agreement with two debtors to reduce the interest charged to all three debtors, from taking advantage of it. It is consistent in its general approach with the cases in which the High Court held that the common law doctrine of privity is not part of Myanmar law.

[84] *Ma E Tin v Ma Byaw* AIR 1930 Ran 172, (1930) ILR 8 Ran 266 (right of spouse to enforce ante-nuptial agreement made by parents for her benefit, following on this point *Khwaja Muhammad Khan v Hussein Begum* (1910) 37 Ind App 152, which may be considered to limit the scope of the decision to the enforcement of matrimonial contracts, though there is no real reason to support this. The fact that the spouse may be a minor does not appear to matter, because he or she is not a party to the contract); *Daw Po v U Po Hmyin* AIR 1940 Ran 91, (1940) RLR 237; *Burma (Government Security) Insurance Co Ltd v Daw Saw Hla* (1953) BLR 350 (HC).

[85] Or with what English lawyers at the time argued that the English common law should be.

[86] The Privy Council appears to have held that the doctrine of privity is part of the law of India (*Jamna Das v Ram Avtar* (1911) 30 Ind App 7) and of Malaysia (*Kepong Prospecting Ltd v Schmidt* [1968] AC 810). These decisions have no formal status in Myanmar.

[87] *Burma (Government Security) Insurance Co Ltd* (n 84) 356.

One would assume that the contract would need to specify, by an express or implied term, that C should be entitled to do this, but it cannot be said that this is yet established. For another, if C does enforce the contract, or seeks compensation for non-performance of the contract, it may be necessary to consider whose loss—C's or B's—determines the measure of compensation. If C did not provide consideration,[88] some may argue that C suffers no loss if the promise made by A to B is not performed, or that if he did provide consideration, the consideration is all that is lost. But one would assume that C should be able to say that what C has really lost, the interest which C has lost, is the performance of the promise, and the value of this to C is what needs to be calculated. However, if C brings a suit against A for specific performance[89] of the promise made by A to B, there will be no need to assess compensation, and some at least of these problems will not arise.

There are different problems if B sues A when A fails to perform. B, after all, accepted and provided consideration for A's promise. That might suggest that B should be entitled to sue A if A does not perform. However, if A had performed the promise exactly as promised to B, B would not have received anything: this may mean that A's failure to perform causes B no loss, so that B is not entitled to any compensation. Issues of this kind have proved to be tricky in many systems, and legislation has been required to provide answers to some of them. But the essential starting point in dealing with these issues is that in Myanmar the question as to who can enforce a contract is a matter for the interpretation of the contract.

[88] Though C may have been the person who provided consideration: Contract Act 1872, s 2(d).

[89] It is not clear that C may. He is not within the class of persons listed in Specific Relief Act 1877, s 23, but he is not listed among those in s 24 of that Act in whose favour a decree may not be ordered.

23

Insights from Comparing the Contract Laws of Asia on Formation and Third Party Beneficiaries

*Alexander LOKE**

I. Why Compare?

A read through of all the chapters reveals something very striking. The geographical proximity of the covered jurisdictions notwithstanding, there is very little cross-reference made between jurisdictions situated in different legal traditions. The Singapore and Malaysian chapters make no reference to either Thailand or Indonesia. The civilian jurisdictions in East Asia—China, Japan, Korea, and Taiwan—make no reference to developments in Hong Kong. Rather, the source jurisdiction from which their contract laws were transplanted or which formed the model for their contract laws tends to be the primary reference point for comparative purposes, with developments in other jurisdictions within the same legal tradition forming the secondary reference points. The former comes through saliently in almost all the chapters. The civilian jurisdictions of East Asia are acutely aware of German legal developments, while the common law jurisdictions cite English legal developments as a matter of course. There is some, if limited, reference to developments in other jurisdictions located in the same legal tradition. Strikingly, this obtains even in Malaysia, whose Contracts Act 1950 is virtually a copy of the Indian Contract Act 1872.

If one is to draw a network diagram akin to the undersea fibre optic cables that connect these jurisdictions, the densest network would run to three nodes in Europe—the source jurisdictions of England and Germany and, to a lesser extent, France. The next densest network would have its node in Japan, whose Civil Code was transplanted into Korea and more recently into Cambodia, and which often serves as reference for Taiwan and China. The network connecting the common law jurisdictions in Asia would not reveal any node having a particularly strong influence on other nodes. Yet it would be a fairly robust network. That English continues to be the language of the law in these jurisdictions and that there continues to be a strong tradition of reporting judicial decisions contribute in no small part to the maintenance of conversations between these jurisdictions.

To the extent that the network map above reveals that there is a paucity of network links between the covered jurisdictions, it is indicative of a gap in mutual understanding between the legal elites in the legal systems represented by these nodes. The paucity of references between these nodes may of course be explained by the difficulty of transplanting legal doctrines or legal solutions to a different legal tradition. However, it is also consistent with the experience of at least two of the editors when they participated in the Principles of Asian

* Cite as A Loke, 'Insights from Comparing the Contract Laws of Asia on Formation and Third Party Beneficiaries' in Chen-Wishart, Loke, & Vogenauer, *Studies in the Contract Laws of Asia Vol II: Formation and Third Party Beneficiaries* (Oxford: OUP 2017) ch 23.

Conclusion. Alexander Loke.

Contract Law Project—Asian jurisdictions have some way to go in understanding how their geographical neighbours situated in a different legal tradition think about contract law and analyse contract problems. This is the knowledge gap that this series seeks to fill. The concluding chapter to the first volume began by quoting Samuel Johnson:[1]

> A generous and elevated mind is distinguished by nothing more certainly than an eminent degree of curiosity; nor is that curiosity evermore agreeably or usefully employed, than in examining the customs of foreign nations.

There is much material to excite the curious mind. Indeed, the generous and elevated mind may well exclaim as Alice did in her *Adventures in Wonderland*, 'Curiouser and curiouser!'[2] How many of Indonesia's Asian neighbours know that the Indonesian civil code in force is in Dutch and that there is no official code in Bahasa Indonesia? How many common lawyers know when they are negotiating in a civil law jurisdiction that the protean principle of good faith means that they cannot maintain the same expectations of freedom *from* liability as they would when negotiating in a common law jurisdiction? And how many civil lawyers understand the breadth of the presumption to confer enforceable rights on third parties predicated by the clause, '[a term that] purports to confer a benefit' on third parties?[3]

Beyond exciting the curious mind, this volume hopes to contribute to the wider legal community in a number of ways.

First, the better understanding of how lawyers in a foreign legal system think and analyse problems heightens one's sensitivity to the different premises that might obtain, and thus the potentially different outcomes. It exposes unwarranted assumptions and matters that one might trip over unawares. This is of enormous practical importance if one desires to avoid stumbling into liability. The promise to hold an offer open for a fixed period—or for that matter, an offer without a specified period for acceptance—has in Japan ramifications which are different from those in Hong Kong. Nuances between jurisdictions in the same legal tradition may be slight yet significant. The promise to provide a service as a gift in Indonesia has a different legal effect from the same promise made in Taiwan. The best way not to be tripped by unknowns is to know them, or at least to be aware of what these might be, so that suitable guidance can be obtained to navigate round them. Awareness of the differently contoured frontiers of liability would thus facilitate transaction design so that the undesired incidents are excluded or avoided.

Second, a better understanding of other systems promotes deeper conversations, whether they are about harmonization, formulation of minimum common standards, or developing one's own legal system. A holistic understanding of contract law requires not only knowledge of the doctrinal elements but also how the doctrine functions. The elements of offer and acceptance can be found in all common law jurisdictions and some civil law jurisdictions. While conceptually similar (the offer, for example, involves a serious intention and readiness to enter into a legally enforceable agreement), the philosophical foundations on which the elements rest portend different ways of working out whether there is indeed agreement and if there is, what the terms are. The way they are worked out depends critically on the theoretical foundations of contract law. The tension between objective and subjective theories of contract are not mere scholarly musings; instead, they carry very real implications for the

[1] M Chen-Wishart, 'Comparative Asian Contract Law on the Remedies for Breach of Contract: Transplant, Convergence, and Divergence' in Chen-Wishart, Loke, & Ong, *Studies in the Contract Laws of Asia: Remedies for Breach of Contract* (Oxford: OUP 2016) ch 17, 400.

[2] L Carroll, *Alice's Adventures in Wonderland* (Chicago: VolumeOne Publishing 1998) 15.

[3] Singapore: s 2(1)(b), Contracts (Rights of Third Parties) Act 2001. Hong Kong: s 4(1)(b), Contracts (Rights of Third Parties) Ordinance (Cap 623).

determination of contractual liability. The hypotheticals posed to all contributors are therefore valuable in drawing out how a legal system operationalizes doctrine. Through them, we obtain a deeper insight into whether there are functional equivalences, and if the outcomes are different, why they are so. Deeper questions of values are necessarily implicated. These deeper conversations should also prompt a re-examination of certain orthodox positions. An example is the English rule that promissory estoppel cannot be a cause of action, a position embraced by both Hong Kong and Singapore. That Australia takes a different position is well known and, indeed, referred to in these jurisdictions though more for the completeness of research. That India similarly allows for it to be a cause of action renders Australia no longer an outlier. Rather, serious questions should be asked whether the English position should be maintained in Singapore and Hong Kong. Added to this is the fact that there is no general rule against estoppel as a cause of action; certain estoppels (eg proprietary estoppel) can be used as a cause of action. Even if the current legal position is maintained, it should pave the way for a satisfying rationalization of why certain kinds of estoppel can and others cannot be causes of action.

Third, this volume makes a contribution to the scholarship on legal transplantation. As all the covered jurisdictions in this volume can trace the genealogy of their contract laws to source jurisdictions in Europe, they provide interesting studies on how the source laws have been received—oftentimes embraced, sometimes adapted—and further developed. We have therefore gone beyond the Legrand–Watson debate whether legal transplant is *possible*. Legrand's argument that it is impossible conceives of transplantation as an exact replication of the source law.[4] It is clear that the Asian jurisdictions were never wedded to producing an exact replica of the European source law. The drafters of the Japanese Civil Code were intentionally pluralistic in receiving Western law. The French influence in the original draft was supplanted, but not totally, by German law. The mailbox rule found in Article 526(1) is drawn from English law. Similarly pluralistic is the Chinese Contract Law 1999 which draws from a variety of sources, including international contract codes. In Singapore and Malacca, the general reception of English law by the Second Charter of Justice 1826 was qualified by local circumstances.[5] As underscored by Maxwell CJ in *Chua Choon Neoh v Spottiswoode*:[6]

> [I]n this colony, [the general reception of English law] is subject, in its application to the various alien races established here, to such modifications as are necessary to prevent it from operating unjustly and oppressively on them.

What is more interesting are the adaptations made to the source law, and the subsequent developments of the received law—for these often reveal the value choices made and the conceptions of justice held by that jurisdiction. What accounts for the divergences and the unique accents in a jurisdiction is, thus, a deeply interesting question that is as important for scholars as it is for practitioners.

Fourth, a close study of how the different legal systems solve common problems often reveals that, despite the different theoretical premises and analytical frameworks, the outcomes are not as disparate as might be expected. Similar solutions are often arrived at

[4] P Legrand, 'The Impossibility of "Legal Transplants"' (1997) 4 Maast J Eur & Comp L 111.

[5] The Second Charter of Justice did not expressly provide that English law was to apply in the Straits Settlements. Rather, it set up a court having the jurisdictions and authority of the English courts (King's Bench, Chancery, Common Pleas, and Exchequer). This was interpreted in *R v Willans* (1858) 3 Ky 16 to entail the general reception of English law. The imperative to give due regard to local circumstances can be found in the text of the Charter. In administering criminal justice, eg, the court was given this direction: 'due attention being had to the several religions, manners and usages of the native inhabitants'.

[6] (1868) 1 Ky 216, 221.

despite the very different starting points. This chapter will draw out some of the broader considerations which conduce to such convergence, just as it will also discuss the underlying reasons for divergent development of the law.

II. Legal Genealogy, Legal Transplantation, Contextual Adaptations, and Developmental Trajectories

The legal genealogy of the contract laws of the covered jurisdictions may be said to fall *broadly* into the common law tradition and the civil law tradition. The common law jurisdictions—India, Malaysia, Hong Kong, and Singapore—were all former British colonies into which English law was transplanted by the establishment of legal institutions modelled on the English legal system. These included the establishment of courts and a legal profession modelled on that found in England, the application of English statutes and case law, and the adoption of English as the legal language.

Soon after the Treaty of Nanking ceded Hong Kong to the British, the colony of Hong Kong was created by the proclamation of the Charter of the Colony of Hong Kong on 5 April 1843. English law may be seen to apply upon the inception of the colony,[7] or when the legislature established the law courts and provided that 'the Law of England shall be in full force in the said Colony of Hong Kong…'[8] While sovereignty over Hong Kong was returned to China in 1997, Article 8 of the Basic Law maintains the continuance of the existing law, including the common law and the rules of equity. In applying and developing the common law, the Hong Kong courts are expressly empowered to consider the developments in other common law jurisdictions.[9] While such reference does take place, the common law of Hong Kong continues to track closely the developments in English law.

The reception of English law into Singapore took place through the Second Charter of Justice 1826, which was interpreted to import English statutes then existing and the common law.[10] Until the repeal of section 5 of the Civil Law Act (which creation can be traced to 1878), the law to be applied to issues relating to 'mercantile law generally…was to be the same as would be administered in England in the like case…' This portended a rather odd situation where there was continuing reception of statutes made by a foreign legislature, albeit in specified subject areas and mercantile law generally. This was brought to an end by the Application of English Law Act 1993,[11] some 28 years after Singapore obtained its independence. The applicable English statutes (13 in total) were specifically listed.[12] At the same time, the Act provided that the common law of England before its commencement shall continue to be part of the law of Singapore.[13] The Singapore judiciary has demonstrated confidence and erudition in articulating its distinctive views of how contract law doctrines should develop. Nonetheless, it continues to draw from the deep wells of English case law.

[7] JW Norton-Kyshe, *The History of the Laws and Courts of Hong Kong* (reissue of 1898 edn, Hong Kong: Vetch and Lee 1970) vol I, 23–24.

[8] s 3, Supreme Court Ordinance (No 15 of 1844) (HK). See P Wesley-Smith, 'The Reception of English Law in Hong Kong' (1988) 18 HKLJ 183. This latter view is consistent with how English law was received into the Straits Settlements: see *R v Willans* (1858) 3 Ky 16.

[9] Art 84, Hong Kong Basic Law.

[10] The Charter did not expressly state that English law was to be applied. Instead, it merely directed that the court was to give 'judgment…according to Justice and Right'. In *R v Willans* (1858) 3 Ky 16, Sir Peter Benson Maxwell ruled (at p 37) that, 'The words are…in jurisprudence mere synonyms for law…and a direction in an English Charter to decide according to justice and right…is plainly a direction to decide according to the law of England.'

[11] Cap 7A (Act 35 of 1993) (Singapore).

[12] These English statutes included the Misrepresentation Act 1967, Unfair Contract Terms Act 1977, and Sale of Goods Act 1979.

[13] s 3(1), Application of English Law Act 1993 (Cap 7A (Act 35 of 1993)) (Singapore).

The story of how English law was received into Malaysia is somewhat more involved. Penang and Malacca, which together with Singapore constituted the Straits Settlements, received English law through the First and Second Charters of Justice respectively. The Federated Malay States, comprising Perak, Selangor, Pahang, and Negeri Sembilan, were constituted in 1895; by treaty, the sultans of these states were obliged to follow the advice of the British Resident General. Accordingly, law courts were set up and statutes modelled on English law were enacted. These statutes included the equivalent of the Indian Contract Act 1872 which was enacted in Perak, Selangor, and Negeri Sembilan in 1899 and Pahang in 1900. These statutes were the antecedents of the Malaysian Contracts Act 1950, which covered all the states of the Federation of Malaya. These states included the former Unfederated Malay States[14] which joined the Federated Malay States to form the Malayan Union in 1946 and which, in turn, became the Federation of Malaya in 1948. Continuing reception takes place through a few sources. Section 5(2) of the Civil Law Act 1956,[15] which applies to Penang, Malacca, Sabah, and Sarawak, is the cognate provision to the Singapore provision repealed in 1993; it provides for the continuing reception of English law in specified subjects and 'mercantile law' generally. The only difference from section 5(1) (which applies to the rest of Malaysia) is that section 5(1) has a cut-off date—1956. As demonstrated in the Malaysian chapters in this volume, Malaysian lawyers are acutely aware of developments in the English common law. Further testament to the continuing strong influence of English law can be found in the citation of English case law on any matter not covered or left open by statute.

The reception of English law in India proceeded along a similar path: the acquisition of control over territory, legislation providing for the administration of justice through courts similar to those found in England, and the transplantation of the common law and English statutes. Starting with Bombay, Calcutta, and Madras,[16] the influence of English law grew in tandem with the rise of British influence in the Indian subcontinent. English law, consisting of the common law and diverse kinds of written law,[17] applied alongside Hindu and Mohammedan law and usage, as well as the laws of the local sovereigns. The complex and confusing 'medley of laws'[18] led to the Charter Act of 1853, which provided for the establishment of the first Law Commission of India. At the second reading of the bill in Parliament, Lord Macaulay (who was later responsible for the Indian Penal Code) said: 'I believe that no country ever stood so much in need of a code of law as India, and I believe also that there never was a country in which the want might be so easily supplied.'[19] The Indian Contract Act 1872 constitutes one of the achievements of the third Indian Law Commission. A draft was completed by 1866, but opposition arose both in England and India to the clauses relating to specific performance; this explains why the Contract Bill remained before the Legislative Council in the years 1867–72.[20] It was only with the removal of these provisions for later consideration under the Specific Relief Bill that the Contract

[14] The Unfederated Malay States comprised five states which were British protectorates: Kedah, Terengganu, Perlis, Kelantan, and Johor. Each had a British resident 'advisor' whose advice had to be adhered to and whose consent had to be sought for any matter of significance.

[15] Act 67 (Malaysia).

[16] Significantly, the Letters Patent of 24 September 1726 is taken to have introduced into the three Indian Presidencies of Bombay, Calcutta, and Madras all the common law and statutes extant in England on that date: G Rankin, *Background to Indian Law* (Cambridge: The University Press 1946) 1.

[17] This included Charters and Letters Patent of the Crown, and regulations of the government (whether under powers expressly conferred by an Act of Parliament, general powers entrusted to the East India Company by Parliament, or powers which follow as successor to the native government).

[18] MC Setalvad, *The Common Law in India* (London: Stevens & Sons Ltd 1960) 27.

[19] Cited by W Stokes, *The Anglo-India Codes* (Oxford: Clarendon Press 1887) vol I, x.

[20] MC Setalvad, *The Common Law in India* (London: Stevens & Sons Ltd 1960) 71.

Act 1872 was passed. This Act was subsequently extended to territories comprising present-day Myanmar after they were annexed and designated part of British India.

Whereas the transplantation of English law into the covered jurisdictions was uniformly carried out through the control that an imperial power had over these territories, the process of transplanting European civil law into Asia is more varied.

The Indonesian Civil Code is a relic from its colonial past. The official version is in Dutch, and it was enacted by the Dutch colonial authorities in 1847. It is modelled on the then existing Dutch Civil Code which, in turn, was based on the French Civil Code of 1804. Whereas the legal elites in the Asian common law jurisdictions continue to be in close conversation with their counterparts in England, the same cannot be said of the Indonesian legal community. Dutch is now an unknown language not only to the general populace, but also to the overwhelming majority of legal professionals. Moreover, both the Dutch and French Codes have evolved; their jurisprudence is thus of limited utility to a code tethered to the nineteenth century.

The transplantation of European civil law into Japan, on the other hand, was very much one carried out by its own elites, even if the initiative was set into motion by Western imperialist threats. Indeed, Boissonade's draft civil code, which closely tracked the French Civil Code and was completed in 1890, was done at the invitation of the Japanese Government. The Japanese Civil Code of 1898 ('JCC') was the product of Japanese legal scholars who had studied in Europe. The criticism against Boissonade's draft—that it was too individualistic and at odds with the Japanese familial system—was addressed through provisions reflecting traditional family law. While the 1898 Code was modelled on the most recent draft of the German Civil Code (*Bürgerliches Gesetzbuch*, 'BGB') and adopted the Pandectist system, the influence of French law can also be found in its substantive provisions. Slight English law influence can be found in the mailbox rule. The JCC can thus be said to be a product of comparative law. Nonetheless, the strongest foreign influence today is without doubt German law and German legal theories.[21] Indeed, it has been said that, 'In term of legal interpretation, Japanese Civil Code has become a genus of German Civil Code.'[22] The German influence notwithstanding, Japanese jurisprudence on the interpretation of the Code is rich, reflecting both the amount of scholarly work on the Code as well as the well-developed system of reporting judicial decisions.

The JCC was transplanted into Korea when the latter became its colony. Work on the Korean Civil Code ('KCC') began in 1948 soon after it was liberated from Japanese rule. Nonetheless, the KCC enacted by the National Assembly in 1958 bears the strong imprint of the JCC. As the product of a double transplant, it is unsurprising that the strongest influences on the development of Korean civil law are German and Japanese law. A more recent instance of a jurisdiction to which the JCC has been transplanted is Cambodia. The enactment of the Cambodian Civil Code in 2011 is the culmination of years of effort by the Japanese International Cooperation Agency ('JICA') which began in 1999.[23] These efforts included sending Japanese legal experts to Cambodia to hold seminars, provide training, and conduct discussions of the proposed new law. JICA also helped to design the curriculum

[21] A distinction should therefore be made between the source of a code provision and the influence in the interpretation and expounding of the JCC: Z Kitagawa, 'Japanese Civil Law and German Law—From the Viewpoint of Comparative Law' in Z Kitagawa and K Reisenhuber (eds), *The Identity of German and Japanese Civil Law in Comparative Perspective* (Berlin: De Gruyter Recht 2007) 33–34.

[22] Kitagawa Zendarou, *Minpo no Riron to Taikei* [*Theories and Systems on Civil Code*] 3, as interpreted by Tsung-Fu Chen, 'Transplant of Civil Code in Japan, Taiwan and China: With the Focus on Legal Evolution' (2011) 6 NTU L Rev 389, 397.

[23] 'A New Civil Code for Cambodia is Readied as Another Major Milestone is Reached', JICA News Release, 18 August 2011: <https://www.jica.go.jp> accessed 25 January 2017.

for the Royal School for Judges and Prosecutors and to write its educational material.[24] While Cambodian jurisprudence may be thin, it can assuredly draw on the thick jurisprudence from Japan. However, given that Japanese is a foreign language unknown to most Cambodians, the continuing influence of Japanese law and scholarship will depend critically on the capacity of its legal elites to access Japanese legal materials.[25] The Indonesian experience offers lessons on what is likely to happen if the language barrier presents an obstacle to legal elites drawing on the source jurisdiction. The experience of Thailand accentuates the point.

The 1925 Civil and Commercial Code of Thailand ('Thai CCC') draws principally from the BGB and the JCC. Two significant points should be noted in its transplantation of foreign law. First, the draftsmen of the Thai CCC relied on English translations of the BGB[26] and JCC.[27] An earlier draft of the Thai CCC (1923) based largely upon French law was compared against these. Where there were inconsistencies, the preference was for the BGB/JCC provisions to supplant the 1923 draft provisions. Nonetheless, many provisions in Books I and II of the Thai CCC can be traced to the French Code. Second, the draftsmen, following the then prevailing view of the sources for the JCC, believed the JCC to be a mirror of the BGB.[28] As such, there was little appreciation of the conceptual differences between them. This is explicable by the imperative to enact modern (Western-styled) codes demanded by the Western powers for the cancellation of the extraterritorial jurisdiction treaties.[29] As such, the Thai CCC 1925 consists of an eclectic mix of provisions sourced from German, Japanese, and French law—without the intricacy and depth of its models.[30]

The Taiwan Civil Code ('Taiwan CC'), which took effect shortly after Taiwan was handed back to China at the end of the Second World War, is essentially the Nationalist Civil Code 1930 intended for mainland China. By one estimate, about '95 percent (of the provisions) were either completely copied or slightly revised' versions of the BGB and the Swiss Code.[31] The influence of French, Japanese, and Russian law is also discernible. Given this, the interpretation of the Taiwan CC draws on diverse sources of scholarship, though German legal theories are undoubtedly the most influential.[32]

The drafters of the Contract Law 1999 ('CCL 1999') of the People's Republic of China intentionally drew from a diversity of sources. The CCL 1999 represents a decisive move away from the Soviet–East European socialist influences that earlier pervaded the contract laws of the post-Mao era.[33] Although principally based on continental civil law, there was a conscious decision to look beyond the German model. While the influence of German law is palpable—for example, the good faith provision and the specific provision for

[24] ibid.

[25] Initiatives like the setting up of a satellite campus by Nagoya University help sustain the links to Japan: <http://asci.nagoya-u.ac.jp/campus/cambodia/> accessed 25 January 2017.

[26] Chung Hui Wang, *The German Civil Code: Translated and Annotated* (London: Steven & Sons 1907) and EJ Schuster, *The Principles of German Civil Law* (Oxford: Clarendon Press 1907).

[27] JE de Becker, *Annotated Civil Code of Japan* (London: Butterworth 1909) and JE de Becker, *The Principles and Practice of the Civil Code of Japan* (London: Butterworth 1921).

[28] M Pongsapan, 'Remedies for Breach of Contract in Thai Law' in Chen-Wishart, Loke, & Ong, *Studies in the Contract Laws of Asia: Remedies for Breach of Contract* (Oxford: OUP 2016) ch 16, 372.

[29] Tudsri and Pinkaew, ch 19, text accompanying n 10 et seq.

[30] ibid.

[31] Jing-Xiong Wu, 'Xin Minfa he Minzu Zhuyi' ['New Civil Code and Nationalism'] in *Falu Zhexue Yanjiu* [*Legal Philosophy Research*] 27, cited in Wei-He Pan, *Zhongguo Jindai Minfa Shi* [*Chinese Modern Civil Law History*] 99 (Taipei: Hanlin 1982), as translated by Tsung-Fu Chen, 'Transplant of Civil Code in Japan, Taiwan and China: With the Focus on Legal Evolution' (2011) 6 NTU L Rev 389, 400.

[32] This is in no small part due to the pre-eminent scholar on Chinese civil law, Wang Tze-chien, whose prolific scholarly writings reflected his deep knowledge of German law.

[33] These contract laws include the Economic Contract Law 1981 (China); Third Draft of the Civil Code 1982 (China); Economic Contract with Foreigners Law 1985 (China); and General Principles of Civil Law 1986 (China).

pre-contractual liability—the drafters borrowed additionally from French, Japanese, and Anglo-American law, as well as international contract codes such as the UNIDROIT Principles of International Commercial Contracts ('PICC'), the UN Convention on Contracts for the International Sale of Goods ('CISG'), and the Principles of European Contract Law ('PECL').[34]

The Vietnamese Civil Code ('VCC') is yet another example of a conscious attempt at selectively borrowing from a variety of sources to create a code considered suitable for its circumstances. The VCC 1995 was a signature piece of legislation resulting from the *Grand Change*; but as one approaches it, the fact that Vietnam seeks to maintain a socialist market economy must be borne in mind. First, the drafters of the VCC 1995 were trained in the socialist legal tradition. The VCC 1995 represented a cautious if significant step by Vietnam towards a code that catered to a market economy. The major revisions to the VCC which have taken place every ten years since then may thus be regarded as further revisions to incorporate further concepts or rules that Vietnam sees as necessary and which comport with its conception of market socialism. Second, whereas the civil code in a capitalist jurisdiction might typically resolve a legal issue with finality, this would not be a safe premise when operating in Vietnam since the reality of socialism invites the further question of how state interest regards a particular contract. Thus, one has to be on the lookout for further regulations that affect the acquisition or enforceability of contractual rights.

III. Legal Concepts and Analytical Frameworks

1. Different Philosophical Foundations of Contract

What do we mean when we refer to the formation of a contract? Do the jurisdictions have a common understanding of what constitutes a contract? Well, isn't it obvious? It is about agreements. More specifically, since the subject matter is the law of contract, a contract would involve the question of when the law regards such an agreement to be legally enforceable. And the way to constitute a contract is to have an offer to which an acceptance is given. This is a good starting point. Yet, before going into the doctrinal elements for the formation of a contract, it is useful to take a step back to understand the philosophical underpinnings of the concept of a contract. To the common lawyer, a contract is about exchanges and bargains. One must give something to secure the promise that one is given. That is the core idea behind the essential element of consideration. While the civil lawyer would agree that exchanges and bargains count as contracts, they do not fully capture the notion of what the contract is about. Since many of the subject jurisdictions follow the Pandectist tradition, it is apposite to understand the nature of the contract as conceived by the BGB. A contractual relationship is constituted by a legal transaction, which in turn consists of two corresponding declarations of will, or in the words of the Taiwan CC, constituted by the parties 'reciprocally declaring their concordant intent'. As Kwon explains in the Korea chapter,[35] the civilian concept of the contractual relationship underpins Article 533 of the KCC and admits cross-offers—two identical offers sent by contracting parties to each other—constituting a contract; this is precluded under the common law which regards the response to the offer as fundamental to the concept of the acceptance.[36] Hence, though offer and

[34] Hui-Xing Liang, 'Zhongguo Dui Waiguo Minfa de Jishou' ['The Reception of Foreign Laws in China'], Special Issue of the Yuedan Minshangfa Zazhi [(2003) Cross-Strait Law Review 4, 7], cited in Tsung-Fu Chen, 'Transplant of Civil Code in Japan, Taiwan and China: With the Focus on Legal Evolution' (2011) 6 NTU L Rev 389, 417.

[35] Kwon, ch 14, text accompanying n 25 et seq.

[36] *Tinn v Hoffman & Co* (1873) 29 LT 271.

acceptance inhabit both the Pandectist and the common law analytical frameworks, the different foundational concepts give a different complexion to these terms.

The difference in philosophical foundations of the contract is of no small moment. A concept of contract as a bargain will require something to be given in return. Legal consideration, which emphasizes the exchange of something of value in the eyes of the law, is a natural outworking of this bargain notion. On the other hand, a concept of contract stemming from the declarations of will admits as a contract an offer of a gift which is accepted. Article 554 of the KCC is illustrative: 'A contract of gift shall become effective when one of the parties declares his intention to transfer property of his own gratuitously to the other party and the other party agrees to accept it.' The common lawyer's puzzlement at the characterization of a gift as a contract should resolve once it is appreciated that the civilian concept of contract rests not on exchange, but on concordant intent. Yet, that an accepted offer of a gift can be regarded as a contract does *not always* mean that the intended recipient is *ipso facto* entitled to require the performance of the promise. Often, though not always, further elements need to be demonstrated before the recipient acquires enforceable rights. To be enforceable, an Indonesian contract involving the gift of a thing must be in the form of a notarial deed (*akta notaris*); the formal requirement performs the cautionary, evidential, and channelling functions. A loan is classified as a 'real contract', with the consequence that the contract is regarded as complete only upon the delivery of the subject matter.[37] Nonetheless, under Indonesian law, a gratuitous promise to perform a *service* attracts no formality requirements and becomes binding once accepted. The instinct that gifts are not binding to the same degree as onerous (bargain) contracts is reflected in the provisions often found relating to revocability of the gift. In China and Taiwan, the promise of a gift, though characterized as a contract, is revocable until the subject matter has been transferred.[38] The qualification to the enforceability of the gift is a good example of words having different connotations in different contexts. Though the promise of a gift is characterized as a contract, the characterization tells us very little about how secure the promisee's expectations are. Any generalization is apt to be inaccurate. It certainly does not portend enforceability in the manner predicated by the common law. Rather, the diversity in the legal positions directs us to frame our questions in terms relating to the strength of the entitlement to enforce the promise.

The emphasis on honouring promises in the civilian law tradition, which can be traced to religious origins, will also explain why an offeror is bound to honour his promise to hold his offer for a stated period of time. The different premises for holding promises to be binding signal a more extensive obligations regime, though countervailing considerations do serve to check on overreach.

The different philosophical foundations of contract will also explain why the civil law jurisdictions have little issue with enforcing the subsequent promise to pay more for what the promisee has already promised to do under the original contract in the Delayed Building Work hypothetical.[39] The mutual declaration of wills creates the contract—provided, of course, that the terms are precise and complete in the essential elements. By contrast, the matter is less straightforward in the common law. As Tan notes in Chapter 8, *Stilk v*

[37] Bell, ch 18, text accompanying n 57 et seq. cf China where the position differs depending on whether the loan is between natural persons, or involves a juridical person. In a loan between natural persons, the loan contract is effective only when the loan is provided: Art 210, CCL. However, Art 201 specifically provides that the lender who fails to provide the loan is liable for losses suffered by the borrower; similarly, the borrower who fails to take up the loan is liable for the interest chargeable according to the agreement.

[38] China: Art 186(1), CCL. Taiwan: art 408, Taiwan CC.

[39] See eg Bell, ch 18, text accompanying n 91; Ly, ch 17, text accompanying n 16 et seq.

Myrick[40] held that such a promise to pay more is unenforceable. The more usually accepted explanation is that the promisee's promise to render the performance promised under the original contract does not have value in the eyes of the law, that is, it is not good *legal consideration*. The value judgment made by the common law rendered the subsequent promise unenforceable. It was only in *Williams v Roffey*,[41] when the English Court of Appeal adopted the notion of *factual consideration*, that this obstacle to enforcing parties' intention to create a legal relationship was undercut. The notion that a practical benefit qualifies as good consideration comports with the urge to honour parties' intention to create a legal relationship; unsurprisingly, the development in *Williams v Roffey* has been embraced in Singapore,[42] Hong Kong,[43] and Malaysia.[44]

2. Subjective Theory of Contract vs Objective Theory of Contract

What do we mean by the parties are in agreement? The common lawyer will unhesitatingly reply that intention is constructed from a party's words and conduct. Ergo, an objective theory of contract undergirds the interpretation of intent, whether of offer, acceptance, or the terms which the parties have agreed to. It is a pragmatic approach, taking as its starting point verifiable facts from which inference is drawn about what a person intends or means.

Yet, the subjective theory is the starting point for many of the civilian jurisdictions. Article 98 of the Taiwan CC prescribes, 'In the interpretation of a manifestation of intent, the real intention of the parties must be sought rather than the literal meaning of the words.' This tracks § 133 of the BGB, where one is instructed to ascertain the real intention of a party when interpreting a declaration of will. A classic application of this subjective approach is seen in the famous *Haakjoringskod* case[45] where the parties to a sale mistakenly believed that *haakjoringskod* is the Norwegian term for whale meat when it in fact means shark meat. The court upheld the parties' subjective shared understanding and found that the delivery of shark meat constituted a breach of contract, even though the performance would satisfy the objective meaning of the term. The analogous case in the common law is *Rose v Pim*,[46] where the parties laboured under a common mistake that 'feveroles' referred to horsebeans. The claimant-purchaser sought to fill a customer's order for horsebeans; upon inquiry, the defendant-vendor thought feveroles meant horsebeans. Accordingly, the parties entered into a contract for the sale of 'horsebeans'. That the claimant-purchaser failed in his attempt to apply the doctrine of rectification for common mistake demonstrates that although rectification at common law *might* functionally overlap with the subjective theory of interpretation under the BGB, it operates under different conditions and does not necessarily yield the same result. Rectification deals with an inaccurate record of a previous oral agreement; if the contractual document accurately records the oral agreement, as it did in *Rose v Pim*, there is no room for its application.

While a subjective theory of contract portends a search for the shared intentions of the parties, the normative inquiry is in practice tempered by the pragmatic concern that proof of a contract might too easily be undermined by assertions that a contracting party had a different subjective understanding of what obligations were entered into. Where this has happened, for example in the Japanese Supreme Court decision on the licence of silk

[40] (1809) 2 Camp 317, 170 ER 1168. [41] [1991] 1 QB 1 (CA).

[42] *Sea-Land Service Inc v Cheong Fook Chee Vincent* [1994] 3 SLR(R) 250 (Singapore CA); *Teo Seng Kee Bob v Arianecorp Ltd* [2008] 3 SLR(R) 1114 (Singapore HC).

[43] *UBC (Construction) Ltd v Sung Foo Kee Ltd* [1993] 2 HKLR 207.

[44] *Aspac Lubricants (M) Sdn Bhd v Ketua Pengarah Hasil Dalam Negeri* [2007] 6 MLJ 65 (Malaysian CA).

[45] RGZ 99, 147 case no 44. [46] [1953] 2 QB 450 (CA).

production, it has attracted much criticism.[47] A balanced approach is usually taken. For example, the Taiwan Supreme Court has indicated that the subject matter of interpretation is not the subjective intention in the mind of the contracting party; rather the exercise involves an inquiry into the purpose of the contract, the conventions and customs of the market, default rules, and, lastly, the good faith principle.[48] This comports with the approach under the BGB, where the good faith principle found in § 157 of the BGB serves as a basis for the court adopting an objective approach to ascertain the meaning of terms found in a contract. Thus, while the parties' subjective intentions frame the inquiry, the actual ascertainment of parties' intentions is likely to involve an interpretative exercise that looks at objective elements external to the thoughts of the parties. The precise working out of the tension between the subjective intentions and the objective indicators of intention, however, is likely to differ between jurisdictions. The guidance offered by the Taiwan Supreme Court should be contrasted with the uncertainties flagged by Yamashita in the case of Japan.[49]

The picture of a dominant approach mitigated by the alternative approach is also found in the common law jurisdictions where the starting point is the objective theory of contract. Whether a person is to be regarded as making an offer is determined by his words or conduct; that which a contracting party subjectively intends in his mind is prima facie irrelevant. However, where one subjectively knows that the counterparty is mistaken as to the terms of the contract, one cannot rely on the objective appearance of agreement to assert the existence of a contract. Thus, in *Chwee Kin Keong v Digilandmall.com Pte Ltd*,[50] the Singapore Court of Appeal held that a purchaser who knew that an online vendor did not intend to sell sophisticated laser printers at a ridiculously low price was unable to take advantage of the acceptance of the purchaser's orders.

The chapters reveal that while the subjective theory of contract *generally* forms the starting point in civil law jurisdictions[51] and the objective theory of contract the starting point in common law jurisdictions, the precise analytical approach to be employed will invariably involve a mix of objective and subjective approaches to ascertaining the contractual intent and terms. The exact balance between the objective and subjective approaches will vary between jurisdictions, as will the correct approach to be applied to the circumstance in question.

A notable outworking of the precept that the court should find the 'real intentions' of the parties is found in the chapter on Thailand—the risk of re-characterization. This potentially creates the risk that the legal form chosen by the parties will be disregarded by the court and re-characterized as another kind of legal transaction. Wielding the broad interpretative powers conferred by the Thai CCC, the courts have re-characterized sale and buyback agreements as loans. In one case, the purchaser's motion to register the conveyance was rejected.[52] In another case, the sale and buyback agreement was enforced as a loan, and the court rejected the purchaser's motion to evict the vendor.[53] Instead, the title deeds were regarded as collateral pledged to secure the loan. Lest it be thought that the risk is peculiar

[47] Japanese Supreme Court, 28 June 1944. See Yamashita, ch 12, text accompanying n 4.

[48] Wu, ch 15, text accompanying n 37 et seq.

[49] Nonetheless, Yamashita submits that the uncertainties are mitigated by the rule on negotiation in good faith: ch 12, sections II.3 and IV.1.

[50] [2005] 1 SLR(R) 502 (Singapore CA).

[51] As always, generalizations should be taken with caution. A notable exception is China where there is no equivalent of art 98, Taiwan CC and the approach is overtly objective. See Ding, ch 2, text accompanying n 13 et seq.

[52] Thai Supreme Court Decision No 1050/2536. See Tudsri and Pinkaew, ch 19, text accompanying n 31.

[53] Thai Supreme Court Decision No 1441/2545. See Tudsri and Pinkaew, ch 19, text accompanying n 31.

to Thailand, the readers' attention is drawn to the seventh issue of the 2015 Opinions of the Supreme People's Court ('SPC' China), in which the SPC discussed the re-characterization of a factoring arrangement as a loan on the basis of ascertaining the parties' hidden subjective intentions.[54]

The precept that the court should seek the parties' 'real intentions' brings up the conceptual question of what this phrase means. It is difficult to divorce the business purposes that the contracting parties seek to achieve from the legal form employed to achieve those purposes. The provision of finance for a car purchase may be structured as a hire purchase or a loan with a chattel mortgage. The real intentions cannot merely be seen as the provision of finance, for in choosing a particular legal form, a contracting party may be taken to intend to have the benefit of the legal incidences associated with that particular legal form. Thus, it is not surprising that even as the Thai courts have exercised their powers of interpretation to re-characterize transactions on the basis of the parties' 'real intentions', they have also acknowledged parties' freedom to choose between legal forms. Materially, the Thai courts have indicated that they will not intervene unless the express juristic act is not the transaction intended by the parties. Nonetheless, the spectre of re-characterization does loom over attempts at creatively using legal forms to achieve purposes not traditionally associated with those forms. The uncertainty that attends the risk of re-characterization might therefore chill legal innovation and the design of novel products which involve the creative employment of existing legal forms to achieve new purposes. The risk of re-characterization, which has linkages to but is not synonymous with sham transactions,[55] exists in common law too;[56] however, the objective theory of contract, which requires the court to give premium to the objective interpretation of, inter alia, the words used portends a careful sifting of the documentation for a correct characterization of the transaction even though the conduct of the parties may be relevant.[57]

How real that risk is in any jurisdiction will depend on how its courts approach the allegation that a transaction does not reflect the true intention of the parties; this, in turn, raises difficult questions involving the slippery boundary between form versus substance, as well as how its courts address the contention that parties should have the freedom to structure existing legal forms for novel ends.

3. Charting Contours of the Line between Liability and No Liability

The first principal question which this volume investigates—the formation of contracts—is fundamentally about charting the contours of the line between liability and no liability. This is a question of no small moment for transaction planners, for the zone of freedom of action without attracting liability is just as important as the moment of responsibility. As this commentator has pointed out elsewhere:[58]

[54] Ding, ch 2, text accompanying n 20.

[55] Recharacterization may merely involve a *more precise* characterization of the transaction. This is the sense in which it was used by the English Law Commission, *Registration of Security Interests: Company Charges and Property other than Land* (Law Com CP No 164, June 2002) (UK) paras 6.8–6.10 and 6.34–6.35.

[56] *Cheah Geok Tuan v Lie Khin Sin* [2006] 1 SLR(R) 340 (HC). See comment by H Tjio, 'When is an Elephant a Bird?' (2006) 18 SAcLJ 473. More generally, see Law Commission, *Registration of Security Interests: Company Charges and Property other than Land* (Law Com CP No 164, June 2002) (UK).

[57] *Thai Chee Ken v Banque Paribas* [1993] 1 SLR(R) 871 (CA). Nonetheless post-contractual behaviour has been used as evidence to indicate the parties' state of mind though not as an aid to the construction of the document: *Cheah Geok Tuan v Lie Khin Sin* [2006] 1 SLR 340 (HC) [22].

[58] 'Pre-Contractual Liability through the Looking-Glass of the Common Law' in Di Matteo and Chen, *Chinese Contract Law: Civil and Common Law Perspectives* (Cambridge University Press, forthcoming) text accompanying n 1 et seq.

> In the contracting space, we can term this freedom *from* contract—the space allowed for deliberation, for hard bargaining, for backing away due to changed circumstances or simply, the freedom to change one's mind. This is an important value running through the rules of contract law. It explains the latitude given to the many instances of invitations to treat, which, in contrast to the offer, attracts no legal consequences for the purposes of contract formation…It also informs us why the court requires strong evidence to be convinced that a 'subject to contract' clause is no longer operative…Importantly, it informs us…what is regarded as fair, reasonable or legitimate self-interested conduct.

A document marked 'subject to contract' indicates that the parties are not yet prepared to assume contractual responsibility. While parties have reached agreement on certain terms, other terms integral to the deal may still be in the process of negotiation. Even if all the terms have been agreed upon, 'subject to contract' indicates parties' presumptive intention that contractual responsibility is contingent on the parties executing the formal contract. It is, therefore, not surprising that strong evidence is needed to prove that 'subject to contract' no longer applies. Similarly, a letter of intent indicates, by industry practice, that the parties do not as yet intend to be bound. It is not surprising that the parties' intentions are likely to be respected, whether in a common law or a civil law jurisdiction. Though the precise doctrinal mechanism by which this is achieved may differ—for example, through the element of intention to enter into legal relationships (common law), the serious intention/readiness to be bound (both common law and civil law), or the requirement for completeness (both civil law and common law)—the outcomes should converge, reflecting the parties' intentions on the anticipated moment of responsibility. Indeed, it may not matter that a legal system does not employ the notion of an invitation to treat (as in Indonesia), as long as a legal distinction is made between an offer (where one is ready to assume contractual responsibility) and a non-offer (where one is not yet ready to do so).

Accompanying the conceptual distinction between an offer and an invitation to treat (or to use a more generic term, a non-offer) is how this is put into operation in a given jurisdiction. While jurisdictions of the same legal tradition may adopt the same starting legal position for common fact patterns, this is by no means assured. Article 154(2) of the Taiwan CC deems a display of goods with price to be an offer, but the German position, it appears, has yet to be fully resolved by the courts.[59] More important than the starting point is the porosity of the line that separates an offer from an invitation to treat. Notwithstanding the presumptive starting points for analysis, what is perhaps most material is what the courts take into account in determining the exact legal nature of a given pre-contractual statement. The notorious *Carlill v Carbolic Smoke Ball Co*[60] is a good illustration of how, despite the usual practice of treating advertisements as invitations to treat, the precision and specificity of the advertisement invested it with the character of an offer. The result was arrived at by using an objective approach to interpret the intent of the advertiser. In a civil law jurisdiction, the outcome will be intimately connected with how the courts work out the balance between the subjective theory, legitimate reliance, and fair conduct. This underscores the importance of understanding how a legal system constructs the moment of contractual responsibility. Beyond the elements that constitute a contract, one should seek an understanding of how these elements are operationalized, and the related doctrines that shape the application of these elements.

Yet, as the chapters demonstrate, the notion of freedom *from* contract would not fully capture the freedom of action without liability in the period preceding the formation of the agreement—for the freedom of action without liability is circumscribed not only by the

[59] BGHZ 66, 51, 55. [60] [1893] 1 WLR 1204 (CA).

moment of contractual responsibility. Ancillary rules pertaining to pre-contractual conduct may very well circumscribe one's freedom of action. The civil law and common law jurisdictions covered in this volume reveal the divide over whether an offer to hold an offer open for a fixed period may be revoked. A party used to contracting in a common law jurisdiction is in for a rude shock if he thinks that he may freely revoke such an offer made in Japan[61] or Korea.[62] Legal advisors, therefore, need to be sensitive to such nuances relating to the revocability of offers.

(a) Revocability of an offer

A strong contrast between the civil law jurisdictions and the common law jurisdictions lies in the treatment of the offer. Beyond the common notion that the maker of the statement is ready to enter into a legally enforceable agreement upon the acceptance of his proposal, jurisdictions in the two traditions give contrasting answers to whether the offer as stated is binding. All the common law jurisdictions see the offer as giving rise to a legal obligation only upon acceptance; prior to that, however, the offer is revocable at will. This is so even if the offer states that it will be held open for acceptance for a fixed period of time. The common law regards such an offer as a gratuitous promise, and hence a promise which is not legally binding. This comports with the bargain theory of contract, and also with the fundamentality of consideration to render promises binding. The unaccepted offer is, thus, placed in the no-liability space.

The civil law jurisdictions covered in this volume reveal a very different approach. Japan takes the position that an offer specifying a fixed period for acceptance is irrevocable for the period specified;[63] if the offer does not specify a time period for acceptance, revocation may only be made after the lapse of a reasonable period of time.[64] This legal position similarly obtains in both Korea and Taiwan. This is no surprise since the civil codes of both these jurisdictions were modelled (if to different degrees) on the Japanese Civil Code. Notably, the same position obtains under the Thai Civil and Commercial Code 1925,[65] which draws heavily on the BGB and the JCC.

The common law position relating to the offer to form a unilateral contract (namely, a promise in return for an act) is more nuanced. Is the promise revocable upon the offeree beginning performance? There are two possible legal strategies for addressing the unfairness that might result from the promisor revoking the promise in such a circumstance. The first, suggested by Treitel,[66] is that the offer is accepted by the commencement of performance, and that it is upon the completion of performance that the promisor is obliged to carry out his promise. The second involves a two-contract analysis. The essence of this two-contract analysis, embraced in Singapore by *Dickson Trading (S) Pte Ltd v Transmarco Ltd*[67] following *Daulia v Four Milbank Nominees Ltd*,[68] is that the offer to enter into a unilateral contract contains an *implied* offer not to prevent the condition from being satisfied once performance has begun. Neither strategy is without problems. The first suffers from a reconstruction of the offeror's terms. If the offeror's promise is to pay a reward for the return of his dog, the consideration he seeks is an outcome, not the beginning of the process. The second involves

[61] JCC, Arts 521 (duration of offer fixed) and 524 (duration of offer not specified). [62] Art 527, KCC.
[63] Art 521, JCC. [64] Art 524, JCC. [65] Arts 354 and 355, Thai CCC 1925.
[66] E Peel, *Treitel on the Law of Contract* (14th edn, London: Sweet & Maxwell 2015) para 2-053. This is consistent with Lord Denning's judgment in *Errington v Errington* [1952] 1 KB 290 (CA) 295, where he held that the promisor could not revoke the promise once the promisee had acted on the promise. See also *Soulsbury v Soulsbury* [2008] 2 WLR 834 (CA).
[67] [1987] SLR(R) 674 (Singapore HC) [39] (Chan Sek Keong J). [68] [1978] 1 Ch 231 (CA) 239 (Goff LJ).

the finding of a collateral contract, through an implied promise. This can attract the accusation that the court is inventing a contract. However, given that the common law operates by the objective theory of contract, a credible reply is that the implied promise is inferred from the words articulated or the conduct observed. The contingent nature of the collateral contract will also address the criticism by the Federal Court of Australia in *Mobil Oil Australia Ltd v Lyndel Nominees Pty Ltd*[69] that it is not always unjust for the offeror to revoke the offer. On this basis, the Federal Court rejected the existence of a universal proposition that an offeror is not at liberty to revoke the offer once the offeree 'commences' or 'embarks upon' performance. The contingency inherent in the two-contract analysis allows for its disapplication if the circumstances do not suggest the existence of an implied promise.

The nuanced position relating to the revocability of an offer to form a unilateral contract at common law is noteworthy in a number of regards. First, there is a concern with fairness, one that is prompted by detrimental reliance on the part of the offeree. Beyond the simple notion that 'the requested consideration is the act', one needs to inquire whether the outcome predicated by the simple proposition will prevail, or whether one should expect a different outcome from a sophisticated marshalling of related doctrines. Second, it demonstrates the imperative of going beyond the foundational rules to investigate how ancillary doctrines are very often harnessed to shape the application of foundational rules. Third, it demonstrates the suppleness of the collateral contract, though the court might find or 'invent' a contract by an objective construction of the words employed, conduct manifested, or the context in general.

(b) Pre-contractual liability

The question of pre-contractual liability invariably accompanies the discussion of contractual liability in civil law jurisdictions. *Culpa in contrahendo*, or fault in contracting, is a quintessentially German doctrine and serves a number of disparate purposes. Developed by scholars and embraced by judicial decisions, it is probably fair to describe it as an elastic doctrine providing solutions to gaps revealed in the space between contract and tort. Growing initially from the concern to protect parties whose agreement is found to be void in law, the doctrine has grown to cover diverse scenarios: misrepresentations made in the lead-up to the contract (whether by the contracting party or by an intermediary); misconduct relating to confidential information provided in the course of negotiations; contumelious breaking off of negotiations; failure to warn that a contract was subject to a licence; and occupier's liability for injury sustained by potential customers and their family on one's premises.[70] While the doctrine uses fault as the basis of liability for obligations generally (§ 276 of the BGB), the restrictive stance of German law towards tortious liability for economic losses goes a long way towards understanding the absence of a coherent theory underlying the doctrine.[71] It was only in 2001 that the BGB was amended to provide an explicit statutory basis for the doctrine.[72] Interestingly, the influence of *culpa in contrahendo* found statutory expression earlier in Asia. Article 42 of the Chinese Contract Law, for example, provides:[73]

[69] [1998] FCA 205 (Australian FC).

[70] B Markesinis, H Unberath, and A Johnston, *The German Law of Contract, A Comparative Treatise* (2nd edn, Oxford: Hart Publishing 2006) 72.

[71] Compare the less restrictive position towards torts resulting in economic losses, discussed in Korea (ch 14) and Taiwan (ch 16), and hence, creating room for tort law to play the function performed by *culpa in contrahendo*.

[72] § 311 BGB 1.2001 I, 3183.

[73] See also art 245(1), Taiwan CC. cf Japan: principle of good faith (Art 1(2), JCC) extended to contractual negotiation by the Japanese Supreme Court, 18 September 1984. See Yamashita, ch 12, n 14.

A party shall be liable for compensation if he, in the course of concluding the contract, causes damage to the other party in one of the following situations:

(1) he negotiates in bad faith under the pretext of concluding a contract;
(2) he intentionally conceals a material fact relevant to the conclusion of the contract or gives false information;
(3) he engages in other acts that violate the principle of good faith.

In addition, Article 43 proscribes the improper use or disclosure of trade secrets revealed in the course of contractual negotiations.

The setting out of the actual text serves a number of purposes. First, it illustrates the style of codification adopted. *Culpa in contrahendo* is framed in fairly concrete terms. This stands in marked contrast with the abstract formulation found in § 311 II and III of the BGB, introduced in 2001, which merely provides for the possibility of liability from the opening of negotiations but which does not detail the circumstances that give rise to such liability. Second, the background to the origins of *culpa in contrahendo* and the corrective role it has played in addressing the various gaps in coverage revealed by German law explains what appears at first sight to be a diverse collection of rules comprising a codification of *culpa in contrahendo*. Once it is appreciated that the categories comprising *culpa in contrahendo* developed as solutions to discrete types of scenarios—in a manner akin to case law development familiar to the common lawyer—the mystique surrounding *culpa in contrahendo* should dissolve. The question transforms from what *is culpa in contrahendo* to what *kinds of pre-contractual behaviour* attract liability.

From a comparative law perspective, this leads to a search for functional equivalences, whether the functionally equivalent doctrines are exactly congruent or whether there are disparities in coverage. The concealment limb of Article 42(2) would not, *ex facie*, fall within the ambit of the common law of actionable misrepresentation, for the starting point for *mis*-representation is words or conduct which mislead. Non-disclosure is, *ex facie*, beyond the scope of misrepresentation. However, the gap between Article 42(2) and the common law may not be as wide as it first appears. There are at least three ways by which the common law undercuts the starting proposition that a party owes no duty of disclosure. If a negotiating party makes a partial statement, that which is not disclosed may be necessary to render what is said accurate; the half-truth is therefore a misrepresentation as it conveys a misleading impression.[74] A second way is to infer an implied statement from conduct. This was vividly illustrated by *Spice Girls Ltd v Aprilia World Service BV*,[75] where the dispute concerned a contract under which Aprilia World Service BV ('AWS') agreed to sponsor a Spice Girls concert tour; in return, the Spice Girls would endorse and promote AWS products. The value of the endorsement depended critically on the band remaining intact. At the date the agreement was signed, one of the band members had decided to leave the band. This was not disclosed to AWS. The trial judge found that, by the band members' participation in a commercial photo shoot prior to the contract, they represented that there was no declared intention on the part of any member to leave the band. Once such a representation was found, it followed that there was a misrepresentation. A third way is through the concept of the continuing representation. A statement made for the purpose of an intended transaction can be taken to continue until the transaction is completed or

[74] *Nottingham Patent Brick and Tile Co v Butler* (1866) 16 QBD 778 (CA).

[75] [2002] EWCA Civ 15. The implied representation proposition is referred to in *Thode Gerd Walter v Mintwell Industry Pte Ltd* [2009] SGHC 44 [29]. The legal propositions articulated in *Spice Girls* are uncontroversial; this may explain why the leading Singapore text on contract law refers to them without reservation: A Phang Boon Leong (gen ed), *The Law of Contract in Singapore* (Singapore: Academy Publishing 2012) [11.013], [11.024], [11.215].

abandoned; as such, if subsequent events falsify the truth of the statement made earlier, a failure to correct constitutes a misrepresentation.[76] Even if the common law on misrepresentation starts from different premises and does not exactly overlap with Article 42(2), its ambit is capable of covering that which is contemplated by Article 42(2). The key lies in whether there is a context which is capable of investing silence or conduct with an unambiguous message. Similarly, Article 42(1) may be readily accommodated under the common law on misrepresentation, since it is misrepresentation (indeed fraud) if one falsely represent one's true intentions.[77]

The notion of good faith in negotiation, *ex facie*, runs up against the infamous repudiation of a duty to carry on negotiations in good faith articulated by the House of Lords in *Walford v Miles*,[78] '[T]he concept of a duty to carry on negotiations in good faith is *inherently repugnant* to the adversarial position of the parties when involved in negotiations.' Given such a strong statement of the common law position, what room might there be for finding functional equivalence? To begin with, the statement in *Walford v Miles* rests on a factual premise—that the parties are in an adversarial position. Where the context reveals that the factual premise does not hold, the context may yet supply sufficient certainty to the content of an obligation to negotiate in good faith. Such was the case in *HSBC Institutional Trust Services v Toshin*,[79] where the parties to a tenancy agreement were under an obligation 'in good faith [to] endeavor to agree on the prevailing market rental value of the demised premises'.[80] There was an overarching contractual framework which gave definition and content to the parties' obligation 'in good faith . . . to agree'. Given the context of the relationship between the parties, the Singapore courts found that it was possible to ascertain what reasonable commercial standards of fair dealing required and, hence, the boundaries of permissible conduct. If context can supply definition and precision to the obligation to negotiate in good faith, it can also generate an implied term of like effect.

Two matters stand in the way of the common law embracing the notion that parties have a duty to negotiate in good faith. The first is the premise that the parties are in an adversarial position; this is inherently at odds with the general notion that one has a duty towards another party and to negotiate in good faith. The second is the *ex facie* free-floating nature and hence breadth of the notion that one should negotiate in good faith. This runs up against the emphasis on precision and the desire that duties be defined with as much precision as possible. Thus, while the common law may be prepared to allow for a specific negotiating context to generate specific implied duties, its methodology and instinct argue against a general obligation to take care of the interests of the counterparty. It is important to appreciate that *Walford v Miles* does not portend the common law condoning sharp conduct. Rather the response of the common law to sharp conduct depends on the behaviour in question and the context; to the extent that the conduct is regarded as unacceptable, existing doctrinal devices may be deployed to obtain a fair result.

What, then, are the functional equivalents? In India, promissory estoppel has shaken off the restriction in English law that it cannot be used as a cause of action. A negotiating party who actively encourages the counterparty to believe that the conclusion of the contract is a certainty will probably be estopped from denying the promise and indeed be held to it, so that the counterparty may at least obtain a remedy for the detriment suffered. Indeed, in *Walton Stores v Maher*,[81] the High Court of Australia decided that the right response in that case was to hold the parties to the contemplated contract; thus, it went beyond addressing a

[76] [2002] EWCA Civ 15 [51].
[77] *Edgington v Fitzmaurice* [1885] 29 Ch D (CA) 459.
[78] [1992] 2 AC 128 (HL) 138.
[79] [2012] 4 SLR 738 (Singapore CA).
[80] Clause 2.4(c)(i) of the Lease Agreement: ibid [29].
[81] (1988) 164 CLR 387 (Australian HC).

reliance interest to honouring the counterparty's expectation interest. Even though the Singapore and Hong Kong courts follow the English position in not allowing promissory estoppel to be used as a cause of action, cases such as *Goh Swee Fang v Tiah Juah Kim*[82] (discussed in the relevant Singapore chapter) and *Luo Xing Juan Angela v The Estate of Hui Shui See Willy (Deceased)*[83] (discussed in the relevant Hong Kong chapter) suggest that some undercurrent of subversion is taking place beneath the surface of orthodoxy.[84]

Strategies for addressing unfairness in the pre-contractual stage need not necessarily be wrongs-based. Even if the contemplated contract was not formed, there may yet be room for the court to find that the parties have made a contract of a more limited scope. Thus in the tender context, though the party who invites the tender is taken to have invited offers from bidders and is free to choose any or none of the bidders with whom to enter into a contract, the circumstances of the invitation to tender may create a contractual obligation to *consider* all conforming bids, even if it is under no obligation to contract with any particular bidder.[85]

That the common law does not have a doctrine of *culpa in contrahendo* or a general obligation to negotiate in good faith should not be taken to mean that the common law condones the kind of conduct proscribed by the doctrine. It is necessary to inquire how the common law would respond to the scenarios covered by *culpa in contrahendo*. Once this is done, it will be observed that many of the scenarios covered by *culpa in contrahendo* are addressed by existing common law doctrines. This is not to say that the outcomes will be identical, for the conceptions of permissible hard bargaining and the limits of self-interested behaviour which underpin pre-contractual liability can be expected to be different.[86] Rather, one should be alert to functional equivalences, even if the terrain covered will not be totally congruent.

(c) Acceptance and the battle of forms

The problem relating to the battle of forms proceeds from the precept that acceptance of an offer must be clear and unequivocal. This mirror image rule, as common lawyers term it, means that the introduction of a new term or any qualification to the terms in the purported acceptance would not qualify as legal acceptance. Rather, it would in law be treated as a counter-offer, which the counterparty might accept. The battle of forms occurs when each of the contracting parties insists that the contract is formed on his own standard terms of contract. An offeree purports to accept the offer made on the offeror's standard terms, but the acceptance refers to and is premised on the offeree's standard terms. There is, strictly speaking, no legal acceptance. Had performance not been rendered, a court would have little reservation in declaring that no contract was formed. However, where the parties have proceeded on the assumption that a contract was indeed formed and have rendered performance, a finding that no contract was formed would be at variance with the legitimate

[82] [1994] 3 SLR(R) 556 (Singapore CA) (whether the action was really one in proprietary estoppel or one properly involving promissory estoppel: SY Tan, 'A Tale of the Tiahs and the Flexibility of Equity' (1995) 7 SAcLJ 195; H Tjio, 'Undue Influence, Unconscionability and Good Faith' (1996) 8 SAcLJ 429).

[83] [2008] HKCU 918 [58].

[84] ibid.

[85] *City University of Hong Kong v Blue Cross (Asia-Pacific) Insurance Ltd* [2001] 1 HKC 463 applied *Blackpool and Flyde Aero Club v Blackpool Borough Council* [1990] 1 WLR 1195 (CA). In *Hiap Huat Pottery (S) Pte Ltd v TV Media Pte Ltd* [1998] 3 SLR(R) 734, the Singapore Court of Appeal emphasized that *Blackpool* should be seen as a case where the circumstances revealed an implied offer on certain terms.

[86] Thus, while the common law of misrepresentation might functionally overlap with Art 42(1) and (2), CCL, there might yet be gaps; it may very well be that the circumstances of non-disclosure fall within the ambit of Art 42(2) but not within the extended ambit of misrepresentation.

expectations of the parties. As such, courts tend to construct the agreement either by regarding the performance in response to the last counter-offer as acceptance, or by interpreting a response as sufficient to constitute acceptance. The last-shot rule constitutes the common approach of all the covered common law jurisdictions.

In theory, the civil law approach is symmetrical with this. If a contract is to be formed by the concordant declaration of wills, there should be perfect identity between the offer and the acceptance.[87] Whether this is indeed how courts in Korea and Japan will resolve the problem is difficult to tell since the matter has not been presented before their courts. As Tudsri and Pinkaew indicate in the Thailand chapter, a more nuanced approach may be taken if the system makes a distinction between essential and non-essential terms.[88] If the disagreement relates to an essential term, there is *ex hypothesi* no agreement. However, where the lack of agreement relates to a non-essential term, there might yet be room for the rule relating to hidden lack of agreement to apply.[89] This relates to a scenario where the parties consider themselves to have an agreement when there is in fact no perfect concordance of their wills. In such a scenario, the common points of agreement will form the core of the contract; this contract is supplemented by terms which the court considers to be reflective of the parties' mutual intention.[90] This comes close to Lord Denning's (minority) approach in *Butler Machine Tool Co Ltd v Ex-Cell-O Corp Ltd* where he suggested that, in a battle of forms scenario, the terms which the parties have agreed on can be supplemented by judicially implied terms.[91] In the view of Tudsri and Pinkaew, Thai courts hesitate to find terms to be non-essential when parties contest the point, unless there is good evidence that it is so regarded by the custom and usage in the particular trade. This highlights the key role that judicial attitudes play in determining how the battle of forms problem is resolved.

The distinction between essential and non-essential terms similarly informs the approach taken in China, which has adopted the rule in Article 19 of the CISG.[92] If the acceptance contains material modifications of the offer, it is taken as a new offer. Contrariwise, if the modifications are considered non-material, the acceptance is presumptively effective and the contract is taken to be concluded on terms which include the non-material alterations; the presumptive position does not apply if the offeror objects in a timely manner to the introduction of new terms. A similar approach is adopted in Cambodia, which models its rule on Article 2:208 of the PECL.[93]

IV. Convergences and Divergences

1. Convergences Forged by the Imperative to Honour Parties' Expectations

Beyond the doctrinal devices and analytical frameworks, it is important to appreciate the broader forces that serve to bring about functional convergence. A key undercurrent driving this convergence is the imperative to honour contracting parties' expectations.

The Roman–French law influence in Japan and Indonesia explains the notion of the loan as a 'real contract' which is complete only upon the transfer of the subject matter. The market demand that the agreement to lend should be complete and capable of enforcement led the Japanese Supreme Court to change the Roman law position.[94] In Indonesia, where both

[87] Yamashita, ch 12, text accompanying n 20; Kwon, ch 14, text accompanying n 61 et seq; Wu, ch 15, text accompanying n 34.

[88] Art 366, Thai CCC. cf § 154 I BGB.

[89] Art 367, Thai CCC. cf § 155 BGB.

[90] B Markesinis, H Unberath, and A Johnston, *The German Law of Contract, A Comparative Treatise* (2nd edn, Oxford: Hart Publishing 2006) 72.

[91] [1979] 1 All ER 965 (CA) 968.

[92] Art 31, CCL.

[93] Art 342, Cambodian CC.

[94] Yamashita, ch 12, text accompanying n 2.

the jurisprudence and judicial precedents are silent on the matter, the Roman law position prima facie prevails. Nonetheless, Bell predicts that French jurisprudence giving effect to market expectations will probably be persuasive in avoiding an outcome that undermines confidence in concluded agreements to lend.[95]

The story of the privity rule in the common law jurisdictions vividly illustrates the nature of the undercurrent. Though the civilian jurisdictions have an equivalent concept—the relativity of contractual relationships—the allowance for a third party to enforce rights under a contract if it is so intended by the parties is fairly uncontroversial. In contrast, the common law privity rule takes an especially astringent form, creating in effect a doctrinal obstacle to the effectuation of parties' intentions. The enactment in Singapore and Hong Kong of legislation equivalent to the UK Contracts (Rights of Third Parties) Act 1999 is, thus, highly significant. It changes the paradigm of the contract law regime from confining the enforceability of contractual rights to the contracting parties, to one that facilitates parties' intentions to confer enforceable rights on third parties. Indeed, the question which arises in these jurisdictions is whether the legislation goes too far to presume that parties intend to confer *enforceable* rights on third parties when it merely purports to confer a benefit on third parties.

Legislation facilitating the circumvention of the privity rule may yet come about in India and Malaysia.[96] But for the moment, contracting parties wishing to confer rights on third parties will have to contend with the privity rule and finesse the toolbox of circumvention devices to achieve their intentions. The reader with a civilian law background would be forgiven for feeling bewildered by the plethora of circumvention devices and for feeling lost amongst the thicket of exceptions which puncture the privity doctrine. The stevedores hypothetical posed to contributors is taken from a real problem posed to the English courts for a good number of years until its resolution in *The Eurymedon*.[97] May the stevedore who is not a party to the contract of carriage between the shipper and the carrier take advantage of a clause which limits the liability of those who handle the goods? The shipping industry had an interest in restricting the liability of stevedores. This was not born out of charity. Rather, by limiting the liability of stevedores, the charges would be the cost of the services plus the extent of the limited liability contemplated. Shippers who desire full coverage for damage should thus do so through insurance. Without a limitation of liability, shippers of lower value goods would in effect be subsidizing those who ship goods of higher value. The limitation of liability is, thus, a component in a more complex contract web that seeks more precisely to align risk with transaction costs. The imperative to honour the commercial expectations explains the detailed guidance given in *Scrutton Ltd v Midland Silicones Ltd*[98] to facilitate the creation of a contractual relationship between the shipper and the stevedores. It also explains the inventive manner by which the court in *The Eurymedon*[99] construed the formation of the contract. If the rationalization seems somewhat contrived and puzzling, the desire to uphold the risk-allocation arrangement desired by the shipping industry would go some way towards rendering the contortions more understandable. Even as the legitimate expectations of the shipping industry were finally realized by *The*

[95] Bell, ch 18, text accompanying n 58.

[96] Although the Myanmar Contract Act 1872 is *in pari materia* with the Indian Contract Act 1872, Myanmar courts have held that the privity doctrine does not apply in Myanmar: *Daw Po v U Po Hmyin* (1940) RLR 239 and *Burma (Government Security) Insurance Co Ltd v Daw Saw Hia* (1953) BLRHC 350.

[97] *New Zealand Shipping Co Ltd v AM Satterthwaite & Co Ltd (The Eurymedon)* [1975] AC 154 (PC).

[98] [1962] AC 446 (HL).

[99] The bill of lading was construed to bring 'into existence a bargain initially unilateral but capable of becoming mutual, between the shipper and the [stevedore], made through the carrier as agent. This became a full contract when the [stevedore] performed the services by discharging the goods': ibid 167–168 (Lord Wilberforce).

Eurymedon, it should be noted that the problem of the *Himalaya* clause dates back to October 1954[100] and that it was not until February 1974 (the date of the judgment for *The Eurymedon*) that the Privy Council settled on what amounts to an adequate clause for conferring limited liability on stevedores. The desired outcome was achieved only after almost 20 years of uncertainty, frustration, and legal costs. It is a rare but notable instance where the pragmatism of the common law struggled long before overcoming an inconvenient doctrinal obstacle.

A similar struggle, but one which was ultimately less fruitful, is seen in the employment of the trust of a promise to circumvent the privity rule.[101] This entails the creation of a property right in the third party, which variation will require the consent of the third party. If the parties in fact intended the creation of such strong rights, their intentions should be given effect to. However, it is not a matter to be lightly inferred. The reiteration of the certainty of intention—one of the three essential 'certainties' for constitution of an express trust—is a cautionary step back to ensure that the creation of a property right in the nature of a trust is truly intended. The ebb and flow of this device serves to demonstrate the imperfect nature of circumvention devices in the common law's attempt to honour the expectations of parties. In the case of the express trust of a promise, the device risked overreaching parties' intentions to create strong entitlements beyond what the parties intended.

The desire to honour parties' intentions and to uphold party autonomy notwithstanding, the chequered success of the devices employed to overcome the privity rule demonstrates that the doctrine may yet frustrate parties' desires. The same undercurrent runs through the China chapter on third party beneficiaries. Given that an express provision enabling the conferral of third party rights was included in drafts of the CCL 1999, its omission in the enacted legislation is a mystery that awaits unravelling. In the meantime, scholars argue courageously in the face of the lacuna, that the law should recognize parties' intentions to create in third parties enforceable rights. Whether scholarly rationalization will suffice, or whether the convergence towards the position of majority jurisdictions requires a statutory amendment or judicial interpretation of the Supreme People's Court—the position is still an open one.

2. Convergence Forged by International Norms

The rise of information technology and its use in commerce threw up a whole variety of questions. May one form contracts by electronic communications? Can it constitute writing? Or satisfy the requirement for a signature? To place electronic transactions on secure ground and further the progressive harmonization and unification of international trade law, the United Nations Commission on International Trade Law ('UNCITRAL') produced the Model Law on Electronic Commerce 1996.[102] Its provisions now find effect in many of the covered jurisdictions. Amongst these provisions is Article 15, which provides for the time and place of dispatch and receipt of data messages. This provision does not prescribe when a contract is formed. That question is left to the contract laws of member states. What it does do is define when a data message is dispatched and received. Hence, if by the law of the member state, acceptance takes place when it is dispatched, such dispatch occurs when the data message 'enters an information system outside the control of the originator...'[103] On the other hand, if acceptance takes place when it is received, the time of receipt is

[100] *Adler v Dickson* [1954] 2 Lloyd's Rep 267. [101] See eg account in Fung, ch 7.
[102] Available at <http://www.uncitral.org/> accessed 30 January 2017.
[103] Art 15(1), UNCITRAL Model Law on Electronic Commerce 1996.

determined by whether the addressee has designated an information system for the purpose of receiving data messages; where there is such designation (eg a designated email for communication), receipt occurs when it enters the designated information system.[104] While not prescribing the rules for *when* a contract is formed, it does prevent further fragmentation in the legal treatment of electronic communication. Thus, to the extent that two legal systems have the same rules on offer and acceptance, the adoption of the norms found in Article 15 of the Model Law means that electronic transactions will continue to have the same outcomes.

Occasionally, the scope of a norm in an international instrument is not only adopted but also expanded into a general norm. The most salient example is Article 31 of the CCL 1999 and Article 342 of the Cambodian Civil Code, which are both modelled on Article 19 of the CISG. The provision, which deals with the battle of forms problem, prescribes that an acceptance with non-material alterations to terms contained in the offer is valid. This rule, thus, extends beyond the international sale of goods to contracts in general, whether or not involving goods. Whether it is an international transaction is also irrelevant.[105]

3. The Continuing Influence of the Source Jurisdiction and Jurisdictions in the Same Legal Family

That the source jurisdictions and jurisdictions within the same legal tradition continue to exert the strongest influence is only to be expected. The transplantation of a legal culture and its methodology also carries with it the implication that legal developments which grow out of that legal culture can be more naturally grafted on. Thus, it is no surprise that in both India and Malaysia similar techniques and doctrines are employed to overcome the obstacle that the privity rule poses to parties' intention to confer enforceable rights on third parties. These include the following: express and constructive trusts, the construction of a contractual relationship through agency, and the allowance for restrictive covenants on land to bind successors in title.[106] It is also unsurprising that when the desirability and suitability of certain devices are doubted, for example the trust of a promise, similar critical examination will take place in the host jurisdiction.[107]

That subsequent legal reforms in the source jurisdiction continue to be influential is also to be expected. The transplantation of the UK Contracts (Rights of Third Parties) Act 1999 into Singapore (2001) and, more recently, into Hong Kong (2015) is par excellence an example of host jurisdictions transplanting subsequent legislative reforms initiated in the source jurisdiction. The UK Contracts (Rights of Third Parties) Act 1999 represents the fruits of a fairly long process of thought relating to the reform of the privity rule. In addition to facilitating contracting parties' desire to confer enforceable rights on third parties, it addresses many of the ancillary issues, for example the promisor's right to assert defences, set-offs, and counterclaims; the effect of an arbitration agreement; and the applicability of the Unfair Contract Terms Act 1977. It therefore represents a ready template for the reform of the privity rule in other jurisdictions, which can make such adaptations to the template as they desire fit to suit their policy preferences.

[104] Art 15(2)(a), UNCITRAL Model Law on Electronic Commerce 1996. Where there is no designated information system, receipt occurs when the message enters 'an information system of the addressee': Art 15(2)(b).

[105] No similar extension is found in the laws of the other covered Asian jurisdictions.

[106] *Tulk v Moxhay* [1843–60] All ER Rep 9, followed in *Datuk M Kayveas v See Hong Chen & Sons Sdn Bhd* [2014] 4 MLJ 64 (Malaysian FC).

[107] See eg Fung, ch 7, text accompanying n 64.

Contrariwise, the different philosophical premises and the different theoretical frameworks which inhabit different legal traditions render it more difficult to fit doctrinal tools developed in one legal tradition into another legal tradition. An example is the problem relating to the unfairness of an offeror seeking to revoke an offer stipulated to be open for a fixed time. As the covered civil law jurisdictions demonstrate, the solution is a fairly simple one of rendering such revocation ineffective. It comports with the premium given to promise-keeping in the civil law. However, the consideration doctrine and the underpinnings of the bargain theory preclude the adoption of such a solution in common law jurisdictions. Instead, the fair solution can be arrived at only through a more sophisticated marshalling of the notion of an ancillary implied offer or a collateral contract.

This should not, however, convey the impression that the room for influence across legal traditions is limited. While the style of legislative drafting employed in the UK Contracts (Rights of Third Parties) Act 1999 may be different from that employed in civil law jurisdictions, the many issues that it addresses offers a checklist of matters to be considered in legislation providing for the conferral of enforceable rights on third parties. These issues include: how parties' intentions are to be determined, whether there should be a presumptive intention to confer such rights when a term purports to confer a benefit on third parties, what amounts to sufficient identification of the third party, the conditions that circumscribe the third party's acquisition of rights, the reservation of the right to vary the benefit to be conferred, and the assertion of vitiating factors against the promisee or the third party. Whether specification of the details found in the UK legislation is necessary is undoubtedly a matter of value judgment; nonetheless, the legislation does surface many of the parameters that attend a holistic reform of the privity rule. If and when China takes steps to make specific provision to facilitate the conferral of rights on third parties, the policy choices made in the UK, Singapore, and Hong Kong relating to the basic model and the ancillary issues will be useful reference for drafting comprehensive legislation on the subject matter.

4. Functional Convergence and Common Parameters

Legal problems often require the aid of similar conceptual tools for their solution. Insofar as a legal system permits parties to confer upon a third party a benefit which he can enforce, a necessary question is how the law draws a line between enforceable and unenforceable benefits. In Japan, this is demarcated by inquiring whether the parties intend to confer a right or only a factual benefit. In Taiwan, the inquiry is framed in terms of a 'genuine contract to confer a benefit' and a 'spurious contract' to do the same, while in Korea, the distinction lies in 'intended beneficiaries' and 'incidental beneficiaries'. The outcome of the Selling Bread hypothetical depends critically on how one interprets the parties' intentions. The variance in predicted outcomes is perhaps more reflective of contributors' interpretation of parties' intentions than prescribed outcomes by the legal system in question. In this regard, the inclination of a legal system towards or against the conferral of enforceable rights would make a material difference. In Singapore and Hong Kong where there is a statutory presumption that enforceable rights are intended when a contract purports to confer a benefit on a third party, the outcome is likely to be different from that in Thailand, where judges require strong evidence before finding that parties intend to confer enforceable rights on third parties.

What may be broadly termed the 'intended beneficiary–incidental beneficiary' distinction will similarly inform the outcome in the Stolen Shop Takings hypothetical. Although it is unlikely that parties intend by their contract to confer on Z store rights against Y security company, the right of action may yet be located in tort law.[108]

In the Exemption Clauses for Stevedores hypothetical, the parties' intentions are clear. The material issue is whether an exemption of liability falls within the coverage of the rule facilitating the conferring of rights upon third parties. In Singapore and Hong Kong, it clearly does.[109] In Korea, it is a good question whether an exemption of liability falls within the notion of 'right' under the Korean Civil Code. While the benefit does not exactly fit Article 539 of the KCC, the Korean Supreme Court has held that it is analogous to a right and that Article 539 can be extended to it. Specific legislation on this question in Japan addresses the issue without the need to consider the applicability of Article 537 of the JCC.[110]

5. Divergences

(a) Intentional mix and match

(1) Mailbox rule in Japan and Korea

A recurrent feature in the transplantation of foreign legal rules into the covered civil law jurisdictions is the purposeful selection of rules from different jurisdictions. An example of a rule that has crossed the legal traditions divide is the mailbox rule represented by *Adams v Lindsell*,[111] namely, in *inter absentes* transactions, the time of acceptance is at the point the acceptance is placed into the mailbox and not when it is received by the offeror. The adoption of this rule in Japan can be found in Article 526(1) of the JCC, which uses the time of dispatch as the determinant for the time of acceptance. Though the draftsmen of the Korean Civil Code had the liberty to change the rule on the ground that they prefer the German rule that the acceptance takes place when the reply comes within the offeror's sphere of influence, the choice was made to adopt the mailbox acceptance rule.[112] Consequently, Korean scholars had to grapple with how to reconcile this provision with Article 111 which prescribes the time that a declaration of intention *takes effect*. In an age where instantaneous communication is possible even between parties dealing *inter absentes*, the rule has probably outlasted its usefulness. Its expected deletion at the next round of amendments testifies to the continued scrutiny exercised by legislators and scholars in these jurisdictions over the relevance and desirability of the transplanted rules. Indeed, the omission of the mailbox rule when the Japanese Civil Code was transplanted into Cambodia reflects current thinking on this question.

(2) Payment of lesser sum in discharge of debt owed under Indian Contract Act 1872 and Malaysian Contracts Act 1950

The codification of the English rules on contract in the Indian Contract Act 1872 similarly displays the alteration of the source rules and the formulation of 'better rules'. A sterling example is the rule in *Pinnel*'s case[113] and *Foakes v Beer*[114] which prescribes that payment of a lesser sum does not constitute good consideration to bind the promise to forgive the rest of the debt. As can be seen in the Hong Kong and Singapore chapters on formation, this rule continues to be an issue. The fundamental problem with the rule is that it stands in the way of considered compromises arrived at by the parties. The two principal devices for circumvention

[108] See eg ch 13 (Japan: Third Party Beneficiaries) and ch 16 (Taiwan: Third Party Beneficiaries).

[109] Singapore: s 2(6), Contracts (Rights of Third Parties) Act 2001. Hong Kong: s 4(1), Contracts (Rights of Third Parties) Ordinance (Cap 623).

[110] Art 20–2, International Carriage of Commodities by Sea Act (Japan).

[111] (1818) 1 B & Ald 681, 106 ER 250 (KB).

[112] Art 531, KCC.

[113] (1602) 5 Co Rep 117a, 77 ER 237.

[114] (1883–4) LR 9 App Cas 605 (HL).

of the rule—factual consideration and promissory estoppel—reflect the inventiveness of the common law in arriving at a just solution when the rationale for not honouring the parties' intentions is based on little more than precedent. Such convolutions have been avoided by section 63 of the Indian Contract Act 1872 and section 64 of the Malaysian Contracts Act 1950, which specifically reverse the rule in *Pinnel's* case. Nonetheless, one must at this point pause to note that in India judicial decisions have narrowed the scope of the provision to apply only to remission *in praesanti* and not agreement to remit in the future. Such a limitation does not seem to exist in Malaysia. A good question which arises will be whether Indian courts will, after surveying how English common law has systemically neutered *Pinnel's* case through factual consideration and promissory estoppel, choose to adopt those devices or consider giving full force to the text of section 63.

(3) Requirement for third party to accept benefit before rights accrue in Japan: adaptations to suit cultural sensitivities

The formulation of the provisions on third party beneficiaries in Japan demonstrates, first, the conscious choice in selecting the preferred rule from amongst the European models and, second, the further fashioning of the rule to cater to Japanese cultural sensitivities. The third party beneficiary provision in Boissonade's draft code was modelled on that found in the French Civil Code. This provided for limited circumstances in which a third party may acquire rights under a contract to which he is not privy—where it is for the promisee's benefit, or where it is a condition of a gift made to the promisor. The drafters of what ultimately became the Japanese Civil Code 1898 regarded the French-inspired provision to be unduly narrow, and preferred a broader recognition of contracting parties' intention to confer enforceable rights on third parties. They, therefore, preferred the positions taken by the draft BGB and the Swiss Law of Obligations. However, whereas these two European models provide that the third party's right accrues immediately, the Japanese drafters felt that such a legal position did not comport with the 'Japanese way of thinking'.[115] It was considered to be against the 'samurai spirit' to confer a benefit without the recipient acknowledging his consent to receive the benefit. This explains the requirement under Article 537(2) of the JCC that, as a general rule, the third party's right accrues only upon the third party acknowledging his intention to accept the benefit. Interestingly, the 'samurai spirit' did not extend to beneficiaries under a trust, or under a life insurance contract.

Article 539(2) of the KCC, which is a transplant of Article 537(2) of the JCC, has thus embedded within it this Japanese cultural value. Nonetheless, the true test of whether Korean law embraces this cultural value will be found in working out whether parties may by contract dispense with this acceptance requirement—an issue that Korean law has yet to resolve.[116] If the notion of allowing rights to accrue without the beneficiary indicating willingness to accept the benefit is truly repugnant to the culture, acceptance should be a mandatory requirement; contracting parties should not have the liberty to dispense with the requirement. If Korean law allows for contracting parties to dispense with third party acceptance, it would signal a premium for party autonomy and that the traditional Japanese cultural value which underpins the provision does not similarly obtain in modern day Korea.

(b) Institutional and contextual differences

Legal institutions play a critical role in determining the shape and form of the transplanted legal rules and norms. It should be firmly borne in mind that the reception of English law

[115] Okino, ch 13, text accompanying n 7. [116] See Kwon, ch 14, text accompanying n 76.

into the covered jurisdictions did not merely consist of the copying out of English rules; the establishment of English-style courts and a legal profession deeply immersed in the English legal culture played significant roles towards the embedding of English law in the transplant jurisdictions. Contrariwise, the absence or inability to host supporting institutions will mean that adaptations will have to be made to the rule sought to be transplanted. A good illustration is the institution of the public notary, which is a key institution in Germany for overseeing compliance with the formalities that attend certain transactions, for example a contract for the sale of land. The absence of an equivalent institution in Thailand, together with the impracticability of setting up the institution of a public notary given the pressing need to enact the Thai CCC 1925, meant that adaptations had to be made. In the words of Tudsri and Pinkaew, the institution was an 'unaffordable luxury'.[117] This explains the different formality requirements in Thailand. Whereas the validity of a contract for sale of land in Germany depends on its registration by the notary public, a contract in writing suffices for its enforceability in Thailand.[118] The absence of the institution of public notary will also explain why a gift of land (but not other gifts) attracts the formality requirement in Thailand.[119] The creation of such a legal institution comes at a cost. This explains why despite legislative amendments to the Taiwan CC in 1999 providing that contracts involving land must be notarized, the amendments have not yet come into force. In the absence of a glaring problem with the existing system requiring only writing for such a contract to be enforceable, the Taiwanese people are unwilling to move to a system that entails greater expense.[120]

The different cultural context may also mean that a problem which exists in one jurisdiction is a non-issue in another jurisdiction. A good example of this is the battle of forms. According to Yamashita, forms are not exchanged till the conclusion of negotiations. In Yamashita's succinct words, 'no form, no battle'.[121] This goes some way towards explaining why the battle of forms has not been litigated in Japan.

(c) Unique accents and policy choices in the subsequent development of the law

That divergences emerge after transplantation should not be surprising. Adaptations of the rules to suit the circumstances of the host jurisdiction should be expected. The Hong Kong position on what is sufficient memorandum of writing for the purposes of satisfying the formalities requirement in a contract involving land is a good illustration. Given the volatility of the real property market, it was thought necessary to add on the requirement that the time for completion must also be specified in addition to the property, parties, and price.[122] One would also note the nuances in the application in Hong Kong of the presumptive rule that family members do not intend to enter into legally binding contracts in their agreements.[123]

A clear instance of the legal elites taking a different path from the source jurisdiction lies in the example of promissory estoppel. As the Indian Contract Act 1872 is not created as a complete code, there continues to be room for the common law to apply where it is not in conflict with its provisions. There was, thus, little issue with accommodating a common law development subsequent to its enactment. What is noteworthy is how the Indian Supreme

[117] Tudsri and Pinkaew, ch 19, text accompanying n 77. [118] Art 456(2), Thai CCC.

[119] Tudsri and Pinkaew, ch 19, text accompanying n 76. The formality requirement extends to other kinds of property, eg ships and vessels above 6 tons, steam launches and motors above 5 tons, and beasts of burden.

[120] Wu, ch 15, text accompanying n 54. [121] Yamashita, ch 12, text accompanying n 22.

[122] *Kwan Siu Man Joshua v Yaacov Ozer* (1997–8) 1 HKCFAR 343. See Ho, ch 10, text accompanying n 78.

[123] See Ho, ch 10, text accompanying n 39.

Court went on to develop promissory estoppel and to permit its use as a cause of action. Thus, whereas promissory estoppel cannot be a cause of action and can only be a defence in England, Hong Kong, and Singapore, Indian law on the matter is broader.[124] Significantly, this took place in 1979, almost ten years before a similar move by the High Court of Australia in the better known decision of *Walton Stores v Maher*.[125] While not recognizing promissory estoppel as a cause of action, the Federal Court of Malaysia has signalled a liberal attitude to its use, for example to assist in the main cause of action.[126]

(d) Gaps in transplant process

Sometimes gaps occur in the process of transplantation. Under section 4 of the Indian Contract Act 1872, the rule for when communication of acceptance is deemed complete differs between the proposer (offeror) and the acceptor (offeree).[127] In the case of the offeror, the communication of an acceptance is complete when it has been put in the course of transmission. In the case of the offeree, the communication of acceptance is complete when it comes to the knowledge of the offeror. The first problem with this 'codification' of the mailbox rule is that in positing two times for the completion of the communication of acceptance, there are two equally plausible answers to the question of when the contract is formed. The determination of this question impacts on whether the doctrine of frustration or mistake applies if an extraneous event occurs during the course of transmission which is said to affect the agreement. Second, section 4 allows the offeree to blow hot and cold—there is nothing to prevent the offeree withdrawing his acceptance by a faster means of communication. In effect, therefore, section 4 creates such an option for the benefit of the offeree. Third, as there is no equivalent of the instantaneous communication rule in the Indian Contract Act 1872, an issue arises whether this represents the general rule for the formation of contracts, or whether it is merely an exceptional rule operating against an instantaneous communication rule at common law. The matter was resolved by the Indian Supreme Court in favour of the latter position in 1966.[128] If the codification stated the general rule clearly, no mere detail, the litigation to resolve such a fundamental question would not have been necessary.

Another possible gap is the absence, in China, of a provision dealing with the right of a third party to enforce a contract made to confer a benefit on him. The matter was discussed at the preparation stage of the CCL 1999. Indeed, a draft article was prepared. Curiously, the CCL 1999 as enacted does not contain such an article—all the more so because all the other civil law jurisdictions in East Asia have a provision on the matter. A third party should not be entitled to acquire rights in a contract to which he is not a party—was that the intention? Or, was it an oversight (as suggested by Chen in Chapter 3)? This gap points to the question of how the courts will decide when parties unequivocally intend to confer enforceable benefits on third parties. It is possible that some of the circumvention techniques used by the common lawyers might inspire similar strategies, for example the use of the collateral contract or through co-opting agency principles. Or perhaps, as Chen suggests, the protean good faith principle will be employed to generate the correct responses. While the mystery of why the draft provision did not make it to legislation might be revealed one day, there

[124] *Motilal Padampat Sugar Mills v State of Uttar Pradesh* (1979) 2 SCR 641, AIR 1979 SC 621.
[125] (1988) 164 CLR 387 (Aus HC).
[126] *Boustead Trading (1985) Sdn Bhd v Arab-Malaysian Merchant Bank Bhd* [1995] 3 MLJ 331 (Malaysian FC).
[127] Similarly, s 4 of the Malaysian Contracts Act 1950 and s 4 of the Myanmar Contract Act 1872.
[128] *Bhagwandas Goverhandas Kedia v Girdharilal Parshottamadass* AIR 1966 SC 543. Cf Malaysia: *Mega First Corporation Berhad v Tepat Intan Sdn Bhd* [2010] MLJU 927 (HC).

exists the more pressing issue of how one should structure the transaction when it calls for the conferring of enforceable rights on third parties.

(e) Isolation

Amongst the jurisdictions which have received the common law, Myanmar stands out for the isolationist policy which the government pursued from 1962. The 'Burmese Road to Socialism', which lasted from 1962 to 1988, saw Myanmar looking inward and systematically disengaging itself from international engagements. Foreign legal influence was frowned upon. Writing in 1973, the Minister for Judicial Affairs Dr Maung Maung indicated that 'since the circumstances vary from case to case depending on social and historical factors, reliance on previous ruling which were from different times should not be made. *Foreign ruling should not be cited at all*' (emphasis added).[129] Coupled with the designation of Burmese (the 'Myanmar language' in present-day terms) as the official language, the isolationist policy resulted in the insulation of Myanmar from foreign legal influences. Pertinently, the isolation did not end in 1988 as military rule—which lasted from 1962–2011—resulted in Myanmar being treated as a pariah state by the international community.

While Myanmar has since re-engaged with the international community, it is unclear how foreign law influences its contract law today. The chapter on Myanmar highlights judicial precedents which determined that as the Contract Act 1872 does not refer to the privity doctrine, it does not exist in Myanmar.[130] Significantly, these decisions were decided prior to 1962. With both India and Malaysia having settled on the position that the privity doctrine forms part of their contract law notwithstanding no mention of the doctrine in their respective Contract Acts, Myanmar courts may very well revisit these earlier decisions. This is especially so given the fact that civil law jurisdictions have a similar principle in the form of the relativity of contractual relationships. If the Myanmar courts do indeed affirm the non-existence of the doctrine, it will need to be prepared to tackle the related issues. These include: the circumstances in which the third party acquires enforceable rights under a contract, and the freedom of contracting parties to alter or extinguish such rights. A similarly interesting matter is whether Myanmar courts will give a broad interpretation to the phrase 'at the desire of (the promisor)' found in definition of consideration,[131] or whether they will adopt a narrower interpretation which aligns Myanmar law with the position of other common law jurisdictions.

V. Conclusion

For the comparative lawyer, this volume provides a treasure trove of material on how the covered jurisdictions approach issues relating to the formation of contract and the conferral by contract of enforceable rights on third parties. While the legal tradition in which a legal system is located explains the analytical framework and starting positions for how it addresses legal issues, the nuances in how the problems are resolved are intriguing for what they reveal about the legal culture and the implicit value choices made in working out the solutions. The chapters reveal that a broad divide in the philosophical foundations of contract can be found in the bargain theory of contract and the theory of contract as the concordant expression of wills. These theories help make sense of the divide in how the

[129] Foreword to the Courts Manual (Rangoon: Chief Court Press 1973).

[130] *Daw Po v U Po Hmyin* (1940) RLR 239 and *Burma (Government Security) Insurance Co Ltd v Daw Saw Hia* (1953) BLRHC 350. See discussion in Briggs and Burrows, ch 22, text accompanying n 84.

[131] s 2(d) of the Myanmar Contract Act 1872. See Briggs and Burrows, ch 22, text accompanying n 46.

revocability of offers is handled by common lawyers and civil lawyers, just as they explain why the civilian jurisdictions have little issue with enforcing a subsequent agreement to pay more or take less when the counterparty does no more than that promised under the original agreement. Similarly, the presumptive starting points in the objective or subjective theories of contract frame the way in which the legal system determines whether a legally enforceable agreement has been made and, if so, on what terms. Even so, the chapters highlight the fact that these often form no more than starting points. In actuality, elements of both the objective and subjective theories are employed, in intriguing and varied ways such that it is unsafe to predict outcomes merely from the legal traditions. Each jurisdiction reveals unique accents and elements to tease the intellectually curious; for the practitioner, the chapters serve to signpost subtle yet significant differences that one should be mindful of when approaching a particular legal system.

A key theme which underpins the subject matter covered in this volume is how the law gives effect to and honours the parties' intentions, whether in circumscribing when an agreement takes effect or in conferring enforceable rights on third parties. Thus, while the doctrinal elements for the formation of contract may differ between jurisdictions, they are united by the common aim of ensuring that parties are ready to enter into a legally binding agreement. As such, contracting parties have a certain assurance that qualifications such as 'subject to contract' will be given like effect in different jurisdictions and that they will not be found to have assumed contractual responsibility before the moment contemplated. Parties' qualifications in offers and other pre-contractual statements should also serve to modify the presumptive legal consequences ascribed by the contract law, though whether it actually does so will ultimately depend on whether the rule is regarded to be of a supplemental or mandatory nature. This points to another important policy value in contract law—fairness in dealings. While there may be some variation in the conception of what amounts to fair dealing, one can expect a certain degree of commonality in outcomes. As such, even if the common law does not recognize the doctrine of *culpa in contrahendo*, it does have functionally equivalent doctrines which together broadly cover the terrain of the doctrine. The necessary and important qualification is that one should not expect exactly the same outcomes; rather, one should be on the lookout for functionally equivalent devices and ask whether a different outcome is indeed predicated by the other legal system. A useful operating precept is to be conscious of the forces of convergence while being alert to the values and policy considerations which finally determine the legal outcomes.

This principle applies equally when analysing the material from the perspective of legal transplantation and legal traditions. The legal tradition in which a legal system is situated provides the basic analytical framework by which one should approach legal problems; the values and methodology embedded in the framework can be expected to have a continuing influence as the legal system develops and reforms the law to better reflect its values and cater to its needs. This points to the greater ease with which reform initiatives can be transplanted within jurisdictions of the same legal tradition. Yet, as the discussion on legislation facilitating the conferral of enforceable third party rights demonstrates, the lessons can sometimes be readily portable across legal traditions. Different legal traditions and legal values notwithstanding, common parameters are often used in approaching legal problems. Moreover, there is room for transplantation of ideas across legal traditions when one allows solutions adopted in another legal system to prompt a radical re-examination of one's usual mode of approaching a legal problem. While one should not expect a common law system to embrace a free-floating notion of good faith in contractual negotiations, the common law can be expected to be responsive to the legitimate expectations of fair play of the parties and of the particular business community. Whether it chooses to do so by using the usual doctrinal devices, or by using good faith to inspire a creative use of the existing toolkit will depend as much on the persuasiveness of counsel as on the inclination of the judges.

We have sought to present the subject matter in as holistic a manner as possible: the analytical framework, the doctrinal elements, their philosophical underpinnings, and the way in which the law operates when confronted with real-life problems. In the process, we observe interesting adaptations made in the transplantation of contract laws as well as the means by which they were applied and further modified in the host jurisdictions. We trust that the rich comparative material presented in this volume will go some way towards fulfilling our aims of facilitating richer conversations between Asian jurisdictions, as well as between Asian jurisdictions and Western jurisdictions.

Bibliographies

CAMBODIA

A. Major Texts

Avillaneda Loic, Theng Chansang-var, Kan Chanmeta, and Keout Rith, *Introduction au Droit Cambodgien* (Phnom Penh: Royal University of Law and Economics 2003)

Jennar Raoul M, *The Cambodian Constitution (1953–1993)* (Phnom Penh: White Lotus Press 1995)

Phallack Kong, Peng Hor, and Menzel Jorg (eds), *Introduction to Cambodian Law* (Phnom Penh: Konrad Adenauer-Stiftung 2012), <http://www.kas.de/wf/doc/kas_31083-1522-1-30.pdf?120720080906>

B. Other Relevant Materials

The Code of Civil Procedure, Draft Ancillary Laws (with commentary on each article) and *Textbook on the Code of Civil Procedure of the Kingdom of Cambodia*, International Cooperation Department (ICD), Research and Training Institute, Ministry of Justice, Japan (January 2007)

The Civil Code of Cambodia, Tentative English Translation (17 September 2008)

Explanatory Notes on Each Article of the Code of Civil Procedure, Ministry of Justice (2007)

Explanatory Notes on Each Article of the Civil Code, Ministry of Justice (2010)

Explanation of the Civil Code, Part II, prepared by the Working Group for Future Trainers of the Royal Academy of Judicial Profession, Phnom Penh (2013)

C. Online Resources

<http://www.cambodiainvestment.gov.kh/laws-regulation.html> (unofficial English translation of laws and regulations published on the website of the Council for the Development of Cambodia)

CHINA

A. Major Texts

韩世远，'合同法总论(第二版)' (北京：法律出版社 2008) (Han Shiyuan, *The Law of Contract* (2nd edn, Beijing: Law Press 2008))

韩世远，'合同法总论(第三版)' (北京：法律出版社 2011) (Han Shiyuan, *The Law of Contract* (3rd edn, Beijing: Law Press 2011))

Hart HLA and Honoré T, *Causation in the Law* (2nd edn, Oxford: Clarendon Press 1985)

胡康生，'中华人民共和国合同法释义' (北京：法律出版社 1999) (Hu Kangsheng (ed), *The* Liang Huixing, *Interpretation of Contract Law in the People's Republic of China* (Beijing: Law Press 1999)

梁慧星, '梁慧星教授谈合同法'(成都：四川省高级人民法院印 1998)

Ling Bing, *Contract Law in China* (Hong Kong: Sweet & Maxwell Asia 2002)

Markesinis BS, Unberath H, and Johnston Angus, *The German Law of Contract* (2nd edn, Oxford: Hart Publishing 2006)

McKendrick Ewan, *Contract Law* (11th edn, Basingstoke: Palgrave Macmillan 2015)

王利明,'合同法研究'(第一卷)(北京：中国人民大学出版社 2002) (Wang Liming, *A Study on Contract Law* (1st vol) (Beijing: Renmin University of China Press 2002))

王利明，'合同法研究', (第一卷修订版)(北京：中国人民大学出版社 2011) (Wang Liming, *A Study on Contract Law* (1st vol, revised edn, Beijing: Renmin University of China Press 2011))

王泽鉴，'债法原理第一册' (台北：三民书局 1999) (Wang Zejian, *Principles of Civil Obligation Vol 1* (Taipei: San Min Books 1999))

王泽鉴，'民法总则' (台北：三民书局 2000) (Wang Zejian, *General Provisions of Civil Law* (Taipei: San Min Books 2000))

奚晓明, '最高人民法院关于买卖合同司法解释理解与适用' (北京：人民法院出版社。 2012) (Xi Xiaoming (ed), Understanding and Applying the Judicial Interpretation of the Sale of Goods Contract by the Supreme People's Court (Beijing: People's Court Press 2012))

张家勇, '为第三人利益的合同的制度构造' (北京：法律出版社 2007) (Zhang Jiayong, *Designing a Third Party Contract Rule* (Beijing: Law Press 2007))

郑玉波，'民法债编总论'(第十五版) (台北：三民书局 1996) (Zheng Yubo, *Civil Obligations* (15th edn, Taipei: Sanmin Bookstore 1996))

B. Major Articles

Burrows Andrew, 'The Contracts (Rights of Third Parties) Act 1999 and Its Implication for Commercial Contracts' [2000] LMCLQ 533

陈磊, '纯粹经济损失：普通法系的视角'《清华法学》2010年 第5期,第116页 (Chen Lei, 'Recovery of Pure Economic Loss: Experiences and Lessons from Common Law' (2010) 5 Qinghua Faxue (Tsinghua Law Journal) 116)

Chen Lei, 'The Historical Development of the Civil Law Tradition in China: A Private Law Perspective' (2010) 78 Legal History Rev 159

崔建远,'为第三人利益合同的规格论'《政治与法律》2008年 第1期，第68页 (Cui Jianyuan, 'A Discussion of Third-Party Contracts—From the Perspective of Article 64' (2008) 1 Zhengzhi yufalü (Political Science and Law) 68)

樊启荣，'保险合同成立疑难问题研究',《法商研究》2008年，第126期，第61页 (Fan Qirong, 'Issues Concerning the Formulation of Insurance Contracts' (2008) 26 Fashang yanjiu (Study on Law and Commerce) 61)

韩世远,'试论向第三人履行的合同—对我国<合同法>第 64 条的解释'《法律科学》2004年，第6期，第100页 (Han Shiyuan, 'A Discussion on Contracts with regard to Third Parties' (2004) 6 Falü kexue (Science of Law) 100)

Han Shiyuan, 'A Snapshot of Chinese Contract Law from an Historical and Comparative Perspective' in Lei Chen and CH van Rhee (eds), *Towards a Chinese Civil Code: Comparative and Historical Perspectives* (Leiden: Brill 2012) 247–248

Keating Daniel, 'Exploring the Battle of the Forms in Action' (1999–2000) 98 Mich L Rev 2678

MacQueen Hector, 'Third Party Rights in Contract: A Case Study on Codifying and Not Codifying' in Lei Chen and CH van Rhee (eds), *Towards a Chinese Civil Code: Comparative and Historical Perspectives* (Leiden: Brill 2012) 309

Poggi Christopher T, 'Electronic Commerce Legislation: An Analysis of European and American Approaches to Contract Formation' (2000–1) 41 Va J Int'l L 224

Smith SA, 'Contracts for the Benefit of Third Parties: In Defence of the Third Party Rule' (1997) 17 OJLS 645

Sutherland Philip, 'Third-Party Contracts' in HL MacQueen and R Zimmermann (eds), *European Contract Law: Scots and South African Perspectives* (Edinburgh: Edinburgh University Press 2006) 203

Vergne Franqois, 'The "Battle of the Forms" Under the 1980 United Nations Convention on Contracts for the International Sale of Goods' (1985) 33(3) Am J Comp L 233

Vogenauer S, 'The Effects of Contracts on Third Parties: The Avant-projet de réforme in a Comparative Perspective' in J Cartwright, S Vogenauer, and S Whittaker (eds), *Reforming the French Law of Obligations* (Oxford: Hart Publishing 2009)

Vural Belkis, 'Formation of Contract According to the CISG' (2013) 6 Ankara Bar Rev 125

王利明， '统一合同法制订中的若干疑难问题的探讨(上)'《政法论坛》1996年第4 期，第49页 (Wang Liming, 'Issues in the legislative Process of Unified Contract Law (1st Volume)' (1996) 4 Zhengfa luntan (Journal of CUPL) 49)

吴旭莉， '合同第三人存在情形的实证分析——兼评第三人利益合同在我国存在与否之争'《厦门大学学报(哲学社会科学版)》2001年 第5期，第75页 (Wu Xuli, 'A Case Analysis of the Third Party of Contract—A Review of the Debate (2012) 5 Xiamen daxue xuebao (Journal of Xiamen University (Arts & Social Sciences)) 75)

薛军, '利他合同的基本理论问题'《法学研究》2006年第4期第116页 (Xue Jun, 'The Basic Theory of Third-Party Contract' (2006) 4 Faxue yanjiu (CASS Journal of Law) 116)

薛军， '意思自治与法律行为涉他效力的模式选择'《上海财经大学学报(哲学社会科学版)》2008年 第5期 第25页 (Xue Jun, 'Private Autonomy and the Third-Party Effect on Legal

Behaviour (2008) 5 Shanghai caijing daxue xuebao (Journal of Shanghai University of Finance and Economics (Arts and Social Science edition)) 31)

薛军,'<中华人民共和国合同法>第64条的定性与解释'《法商研究》2010年第2期，第51页 (Xue Jun, 'The Nature and Interpretation of Article 64 concerning Contract Law of the People's Republic of China' (2010) 2 Fashang yanjiu (Studies in Law and Business) 51)

叶金强,'第三人利益合同研究'《比较法研究》2001年 第4期，第70页 (Ye Jinqiang, 'A Study of the Third Party Beneficiary Contract' (2001) 4 Bijiao fa yanjiu (Journal of Comparative Law) 70)

Yeo Tiong Min, 'When Do Third Party Rights Arise under the Contracts (Rights of Third Parties) Act 1999 (UK)?' (2001) 13 SAcLJ 34

尹田, '论涉他契约——兼评合同法第64条、第65条之规定' 《法学研究》2001年第1期，第33页 (Yin Tian, 'A Discussion on Contracts Involving Third Parties—And a Discussion on Articles 64 and 65' (2001) 1 Faxue yanjiu (CASS Journal of Law) 33)

张新宝,李倩,'纯粹经济损失赔偿规则'《法学论坛》2009年第1期，第7页 (Zhang Xinbao and Li Qian, 'The Compensation Rule of Pure Economic Loss: Theory, Practice and Legislative Choice' (2009) 1 Faxue luntan (Legal Forum) 7)

朱岩,'利于第三人合同研究'《法律科学》2005年第5期,第55页 (Zhu Yan, 'Studies on Contracts in Favour of the Third Party' (2005) 5 Falü kexue (Science of Law) 55)

C. Major Cases

中国人民银行儋州市支行、中国建设银行股份有限公司儋州支行、羊东广与儋州春江南华糖业有限公司买卖合同纠纷案，最高人民法院，(2011)民提字第318号 (*Danzhou Branch of Bank of China Corporation & Danzhou Branch of China Construction Bank Corporation & Others v Danzhou Chunjiang Nanhua Tangye Co Ltd* in relation to a sale contract), the Supreme People's Court (2011) Min Ti Zi No 318: construction of intentions to be legally bound

昆明风情国际旅游(集团)有限公司与北京市华远国际旅游有限公司成都分公司、北京市华远国际旅游有限公司旅游合同纠纷案，四川省高级人民法院，(2013)川民申字第2525号 (*Kunming Fengqing Guoji Lvyou (Group) Co Ltd v Beijingshi Yuanhua Guoji Lvyou Co Ltd* in relation to a travel contract), the High Court of Sichuan Province (2013) Chuan Min Shen Zi No 2525: augmenting essential elements of a contract based on soft laws

成广义与黑龙江兴运房地产开发有限公司房屋买卖合同纠纷案，黑龙江省佳木斯市东风区人民法院，(2014)东民初字第120号 (*Cheng Guangyi v Heilongjiang Xingyun Fangdichan Kaifa Co Ltd* in relation to a property sale contract), Dongfeng District Court of Jiamusi City of Heilongjiang Province (2011) Dong Min Chu Zi No 120: augmenting essential elements of a contract based on the nature of a contract

射阳元新服装有限公司与江苏苏豪泓瑞进出口有限公司管辖纠纷案，江苏省射阳县人民法院，(2015)射商初字第00731号 (*Sheyang Yuanxin Fuzhuang Co Ltd v Jiangsu Suhao Hongrui Jinchukou Co Ltd* in relation to a dispute over forum), Sheyang County District Court of Jiangsu Province (2015) She Shang Chu Zi No 00731: a contract made by the parties' conducts of performance

东莞市欣宇超声波机械有限公司与深圳市安科讯电子制造有限公司试用买卖合同纠案，广东省深圳市中级人民法院，(2013)深中法商终字第1332号(*Dongguanshi Xinyu Chaoshengbo Jixie Co Ltd v Shenzhenshi Ankexun Dianzi Zhizao Co Ltd* in relation to a sale on approval contract), Shenzhen Intermediate Court of Guangdong Province (2013) Shen Zhong Fa Shang Zhong Zi No 1332: an acceptance by the conduct of performance in more situations than Article 22 of the CCL allows

张成林与大连顺达房屋开发有限公司房屋买卖合同纠纷案, 辽宁省高级人民法院, (2014) 辽审四民申字第577号 (*Zhang Chenglin v Dalian Shunda Fangwu Kaifa Co Ltd* in relation to a property sale contract), the High Court of Liaoning Province (2014) Liao Shen Si Min Shen Zi No 577: means of a notice of the revocation of offer

褚江与凯丹置地(成都)有限公司不当得利纠纷案, 成都高新技术产业开发区人民法院, (2013)高新民初字第2135号 (*Chu Jiang v Kaidan Zhidi (Chengdu) Co Ltd* in relation to a unjust enrichment dispute), the District Count of the High-Tech Industrial Development Zone of Chengdu (2013) Gao Xin Min Chu Zi No 2135: late acceptance ratified by conduct under Article 28 of the CCL

张穗红与陆奇玲、广州市德诚综合市场有限公司股权转让纠纷案, 广东省高级人民法院, (2013)粤高法民二申字第560号 (*Zhang Huihong v Lu Qiling and Guangzhoushi Decheng Zonghe

Shichang Co Ltd in a relation to a transfer of shares dispute), the High Court of Guangdong Province (2013) Yue Gao Fa Min Er Shen Zi No 560: timely arrival of a notice of the rejection of late acceptance under Article 29 of the CCL

兴业全球基金管理有限公司与江苏熔盛重工有限公司缔约过失责任纠纷案， 最高人民法院，(2013)民申字第1881号 (*Xingye Quanqiu Jijin Guanli Co Ltd v Jiangsu Rongsheng Zhonggong Co Ltd* in relation to a breach of pre-contractual obligations dispute), the Supreme People's Court (2013) Min Shen Zi No 1881: a two-stage analysis on breach of pre-contractual obligations

安徽水利开发股份有限公司与怀远县城市投资发展有限责任公司缔约过失责任纠纷案，安徽省高级人民法院，(2014)皖民二终字第00659号 (*Anhui Shuili Kaifa Co Ltd by Shares v Huaiyuanxian Chengshi Touzi Fazhan Co Ltd* in relation to a breach of pre-contractual obligations dispute), the High Court of Anhui Province (2014) Wan Min Er Zhong Zi No 00659: compensation of reliance interests for breach of pre-contractual obligations

华夏银行股份有限公司常州分行与常州市申利模具有限公司、常州亚泰纺织染整有限公司等金融借款合同纠纷案，江苏省高级人民法院，(2013)苏商终字第0078号 (*Changzhou Branch of Huaxia Bank Co Ltd by Shares v Changzhoushi Shenli Moju Co Ltd and Changzhou Yatai Fangzhi Ranzheng Co Ltd* in relation to a loan contract), the High Court of Jiangsu Province (2013) Su Shang Zhong Zi No 0078: application by analogy of the doctrine of contributory fault in pre-contractual obligation cases

盛巧洪等与储文化股权转让纠纷上诉案， 重庆市高级人民法院 (2011)渝高法民终字第00119号民事判决书 (*Sheng Qiaohong & Ors v Chu Wen Hua*, the Judgment of High Court of Chongqing Province (2011) Yu Gao Fa Min Zhong No 00119)

中国太平洋财产保险股份有限公司海南分公司与中远航运股份有限公司、第三人海南一汽海马汽车销售有限公司水路货物运输合同货损赔偿纠纷案， 最高人民法院， 民事判决书2011民提字第12号 (*China Pacific Insurance (Group) Co, Ltd v China COASCO Shipping Corporation Ltd and Hainan Office of Haima Automobile Group Co Ltd*, the Judgment of Supreme Court of People's Republic of China (2011) Min Ti Zi No 12)

张勇诉广西恒鑫轻钢活动房有限公司股权转让纠纷民事判决书， 南宁市中级人民法院民事判决书2011南市民二终字第132号 (*Zhang Yong v Guangxi Hengxin Movable Housing Co, Ltd*, the Judgment of Nanning Intermediate People's Court (2011) Nan Shi Min No 2 Zhong No 132)

福建顶益食品有限公司诉中远集装箱运输有限公司等海上货物运输合同货损赔偿纠纷案(2003)广海法初字第171号 (*Contractual Disputes over Goods Damage between Fujian Dingyi Food Co v COSCO Container Lines Co, Ltd*, Guangdong Maritime Trial Court Judgment No 171)

福建顶益食品有限公司诉中远集装箱运输有限公司等海上货物运输合同货损赔偿纠纷案，广东省高级人民法院民事判决书第广高法二字第233号 (*Contractual Disputes over Goods Damage between Fujian Tingyi Food Co, COSCO Container Lines Co, Ltd v Guangzhou Maritime Transportation Bureau* (2003), Judgment of Guangdong High Court (Second) No 233)

D. Other Relevant Materials

(a) Legislation

Civil Aviation Law of the People's Republic of China (effective 1 March 1996) 中华人民共和国民用航空法 (1996年生效)

Contract Law of the People's Republic of China (effective 1 October 1999) 中华人民共和国合同法(1999年生效)

General Principles of Civil Law of the People's Republic of China (effective 1 January 1987) 中华人民共和国民法通则 (1987年生效)

Insurance Law of the People's Republic of China (2015 Amendment) (effective 24 April 2015) 中华人民共和国保险法(2015年修正)(2015年生效)

Interpretations I of the Supreme People's Court of Several Issues concerning the Application of the Contract Law of the People's Republic of China (Fa Shi [1999] No 19, effective 29 December 1999) 最高人民法院关于适用《中华人民共和国合同法》若干问题的解释(一)法释〔1999〕19号(1999年生效)

Interpretations II of the Supreme People's Court of Several Issues concerning the Application of the Contract Law of the People's Republic of China (Fa Shi [2009] No 5; effective 13 May 2009) 最高人民法院关于适用《中华人民共和国合同法》若干问题的解释(二)法释〔2009〕5号(2009年生效)

Interpretations of the Supreme People's Court of Issues concerning the Application of Law in the Trail of Cases on Sale Contract Disputes (Fa Shi [2012] No 7; effective 1 July 2012) 最高人民法院关于审理买卖合同纠纷案件适用法律问题的解释法释〔2012〕7号 (2012年生效)

Law on Electronic Signature of the People's Republic of China (effective 1 April 2005) 中华人民共和国电子签名法 (2005年生效)

Maritime Law of the People's Republic of China (effective 1 July 1993) 中华人民共和国海商法 (1993年生效)

Property Law of the People's Republic of China (effective 1 October 2007) 中华人民共和国物权法 (2007年生效)

Succession Law of the People's Republic of China (effective 1 October 1985) 中华人民共和国继承法 (1985年生效)

Tort Liability Law of the People's Republic of China (effective 1 July 2010) 中华人民共和国侵权责任法(2010年生效)

Trust Law of the People's Republic of China (effective 1 October 2001) 中华人民共和国信托法 (2001年生效)

E. Online Resources

<http://wenshu.court.gov.cn> (China's Judgments Online (中国裁判文书网), initiated by the Supreme People's Court, Chinese only)

'The Report on the Consensus of the Contract Law (Draft)' by the Legal Committee of the 9th National People's Congress of the People's Republic of China in March 1999 <http://www.npc.gov.cn/wxzl/gongbao/2000-12/06/content_5007083.htm> accessed 22 November 2015

The Consultation Paper by the Hong Kong Law Reform Commission on the Privity of Contract, 2005, available at <http://www.hkreform.gov.hk/en/publications/privity.htm>

HONG KONG

A. Major Texts

Course Lindy et al, *Butterworths Hong Kong Contract Law Handbook* (3rd edn, Hong Kong: LexisNexis Butterworths 2013)

Fisher Michael J, *The Legal System of Hong Kong* (Hong Kong: Blue Dragon Asia Ltd 2010)

Fisher Michael J and Greenwood Desmond G, *Contract Law in Hong Kong* (expanded 2nd edn, Hong Kong: HKU Press 2011)

Hall Stephen, *Ho & Hall's Hong Kong Contract Law* (3rd edn, Hong Kong: LexisNexis 2013)

Hall Stephen, *Law of Contract in Hong Kong: Cases and Commentary* (3rd edn, Hong Kong: LexisNexis 2011)

Mason Lee, *Contract Law in Hong Kong* (Hong Kong: Sweet & Maxwell 2011)

Ribeiro Robert (ed), *Chitty on Contracts: Hong Kong Specific Contracts* (3rd edn, Hong Kong: Sweet & Maxwell 2013)

Wesley-Smith Peter, *An Introduction to the Hong Kong Legal System* (3rd edn, Oxford: OUP 1998)

B. Major Articles

Bateson David and Barton Kim, 'Hong Kong: Enforceability of Agreements to Negotiate and Mediate—Where Does Hong Kong Stand?' (2006) 23 ICLR 266

Chan Ming K, 'The Imperfect Legacy: Defects in the British Legal System in Colonial Hong Kong' (1997) 18 U Penn J Int'l Econ L 133

Kowalski Mitchell E, 'Good Faith, Greed and Time of the Essence' (2000) 30 HKLJ 476

Marcks Eric, 'English Law in Early Hong Kong: Colonial Law as a Means for Control and Liberation' (2000) 35 Texas Int'l LJ 265

Seng Daniel, 'The Singapore Electronic Transactions Act and the Hong Kong Electronic Transactions Ordinance' (2008) 5 DE & ESLR 7

C. Major Cases

Anstalt Nybro v Hong Kong Resort Co Ltd [1978] HKLR 414 at 428: specific performance of a personal service

Attorney General of Hong Kong v Humphreys Estate (Queen's Gardens) Ltd [1987] HKLR 427: estoppel
B + B Construction Ltd v Sun Alliance and London Insurance Plc [2000] 2 HKC 295: privity doctrine stands firm despite developments elsewhere
Bewise Motors Co Ltd v Hoi Kong Container Services Ltd [1998] 2 HKLRD 645: using a *Himalaya* clause
Bonus Garment Co v Karl Rieker GmbH & Co KG [2001] HKCA 335: agent acting with usual authority
Chan Kam Ming (No 2) v Kwong Lin [1959] HKLR 544 at 556: specific performance and mutuality
City University of Hong Kong v Blue Cross (Asia Pacific) Insurance Ltd [2001] HKCFI 1356: revocation of offer before acceptance
Chong Cheng Lin Courtney v Cathay Pacific Airways Ltd [2010] HKCA 338: consideration
Greatworth Industrial Ltd v Sun Fook Kong Construction Ltd [2006] HKCA 460: agent with usual authority
Hong Jing Co Ltd v Zhuhai Kwok Yuen Investment Co Ltd [2012] HKCA 296: duty to negotiate in good faith
Hyundai Engineering and Construction Co Ltd v Vigour Ltd [2004] HKCFI 205, [2006] HKCA 52: duty to negotiate in good faith
JN Roland Deneault v Yangtzekiang Garment Manufacturing Co Ltd [1977] HKLR 320: formality for contracts to sell land
Kanematsu-Gosho (HK) Ltd v Lee Boon-Chean [1986] HKLR 59: stay of proceedings to enable a promisee to enforce a promise for the benefit of a third party
Kinetics Medical and Health Group Co Ltd v Dr Tse Ivan Cheong Yau [2013] HKCFI 1645: promisee recovering damages for losses suffered by a third party
Kowloon Development Finance Ltd v Pendex Industries Ltd (2013) 16 HKCFAR 336: objective test of formation
Kwan Siu Man Joshua v Yaacov Ozer (1997–8) 1 HKCFAR 343: formality for contracts to sell land
Leon Engineering & Construction Co Ltd v Ka Duck Investments Ltd [1989] 2 HKLR 537: economic loss to a third party
Mahkutai, The [1996] 2 HKLR 199 (PC): fully developed exception to the privity doctrine considered; using a *Himalaya* clause
New World Development Co Ltd v Sun Hung Kai Securities Ltd (2006) 9 HKCFAR 403: formality in formation
Newmark Capital Corp Ltd v Coffee Partners Ltd [2007] HKCFI 113: estoppel
OKA Electronics Ltd v Manohar Chugh (t/a Electric & Electronic Industries) [1991] HKCA 266: battle of forms
Real Honest Investment Ltd v Attorney-General [1997] HKLY 490: variation of a restrictive covenant
Shanghai Tongji Science & Technology Industrial Co Ltd v Casil Clearing Ltd (2004) 7 HKCFAR 79: objective test of formation; restitution for total failure of consideration
Shiu Yeuk Yuen v Hong Kong Solicitors Indemnity Fund Ltd [2010] 4 HKLRD 296: trust of a contractual right
Siu Yin Kwan v Eastern Insurance Co Ltd [1994] 1 HKLR 77 (PC): undisclosed identity of principal; promisee recovering damages for losses suffered by a third party
Sunface International Ltd v Meco Engineering Ltd [1990] 2 HKLR 193: economic loss to a third party
Solicitor (24/07) v Law Society of Hong Kong (2008) 11 HKCFAR 117: precedent status of UK Supreme Court and Privy Council decisions in Hong Kong
Take Harvest Ltd v Liu [1994] 1 HKLR 32 (PC): part performance of contracts
THH and TWK v The Commissioner of Estate Duty [1990] 2 HKLR 333: trust of a contractual right
UBC (Construction) Ltd v Sung Foo Kee Ltd [1993] HKCFI 261: consideration
Union Eagle Ltd v Golden Achievement Ltd [1997] HKLRD 366 (PC): time of the essence in conveyancing contracts
Unruh v Seeberger (2007) 10 HKCFAR 31: estoppel
Wong King Lim v Incorporated Owners of Peony House [2013] HKCA 256: third party enforcing a land covenant
World Food Fair Ltd v Hong Kong Island Development Ltd (2006) 9 HKCFAR 735: part performance of contracts

Wu Koon Tai v Wu Yau Loi [1996] 2 HKLR 477 (PC): part performance of contracts
Yuen Kun-yeu v Attorney General of Hong Kong [1987] HKLR 1154 (PC): economic loss to a third party

D. Other Relevant Materials

(a) Constitutional document

The Basic Law of the Hong Kong Special Administrative Region (adopted on 4 April 1990 by the Seventh National People's Congress of the PRC, effective from 1 July 1997): <http://www.basiclaw.gov.hk/en/basiclawtext/images/basiclaw_full_text_en.pdf>

(b) Legislation

Arbitration Ordinance (Cap 609)
Bills of Exchange Ordinance (Cap 19)
Bills of Lading and Analogous Shipping Documents Ordinance (Cap 440)
Building Management Ordinance (Cap 344)
Companies Ordinance (Cap 622)
Contracts (Rights of Third Parties) Ordinance (Cap 623)
Control of Exemption Clauses Ordinance (Cap 71)
Conveyancing and Property Ordinance (Cap 219)
Copyright Ordinance (Cap 528)
Electronic Transactions Ordinance (Cap 71)
Enduring Powers of Attorney Ordinance (Cap 501)
High Court Ordinance (Cap 4)
Law Amendment and Reform (Consolidation) Ordinance (Cap 23)
Marine Insurance Ordinance (Cap 329)
Married Persons Status Ordinance (Cap 182)
Motor Vehicle Insurance (Third Party Risks) Ordinance (Cap 272)
Powers of Attorney Ordinance (Cap 31)
Third Parties (Rights Against Insurers) Ordinance (Cap 273)

(c) Reports and Bills Committee Papers

Law Reform Commission of Hong Kong, Report on Privity of Contract (2005), available at <http://www.hkreform.gov.hk/en/docs/rprivity-e.pdf> (third party rights)
'Further Views on Consultation Paper on the Contracts (Rights of Third Parties) Bill 2013' (Hong Kong Bar Association, January 2014), LC Paper No CB(4)328/13–14(01): <http://www.legco.gov.hk/yr13-14/english/panels/ajls/papers/aj1126cb4-328-1-e.pdf> (third party rights)
'Comments on the Bill' (Lee Mason, May 2014), LC Paper No CB(4)672/13–14(01): <http://www.legco.gov.hk/yr13-14/english/bc/bc102/papers/bc1020507cb4-672-1-e.pdf> (third party rights)
'Administration's Responses to the Written Submissions of (1) Mr. Lee MASON, Faculty of Law, the University of Hong Kong; (2) the Law Society of Hong Kong; and (3) the Hong Kong Association of Banks' (Department of Justice, June 2014), LC Paper No CB(4)815/13–14(01): <http://www.legco.gov.hk/yr13-14/english/bc/bc102/papers/bc1020616cb4-815-1-e.pdf> (third party rights)
'House Committee Meeting Paper: Report of the Bills Committee on Contracts (Rights of Third Parties) Bill' (November 2014) (Legislative Council Secretariat, November 2014), LC Paper No CB(4)145/14–15: <http://www.legco.gov.hk/yr14-15/english/hc/papers/hc20141114cb4-145-e.pdf> (third party rights)

E. Online Resources

<http://www.hklii.org> (Hong Kong legislation, case law and some official documents)
<http://www.legislation.gov.hk> (Bilingual Laws Information System, database of Hong Kong legislation maintained by the Department of Justice)

INDIA

A. Major Texts

Beale Hugh, *Chitty on Contracts* (Vol I, 31st edn, London: Sweet & Maxwell 2013)

Beatson J, Burrows A, and Cartwright J, *Anson's Law of Contract* (29th edn, Oxford: OUP 2010)

Bijay Kisor Acharyya, *Codification in British India* (Calcutta: SK Banerji and Sons 1914)

Daruvala Pherozeshah N, *The Doctrine of Consideration treated Historically and Comparatively* (Calcutta: Butterworth & Co (India) Ltd 1914)

Furmston MP, *Cheshire, Fifoot and Furmston's Law of Contract* (16th edn, Oxford: OUP 2012)

Gupta Apar, *Commentary on Information Technology Act* (2nd edn, Haryana: LexisNexis Butterworths Wadhwa Nagpur 2011)

Halsbury's Laws of India, Vol 9, *Contracts* (2nd edn, Gurgaon: LexisNexis 2015)

Ilbert Courtney, *The Government of India: Being a Digest of the Statute Law relating thereto with Historical Introduction and Explanatory Matter* (3rd edn, London: Clarendon Press 1915)

Kamath Nandan, *Law relating to Computers Internet & E-commerce* (4th edn, Delhi: Universal Law Publishing 2009)

Krishnamachari V and Gogia Surender, *TS Venkatesa Iyer's The Law of Contracts & Tenders* (Vol 2, 10th edn, Hyderabad: S Gogia and Co 2011)

Macpherson William, *Outlines of the Law of Contracts as administered by the Courts of British India not established by Royal Charter* (London: RC LePage and Co 1864)

Pollock Frederick and Mulla Dinshah, *The Indian Contract Act* (2nd edn, Bombay: NM Tripathi & Co 1909)

Pollock Frederick and Mulla Dinshah, *The Indian Contract and Specific Relief Acts* (14th updated edn, Gurgaon: Lexis Nexis 2014)

Raman A, *MLJ: Law of Contract and Specific Relief* (Vol I, 2nd edn, Nagpur: LexisNexis Butterworths Wadhwa 2009)

Rao SV Joga, *Computer Contracts and Information Technology Law* (Part 1, 1st edn, New Delhi: Wadhwa and Co 2003)

Saharay HK, *Dutt on Contract: The Indian Contract Act, 1872* (9th edn, Calcutta: Eastern Law House 2000)

Sarkar Sudipto and Kannan K, *Sarkar on Specific Relief Act* (16th edn, Gurgaon: LexisNexis Butterworths Wadhwa Nagpur 2007)

Setalvad MC, *The Common Law in India* (London: Stevens & Sons 1960)

Singh Avtar, *Contract and Specific Relief* (11th edn, Lucknow: Eastern Book Co 2013)

Stokes Whitley, *Anglo-Indian Codes Vol 1* (London: OUP 1888)

Treitel GH, *The Law of Contract* (11th edn, London: Thomson Sweet & Maxwell 2003)

Venkatraman S and Ramamoorthy K, *TS Venkatesa Iyer's The Law of Contracts* (Vol 1, 4th edn, Hyderabad: Asia Law House 1983)

B. Major Articles

Abhilash CM, 'E-Commerce Law in Developing Countries: An Indian Perspective' (2002) 11 Info & Com Tech L 269–281

Ahmad Farooq, 'Electronic Commerce with an Indian Perspective' (2001) 9 Int'l JL & Info Tech 133

Atiyah P, 'Consideration: A Restatement' in (ed) *Essays on Contract* (Oxford: Clarendon Press 1986)

Capper David, 'Common Mistake in Contract Law' (2009) Singapore Journal of Legal Studies 457–473

Chatterjee Bimal Kumar, 'Pre-Contract Negotiations: Are they Enforceable?' (2011) AIR 54–58

Jain MP, *The Law of Contract before its Codification* (1972) 14 (Special Issue) JILI 178

Kamat Devadatt, 'Information Technology Act, 2000: A Contractual Perspective' (2004) 1 SCC (Jour) 11

Mishra Sachin, 'Determining Jurisdiction over E-Commerce Disputes in India' <http://docs.manupatra.in/newsline/articles/Upload/FE4BA350-DBEF-49DA-97D4-09E54ED8B813.pdf> accessed 24 November 2014

Palmer Vernon Valentine, 'Contracts in Favour of Third Persons in Europe: First Steps Toward Tomorrow's Harmonization' (2003) 11(1) European Review of Private Law 8

Pandey Ashalika, 'Doctrine of Privity of Contract Under Indian Law: Should it Be Abolished in Toto or Subject to Certain Proviso?' (7 April 2013). available at SSRN: <http://ssrn.com/abstract=2246273> accessed January 2016

Pandey Atul Kumar, 'E-Contracts: Mail Box Rule and Legal Impact of the Information Technology Act' (2000) I(IV) RLR <http://rostrumlegal.com/blog/e-contracts-mail-box-rule-and-legal-impact-of-the-information-technology-act-2000-by-atul-kumar-pandey/> accessed 31 October 2014

Patra Atul Chandra, *Historical Background of the Indian Contract Act, 1872* (1962) 4 JILI 373

Sharma Priyesh, 'Treatment of Doctrine of Privity by Indian Judiciary' <http://www.mondaq.com/india/x/243778/Contract+Law/Treatment+Of+Doctrine+Of+Privity+By+Indian+Judiciary> accessed January 2016

Swaminathan Shivprasad, 'Eclipsed by Orthodoxy: The Vanishing Point of Consideration and the Forgotten Ingenuity of the Indian Contract Act 1872' (2017) 12 Asian J Comp L 141

Tavella David F, 'Is Privity Dead? Should it Be?' (2012) 8 NYU J L and Bus 505

Teeven Kevin M, 'Consensual Path to Abolition of Preexisting Duty' (1999) 34 Val U L Rev 43

Treitel GH, 'Consideration a Critical Analysis of Professor Atiyah's Fundamental Restatement' (1976) 50 ALJ 439

Vogenauer Stefan, 'The Effects of Contracts on Third Parties: The Avant-projet de reforme in a Comparative Perspective' in J Cartwright, S Vogenauer, and S Whittaker (eds), *Reforming the French Law of Obligations* (Oxford: Hart Publishing 2009)

C. Major Cases

AR Iswaran Pillai v Sonnivevaru V Tharagan (1914) 38 Mad 753, AIR 1914 Mad 701: the promisee is the proper person to enforce a contract because his right is violated

Balasundra v Ranganath AIR 1929 Mad 794: s 63 of the ICA applies to unilateral remissions and not agreements

Bhagwandas Goverdhandas Kedia v Girdharilal Parshottamdass AIR 1966 SC 543: offer and acceptance by telephone

Chinnaya v Ramayya (1881) 4 Mad 137: in Indian law, consideration can move from a third party; hence the promisee can sue if consideration has moved from a third party, but the third party cannot sue on the contract

Commissioner of Wealth Tax, Bhopal v Abdul Hussain Mulla Muhammad Ali AIR 1988 SC 1417: test of intention to create legal relations

Deb Narayan Dutt v Chunilal Ghose (1914) ILR 41 Cal 137: Indian courts should apply the principles of equity, justice, and good conscience to achieve 'complete justice'

Dhanrajamal Gobindram v Shamji Kalidas AIR 1961 SC 1285: s 29 of the ICA accounts for contracts that are 'capable of being made certain'; consequently additional evidence could be allowed to make clear those clauses of the contract that are unclear at first blush

Dorasinga Tevar v Arunachalam Chetti (1898) 23 Mad 441: the promisee can recover from the promisor the amount that the promisor has promised to pay to a third party

Doraswami Iyer v Arunachala Ayyar AIR 1936 Mad 135: a promise is not supported by consideration unless the promisee has done something at the request of the promisor

Enercon (India) Ltd v Enercon Gmbh AIR 2014 SC 3152: legal effect of an arbitration clause even though the arbitration clause was part of an agreement the existence of which was in dispute

Jamna Das v Ram Autar Pande (1911) 39 IA 7 (PC): a mortgagee cannot sue to recover the amount promised by the purchaser to the seller (mortgagor) in a sale of mortgaged property to which the mortgagee is not a party

JK Enterprises v State of Madhya Pradesh AIR 1997 MP 68: postal rule; the proposer cannot revoke his offer after the acceptance has entered the course of transmission

Khardah & Co Ltd v Raymon & Co (India) Pvt Ltd AIR 1962 SC 1810, [1963] 3 SCR 183: an assignee of a contract can sue to enforce it

Krishna Lal Sadhu v Promila Bala Dasi AIR 1928 Cal 518: the use of words 'promisor' and 'promisee' in the ICA clearly do not allow a person to sue on a contract to which he is not a party

Life Insurance Corporation of India v Raja Vasireddy Komalavalli Kamba AIR 1984 SC 1014: without communication of an unconditional acceptance from the insurers, there was no binding agreement

Lothamasu Sabasiva Rao v Thadwarthi Balakotiah AIR 1973 AP 342: an unstamped promissory note not admissible in proof of a loan nor could the loan be proved through oral evidence
Mahabir Auto Stores v Indian Oil Corporation (1990) 3 SCC 752: contracts with public authorities
MC Chacko v State Bank of Travancore AIR 1970 SC 504, 1969 (2) SCC 343: except in the case of a beneficiary under a trust created by a contract or in the case of a family arrangement, no right may be enforced by a person who is not a party to the contract
Mirriyala China Subbaraidu v Kallarsu Mahadeva Rao AIR 1965 AP 171: application of s 63 of the ICA
Monnet Ispat & Energy Ltd v Union of India 11 SCC 1 (2012): promissory estoppel
Motilal Padampat Sugar Mills v Union of India 1969 SCR (3) 75: promissory estoppel
Muthukaruppa Mudali v Pi Mu Kathappudayan (1914) 24 MLJ 249: consideration must consist of benefits that are 'real' rather than illusory
Nair Service Society v Krishna Pillai Kunjukrishna Pillai AIR 1964 Ker 265: promissory estoppels in the context of subscription to charities
Nalini v Somasundaram AIR 1964 Mad 52: intention to create legal relations
Nandganj Sihori Sugar Co Ltd v Badri Nath Dixit AIR 1955 SC 1525: intention to create legal relations
Naresh Chandra Guha v Ram Chandra Samanta AIR 1952 Cal 93: disputes on matters not covered by the ICA should be decided on 'established English principles not inconsistent with principles of equity, justice and good conscience'
National Petroleum Co v Popatlal Mulji AIR 1936 Bom 344: the rule of privity must be introduced by the legislature, and not by the courts. The ICA 1872 supports the doctrine of privity because under its provisions, a promise is an agreement when the proposal made by the promisor is accepted by the person to whom it is made, the promisee
Nawab Khwaja Muhammad Khan v Nawab Husaini Begam (1910) 37 IA 152 (PC): rule of privity must give way to special circumstances in India where marriages are contracted for minors by their parents must be reckoned; hence, contracts between parents of married persons can sue on the contract. A charge can be enforced by the charge holder, even if not party to the transaction creating it
New Bank of India Ltd v Union of India (1977) 2 Del 672: the third party cannot enforce where the parties to the contract, while referring to a third party, have expressly declined him any benefit under the contract
NK Giriraja Shetty v NK Parthasarathy Shetty AIR 2006 Kant 180: agreements which are too uncertain will not be enforced
Raja Burdakanth Roy v Aluk Munjooree Dasiah (1848) 4 MIA 321 (PC): a third party cannot sue on contract, but can sue in tort
Raja of Venkatgiri v Krishnayya Rao (1948) 50 BOMLR 517: consideration can neither move pursuant to the recipient party's desire nor move voluntarily from the supplier of the consideration. If consideration falls in this twilight zone between desire and volition, it cannot support a contractual obligation
Rajasthan State Electricity Board v Dayal Wood Work AIR 1998 AP 381: offer and acceptance must match each other
Rajendra Kumar Verma v State of Madhya Pradesh & Ors AIR 1972 Madhya Pradesh 131: revocation in case of tender offers
Rajkishor Mohanty v Banabehari Patnaik AIR 1951 Ori 291: where there is clear intention the court will imply reasonable terms to give effect to the parties' intention
Ramachandra Chintaman v Kalu Raju (1878) ILR 2 Bom 362: contractual effect of promises that provide benefits in return for existing contractual obligations not recognized
Ramji Dayawala & Sons (P) Ltd v Invest Import AIR 1981 SC 2085: silence as acceptance of a contractual bargain
Rudra Pratap Singh v Ballabh Das AIR 1956 Pat 116: agreement without consideration lacks contractual force
Secretary of State v S Rangaswamy AIR 1928 Mad 198: unjust enrichment
Shuppu Ammal v Subramaniyan (1910) 33 Mad 238: a family member not a party can enforce a promise made in his favour in a partition of properties between other family members

SMS Tea Estates Pvt Ltd v Chandmari Tea Co Pvt Ltd (2011) 4 SCC 66: validity of the arbitration clause is not affected by the validity of the overall contract of which it is a clause

Somasundaram Pillai v The Provincial Government of Madras AIR 1947 Mad 366: an offer can be withdrawn even if an offer has been provisionally accepted

Sonia Bhatia v State of UP AIR 1981 SC 1274: transactions that involve consideration in order to distinguish such transactions from gifts

Sri Rajah Inuganti Kasturamma Bahadur Zamindarini v Chelikani Venkatasurayya Garu (1915) 29 Mad LJ 538: the existence of an obligation in the nature of a trust in favour of the third party can be inferred from the many circumstances including the conduct of the parties and the third party

State of West Bengal v BK Mondal and Sons AIR 1962 SC 779: party's right to compensation under an invalid contract

Suradhani Debi v Hari Charan Mahton AIR 1922 Pat 337: s 69, on reimbursement of person paying money due by another, in payment of which he is interested

Tirumulu Subbu Chetti v Arunachalam Chettiar AIR 1930 Mad 382 (FB): a person not party to a contract cannot sue even if all parties to the contract are parties to the proceedings

Trimex International FZE Ltd Dubai v Vedanta Aluminimum Ltd, India (2010) 3 SCC 1: email communications of acceptances ought not to be treated on a par with instantaneous communications

Union of India v Kishorilal Gupta & Bros AIR 1953 Cal 642: s 62 requires an agreement which necessarily implies consideration

UP Rajkiya Nirman Nigam Ltd v Indure Pvt Ltd AIR 1996 SC 1373: where the relationship between the parties could not achieve the status of a legally enforceable agreement, the arbitration clause did not have any force either (position has since changed)

W Srinivasavaradachariar v Dasu Reddiar AIR 1944 Mad 330, (1944) 1 Mad LJ 269: the promisee can claim compensation for breach of promise made in favour of third party

D. Foreign Cases

Butler Machine Tool Co Ltd v Ex-Cell-O Corp (England) Ltd [1977] EWCA Civ 9, [1979] 1 WLR 401, [1979] 1 All ER 965: battle of forms

Central London Property Trust Ltd v High Trees House Ltd [1947] KB 130: a mere promise, unsupported by consideration, can nevertheless lead to a judicially enforceable obligation on the party making the promise if certain conditions are satisfied

Collier v P & MJ Wright (Holdings) Ltd [2007] EWCA Civ 1329: promissory estoppel

Courtney & Fairbairn Ltd v Tolani Bros (Hotels) Ltd (1975) 1 WLR 297: contract to negotiate is not enforceable

Entores Ltd v Miles Far East Corporation [1955] EWCA Civ 3: postal rule was not applicable to instantaneous communications

Felthouse v Bindley (1862) EWHC CP J 35: silence does not lead to acceptance

Foakes v Beer [1884] UKHL 1: a promise to accept a lesser sum in repayment of the debt would not be binding if there is no other consideration for such a promise

Kepong Prospecting Ltd v Schimdt [1968] AC 810 (PC) (appeal from Malaysia): paras (a), (b), (c), and (e) of s 2 of the Act supported the English conception of a contract as an agreement on which only the parties could sue (provisions of the Malaysian law are the same as the ICA)

Paul Wilson & Co v Partenreederei Hannah Blumenthal (The Hannah Blumenthal) [1983] 1 All ER 34 (HL): relevant test of an intention to enter into a legal relationship is that which would be understood by a reasonable person in the shoes of the person receiving the proposal

Penny v Cole (*Pinnel's* case) (1602) 5 Co Rep 117a: a promise to accept a lesser sum in repayment of the debt would not be binding if there is no other consideration for such a promise

Scammell v Ouston [1941] AC 25: a contract with uncertain terms will not be enforced

Sudbrook Trading Estate Ltd v Eggleton [1983] 1 AC 44: uncertainty in pricing did not nullify the contractual obligations of the parties

Tweddle v Atkinson (1861) 1 B & S 393

Walford v Miles [1992] 2 AC 128: duty to negotiate in good faith not recognized

Williams v Roffey Bros & Nicholls (Contractors) Ltd [1989] EWCA Civ 5: benefits version of contractual obligations

E. Statutes/Acts

Arbitration and Conciliation Act, 1996, s 45
Consumer Protection Act, 1986, ss 2(d), 14
Indian Bills of Lading Act, 1856, s 1
Indian Contract Act, 1872
Indian Evidence Act, 1872, s 115
Indian High Courts Act, 1861
Indian Trusts Act 1882, s 6
Information Technology Act, 2000
Insurance Act, 1938, ss 38, 39
Insurance Laws (Amendment) Act 2015
Marine Insurance Act, 1963, ss 16(2), 52(2)
Married Women's Property Act, 1874, s 5
Motor Vehicles Act, 1988, ss 146, 147, 149
Negotiable Instruments Act, 1881, ss 8, 9, 36, 46, 48
Railways Act, 1989, s 74
Registration Act 1963, s 17
Specific Relief Act, 1963, ss 15, 38(2)
Transfer of Property Act, 1882, ss 39, 40, 109, 130, 135

F. Law Reform Efforts

Law Commission of India, Thirteenth Report, Ministry of Law, Government of India, 1958 <http://lawcommissionofindia.nic.in/1-50/report13.pdf>

Law Commission of India, Sixty-Seventh Report on the Indian Stamp Act, 1899 (1977) pp 3–4 http://lawcommissionofindia.nic.in/51-100/report67.pdf>

INDONESIA

A. Major Texts

Bell Gary F, 'Indonesia: The Challenges of Legal Diversity and Law Reform' in E Ann Black and Gary F Bell (eds), *Law and Legal Institutions of Asia—Traditions, Adaptations and Innovations* (New York: Cambridge University Press 2011)

Bell Gary F, 'Codification and Decodification: The State of the Civil and Commercial Codes in Indonesia' in Wen-Yeu Wang (ed), *Codification in East Asia—Selected Papers from the 2nd IACL Thematic Conference* (Heidelberg: Springer International 2014)

Budiono Herlien, *Asas Keseimbangan bagi Hukum Perjanjian Indonesia* (Bandung: Citra Aditya Bakti 2006)

Darus Badrulzaman Mariam et al, *KUH Perdata, Buku III—Hukum Perikatan dengan Penjelasan* (3rd edn, Bandung: Penerbit Alumni 1996)

Darus Badrulzaman Mariam et al, *Kompilasi Hukum Perikatan* (Bandung: Citra Aditya Bakti 2001)

Dewi Gemala et al, *Hukum Perikatan Islam di Indonesia* (Jakarta: Kencana 2007)

Fuady Munir, *Hukum Kontrak Dari Sudut Pandang Hukum Bisnis* (Bandung: Citra Aditya Bakti 2007)

Gautama Sudargo, *Indonesian Business Law* (3rd edn, Bandung: Citra Aditya Bakti 2006)

Gautama Sudargo and Hornick Robert N, *An Introduction to Indonesian Law—Unity in Diversity* (Bandung: Penerbit Alumni 1983)

Harahap M Yahya, *Segi-Segi Hukum Perjanjian* (Bandung: Penerbit Alumni 1986)

Hardjowahono Bayu Seto (ed), 'Naskah Akademik Rancangan Undang Undang Hukum Kontrak' (Academic Paper for a Draft Legislation on the Law of Contract) (National Law Reform Commission of the Ministry of Law and Human Rights, 2013)

Hasan A Madjedi, *Kontrak Minyak dan Gas Bumi Berazas Keadilan dan Kepastian Hukum* (Jakarta: Fikahati Aneska 2009)

Hooker MB, *Adat Law in Modern Indonesia* (Kuala Lumpur: OUP 1978)

Muhammad Abdulkadir, *Hukum Perikatan* (Bandung: Citra Aditya Bakti 1992)

Muhammad Abdulkadir, *Hukum Perdata Indonesia* (Bandung: Citra Aditya Bakti 2000)

'Naskah Akademik Peraturan Perundang-Undangan Tentang Hukum Perikatan' (Academic Paper on the Legislative Regulation on the Law of Obligations) (National Law Reform Commission of the Ministry of Justice, 1994)

Panggabean Henry P, *Penyalahgunaan Keadaan (Misbruik van Omstandigheden) Sebagai Alasan (Baru) Untuk Pembatalan Perjanjian (Berbagai Perkembangan Hukum Di Belanda)* [*The Abuse of Circumstances (Misbruik van Omstandigheden) as a (New) Ground for the Nullity of Contracts (Different Legal Developments in the Netherland)*] (Yogyakarta: Liberty 1992)

Panggabean Henry P, *Peranan Mahkamah Agung Melalui Putusan-Putusan Hukum Perikatan* (Bandung: Penerbit Alumni 2008)

Prodjodikoro R Wirjono, *Azas-Azas Hukum Perjanjian* (Bandung: Mandar Maju 2000)

Salim HS, *Hukum Kontrak—Teori dan Teknik Penyusunan Kontrak* (Jakarta: Sinar Grafika 2003)

Satrio J, *Cessie, Subrogatie, Novatie, Kompensatie dan Percampuran Hutang* (Bandung: Penerbit Alumni 1999)

Satrio J, *Hukum Perikatan—Perikatan Yang Lahir Dari Perjanjian—Buku I dan II* [*The Law of Obligations—Obligations Arising from Agreements—Book I and II*] (Bandung: Citra Aditya Bakti 1995)

Simamora Yohanes Sogar, *Hukum Perjanjian—Prinsip Hukum Kontrak Pengadaan Barang dan Jasa oleh Pemerintah* (Yogyakarta: LaksBang PRESSindo 2009)

Simanjuntak PNH, *Pokok-Pokok Hukum Perdata Indonesia* (Jakarta: Djambatan 2005)

Subekti, *Aneka Perjanjian* (10th edn, Bandung: Citra Aditya Bakti 1995)

Subekti, *Hukum Perjanjian* (Jakarta: Penerbit Intermasa 2001)

Subekti, *Pokok-Pokok Hukum Perdata* (30th edn, Jakarta: Intermasa 2002)

Suharnoko, *Hukum Perjanjian—Teori dan Analisa Kasus* (Jakarta: Kencana 2008)

Syaifuddin Muhammad, *Hukum Kontrak—Memahami Kontrak dalam Perspektif Filsafat, Teori, Dogmatik, dan Pratik Hukum* (Bandung: Madar Maju 2012)

JAPAN

A. Major Texts

平井宜雄『債権各論Ｉ上契約総論』182–187頁(弘文堂、2008) (Hirai Yoshio, *Law of Obligations in Specific, I-1 Contracts in General*, pp 182–187 (Tokyo: Kobundo 2008))

Kihara Hiroyuki, *Tort Law in Japan* (Alphen aan den Rijn: Wolters Kluwer 2015)

能見善久、"民法総則"(第８版、2010年　弘文堂) (Nomi Yoshihisa and Shinomiya Kazuo, *General Provisions of the Civil Code* (8th edn, Tokyo: Kobundo 2010))

内田貴、"民法　２" (第3版、2011年、東京大学出版会) (Uchida Takashi, *Civil Code II* (3rd edn, Tokyo: Tokyo University Press 2011))

大村敦史、"新基本民法５　契約編" (2016年、有斐閣) (*New Fundamental Civil Code 5 (Contract)* (Tokyo: Yuhikaku 2016))

B. Major Articles

春田一夫『第三者のためにする契約の法理』(信山社、2002年) (Haruta Kazuo, *The Theory of Contracts for the Benefit of Third Parties* (Tokyo: Shinzansha 2002))

Kamo Akira, 'Crystallization, Unification, or Differentiation? The Japanese Civil Code (Law of Obligations) Reform Commission and Basic Reform Policy (Draft Proposals)' (2010) 24 Columbia J of Asian L 171

柏木昇 "日本の取引と契約法(上・下)" NBL (New Business Law) 500号16頁、501号16頁 (Kasiwagi Noboru, 'Japanese Transaction and Contract Law' NBL (New Business Law) No 500, p 16, No 501, p 16)

奥田昌道編『新版注釈民法(10)II』250–255頁(北川善太郎・潮見佳男)(有斐閣、2011) (Okuda Masamich (ed), *Japanese Civil Code Annotated*, Vol 10-II, pp 250–255 (written by Kitagawa Zentaro and Shiomi Yoshio) (2nd edn, Tokyo: Yuhikaku 2011))

新堂明子「第三者のためにする契約法理の現代的意義(１)(２・完)」法学協会雑誌115巻10号、11号(1998) (Shindo Akiko, 'On the Doctrine of Contracts for the Benefit of Third Parties—A Comparison Between Common Law and Japanese Civil Law' (1998) 115(10) Journal of the Jurisprudence Association 11)

Sono Hiroo, 'Integrating Consumer Law into the Civil Code: A Japanese Attempt at Re-codification' in Mary Keyes and Therese Wilson (eds), *Codifying Contract Law: International and Consumer Law Perspectives* (Aldershot: Ashgate 2014)

谷口知平・五十嵐清編『新版注釈民法(13)』(補訂版)695–792頁［中馬義直・新堂明子］(有斐閣、2006年) (Taniguchi Tomohei and Igarashi Kiyoshi (eds), *Japanese Civil Code Annotated*, Vol 13, pp 695–792 (written by Chuma Yoshinao, and Shindo Akiko) (2nd revised edn, Tokyo: Yuhikaku 2006))

Uchida Takashi, 'Contract Law Reform in Japan and the UNIDROIT Principles' (2011) Uniform L Rev 705

山本豊「免責条項の第三者効——履行補助者保護効を中心に」同『不当条項規制と自己責任・契約正義』(1997)201頁以下 (Yamamoto Yutaka, 'The Effect Against Third Parties of Exemption Clauses' in Yamamoto Yutaka, *Regulation of Unfair Terms and Self Responsibility and Contractual Justice*, pp 201–229 (Tokyo: Yuhikaku 1997))

民法(債権法)改正検討委員会『詳解債権法改正の基本方針Ⅴ』363–399頁(商事法務、2010)(The Japanese Civil Code (Law of Obligations) Reform Commission, the Draft Proposals of the Reform of the Law of Obligations, Full Account, Vol V, pp 363–399, Commission)

C. Major cases

大判明治41年9月22日民録14輯907頁 (Former Supreme Court, judgment, 22 September Meiji 41 (1908), Civil Reports, Vol 14, p 907): a third party beneficiary acquires property rights as well as a claim based on a contract for the benefit of the third party in which A and B agree to transfer the ownership of B's land to C (the beneficiary)

大判大正3年4月22日民録20輯313頁 (Former Supreme Court, judgment, 22 April Taisho 3 (1914), Civil Reports, Vol 20, p 313): the promisee's right arises at the time of the conclusion of contract even before the acknowledgement by the third party beneficiary, unless any time of commencement or condition precedent is set to the contract

大判昭和10年10月10日新聞3909号18頁 (Former Supreme Court, judgment, 10 October Showa 10 (1935), Law Paper, no 3909, p 18): a (an obligor) and B (an acceptor) may agree that B shall assume A's obligation against C jointly and severally as a contract for the benefit of the third party obligee C

大判昭和11年7月4日民集15巻1304頁 (Former Supreme Court, judgment, 4 July Showa 11 (1936), Civil Reports, Vol 15, p 1304): a contract is not a contract for the benefit of the third party unless it is agreed that the third party shall acquire a right to demand directly against the promisor to perform

最判昭和43年12月5日民集22巻13号2876頁 (Supreme Court, judgment, 5 December Showa 43 (1968), Civil Reports, Vol 22, no 13, p 2876): a contract between a bank and its customer to transfer money electrically is not regarded as a contract for the benefit of the third party recipient based on the practices of the banks

Supreme Court 8 May 1913: the transfer of money and the agreement need not be made at the same time to make a loan contract

Supreme Court 28 June 1944: internal disagreement makes no contract

Supreme Court 18 September 1984: there may be responsibility for breaking off contractual negotiations

Supreme Court 29 November 1985: an irrevocable gift contract requires writing that represents the intent of the donor but it does not have to be a formal document

Supreme Court 25 April 1935: refusal to enforce a formal gift contract

D. Other Relevant Material

潮見佳男、"民法(債権関係)改正法案の概要、金融財政事情研究会、2015年 (Shiomi Yoshio, 'Outline of bill to revise the Civil Code (Relationship)', Kinzai Institute for Financial Affairs (2015))

E. Online Resources

<http://law.e-gov.go.jp/cgi-bin/idxsearch.cgi> 法令データ提供システム(Japanese Civil Code in Japanese)

<http://www.japaneselawtranslation.go.jp/?re=01> 日本法令外国語訳データベース (Japanese law database in English and Japanese)

<http://www.japaneselawtranslation.go.jp/law/detail/?ft=2&re=01&dn=1&yo=%E6%B0%91%E6%B3%95&ia=03&kn[]=%E3%81%BF&x=64&y=13&ky=&page=1> (the Civil Code Parts I, II, and III)

<http://www.moj.go.jp/content/000056024.pdf> (Translation of the Japanese Civil Code)

<http://www.moj.go.jp/MINJI/minji07_00175.html> 民法の一部を改正する法律案 (第189回国会提出)および関連資料 (A bill to revise the part of the Civil Code, presented to the 189th session of the Diet, with related materials in Japanese)

<http://wwr7.ucom.ne.jp/sh01/> a民法(債権法)改正検討委員会(Japanese Civil Code (Law of Obligations) Reform Commission (work by academics))

<http://wwr7.ucom.ne.jp/sh01/english/draft_en.html> 「債権法改正の基本方針」(Draft Civil Code proposal, in English)

<http://www.moj.go.jp/shingi1/shingikai_saiken.html> 法務省 法制審議会 民法(債権関係)部会 (Homepage of the Legislative Council of the Ministry of Justice, Reform of the Civil Law (obligation))

MALAYSIA

A. Major Texts

Cheong May Fong, *Contract Law in Malaysia* (Petaling Jaya: Sweet & Maxwell 2010)

Krishnan Arjunan and Abdul Majid Nabi Bakhsh, *Contract Law in Malaysia* (Petaling Jaya: Malayan Law Journal 2007)

Mohaimin Ayus, *Law of Contract in Malaysia* (Petaling Jaya: Sweet & Maxwell 2009)

Nilima Bhadbhade, *Pollock & Mulla: The Indian Contract and Specific Relief Acts* (updated 14th edn, Bombay: LexisNexis 2013)

Phang Andrew BL, *Cheshire, Fifoot and Furmston's Law of Contract* (2nd Singapore and Malaysian edn, Singapore: Butterworths Asia 1998)

Syed Ahmad SA Alsagoff, *Principles of the Law of Contract in Malaysia* (3rd edn, Petaling Jaya: LexisNexis: 2010)

Visu Sinnadurai, *Law of Contract* (4th edn, Petaling Jaya: Sweet & Maxwell 2011)

B. Major Articles

Edwin C, 'Contracts for the Benefit of Third Parties—Will Our Common Law See the Demise of Privity of Contract?' [2000] 4 MLJ i

Edwin C, 'Judicial Interference with Standard Form Contracts—A Critique on *Ho Lai Ying v Cempaka Finance Bhd*' [2005] 5 MLJ xiii

Kadir Rokiah, 'Old Law and New Environment: The Basis of the Determination of Place of Contract for Acceptance via Electronic Mail' [2008] 3 MLJ lxiii

Kadir Rokiah, 'Websites: The Best Policy Approach' [2009] 3 MLJ cliv

Matta Ali Mohammad, 'Promissory Estoppel: Does Malaysia Need this Doctrine?' [2006] 6 MLJ lxviii

Munir Abu Bakar and Mohd Yasin Siti Hajar, 'Electronic Commerce Bill 2006: An Oversight or Wanting a Different or…?' [2006] 4 MLJ i

Tan Pei Meng, 'Circumventing the Privity Rule in Malaysia' (2009) 4 JICLT 262

Trakic Adnan, '"Offer" and its Significance for Formation of Contracts: The Malaysian Perspective' [2012] 5 MLJ cxlvii

C. Major Cases

Aseambankers Malaysia Bhd & Ors v Shencourt Sdn Bhd & Anor [2014] 4 MLJ 619 (Court of Appeal): there is no duty placed on parties to negotiate in good faith because it is unworkable in practice and inherently repugnant to the adversarial position of the parties when involved in negotiations

Aspac Lubricants (M) Sdn Bhd v Ketua Pengarah Hasil Dalam Negeri [2007] 6 MLJ 65 (Court of Appeal): consideration must be sufficient but need not be adequate

Ayer Hitam Tin Dredging Malaysia Bhd v YC Chin Enterprises Sdn Bhd [1994] 2 MLJ 754 (Supreme Court): where an agreement contains the phrase 'subject to contract', the court will examine the parties' communications to determine whether there was an intention that no contract is to come into existence until a formal sale and purchase agreement has been executed

Badiaddin bin Mohd Mahidin v Arab Malaysian Finance Bhd [1998] 1 MLJ 393: Federal Court's ruling that privity doctrine is entrenched and fundamental in Malaysia

Bank Negara Indonesia v Philip Hoalim [1973] 2 MLJ 3 (Privy Council): the existence of a contractual relationship is not necessary for promissory estoppel to apply

Beca (Malaysia) Sdn Bhd v Tan Choong Kuan & Anor [1986] 1 MLJ 390 (Court of Appeal): unlike English law, Malaysian contract law makes a distinction between an agreement and a contract

Boustead Trading (1985) Sdn Bhd v Arab-Malaysian Merchant Bank Bhd [1995] 3 MLJ 331 (Federal Court): the doctrine of promissory estoppel is not limited to defendants only and plaintiffs can have recourse to the doctrine in order to assist the main cause of action. A defendant who invokes the doctrine of promissory estoppel need not prove that in relying on the promise or representation, he had acted to his detriment. In addition, the defendant need not prove that he was induced by the conduct of the promisor or representor to act in a particular way. It is sufficient for him to prove that he was influenced by the encouragement or representation such that it would be unconscionable for the representor or promisor thereafter to enforce his strict legal rights

Cipta Cermat Sdn Bhd v Perbandaran Kemajuan Negeri Kedah [2007] 2 MLJ 746 (Court of Appeal): the court can adopt an objective approach in analysing whether a contract exists

Datuk M Kayveas v See Hong Chen & Sons Sdn Bhd [2014] 4 MLJ 64 (Federal Court): use of the constructive trust in enforcing proprietary rights

Government of Malaysia v Gurcharan Singh [1971] MLJ 211 (High Court): agreements entered into with minors are void

GR Nair v Eastern Mining & Metals Co Sdn Bhd [1974] 1 MLJ 176 (High Court): trust of a promise was not established because of lack of intention to create a trust

Guthrie Waugh Bhd v Malaippan Muthucumaru [1972] 1 MLJ 35 (High Court): contracts under seal are not recognized under the CA 1950 unless the exceptions to s 26(a) apply

Kepong Prospecting Ltd & Ors v Schmidt [1968] 1 MLJ 170 (Privy Council): consideration may be given by the promisee or someone else who is not a party to the contract but the privity doctrine is entrenched and fundamental in Malaysia

Macon Works & Trading Sdn Bhd v Phang Hon Chin & Anor [1976] 2 MLJ 177 (High Court): an offer would lapse after a reasonable time because failure to accept within a reasonable time implied rejection by the offeree

Madam Loh Sai Nyah v American International Assurance Co Ltd [1998] 2 MLJ 310 (Court of Appeal): an offer must be communicated to the offeree before acceptance can take place

Mahomed Syedol Ariffin v Yeoh Ooi Gark [1916] 2 AC 575 (Privy Council): a minor is not estopped from pleading his minority even though he had misrepresented his age to the other party

Malaysian Australian Finance Co Ltd v The Law Union & Rock Insurance Co Ltd [1972] 2 MLJ 10 (High Court): trust of a promise to enforce third party's right

Preston Corporation Sdn Bhd v Edward Leong [1982] 2 MLJ 22 (Federal Court): an offer is an intimation of willingness by an offeror to enter into a legally binding contract and, hence, is synonymous with the word 'proposal' which is used in the CA 1950

Rajeswary & Anor v Balakrishnan & Ors (1958) 3 MC 178 (High Court): a minor can sue or be sued for a breach of promise to marry

Sim Siok Eng v Government of Malaysia [1978] 1 MLJ 15 (Federal Court): the doctrine of promissory estoppel is applicable in Malaysia and its effect is suspensory in nature

South East Asia Insurance Berhad v Nasir Ibrahim [1992] 2 MLJ 355 (Supreme Court): past consideration is valid in Malaysia only to the extent that the past act was done at the desire of the promisor but not if it was done voluntarily

Takako Sakao v Ng Pek Yuen [2009] 6 MLJ 751 (Federal Court): a constructive trust was imposed for breach of fiduciary duty by a partner; the equitable interest in the property which is protected under the constructive trust was enforced by the beneficial owner against a third party who is not a bona fide purchaser of the trust property

YK Fung Securities Sdn Bhd v James Capel (Far East) Ltd [1997] 2 MLJ 621 (Court of Appeal): a contract that is made by way of instantaneous communication is deemed to be made at the place where the offeror hears from the offeree about the acceptance

D. Other Relevant Materials

(a) Statutes

Age of Majority Act 1971
Consumer Protection (Amendment) Act 2010
Contracts Act 1950
Contracts (Amendment) Act 1976
Civil Law Act 1956

SINGAPORE

A. Major Texts

Phang Andrew BL, *Cheshire, Fifoot and Furmston's Law of Contract* (2nd Singapore and Malaysian 2nd edn, Singapore: Butterworths, 1998)

Phang Andrew BL, *From Foundation to Legacy—The Second Charter of Justice* (Singapore: Singapore Academy of Law 2006)

Phang Andrew BL (ed), *The Law of Contract in Singapore* (Singapore: Singapore Academy of Law 2012)

Phang Andrew BL and Goh Yihan, *Contract Law in Singapore* (Alphen aan den Rijn: Kluwer Law International 2012)

Tan Cheng Han, *The Law of Agency* (2nd edn, Singapore: Academy Publishing 2017)

B. Major Articles

Kwek ML, 'Law, Fairness and Economics—Unilateral Mistake in Digilandmall' (2005) 17 SAcLJ 411

Loke Alexander, 'The "Broad Ground" and the Not-so-narrow Ground in Singapore: *Chia Kok Leong v Prosperland Pte Ltd*' (2007) 23 JCL 148

Phang Andrew BL, 'Cementing the Foundations: The Singapore Application of English Law Act 1993' (1994) 28 UBC LR 205

Phang Andrew BL, 'Contract Formation and Mistake in Cyberspace—The Singapore Experience' (2005) 17 SAcLJ 361

Phang Andrew BL and Seng D, 'The Singapore Electronic Transactions Act 1998 and the Proposed Article 2B of the Uniform Commercial Code' (1999) 7 Int'l J Law & IT 10

Tan CH, 'Contract Modifications, Consideration and Moral Hazard' (2005) 17 SAcLJ 566

Tan KH, 'Breaking New Ground: The Electronic Transactions Act 1998' (1999) Asia Business L Rev 64

Tan Sook Yee, 'A Tale of the Tiahs and the Flexibility of Equity' (1995) 7 SAcLJ 195

Tan Yock Lin, 'Choses in Action: Still More Contract than Property?' (2010) 26 JCL 160

Tjio Hans, 'Undue Influence, Unconscionability and Good Faith' (1996) 8 SAcLJ 429

Woon W, 'The Applicability of English Law in Singapore' in KYL Tan (ed), *The Singapore Legal System* (Singapore: Singapore University Press 1999)

Yeo Tiong Min, 'When Do Third Party Rights Arise under the Contracts (Rights of Third Parties) Act 1999 (UK)?' (2001) SAcLJ 34

Yeo Tiong Min, 'Unilateral Mistake in Contract: Five Degrees of Fusion of Common Law and Equity' [2004] SJLS 227

C. Major Cases

Aircharter World Pte Ltd v Kontena Nasional Bhd [1999] 2 SLR(R) 440: when construing if offer and acceptance has taken place, the courts will look at the objective circumstances and not give effect to the unexpressed intentions of the parties

Alrich Development Pte Ltd v Rafiq Jumabhoy [1995] 2 SLR(R) 340: an offer need not be made to specified individuals but can be made to the world or a class of persons

Anwar Patrick Adrian & Anor v Ng Chong & Hue LLC & Anor [2014] SGCA 34: solicitor found to owe duty of care in tort of negligence for economic loss caused to non-client third party

Brader Daniel John v Commerzbank AG [2014] 2 SLR 81: generally, acceptance must be communicated to the offeror unless this requirement has been waived

Chia Kok Leong v Prosperland [2005] SGCA 12: availability of substantial damages to the promisee when promisor's breach of contract causes loss to third party, broad ground principle regarded as more consistent with 'principle'

Choo Tiong Hin v Choo Hock Swee [1959] 1 MLJ 67: notwithstanding offer and acceptance, and consideration, no enforceable contract arises if there is no intention to create legal relations between the parties
Chwee Kin Keong v Digilandmall.com Pte Ltd [2004] 2 SLR(R) 594 (High Court): offer and acceptance in the context of electronic transactions
Chwee Kin Keong v Digilandmall.com Pte Ltd [2005] 1 SLR(R) 502: discusses the doctrine of unilateral mistake
CLAAS Medical Centre Pte Ltd v Ng Boon Ching [2010] 2 SLR 386: judicial interpretation of ss 2(1)(b), 2(2), and 3 of the Contract (Rights of Third Parties) Act
Cooperatieve Centrale Raiffeisen-Boerenleenbank BA (trading as Rabobank International), Singapore Branch v Motorola Electronics Pte Ltd [2011] 2 SLR 63: contracts should not be implied lightly
Dickson Trading (S) Pte Ltd v Transmarco Ltd [1987] SLR(R) 674: an offeror in a unilateral contract has an obligation not to revoke the offer after the offeree has embarked on the performance of the condition
Family Food Court (a firm) v Seah Booh Lock [2008] SGCA 31: protection of the promisee's performance interest, availability of damages to the promisee under the 'broad' and 'narrow' ground principles
Fong Holdings Pte Ltd v Computer Library (S) Pte Ltd [1991] 1 SLR(R) 834: the conferment of a practical benefit on a party can amount to consideration even though the party conferring the benefit was already under a legal obligation to perform the act
Gay Choon Ing v Loh Sze Ti Terence Peter [2009] 2 SLR(R) 332: distinction between an offer and an invitation to treat, and outlines a coda on the doctrine of consideration
Jiang Haiying v Tan Lim Hui [2009] 3 SLR(R) 13: English law collateral contract principles endorsed
Lam Chi Kin David v Deutsche Bank AG [2011] 1 SLR 800: doctrine of promissory estoppel may prevent a promisor from resiling from the promise even though such promise was not supported by consideration from the promisee
Midlink Development Pte Ltd v The Stansfield Group Pte Ltd [2004] 4 SLR(R) 258: whether there has been acceptance of an offer is to be determined objectively and acceptance can be inferred from conduct where such conduct objectively points towards an unequivocal acceptance
Overseas Union Insurance Ltd v Home and Overseas Insurance Co Ltd [2002] 2 SLR(R) 1: enforceable contract requires an offer from one party to be accepted by another
RSP Architects v MCST Plan 1075 (Eastern Lagoon) [1999] 2 SLR 449: duty of care in tort of negligence for pure economic loss
RSP Architects v Ocean Front [1996] 1 SLR 113: duty of care in tort of negligence for pure economic loss
Sea-Land Service Inc v Cheong Fook Chee Vincent [1994] 3 SLR(R) 250: consideration is required for an agreement to be enforceable
Spandeck Engineering (S) Pte Ltd v Defence Science & Technology Agency [2007] SGCA 37: single test for duty of care under tort of negligence applicable to all kinds of loss
Tribune Investment Trust Inc v Soosan Trading Co Ltd [2000] 2 SLR(R) 407: where a person accepts an offer though such person knows that the offeror did not intend to make an offer despite the objective appearance of such offer, the offeror is not bound
Vaswani Lalchand Challaram v Vaswani Roshni Anilkumar [2005] 3 SLR(R) 625: distinction between privity rule and consideration rule
Yusen Air & Sea Service (S) Pte Ltd v Changi International Airport Services Pte Ltd [1999] 3 SLR(R) 95: collateral contract reasoning applied to allow third party to enforce a limitation of liability clause

D. Other Relevant Materials

(a) Legislation

Electronic Transactions Act, Cap 88, 2011 Rev edn
Civil Law Act, Cap 43, 1999 Rev edn—ss 6 and 7
Contract (Rights of Third Parties) Act, Cap 53B, 2002 Rev edn
Conveyancing and Law of Property Act, Cap 61, 1994 Rev edn—s 53

(b) Law Reform Committee Reports

Report on the Contracts (Rights of Third Parties) Bill (2001)

E. Online Resources

<https://www.lawnet.sg/lawnet/web/lawnet/home (Database of Singapore judicial decisions)

<http://www.singaporelawwatch.sg/slw/judgments.html> (Recent judicial decisions. The Singapore Law Watch website provides free access to recent judgments for three months from their date of publication)

<http://statutes.agc.gov.sg> (Singapore statutes)

SOUTH KOREA

A. Major Texts

김형배, "채권각론" (2판, 박영사. 2001) (Kim Hyeong Bae, *Special Part of Obligation Law* (2nd edn, Seoul: Pakyoungsa 2001))

김재형, "법률행위의 확정과 그 기준" 《서울대학교 법학》 *2001*년, *41*권, *1*호 (Kim Jae Hyung, 'Standard of Determining the Meaning of a Juridical Act' (2001) 41(1) Seouldaehakgyo beobpak (Seoul National University Law Journal))

김증한, "채권각론" (박영사. 1988) (Kim Jeung Han, *Special Part of the Obligation Law* (Seoul: Pakyoungsa 1988))

김주수, "채권각론" (2판, 삼영사. 1997) (Kim Joo Soo, *Special Part of Obligation Law* (2nd edn, Seoul: Samyoungsa 1997))

김상용, "채권각론" (2판, 법문사. 2003) (Kim Sang Yong, *Special Part of Obligation Law* (2nd edn, Seoul: Beopmoonsa 2003))

곽윤직, "채권각론" (6판, 박영사. 2005) (Kwak Yoon Jik, *Special Part of Obligation Law* (6th edn, Seoul: Pakyoungsa 2005))

이은영, "채권각론" (5판, 박영사. 2005) (Lee Yeun Young, *Special Part of Obligation Law* (5th edn, Seoul: Pakyoungsa 2005))

박준서 편, "민법주석" (3판, 한국사법행정학회. 1999) (Park Joon Seo (ed), *Annotated Civil Law* (3rd edn, Seoul: Hankgooksabeobhaengjeonghakhoe 1999))

송덕수, "신 민법강의" (5판, 박영사. 2012) (Song Deok Soo, *New Civil Law Lecture* (5th edn, Seoul: Pakyoungsa 2012))

B. Major Articles

최희섭, "원시적 불능론과 민법 535조", 《재산법연구》 1992년, 9권, 1호 (Choi Heung Seop, '*Culpa in Contrahendo* and Article 535 of the Civil Code' (1992) 9(1) Jaesanbeob Yeongoo (Studies on Property Law))

Kwon Youngjoon, 'Korea: Bridging the Gap between Korean Substance and Western Form' in E Ann Black and Gary F Bell (eds), *Law and Legal Institutions of Asia* (Cambridge: Cambridge University Press 2011)

Kwon Youngjoon, 'Civil Law and Civil Procedure Law' in Korean Legislation Institute (ed), *Introduction to Korean Law* (Heidelberg: Springer 2013)

Kwon Youngjoon, 'Pure Economic Loss: A Korean Perspective' (2011) 10(2) J Korean L

양창수, "원시적 불능론", 《민법연구》 1995년, 5권 (Yang Chang Soo, '*Culpa in Contrahendo*' (1995) 5 Minbeob Yeongoo (Studies on the Civil Law))

C. Major Cases

Supreme Court Decision, 26 October 1993, *93Da2629, 2636*: regarding natural interpretation, the interpretation of a contract based on the actual intention of the parties

Supreme Court Decision, 14 May 2009, *2008Da90095*: regarding normative interpretation, the interpretation based on the objectively understood intention of the parties

Supreme Court Decision, 23 November 2006, *2005Da13288*: regarding supplemental interpretation, the interpretation based on the hypothetical intention of the parties where parties have failed to make an agreement on a certain issue

Supreme Court Decision, 11 April 2003, *2001Da53059*: stating that a party may bear tortious liability for breaking off negotiations in a manner contrary to good faith and fair dealing

Supreme Court Decision, 26 January 1996, *94Da54481*: suggesting the factors to be considered when determining the existence of a third party beneficiary clause

Supreme Court Decision, 22 July 2005, *2005Da7566,7573*: stating that the promisee in a third party contract cannot seek the return of what he performed to the third party based on the claim for restoration or unjust enrichment

D. Other Relevant Materials

법무부 편, 2013년 법무부 민법 개정시안 – 조문편 – (법무부. 2013) (Ministry of Justice (ed), *2013 Civil Code Amendment Draft by Ministry of Justice—Provisions* (Ministry of Justice, 2013))

E. Online Resources

<http://elaw.klri.re.kr/kor_service/lawView.do?hseq=29453&lang=ENG> (English version of the Korean Civil Code)

TAIWAN

A. Major Texts

陳忠五，“民法(第十二版)”(台北：新學林。2013) (Chen Chung Wu (ed), *The Civil Code* (12th edn, Taipei: New Sharing Publishing 2013))

陳自強，“契約之成立與生效”(台北：元照出版社。2014) (Chen Tzu-Chiang, *Contract Formation and its Effects* (Taipei: Angle Publishing 2014))

鄭玉波，“民法債編總論(修訂二版)”(台北：三民書局。2002) (Cheng Yu Po, *General Principles of the Law of Obligation* (2nd edn, Taipei: Sanmin Publishing 2002))

邱聰智，“新訂民法債編通則(新訂二版)”(台北：承法數位文化有限公司。2013)(Chiu Cong Chie, *General Principles of the Law of Obligations* (2nd edn, Taipei: Lawbooks Publishing 2013))

林誠二，“債法總論新解(上)”(台北：瑞興圖書股份有限公司。2010) (Lin Cheng-Erh, *General Principles of the Law of Obligations (Vol 1)* (Taipei: Juihsing Publishing 2010))

孫森焱，“民法債編總論 (修訂版)”(台北：自刊。2013) (Sun Sen Yen, *General Principles of the Law of Obligations* (Newly Revised edn, Taipei: Wang Mu Hua 2012))

內田貴“債権各論(第3版)”(東京：東京大学出版社。2011) (Uchida Takashi, *Special Provisions of Obligations* (3rd edn, Tokyo: Tokyo University Press 2011))

王澤鑑，“債法原理(一)”(台北：自刊。2012) (Wang Tze-Chien, *Principles of the Law of Obligations I* (Taipei: Wang Mu Hua 2012))

王澤鑑，“民法物權”(台北：自刊。2011) (Wang Tze-Chien, *Property Law* (2nd edn, Taipei: Wang Mu Hua 2011))

王澤鑑，“侵權行為”(台北：自刊。2011) (Wang Tze Chien, *The Law of Torts* (Taipei: Wang Mu Hua 2011))

姚志明，“契約法總論”(台北：元照。2014) (Yau Chih-Ming, *General Principles of the Law of Contract* (Taipei: Angle Publishing 2014))

B. Major Articles

張永健，“購物網站標錯價之合約糾紛與行政管制—經濟分析觀點”，《政大法學評論》2016年，第144期，第155頁(Chang Yun-Chien, ‘Misquoted Prices in Online Retailing Websites: An Economic Analysis’ (2016) 9 ZhengDa FaxuepingLun (Chengchi Law Review) 155)

邱慧洳，“「指示給付關係」之不當得利—評最高法院95年度台上字第2610號判決”，《中正大學法學集刊》2006年，49期。(Chiu Hui-Ju, ‘Unjust Enrichment and Instruction Payment Relationship—An Analysis of the case TSC 95 Tai-Shangzi Case No. 2610’ (2006) 49 Zhongzhengdaxeu Faxuejikan (National Chung Cheng University Law Review) 143)

洪瑞君，“論第三人利益契約—以實務適用之綜合探討為中心”(國立臺灣大學法律學院碩士論文。2006) (Hung Jui-Chun, ‘Contracts for Third Parties—Practical Applications’ (National Taiwan University, College of Law, Master’s thesis, 2006))

曾品傑，“論契約之成立——從臺灣最高法院九十七年度台上字第二六七八號民事判決談起”，《月旦民商法雜誌》2013年，第41期,第107頁。(Jseng Pin-Chieh, ‘Formation of Contract—An Analysis of the case TSC 98 Tai-Shangzi Case No. 2678’ (2013) 41 Yuedan Minshangfa zazhi (Cross-Strait Law Review) 107)

林大洋，“給付型不當得利－以「指示給付關係」及「第三人利益契約」為例”，《法令月刊》2011年，第62卷7期。(Lin Da-Yang, ‘Unjust Enrichment and Contracts for Third Parties’ (2011) 62(7) Falingyuekan (The Law Monthly) 84)

林麗真，"網路交易標價錯誤之契約法律問題探討"，《東吳法律學報》2011年，第22卷4期，第126頁。(Lin Lih-Jen, 'A Study on the Legal Issues of Price Indication on the Internet' (2011) 22(4) Dongwu Falüxuebao (Soochow Law Review) 126)

蔡承育，"歐陸法下第三人利益契約制度之發展"(國立臺灣大學法律學院碩士論文。2015) (Tsai Cheng-Yu, 'The Historical Developments of Contracts for Third Party in the Civil Law Tradition' (National Taiwan University, College of Law, Master's thesis, 2015))

蔡晶瑩,"契約之成立與效力——錯誤"，《月旦民商法雜誌》2012年，第36期，第35頁。(Tsai Ching-Ying, 'Formation of Contract and Mistake' (2012) 36 Yuedan Minshangfa zazhi (Cross-Strait Law Review) 35)

蔡胥捷，"英美法上第三人利益契約與我國民法規定之比較研究-以美國法為比較重心"(東吳大學法律學院碩士論文。2001) (Tsai Hsu-Chieh, 'A Comparison of American and Taiwanese Law of Contracts for Third Parties' (Soochow University, School of Law, Master's thesis, 2001))

王澤鑑，"第三人利益買賣契約之解除及其效力"，《法令月刊》1992年，第43卷3期，第8頁。(Wang Tze-Chien, 'The Termination of a Contract for Third Party and its Effects' (1992) 43(3) Falingyuekan (The Law Monthly) 8)

C. Major Cases

Taiwan Supreme Court Decision 58 Tai-Shang No 715: an offer takes effect once it arrives at a place that is under the other party's control

Taiwan Supreme Court Decision 88 Tai-Shang No 1671: the subject matter of the interpretation is not the intention kept in the parties' minds, but that expressed *outwardly*

Taiwan Supreme Court Decision 73 Tai-Shang No 2540: an invitation to treat is a preliminary proposal to attract a person to make an offer. A good example is a newspaper advertisement

Taiwan Supreme Court Decision 82 Tai-Shang No 1850: an announcement of items for sale at an auction is regarded as an invitation to treat

Taiwan Supreme Court Decision 100 Tai-Shang No 1906: if contracts are successfully formed, no pre-contractual liability can arise

Taiwan Supreme Court Precedent 20 Tai-Shang No 2405: a sale contract does not give rise to an effect against a third person who is not a party to the contract

Taiwan Supreme Court Decision 69 Tai-Shang No 244: if parents, upon their divorce, make clear in their agreement that their children shall be entitled to demand certain benefits, a contract for the benefit of a third party is deemed to have been concluded

Taiwan Supreme Court Precedent 83 Tai-Shang No 836: both the creditor (promisee) and the third party beneficiary of a contract for a third party can claim compensation for their own loss resulting from the debtor's breach of contract

Taiwan Supreme Court Decision 87 Tai-Shang No 180: the debtor of a contract for a third party is entitled to refuse to render the performance to the third party if the contract is void, rescinded, or revoked

Taiwan Supreme Court Decision 72 Tai-Shang No 3887: once the third party beneficiary of a contract for a third party declares his intent to enjoy the benefit, the parties to the contract are no longer permitted to modify or revoke the contract

THAILAND

A. Major Texts

จิ๊ด เศรษฐบุตร, หลักกฎหมายแพ่งลักษณะนิติกรรมและหนี้ (พิมพ์ครั้งที่ 2, กรุงเทพ: คณะนิติศาสตร์ มหาวิทยาลัยธรรมศาสตร์ 2522) (Sethabutr Chit, *The Law of Juristic Acts and Obligations* (2nd edn, Bangkok: Faculty of Law, Thammasat University 1979))

จิ๊ด เศรษฐบุตร, หลักกฎหมายแพ่งลักษณะนิติกรรมและสัญญา แก้ไขเพิมเติมโดย ดาราพร ถิระวัฒน์ พิมพ์ครั้งที่ 7 (กรุงเทพ: โครงการตำราและเอกสารประกอบการสอน คณะนิติศาสตร์ มหาวิทยาลัย ธรรมศาสตร์, 2556) (Thirawat Daraphon (ed), *Sethabutr on the Law of Juristic Acts and Obligations* (7th edn, Bangkok: Faculty of Law, Thammasat University 2013))

จิตติ ติงศภัทิย์, ประมวลกฎหมายแพ่งและพาณิชย์ บรรพ ๒ มาตรา 354 ถึง 452 ว่าด้วยมูลแห่งหนี้ พิมพ์ครั้งที่ 5 แก้ไขเพิมเติม (นิติศาสตร์ ธรรมศาสตร์, 2526) (Tingsabadh Chitti, *The Civil and Commercial Code Book II: Sections 354 to 452 on the Sources of Obligations* (5th edn, Bangkok: Faculty of Law, Thammasat University 1983))

ชาญชัย แสวงศักดิ์, อิทธิพลของฝรั่งเศสในการปฏิรูปกฎหมายไทย (กรุงเทพมหานคร: สำนักพิมพ์นิติธรรม, 2539) (Sawaengsak Chanchai, *Influence of France on the Reformation of Thai Law* (Bangkok: Nititham Publishing 1996))

ไชยยศ เหมะรัชตะ, กฎหมายว่าด้วยสัญญา (พิมพ์ครั้งที่ 2, **กรุงเทพ: สำนักพิมพ์จุฬาลงกรณ์มหาวิทยาลัย** 2539) (Hemaratchata Chaiyos, *The Law of Contract* (2nd edn, Bangkok: Chulalongkorn University Press 1996))

ไชยยศ เหมะรัชตะ, คำอธิบายกฎหมายว่าด้วยสัญญา, พิมพ์ครั้งที่ 3 **(กรุงเทพ: สำนักพิมพ์แห่งจุฬาลงกรณ์มหาวิทยาลัย,** 2547) (Hemaratchata Chaiyos, *The Law of Contract* (3rd edn, Bangkok: Chulalongkorn University Press 2004))

ปรีดี เกษมทรัพย์, เอกสารประกอบการศึกษาวิชานิติปรัชญาชั้นปริญญาตรี ภาคหนึ่ง : บทนำทางทฤษฎี (กรุงเทพมหานคร: โรงพิมพ์และทำปกเจริญผล, 2526) (Kasemsup Predee, *Introduction to Jurisprudence for First Year Undergraduates I* (Bangkok: Jaroenpol Press 1983))

ปัญญา ถนอมรอด, คำอธิบายประมวลกฎหมายแพ่งและพาณิชย์ ว่าด้วย ยืม ค้ำประกัน จำนอง จำนำ (พิมพ์ครั้งที่ 9, **กรุงเทพ: กรุงสยาม** 2556) (Thanomrod Panya, *Loan, Surety, Mortgage, Pawn* (9th edn, Bangkok: Krung Siam 2013))

โรแบรต์ แลงกาต์, ประวัติศาสตร์กฎหมายไทย, เล่มที่ 2 **(กรุงเทพมหานคร: สำนักพิมพ์ไทยวัฒนาพาณิชย์,** 2526) (Lingat Robert, *The Thai Legal History Vol II* (Bangkok: Thai Watana Panich Press 1983))

ศนันท์กรณ์ โสตถิพันธุ์, หลักความรับผิดก่อนสัญญา (พิมพ์ครั้งที่ 3, **กรุงเทพ: วิญญูชน** 2548) (Sotthibandhu Sanunkorn, *Pre-Contractual Liability* (3rd edn, Bangkok: Winyuchon 2005))

ศนันท์กรณ์ โสตถิพันธุ์, คำอธิบายประมวลกฎหมายแพ่งและพาณิชย์ เรียงมาตรา ว่าด้วยสัญญา (กรุงเทพ: กองทุนศาสตราจารย์จิตติ ติงศภัทิย์ คณะนิติศาสตร์ มหาวิทยาลัยธรรมศาสตร์, 2552) (Sotthibandhu Sanunkorn, *An Explanation on the Civil and Commercial Code in Order of Sections: Contracts* (Bangkok: Professor Sethabutr Fund, Faculty of Law, Thammasat University 2008))

ศนันท์กรณ์โสตถิพันธุ์, คำอธิบายกฎหมายเช่าทรัพย์ – เช่าซื้อ (พิมพ์ครั้งที่ 5, **กรุงเทพ: วิญญูชน** 2554) (Sotthibandhu Sanunkorn, *Hire—Hire-Purchase* (5th edn, Bangkok: Winyuchon 2011))

ศนันท์กรณ์ โสตถิพันธุ์, คำอธิบายซื้อขาย แลกเปลี่ยน ให้ (พิมพ์ครั้งที่ 6, **กรุงเทพ: วิญญูชน** 2556) (Sotthibandhu Sanunkorn, *Sale, Exchange, Gift* (6th edn, Bangkok: Winyuchon Publication 2013))

ศนันท์กรณ์ โสตถิพันธุ์, คำอธิบายนิติกรรม – สัญญา (พิมพ์ครั้งที่ 18, **กรุงเทพ: วิญญูชน** 2557) (Sotthibandhu Sanunkorn, *Juristic Acts—Contracts* (18th edn, Bangkok: Winyuchon Publication 2014))

ศักดิ สนองชาติ, คำอธิบายประมวลกฎหมายแพ่งและพาณิชย์ว่าด้วยนิติกรรมและสัญญา,พิมพ์ครั้งที่ 11 **(กรุงเทพ: นิติบรรณการ,** 2557) (Sanongchart Sak, *The Civil and Commercial Code: Juristic Acts—Contracts* (11th edn, Bangkok: Nitibannakarn 2014))

เสนีย์ ปราโมช, ม.ร.ว., ประมวลกฎหมายแพ่งและพาณิชย์ว่าด้วยนิติกรรมและหนี้ เล่ม 1 **(ภาค** 1–2), **พิมพ์ที่ครั้งที่** 2 **(กรุงเทพ : นิติบรรณการ,** 2505) (Pramoj Seni, *Civil and Commercial Code: Juristic Acts and Obligations (Parts I–II) Vol I* (2nd edn, Bangkok: Nitibannakarn 1965))

เสนีย์ ปราโมช, ม.ร.ว., ประมวลกฎหมายแพ่งและพาณิชย์ว่าด้วยนิติกรรมและหนี้ (ภาค 1–2) **พุทธศักราช** 2478 **แก้ไขเพิ่มเติม พ.ศ.**2505, **เล่ม** 1–2 **(กรุงเทพมหานคร: โรงพิมพ์แสวงสุทธิการพิมพ์,** 2520) (Pramoj Seni, *Civil and Commercial Code: Juristic Acts and Obligations (Parts I–II)*, vols 1, 2 (Bangkok: Sawaengsutthikanphim Painting 1978))

อัครวิทย์ สุมาวงศ์, คำอธิบายประมวลกฎหมายแพ่งและพาณิชย์ว่าด้วยนิติกรรม-สัญญา (กรุงเทพ: สำนักอบรมศึกษากฎหมายแห่งเนติบัณฑิตยสภา, 2555) (Sumawong Akarawit, *Explaining the Civil and Commercial Code: Juristic Acts—Contracts* (Bangkok: Institute of Legal Education of the Thai Bar 2012))

B. Major Articles

กิตติวัฒน์ จันทร์แจ่มใส, 'สัญญาเพื่อประโยชน์ของบุคคลภายนอก: The UNIDROIT Principles of International Commercial Contracts (2004)

กับกฎหมายไทย', วารสารนิติศาสตร์ มหาวิทยาลัยธรรมศาสตร์ ปีที่ 39 **ฉบับที่** 2 **หน้า** 339–356 (Chunchaemsai Kittiwat, 'Contracts in Favour of Third Parties: The UNIDROIT Principles of International Commercial Contracts 2004 and Thai Laws' (2010) 39 Thammasat Law Journal 339)

พิชาญ บุญยง, 'การตรวจชำระและร่างประมวลกฎหมายในประเทศไทย (ตอนที่ 2)', **ไพจิตร ปุญญพันธ์ และจำรัส เขมะจารุ ผู้แปล, ดุลพาห เล่ม** 5 **ปีที่** 6 **(พฤษภาคม** 2502) (Guyon René, 'Revision and

Drafting of the Thai Codes (Part II)' translated by P Punyapan and C Kemacharu (1959) 6(5) Dulapaha)

Kasemsup Predee, 'Reception of Law in Thailand, A Buddhist Society' in M Chiba (ed), *Asian Indigenous Law* (London: KPI Ltd 1986) 267

C. Major Cases

Supreme Administrative Court Decision No อ 80/2548: lost profits recoverable by person submitting best quotation in a call for price inquiry

Supreme Administrative Court Decision No อ 154/2547: consequential loss not recoverable by best tenderer in a call for competitive bidding

Opinion of Attorney-General Case No 125/2533: suggesting delictual claim available in tandem with breach of tender contract

Supreme Court Decision No 3801/2555: promise to renew lease with price and duration 'fairly adjusted in accordance with customary practice' not sufficiently precise to constitute binding promise

Supreme Court Decision No 2952/2554: fictitious intention affecting only main contract and not collateral contract

Supreme Court Decision No 6342/2552: gift of land concealed as contract of sale; registration of sale valid as of gift

Supreme Court Decision No 3827/2552: strong presumption of no contract when essential terms not agreed upon

Supreme Court Decision No 657/2549: acceptance by conduct

Supreme Court Decision No 7308/2545: legitimate use of hire purchase of future property as secured financing; not concealing simple loan

Supreme Court Decision No 3942/2545: conduct of parties as well as trade practice relevant in determining what terms are regarded as essential

Supreme Court Decision No 2899/2545: legitimate use of hire purchase as secured financing; not concealing simple loan

Supreme Court Decision No 1441/2545: loan concealed as sale with the right of redemption

Supreme Court Decision No 8898/2544: suggesting delictual claim for refusal to conclude principal contract with best bidder

Supreme Court Decision No 6532/2544: sale prohibited by law concealed as mortgage together with granting of right of superficies

Supreme Court Decision No 5343/2542: existence of written contract not necessarily implies that parties regard written form as essential in agreeing new contract

Supreme Court Decision No 2036/2542: agreement 'subject to contract in writing' binding as contract when both parties agree on commencement of performance despite no written contract

Supreme Court Decision No 2286/2538: agreement to register mortgage on a later date is void; preliminary agreement to mortgage not recognized

Supreme Court Decision No 596/2538: rule of good faith interpretation applies in determining contents of 'trivial' points not agreed upon by parties; performance substantially completed despite hidden *dissens*

Supreme Court Decision No 1931/2537: unregistered but written promise to make a gift of land on a later date is incomplete

Supreme Court Decision No 4696/2536: loan concealed as sale; sale document treated as written evidence for purpose of loan

Supreme Court Decision No 848/2534: fictitious intention cannot be set up against third party acting in good faith

Supreme Court Decision No. 1418/2529: term for successful bidder to compensate for difference with price charged by alternative supplier considered object of contract of sale, not of tender contract

Supreme Court Decision No 378/2525: invalid sale of land 'transformed' as contract for delivery of possession for price

Supreme Court Decisions No. 1213/2517 (General Assembly): lessor's promise to renew lease must be accepted before lessee knew of lessor's death

Supreme Court Decision No 1124/2512: contract considered as having a lawful object when illegal motive by one party is not known to the other
Supreme Court Decision No 1170/2506: lessor's promise to renew lease must be accepted before end of original lease
Supreme Court Decision No 146/2495: unregistered but written lease of three years with an agreement to contract for lease for additional three years is enforceable up to three years only
Supreme Court Decision No 1004/2485: sale with a 'promise' to re-sell; a 'promise' binding for an indefinite period
Supreme Court Decision No 931/2480: disappointed caller entitled to confiscation of bidder's deposit but not compensation for other consequential loss
Supreme Court Decision No 12616/2555: single set of events giving rise to (1) assignment of debt and (2) contract for the benefit of third party
Supreme Court Decision No 7894/2553: tenant in unregistered lease enforcing agreement between landlord-vendor and purchaser—enforcement refused due to no proof of agreement even though purchaser had notice of lease
Supreme Court Decision No 7355/2553: testator's unpaid creditor enforcing compromise agreement between heirs
Supreme Court Decision No 2675/2551: cancellation of transfer of land in breach of divorce settlement was ordered in favour of the settlement beneficiaries
Supreme Court Decision No 277/2551: beneficiary need be determinable but need not be in existence at the time of the contract; beneficiary company incorporated after conclusion of contract
Supreme Court Decision No 2468/2549: 'assignment of contract' analysed as assignment of debt (transfer of assignor's rights) together with contract in favour of third party (transfer of assignor's obligations)
Supreme Court Decision No 987/2549: financial contributors enforcing contract between landowner and developer to register long lease in favour of prospective contributors
Supreme Court Decision No 3702/2545: contract for benefit of third party distinguishable from assignment of debt; no requirement that it be made in writing
Supreme Court Decision No 1950/2543: residual benefit reverts to promisee when beneficiary declines to accept the benefit
Supreme Court Decision No 778/2541: no residual benefit for promisee if the benefit can only be legally performed for beneficiary; agreement to create easement
Supreme Court Decision No 3467/2535: prospective transferee cannot demand lease transfer where lease agreement conditions transfer on landlord's approval
Supreme Court Decision No 6104/2534: modification/revocation of third party's right must be agreed upon by all original contracting parties prior to assent being given by third party
Supreme Court Decision No 639/2530: third party has no right of enforcement where agreement gives discretion to promisor whether to make performance in favour of third party
Supreme Court Decision No 489/2524: promisee entitled to take the benefit for himself if beneficiary has not given assent
Supreme Court Decision No 2873/2519: outsiders enforcing agreement between vendor and purchaser to respect a pre-existing arrangement to re-convey property to outsiders
Supreme Court Decision No 2733/2517: burden imposed on third party as condition for receiving benefit
Supreme Court Decision No 1366/2516: beneficiary given option to adopt hire purchase after purchaser's death; beneficiary obtaining direct right against vendor; property not forming part of purchaser's estate
Supreme Court Decision No 2401/2515: beneficiary's right uncrystallized as no assent given prior to beneficiary's death; benefits reverting to promisee or promisee's estate

D. Legislation

Act on Establishment of Administrative Courts and Administrative Court Procedure, B.E. 2542 (1999), s 9(3)
Civil and Commercial Code of Thailand, ss 149, 152, 154–155, 168–169, 174, 354–355, 360, 366–368, 454, 456, 523, 525–526, 538 (Contract)

Civil and Commercial Code of Thailand, ss 159, 306, 308, 314, 374–376, 627, 850, 881, 891 (Third Parities)
Civil Procedure Code of Thailand, s 57(1) (Third Parities)
Electronic Transactions Act B.E. 2544 (2001), ss 22–23

E. Other Materials

รายงานการประชุมร่างกฎหมาย วันที่ 25 **พฤษภาคม พระพุทธศักราช** 2468 (**ห้องสมุดสำนักงานคณะกรรมการกฤษฎีกา**) (*Reports of the Drafting Committee Meeting on 25th May 1925* (Library of the Office of the Council of State, 1925))
บันทึกคำสัมภาษณ์ พระยามานวราชเสวี (**ภาควิชานิติศึกษาทางสังคม ปรัชญาและประวัติศาสตร์ คณะนิติศาสตร์ มหาวิทยาลัยธรรมศาสตร์**, 2525 **เอกสารอัดสำเนา**) (*Transcription of the Interview with Phraya Manawaratchasewi* (Division of Social, Historical and Philosophical Law Study, Thammasat University, copy of 1982))

VIETNAM

A. Major Texts

Đỗ Văn Đại, *Vietnam Contract Law—Cases and Comments* (Hanoi: National Political Press 2009) (Luật Hợp đồng Việt Nam, Bản án và bình luận bản án, NXB. Chính trị quốc gia, 2009)
Ho Chi Minh City University of Law, *Textbook on Civil Law, Part III—Contracts* (Ho Chi Minh City: Ho Chi Minh City University of Law 2011) (Giáo trình Luật Dân sự, Phẩn III—Hợp đồng), NXB Công an Nhân dân
Lê Nết, 'Contracts' in J Herbots (ed), *International Encyclopedia of Laws: Contracts* (1st edn, 1999, 2nd edn, 2011, 3rd edn, 2014, Boston, MA: Kluwer Law International)
Lê Nết, *The UNIDROIT Principles of International Commercial Contracts* (Ho Chi Minh City: Ho Chi Minh City Publishing House 1999) (translated into Vietnamese—Nguyên tắc của UNIDROIT về Hợp đồng thương mại quốc tế, NXB TP Hồ Chí Minh 1994)
Lê Nết, *Vietnam Contract Law* (Ho Chi Minh City: HCMC National University Press 2007) (Luật Hợp đồng Việt Nam, NXB Đại học Quốc gia TP HCM)
Phạm Duy Nghĩa, *Cases and Materials on Economic Laws* (Hanoi: Hanoi National University Press 2004) (Chuyên khảo luật kinh tế, Nxb. Đại học Quốc gia Hà Nội)

Index